SOCIAL WORK AND FRAUD

MALCOLM JORDAN

Copyright © 2023 Malcolm Jordan

All rights reserved. No part of this publication may be reproduced, stored in a database or retrieval system, or transmitted, in any form or by any means, without the prior permission in writing of the author, nor be otherwise circulated in any form or binding or cover other than that in which it is published and without a similar condition including this condition being imposed on the subsquent purchaser.

The majority of the images in this book are from the author's collection. Every attempt has been made to gain permission for the use of images not from the author's collection in this book. Any omissions will be rectified in future editions.

ISBN (Paperback): 978-1-913012-82-3

ISBN (Kindle): 978-1-913012-83-0

The moral right of the author has been asserted.

A full CIP record for this book is available from the British Library.

First published in 2023 in association with Riverside Publishing Solutions, Salisbury, UK

www.riversidepublishingsolutions.com

Printed and bound in the UK.

*This book is dedicated to
my late wife,*
ANN

CONTENTS

	Acknowledgements	vii
	Introduction: A Guide for the Reader	ix
Part One	**Clearing the Ground: 1850–1954**	
	Chapter 1 A Modern Empire 1850–1900	3
	Notes and References	18
	Chapter 2 A New Century 1900–1934	21
	Notes and References	63
	Chapter 3 The Nazi Advance 1934–1942	68
	Notes and References	114
	Chapter 4 Two Great Victory Celebrations: Home and School 1942–1945	120
	Notes and References	152
	Chapter 5 The Less Than Shining Years 1945–1950	157
	Notes and References	203
	Chapter 6 Colonial Adventures 1950–1954	211
	Notes and References	256
Part Two	**Engagement: 1954–1980**	
	Chapter 7 The Tectonic Plates Start to Shift 1954–1961	265
	Notes and References	301
	Chapter 8 Hope and Despair 1961–1969	308
	Notes and References	353
	Chapter 9 Transitions 1969–1975	358
	Notes and References	391
	Chapter 10 Radical Social Work Education (Maidstone) 1969–1976	396
	Notes and References	422
	Chapter 11 Research on a Shoestring 1969–1976	429
	Notes and References	457
	Chapter 12 The Counter Revolution – Monetarism 1977–1980	458
	Notes and References	490

Part Three	**Pushing Onwards: 1980–2021**		
	Chapter 13	Traumas 1980–1987	495
		Notes and References	529
	Chapter 14	Radical Changes 1987–2001	531
		Notes and References	576
	Chapter 15	Closing Time 2001–2008	581
		Notes and References	621
	Chapter 16	On the Edge (Making us Great – Again) 2009–2019	625
		Notes and References	700
	Chapter 17	Alarm 2019–2021	704
		Notes and References	723
Part Four	**The Last Post 2021–2022**		
	Chapter 18	What Future?	727
		Notes and References	741
	About the Author		743

ACKNOWLEDGEMENTS

My thanks are due to my daughter Juliet and my son-in law Rod Edge, without whose help this book could not have been published.

Also my granddaughter Aella and grandson Duke, my close family and friends, and all of who have put up with me and patiently offered help and advice during the thirty plus years of the book's creation.

Publisher

Riverside Publishing Solutions
Duncan Potter

Editors

Irene Pizzie
Sally Poulson
Sophie Gillespie
Andrew Goode

Cover Design

Alberta Jones

Contributors

Don Brand
Stephanie Davies
John Durham
Luke Edge
Myra Garrett
Mary Gordon
Gay Golding
John Golding
Anne Gulliford
Juliet Jordan
Aella Jordan-Edge

Duke Jordan-Edge
Mary Langan
Angi Naylor
Shahid Naqvi
David Pithers
Kathleen Ralphs
Pat Rostron
Colin Schofield
Alex Turner
Richard White

INTRODUCTION
A GUIDE FOR THE READER

His early wakened sensibilities and reflectiveness had developed into a many-sided sympathy, which threatened to hinder any persistent course of action … His imagination had so wrought itself to the habit of seeing things as they probably appeared to others, that a strong partisanship, unless it were against an immediate oppression, had become an insincerity for him. With the same balance he was fervently democratic in his feelings for the multitude and yet, voracious of speculations on government and religion, yet loath to part with long-sanctioned forms which, for him, were quick with memories and sentiments that no argument could lay dead.

– George Eliot, *Daniel Deronda*[1n]

Sometime in the late 1980s, at a challenging time in my career and with an interest in family history, I was relaxing in a small family hotel on the east coast of Turkey. It occurred to me that I might follow my late mother's example of writing and review the 170 plus years of my family history, which coincides with the story of social work, and eventually my own career. The final result is this book, completed over thirty years later!

Social Work and Proud reflects my understanding of social work history over the past one hundred and seventy years. Social work is a profession shaped inevitably by the society and culture in which it develops, that itself being influenced by international events. All of this is reflected in my own family's history, and this all fed into my sixty-six-year career 'doing social work.'

This is a book about social work and me; how we discovered each other, explored ourselves for over half a century through political, economic, social and cultural upheavals to reach a point where our ways can finally part. Time to try and make sense of the forces that brought us together and shaped our journey.

I hope that these chapters help illuminate the question 'Why social work?' Having developed an interest while still at school, it turned out that I had joined a profession where the practitioners have been described as human shape shifters. How else can we effectively work with such a wide range of personal circumstances? While our aim is always 'to start where the client is' in order to craft mutual solutions, our profession also requires us to abide by well-defined codes of practice and values.

As boundaries have always been a problem for me, it turns out I was a good fit for such a flexible profession. Friends in other professions seem to me to be so clear about their identity and the boundaries between themselves and others are so easily drawn.

I admire them greatly, but that is not me or my profession. Most social workers have experienced many roles and careers before entering the profession. Wars meant that many of my previous colleagues would have been disciplined in their youth into becoming efficient killing machines. In addition, my social work career has seen me dipping in and out of high commerce, being black-listed as too subversive an educator, too loyal a bureaucrat, too keen a social worker. I have been instructed in how to hang or birch a prisoner, and I have sat comfortably with the great and the good as well as the most desperate in society.

If all this requires a chameleon-like personality I content myself with the belief that even a chameleon must know it is always a chameleon determinedly following its core values, despite the particular colour of its current surroundings. Two small light hearted but by no means unique incidents may illustrate the point. My extrovert business partner had been more than pressing in his attempts to see a minor but famous author and actress so that they may share memories of long lost schooldays in Wales, although she has been remarkably reluctant to meet him. We climbed into a taxi for a hectic ride through central London to her flat, although there was no guarantee that she would open the door. As he rang the bell an idea occurred to him, 'I'll tell her that you're a TV producer, that'll do the trick. Let's face it, you could be anyone.' When a guest at a more recent gala dinner asked our host to identify that 'tall white-haired chap at the top table,' the role of 'Brigadier Jordan of Mogadishu' was mine to act out for the rest of an uncomfortable evening. Whilst it may have been true that I had the vague remnants of a military bearing left over from National Service and also that I had been trying to persuade television companies that my series on social work was a sure shot winner, neither are truly me.

I have always felt an integral part of my extended family, of friendship networks and of those beyond with whom I readily empathise. More recently, I have been wondering what this feeling has in common with the Muslim concept of 'ummah,' the brotherhood which shares a common identity so that if one is damaged, so are all. For me, however, this is a secular concept, based in class or a natural identification with the underdog, or perhaps just a reflection of core British values.[2n]

It may help the reader if I now outline the principal families whose genetic or historical twists have shaped much of my life and whose stories add a degree of continuity to this tale. The Jordan and Wood families were rooted in South London, my paternal forbears from Peckham being marked by their slight build and rather grey outlook on life, in contrast to the Woods from Lambeth who were extroverts, jolly and happily plump. The Glovers were based in Hands Cross, Sussex, but whether from rural or urban environments they would all have been classed as 'humble stock,' poorly educated and well used to the daily struggle required to make ends meet. This could also be said of the large Howard family from Clapham, where they had once been able to see the sheep herds grazing daily on the Common.

Further afield and with a late but vast influence was the Wickett family from Cornwall, comfortable dairy farmers establishing their pork butcher business in Launceston, and the Tomlinsons from the New Forest in Hampshire. Waiting in the wings were the Adams family from Suffolk: four boys and their parents Grace and Reverend Corben Adams, who moved to near Chicago in the 1920s. To my grandchildren comes an inheritance from the Edges of Staffordshire and the Rossi families with roots in Genoa.

Social Work and Proud is neither academic nor authoritative in respect of historical events, but hopefully will be a spur to those who wish to do further research. Most chapters are laid out so that, in the best social work tradition, the readers can choose which aspect to pursue in detail and which to give a lighter touch: world events, social history and culture, family or career.

If the reader wonders why minor or major events are included then I ask for patience as most such items reoccur to have a greater significance later in the story. Perhaps I have been too obsessive in making links across the years, but for me that is what makes history come alive. For example, not only does the assassination of General Gordon in Khartoum in 1886 link with my own time there 63 years later, but my son-in-law's Italian great-grandfather reported the incident for one of the Rome papers.

I do not possess the honed ability of a professional historian, social scientist or politician, but I have written my understanding of these events, and checked them wherever possible. Any errors therefore are mine alone. I hope that others may be able to study these histories and draw their own answers, hopefully to confirm the essential role that social work plays in society.

NOTES AND REFERENCES

1. Eliot, G. (1995). *Daniel Deronda*. London: Penguin. First published in 1876. There is no claim to the virtues of that fictional character although it is as good a portrait as any of many fellow professionals.
2. The concept of class is permanently embedded in British society. It has been suggested that this would have changed had the social structure been challenged by revolution, as in America, France and Russia. Whilst there may be some truth in this, my experience of these countries is that similar structures persist. Definitions and perceptions have changed throughout the period covered in this book, usually related to inheritance, occupation, income and education. Perception is also important in everyday interaction so that although, at the time that I started writing this book, I lived in a comfortable stone barn, shared the ownership of a second home, owned four family cars and enjoyed a wide range of cultural activities, once I open my mouth I reveal my class as decidedly below middle. Deep inside my psyche of course I remain working class, but then I am still a teenager in there! A review of this subject is available in Cannadine, D. (2000). *Class in Britain*. London: Penguin, or more entertainingly in the John Cleese, Ronnie Barker and Ronnie Corbett classic 1966 sketch from *The Frost Report* readily available on You Tube. The subject inevitably runs throughout this book.

PART ONE

1850–1954

CLEARING THE GROUND

ONE

1850–1900
A MODERN EMPIRE

To be ignorant of what occurred before you were born is to remain a child. For what is the worth of human life, unless it is woven into the life of our ancestors by the records of history?
— Cicero[1]

Men are born free and equal in rights. These rights are liberty, property, security and resistance to oppression: My country is the world and my religion is to do good.
— Thomas Paine[2n]

THINKERS

By the early part of the 19th century, the full consequences of the Enlightenment for the west were becoming clear. Religious belief as a central driving force had given way to rationality, and power had moved from established churches to secular organisations, now forming the nation states that were establishing themselves in Europe. The certainties of science had encouraged major developments in industrial methods of production and consequent urbanisation, and Britain was well poised economically, benefiting from its colonies and a certain buccaneering spirit revelling in minimum intervention by the state, the central tenet of the doctrine of Laissez-faire. Intellectually this was a time to be alive; the upheavals of the French Revolution were still being assimilated throughout the 19th century, and the people of Britain were worried whether that could happen at home. Liberalism as a political belief and the old pamphleteering of activists such as Thomas Paine (1737–1809) had been carried forward into a Britain where the newly created urban poor, suffering the full impact of industrialisation, were seen as a threat to be kept down at all costs.

The turn of the century had seen the influence of the romantic poets, themselves influenced by revolutionary ideas and achievements in post-revolutionary France. The 'Cockney Nutcase' William Blake (1757–1827) could conjure up his hallucinatory vision in etchings and poetry. As a child he had clearly seen angels in the trees on Peckham Rye, preached liberation and, well ahead of Freud, could recognise child sexuality: 'Infancy, fearless, lustful, happy! Nestling for delight in laps of pleasure.'[3] On the streets of Lambeth, where he lived a highly eccentric life, he railed against the oppressions of the urban poor.

> I wander through each charter'd street
> Near where the charter'd Thames does flow

> And mark in every face I meet
> Marks of weakness, marks of woe
> In every cry of every Man,
> In every infant's cry of fear,
> In every voice, in every ban,
> The mind-forg'd manacles I hear[4]

Among Blake's admirers was William Palmer, who lived in the small village of Shoreham in Kent. Here, in the mystical Darenth Valley, he and fellow Romantics established a group known as 'The Ancients.' It is thought that Blake gained inspiration for his poem 'Jerusalem' from the village setting. When my family moved there one hundred and fifty years later, stories of the eccentric goings on at the house still abounded. Beyond the darker effects of industrialisation, the Romantics could see a New Age in which intellect and emotion could be expressed openly. Wordsworth (1770–1850), on returning from France, could say 'Bliss was it in that dawn to be alive. But to be young was very heaven.'[5]

The census of 1801 had indicated a population of 10.5 million in the British Isles; by 1851 the total population had doubled to 21 million,[6n] with the urban population rising to 9% (although life expectancy was forty years). Of the working population (all those over the age of 10 years), some 10% worked in industry, 11.4% were still in agriculture and 7% worked in domestic service. Such rapid expansion reignited the arguments around the ideas of Thomas Malthus (1766–1834). He saw how population increased as people were better fed (quoting America as a clear example). This led to a shortage of resources with disastrous consequences for economies and the poorer strata of society. Thus, the control of population growth was the key to prosperity. However, the practical political and economic problem of the late 19th century was how such an expanding population, increasingly living in poor urban environments, could be contained with minimum state intervention.

Jeremy Bentham (1748–1832) developed the ideas of utilitarianism, the greatest happiness of the greatest number, and related them to various social problems, including the penal system. One example was his design of the Panopticon, a circular prison, only one example of which, Millbank Prison,[7n] was ever built in the UK. Several were built in the USA, Argentina, New Zealand and Cuba. The principle of this design was a central core which enabled the warders to watch every prisoner in the radiating wings without them being able to tell whether they were being observed or not, thus conveying a 'sentiment of an invisible omniscience.'[8n] His statue stands in the entrance hall of University College, London, founded in 1828 by a group of secularists determined to see one new seat of learning bound to science rather than the classics and the 39 religious Articles. As I write this, at the start of the 21st century, I attend meetings of the Social Work History Network in that College.

Edwin Chadwick (1800–1890), a man heavily influenced by Bentham and described as 'full of propellant zeal,' had been appointed a Commissioner under the Poor Law

Amendment Act (1834). This Act had made all poor relief outside the workhouse unlawful and held that benefits inside should always be less than the conditions outside – the principle of 'less eligibility.' From his position as secretary, Chadwick examined the health and housing of the poor and, aided by outbreaks of cholera, he argued that disease could be prevented by proper drainage, sewage disposal and basic housing. In a call to the age, he argued that the terrible unsanitary arrangements he had discovered led to bad moral habits in the poor. Against opposition from all the vested interests and the continued belief in limited state intervention, the Public Health Act (1848) was passed as a temporary, but important, precursor to all subsequent legislation on health and public housing.

DEVELOPMENTS

The Public Health Act called for local boards, which would have power over water, sewage and paving, but the legislation was permissive only. These few, but key, provisions were met with considerable opposition, partly as resistance to yet another set of structures similar to the much-despised Poor Law Boards. *The Times* of London declared that it would rather take its 'chance of cholera and the rest than be bullied into health by these Boards.'[9] The London Board (the forerunner of the London County Council) employed a young engineer, Joseph Bazalgette, as Chief Engineer. Action became urgent in the hot summer of 1858 when the outflow from slaughterhouses and domestic cesspits emptying into the Thames created the 'great stink.' One thousand miles of capacious underground sewers were built which still serve London today.[10n] Bazalgette was also responsible for the construction of the Victoria, Albert and Chelsea Embankments to the Thames, some main London thoroughfares and the bridge over the River Medway at Maidstone. This latter location and Joseph's descendants come together in this story a hundred years later.

By the middle of the 19th century, Charles Dickens (1812–1870) had become an established writer and social campaigner in the company of Lord Shaftesbury and Chadwick. Bringing his own childhood experiences as a wretched blacking boy visiting his father in Marshalsea debtors' prison every week, he brought the attention of the literate classes to the plight of people in poverty, in private boarding schools and in the workhouses. His complex novel *Bleak House* was published in 1852, although by the time of publication, and certainly by the time his writing was read by the lower classes, many of the conditions were marginally improved.

By the mid part of the 19th century one branch of the Wood family had shipped to Australia, not to my knowledge via Millbank Prison; another was busy in London with their twenty-three children. The next generation, perhaps in response to the pressures of the day, numbered only five, the third of whom was my maternal grandmother, Edie Wood. Although the Jordan family of that time numbered eight, by the dawn of the next century the eldest had commenced a line of eleven children, of which my father Harry was the sixth. This simple outline may go some way to explain why, with such an age range between first and last born, the life stories of my uncles, aunts and cousins make so much history and geography come alive for me.

From 1825 the railway had started to develop and spread its network across the land. In 1838 the line from London to Bristol (later the Great Western Railway) was laid as part of the 500 miles of track then completed. Ten years later 5,000 more miles had been laid and the train had started to outgrow the canal barge as the main carriers of goods. By 1870, 13,600 miles were laid, and by the end of the century this had increased to an amazing 20,000 miles.[11n] Financial speculation on railway development was a fascinating story as money pressed upon vested land and legal interests. Sometimes large landowners were bought off; sometimes they forced the line to take roundabout routes. An associated problem was the manual workers upon whose hard labour the development relied. Often these navvies (who had dug the canals, originally called navigations, across the country) were local men, but large numbers also came from abroad, notably Ireland. Government lack of intervention in these developments and the consequent human problems was slow, but in 1847 a government committee examined the working conditions and high accident rates of these navvies. Accidents were not confined to the workers. The first man killed in a railway accident in 1830 had been Thomas Huskisson, MP for Liverpool, who had stepped off the train onto the track of an oncoming train, having completely failed to appreciate the speed of the new invention and the distance required for the train to stop.

In 1851 The Great Exhibition was held in Hyde Park in London in and around the vast 'Crystal Palace.'[12n] This was a wonderful example of Victorian pride and optimism, showing off products from home and Empire. A special place was reserved to display the fabulous Kohinoor diamond, famous since the 14th century and a central part of the Shah of Persia's throne until 'acquired' by the British (and now part of the Crown Jewels of the United Kingdom). Over 7,000 British exhibitors took part, but an almost equal area was taken by foreign exhibitors. News of the event travelled fast, in part thanks to the recently introduced Penny Post, and access was helped by train travel and the popularity of the horse-drawn omnibuses. Thus a cross section of the population could visit the Exhibition; for large numbers this would be their first long journey from home and certainly to London. One observer remarked that 'The Exhibition engrosses everybody and disarranges everything; it has literally driven all the London world mad.'[13]

My growing family witnessed the consolidation of the Empire; for them and through to my early years a hundred years later there was no doubt about the 'Great' in Great Britain and her Empire. It was a period in which the self-evident virtuous values of the country were exported, a time of minor war, gunboat diplomacy and complex treaties. There was great pride in the industrial achievements which, together with overseas conquests and unfair trade (the large part of which had derived from slavery), had made the nation rich. In fact the slow decline in our economic leadership had already commenced, as America, with the Civil War settled, and India were challenging us in the production of machine tools and cotton goods.

It is somewhat ironic that while blockades of southern American ports deprived the Lancashire Mills of raw cotton, leading to unemployment, the workers bore the hardship as they supported freedom for the slaves. A certain restlessness was evident in some colonies, which were perhaps beginning to question our natural right to rule, but to the general public at home it must have seemed that the adventures and achievements of Empire would go on forever, if only because they were so evidently God's will. This was the general Victorian attitude of pride in the nation and its achievements, a clear sense of right and wrong, the duty to country and sometimes to those less privileged members together with an overriding optimism (God's in his heaven and all's right with the world) that came down to my parent's generation.

These political aspirations, the underlying financial power of the city and self-belief can be illustrated by the building of the Suez Canal, a joint Anglo-French enterprise, which opened in 1869 allowing faster access to the eastern colonies, the largest of which was facing trouble. The East India Company maintained three armies, but as the 19th century advanced a combination of poor leadership, historic grievances and misunderstandings led to discontent in the Third Army based in Meerut. The final spark was the mistaken belief that new ammunition arriving from Britain was coated in pig and cow fat. When soldiers of the Bengal Light Cavalry refused to touch this ammunition, they were imprisoned for ten years with hard labour. In May 1887 colleagues released them, whereupon the mutiny rapidly spread across Bengal, where it built on rising anti-colonial feelings among the Indian aristocracy and their subjects.

Delhi was the first city to fall, and the 30,000 mutineers managed to hold the city for four months. The mutineers attacked Lucknow, killed the Commander and held the garrison until November 1857 when the relieving troops restored order to the province but butchered virtually all of the 2,000 mutineers in Lucknow. This was in revenge for the atrocity of Cawnpore where 200 women and children had been butchered by the mutineers. The mutiny caused great concern in London, where Dickens, he so sympathetic to the poor, reflected the public mood by calling for the extermination of the responsible race! The East India Company was abolished, and the Crown took direct responsibility for the colony; Queen Victoria became the Empress of India, and the Governor-General (designated Viceroy), Viscount Canning, instituted immediate reforms by bringing selected Indian nationals into the civil service and generally rowing back westernisation programmes. Thus, a middle class of civil servants developed to serve the new British Raj, although the underlying caste systems remained, as did the knowledge that the British could be beaten.

Unfortunately, the Suez Canal crisis also focussed nationalistic feelings across Egypt and the Sudan, culminating in open rebellion, crushed by the British Army at Tel-el-Kebir in 1882. Only three years later, General Gordon, Governor of Sudan, found himself besieged and defeated by the jihadist Mahdi's Dervishes outside

Khartoum. His own pride and political uncertainties at home led to his capture and beheading on the steps of the Governor's Palace. General Horatio Kitchener led the expedition to regain control of the Sudan and avenge Gordon's death, which he did by deploying overwhelming fire power at Omdurman. Gordon and Kitchener were inexplicably, but in typically British style, both hailed as victorious national heroes, the latter's fierce face calling for volunteers for the Great War with the slogan 'Your Country Needs You.'

Further afield on the borders between the Indian subcontinent and Afghanistan, Britain faced Russia in the 'great game' of Empire.[14n] Lord Curzon, Viceroy of India, who paid great attention to the North-West Frontier Province, was concerned about Russian ambitions as they built railways south through the Karakum Desert and towards Persia. Curzon sent missions and expeditions into Tibet and Persia in order to sustain British superiority. Britain's brilliant capacity for drawing false boundaries divided the ancient and powerful Pashtun people between India and Afghanistan. Despite his great enthusiasm, Curzon baulked at bringing order to the wilder parts of Waziristan. From these adventures came tales of derring-do and of fighting the wily tribesmen of the Khyber Pass from authors Kipling and Masters.[15] In 1897 the young Winston Churchill fought against the Pashtun tribe, sending dispatches and articles home for publication.

SOCIAL SCIENCE AND ACTION

Closer to my family's situation and an example of other Victorian values was the work of Octavia Hill,[16n] a relatively wealthy lady with a long-standing interest in housing provision. Maintaining that 'you cannot deal with a person and their housing separately' she purchased increasing numbers of houses, which she let out to families in need for as low a rent as possible.[17n] Having achieved this, she insisted that the rent was paid and would evict a family who ran into arrears. Later, following the formation of local cadet militia units, Octavia Hill founded Cadet Corps units in the belief that discipline, adventure and training towards a military career was a helpful route out of poverty for young boys.

It was the pursuit of the application of science to history that led Karl Marx (1818–1883) to attempt the construction of 'laws' which would inevitably confirm the economic conditions that would replace capitalism. Marx had been approached by the League of the Just[18n] to write a manifesto following two long congresses held in London, which also led to the League's re-designation as the Communist League. The Communist Manifesto was completed by Marx and his financial sponsor Friedrich Engels and published in 1848. 'It is high time that Communists should openly in the face of the whole world, publish their views, their aims, their tendencies ...'[19n]

The power of the document and the movement was directed primarily at Germany, but the following year, faced with a charge of high treason there, Marx and his family arrived in London as political refugees, where they lived for many years in poverty while he worked in the Reading Room of the British Museum. His ideas were slow to gain ground in this country and in fact his major works, including *Das Kapital*, were not published until after 1867, shortly before he suffered a stroke, which severely curtailed the enormous drive and energy that had been the mark of the man. He died in March 1883, a sad and lonely man, although some of his last correspondence had indicated his doubts that Russia could move from a feudal to a communist regime without passing through the capitalist stage.

On a more immediate level the less well-off members of society were being pressed to improve themselves through thrift and 'self-help.' These twin virtues had been promoted by Samuel Smiles in popular books published in 1859 and 1875. The spirit of the times can be seen by an extract from *Self-Help*:

> That there should be a class of men who live by their daily labour in every state is the ordinance of God and doubtless is a wise and righteous one; but that this class should be otherwise than frugal, contented, intelligent, and happy is not the design of Providence, but springs solely from the weakness, self-denial and perverseness of man himself. The healthy spirit of self-help created among working people would more than any other measure serve to raise them up as a class, and this, not by pulling down others, but by levelling them up to a higher and still advancing standard of religion, intelligence and virtue.[20]

An alternative and more deterministic view was advanced by an Italian surgeon Cesare Lombroso (1835–1909) who had developed an approach to criminology which relied on exact measurements of features of the face, skull and body. He believed that violent criminals were less evolved so that recognition of their characteristics (shifty eyes, handle-shaped ears, high cheekbones, low sloping foreheads, etc.) would enable them to be identified and isolated for the protection of society. He advocated humane treatment for such individuals. Through a study of the art of the insane, he also believed that genius was a form of hereditary insanity.[21n]

In 1844 the Rochdale Society of Equitable Pioneers had been registered as a 'friendly society,' although its prime purposes were the establishment of a store for the sale of provisions, clothing etc., the building of houses and the manufacture of such articles as the society determined. Local friendly societies and co-operative societies were being formed across the country as a means of helping poor people to save, to insure themselves against sickness and, as far as the stores were concerned, to cut out the middleman and pay purchasers a dividend to aid savings. By 1863 the English Co-operative Wholesale Society was formed. From an original membership of 28 members in Rochdale, by 1900 the Co-operative movement had 1.7 million members with sales in excess of £50 million.

By 1834 the unions of working men had become dormant following the exile of the Tolpuddle Martyrs to Australia for swearing a secret oath to form a friendly society in their village. From the middle of the century, trades unions were revived, acting under friendly society rules. The Society of Boilermakers sought action against its secretary for allegedly withholding funds. Much to their surprise, the judge hearing the case in 1867 not only rejected their action, but also held that the society was not a friendly society and although not criminal it was so far acting in restraint of trade as to be illegal. The Royal Commission into the Organisation and Rules of Trades Unions reported in 1869, and recommended the registration of unions under the friendly society rules and supported workers coming together in combinations, but that molestation and obstruction by means of picketing should remain as offences. That the Liberal Party should support the subsequent legislation came as a profound shock to the leaders of the trades unions, and in 1869 the Labour Representation League was formed. In 1874 fifteen working men stood for election to Parliament and two miners were the first to be elected, although taking their seats with the Liberals in opposition to the Tories.

The year of the birth of my maternal grandmother, Edie Wood, 1878, had seen Britain buying a major shareholding in the Suez Canal Company. The Factory Act (1878) had imposed a maximum 56-hour working week and introduced some minor safeguards for the small boys who were employed to climb up the inside of chimneys to scrape off the soot. Less noticed was the sinking of the first borehole to explore the feasibility of a tunnel under the English Channel. Meanwhile, W. G. Grace was continuing to break cricketing records at Lords and The Oval cricket grounds (in the season of 1871 he had scored 2,739 runs); Gilbert and Sullivan were mocking the establishment in their brilliant operettas; and music hall songstresses such as Marie Lloyd were providing the popular tunes of the day. Edie was born in Lambeth just as Cleopatra's Needle arrived on the opposite bank of the Thames; two years later the Embankment was the first public place to have electric lighting installed. Domestic installation was some time away, and telephones, radios and petrol driven vehicles, together with all the other facilities of modern living that are now taken for granted, were not in sight. In 1879 the first telephone exchange was installed in London with ten subscribers. *The Times* noted that 'By its means the human voice can be conveyed in full force from any one point to another five miles off, and with some loss of power to a very much more considerable distance.'[22]

Edie was the fourth child of Alfred and Elizabeth Wood. She had two younger brothers, Jack (whose daughter we corresponded with) and Charlie, whose American adventures we will return to later. The politics that surrounded Edie's early years were dominated by Gladstone (1809–1898) and Disraeli (1804–1881) as the Liberal and Tory parties see-sawed in and out of power following the tragedies of the potato famine unrest in Ireland. The issue of Home Rule was to bring down more than one government, and in the provinces of South Africa there were the first rumblings of discontent, which would soon lead to the Boer War as the Dutch Protestant settlers challenged British rule.

As Edie grew up, adventures abroad must always have seemed to be in the news. In addition to being told of the great adventure that led Henry Morton Stanley, as a reporter for *The New York Times*, to find the medical missionary David Livingstone, whose expedition was for *The Daily Telegraph*, with the famous greeting 'Dr Livingstone, I presume?'[23n] in Australia, the outlaw Ned Kelly, whose self-made armour failed to stop all the police bullets, was captured and hanged in 1880. Nearer to home, as Edie was finishing her basic schooling, *The Adventures of Sherlock Holmes*, the writings of Oscar Wilde and Kipling's patriotic stories including *The Jungle Book* would all have been available, as was H. G. Wells' *War of the Worlds*. Edie and her family would certainly have enjoyed Queen Victoria's Golden Jubilee celebrations in 1897, although they probably would not have registered the mentioning in dispatches of a young officer, Winston Churchill, for action against the Afghans on India's North-West Frontier. By 1899, when Edie was 21, the pneumatic tyre invented by Dunlop was coming into use and the first motor buses were appearing on the streets of London. The next innovation was the 'Twopenny Tube' ride on the underground in Central London.

In 1888 the young women who were employed to make matches for Bryant and May in East London went on strike in protest at the poor working conditions which led to the disfigurement 'phossy jaw' from the phosphorous they had to handle. Their cause was taken up by Annie Besant (1847–1933),[24n] an outspoken activist for socialist ideas, a divorced single parent and a founder member of the Fabian Society, a sort of early left-wing 'think tank' whose membership included George Bernard Shaw (1856–1950), who wrote many of his early plays while rushing between public meetings in working men's clubs, trade councils and smoke filled bars where he energetically promoted the cause of socialism to be achieved by human will and conscious choice. He and Besant shared the feminist cause with H. G. Wells, another fierce campaigner for early socialism, whose urgent call to establish a New Jerusalem set him in conflict with the best known Fabians, Beatrice (1858–1943) and Sidney (1859–1947) Webb.

Wells, in common with other thinkers of his time, developed an interest in birth control based on the science of eugenics, which would avoid the human species mutating downwards until it destroyed itself. The answer, according to that science, was to secure mankind's future by breeding a superior race. These views hardly endeared him to his fellow socialists, particularly the Webbs, who in any event were more concerned with the mechanics of a socialist state and advancing policies based on evidence. The Fabian belief in the inevitability of gradualism suited them well (as Beatrice once counselled her ardent fiancée), but their contribution to the cause of the underprivileged was great. In 1894, together with H. G. Wells, Octavia Hill and Graham Wallas, they founded the London School of Economics with the motto 'To know the causes of things' and the purpose of studying poverty and inequality for the betterment of society. This major achievement by the Webbs went alongside a leading role in government initiatives together with their service on the London County Council. All this they saw as paving, in a practical if mundane way, the route by which socialism could advance.

Despite amendments to the 1834 Poor Law, the problems resulting from the denial of out-relief were causing increasing economic problems. Faced with the reality of desperate poverty, the churches and other charities had acted, but despite their best intentions the proliferation of different charities meant that some families received no help while others benefited from the lack of co-ordination and got relatively excessive help. Thus in 1869 a familiar grouping of the Webbs, Octavia Hill and others established the Charity

Organisation Society (COS) with the express purpose of regulating the charitable flow of help by assessment of need and application of appropriate help. While it achieved a degree of success, and some staff were called social workers, the application of these investigative methods was much disliked by the poor. The Labour MP George Lansbury (1859–1940) called the methods brutal. In 1870 the COS established the first labour exchange to help unemployed men find work.

In 1865 William Booth (1829–1912), an evangelical Christian missionary working in the East End of London, established The Salvation Army as a spiritually based organisation which would bring relief to the poor. Fifteen years later he was installed as the first General of that Army, publishing in 1890 a treatise *In Darkest England*, echoing the appalling conditions described in Stanley's recent novel *In Darkest Africa*. The Salvation Army later transferred its headquarters, by then a worldwide movement, to Denmark Hill in South East London, a short distance from the ill-fated Jordan family home at Goose Green.

In 1881 the *Liverpool Mercury* published a letter from Rev George Staite, who was concerned about the neglect and abuse of children. He asked why there was already a Society for the Protection of Cruelty to Animals, but nothing for children. The resistance of course was the enduring belief in Laissez-faire and the absolute power and rights of parents. The reformer Lord Shaftesbury conceded that although the evils of child abuse were enormous and indisputable, they were of such a private and domestic nature that Parliament would not entertain any action. Similar concerns were being raised in America, and in New York a Society for the Protection of Cruelty to Children had been formed in 1875. This model was brought to Liverpool by a wealthy banker, Thomas Agnew, who formed a local society in 1883. Similar local societies were formed, and by 1889 the London Society had 32 local committees; in that year the NSPCC was formed with Queen Victoria as patron. That same year Parliament passed the first Act on the subject, which came to be known as the Children's Charter, which empowered the police to arrest anyone found ill-treating a child. One of the early funders, the rich aristocrat Angela Burdett-Coutts, who had also funded David Livingstone's expeditions and worked with Charles Dickens, caused a scandal when at the age of 66 she married an American man aged 29, thus provoking a society scandal and Queen Victoria's comment that the marriage was 'ridiculous.'

George Sims (1847–1922), a journalist who saw the slum conditions for himself, campaigned for improved housing and public health. In 1883 he published the first of his 'Horrible London' articles in the *Daily News* and pamphlets which described the degradation and immorality in the heart of London in

> … pestilential human rookeries … where tens of thousands are crowded together amidst horrors which call to mind what we have heard of the middle passage of the slave ship. To get into them, you have to penetrate courts reeking with poisonous and malodorous gases arising from accumulations of sewage and refuse scattered in all directions and often

flowing beneath your feet … Then … you may gain admittance to the dens in which these tens of thousands of beings … are herded together. Walls and ceilings are black with the accretions of filth which have gathered on them through long years of neglect. Every room in these rotten and reeking tenements houses a family or two.[25]

Unfortunately, three subsequent Acts directed to cure these ills had little effect in the face of intransigent landlords, and as the century ended Sims' conditions could still be experienced. These concerns were echoed at the old universities, initially under the influence of T. H. Green (1836–1882) who took the lead in developing the idealist school of English philosophy which influenced many leading reformers and politicians. To the liberal belief in the removal of restraint they were able to oppose the positive conception of action by the state to enable its citizens to grow in 'freedom in the positive sense … the liberation of the powers of all men equally for contribution to a common good.'[26]

In 1884 Rev Samuel Barnett (1844–1913), combining the work of priest and social worker in the East End of London, founded the first University Settlement, which he named as Toynbee Hall in honour of Green's young associate, Arnold Toynbee, the brilliant historian and ardent social reformer who had died at the age of 31 in 1883. This was followed by the Cambridge Settlement, and in 1887 the Oxbridge and London women's colleges established their own Settlement at 44 Nelson Square, at Blackfriars just south of the Thames. The purpose of these settlements was to offer undergraduates and graduates a chance to live with and observe the conditions around them, to research and to intervene. All these settlements still function today. In particular, Toynbee Hall came to boast William Beveridge (1879–1963) and R. H. Tawney (1880–1962) among its alumni, and in 1910 an experience there turned the Conservative barrister C. R. Attlee (1883–1967) into a socialist, later becoming the father of the modern Welfare State.

In 1886 a wealthy Liverpool ship owner Charles Booth (1840–1916), who had a long-standing interest in social problems, commenced his massive investigation into the life and labour of the people of London, a work which took him 17 years to complete.[27]

His 17 volumes presented impressive facts and figures, 'an instantaneous picture' to support the plight of the poor and were used by many reformers and politicians. In general, Booth attempted no explanations and offered few remedies, but in Beatrice Webb's words his reports 'reverberated in the worlds of politics and philanthropy.' Booth demonstrated that charity was largely irrelevant and that when it had been applied, most thoroughly by the COS, 'the people are no less poor … there are fewer paupers but not any fewer that rely on charity. In fact, charity was doing little more than relieve the rates.' As the facts about poverty accumulated, Booth concentrated his attention on the overcrowding, ill health, child neglect and moral decay of the bottom ten percent who, particularly due to irregularity of employment, were incapable of supporting themselves and their families. In Booth's view the community, in its own interest, should 'take charge of the lives of those who are incapable of independent existence up to the required standard.'

Some thirty years earlier, the 1854 Youthful Offenders Act, by recognising that lawbreakers under the age of 16 should not be sent to adult jails, had given philanthropic magistrates an opportunity to establish an alternative reform programme, originally on two training ships moored in the River Mersey. These ships, which relied on naval routines and discipline to reform their young charges, would continue for some fifty years, offering boys a basic education and the opportunity to learn a trade (mostly towards a naval career) in the context of a rigid disciplinary framework. Although offering care and kindness, punishments for misbehaviour were severe. A 13-year-old boy was given three months hard labour and a whipping for stealing two biscuits; an 11-year-old lad suffered one day's hard labour and a whipping for stealing one penny's worth of potatoes. Those who misbehaved in class might have their hands tied and a placard with derisory remarks put round their neck. Others might have 12 strokes of the birch. Very soon after setting up the ships, the Liverpool Juvenile Reformatory Association searched for a suitable site inland, and by 1867 a new school had been built as Bridge Park Farm School, which would wind itself in and out of my history 100 years later, renamed as Red Bank School.[28]

Emile Durkheim (1858–1917) in France, followed by Max Weber (1864–1920) in Germany, were applying the scientific method to society itself. Each struggled to use their philosophical training to understand how to objectivise the study of their fellow man. Each was clear that the scientific approach was the only one applicable in that historical period. Durkheim's three major publications in the 1890s (on the division of labour, sociological method and suicide) marked the foundations of sociology as a modern discipline.[29] He examined aspects of modern and traditional societies from a functionalist perspective, with particular reference to the relationship between the individual and society. He wondered how the multiplicity of individuals make up a society, and how individuals achieve the consensus necessary to form a society.

Durkheim considered how the existence of organised societies leads to a natural specialisation of roles, a phenomenon which is taken to extremes in modern industrialised societies through the creation of dependencies with access to the products of skilled labour accessed through the exchange of money. He saw religion as a mechanism which shored up the social order, as an outward expression of the fact that 'society has to be present within the individual.' As the pace of change in a society increased, it became more difficult for individuals to maintain internalised norms. There is an inevitable drift into normlessness, which Durkheim termed 'anomie,' a significant cause of suicide. Durkheim's approach was evolutionary, and his socialism was a moral one. His ideal society was one where respect for the human person and fulfilment of personal autonomy reigns. The role of sociology is to justify rationalist individualism balanced by respect for collective norms.

Weber, whose major works were not published in English until after his death in 1920, adopted a more individualistic approach as he was more interested in what motivated individual actors in society – a less positivistic approach which sought to differentiate the social from the natural sciences. Weber considered that individuals act rationally in accordance with social customs and norms, which become habituated so that we act by conditioned reflexes rather than the achievement of specific goals. (For example, we rationally accept a challenge to a dual because to refuse would be to act dishonourably by the customs of the time.) His later work examined the impact of cultures and religions on the development of economic systems in different societies. These studies led to his best known work *The Protestant Ethic and the Pursuit of Capitalism*.[30]

Weber wondered why, although forms of capitalism were established elsewhere, the combination of the unlimited quest for profit and rational discipline of work had appeared only once, particularly in western societies where the protestant religion was paramount. He concluded that there exists a spiritual affinity between certain visions of the world and a certain style of economic activity. In particular, Calvinism gave spiritual and moral meaning to the pursuit of economic gain. Calvinistic asceticism has a strange coincidence with capitalism's aim to make profits that are re-invested rather than spent. In time, as the religious foundations fall away, the pursuit of the work ethic and capital gain became the central force in society. To quote Marx in *Das Kapital*, 'Accumulate, accumulate, this is the law and the prophets.' These dynamics are, of course, most powerful in America, from the settlement of the Founding Fathers to the present day. It was the excess of unregulated markets, rather than market mechanisms per se, that lay at the root of the critique of capitalism advanced by Marx and Engels.

> Capitalism has left no other nexus between man and man than callous 'cash-payment' ... It has drowned the most heavenly ecstasies of religious fervour ... in the ice water of egotistical calculation. It has resolved personal worth into exchange value, and in place of numberless indefeasible chartered freedoms, has set up that single unconscionable freedom – Free Trade.[31]

In 1881 the Democratic Federation was founded by Henry M. Hyndman (1842–1921), a wealthy radical influenced by Marx; two years later, William Morris (1834–1896), whose interests included poetry, painting, design and managing his craft workshop, joined the Federation and devoted his energies to preaching socialist ideas across the country. Their efforts were targeted at the rising numbers of unemployed, and for this purpose it changed its name to the Socialist Democratic Federation, although very quickly Morris broke away to form the Socialist League, which opposed Parliamentary action, believing that this would only be appropriate when the working classes were thoroughly imbued with the spirit of socialism.

In general terms, the League demanded universal suffrage, abolition of the House of Lords, widespread state intervention to aid the poor and nationalisation of the land, the railways and the mines. In 1887 James Keir Hardie (1856–1915) stood as Labour candidate in Mid Lanarkshire against a Liberal; he asked voters to support him as 'a man of yourselves who being poor can feel for the poor and whose whole interest lie in the direction of securing for you a better and happier lot.' Although not elected, he became

Secretary to the newly formed Scottish Labour Party and in the following years local Labour Parties were formed. In 1892 Hardie was one of three Independent Socialists elected to Parliament with the declared intention of forming an Independent Labour Party (ILP). In January 1893, at a conference which brought together trades unions, the SDF, Labour Clubs and the Fabians, the ILP was formed with Keir Hardie as its Chairman. In 1900 agreement was reached to form a Labour Party in the House of Commons.

With the benefits of Empire, the exploitation of people and raw materials across the world, with manufacturing at home and export for profit continuing, the reality was that the country's fortunes were already on the turn and these closing years of the century were years of relative economic depression. Political rivalry and commercial competition between the European powers were coming to a head, exacerbated by the race for colonial conquest. Germany (and certainly the USA) were clearly overtaking Britain in industrial production. By 1897 Queen Victoria had been on the throne for 60 years, during which time the Empire had expanded ten times: it covered one-fifth of the earth's surface and comprised a quarter of the world's population. Victoria's eldest son Edward would soon become King, his cousin the Tsar of Russia was struggling with the modernisation of his vast country, whilst Germany was ruled by cousin Kaiser Wilhelm II (1859–1941), generally portrayed as a blustering fool. His perception of a Great Britain busy re-arming led him to stir up trouble wherever he could, and particularly by supporting the South African Boers in the run up to that war which started in 1899.

The dynamic that would lead to the tragedy of war two decades later was already underway.[32n] Worried by what he saw as encirclement by France and Britain, the Kaiser signed a Triple Alliance with Austro-Hungary and Italy, by which they agreed to support each other militarily if attacked by two or more of the great powers. Fourteen years later, France and Russia signed an Alliance which committed them to consultations in the case of war. In 1904 Britain entered the Entente Cordial with France, and soon after an agreement with Russia was made. The main purpose of these two treaties was to reduce conflict between the nations by settling long-standing disputes about interests in the colonies and spheres of influence from Newfoundland to Afghanistan and Siam to Morocco. Whilst the effect of these agreements was to bring the nations closer together, there was no mention of military conflict in Europe, and indeed there was no military agreement with France until after the outbreak of war in 1914. As the 19th century drew to a close and in the early years of the next century, these alliances, although by no means completely binding, increasingly formed the basis of mutual suspicions and defensive preparations.

Probably unknown by most of the population, the certainties that had underpinned the age were being undermined by new ideas and developments. In the Paris of the late 1880s a young neurologist Sigmund Freud (1856–1939) was studying the effects of hypnotism on patients suffering from hysteria. Freud and his mentor Charcot were puzzled by the fact that traumatised patients who complained of disability of a limb do so with no relationship to known anatomical and neurological facts. It seemed that 'hysteria' behaved as though anatomy did not exist, or as though it had no knowledge of it. The symptoms, for example paralysis of a leg but only below the dress line, could be both induced and removed by hypnosis. The next fifteen years were spent exploring, by scientific observation, experiment and logical thought, and the relationship between the physical structures of body and the mind. By 1896 Freud had used the term 'psycho-analysis,' and in the following three years he was contemplating the issue of infantile experience, sexuality and the role of dreams, ideas abhorred by the Victorians.

In the margins of everyday life, other ideas that would transform the world were just coming to light. The traditional divisions of political action were having to struggle with the impact of Marx and the expansion of communism. Freud's writings were opening up the world of the unconscious as a major dynamic in what had hitherto been seen as rational action. The shock of these ideas, and the courage needed to develop them, were much later clearly summarised by the child psychiatrist Donald Winnicott:

> Courage was needed because once we accept the unconscious, we are on the path which sooner or later takes us to something very painful – the recognition that however much we try to see evil, beastliness, and bad influence as something outside ourselves, or impinging on ourselves from without, in the end we find that whatever things people do and whatever influences actuate them, these are in human nature itself, in fact in *ourselves*.[33]

Ernest Rutherford (1871–1937) in Cambridge had discovered the structure of the atom, and Marie Curie (1867–1934) had started her exploration of radioactivity. These phenomena, the creation of energy without loss of size or detectable changes, came to be explained via Max Planck's exploration of entropy and by the genius of Albert Einstein (1879–1955) in papers published at the start of the 20th century. The firm certainties of 19th century Newtonian science, Victorian values and Britain's role in the world were quietly being undermined, although the effects of these changes would take many decades to be fully realised.

Edie Wood married Herbert Glover in 1898. He was a sawyer who had moved to London from Handcross in Sussex seeking work; they had three daughters, although the marriage did not last. When I met Herbert some fifty years later, despite the ravages of alcohol and destitution he impressed me as a wonderful example of the proud Victorian male. His dark suit and bowler hat set off his great frame and waxed moustache, and across his chest was the gold chain holding his 'Hunter' watch. I could see him standing beside the great industrial machines and showing visitors how his mastery of the machine caused the whole weight to stop that minute fraction before it crushed his precious watch. The last year of the century was marked by the birth of Edie and Herbert's first daughter, Edie Elizabeth, a frail child whose succession of illnesses was to produce a flower-like beauty and great gentleness.

Life in Britain would not continue in the comfortable certainties that had marked the dying century, although as the century turned the old certainties in Britain's pre-eminence were being reinforced by the relief of Mafeking and the end of the Boer War in 1902. (Much later we learnt that Lord Kitchener, in an effort to contain elements of the population sympathetic to the Boers, had concentrated people in large camps, the first use of concentration camps by a European power.) During the general election of 1900, much influenced by the 'khaki vote' but still on a restricted franchise of householders, about 60% of the male population, Winston Churchill was elected MP for Oldham representing the Liberal Party. But as far as most Londoners were concerned that could have been happening in a far-off land. The Census of 1901 put the population at some 35 million, some 27% of whom lived in an urban environment.

The processes of industrialisation and urbanisation had made both the exploitation of workers and the plight of the poor more visible and the search for solutions in terms of public health, education and welfare more urgent. Whilst governments and higher levels of society feared the increased numbers of the lower classes and their potential for violence, others sought to mitigate the situation that actually confronted them on a daily basis. In that mixture of zeal, often based on religious or political values and direct action, one can see the threads that were soon to be woven together to shape the new profession of social worker. Fierce reformers such as Chadwick, along with the careful research of Charles Booth and the combination of the academic analysis and action of the Webbs, were working alongside the practical work of the university settlements, the housing schemes of Octavia Hill and the methods of the COS. The creative links between literature, poetry and social action from the Romantics through Blake and Dickens to Shaw and Wells were to be relegated to the background of this new profession, perhaps until the advent of popular TV and the 1960s. But at the time these other more practical elements were coming together as the necessary mark of professionalisation.

NOTES AND REFERENCES

1. Cicero as quoted in Harris, R. (2006). *Imperium*. London: Hutchinson, p. 264.
2. Thomas Paine, in *The Rights of Man* (1792) and *Common Sense* (1776), had defended the French Revolution and the War of American Independence. His *Age of Reason* (1794), 'a march through Christianity with an Axe,' turned him from feted hero of the war in America to a hated antichrist. A hundred years after his death (in 1809, in obscurity in Greenwich Village, New York), Theodore Roosevelt referred to him as that 'filthy little atheist.' It has been said of him that, as the inspiration behind modern western society we are all Paine's children. He is memorialised in America and France, and in 1964 a statue of him was erected in his hometown of Thetford, Norfolk.
3. Blake, W. (1793). 'Visions of the Daughters of Albion.' Published as an illustrated book.
4. Blake, W. (1986). 'In Wain, J., ed. (1986). *The Oxford Library of English Poetry*. Vol. II, *Songs of Innocence and Experience*. Published in 1789 as illustrated books.
5. Wordsworth, W. (1850). 'The Prelude: Residence in France and the French Revolution,' stanza 11, line 4. In Wain, *op. cit.*
6. By contrast, it had taken some 200 years until 1801 for the population to double.

7. Millbank Prison opened in 1821 but was demolished in 1890. Tate Britain now occupies part of the site, although one buttress still stands by the river marking the point where convicts sentenced to transportation embarked for their journey to Australia.
8. Foucault, M. (1977). *Discipline and Punish – The Birth of the Prison*. London: Penguin. In this book Foucault saw these principles as a metaphor for all hierarchical societies and structures where the constant observance of the citizen or member is of increasing importance. Clearly a current issue. The UK is seen as a country with the highest level of CCTV coverage, speed cameras, reality TV shows, etc.
9. *The Times*, August 1st 1854, as quoted in Gregg, P. (1971) *A Social and Economic History of Britain 1760–1964)*, Third Edition. London: George & Harrop, p. 204.
10. By January 2011, plans were completed to ease the sewage problems of the enlarged city by building a twenty-four-mile super sewer from Hammersmith under the Thames to Beckton. Work commenced in 2014 and is scheduled to last until 2024. In contrast to 1858, local residents and conservationists are campaigning against the use of public parks, squares and facilities for access and disposal of soil, working day and night.
11. By 1990, the mileage had been halved.
12. The Crystal Palace was some 1,848 feet long and 68 feet high with a vast vaulted glass dome on top. It was later removed to high ground in Sydenham, South London, where it suffered a series of disasters by gales, fire and bankruptcy of its Trust. New design and development remain uncertain.
13. From *The Journal of Gideon Mantell* (1851). Quoted in Mitchell, R. (1963). *A History of London Life*. London: Penguin, p. 310.
14. The battle was commemorated by Sir Henry Newbolt's poem, 'Vitai Lampada,' which transposed the playing field of Eton to the great game of Empire, a poem quoted again at the start of the Great War, although that experience overwhelmed any idea that war was a game.

> The sand of the desert is sodden red,
> Red with the wreck of the square that broke:
> The Gatlings jammed and the colonel dead,
> And the Regiment blind with dust and smoke.
> The river of death has brimmed his banks,
> And England's far, and Honour a name
> But the voice of a schoolboy rallies the ranks:
> Play up! Play up! And play the game.

15. See Kipling's *The Man Who Would be King* (1888) and *Kim* (1901) in Kipling, R. (1994). *The Man Who Would Be King and Other Stories*. London: Wordsworth Classics; and Masters, J. (1951). *Night Runners of Bengal*. London: Michael Joseph. Masters J. (2000). *Nightrunners of Bengal*. London: Souvenir Press; and Masters, J. (1965). *Bhowani Junction*. London: Penguin.
16. In addition to this work, Octavia Hill was instrumental in founding the London School of Economics, the Charity Organisation Society and the National Trust.
17. It is interesting to note that the social reformer Beatrice Webb career had started her career as a volunteer in the East End of London in a block of flats which she described as 'catering for the aboriginals of London.'
18. The League of the Just was a group of German working men and communist groups originating in Paris. Its motto was 'All Men Are Brothers.' Its goals were 'The establishment of the Kingdom of God on Earth, based on the ideas of love of one's neighbour, equality and justice.' Gregg, *op. cit.*, p. 315.
19. Engels gave a clear definition of Communism in 1847. 'Communism is the doctrine of the conditions of the liberation of the proletariat. What is the proletariat? The proletariat is that class

in society which lives entirely from the sale of its labour and does not draw profit from any kind of capital; whose weal and woe, whose life and death, whose sole existence depends on the demand for labour...' Engels, F. (1914). 'Principles of Communism,' in *Selected Works, Vol. 1*. Moscow: Progress, pp. 81–97. Originally published in 1847.
20. Smiles, S. (2008). *Self-Help*, Oxford World's Classics. Oxford: Oxford University Press. First published in 1859.
21. Lombroso published *L'Uomo Delinquente* (1876) and *The Man of Genius* (1889). It is interesting to note that when studying female criminals he deduced that they were rare and showed few signs of degeneration because they had evolved less than men. He advocated that it was the female's natural passivity that withheld them from breaking the law, as they lacked the intelligence and initiative to become a criminal.
22. *The Times*, 8th September 1879, as quoted in Mitchell, R., *op. cit.*, p. 311.
23. It was these adventures that developed the mystery of 'Darkest Africa' from Stanley's account of his journey *In Darkest Africa* published in 1890. Since the Congo became independent and subsequently descended into chaos, another *Telegraph* journalist set out to retrace Livingstone's journey, although he had to travel independently as the paper would not insure him. His book, Butcher, T. (2008). *Blood River: A Journey to Africa's Broken Heart*. London: Vintage, was reviewed as a masterpiece. The film *Apocalypse Now*, Dir. Francis Ford Coppola, Omni Zoetrope, 1979, starring Martin Sheen, Marlon Brando and Robert Duvall, although set in Vietnam/Cambodia, develops the same theme and was based on Joseph Conrad's novella *Heart of Darkness*.
24. Like Catherine Booth of The Salvation Army, Annie Besant was concerned about the health of young women workers at the Bryant & May match factory. On June 23rd 1888, Annie published in her newspaper *The Link* an article, '*White Slavery in London*,' where she drew attention to the dangers of phosphorus and complained about the low wages paid to the women who worked at Bryant & May. The women who provided information for Annie's article were sacked. Annie responded by helping the women to form a Match Girls Union. After a three-week strike, the company was forced to make significant concessions, including the re-employment of the three victimised women.
25. Sims, G. R. (1899). 'Horrible London,' published in *The Daily News* and later as *How the Poor Live and Horrible London*. (2016). Guildford: Billing and Sons. Sims is generally remembered for his satirical monologue 'It is Christmas Day in the Workhouse.'
26. Cookson, M. D. (2001). *Green's Moral and Political Philosophy. A Phenomenological Perspective*. Oxford: Palgrave, p. 105.
27. Booth, C. (1902–03). *Life and Labour of the People in London*, Third Edition. London: Macmillan.
28. Rimmer, J. (1986). *Yesterday's Naughty Children. Training Ship, Girl's Reformatory and Farm School*. Manchester: Neil Richardson.
29. Durkheim, E. (1893). *The Division of Labour in Society*; (1895). *Rules of the Sociological Method*; (1897). *Suicide: A Study in Sociology*. Paris: University of France.
30. Weber, M. (2001). *The Protestant Ethic and the Spirit of Capitalism*. Like many of the early leaders of the Labour Party, Keir Hardie was a lay Methodist preacher. New York: Roxbury.
31. *The Communist Manifesto* (1848).
32. Some clarity about the lead up to World War I has been afforded by my granddaughter Aella Jordan-Edge whilst studying at the United Nations International School in Manhattan.
33. Winnicott, D. W. (1964). *The Child, the Family and the Outside World*. London: Penguin, p. 199.

TWO

1900–1934

A NEW CENTURY

> Land of hope and glory, mother of the free,
> How shall we extol thee, who are born of thee?
> Wider still and wider shall thy bounds be set;
> God, who made thee mighty, make thee mightier yet.
> – *Land of Hope and Glory*, lyrics by A. C. Benson[1n]

> The mode of production conditions the social, political and intellectual life processes in general. It is not the consciousness of men that determine their being, but, on the contrary, their social being that determines their consciousness.
> – Karl Marx (1859)[2]

> Good morning; good morning!' the General said
> When we met him last week on our way to the Line.
> Now the soldiers he smiled at are most of them dead,
> And we're cursing his staff for incompetent swine.
> "He's a cheery old card" grunted Harry to Jack
> As they slogged up to Arras with rifle and pack,
> But he did for them both with his plan of attack.
> – Siegfried Sassoon, 'The General' (1917)[3n]

INTERNATIONAL EVENTS

(*This chapter follows the First World War in a rough chronological sequence.*)

Unlike the democracies of Britain, France and America, in Germany, Russia and Austria-Hungary power was in the hands of individual rulers and perhaps therefore more prone to take a dramatic nationalistic stance in the face of real or perceived threats or actual disputes. In Germany and Russia, rulers were imposing more repressive domestic measures against the growing tide of Marxist inspired socialist movements, while also building up the idea of external threat to increase national unity. Events far away, for example a military defeat of Russia by Japan, the diplomatic defeat of Germany's bid to control Morocco and the increasing tensions in the Balkans, were paving the way to the greater conflict. Some alarms had led to action at home; the Royal Navy was strengthened, which, of course, increased suspicion in Germany, and in 1909 the Territorial Army and MI5 were established. Following an early initiative from Octavia Hill, more Army Cadet Corps were established, often in boys' schools. The shooting club started by Captain F. Richmond Coggan at Haberdashers' Aske's Hatcham School in South London in 1912 became a Cadet Corps in 1914 affiliated to the 8th Battalion Royal Fusiliers, a corps which would come to play a significant part in my life some 45 years later.

Further afield, in 1903 the King of Serbia had been assassinated and a more nationalistic, anti-Austrian feeling established. The spark that ignited the great conflict was provided on June 28th 1914 in Sarajevo by the young Serb Gavrilo Princip, who assassinated Archduke Franz Ferdinand, heir to the Austrian throne, and his wife. The treaties signed towards the end of the 19th century then formed a chain reaction which led to the Great War. In July, Austria declared war on Serbia, which led Russia to mobilise in Serbia's support. Russia saw itself as leader of the Slav nations whose security would be compromised if Austrian troops occupied the Dardanelles. Russia's rapid mobilisation was seen as a threat by Kaiser Wilhelm, who sought dominance in Europe and the empires across the world, then ruled by rival European nations. The German assumption that Russia would remain passive in its initial support of Austria was just one, but perhaps the determining one, of the tragic miscalculations that led to the first modern war. Germany declared war on Russia and France on August 1st and 3rd 1914. Moving quickly, German troops invaded Belgium in order to attack France. Britain, who had guaranteed Belgium neutrality, declared war on Germany on August 4th. Within the space of six weeks the nations of Europe had drifted into a war that would see death and mutilation on an unprecedented scale, Europe lose its pre-eminent place in the world to America and the seeds sown for further tragedies in the next hundred years.

Historians still debate the actual causes of the First World War and the post-war settlement. Did sensible established nations really just drift into such a tragic war? If the grip of the old 19th century alliances were neither a sufficient nor powerful enough explanation, then can the actions of both Russia and Germany be viewed as reactions to increasing pressure of discontent from poorer sections of their population being wooed by socialist or communist ideas? Troops were called from across the empires of the main combatants and of course the fighting extended to all but a few neutral states, with America drawn in decisively late in 1917.[4n] Industrialisation gave war a new meaning as weapons and ammunition could be made in unprecedented quantities, with a greater destructive power and greater profits for the manufacturers. A war which had commenced with the use of horses, airships and balloons, using strategies and tactics based on civilised war between the defined military forces, saw mechanised innovations as the Germans used poisonous gas and the Allies used tanks and aircraft (initially used for reconnaissance by both sides, but planes were soon developed as fighters and bombers with inevitable implications for civilian casualties). By 1916 the life expectancy of a pilot in France was 11 days, but Haddon Adams, who had volunteered for the Royal Flying Corps, gained a Military Cross for gallantry as a pilot in battle, survived. Although the slaughter of the trenches has carried forward in our communal memories, perhaps there was a more insidious outcome as mechanisation meant that a more impersonal means of delivering death was available. The long distance gunner, the well protected tank crew and, above all, the high level bomber could blot out the human consequences of the command to fire or the release bombs that could eliminate hundreds of other humans from the planet.

It was widely expected that, like other recent wars, this one would be quick, 'all over by Christmas,' and perhaps the speed with which it had started supported this optimistic view. This, and the strong patriotic feeling that our country and our great Empire (which now had a population of over 450 million) had to be defended, led to a rush by young, and not so young, men in Britain to join the Services. The national hero, Lord Kitchener, now serving as a government minister, used his image to run a very successful recruitment drive.[5n] Some four and a half million men volunteered for service. Most were fired by sheer patriotic determination to defend the Empire and all that it stood for; young men from small colonies and commonwealth countries were equally determined to defend the motherland. Some needed a push from their friends, 'Get in early before the rush,' and some a push from their fathers.[6n]

In June 1915 London was bombed by a Zeppelin raid and the following year one was shot down during a mass raid on the east coast by 14 airships. As a contrast to later experiences there is an account of a raid by the author H. M. Tomlinson (a relative of my wife) who was at home when he heard a sound he had heard in the trenches as a Zeppelin manoeuvred to drop bombs on suburban London. It seems to me to sum up the realisation of total war, a massive change in the history of war political morality and a glimpse of things to come.

> Guns, I said to myself, and went to the front door.
> Beyond the vague opposite shadows of some elms. Lights twinkled in the sky, incontinent sparks, as though glow lamps on an invisible pattern of wires switched on and off by an idle child. That was shrapnel … I heard the guns easily enough now, but they were miles away …
> A slender finger of brilliant light moved slowly across the sky, checked, and remained firmly accusatory, at something it had found in the heavens. It was a Zeppelin! … a celestial maggot stuck to the round of a cloud like a caterpillar on the edge of a leaf … War now would be not only between soldiers. In future wars, the place of honour would be occupied by the infants in their cradles. For war is not murder. Starving children is war, and it is not murder … Men will now creep up after dark, ambushed in safety behind the celestial curtains, and drop bombs on sleepers beneath, for the greater glory of some fine figment or another.
> It filled me not with wrath at the work of Kaisers and Kings, for we know what is possible with them, but with dismay that one's fellows are so docile and credulous that they will obey any order, however abominable. The very heavens had been fouled by this obscene and pallid worm, crawling over those eternal verities to which eyes had been lifted for light when night and trouble were over dark. God was dethroned by science. The eruptions

ceased … We found ourselves gazing at the familiar and shadowy peace of our suburb as we have always known it. It was not and never could be again, as once we had known it. The security of our own place had been based on the goodwill or indifference of our fellow-creatures everywhere. Tonight, over that obscure and unimportant street, we had seen a celestial portent illuminate briefly a little of the future of mankind.[7n]

British nurse Edith Cavell, who had been living in Belgium, soon found herself caring for wounded soldiers regardless of nationality. She also saw it as her duty to help British and French troops to escape the German occupation. She was arrested, and at 2am on October 12th 1915 she was shot. This was despite frantic efforts by American diplomats, the more passive British Foreign Office taking the view that Germans would never shoot a woman! Her last words, recorded by the chaplain as she stood before the firing squad, were 'I expected my sentence and believe it was just. Standing, as I do, in the view of God and eternity I realise that patriotism is not enough. I must have no hatred or bitterness to anyone.' The barbarity of her execution whipped up anti-German sentiment and increased the flow of volunteers. Her remarkable bravery ensured that she became a national heroine, and she was commemorated by a statue erected outside St Martin-in-the-Fields by Trafalgar Square, one of the London sites which helped inspire my own early anti-German feelings.

British and French territories in Egypt, North and Eastern Africa and Russia's southern borders were being threatened by the Ottoman Empire's alliance with Germany. The vast Ottoman Empire, already threatened from within by Turkish, Armenian and Arab revolts, suffered early defeats by the Russians in the Caucasus. The core Armenian resistance group formed an independent provisional government in May 1915; this served to exacerbate the suspicions and killings of Christian Armenians by the newly established Turkish government. While Turkey was allied with Germany, a core group feared that the Armenians would side with Russia. This was used as an excuse to attack them further, and between 1915 and 1920 some 1.5 million Armenians were massacred. The details of the exact authorisation, and the role of General Mustafa Kemal Atatürk, is heavily disputed. Within Britain and her Empire, however, such issues have been vastly outweighed by their defeat by Turkish troops defending the peninsular of Gallipoli which overlooked the Dardanelles Straits leading through the Bosphorus to the Black Sea.

Europe

The German Army met much stronger opposition than expected in Belgium, thus giving Britain time to launch the Expeditionary Force through the French Channel ports. Thus, instead of advancing directly to Paris, the Germans were pushed eastwards, where, exhausted by long marches in the heat of summer, they were driven back by the French army to the River Marne. Here the armies became bogged down in trench warfare for the winter. The next four years would see the horrors of prolonged trench warfare; years of close fighting over yards of territory gained or lost, initially with equipment and tactics more suited to the previous century. The young doctor and poet John McCrae patched up a close friend at his advanced post, but the guy was killed en route to the rear hospital. McCrae immediately wrote his well known poem 'In Flanders Fields.' McCrae was killed in 1918 having written the poem that would inspire remembrances on every anniversary:

> In Flanders fields the poppies blow
> Between the crosses, row on row,
> That mark our place; and in the sky
> The larks, still bravely singing, fly
> Scarce heard amid the guns below.
>
> We are the Dead. Short days ago
> We lived, felt dawn, saw sunset glow,
> Loved and were loved, and now we lie
> In Flanders fields.
>
> Take up our quarrel with the foe:
> To you from failing hands we throw
> The torch; be yours to hold it high.
> If ye break faith with us who die
> We shall not sleep, though poppies grow
> In Flanders fields.[8]

In Europe, some four hundred miles of trenches, stretching from the coast of Flanders to the Swiss border, became the avenues for a massive machine of repeated massacres of young men, the 'Flower of Europe.' In 1916 at Verdun the German attempt to break out involved two million men, half of whom became casualties together with 450,000 Frenchmen. The British counterattack on the Somme saw 420,000 dead, 20,000 on the first day. Lloyd George described it as 'The most gigantic, tenacious, grim, futile and bloody fight ever waged in the history of war.'[9] The film *All Quiet On The Western Front* gives a good picture of trench warfare, as does Robert Graves' 'Goodbye to All That,'[10n] but one of my precious possessions is *Bullets and Billets*[11] by Bruce Bairnsfather, whose realistic but humorous sketches of 'Old Bill' and his laconic sayings captured the public imagination. Bill, with his drooping moustache and wrapped in his greatcoat and balaclava, can often be seen surrounded by dead soldiers and horses. One cartoon (not reproduced in my book) shows Bill and his mate in a trench, shelling and gunfire all around. 'Well,' says Bill, if you knows of a better 'ole, go to it.' That saying was used as a play based on his accounts of the British soldier in the trenches. The phrase became a byword in my family, and many others, particularly when dodging bombs in WWII. Above all, of course, were the poets Sassoon,

Owen and Brooke who brought the horror of the trenches back home. One example of Siegfried Sassoon's bitter poetry will suffice:

> I knew a simple solider boy
> Who grinned at life in empty joy,
> Slept soundly through the lonesome dark
> And whistled early with the lark.
>
> In winter trenches, cowed and glum,
> With crumps and lice and lack of rum,
> He put a bullet through his brain.
> No one spoke of him again.
>
> You smug-faced cowards with kindling eye
> Who cheer when soldier lads march by,
> Sneak home and pray you'll never know
> The hell where youth and laughter go.[12]

Among those who survived to pursue an anti-war agenda was Vera Brittain, who had left her studies at Oxford to be a nurse throughout much of the war in which both her brother and fiancé were killed. Her experiences were published in her autobiography *Testament of Youth*, which became a best seller.[13] Before the Second World War she became a leading member of the Peace Pledge Union, criticising the saturation bombing of German cities. After the war she joined the Labour Party, but married and moved to America, where she had a son and daughter. Her daughter was Shirley Williams, who would become a cabinet minister in the Labour government of 1974.

Not surprisingly, 1916 saw the introduction of conscription in Britain for men between the ages of 18 and 41. Stalemate in the trenches and the heavy loss of men on both sides led to increased reliance on technical inventions to win, hence the poison gas, tanks and U-boats patrolling the eastern Atlantic in an attempt to starve civilian populations. In June 1917 London was bombed by 14 German aircraft. A postcard in my collection shows the U-boat UC95, the *Hun Pirate*, which was mined in the Dover Straits and exhibited on the Thames. On the Eastern Front, German troops conquered Poland and were forcing Russia out of the war, and into revolution. Troops and resources were therefore free to move westwards and may well have had an unbeatable effect on the Allies had the American troops, with their vast resources, not arrived in April 1917. On May 7th 1915 U-boats had sunk the passenger liner *Lusitania* sailing from New York to Liverpool. One thousand, one hundred and ninety-five people were drowned. The event caused a storm of protest across the world, particularly in the UK and USA (128 Americans were drowned). It was the increasing anti-German feelings and this tragedy that finally persuaded King George V to change the royal family's name from Saxe-Coburg and Gotha to Windsor in 1917.

Russia

With the German plan to capture Paris within six weeks abandoned, and the objective of quick victory in the west foiled, Germany decided to attack Russia, who was known to be weak and unprepared. The autocratic Tsar Nicholas II, faced with civilian and military disquiet following defeat by Japan, was forced in 1905 to publish the October Manifesto setting up a parliament (Duma) which proceeded to publish a sensible programme to democratise Russia and ease the incredible financial pressures on the rural poor. Faced with such radical proposals, Nicholas disbanded the Duma and subsequent bodies until a limited franchise of landowners elected a conservative and compliant body. Meanwhile, industrial disputes had risen from 2,000 in 1912 to 4,000 in 1914. These were met with fierce repression, including the shooting of 270 strikers in April 1912. The secret police then determinedly set about rooting out any revolutionary groups across all sections of society. By then Leon Trotsky had been exiled to Siberia and had escaped to the west and Vladimir Lenin had exiled himself. Thus by the time Germany declared war, fear and discontent had gripped peasants, the middle classes and the intelligentsia, who all looked more and more to the ideas of Marx as a model for a new society. The Tsar's standing was not helped by the eccentric behaviour of his wife and the malign influence of the priest Rasputin, or by the fact that he was under increasing pressure from revolutionary groups, strikes and public demonstrations, culminating in a general strike. In March 1917, the Tsar's troops refused to fire on strikers. When he tried to rally his troops for a counterattack against the advancing Germans, his troops preferred to go home and gather the harvest, events which led inevitably to his abdication.[14n]

In the absence of all authority, chaos ensued as different sections of the population sought to achieve their own ends by forming local groups, termed 'Soviets.' Broadly speaking, the rural poor sought land, the urban poor wanted food and workers wanted fair wages and fewer hours. As anarchy continued, the only thing that united the people was the search for resolution at home and peace on the military front. Late in 1917 the Germans agreed that Lenin and his group could cross Germany en route to Petrograd – anything to help the collapse of Russia. Trotsky then joined them from New York. It was the supreme skill of Lenin that he melded the demands of the different populations with the yearning for peace, thus seeming to meet the needs of each group. The Bolsheviks simply adopted the peasant's slogan 'Bread, Peace, Land.' The way was open for them, not so much to seize power, but to pick it up, a process completed on November 7th with the so-called storming of the Winter Palace. Subsequent divisions in the revolutionary movement brought together Lenin, Trotsky and the increasingly powerful Stalin. Lenin promoted Stalin to the post of General Secretary of the Communist Party in 1922, a post which he held for thirty-one years until his death in 1953, but following Lenin's stroke and subsequent death Stalin manipulated the different factions to enhance his power and establish himself as supreme leader (and effectively dictator), and he turned into a paranoid, vengeful and cruel leader. Trotsky, who had been Commander of the Red

Army with a reputation for bloody revenge, opposed Stalin and the increased bureaucracy of the new state and was exiled. He continued to oppose Stalin and urged action against the rise of fascism and therefore Stalin's pact with Hitler. He was killed on Stalin's orders in Mexico on August 20th 1940,^{15n} an early example of the long arm of the Russian State pursuing those seen as traitors.

The Middle East and Turkey

Early in the war, as the stalemate on the Western Front was fully understood, consideration was given to starting an Eastern Front which would divide German resources, attack its ally Turkey and thus secure Russia's continued use of its Black Sea ports, which required access through the Dardanelle Straits and Bosphorus. Constantinople had to be captured. A suggestion to bribe the Turks (whose nationalistic ideas were weakening their allegiance to the Ottoman rulers) was put aside, and, when an intelligence report from a Lt T. E. Lawrence stated that there were few troops defending the Dardanelles, Churchill (then First Lord of the Admiralty) supported the French proposal to use old naval vessels, proving useless against the German fleet in the Atlantic, in a bombardment that would then require minimum ground troops to occupy the peninsular of Gallipoli. The bombardment started in February 1915 but was defeated in March when three battleships were sunk by mines, a further three being badly damaged, with hardly any ships remaining effective. It was clear that ground troops would be required to silence the coastal gunners that had seen off the Allied Navy.

The invasion itself commenced in April 1915 on several beaches at the tip of the peninsula, with Australian and New Zealand troops landing further north in order to cut off a Turkish retreat or a deployment of reinforcements. Contrary to intelligence, the peninsula was actually defended by some 84,000 Ottomans commanded by a very able German general, with the central Turkish element led by Mustafa Kemal (later known as Atatürk) so that, in a chilling replay of the western trenches and a rehearsal of Dunkirk twenty-five years later, some Allied troops (most notably the Lancastrians and Irish) were mown down by well-placed machine-gun fire as they landed. Four months later the Allies decided to open a new front on Suvla Beach but the strategy never succeeded. In one engagement, while attempting to take and hold a particular piece of high ground, the Wellington Battalion of the New Zealand troops suffered 711 casualties from an original count of 760 men. The decision was taken to evacuate the peninsular and the last British troops had left by January 1916. The eleven-month campaign had cost just short of 100,000 lives with a further 237,000 wounded. Although the Ottomans lost nearly 56,000 lives, with 140,000 wounded, the Anzac forces had suffered over 10,000 dead with nearly 25,000 wounded, a toll that would cause lingering resentment and damage trust between these nations and Britain for many years. Anzac Day on April 25th is now a national holiday in both Australia and New Zealand.

The political consequences of this major defeat were significant for both sides. The UK Prime Minister, H. H. Asquith, was forced to accept a coalition government with

Conservative participation (a condition of which was Churchill's demotion) and had to concede the premiership to David Lloyd George. The fact that Labour now had six ministers appointed helped the feeling that all classes were fighting together in a common cause. (In fact, the Independent Labour Party (ILP) had been opposed to the war and the Labour group split in 1917 to form the National Labour Party, pledged to socialism and the common ownership of the means of production.) Victory at Dardanelles boosted the Ottoman morale and led to further victories, including the British surrender in Mesopotamia and the invasion of Sinai with the aim of pushing the British from the Suez Canal and Egypt – in 1917 in Palestine the Allies had suffered terrible losses in a failed attempt to capture Gaza. Of 800 men in the Isle of Wight Rifles, only 62 survived.[16n]

The Sharif of Mecca, forming a pan-Arabic nationalist challenge to Ottoman rule, sought to ally himself with the French and British, the latter giving him written assurances that assistance in the war would be rewarded with an Arab empire when hostilities ceased. The British then sent the newly promoted Captain T. E. Lawrence to advise and support. By using his extensive knowledge of Arabia, local languages and cultures, Lawrence persuaded the separate tribal leaders to co-ordinate their actions in line with British strategic objectives. In 1917 the port of Aqaba fell to them, thus providing the Allies with an important supply base. In December General Allenby walked through the Jaffa gate of Jerusalem. By September 1918 the Arab forces had gained in strength, enabling Australian troops to occupy Damascus and 'Lawrence of Arabia' to lead the Arab troops to receive the Ottoman surrender.

In the middle of all this, the Bolsheviks, having delved into the Russian archives, published a document that provided clear evidence of how the evil imperial powers operated. (A major precedent for the WikiLeaks of the 21st century.) This was the infamous Sykes–Picot agreement of 1916, by which the Foreign Office and France, anticipating the collapse of the Ottoman Empire (and with Russia's agreement), had arranged a secret agreement as to how the territories would be divided up. In placing parts of Arabia under French or British mandate and leaving Palestine for international administration, it bore no relation to the assurances already given to the Arabs by the British Army and so emotionally carried forward by Lawrence. The Anglo-French agreement is said to have been in part due to the need to gain the sympathy of the Jewish lobby in the hope that America's entry to the war would be eased.

Similar motivations lay behind the formal declaration made in November 1917 by the British Foreign Secretary A. J. Balfour to Lord Rothschild, leader of the Jewish community in Britain. This short letter expressed sympathy with Zionist aspirations to establish a national home in Palestine and promised the government's best endeavours to facilitate this objective provided that 'nothing shall be done which may prejudice the civil and religious rights of existing non-Jewish communities in Palestine.'[17n] Lawrence emerged from the war as a significant hero, publishing *Seven Pillars of Wisdom* then retreating into a series of alter egos before his death at the age of 46 in a motorcycle accident.[18n] Examination of his life, his actual role in the war and subsequent downfall have carried forward to the present day by historians, playwrights[19n] and film makers, but in no way do they bear comparison or proportion with the bloody conflicts that have consumed the region in subsequent years: the deterioration in western/Arab relations in the light of the different 'dishonest' assurances given, and the result of Jewish immigration and the establishment of Israel after WWII.

Peace

Eventually the heavily defended last German line of defence, the Hindenburg Line, was breached, and, although there had been no significant invasion of German soil, the Armistice was signed on November 11th 1918. The Allies came together to sign a series of peace treaties, the most important of which was the Versailles Treaty in June 1919. The American Congress refused to ratify the treaty.

Some eight million Allied troops had lost their lives: America lost 126,000, Britain lost more than 500,000, most of whom were under 30 years old and disproportionally from the upper social classes. The Axis powers lost four million troops. If civilian casualties and all operations are included, the final death toll was about 40 million. This was described as 'the greatest sexual catastrophe ever suffered by civilised Man.'[20] In Germany alone there were over half a million war widows, most of whom would never re-marry. To appreciate the full impact of these deaths, the effects of the deadly influenza pandemic that started early in 1918 should be added. Partly due to the demobbed troops returning home from across the globe, some 50 million people died, one-fifth of the total world population.

Many of the troops who returned were so traumatised by their experiences that they were 'destroyed men,' incapable of fully reintegrating themselves into civilian life, or keeping their traumas hidden within a lifelong depressive state. The nations turned to mourning and memorials. The Cenotaph was erected in Whitehall and the idea of a tomb for an unknown soldier was developed, with some hesitation. A body was found, so decomposed that it could not be identified, and transported with six barrels of Flanders earth from France across the Channel and by train to London.[21n] After a two-minute silence following the chimes of Big Ben at 11 o'clock on November 11th 1920, the special coffin paused at the Cenotaph and the King placed his wreath watched by the largest crowd that London had ever seen. In Westminster Abbey the coffin was buried under the imported earth in the presence of 100 holders of the Victoria Cross. The inscription 'The Unknown Warrior' was agreed rather than the original 'Unknown Comrade,' which was thought to smack of Bolshevism. The tomb also carries an adaptation of a biblical quote (2 Chronicles 14–16): 'They buried him among the kings, because he had done good toward God and toward his house.' In the first week, a million and a quarter people filed past the grave and it remains one of the most visited graves in the world. Every night since November 11th 1929 at the Menin Gate memorial at Ypres, the great memorial to the unknown dead, a trumpeter sounds the 'Last Post.'

As peace was declared and the terrible cost of this unnecessary war started to be calculated, the nature of the political and economic risks emerged. As troops on both sides had become weary of trench fighting and had lost confidence that their commanders would ever find a solution, some started to look towards socialist ideas, and perhaps the revolutionary leaders in Russia, as offering possible ways out of the slaughter. To some extent this was a realisation that total war had undermined the individual freedoms of old Laissez-faire beliefs as governments had of necessity taken control of all aspects of life. Western politicians of course saw events in Russia as dreadful forebodings that revolution may spread, and in fact in some governments were already being openly challenged by Marxist or socialist movements. The socialist or communist ideas discussed at the front led to mutiny by troops in Folkestone, the creation of nascent 'Soviets' in the Service Corps at Grove Park and Kempton, riots in Glasgow and Belfast and the deployment of divisional troops in Calais to control a mutiny.

Peace was agreed through a variety of treaties, but the German Treaty limited Germany's ability to raise an army to 100,000 men, demanded the removal of all Germany's colonial territories and fixed vast financial penalties at the totally unrealistic sum of $33 billion. There existed a significant need for such payments to enable the Allied powers to repay the money borrowed from America in order to fund their own war efforts. Advice that the economic power of Germany should be incorporated into a post-war settlement was ignored, so the world went forward as if Germany and Russia did not exist, a formula that inevitably led to growing discontent in the defeated nations and an increased risk of future conflict. President Woodrow Wilson determinedly sought a mechanism that would prevent yet another European war and collapse of world trade while also spreading the values of equity and democracy across the world by writing these values into every treaty and territorial mandate. The Council of the League of Nations met in St James's Palace, London, early in 1920, while the League Headquarters was established in Switzerland, which had remained neutral. Although its aims of world peace, welfare and the spread of positive values were laudable, the League was severely limited by the fact that isolationist America, fearing communist Russia and a disgraced Germany, were not members. The League had limited powers, and no access to military might which could enforce its rulings, an impotent position made clear in 1923 when France and Belgium invaded the industrial area of Germany as a result of Germany's failure to pay the post-war compensation. How could the League be credible if one of its leading nations ignored it? It has been argued that, by accepting the power and boundaries of nation states, the post-war settlements presaged future problems. If the traditional concept of dynastic loyalty now gave way to a state deriving its sovereignty from the people, it was possible that significant minorities would seek to exclude residents who did not 'belong.' Point four of the Nazi Programme, launched by Hitler on November 24th 1920 stated that 'None but members of the nation may be citizens of the state.' As so many future conflicts would show, groups who, whether for religious or ethnic reasons, owed loyalty beyond national boundaries would cause trouble.[22]

It was the League which sanctioned the territorial divisions in Europe and granted mandates in the Middle East. Although not granting permanent territorial ownership, mandates basically allowed the mandated powers to run the new countries under the rather weak supervision of the League. The addition of these territories marked the zenith of Britain ruling other lands. From 1920, the reach of the Empire shrank. A condition of the Ottoman Caliphate's retention of Turkey was the occupation by Allied troops of Constantinople, a situation which provided impetus to the Turkish National Movement led by Kemal Atatürk through the Turkish War of Independence. Having ousted the Ottomans, and seeing British troops leave Constantinople, Atatürk set about creating a new secular state in 1923. He banned the wearing of the fez as it had been a mark of religious subjugation, insisted that the linguistic professors create an entirely new language in six months and created the new structures of state underpinned by free education for all. In short, he is quite a hero of mine, not least because of the remarkable memorial he had erected above Anzac Cove, the inscription on which reads

> Those heroes that shed their blood and lost their lives … you are now lying in the soil of a friendly country. Therefore rest in peace. There is no difference between Johnnies and the Mehmets where they lie side by side here in this country of ours … You the mothers who sent their sons from far away countries, wipe away your tears. Your sons are now lying in our bosom and are in peace. Having lost their lives on this land they have become our sons as well.

There was much concern across Europe that the physical conditions of the population should be raised; housing standards were improved, clinics opened and, as just one example in 'Red Vienna,' Marxist councillors offered clothing and other hygienic aids to 'incurable families' in exchange for contracts that enforced good standards of parenting.[22] The fact had to be faced that the countries that had fought so determinedly had not only bankrupted their stock of manpower, but also risked total financial ruin. The aim of the victors, particularly France, was to seek recompense from Germany and prevent any further desire by that country to invade neighbours again, then, with Britain, to carve up the disrupted territories in such a way as to increase their world power, maintain their empires and secure a lasting peace. Britain, aware of growing discontent with her rule in the Indian subcontinent and the East, sought to strengthen her influence in the Middle East. The defeated Ottoman Empire was carved up, and the states of Turkey, Lebanon, Palestine, Iran (Persia) and Iraq were created under the mandates of France (Lebanon) and Britain (all the rest).

The British position in Palestine had of course already been compromised by conflicting promises and declarations, and from 1921 onwards Britain was increasingly engaged in quelling Arab protests at Jewish immigration. In that same year, the British promoted the cause of Reza Khan, Commander of the Persian Cossacks, who in 1925 established himself as Shah of Persia, instituting a repressive regime against religious sects (thus earning enmity against Britain), although by the Second World War he favoured Germany, which naturally enough led Britain to re-occupy the country, depose the Shah and appoint his son to reign. Yet another section of Iranian society had good reason to hate the British.

Russia

In Russia the Bolsheviks held on to power until the end of the war but then had to withstand counterattacks from royalist and right-wing groups, quietly financed by Britain, France, America and other western powers. However, by 1920 a much reduced Russia emerged as a powerful country under the leadership of a well organised and structured Communist Party. It is not difficult to see how the intellectual appeal of communist ideology, the achievement for the long oppressed working people of Russia, the rosy reports given by returning prisoners of war and the pain imposed by what was seen as an imperial war, where the long term interests of capitalism were paramount, led to a wide acceptance of that ideology and the relative popularity of communism as a legitimate political activity. As the post-war economic catastrophe removed many of the political and intellectual certainties, the main choices seen by many were communism, which seemed to be working well, and fascism, which espoused an abhorrent set of values. Thus, many intellectuals joined the Communist Party as a counter to more right-wing movements.

An account of such a commitment is the three-part novel *The Spiral Ascent*, which charts the career of the fictional poet Alan Sebrill first caught by Marx's comment that 'Philosophers hitherto have merely interpreted the world. The thing is to change it.'[23] After the 1917 revolution, journalist and author Arthur Ransome became drawn into the movement – he fell in love with Trotsky's personal secretary and they married back in England. It was, however, the central control and organising power of the Party itself as a tool that was to be copied in many revolutionary movements, which spread across the world for the next sixty years. In Russia the peasants gained the land, but the Party had to face the task of converting, governing and modernising the vast population that it now commanded.

Post-War Britain

In Britain, trade union membership rose from 4 million in 1914 to more than 8 million in 1920. The same year saw the formation of the Communist Party of Great Britain with a membership of 2,500 rising to 10,000 during the 1926 general strike and to more than 50,000 by the end of World War II. Many leading intellectuals subscribed to the cause and held up the social and political achievements of Russia as models of a successful society. Stalin, who now ruled with an iron fist, had enforced collectivisation across agriculture and industry. As devastating as these policies were to the workers, the obsessive commitment to successive 'five-year plans' helped Russia avoid the worst effects of the coming economic crash. In 1932–1933 central government intervention in agriculture produced a famine which led to between five and ten million deaths, a fact which was suppressed and certainly not acknowledged by visitors, including H. G. Wells and the Webbs, who continued to promote the virtues of Soviet life. These very widely held views were to play a significant part in British life for many years, among other things providing the climate from which the major so-called Cambridge Soviet spies were recruited and worked until late in the 20th century. The Party continued to be politically active until, some 30 years later, news of Stalin's cruel repressions in Russia and its satellite states caused a major drop in membership and credibility, finally moving to the margins after the fall of the Berlin Wall in 1989.

The Great Depression

Before the war, Britain's industrial exports and surplus population had gone to her Empire and the USA, but in 1918 America, whose farmers and industrialists had benefited greatly during the war years by Europe's need to stave off starvation and have an endless supply of military equipment and ammunition, decided to resume the isolationist policies that had been breached by participation in the war. By 1929 America contributed 42% of the world output, while that from the three major European countries together was reduced to 28%. America was also the greatest creditor as other Allies had had to borrow to pay the costs of war; indeed, it is impossible to consider the forthcoming collapse without America. It was the greatest exporter and, next to Britain, the leading importer. The boundless prosperity of the immediate post-war years, the satisfaction of instant gratification by consumption of radios (boosted by the total availability of electricity), cars, air travel and, perhaps most significantly, bonds and stocks, had all been financed by credit. My uncle Ernie, who was struggling to support his family in Canada, worked as a salesman, but had an early success criticised as it was a cash sale – the company could make more out of credit.

Banks and finance houses had used the public's willingness to buy wartime 'Liberty Bonds' to persuade people that post-war stocks would be just as safe. Celebrities led the way. Everyone could make a fortune and the American Dream would come true. The value of stocks went up and up, inflating a great financial bubble. As the slump took hold, both American imports and exports fell by 70%, with devastating effects on its own economy and that of the rest of the world. A policy of unlimited credit by small local banks, which had boosted demand beyond any normal market expectation and with no tradition of central control, meant that decisions were made by local managers with only a limited view of wider economic conditions. (Although a Federal Reserve facility had been put in place early in the century, it chose not to intervene, the Republican government believing that market forces would resolve the issue.)

In September 1929, a sudden loss of confidence led to the collapse of stocks and share prices, later known as the Wall Street Crash. On 'Black Thursday' (October 24th), many investors panicked. Ultimately, this led to the suicide of bankers and businessmen who were unable to face the sudden loss of self-belief and faith in American capitalism. (For the religious values set so deeply in the American psyche, it followed that if success was earned, failure was deserved.) Winston Churchill walked down Wall Street having lost a fortune. Some $25 billion of personal wealth was lost and 3,000 banks closed. A stock trader at the time recalled the events:

> In 1929, it was strictly a gambling casino with loaded dice. The few sharks taking advantage of the multitude of suckers ... I saw shoe-shine boys buying $50,000 worth of stock with $500 down. Everything was built on hope. Now if you want to buy $100 of stock you have to put up $80. In those days you could put up $8 or $10. That was really responsible for the collapse. The slightest shake up caused calamity because people didn't have the money required to cover the other $90 or so.
>
> Jesse [who was in his late 60s but refused to retire on $50,000 a year traded short on grain] Ben ... who was in Europe told him there was not going to be a war. When I was in Argentina I learnt that Germany had invaded Poland. Poor Jesse was on the phone. 'Art you have to save me.' I refused being so far away. A couple of months later I was back in New York with Jesse waiting for me in my office ... he had lost everything he could lay his hands on. He asked me for a $5,000 loan which I of course gave him. Three days later Jesse had gone to eat breakfast ... went to the lavatory and shot himself. They found a note made out to me for $5,000. This was the man who said, 'What's the use of having ten million if you can't have big money?'[24n]

While every country in the world was badly hit by the Great Depression, the actual and psychological consequences for America probably lasted longer. The plight of the urban poor in soup kitchens in shanty towns such as Hooverville and the plaintive song 'Brother, Can You Spare A Dime?' was a shameful thing to accept for a country with such complete faith in the virtue of capitalism. In addition, the rural population suffered badly in 1930 when a severe drought blew soil away from the vast over-farmed and over-grazed prairies of the southwestern plains. Some 400,000 people were forced to move westwards to the promise of a new life in the rich coastal areas. The experience of these people is well captured by John Steinbeck in his novel *The Grapes of Wrath*:

> And then the dispossessed were drawn west ... families, tribes, dusted out, tractored out ... They streamed over the mountains hungry and restless, restless as ants, scurrying to find work to do, to lift, to push, to cut anything, any burden to bear, for food. Like ants scurrying for work, for food and most of all land.[25]

For most of this period, President Hoover had remained opposed to any intervention by the promotion of public works. The 1932 election saw a landslide victory for Franklin D. Roosevelt, the rich governor of New York. In March 1933 he immediately passed legislation to stabilise the banking system and launched his New Deal of public works in close association with labour unions and minority groups. A man described as ordinary and very pleasant gave hope and leadership to a nation in distress. Stable institutions had very rapidly collapsed, and with no ready answers to a totally new situation he determined to try a radical solution and, in the best American tradition, to try another if the first one failed. In his inaugural speech on March 4th 1933, he proclaimed that this was the time to 'speak the truth, the whole truth,' and promised that America would revive and prosper again: 'So first of all, let me assert my firm belief that the only thing we have to fear is fear itself, nameless, unreasoning, unjustified terror which paralyses needed efforts to convert retreat into advance.' Excoriating the financiers and money changers, he pledged himself and the nation to restore the true social values in place of profit. 'Small wonder that confidence languishes, for it thrives only on honesty, on honor, on the sacredness of obligations, on faithful protection, and on unselfish performance; without them it cannot live.' To my mind, there have been only two inaugural addresses since then that have so uplifted the spirit of that great nation. The new administration strengthened the regulating authorities, which in turn would be relaxed fifty years later to allow the great financial crisis in the early years of the 21st century.

The ability of other countries to protect their own economies was severely restricted by the fact that the value of their currencies was tied to gold. Governments therefore had to face a decision whether or not to abandon the internationally recognised and valued gold standard or to expose their citizens to the full effects of the Depression. In general, those countries that abandoned the standard early suffered less.

India

An Imperial Conference took place in 1926 that gave the major white colonies dominion status within the British Commonwealth. The exclusion of India, partly due to the Balfour letter of 1917 (see Reference 22) and the fact that one-third of the British Army was garrisoned there, divided Indian opinion between those that would settle for dominion status and those that sought complete independence. Four years later, the Indian lawyer and civil rights campaigner Mahatma Ghandi started his campaign for independence; this would last for seventeen years and end in his assassination, with the Indian subcontinent divided along religious grounds into the independent states of India and Pakistan.

NATIONAL EVENTS

The new century saw a quickening in the pace of social change. First the country faced the death of the long-serving Queen Victoria, dying in the arms of her grandson Kaiser Wilhelm II, who had resisted the family's requests to stay away. This irritation and lack of civility between the Kaiser and the new King continued throughout the nine years of Edward's reign. As the news of Victoria's death circulated through London, silent crowds came out to walk the streets to try to come to terms with the end of her sixty-three-year reign. The crowd's reactions included, 'Ah, she felt the war too much,' or 'What a pity she can't know how sorry we are – she'd be glad to know we were so very sorry,' or 'She's been a good Queen.' Edward VII was crowned in August 1902, the ceremony having been delayed by an operation for appendicitis supervised by Lord Lister (the founder of sterile procedures, a key figure at King's College Hospital) who thus became a national hero. Edward was crowned with Alexandra his Queen, although he resolutely refused to give up his mistress, the socialite Alice Keppel.

The young, socially remote, Somerset Maugham was then working in the slums of Lambeth as a trainee doctor. He remembers,

> For here I was in contact with what I most wanted, life in the raw. In those three years I must have witnessed pretty well every emotion of which man is capable. It appealed to my dramatic instinct ... I saw how men died. I saw how they bore pain. I saw what hope looked like, fear and relief; I saw the dark lines that despair drew on a face; I saw courage and steadfastness. I saw faith shine in the eyes of those who trusted in what I could only think was an illusion, and I saw the gallantry that made a man greet the prognosis of death with an ironic joke because he was too proud to let those about him see the terror of his soul.[26]

The novelist E. M. Forster drew on the strict class divisions in Britain at this time. Detailing the relationship between the gentile orphaned Schlegel sisters and the poor clerk Leonard in *Howards End*, he dramatically illustrated the fragile nature of life in the growing and widening middle class, the near impossibility of upward mobility and the fear of failure:

> We are not concerned with the very poor. They are unthinkable, and only to be approached by the statistician or the poet ... The boy, Leonard Best, stood at the extreme verge of gentility. He was not in the abyss, but he could see it, and at times people whom he knew had dropped in, and counted no more. He knew that he was poor, and he would admit it: he would have died sooner than confess any inferiority to the rich ... Had he lived some centuries ago, in the brightly coloured civilisations of the past, he would have had a definite status, his rank and his income would have corresponded. But in his day the angel of democracy had arisen, enshadowing the classes with leathern wings, and proclaiming 'All men are equal – all men, that is to say, who possess umbrellas' and so he was obliged to assert gentility, lest he slipped into the abyss where nothing counts, and the statements of democracy were inaudible ...[27]

The mourning period following Queen Victoria's death came to an end; the return of troops from the Boer War and the crowning of a king who enjoyed the whirl of the social scene signalled party time, a situation graphically described to my daughter 82 years later by Edie Glover's young brother Charlie at his home in Florida. Victory against the Boer restored the national sense of security and Britain's continued dominance of the world was no longer in doubt, a feeling perhaps justified by the fact that one-quarter of the population of the world was then under British rule. It is interesting to note that this sense of power was enhanced by the growing power of the City of London as a principal financial centre. In Edward's reign, London was responsible for an amazing 44% of global investment, an outward looking view which worked against investment in domestic industry and consequently future prosperity. My family no doubt shared the feeling that to be British was to be on top of the world. How could anything possibly go wrong?

Elsewhere, aspiration to nationhood was slowly replacing the dynastic or religious loyalties of the previous century, uprisings were challenging Imperial Russia and the Ottoman Empire was divided to form the Balkan States of Bulgaria, Serbia, Greece and in due course Turkey. The new nation states, defined by geographical boundaries and common cultures, 'looked to their populations for their sovereignty and legitimacy, thus the presence of other ethnic groups inside its borders could not but seem a reproach, threat or challenge to those who believed in the principle of national self-determination.'[28] Europe, before, during and after the two world wars, and Africa, the Balkans and the Middle East into the 21st century, would certainly witness the tragic results of that process.

As the new century became established, urbanisation, the migration of the population within Europe and increased education all played a part in the dissemination of Marx's ideas and the establishment of socialist and labour movements across the continent. In the democratic nations, where classic liberalism had already given way to some state intervention, welfare measures were taken to relieve the plight of the poorest people. Revolution had to be avoided at all costs, particularly as economic decline was making workers less secure and liable to search for alternative economic and political ideas. Britain moved piecemeal into such provision, moving forward or pausing in relation to the need to deal with a series of crises across the Empire which demanded government attention abroad. As the journalist George Sims asked, 'Is it too much to ask that in the intervals of civilising the Zulu and improving the conditions of the Egyptian fellah the Government should turn its attention to the poor of London to see if it could remedy this terrible state of things.'[29]

The Town Planning Act (1909) stopped any further building of the back-to-back dwellings which housed so much dire poverty. New ideas for urban living were implemented in Hertfordshire with the first Garden City at Letchworth, which, unlike the entirely residential Hampstead, had been planned complete with its own industries. The Workers Educational Association (WEA) was formed and charters were granted to Birmingham University in 1900 and to Leeds in 1904. Robert Baden-Powell, returning from South Africa as the Hero of Mafeking (see Chapter 1), launched the Boy Scout movement, writing *Scouting for Boys* in 1908 (reprinted in 2004). The idea borrowed heavily on the public school system of monitors and prefects, where boys carried responsible roles, and was built around well established Victorian values of fair play, honesty and service to society. The movement started with a trial adventure camp on Brownsea Island in Poole Harbour with twenty boys from a cross section of society, and his insistence on a social mix remains central to the movement. Baden-Powell himself thought that 'we are all Socialists,' although he did not see this in the normal political sense; rights were important but only after duty had been fulfilled. Although latterly criticised as grooming boys for the 'great game' of Empire, my view is that Baden-Powell's values were more naïve and his motivation more straightforward. In part he was responding to the revelation about the poor state of health among army recruits, concern about the increasing numbers of relatively poor urban underclass and the need for meaningful leisure activities. Let's have fun and fair play. Soon after the First World War, the movement had been enthusiastically joined by over half a million boys worldwide from 'any nation, any class, any colour'.[30n]

In Britain, the newly formed ILP was a new actor on the political stage between the old Liberal and Conservative Unionist parties. Under the leadership of Keir Hardie it was not explicitly socialist, not avowedly trade unionist ('more Methodist than Marxist'[31n]), but it was determined to fight for an independent representation in Parliament which would campaign for better conditions for the working class. Any candidate standing as a representative of the ILP, the trades unions or the various socialist groups agreed that if elected they would generally obey a Labour whip. In 1906 this grouping became simply the Labour Party. It has been argued, and with the benefit of hindsight I see the virtue in it, that the core weakness of the new party was its failure to spell out and commit to a clear philosophy. Thus it defined itself in relation to the underdog in a capitalist society, fighting for the poor in a reactive manner rather than spelling out any clear vision of a New Jerusalem.

In the election of 1906, twenty-nine members, including Hardie and Ramsay MacDonald, were returned to Parliament, albeit one with a Liberal majority of 346. Even the defeated Conservative leader perceived the change in public attitude: 'We are face to face (no doubt in milder form) with the socialistic difficulties which loom so large on the continent. Unless I am much mistaken the election of 1906 inaugurates a new era ... a new order coming from the people of this country ... It is a quiet, but certain, revolution, as revolutions come in a constitutional country.'[32] This public mood and the effect on the Labour representatives and allies in both the Liberal and Conservative parties was felt immediately. The Liberal Government had to abandon the original Trade Dispute Bill for the more radical Act passed in 1906 which gave trades unions immunity from prosecution.[33n] Two ministers played a key role in these pre-war years: David Lloyd George, in his mid 40s, an emotional reformer and great Welsh non-conformist orator from a poor family, and Winston Churchill, some ten years his junior, born in Blenheim Palace, part of the Duke of Marlborough's family. He had entered Parliament in 1901 as a Conservative, but moved steadily to the left and joined the Liberal Party in 1904.[34n]

The Suffragettes

A striking example of socialistic ideas adopted within 'families of quality' and another facet of radical ideas developed in Manchester was provided by Richard and Emmeline Pankhurst, who moved there from London in the 1890s with their son and three daughters so that Richard could expand his work as a barrister. Emmeline was an early member of the ILP and friend to Keir Hardie, Tom Mann and other leading members. Following Richard's death in 1898, Emmeline took a job as local registrar, also opening a fancy goods shop selling William Morris prints among other items.[35] Possessing remarkable energy, Emmeline was elected to the National Council of the ILP, taking two of her daughters to their annual conference in 1901, an event which brought daughter Christabel out of her long period of mourning. Being denied entry to her chosen legal profession led to a high level of resentment, which, with the help of more radical women working with factory girls, propelled her into the cause of women's suffrage.

In 1901 the ILP conference had unanimously passed Christabel's motion that 'In order to improve the economic and social condition of women, it is necessary to take immediate steps to secure the granting of the suffrage to women on the same terms as it may be granted to men.'[36] Following a series of rather personal disputes and the recruitment to the cause of her mother, the Women's Social and Political Union was formed as a separate organisation in 1904. In the following years the women became increasingly convinced that the male dominated Parliament would never accede to their cause and thus became more determined to take direct action. On October 13th 1905 Christabel and a colleague disrupted a meeting addressed by Churchill, who, when they both chose to go to prison rather than pay the fine, said he 'hoped the quiet and seclusion may soothe their fevered brain.'[37]

When it became certain that the new Liberal Government was not going to act, the women invaded both the Prime Minister's car and residence. Their arrest caught the attention of the national press, who named them 'suffragettes.' By the end of 1906 there were twenty-one suffragettes in prison. The following year, Labour's annual conference rejected a motion in support of women's suffrage not because they disagreed with the principle but because they found the proponents intolerable. Emmeline and Christabel resigned. The following year there was a mass demonstration in Hyde Park attended by nearly half a million supporters and addressed by H. G. Wells, Thomas Hardy and George Bernard Shaw. When the Prime Minister, Herbert Asquith, refused to meet them, stones were thrown through the windows of 10 Downing Street with the cry that it will be bombs next time.

Emmeline and her daughter served twelve and ten weeks in prison, respectively, which only served to whip up more public support. In late 1910, further frustrated by the Government's refusal to pass legislation, a group of women vandalised their way through Central London, leading inevitably to further prison sentences. In 1913 Emily Davison was killed as she ran on to the Epsom Derby racecourse trying to interfere with the King's horse 'Anmer.' Christabel fled to Paris where she stayed until 1914. While raising funds in America, Emmeline Pankhurst delivered a fierce speech justifying militant action:

> As long as women consent to be unjustly governed, they can be, but directly women say 'we withhold our consent, we will not be governed any longer so long as that government is unjust.' Not by the force of civil war can you govern the weakest woman … No power on earth can govern a human being, however feeble, who withholds his or her consent …

we have brought the government of England to this position, that it has to face this alternative: either women are to be killed or women are to have the vote … Human life for us is sacred, but we say if any life is to be sacrificed it shall be ours; we won't do it to ourselves, but we will put the enemy in the position where they will have to choose between giving us freedom or giving us death.[38n]

As war broke out, the women's movement realised that agitation would be futile while men were being killed in France, and therefore turned their attention to supporting the war effort by volunteering for tough jobs vacated by the men now fighting abroad. By the end of the war it was politically impossible to resist an argument that women should have the same voting rights as men. In 1918 the suffrage was extended to all men over the age of twenty-one and women over the age of thirty. It was a further ten years before women and men achieved equal voting rights at 21 years of age and 1949 before the principle of one person one vote became a reality.

Monarchy

In May 1910 it was 'King Edward is dead, God save King George V,' and another good reason for celebration. The Wood and Glover families would certainly have followed the well established tradition that any event happening in London called for their participation and a good old 'knees-up.' King George would see the most dramatic and violent changes of any modern monarch in the 26 years of his reign. The new King, who had at least actually visited the colonies, travelled to India to be crowned Emperor of India and attend the extraordinary last Great Durbar in December 1911, but by the time of his death the concept of British rule over an Empire was a ghost, his subjects devastated by war, economic depression and political upheavals. Within seven years his first cousins Tsar Nicholas of Russia and Kaiser Wilhelm of Germany had both been removed from power by popular revolution.

Ireland

Having virtually ended the career of Gladstone at the end of the previous century, the 'Irish Question' smouldered on as the majority Catholic population, faced with the political and economically powerful and intransigent Protestant minority, became more nationalistic. The nationalists, boosted by migrants overseas, particularly in America, who deeply resented the rich 'asset stripper' British who had forced them to quit their native land, moved to the more radical and militaristic position of Fenianism. The awful history of the English and their first and closest colony was characterised by the lack of any appreciation of local culture that had been one positive aspect of rule of the 'lesser breeds without the law' in distant lands. A possible Jungian explanation is the effect of the imaginative, romantic and expressive Irish personality on the repressed English. Whatever the explanation, it appears that Parliamentarians failed to grasp the high levels of feeling on both sides in Ireland and the extent to which both were preparing for violent action. So the Home Rule Bill, introduced in 1912 and eventually passed in 1914 (although implementation was delayed until after the war) solved nothing; faced with its implementation the Protestants demanded partition and formed the Ulster Volunteer Force, which by 1913 had 90,000 members – a move which naturally led the Catholic population to form the Irish Voluntary Army.

Due to a high degree of sympathy and close personal relationships with Unionists, insisting that the law must be obeyed led to something approaching mutiny from the higher echelons of the British Army. The King could see partition as the only solution. It seemed that the future of Ireland was more likely to be settled by violence on the ground rather than any parliamentary process, although, in another strange twist in this local conflict, when war was declared millions of Irishmen joined up to fight for the Empire that they so longed to leave.

The names associated with the Irish conflict have passed into legend, whether romantically like the poet W. B. Yeats and the playwright J. M. Synge, or politically and militarily like Edward Carson, who led the Protestant Union movement, or Maud Gonne (who had started doing social work among the starving peasantry in the western counties and had returned to Ireland after active anti-British action in the Boer War), Roger Casement, Patrick Pearse, Michael Collins, James Connelly and Eamon de Valera. On Easter Monday 1916 the decision was taken by the republican movement to attack key buildings in Dublin in the belief that British forces were occupied in Europe. Action would increase support for the cause and there was an expectation that Germany would supply arms. In the event the supply ship was blocked, but at midday Pearse led his followers to the General Post Office where he announced the formation of the Republic of Ireland. Two days later, on Wednesday April 26th, the British Army counterattacked using artillery, and by the Saturday the rebels had surrendered, although 500 soldiers had been killed. The prisoners were marched through Dublin to the sounds of booing and jeering, more than twelve of the leaders were quickly tried by Field Court Martial and executed, including the leader James Connolly. As news of this filtered out, the general mood of the population changed to support for the martyrs, the dynamic for an independent state increased and the nationalist movement flourished.

The intervention of the war had been marked by competition and conflict between different movements among the nationalists, a situation not eased by the creation of a legislature for Northern Ireland (the six Unionist Provinces) and an Irish Free State (by the Government of Ireland Act of 1920); this legislature was included as part of the British Commonwealth, members of the Executive Council having to swear allegiance to the King, which would have been totally abhorrent to those fighting for an independent state, thus further splitting the national movement. Civil war broke out in June 1922 and was fiercely fought until May 1923. During that time, 5,000 militiamen were killed and Collins, one of the early heroes who had managed to escape British custody, was ambushed and killed.

The whole situation was exacerbated by the fact that the Royal Irish Constabulary had insufficient manpower to cope with the conflicts that surrounded them. An urgent recruiting campaign in Britain with the promise of good pay for 'a rough and dangerous task' attracted some 10,000 men, among whom were veterans of the trenches and criminals. Faced with a shortage of uniforms, they wore old khaki trousers and dark green RIC tunics; they were nicknamed the 'Black and Tans,' which quickly became a term of abuse as they lacked leadership, which led to them becoming undisciplined, drunk and brutal. The atrocities committed by some of these troops (including a reprisal massacre of 13 football spectators at Croke Park on Bloody Sunday in 1920) added to the complex bitter feelings that would continue to bedevil intra-Irish and Irish–British dealings for many, many years. Eamon de Valera took steps to resolve the internecine conflict by opening negotiations with the Executive. Two years later, in return for the abolition of the vast debts incurred by the war, the Executive had to concede a defined boundary of Northern Ireland which would include nationalist enclaves. The bitter legacy between rival nationalist groups continued to fester, despite the formal creation of the Independent State of Éire in 1937 with de Valera as the first President. Having lost so many able and brave leaders on all sides, their sons and daughters continued to take an active part in the conflicts of Irish politics for many years, and their grandchildren continued to play their part in the renewed struggle for a united Ireland, which brought so much death and distress to Northern Ireland for over forty years, from the 1960s into the 21st century.[39n]

Britain – The Great Depression

The global economy had been in decline before the war, and it was not long before many chronic problems came to a head. With no international mechanism or sufficient expertise to manage the global economy, the world drifted into another period of human suffering. The prevailing economic policy at that time, based on the experience of two minor recessions in the late 19th and early 20th centuries, was that economies were self-adjusting. So it was expected that the immediate post-war boom and consequent deflation would lead to the economy correcting itself in terms of lower wages and prices. The first years of world peace saw a significant economic boom: middle-class families retained their maidservants and as production was resumed consumers, happy that the horrors were behind them, celebrated by spending the earnings that high levels of employment offered. The great sense of being British prevailed. Lloyd George's view was that 'our bloodstained stagger to victory' should be rewarded with a range of social benefits to create a 'country fit for heroes.' The Budget of 1918 was, with little forethought, five times that of 1914. However, the return of troops in the years after 1918 led to significant levels of unemployment or low paid work, and consequently there was insufficient money to spend on the goods now being produced.

Throughout the coming period the proportion of the population who had secure employment saw only a slight dip in their family finances. Only 34 of the 631 Poor Law Unions were significantly affected; the workers in most of the country were busy going to the cinema and buying better clothes, radios and, for the better off, motor cars – indeed all the advantages that modern technical advances had promised.

Politics

Addressing the Labour Party Conference in 1922, the chairman complained that the £200 million spent every year on pleasure motoring was enough to build the million houses that were needed. The post-war election of 1922 returned 258 Conservative, 159 Liberal and 192 Labour members, and Ramsay MacDonald became the first Labour prime minister. Pressure of events however soon broke up the Liberal–Labour pact and the Tories took power under Stanley Baldwin. Two years later, although Labour polled a million more votes, their members were reduced to 151 and Liberals to 40 while the Conservatives won with 413.

The charismatic orator Oswald Mosley (described by Beatrice Webb as the most brilliant man in the Commons, although her intuition warned her that so much perfection indicated rottenness somewhere) was elected as a Coalition Unionist with a policy of socialistic imperialism.[40n] He joined Labour, and as a member of the 1929 Government supported the new ideas put forward by the economist J. M. Keynes. Keynes had correctly seen that the punitive economic conditions imposed on the defeated nations would destabilise the world economy. A central feature of his economic theory was that demand led production, and consequently, as the depression developed, he argued that the way forward was for the government to pump money into the economy, thus stimulating demand. His recommendations were largely ignored.

Mosley, frustrated by this failure to repair the economy through public works, as per the German and later American solution, launched his own 'New Party,' which attracted several highly intelligent social thinkers. Mosley's dictatorial attitude soon drove these away, but he marched on until 1932 when he formed the British Union of Fascists, funded by Mussolini and the Nazi Party and regulated by his notorious Blackshirts. By 1934 the BUF had 50,000 members ('Hurrah for the Blackshirts' cried the *Daily Mail*[41n]), but after the Blackshirts had exceeded their own brutal reputation at the first national rally the movement declined to 15,000 and then 5,000. The BUF remained active until 1940 when it was proscribed, with Mosley and its remaining members interned for the duration of the war. Sometime after the war Mosley started a new party with a declared European agenda, which at one point considered amalgamating with the emerging British Union Party. The Party ceased in the 1990s. Sometime in the late 1940s I encountered one of their candidates speaking in the midst of Brixton Market. There was a fierce fight and, as the lorry carrying the candidate drove through the crowd, the driver received a face full of well aimed spit from a very determined dissenter. Politics was alive and real indeed!

Poverty

As production slowed, it was those employed in the basic industries and the unemployed that were hardest hit, and it is the fate of this section of society that is recalled by the main events, pictures and accounts of the Great Depression. The industries that had increased production during the war faced the need to redesign and re-tool, but nonetheless in the five years from 1920 one million men lost their jobs, while transfer of skills was not easy given the difficulties of relocation. George Lansbury led a group of local councillors in the London Borough of Poplar to take direct action. Faced with the poverty and distress caused by unemployment, they decided to divert money from the rates to provide food vouchers for the most needy. Their argument was that as the London rate was set at a standard, rate money collected in poor Poplar was made available to rich boroughs in the West End. Therefore, when times were hard a reverse flow would be appropriate. Such action was illegal, and in March 1921 the councillors attended the High Court supported by 2,000 supporters and displaying a banner reading 'Poplar Borough Council, Marching to the High Court and Possibly to Prison, To Secure The Equalisation of Rates For Poor Boroughs.' On September 30th the councillors were jailed, but they were released six weeks later, having won their case, following an energetic campaign for their release. Poplar had also decided to pay their staff a working wage for which they were held personally responsible, Lansbury being threatened with a personal surcharge of £43,000.[42]

The unemployment rate rose from 3.9% in 1920 to 22.1% in 1932, which reflected a total of 2.7 million unemployed, and fell back to 10.8% by 1937. The cotton mills of Lancashire now faced major competition from India, China and Japan. One small compensation as the mills closed was the trade in exporting old looms and associated machinery. When we moved to Lancashire some sixty years later the trade still continued, although by that time it was in spare parts! Similar situations faced the iron and steel foundries. The coal mines were particularly hard hit, both by the reduction in domestic demand and fuel for shipping, exports having diminished by 50% between 1913 and 1934. The worst effects of the depression were held at bay to some extent by the Bank of England printing more money, but this backfired when in 1925 Churchill, then Chancellor of the Exchequer, returned Britain to the gold standard without significantly devaluing Sterling, thus making exports more expensive to the further disadvantage of British industry. Pride in our world reputation thus denied us the solution that had helped other European countries work their way out of their problems.

The General Strike

Four years later, Britain abandoned the gold standard again. For workers in the basic industries, including railways, these years had seen repeated attempts to lower wages, a situation which came to a head in 1926 when the mine owners (now free of government wartime control) tried to reduce wages and lengthen hours. Resistance by miners led to the owners locking the men out. The Trade Union Council (TUC) demanded that the government intervene to open the mines. As this was refused and contingency plans having been laid, the TUC declared a general strike on May 3rd 1926. Almost total support in all industries brought the country to a standstill. The government opened recruiting stations for volunteer special constables and people to keep the nation moving. The strike spread to second level industries including the print workers. Unfortunately, this left the government propaganda machine free to use the new media of radio to portray the strikers as a threat to the constitution, running an illegal strike and severely damaging the nation's economy.

The state newspaper the *British Gazette* announced 'Either the Country will break the General Strike or the General Strike will break the Country.' I have a wonderful collection of the government's daily *British Gazette* and the *British Worker* published by the TUC, as well as single page, sometimes handwritten, headlines of the *Daily Mail* and *Daily Mirror*. The *Gazette* pushed the line that the strike was a challenge to the democratic constitution and a gift to countries which would steal British trade, while the *Worker* insisted that it was an industrial dispute precipitated by the government's refusal to intervene in the miners' dispute. Each claimed success for their campaign. The government offered protection and compensation for anyone breaking the strike. By the fifth day, the government was screaming via the *Gazette* that the strike was an 'Organised Attempt to Starve the Nation.'[43] The *Worker* concentrated on the country-wide success of the stoppages and attributed the walkout of the printers at the *Daily Mail* as evidence of the government's refusal to continue with the negotiations.

Volunteers, many being middle- and upper-class university students with little understanding of the poor conditions facing the strikers but pumped up by a vague fear of socialism and communism, rushed to the government's aid. After nine days the TUC accepted the terms of a settlement, which the miners refused. The hard pressed strikers were furious and many never trusted their national leaders again. It is believed that one of the main reasons that the TUC surrendered was the threat posed by the outcome of a legal judgement that secondary striking was illegal, thus threatening the seizure of all trade union assets. In 1927 the government Trade Disputes Act outlawed sympathetic strikes, forced workers to 'contract in' to trade union subscriptions and outlawed mass picketing.

Unemployment in Britain proved to be a long term problem. Initially put out of work by falling demand, men became depressed by the loss of self-identity that work afforded them. As time went by, they faced difficulties in becoming re-employed, either because they had no work record or because they had adjusted to life on what by those standards was a fairly generous unemployment benefit. Unfortunately, these benefits expired after twenty-six weeks, after which time families reverted to Poor Law rules. In the North East of England, shipbuilding was badly hit by the complete lack of orders. Faced with chronic and extreme poverty and the dismantling of the cranes at Palmers Yard on the Tyne, 207 men decided to march the 300 miles from Jarrow to London to present a petition to Parliament to draw attention to their plight and that of many others in similar circumstances. The Conservative Prime Minister, Stanley Baldwin, refused to see the marchers, and the TUC and Labour opposed the march, although it is generally portrayed as a historical triumph of the Left. The National Government, established in 1931, saw the marches as an attempt by Moscow to promote a communist inspired revolution. Ramsay MacDonald, the much reviled Labour leader who had agreed to serve in the National Government, supported by George Lansbury and others, pressed for the release from prison of some trade union leaders who were former colleagues during the formation of the Labour Party. The North East continued in a depressed state until the start of the Second World War.

The horrific experiences of this long war have been so well documented, initially by the more powerful or expressive, but more recently by the publication of accounts from ordinary soldiers, that they do not need repeating here. Some eight million men died in this war, many from the Colonies and the USA, and with the influenza pandemic that spread across Europe in 1918 a total of thirteen million people died. (In London alone, 2,200 died in one week in late October.) In addition of course were the physical and mental injuries suffered by many survivors, the so-called 'destroyed men' who lingered on hidden by the celebrations, culminating in the victory parades of 1919 and the erection of noble memorials in practically every parish and town in Britain. Rudyard Kipling, the most patriotic of poets, wrote his angry poem 'Tommy':

> You talk o' better food for us, an' schools, an' fires an' all:
> We'll wait for extry rations if you treat us rational.
> Don't mess about the cook-room slops, but prove it to our face
> The Widow's Uniform is not the soldier-man's disgrace.
> For it's Tommy this, an' Tommy that, an' 'Chuck him out the brute!'
> But it's 'Saviour of 'is country' when the guns begin to shoot;
> An' it's Tommy this an' Tommy that, an' anything you please;
> An' Tommy ain't a bloomin' fool - you bet that Tommy sees![44n]

The memorials would be used and the neglect of soldiers after conflict would recur after the Second World War and after all major conflicts up to and including those in Iraq and Afghanistan in the 21st century.

CULTURE

Despite rumours of troubles elsewhere and a dip in the economy, the good times still rolled on and the popular songs from music hall stars such as Florrie Forde, Marie Lloyd and Lilly Langtry were overtaken by American bands which crossed the Atlantic to bring exciting new sounds such as the cakewalk, jazz and ragtime. Stanley Holloway was popularising his humorous musical monologues, the most popular of which was 'Old Sam,' the poor soldier who dropped his rifle on parade and refused to pick it up until asked nicely by the Duke of Wellington. Definitely a family favourite. Most popular were Scott Joplin's 'Maple Leaf Rag' and 'Pineapple Rag' and perhaps above all 'Alexander's Ragtime Band' and 'Balling The Jack.' Al Jolson's 'You Made Me Love You' and 'Shine On Harvest Moon' were popular ballads. By now Charlie Chaplin had moved from Walworth to the USA, where, after touring with Fred Karno's troupe of musical artists and having been spotted by the film producer Mack Sennett, he joined the Keystone Film Company. By 1918 he had formed his own studio, producing his first full length film *The Kid* in 1921, which took a massive $2.5 million on first release.

In England, the film studios of Pinewood and Ealing were producing good popular films and did so for many years; the early stars tended to resist the lure of Hollywood, so the publicity fell on Jean Harlow, Bette Davis and Gloria Swanson, matched by Douglas Fairbanks, James Cagney and Clark Gable, who led the way into the modern era of 'the talkies'.

In Detroit, Henry Ford had developed his system for the mass production of inexpensive motor cars, one of the first being the famous Model T Ford (the Flivver) on the basis that 'no man making a good salary will be unable to own and enjoy one and can enjoy with his family the blessing of hours of pleasure in God's great open spaces.'[45] The method of production, by which the workers' tasks were divided up into small specialisms applied to the vehicle as it travelled along a conveyor belt, came to be known as Fordism. It formed the basis of mass production of equipment in both world wars, was adopted by the Soviet Union and parodied by Chaplin in a hit film *Modern Times* released in 1933. The system, of course, perfectly illustrates the depersonalisation of industrial processes and the Marxist view of worker alienation. Not all was doom and gloom. In particular, Berlin, benefiting from the Weimar Republic's abolition of censorship, had become the city where anyone could have a good time, an anarchistic bohemian culture. Something of the atmosphere of the times can be gleaned from the 1972 film *Cabaret* based on the autobiographical novel *Goodbye to Berlin* by Christopher Isherwood.[46n]

As the Nazi Party took power, they abolished the culture which they correctly saw as threatening to an authoritarian regime; many of the leading players were eventually sent to the concentration camps. After the war, artists who had lived through it would emerge with a new style that reflected an age of cataclysm. Brecht and Weill staged their harsh *Threepenny Opera* featuring the song 'Mack The Knife,' Sergei Eisenstein's iconic film *Battleship Potemkin* was released and Kafka's dark novels were published after his death in 1924. In the fields of architecture and art, the Bauhaus movement, emphasising simplicity and sharpness, spread its influence across the west. Popular music imported from America was the latest fashion. Swing arrived with the 'big bands' of Duke Ellington, Count Basie, Benny Goodman and Glenn Miller. This music, supplemented by faster jazz groups and the mad 'jitterbug' and 'boogie-woogie' dances would carry forward into the Second World War led by Charlie Parker, Dizzy Gillespie, Miles Davis and many others.

In 1901 Marconi had made the first radio link from the Lizard Peninsular in Cornwall to America, residing at the Housel Bay Hotel, as had the King. Trams and the 'Twopenny Tube' soon arrived in London.[47n] The London Coliseum was opened with the first revolving stage in 1904, and a campaign to build the National Theatre was launched. The cinema was becoming popular.[48n]

In 1929 the sculptor Jacob Epstein unveiled his very large modern nude statues 'Day and Night' at the Headquarters of London Transport near St James Park. A storm of abuse met his creations, thought to be ugly, obscene and barbaric. I love them for their boldness and vision.[49n] Communication was moving forward. The first public telephone boxes had been set up at the end of 1929. In July 1930 Mr John Logie Baird was in London to demonstrate his new television apparatus, elementary and with no clear picture, but a whole new media. Radio had come into its own as more households bought sets. My newly married parents, starting with a small crystal set which had to be tuned by stroking it with a 'cat's whisker,' moved to a small valve set then upgraded to acquire a broadcasting licence to send out their own programmes. The British Broadcasting Company[50n] was formed in 1923, and in 1932 they moved into its new headquarters in Portland Place where the modern statue by Eric Gill over the entrance ran into a storm very similar to that faced by Epstein.

A particular long term cultural impact was the founding in 1935 of Penguin Books by Allen Lane, a director of The Bodley Press. Their cheap paperback books (originally sixpence) from the best authors were made available to ordinary people, right up to the present day. With as much impact on my family was the development of the London County Council. Originally formed in 1889 it had matured by raising education standards throughout the capital, offering a vast range of evening classes, building the extensive network of tramways and facilitating leisure activities. In 1933 the LCC moved into its new buildings opposite the Houses of Parliament, and in 1934 the Labour Party, with Herbert Morrison as leader, won power in London. They retained the LCC, known later as the Greater London Council, until 1986 when Mrs Thatcher closed it down.

Unfortunately, the errors of the post-war settlements were already undermining the desire for peace; this was perhaps evidenced by the debate held on February 9th 1933 in the Oxford Union when students voted 275 to 153 that 'This house will in no circumstances fight for its King and Country.' The vote was attributed to 'student practical jokers and sexual indeterminates.' Fourteen days later, Churchill, in a speech to the Anti-Socialist and Anti Communist Union, called it 'an abject, squalid and shameless avowal.' There is some evidence, however, that Hitler, being less familiar with free expression, took it as serious evidence that the British were not inclined to fight.

In 1927 Charles Lindbergh had flown across the Atlantic from New York to Paris, taking thirty-three and a half hours. In August 1937 a commentator, watching the great German Zeppelin airship *Hindenburg* land in New Jersey at the end of a trans-Atlantic flight, described the magical picture as the vast hydrogen filled ship turned towards the docking masts. A few minutes later he was screaming. 'It's burst into flames … Oh God, Get out of the way PLEASE! This is the worst of the worst catastrophes in the world! Oh, the humanity and all the passengers screaming around here.' Surprisingly, of the 97 people on board 62 escaped alive, although clearly the American commentator had forgotten the catastrophes of the recent war. The BBC, determined to give full justice to the incredible Jubilee Review of the Fleet in May 1937, asked a retired naval officer to commentate. Unfortunately he was somewhat drunk, so listeners heard a historical ramble which started

> At the present moment, the whole fleet is lit up. When I say 'lit up' I mean lit up by fairy lights ... It's fantastic, it isn't the fleet at all. It's just ... it's fairyland ... I'm sorry I was telling some people to shut up talking. In a second or two we're going to fire rockets, we're going to fire all sorts of things. This colossal fleet all ... lit up. And as I say it ... It's gone! It's gone! There's no fleet. It's disappeared ... We had a hundred, two hundred warships around us a second ago and now they've all gone ... There's nothing between us and heaven. There's nothing at all.[51n]

As he was among fellow officers on board HMS *Nelson*, the BBC could not prove he was drunk, so they apologised that their commentator was 'tired and emotional,' a useful phrase that has been used many times since in very different circumstances!

WELFARE AND SOCIAL WORK

It was said of Lloyd George that he had such a spirit of the times that he could make the Liberal's moderate aims sound like trumpet blasts against the Jericho walls of Conservatism and industrial neglect.[52] The Royal Commission, which had struggled for four years to redesign the ancient provisions centred on the parish workhouse for the industrial urban age, reported in 1909. The Commissioners recommended the abandonment of the deterrent principles that had held sway for over a hundred years in favour of a system that was preventive and curative. The newly introduced pensions were agreed, and it was suggested that the rudimentary system of free hospitals and infirmaries for the poor should be extended, 'mental defectives' were to be separated and cared for in special institutions and poor children and bad parents should have increased access to special schools, orphanages and foster or boarding out systems.[53]

Beneath these recommendations the Commissioners were split, the majority recommending that a Public Assistance Division of the existing Local Government Board should manage these new systems. The minority report (led by Beatrice Webb and signed by George Lansbury and two others) proposed the total breakup of the old system, wherein provision for each group was to be the responsibility of separate Committees of County or Borough Councils. In general terms, as the new approach was implemented in the following years, it was the minority report which was adopted. For some reason George Lansbury was a hero of my family; his name was always spoken with pride. He was seen as a true socialist, loved and elected by the people of London. He had sacrificed his seat in the cause of women's suffrage. As editor of the Labour newspaper the *Daily Herald* he sustained the socialist cause through the most difficult years and played a key role in preparing for the 1945 Labour electoral victory.[54n]

The year 1909 saw the first actual payments of a State Pension for those over 70 years of age, means tested to between one and five shillings a week. It is an insight into both the innovative nature of this provision and the manners and perceptions of the day that in the more rural areas pensioners arrived at their local post offices with a small bunch of flowers to thank the post office clerk and Mr Lloyd George for the weekly payment. Was it a coincidence that this was an election year? Labour exchanges were opened the following year,[55n] and in 1911 a National Insurance scheme to cover sickness, unemployment and maternity benefits was introduced. This followed a report by William Beveridge, who used the German model of state benefits and had been strongly supported by that most unlikely duo Winston Churchill and Lloyd George.

Social work, if defined by the great personalities discussed in Chapter 1, went through a relative period of retreat in the face of this rush of social legislation. It seems to have continued to stagnate through the war years, although of course a small civilian army was required to administer the new benefits and services, and hordes of volunteers were called upon to help when civilian populations were bombed and families evacuated. In some contrast (although sharing the same ideals), and a little ahead of the high society led suffragette movement, small but very active groups of women in some northern towns, for example Bolton, were moving resolutely to influence local welfare provision through gaining membership of local committees or established women's organisations which ran parallel to the male dominated services. A selection of such organisations established by Mary Haslam and other 'ordinary' women included The Bolton Sanitary Society, The Bolton Women Ratepayers Association, the Women Citizens Association and the Bolton Ladies Workhouse Visiting Committee. In this latter example they achieved dedicated birthing rooms, the classification of the mentally ill, segregated places for consumptives and a halfway house for young women when they left the workhouse together with support to find work and continuing friendship groups. In time they came to form a seamless philanthropic web between private charity, organised charity and the Poor Law. In February 1910 the *Bolton Journal* commented on

> … the increasing influence for good brought about by the appearance of women in practically every department of public life. Able, businesslike and active, they were showing themselves ready and willing to take their share in public labours … the work done … was not only practical, carefully considered and wise, but a great blessing to all concerned.[56]

New ideas, promoted by Labour and Liberal representation, were changing the view that children were the exclusive responsibility of parents, and that instead there should be a joint involvement between state and parents. Discussing school meals in 1905, an MP commented that 'the future of the Empire, the triumph of social progress and the freedom of the British race depend not so much upon the strengthening of the Army as upon fortifying the children of the State for the battle of life.'[57] Two Education Acts in 1906 carried the principles forward by the provision of school meals for the 'necessitous poor' and regular medical inspections. The 1908 Children Act set up separate courts for children and separate detention in Borstal Institutions (named after the village in Kent where the first establishment was opened) for delinquents rather than adult prisoners. It also made child neglect a criminal offence for the first time.

While a positive view of childhood was one dynamic, another was a fear that the efforts of the growing middle class to limit the size of their families were being overtaken by a fear that 'The feeble-minded, the insane and the epileptic have been allowed to mate to such an extent with healthy stocks that … the vigour and competence of many families has been undermined and the aggregate capacity of the nation has been seriously reduced.'[58] It is no surprise therefore that there was widespread support for the construction of large institutions that would 'care' for these people well removed from centres of normal population. A remarkable experiment in preventive medicine was established in Peckham. The founders believed that health could be conceived as contagious, in the same way as a disease. In the right environment people could 'infect' themselves with 'wellbeing' or happiness. Within a large building was established a club where, for a small subscription, people could use the gym, eat carefully prepared organic fresh food and take advantage of a swimming pool, a crèche and regular medical examinations to forestall ill health.[59n]

The relationship between humans and their environment was under increasing study by the newly found disciplines of psychology, sociology and anthropology. Early in the 20th century, the French government sought advice on the education of 'feeble-minded' children, so in 1905 two physicians with an interest in psychology, Alfred Binet and Theodore Simon, investigated the problem-solving ability of children at different ages, developing a scale of 'mental age' against chronological age. By 1911, by which time Binet had died, the first standardised test was published. The work was taken up by Lewis Terman, a psychologist at Stanford University in America, and in 1916 the first standardised Stanford–Binet Intelligence Test was published and welcomed in a country where individual competitive success was valued. This work was of particular interest to the US military, who by 1919 had formed a psychology division which repeatedly discovered that white soldiers had a higher IQ score than 'Negro' soldiers. It took many years to invalidate these results and to realise that the tests themselves were culture specific, but by then considerable damage had been done.

The psychiatrist Ernest Jones is credited with introducing psychoanalytic methods into British psychiatry, particularly through the treatment of soldiers during and after the First World War. He was the first among those psychiatrists who adapted Freud's principal tenets to a more pragmatic and eclectic approach, which became a characteristic of the British School. A second important contribution was that of the eminent psychiatrist Maxwell Jones, who concentrated on the treatment of psychopaths by group methods at Belmont Hospital in South London. In 1939 Henderson categorised patients with psychopathic personalities as either aggressive, inadequate or creative, incidentally quoting Lawrence of Arabia as an example of the latter, a categorisation which remains valid today, while the work started by Jones and Henderson continues in the Henderson Hospital on the site of the old Belmont Hospital. In a belief that reliable delineation would lead to effective treatment, as in physical medicine, from 1909 Ernst Kraepelin, seen as the founder of modern scientific psychiatry, published his key categorisation of mental illness; apart from schizophrenia and psychopathy, he delineated manic-depressive psychosis, dementia praecox. In the absence of any effective drug treatments, psychiatrists had to rely on psychotherapy and more aggressive treatments including, from 1933, the induction of long comas induced by insulin over many days (mostly for depressive or borderline schizophrenic patients) and from the same year the application of electric shock to induce convulsions. This latter treatment, mostly prescribed for severe depressive conditions, carried severe risks until the introduction of muscle relaxants to modify the severe thrashing of limbs during the seizure.

Child psychiatry was first developed in America, where the first Child Guidance Clinic was opened in Boston in 1921. In 1925 the physician Ernst Kretschmer, working in large mental hospitals in Germany, developed his theory of typologies, linking body types to personalities and mental symptoms. The frail, thin 'asthenic' types he associated with schizophrenic symptoms; soft round 'pyknic' bodies related to manic-depressive tendencies; and mixed body shapes gave mixed diagnostic categories.

In 1927 the Russian physician Ivan Pavlov, while researching the digestive system of animals, noticed that under certain conditions salivation occurred before food reached them. Further intensive research led to the discovery that if a buzzer were routinely sounded before food was produced a dog would salivate on just hearing the buzzer. Thus, the researcher had caused a response conditional on stimulation other than the natural one. From 1913, J. B. Watson, exploring the application of this work to human behaviour, reported that in his objective study of man

> ... no behaviourist has observed anything that he can call consciousness, sensation, imagery, perception, or will. Not finding these so called mental processes in his observations he has reached the conclusion that all such terms can be dropped out of any description of man's activity.[60]

This was to be developed further by Skinner from 1958, who worked with rats trained to make required responses by rewarding only those acts. It was not until 1971 that Skinner published his seminal work that firmly established behavioural psychology as a major contribution to modern thought and the treatment of people in distress, while distancing himself from the growing psychologists and therapists exploring the emotional and sensate aspects of the whole human being.[61]

In this same period, anthropology was drawing attention to the way behaviour, social norms and roles differed between societies. In 1934 and 1935 Margaret Mead was publishing her early findings, the first of which concerned the Tchambuli tribe of New Guinea.[62] Here, the women made the world go round, undertaking all the active and executive activities, while the men, seen as the weaker sex, excelled in artistic activities such as dancing, flute playing, painting and gossiping. So it appeared that scientific measuring and judging of individuals did not meet the universal verification required of true science. They always had to be weighed with the local culture in mind.

The growth of sociology as a discipline separate from anthropology and social philosophy and politics (the leading examples of which were Durkheim, Weber and Marx) was not straightforward or hurried. Early work tended to concentrate on statistical studies of society at a macro level, but as the 20th century moved forward attention turned to the evolution and functioning of societies and individuals within them. An early American study that struggled with the demands of objective measurement and local culture was *Middletown: A Study in American Culture*, which placed statistical information alongside 'the rattle of conversation that goes on around a luncheon table, on street corners ... is here presented, not because it offers scientifically valid evidence, but because it affords indispensable insights into the moods and habits of thought in the city.'[63] Another early approach was that of G. H. Mead, published in 1934, as *Mind, Self and Society*. His view was that the 'Self', as that which can be an object to itself, is essentially a social structure and that it arises in social experience ... The 'I' is the response of the organism to the attitude of others: the 'Me' is the organised set of attitudes of others which one himself assumes ... Social control is the expression of the 'Me' over against the expression of the 'I'. So much change in so short a time and now the certainties of science were being undermined by cultural relativity!

Whilst this new discipline flourished in America, progress in Europe was slower due partly to conservatism among British universities. In Britain, the London School of Economics (LSE) was practically alone in embracing the new ideas, and it was there, of course, that social workers were receiving their first full professional training. The settlements continued to provide a range of support to local communities, particularly in deprived areas of the major cities. Between 1914 and 1922, the number of settlements across Britain had increased from 46 to 60. They continued to combine direct social action with research linked to the main universities. In 1920 Clement Attlee had published *The Social Worker*, which was based on his settlement experiences. He developed the argument that the war, with military devotion to duty, had finally killed off the old belief in Laissez-faire in favour of an acceptance of widespread public service. In this:

> The Social Worker is one who feels the claims of society upon him more than others, he brings to all his work this conception of duty as a member of civilised society to make his contribution to the wellbeing of his fellows.[64]

Attlee was very clear that training should include a knowledge of social conditions, social and industrial history, economics and social philosophy, social psychology and a 'study of the minds of the people who you are dealing with. Above all else the first thing that a would-be social worker must learn, is a thorough appreciation of the outlook of those with whom he will come into contact. The social worker must try to put himself on a level with those who he is helping as they must become his fellow workers in creating a better state of affairs.' East End boys had carefully explained to him that 'A pal is a bloke that knows all about yer, and yet loves yer' but 'A gentleman is a bloke that is the same to everybody.'[65] Attlee saw the social worker as a pioneer discovering new social groupings and needs, a social investigator to build the present low level of knowledge results to form well meaning legislation, and certainly an agitator, exercising full rights as a citizen to concentrate attention on a particular aspect of a social problem.

Organisations such as the COS, the Salvation Army, the NSPCC and a wide range of Church organisations continued to support families and children caught in poverty. Frustrated by the Tory government's failure to sort out high unemployment, the election of 1929 returned Labour to power with Ramsay MacDonald as Prime Minister. Laissez-faire had given way to a recognition that state intervention was essential in an urban industrialised society, and the welfare legislation provided more formal roles for welfare workers, who were increasingly linked with local government. In succession these were the Local Government Act (1929), the Mental Treatment Act (1930) and the Children and Young Persons Act (1933). The latter, moving from rescue to treatment, set new responsibilities for probation officers (previously court missionaries) and established the role of school attendance officer.

Concern for children, particularly delinquents, led to social workers going to America where training was available for psychiatric social workers at Smith College, Boston. There and in the UK the academic disciplines of psychology and sociology, combined with a consideration of the differing organisational and political context of welfare work, were merging with new ideas about methods of working. Mary Richmond, working in America from 1917 to 1922, is usually credited with the first publication[66] to lay out a process of study of all facts, diagnoses and treatment plans by which social workers, drawing on the new academic disciplines, could have an identity separate from the agency in which they worked. Recognising that although intervention at a social level should not be neglected, the new profession drew more and more on psychoanalytic concepts to understand the dynamics that drove individuals and families. In 1929 the LSE started the first mental health course, and in the following year the Association of Psychiatric Social Workers was formed. There were twelve students on the first course, and in 1962, when I was working on a sessional basis at the local Residential School for Maladjusted Boys, the social worker swept into the Head's study announcing that she was 'one of the original twelve!' This gives some indication of the long-lasting feeling of superiority retained by this specialist group of social workers (closely followed by almoners and probation officers and, in the course of time, children's officers) who held the great secrets of psychodynamic intervention. The Head was inclined to feel that the next person to walk in would be walking on water!

In Vienna, Sigmund Freud, expanding his ideas about the structure of the psyche, developed the concept of the 'super-ego' (the centre of internalised authority) as an added task for the ego (that modern sense of self) which already had the task of balancing the conflicting basic desires of the id and the demands of external events and environment. By 1914 he was linking these concepts with political authority and the attraction of powerful charismatic leaders, who, he considered, enabled followers to get relief from their own internal conflicts. By 1923 Freud had been diagnosed with oral cancer and, with his family harassed by the Nazis, he moved to London with his daughter. He died in the September of the following year, leaving his daughter Anna to continue his great work, although she tended to specialise in the treatment of children. The poet W. H. Auden's 'Tribute to Sigmund Freud' made the point: 'To us he is no more a person now but a whole climate of opinion.'[67] The division between the psychoanalytic and behaviourist approaches to human behaviour continues to this day in philosophy, academia and therapeutic work with patients. To some extent this derives from Freud's use of abstract concepts, which he himself saw only as 'mind holds' which may one day be replaced by scientific explanations based on neurology and medical research. The psychologist George Allport commented in 1937

> Psychoanalysis ... has made no contact with other branches of psychology. The somewhat fantastic metaphors it employs show how little it has profited from the antecedent labours of psychological science. Much is known to general psychology about the unconscious operations of the mind, the processes of remembering, forgetting, dreaming ... and all this knowledge psychoanalysis should but does not employ. No school of psychology can afford such splendid isolation.[68]

This criticism may be less applicable today, but psychoanalytic theories remain open to the criticism that by their all or nothing bundle of tightly inter-related ideas it is impervious to objective experiment, verification and logical challenge. Although it was originally developed from the neurotic complaints of middle-class Viennese people at a particular point of cultural history, it has branched out and been developed to help many millions of ordinary men and women; quite the opposite can be said of the other ideas developed in Vienna at the same time: Nazism!

THE FAMILY

In July 1901, a second daughter, Mabel Doris, joined the Glover family, bouncing lustily and determinedly into the new century. At that time the family house backed on to Lambeth Walk, where the Pearly Kings and Queens reigned and the noise of the market and cries of the sellers could disturb the Archbishop's Palace up by the Thames. A keen observer of life, Mabel, my mother, later described the environment that had embraced her early years:

> The railway from Vauxhall crossed above the walk. Beneath the arches were very particular activities that held a great fascination for me: one a blacksmiths, had a small surrounding wall so convenient to sit on; beyond the wall a blazing fire that seared and choked, the ring of hammer on red hot iron, the sizzle of the iron being cooled, the quiet

sighing of the patient horses waiting to be shod, occupied all one's senses. In the next arch were the glass blowers, another searing fire with a cauldron where the practiced hand of the glass blower dipped his long pipe, twisted and blew again and again, then the finished magical beauty - a bottle, a vase, an animal; with what nonchalance they produced such art.

Our house was in a Georgian terrace set well back from the road which was wide and very noisy. The last of Tillings horse buses rocked and shook on their iron rims along the cobbled road; the open tops offered a good wind-blow and a good view to those young enough to climb the stairs. Soon the triple lines were to be laid for the trams, a tram and trailer adding to the far from concerted medley of road noises.[69]

Then there was A. Wood Confectioners. This was my maternal grandmother's business and abode where he and his wife strove to make a living. They sold sweets, cigarettes and a large variety of haberdashery on the side. The window was large and the goodies tastefully arranged, the sweets mostly priced at 4 oz for one penny and one delicious sweetmeat called honeycomb was 8 oz for a penny so for a farthing you got a huge 2 oz bag, a scrumptious treat. A farthing too for a pair of liquorice bootlaces or a taster of ice cream, a generous dab on a piece of paper. The ice cream was made by hand, a custard like mixture poured into drum packed with ice. The drum had to be turned by hand for hours and hours until the 'custard' was frozen into ice cream. The ice was delivered by horse and cart the water dribbling along the road; the children grabbed for chippings as the ice chipped beneath the carter's huge tongs … The area abounded with theatre folk who had a difficult time, so often 'resting'. My family well remember the young Charlie Chaplin whiling away the time on the street corner or looking in the shop window, having not even a farthing with which to buy.[70]

Herbert Glover bought some shares in the 'Bioscope Palace' near The Nelson public house in the Old Kent Road, a problematic location as Herbert's taste for alcohol was causing marital arguments and a series of moves, generally in Peckham, which ended up in a flat in Paulet Road, near Camberwell Green. The area was busy and poor. Some 60 years previously, Felix Mendelssohn had, while staying at Ruskin Park, composed a delightful rural idyll which he named 'Camberwell Green,' having heard the birdsong there. It became popular when he changed the name to 'Spring Song.' Today, as a major road junction, it would be impossible to hear a bird sing!

At the age of three, Mabel fell and broke her arm, which, she records, was mended by the doctor: 'Dr. Salter was one of the leaders of the Independent Labour Party, a socialist who did not charge the poor for treatment and as far as I can remember his maximum charge was sixpence.'[71n] During the 1909 election, Mabel recalled the soapbox meetings on the street corners, true meetings for the citizens where the candidates met the people and the people knew who and what they were voting for. Mabel notes that for the first time campaign photographs were projected onto the blank sides of buildings in the Old Kent Road. New media at work!

The young Mabel's main concern at this time was that she caught scarlet fever from her poorly sister Edith, but she determinedly carried on playing her violin in the school orchestra until she became so ill that she was packed off to an isolation hospital for twelve weeks. She comments that, totally institutionalised, she was reluctant to return to the 'poor beetle infested flat' where the family was then living. Much more disappointing for her was the loss of the much prized silver medal for seven years' 100% attendance at school. How much of her subsequent determination to give her children a good education and her energetic pursuit of theatre, musicals and concerts stemmed from this halt to her own musical development and education?

The Glover family now found lodgings in a house backing on to the Surrey Canal at Camberwell Green, next to the wood yards where Herbert worked (the yards being supplied by barge from Shoreham-by-Sea). This was where, in 1904, their third daughter Lola Aileen was born.[72n] This event coincided with a fire on the canal bank at the Hatherways timber yard. My mother recalls:

> What a blaze that was! The deafening noise of the crackling wood, the flames leaping into the September night, the fire engines drawn by fiery steeds sometimes a pair, occasionally four in hand, the horses eyes blazing bald and red in anticipation and effort, their nostrils belching steam and their shoes clattering pyrotechnical sparks from the flints of the road … I stood at the window at the head of my mother's bed where she lay with the day old Lola, my excitement and fear intense, gripping the iron rail, and with desperate and agonizing excitement screwed and unscrewed the large brass knobs with which her bed was adorned. Of course a wider blaze would soon engulf family and nation.[73]

At the start of the war, Herbert Glover, true to his Sussex roots, joined The Sussex Regiment and left for the front from Liverpool Street Station, which, according to his daughter, was 'a sea of khaki with a festive mood of laughter, joking and singing as they said their goodbyes [and he was] propelled into the foulest four years through which man could exist.'[74] Wife and daughters went home to knit every evening, making khaki socks for the soldiers, heavy blue socks for the sailors and balaclavas. Popular songs of the time were 'It's A Long Way To Tipperary' and 'Pack Up Your Troubles In Your Old Kit Bag And Smile, Smile, Smile'. Edie's younger brother Charlie, a male replica in build and jolly humour, had finished his apprenticeship as a stone and wood carver with John Daymond & Sons at Vauxhall and joined the Royal Flying Corps, and while stationed near Folkestone had been busy designing new tail-fins for airships. He was a strikingly handsome young man who married young: his bearing and uniform attracted the passionate dreams of the teenage daughter of an established local newsagent Percy Peppin, and as soon as possible they eloped to Canada, a story which can be returned to later.

Bitter conflict hit the family as Herbert's elder brother Fred declared himself a communist and refused to fight a capitalist war. This enraged the rest of the family who were all loyal royalists. Unfortunately, Fred and his young family lodged in the family house so furious rows developed as registered conscientious objectors had to be arrested, taken to prison, strip searched and serve a short sentence. Immediately Fred returned home he would be rearrested (many of the relatives' houses having been searched as well) and the process started again, thus bringing more fury within the household and shame without. A permanent breach was formed in the family.

In Cornwall, William W. Wickett was progressing conscientiously through secondary school, firstly Bude County and then Horwell Grammar School for Boys in Launceston. Although he held a position in the top half of the form, the interesting feature of his reports is that at Bude there were never more than fifteen boys in the class and at Horwell never more than five. He left school in 1919 having passed the Cambridge entrance exam, but for some reason he was never to pursue a university education. In 1913 Edith Glover's sister Lizzie was so disgusted that her daughter Clara had become pregnant to Bob Little, fishmonger of Billingsgate, that she threw her out of home. Edith took her in and soon Clara and Bob emigrated to Canada, remembering that Edith, Mabel and Lola were the only people to see them off. The Jordan family from their base in Peckham had sent all three of their sons to the front, joining the 'poor bloody infantry,' naturally the local City of London regiment, The Royal Fusiliers, the 3rd (Territorial) Battalion. Jack and Harry served together, Jack obtaining promotion to Sergeant and then Acting Company Sergeant Major in the line. His account, which he sent back to the *News of the World* from Neuve Chapelle, could have been repeated tens of thousands of times:

> It may be said with truth that this life is not all honey, but what we have endured – perhaps what we are about to go through – will remain in the memory as life's most thrilling experience. Times come when we feel a bit 'fed up' with soldiering, but a spell in the trenches and a spell out of them have the curious effect of making one anxious to go back to the firing line. Our second time in the trenches was the occasion of the big bombardment. My God, it was hell upon earth; startling, thrilling yet all very wonderful. Then the slow advance with fixed bayonets to 'Port Arthur.' Here we formed up and waited the signal to charge that portion of the German trenches still held by the enemy. When the word came, every man went over the barricade like lightning. The brave boys fell, killed or wounded, in dozens, for the Germans met us with an awful fire, but we held on to the barbed wire. Sixty-three Germans, all that was left of them, surrendered to us, the 'Saturday Night Soldiers' and we only numbered seventy. Poor Bill Parsons [a *News of the World* employee] fell in the fight, and we shall miss him here and at work.

Returning for supplies, Jack was killed at Hebuterne, near Arras, on June 26th 1916, a field away from Harry. Although both Harry and his younger brother Ernie survived, the psychological effects were evident in a certain closedness and sadness of manner. Harry, with a heart weakened by rheumatic fever contracted in the trenches, survived with ill health for another 34 years. So eventually Harry and Jack, who had no doubt shared the view that their generals must be right because of their natural superiority, were both done for, although I never remember Ernie or my father Harry ever mentioning their war experiences. Herbert Glover was discharged from hospital in Aberdeen having been shot in the abdomen whilst serving on the Hindenburg Line.

They returned to their large family in an end of terrace house at Goose Green in South London. There, as the effects of Jack's death and the post-war depression started to take their toll, the population in the house escalated beyond any tolerable level. Added to the deaths and accidents that marked that house, Jack's three children had to be given up to Spurgeon's Homes, although his small son Jack had already lost a leg in a road traffic accident right outside the house. Some members of the family thought it best to try their luck in Canada, South Africa and Australia. Some came back in greater poverty than they left; some prospered. Harry's brother Ernie returned from Canada with his Canadian wife Ada and their children. He had written home to say that 'We shall all be on the streets soon. The government will take the kids, but Ada and I will go to the dogs.'

Harry's sister Maud returned having been married to a handsome Swedish engineer Charles Kjellberg who, as the depression had worsened had committed suicide. The consequent penury resulted in her four children entering an orphanage in Nunhead. As with many in those years, experience gave way to a quiet determination to survive against all odds. There was no prospect anyway to improve one's lot in life, but there was a quiet sense of humour, and when my father's family were together they would recount happy times and even laugh at the circumstances of the tragedies at the house of horrors in Goose Green. Mabel enrolled herself in a French class and visited Paris, where she and her friend's dowdy post-war clothes stood out against the brilliance of the new fashionable social scene. Grenadines with water were very much enjoyed. Four years after the war, Mabel Glover married Harry Jordan in St John's Church, Goose Green, and, following the rule in government offices, she received a 'dowry' of £20 and was dismissed due to her marriage! She invested the money in a Singer sewing machine. Two years later on August 26th 1924 their first son John was born; three days later, Mabel's sister Edith, who had joined the Land Army, working in Sussex and Dorset, wrote urgently to be sent money for the fare to London.

Edith had been kicked by a cow then developed lockjaw and cowpox followed by diabetes. The only way to save her life was access to King's College Hospital where a new treatment by insulin was being developed. For the rest of her life she had to attend twice a day for injections as well as having hospital treatment for tuberculosis. My parents' early happiness came to an abrupt end a few years later. Harry had a good job as an engineer maintaining the printing machines for the *News of the World* newspaper, but some misunderstanding gave the new chief engineer the chance to arbitrarily dismiss him. Mabel remembers:

> When a great tragedy befalls, the human mind quickly wraps itself in a protective layer of unbelief, lest the shock prove more than can be borne … Harry came home and went to bed, where he stayed for several days, speaking very little until the humiliation slowly passed and the protective layers peeled off. He had rejected all help from friends … Now it was too late to get decisions altered. All the Jordans are quiet, retiring people … inevitably at the end of the week he joined the million other unemployed. He never recovered from this experience completely and change was now to be an ever presence in our lives. In retrospect, I know I could have made a living for us but reason did not work that way in the twenties, schooled as we were in the ethics of Miss has a job, but Mrs. is a housewife.[75]

The children, who had been sent into care, returned to a life in service to the prosperous middle class or to practice the skills they had been taught. Doris worked as a seamstress in the top fashion houses in London and Jack repaired clocks and watches. Nonetheless, among the stockpile of archives bequeathed to me is a carefully mapped out family tree that extends through some three hundred years.

As the branches extend down through the 20th century to show more and more offshoots, there remain an uncomfortable number of male entries which never grow. These were the hidden casualties of World War I whose gifts to the future were never realised. In her autobiography written in 1994, the author Doris Lessing was to write angrily of the

> Unlived lives, Unborn children. How thoroughly we have all forgotten the damage that war did to Europe, but we are still living with it.
> Perhaps if The Flower of Europe (as the young men were called) had not been killed, and those children and grandchildren had been born we would not now, in Europe be living with such second ratedness, such muddle and such incompetence?[76]

In the early part of the war, at the age of 14, Mabel Glover, working as a seamstress, soon moved to work for the Post Office as a telegram girl, which gave her the freedom of fresh air and enabled her to travel all over South East London. She records how

> ... the public resented girls taking the place of boys and we were subject to a good deal of abuse. The flats at the back of Lambeth Underground Station were a special hazard; most unwholesome refuse was showered down on us from the upper flats ... one day a girl was hit in the face with a kipper. The Post Office were sensitive to these difficulties and to the emotional cost to their young employees of the daily delivery of wounded or 'killed in action' telegrams to distraught families. They set up a club and after each girls only nights there would be a string of boy messengers (called 'Piccaninnies') waiting to escort the girls' home. Unfortunately, this involved a walk down Union Street, a slum riverside street probably not changed since Dickens [sic] days; it boasted several pawnbroker shops outside each of which hung three brass balls. These were open until late at night and many a fight took place where perhaps father's trousers or boots were for a meagre sum. It was one of these most viscous attacks we witnessed one night and the young woman was in a cringing poorly state. I begged my escort Harold, to intervene and he shocked me by saying 'Not likely, he's telling her he loves her.'[77]

Soon after, Mabel was promoted to indoor messenger, which required attending the Civil Service School where

> English was the major subject and we were taught to say 'Have you not heard?', 'Do you not know' instead of 'Aint yer erd?' and 'Doan cher no?'[78]

This was clearly the start of my mother's 'telephone voice' which led long-standing suspicion from the wider family that she was a little 'above herself.' The resentment shown towards the telegraph girls was but a small part of the public feelings towards women taking men's jobs during and after the war, not least by men returning home. A more significant problem was the fate of women who had outnumbered men before the war, a balance made worse by the loss of some 700,000 British men slaughtered in the war. In 1917 the headmistress of Bournemouth High School for Girls announced to her assembled sixth form that 'Only one out of ten of you girls can ever hope to marry. You will have to make your own way in the world. But there will be prejudice. You will have to fight you will have to struggle.'[79] She was right on both counts, but may not have approved of how young women were to embrace the new American dance crazes of the 1920s to help fight for a man.

By 1919 the Rev Corbyn Adams had moved from Ipswich to the small town of New Milton some 120 miles north west of New York, although he returned ten years later. In Clapham, South London, the Howard family was growing towards the total of five children, one of whom, Jim, would marry Mabel's sister Lola. Jim started work at the age of 14 for a Mr Hambling who made the fragile electronic valves forming the essential power base for the new radio craze. The valves ranged from small (about 4 cm) to those nearly a metre tall used by the broadcasters, most notably the BBC. As this trade decreased, Mr Hambling decided to pursue his hobby of creating small precise model railways. He opened a shop in Cecil Court, between Charing Cross Road and St Martin's Lane in London, where Jim worked until 1980 after 65 years in the shop. Elsewhere, players that would fill key roles in my family history were entering the field. In the Turin area of Northern Italy, a family named Rossi, of either Italian/German or Italian/Albanian descent, produced a son who would move to England, marry and have seven children, one of whom, Catherine, having married Kenneth Edge, would step into our family history towards the end of the 20th century. We share grandparent duties. In America the reverend Corbyn Adams and his wife Alice had welcomed the arrival of their first son, Haddon, to be followed by five more. The third, Hugh Stanley, born in 1905, would play a significant part in my life some sixty years later. When their parents returned to England, both Haddon and Hugh remained to study civil engineering at American universities, then returned with expertise in the newest techniques of reinforced concrete design. They lived in Chicago during the prohibition of alcohol and the gang warfare most famously remembered for Al Capone's cruel leadership. Far from using their Ford Model T cars to enjoy the countryside, they would enjoy what they saw as a sport of venturing into the poor areas hurling abuse and empty beer bottles at black pedestrians. I very much hope this no longer happens, although in such cities prejudice and violence are still in evidence every day.

Of more significance are the continuing adventures of Keziah Grace Polkinghorne, who, having given birth to Violet in 1898, moved to London with one Robert Jackson, an engineer (from the same small Devon village of Bere Alston). In 1906 Grace married Harry Lang Tomlinson, an engineer, and by 1911 they had settled in West Moors, Dorset, where they registered Violet as 'adopted' French! Grace and Lang were much travelled and lived in some style. Grace had an original three-wheeler Morgan car which had no reverse gear; consequently, if she needed to perform that manoeuvre she would summon the nearest policeman to manhandle the car round, such were the assumptions of the class that saw themselves as superior. By this time the Wickett family had established a successful farm at Launceston in Cornwall. The Tomlinson's daughter, Violet, would come to marry the eldest Wickett son William Wilfred (born 1902) and, after a divorce after World War Two, Hugh Stanley Adams.

As 1933 turned to 1934, two totally insignificant events occurred at opposite ends of the country. In the St Barnabas Nursing Home, which clings to the Cornish side of the Tamar under Brunel's great Royal Albert bridge, a baby girl, named Ann, was born to Violet (née Tomlinson) and William Wickett. In the confines of Lister's hospital, King's College in Camberwell, I arrived as a bouncing boy, laying my mother near death with fever. Ann and I would marry thirty years later.

NOTES AND REFERENCES

1. Sung to the music of the first Pomp and Circumstance March composed in 1901 by the great English composer Edward Elgar, this has become a standard patriotic song sung on significant occasions. A version was originally sung at the coronations of Edward VII and King George V.
2. Marx, K. (1859). *A Contribution to the Critique of Political Economy*. Preface. See also Marx, K. and Engels, F. (1971). *Historical Materialism*. London: Pluto Press.
3. Sassoon, S. (1917). 'The General', in Wavell, A. (1960). *Other Men's Flowers*. London: Penguin Books. This book contains some 380 pages of poetry of many genres all memorised by Field Marshal Earl Wavell (1883–1950). In WWII he was commander in chief in North Africa, the Middle East and the Far East. Sassoon was an established poet whose active protest against the conduct of the war caused so much embarrassment that he was placed in a special hospital for shell-shocked victims near Edinburgh. There he met fellow officer Wilfred Owen whom he mentored. Owen, who returned to the front, fought gallantly, and was awarded a Military Cross. He was killed a few days before Armistice day on November 11th 1918. Few of his poems were published, but his ability to transmit the horrors endured by fighting men in the front line were eventually recognised, set to dramatic effect by Benjamin Britten in his War Requiem which had its premiere at the opening of the new Coventry Cathedral in 1962. Owen's poetry became very popular in the anti-war movements of the late 1960s and he is probably now recognised as the greatest war poet of the 20th century. Had Wavell published his book later, I am sure he would have included Owen and Sassoon. In 2009 a campaign was launched for £1.25 million to save the original of Sassoon's 'Soldier's Declaration' for the nation.
4. Allies in WWI were:

    Britain and her Empire (including troops from Australia, Canada and New Zealand)
    France
    Russia (until December 1917)
    Italy (entered May 1915)
    Serbia
    Belgium
    Romania (from August 1916)
    USA (entered April 1917)

Japan

The Central (Axis) Powers were:
Germany
Austria-Hungary
Turkey (entered November 1914)
Bulgaria (entered October 1915)

5. Lord Kitchener of Khartoum had run the recruiting drive from his position in the Ministry of Defence. In due course he became the victim of political intrigue. His reputation as the nation's unbeatable hero severely dented, he drowned in June 1916 when HMS *Hampshire* hit a mine off the Orkney islands.
6. *Oh! What a Lovely War* was an extraordinary satirical musical developed by Joan Littlewood in her East London Theatre Workshop in 1963. In 1969 it was made into a very popular film starring Maggie Smith, Laurence Olivier, John Mills, John Gielgud, Ralph Richardson and Dirk Bogarde.
7. See Tomlinson, H. M. (1930). *A Night Raid*, in Blunden, E., ed. *Great Short Stories of the War*. London: Eyre and Spottiswoode, p. 35. H. M. Tomlinson was an uncle of Violet Tomlinson, my late wife's mother. See also Tomlinson, H. M. (1922). *Waiting for Daylight*. London: Cassell, Section 15.
8. In Wavell, *op. cit.*, p. 367.
9. Lloyd George, D. (1930). *War Memories*. London: Odhams Press.
10. Graves, R. (2000). *Goodbye to All That*. London: Penguin. The film *All Quiet on the Western Front*, released in 1930, was based on a book of that title written from the German perspective: Remarque, E. M. (1984). *All Quiet on the Western Front*. London: Methuen. Originally published in 1929.
11. Bairnsfather, B. (1916). *Bullets and Billets*. London: Grant Richards.
12. Sassoon, S. (1918). *Counter Attack and Other Poems*. New York: Dutton & Co.
13. Brittain, V. (2005). *Testament of Youth*. London: Penguin. First published in 1933.
14. Nicholas and his family hoped to go into exile in Britain, a request that caused alarm. It was suggested that he seek residence in a neutral country. France also refused. They were moved to a minor palace in the Urals, where it was hoped that they could move to Japan. However, following a change of government, on March 1st 1918 all luxuries were removed from them and they were moved to a house in Yekaterinburg, where, on July 18th 1918, they were all executed.
15. For a good account of the circumstances and murder, see the film *Frida*. Dir. Julie Taymor, Lionsgate (2002), starring Salma Hayek, Alfred Molina and Geoffrey Rush. The film is a biography of the artist Frida Kahlo, who had an affair with Trotsky.
16. Their graves are in the Commonwealth Graves Cemetery in Gaza and were badly damaged during Israeli attacks in 2004.
17. In the same year, Balfour gave India a promise that Indians would be involved in every branch of administration in preparation for responsible government in India as an integral part of the British Empire.
18. Paying tribute after his death, Field Marshal Lord Allenby said 'He was the mainspring of the Arab movement and knew their language, their manners and their mentality. He shared with the Arabs their hardship and dangers ... not a few lost their lives in devotion to him and in defence of his person. He was a shy, retiring scholar, archaeologist, and philosopher swept by the tide of war into a position undreamt of.'
19. In 1960, Terence Rattigan's play *Ross* became a considerable success. It examined Lawrence's complex personality, including his underlying homosexuality. In 1965 I saw the play staged by the pupils of Chislehurst Comprehensive School. It was a tribute to pupils and staff who faced the sexual undercurrents bravely. As a teacher there, my brother John provided the music. A more

iconic view was given in David Lean's 1962 epic film *Lawrence of Arabia*, which brought Peter O'Toole and Omar Sharif to fame and has recently been voted one of the best films of all time.
20. Mazower, M. (1998). *Dark Continent: Europe's Twentieth Century*. London: Allen Lane, p. 82.
21. Ninety years later to the day, on December 23rd 2010, the Original Carriage (Number 132), which had also carried the body of Nurse Cavell, was opened as a museum in Tenterden, Kent.
22. Mazower, *op. cit.*, p. 90.
23. Upward, E. (1962). *The Spiral Ascent. Vol. 1 In the Thirties*. London: Heinemann. This was a three-book series. The quotation is from Marx's 1845 'Theses on Feurbach' in *The German Ideology*.
24. Terkel, S. (2005). *Hard Times. An Oral History of the Great Depression*. New York: The New Press, p. 99. This rich book of oral history, written across a vast span of time, class, occupation and wealth, provides a unique insight into the American experience. It is a valued example of rigorous intellect and sociological imagination. It was a very welcome Christmas present from my family in 2008.
25. Steinbeck, J. (2000). *Grapes of Wrath*. London: Penguin Classics. Originally published in 1939.
26. Maugham, S. (1990). *The Summing Up*. London: Mandarin. First published in 1938. His novel *Liza of Lambeth* (1897) launched his career.
27. Forster, E. M. (1961). *Howards End*. London: Penguin, pp. 39, 44. First published in 1910.
28. Mazower, *op. cit.*
29. Sims, G. R. (1883). *How The Poor Live*. London: Chatto & Windus, Chap. 13, p. 18.
30. Baden-Powell's motivation and political views came under scrutiny as the scouting movement expanded. He was accused of training boys to be ready recruits in the great game of Empire and his interest in some Nazi ideology has been questioned. Based on his treatment of black South African troops during the Siege of Mafeking there have been calls for his statue to be taken down.
31. A phrase describing the early Labour Party attributed to its General Secretary, Morgan Phillips.
32. David Lloyd George quoted in Bruce, *op. cit.*
33. In 1901, following a trade dispute, the Taff Vale Railway Company sued and won an action against the Amalgamated Society of Railway Servants, the result of which would be to ruin the Society. The realisation that, despite previous legislation, trade union funds were unprotected led to a pressure on the newly formed ILP, whose increasing popularity and representation in Parliament forced the Liberal Government to pass the Act.
34. In 1924, following the loss of his seat (after the Dardanelles disaster) and being re-elected as a Conservative, Churchill commented 'Anyone can rat but it takes a certain amount of ingenuity to re-rat.' Stanley Baldwin, faced with the likelihood of having a dangerous back bencher, made him Chancellor of the Exchequer.
35. Hattersley, R. (2004). *The Edwardians*. London: Little Brown, p. 203.
36. Hattersley, *op. cit.*, p. 207.
37. See the film *Suffragette*. Dir. Sarah Gavron. 20th Century Fox (2015), starring Carey Mulligan, Anne Marie Duff and Helena Bonham Carter.
38. From a speech given by Emmeline Pankhurst on November 13th 1913 in Hartford, Connecticut. Reproduced in a series of Great Speeches by *The Guardian* in 2007.
39. Dan Keating, an iconic last survivor of these wars, lived to the age of 105. He remained an 'Irish republican irreconcilable' still supporting the all Irish republic proclaimed by Patrick Pearse from the GPO steps in 1916. Interviewed shortly before his death in 2007, he described Tony Blair's peace process as a joke because 'There will never be peace until the people of the 32 counties elect one parliament without British interference.' McCann, E. (2007). *Guardian Obituaries*, 15.10.07. Available at https://www.theguardian.com/news/2007/oct/15/guardianobituaries.northernireland (accessed October 2007).

40. Mosley married the daughter of a high Tory grandee and was highly promiscuous (sleeping with his wife's two sisters and many other aristocratic ladies who were part of the dying decade of aristocratic power). Nancy Mitford was the most loyal of his conquests. Nonetheless she certainly did not share her sisters' Diane and Unity's devotion to Mosley and Hitler.
41. *Daily Mail*, January 14th 1934, headline by the owner Harold Harmsworth 1st Viscount Rothermere, whose family continue to control the paper. The *Mail* was by no means the only paper to support Mosley.
42. Lee, S. (2005). *Aspects of British Political History 1914–1995*. London: Routledge.
43. *British Gazette*, Thursday May 6th 1926. London: HMSO.
44. Kipling, R. (1890). 'Tommy', in Wain, J. (ed.) (1990). *The Oxford Library of English Poetry, Vol. III*. London: BCA, p. 276. This is the last and most popular verse as the original, Tommy Atkins, referred to Red Coats.
45. Casey, R. (2016). *The Model T: A Centennial History Paperback*. New York: John Hopkins University Press.
46. Isherwood, C. (1989). *Goodbye to Berlin*. London: Vintage Classics. Originally published in 1939, the novel was adapted for the award winning musical *Cabaret*, starring Liza Minnelli, Michael York and Joel Grey
47. The Circle Line had been completed in 1863 and the Central Line was opened in 1913; both were sub-surface lines built about 5 metres below ground. The 'Twopenny Tube' became possible only by the rationalisation of competing companies in 1913. The Jubilee Line Extension, which opened in 1979, is at a depth of 32 metres as it passes under the Thames near Westminster.
48. The first purpose-built cinema was opened in Calne, Lancashire, in 1908. The following year the Provincial Cinematograph Theatre Company commenced a five-year programme to open 3,000 'moving picture houses.'
49. During the war, Epstein served in the 38th Battalion of the Royal Fusiliers. His daughter Kitty married the painter Lucian Freud in 1948. Unfortunately, he was not offered major commissions until well after the war.
50. The Company became the British Broadcasting Corporation (BBC) in 1927. The earlier call sign, 2LO, which my parents would have searched for, was broadcast from Marconi House in the Strand.
51. Following protests, the BBC concluded that, as he was not one of their employees, there was no action they could take. As a Naval officer he was entitled to hospitality in the Mess, which he had obviously taken full advantage of. The recording is available on YouTube.
52. Bruce, *op. cit.*, p. 171.
53. *The Royal Commission on the Poor Law and Relief of Distress 1905–09*.
54. As I write this over one hundred years later, the actress Angela Lansbury, interviewed on TV, reveals that she is George Lansbury's granddaughter. Further research then reveals that, in addition to the well known *Murder, She Wrote* series, she starred in the 1944 thriller *Gaslight*, which I was taken to see age ten, at Letchworth Golf Club that same year. The suspense (the victim knows that a threat is coming because the gaslight goes down every time someone else turns another light on) frightened me considerably! Also starring in the film were Ingrid Bergman, Joseph Cotton and Charles Boyer – quite a list. I note that 'gaslighting,' a form of manipulation using psychological means of making someone doubt their own sanity, is currently a term for the calculating systematic frightening of a person. Angela Lansbury, born in 1925, has had an extraordinarily film and stage career since *Gaslight*. My wife and I saw her in the leading role in the musical in 1966. She took the leading role in the TV series *Murder, She Wrote* until 1996. Her most recent film was *Mary Poppins Returns* (2018).
55. The Labour Exchanges Act of 1909 implemented the recommendation of both Royal Commission reports by establishing a national network of Labour Exchanges. In the following two years the whole nation was covered and by 1914 a million vacancies were being filled annually.

56. Burnham, D. (2012). *The Social Worker Speaks: A History of Social Workers Through the Twentieth Century*. Aldershot: Ashgate.
57. Hansard HC Deb. Vol 148 Col 1251 et seq. March 27th 1905. A fascinating debate.
58. Recently appeared in Cunningham, H. (2006). *The Invention of Childhood*. London: BBC Books.
59. Stallinbrass, A. (1989). *Being Me and Also Us*. Edinburgh: Scottish Academic Press. The Foundation responsible for the project continues to exist as phf.org
60. Sanford, F. H. (1961). *A Scientific Study of Man*. New York: Wadsworth, p. 390.
61. Skinner, B. F. (1971). *Beyond Freedom and Dignity*. New York: AA Knopf Inc.
62. Mead, M. (1950). *Sex and Temperament in Three Primitive Societies*. New York: Mentor. Originally published in 1935.
63. Lynd, R. and Lynd, H. (1929). *Middletown: A Study in Contemporary American Culture*. New York: Harcourt Brace.
64. Attlee, C. R. (1920). *The Social Worker*. London: Bell & Sons. Part of The Social Service Library, in conjunction with the University of London, Ratan Tata Department, p. 27.
65. Attlee, *op. cit.*, p. 237.
66. Richmond, M. (1917). *Social Diagnosis*. New York: Russell Sage.
67. Auden, W.H. (1940). 'In Memory of Sigmund Freud,' *Another Time*. London: Random House.
68. Allport, G. (1937). *Personality: A Psychological Interpretation*. New York: Holt, Rinehart & Winston.
69. Jordan, M. (1986). *An Autobiography*. Preston: Nemco Press, p. 1.
70. Jordan, *op. cit.*, p. 2.
71. Dr Alfred Salter was a GP whose practice was based in the Bermondsey Methodist Settlement, established as a community of social workers who come to a poor neighbourhood to assist by methods of friendship and cooperation those who are concerned with upholding all that is essential to the wellbeing of the neighbourhood. Dr Salter treated thousands of patients, particularly those suffering from TB. In 1922 he was elected as an MP to represent that area. He and his wife Ada devoted their lives working in that area. A statue was erected to him in 1991 but was stolen by metal thieves in November 2011 to the consternation of the community. Dr Salter died in August 1945.
72. Jordan, *op. cit.*, p. 4. Lola's full name (Lola Aileen) caused an issue. While the registrar accepted the names without question, a problem was encountered at the christening when the vicar refused to accept such heathen names. Her mother had to explain patiently the Spanish and Irish derivation of the names, although quite why this derivation was relevant remains a mystery.
73. Jordan, *op. cit.*, p. 3.
74. Jordan, *op. cit.*, p. 6.
75. Jordan, *op. cit.*, p. 21.
76. Lessing, D. (1994). *Under my Skin*. London: Fourth Estate. This is Lessing's autobiography from 1919 to 1949.
77. Jordan, *op. cit.*, p. 7.
78. Jordan, *op. cit.*, p. 7.
79. Nicholson, V. (2008). *Singled Out: How Two Million Women Survived Without Men After The First World War*. London: Penguin.

THREE

1934–1942

THE NAZI ADVANCE

If one side clearly did not want war and did everything possible to avoid it, and the other side glorified in it and, in the case of Hitler, certainly actively desired it, none of the aggressors wanted the war they got, at the time they got it, and against at least some of the enemies they found themselves fighting.

– Eric Hobsbawm[1]

I, WHO am known as London, have faced stern times before,
Having fought and ruled and traded for a thousand years and more;
I knew the Roman legions and the harsh-voiced Danish hordes;
I heard the Saxon revels, saw blood on the Norman swords.
But, though I am scarred by battle, my grim defenders vow
Never was I so stately nor so well-beloved as now.
The lights that burn and glitter in the exile's lonely dream,
The lights of Piccadilly, and those that used to gleam
Down Regent Street and Kingsway may now no longer shine,
But other lights keep burning, and their splendour, too, is mine,
Seen in the work-worn faces and glimpsed in the steadfast eyes
When little homes lie broken and death descends from the skies.

– Greta Briggs[2]

Sweet Auburn! loveliest village of the plain,
Where health and plenty cheer'd the labouring swain,
… Dear lovely bowers of innocence and ease,
Seats of my youth, when every sport could please,
How often have I loiter'd o'er thy green,
Where humble happiness endear'd each scene.

– Oliver Goldsmith[3]

'Easy,' she said. 'You've got to have patience. Why, Tom – us people will go on livin' when all them people are gone. Why, Tom, we're the people that live. They ain't gonna wipe us out. Why, we're the people – we go on.'

– Ma Joad in John Steinbeck's *The Grapes of Wrath*[4n]

INTERNATIONAL EVENTS

Japan

The first steps in a long war had, in fact, already been taken late in 1931 when an overcrowded Japan, pressed hard by the worldwide economic depression and under the control of its army, occupied Manchuria, an underpopulated region on the eastern coast of China. The League of Nations decided it was powerless to intervene where a country was no longer in control of its legitimate government. Thus began a war which was, for the Japanese, to last fourteen years. In December 1937 the Imperial Japanese Army entered the capital city of Nanking. Seeking revenge for fierce Chinese resistance en route, they had orders to kill all captives. Surrender being unthinkable in the Japanese military code, slaughter commenced with the filmed torture and execution of the 90,000 Chinese soldiers but then moved to the sexual abuse of all female residents from the aged to small children. After six weeks of carnage, some 300,000 of the city's 600,000 residents had been killed. The 'Rape of Nanking' remained the worst single atrocity of the long war. As Churchill was outlining the bleak task ahead of Great Britain in 1940, the Japanese were dropping contaminated food such as wheat and rice on China, and the dropping of fleas caused outbreaks of bubonic plague. The combination of fierce fighting, excessive cruelty and refusal to surrender were to mark the western powers' experience of the Japanese military throughout the coming world war and finally led to the dreadful extreme response by the USA in 1945.

Ethiopia

Late in 1934 the fascist Italian dictator Benito Mussolini, seeking to restore national pride following the humiliating military defeat by the Abyssinians eight years earlier and wishing to rebuild an Italian empire, moved troops from the Italian colonies of Somalia and Eritrea into Abyssinia. A full invasion was launched in October 1935, and six months later the Emperor Haile Selassie, 'The Lion of Judah,'[5n] was deposed in favour of King Victor Emmanuel III of Italy. The exiled emperor moved to Bath in southwest England, where he continued his campaign to free his country. In January 1941 he was to re-enter his realm, rally his loyal troops to fight with British forces under the command of the maverick General Orde Wingate and drive the Italians out. The Emperor was able to address his people from the capital Addis Ababa exactly five years after his exile. Although the League of Nations had condemned Italy's invasion and passed resolutions imposing sanctions, member nations failed to act despite a dramatic address by the Emperor in which he made it clear that Italian forces had used chemical weapons against his people. The Italian campaign in Abyssinia not only destroyed any credibility left in the League, but also carried a further warning of the atrocities that modern warfare would soon bring home to us all. At home, it had been claimed that Abyssinia was too far away to be of immediate concern, rather ignoring the fact that the aggressor was Italy. The same argument would be used again within four years. The next marker on the road to war was within another European country, where the clash of ideologies drew men and women from across the world to fight for democracy against dictatorship.

Spain

Spain, with a long history of political unrest and military coups, including the ceding of power from King Alfonso XIII to form a virtual republic in 1923, suffered badly in the economic depression, which a weak liberal government had been handled ineptly. Consequent demonstrations and strikes by workers led the right wing, in close alliance with the Catholic Church, to fear Bolshevik influences. Steps taken by one side to counter actions by the other escalated tension step by step until, in July 1936, a military coup led by General Francisco Franco toppled the central government and commenced a three-year civil war, ending in the surrender of the most independent and republican of regions of Basque and Catalonia. This intense conflict remained geographically isolated, having no global consequences, except that both Spain and Portugal remained nominally neutral during the approaching world war. The Spanish Civil War (1936–1939) foreshadowed coming events in that it was essentially a clash of deeply held values: fascism vs democracy. It demonstrated for the first time how the rapid communication of radio and film could immediately spread news across the world, and it showed the destructive power of aerial bombardment. In those three years, the clash of values and beliefs split families, corrupted the Catholic Church and featured terrible atrocities, all of which continued after the war and left deep scars that continue to this day.[6n]

Some 40,000 volunteers from fifty countries were drawn to fight, mostly for the republican side, recruitment being largely organised through communist international organisations. The majority were of left-wing persuasion, including members of national communist parties, many disturbed by the growing right-wing movements at home. It was the sight of Mosley's 'Blackshirts' parading openly in the streets that encouraged many British volunteers to head for Spain. Among them was the writer and poet Laurie Lee, who explained

> I believe we shared something else unique to us at that time … the chance to make one grand and uncomplicated gesture of personal sacrifice and faith which may never occur again … few of us yet knew that we had come to a war of antique muskets and jamming machine-guns, to be led by brave but bewildered amateurs. But for the moment there were no half-truths and hesitations, we had found a new morality, and discovered a new Satan – Fascism.[7]

The exploits of the volunteers fed back into popular culture,[8n] and the personal accounts of their involvement in modern close encounter warfare seemed to indicate that individuals could make a difference. Jack Jones, who was to lead the trade union opposition to the government of Ted Heath resulting in the national crises of 1972 and 1974, recalled that

> For many men who went, it wasn't a sense of adventure by any means. It was a feeling that we were on the right side – the side of justice. For us it was the battle against fascism, including our local Mosley crowd, and that inspired me and encouraged me to do what I could against it,

even if it meant laying down my life for it … Before the battle of the Ebro I met up with young Ted Heath (later the Tory Prime Minister). As chairman of the Federation of Conservative Associations he came out with a small group of students while we were in training. I suppose he reflected a strand of Conservative thinking that had some sympathy for the Republic – a line more prominently followed by the Duchess of Athol and even occasionally by Winston Churchill. I established a link with him which I maintained afterwards.[9n]

Few foreign volunteers fought on the fascist side, but Franco was supported by Hitler, most strikingly on the afternoon of April 28th 1937 when wave after wave of German bombers destroyed the undefended Basque town of Guernica, flying in at 600 feet. The increased speed of communication meant that the atrocity was reported effectively by newsprint and radio, strengthening worldwide anti-fascist sentiment,[10n] while Pablo Picasso's iconic painting *Guernica*, first shown at the 1937 Paris Exhibition, ensured a lasting memorial.[11n] While the Spanish experience persuaded the British to modernise their air force, it also put political pressure on some western governments to introduce economic and social reforms as a matter of considered policy rather than those previously introduced for fear of popular uprisings. More generally it could be claimed that this early 'success' of fascism led directly to its eventual downfall as the campaign had alerted people everywhere of the threat to the essential values of a democratic and open society.

Germany

Since his appointment as German Chancellor in 1933, Hitler had proclaimed his programme of aggressive geographical expansionism (requiring massive military expenditure) and Aryan ethnic purity. As the central determining features of both of these policies became clear to the outside world, it was obvious that no liberal democracy could realistically consider compromise. Nonetheless, in the five years before the final outbreak of war many governments, fearing a return of the horrors of WWI and well aware of the poor state of their economies and the war weariness of their citizens, attempted to appease the ambitions of the Reich. In August 1936, with great hopes that the occasion would act as a showcase for its new Aryan ideals, Germany hosted the Olympic Games in Berlin. Much to Hitler's fury, both the 200 metre race and the long jump were won by Jesse Owens, an African-American. On March 12th 1938, a bare six months after Franco's victory in Spain, Hitler crossed the border into Austria, and a month later he incorporated Austria under full German control, thus gaining immediate access to valuable mineral resources and a supply of labour. Although regretting the brutality of the event, Conservative Prime Minister Neville Chamberlain reflected the views of many when he told the Cabinet that he did not think anything that had happened should cause the government to alter their present policy of seeking a general settlement of Europe's problems through the appeasement of Germany. Given the rising independence movements and some actual revolts in British colonies, it was considered that a war in Europe would threaten British world domination. The British view of looking beyond instead of at Europe was to prove fateful for the second but not the last time.[12]

Anti-Jewish propaganda in Germany had steadily raised racial tension since Hitler's accession. The 1935 Nuremburg Laws had forbidden sexual intercourse between a Jew and an Aryan, leading to the breakup of families and the turning of a blind eye to the harassment of Jews and other minorities, events which acted as a clear warning and encouraged many Jewish families to emigrate. The drive to promote a pure Aryan German race demanded that all Jews be driven out of any positions of influence and expelled from the Reich. On the night of November 9th/10th 1938 Nazi thugs carried out coordinated raids on Jewish property. Some 100 Jews were killed, and synagogues were ransacked throughout Germany and Austria. Around 30,000 Jewish men were sent to concentration camps to work and await expulsion. In a crazy counterpoint, the young Orson Welles' Halloween radio production of H. G. Wells' *War of the Worlds* was so realistic that people panicked, jammed telephone and police lines and fled on crowded roads to escape these Martian warriors. In Indianapolis a church service was interrupted by a man who rushed in shouting 'New York is destroyed. It's the end of the world. We might as well go home to die. I've just heard it on the radio.' What a good illustration of both the degree of international nervousness and the power of a new medium. In late 1938 *Story* magazine caused another sensation in the USA when a fictional series of letters was published exposing the poison of the Nazi regime in Germany. Letters from a Jewish businessman who had returned to Germany sought to explain the feeling abroad in that country, while the replies sought to halt his moral corruption and loss of critical thought. The last letter to Germany was returned 'Address Unknown,' which is the title under which the novel was eventually published:[13n]

> [Hitler] is like an electric shock … there is a surge. The people everywhere have had a quickening. The old despair has been thrown aside like a forgotten coat. No longer the people wrap themselves in shame. A leader is found! Yet cautiously to myself, I ask a leader to where?
>
> If I could show you, if I could make you see – the rebirth of this new Germany under our Gentle Leader … In defeat for fourteen years we bowed our heads. We ate the bitter bread of shame and drank the thin gruel of poverty. But now we are free men. Once pride is shown I put my back and shoulders behind the great new movement. I am a man because I act … I do not question the ends of our action. It is not necessary. Men are not drawn into bad things with so much joy and eagerness.

The early indications were that Jewish communities were divided between those who quickly left Germany and those who stayed, either out of the habit and connections of daily life – or perhaps they could not believe the reality of what lay ahead.[14n]

Czechoslovakia's rich mineral and heavy industrial plants were too tempting a target for Hitler, particularly as some three million ethnic Germans lived in the Czech

Sudetenland. A propaganda campaign was launched demanding that they be brought home to the Reich. France and Russia had direct treaty obligations to Czechoslovakia, and Britain was bound to assist France. Hitler could have chosen to ignore these and march his troops across the border, but he knew that most Germans were horrified by the prospect of another war, a view shared by many senior politicians and military commanders. In fact, some consideration was given to deposing the Chancellor should he attack Czechoslovakia. September 1938 saw Chamberlain's last desperate attempts to preserve peace in Europe by negotiation, leading to the infamous Munich Agreement which forced the Czechs to cede the Sudetenland. It is difficult, with the knowledge of what was to follow, to understand the policy of appeasement in Europe, but in addition to the fresh memories of the recent war, governments knew that they were at this time too weak to beat the massively re-armed Germany; Allied troops were still engaged across the world (in the British case policing an increasingly restless Empire) and their foreign policies were in turmoil with rearmament programmes, in the case of Britain resisted by both the Labour and Liberal parties.

Europe

Before September 1938 was out, America had declared its neutrality. Russia, reassured from the east by its Sino-Japanese Treaty and having signed a non-aggression pact with Germany, invaded Poland from the east, incorporating Belarus into the USSR en route. The two powers then divided Poland as previously agreed.[15n] The Polish forces fought bravely but were denied the expected support from France and Britain. The campaign was short and gave a further taste of total war. Fifty thousand people were killed in the intensive bombing of Warsaw. Civilians attempting to escape were strafed on the roads by the Luftwaffe. Twenty thousand civilians were killed in reprisals. Europe had never seen anything like it. Joint victory parades were held in Warsaw for Stalin and Hitler on October 10th 1939. The previous day, Hitler had ordered his generals to prepare their plans for the invasion of Western Europe.

More detail should now be added to the opening quotation from Eric Hobsbawm. After the First World War all European countries had suffered from the economic depression and the influenza pandemic, which had killed more people than the war. People were tired and fearful of more conflict. Now an ambitious Germany was seen to have achieved so much at so little cost. It had a well-trained, well-equipped and well-prepared army, air force and navy. Hitler, the 'Hun in a hurry,' could see his overblown ambitions being quickly realised. With 2,730,000 troops (having ignored the 1918 imposed limit of 100,000), 2,916 planes, 28 warships and a fleet of U-boats, he could turn on Russia if he chose, then look to see France and Britain sue for peace. Although Russia had more troops and the capacity to enlist vast numbers, her services had been prejudiced by Stalin's successive brutal purges, including the recent killing or exiling of more than half of the officer corps. Poland had a sound army of some 1,200,000, with 670 planes. France had 900,000 soldiers, 950 planes and 97 warships in September 1939 but were over-reliant on the heavily fortified defensive Maginot Line built specifically to protect the eastern border from a German invasion. Britain had only 403,000 troops and 1,660 warplanes boosted by a strong navy of 251 ships, wonderful for defence across the Empire rather than fighting in Europe. America, determined not to get involved in another European war, had a similarly strong navy but only 175,000 full-time troops. These opening positions go a long way to explain the conduct of the coming war. The Allies, faced with the need to recruit and equip a force strong enough to halt Hitler, could only look to 1942/3 as a target date for any decisive campaign. Before then, and for some time afterwards, battles would have to be joined conservatively to avoid waste of precious trained manpower and valuable equipment.

In the Allies' view, if this turned out to be a long war, Poland could be sacrificed for a while, and it remained to be seen how long the USSR/Germany partnership would last given their fiercely opposing ideological beliefs. Uniquely, Britain and the Allies would have to rely on amphibious landings, a skill which was completely undeveloped.[16n] The necessity for such a slow build up was frequently to enrage Stalin, once he had changed sides, as he had the vast eastern area of the USSR (well out of range of German attack) in which to manufacture equipment and enlist manpower. In addition of course he had the resources of millions of slaves labouring in the remote Gulags, the existence of which was unknown in the west. Seven European countries were not directly involved in the war.[17n]

The war aims of the major combatants can readily be summarised: Germany sought expansion and the establishment of a united Europe of racial purity; Russia wanted to regain the territories that it had been forced to give up after the previous war; Poland and France wanted to live independently in peace. Britain, in common with others, wanted to defeat fascism and retain its Empire (and thus its prime role in the world). None of these aims remained intact as the war progressed. Stalin described Europe in 1939 as a 'poker game' with three players, in which each hoped to persuade the other two to destroy one another, leaving the third to take the winnings, the three players being the fascists (Nazi Germany), the capitalists (Britain and France) and the Bolsheviks (USSR). America, once it entered the war and Germany was defeated, could anticipate a weakened Britain and Russia, and thus assume its manifest destiny as the world's sole superpower. In the meantime it could turn its depressed economy to boom time by supplying arms and equipment to the Allies. It would be true to say that while the American public and their President were generally sympathetic to the British position, especially following the American Ed Murrow's emotional reporting on London's suffering under nightly bombing,[18] Congress remained resolutely isolationist. The American Ambassador to London, Joseph Kennedy, was reporting that in his view the British could not withstand the Germans and a Nazi victory was certain.

The early months of 1940 became known as the 'Phoney War' when both sides were preparing for the next moves in Europe and there were only two local military engagements. This was not entirely phoney as the first civilian deaths happened on March 16th 1940 when bombs, targeted at the naval base, were dropped on the Orkneys. On April 30th

1940, two people were killed at Clacton on England's east coast when a German bomber crashed after having been disabled by an RAF fighter. The German crew of four were killed. They were buried with full military honours, and flowers were sent from the RAF base 'With deepest sympathy' and from local women 'Knowing you have lost someone dear to you.'[19] Certainly not fully appreciated by those at home at the time was that in the Atlantic German battleships and U-boats were determinedly and successfully attacking Allied ships with the strategic aim of cutting supplies of food, equipment and ammunition, thus hoping to force an early surrender. Some 800,000 tons of Allied shipping was sunk in these early years.

An early disaster occurred on October 14th 1939 when a German U-boat sailed, on the surface, into the secure Scottish base at Scapa Flow and sunk the battleship HMS *Royal Oak* with the loss of 833 crew (including 122 boy sailors) then used the confusion to escape so that the U-boat crew could enjoy a celebratory lunch with Hitler. At the close of 1939 in the South Atlantic, Royal Navy success had come from a determined and cleverly fought campaign which trapped the German heavy cruiser *Admiral Graf Spee* (which had featured in the Coronation Review of 1937) in the neutral harbour of Montevideo while Admiral Harwood's two under-armed ships waited in the mouth of the River Plate. British diplomats in Uruguay successfully pressed for the *Graf Spee* to leave this neutral port. As the ship prepared to leave, false information from the British Navy led the captain to believe that a strong force awaited him if he left. On December 17th he scuttled his ship, one of the premier German ships, in order either to save the life of his crew and to avoid certain internment by the British.[20]

In March 1940 Germany, Italy and Japan signed the Tripartite Pact, and on May 10th Germany launched its vast three-pronged attack on France. The northern divisions rolled through the Netherlands towards Belgium, where they drew the main force of the French Army and the small British expeditionary force. Meanwhile, the central attack drove through the mountains and forests of Ardennes, where the French, assuming that to be impenetrable, had not fortified the Maginot Line. By May 16th, German troops had cut Allied communications and were approaching the English Channel, corralling Allied troops in the Calais to Dunkirk area. In the belief that Britain would sue for peace, Hitler ordered his troops to halt. What followed during the nine days from May 20th was the chaotic, but miraculous, rescue of a significant number of Allied troops by naval vessels and many small ships that were capable of crossing the English Channel.[21n]

The loss of essential men and equipment in this humiliating retreat was hailed as the victory of Dunkirk. The returning troops were at rock bottom; the last thing they wanted to do was face the public. However, the pride in this event served to raise their morale – there were crowds waving flags of welcome, and all the way to London people lined and ran alongside the tracks cheering the returning troops. Every time they pulled into a station, tea and cigarettes were passed through the windows of the locked carriages.

Paris fell on June 10th 1940, and on the 16th the French Government surrendered in humiliating circumstances. For a nation who had put their trust in the best and most prepared army in the world, this was unbelievable. Marshal Philippe Pétain, a great hero of the First World War, declared a new government and negotiated a peace settlement which allowed him continued authority over French citizens across France, more particularly in the southern third that Germany then considered it would be too costly to occupy. In taking this step Pétain was supported by the majority of the population, for whom the prospect of another war had been intolerable, as well as those on the political right who had some sympathy with national socialism. The new government established itself in the spa town of Vichy, replacing the established motto of 'Liberty, Equality, Fraternity' with 'Family, Work, Fatherland,' and took an authoritarian stance, particularly against those who by popular belief were thought to bear some responsibility for the military defeat: the Jews, the Left and those who had softened French culture during the inter-war social heyday. Pétain's government was soon to learn their subordinate position as they were required to collaborate in the forced supply of labour (naturally Jews and communists first), and fear, a poor food supply and powerlessness produced a demoralised and divided population.

Successive Vichy prime ministers sought in vain to negotiate better terms for the occupation, but Hitler's main motivation remained revenge for the punitive terms imposed in 1918; he would never see France as an ally. In late 1942, as German troops spread out to occupy the whole of France, the Vichy government were clearly seen as mere Nazi puppets. More resistance groups established themselves to fight the occupiers. For one German soldier killed, the Nazis required six French hostages, supplied by Vichy, a ratio which quickly rose to fifty. Faced with a threat to suspend Pétain's government in mid 1942, his police fully co-operated in the rounding up of Jews for extermination.

The humiliating peace agreed by Pétain was never accepted by a small group of army officers led by General de Gaulle. On June 17th 1940 they had flown in a small biplane to England, thus placing themselves in rebellion against the French Government and becoming deserters of the French State. A brief meeting with Churchill gave access to the BBC, and on June 18th the General gave the first of three speeches calling on all French people to resist the German invasion and reassuring them that the cause of France was not lost:

> I General de Gaulle now in London am fighting for you for France does not stand alone. Behind her is a vast empire, and she can make common cause with the British empire, which commands the seas. Like England she can draw on the immense industrial resources of the United States … Whatever happens the flame of France must not and shall not perish.

As the details of Pétain's deal became better understood, de Gaulle became more aggressive in denouncing them for the complete demobilisation of French forces and the total capitulation of France and the placement of her people in slavery. His next broadcast

> [called] upon all the leaders, together with all soldiers, sailors and airmen of the French land sea and air forces, wherever they may now be to get in touch with me. I call upon all Frenchmen who want to remain free to listen to my voice and follow me.[22]

Whilst it is impossible to underestimate the contribution made by de Gaulle and the Free French troops, he was not an easy man to deal with. Although he was determined and possessed an obsessive national pride, he was disadvantaged in London against the representatives of Poland, Norway and the Benelux countries whose legitimate governments were in exile. De Gaulle was a sole military commander who presented difficulties for the formalities of diplomatic protocol. This proud man thus often felt slighted and humiliated, feelings which were to cause us problems for many years to come.[23n]

Italy, whose occupied territories bordered Egypt and whose navy dominated the Mediterranean, declared war on Britain in June 1940. To prevent valuable assets falling into Axis hands, the British Navy at Algiers sunk the French Fleet with all hands when the commanding admiral refused to cooperate. The message was 'Don't mess with the British,' although condemnation came from around the world. This was war. On June 16th 1940 Britain suffered its worst ever maritime disaster when the Cunard liner RMS *Lancastria* with up to 9,000 troops and evacuees escaping France was sunk off Saint-Nazaire; only 2,500 were saved. Churchill imposed a complete news blackout.

Now was the time that 'Britain stood alone,' as reflected in the report of Cordell Hull, President Roosevelt's Secretary of State:

> Never have I admired a people more than I admired the British people in the summer and autumn of 1940. Even the children seemed to realize that upon their indomitable spirit depended not only their own fate, but that of the whole democratic world.[24]

Commonwealth and Colonies

The portrayal of Britain as standing alone should never obscure the strength, determination and size of the support given by the Empire. The principal dominions were first to declare their complete support. The Prime Minister of Australia, Robert Menzies, summed up the spirit of the times by announcing

> We are in this most holy war with you, everything that we have of manpower or treasure or skill or determination is pledged to work and fight for you until victory is attained. One King, one flag, one cause.[25]

The first contingent of Canadians had arrived in the UK by September 1939; conscription was introduced late in the war and then only for support roles. Throughout the war all Canadian and Empire soldiers were volunteers. In total, some 8,700,000 men from the Empire fought in the war: 450,000 were killed. India contributed 2,250,000 men, despite the fact that the Viceroy had declared them at war without any consultation with the government. Pandit Nehru (the leader of the Indian Independent Movement) deplored the proclamation, but both he and Mahatma Gandhi (the leader of the Congress Party) agreed with the sentiment. Both had campaigned for Indian independence, but they considered that the best interests of the campaign lay in a British victory. Nehru allied himself for a period with Chandra Bose (the president of the All India Forward Bloc), who took a more militant stand and raised troops to fight against the British.

Air Raids

German air raids on Britain started with RAF and communications targets, but in June 1940 the German bombers and their escorting fighters were met by the faster and more manoeuvrable Spitfires and Hurricanes, planes piloted by young extraordinarily brave British, Commonwealth, Czechoslovakian, Polish, French and American pilots. The famous Battle of Britain, when so much depended on so few, quickly increased the German losses, forcing the Luftwaffe to move both to urban targets and night-time raids by September. In those three critical months the Luftwaffe lost 1,733 planes, the RAF 915. The success of the RAF, both the famous few fighters but also the brave bomber crews who were decimating German airfields, deprived Hitler of the aerial superiority that was an essential prerequisite to any cross-Channel invasion, which he cancelled that month. In fact, 'the few' had forced a situation that would foretell the end of the war. Hitler's response was to turn eastwards and plan his attack on Russia, his greatest strategic mistake.

Northern Africa

Italy was building up its strength in the Mediterranean. Italian and German troops had moved across northern Africa to the Egyptian border where British troops were outnumbered five to one, causing the government to consider abandoning this part of the Empire in order to concentrate on defending the home islands. It was, however, essential to maintain domination of the Mediterranean in order to keep essential links with the eastern colonies through the Suez Canal. In November 1940 Britain sunk a significant part of the Italian Fleet, and the Allied land forces were able to force Italian troops back along the coast to Benghazi. The very able German General Erwin Rommel then took command and took his troops back to the Egyptian border, with the exception of the Tobruk garrison which was extraordinarily defended by British, Australian and Polish troops.

As the year ended, President Roosevelt was re-elected on a campaign promise of 'No war,' although in fact America was re-arming and producing vast supplies of ammunition and equipment for the Allies. It had become the great arsenal for democracy, and the dreadful level of pre-war unemployment was falling fast. At the start of 1941 Roosevelt bypassed the Neutrality Acts by declaring 50 destroyers and ammunition surplus to American requirements and transferred them to Britain in exchange for a long list of leased bases in the Caribbean and Newfoundland. A Lend–Lease agreement was negotiated between the United States and the Allies, Britain getting the major part. Although Roosevelt described the arrangement as 'lending one's hose to a neighbour so he can put out the fire,' the truth was that Britain was no longer an entirely independent state. Early in 1941, Wendell Willkie, as the newly appointed Ambassador to the UK, brought with him a hand-written letter from the President, quoting Longfellow:

> Sail on, O Ship of State!
> Sail on, O Union, strong and great!
> Humanity with all its fears,
> With all the hopes of future years,
> Is hanging breathless on thy fate![26]

Nazi–Soviet Pact

By late 1940, while Britain was desperately building up its stocks of aircraft, ships, arms and equipment towards the coming fight, Hitler could consider his options now that his forces had conquered all of contested Europe. His enemies did not include Russia and America, although both were growing in military might. Although it was tempting to attack the United Kingdom, a sea and airborne invasion would be difficult while the RAF was so strong. In the meantime a critical issue was whether to prolong the Nazi–Soviet Pact, which might still pay dividends by concessions yet to be wrung from a Russia, faced with an all-powerful Germany and promises of joint planning to conquer and divide the world. If Germany fought and conquered Russia, the British would be most likely to surrender without a fight. In November 1940 Vyacheslav Molotov, Russia's Foreign Minister, arrived in Berlin to confer. Hitler proposed that Russia could rule the Middle East as Britain, following Dunkirk, was virtually defeated. Molotov reportedly said little of consequence except 'No' (for which he was to become famous in all post-war negotiations) but did wonder why, if Britain was no longer to be feared, the meeting was being held in an air-raid shelter. The Germans followed this meeting with a written proposal which in broad terms kept Russia out of Europe but offered her new territories in the Eastern Mediterranean and the Persian Gulf. Stalin never replied. One month later Hitler ordered plans to prepare for the invasion of Russia, called Operation Barbarossa. Preparations were to be completed by May 1941. In the meantime he could attack the Middle East where the UK's hold was weak, a course which would also please Stalin. However, although the Soviet military was numerous, it was still disabled as a result of Stalin's continuing purges of the officer class. If the completed plans for Operation Barbarossa were activated, the next move could be eastwards. Hitler gave successive assurances to Stalin that their relationship as allies was firm, that the growing German forces assembling in the east were both a feint to confuse the British and a chance to train and strengthen the troops out of range of British bombers. Stalin, for reasons still unclear, refused to accept intelligence from within his own forces and from Churchill, who was able to decode German directives using the Ultra code-breaking system indicating that Germany was preparing to invade.

Betrayal and Revenge

Saturday June 21st 1941 was a warm but uneasy day in Moscow: the schools had broken up for holidays; Dynamo Moscow, the football team, lost their match; and the theatres were showing *Rigoletto, La Traviata* and Chekhov's *Three Sisters*. Stalin and the Politburo sat all day, coming and going. By early evening Stalin was deeply disturbed by the persistently ominous reports that even his Great Terror could not disperse. Just after midnight, Stalin was told that yet another German deserter had swum from Romania to Ukraine to warn his communist comrades that they had orders to attack at dawn. Stalin ordered him shot for disinformation. At 03.00 hrs on June 22nd 1941 German troops invaded, thus marking, in the words of the great historian A. J. P. Taylor, the greatest event of the Second World War. The troop and equipment resources involved were on a scale vastly in excess of anything before or since, and the campaign was to last some 46 months. At first all seemed well for the German troops as they swept east towards Moscow, north towards Leningrad and south towards Kiev. The German forces were intent on conquering territory and the resources of the land, and were not in the least concerned with capturing the hearts and minds of the population, who were seen only to be exploited.

Despite fierce resistance by Russian troops, who either fought to the last man with no retreat or moved back to be shot by their own officers and the infamous People's Commissariat for Internal Affairs (NKVD), some two million Russian troops were taken prisoner (thus strengthening the number of slave labourers for the German war effort) and thousands of tanks and aircraft were lost. It was however also true that Hitler's war machine was now having to face both east and west. In the west of course he was playing a waiting game, gambling that with a Russian defeat Britain would surrender rather than stand alone, but his eastern drive was consuming vast resources with extraordinarily extended supply lines. Within eight or so weeks Stalin's military were able to stiffen their resistance at least to slow the German advance. By August the German army in the north had no option but to blockade the city of Leningrad, a siege which was to last for nearly 900 days and cost a million lives. (Leningrad restored its original name of St Petersburg in 1961.) In December, in heavy snow and temperatures of minus 40 degrees centigrade, the Russian army counterattacked to drive the enemy's central force from near Moscow. Hitler's army had been checked for the first time in more than two years. An element that emerged in August 1942 in Leningrad was the power of music on Russian morale. By this time the inhabitants of the city were exhausted and starving, but the composer Dmitri Shostakovich, who lived among them, had completed his immense Seventh Symphony. The authorities allowed all musicians, including military personnel, to rebuild the Bolshoi Theatre Orchestra to perform the world premiere. Poorly dressed and with hardly enough strength to hold instruments, let alone play with such damaged and calloused hands, the orchestra completed a fifteen-minute rehearsal and performed the symphony which was broadcast by loudspeaker and radio throughout the city.

Russian morale was strengthened, and in fact the city was never defeated. A German soldier having heard the music realised that victory would be impossible, so he surrendered. He was not alone. The forthcoming battles at the Eastern Front would drain both nations of manpower and resources to a greater extent than would the forthcoming situation at the Western Front, hence the importance of these events in the eventual defeat of Germany.

The Mediterranean

If Germany were to act in the Middle East, the need to dominate the Mediterranean and cut off the Allies' supplies was essential; with this in mind, Luftwaffe reinforcements were sent to Sicily to support Italian efforts. Attacks were launched on Allied convoys and the attacks on the 'British Fortress' of Malta were intensified. The skills of the Royal Navy, the RAF fighters and the loyalty and long personal relationship between the Maltese, these forces and the Crown were underestimated. The bombing reached unbelievable levels as war proceeded, and the importance of the island for the Royal Navy and Allied supplies became critical. This virtual 'Siege of Malta' continued for two years.[27n] With only three weeks' food left, the British Cabinet decided to send a huge convoy escorted by the largest naval ships available. Unfortunately news of its departure and destination reached Berlin before the ship left Britain; consequently, German and Italian forces were waiting in strength and a major naval battle was in store. Central to the convoy was the tanker SS *Ohio* carrying 11,000 tons of aviation fuel. The main battle was engaged on August 12th 1942 and lasted for four days. Many Allied ships were lost, and the slow-moving *Ohio* (an American ship with a British crew) was hit by a torpedo, five bombs and a crashing plane; unbelievably the aviation fuel never caught fire! The few ships that remained in the convoy were sufficient to ease the needs of the island, and on August 15th the *Ohio*'s arrival, kept afloat by destroyers on either side, ensured that the fighter and bomber planes based at Luca and other bases on Malta could continue their attacks on enemy ships that were carrying troops and equipment retreating from North Africa to Sicily and Italy. From then until May Malta suffered almost continuous bombing, shelling from German warships and submarine attacks on all vessels that strove to keep the island supplied.[28n]

Politics

Britain, whose only formal ally was occupied Poland (Poland's government and military leaders in England were calling on all Polish citizens living abroad to join the Allies), was increasingly reliant on America for sustenance and support. Churchill continued to press Roosevelt for a more formal alliance, but all that could be agreed was a statement of principles known as the Atlantic Charter (declared in August 1941), the core values of which were to morph into the formative document for the post-war United Nations Organization. As the USSR changed sides, Lend–Lease had been extended to it;

in fact America was now actively supporting Britain, Russia and China in their war with Japan, and the American Navy was fighting German U-boats in the Atlantic. Although Germany, Italy and Japan had declared war, it remained beyond President Roosevelt's power to formally respond in the face of an isolationist Congress and the fact that the economy was booming with no immediate risk to their own forces. Churchill had been quick to exploit Stalin's change of sides. Before the formal signing of any Anglo-Soviet treaty (on May 26th 1942), the first of the brave but relatively unsung Arctic convoys had left Scapa Flow in August 1941 for Murmansk loaded with arms and ammunition. In Churchill's view when times were hard we would sup with the Devil, even if one had to use a long spoon. In Britain at last the suspicion and distrust aimed at supporters of communism was easing as all political constituencies could now rally behind an anti-fascist call. The pre-war support for communism now seemed justified, and the fearful Stalin in league with Hitler was transformed to good old Uncle Joe fighting with us.

North Africa

In Egypt General Claude Auchinleck was carefully preparing to attack the Italian and German forces, once again pressing the Egyptian borders. In November, the Eighth Army made a western thrust and managed to relieve the besieged garrison at Tobruk. The Germans, under the command of Rommel, counterattacked, capturing some 38,000 troops and returning to the Egyptian border. General Auchinleck was replaced by General Bernard Montgomery.

Lieutenant, Royal Ordinance Corps, W. W. Wickett, my future wife's father, was attached to the Royal Artillery and had experienced the retreat from Rommel's forces. He was not a happy man and was sending letters home to his wife, who had a distant relative in the War Office, to please get him home, but before the next campaign started he caught a bad dose of dysentery and at the age of 40 was declared unfit for active service and sent on the long voyage home. This involved a route via the Southern Ocean and the West Indies with a shipload of similarly 'crocked' servicemen of various nations.

The Far East

America, with Britain and the Dutch government-in-exile, concerned at the Japanese aim of expansion across the Pacific, had imposed complete trade sanctions in the summer of 1941. The shortage of fuel oil hit the Japanese hard and presented them with a sharp dilemma: either withdraw their ambitions or attack British, Dutch and American territories in the Far East. On December 7th 1941 Japan invaded Malaya, quickly destroying the British air force, then advanced into the New Territories of Hong Kong, which surrendered on Christmas Day. The main defence plan had relied on reinforcement by the Royal Navy, but at this time they were fully occupied in the Atlantic. The same strategy failed for the defence of Malaya, and in fact in the Far East generally British troops were poorly trained and led. They had relied on the historically superior status of 'the Empire' and had been relatively out of touch with modern military developments. In the autumn of 1941 the Malaya garrison consisted of a small British presence, one Australian and one Indian division plus local Malay troops. They were harassed right down the Malayan peninsula by an overwhelming Japanese force. The mainland was surrendered on February 1st 1942. The command to hold Singapore at all costs became impossible to obey, and this major garrison and emblem of the British Empire surrendered on February 15th. As the sound of the Japanese bombs fell, a young Lee Kwan Yew, the future Prime Minister of Singapore, was said to have remarked, 'That noise is the end of the British Empire.' British prisoners, however, were to be subject to the utmost cruelty in captivity.[29n]

In June, the Japanese Prime Minister Major General Hideki Tojo attended a rally in Singapore and was joined by Subhas Chandra Bose, a radical member of the Indian Congress Party, who had campaigned for independence from Britain and had formed a nationalist army to fight the British, particularly in Burma at Imphal. The fight was on to save the Indian subcontinent, the 'Jewel in the Crown' of the Empire. Between Malaya and India lay Burma, suffering the same defensive shortfalls as Malaya and Singapore. Some reinforcements were dispatched from Europe and China with America playing a significant part in the campaign to resist Japanese advance. The RAF had superiority in the air throughout the campaign. Having faced the invasion in January 1942, the British were soon forced into the long 1,000 mile retreat towards the Indian border with 13,000 casualties, 4,000 of which were fatal. This terrible defeat in the Far East was followed almost immediately by Rommel's attack in North Africa. These were bad times.

Churchill reacted by changing the command of the Fourteenth Army to the charismatic and much respected Lt General Sir William Slim.[30n] Slim commanded the instant respect of his men, having worked his way up from the ranks. Addressing troops who saw themselves as the forgotten army, he assured them, 'What do you mean forgotten? No one's fucking heard of you.'[31] He was one of the few commanders brave enough to deploy the eccentric and daring Major General Orde Wingate (of Ethiopian fame), and they both served under the general command of Vice Admiral Lord Louis Mountbatten.[32n] As Supreme Allied Commander in the Far East, Mountbatten was concerned not only with the coordination of British, American and Chinese forces, but also with the delicate political issues facing the British Raj in India, including a major threat of civil disobedience and some military nationalists supported by Chinese communists seeking to end British rule. The Indian National Congress, including Nehru, joined the 'Quit India' campaign started by Gandhi in 1942, which demanded independence as a condition for further wartime support. Gandhi was imprisoned for two years, but was released in 1944 as his health had deteriorated so much that it was feared his death in jail would provoke complete upheaval. Nationalist movements in Burma, Indonesia, Vietnam and some countries in Africa were also increasing their activities at this time. At one time, fifty British battalions had to be deployed in India to contain these internal threats.

The Pacific

On December 7th 1941 the Japanese air force bombed the American fleet at Pearl Harbour in Hawaii killing 2,400 and sinking or damaging eight ships. Fortunately, the aircraft carriers had left port on exercise. Disputes continue to this day as to whether Roosevelt or Churchill had advance warning of this attack then delayed action knowing that such an attack would bring America into the war. The next day, Congress declared war on Japan but remained silent about Germany and Italy. In fact, as these countries were allied with Japan, the USA had now in practice joined the war, although its formal declarations were limited to Bulgaria, Hungary and Romania! Hitler, in a bid to impress Japan, declared war on the USA. China declared war on Japan now that they could be assured of American help. Although the nationalist forces, commanded by Chiang Kai-shek, and the communists had resolved to fight Japan together, the partnership had already broken down. Chiang Kai-shek established himself in a dictatorial position, renounced communism and was thus supported by America, who supplied his forces with arms and equipment.

Seizing a golden opportunity, Churchill arrived in Washington four days after the attack on Pearl Harbour. He stayed until early in 1942 to work out the formal structures of a joint command, gaining a resolution that Germany must be defeated before a full attack on Japan. Stalin was not included in these discussions, and in any event he was fully occupied in chasing the Germans from Moscow. On Roosevelt's initiative, a 'United Nations Declaration of Allied war aims,' incorporating the values of the Atlantic Charter, was signed by 26 nations in January 1942.

Joint planning was not without major disagreement; in general terms, America was for an early attack in Europe whereas Churchill was more cautious. This was in part due to the toll on shipping by German U-boats, which were at the height of their power; they were approaching their target of 700,000 tons of shipping sunk every month, thus preventing the transportation of arms and manpower across the Atlantic and forcing Britain to adopt stricter rationing of fuel and food. Some examples of rationing at this time were sugar, reduced by half to 8 ounces per week, tea to 2 ounces per week and sweets to 12 ounces per month. (One ounce equals 28.35 grammes – a standard 250 g pack of butter is therefore equivalent to just under 9 ounces.) Dried milk, dried eggs and whale meat crept into use. The government, through the Minister of Food Lord Woolton, urged complete economy in the use of basic products, giving rise to a popular ditty:

> Those who have the will to win
> Cook potatoes in their skin
> Knowing that the sight of peelings
> Deeply hurts Lord Woolton's feelings

In March 1942 America ordered 120,000 Japanese American citizens to go to special camps.[33n] The vast battle of the Pacific, which was to range across all the island communities to Australia, Malaya and India and would last for nearly four years, commenced.

For some nine months the Japanese held the initiative, sinking key American carriers and battleships, occupying islands, including Dutch Java, and bombing Darwin in Australia in February 1942. The so-called 'Yellow Peril' was let loose. The following month, a foretaste of Japanese military values and operational cruelty was experienced in the Philippines, where 76,000 American and Filipino prisoners of war were forced to march sixty miles in unbearable heat with no food or water. The march, which lasted a week, was characterised by wide-ranging physical abuse and murder; beheadings, cut throats and casual shootings were the more common and merciful actions, compared to bayonet stabbings, rapes, disembowelments and numerous rifle butt beatings. Falling down or being unable to continue moving was tantamount to a death sentence, as was any degree of protest or expression of displeasure. It is estimated that only 54,000 prisoners reached the destination; 5,000 Americans died.[34n]

In June 1942 squadrons of US torpedo planes destroyed four Japanese carriers, complete with all their aircraft, as well as a cruiser at Midway Island, marking a turning point in the Pacific campaign. Two months later, the extensive and fiercely fought battle of Guadalcanal in the Solomon Islands commenced, and this lasted right through to the major land battle of Bloody Ridge and the defeat of a Japanese naval task force. Further major land battles against a determined enemy lasted until December 1942 when, extraordinarily, Emperor Hirohito gave permission for his troops to leave Guadalcanal. Over 7,000 American and 31,000 Japanese troops had died.

New Technology

The combined Allied naval power had to be concentrated on essential supply convoys in the North Atlantic to the UK and Russia. The Battle of the Atlantic would continue throughout 1942, but Allied ability to deploy the new technologies of radar and ASDIC (the ability of submarines to detect other vessels) as well as signal intercepts would turn the tide and force the Germans to a slow but sure naval defeat by 1943. Britain urgently needed to break the Axis codes, particularly those used by the powerful German Enigma machine.

Admiral Hugh Sinclair, head of MI6, having failed to convince the government to spend money on proper premises, purchased Bletchley Park in Buckinghamshire with his own money. Here gathered an extraordinary mixture of mathematicians, engineers and military experts, all tasked to build on the information originally provided by Polish intelligence, who had broken the original Enigma code. By the end of the war no less than 9,000 people worked in or around Bletchley, the most frequently used recruitment test being the ability to solve a difficult crossword in less than 12 minutes. Among them was Alan Turing, who is credited with the invention of the modern computer.[35n] Throughout the war Bletchley Park provided vital information which, it has been estimated, shortened the war by at least two years.

In December 1942, Enrico Fermi achieved the first nuclear chain reaction in a squash court underneath the stadium at the University of Chicago. Development quickly moved to a large but temporary site at Los Alamos, New Mexico, where some 6,000 men and women were led by the enigmatic but inspiring genius J. Robert Oppenheimer, whose two great loves were physics and New Mexico. After the atomic bombs were dropped on Japan, Oppenheimer was haunted by the event and opposed further development. In the demonic hunt for communist spies by Senator Joe McCarthy, Oppenheimer's previous associations with members of the American Communist Party were exposed and his security clearance was cancelled. He remained an isolated and unhappy man. Throughout the 1950s he continued his campaign on the control of atomic weapons and peace, lecturing at many American universities. He was finally rehabilitated by President Kennedy with the award of the Enrico Fermi Award in 1963. Oppenheimer, together with Albert Einstein, Bertrand Russell and other eminent scientists and academics, established what would eventually become the World Academy of Art and Science in 1960. He had been a chain smoker all his adult life and died of throat cancer in 1969 at the age of 63.

Carpet and Precision Bombing

Partly under pressure from Stalin for action, although still nursing a damaged army, Churchill agreed early in 1942 to the use of 'carpet bombing' on major German industrial cities by day and night. These raids were planned by Air Vice Marshal Arthur Harris, who had used this deadly system against insurgents in pre-war Iraq. A memo dated October 12th 1942 revokes the existing rules, including restriction to military objectives, then confirms that, 'Consequent upon the enemy's adoption of a campaign of unrestricted air warfare, the Cabinet have authorised a bombing policy which includes the attack on enemy morale.'[36] The bombs were dropped with the clear intention of causing a firestorm; indeed, one of the first raids on Lubeck was chosen because of the large number of wooden houses. Once the first wave of bombers struck, the fires led subsequent waves to an easy target. In August 1943 43,000 residents of Hamburg were incinerated in one night. The raids, which were carried out relentlessly night after night, continued for some eighteen months against increasing opposition from those who saw the lack of distinction between military and civilian casualties as a clear breach of the Geneva Convention and therefore a stain on our national character.[37n] The programme took a heavy toll on bomber crews. In the initial four and a half months almost a thousand aircraft were lost. Flight Lieutenant Denis Hornsey of 76 Squadron explained his dark but realistic philosophy thus:

> If you live on the brink of death yourself, it is as if those who have gone have merely caught an earlier train to the same destination, and whatever that destination is, you will be sharing it soon, since you will almost certainly be catching the next one.[38]

In fact, apart from direct damage, death and casualties, the air raids were tying down about a million German troops who were manning the anti-aircraft guns and factories that were having to produce more night fighters while under severe pressure to equip the Nazi air force on the Eastern Front. Further destruction of the German industrial infrastructure in May 1943 resulted from the breaches in the dams at Möhne, Eder and Sorpe by the 'Dambusters' (RAF 617 Squadron), a daring raid which required a round 'bouncing bomb' invented by Barnes Wallis[39n] by flying over the heavily defended reservoirs at 60 feet. The leader of the mission Wing Commander Guy Gibson's bomb failed to breach Mohne dam, but the third and fourth bombs succeeded. Gibson recalled:

> There was a great breach 100 yards across ... with water gushing out into the Ruhr Valley. The whole valley filled with fog from the steam of the gushing water, and we saw cars speeding along the road in front of this great wave which was chasing them faster than they could ever hope to go. The floods raced on carrying with them as they went viaducts, railways, bridges and everything in their path.[40n]

El-Alamein

If late 1942 and early 1943 were to mark a turning point in the war for the Allies, for Britain the most significant and newsworthy event was the removal of Axis forces from northern Africa. On October 23rd, General Montgomery scored a major victory at El-Alamein by sending in his massed tank and infantry troops after one of the heaviest artillery barrages in history had crippled the German defences. The following month, American troops landed in Morocco and Algiers, thus catching German forces in a pincer from which their only retreat was seaward towards Sicily and Italy. A lively picture of chaos in North Africa appears in the diary of that extraordinary comedian Spike Milligan, who was serving time in an artillery unit entering the newly captured Tunis:

> We set off across the Goubellat Plain to Tunis, following the wake of the victorious 6th and 7th Armoured. We passed smouldering tanks, dead soldiers in grotesque ballet positions, Arab families emerging from hiding, baffled and frightened, and the children, always the children, more baffled and frightened than the rest.
> In Tunis we motored slowly through the crowded streets, being kissed several times by pretty girls and once by a pretty boy. 'No one's kissed me,' complained Gunner Holt, his face like a dog's bum with a hat on. 'Never mind – ere comes one now – I'll stamp on her glasses!'
> A fat lady with revolving bosoms shouts 'Vive les Americans.' 'She thinks we're American,' says Holt. 'We'll slip one up her, then blame them,' says Devine.
> A group of 'Ities' insist they be taken prisoner or they'll surrender. 'Sorry,' I explain. 'We British Army prisoners.'[41]

Six months later, Allied troops would land on Sicily and then commence the hard fight northwards up the Italian mainland: another campaign brought forward to ease the pressure on Stalin's Eastern Front. The tide had turned.

DOMESTIC EVENTS

In January 1936 the energetic new King Edward VIII faced a nation in the grip of a depression. He toured widely, visiting the slums of Glasgow and London, the coalfields of South Wales and closed steelworks assuring gatherings of the unemployed that 'something must be done,' although his position dictated that he could do nothing. However, the public had seen a monarch who, for the first time in living memory, had stepped out from the trappings of his court and engaged actively with his people. These acts, and the communication demanded by the new media of broadcasting, marked a new role and style for the royals. His energies and sharp enthusiasms were not confined to his formal duties, and soon after came the rumours of his relationship with the American divorcee Mrs Simpson; within a year, on December 11th 1936, Edward had abdicated. His famous final broadcast was, as he pointed out, heard 'In the Empire and throughout the world – in the jungle and in Arctic wastes, in crowded cities and desolate homesteads.' Theatres, cinemas and cabarets stopped to listen to the broadcast. The couple then left to pursue a life in virtual exile, frustrated that the royal court would never accept Mrs Simpson or afford Edward a useful role. Further insight into these times comes from my copy of the *Daily Mail* dated December 12th, which headlined Queen Mary's statement:

> I need not speak to you of the distress which fills a mother's heart when I think that my dear son has deemed it to be his duty to lay down his charge, and that the reign that had begun with so much hope and promise has so suddenly ended ... I commend to you his brother, summoned so unexpectedly, and in circumstances so painful, to take his place ... With him I commend my dear daughter-in-law who will be his Queen. May she receive the same unfailing affection that you have given to me for more than six and twenty years. I know that you have already taken her children to your hearts.[42n]

The Free State of Southern Ireland took the opportunity to pass legislation which would abolish the role of governor and remove the British monarchy from all domestic functions and documents of the Dáil.

In Britain, the British Union of Fascists, led by Oswald Mosley, was drawing support from right-wing groups and some discontented working-class areas by blaming the problems of unemployment and lack of accommodation on immigrants and the Jews. Mosley gained some 40,000 members, and on June 4th 1936 the members, dressed in Nazi type uniforms, decided to march through the poorer areas of the East End of London, specifically targeting the Jewish area. Marching down Commercial Road, the 'Blackshirt Army' turned into Cable Street, where they were met by 300,000 people shouting the communist motto of the Spanish Civil War 'They shall not pass.' The fascist marching song was:

> Onward Black Shirts! Form your legions
> Keep the flag for ever high
> For a free and greater Britain
> Stand we fast to fight or die!

The Cockney response came:

> Hitler and Mosley, what are they for?
> Thuggery, buggery, hunger and war!
> Two, three, four, five
> We want Mosley, dead or alive.[43]

Barricades were erected, lorries overturned and horses in the march were attacked by throwing pepper bags in their faces and marbles under their feet. The defenders, a mixture of young and old, Catholic and Jew, communists and socialists, forced the Blackshirts to retreat. The 'Battle of Cable Street' had been won by ordinary people standing up against fascism.

Following a last attempt to negotiate with Hitler, the Prime Minister Neville Chamberlain returned from Munich on September 30th 1938 to be greeted by cheers in Parliament, with people eager to shake the hand of the man who had prevented a second terrible war. The League of Nations, after Abyssinia, had in any event lost all power to act. Speaking in the House of Commons, Chamberlain conceded that, as far as Britain was concerned, Czechoslovakia was, like Abyssinia, 'that far away country of whom we know nothing.' Celebration turned to national ignominy when Hitler proceeded to occupy the whole of Czechoslovakia and threaten Poland in the mistaken belief that European powers would again accede to his ambitions. Britain and France were bound by treaty to defend Poland when Germany invaded at dawn on September 1st 1939 by shelling the Polish port of Danzig (now Gdansk). War was consequently declared on September 3rd 1939. Announcing this to the House of Commons, the elderly Chamberlain commented

> This is a sad day for all of us, and to none is it sadder than for me. Everything that I worked for, everything that I hoped for, everything that I believed through my public life, has crashed into ruins.[44]

In this grave hour, the King addressed his people,[45n] and a copy of his statement was delivered to every house in the country:

> For we are called with our allies to meet the challenge of a principle which if it were to prevail would be fatal to any civilised order in the world … the freedoms of our own country and the whole British Commonwealth of Nations would be in danger … For the sake of all that we ourselves hold dear and of the world's order and peace it is unthinkable that we should refuse to meet the challenge.

In addition to the frantic drive to re-arm and build up land, naval and air forces, the British government had formed civil defence networks, appointed air-raid precaution wardens (ARPs) and, following the sharp lesson of Guernica, manufactured air-raid shelters and gas masks which would hopefully protect people from bombs and the anticipated poison gas as used by Germany in the previous war. Before the official declaration of war, these had been issued to the most vulnerable populations: those in the main cities and those near docks and manufacturing centres. In late 1938, 38 million masks were issued. If the task of fitting these awful smelly things was distasteful, the fact that everyone had to do it at least reinforced a great sense of democracy in action. Beautiful parks were rudely dug up; one excavation in Hyde Park went so deep as to expose the foundations for the Great Exhibition of 1851.[46n] Blackout was imposed every night for the rest of the war; thick blinds had to be used to ensure that no light emerged that might help enemy aircraft find their target. ARP wardens patrolled to ensure compliance, and whether in cities or small villages the slightest careless error would bring down the loud command 'Put that light OUT!' If a vehicle had to move, the lights were fitted with close louvred covers to reduce the amount of emitted light. On September 4th 1939 the BBC news included an item that stated: 'Motorists who claim in future to have seen zebras in the forests should not be disbelieved.'

Arrangements were also made to compulsorily evacuate all children from vulnerable areas, either individually or as whole schools. In recognition of the distress caused, the first Citizens Advice Bureaux (CAB) were opened; 200 were opened the day after war was declared. From 1940 pacifists offered direct practical aid to distressed families, leading to the establishment of Pacifist Service Units across the country.[47n] Government, haunted by the casualties of the limited bombing in the previous war, had calculated the possible effects of a re-armed Germany. About half of the 48 million population of the UK lived in six main urban centres. If Germany embarked on an immediate and continuous bombing campaign of these areas, in 60 days 600,000 deaths and 1,200,000 casualties could be expected. Panic and social upheaval could result.

In reviewing the inter-relationship between social policy and war, Richard Titmuss picked up this reaction to the Dunkirk evacuation, evidencing *The Times* leader of the following day which called for social justice, for the abolition of privilege, for a more equitable distribution of income and wealth and for drastic changes in the economic and social life of the country. Titmuss comments that such cries stem from the very nature of total war, where the boundaries between military and civilian involvement are diffused. The 1942 Beveridge Report, which launched the welfare state, and the sweep of post-war social legislation were, he stated,

> ... in part an expression of the needs of a war time strategy to fuse and unify the conditions of life of civilians and non civilians alike. In practice ... this involved the whole community in accepting an enlargement of obligations – an extension of social discipline – to attend to the primary needs of all citizens.[48]

Some disasters put heavy pressure on Chamberlain's government, which was forced out of office following the 'Norway Debate' of May 8th 1940. From a poor position, Chamberlain's announcement of a British withdrawal in Norway had caused uproar in the House of Commons and it was attacked by Clement Attlee, whose deputy suddenly called for a vote of confidence. Chamberlain foolishly made the issue personal by stating that his friends would back him, but this brought many of his own side (including the maverick Robert Boothby and the most recently elected MP John Profumo) to desert him and call for a National Coalition Government. The elderly Lloyd George, who had led the country through the previous war, reminded the Prime Minister how he had called the nations' men to sacrifice, concluding that he should now follow that example.

The loyal Conservative MP Leo Amery used Cromwell's famous phrase to demand of Chamberlain, 'In the name of God, go.'[49n] Clement Attlee, leader of the Labour Party, refused to serve under either Chamberlain or Lord Halifax (the Foreign Secretary and a leading appeaser), but agreed to serve under Churchill. Consequently, on May 10th 1940 Winston Churchill became Prime Minister, one imposed on the Conservative Party by the mood of the nation, imposed that is by Labour leader Attlee and a brave group of Tories who refused to follow the party whip. R. A Butler, who was to serve in the War Cabinet, is said to have commented that Chamberlain and his supporters had 'weakly surrendered to a half-breed American.'[50] The Labour politician Michael Foot commented thus, speaking about 1940,

> That was the year of years, the hour of hours, the moment when the British people much more surely than their leaders (on Churchill's own testimony) decided to expiate all the crimes and follies of those who had fed the fascist monster. It was done magnificently and, more than ever before or after, Churchill's language fitted the time.[51]

When it was suggested that an official inquiry be held into Chamberlain's record, Churchill said, 'If we open a quarrel between the past and the present we shall find that we have lost the future.' The appointments to his government broke with all the old divisions and stereotypes. He formed a War and Defence Cabinet (which he chaired) with all other matters delegated to The Lord President's Committee, chaired by Attlee (who also attended many other Cabinet Committees). The newspaper magnate Lord Beaverbrook (who had been responsible for Allied propaganda in WWI and was a great friend of Churchill) was appointed Minister of War Production, where he was teamed up with Ernest Bevin, a radical left-wing Labour MP who served as the Minister of Labour and National Service. Lord Woolton (Conservative) was Minister of Food (and later of Reconstruction), Herbert Morrison (Labour) was the first Minister of Supply (later of Home Affairs) and Anthony Eden was Foreign Secretary, where one of his ministers was R. A. Butler (Conservative), a great liberal educationalist. This diverse group of men with widely differing social backgrounds and political beliefs worked tirelessly together for the next five years. Attlee, as Deputy Prime Minister, in particular was completely loyal throughout the war to Churchill, by no means the easiest man to work under.

Within a few days, the formation of the 'Local Defence Volunteers' was announced, and within six weeks one and a half million men had volunteered for what Churchill promptly renamed the 'Home Guard,' equal in size to the regular army. The purpose was to have a body of men offering stout resistance in every district to prevent landing parties, to maintain communication by signals or runners, to supply guards for vital points including petrol stations (or to make them useless if abandoned) and to maintain order and morale in their district. In the *Home Guard Manual 1941*,[52] ready advice is given on tank hunting:

> Tanks are big, strong and bullying in their use and, like most bullies, have some vulnerable points – once a tank is found it must be a point of honour not to let it escape.

One handy weapon in this unequal contest would be five or more home-made 'Molotov cocktails' consisting of a two-pint beer bottle filled with tar, diesel and petrol; a cloth and a cork would be inserted in the neck, then it would be set alight and thrown at a tank. Volunteers could progress to special training where they were taught the techniques of guerilla warfare, the plan that would become operational if Britain were occupied (in which event the volunteers would have a very short life expectancy). The instructors were drawn from the army, but the skills required had been practised by the volunteers who had fought Franco and were familiar with the fieldcraft second nature to the Boy Scout movement. Among the motley crew of instructors was Stanley White, already a veteran and much honoured Scout Commissioner, a man who was to become a friend of mine and to have an influence on my life.

Addressing the House of Commons on June 4th 1940, Churchill, described as standing like 'an obstinate ploughman' and using all his powers of rhetoric so that his listeners 'felt the whole massive backing of power and resolve behind him, like a fortress,' delivered his most memorable speech. It sent shivers down everyone's spines. Following a review of the retreat from Dunkirk (see above), he thanked and admired the 250 light warships and 650 other vessels that 'strained every nerve' to rescue the troops, he admired the RAF who proved superior in the air which provided confidence for the coming battle, and he laid out the impoverished state of the troops, who had lost 30,000 souls, 1,000 guns and all the transport and armoured vehicles that were with the army (a colossal military disaster that would delay any proposed counterattack). More stringent methods would be taken against 'enemy aliens and suspicious characters of other nationalities, but also against British subjects who may become a nuisance should the war become transported to the United Kingdom.' He then turned to more positive aspects, and that dramatically aggressive and determined growl rose before he repeated the resolve of His Majesty's Government to fight on to defend these islands, that is the will of Parliament and the nation:

> We shall go on to the end, we shall fight in France, we shall fight on the seas and oceans, we shall fight with growing confidence and growing strength in the air, we shall defend our island, whatever the cost may be, we shall fight on the beaches, we shall fight on the landing

grounds, we shall fight in the fields and in the streets, we shall fight in the hills, we shall never surrender, and, even if, which I do not for a moment believe, this island or large parts of it were subjugated and starving, then our empire beyond the seas, armed and guarded by the British fleet, would carry on the struggle, until, in God's good time, the new world, with all its powers and might, steps forth to the rescue and liberation of the old.[53]

No more phoney war: obvious facts were stated honestly. The experience of defeat, and a government where all interests were involved and oratory such as this prevailed, seemed to be a turning point in bringing trades unions, businesses, government workers and wives together to demand increased production for war. Inspiration was preferred to re-organisation, which would take time and thus cause delays.

We all knew that our backs were against the wall and that there were tough times ahead. I think it was clear then that, although we were defending our land and our Empire, the important point was a fight for our values and beliefs; what I now understand to be the values of enlightenment, reason, the promotion of equality, democratic government and openness. The Nazis, by contrast, sought racial purity, territory and revenge for past humiliations.

It seems almost unbelievable that, amidst the immense effort required to fight a total world war, the government was devoting resources to plan the sort of social provision that would be required after victory had been won. In large part it was the unprecedented scale of the conflict that justified the initiative. As the First World War drew to a close, people had dreamt of a return to society as it had been before the war. Now such a thought was impossible, and the members of the Cabinet were well aware that those dreams had been shattered in the inter-war years. As the pain of the economic depression eased and the foothills of the war were approached, support grew for a move from the hated means-tested to universal benefits. From 1934 school milk was subsidised so the daily third of a pint became a regular feature of the school day for all pupils. The previous year, the need to focus on child welfare had been enshrined in the Children and Young Persons Act (1933), which required that

> Every court in dealing with a child or young person who is brought before it, either as being in need of care or protection or as an offender or otherwise, shall have regard to the welfare of the child or young persons and shall in a proper case take steps for removing him from undesirable surroundings, and for securing that proper provision is made for his education and training.

As war began, the economic strains on the elderly forced many to consider applying for means-tested benefits. Their plight was eased, with little political conflict, by the introduction in 1939 of supplementary allowances aimed at the anticipated 275,000 pensioners thought to be in need. In short time a million applicants had been found eligible. Politicians of all parties recognised that the demands of a major war on the total population called for a united response. There emerged an implied contract that the people would accept hardship providing that things would improve when it was all over.

It was this spirit that helped the Labour members of the coalition government push for the abolition of the hated household means test in 1941, which they had struggled for so bitterly and for so long. This group also inserted the words 'improved labour standards, economic advancement and social security' into the Atlantic Charter.[55]

In the wake of Dunkirk, and as the realisation that stark class differences were no longer acceptable, free milk was made available to mothers and babies and free concentrated orange juice was given to young children. The future raw material of the nation must not be put at risk. As state planning became commonplace and post-war planning was seen as essential, the formation of a Ministry of Town and Country Planning was accepted. The fact that these initiatives, with an acceptance of universal provision, were generally supported by all political parties prepared the ground for the raft of post-war legislation, generally seen as the start of the welfare state. In fact, it started in 1941.

The abolition of the household means test, the prompt payment of a supplementary pension and the issue of reduced price or free milk within weeks of the Dunkirk defeat signalled that, in desperate times, the state accepted responsibility for all. The Labour members of the coalition government were determined to achieve a more equal society and knew that the idea that the government could effectively run a broad range of social institutions now seemed to be acceptable. If for warfare, why not for welfare? In the services and at home the early stages of the war had seen an unprecedented mix up of the social classes. Evacuation had brought children, many from the poorest, most densely parts of cities where chronic unemployment had been a feature, to the attention of the middle and upper classes, who had assumed that such conditions no longer existed. They came face to face with dirty habits, bed-wetting and children needing medical attention and with no social training. This was unbelievable and stirred social conscience that something must be done.

In 1940 Churchill had appointed the Labour leader Arthur Greenwood, who had been part of the reconstruction work after WWI, to the Cabinet. Churchill asked him to plan 'a number of practical steps which it is indispensable to take if our society is to move forward.' It was Greenwood who set up an inter-departmental committee to examine social insurance and allied services under the chairmanship of William Beveridge (previously of Toynbee Hall, Head of Employment Exchanges, then Director of the London School of Economics). It was agreed that as the system only needed some technical adjustment the self-effacing Beveridge would be the man for such a tedious task. How wrong both assumptions proved to be. The report was issued in late November 1942, marking a 'British Revolution.' The underlying political climate was twofold. One, emphasised by the Labour element in the coalition government, was the divisive social structures of pre-war Britain highlighted by the depression. (In 1929, 1.5% of the population took 23% of total personal income, and under 2% of the population owned 40% of the property, with 6% owning 80%.) The outspoken Archbishop of Canterbury, William Temple, who argued before his promotion that the private ownership of the means of production was anti-Christian, was to publish his radical views on the urgent need for a welfare state. He also insisted that the 1944 Education Act included compulsory religious education in all schools. The other theme was fear that, given the new alliance with communist Russia, troops returning from the war would expect a different society to the class-dominated one that they had left behind. In fact, the political consequences of the extensive cross-class and cross-culture experiences of military service and the effect of the Military Education Corps lessons in citizenship were difficult to calculate. The Beveridge Report was a sensation, selling 650,000 copies, an all-time record, with summaries distributed to all households and service units. Publication, against the background of victory at El-Alamein and Stalingrad, boosted morale as it painted a picture of a promised future for which the troops had long hoped that they were fighting.

The Beveridge Report

The Beveridge Report sought to achieve 'revolutions' rather than to patch up old systems now that war was abolishing old landmarks. In spelling out a comprehensive system of social insurance as an attack on the giant 'Want' required that social progress attacked the others, namely 'Disease,' 'Ignorance,' 'Squalor' and 'Idleness.' All this was best achieved by co-operation between state and the individual. Want would be countered by a comprehensive system of National Insurance, contributed to by employers and employees as a bulwark against periods of unemployment, sickness and retirement. Such a system would elevate benefits drawn as a right and abolish once and for all the old attitudes of the Poor Law and the need for the degrading assessment of means. The system would cover individuals from cradle to grave. Disease required the establishment of a free system of National Health, Ignorance by a reformed education system, Squalor by new house building programmes and the demolition of old slum areas, and Idleness by achieving full employment. In conclusion, Beveridge commented that, 'If the united democracies today can show strength and courage and imagination even while waging total war, they will win together two victories which in truth are indivisible.'[56]

Supported by Attlee and welcomed by wide sections of the population, who had perceived that state control of many aspects of industry and society had worked in the war effort, nevertheless resistance came from insurance companies with their vested interest and the medical establishment. The majority of social workers feared that, by abolishing the need for assessment of need and ability to pay, the report would damage the newly established profession. Others saw the ideas as charting a road to moral ruin or as a seductive opiate, and Churchill, in a moment of political miscalculation, gave a somewhat cool reception. His view, shown in a note to Cabinet, was that as he did not feel able to make promises about the future, and he could not hold out false hopes and airy visions of Utopia and Eldorado.

The 1944 Education Act

The Conservative Minister R. A. Butler, appointed as President of the Board of Education in 1941, had worked steadily to produce a radical landmark piece of legislation, the Education Act (1944), which pulled together the untidy pattern and uneven standards of state, independent, voluntary and denominational schools. The Act introduced free education for all from the age of five to fifteen (with nursery school provision from two years of age and further education from fifteen to eighteen). The school leaving age was fixed at fifteen (a provision of the 1936 Act not implemented due to the war), with provision divided into primary, secondary and further education. Butler explained to Parliament that the Bill attempted:

> [a] synthesis ... between order and liberty, between local initiative and national direction, between the voluntary agencies and the state, between the private life of the school and the public life of the districts which it serves, between manual and intellectual skills and between those better and those less well endowed.[57]

Secondary schools were classified as grammar (continuing the highest traditions of an academic education), modern (more general education to match the interests of the pupils) and technical (linking education with industry, agriculture or commerce). One commentator wondered how marvellous it was that the Almighty had benevolently created three types of child in just those proportions that would gratify educational administrators. The administration of all state schools was to be the responsibility of county and borough councils under the control of a Minister for Education, and the new arrangements would be implemented on April 1st 1945. Within a few years, the division of secondary education by type would become a matter of political and public conflict, but the main parts of the Act, including daily worship, free medical care and a national pay scale for teachers, would remain in place for more than fifty years.

CULTURE

The only films I remember were from the Disney Studio: the weird and wonderful *Fantasia* in 1940, and the enjoyable *Dumbo*, with that delightful baby elephant, the following year. More grown up was the legendary *Gone With The Wind* released in 1939, although it did not reach me until years later. Orson Welles struck again in 1941 with the now iconic *Citizen Kane*, which portrayed the career of the powerful media magnate William Randolph Hearst. These involved a trip from Willian, the village to which I had been evacuated, to the one cinema in Letchworth.

Paul Robeson was an African-American actor and singer who came to notice in the late 1920s in the UK for his presentation of so-called 'negro spirituals.' In 1928 his strong bass-baritone voice won him the lead role in the musical *Showboat*, from which the song 'Ol' Man River' became immensely popular. In 1930 he took the part of Othello in

London to great acclaim. Robeson was a fierce anti-fascist (he toured for the republican fighters in Spain) and anti-racist, who supported a number of left-wing causes, including the Welsh miners during the inter-war depression, from which came a lasting and deep relationship of mutual respect. Robeson attributed his militancy and his politics to the British Labour movement.

SOCIAL WORK

As the social dimension of evacuation became clear, there was a search for the services of qualified social workers. Regional organisations had been established to oversee welfare provision, and many were headed by qualified social workers. Lucy Faithfull, who had worked as a psychiatric social worker (PSW) in child guidance clinics, was a London Region Organiser for Nottinghamshire and Derbyshire.

As those fostering evacuated children ran into difficulties, facing bed-wetting, disturbed behaviours, foul language and stealing, social workers were called in to help, to refer children to child guidance clinics and to set up hostels and children's homes, of which there were eventually some 700. Clare Britton, a qualified PSW, managed the hostels in Oxfordshire, where she welcomed the support of psychiatrists and encouraged research. Psychiatric support for the hostels was provided by Donald Winnicott,[58n] who established a strong reputation advising parents and carers faced with separation and the consequent problems. Such was the level of concern that researchers became involved, one of the most interesting being Susan Isaacs, who in 1924 opened her own boarding school, Maltings House, with a child centred approach to young children; unfortunately, it failed within a few years. More successful were Summerhill, founded in 1921 by the educationalist A. S. Neil, and Finchden Manor, opened as a therapeutic community soon afterwards by George Lywood.[59]

FAMILY

My arrival early in 1934 caused a degree of turmoil in the family. Although I was declared a bouncing healthy 10 lb boy, my mother Mabel developed puerperal fever, a serious complication at that time. This infection had a mortality rate of 5 in 1,000 in the early 1930s and was known to be highly contagious. Effective treatment by sulfonamide drugs was only slowly introduced in that decade. (The current mortality rate is less than 1 in 10,000.) The realisation that aseptic techniques could prevent the infection had led to the first training scheme for midwives in 1933. My mother recalls that admission to hospital was immediately followed by the arrival of the borough isolation teams at our house in Peckham,

> ... to take bedding, clothes and everything I had touched for purification. They went to the house of the nurse and demanded her clothes that she had worn when attending me. She was angry and difficult, and finished the argument by going into the bedroom, divesting herself of her clothing and throwing the articles one by one to the waiting isolation team. The fumigated but rotted bundles were returned next day.[60]

One result was that my immediate care, and presumably that of my nine-year-old brother John, became the responsibility of my indomitable maternal grandmother Edith Glover until mother's strong constitution and dogged determination restored her to health. Meanwhile, I went downhill fast by refusing all sustenance. I lost weight and became a frail child who tried everyone's patience. Quite why there was such an age gap between my brother and I was never explained. Neither was the fact that my slightly built father produced two sons who grew to be well over six feet tall. My grandchildren, now growing up in North London and New York, have easy access to a wide range of comparators, directly and via a wide choice of media from across the world, by which they can appreciate and readily articulate difference and similarities. In 1934 any understanding of family status, dynamics or economics was impeded by the narrow compass of our immediate South London world. The low level of verbal communication in my immediate family was a further problem. We lived by glances and body language and a rule that spelt out the dire consequences on my father's health if anyone were ever to raise their voice or express a firm opinion which might possibly provoke an argument. It has however been possible bit by bit to reassemble key pieces of the puzzle and set them down, although others remain clouded by the passage of time and failure or blockage of memory.

I soon came to recognise the family characteristics. My father, like all the Jordan relatives, was kind and retiring; all had a rather grey, tired appearance with a depressive air about them, quite common among those who had never expressed the horrors of their experiences in the Great War. The Glover family was quite different. My maternal grandmother Edith (who cooked for the moderately wealthy gentleman's clubs in London) was extrovert with a love of life, a big heart and bellowing laugh, ready to express a view on anything to anyone, preferably in Cockney rhyming slang. My mother Mabel, Edith's daughter, loved the whole extended family and took any excuse to organise a grand get together, but she was more restrained than her mother, more 'bookish,' but thoughtfully determined. Such a brief glance at my genetic pool hardly does justice to the complexities of the times and the interaction of each element on the other. With the benefit of hindsight, it does throw some light on a central piece of the puzzle that was to shape our future. Loss of status, chronic illness, awareness of unrealised potential and lack of secure income had put survival at the top of family life. There being no state support, my father's frequent indispositions placed an enormous emotional and financial strain on my mother, who worked wherever and at whatever on a full-time basis until her retirement in 1961. As the family battled on, another theme became more marked and more important. This was a determination, most strongly evident in my mother, that ground had to be regained, that progress had to be made, that her boys and their children deserved better. So, survival and determination were the dynamics of this close bound and loving family. This was a good situation in which to be born and nurtured, particularly as early in my fifth year the family was to be broken up. Our skills and determination were to be put to the test by war and the aftermath of war. Mabel wrote:

> As the promise of spring arrived so Malcolm and I regained our strength. We all rejoiced in the sunshine, the garden and the fullness of life, yet the rumblings of war were already threatening and sometimes my heart was heavy for the future of my two wonderful sons. I expressed this foreboding to one of the teachers at the school and she said 'Oh now we have young men like Anthony Eden in the Cabinet, there will be no more war.' How wrong she proved to be.[61]

Two small incidents illustrate the basis of family legend in the years when there was talk, talk, talk of war. For the Jubilee of King George V and Queen Mary in May 1935, my parents untied my baby swing and created handles so that they could carry me between them throughout the celebrations and parades in London. They became convinced that a passer-by had seen the prototype and produced the carrycot which hit the market soon afterwards. The Jubilee programme, which I still have, lists 150 cars for the diplomatic corps, 20 for the Cabinet and 40 for the royal household. The main carriage procession was led by carriages with the prime ministers of the UK and Commonwealth countries, the Speaker of the House of Commons and the Lord High Chancellor and Lord Mayor. Then followed the six carriages with the royal family. They went up the Strand to St Pauls and returned via the Embankment. It was about this time that the BBC's early experiments with television had reached the point where reasonable images could be transmitted to the 2,000 sets in London (each set costing as much as a small car). Early programmes featured talent shows, one of which included a young man called Bruce Forsyth.[62n] The next brush with fame followed a photograph taken of me as a happy golden curly haired babe by 'Barr,' a commercial photographer whose shop then stood near Camberwell Green in South London. He decided his trade could be increased by enlarging the photo, gluing it to plywood about 6 ft square, then varnishing and hanging it on the wall above his shop. Mother was so proud. Pushing me round Ruskin Park she thought her pride justified when more than one lady recognised that this was the baby on display at Camberwell Green. It transpired that they had recognised not the child but the clothing and were only interested in what stitch mother had used to knit my cardigan! A suitable fate awaited the portrait when it was cut up and sections used as a backing to catch the poorly aimed darts during the endless family competitions, though we did have the decency to use the reverse.

Within eight months of the Jubilee, the sombre perfectly modulated voice of BBC newsreader Stuart Hibbert announced that the King's life had drawn peacefully to a close and that his son Edward had started his reign. It was going to be brief. Typically, Mabel and my brother John found an early morning spot on the corner of Downing Street and Whitehall from which to view the heartrending funeral procession as it passed slowly by with the new King walking behind his father's coffin. The same month saw the death of my mother's elder sister Edie, who died of tuberculosis after prolonged treatment. While she had been in hospital the 'secretary and social worker' had arranged a grant for extra nourishment from public assistance. While Edie was in hospital, special permission had to be sought to make enquiries about her progress by telephone. A severe note from Grove Park Hospital (run by the London County Council) allowed 'no more than two calls a day, when only general information will be given.'

Five years old in 1939 I was far too young to appreciate world events. But I was made ready with my label to gather at Coldharbour Lane School, near Camberwell Green, and, grasping my big brother's hand, I followed the crocodile of other children through the gates onto a waiting tram and thence to the train. At the time it all seemed an exciting adventure, a trip on a train and whatever happened I would be safe with John. Not many knew that at the same time the first Kindertransport trains were leaving Berlin. This escape route, mostly for Jewish children, was organised by a (non-Jewish) English solicitor and carried some 10,000 children to safety. They were, of course, most unlikely ever to see their parents again. A young Jewish banker, Nicholas Winton, also financed and organised eight trains from Prague to London that carried 669 Jewish children to safety. My mother clearly records her London experience:

> Now the war was imminent and the greatest decision of a lifetime had to be faced – our dear John and Malcolm – should we let them go? ... To our great comfort Loughborough School agreed to take Malcolm along with them. Whatever was ahead at least the boys would be together. We packed them off early on that unforgettable morning with sandwiches for the day, a drink and a pitifully small valise because John would have to do most of the carrying, and, most important of all, each carried a gas mask in a small box. We left them at the school gates and were told that it would be better for the children if we left them immediately; this we did, but I remember as if it were yesterday standing for hours in Coldharbour Lane, watching tram after tram full of children being taken to the London main line stations. I doubt whether through tear soaked eyes I would have seen the Loughborough children pass; there I stood in shivering misery until afternoon when normal passenger traffic resumed. In utter despair I at last went home to try to rest. Early next morning we were at the school gates begging for news; the destination of the children was to be posted on the gates as soon as the news arrived. No news, no news, so back home I went to tell Harry ... [he] at last came home having waited all day with the Griffin family; they had three children in the evacuation. At last he had news – the children had gone to Swanage in Dorset.[63]

Some sixty years later, giving an account of 'being an evacuee' to my granddaughter's class of ten-year olds, I made the mistake of reading this extract out loud. I burst into tears to be so sharply reminded of the real meaning of that exciting day. The children of the late 1990s were very polite. Several class members were themselves refugees from oppressive regimes across the world and empathised entirely with this blubbering old man; they later wrote to reassure me that they fully understood.

Arriving at the seaside town of Swanage in Dorset in the pouring rain, we were put in the hands of the 'Welfare Ladies,' and walked round several houses, but it seems that no one wanted two brothers, certainly not a young teenager plus a five-year-old. We ended up in what I can only think was a temporary hostel, crammed to the roof with distressed and anxious London adults and kids like us. The noise and the overcrowding had a comforting effect on me. I recall enjoying the closeness and the evening singsongs to cheer us up. Mother took a different view when the landlady's explanation was that she had had to let us in, stating 'I couldn't have left a dog out in that weather.'

A contrasting experience of war was happening in Cornwall, where William Wilfred Wickett had broken with his family's farming tradition, completed his teacher training in Exeter and had spent four years as Head of the primary school at Ruan Minor/Cadgwith on the Lizard Peninsular in Cornwall. He had married Violet Tomlinson of West Moors in Hampshire, and in 1925 their first daughter Joan had been born at a time when 'WWW' was taking further training in Suffolk. In 1932 he had been promoted to take up position as Head of Sir Robert Geffrey's Primary School at Landrake, near Saltash, on the Cornish side of the River Tamar (which separates Cornwall from Devon and the city of Plymouth). The school was under the patronage of the Worshipful Company of Ironmongers and was consequently well endowed with adjoining land where pupils could learn horticulture and the care of animals. The family lived in the school house immediately adjacent to the playground, and while here the couple's second daughter Ann, who would in due course become my wife, was born. She always believed that she had been conceived when her parents were camping behind Kennack Sands, which lies in the parish of Ruan Minor. Unfortunately the marriage ran into trouble and the home became the scene for some pretty violent disputes. Despite this, the ambitious headmaster became a well-respected local figure and tried his hand as a poet and local historian. Some six years after taking up this appointment, he sought further promotion and a wider field as a schools inspector with the Department of Education. This plan was stymied by the approaching war. In August 1937 he joined the Officers Emergency Corps with a temporary commission. Whether this decision was prompted by patriotic zeal or domestic pressure is now impossible to judge, but I doubt whether it pleased his wife. As the inevitability of war approached, he volunteered for the Territorial Army but was rejected on grounds of age. It seemed that such determination to escape civilian life further infuriated Violet who decided to volunteer as a nurse, which meant that both children were placed as weekly boarders at Pendruccombe School in Launceston. The difference in age between Ann and her sister Joan was about the same as that between John and me, but whereas I had felt loved and supported Ann felt deserted and angry. Her extrovert and assertive personality led to the role of rebel, and consequently she spent time locked in a room served only with bread and water, which she rolled into balls to stick to the ceilings. Luckily these very negative feelings were relieved at weekends when she spent time at Northumberland House Farm in the same town. Here she spent time with her beloved grandparents, riding the old horse Flossy and collecting small cash funds from Joan to deter her from following her and the boyfriend into the fields. Unfortunately, the fear of desertion and the future experience of parental warfare were to be carried into her adult life.

In these early days of war I remember only those things that were real to a five-year-old. Declarations, news bulletins, conscription and casualties were I suspect kept from us. In Swanage, just under one of the main flight paths, we had been moved from the hostel to the other end of the social scale. Presumably under duress, the Misses Gaye, kindly gentle ladies living in a beautiful house with a maid and a gardener, accepted us. There were elegant toys and a peaceful lifestyle, although the admonition to behave and not to touch were too frequent for my comfort. I think the same applied between my brother and the maid, and consequently we were soon scheduled for re-location. Eventually we were settled with the Grant family, a local builder, sign writer and part-time policeman and his wife and children, where I recall being made welcome and eventually feeling at home. We have been grateful for their care ever since. Of school, I remember nothing. I do remember 'our gang' of miniature Londoners racing round the cobbled streets of this quiet town and making a general nuisance of ourselves. Quite how the burden of care affected my brother and his relationships is difficult to gauge, except for a contribution to his school magazine:

'I want John,' a plaintive voice issued from a small form huddled up in the corner of the bed. 'He won't be long,' came a voice from the downstairs room ... after much ado the small form was washed and dressed. As soon as he felt the morning air on his face he wanted his breakfast, demanded to be taken for a walk, to be bought some sweets or an ice, to go for a swim, to wear his best clothes, to get some toys, and many other desires were voiced and naturally not carried out.

In the course of doing my duty by taking this young brother for a walk, yours truly nodded to a friend, who was passing. I was bombarded with questions, 'What's his name? How old is he? How did you know him? Has he any brothers?' At last I managed to divert his attention, but soon he started again with 'Where did you go last night? How much money have you got? Is it nearly tea time? Can we go on the beach? Are there any steamer trips?' Will he ever stop?

Soon we halted and talked to another of my friends who had a small sister, perhaps even more inquisitive. This proved to be a comforting talk as my small brother for once didn't scream or throw things about, but simply left us talking. Then I discovered him a little way off in a free fight and decided to set out for home. But after comparing notes with my friend with the sister I mused:

> He's not so bad as I made out,
> And now that we're at war;
> I'll care for him without a doubt,
> Thankful I've got no more[64]

I certainly remember watching aerial dogfights as Spitfire and Hurricane planes attacked incoming bombers with their Messerschmitt and Heinkel fighters fought over the Dorset downs. I know that we cheered 'our lads' (we had all immediately acquired expertise aircraft recognition by engine noise and profile), but what really counted to us was who could collect the most used hot shell cases and ammunition clips from the thousands that rained down around us. Concrete 'tank traps' appeared along the shore and whole areas where we had previously roamed became out of bounds. Amazingly, on an early visit my parents carried down a large birthday cake in the shape of Old Mother Hubbard's shoe. On one of mother's visits we were pulled up short by a soldier with rifle at the ready for crossing some newly drawn boundary across the cliffs. The encounter ended in a friendly fashion, but elsewhere an encounter was reported between a sentry and a motorist: 'Halt. Halt!' said the guard. 'I have halted,' said the motorist. 'What do you want me to do next?' 'I don't know,' said the guard. 'My orders are to say halt three times then shoot.'[65] Another quite different memory is of Wall's water ices, triangular tubes of fruity ice wrapped in cardboard. I note that they have reappeared more than fifty years later. Model military trucks made of tin in Japan were still on sale and I longed for such toys, but they soon fell apart, which was exactly the reputation for anything made in Japan at that time.

In Cornwall, W. W. Wickett was still determinedly fighting his way into the Royal Artillery; this involved officer training at Llandrindod Wells in Wales, which was 'messed up due to sickness and badly fitting dentures which detracted from my personal appearance.' A dispute about his future ended when by March 1940 the War Office gave in: 'A vacancy had unexpectedly occurred to which your qualifications appear to be suited.' Service life was not to run smoothly as five months later his commission was terminated again. He appealed to the Army Council, begging for reconsideration: 'It will be a serious thing for me if I have to return to civil life with a stigma upon me.' Whether his appeal succeeded or he was routinely conscripted is not clear, but by March 1941 he was stationed at the Ordinance Depot in London, and three months later he was in Egypt.

What it Felt Like for my Family in London

The greatest fear, day by day, was of an imminent invasion, which we now know was scheduled for late October 1940. On September 15th the Commander of Land Forces, General Alan Brooke, was certain that Hitler could not hold back. Thinking, erroneously, that the RAF was still too strong, the invasion was finally cancelled on October 12th. The first major daylight raid on London was on September 7th 1940 when a massive fleet of bombers and escorting fighters twenty miles wide and forty miles long crossed the coast to undermine morale by destroying property and terrorising the civilian population. One account of that first raid describes the experience of those rushing for shelter in the school in Glengall Road in South London:

> I remember so vividly walking up to that school carrying one of my neighbour's children wrapped in a blanket. Great canopies of billowing smoke blotted out the sun, and barrage

balloons were falling down in flames. We were obliged to slap out sparks that alighted on us from all directions … Everybody settled as comfortably as conditions would allow on that cold concrete floor and the people sat facing each other with our backs against the rough surface of the wall … It was the awful helplessness that was the hardest to bear. We felt like sitting ducks … sticks of bombs whistled down and the air was literally torn apart in a loud rushing noise as they sped earthwards. Everybody instinctively crouched. Holding my breath in an agony of suspense I waited for the blast fully expecting to be blown to pieces. The bombs exploded, rocking the great building to its foundations but by some miracle the school escaped unscathed and nobody was hurt. But the awful expectancy had been too much and I sensed a rising panic as the overwrought women burst into tears and the little ones sensing their fear began to scream.[66]

The next morning, Churchill, who had been at Chequers, visited the East End of London, worst hit because of the proximity of the docks. The King and Queen visited during the next day. On September 8th the writer J. B. Priestly pinpointed in a radio talk a phenomenon that would have great significance on the conduct of the war and the determination of the peace:

The fact that we are all at least within reach of danger seems to me of one the better and not one of the worst features of the war. I consider this an improvement on the last war, in which civilians, who developed some most unpleasant characteristics, lived in security while young men were mown down by the millions … We are much better off now. At least we are sharing the danger as there is, and are not leaning back watching all our young men wither away.
   … We see now, when the enemy bombers come roaring at us at all hours, and it's our nerve *versus* his, that we are not really civilians any longer but a mixed lot of soldiers – machine-minding soldiers, milkmen and postman soldiers, housewife and mother soldiers … Instead of being obscure and tucked away, we're bang in the middle of the world's stage with all the spotlights trained on us; we're historical personages…[67]

The first raid finished in the early evening, but just after 8pm the second raid started. These night raids would continue relentlessly every clear night until May 1941. Often, there was more than one raid; they just went on and on. The night raids included incendiary bombs which would cause the fires and lit the way for further bombers and allowed anyone for many miles to witness the horror of London's nightmares by the distant unmistakable glow. Locally the scout hut of the 34th Camberwell Group, which so many had laboured to build in 1932 and was used as the neighbourhood wardens' HQ, received a direct hit, killing the vicar, Rev Tolley, and five wardens. At the other end of the social scale, the Café de Paris in Soho, which had promoted itself as a safe place for the wealthy and fashionable to party as it was twenty feet underground, suffered a direct hit. Unbelievably two bombs had come down the ventilation shaft, exploded in front of the band and killed 34 people instantly. There were rich pickings for the criminals who roamed bombed buildings, often disguised as wardens, in order to remove rings and other jewellery from the dead.[68n]

On November 14th a massive raid on an undefended Coventry dropped 30,000 incendiary and 500 tons of high explosive bombs, causing over a thousand casualties, obliterating 75% of all buildings (33% of the factories and 50% of the houses) and incinerating Coventry Cathedral. The pictures of this gutted medieval structure hit the front pages in America and may have hastened that country's entry to the war. Controversy still rages as to whether Churchill knew of this raid but gave no advance warning for fear that such preparations would alert the Germans to the fact that their codes had been broken. More than 100,000 people fled the city in fear of the next raid, causing the government to mount a campaign to rally workers to return. The King and Churchill visited on November 16th as low morale turned to defiance; factories were repaired and soon productivity had far exceeded the pre-Blitz level. One of the last raids on the East End of London on May 9th 1941 killed 5,000 people. By the end of the war, 28,000 Londoners had been killed and similar raids on other cities brought the total killed to 60,000.

Re-evacuation

As my brother John approached 15, my health deteriorated and, in common with many parents, the decision was taken to bring us home.[69] Thus at the age of 6 I became aware of the vast apparatus of the state and the scale of the conflict that was embracing us. Unfortunately, this return in September 1940 saw the start of the German raids on London. On the first night-time raid on the London Docks on September 7th 1940, 2,000 Londoners were killed. Shelters had been issued for the protection of those still living in London. Ours was an 'Anderson' shelter, which we had to dig into the garden. Others in the family network were given 'Morrison' shelters, large metal tables that they could get under in the event of a raid. Everything was rationed. Men were getting their 'call-up' papers and disappearing from the local scene. More immediately, money was short, Dad looked weak and weary and Mum was always tired. Despite everything, life went on and I remember this as an adventurous period. I have a clear recollection of my brother's 15th birthday celebrations. The air-raid warning went and into the shelter we all tumbled together with Edith Glover, my Gran. Once there was a lull in the bombing, Mum and I ran up the road, keeping close to the hedges, and bought a small cake from the local shop (the local branch of United Dairies).[70n]

After a quick run home and a dive into the shelter as a bomb fell nearby we could all sing 'Happy Birthday' to keep the terrors away. Houses near us disappeared into rubble, large pieces of shrapnel fell in the garden, relatives were hurt and made homeless, but none were killed that time. Once again attention was focused on getting the children out of London. My health again became an issue. I developed glandular fever, which required our wonderful GP Dr Escovar to be in constant attendance. On every occasion he berated my mother for ever sending me away, lifting a warning finger appealing to her never to be so foolish again. Eventually as the bombing got worse arrangements had to be made for us to be re-evacuated.

For our second evacuation the family made its own plans. John and I were going to the village of Willian some two miles from the Garden City of Letchworth in Hertfordshire. A village still controlled by the squire, the rich farmer and the parish priest, 'Sweet Auburn' indeed. Willian's claim to fame was that it contained three pubs that attracted eager customers across the fields from Letchworth which was a 'dry' town.[71n] After a brief spell with family friends, the welcoming Tucker family, we were unexpectedly joined by Gran who we had left working in the Woolwich Arsenal where she had made munitions during the First World War. I remember hearing her laugh as she came round the corner, and I just ran and threw myself bodily at her large frame. She was to care for me for the next five years. Four of us were housed, together with other London evacuees, in a terrace of six condemned farm worker cottages overlooking the churchyard and the school playground and adjoining the squire's parklands. Our position in the village structure had been predetermined. There was no fuel supply. Cooking was by a small built-in coal-fired range; light was from candles or an oil lamp. The two rooms were connected by a rough open staircase and the whole building was in a state of near collapse. Each room measured some 7 feet square at the maximum. My aunt Lola (who had married a dance band drummer Jim Howard, soon to be conscripted and sent to West Africa as an engineer) came down to help get the cottage fit for human habitation. Throwing herself on the bed exhausted brought all four legs through to the downstairs room. If we were in bed when the postman called he just pushed the letters directly up to the bedroom through gaps above the front door!

The Bell family with their three children lived in a similar space and we shared two cold stone-floored back rooms, which contained a stone sink, a single cold water tap and a copper-lined coal-fired laundry boiler. The single lavatory was reached via the back yard. On the other side of us lived the Shires family, who had two children in their early teens and a severely disabled younger child, Tony, whose chief fascination for us younger children was his continued dribbling and sucking of his thumb, to the stage where it resembled a small wet sponge. Tony was to spend the whole war walking obsessively but uncertainly along the frail railing that ran along our half of the terrace. Gardens were dug up and vegetables grown (the 'Dig for Victory' campaign was running to cut down the need for imported food). The backdrop to all this was the continued throb of night bombers overhead, the sound of the guns defending London and even, occasionally, the dropping of bombs. When things got bad we could walk a few miles to the top of a hill and actually see London burning in raid after raid, 33 miles away. Often our information came from just a snatched piece of conversation: 'London got it bad again last night.' 'Where?' 'Who?' 'Was X or Y's family safe?' A constant state of anxiety was broken by occasional grief as bad news filtered through. My dad was in there watching for fires whenever he was able, but remained too ill to work throughout the war.

The only income for him was from the small weekly payments due from his membership of the Oddfellows Society.[72n]

Time went by and it occurs to me now that Mum, with memories of all those lost in the previous war, must have been increasingly preoccupied with the short time before her oldest son would be conscripted for battle. She split her time between Willian, Baldock and Peckham, where Dad was refusing to leave. At home she was always reduced to tears when the friendly voice of Uncle Mac ended the daily *Children's Hour* broadcast with the words 'Goodnight children, *everywhere*.' She cycled the three miles to Letchworth then seven miles from Kings Cross to home, often through air raids and exhausted. Once, passing a local Franciscan priest's house, one of them stopped her and invited her in for a reviving tea which she politely refused as she was so close to home.[73n] On another occasion she recalls:

> I had reached home and opened the gate when right in front of me was the most fantastic firework display breaking in the sky. I stood transfixed by its beauty, holding the gate with one hand and my bicycle with the other; the enchantment lasted but a second or two, the time difference of travel of light and sound, then the terrific sound of the mine exploding in the air projected me to crouch in the shelter of the tiny porch just in time before the debris tumbled all around me.[74]

John got a job in various factories in Letchworth, but he found the noise and environment distressing. Mother took an all-night job in Knebworth to add to her day duties in Willian. For this she needed a permit to travel by night in a dark train past unlit stations, requiring everyone to count the stops. Mistaking the gender of a long-haired carriage occupant, buried deep in piles of paper and deciding this was a safe seat, she discovered that her fellow passenger was Herbert Morrison, Labour leader and Minister for Supply. These journeys came to an end when, taking me for a routine school medical, the doctor said 'The child is perfect but you are not going to live to take your children back to London unless you consult a doctor for yourself.' She was far too exhausted and stressed. My first direct experience of death came when the Tucker's youngest child Verity died of diphtheria in November 1940 and was buried in the cemetery immediately across from our cottage.[75n]

In Willian, in order to relieve the terrible overcrowding in the cottage and reduce her commutes, Mother and John moved to nearby Baldock and fell into the hands of a tyrannical landlady. Mum worked on the emergency telephone system, John took a post as an assistant billeting officer and Gran was cook and cleaner in the squire's house, where I was occasionally allowed to glimpse the children's nursery and toys, a wonderland way above anything I had ever seen in my life. Gran also worked as a cleaner at the Fox Inn in the village, where she developed a friendship with the landlords Mr and Mrs Royle. The ARP was well organised with a democratic membership of the squire, the vicar, four women and a total of five men (plus two messengers and a fire guard leader), each taking turns to keep this small village safe if bombs dropped. I still have a summons for them to take part in an invasion exercise, and to attend at

> ... 9am and proceed to their stirrup-pumps and then to the scene of any fire. On hearing the short sharp blasts on the whistle, wearing brassards, steel helmet and carrying whistles, which should be used freely to spread the news of any fire.

Quite what invading troops would have made of that was never recorded. John joined the Home Guard, by now supplemented by the Army Cadet Force with recruits from the age of 14 years. My only contribution was to work the hand pump for the church organ where John had permission to practise and play for Sunday services. Every Saturday evening I acted as pot-boy in the Fox Inn. Apart from acquiring an early taste for a wide variety of beer dregs, I recall happy Saturday nights as people walked the two miles across the fields from Letchworth, lost their worries and sang and sang. The favourite of the time was 'Roll Me Over In The Clover' with its lyrics 'Roll me over, in the clover. Roll me over, lay me down, and do it again,' the clear sexual meaning of which was entirely lost on me. Other favourites were the patriotic 'There'll Always Be An England' and the sentimental 'We'll Meet Again,' both popularised by Vera Lynn, and sometimes 'I'll Be Seeing You,' one of Bing Crosby's songs. On Saturday afternoons we delivered bottled beer to better off homes in Letchworth. We had an allotment, and Dad would visit at weekends if he were well enough, during which time we became, however briefly, a more united family.

I was certainly very well cared for and never lacked love. Discipline, structure and formal education were, however, entirely missing throughout these years. By and large we were adapting well to rural life and were welcomed by the villagers. We joined in the activities in the small village hall, which by now had become a 'British Restaurant' (a type of communal kitchen) so we were kept busy washing up in the kitchen, taking it in turns at the crack of dawn to run down and make sure that the fire under the boiler had not gone out. At least this meant that the village children got one meal with meat a day, rations being supplemented by local caught game. This was an introduction to community service in the back room that was to be lifelong for all of us. Stress was affecting us all. As Mother finished work in the morning she would sit exhausted in the local church and pray for our safety and for relief from the debilitated state that she could not shake off. On one occasion the verger tapped her on the shoulder and advised her not to leave her bag unattended as 'Them evacuees from London will pinch it. They pinch anything.' She was too weary to explain.

My gang, which was complete with secret codes and names, consisted mainly of fellow evacuees, particularly the Bell family, which seemed to add another member soon after each of Mr Bell's leave visits. So there was a constant supply of babies in small prams which could be pushed around the village at high speed with an occasional spill usually resulting in a heavily bruised head. Trees were there to be climbed to the highest conceivable point and wild animals were there to be tracked. Haystacks, that essential part of harvest, were not only enjoyable to help build but also a delightful source of fun, as was the debris left by friendly Gypsy encampments as they moved to the next predetermined site. My memory of those summers is that they were long and very warm. In winter the village pond froze deeply, so skating was added to our skills, although Gran was horrified one year when I returned home with the most enormous egg-shaped bump on my forehead. When I teamed up with older village lads, tracking included following American servicemen and the local girls as they crept away to secluded spots for some strange activity which would leave evidence in terms of used 'French letters,'[76n] which caused much excitement among the older lads. One of the girls, being a year or two older than me, used to enjoy playing 'lions and meat,' which involved her stripping naked in the field and me licking and chewing her all over, innocent country pastimes indeed. Fruit orchards were of course there to be scrumped, ensuring a regular supply of fresh fruit. Whether I was more adventurous or on one occasion a slower runner I do not recall, but when I was caught I had my full paper bag of stolen blackcurrants squashed in my face. The trick was to get home and to wash your face, hands and then hair under the tap that released the soft sweet smelling rainwater from the rain barrel before Gran found out. Some chance!

A partridge rising suddenly and vertically a few feet away as I raced across the fields certainly sent the adrenaline running, but this could be outdone by the owl, perching on a gravestone which took off just as you ventured through taking a short cut as darkness fell. We had our secret dens, hidden deep in the bracken covered ditches where we could hide undetected in the event that the Nazis came. We practised parachuting from trees so that we could do surprise attacks. I once narrowly avoided giving my father a heart attack as he approached across the meadow just in time to see me launching myself from a treetop using an old tent *underneath* me in the belief that it would break my fall. Somehow I survived with a few bruises.

As time went by, our school day excursions were extended up Bluebell Hill and to Baldock, where being bored one day we decided to search out my mother, who I guessed to be working at the emergency telephone exchange in the Town Hall. We called and called down the fortified embrasures without result. Some two days later I came home to find Mother in tears, nearing on hysterics, but not letting me know the reason. News eventually reached me that our behaviour had been so disgraceful in the eyes of the Town Clerk that Mother had been immediately sacked, with the inevitable result that she and John would have to return to London. Back there, Mother soon found the job that she would keep until her retirement, as a telephonist taking the calls from distressed customers of the South Metropolitan Gas Company in the Old Kent Road. This was a walk of over five miles a day which she did for the next twenty years. Never one to spare herself, she got involved in running the 34th Camberwell Cubs and Boy Scout troop for the few local children still in London. She took her part in fire watching, and during one Scout meeting in the old wooden hut situated in the sports ground of Haberdasher Aske's School she describes a raid on the barrage balloon unit based in those grounds:

> One Saturday morning we were on Aske's field, the danger soon passed, when, without warning, German planes hedgehopped their way across London, popping off the barrage balloons. There was one in the next field, and as two planes roared towards us we could clearly see the airmen firing the machine guns as they flew across the field. We flew too, to the only shelter which was the turnstiles, with heads tucked under the iron turnstile arms, the danger soon passed, the cubs ran onto the field to pick up the spent bullets, and were surprised to find them still hot – well I too was surprised as some balloons were on fire. We hustled into a nearby house and grabbing the nearest tin helmet, which happened to belong to a policeman, I went to the balloon field where the company of young girls who manned the site were unhurt but badly shaken, except one who had completely collapsed, and had to be taken to hospital.[77]

Mother records a striking experience when a 10-year-old cub came visiting, shaken by the fact that the block of flats where he lived had been demolished by a mine with many casualties. As he eagerly drank his tea he casually explained that, 'When you've touched one stiff it doesn't matter how many more you handle.' Meanwhile John got a job collecting rents in the council flats in Lambeth, not an ideal job for such a shy and sensitive lad. Somehow he survived the demanding work including the threats and dubious invitations sometimes handed out by desperate tenants. He actually managed to collect record weekly amounts by the simple expedient of calling when tenants had their wage packet in their hand rather than at the regular day and time set by the council.

From time to time, Gran and I would make a trip home, always an exciting event travelling in old railway carriages where the soot particles from the engine would cover all surfaces including our hands and faces. These were the carriages with no corridors that had drop windows opened by leather straps. The overhead structures being somewhat primitive, you were in danger of losing your head if you leaned out too far. If a troop or equipment train went through, we would be shunted to a side line, eventually arriving at a dirty Kings Cross Station where the smoke and steam of the engines enveloped the drab civilians, vastly outnumbered by the khaki or blues of the troops. A small diversionary thrill awaited me as there were usually long queues of people waiting to use the ranks of telephone boxes in the station entrance hall. By employing my small size and speediness I could nip into each booth between occupants, and by pressing 'button B'[78n] I could collect any pennies that the previous caller had left unclaimed. This was a relatively profitable activity compared with our family circumstances, although I can only think that I spent the money on comics as sweets were non-existent and no money was required or sought for our rural adventures. As the war progressed, the journey across London changed as the extent of the destruction increased: large bomb craters became sites for a profusion of weeds and wildlife or, if cleared, huge emergency water tanks and eventually the amazing 'prefabs' offering temporary homes for the increasing number of 'bombed-out' Londoners. Every visit included regular nights in the damp and dark shelter as bombs and bits of bombs fell all around. Any lull would encourage us to poke our heads out, and I vividly recall one clear dark night looking up at the brilliant stars and the amazing criss-cross patterns formed by searchlight beams as they wove in and out looking for the enemy aircraft that the gunners could then hit. Five in the shelter added to the sense of claustrophobia that affected both my dad and John, leading them to spend more and more time out of the shelter. Gran's concern led to another of her famous sayings. 'Don't do it, Harry! Don't let him, Mabel!' she would wail. From time to time we would have to scramble into a public shelter if the warning went, but as bombs were replaced by rockets a new hazard had to be faced from June 1944. The V1 rockets (Vergeltungswaffe Revenge Bomb) brought little or no warning except the drone of their strange two-stroke engine from which one could guess their direction and trajectory to their target. Much more scary was the V2, a ballistic missile, which you would hear overhead but would then cut out and fall directly and ramdonly. A real horror. Immediately the war ended, nations competed to get the best scientific research from the Nazi physicists.[79n] As the post-war space race developed between Russia and America, the comedian Bob Hope joked 'Of course our rockets are better than the Russians, our Nazis are better than their Nazis.'

Finances dictated that return journeys started by catching the extraordinarily early morning 'workman's' tram that started from the terminus at the top of Peckham Rye. Through senses only half awake, I tucked myself into a seat in the fug of stale breath and cigarette smoke, feeling warm and welcome among the char ladies and shift workers as they recounted their personal and war experiences of the previous night. Willian may have been a place of freedom and fresh air, but this was where I felt most at home, with these workers whose daily lives were such a challenge to be met with such good humour and commitment, with the survival of their families and as many of their neighbours that could be managed. In common with my mother and grandmother they were the inheritors of the fictional Ma Joad determinedly seeing her family across America in the Depression (see the quotation at the beginning of this chapter). I write this in the lounge of my family's house in Brooklyn, New York, where on the wall is a framed replica of a wartime poster which simply says 'Keep Calm and Carry On.' Exactly.[80n] At the end of a long trip back lay the rare treat of a visit to the Letchworth branch of the British Restaurant (another aspect of life under government control) where beans on toast revived our spirits.[81n] Leaving the restaurant one day, my early masculinity was shocked to find a large double-decker bus being driven by a woman! This was of course one small example of how war service, whether in the forces, land army, factories or services, had emancipated women. The pressure of work while caring for the family may have exhausted them, but a return to the limiting pre-war stereotype was unthinkable.

I am sure that every adult followed every available scrap of news and rumour about the progress of war, but I cannot recall having an awareness of the great issues or minor events. The only radio was with our neighbours, the Shire family. It was powered by a glass accumulator battery which their son would frequently have to take to Letchworth to be recharged. The censored news came through and sometimes we got 'Lord Haw-Haw' propaganda messages in that strange voice and with the call sign 'Germany calling. Germany calling,' only to be thoroughly laughed at[82n]. My concerns were more with the immediate world of childhood. The gang, which I led, roamed far and wide; indeed, the whole period of life in Willian was of freedom to explore nature. We just ran wild, out early and back before nightfall. In post-war social work terms, the Bell family who shared our washing area would have been classified in the socio-economic grading as 'DE' – the lowest.[83n] In any event, we were all in the same boat and shared a great sense of community. The Bell children were incontinent, so in the morning a pile of soiled sheets in the boiler room imbued both cottages with a distinct aroma. There were the occasional disputes and upsets, and a small fire on one occasion when Mr Bell was home from leave and left his rifle and ammunition propped up beside the stove. A small crisis! In time we all had 'nits,' horror of horrors discovered by the school nurse, combed out with the special comb and the first secret to be kept from my mother when she visited.

The families gave all the support and care that they could as they went back and forward to London. Gran, approaching the age of 60 and faced with the care of an extrovert, lively and overactive boy, gave unconditionally of her energy and love. She became a significant local 'character,' the cheeky bright Londoner who could cope with anything that circumstances or the war could throw at her. An original live example of the famous Giles cartoon character. Dressed in a set of overalls she was a dead ringer for Churchill; regretfully, the only photo of her was destroyed. Love and jollity were received from all. If you couldn't beat it, then laugh at it seemed to be the motto. Evenings were preoccupied with lighting the oil lamp; if you turned the flame up too fast the delicate glass globe would shatter (it was very difficult to replace), but if you did it too slowly there was what seemed like an interminable delay before any activity could begin. Once settled down, Gran and I would start work. If socks or balaclavas were to be knitted for the troops then an old garment had to be found and unthreaded round a chair back. I would then hold the skein while Gran wound a ball of wool from which to knit. Alternatively my job was to cut old clothing into strips about 4 inches long and one inch wide. Once we had a sufficient quantity and variety of colours, the job of making a rug would begin. Having acquired a piece of hessian a design would be roughly drawn and then the coloured strips would be forced through the hessian and doubled over, each piece being as close as possible to its neighbour. When such a long project was finished a second piece of hessian was sewn on the back, resulting in a hard wearing and warm rug for the earth floor to keep us warm in the winter.

Gran slept on a large feather bed supported by a succession of strong springs; she seemed to disappear into it every night, while I had a simple narrow board bed. The 'po' for any night-time calls of nature I think started my lifelong bad habit of retention.

If the neighbours' friendly teasing became too much, Gran would lean out of the upstairs window and threaten to empty the contents over them.

Gran was much given to telling your future by reading your palm or the pattern of tea leaves left in the bottom of your cup. From time to time Gran and friends would attend a séance, where the medium would summon spirits from the dead and Gran would return home upset by some personal revelation that the medium could only have known from a dead relative. Such séances and the supernatural beliefs behind them were not uncommon. In April 1944 a well established medium Helen Duncan (whose eminent clientele was said to include Winston Churchill and George VI) was found guilty at the Old Bailey of spying and was branded a witch under the 1735 Witchcraft Act. Part of the case against her was that during a séance she had told a woman that her son, serving in the Navy, was dead. Although this was true, the loss of his ship had been suppressed as a state secret.[84n]

While these global events were taking place, Lt W. W. Wickett was nearing the end of his long cruise home from Egypt. The journey had crept slowly down the eastern coast of Africa, docking from time to time to refuel, discharge some troops, including Vichy prisoners, and to take on others while being dive-bombed. At Durban there had been a change from the Dutch ship *Indrapoera* to the MRS *Strathnaver*, but although WWW's dysentery had more or less cleared, he was deeply depressed and homesick. His diary details both his unhappy state of mind and life on board:

> What a long, wearying voyage this is! It seems such a long time since I saw my little wife – the only woman who matters and my two precious daughters. Please God take care of them.

As they crossed the equator, the service wives picked up in South Africa and the Caribbean were really irritating him:

> They seem so prosperous and so utterly callous, & show no signs of ever intending to help the war effort. When I think of the sacrifice my own darling has made, I become bitter and hate them!

The ship had no escort for the next eleven days back across the Atlantic, and a torpedo narrowly missed them in mid Atlantic. When in the greatest danger, they slept fully dressed for six nights dodging U-boat attacks while tremendous seas threatened to overturn the top-heavy old ship. Approaching the west coast of Scotland, two flying-boats came out to greet them, then they went up the Clyde to King George Dock in Glasgow. After quick disembarkation and a train trip via St Pancras out to Sevenoaks, where his wife Violet was working as a nurse in that part of Guy's Hospital evacuated to nearby Seal, he writes: 'I took her in my arms (heaven again). I thank God for all his mercies & a safe landing home.' They divorced eighteen months after the end of the war.

NOTES AND REFERENCES

1. Hobsbawm, E. (1994). *Age of Extremes: The Short Twentieth Century, 1914–1991*. London: Abacus, p. 37.
2. Briggs, G. 'London Under Bombardment,' in Wavell, A. P. (1960) *Other Men's Flowers*. London: Penguin, p. 67.
3. Goldsmith, O. (1770). 'The Deserted Village,' in Wain, J. (ed.) (1990). *The Oxford Library of English Poetry, Vol II*. Oxford: Oxford University Press, p. 155. I have not succeeded in tracking down a BBC production called 'The Tuppenny Ha'penny Opera' after Kurt Weil. The vicar recites these lines as a gang of East End kids spills out of the coach at the village. Their leader Mac says 'Wot, no fish and chip shop, no flicks, no pubs. Get back in the coach we ain't staying 'ere.'
4. Ma Joad says these words to her family when their backs are against the wall. Steinbeck, J. (2000). *The Grapes of Wrath*. London: Penguin Books, p. 293.
5. Before succeeding as Emperor, Selassie was known by his own name and as a Prince, Ras Tafari Makonnen. During the 1930s in Jamaica, Rastafarianism developed as a new religion. Haile Selassie is seen by Rastafarians as the second coming of Christ (as God incarnate) or as a human prophet who recognises the inner divinity in every individual.
6. The conflict claimed at least half a million lives. In 2008, a Spanish judge, Baltasar Garzón, opened an investigation into the executions and disappearances of 114,266 people between July 17th 1936 and December 1951; this included the execution of the poet Federico García Lorca. This action was in contradiction to the 1977 amnesty, by which time the government had hoped to put the terrible past behind the nation. In 1998 he had issued an international warrant against the Chilean dictator Pinochet. Garzón was subsequently indicted and suspended before any cases could be brought. While awaiting trial in 2010, he worked at the International Criminal Court in The Hague. In 2012 he was summoned by the Spanish Supreme Court. In that year he also became a legal advisor to WikiLeaks. His appeal to the Supreme Court on the 2008 investigation was cleared. In 2019, in view of the increase in right-wing activity in Europe, the Spanish government finally agreed to remove Franco's body from the elaborate mausoleum in which he had been buried. He now lies next to his wife and ministers.
7. Lee, L. (1961). *A Moment of War*. London: Penguin.
8. See Ernest Hemingway's best seller *For Whom the Bell Tolls* centred on the brave spirit of the American volunteer Robert Jordan. It is interesting to note that more than seventy years later both candidates in the 2009 USA presidential campaign, John McCain and Barack Obama, considered Jordan to be one of their iconic heroes.
9. Interview with historian Max Arthur: Arthur, M. (2009). *The Observer*, 26.04.09, p. 21. Printed on the occasion of the death of Jack Jones at the age of 96.
10. This included early war photos by Robert Capra.
11. Now in the Museo Nacional Centro de Arte, Madrid. A tapestry copy is in the United Nations Building in New York.
12. Kershaw, I. (2008). 'The crisis of 1938,' *The Guardian*, 23.08.08.
13. Kressmann Taylor, K. (2003). *Address Unknown*. Stuttgart: Reclam. The original book sold 50,000 copies in America. A further issue coincided with the 50th anniversary of the discovery of the concentration camps, and a French edition in 1999 sold 100,000 copies. The 2003 edition is the first in German.
14. From these early days throughout the war many individuals acted with incredible bravery to help Jews escape. After the war some individuals were identified with some very daring schemes. The most famous of these was probably Oskar Schindler, who was able to exploit his position as a member of the Nazi party to save many of his Jewish 'employees.' Poles, Germans, Austrians,

Italians, Spanish, Dutch, British, American, Chinese, Swiss, Lithuanian and French individuals acted out of a variety of motives, at the risk of instant death, to spare Jewish individuals and families. After the war some 20,000 people received the award of 'Righteous among the Nations' from the State of Israel. See Grunwald-Spier, A. (2010). *The Other Schindlers*. London: The History Press. This is a very detailed study exploring both the deeds and motivations of a selection of these brave people. It was my pleasure to work with Agnes, who was saved from being tossed alive into a concentration camp furnace, the routine fate of small babies arriving in camps, by an unknown official who decided to send all families with babies home rather than board the fatal train. She makes the important point that no one will ever know how many more helpers failed. The film *Schindler's List*, directed by Steven Spielberg and released in 1994, won seven Oscars.

15. Signing the German–USSR Pact on August 23rd 1939, Hitler had commented 'Now I have the world in my pocket.' See Davies, N. (2007). *Europe at War, 1939–1945, No Simple Victory*. London: Pan Macmillan, p. 57. A secret protocol to this pact gave Germany and Russia shares of all Eastern European countries. Such a division seems to have contributed to the post-war and continuing Russian belief that these territories form a natural area of influence for Russia.
16. A practice D-Day landing was held at Slapton Sands in Devon on the night of April 28th 1944, many families having been moved from the hinterland. An attack by German E-boats led to disaster and the loss of nearly 1,000 American troops. News was suppressed and relatives sent misleading information. See Davies, *op. cit.*, p. 221. After many difficulties the relatives succeeded in raising sufficient funds to erect a memorial on the site. It was opened on April 28th 1984, 40 years after the event.
17. These were Spain (sympathetic to fascism), Portugal, Sweden, Switzerland and Vatican City. Eire was the only British Dominion to refuse to support Britain. Turkey, anxious about Russian domination, allied themselves to whichever side fought Russia.
18. Bliss, E. (ed.) (1968). *In Search of Light: The Broadcasts of Edward R. Murrow 1938–1961*. London: Macmillan.
19. Stansky, P. (2007). *The First Day of the Blitz*. New York: Yale, p. 56.
20. A good account of these events is given in the Powell and Pressburger 1956 film *The Battle of the River Plate*.
21. The evacuation of British, French and Belgian troops from France and Germany was accomplished by 222 British naval vessels and 665 small craft. In the early days of the war the Admiralty had obtained full details of all available small vessels, which considerably helped the very rapid response. Despite intense shelling, bombing and submarine attacks, only six destroyers and 24 small craft were lost. German ships and submarines were destroyed and several major ports blocked. A large number of French naval and merchant ships also took part in the evacuation. Kerr, M. (ed.) (2010*). Bon Voyage: The Telegraph Book of River and Sea Journeys*. London: Aurum Press, p. 217.
22. Beevor, A. (2008). *Great Speeches of the 20th Century. The Flame of French Resistance: Charles De Gaulle June 18,19, 22 1940*. London: Guardian News and Media Ltd.
23. Proud, unbending, infinitely touchy, obstinate and lacking gratitude – he felt humiliated, etc. Paris August 25th 1944: 'Paris outraged, Paris martyred, but Paris liberated! Liberated by herself, liberated by her people, with the help of the whole of France, that is to say a fighting France, the true France, the eternal France.' Excessive and obsessive national pride would not allow mention of British and American armies or Britain's role in giving him shelter.
24. Cordell, H. (1948). *The Memoirs of Cordell Hull*. London: Hodder & Stoughton.
25. *The Empire and the Second World War*. BBC Broadcast, June 14th 2006, Episode 88.
26. Longfellow, H. W. (1849). 'O Ship of State,' quoted in Eade, C. (ed.) (1946). *Victory: The Sixth Volume of Winston Churchill's War Speeches*. London: Cassell.

27. Attard, J. (1988). *The Battle of Malta*. London: Hamlyn. An interesting item of naval history concerns the actions of Lt Commander Alister Mars, who objected to the position allocated to his submarine in the preparations for the defence of the convoys. His objections having been overruled, he proceeded to his station where he was promptly located and attacked. By the time he had shaken off his attackers he was some 15 miles from his position, so decided to risk his career and a charge of disobeying orders in the face of the enemy by taking up a new position. His intuition paid off as he was the sole vessel in a position to stop the Italian ships that broke cover determined to finish off the vessel. He was able to save the day.
28. This resulted in the whole island being awarded the George Cross for exceptional gallantry.
29. For a clear first-hand account of the Japanese treatment of prisoners, their mental trauma and recovery, see two accounts by the Australian author Russell Braddon: *The Naked Island* (1953) and *End of a Hate* (1960), both published by Pan Books.
30. An illustrative example of Slim's leadership is reported that when he arrived, monocle in place, at a large parade of Australian troops. Not known for showing undeserved respect, the troops could be seen to each have a coin balanced in one eye. Slim took the stand, removed his monocle, tossed it in the air, caught it in his eye and said 'Now try that you bastards!'
31. Fowler, W. (2009). *We Gave Our Today: Burma 1941–1945*. London: Weidenfeld & Nicolson.
32. The Mountbatten name had been invented in 1917 in the face of public dislike of the German Battenburg family name. Lord Louis Mountbatten was a favourite of Churchill and uncle to the late Prince Philip.
33. Some 17,000 Japanese Americans had volunteered for the forces and fought bravely in Europe.
34. After the war, Japanese Commander General Homma was tried for the war crime of the Bataan Death March (and others) and was executed on April 3rd 1946.
35. In 1952, Turing was tried for homosexuality, which was then a criminal offence, and sentenced to chemical castration. His security clearance was removed, which ended his career as a computer designer and code breaker (then at Government Communications Headquarters (GCHQ) in Cheltenham). He committed suicide on June 7th 1954. In September 2009 the Prime Minister, Gordon Brown, responding to a public petition, stated 'It is no exaggeration to say that, without his outstanding contribution, the history of World War Two could well have been very different. The debt of gratitude he is owed makes it all the more horrifying, therefore, that he was treated so inhumanely. I am pleased to have the chance to say how deeply sorry I and we all are for what happened to him. But even more than that, Alan deserves recognition for his contribution to humankind. For those of us born after 1945, into a Europe which is united, democratic and at peace.' After the war much equipment was destroyed and the Bletchley Park buildings fell into disrepair. A substantial donation was given by an American millionaire to save some equipment, and there is now a museum on the site. In 2009 desperate appeals were being made to prevent the collapse of many historic buildings on site. The Museum and Park opened in 1991. Appeals are being made to repair some of the buildings.
36. Hastings, M. (1979). *Bomber Command*. London: Pan Books, p. 170.
37. In a debate in Parliament as late as January 27th 1944 the government's reply to criticism was to reject the charge of terror bombing but to declare that 'The air offensive is carefully planned to achieve victory at the earliest possible moment and that was the only way to end the present horrors.'
38. Hastings, *op. cit.*, p. 196.
39. In addition to designing even more destructive bombs, Wallis was responsible for developing the lightweight frames important in the construction of early airships and aircraft, including the Wellington bombers, a design that enabled many to keep flying even though large sections of the aircraft had been shot away.

40. Arthur, M. (ed.) (2008). *Dambusters: A Landmark Oral History*. London: Virgin Books. Although two dams were breached and the raid raised national morale at home, the dams were rebuilt within three months and the interruption in industrial output was much less than anticipated, although the floods badly affected food supplies. The entire mission from take-off to return lasted around seven hours, but eight of the nineteen aircraft had been shot down and fifty-six highly valued aircrew lost. The role of Bomber Command has never been given the same recognition as the more romantically portrayed fighter crews. Sixty-seven years after the end of the war, a memorial to the 55,573 crewmen killed during the war (the average age of those killed was 22 years) was unveiled in Green Park, London.
41. Milligan, S. (1978). *Monty: His Part in My Victory*. London: Penguin, p. 16.
42. The former King Edward (relegated to Duke of Windsor) and Mrs Simpson were to spend the rest of their lives based in Paris, resentful and frustrated during the war that he was denied any useful role. Caught between a fear that their capture would be a Nazi prize and concern at their alleged Nazi sympathy, the Duke was made Governor of The Bahamas. Queen Mary's acute disappointment that her son had evaded his duty, and Queen Elizabeth's feeling that he bore responsibility for the burden placed on her husband and his early death, meant that he was denied attendance at any state occasion, including the coronation of her daughter Queen Elizabeth II in 1953. With the death of the Queen Mother in March 2002 there was some easing of tension. When the Duke died in 1972, his state funeral in Windsor Castle was attended by the Queen. When Edward's wife died fourteen years later, she was buried beside him with the simple inscription 'Wallis, Duchess of Windsor.'
43. Woodruff, W. (2003). *Beyond Nab End*. London: Abacus, p. 99.
44. Reported in *The Manchester Guardian*, Monday, 04.09.39.
45. King George VI had a nervous stutter which handicapped him when speaking in public or broadcasting on the newly available radio. It was almost unnoticeable after treatment by an Australian therapist Lionel Logue. These events were excellently portrayed in the film *The King's Speech*. Dir. Tom Hooper (2010), starring Colin Firth as King George, Geoffrey Rush as Logue and Helena Bonham Carter as Queen Elizabeth.
46. In time the excavation was filled in with the rubble from bombed buildings. The ensuing pile reached a height of forty feet before being transported to extend RAF runways to take the large American aircraft.
47. In 1946, this became the Family Service Units, which provided a model of intensive casework and practical intervention for families facing complex problems.
48. Titmuss, R. M. (1950). *Problems of Social Policy*. London: HMSO, p. 289.
49. Leo's younger brother went to Germany as a fascist and was involved in the proposal to develop a British branch of the SS. He was hanged in Wandsworth Jail in December 1945.
50. See Colville, J. (1986). *The Fringes of Power: Downing Street Diaries, 1939–1955*. New York: Norton.
51. Foot, M. (2003). *The Uncollected Michael Foot: Essays Old and New 1953–2003*. London: Politico, p. 308.
52. Tempus Publishing UK (2006). *Home Guard Manual 1941*. Stroud: Tempus Publishing.
53. Hansard HC Deb. Vol. 148 Col 796. June 4th 1940.
54. Brinkley, D. and Facey-Crowther, D. (eds.) (1964). *The Atlantic Charter*. Basingstoke: Palgrave Macmillan.
55. Titmuss, R. M. (1958). 'War and Social Policy,' in *Essays on the Welfare State*. London: Unwin.
56. Mazower, *op. cit.*, p. 190.
57. Stansky, *op. cit.*, p. 151.
58. Winnicott, D. W. (1964). *The Child, the Family and the Outside World*. London: Penguin.

59. See Neill, A. S. (1960). *Summerhill: A Radical Approach to Child Rearing*. With a Foreword by Erich Fromm. London: Hart. See also Burn, M. (1956). *Mr Lyward's Answer*. London: Hamish Hamilton.
60. Jordan, M. (1986). *An Autobiography*. Preston: Nemco Press, p. 22.
61. Jordan, *op. cit.*, p. 22.
62. Bruce Forsyth commenced his career in 1942 aged 14 with a song and dance act in Bilston. His first big break was hosting *Sunday Night at the London Palladium* in 1958. This was followed by film and TV appearances until *The Generation Game* (which he hosted from 1971 to 1994), a show based on family competition. Forsyth's strength was in his ability to work with audience members on stage, using his quick wit to create fun while not ridiculing the competitors. His catch phrase was 'Didn't he do well,' interspersed with his pose as 'The Thinker.' His last great success was as presenter for *Strictly Come Dancing* (2004–2013), where all his skills were on display. He gained many awards and was created a Knight Bachelor in 2011. He died in August 2017.
63. Jordan, *op. cit.*, p. 25.
64. Jordan, *op. cit.* p. 26. Jordan, J. (1940). *Loughborough Central School Magazine*, July.
65. *Sunday Times Magazine* (1965). Special edition: 'Reliving 1940,' p. 38.
66. Stansky, *op. cit.*, p. 15.
67. Savarid, E. (1967). *All England Listened: The Wartime Postscript of J. B. Priestley*. New York: Chilmark Press.
68. This event was reconstructed as the Grand Ball in Mathew Bourne's ballet *Cinderella*, which I saw in 2017. It was the only time I was alone in anticipating the climax.
69. Having just rediscovered the sweet notes that my classmates at Herston School wrote when I left Swanage, I was, in 2009, able to take them back to the school and the local museum.
70. These local stores, together with Sainsburys and Home and Colonial (in Rye Lane), were part of a combined campaign to spread 'middle-class' goods to the lower classes. After the war, United Dairies joined Cow and Gate to form Unigate, now Dairy Crest.
71. Residents of Letchworth voted against the sale of alcohol in the town many times. The first pub was opened in 1960. Letchworth Garden City has had its critics: George Orwell, who lived nearby, dismissed it as a magnet for 'every fruit-juice drinker, nudist, sandal-wearer, sex maniac, Quaker, Nature Cure quack, pacifist and feminist in England.' See Orwell, G. (2001). *The Road to Wigan Pier*. London: Penguin Modern Classics. Originally published in 1937.
72. This was the largest of the affiliated societies which enabled working-class families to ensure against the cost of sickness. For a weekly subscription of about 4d, the Oddfellows Society would pay doctor's bills and an income of ten shillings a week in case of long term illness.
73. This was Father Potter of Peckham. See Potter, The Rev Canon G. (1955). *Father Potter of Peckham: A South London Saga*. London: Hodder & Stoughton.
74. Jordan, *op. cit.*, p. 31.
75. As observed on a recent visit, this small grave still sits alone but in good condition.
76. Condoms.
77. Jordan, *op. cit.*, p. 35.
78. Having put your money into the telephone box and dialled the number, you waited to be connected. If the connection were made, you pressed button A and could be heard. If the call failed, you pressed button B to get your money back. Unless of course you were in a hurry!
79. This rocket was developed by Werner von Braun. In March 1945 he led a group of 500 scientists across Germany in a stolen train to surrender to the Americans. He became Director of the American Space Flight Center. The V2 rockets were launched from The Hague from September 8th 1944 to March 1945.

80. This was one of the many posters designed to raise morale, but there seems some doubt that it was ever used as it implied that it was just a statement about what everyone was doing anyway. It became fashionable many years later when it was rediscovered.
81. Meals away from home were off the ration. The rich could therefore avoid food rationing. The British Restaurants were an extension of the meals service provided by local councils for people who had been bombed out. A three course nutritious meal would cost about 9d (equivalent to 3p).
82. William Joyce, nicknamed Lord Haw-Haw, was an American-British man who had been a leader of Mosely's British Union of Fascists but fled to Germany rather than be interred on the Isle of Wight with other undesirables. After capture he was tried for treason and was hanged in January 1946. In the Far East, Japanese broadcasters known as 'Tokyo Rose' broadcast propaganda to Allied troops.
83. My understanding is that the category D5/E was the lowest/poorest band in demographic ratings.
84. Descendants and supporters have campaigned for a posthumous pardon for Helen Martin, which has been rejected three times by the Scottish Parliament, the latest in 2012. See the website helenduncan.org.

FOUR

1942–1945

TWO GREAT VICTORY CELEBRATIONS: HOME AND SCHOOL

Our victory in Europe was more than a victory of arms. It was a victory of one way of life over another. It was a victory of an ideal founded on the right of a common man, on the dignity of the human being, and on the conception of the State as the servant, not the master of its people.

– *Winston Churchill*[1n]

If, as was once claimed … the British Empire was created in a fit of absence of mind, the Welfare State has been no less the result of a fit of conscience. In this last stage, under the pressure of the great levelling influences of total war, conscience rounded off, between 1940 and 1948, the long process by which an elaborate series of social services … was at last consolidated and extended into a pattern of welfare provision which could reasonably be styled a 'Welfare State.'

– *Maurice Bruce*[2]

Now I am become death, the destroyer of worlds.
Bhagavad Gita, attributed to Robert Oppenheimer[3n]

WORLD EVENTS

Europe

On the Eastern Front the German armies had continued their advance to the south and east, these two spearheads drawing further apart, thus limiting their ability to support each other and increasing the problems of supply. In September 1941, the SS commander in Kiev had been ordered to eliminate Jewish residents, and during the closing days of that month 33,771 Ukrainian Jews were systematically machine gunned, their bodies thrown into the Babi Yar ravine. The same site was used until the Nazi retreat, and it has been estimated that a further 170,000 Russian prisoners of war, Roma, resistance fighters, homosexuals and mentally ill or disabled people died in the same ravine.[4n] Such massacres were part of the Nazis' drive for a pure Aryan race and the complete expulsion of the Jews. As the implementation of that policy became a priority, a specific organisation was required, and Adolf Eichmann was placed in charge. In January 1942, Heidrich and Eichmann[5n] called the infamous conference at Wannsee to meticulously plan the extermination of Jews in mainland Europe. The minutes of the meeting comment how many Jews had already emigrated with the help of some $9.5 million raised by wealthy Jews:

> Another possible solution of the problem has now taken the place of emigration, i.e. the evacuation of the Jews to the East ... practical experience is already being collected, which is of the greatest importance in relation to the final solution of the Jewish question. Approximately 11 million Jews will be involved in the final solution of the European Jewish question.[6]

The decision to exterminate rather than rely on exile (to a slow death in slave camps) was made following the defeat of German troops at Moscow. Records show that Eichmann had previously visited both Palestine and Madagascar as possible destinations for a mass forced exodus from Germany.

Russia

By the autumn of 1942, five German armies were approaching Stalingrad (now Volgograd) while the Luftwaffe started to raze the city. An easy surrender was in prospect. With the city having a population approaching 700,000, being well defended and bearing the name of the Great Leader himself, a victory would be a military and propaganda prize of great value to the German cause. With the city besieged, the defending troops fought fiercely, then the neighbouring Russian commanders (Generals Vasilevskiy and Zhukov), with well-supplied troops, painstakingly drew a ring round the German army. The besiegers were now being besieged. On November 19th the Russians launched their major attack, and four days later the ring had been sealed: the German army was now completely surrounded. The German commanders decided to sit tight, believing that they could be supplied from the air until help arrived to pierce the encircling Russians. Both sides had been given orders forbidding retreat or surrender. The ensuing battle between these two great armies lasted for eleven weeks, each side throwing all the resources of modern warfare against their enemy.

As winter advanced, the Russians piled on the pressure by damaging the temporary runways used by the Luftwaffe and restricting the movement of heavy weapons. The German army despaired, froze and died. There was no evacuation for injured or weak soldiers. Within the city, civilians, hidden in cellars, caves and sewers, ate meat carved from dead horses and eventually from dead humans. The alternative was starvation. Slowly the outer ring of Russian troops tightened the circle, and at the end of a month, with the temperature down to minus 20 degrees Celsius, German soldiers were waving white flags or shooting themselves. When General Friedrich Paulus finally surrendered, he did so with only 90,000 men left from the 250,000 he had commanded three months earlier. Only 4,500 would survive the Russian camps to return home. It is estimated that 973,000 people died in this battle. This included 13,500 executions of Russians perceived as cowards or traitors, carried out by the NVKD (the feared secret police with the power to carry out extra judicial executions). It cannot be said that Stalingrad was the decisive battle of the war in Europe, but the very fact that the mighty German army could be defeated by effective and well-led Russian troops was a message which was not lost in Berlin, London or Washington.

By now it was clear to both sides that a decisive battle would have to be fought at Kursk, towards the border with Ukraine. This encounter, where both sides used tanks in a style reminiscent of old cavalry battles, was the biggest tank battle of all time, costing the Germans 70,000 men and 3,000 tanks. They were pitched against Russian troops who had called on all their reserves of men and materials. General Zhukov had laid concentric circles of mined defences, and for every German tank he responded with 3 anti-tank weapons, 9 assault guns, 50 Katyusha rockets every hour and 150 mines. As the Russians launched their final assault at the end of July 1943, their allies had still not landed one soldier on the mainland. Kursk was decisive, both militarily and psychologically. It was a major turning point in the war. The Germans had been broken to the extent that they were unable to mount another grand blitzkrieg. It also allowed the Russians to advance on Berlin with all the military and political consequences feared by Churchill, but not fully appreciated by the USA. D-Day ('D' for deliverance), the vast landing of Allied troops across the English Channel, was still ten months away.

Casablanca

In January 1943, as the siege of Stalingrad was in its final stages, Churchill and Roosevelt met at a pre-arranged conference at Casablanca to decide the strategy for the European campaign. America, now financially supporting most of the Allied countries and anticipating a devastated Europe, saw itself emerging as the one world superpower. The leaders decided that it was necessary to postpone invasion plans until the following year, but agreed that the programme of intensive bombing of German cities would now move further east. The most notorious culmination of these bombing raids, one argued over to this day, was in February 1945, when RAF Bomber Command sent 796 Lancaster bombers over the undefended city of Dresden, loaded with 1,500 tonnes of high explosives and 1,250 tonnes of incendiaries. They were followed the next morning by a similar wave of American B-17 planes. In addition to the resident population, many of the 600,000 refugees forced from Breslau by the Nazis were sheltering in the city. Estimates of civilian casualties vary between 30,000 and 120,000. Among the Allied prisoners in the area was the American writer Kurt Vonnegut, who later included his experiences in his novel *Slaughterhouse Five*:

> When the Americans and their guards did come out, the sky was black with smoke. The sun was an angry little pinhead. Dresden was like the moon now: nothing but minerals. The stones were hot. Everybody else in the neighbourhood was dead. So it goes.[7]

At the concluding Casablanca press conference, and with no prior notice, Roosevelt announced that only an unconditional surrender by the Axis powers would be accepted, later urging Churchill to accept that Germany should be forced back to an agricultural economy, with no military power, and certainly never to become a future industrial competitor to the USA. By now, the Allies were winning the Battle of the Atlantic, much helped by the American production of two new ships *per day*. Russian troops were engaged in the continued push westwards to drive both the remaining German thrusts back. In July 1944, as the war turned against Germany, senior officers, some of whom had long resisted Hitler's ambitions, planned to assassinate him by placing a bomb under a conference table. Although the bomb exploded and killed some officers, Hitler escaped injury. Nearly five thousand people died in the subsequent purge, and false accusations against General Rommel forced him to commit suicide.

Italy

Italy surrendered on September 8th 1943, and their troops were ordered to change sides.[8n] Allied troops landed in southern Italy at Salerno that same month and then further north at Anzio in January 1944. The first, which was American led, met with fierce defensive fire and led to high casualties. The landing officer at Anzio was Major Denis Healey (the Labour Party politician). He described the operation as going like clockwork, unlike that at Calabria where troops were held on the beach under heavy machine gun, mortar and air attack. Between these events Healey was able to attend the opera in Naples and work with fellow officers Jack Donaldson (who later helped set up the Peckham Health Centre) and Marcus Sieff. Also there was Richard Hoggart, an intelligence officer at Cassino, who was producing an excellent cultural magazine, and had helped establish the Three Arts Club in Naples where men and women from all services could meet regardless of rank or status. He was also contributing to issues of ABCA.[9n] Hoggart, who was to become a major cultural figure eleven years later, recognised the influence of the ABCA pamphlets because they were written in a balanced and ordinary language that made troops think about and discuss topical issues in a manner directly relevant to them, for many a new experience. He also comments, however, that by this late stage in the war troops were expressing a resolution that 'We didn't go through all this just to settle back where we were' or 'Things have got to change.'[10] In contrast, army experiences turned Healey away from academia and the arts to politics as the only means of avoiding another war. He was to become Chancellor of the Exchequer in the 1974 Labour Government and subsequently narrowly missed becoming Prime Minister.[11] Sieff would follow his father Israel to own Marks and Spencer. Probably the most famous was Spike Milligan, then a lance bombardier in Italy, shell shocked and exhausted, working his way northwards to battle fatigue and a discharge on health grounds having been wounded at Cassino.[12n] We catch up with him in late October 1943:

> No sleep. Feeling tired. During the day the guns arrived and spread themselves about in their unexplainable pattern, two were ahead of us and two behind with their backs to the wood. The Command post was not to the liking of the Major…

All hell is let loose, Ack Ack starts blazing away, we all go head first to the deck, a swarm of MEs [Messerschmitt planes] roar over the position at nought feet. We hear the major shouting 'Tommy Guns … Tommy Guns' Edgington was first to rise to his feet … He knelt over me, made a sign of the cross and then started to feel in my pockets for fags. I am notoriously ticklish, and using one hand to tickle and convulse me he withdraws my fags. There follows a friendly struggle during which Major Jenkins appears and says, 'What is going on, this isn't a nursery, Bombardier you ought to know better'… 'Did any of you men fire at those planes?' he asked. We admit we didn't. I explained. 'It's not easy to shoot down planes with shovels, sir.'

'You will keep your side arms within reach, next time I expect to hear a volley.'

'Very good Sir.'

In an hour the planes flew over and we let fly. The major is running up waving his arms. 'No, no, bloody fools, they're ours.'

'Don't worry, sir when they fly back again, we'll apologise,' I said.

He didn't know how to take me; he stood there clenching his fists, his face a mask of frustration.

It was a mixed day of planes, one moment Jerry, then the RAF, then Jerry. The Ack Ack boys took no chances and fired at the lot. The Major was out of his mind by day's end, trying to co-ordinate all our efforts for maximum retaliation. That night, we heard him mournfully playing Schubert's Serenade on his clarinet. Later, Smudger Smith … answered it by howling like a dog. The Major sent Woods, his batman, to find out who the offender was. As fast as he silenced one howl another one would start somewhere else; the pay-off was an actual farm dog behind us who took up the howling and no one could stop him.[13n]

Cassino

Advancing up the mountain spine of Italy, Allied troops met their toughest challenge at Monte Cassino, a monastery topped mountain 1,700 feet high that formed a major physical and psychological obstacle to the advance on Rome. The Germans were heavily defended both on the mountain and in the town of Cassino, as well as in the surrounding mountains which overlooked the monastery. In winter, and in terrain which severely limited the deployment of tanks or other mechanised vehicles, the battle fell to the infantry to capture the heights with little ground cover, steep rocky climbs and using narrow hairpin tracks.[14n] Approaching the area, the Allied commander, Field Marshal Harold Alexander, found himself leading 25 divisions: seven American, five British, four French, three Indian, two Canadian, one each from South Africa and New Zealand and two Polish. The latter were led by the impressive General Wladystaw Anders. His troops joined those who had earlier responded to the call to leave Poland and regroup in the Middle East. They had fought bravely for the Allies ever since. Cassino was truly to be a battle of the nations.[15]

The first attempt, in January 1944, to break this German stronghold had been brought forward to take pressure off the Anzio landings. It failed, as American and New Zealand troops came under withering fire. There followed an agonising discussion about whether

German troops were actually using the monastery.[16n] Faced with differing reports, but with the knowledge that advance was impossible while troops could be fired on from above, a decision was made to bomb the monastery, which was known to contain many refugees from the surrounding villages. Pamphlets were dropped and most civilians left; on February 15th, just as the monks had commenced their prayer 'Beseech Christ on our behalf', the first bombs struck to mark the start of the second battle This and a third attack failed in terrible weather. The Allies had failed, and in the process had attacked a venerable monastery which was protected by the rules of war. Future attempts would call for more concentrated and better co-ordinated infantry attacks, supported by heavy artillery and air support. An extraordinary decision was taken by Allied Command that in these desperate circumstances heavy bombers would be used in close proximity to an infantry assault. On March 15th 455 aircraft poured bombs into the small town of Cassino and its immediate area; the bombs fell for over three hours. One observer commented:

> I remember no spectacle of war so gigantically one sided. Above the beautiful, arrogant, silver-grey monsters performing their mission with what looked from below, like a spirit of utter detachment; below, a silent town suffering all this in complete passivity.[17]

Immediately the last bomb fell, 610 artillery pieces opened fire. On the ground there was fierce close-quarter fighting with New Zealand and Indian troops pitched against the German 1st Parachute Regiment in the ruins of the town. Within two days, Allied troops held key positions. Two days later, the Germans launched a counterattack with paralysing machine gun fire as they swept down the mountain onto the Allied infantry. A few days later, the attack had to be called off, although the Allies had secured some important sites. Clearly the only way to eventually break this stronghold was to marshal sufficient troops to outnumber the enemy and to wait for better weather. The final assault commenced on May 4th following the masterful deployment of troops under the cover of darkness and in secret, with no radio traffic so that the assault would have a large element of surprise. There can be no doubt about the bravery of all the troops involved, but it had been recognised that French and Polish troops had an additional motivating force: revenge. This time, the overwhelming numbers served to ensure success, although casualties were high, particularly for the Poles who fought their way up the mountain, inch by inch against heavy fire. In this they were supported by specifically skilled French Moroccan mountain troops. Three long weeks later, victory was declared, but by then the heavy troops had started to by-pass Cassino, and the beachhead at Anzio was left behind as all roads now led to Rome. On Hill 593, one that had seen much bloody fighting, stands a memorial to the gallant Poles:

> We Polish soldiers
> For our freedom and yours
> Have given our souls to God
> Our bodies to the soil of Italy
> And our hearts to Poland.[18]

On June 4th 1944 the Allies were in Rome, then driving north through territory heavily defended by German troops. They would reach the Alps in the Spring of 1945, but would never cross them.

Tehran

At the close of 1943, with the Axis powers severely damaged, the three major Allied leaders held their first joint meeting in Tehran to review progress, clarify their joint purposes and set objectives for the next phase and post-war issues. Recognition had to be given to Stalin's great success in the east, a capacity which America was anxious to use in their fiercely fought Pacific campaign. Roosevelt and Churchill had not yet finished planning Operation Overlord, the invasion across the English Channel. In particular, Churchill's influence was relatively diminished by the obvious fact that his two major Allies commanded resources far beyond his own. Given the strong position of a booming and fully armed America, it seems that Roosevelt decided to distance himself from that old imperialist Churchill and move closer to the magnificent dictator now forging his new empire. It helped that Stalin took the opportunity to indicate that communist Russia could conceivably live with and cooperate with capitalism, thus apparently closing off the communist historical commitment to promote permanent international revolution. Consequently, while operational decisions were taken quickly, no firm discussion took place about post-war 'spheres of influence.' In particular, Roosevelt assured Stalin that the fate of Poland would cause no difficulty, hence the latter's assumption that he had a free hand in Eastern Europe once his troops had crossed from their homeland. In historical terms, the 'Cold War' started in Tehran in November 1943.

As the Allied campaigns gathered pace, new problems came to the surface whereby competing political and ethnic groups sought to gain power in countries weakened by war and occupation. In Yugoslavia the Allies supported the communist partisans led by Josip Tito, who managed to tie down 35 German divisions, preventing them from strengthening the Italian and German defences.[19n] In Greece, by the winter of 1943, the two broadly republican movements were in fierce conflict, eventually leading to an uprising against the royalist government in exile. By December 1944, British troops were called on to support the Greek government and the non-communist partisan movement in suppressing the communist controlled Greek People's Liberation Army (ELAS).

Montgomery

In the spring of 1944, with the three-year siege of Leningrad broken, Stalin could concentrate his forces on a westerly drive into Germany, crossing the border in June. Meanwhile, all the detailed preparations for the cross-Channel invasion were going ahead. Field Marshall Montgomery (Monty) returned to England to play a key role in the campaign. Having satisfied himself that the major issues were clarified, he let his staff sort out the details and embarked on a campaign to raise the morale of the troops now waiting for the 'off'. Monty toured the whole country, addressing troops of all nationalities to make them feel that they had a special status as commanding human beings, without doubt equal to the enormous challenges ahead. He became immensely popular, which was not always appreciated by the War Office, who feared a personality cult. He concluded with an address to the high and mighty of the land at Mansion House. Given the memories of the previous war and the disaster of Dunkirk, his address illustrates the mood, feelings and ambitions of the day expressed by a leader who put so much store by the welfare and morale of all his troops and the civilian army producing the essential arms and ammunition:

> It must forever redound to our shame that we sent out soldiers into this most modern war with weapons and equipment that were hopelessly inadequate; we have only ourselves to blame for the disasters that early overtook us in the field. Surely we must never let this happen again. Nor will we. But it is the man that counts and not the machine. If you have got men that are mentally alert, who are tough and hard, who are trained to fight and kill, who are enthusiastic, and have that infectious optimism and offensive eagerness that comes from physical well being – and you then give these men the proper weapons and the equipment – there is nothing you cannot do. *Nothing. Nothing* … Only from an inspired nation can go forth an inspired army.
>
> *It will be when our men go forth into battle on this great endeavour*. The tide will flow *then* or not at all. That is the time when there must swell up in the nation every noble thought, every high ideal, every great purpose which has waited through the weary years. And then, as the sap rises, the men will feel themselves to be the instrument of a new born national vigour…
>
> Can you image this conversation in after years? 'What did you do in the World War?' I pulled hard to start with; but after a time I began to lose interest and let go the rope. I thought I wanted a rest; … 'And did you win?' 'No. We lost. I let go the rope and we lost the match. God forgive me; we lost the match.'
>
> Is it possible that that such a conversation could apply to us British? *No. It is impossible*. Thank God it is impossible. Then let us stand-to and get on the rope … And we shall win.[20n]

France

June 6th 1944 saw the massive landing by Allied troops across the Channel to five beach-heads, under the command of the American General Dwight Eisenhower. D-Day had arrived. The extraordinary engineering feats of the 'Mulberry Harbour' (huge concrete blocks floated across the Channel to form effective harbours) and Operation Pluto (a pipeline under the ocean which supplied fuel) both worked excellently. In total, some 156,000 men boarded around 7,000 ships and were landed by 1,200 landing craft under superb air cover and massive naval bombardment with parachutists landing behind enemy defences at Pegasus Bridge.

Given that approximately 380,000 German troops were deployed along the coast, the British casualties were light at 2,700, and the total Allied casualties were less than 10,000. The Americans, many setting sail from Cornwall, met the fiercest opposition on Omaha and Utah Beaches, where they met with withering fire from strong German machine gun emplacements.[21n]

Only two months later, the Normandy campaign, the fiercest fighting of the whole western invasion and the only period when comparison could be made with the Eastern Front, ended at Falaise, where the retreating Germans were bottled between the Canadian army to the north and the Americans from the south,[22n] while the Polish Armoured Division kept the cork in the bottle. In this one battle the German army lost 60,000 troops: 10,000 were killed and 50,000 captured. The way eastwards seemed clear. In August, Allied troops landed on the Riviera heading north. This horrendous war would surely be over by Christmas! In addition to this firm military forecast, my copy of *The Manchester Guardian* dated June 7th and the *Observer* dated June 11th 1944 have extensive (but censored) accounts of all the battles, reporting that everything 'is proceeding in a thoroughly satisfactory manner,' and include a report that the Polish government had broadcast commands to the 'several hundred thousand' Poles forced to serve in the Nazi army not to open fire on Allied troops. Now that the forces were at their maximum strength, more men could be sent to work in the mines and industry. Between 1943 and 1948, some 48,000 young men, known as Bevin Boys, were sent down the mines.

Warsaw, having witnessed the brave uprising from the Jewish ghettos of those who faced certain death in 1943, now became the scene of successive terrors. On August 1st 1944, the lightly armed Polish 'Home Army' of 50,000 took on the might of the occupying German troops, tanks and air force. Their hope was that, with help from the approaching Russian troops and air support from Britain, they could free the city in six days. No help came.[23n] They fought on for ten weeks with incredible ingenuity and bravery. In the end, 50,000 civilians were slaughtered by the SS (including the sick who were killed in their hospital beds), 100,000 were killed by German bombing and 500,000 were taken to camps, where the majority perished. The city, which in the Nazis' view had blocked their eastern ambitions and prevented the spread of the Aryan race for 700 years, was completely razed to the ground.

In contrast, great rejoicing followed the liberation of Paris on August 25th, where an uprising was supported by Allied troops. Two other individuals helped or complicated the situation in Paris. The German commander Dietrich von Choltitz disobeyed Hitler's orders to destroy the city and then, as conflict threatened between the communist partisans and the Free French Army, General De Gaulle appeared as mediator. On August 26th 1944 he marched down the Champs-Elysees avoiding sniper's bullets to announce that the Republic was now re-established.[24n] These events precipitated the approaching American troops to enter, secure and confirm the liberation of the city. French troops were to lead their American allies in the celebratory march past. This proved controversial as the American Army had, until late in the war, segregated its forces, thus they insisted that the French contingent must be all white. As the main fighting force of the free French was 40% black from the West African colonies, these men were stood down and white troops were flown in from units in Egypt and North Africa. This was a war in which colonial troops had made a vast contribution with high casualty rates and where many had fought against the Nazi persecution of the Jewish race.

In May 1945, the town of Sétif in the French colony of Algeria was the scene of a massacre when victory celebrations developed into a pro-independence demonstration after some French settlers ('Pieds-Noirs') were killed. French military and police reprisals by bombing and shooting killed some 9,000 Algerians. A sign of things to come. In the immediate aftermath of liberation, some 9,000 alleged French collaborators were killed. As full trials were established, a further 1,600 death sentences were carried out and 38,000 collaborators were sent to prison. Marshall Pétain himself was sentenced to death, but this was commuted to life imprisonment. In the early 1950s, amnesty laws led to the rehabilitation of most of the remaining prisoners.

Arnhem

Brussels was liberated on September 3rd 1944. As the German troops were forced back towards their own country, their resistance strengthened, slowing the Allied advance. General Montgomery, under some pressure to speed up his advance, opted for an airborne strike behind enemy lines to prevent the destruction of vital bridges crossing the subsidiaries of the Rhine at Grave, Nijmegen and, furthest from the main troops, Arnhem. The way would thereby open to strike eastwards into the heart of the Ruhr. This was a brilliant strategic plan, which proved a disaster on the ground due primarily to poor intelligence and communications, terrain which severely limited movement and bad weather which delayed reinforcements. Between 15,000 and 17,000 British, Polish and American troops were lost and an advance into the Ruhr was delayed for four months.

It was at this low point in the war that my brother John, aged 20, landed in Normandy, on D-Day plus 10, en route for Holland to join the 79th Division. He was fully equipped with a booklet of helpful phrases in German, such as *Ich bin ein Freund* (I am a friend) and *Wohin sind die Deutschen gefahren?* (Which way have the Germans gone?). En route, he and his friends got a lift into a French town in a comfortable car. Discovering it to be a taxi, there was high anxiety about the fare and much misunderstanding during the journey, there being no handy book of French phrases. Arriving in the town square, the driver held out his hand. But what were they to pay him? All he wanted was to shake these saviours by the hand. In the same area, but unbeknown to them, was our cousin Ron Lane. Ron (aged 18 at the time) was from Toronto and had lied about his age to join the Canadian Royal Artillery. He was now a 'spotter' using the small Auster planes to hover above the battlefields seeking out enemy positions.[24n]

Within the 79th Division, John was involved in the relief of Breda and Walcheren and in the reopening of the port of Hamburg, which shortened the Allies' supply lines (until then everything had been landing in Normandy). By this time his popularity in whichever unit he was with was high. Whatever casualties were suffered they always missed my brother so, not unusually in wartime, he gained the nickname 'Lucky Jordan,' a good guy to be with.[25n] He was also making friends in Ghent with girls and families, one of which wrote:

> [It] was a favour to make knowledge with you, especially as Boy Scout, young and pianist. Our all family has a good remembrance from you and hope you see again and soon as possible ... We wish you again all the best and please John to receive many greetings of all our family who will remember you ... we wish you again and reciprocate the best of health and much courage, because the war can't endure. All the best and cheerio from all the family. Andre.[26n]

This clarifies a picture that I have always had of my dear brother. Among all the noise and horror of war, or during whatever life held for him thereafter, he was the quiet one. It brings to mind the portrait drawn by the poet James Elroy Flecker:

> There lived a king, I know not where
> Perhaps in Mirascower
> Whose daughters grew so deadly fair
> He shut them in a tower.
>
> There lived three bright and handsome boys
> Not far from that country
> The first one's name was Forest Noise
> The second Sound of Sea.
>
> The third one had no name like this
> For girls to dream upon
> His was a face you had to kiss
> And yet they called him John.
>
> Forest Noise made a rope of his curls
> Sound of the Sea he threw it
> and John went up to get the girls
> and nobody ever knew it.[27n]

The reference to scouting is interesting because on reading through John's letters the overlap between enlisted men and their previous scouting membership is very clear. Given the rate at which men were posted from unit to unit, moved abroad or became casualties, contact could only be maintained by reference back to families at home who were members of the vast scouting community and were in touch with each other. As I look through the songbook that was used in the famous 'Gang Shows' produced by every troop once a year, regionally and nationally, the sheer optimism of the whole enterprise shines through; perhaps that was another reason to stay with it.[28n] Towards the end of 1944, John was moved to 'Shepherd Force,' which was charged with assisting Scottish troops in a classic joint attack on the German stronghold of Blerick.

On December 14th 1944 John kept a copy of the local paper, which, in addition to news of the war (including Joseph Goebbels' visits to the cities that the RAF and US Air Force had carpet bombed, during which he commented that such brutality 'had never been experienced before') were the usual small ads and personal notices, mostly women looking for marriage partners. Also included were the lyrics to a marching song entitled 'We Are Marching To England.' Later, a report appeared in the South London paper under the headline 'The Tank That Did Its Job':

> Trooper John Jordan, 22 Lanbury Rd., Nunhead, was a member of a tank crew which recently led an attack on Blerick, the last German stronghold before Venlo, the Dutch-German frontier town. The task was to 'flog' a minefield across a deep and wide anti-tank ditch and then clear another minefield at the edge of the German fortifications … The flog was accomplished, and a tall chimney stack used by the enemy as an O.P. was shot down to the ground.
>
> The Huns had turned the houses at the edge of the second minefield into a row of fortifications so the crew fired round after round at them, bringing down the dwellings on the German defenders. By this time the infantry were preparing to go in for the final assault. The tank crew took up the best position that they could, laid down covering fire for the advancing infantrymen, and having completed their task, made back to harbour.[29]

Moscow and Yalta

In the closing stages of the war in Europe, with America heavily involved in fighting the fierce Japanese resistance in the Pacific, and Britain and the Allies still heavily engaged in Burma, political strategies were moving to the fore. In October 1944, as the recapture of the Philippines put mainland Japan in range of heavy US bombers, Churchill visited Moscow in an attempt to clarify the long neglected question of post-war spheres of influence. He and Stalin agreed, reputedly on the back of an old brown envelope, some percentage interests in the occupied countries. Greece, Churchill's main concern, was to be 90% British interest, Bulgaria 90% Russian, Yugoslavia 50/50 and so on. Achieving this meant that the Poles had to be sacrificed to Russia, who already occupied Poland and showed no willingness to relinquish control. By February 1945 when the 'Big Three' met in Yalta, Stalin's position was at its height as his forces occupied most of Eastern Europe while western forces had not yet achieved the agreed goals. Churchill was relatively powerless, having to settle for a weak agreement over Poland, while Roosevelt, who was to die two months later, seemed prepared to agree to practically anything in Europe in exchange for Stalin's help in the war against Japan. Roosevelt's closest advisor concluded that

> [This] was the dawn of the new day that we had all been praying for … The Russians have proved that they could be reasonable and farseeing, and there wasn't any doubt in the mind of the President or any of us that we could … get along with them peacefully for as far into the future as any of us could imagine.[30]

Bretton Woods

Anticipating the inevitable economic problems that would be faced after the war, the Allied powers had met at Bretton Woods in New Hampshire on July 1st 1944 to decide the mechanism for management of fixed exchange rates and to propose the establishment of the World Bank and the International Monetary Fund, steps which enabled rapid post-war industrial recovery. Forty-four nations attended, including China (then pre-communist) and India (not yet independent), but the running was clearly made by the USA as they were the nation to whom most other countries owed money.

Europe

Further south from John, American troops had problems of their own as the Nazis used bad weather to launch a surprise attack by two armies, including Panzer divisions on the Allied positions in the Ardennes Mountains. The attack was preceded by dropping pamphlets asking why American troops were fighting for greedy Britain who only wanted to protect her empire. Hoping to repeat their initial attack on France, they succeeded in forcing a significant 'bulge' in the American lines, resulting in fierce combat along a complex front until, after two weeks, the skies cleared and Allied planes could strafe the German tanks and infantry. Nineteen thousand Americans were killed,[31n] but 100,000 German troops were killed, injured or captured, and 800 of their tanks and 1,000 aircraft were lost. Although the losses had crippled any further major German counterattacks, the western Allies had not yet reached German soil. Christmas was approaching and there was still a long way to go. While the Western Front was advancing, the Soviet command was preparing for a major offensive on Berlin which involved 3.8 million troops, ensuring an overwhelming majority of 10 to 1 in the critical sectors of the advance. At Churchill's request, the attack was brought forward to January 13th 1945 in order to take the pressure off the Americans in the Ardennes. By Stalin's special order, no prisoners were taken: all German civilian men were murdered and the women were gang raped; the 'Red Terror' was in full spate. Five days later, Russian troops passed the ruins of Warsaw and unveiled to the world the horrors of the death and work concentration camps.[32n]

The impact of the scenes that met the troops went beyond any previous experience. Immediate steps were taken to feed those barely alive and to separate the thousands in the advanced stages of typhoid and tuberculosis. One officer described driving round the camp: 'We saw compounds filled with dead and dying ... one pit was chocked with blackened bodies, there were several piles of unclothed dead.' At home I saw these scenes on the news reels in the cinema and they had a profound effect on me. While the short term effect was distress and horror, the long term result was to deny me any sympathy or willingness to understand Germans for many years. By the end of January, Berlin was in sight. There, Hitler had made his final move to the bunker. From the west, American and British troops crossed the Rhine, moving cautiously. In March 1945, with America anxious to lower casualties for an anticipated transfer of troops to the Pacific, Eisenhower called a halt, leaving the Soviets to take Berlin and meet the western advance beyond Dresden. Churchill was furious but powerless to change the decision. John's unit spent Christmas 1944 in Vessem before the brigade moved south, leading the attack on Kranenburg. Tank attacks were helped, when the conditions were right, by the technique of 'natural light' developed by Brigadier ap Rhys Pryce of the Royal Welsh Fusiliers who had served with the Indian Army. By calculating the correct elevation angles, searchlights, placed well behind the lines, could reflect the light off clouds in front of the advancing tanks. Units were approaching the northern part of the long line of tank-traps, concrete barriers and other major defensive structures built by Germany and known as the Westwall, but known to the Allies as the Siegfried Line, as it followed a similar route to the defences of WWI. This started at Kleve, and John's unit were involved from February 9th in the assault on that town using flails and flame throwers which lasted for three days. Fighting through Nütterden and Pfalzdorf, the next major obstacles were Weeze and Wesel across the Rhine where the amphibious DD tanks started their swim across under relatively light fire. John's squadron was included in the biggest shelling barrage of the war (bigger than El Alamein) involving 1,000 guns of every type. A tank usually carried 100 75 millimetre shells and 100 gallons of fuel in gallon cans, all of which had to be manhandled from packed crates. For this barrage each tank had 300 shells, a total weight of 4 tons (over 4,000 kg) that had to be lifted before battle commenced. Heavy bombers then hit the town of Wesel, which surrendered soon afterwards when the heavier tanks, including the flails, crossed using wobbly bridges of rafts tied together. On February 26th 1945 tanks of the division carried Churchill and the top military brass to the front line east of the Rhine. Casualties for the whole division for this major crossing were 5 killed and 49 wounded. At some time during this campaign, John's unit entered the evacuated offices of senior Nazi officers. This very moral guy emerged with a beautiful leather document case as his personal war prize.[33n]

Stalin saw the big prize now within his grasp. With 2.5 million men and vast numbers of tanks, the assault on Berlin was launched on April 16th. His troops had met with fiercer than expected resistance (the Military Police were shooting any Berliner who was thought not to be energetically defending the city). By the end of April Berlin was encircled, and on April 30th 1945 Russian troops were on the Reichstag. Hitler committed suicide.

On May 4th General Montgomery received a German delegation on Luneberg Heath, after which all German forces in northern Germany surrendered unconditionally. John's unit had moved to the port of Bremerhaven where amid great uncertainty the following historic signal arrived:

> Top secret STOP Germans surrendered unconditionally at 18.30 hours STOP Hostilities on 2nd Army fronts will cease at 08.00 hours tomorrow 5 May STOP No repeat no advance beyond present positions until further orders from this HQ STOP All informed STOP.[34n]

Two days later, all German troops surrendered unconditionally to General Eisenhower and May 8th 1945 was declared Victory in Europe, VE, Day. More than one million civilians had died in bombing raids, over six million had died in the Russian gulags and German camps, and over three million military personnel had perished. Altogether, twenty-six million lives had been lost in Europe out of a total population of five hundred million.

Tanks were taken to the mechanical engineers' base as they were no longer required. The following month John was to be posted to the 4/7th Royal Dragoon Guards for an unknown future. To join the forces occupying Germany? To transfer to the Far East where the war against Japan was still being fiercely fought? No one knew, but what lay ahead was months of movement from unit to unit and back again to Ochtrup as an army of occupation. His letters home saw him 'having a smashing time' celebrating in Brussels where all troops were welcomed, especially by the girls, and everything was free. In December 1945, John was the accompanist for the unit show 'Black-Beret Pie – A Laugh! A Song & A Basin Full of Fun.' This was followed by 'Christmas dinner of goose and pork with all the trimmings, followed inevitably by Christmas pudding and custard.'

The Pacific and the Far East

The war, of course, was only half over. The Japanese were resisting all Allied advances in the Pacific and Burma. In August 1943, south of the Solomon Islands, an attempt by a group of small US Naval ships to blockade Japanese ships failed with severe American casualties. A young Lieutenant John F. Kennedy, in charge of one of the boats, succeeded in helping his crew to swim to a safe island, personally carrying a badly injured crew member. For this he was awarded the Marine Corps Medal with a citation stating:

> Unmindful of personal danger, Lieutenant Kennedy unhesitatingly braved the difficulties and hazards of darkness to direct rescue operations, swimming many hours to secure aid and food after he had succeeded in getting his crew ashore. His outstanding courage, endurance and leadership contributed to the saving of several lives and were in keeping with the highest traditions of the United States Naval Service.[35]

The American campaign was to progress across the Pacific islands for a further two years against Japanese forces who employed kamikaze pilots to attack American ships and carried out mass executions of American prisoners of war. In February 1945, the Americans invaded the small Japanese mountainous island of Iwo Jima, where Japanese troops occupied well-prepared advantageous positions. The landing of 30,000 American marines was preceded by intensive bombing and followed by 40,000 more troops. The battle comprised twenty-four days of vicious close fighting with 6,800 American dead and over 19,000 wounded, while over 99% of the Japanese force of 22,800 died. Among striking photographs of the battle was the iconic shot of marines hoisting the American flag on top of the mountain. Although it later emerged that the photo had been posed, I am not sure that that fact reduces the impact.

In Burma General Slim had taken Major General Orde Wingate under his command. Wingate formed the view that the method most likely to be effective in the wild and inaccessible jungle terrain was to get behind Japanese lines, disrupt their communication systems and conduct guerrilla raids against troops and supplies. To this end, he formed British, Indian and Gurkha troops into long range penetration units, christened 'Chindits' after a Burmese mythical beast. Having committed himself to this strategy, Wingate set about it with the obsessive fanaticism. He was described as

> [A] man whose energy and faith were as demonic as his temperament was difficult … He had a formidable and aggressive persecution complex. He impressed as one with total self confidence, sure of his task, destiny and abilities; but one without pity or remorse. He was bold and original – a visionary. He was one of those who, with a thousand faults, nevertheless enrich an entire generation by their quality … while Wingate was anathema to some, his claims unsubstantiated, his methods outrageous and his manners vile, to others the pity was that there was only one of him.[36]

The attack to drive the Japanese from Burma would be launched in the dry season, well before the monsoon. The Chindits would be flown behind enemy lines at the same time as Slim's infantry divisions would advance eastwards and the Chinese Army, advised by the American General Stilwell, attacked from the south. America had made 348 aircraft available for this operation, including 150 gliders escorted by fighters in case of an air attack. This vast manoeuvre commenced on March 5th 1944 and was a remarkable success, transporting two whole brigades complete with artillery, supplies and animal transport over the Himalayas well behind Japanese lines without their knowledge or interference. Surprise operations on airfields, ammunition dumps and enemy headquarters were carried out successfully, but on March 24th 1944 Wingate was killed in an air accident. Thereafter, under a new command, the brigades continued to achieve considerable success.

> The Chindit Operation was jungle warfare at its most grim … Moving through jungle against Japanese who were masters of concealment and often tied themselves to trees to shoot downwards, the soldiers of the Chindit columns could expect no pity if found wounded and, because of the terrain were sometimes impossible to carry by stretcher, so that a commander's merciful bullet was the only way to help a fallen comrade.[37]

Meanwhile, the Chinese advance had been stalled and the initial success of Slim's forces was reversed by the heavily reinforced Japanese troops. This retreat, however, was an aggressive one, with Allied troops carrying out many counterattacks along the way against an increasingly exhausted Japanese army. The turning point came in the mountain ridges of Kohima and Imphal where infantry fought fiercely at close quarters. Completely surrounded in Kohima (the 'Stalingrad of the East'), the encounter lasted from April to June 1944 with soldiers of the Royal West Kent Regiment and the Japanese 31st Division facing each other across the District Commissioner's tennis court.[38] By the summer of 1944, the tide had been turned. Once the captured prisoners of war in Mandalay were freed by troops led by General William Dimoline, the Japanese started to withdraw slowly across the continent.[39n] By January 1945, the Burma Road was reopened for essential supplies to support the Pacific campaign. By June 1945 Burma had been cleared, and in August Hong Kong was relieved. Mountbatten held a glorious victory campaign in Rangoon in

June, taking the salute as the army marched past, although for them the occasion was bitter sweet as their much loved and respected leader Bill Slim had been 'excused' from the parade. The only British general to have fought a first-class enemy throughout the war, transformed an army of beaten refugees into a war-winning machine that bounced back from defeat and masterminded the eventual victory had been denied his place of honour.[40]

Dumbarton Oaks and Potsdam

The Bretton Woods proposals were confirmed at the Dumbarton Oaks conference, which also finalised preparations for the United Nations Organization, the opening ceremony of which was held on October 24th 1945 in San Francisco under the victorious permanent members of the Security Council: China, France, the USSR, the UK and the USA. Now the rich United States had risen to be the pre-eminent world power. For the final meeting of the Allied war leaders, held for two weeks in July 1945 in Potsdam, President Truman represented the United States; halfway through the conference, Clement Attlee replaced Churchill. The main subject was the conduct of the war and surrender terms for Japan, and it was at this conference that Truman revealed that, with the successful completion of a test, the USA had become the first atomic power in the world. The Conference Declaration called for surrender, which, true to their culture and tradition the Japanese refused.

Hiroshima and Nagasaki

Two weeks later, the first atomic bomb was dropped on the military base and port of Hiroshima causing unimaginable death and horror, but still there was no surrender. President Truman warned that his planes were prepared to

> ... obliterate more rapidly and completely every productive enterprise the Japanese have above ground in any city ... If they do not accept our terms (unconditional surrender) they may accept a rain of ruin from the air, the like of which has never been seen on earth.[41]

Three days later, the second bomb was dropped on Nagasaki, after which Emperor Hirohito decided to seek an immediate surrender. Within some ten days the Japanese troops occupying Burma, Hong Kong, Singapore, the Philippines and Korea had surrendered. President Truman described the bomb as

> ... harnessing the basic power of the universe. The force from which the sun draws its power has been loosed against those who brought war to the Far East. We have spent $2,000,000,000 on the greatest scientific gamble in history, and we have won.[42]

Although Tokyo had been carpet bombed to destruction, inevitably a time-consuming process, the devastation of these two cities, where over 100,000 people had been killed and virtually all buildings turned to dust, had taken seconds. The long term effects of the blast and the radiation that caused early injuries and deformities would be passed down to subsequent generations. Group Captain Leonard Cheshire, whose decorations for outstanding bravery included the Victoria Cross, was flying as an RAF observer of the bombing of Nagasaki. This experience, coming as it did at the end of a long and demanding war, led him to establish a community for former servicemen and their families. This evolved to become the first Leonard Cheshire home for the care of disabled people, now a worldwide charity.[43n]

Japan formally surrendered to General MacArthur aboard the US battleship *Missouri* on September 2nd 1945, the first time that the Japanese nation had lost a war for 2,000 years. Surrender, however, was not part of the Japanese psyche, and consequently small groups of soldiers or individuals who had been bypassed by the fighting continued to live and slowly emerge from jungle hideouts for the next nineteen years, often weeping for the disgrace to the Emperor for having surrendered. Most were captured, but in 1974 the most famous, Hiroo Onoda, emerged in the Philippines. He was regarded as quite a hero and in fact wrote a book about his 'adventures,' although it later emerged that during his time in hiding he had probably killed some 60 Filipinos.[44n]

Europe

Hitler had provided the remarkable catalyst that was to sweep away the old class-based order throughout Europe and beyond. Although a few fascist groups remained, for example in northern Italy, Czechoslovakia elected a communist government, and Yugoslavia welcomed Tito as a communist leader who could hold the Serbs, Croats and Montenegrins together. Russia, newly expanded to the Union of Soviet Socialist Republic (USSR), and America were the only two nations to remain relatively untouched by political upheaval. In Britain, and perhaps France, the enthusiastic commitment to the concepts of equality and shared power led naturally to a reconsideration of the whole concept of empire and their relationships with the colonies.

The immediate concern, however, was post-war reconstruction, so there was little time for debate. If state control got things done, then so be it. In 1944, however, the emigré Austrian economist Friedrich von Hayek published *The Road to Serfdom*, a cry from the wilderness questioning why the people in power were all socialists heading for state intervention and a planned economy.[45n] He feared a new totalitarianism, asking why have we fought the Nazis if we are now stamping out freedom at home? He urged people to turn away from the mirage of the great utopia and head for the individualistic economic liberalism. His views gained no hold in Europe, at least not for thirty years, but they were widely promoted in America. It was argued that central planning was not of itself wrong, there was just good and bad planning. George Orwell's response illustrated the feelings of the time:

> In the negative part of Professor Hayek's thesis there is a great deal of truth. It cannot be said too often – at any rate, it is not being said nearly often enough – that collectivism is not inherently democratic, but, on the contrary, gives to a tyrannical minority such powers

as the Spanish Inquisitors never dreamt of ... [yet a] return to 'free' competition means for the great mass of people a tyranny probably worse, because more irresponsible, than that of the state.[46]

The immediate and very practical problem, which forced a degree of continued cooperation between the Allies, was the administration of Germany. The infrastructure had collapsed, the population were short of food and millions of refugees were on the loose. The answer was to divide the country into 'administrative zones' run by Russia, America, Britain and France. Faced with Russian intransigence, the Potsdam meeting had decided that the German minorities in Poland, Hungary and Czechoslovakia were to be deported wholesale. The consequences of these high level decisions in the short term was to further exacerbate the degree of actual chaos on the ground throughout Europe as some thirty million refugees, freed prisoners of war and ex-soldiers sought either to return home or avoid the consequences of such an event. There was no administration that could deal with such huge numbers. The scale of any resettlement, and the conditions in which it took place, were without precedent in history. It seemed a crime against humanity.

Millions throughout Europe were scrambling around on rubbish dumps for food and the necessities of life. The Dutch were down to eating tulip bulbs. Often troops or agencies called in to help failed to appreciate the horrors that drove these refugees. The writer Geoffrey Moorhead, who had reported throughout the war, wrote:

> The Germany in which we found ourselves presented a scene almost beyond comprehension. Around us, 50 great cities lay in ruins ... many had no electric light or power or gas or running water, and no coherent system of government. Like ants in an ant-heap, the people scurried over the ruins, diving furtively in to cellars and doorways in search of loot ... Life was sordid, aimless. [Germans] had an immense sense not of guilt, but of defeat. One saw few tears. For the Germans, the catastrophe had gone far beyond that point.[47]

As British and American forces released the millions of Eastern Europeans from Nazi slave camps, they soon discovered their reluctance to be deported back to Russian control. Escapes and suicides were common, but the process continued even when it became clear that mass executions as deserters often awaited them. The fear was that Russia would withhold British and American prisoners from repatriation. In April 1945, British troops had to use force to send back the Cossack Brigade and their families who had originally sided with the Tsar. The result was mass suicide on the border bridge at Lienz.[48] In May the British Army sent 10,000 Slovenian soldiers and civilians who had fled to Austria back to Yugoslavia. Most of them were trucked to the Kočevje forests and shot. In due course, Nazi officers and collaborators were brought to justice. By late 1945 over 200 prisoner of war camps had been established, mostly financed by America, Britain and Canada. A distressing problem occurred near Dusseldorf in 1945 when the American provision was overwhelmed by over a hundred thousand German POWs who were left in the open for many months to suffer high levels of mortality due to disease and poor hygiene. In order to avoid inspection by the International Red Cross, the prisoners were re-classified as 'disarmed enemy personnel.' Eisenhower, the Supreme Commander in Europe, reported to President Roosevelt that his troops had had to change from combat to repatriation to welfare in quick time, but that in certain instances 'we have fallen below accepted standards.' As soon as possible the whole problem became the responsibility of the newly created United Nations Relief and Rehabilitation Administration (UNRRA), which was one of the agencies financed by the main western powers. This vast population crossing Western Europe was categorised either as 'displaced persons' (DPs), who had a home somewhere to go to, or as refugees, who were homeless. Whatever group they fell into, most wanted to go anywhere except home. Many Allied countries were, thanks to the slaughter, short of manpower and were willing to accept able-bodied men. Britain needed miners, builders and farm workers and accepted 86,000 refugees; other European countries accepted 60,000, America 600,000, Canada 157,000 and Australia 182,000 within ten years. After 1948, 332,000 Jews went to Israel. While the distress of this episode cannot be underestimated it was possible to close the last camp in 1957 and, in great contrast to WWI, there had been no serious outbreak of disease which could have decimated overcrowded camps full of undernourished and sick people. One side effect of this situation was that the British, already on wartime rations, had their ration and fuel cut further as supplies were diverted to Europe.

SOCIETY

Election

The foundations of the post-war welfare state were being put in place, but for a society much changed Churchill recognised that the co-operation of the trades unions throughout the war had placed them in a position as a vital estate of the realm. Science had moved up to centre stage as the wartime inventions fed into manufacture and design for the post-war world. In 1937, the government had invested £2.5 million in scientific research; by 1945 this had risen to £315 million (a high proportion of which remained on military work). In six years the role and status of women had changed, as had the occupational pattern of the nation (see Table 1).

Table 1 Occupational comparisons in 1939 and 1945[49]

	1939	1945
Forces	480,000	5.1 million
Agriculture	711,000	887,000
Industrial and chemical	3.1 million	5.2 million

While these events were unfolding, an event of far greater significance was happening in Great Britain. As victory seemed certain, the Parliamentary Labour Party decided to withdraw from the National Government, a move that triggered a general election, the first for ten years, to be held on July 5th 1945. Parties published their manifestos and conducted their campaigns by local election meetings (sometimes challenging and disruptive), by radio and by house-to-house canvassing within the limits of the scarce resources available. The Labour Party, led by one of its most uncharismatic leaders Clement Attlee, promised a post-war world of full employment, a free National Health Service and 'cradle to grave' welfare, plus control of all the major services and economic institutions.

The Conservatives pointed to the cost of such promises at a time when the country was completely bankrupt, and they relied heavily on the goodwill and extraordinary loyalty to Winston Churchill who had led the country to victory. The electorate, however, took a different view, although throughout most of the campaign Churchill sustained an 83% approval rating. Memories of Conservative failures in the dreadful inter-war years, and those Conservatives and Liberals who had favoured appeasement with Hitler, made people suspicious that they would not once again cause a slump when times were already bad and thus not implement the Beveridge proposals. Quite late in the campaign, Churchill blundered by stating that such widespread social provision could only be achieved if Labour fell back on some form of 'Gestapo' to impose socialism on Britain, an unkind slur on Attlee, his loyal and able deputy throughout the war.[50n]

Attlee responded the next night by sarcastically thanking the Prime Minister for demonstrating to people the difference between Churchill the great wartime leader and Churchill the peacetime politician. Labour had a proven track record in power and offered a programme that met the needs of both civilian and service personnel. The latter particularly feared that demobilisation would be followed by unemployment and lack of sufficient housing.

The motto was 'We are facing a new era – Labour can deliver the goods.' Nonetheless, the result when it was announced was a shock to both parties. Not only had the electorate abandoned the man that had led the country to victory, they had done so in a devastating way, reducing the Conservative representation in the House of Commons by nearly two hundred and increasing the Labour seats by nearly two hundred and fifty, cutting the small Liberal Party by half. Labour, with 393 MPs, had nearly 50% of the votes cast, and among the MPs from minority parties over 20 were sympathetic to the left and 21 had been elected on a communist manifesto. For the first time there was a majority of Labour MPs not directly sponsored by trades unions. Meeting in Downing Street, a shocked Party leadership were less than united. There was intense rivalry between many who had served so loyally and well in the War Cabinet. In particular, Herbert Morrison challenged Attlee's position, arguing that leadership of the Party did not automatically entitle him to become Prime Minister. The argument went on for some time, only coming to an end when Attlee announced that as he had already been to the Palace, kissed hands and been invited by the King to form a government, further argument was pointless! He was my sort of man.

Fifty years later, when challenged by that party game that demands that you instantly say who you would most like to have been, I replied Attlee, although I was not aware of having given him a thought for decades. Apart from the opening of Parliament, his first urgent appointment was to replace Churchill at the Potsdam Conference, which was already underway, charting the shape of the post-war world. The MPs assembled on August 15th amid great scenes of celebration as this was also VJ Day and the King and Queen drove to Westminster in an open carriage. The emotion of the occasion was enhanced when the Labour benches raised the ancient rafters by singing 'The Red Flag,' the song adopted by communist movements across the world, two verses of which are:

> The people's flag is deepest red,
> It shrouded oft our martyred dead,
> And ere their limbs grew stiff and cold,
> Their hearts' blood dyed its ev'ry fold.
>
> *Then raise the scarlet standard high.*
> *Within its shade we'll live and die,*
> *Though cowards flinch and traitors sneer,*
> *We'll keep the red flag flying here.*
>
> It well recalls the triumphs past,
> It gives the hope of peace at last;
> The banner bright, the symbol plain,
> Of human right and human gain.[51n]

A glance through the list of honourable members indicates traditional Conservative groups, which included many individuals who had held their seats for a long time. The only well known names to me would be Winston Churchill, of course, Anthony Eden and R. A. Butler. On the other hand, the following names stand out from the Labour benches: Barbara Castle had been elected in Blackburn; Jim Callaghan, from a poor educational background and serving in the Royal Navy, was appointed a junior minister; Aneurin Bevan, a great orator first elected in 1929, was to found the NHS; Bevan's wife Jenny Lee had also served from 1929 and was to become Minister of Arts (later with Harold Wilson to become a founding member of the Open University); Ernest Bevin, who had served in the War Cabinet; Richard Crossman, the educator and writer, with a good war record, including a Military Cross; Lewis Silkin represented Peckham; the more radical pacifist Sydney Silverman, who had served three prison sentences and was later to found the Campaign for Nuclear Disarmament with Michael Foot; the veteran Manny Shinwell; and a certain Harold Wilson, who had worked brilliantly in the Statistical Office throughout the war.

The new government set a radical and ambitious schedule of reform, committing itself to an urgent programme to nationalise the commanding heights of the economy following Clause 4 of the Party's aims to achieve the common ownership of the means of production, distribution and exchange; the best obtainable system of popular administration and control of each industry or service. The British were not alone in moving to left-wing politics. The fight against fascism led to leftward shifts in the victorious countries, all of which were secular states.

> Ideologically it was based on the shared values and aspirations of the Enlightenment and the Age of Revolution: progress by the application of reason and science; education and popular government; no inequalities based on birth or origin; societies looking to the future rather than the past … As all three regions of the world advanced into the post-war world with the conviction that victory over the Axis, achieved by political mobilisation and revolutionary policies as well as by blood and iron, opened a new era of social transformation.[52]

CULTURE

The general feelings of austerity and anxiety remained throughout this period, although during 1944 these eased as the possibility of an end of these dreadful years began to give us hope. In 1944 the severe blackout laws began to be withdrawn. Of course, the performers mentioned in previous chapters continued to entertain us on the radio, but there were a few newcomers. June 1942 brought us *Desert Island Discs* (still broadcasting every week into the 2020s), while *The Brains Trust* kept us on our intellectual toes by discussing topical questions sent in by listeners (about one-third of the adult population, there being no real choice of other programmes) in an intellectual but often amusing way. It was pretty high powered; the most popular figures were Professor Joad, Julian Huxley and Hannen Swaffer. Guests over the whole run included Noel Annan, Isaiah Berlin, Jacob Bronowski and Violet Bonham Carter.[53n] If our bodies needed attention, the sonorous voice of Charles Hill, the 'Radio Doctor,' regularly advised on how to keep our bowels healthy and regular.[54n]

Cinema was producing a steady stream of popular films, drawing on the experience of war, some commissioned to boost morale. Among these were iconic films such as *Casablanca*[55] in 1943, a masterly spy story set in Morocco, and two years later *Brief Encounter*, a painful romance in times of war.[54] More direct propaganda was clear in Noel Coward's *In Which we Serve,* a display of British stiff upper lips in the Royal Navy.[56]

On a lighter note, St Francis Convent in Letchworth had a theatre which was used from time to time by travelling music hall companies. I particularly remember two acts which made me convulse with laughter. The first was a simple routine set in a boarding house where sleepy residents shuffle in, push the bathroom door (which will not open) and form a dull queue. Enter the happy singing man who slides the door open and waltzes in. I have always thought that it was a Harry Secombe sketch, it was certainly exactly his style. Maybe there was an accordion and tap dancing act by the up and coming Bruce Forsyth. The second act was a slow silent act of a man pretending to be a woman very very slowly peeling off her newly acquired nylon stockings without damage. Pure pantomime, but Gran and the rest did wonder why an innocent nine-year old found this so extraordinarily funny. I missed the point of one of the most popular jokes which managed to combine utility, sexual innuendo and resentment at the popularity of the GIs: 'Have you heard about the latest utility underpants? One Yank and they're off.'

SOCIAL WORK

Social workers continued to be deeply involved at all levels of intervention during the war, helping local communities who were facing the fact that nearly four million evacuees and their families revealed the poor conditions and individual problems of ill health, enuresis, etc., along with a lack of parental structure of many city children. Some evacuees returned home, but in 1944 families, especially those in London, were re-evacuated as a result of the much feared V1 rockets. Social workers remained active in local welfare and child care services, as well as in the cities as families became homeless or lost relatives. In this they worked side by side with the vast Royal Voluntary Service (RVS, later the WRVS). Many qualified and experienced social workers held key posts in regional and national organisations.

Towards the end of the war, Lucy Faithfull's responsibilities had changed from working with London children in Derbyshire to care for elderly people in Plymouth. She recounted one incident which illustrated some aspects of the problems encountered:

> We requisitioned a very prestigious hotel and used it for forty to fifty old people. A town clerk phoned me to say that he had a terrible problem. The billeting officer could not find anywhere for an old lady who was a lavatory cleaner in London, who was absolutely filthy, crawling. I rang up the matron at the hotel and said 'You must take her but have a bath ready.' I picked up the old lady and told her she must have a bath. 'I've never had a bath,' she said 'and I'm not going to start now.' I stopped the car and told her that if she would not have a bath, then I would leave her at the gate. So she agreed. When we arrived, matron whisked her upstairs to the bathroom. She was amazed to see her whip off a wig with the words 'The young lady said I must wash from top to toe.' So she washed herself and her wig. She was in a room with a balcony. Suddenly we heard this terrible scream and rushed upstairs. She had hung her wig on the balcony and a seagull and swooped and made off with it. There she was as bald as a coot. I fetched my hat and put it on her. She looked rather nice. It took me six months to get the money out of the ministry to replace her wig.[58]

In 1944 domestic health services from pregnancy to the elderly and the provision of school meals had risen from a pre-war 300,00 to 1,650,000. The growth of public awareness, particularly the realisation that the pre-war services were so inadequate and the development of these initiatives meant that the government came under more pressure to go further. As the lack of trained child care staff became evident, more letters were written to *The Times* about child deprivation than about any other subject. Winnicott, whose central concern was to reassure young mothers to rely on their natural self-reliance, about which he tried to provide helpful ideas, regularly broadcast towards the end of the war and afterwards. These formed the basis for books published in 1957. Seven years later they were brought together in one volume which fed into the psychoanalytic ideas so prevalent in the 1960's 'Summers of love.' All these campaigners, including the skilful Lady Allen of Hurtwood, leading member of the Independent Labour Party and fierce campaigner for children, used her authority to press for the full implementation of the Beveridge Report.

FAMILY

Willian During the War

In Willian we dug for victory, we watched what we said in public for fear that a spy might be within earshot ('Careless talk costs lives'), we lived simply and spent little ('Don't be a Squander Bug'). Each of these 'propaganda' messages, from the Ministry of Information, were accompanied by a striking picture. Careless talk showed Hitler and Mussolini eavesdropping on two gossiping women and The Squander Bug was a horrible greedy monster. Troop convoys passed through the village from time to time (to the sound of cheers from us all), and at least one American tank unit camped out in the Squire's land right next to our cottages. As they drove out, they took a small chunk out of a corner building, but it was accepted as part of the war. The first question was always the same, 'Where are we?' The absence of any signposts was meant to confuse invading forces, but we could only be of limited help as at the age of eight we knew only the village name but hardly where it lay within a European theatre of war. With the signposts went all the metal railings and anything that could be converted into fighting vehicles or weapons.

This might be a good time to state that, apart from on film, we had yet to meet a black person. Although some Caribbean men were fighting in all three services, they were vastly outnumbered by black American troops serving in a segregated army. These troops were not admitted to combat units, so were used as drivers and in service units. Commanders drew up leisure rotas which ensured segregation even when troops visited local towns. In general, the British found this separation difficult to take and were hospitable to anyone who was on 'our' side. Conflict did arise in pubs and cinemas, and unhappy incidents occurred when a British Caribbean soldier arrived at a white American base to deliver supplies and would be refused admission. Some fact based incidents are included in *Small Island*, the wonderful novel by Andrea Levy.[59] While the lockers of white troops might be covered in pin-ups such as Ginger Rogers, Betty Grable or Judy Garland, one of the main pin-ups found on the lockers of African-American personnel was the actress and singer Lena Horne. While singing to troops she noticed that white troops and POWs were seated in front of the black troops. She furiously marched to the back and sang from there.

For us there was an overwhelming feeling of common purpose that we knew was more important than our ongoing fight with any village kids. On occasional train journeys home or standing on the nearest railway bridge, we saw troops, equipment and vehicles all moving south in long lines of up to 90 wagons, pulled by a single aged and under-powered steam engine which would puff out black smoke and (if we had leaned over the parapet for too long) would lead to a punitive wash when we got home.

John

Although I am sure that my family welcomed the publication of the Beveridge Report, such future hopes were crowded out by the fact that John had received his call-up papers and was to report for basic training to Beverley in Yorkshire in December 1942. In preparation for the assault on Western Europe, a decision had been taken to strengthen the Allied armoured regiments by forming a new division to develop and deploy all specialised equipment; this became the 79th Armoured Division under the command of Major General Hobart based at Catterick, in North Yorkshire. The Division, which included elements of the Royal Armoured Corps (RAC) the 4/7th and 22nd Royal Dragoon Guards and the Westminster Dragoons, as well as American and Canadian units, operated such terrifyingly useful equipment as tank mounted flame throwers, tanks with a protruding revolving drum, attached to which were heavy chains designed to be first into a minefield with the chains detonating mines as it went (flails), and tanks that could navigate themselves in the sea (DD tanks), etc. What could be more natural than allocating a tall, claustrophobic, sensitive recruit to this Division, but that is where John would serve as tank driver/operator for the next three years. Although he moved between regiments within the Division, he spent those three years training; then, from September 1943, he was flailing his way through minefields across Northwest Europe. Though always a conscientious soldier, John never took fully to military life; however, he accepted all the terrible tasks allocated to his unit and became more and more proud to wear the black beret, which was the mark of the armoured forces. John became Gran's favourite 'Blackberry,' being injured only once during a training exercise using live ammunition when a bullet fired by the 'enemy' unbelievably travelled down the barrel of the gun hitting the closing mechanism just as John was about to shove the next round in. It was recorded as a 'Minor Casualty, injury to chest, No Board of Inquiry needed.'

Willian at Peace

Swinging my legs on the outside loo in Willian, I mused over the news of surrender, even managing to work out why everyone was so excited by the phrase 'unconditional.'

It felt good. For some time, news items about the atrocities inflicted by the Japanese on their prisoners had afforded rich material for nightmares. Not only could one be bayoneted in such a way that all your guts fell out while you were still alive, but also they could drip water on you for days until you drowned or plant a fast growing bamboo under you and make it grow up through your arse until it enveloped all your internal organs. Such thoughts could be kept away by magical thinking. If they ever caught me, I argued to myself, I could avoid torture or summary beheading by invoking my ability to accurately guess how many peas in a jar or nails in a pile!

American relatives had sent aid parcels where the goodies were packed with comics, which I remember far more for their graphic horror stories than for anything amusing.[60n] These comics usually included a moral tale, and I particularly remember one of these. The graphics showed two scenes. The first told the story of a popular school athlete winning his race in record time and gaining the prize and the adulation of his peers. The second showed an almost identical boy, this time from the wrong side of the tracks, challenged by the police, running and being shot dead. The cops were so impressed that they measured the distance he had run and the time he took to do it, and found that he had broken the world record.[61] What a waste of talent! At the age of eight I must have been more deeply affected than I realised. Forty years were to pass before this memory came rushing back to mind when I was musing over that frequently asked question, 'Why did you choose social work?'

In one parcel a small battery-operated slide lantern and a few slides arrived, also of the horror variety. I had also somehow seen an Abbot and Costello comedy film about a 'haunted' house, in which one of them makes the mistake of standing too close to a paneled wall where mysterious hands come out and pull them in. It was a long time before I would be caught standing with my back against a wall! So, anxiety ('fear spread thin') seemed always to be present.

School, although less than fifty yards away from the house, had not impinged greatly on my life, although free milk and later free bottles of highly concentrated orange juice were an attraction.[62] The temporary teacher allocated to the task had far to travel and no transport. The day started whenever the coal lorry or other utility vehicle on which she happened to hitch a ride arrived. One way in which she coped with the mixed range of age and abilities was to dispatch small groups into the countryside to aid the war effort. This entailed gathering leaves or any form of compost, loading it into a wooden handcart and wheeling it to the local market garden and allotments where everyone was busy growing vegetables. I never knew whether it was my overactive behaviour or my natural curiosity and constant questioning that resulted in my daily inclusion in these errands. I was probably bored and had developed a bad habit, which has lasted all my life, of managing two things at the same time but inevitably missing something of each. Sitting in the back of the class, I would be daydreaming or reading a comic under the desk. Summoned to the front to be made an example of when asked to repeat what the teacher had just been saying, I was able, infuriatingly, to repeat it exactly. What I strongly recall was the unexpected but enjoyable freedom of the countryside and its total availability to our gang of very young refugees. We roamed throughout the seasons and got up to all kinds of adventures and mischief, either in league with or against the village lads. A minor crisis point occurred when Gran, presumably worried about my lack of education, hailed me as I returned to school one afternoon. The exchange, bellowed across the playground, achieved legendary status in the family: 'Malcolm, where have you been?' 'Been out leaving, Gran.' 'You ain't leaving,' she yelled. 'You've left! Come home, now!'

At some point, presumably following my sudden removal from the village school, a decision had been taken that I should travel to Letchworth for my education. I spent a short time at St Francis Convent School being taught by nuns, then I moved to the secondary school, where other friends from the village had also arrived. No explanations were ever given of course, and consultation with a child was unthinkable. The daily school trip was made by a creaky old bus, starting each morning by the driver chatting up the mothers and ending in the exuberance of after school freedom. At least once my excitement must have been too much as I was ordered off the bus to walk across the fields home – the thought that I may come to harm was not a consideration, certainly not to me. Not surprisingly, school was not a success. An early interest in football came to a quick end when the sports master yelled at me to kick the football with my instep. Such authority and such a literally minded boy combined to ensure the perfect way to fall hard on your bum and avoidance of sports for many years to come. This was the first in a long line of misunderstandings that convinced me that, although I was naturally able and athletic, there was somehow some hidden knowledge or rules that were known to everyone else but me. One other memory illustrates a similar point. On a rare visit to the unheated open-air swimming baths, the gang in the charge of a young mother, it was decided that a game of 'Ring a ring of roses' would be fun. Great, except that on the line 'All fall down' I was the only one obedient enough to go right under water, but I apparently lacked the automatic response of holding my breath! No football, No swimming, forever. A certain skill in taking matters literally, if to excess, along with a naivety and a desire to please seemed to be emerging at an early age. Soon after joining this school I was sat in a cold cloakroom alone and told to take a test (actually, the 11+), the likes of which I had never seen before. Not surprisingly, I failed. An idea of my educational standard can be gained from a letter written to John telling him how Mum and I had gone to 'Whipenade zoo on my biche and we had a conset at scool … in aid of salut the soldie week.' Clearly, there was no chance of any academic success. My last school report from Hillshott School, placing me 37th out of 44 pupils, rather confirmed that prediction. While all those comics must have helped me achieve full marks in reading, my writing and spelling were marked as 2 out of 10 and 6 out of 20. I recall the Whipsnade trip as a first encounter with the long arm of the law. When Mum and I were halted by annoying traffic lights, we put our rusty old cycles on the pavement and walked them across the junction. 'Oh no you don't,' said the large policeman. 'You are either vehicles or pedestrians. You can't be both.'

In the final few months in Willian we stood with the farm workers to see a new invention imported from America, the combine harvester. This amazing machine not only cut the wheat, but also, within the same machine, shook out the corn and tied the hay bales, dropping these in straight lines and filling a large sack with the corn. Amazing, but worrying for the workers who could see the time spent on tractors and hand gathering the stoops of wheat resulting in unemployment. It took only a few years for the combine harvester to be used across the country, severely reducing the manpower required and encouraging farmers to remove the hedgerows to develop larger fields, forever changing the landscape and altering the patterns of wildlife.

Home At Last

In the spring of 1945 we returned home to London to join in the celebrations. I have a clear memory of Gran and I, with our pathetic luggage, standing at the bus terminus in Peckham waiting patiently for the single-deck bus that carried us for the last stage of the journey. After an hour we ventured to ask when it would come. It now had a proper number and was a double-decker, several of which had already pulled out while we stood there. Things had changed! Street parties to celebrate VE Day were hurriedly arranged, despite the rationing (there was lots of jelly and custard), parades were cheered and joyous crowds were everywhere. On VE Day we were in Whitehall cheering Churchill, who led us all in 'Land of Hope and Glory'. *The Guardian* of May 9th 1945 reported his stirring speech where he recalls the year when Great Britain stood alone: 'There we stood alone. Did anybody want to give in?' The crowd roared back a terrific 'No!' 'Were we downhearted?' 'No!' came the answer. I remember it well. Then, we went over to the Palace to yell until the King and Queen came out on the balcony. We experienced a tremendous feeling of togetherness; privations had been rewarded and victory achieved for monarch, government and all the people. Such simple joy, so unrestrained. A great weight had been lifted from everyone's shoulders and the celebrations brought us all together. All this was set against the austerity of the time.[68] Two diarists recorded the feeling of the time. The wonderful amateur diarist Nella Last records how she and her husband heard the news of victory, and Anthony Heap gave his observation of how life failed to live up to expectations:

> [May 7th 1945] When Stuart Hibberd on the wireless said so unemotionally that tomorrow was to be VE Day, we just gazed at each other. We felt no pulse quicken, no sense of thankfulness or uplift of any kind. I rose placidly and put on the kettle. I looked on my shelf and said, 'Well dash it, we must celebrate somehow – I'll open a tin of pears.' And I did.[63n]
>
> Housing, food, clothing, fuel, beer, tobacco – all the ordinary comforts of life that we'd taken for granted before the war, and naturally expected to become more plentiful again when it ended, became instead more and more scarce and difficult to come by.[64]

No one forgot the sacrifices or that so many families that had lost loved ones, neither did we push too far from our minds that Japan was still a terrifying enemy, but it was, of course, further away, and we had really almost forgotten the 14th Army's battle in Burma. By no means were all our family travails over. My brother John was still in khaki. I have, to this day, no idea how such a gentle soul managed to cope and survive the horrors of tank warfare, but he did. Throughout the years his welfare was always a major concern as reports of European victories and withdrawals were given out by the sonorously measured tones of the BBC announcers, when we were left to deduce that 'tactical withdrawal' really meant defeat; a word never to be spoken. In all his life the only thing I ever knew John to hold a grudge about was that, having gone through all that trauma, everyone in his regiment was required to surrender their 'pay books' to have them returned with the clause 'for the duration of the war' replaced by 'for the duration of the emergency'. Such an arbitrary change of contract came hard after so much exhausting conflict. Off to Palestine they went, and more chronic anxiety and fearfulness resulted for us about his fate at the hands of Israeli guerrillas fighting for their homeland. It would be late 1946 before he came home.

Although VJ Day on August 15th 1945 marked the end of the war, it was a more moderate celebration in Britain than VE Day had been. Clearly, for those many people that still had family members fighting in the Far East, or even worse starving in prisoner of war camps, the relief was enormous, as was the feeling of freedom from exhaustion and fear balanced by some hope of a positive future. I clearly remember different opinions about the manner of the final victory. The majority, myself included, were of the view that the cruelty of the Japanese combined with their fierce creed never to surrender justified such a dreadful end given the many Allied troops that would have been killed fighting every last determined Japanese soldier (although we were only dimly aware of the reality of the horror of the atomic bomb, and certainly had no concept of the long term effects of radiation). Others were fearful about the power of a single bomb, each with the immediate power equal to two thousand of the biggest bombs used so far in the war. There was much debate in the press. The Dean of Saint Albans Abbey forbade any bells to be rung as a protest against this inhuman weapon, and there was no civic service to celebrate the final victory. Nella Last records:

> Old Joe called upstairs, brandishing the Daily Mail: 'By God, lass, but it looks as if some of your daft fancies are reet. Look at this.' I've rarely seen him so excited – or upset. 'Read it – why this will change all t'world.' I felt sick – I wished I was 30 years older, and out of it all. This atomic bomb business is so dreadful.[65]

My Personal View

My family had survived, tired and changed by the experience of war and the knowledge of the losses to our community and country. While I had experienced sudden and unexplained separation, I always had close family to love and support me, but I had now began to see how things had worked out. We may have been near the bottom of the pile, but I now had a dim view of what those above me took for granted, how they behaved and how their power influenced me and mine. Our heroes were the King and Queen, Churchill, Monty, Eisenhower, Alexander, Slim, the dockers, the miners, all service men (especially those wearing the light blue uniforms of the wounded), and most Cabinet members. We respected Rommel, hated Hitler and laughed at Goebbels and Mussolini. Above all, we admired John as our own quiet and courageous hero. I do not believe that anyone had yet calculated, and certainly had not grasped, the fact that the whole conflict had cost the lives of sixty million people plus countless injured and traumatised, the consequences of which would work themselves out across the world in the next decades. I had seen how everyone pulled together for the common cause, despite the widespread black market and the 'spivs' who could get anything for a price.

Hope was supreme. I have a vivid memory of standing outside Central Hall Westminster in January 1946 fascinated by the spectacle of all these great men in exotic national costumes assembled for the first meeting of that symbol of a new and hopeful world, the United Nations Assembly. Perhaps I thought that such a powerful body would soon sort out the problems of the Middle East, where my cherished brother was trying to keep the peace. We were unaware of the way in which the tectonic plates of global power had shifted. American financial demands on Britain and our complete exhaustion had effectively ended our ability to retain an empire. America's inclination to recognise and deal with Russia and that country's occupation of the countries of Eastern Europe had ensured the creation of a great power that would challenge America at every turn. The insistence on unconditional surrender had reduced Germany and Japan to poverty, which would determine their populations to rebuild their flattened infrastructures using the most modern techniques so that they would soon outpace Britain and, to a lesser extent, America, whose capacities still relied on increasingly outdated machinery and systems. This fearful war had started to 'save' Poland and ended sacrificing it to years of oppression under Soviet Russia. Poland had maintained the fourth largest army to fight in Europe. Their troops had no place in the victory parades, and some trades unions set themselves against Polish workers in Britain, seeing them as anti-communists stealing British jobs. Some Polish ex-pilots who had been part of the RAF were spat on.[67n] Their sacrifice for Britain was not marked until September 2009 when a memorial to all 500,000 who fought with the Allies, largely financed by public subscription, was erected at the National Memorial in Staffordshire. A privately financed memorial to Polish airmen who fought in the Battle of Britain is now at RAF Northolt.

Although the toll of the war in Europe was truly terrible, it has to be seen against the total catastrophe of the worldwide war which had resulted in some 77 million deaths. Of these, nearly 18 million were from the Soviet Union (Russia plus Eastern Europe), 12 million were from China (3.4% of the population), over 8 million were from Germany (8.2% of the population), over 6 million were from Poland (17% of the population), 460,000 were from the UK (0.9% of the population), over 400,000 were from America (0.3% of the population) and over 3 million were from Japan (4% of the population).

History would be told according to the perspective of the participating countries. Whilst the western powers saw a victory of democratic values, Stalin would say that it demonstrated the superiority of the communist regime, ('The Great Patriotic War' of 1941 to 1945) forgetting the early alliance with Germany, and China saw their many years of suffering as a prelude to the glorious revolution which ushered in a new order (forgetting the part played by Chiang Kai-Shek's regime). American memorials and early history lessons refer to 1941–45 (forgetting the two years of Nazi aggression before Pearl Harbor). Many countries under the yoke of colonial masters saw it as an opportunity to throw off their shackles. Stalin may have provided a good summary when he commented that 'Britain provided the time, America provided the money and Russia provided the blood.'[66] While local uprisings, decolonisation and the consequences of war changed borders across the world, Russia and America remained unchanged. Jock Colville, Churchill's wartime Private Secretary, wrote 'Sadly, I reflect how much easier it will be to forgive our present enemies in their future misery, starvation and weakness than to reconcile ourselves to the past claims and future demands of our two great allies.'[68]

Grammar School

In these years I had developed a love of rural life as well as defences against anxiety. Full of life, bright eyed, keen but entirely uneducated, I returned home to London in the closing days of the war. Unfortunately, some phrenological crone had once said that the bumps on my head showed that I would be some sort of mathematical genius.[69n] That, the general feeling that the hardship of war was to be rewarded and, I now think, a determination that lost ground had to be regained drove my mother to aim high in her plans to get me a good education. I had been enrolled at the local grammar school by means of savings from mother's meagre earnings. The place would become free once the 'Butler' Education Act came into effect a year later. The gap between the starting point expected by the school and my wild unstructured non-education in the fields of Hertfordshire was not apparently seen as a problem – my natural brightness would soon cope!

Luckily, when I arrived at the imposing buildings of Haberdashers' Aske's Hatcham Boys School at the top of Telegraph Hill, between Nunhead and New Cross, only a small remnant of the school operated in the bomb-damaged buildings. I remember a short interview with the kindly headmaster Mr Richmond Coggan and I was in, starting halfway through the academic year 1944/45. I guess something about my wildness must have been seen as enthusiasm, curiosity or potential. Perhaps the school was badly in need of pupils, or it believed in its own ability to overcome my appalling lack of basic knowledge. Perhaps I was a social curiosity, an experiment since reflected in books and dramas illustrating the pain and anger engendered by the forcible mixing of two widely differing classes and cultures. Time seems to have removed the memory of any pain or anticipatory fear that accompanied the rapid transition from village wild boy to first day pupil dressed, at extraordinary strain on the family exchequer, in neat school uniform including beginner's cap. Probably my lifelong hatred of hats stems from that time – it certainly got me into enough trouble in later school and army days. I suspect that by the age of eleven I just accepted the effect of outside events on my life as normal, and certainly not in my power to question. The fact that I ended up at the end of the year only 7th in class reflected either some progress or smaller classes than Letchworth. I had no idea what was in store for me. Mother comments as follows:

> Malcolm was reluctant to leave the freedom of his country life to be dressed in the formal uniform that the London school required. The summer uniform was restricting enough, but the heavy black winter suit was a torment. Above all was the irksomeness of having to wear a cap … a capital crime … It took him a long time to re-adjust to town life, and only in retrospect can I appreciate the effort he had to make. The school emulated the public schools, the younger boys subject to humiliation of all kinds by the prefects, which Malcolm's experience and his own particular forthright nature found hard to endure, the great a toll this took upon his extravert nature one can only imagine.[70]

For me this includes so many masterly understatements!

NOTES AND REFERENCES

1. Winston Churchill's final review of the war, and his first major speech in the House of Commons Has Leader of the Opposition, August 16th 1945. Eade, C. (ed.) (1946). *Victory, the Sixth Volume of Winston Churchill's War Speeches*. London: Cassell.
2. Bruce, M. (1968). *The Coming of the Welfare State* (4th edn). London: Batesford, p. 291.
3. This, from the Hindu text the *Bhagavad Gita*, was said to have been quoted by Robert Oppenheimer, reputedly the father of the atom bomb, as he watched the detonation of the first test bomb at Alamogordo, New Mexico, on July 16th 1945.
4. Although a memorial was erected in 1976 to the Russian dead, a Jewish monument could not be erected in the park until 1991 after the collapse of the Soviet Union. Further conflict developed in late 2009 when it was proposed to build a large hotel next to the site in preparation for the Euro 2012 football tournament in Kiev.
5. Heidrich (the main architect of the Holocaust) was assassinated in Prague by British trained Czech and Slovak soldiers in May 1942. The Village of Lidice was razed and all villagers killed as a reprisal. Eichmann (the main organiser) escaped to Argentina but was found by Israeli agents, tried there and hanged in 1962.
6. Bruce, *op. cit.*, p. 301.
7. Vonnegut, K. (1969). *Slaughterhouse Five*. New York: Delacorte.
8. The surrender had followed Mussolini's removal from power and imprisonment in the Abruzzo mountains. He was released by German troops, who restored him to power in Northern Italy, where in April 1945 he was murdered by partisans who left his body hanging in a petrol station in Milan.
9. ABCA (the Army Bureau of Current Affairs) required all units to devote a set time every week to discussions of current affairs. Its purpose was general education and to emphasise the post-war world for which the troops were fighting. These sessions were reputed to be a significant factor in

the post-war landslide Labour victory. (It is thought that some 80% of Army votes were for the Labour Party.)
10. Hoggart, R. (1990). *A Sort of Clowning: Life and Times 1940–59*. London: Chatto and Windus, p. 60.
11. Healey, D. (1989). *The Time of My Life*. London: Michael Joseph.
12. Milligan had been born in India to an English mother and an Irish NCO in the British Indian Army. As Spike commented, 'My father had a profound influence on me. He was a lunatic.'
13. Milligan, S. (1980). *Mussolini: His Part in My Downfall*. London: Penguin, p. 81. An American view of the black humour and madness of war, set in this same campaign, is the novel *Catch 22* by Joseph Heller, which achieved an iconic status following its publication in 1961.
14. For a fictionalised account of a very wet 24 hours in the life of a small American infantry unit at Cassino, see Baugch, R. (2008). *Peace*. New York: Vintage.
15. Majdalany, F. (1999). *Cassino. Portrait of a Battle*. London: Cassell and Co., p. 87.
16. Majdalany, *op. cit.*, pp. 122–124.
17. In fact, there were no German troops in the monastery.
18. Majdalany, *op. cit.*, p. 254.
19. They may have been less supportive had they realised that 60% of the 1.7 million deaths were caused by Tito's followers fighting their Serb/Chetnik rivals.
20. Moorehead, A. (1946). *Montgomery*. London: Hamish Hamilton, p. 189. It may help when reading these quotes to remember that Montgomery had a slight trouble pronouncing his 'r's. His concern that no detail should be overlooked can be illustrated by one of his extensive briefings to officers in a large cinema started with the command 'There will be no coughing,' but he had taken the precaution to issue cough sweets to everyone beforehand. He ran into controversy later by commanding that every man be issued with condoms before entering a captured town.
21. Discussing these events in 2009 with residents on the Lizard Peninsula, they were sad to see that through all the anniversaries none of the American troops ever returned, only ever their families. Among the troops landing on Utah Beach, fighting in the Battle of the Bulge and among the first to enter the liberated concentration camps was J. D. Salinger. Soldiers emerging from the landings and early battles were often unfit for front line duties for some weeks. Salinger certainly suffered some form of battle fatigue. In *Catcher in the Rye* his disaffected hero Holden Caulfield, a seventeen-year-old boy whose innocence is challenged by the corruption and brutality of his age, says 'I'm sort of glad they've got the atomic bomb invented. If there's ever another war I'm going to sit right on top of it. I swear to God I will.' When the unique and remarkable lyricist and performer John Lennon was shot in December 1980, his assassin had a copy of this book in his pocket. See McCrum, R. (2010). 'J. D. Salinger: From Boy of War, to Modern Man of Letters.' *Observer*, 31.01.10.
22. Russia refused landing rights which would have enabled British planes access to the city. When Churchill, well aware of the extraordinary Polish contribution in the campaigns, pleaded with Roosevelt to join him in pressing Stalin to change his mind, Roosevelt refused.
23. An increasingly arrogant and protectionist de Gaulle led the new Republic. In subsequent years he was able to establish the myth that the French had freed the city alone. At a subsequent low point in Franco-American relations he demanded that President Truman remove his troops from France, to which Truman fired back 'Does that include the dead ones?'
24. Discussing these events in April 2009, Ron was both proud of his service and the fact that his unit had gone through all the campaigns without serious casualties. He put this down to smart tactics and the ability of his small plane to turn so quickly that they could avoid the more modern attacking aircraft. Discharged at the end of the war, he was a veteran at the age of 21. Through the next sixty years he asked many war museums if they had an Auster plane, but with no success.

Moving to a retirement community in January 2009 he visited the local museum to find that not only did they have an Auster but also that it was the very one that he had used all those years ago!

25. Derived also from the 1941 film *Here Comes Mr Jordan*, in which a boxer who dies 'mistakenly' is sent back to earth for a second chance to fulfil his true destiny.
26. In conversation in 2009 with cousin Ron Lane, he mentioned that his daughter, when visiting Belgium many years after the war, was given a new camera in exchange for her own damaged one, once she had casually mentioned that her father had been stationed there during the war. Ron contrasted this recognition and memory with the lack of interest in contemporary Canada. Much the same I think applies in the UK among younger generations, a contrast readily seen at anniversary ceremonies on the continent where the children seem to recognise what they owe to this generation and while at school tend the war graves.
27. Flecker, J. E., 'A Fable,' in Squires, J. C. (ed.) (1919). *The Collected Poems of James Elroy Flecker*. London: Secker. It took me several years to locate this poem. Finally I put a call out online and two years later I had the answer.
28. Songs such as 'It's Great To Be Young' and 'Scouting Must Go On,' and the iconic finale, with audience participation of 'Crest Of A Wave': 'We're riding along on the crest of a wave, and the world is OURS!'
29. *South London Observer*, Friday 22.12.44. See also Anon (1945). *The Story of the 79th Armoured Division 1945*. Hamburg: Publisher unknown, p. 195.
30. Davies, N. (2007). *Europe at War 1939–1945: No Simple Victory*. London: Pan, p. 122.
31. This high loss forced a decision to arm African-American troops 'en masse' to fight. Up to this point they had been used for transport and supplies, and in any event segregated. BBC (2001). Documentary *Letter from America*, 16.12.02; broadcast by BBC2.
32. Whilst the former were operated with the sole purpose of mass killing (for example, Treblinka), the latter were for slave labour, where the majority died anyway (for example, Dachau and Belsen). Auschwitz was a mixture of the two, and is now the most visited as a memorial and museum. The cartoonist Carl Giles, who created the wonderful Giles family complete with Grandma, was so shocked by the piles of skeletons and corpses that he was unable to draw anything whilst there.
33. I used this beautiful case to keep my certificates in from school onwards. It was seldom used, but over time it deteriorated badly. In 2019 I contacted the BBC programme *The Repair Shop*, a great programme where true craftsmen repair treasured family objects. They accepted my submission, and my case appeared in the programme shown in the autumn of 2020. During its restoration, a 1939 newspaper was found detailing Nazi plans for the future.
34. Copies of this and other related messages are retained in my collection.
35. See Roos, D. (2018). 'The Navy Disaster That Earned JFK Two Medals for Heroism,' history.com; accessed 2002.
36. Fraser, D. (1983). *And We Shall Shock Them*. London: Hodder & Stoughton, p. 317.
37. Fraser, *op. cit.*, pp. 312–315.
38. Swinson, A. (1966). *The Battle of Kohima*. London: Cassell. Keane, F. (2010). *Road of Bones: The Epic Siege of Kohima 1944*. London: Harper Press.
39. General Dimoline was later appointed as Chairman of the Army Cadet Force Association, and it was my pleasure to work with him on the King George VI Leadership courses. (see Chapter....)
40. Slim, W. (1956). *Defeat into Victory*. London: Pan (reprint).
41. Nimmo, W. F. (2001). *Stars and Stripes Across the Pacific: The United States, Japan, and the Asia Pacific Region 1895–1945*. Westport: Greenwood Publishing.
42. Yellin, E. (2004). *Our Mothers' War. American Women at Home and at the Front During WWII*. New York: Simon & Schuster.

43. This became the Ryder–Cheshire charity, which has grown to include 50 homes in the United Kingdom, with many homes and projects overseas. A unique footnote to history is the unfortunate Tsutomu Yamaguchi who was in business in Hiroshima when the bomb was dropped. The next day he took the train to Nagasaki to be hit by the second bomb. He survived to the age of 93. In 2011, a light-hearted comment was made on a BBC quiz show by Stephen Fry to the effect that he must have been the unluckiest man on the planet, but how extraordinary that the trains were running the day after such a disaster, not something that the poor British network would have achieved. Fry's plans to film a documentary in Japan shortly after the show had to be cancelled due to threats for treating the bomb lightly.
44. Many Japanese soldiers were stranded in remote places, continuing to obey the last order never to surrender. On the Philippine island of Mindoro a captain was discovered still holding out in 1980, and the sole remaining member of a group surrendered in 1997.
45. Hayek, F. (1944). *The Road to Serfdom*. London: Routledge. The book was originally published in the UK and then by the University of Chicago Press in September 1944. A condensed version of the book written by Max Eastman was then published as the lead article in the April 1945 issue of *Reader's Digest*, with a press run of several million copies. This condensed version was then offered as a Book of the Month selection with a press run of over 600,000 copies. In February 1945 a picture-book version was published in *Look* magazine; this was later made into a pamphlet and distributed by General Motors.
46. Orwell, G. (2007). *As I Please, 1943–1945. Vol. 3: The Collected Essays, Journalism and Letters*. London: Godine.
47. Moorehead, A. (2000). *Eclipse*. Oxford: Granta.
48. Davies, *op. cit.*, p. 313.
49. Wilkinson, E. (1941). 'Social Justice,' in *Programme for Victory. A Collection of Fabian Essays prepared for The Fabian Society*. London: Routledge, p. 134.
50. Apparently, MI5 had discovered towards the end of the war that Hugh Dalton, responsible among other things for resistance and secret operations, was using his department to bug a fellow Cabinet minister. Churchill immediately 'promoted' Dalton out of his post. It was this suspicion about Labour behaviour, not any disrespect for the leaders, that prompted this remark.
51. 'The Red Flag,' lyrics by Jim Connell in 1889. It is normally sung to the tune of the German carol 'Oh Tannenbaum' attributed to the 16th century composer Melchior Franck.
52. Marwick, A. (1971). *The Explosion of British Society 1914–1970*. London: Macmillan.
53. This remarkable group of intelligent people revealed that in a pub one night before a broadcast they decided to explore the possibility of levitation, and, somewhat to their surprise, several of them were able to float towards the ceiling!
54. Dr Charles Hill was elected to Parliament in 1945. In 1955 he became postmaster general. In 1963 he became the chairman of ITV, having been highly critical of the BBC. In 1965 Harold Wilson appointed him as chairman of the BBC governors to 'sort them out.'
55. *Casablanca*. Dir. Michael Curtiz. Warner Brothers (1942), starring Humphrey Bogart and Ingrid Bergman.
56. *Brief Encounter*. Dir. David Lean. Cineguild (1945), starring Celia Johnson, Trevor Howard and Stanley Holloway.
57. *In Which We Serve*. Dir. Noel Coward and David Lean. Two Cities Films (1942), starring Noel Coward, John Mills and Bernard Miles.
58. From a private discussion following research on Lucy Faithfull at the Social Work History Network, 2007; kcl.ac.uk>scwru>swhn.
59. Levy, A. (2004). *Small Island*. London: Headline.
60. This seems to have coincided with the unregulated expansion of such comics in the USA. There had been none in 1933, but twenty years later up to 880 million copies were being circulated.

This led to a series of federal inquiries and some toning down of content. See the novel Chabon, M. (2000). *The Amazing Adventures of Kavalier & Clay*. New York: Picador.
61. Biro, C. (c. 1942). *Daredevil*. DC Comics. New York: Lev Gleason.
62. Bruce, *op. cit.*, p. 300.
63. Broad, N. and Fleming, S. (2006). *Nella Last's War: The Second World War Diaries of 'Housewife 49.'* London: Profile Books. Nella Last was one of the individuals recruited by the Ministry of Information's Mass Observation Project to keep a day to day record of their lives.
64. Kynaston, D. (2008). *A World to Build. Austerity Britain, 1945–1951*. London: Bloomsbury.
65. Marwick, *op. cit.*, p. 107.
66. Quoted in the article 'The day the war finally ended' by Max Hastings, published in the *Daily Mail* and *The Week* on 16.07.05, p. 40.
67. See Correspondence (on the dispute concerning the Gurkhas possibly being allowed to settle in the UK) in *The Times*, reproduced in *The Week*, 02.05.09, p. 22. Polish clubs have continued in many towns across the UK, and Polish newspapers have been sold across the country ever since the war. Both these cultural institutions received a boost in the later years of the 20th century when many Polish workers came to work in the UK.
68. Colville, J. (1985). *The Fringes of Power: Downing Street Diaries 1939–1955*. London: Hodder & Stoughton.
69. The pseudo-science of phrenology (reading the bumps on the head) had been so popular in Victorian times that some employers insisted on a 'reading' before appointing staff. Luckily I was not found to have a bump above the ear (destructiveness) or over the eyebrow (murderer).
70. Jordan, *op. cit.*, p. 80.

FIVE

1945–1950
THE LESS THAN SHINING YEARS[1n]

There was some talk of total war, but no one knew what it really meant. Few if any foresaw what the price of victory would be. The world of six years ago has gone and there is a realisation that there can be no return. For tens of millions of people, the whole basis of existence has gone. They were without homes or hope.

– Edward Murrow[2n]

… through the inventions of science I can do what was not possible for any of them. I can make my solemn act of dedication with a whole Empire listening. I should like to make that dedication now. It is very simple … *I declare before you all that my whole life whether it be long or short shall be devoted to your service and the service of our great imperial family to which we all belong* … But I shall not have strength to carry out this resolution alone unless you join in it with me, as I now invite you to do: I know that your support will be unfailingly given. God help me to make good my vow, and God bless all of you who are willing to share in it.

– Princess Elizabeth 21.04.1947[3n]

It is a fateful moment for us in India, for all Asia, and for the world. A new star rises, the star of freedom in the east, a new hope comes into being, a vision long cherished materialises. May the star never set and that hope never be betrayed!

– Jawaharlal Nehru[4n]

All human beings are born free and equal in dignity and rights. They are endowed with reason and conscience and should act towards one another in a spirit of brotherhood … Everyone is entitled to all the rights and freedoms set forth in this declaration, without distinction of any kind, such as race, colour, sex, language, religion, political or other opinion, national or social origin, property, birth or other status. Furthermore, no distinction shall be made on the basis of the political, jurisdictional or international status of the country or territory to which a person belongs, whether it be independent, trust, non-self-governing or under any other limitation of sovereignty … Everyone has the right to life, liberty and security of person.

– From the United Nations Declaration of Human Rights, 1948[5n]

INTERNATIONAL EVENTS

Europe

The Nuremburg trials meted out a welcome form of justice to the Nazi leaders: twelve leading Nazis were sentenced to death and seven to long periods of imprisonment, among whom was Rudolf Hess who had been Hitler's deputy.[6n] Traitors were similarly dealt with – some were shot in the Tower of London, and William Joyce (Lord Haw Haw) was hanged in Wandsworth Prison.

It would take some time before the spies, so well placed by Stalin, were discovered. In Britain these included the 'Cambridge Five' spread across all areas of government.[7n]

America

In America, the spies Alger Hiss in the state department and Julius and Ethel Rosenberg in atomic research were discovered, and later others were revealed in all sections of Congress. Klaus Fuchs was a leading atomic scientist and spy in both America and the UK. Throughout the war, the House Committee on Un-American Activities had investigated security threats. Their investigations into right-wing pro-fascist influence in the Ku Klux Klan and overtly fascist groups listed millions of Americans. Towards the end of the war and through to the late 1970s attention turned to fear of communist infiltration, and a publication prepared by the Congressional Library which listed a limited number of pro-communists sold half a million copies.[8n] The list of pro-fascists was never published. The House Committee, which included the young Richard Nixon, continued their investigations and were the committee responsible for investigating the film industry and blacklisting many movie stars. The key question was 'Are you now or were you ever a communist?' Ten key people from the film industry refused to answer that question on the grounds that it infringed their constitutional right of free speech, and they served a year in jail for contempt of Congress. The work of the Committee ended many careers as, once on one of the blacklists held by the studios, you were denied work. Cruel divisions were caused by those who were persuaded to give information against their colleagues. This led Britain, along with other countries, to gain a number of gifted artists, including the musician Larry Adler, the actor/director Sam Wanamaker (who developed The Globe Theatre on the South Bank) and Carl Foreman, who wrote the screenplay for the film *The Bridge on the River Kwai*.[9n] The right-wing senator Joseph McCarthy drew massive publicity for his anti-communist campaigns which included sensational claims that President Truman's administration, the State Department and Voice of America were riddled with communists, none of which he was ever able to identify. His investigation of the US Army eventually led to a loss in popularity, and in December 1954 he was censured by the Senate and died three years later at the age of forty-eight.

Churchill

Relieved of the burden of office, Churchill, whose mother was American, was free to express his fears and hopes for the future of the world. In March 1946 he was at Westminster College in Fulton, Missouri, to receive an honorary degree. He used the occasion to give the audience his view of possible futures based on the current chaos in Europe and his long experience of world affairs. In many ways his predictions were accurate, and confrontation came quickly in Berlin, but no nation was prepared to arm the United Nations. Many saw his speech as that of an old warmonger; many had not yet grasped the true nature of Stalin's regime. His speech ran as follows:

> Our supreme task and duty is to guard the homes of the common people from the horrors and miseries of another war ... I have, however, a definite and practical proposal to make for action ... The United Nations Organization must immediately begin to be equipped with an international armed force ... I propose that each of the Powers and States should be invited to dedicate a certain number of air squadrons to the service of the world organisation ... Now ... I come to the crux of what I have travelled here to say. Neither the sure prevention of war, nor the continuous rise of world organisation will be gained without what I have called the fraternal association of the English-speaking peoples. This means a special relationship between the British Commonwealth and Empire and the United States of America ... Fraternal association requires ... the continuance of the intimate relations between our military advisers.
>
> [W]e welcome Russia to her rightful place among the leading nations of the world. We welcome her flag upon the seas ... It is my duty however ... to place before you certain facts about the present position in Europe. From Stettin in the Baltic to Trieste in the Adriatic an *iron curtain* has descended across the continent. Behind that line lie all the capitals of the ancient states of Central and Eastern Europe ... and the populations around them lie in what I must call the Soviet sphere, and all are subject in one form or another, not only to Soviet influence but to a very high and, in some cases, increasing measure of control from Moscow ... From what I have seen of our Russian friends as Allies during the war, I am convinced that there is nothing for which they have less respect than for weakness, especially military weakness. If the Western Democracies stand together in strict adherence to their principles, no one is likely to molest them. If however they become divided or falter in their duty and if these all-important years are allowed to slip away, then indeed catastrophe may overwhelm us all.[10]

In September he made an equally remarkable speech in Zurich on the future of Europe:

> I am now going to say something that will astonish you. The first step in the re-creation of the European family must be a partnership between Germany and France. In this way only can France recover the moral and cultural leadership of Europe. There can be no revival of Europe without a spiritually great France and a spiritually great Germany. The structure of the United States of Europe, if well and truly built, will be such as to make the material strength of a single state less important ... And the first practical step would be to form a Council of Europe. Great Britain, the British Commonwealth of Nations, mighty America and I trust Soviet Russia – must be the friends of the new Europe and must champion its right to live and shine. Therefore I say to you: let Europe arise![11]

These speeches are of particular interest, quite apart from the first formal use of the term 'special relationship,' which has caused so much controversy in the subsequent years on both sides of the Atlantic. The fear of Russian imperialism, the need to prepare both economically and militarily and the future shape of Europe would, under pressure of post-war poverty and chaos in Europe, shape four main inter-related structures that played such an important role in post-war recovery and the world as we now know it. The speeches also reveal how Britain, failing to recognise how significantly its standing had been reduced, strove to set itself apart, a special power, certainly part of Europe but caught between it, the Commonwealth and America. Britain would have a key role at the centre of all three power groups. Unfortunately, the rest of the world did not quite see it that way. One institution which directly related to Churchill's speech was the formation of the Council of Europe. Agreement was reached at The Hague in May 1948 that a Council should be set up to protect the virtuous values and culture of Europe from outside influence, meaning Bolshevism. Britain was cautious about joining such a euro-centred body. The Foreign Secretary Ernest Bevin's 'bon mots' reached record levels. Although his view was that, 'If you open that Pandora's box, you never know what Trojan 'orses will jump out,' he was eventually persuaded to agree, magnanimously conceding to his deputy, 'Well you know Chris, we've got to give them something and I think we'll give them this talking shop in Strasbourg – the Council of Europe – we'll give them this talking shop.'[12] The objective of the Council was 'to achieve a greater unity between its members for the purpose of safeguarding and realising the ideals and principles which are their common heritage and facilitating their economic and social progress.' The Council still exists, having grown from ten to forty-six states, building on the European Conventions on Human Rights, drafted by Churchill, to establish the European Court of Human Rights and the iconic blue flag with twelve gold stars. (This body is not to be confused with the European Union, which was not founded until 1993, but uses the same flag.)

The Marshall Plan

Early in 1947, President Truman appointed the war hero General George Marshall as Secretary of State. It would be Marshall who conceded that America would take financial responsibility for Greece and Turkey when Britain ran out of resources. Marshall fully appreciated how desperate the post-war situation was in Europe, and that large numbers of desperate refugees were susceptible to communist propaganda.[13n] In March, returning from a failed Moscow conference, Marshall did not talk about armies and ideologies but of shortages of food and fuel and their relationship to production. He fully approved what became known as the established 'Truman Doctrine', that 'it must be the policy of the United States to support free peoples who are resisting attempted subjugation by armed minorities or outside pressures,' a policy that understandably alarmed the Russian authorities.[14n] Marshall accepted that Europe's need for the essentials of life far exceeded the ability to pay for them. His generous plan therefore made development funds available to European countries. Under the plan, American goods would be paid for in dollars from the new Organization for European Economic Cooperation, and the receiving country would pay an equivalent amount to a national fund in its local currency. Eventually these payments would be absorbed into the country's budget, but the original American sum would not have to be repaid. The scheme would run for four years from August 1947, would be funded by $13 billion and would be conditional upon the European nations deciding their priorities together. The scheme was offered to Russia on the same terms but, as anticipated, they were not prepared to share details of their economic plans. However, whether viewed as an act of extreme generosity or a cynical move to get US manufacturers tied into Europe, the plan was a great success, reviving key European industries until, when aid stopped in 1951, they were on the edge of boom time. *Pravda*, following the party line, commented that having already bought up several small European States America had now bought the lot.[15n]

International Pressures

In Palestine the fighting between Arabs and Jews continued with no sign of a solution, but it was only one of a range of conflicts across the world as anti-imperialism and communism combined in various mixtures to challenge the old order. Stalin's grip on Eastern Europe rapidly swept up Bulgaria, Czechoslovakia, East Germany, East Poland, Hungary and Romania. In Yugoslavia Marshal Tito determined his own brand of communism designed to hold together the differing cultures, traditions and rivalries of Bosnia and Herzegovina, Croatia, Macedonia, Montenegro, Serbia (including Kosova) and Slovenia. Tito's so-called 'National Communism' caused a split from Moscow. Communist China was extending its influence to Malaya, Korea, Laos, Cambodia and eventually Vietnam, in fact anywhere else that anti-imperialist movements could be supported.

Greece

The divisions between the Greek guerrilla movements, supported by the Allies during the war, eventually broke into civil war, with both factions challenging the right-wing royalist government elected in 1946. Although supported by Yugoslavia, Bulgaria and Albania, it seems that Stalin withheld direct support following the informal 1944 agreement with Churchill, which had nominated Greece to be within the British sphere of influence. Britain had re-trained and equipped the Greek Army, but as the economic situation deteriorated America agreed to take over this task – anything to keep the communists out of a key Mediterranean country. The success of these efforts coincided with some reduction of support from the north as the Tito versus Stalin dispute escalated. By late 1947 the communist forces changed from guerrilla tactics to more traditional open warfare, one major result of which was that many civilians were caught in the crossfire with consequent loss of life, injury and destroyed villages. The Greek Army succeeded in a series of major battles across Greece, and by December 1948 most leaders of the uprising had sought refuge in Yugoslavia and other friendly states. By early 1949 the civil war was over, with the royalist government once again in control. Costly in terms of death and injury, economic development and financial support from outside, the Greek Civil War was seen in the west, particularly in America and Britain, as the first successful fight to contain the spread of communism. By the early 1940s, a third of the world's population were already living under a communist regime. The next rounds, including Korea and Vietnam, would not be as short lived or certain.

Africa

From the opposite political position, the right-wing African Nationalist Party in South Africa came to power intent on reversing the racial assimilation policies that had been followed during the war, a special commission having decided that further integration would result in the loss of personality for the nation. Mixed marriages were outlawed in 1949, and in the following year sexual relations between different races became a criminal offence. Identity cards, which classified the holder by race, were imposed, and the Group Areas Act defined where different races lived. Resistance was suppressed by outlawing any communist organisations, which included any that the government decided were communist. Three years later so-called 'coloured' people (black and Indian) were banned from 'whites only' beaches, buses, hospitals and other social amenities. The issue of racial prejudice came home to my family and many others in the romance that somehow caught the public imagination: the engagement of the young Oxford student Prince Seretse Khama, heir to the Kingship of the Bangwato people (part of the British Protectorate of Bechuanaland, which bordered South Africa), to Ruth Williams, a white British woman. They were forced to marry in a civil ceremony after the Bishop of London had barred them from having a Church wedding. Late in 1947, Seretse returned home, where thousands of his people supported his marriage and set about welcoming his bride as their future Queen. Much to their shame, the British government, under pressure from South Africa, agreed to intervene. Although judged eminently suitable to be King, it was agreed that South Africa's opposition was sufficient reason to prevent what the tribe wanted. Summoned to Britain, he was told that he would be banished from his homeland for at least five years. It was to be seven years before the government gave way to a continuous campaign by journalists, celebrities and politicians of all parties. The dignity of the couple won them many friends; certainly my family were on their side. The return home in 1956 was on condition that he renounced his chieftainship. As a highly successful politician and in a wonderful, typically British, action, Queen Elizabeth appointed him a Knight Commander of the Most Excellent Order of the British Empire![16n]

Germany

While western leaders were considering how they could strengthen their response to a determinedly expansionist Soviet Union, tension was rising in Berlin. The Allies had right of access from their control zones to their respective areas of Berlin, and on June 21st 1948 they announced the introduction of a new Deutsche Mark; this was opposed by Moscow, who saw this as a bid to re-launch the German economy and thus perceived the action as a threat. The Allies had also stated their intention to establish a West German state. From the Russian point of view, the only response to such provocative acts seemed to be to force the Allies out of Berlin. Near midnight on June 23rd The Kremlin announced the closure 'for technical reasons' of all western routes to Berlin from 6am the following morning. Two days later they withdrew food supplies to the non-Soviet zones of Berlin. The first great crisis of the Cold War had started, prompting fear that this might be the start of a Third World War. The Allies' response was to exploit the only route left, which was an agreed air corridor into Tempelhof Airport which lay outside the Soviet zone. If unarmed cargo planes were sent in, they could only be stopped if the Soviets shot them down, which would certainly precipitate open warfare. Calculations showed that if the population of two million were to be fed and supplied with water and fuel for transport and heating, some five thousand tons of supplies would be needed every day.

The RAF calculated that sufficient American and British planes could be marshalled to start an airlift quickly for an operation that was anticipated would last a few weeks. The many wartime examples of Russian determination were not fully appreciated. The airlift began on June 26th and soon settled down to a routine; by the end of August, 1,500 flights a day were meeting the total requirements of the population. Some flights went direct from Britain to the British controlled airport of Gatow in Berlin. Flying boats were also used. As winter set in, the need for fuel increased, but the demand was met. In April 1949, the increased skills of pilots flying in shorter intervals, quicker turn round time and the use of heavy aircraft, enabled the daily lift to be raised to nearly 9,000 tons a day, with planes landing every thirty seconds. This seems to have proved to Stalin that his blockade could not be maintained, and on May 12th 1949 the blockade was lifted, although supplies were delivered until September. The operation had lasted for fifteen months, ninety-two million miles had been flown and twenty-five aircraft had crashed with the loss of 101 crew. The cost was in excess of $224 million. My belief is that the experience and income generated by the airlift, and the availability of planes when it finished, aided the development of some travel companies which were well placed to meet the interest in cheap foreign travel as the post-war austerity came to an end.

The European Coal and Steel Community

America played an important role in developing the European Iron and Steel Community, pursuing their general policy that a united Europe, including Britain, would be more able to resist communism and any future military threat. This was effectively a revival of an idea that had been discussed intermittently over the previous twenty-five years. The key players were the Prime Minister of France, Robert Schuman, and Jean Monnet, his Head of Planning, who was a very experienced international civil servant who had worked in Britain in the early war years. Immediately the war ended, Monnet proposed that France should use German coal from the Ruhr and Saar regions in order to restore the French steel industry. The scheme was implemented with American agreement. Monnet considered that the Marshall Plan should be matched by an equally imaginative European plan, and informal talks in early 1949 put forward his view that Europe was now a vacuum on either side of the great dynamic forces of communism and capitalism. It might be inevitable that the vacuum would be filled by one or the other unless the European nations worked together to sustain the 'Western European Way of Life.'[17n] Despite Churchill's proposal, spelt out above, it quickly became clear that the British government had no intention of entering into any union with France or anyone else. Further negotiation led Schuman to get agreement from West Germany, Italy and three other nations to form the European Coal and Steel Community who pledged to pool these key resources. The Community, formed in March 1951, would prevent war between the participants, create the world's first supranational authority and mark the birth of a united Europe. Britain stood aside, still committed to strengthening Sterling, looking across the Atlantic to that 'special relationship' and comfortable with its worldwide role leading the Commonwealth. In any event, it would have been impossible to link together the newly nationalised British Steel and commercial companies abroad. Monnet, an Anglophile, commented that, having not suffered defeat and occupation, 'Britain felt no need to exorcise history ... it was the price of victory – the illusion that you could maintain what you had, without change.'[18]

North Atlantic Treaty Organization (NATO)

Overtly, NATO would be concerned with security and defence. It was formed in the shadow of the communist coup in Czechoslovakia, the expulsion of Tito's Yugoslavia from the Cominform,[19] the Berlin Blockade and the threatened aid to North Korea, which certainly raised the anxiety levels in France and Germany. Our Foreign Secretary Ernest Bevin, determined to ensure that if another war came America would be bound in from the start, launched his manoeuvres. In December 1947, in an informal chat with General Marshall, he talked airily about a spiritual union of the west (America, Britain and the Dominions, France, Italy and so on). In the British tradition, nothing was written, nothing was too formal, but an understanding backed by power ensued that the Kremlin got the message 'So far but no further!' One suspects that Bevin also had more than a thought that the development of his scheme would buy time for Britain to gain strength back to her rightful place in the world. It took less than eighteen months for this seed to become NATO, whose treaty was signed by twelve western nations to agree that:

> An armed attack against one or more of them in Europe or North America shall be considered an attack against them all. Consequently they agree that, if such an armed attack occurs, each of them, in exercise of the right of individual or collective self-defence will assist the Party or Parties being attacked, individually and in concert with the other Parties,

such action as it deems necessary, including the use of armed force, to restore and maintain the security of the North Atlantic area.[20]

The Treaty was signed on April 4th 1949 in Washington, with a clause that it would last for ten years, and effectively confirmed America as a superpower. Bevin saw it as a personal triumph; America was firmly tied into the defence of Europe. The Americans saw all three of these developments as encouraging the European powers to recover to a point where they could manage their own affairs and be strong enough to resist communism. It would be very helpful if Britain could be tied into Europe and be less concerned with her old empire. General Lord Ismay, Churchill's former Chief of Staff who was to become NATO's first General Secretary, summed up the British view. The purpose of NATO, he averred, was 'to keep the Russians out, the Americans in and the Germans down.'[21] Attlee was delighted – it gave him the chance to move Montgomery, who was not adapting well to peacetime, to be Deputy Commander for NATO under Eisenhower and rehabilitate Bill Slim, the Burma hero and a man who had a similar background to Attlee, by appointing him Chief of the General Staff.

Burma

In addition to its very busy radical domestic programme, the UK government had to solve the urgent challenges pressing across the world from the desire of its colonies for independence, the perceived threat posed by communist expansionism, the developing Cold War and the Middle East. The most significant of these was India, but in the event Burma became the first to achieve independence. Attlee accepted that, in the post-war political climate, colonies would seek to be independent and anyway maintaining them could no longer be afforded. He put his faith in a strong Commonwealth which ex-colonies could join as a strong cultural, political and economic group which might influence world affairs. In this he found an ally in Mountbatten of Burma (whose nephew Philip married Princess Elizabeth, heir to the British throne in November 1947), who supported indigenous nationalism and opposed any handover to rich and possibly corrupt elites. As the commander of all troops in the Far East, he held a strong position. Unfortunately, at the same time the Colonial Office resumed their pre-war imperialist attitudes and were totally unprepared for any concessions that might reduce the Empire. The post-war Governor of Burma naturally enough supported the Colonial Office and favoured politicians who had been loyal during the war to form the first new government, although they had not won the first election. Mountbatten favoured Aung San, a lively student leader who had led the resistance to the Japanese (despite the fact that he had earlier supported them as anti-colonialists) and whose party had won. Attlee backed Mountbatten's judgement, much to the horror of the Colonial Office. The Governor was replaced and Aung San formed a democratic Cabinet; by the end of January 1947 an independence agreement had been signed. The whole future course of Burma's subsequent history changed when in July 1947 Aung San and six of his Cabinet were assassinated at the instigation of political rivals. The party split, but a socialist government was formed which carried forward to Independence Day in January 1948, whereby Burma opted to refuse membership of the Commonwealth.[22n]

India

Next was the British Empire's 'Jewel in the Crown.' The Cabinet was negotiating with the three main moral leaders of India: the ascetic Mahatma Gandhi, who had led the non-violent independence campaign since returning from his legal and political work in South Africa; Muhammed Jinnah, who had practised as a barrister in London's exclusive Lincoln's Inn; and Pandit Nehru, the elegant, charming product of Harrow and Cambridge. Post-war elections in India had seen the mostly Muslim areas returned Jinnah's party to Congress, while the Hindu areas voted for the left-wing Congress Party of Nehru and Gandhi. Meanwhile, negotiations were underway with a physically and economically weakened Britain, whose Labour Government lent towards anti-colonialism. Inter-racial riots spread throughout this vast country with many thousands killed. When India was on the Cabinet agenda, it is reported that Attlee stopped doodling and took the firm leadership line that independence must be granted during the lifetime of his leadership. In March 1946 a Cabinet committee, sitting in India, concocted a sort of federal structure loosely based on ethnic and religious groupings with a central government responsible for foreign affairs and defence. Jinnah agreed.

In May 1946, the Cabinet voted for an independent united India, whereupon Jinnah quickly changed his position, calling on his Muslim supporters to take direct action to achieve a separate nation for Muslims. In the ensuing riots between all the major religious groups, up to a million people died, often in unspeakable circumstances. Drastic action was required. Attlee appointed Lord Mountbatten as Viceroy with a brief to achieve independence by June 1948 – this in a country with 255 million Hindus, 92 million Muslims and a further 12 million equally divided between Christians and Sikhs. Mountbatten's condition was that he had the power to make decisions on the spot.[23n] The announcement to the House of Commons produced uproar; the majority of the members had not grasped the speed at which the Empire was collapsing. The Conservative Enoch Powell was shocked to the core. Attlee told his biographer that Powell had walked the streets all night in a state of disbelief; the world as he had known it was coming apart. Occasionally he sat in a doorway with his head in his hands.[24] As Attlee saw it,

> The only thing that was clear was that if we let Congress have their own way, the Muslims would start a war to get their Pakistan ... Both parties were asking for everything and blaming us for not getting anything when they should have been blaming themselves. I decided the only thing to do was to give them a deadline ... So you'd better get together straight away. It was the only thing that would bring them together. The next thing was to find the right man ... Dickie [Mountbatten] stood out a mile. Burma showed it. To me the so called experts had been wrong about Aung San, and Dickie had been right.[25n]

The Mountbattens used all their personal charisma and charm on the negotiators once they arrived in March 1947.[26n] Within days he cabled that instant action was the only solution. He proposed a five-month deadline to partition into India and Pakistan as the only way to stop the massacres and force the politicians to face reality. Independence Day would be August 15th 1947. It was July before the Colonial Office lawyer arrived to draw the boundary line between the two new nations, having been warned that time only allowed for butchery not surgery. There was no time to learn from the intelligence gathered by generations of British officers who knew every inch of the country, and no time to visit. He sat in his office with his Indian commissioners sitting in Calcutta and Lahore, but, as he could not sit with both, he sat with neither. Once the boundary was announced, the roads and trains were full of citizens trying desperately to get to the right side of the border before the due date. As whole train loads were slaughtered, the truth of what had been lost and the horror of the events hit the world's press. In those few days some twelve million people moved residence and two million fell victim to the massacres. Gandhi had not been present at the formal ceremony as he was in New Delhi trying to mediate the warring factions. On January 30th 1948 Gandhi was assassinated by a Hindu extremist for daring to suggest that Hindus and Muslims were equal.

Mountbatten was invited to remain as Governor General of the new dominion. Ironically, Muslims remain the largest minority in India. Two days later Pakistan achieved independence with Jinnah as Governor General.[27n] Once the boundary was announced, the 565 princely states that had held a special position in the Empire were given a choice about which country they would join. The Prince of Kashmir opted to join India, although the majority of his population were Muslims. Pakistan launched a series of guerrilla actions to persuade him to change his mind, but he appealed to Mountbatten who honoured the Prince's choice for India. Consequently, Indian troops moved in to drive out the Pakistan invaders. The United Nations was called in to arbitrate, and decided that a referendum should be held, but India only agreed to this once all Pakistan's fighters had left. The referendum has never been held, and India and Pakistan have fought two wars over the territory. Currently, each country controls parts of this area and it remains a permanent source of conflict, as do the tribal lands of the Northwest Passage. There tribal leaders still hold great power, managing to hide the headquarters of the radical Islamist terrorist group Al-Qaeda.

Independence

Ceylon had quietly become independent in 1948, so Britain's furthest colonies had been released, part of a general strategy that increasingly concentrated on Africa as a future power base, although Palestine was also relinquished. At the same time, America released the Philippines and the Netherlands freed Indonesia. Ho Chi Minh had declared Indochina independent in 1945, but France, supported by the USA and the UK, resisted until 1954 when the country split into Laos, Cambodia and Vietnam.

Palestine

The next immediate problem for the government was British Mandated Palestine,[28n] where my brother John and his unit had disembarked in April 1946, the month in which the American Jewish Anglo-American Committee had unanimously recommended the immediate admission of 100,000 Jews to Palestine – an action which would undoubtedly have caused major Arab uprisings. This resolution followed a 1942 conference, financed through the Jewish Agency, in the Biltmore Hotel, New York. The resolution declared:

> That the new world order that will follow victory cannot be established on foundations of peace, justice and equality, unless the problem of Jewish homelessness is finally solved. The Conference urges that the gates of Palestine be opened; that the Jewish Agency be vested with control of immigration … and that Palestine be established as a Jewish Commonwealth integrated in the structure of the new democratic world. Then and only then will the age old wrong to the Jewish people be righted.[29]

In the 1920s the controversial journalist and politician Ze'ev Jabotinsky had formed the defiantly nationalistic and militaristic Revisionist Zionist Movement, from which the Irgun, the fierce paramilitary group which was seen as a terrorist group by Britain, gained inspiration. Jabotinsky urged Jews in Palestine to stop cringing and to tell the *goyim* to go to hell. He perceived that, 'The native population, civilised or uncivilised have always stubbornly resisted change so it will be utterly impossible to obtain the voluntary consent of the Palestine Arabs.' Thus, Zionists should be ready to use force and build an iron wall (actually, now concrete).[30] The Jewish Agency, established with British support in 1929, had, through a variety of organisations, accumulated vast financial support and had been arranging the gradual immigration of Jews into Palestine, a process which increased in the face of Nazi persecutions before and during the war.[31n] The British, denied the extra troops promised by America, decided on a slow process of implementation, eventually agreeing to about 1,500 immigrants a month. In the face of Jewish protests, the British had cracked down hard on the terrorist organisations committed to the Zionist objective of a permanent homeland for the Jewish people. The hold of Zionism can be illustrated by a quotation from David Ben Gurion, a relatively moderate member of the Jewish Agency, who stated that

> If I knew that it was possible to save all the children in Germany by transporting them to England, but only half of them to Palestine I would choose the second because we face not only the reckoning of those children, but the historical reckoning of the Jewish people.[32n]

The British manned Palestine police force had a key role to play in confronting terrorism; many former commando officers and men had been recruited, and there were suggestions that they were forming unofficial 'anti-terrorist' squads which sometimes exceeded ordinary police methods. An extreme example was the case of 'Major Farran's hat.' The Major, a valiant and much decorated intelligence officer, arrested a Jewish teenager whom he tortured to death. Despite the fact that there was clear evidence of Farran's guilt (he had left his hat at the scene), the Court Martial acquitted him. The Irgun swore vengeance and pursued him back to the UK, thus adding a further element to the distrust and deceit that has marked the subsequent history of the Middle East.[33]

In June and July 1946 the terrorists retaliated, in particular by blowing up the King David Hotel in Jerusalem, the headquarters of the British authorities and military. Ninety-one people were killed and more than forty were injured, the majority being local staff and clerks. This was a major escalation of the resistance campaign that swung between Jews and Arabs as different British governments sought to satisfy conflicting demands. British forces now found themselves increasingly caught between the two communities. Montgomery (now Viscount Montgomery of Alamein and Chief of the General Staff), who visited shortly before the attack, had warned the British Commander that the soldiers were 'facing a cruel, fanatical and cunning enemy and there was no way of knowing who was friend and who was foe … men should we warned not to fraternise.' Within hours of the attack the order was issued that all contact between soldiers and civilians must cease and highly unpopular restrictions were imposed on all movement.

Disagreements about the bombing divided the main insurgent groups, and consequently an intense campaign of attacks was carried out in the following months by the Jewish Stern Gang, the Irgun and Hagenah working separately, and, from the British point of view, more unpredictable and complex.[34n] In response to the destruction of the hotel, British intelligence captured Irgun members and sentenced them to death. Irgun's counter was to capture two British sergeants, threatening to kill them if the sentences were carried out, which they were. Irgun killed the hostages and hung their booby-trapped bodies in public, an act which caused widespread condemnation, anti-Semitic demonstrations in Britain and fierce reprisals by troops in Palestine.

None of this was good news to Mum, Dad or me in Lanbury Road! By now, Britain's position was impossible. Consequently, Attlee informed the United Nations that Britain wished to terminate the Mandate no later than August 1948. On the ground, troops were under extraordinary pressure to keep the lid on the explosive situation, and, looking through the intense correspondence between John and home, some resentment at the extension to a traumatic and fierce campaign and exhaustion is increasingly evident. This was enhanced by the fact that, with fewer and smaller tanks needing crews, John was assigned to be a batman/driver to the regimental adjutant! The perfect target for a sniper's bullet.

In early 1947, while John was starting the long journey back to civilian life, the Jewish Agency had financed and organised an old American ship to cross the Atlantic where, re-named SS *Exodus*, it docked in France. *Exodus* took on 4,500 Jews bound for Palestine, shadowed all the way by HMS *Ajax*. Approaching Palestine, the ship was met by other naval ships, which, with some force, boarded and towed the ship to Haifa. The passengers refused to disembark and went on hunger strike for 24 days. Eventually all passengers were transferred to more seaworthy vessels and sailed back to France, where they were subject to a series of long drawn out moves to various camps in Europe. The blockage of the SS *Exodus* was intended to show that, under the terms of the Mandate, Britain would not allow significant Jewish immigration which would inevitably anger the Arabs. Unfortunately, this highly publicised event turned world opinion against Great Britain.

In 1947, the United Nations agreed to partition, giving 56% of the land to the 30% of the population who were Jewish. In May 1948 the independent State of Israel was created with David Ben Gurion as the first Prime Minister. Irgun–Haganah forces carried out a fierce campaign to drive Palestinians from villages and the port of Jaffa. Throughout 1948, Jewish forces forced Palestinians to move to neighbouring Arab countries, where they remain to form a major consideration in any peace process. Villages were destroyed and families massacred, with the aim to ensure that Israel was 'ethnically clean.' Ben Gurion commented that 'We must do everything to ensure that they do not return … the old will die and the young will forget.'[35] Unfortunately, these exiles and the whole Palestinian population have not forgotten.

The Arab nations went to war but, lacking unity and co-ordination against a committed enemy, they lost some 700,000 men. Israel recalls this whole period as the 'War of Independence'; it is known to the Arabs as 'nakba' – 'The Catastrophe.'[36] The UN then imposed an armistice line (the Green Line), with 22% of the land (West Bank and Gaza) under the control of Jordan and Egypt. (In 1967, Israel was to carry out a 'pre-emptive' strike which broke these countries' control of the two areas and also the Golan Heights in Syria and the Sinai Desert.) The unresolved dispute has caused constant international tensions ever since, and the conflict continues to motivate anti-American and anti-British terrorists. Israel continues to receive massive financial support from America.[37n]

China

On October 1st 1949, in Tiananmen Square in Beijing, Mao Zedong, Chairman of the Communist Party of China and commanding the People's Liberation Army, announced victory for his forces and the inauguration of the People's Republic of China.[38n] This dramatic development would have a profound and immediate influence on the post-war world, although the route to this victory had been long and very painful, marked by splits and diversions. Mao was from a peasant family; he had, as a librarian in 1918, established a society to study Marx, and had formed the Chinese Communist Party in 1921, a group which studied and learnt from developments in Russia.

China at that time was under corrupt and harsh imperial rule, which led to great discontent and some uprisings. The Kuomintang (China National Party) under their leader Chiang Kai-shek committed to overthrow the regime, and in 1912, after 2,000 years, the last Emperor of China abdicated. China was now a republic with two leaders and many strong royalist warlords to defeat, a task which the Kuomintang and the newly formed communist Chinese Workers' and Peasants' Red Army cooperated, under orders from Moscow, to achieve. By 1927, the two groups spilt when the stronger Kuomintang, having successfully captured Shanghai, proceeded to massacre communists. At that point, the Kuomintang split into those who were inclined more to nationalism and Chinese culture (and therefore supported Chiang Kai-shek) and those who held more radical left-wing ideas (who inclined to Mao). This effectively marked the start of a civil war between the Kuomintang and the Red Army. Confrontations continued across this vast country in the following years, but by the early 1930s Chiang had successfully encircled the main Red Army units in the south and inflicted heavy casualties. In 1934 the only option for the Red Army was to make a tactical withdrawal on a route to the west and then north, creating an opportunity to recruit more peasants and re-establish themselves in the northern provinces where they had most support.

This historic exercise, usually referred to as 'The Long March,' took 370 days and covered some 8,000 miles over very challenging terrain, and all the while the Red Army were harassed by nationalist forces. En route they were joined by other Red Armies retreating from other eastern provinces. When the armies finally reached relative safety in an isolated province, the 300,000 who had started had been reduced to 40,000. The bravery of such a march, and the behaviour of the troops throughout, earned respect for the Party and has, of course, become an iconic part of modern Chinese history.[39n] As China was under attack from Japan, then and throughout the ensuing war, Stalin ordered both communist sections to work closely together, which they did until soon after Japan surrendered in 1945. The Red Army finally forced the Kuomintang out of mainland China to the island of Formosa (now Taiwan), where they established their own regime. The Republic of China ensued – a very successful industrial power, but under martial law and a Kuomintang dictatorship, supported by America. By the 1970s most countries had recognised the People's Republic of China. In 1950, Mao, now 'Chairman Mao The Supreme Leader' sent a 'volunteer' army into Korea to support the North Korean invasion of South Korea, thus precipitating the second great postwar crisis. In late 1949, China and the USSR formed an alliance, which added to the frightening division between western and communist powers, strengthened the determination to resist the Korean incursion and increased NATO's anxieties that, with his eastern borders more secure, Stalin might now turn his full attention westwards.

Eleanor Roosevelt

The United Nations General Assembly was meeting in Paris when the gracious Eleanor Roosevelt presented the Universal Declaration of Human Rights, which was adopted on

December 10th 1948. Mrs Roosevelt stressed that the document did not represent a legal obligation but hoped that it would become 'an international Magna Carta of all men everywhere.' Some votes were cast against the Declaration, and the Soviet bloc, South Africa and Saudi Arabia abstained, the Soviet representative dismissing the document as 'just a collection of pious phrases.' The genesis of the Declaration clearly came from the previous decade as did the Convention on the Prevention and Punishment of the crime of Genocide adopted by the UN the day before the Declaration. The Convention, the culmination of years of single-handed campaigning by a Polish lawyer Raphael Lemkin, who coined the term 'genocide' for the Holocaust and Armenian massacres. One hundred and forty countries then signed, ratified or acceded to the Convention; these included Burma, China, Haiti, Israel and Russia. The American Senate declined ratification, but each day that the Senate was in session Democratic Senator William Proxmire made a four-minute speech condemning genocide. (It took the Republican President Ronald Reagan to persuade the Senate to ratify the Convention, which it did in November 1988. Only a cynic would say that by then all the ex-concentration camp guards in exile residing in America would be dead.)

NATIONAL EVENTS

As the 1947 demobilisation of men and women from the forces enabled some sort of family life to be resumed, how did we welcome the peace? Much of the communality that had been essential in wartime carried forward, as did the acceptance of central control and government intervention. Horrors had been perpetrated by fellow humans following the orders of perverted dictators, but great evils had been destroyed. Churchill was a strong leader but, despite exhaustion and austerity, the British system of democracy had proved its virtue. In fact, the population had demonstrated this by voting for massive social change under a new leader, Clement Atlee, a politician almost totally lacking charisma. What many thought such a new era would mean can be illustrated by an encounter that the social scientist David Donnison had on a crowded troop train:

> Going on leave for 48 hours when my ship got home, I was standing in the corridor of a train, stuck at Reading station, which was packed with standing service men. Two civilians in dark suits and bowler hats hurried across the platform to see if they could get aboard and turned away, saying they'd better look for a first class carriage. The sailor standing next to me leaned out from the door and shouted 'First class? First class? When this war's over there'll be no more bloody classes!' – his voice echoing through the station. I sensed the unspoken support he gained from men all along the corridor.[40n]

The boost given to the cause of democracy and the belief that nations could work together for peace gave our family a warm inner glow that would see us through the hard times to come. Throughout the west, people were sure that democracy was the preferred system for new nations that were about to be established. Newspapers and, more importantly, newsreels reported that millions of Displaced People were suffering in Europe, so the British public accepted bread rationing (9 ounces a week) for the first time in July 1946 and reduced meat portions five months later. Potatoes were added for the first time in 1947, and the following year the cheese ration was cut back and private motorists were limited to driving 90 miles a month.

Mother and I had our second encounter with the law when we were innocently throwing some broken stale crusts to the pigeons on the steps of St Pauls. A constable came over to warn us that we were breaking the law which forbade the waste of rationed resources. The great victory parade in London was on June 8th 1946, a procession which was nine miles long with contingents from all Allied countries and all services, both military and civilian. Russia was not invited, and despite the fact that the Polish Army had been the fourth largest, fighting so bravely in all theatres, no Polish troops were included as Stalin considered they should march in Moscow! Mother and I could see no chance of getting a good vantage point, so we resolved to see the rehearsal which took place a couple of days before. We cycled up The Mall very early and settled ourselves in a prime spot by the saluting rostrum. It was pouring with rain, so we kept our oilskin sou'westers and capes on. Next day we were amazed to find our photo on the front page of the *Evening Standard* as an example of loyal Londoners who had spent all night in the rain to see the parade. An early lesson not to trust the press.

Industry

Despite the badly damaged industrial infrastructure in the UK, production was resumed, although it would be some time before the many essentials of everyday life were available or free of control. While rationing of food and clothing continued, the government sought to prevent an influx of shoddy goods by introducing the 'Utility' brand, which if displayed on an item was a guarantee of basic quality. Some of this furniture is still in use; some have become collectors' items. Trades unions, having put their power behind the vast war effort, particularly once Russia became an ally, were accepted as a respected estate of the realm and their leaders looked forward to participation in government policy-making now that the Labour Party was in power.

There was little interest in business or unions to invest in the co-operative boards that had helped wartime production, thus the opportunity was lost to develop the strong partnerships that were to be a key feature of post-war European industry as their economy overtook that of Great Britain. The enormous contribution that the natural and social sciences had made to both military and industrial warfare was to carry forward to peacetime in technological and industrial development, and in particular to the policies of the Labour Government, which drew ideas from the London School of Economics, in particular those of Brian Abel-Smith, Peter Townsend and Richard Titmuss.

Atomic Weapons

The fact that the world had now entered the 'atomic age' had to be faced. Having exported our leading scientists to America to take advantage of the vast resources and industrial determination of that country, all out of range of German bombers, the lessons of Hiroshima and Nagasaki had to be weighed against the perceived threat from Russia, especially if it were to develop its own atomic weapon. Agreement was quickly reached that America could base its heavy bombers in the United Kingdom, thus in reach of mainland Russia. In early 1946, RAF planners had already identified 67 Soviet cities as potential targets. In January 1947 Attlee, in a decisive but ingenious manoeuvre, agreed that Britain should have its own atomic bomb, a decision all the more remarkable as the cost was agreed at £100 million when the country was in dire financial straits. As Foreign Secretary, Ernie Bevin fully supported the decision, arguing that in the absence of any effective international system to regulate the proliferation of such weapons we could not afford to acquiesce in an American monopoly. The decision never went to Cabinet.

Against the expectation of western intelligence, Russia detonated its first atomic bomb in August 1949, an event which started the post-war arms race, which was to absorb incalculable sums of money from all three countries. For the foreseeable future the threat posed by nuclear weapons would hang heavily in the minds of everyone. It would provide a constant background of anxiety and in some the development of an attitude that joy should be sought now as we could all be annihilated tomorrow. Certainly, decisions taken on any future military adventures had to weigh up the risk that it could precipitate a nuclear war. The mood was wonderfully satirised by a Professor of Mathematics and musical humorist Tom Lehrer:[41n]

> When you attend a funeral
> It is sad to think that sooner or
> Later those you love will do the same for you
> And you may have thought it tragic
> Not to think of other adject-
> ives to think of all the weeping they will do
>
> (But don't you worry)
>
> No more ashes, no more sack cloth
> And an arm band made of black cloth
> Will someday never more adorn a sleeve.
> For if the bomb that drops on you
> Gets your friends and neighbours too
> There'll be nobody left behind to grieve.
>
> And we will all go together when we go,
> What a comforting fact that is to know.

> Universal bereavement,
> An inspiring achievement,
> Yes, we all will go together when we go...
> We will all fry together when we fry.
> We'll be French fried potatoes by and by.
> There will be no more misery
> When the world is our rotisserie,
> Yes, we all will fry together when we fry ...

The Government's Challenges

The Labour Government took the general sense of national unity to its natural conclusion by putting into place the major pieces of legislation that would bring about a more equal and just society. These developments had an impact either on our own core family or on one part of the vast network of uncles, aunts and cousins that gathered from all across South London from time to time. The national issues seemed to be a natural and intrinsic part of 'our family'; they were developments that were taken for granted and certainly reflected no conscious political activity on our part, although everyone we knew voted Labour as a matter of course. National leaders were accessible and 'like us,' that is to say a cross section of the community. One could post a letter immediately into the front door of No. 10 Downing Street if one felt aggrieved, as one young cousin did. He just cycled up from Peckham and dropped it in. There seemed little distance between 'us' and 'them.' Politicians were known by name, generally respected and trusted to play their part in reconstruction. The Prime Minister Clement Attlee of course epitomised the model; he was modest of dress and habit, self-deprecating to a fault, but driven by a firm determination. He would have stood no chance in the modern media obsessed politics of later years. (Some comparison is possible with the later Labour Prime Minister Gordon Brown who found himself caught between the job, for which he was passionate and able, and presenting a popular image, at which he was poor.) Disrespect for us was confined to those who by inheritance or skullduggery saw themselves as so superior that they could look down on the vast masses of ordinary people. Somewhere in there were the 'spivs' and the 'drones,' petty criminals who ran the black market, from which, it was rumoured, you could get anything if you were prepared to pay for it. While we were aware that there were major criminals somewhere who were beyond the pale, most people were quite ambivalent to low level 'trading.' Certainly, before the end of sweet rationing Dad would, from time to time, bring home a tin of fruit drops, still made to this day by Barker & Dobson. No questions were asked, and they were very welcome.

The domestic problems facing the Labour Government surpassed any previously encountered but were to be implemented in a society where science (and the belief in science) waxed as religious belief waned (although religion was still an important part of family life). Surely, wartime centralised planning and control could carry into peacetime despite dire economic circumstances. The new government determinedly set out to implement 'Clause Four' to nationalise the commanding heights of the economy, to attack the urgent housing problem, introduce a full range of welfare services and rescue the economy!

In 1939, Britain had had overseas assets of some £3,000 million, but by 1945 a third of this value had been lost. The £450 million gold reserve had been reduced by two-thirds and the country had overseas debts of £3.7 billion. Nonetheless in actuarial terms the UK remained one of the richest nations, only behind America and those countries which had remained neutral. Domestic industry had to be rebuilt, although a considerable proportion of our overseas markets had been lost. Bombs had demolished 200,000 houses and damaged 500,000 more. Faced with this situation, and despite a severe shortage of trained labour, the new government promised to build between four and five million houses in the first ten to twelve years after the war.

In March 1946, the government nationalised the Bank of England, and in the same year civil aviation fell under government control, Heathrow Airport having been opened in January. The following year, the coal industry was taken over, together with road haulage companies, canals, railway companies and the Cable and Wireless Company. The year 1948 saw gas and electric companies nationalised, although steel was not taken over until 1951. There were brief strikes in the docks and within transport sectors in London, but fate seemed against the government when, starting in December 1946, Europe suffered the worst winter in recorded history.

The Big Freeze

By January 1947, snow had disrupted all transport, but particularly coal supplies to the power stations, where post-war stocks had been low anyway, thus restricting electricity to homes and much needed industry. A force of 100,000 British and Polish troops and German prisoners of war were put to work clearing snow from the railway lines by hand. Temperatures of minus 21 degrees Celsius were recorded, food froze in the ground only to be retrieved with pneumatic drills, large parts of the potato crop rotted and thousands of chickens froze to death, adding shortages to the already poor rations. All these difficulties naturally damaged the government's reputation as they were now responsible for practically everything. Confidence in Sterling was shaken, which put pressure on the pound. The whole horror lasted through February, when snow fell in some places for 26 of the 28 days; as the thaw set, damaging floods swept across the country with London seriously threatened.

Aid agencies from Australia and Canada sent food parcels and distributed them to villages which had been cut off. By early March ice packs that had formed round the coast began to clear so that supply ships could deliver much needed food and fuel. The same conditions extended to the decimated France and Germany where starvation was reported in Berlin. I certainly remember these extreme conditions, but what my family and most others could not accept was the pressure to eat snoek, a strange fish imported from South Africa, which for some reason was made available. Suspicious at first, once tried it was an experience we did not repeat. In common with most people, we were used to privation; we had suffered worse and could face threats with some equanimity. Perhaps it was the hardening of our skins that would help us in the coming wars from Korea to Afghanistan, during the threat of terrorist incursions and in the Covid-19 pandemic in the 21st century.

Devaluation

By the spring of 1948 the financial markets, not impressed by welfare spending and a tired Chancellor of the Exchequer (Stafford Cripps), were moving against Sterling. The Cabinet was faced with the decision of when to devalue the pound from a value of $4.03. America, well aware of the outstanding loans, advised devaluation, but the Cabinet, still clinging to the belief that Great Britain was a strong world power, hesitated. In September, Bevin went to Washington to meet with the US Treasury Team to argue that in the new climate of the Cold War western nations had to remain strong, and if, as was predicted, a Sterling crisis led to mass unemployment, Britain would be severely weakened. The leader of the US Team launched a broadside that 'England had caused no end of trouble and was costing no end of money.' They thought it was totally unjustified to ask for our help in 'getting out of a problem that we had got themselves into.' Bevin took offence more at the manner of delivery than the content and launched into an emotional tirade at Britain's courage in standing up against the world and the balance of power since. A veteran American diplomat who was present recorded the event; he looked at his strong leader and saw that he now had tears in his eyes. The decision was taken to do what was possible to help.[42] The following year, the US economy ran into a depression, causing concern for British exporters and placing more pressure on the pound. The alternative was deflation of an economy which was now beginning to prosper after the war or devalue. A sick and exhausted Stafford Cripps placed the choice before the Cabinet Committee, but it took another two months before they accepted devaluation with a requirement to agree with America on how far it should be devalued. With mediation from Canada, America agreed to the British terms: lower US tariffs, simplified customs procedures, more US investment abroad and more dollars in order to buy Canadian wheat under the Marshall Plan. In Bevin's mind the issue seemed to rest on the cost of a loaf for the British working man, eventually compromising by fixing a rate (£1 = $2.80) which would give a slight rise in the price of bread, but a guarantee that the loaves would be whiter![43n] At the end of September, Cripps broadcast to the nation, reassuring everyone that this was the only alternative to high unemployment and a cut back in welfare services. *The Manchester Guardian* reported the news with the comment that 'The first effect of devaluation on prices at home is that the 4d loaf will cost 6d.' (This is equivalent to 57p at today's prices.) This development would see the end of our severe post-war economic crises, providing industry increased production for export. Nine other countries devalued on the same day. In fact, austerity Britain had just got grimmer, the ancient class divisions between workers and bosses failed to match the challenge and in 1950 we embarked on another costly war in Korea.

Election

As time was running out for the Labour Government, thoughts turned to the date of the inevitable election. Attlee was advised to call it in the autumn of 1949 or the spring of 1950, but his extremely moral Chancellor Cripps refused to present an annual budget that would inevitably have to be popular whereas in reality the situation was bleak. For some time the government had been under pressure from left-wing Marxist academics, most noticeably Ralph Miliband[44n] of the LSE and the historian E. P. Thompson of Leeds. Thompson, together with intellectuals of all political persuasion, was working hard in extra-mural teaching and the Workers' Educational Association to make a range of exciting ideas available to people of all classes who lacked the requirements of university entrance. To their mind Labour had not been radical enough, for example nationalised industries had retained on their boards the very capitalists that were supposed to have been deposed.[45n]

Controversially, Attlee called the election for February 28th 1950, not a date to ease the general air of austerity and exhaustion or make voting easy. The campaign certainly lacked the fire and impact of a modern election. Mrs Attlee drove her husband around in their rather battered car and, while he made his speech, she sat quietly knitting. The most remarkable aspect of the campaign was the fact that the Conservative Party, still led by Churchill, never questioned any of the radical welfare state initiatives, thus marking a move to the central ground that would be a feature of British politics for many years. Their campaign rested on a promise to restore some nationalised businesses to the private sector, oppose the nationalisation of the sugar and cement industries which were next on Labour's agenda and to cut waste out of the new bureaucracy. The turnout was 84% and, despite boundary changes and adverse weather, Labour was returned but with their large majority reduced to five, although they had in excess of one million votes more than the Conservatives. Emerging from the first Cabinet meeting, Attlee was asked what new programme had been agreed. He seemed somewhat surprised by the question but replied, 'The result of the meeting? Oh, we're carrying on. That's all.'[46n]

It did not quite work out like that, but before the major political, economic and personal storms, a small but significant minor act of low terrorism held the headlines. On Christmas Eve 1950 Ian Hamilton and a small group of Scottish nationalists hid themselves in Westminster Abbey and 'stole' the Stone of Destiny (or Stone of Scone), thereby causing a national scandal. Apart from the shock of losing the stone upon which British kings and queens had been crowned since the Middle Ages, the act brought life back into the diminished Scottish nationalist movement. The group hid the stone until April 1951 when it was left in Arbroath Abbey from where the English police collected it.

As Scottish devolution was proposed, the stone was formally returned to Edinburgh Castle 'on loan.' It is due to be returned to Westminster for the next coronation. We shall see.

With the Education Act already in place, the government proceeded to enact the legislation that would build on the pre-war initiatives to establish the 'Welfare State.' These developments are probably best summarised chronologically.

WELFARE

The interval between the 1944 White Paper 'A National Health Service,' the Legislation of 1946 and the 'Appointed Day' of implementation in July 1948 was a period of conflict and controversy. The White Paper promised 'a publicly sponsored service ... available to all who want to use it.'[47n]

The service would be free to all, to be financed from taxation and would cover all services from the local general practitioner, dentists and community nurses to hospitals and medical consultants. This required a comprehensive organisation which would bring together the services previously run by local authorities, voluntary agencies, doctors and nurses, and had to include buildings owned by these various agencies, including local facilities often raised by public subscription as war memorials. A whole variety of vested interests were to challenge the proposals and the patience of Aneurin Bevan, the responsible government minister. Fortunately he was an able negotiator, blessed from his Welsh roots with an ability to deploy language imaginatively and persuasively and very determined to see his vision become reality. In many ways this was not so much a new initiative as one which drew on the experience of previous legislation and revisited all the arguments that had been voiced for many years. Bevan was driven by socialist principles, verging on Marxism, born of anger at the behaviour of exploitative private owners in the coal mines. Principal among these was the assumption that those working in a government agency would be paid civil servants subject to direction by politicians, and thus accountable to Parliament. This was a central tenet of Bevan's beliefs, even though he recognised that once established he would be called on to explain every mistake and accident anywhere, even 'every time a pail of slops is spilt.' This cut across the doctors' long-established practice as independent self-employed professionals.

Others feared the loss of the voluntary principle, one member of Parliament stating that the Act 'saps the very foundation on which our national character has been built.' The British Medical Association's house journal described the Bill as 'uncommonly like the first steps to National Socialism as practiced in Germany.'[48]

Concerned at the poor distribution of hospitals, particularly between better off rural areas and deprived city areas, Bevan responded that 'It was repugnant that medical care which of all things should be independent of means, should have to rely on charity ... We ought to have left the hospital flag days behind.' Bevan roused could lose some of his more diplomatic skills, and, as his argument with the medical establishment dragged on, suspicions and anger grew on both sides. Eventually mediators emerged and agreement was achieved. Bevan explained that as far as the doctors were concerned the only way he could get the Bill passed was to 'stuff their mouths with gold.' Nonetheless he was a generous enough politician to write a message of goodwill to doctors on the 'Appointed Day':

> There is no reason why the patient–doctor relationship should not be freed from the money factor, the collection of fees and thinking how to pay … My job is to give you all the facilities, resources and help that I can and then to leave you alone … to use your skill and judgement without hindrance.

By this time most of the doctors had joined the service and there were thirty million patients who had signed up using forms obtained at local Post Offices.

The huge popularity and early success of the NHS related to the fact that new treatments and techniques, both pre-war and from wartime practice, were now free. Hence, death from TB fell from 16% of all deaths in the mid 19th century to 0.1% by 1979. Immunisation for the greatest childhood killers of measles, whooping cough, diphtheria and scarlet fever quickly brought them under control, diphtheria falling from 47,000 cases in 1939 to 6 by 1967. When the polio outbreak hit in 1955, immediate vaccination brought the incidence down from 6,000 to 6 by 1970. In Glasgow our dear friend Iain Bryson graduated on the Appointed Day and recalled how many GPs and consultants were unhappy, partly because their income was severely reduced, a situation only partly rectified in 1953. Iain and his wife Moria moved to Lancashire, where Iain practised as a GP for forty years. Later, as a member of the Health Authority, he had many wonderful GP stories to tell.

Five issues would continue to haunt the service: the power of the medical profession; the principle that the service would be free at the point of delivery; the relationship between statutory and voluntary organisations (later to include private companies); the fundamental point that what had been created was a 'sickness' service not one that prioritised prevention and health; and the balance between management and those at the front line. It was confidently expected that once the initial rush was over, the cost would decrease as people were cured!

May 1944 had seen the publication of the White Paper 'Employment Policy,' which, in perhaps an overstated phrase, Beveridge described as marking 'an epoch in the economic and political history of Britain and so of the world.'[48] It was certainly remarkable in accepting the argument that economic recessions should not be left to work themselves out in accordance with market forces but rather that intervention would be 'a new responsibility of the state.' Thus the government committed itself to 'the maintenance of a high and stable level of employment.' The same year had seen the publication of a White Paper on Social Insurance, which had established the new Ministry of National Insurance. The 1946 National Insurance Act which, together with the National Assistance Act (1948), became effective in July 1948 extended the established provisions by introducing a broad subsistence level of benefit, linked to the rise in cost of living and fixed new rates for retirement pensions. The newly appointed Minister for Pensions, Hilary Marquand, declared that this was 'the best and cheapest insurance policy offered to the British people, or to any people anywhere.'

Although the cost of these benefits had, to some degree, to be paid for by increases in National Insurance contributions, the government rejected advice that pension payments should be delayed until the contributory funds had had time to accumulate, as was the case in any private scheme. Attlee insisted that the demands of the poor should take precedence over fiscal probity, a brave decision which of course led to a scheme which was chronically under-funded, a situation which would aggravate the whole basis of pensions provision for decades until, with increasing longevity coinciding with the global economic downturn of the early 21st century, unpopular decisions had to be faced in a crisis situation. This significant post-war legislation was passed with little controversy. While Sir Waldron Smithers could lament to the Commons that the Bill was 'against the natural law that if a man will not work neither shall he eat,' his fellow Conservative R. A. Butler was able to support a government that was able to show the world that, so soon after the war it could produce such a generous Bill. Attlee's approach to the cost of this Act, and in fact all welfare provisions, is illustrated by his contribution to the debate of this Bill in the Commons:

> The question is asked – can we afford it? Supposing the answer is 'no' – what does that mean? It really means that the sum total of the goods produced and the services rendered by the people of this country is not sufficient to provide for all our people all the times, in sickness, in health, in youth and age, the very modest standard that is represented [in this Bill]. I cannot believe that our national productivity is so slow, that our willingness to work is so feeble or that we can submit to the world that the masses of our people must be condemned to penury.[49]

The government urgently needed to solve the shortage of housing, resulting from an accumulation of pre-war economic depression and wartime bombing. In 1944, Churchill's coalition government had supplied pre-fabricated housing to replace bombed dwellings; some 150,000 of these homes were built and came to be known as the much loved 'prefabs,' often being cosier and easier to maintain than the old houses. These concerns, the wish to curtail profiteering by developers and a belief that good homes and infrastructure were essential to personal and economic health led to the Town and Country Planning Act of 1947, an initiative copied across the world and managed by Sam Silkin (MP for Peckham) as Minister for Housing. This nationalised all development rights and extended existing green belts around major cities and ten new towns. The target of 200,000 houses a year was never met; in fact, I don't think that any subsequent target has ever been met. Valiant efforts were made, but the chronic shortage of all materials, the lack of committed leadership (housing was part of the

Health Ministry, busily forming the NHS) and reliance on local authorities defeated this aspect of central planning. Surveys indicated that people would prefer houses to be in a planned environment with green spaces for recreation and industries at some distance. The rather paternalistic New Towns Committee, headed by Lord Reith, the legendary Director-General of the BBC, assumed that people would be healthier and happier away from the dark, dank and damaged inner cities, in new houses, with shops and schools in easy walking distance down leafy avenues. As it turned out, what most people missed was the close community ties in those inner cities, and the new towns would undergo some decades of social problems before settling into more mature communities.[50n]

FINANCE

The social programmes launched by the government, the ongoing battle with the domestic economy and several foreign challenges were all conducted with an elephant in the room: the fact that the country was broke. In addition, the government was committed to a programme of de-colonialisation. In February 1947, the Chancellor had demanded that no more financial aid could go to Greece and Turkey. The war had cost 25% of Great Britain's national wealth, and this percentage was increasing: while Great Britain may have been morally magnificent, economically the country was bankrupt. In August 1947, the Americans made a public announcement that Lend–Lease would end immediately; this came as a severe shock to both the British government and the American Embassy. It transpired that an official in the US Treasury had drawn the inexperienced President Truman's attention to the fact that the legal basis for the whole Lend–Lease programme ceased when hostilities ended. This was a severe, possibly fatal, blow for Attlee's government. Desperate negotiations persuaded America to cancel any debts that would accrue, to buy goods already in transit and to agree to sell off all the American equipment on British soil at a 90% discount. Only the economist Keynes retained any optimism, convinced that he could negotiate a loan of between 5 and 8 billion dollars on favourable terms, an amount that represented about a month's cost of the war for America. The Foreign Secretary Ernie Bevin thought he was deluded. Keynes set sail late in August and addressed the senior figures of the Federal Reserve in the pure gold of perfect English prose. His team could not help noting the contrast between bombed and battered London and untouched Washington. In a faultless Cambridge voice he described the vast complexities of the situation:

> … with the lucidity and good arrangement that only a master mind could have achieved. It was so easy and so light and sparkling, that there was never a dull moment. The most sympathetic and those least sympathetic, agreed on thinking that this was the finest exposition to which they had ever listened or were likely ever to listen.[51]

The expression 'fine words butter no parsnips' was almost borne out. Negotiations went on until November when an exhausted Keynes could see that, although he may not have saved Britain single-handed, he had at least bought time – he called it 'our financial Dunkirk.' The Americans finally agreed a loan of $3.75 billion (£1.7 billion, or £70 billion at current values) plus $650 million for the final payment of Lend–Lease commitments. The terms were that it would be interest and repayment free for five years, then incur 2% interest with repayment over fifty years. A supplementary loan of $2 billion was also made by Canada. The nasty sting in the tail was the stipulation that payment would be in dollars, and all holders of Sterling should be able to convert to dollars within a year. This was a dangerous requirement, and many in the Cabinet thought this less than generous from one victorious ally to another, but in reality there was no alternative but to accept. Many MPs who were ideologically opposed to extreme American capitalism resented the fact that the situation was being used to expand the American financial empire at the cost of our territorial one. The effect of this clause was to extend the loan when in 1949 we were forced to devalue Sterling; thus the end date of the loan was extended from 2002 to 2006. For the moment, the country was credit-worthy again. In 1950, when the first instalment was due, the national debt was 200% of GDP, but the government took a long view. Sixty years later, the credit crunch and the subsequent austerity measures were imposed; the figure was then 37%.

CULTURE

On the same day that Russia closed Berlin, June 22nd 1948, the HMT *Empire Windrush*, carrying 492 men from Jamaica and Trinidad, docked at Tilbury. These men came naively searching for a better life in the mother country, where, as British citizens, they had every right to reside.[52n] This was the first large-scale arrival of black colonial people, all of whom held a British passport. Largely unskilled, they were relatively unprepared for a damaged and impoverished Britain so far from the mythical ideal of the mother country that they had expected:

> The filthy tramp that eventually greets you is she. Ragged, old and dusty as the long dead. Mother has a black eye and bad breath, and one lone tooth in her head when she speaks. Can this be the fabled relation you heard so much of? … She offers you no comfort after your journey. No smile. No welcome. Yet she looks down on you through lordly eyes and says, 'Who the bloody hell are you?'[53]

Those *Windrush* passengers, who had no family or friendly address to go to, were accommodated in a tented camp on Clapham Common or in the Clapham Deep Shelter and were particularly welcomed by the Mayor of Brixton. Unfortunately, wherever they settled most encountered blatant racism, but they eventually found work and settled. Although the impact was local, I cannot remember it making any national impact, no general warning of problems to come. Britain had welcomed waves of immigrants, most recently Poles, who had fought with us, as had many of these men. As one of the passengers commented, 'Surely then, there is nothing against our coming here, for we are British subjects. If there is – is it because we are coloured?'

Although colour prejudice was rife in Britain, it certainly lacked consistency, as can be seen by the treatment of the two most prominent African American singers: the bass singer/actor Paul Robeson and the popular crooner William (Hutch) Hutchinson. Robeson, a dedicated anti-fascist with left-wing sympathies, had made his mark in the depression of the inter-war years, particularly with the miners of South Wales. He was a romantic figure for many British working-class families and was certainly lauded by my family for both his musical talents and political sympathies. Robeson came to support Stalin during the war, spent time in Moscow and entertained Allied troops throughout the world. His remarkable voice led to a very successful radio, concert and recording career, halted in 1949 when he was condemned by the McCarthy Committee on Un-American Activities.[54n] Based in England in 1950, but never accepted by the elite, he continued to tour the world in the 1959 Royal Shakespeare production of Othello. Unfortunately his health deteriorated, and in 1961 he was admitted to The Priory Hospital where he had 54 ECTs. In contrast, 'Hutch,' a smooth operating gigolo was quickly welcomed by the highest levels of society. He had sung to the troops at the D-Day embarkation points and recorded many 'pop' records. He dined at Quaglino's with Prince Charles and Princess Anne and was received by Prince Philip. He reputedly had an affair with the Duchess of Kent. However, his most notorious affair, which lasted for thirty years, was with Lady Edwina Mountbatten. The establishment, including the BBC, only dropped him once the affair became public knowledge. His career declined as The Beatles entered the charts, but by then he had gambled away most of his fortune.[55n]

Summer holidays brought the 'Austerity Olympics' held at Wembley Stadium and opened by the King and Queen at 4pm on July 29th 1948 accompanied by the release of 2,500 doves and a 21-gun salute. My brother and I greatly enjoyed it. Nearly 4,000 competitors (only 10% of whom were women) from 59 countries were housed in a variety of temporary accommodation and arrived for their event by any transport means available. Germany and Japan were not invited, and Russia chose not to take part, so America won the most medals. Great Britain won 23, only three of which were gold. I think our family went twice and were lucky enough to see the wonderful Dutch competitor Fanny Blankers-Koen win one of her four gold medals. My memory is that competitors got off a regular bus, walked on to the field, put on their running shoes and were off. We were also privileged to see the amazing Czech Emil Zátopek run the 10,000 metres.[56n] It was very exciting and reassuring that, in the face of so much hardship, such a wonderful event could be staged with such worldwide involvement.

SOCIAL WORK

March 1945 saw the establishment of a Committee of Inquiry into the care of children; this followed the January death in foster care of a thirteen-year-old Catholic boy, Dennis O'Neil, who had been subject to a regime of violence and neglect, having been placed in Shropshire as there were no Catholic families locally available in his home area. The Committee was chaired by Dame Myra Curtis, Principal of Newnham College, Oxford, and was the first formal national inquiry into a child's death in care. Over two hundred witnesses gave evidence, including the childcare experts John Bowlby (psychologist/child development expert), Susan Isaacs (educational psychologist/psychotherapist), Donald Winnicott (paediatrician/psychoanalyst) and Clare Britton (social worker/psychotherapist). The report of this committee identified over 100,000 children in need of placement in England and Wales. The report recommended that responsibility for deprived children, children's homes, boarding out, adoption and child life protection would be that of the local authorities, each of which would establish a Children's Committee to appoint a Children's Officer responsible for the organisation of services for each local community. If no placement were available with the same denomination, a child could be placed with a family outside their own religion. In 1947, a Central Training Council was established following the publication of the Committee's interim report. The quickly established one-year courses produced the first specialist qualified childcare staff in local authorities. Entry requirements were comparable to those for student teachers or health visitors. Students had to be 21 years of age or over and were selected centrally by representatives of the council, the Home Office and the college. By 1950, 211 women and 5 men were qualified, but after that the number of student places declined due to lack of demand by local authorities for trained staff. (I assume that they could get younger and cheaper untrained staff.)

The Children's Act of 1948 carried these initiatives into a generally welcomed law, stating that committees must show consideration for the best interests of the child and pay attention to their emotional and psychological needs as well as physical welfare. Such children must have the opportunity to mix with ordinary children. The emphasis therefore would be on adoption, boarding out (with visits at least every three months) or institutional care in family homes (maximum nine children) or small homes (fewer than 30 places). A circular issued jointly by the Ministries of Education and Health and the Home Office emphasised the need for co-operation between agencies in the case of children neglected or ill treated in their own homes.[57n] It should not be assumed that the departments thus established bear any resemblance to the children's departments known to most social workers today. Barbara Langridge, finding herself dissatisfied with her work as a factory inspector but moved to tears on reading the Curtis Report, determined to devote the rest of her life to that cause. In 1948 she was appointed as the first Children's Officer in Dudley, faced with the task of implementing the 1948 Act. In the small office allocated to her, she found piles of public assistance files relating to children, but she had no idea quite what to do. In due course, funding was found for a secretary and, in time, two further childcare officers and another clerk. All three officers committed themselves to exhaustingly long days, visiting children already in the care of families in the community, mostly to arrange admission to residential care as the Act made no provision for preventive work.

It was this that became a major preoccupation for the rest of Barbara's long and distinguished career. In 1951 Barbara was appointed to lead the Children's Department in Oxfordshire. Here she encountered initial resistance from the more conservative councillors, who either regretted that children in care should be given ice-cream or had difficulty appreciating why such care should be given to children having a rough time because no one had helped them. Barbara took an early decision which stood her in good stead for the next twenty years in office. She had, she told me, to make a choice between 'being a nice girl or a battle-axe; a nice girl they would pat on the head and ignore; a battle-axe would give them a bit of trouble and they would have to think twice before they dismissed what I said. I chose the latter, what else could I have done if I wanted to achieve anything.' Once established, Barbara became nationally influential in the campaigns to develop preventive work, which she developed in Oxfordshire by appointing specialist social workers to work with 'problem families' and to have properly qualified staff in residential homes. Barbara was influenced by the pioneering work of John Bowlby on the effect of maternal deprivation on young children. In 1955 Barbara married a friend of Bowlby's, Vladimir Kahan, who headed the county's Child Guidance Service. Together they formed a powerful campaigning team from their lively home.[58n] Whilst Barbara Kahan's impact was being felt in the county, Oxford City appointed Lucy Faithfull as Children's Officer in 1958 (she subsequently became the first female Director of Social Services). Although equally powerful in improving services, she was a less extrovert personality than Barbara Kahan. To say that a degree of rivalry developed would be an understatement. In addition to work in the preventive field, Lucy worked intensively with 'battered babies' who were placed with foster carers, the development of which allowed Oxford to close its residential nurseries. As was to be expected in the culture of the time, nearly all the appointments were female. Another powerful woman in Oxfordshire was Barbara Docker-Drysdale, who, with no formal training but wartime experiences with children, opened the Mulberry Bush School in 1948 which provided an intense residential caring environment for severely troubled young children, an establishment still operating today. Docker-Drysdale later qualified as a psychotherapist, working with Donald Winnicott and later Richard Balbernie to develop the Cotswold Community for older children in Wiltshire, which closed in 2011.

Social workers, however loosely defined, had worked at the front line throughout the war. They helped to manage the vast problems posed by children and families uprooted from their home communities, they supported children who had been orphaned or abandoned and they worked with those children and adults hospitalised for physical or mental illnesses. They had little time for contemplation. In the post-war period the profession turned to issues of development and training in addition to finding itself embedded in newly created state structures of welfare, childcare and health, where a whole variety of local and charitable organisations had been swept up into the new NHS. Although there was no longer any need for the almoner to assess the economical means of patients, the standing of hospital social workers increased with the acceptance of the new service. Social work was becoming state social work, although personal concerns were still at the fore. In 1948, a newly qualified almoner at St Thomas's Hospital, Cicely Saunders, cared for and fell in love with a dying Polish patient who had escaped from the Warsaw Ghetto. He left her £500, and her later work in a home for the dying led her to qualify as a doctor. Subsequently specialising in pain control, she opened St Christopher's Hospice, the first purpose designed hospice in the world, to meet the physical, social, psychological and spiritual needs of her patients.

The settings within which most social work was practised had dramatically changed, although the influence of the voluntary agencies, particularly the Family Service Units and the Family Welfare Association, remained significant. There was much discussion therefore about the particular contributions from and the role of social workers as opposed to the administrator of welfare. Possibly now that most social workers were employed by central or local government, they were all primarily just civil servants. In the early 1950s a symposium organised by the Association of Psychiatric Social Workers addressed this issue with presentations from Pauline Shapiro and Miss Hope Wallace from the National Assistance Board. The conclusion seems to have been that, while they had much in common, the prime accountability of the social worker was to the client, whereas that of the administrators was to the employer. Professional social work was additionally characterised by specialist knowledge of both society and individual functioning, full recording, regular supervision and commitment to research.[59]

THE FAMILY

John

Some idea of the strange life led by John and his fellow Dragoons can be gleaned from his diary and letters home. The whole Palestinian scenery clearly appealed to him after so much fighting in Europe: 'Can you wonder why I went so nuts from the mountains overlooking Galilee! It's a good thing that we only want to remember the good and beautiful things in our life.' He sympathised with the reduced bread ration at home and contacted film companies to seek employment as a sound engineer; in this connection he started a correspondence course with BIET.[60] He sent supplies home, including batches of soap and tobacco. Various schemes were available to ex-servicemen, and mother took it upon herself to phone the Ministry for advice for when her son came home. I remember standing outside the telephone box when a very angry and tearful mother came out. They had run through a list of options, but particularly suggested that training as a butcher would be a good job. That anyone should propose such a thing for her gentle boy was too much. She screamed down the phone: 'You've spent four years making him into a butcher, that's the last thing we need!' In October John recorded a visit to Nazareth ('wonderful singing – first time out for months. NAAFI – nice to be with civilians ... not forgetting the 100 Polish girls neat and prim dressed in ATS uniforms and attending the convent next door ... they had strict orders not to speak or have anything to do with British Soldiers, which, on second thoughts, is a very wise instruction.') He and his group waited anxiously for a definite date for a return home and final demobilisation. News of trouble during the split between India and Pakistan elicited fear that their engagement would be further prolonged. As time dragged on, he clearly became more resentful of the army and increasingly found consolation in the Christian heritage surrounding him. His mates looked to him as, close to the adjutant, he should have been a source of information. He records that, 'all I ever find in his pockets are £5 notes!' John found some relief in ENSA shows: 'good, except half the place reserved for the lords and sergeants, but a tonic to see a few white girls tap sentimental songs and a wink – wonderful.' Horlicks was on offer every night. Others felt the strain. A comrade wrote to our mother:

> I must say that I only have John to thank for keeping my mind active and a genuine interest in my career. Several times when Army life became a little overpowering, he helped me to take an interest again. He has been and will always be my firm friend. I hope, and I no doubt you pray, that John will soon be home to stay, and with your guidance, he cannot fail to reach his ambitions.

At Christmas John got on a Music Harmony, History and French course at Carmel College, Haifa. His report said, 'This student has worked steadily and intelligently at all times and produced some very good work.' During the winter months he read books by Lloyd C. Douglas, a writer of novels based on Christian stories.[61n] As part of organised tour groups he visited Jerusalem, Bethlehem, Gethsemane and the Church of the Nativity – noting 'magnificent gold carvings sent by the Czar of Russia, lace of the veils carved so delicately, 6 pictures 2 inches thick solid 18ct gold … Bought bible delicately inlaid with pearl, fascinating bazaars.' He brought home an olive leaf memento and the pearl Bible for me. These more peaceful experiences, a sharp contrast to his battles in Europe, seem to have deepened his Christian belief and, I think, helped him overcome some of the terrible traumas he must have experienced in Europe. He would follow Christianity, mostly through music, for the rest of his life. In the meantime, he was still far from safe. His diary clearly illustrates the situation:

> College truck blown up on mountain road, it appears that terrorists escaped through our camp … Tom and Harry return from HQ, fired on, returned fire … Two dances held in main building. Burnt down our first night on guard. Move to Hadera Jewish settlement.
> Chap blown up on perimeter wire.
> [March] GOC visits camp [for about 15 mins]. Band of 'Loyals' in Naafi solo cornet plays 'American Patrol' … Officer killed in Club … many trucks and jeeps blown up … Corporal K and Hutchinson killed … We now have hedgehog as pet … £14,000 robbery in Tel Aviv: Naafi on fire. Camp attacked at midnight. Bomb throwers shooting at searchlights near loo!
> [April] Terrorist executed. On way for shower in bath-house got mixed up with terrorist incident – shooting of two policemen.

This was certainly different from armoured warfare against a clear enemy but was much more in common with the situations that the British soldier would have to face as colonies fought for independence right up to the campaigns in Iraq and Afghanistan.

In between such events there were periods of leave in Nathanya Leave Camp; these were relaxed but still military. The brochure that John sent home announced: 'Breakfast 07.30/08.30 Lunch 12.30/13.30 Tea 1700/1800. Sheet stealing is prevalent – lock them up or pay. The keynote of your stay is freedom and complete absence of any bovine tendencies.' Here he enjoyed the entertainment: 'Amazing hypnotist show, laughed so much held my side for an hour.' He was volunteered to play for a show which included the budding comedian Arthur English (then a Sergeant in B Company 4/7th Dragoons). Arthur endorsed the programme 'Thanks John for Everything.'[62n]

Visiting The Tel Aviv camp and workshops manned by Arab civilians, John noted:

> … these people are the ones that are really getting terrorized, they are in constant fear of the terrorists, especially the girls and know that they cannot trust the best of friends. They also fear the military and are well disciplined inside the camp. Which obedience I might add is often taken advantage of – i.e. being told to walk not run and take their hat off when speaking to military personnel and it makes the British soldier feel almighty for once.

As John and the rest of his draft started packing, he watched sympathetically as raw new recruits arrived straight from Catterick. (No doubt to the routine challenge from old timers to 'get your knees brown.') The new officers and NCOs were determined to give them a dog's life to break them in. He mused, 'They are all young and have plenty of spirit which they will soon lose … makes me wonder how I did it.' John reports that one recruit was already in jail following a kit inspection, which he reported thus:

> QMS (detestably ignorant individual) shouts: 'Shirts' (meant to be a question)
> Recruit: 'Two.'
> QMS 'Two what' (expecting 'Sir!')
> Recruit 'Two bloody shirts!'
> Exit recruit between two burly soldiers.

Excitement grew as the next five days were spent 'packing and counting (Must remember to say "Two, Sir!")':

> Oh what a funny world. I feel very happy tonight. I shall be trying to control my feelings for the first few days on the boat … Terry went to demob today and it made me very bolshie to see him go … I really get fed up with the present job although it allows me plenty of time and comparative freedom I still feel like throwing his water at him one morning … Give me my ticket and let us get on our way.[63n] This month I will start chucking kit. Who worries? I should care. I'll catch the first boat out next month and catch the rain showers in May.

By Easter the group was demob happy, with just two weeks and six days to go. John resolves, 'I will certainly give New Cross 2000 a call once I get my land legs back. It will be the first thing I do.'[64n]

John embarked at Suez on April 27th 1947 and arrived at Southampton nine days later, thence to camp and was finally demobilised on May 8th 1947. His testimonial read:

> 'Driver Operator' Conduct: Exemplary Served throughout the North West Europe campaign as a member of a tank crew, has since been employed as a batman. He is a smart, trustworthy and loyal soldier. He can drive a vehicle. He can be left to work on his own and he will do the job well and conscientiously. CO A Sqd. 4/7th RDG.

John returned home with the usual three medals and, in common with all such soldiers, was to be held in the Army Reserve until June 30th 1959. His active service had cost him 4 years and 249 days of his life, but he was alive and, thankfully, fit.

My long trek to school had been eased by the arrival of a wonderful bicycle for my 13th birthday. On this I could practise all sorts of tricks and imagine myself as the messenger getting across enemy terrain with the vital message that would save the world! Returning home one evening from the local fish and chip shop, I suspect that I was practising the 'no hands balancing act,' when the front wheel hit a brick and I was catapulted over the handlebars and landed an undignified bleeding mess on the road. Supper was a bit gritty that night. There then came the long awaited day when John was to be demobbed and would be home late in the afternoon. In keeping with the traditions of the time I made a great 'Welcome Home John' board hung in front of the house with floodlighting and my old wooden fort in the small front garden. So proudly did I cycle back from school, persuading a friend to come and admire my handiwork. Mum describes the occasion:

> ... but John arrived early enough to change the John to Malcolm. We watched Malcolm's expression as he cycled up to the house and stood reading the greetings, then hearing John's laughter, with one big long bound he flung himself on him in one big welcoming hug ... We were a family again.[65]

This was, of course, a good reason for a family celebration, which followed the usual pattern of chat, gallons of tea, sandwiches and cake, and John invited Den Hagens and his lovely family.[66n] There was an added dimension as, by now, Dad's nephew Harry Oliver had introduced his new German bride Erna, a very nice, jolly girl who quickly joined in the celebrations and came to be an integral part of the family. While in Palestine, Den and John had developed an act as four hands on a piano; they were very impressive and hugely entertaining. So this was an addition to the usual round of songs, which often started with a group sing song including 'The Man Who Broke The Bank At Monte Carlo' or the more recent 'Daddy Wouldn't Buy Me A Bow Wow,' followed by a small piano piece from me, a performance by Uncle Ernie on his musical saw, then Aunt

Maud would bring her gift to an emotional rendition of Rose's 'Macushla,' Stuart's 'The Lily Of Laguna' and if we were lucky Arthur Sullivan's 'The Lost Chord.' More chat might then be followed by 'Let's All Go Down The Strand' and ending inevitably on 'There'll Always Be An England.' As exhaustion set in there was washing up to do, definitely the men's job, and by now it was my privilege to be counted in. Uncle Jim would normally start washing while one or more of us dried and others stacked. News and views would be exchanged through the ever present cigarette smoke. Extreme and enjoyable bonding. Not long afterwards John and Den were persuaded to enter a national talent competition held at the Trocadero Cinema at the Elephant and Castle. Although they were as brilliant as ever and the music went down well, they had no amplification so did not get the applause required to move through to the next level. Oranges, rare and expensive items, had started appearing in the shops, but John, unaware of austerity Britain and used to an ample and cheap supply in Palestine, proceeded to break the bank by blissfully eating several a day. No one said a word.

Naturally enough, John, who was still on the reserve list and liable to be called up any time for Korea, found the adjustment to civilian life quite difficult, especially as he did not have a clear idea of a career. He eventually decided that, having started the technicians' course, he would pursue a career in the film industry as a sound technician. He drifted a bit in civilian life, at first using his BIET studies to get a job in the sound department of Pathe Pictorial in central London at £5 per week. This proved quite a challenge, not least because his immediate boss was a notorious practical joker; consequently, a whole series of disasters would delay production, once causing a power cut throughout Soho. John quite treasured the reference he got when dismissed because 'his bent does not lie in the direction of electro-mechanical work.' There being no shortage of jobs in the expanding British film industry, he joined the sound technicians at the Pinewood and Elstree Studios, busily producing classic comedies and first-rate dramas, among which were *The Red Shoes* (with Moira Shearer), David Lean's *Oliver Twist* (with Alec Guinness and Robert Newton) and *The Blue Lagoon* (with Jean Simmons), a daring but discrete story, as the censor was always watching, about two child castaways discovering sex. This was a pretty fun time and we were invited to summer garden parties to meet his colleagues and some of the stars. He lost his job in February 1949 when, through no fault of his own, he was made redundant.[67n]

Unfortunately, John seemed to lose his motivation and stopped the long pursued BIET course about two months before he would have got an excellent qualification in sound technology. His enjoyment of the cinema thereafter was limited by his knowledge of what was going on just off the screen – occasionally he would spot the sound boom inching into a frame. His ambitions now returned to music and in 1949 he easily passed the higher grade 5 exam in pianoforte of the Guildhall School of Music. His next work was as college secretary at the City Day College, which trained printers in the complicated techniques of 'setting' lead print blocks ready for printing. The college was just north of Smithfield meat market, so we got a daily report of the state of the meat trade and the antics played by the porters on passers-by. It particularly amused John that most mornings he would pass racks of newly roasted chicken out to cool on a low rack on the pavement, easily in reach of any passing dogs that managed to lift their leg before being chased away. Once cold they were put in bags marked 'untouched by human hand!' Although the College Principal spoke enthusiastically of him as 'a valuable and agreeable colleague in every way,' the job proved less than satisfying but, having worked in an educational establishment, he decided to become a qualified teacher. Late in 1949 therefore he enrolled in the two-year emergency teacher training course at Goldsmiths College, taking advantage of a wartime regulation that enabled ex-servicemen admission without the ordinary entrance requirements. This was an enjoyable time for John; he enjoyed the work and had found his calling, specialising in music and religious education with sport as a secondary subject. He appeared in a great production of *The Mikado* and mastered the great organ that dominated the college's Great Hall.

Gran

Gran had returned to an upstairs flat in Ivydale Road, just round the corner from our house, where she maintained a friendly but often strained relationship with her landlady, Betty. She would regularly bring round the current copy of *Old Moore's Almanac*, an astrological magazine which, apart from some useful information, predicted world and local events month by month. It was then approaching its 250th birthday and is still published annually. Having at some stage in its long history managed to make a true prediction, apparently it could now be relied upon despite the vagueness of the wording. Faced with a major problem Gran would usually say 'Let's see what Old Moore says.' I once showed her how the like poles of a magnet would repel each other and invited her to hold the two magnets. She was horrified that this was some form of strange witchcraft.

A cause for great excitement was the proposed visit by Gran's brother Charlie and his wife Chris from America. I was amazed by Charlie's striking physical resemblance to Gran, and he had the same wonderful sense of humour combined with the great feeling of open warmth that was characteristically American. I do not know whether they had thought of returning home, but it was not to be. They were taken aback by the austerity of the time and very evident signs of bombing and destruction. In addition, they were often confronted with the anti-Americanism stemming from resentment at their late entry to the war and their assumed feeling of superiority now that the UK's 'natural' place in world affairs was being lost. They took a very early flight home.

School

Haberdashers' Aske's Hatcham Boys School stands in South London at the top of the steep hill that separates the industrial and traffic noise of New Cross from the quieter but mixed social strata of Nunhead and Brockley (its title is also a lesson in the use of the apostrophe).[68n] In the main hall were displayed the honours boards naming those who had achieved academic scholarships to Oxford or Cambridge or sporting prowess in rugby or cricket. They seemed to me to be mere decoration, quite unconnected with the small band of returned evacuees that the headmaster Richmond Coggan taught with such gentle care. In fact, we very soon discovered that the tiresome business of French grammar could be stopped by diverting him to his great love, which was philately. One result of this is my collection, full of stamps that he sold us on the understanding that their value would rise exponentially. Not so! As I had no idea even of what a university was for, let alone how you got to into one, it all seemed rather pointless.

These tranquil times soon ended on one Monday morning in September 1945, when the main school, with Nick Goddard as Head, returned from evacuation in Devon. I have a clear memory of the day when the school was first full of hundreds of boys who knew each other through their shared experience of evacuation. I was seated at the desk immediately in front of the door (more indication of naivety) when suddenly the door opened with a bang. In strode a large boy in a striped red, white and blue blazer who brought down his cane hard on my desk. This was the School Captain, not a beast I had ever met before, although had I read anything that a 'normal' boy read I would have immediately recognised a figure straight out of *Tom Brown's Schooldays* and would have had some indication of what lay ahead. I, of course, had no idea what was in store. Masters seemed remote as they swept through corridors in black gowns. Discipline was largely delegated to senior prefects who exercised it through a series of ritualised punishments, often of the painful physical kind. Lessons were of course aimed at the able and well prepared, those who at least knew what the game was.

Those who fell to the bottom were ignored. It slowly dawned on me that you were supposed to join this school knowing why and where you wanted to go. This was no great problem for the majority of my peers as they came from families where progression to university and into a profession were taken for granted as a feature of everyday life. The teamwork of the builder labourers mixing concrete by hand to rebuild the school dining room, which had been flattened by a bomb, appealed to me greatly, but when I later gave this as a possible career choice it was treated with disdain. (Of course, had I done well in the post-war building trade I could probably have retired in comfort at an early age.) The truth was that I naturally understood these men; consequently, as far as the masters and my fellow pupils were concerned, I was an outsider looking in, searching faces and eyes to see what went on in their heads that made them what they were, seemingly so confident and assured in their identity and goals.

I could be and frequently was pulled up for displaying the 'wrong attitude' or behaviour, but it took me many years to find out what the right thing was. Somehow we reached a point where the price of school uniform demanded by the official tailor was too high and so improvisations had to be made; also deprived of any recognition I took to wearing badges from the Butlins holiday camps that John and I had been to. All very much disapproved of. There were many unhappy years ahead before these problems were anywhere near managed, and by then it was too late. I had become the outsider, never able to get inside the close interaction of my peers or those who held the secrets of the culture into which I had been cast. I never remember going to another pupil's home during my whole school career and envied the boys who would tell dirty stories that they had been told by their dads. Just how did that ever happen?[69n]

My lack of primary education had been exacerbated by joining classes in the spring term of 1945, halfway through the school year. A variety of subjects which I had never come across in these discrete forms had to be picked up with no basis for comprehension. English was embarked upon without any knowledge of the basic structures of the language, grammar, syntax or spelling. This vacuum also carried forward to French or German, where I was completely lost without any essential framework. It may be possible to study the past subjunctive of a French verb, but the task is near impossible if you do not know basic written English! The situation was not helped by the fact that German was taught using the old Gothic script.

The report at the end of the first full year was a call to hard work and concentration. My solution was to learn what I could by rote and then surf across the task of putting things together with a mixture of bravado and declared ignorance, the latter always being dismissed with complete scorn by the masters. Something must have worked as by July 1947 I was 9th in a class of 32. There was talk of potential, if only I could do a bit more serious work. There were many disasters when I failed to realise the level of expertise that my classmates had. When the music master called for anyone who could play the piano to accompany group singing, I volunteered on the basis of my many months of elementary piano lessons. I followed the music slowly and not without a few wrong notes. I was summarily replaced by a pupil who I had not realised was already giving classic performances in public![70n] The lesson was, stay in the back row and don't ever volunteer again.

Mathematics and sciences were easier as I could share the start of a new subject or phase. Over time, I must have learned something as I usually came out with average marks in the A or B streams. By the summer of 1948 words like 'very good' appeared next to some subjects, but I note with interest that my form master thought me 'very capable' but warned that I should 'guard against lapses.' This was perceptive as a slight swing between over activity and short spells of depression have caused minor problems throughout my life. However, this only gained the disapproving nickname of 'Master Middling Malcolm' from mother. I assume that my part in the great plan was not moving forward as fast as she had intended, or perhaps she had really believed that phrenologist. My failure to comprehend the skills and rules of any sport was a more significant failure in a school devoted to rugby and cricket and where recognition depended on achievement in these areas.

I do believe that I would have made an excellent athlete given half a chance, but once marked out as marginal in 'games' it seemed impossible ever to regain any recognition. Basically, the whole ethos of individual competition with the objective of beating everybody else in sight was so alien to my own family ethos that the conflict, unrecognised and unmentioned, was getting out of hand as I became increasingly introverted, unhappy and quietly distressed. Shyness, the physical build of a beanpole and tight dark curls (the constant taunt of 'a touch of the tar brush') made me an easy target for constant teasing and regular painful bullying. Approaching 14 and 6 feet tall, I was otherwise a late developer. The terrors on the sports field or gym were nothing compared with the perplexity facing me in changing rooms and group showers. My fellow pupils seemed to be broader, more assured in their masculinity and proud of their new body hair. Deprived of the Biblical comfort that 'My bother Esau is a hairy man but I am a smooth man,' I suffered considerably.[71]

Absence

I must have realised that something was amiss. Adolescence or the hidden strain from living in two completely unconnected worlds must have told, and, for whatever reason, I embarked upon a long episode of truanting or school refusal as it would be termed today. This started easily enough with a few odd days, usually sports or gym days, then progressed by degrees until my absence was permanent and involved daily trips to central London. Although much time was spent in the dirty and disreputable Soho area, it speaks volumes that I had no idea what it was that I was searching for. The only occasion one of the ladies loitering on the curb showed interest, I ran like a hare. Had I had the time to continue my explorations in the evenings I might have discovered the bohemian side of Soho life, the jazz clubs and pubs where new writers George Orwell, Dylan Thomas and many others held court. Unfortunately my adventures were made possible by the fact that both parents and brother John were out at work. I was the last to leave and the first home each day, a so-called 'latch key' child. Occasionally I would treat myself to a cinema visit, once to a 'health and efficiency' film, the nearest one could get to seeing partly naked women.[72n] The last film I saw during one of these absences was Powell and Pressburger's *The Small Back Room*, a gripping drama about bomb disposal, the one and only time in an empty cinema that a man made a point of sitting next to me and keeping his leg uncomfortably close to mine.

Innocence seems to have saved the day and I returned home to be met with the fact that a small bomb had indeed been let off as my dishonest absence from school had been discovered, as had the long series of forged letters sent copying Dad's copperplate writing and signature explaining my various illnesses, together with the misuse of dinner money and various other funds. Great upset ensued, and I was sent back to school with a grovelingly apologetic letter and a slim hope of not being expelled on the spot. Strangely enough, my school reports for this year are missing.[73n] It says a great deal about the school and the headmaster, Nick Goddard, that I was kept on, but by this time my work was so far behind that despite major efforts I was destined for the 'Remove' stream. Any attempt at enthusiasm in class only served to alienate me further as the epithet 'slime' was levelled at anyone who actually showed interest or asked an intelligent question.

Hospital

Soon after this event, a swelling in my neck was diagnosed as tubercular, but at least this enabled my poor mother to rationalise my appalling and deceitful behaviour as the hidden onset of a serious illness. Fortunately, penicillin had just become available and the NHS was now in place, so my life was not seriously threatened. I did however have to go for removal of the gland into King's College Hospital on Denmark Hill where I could witness the working of a democratic health service at first hand.[74n]

The admitting consultant told my mother in no uncertain terms that he was far more worried by the state of her health than mine, an opinion that she totally ignored. At the age of 14, time in the men's ward brought me straight up against serious illness, old age and death. Despite the very large swelling on my neck, I did not feel particularly unwell so enjoyed helping out with some domestic chores or wandering round the hospital in my dressing gown. Both activities attracted the wrath of Matron, that most feared of hospital nurses. My condition was apparently a bit of a rarity. I was therefore sent to central London and used as a test case for doctors seeking promotion. I was examined by the supervising consultants, for it was explained that by this means I would get the opinion of the top medical brains in Britain. After the operation, with the added diagnosis of 'undernourished,' I was sent to a quiet convalescent home near Camberley in Surrey for several weeks. There my daily dose of cod liver oil and malt was poured straight down the drain while yards of green bandaging were pulled out of the hole in my neck. When it stopped being green, I was ready to go home! I did however gain a mild flirtation with one of the young nurses who could then be employed at the age of 16. She seemed to enjoy tucking me in every night. I had no objection at all.

After a three-month break, it was back to school. The fact that I was still not functioning normally was brought home when, in company with another boy, we stretched a wire across the door through which we knew the next master always entered in a rush. Decapitation was narrowly avoided, but the most shameful part of this was that the master in question, A. K. Adams, suffered from a bad attack of Bell's palsy so was often the subject of disrespect. About this time I witnessed a highly distressing scene when a very well built boy, driven to the point of frustrated tears by a teacher's snide remarks about his mother, came very close to hitting out. I met him later when he was administering the IQ tests at army call up and, if my memory is correct, he hit the headlines later by successfully challenging a serious charge of damaging US planes armed with atomic weapons by arguing that he was making UK citizens safer. The case got to the House of Lords where the case was lost.

My recollection of the years from 1945 to 1950 are a strange mixture of close involvement with the extended family and wider social events and relative detachment from my own development in school. The fact that a casual observer might have come to the opposite view would have been due to my chronic shyness and lack of ability to communicate (in any event I had no language that I could use) and the fact that nothing of any consequence was ever discussed within the family. Dad may collapse midway through his evening meal. Mother may be ill with exhaustion from the effort required to run the house and walking or cycling nearly four miles to a full day's work as well as keeping up intensive links with the extended family in London and abroad. John may be the prime target for a terrorist bullet in Palestine. And my hormones might be doing the strangest things. Nothing was ever said. Cups of tea ('a pot every hour on the hour' was the family motto) and denial was relied upon in a display of sangfroid that was both admirable and frustrating.

Sex

Sex in the 1940s was a slow and mysterious thing, at least in an all boys' school. Natural curiosity led to comparisons between belly buttons (whose stuck out, whose went in?). As time passed and, in an American phrase, 'the gonads start sizzling,' investigations inevitably moved south to see if the same strange things were happening. Eventually a 'boy who knew' told us 'the facts of life,' which of course none of us could believe! I have a clear memory of a rainy lunchtime in a classroom when 'a boy who really knew' was trying to explain the basics in as sensitive a way as he could manage to a shy rather religious boy who just could not accept any of it; he just howled as if the whole basis of his life had just been destroyed. How could our parents do that! There could not be a clearer illustration to be made between then and now on the whole issue of sexual understanding, and behaviour. The only way forward from here was to check it out by trying to link together the 'facts' with other rude words and head for the library as a group, where, of course, there were no directly relevant books so we could only resort to finding 'rude' words in the dictionary, which left quite a lot out.[75n] Commentators have seen the withholding of information from girls and boys as deliberate strategies to prolong innocence as a valued social asset, although the boys were expected to actively puzzle their way through the public blanket of silence as a path to manhood. So that's what we were doing! Final confirmation came a short while later when, attending a cadet camp at the Tower of London, we looked over the parapet to see thousands of used condoms floating in the river. So it all really happened![76n]

The most reserved of my close relatives was my father's sister Elsie, her husband Harry and their son Tony, all of whom were deeply involved in the Methodist Church. About this time, during a visit to see them their small terrier dog was apparently so pleased to greet me that it jumped up, took firm hold of my genitals and swung about! It was eventually dislodged amid apologies from its owners and my false assurances that no harm had been done. Even worse was the fact that on our return home my mother insisted on inspecting the damage for fear of rabies or whatever. I could wish no more embarrassing episode on any adolescent boy! One consequence of this was a fear of dogs, many of which laid in wait for me on the long walk to school and back. I never did grasp the fact that the faster I ran the more the dog enjoyed the chase.

Teachers

In school my academic potential had gone from mediocre to disastrous, but luckily two things changed this downward course of action. One was the master in charge of the 4th Remove, P. A. Brown (PAB), whose subject was Geography. A disadvantage of the 'Remove' was that you had no form room but were lodged anywhere a few desks could be found. This was a most painful experience as it emphasised my isolation. I had nothing in common with the other boys in that room, but just longed for them to take some notice of me. Mr Brown taught his subject in a darkened and heated room partly to ward off his frequent bouts of malaria. The whole tropical atmosphere was enhanced by the lingering cornflour odour of mass solo or mutual masturbation once the room was blackened for slide shows. This master taught well and had the true teacher's gift of bringing out hidden strengths in his pupils. If, for example, we were learning about the Yorkshire coal mines we would all be forced to lay under the benches with our hands pressed hard up against the underside until the arm muscles were exhausted. We would then be allowed up to be told how real miners felt having to work in this position for many hours each day.

As nationalisation of the coal mines was on the agenda, PAB staged a debate and I was called upon to put the case for nationalisation. I prepared hard for this, got all sorts of leaflets and posters and wiped the floor with my opponent. One short excursion into politics and perhaps an early career opportunity never followed up. The word must have gone out that one delinquent had been saved as the headmaster was invited to witness the follow up debate. He never came. PAB had seen it all and I have a clear memory of him explaining Britain's place in the world. We are, he explained, 'like a lion which allows all sorts of parasites and smaller animals to peck at its coat or live off its body with comparative equanimity. It would rather sleep than fight, but once eventually roused beware all other animals.' Great stuff for young Empire builders.

The Army Cadet Force

Such a short time after the war, and still in the age when everyone did as they were told, it was a common practice in grammar and public schools that at the age of 14 all boys must join the school Cadet Corps. Drill was seen as a virtuous activity, and in any event it was important to keep up the flow of recruits to the officer class especially as the prospect of a Korean war was threatening. At Aske's it was the army cadets, and the regiment was the Royal Fusiliers, the fruits of the shooting club started by Richmond Coggan in 1912. In those post-war years, with so much khaki still in evidence and the knowledge that all young men would have to undergo National Service, the fact that one afternoon a week plus weekends and summer camps would be devoted to this activity by some 300 lads was quite normal and natural. Much to my surprise I quite enjoyed this activity. In retrospect I think it was the fact that this was the first activity where we all started from the same point, helped by the anonymity of the uniform. With the energy and obsessionalism that was an early indicator of things to come, it became my 'big thing,' although quite why this should be the case I did not then realise. Something about the clear structure of military life and the combination of obedience and loyal service certainly appealed to me. There were well structured examinations in an interesting range of subjects, and I progressed well in both theory and practice and gained promotion apace. Although never entirely sold on the military machine, I certainly enjoyed the majesty of drill, field exercises and manoeuvres when there was much rolling around in the dirt, perhaps a reminder of those wild days in Hertfordshire. Certainly, when it came to call up time the infantry would ensure that we stayed out in the open where there was some chance of using one's own initiative to keep alive, not inside a tank where one shell could turn those trapped inside to minced meat, the horror scene that had played in my head all through John's war. If death came, I would yield more readily to mother earth. I had two more years to redeem myself at Aske's, and this happier time is covered in the next chapter.

Domesticity

In our small front room we continued to listen to the BBC News, the wonderful comedy of *It's That Man Again* (ITMA) and its catch phrases ('Can I do you now sir?' from the char lady and 'I don't mind if I do' from the alcoholic colonel), and the nightly adventures of *Dick Barton – Special Agent*. A daytime alternative was *Mrs Dale's Diary*, a glimpse into the adventures of a nice middle-class doctor's family, or *Woman's Hour*.[77n] John would be practising piano pieces, often in preparation for the Saturday night dance that his band had been booked for. Dad would be completing the leather bound accounts book in which he recorded, in his beautiful copperplate handwriting, the subscriptions to the Vent-Axia Sports Club. Alternatively, he would be gently pedaling away at the fretsaw to make the most detailed and wonderful cut-out designs in thin plywood. An inevitable consequence of following the thin lines drawn painstakingly on the wood was the need to blow away the fine sawdust that built up every few seconds. In time all the surrounding surfaces were covered in a thin layer of dust! Further work meant preparing the glue, sheets of solidified fish bones that were boiled up and smelled disgusting. Application required clamping for 24 hours to set – a far cry from modern instant bonds. If anyone's shoes had worn through, out would come the iron last and new leather soles would be glued and tacked in place. Why pay for anyone else to do it? If our bikes needed stripping down to repair, into the living room they came!

My financial skills were confined to counting out the thin tin replica coins handed out by the Co-op shop on every purchase. These were then paid in to the 'divi book,' which was both a token of your involvement in the Co-operative scheme and could be used as a discount on future purchases. Dealing with these and ration coupons made shopping quite complicated. Mother, having finished all the domestic chores, would either be ironing (a hot iron being heated on the stove for the purpose), knitting sweaters of extraordinary design or writing letters to members of the extended family across the world. Apart from the inevitable homework done or not, in all this business I would most likely be found making a fragile model aeroplane from thin balsa wood and tissue paper, the whole thing being powered by an elastic band. These were usually about 18 inches long with a 24 inch wingspan. Once assembled, the whole structure had to be coated with 'dope,' a foul-smelling acetic acid substance that gave strength and air resistance. The subsequent procession to the Rye Common to launch these crafts had an inevitable conclusion as, anxious to achieve a record flight, I over-wound the elastic causing the plane to concertina into a wreck!

Once through this phase I embarked on the main hobby of my teenage years, my OO gauge model railway,[78n] an activity which brought many joys. It was decided that the track and whole layout would run on a shelf right round my bedroom. Dad set about this structure in his usual thorough, quiet and methodical way, using thick tongue-and-groove wood with elaborately shaped supports. As domestic electric drills had not yet been invented, this involved hours of patient work tapping the rawl into the wall: tap tap, twist, pull, tap tap, twist, pull and so on, creating more and more dust as we went. The completed structure not only prevented access to the room other than climbing under it, but also would have supported an elephant! This was to be the closest I ever got to my patient and wonderful dad, head down, working away and chain smoking his roll-ups with that ever to be remembered smell of his St Julien tobacco.

A further joy was developing a relationship with my Uncle Jim, who ran Hamblings, 'The Home of OO' in Cecil Court near St Martin in the Fields. Frequent trips were necessary to the shop or to the family home in Clapham where, despite my carefully saved cash, payment was always refused. Thus I became an adventurous bus and tram traveller and a regular member of a family more demonstrative and extrovert than my own. (As well as Jim, there was Mother's sister, my Aunt Lola, their son Paul and their daughter Jayne.) Lastly there was the excitement of constructing a whole world, powered by complex electric transformers and switches, which I could control. Before this, however, all the engines, carriages and track had to be built. For the track each minute lead 'frog' which held the nickel line in place had to be hammered onto a Bakelite sleeper. A process which took many, many hours.

Into all this hive of activity, and practically every evening, came Gran with all the local gossip and a demand to know how each of our days had been – a distraction which in time weighed heavily on us, especially on my mother who had little interest in 'idle gossip' and a constant need to 'get on with things.' In time the railway gave way to hours pressing and cleaning my cadet uniform and the whole secret rituals required not only to polish boots, but also to have one pair that resembled the perfect mirror finish of patent leather.

Having blocked off my room, John and I now turned our attentions to the only other space, an upstairs cupboard which was in our parents' bedroom. Out came all the contents and it became a busy dark room for our new hobby of photography. In addition to old Kodak box cameras we acquired a 35 mm, and for this most of the film was end of reel sound (slow) or vision (fast) old stock from Pinewood. This had to be kept in sealed containers and loaded, as with all other activities, in complete darkness, which was almost impossible to achieve. As negatives and prints were developed, the fumes, heat and total lack of any ventilation rather limited our time in the cupboard! Amazingly, the combined expertise of John, Dad and his brother Ernie enabled us to build our own enlarger, so we could print any size of photograph. It was a busy chaos most evenings, but it was wonderful in its warmth and closeness.

The local 34th Camberwell Scout Troop was active again, now based in the church hall. This was the most local place of entertainment, hosting all sorts of money raising events. Here the group staged its annual gang show, and occasionally they might even venture to the national event. The 1950 national production, 'We'll Live For Ever,' caught the feeling of the time, a brave effort of exuberant youth in the face of atomic threats. Although John's involvement was now only as accompanist, it is difficult to underestimate the degree to which this organisation maintained a strong sense of community. It was naturally linked to the church, and in December 1949 I was confirmed as a member of the local congregation.

Important supporters of the 34th Camberwell Troop were Fred and Arthur Gandolfi, rather strange reclusive brothers who had a small workshop making cameras. Visiting them was a real pleasure; the workshop was run down but had the wonderful smell of real craft work. They worked slowly, but very carefully, on the smallest pieces of mahogany or other exotic woods to produce the frames, then went on to create the leather bellows of these masterpieces.[79n]

Music was a constant; a strange mixture of all the old narrative songs, of classical pieces, often related to John's development as a pianist – which also introduced jazz – or dance, and of course the start of popular music thanks to the radio. Dad's all time favourite was the sad ballad which told the life story of 'Little Jimmy Brown.'[80] I seemed to enjoy anything while participating in nothing. Unfortunately, the spring in our gramophone was broken so I resorted to turning each record manually from the centre, trying to keep the correct speed (78 rpm) by means of a strobe disk. This earned me a very sore finger and a lifetime of tone deafness, due I always think to that wobbly form of reproduction. This was confirmed when, in a desperate effort to belong, I joined the school choir. After a few bars the master called a halt and then walked round the group listening to each of us. Once he reached me, his response was brief. 'Get out Jordan!' Such ignominy was in part revenge as it was his class that I had truanted from and he must have resented the long term deception.

Magistrates' Courts

Thumbing through the evening paper, my interest was caught by a regular column which reported the events in the London magistrates' courts, albeit in a rather humorous and patronising manner. Nonetheless, the sheer humanity of daily justice meted out to case after case attracted me. The cases of Roger and Jock might illustrate the style:

> Roger left the RAF still unmarked and uncorrupted by the 'long littleness of life' … The young man, twenty five, hurried home … It was a feather in his cap when the big firm made him manager of the cycle department. True the wage was modest £5 a week plus 10 shillings commission … but the prospects were not inconsiderable … But Roger was driven and consumed by an ambition uncommon in its roots, a burning imperative which made him unable to wait for promotion. Of course there was a woman behind it.
>
> Eight times, between January and August, Roger sold a bicycle and kept the cash. Of course the firm found out … 'The firm think very highly of him,' said the police officer. 'They were most reluctant to bring charges, but they thought it essential that no precedent should be established.' A neat, mild man stepped into the witness box. 'I hardly know how to put it,' said Roger's father to the magistrate … he was grappling with conceptions new in the order of his experience. He's always been a good boy, devoted to his suffering mother. He always runs home and does the housework.
>
> Then the Probation Officer, the man with the mental microscope, the student of the spiritual spectrum said, 'I have visited the home where this boy lives with his mother and father. He has spent a lot of money on this home … His mother, who suffers mentally dotes on the boy. And he – he has a sort of mother fixation.' Roger's turn came. 'No one is more sorry than me. All I was trying to do was tide my mother over until she becomes as normal as possible.
>
> The Magistrate said what he had to say: put society's point of view, re-stated the collective ethic. 'Whatever the motive, what you did to your employers was very wrong. You are liable to six month's imprisonment in this court, but in view of what I have heard I shall bind you over for twelve months. Try to make restitution.' What Roger had been trying to do, of course, was to make restitution to his mother for a loss which no one can make up … To heal a bruised mind by the ministrations of a whole and selfless love.
>
> Jock has not found it a wholly smooth transition from commando to pastry cook. The story of the night operation on which Jock gained the wrong objective reads as a painful little postscript to … St. Nazaire. Perhaps the basic trouble with Jock's post-war operations is that they are not *combined* ops. any more. Jock is out on his own … Jock does not look like a commando, for all he must be six-feet-six. He is one of those men that bend. He stood in the Bow Street dock like a huge question mark, as indeed he is … He was certainly sorry for himself when the policeman, a huge chunk of a man – told the story of Jock's behaviour in an all night café [where] Jock was creating a disturbance, using shocking language. He remonstrated with Jock, who became most violent, and finally arrested him … But when they got him to the police station they found on Jock, a dozen clothing coupons separated from their book.
>
> Jock told Mr Dunne … that he was sitting with a couple of friends when he saw a girl to whom he had lent money. He asked her when she was going to return the money, and she rather taunted him. He had used no obscene language until the police began to use it on him. 'And what's more', said Jock, I was unconscious when they carried me out of the café.'

'Is that true' said Mr Dunne to the policeman? 'He was very violent' he said 'he *did* pass out for few moments.

And what about the clothing coupons?' Mr Dunne asked Jock. 'They came from my own book' said Jock doggedly. 'Where is your book?' 'In my locker back home.' 'If I send you home now with this policeman, will you bring me the book and show me the page from which they were cut?' 'Yes' said Jock unhappily. So Jock left the dock. A few moments later he was back. 'He refused to go home' said the Inspector in charge. 'I did not refuse' said Jock 'I asked if I could have a shave and change my clothes first. This is my working suit. What would the neighbours think if they saw me like this?'

Mr Dunne was not disposed to attach too much importance to Jock's susceptibility to his neighbours' notions of propriety. He found him guilty, and the Inspector read out the list of Jock's six previous convictions. Mr Dunne fined him 20 shillings (or 14 days) for insulting behaviour, 40 shillings (or 28 days) for possessing the coupons unlawfully. The 38 shillings which Jock possessed when he was arrested he would leave behind as a first instalment. But what about my fare home?' asked Jock plaintively. He lived about a mile from Bow Street. 'You can walk' said Mr Dunne. If this is English justice ... mumbled the ex-commando pastry cook, shambling out into the untidy world of peace.[81]

Probation seemed like a really interesting job to me.

NOTES AND REFERENCES

1. In writing this chapter I have enjoyed Peter Hennessy's history of the years 1945–51 which combines strategic, local and personal events and opinions in a way which I cannot hope to emulate. The historian Pauline Gregg refers to this period as 'The Shining Years,' but Eric Hobsbawm places 'The Golden Years' a decade later, a view which reflects the experience of my own family. Hennessy, P. (1992). *Never Again: Britain 1945–51*. London: Cape; Gregg, P. (1962). *Social and Economic History of Britain 1760–1960* (3rd edn.) London: Harrap; Hobsbawm, E. (1995). *Age of Extremes. The Short Twentieth Century (1914–91)*. London: Abacus.
2. Edward Murrow's speech was broadcast on September 2nd 1945. Extract taken from Bliss, E. (1997). *In Search of Light: The Broadcasts of Edward R. Murrow, 1938–1961*. Boston: DeCapo Press.
3. From the 21st birthday speech by Princess Elizabeth on April 21st 1947, broadcast while on tour with her parents in South Africa. A dedication, enhanced by her coronation, which has been faithfully kept ever since.
4. 'A tryst with destiny' – the speech given by Jawaharlal Nehru on August 14th 1947 as India became independent. The speech has become better known for his early phrase that 'At the stroke of the midnight hour, when the world sleeps, India will awake to life and freedom.'
5. United Nations. (1948). *Universal Declaration of Human Rights*. www.un.org universal-declaration
6. Hess was spared execution, having flown solo to Scotland in May 1941, in a mistaken belief that he could arrange a peace settlement. He was imprisoned in the Tower of London. His Nuremburg sentence was served in Spandau Prison in Berlin where he died in August 1987 aged 93. As his guards were shared between the four occupying powers, his continued presence became the only legitimate reason that Soviet troops had to enter Berlin. It is assumed that this was the reason why they resisted calls for his release on humanitarian grounds.
7. Four of the five were Kim Philby, Donald Maclean, Guy Burgess and Anthony Blunt. The fifth member has never been identified beyond doubt.

8. The anti-communist post-war reaction in America, which has always been naturally anti-colonial and the guardian of capitalism, is understandable. Having conceded Eastern Europe to Stalin, the Berlin Blockade, The Prague coup, the uncovering of so many spies, and Mao's victory in China and then Korea (to be followed of course by Vietnam and Cuba) raised concerns to extraordinary levels. In strategic terms it was seen to threaten the 'Heartland' theory first advanced by the geographer Halford Mackinder in 1904. (He was one of the founders and the second Director of the LSE and the founder of geopolitics.) This held that Eurasia was the key to world domination and peace. Whoever held that vast impregnable land mass would be undefeatable. The theory had been distorted by the Nazis to justify their attack on Russia, but was also important in western thinking of how to contain the situation that they now faced with the vastly expanded Soviet Union. Therefore, not only was communism to be contained, and defeated wherever possible (part of which was the domino theory), but also to the present day this explains the ring of weaponry surrounding the Soviet Union from Europe to the Far East. In this context the UK is, in American terms, a moated fortress from which weapons can be launched. The theory underlines NATO, and later SEATO (The South Asian Treaty Organization, and plays a part in the conflict in Afghanistan which started in 2001. Recent archive releases have, naturally enough, shown that the Russian perception of this strategy went some way to explain its suspicions of western intentions and fuelled much of the Cold War.
9. The respected American journalist Andrew Roth, who had served in naval intelligence, wrongly fell under suspicion and moved to London in 1950, where he became a respected parliamentary report writer and biographer for over forty years. In 1963 Roth broke one of the biggest ever Westminster scandals by publishing a letter written by the War Secretary John Profumo to the 'prostitute' Christine Keeler. In 1999, at the age of 90, Roth was scheduled to be interviewed by an American TV company as the last remaining survivor of the McCarthy purges. At the last moment the interview was cancelled with no reasonable explanation. Roth explained that the FBI would have learnt of the interview and leant on the TV company.
10. White, E. (2012). *Churchill's Iron Curtain Speech: How the Iron Curtain Speech Shaped the Post War World.* London: Duckworth.
11. Klos, F. (2016). *Churchill on Europe: The Untold Story of Churchill's European Project.* London: Tauris.
12. Hennessy, op. cit., p. 365.
13. Refugees were also susceptible to corrupt capitalism in the form of a small army of swindlers, con-artists and opportunists ambitious to make money out of chaos. One aspect of this was portrayed in Carol Reed's 1949 classic film *The Third Man* staring Joseph Cotton and Orson Welles with Anton Karas's score. 'The Harry Lime Theme,' music that featured the zither, went on to top the charts, and once heard it seemed impossible to get it out of your head. The film was set in a rubble strewn Europe, where the dead might be better off than the living.
14. This statement was presented to a joint session of Congress in July 1947. It was central to US foreign policy for the next 40 years.
15. During the lifetime of the fund, the greatest beneficiaries were Britain, France, Germany, Italy and the Netherlands. Seventeen countries used the scheme.
16. See Williams, S. (2016). *Colour Bar: The Triumph of Seretse Khama and His Nation.* London: Penguin; Dutfiend, M. (1990). *A Marriage of Inconvenience. The Persecution of Seretse and Ruth Khama.* London: Graymalkin. Khama founded a new political party which came to power in 1965. As Prime Minister, he led Botswana to independence and was elected President of the new country in 1966. Botswana had a very successful economy and was comparatively free from corruption. Khama allowed insurgents fighting for independence of the then Rhodesia to operate from his country, and in the late 1970s he played an important role in the creation of Zimbabwe. His wife Ruth was by his side until his death in 1980. In 2009 their son was elected fourth President of Botswana.

17. These exchanges well illustrate the French commitment to their treasured cultural identity. In the following years, when Britain finally started to realise that the days of Empire were over, De Gaulle froze Britain out of the European Community. That was less than twenty years since he and Monnet had actually urged that Britain and France form a united country. Conflict has arisen from time to time as the French government has restricted the input of American or other nationalities' film and other cultural influences. In 2010 a fierce debate about national identity raged in France provoked by the fact that the iconic French cartoon character Asterix the Gaul accepted sponsorship from that ubiquitous American emblem McDonalds. The fact that only a tiny logo appears occasionally has not lessened the offence.
18. Hennessy, *op. cit.*, p. 392.
19. The Cominform was the central organisation of the International Communist Movement, an alliance of communist parties in Europe. It was closed following in the de-Stalinist period in 1956.
20. North Atlantic Treaty signed in Washington on April 4th 1949, Article 5.
21. Schorr, D. (2009). 'With No Clear Mission, NATO Has Little Power,' *All Things Considered*. National Public Radio. April 1st 2009. Accessed 13th April 2009.
22. In 1962, the government was deposed by a military junta which has ruled the country with an iron hand ever since. Aung San's daughter, Aung San Suu Kyi, has led the National League for Democracy, but has spent most of her political life confined to her house despite widespread support within the country and internationally. For the latest situation, see Chapter 16.
23. Mountbatten egotistically claimed this as a major concession, but in practice his and Attlee's views were very similar. Had he put a foot significantly wrong, Attlee, whose quiet demeanor hid an accurate acceptance of his power, would have withdrawn him immediately.
24. Williams, F. and Attlee, C. (1961). *A Prime Minister Remembers: The War and Post-War Memoirs of the Rt Hon Earl Attlee. Based on his Private Papers and on a Series of Recorded Conversations.* London: Reisman.
25. Hennessy, *op. cit.*, p. 233.
26. It was reported that Nehru and Lady Mountbatten's mutual affection quickly moved to an affair.
27. Nehru continued as Prime Minister until his death in 1964. While history has not always been kind to him, criticising his Soviet style five-year plans for example, his drive for industry and new technology set the national economy on a sound course. Currently, India is recognised as a source of clever, competent and well educated computer experts employed throughout the world. In large part this derives from Nehru's creation of elite technology and business schools. Pakistan originally consisted of East Pakistan and West Pakistan, but following uprisings the eastern part separated out to become Bangladesh in March 1971.
28. The Mandate, which had stood since 1920, covered Palestine and Trans-Jordan, but in 1922 the territory was split into Palestine, west of the River Jordan, and Trans-Jordan, which became Jordan under the rule of the Hashemite King, whose descendants still rule today. In 1946 the population of Palestine was 1,711,000 (including 1,085,000 Muslims, 60,000 Jews and 135,000 Christians). The populations of the main towns were Jerusalem 150,000, Tel Aviv 180,000 and Haifa 130,000. The present population of these three cities now exceeds 1.6 million.
29. Litvinoff, B. (ed). (1975). *The Letters and Papers of Chaim Weizmann (Series A): War Effort; Struggle for Jewish Army; Biltmore Conference; Weizmann in America.* New York: Transaction.
30. Jabotinsky, V. (1923). *Texts Concerning Zionism: 'The Iron Wall.'* jewishvirtuallibrary.org.
31. One of the chief fundraisers in America was Golda Meir, the future Prime Minister of Israel.
32. Kovel, J. (2007). *Overcoming Zionism.* London: Pluto. In 1948, Ben Gurion became Israel's first Prime Minister.
33. Cesarani, D. (2009). *Major Farran's Hat: Murder, Scandal and Britain's War Against Jewish Terrorism 1945–1948.* London: Heinemann.

34. David Ben Gurion, a leading member of the Jewish Agency, became the first Prime Minister. Golda Meir became the fourth Prime Minister. Menachem Begin, who led the Irgun attack on the King David Hotel, became the sixth Prime Minister of Israel. Moshe Dayan had been a member of Haganah, but when they co-operated with Britain during the war, he led an attack on Syria, during which he lost an eye, after which he always wore an eye patch. Dayan led the Israeli troops in the 1948 war and became well known as the Defence Minister during the 1967 and 1973 wars. He was later to become Foreign Minister of Israel. Ehud Olmert, who spent his early years in an Irgun training camp, where his father was leader, became Prime Minister in 2006.
35. Zohar M. (1967). *Ben-Gurion: The Armed Prophet*. New York: Prentice-Hall, p. 157.
36. Nabulsi, K. (2006). 'The Great Catastrophe.' *The Guardian*, 12.05.06, p. 16.
37. The current situation is that Israel maintains close border posts enclosing the small Palestinian areas housing some four million people. Over 400,000 Jews have established settlements in the lands previously designated as Palestinian. Many of these settlers are militant Zionists, but all were encouraged to move there by the Israeli government and now refuse to leave. Israel has ignored many UN resolutions condemning the situation and America has always refused to condemn Israel. Intermittent peace initiatives continue, as do rocket and military attacks across the borders. Both populations see themselves as victims. In December 2017, President Trump announced that he would move the American Embassy to Jerusalem in defiance of diplomatic protocol. In January 2020, Trump produced a 'Peace Plan' grossly balanced in favour of Israel (no Palestinians were invited to participate). A ten-year aid package to Israel worth $50 billion was agreed.
38. Britain quickly recognised the new regime (formally in January 1950) believing that keeping communications open with Mao might help counterbalance Russia. America disagreed.
39. In 2003, two British researchers, Ed Jocelyn and Andrew McEwen, retraced the route in 384 days. In their 2006 book *The Long March* they estimate that the march actually covered about 6,000 kilometres (3,700 miles). Jocelyn and McEwen conclude that 'Mao and his followers twisted the tale of the Long March for their own ends. Mao's role was mythologized to the point where … it seemed he had single-handedly saved the Red Army and defeated Chiang Kai-shek.' They believe that Mao exaggerated, perhaps even doubled, the length of the march. Jocelyn, E. and McEwen, A. (2006). *The Long March*. London: Constable.
40. The opening of David Donnison's address as Emeritus Professor at Glasgow University on October 26th 2005 to mark his 80th birthday. He was a highly respected academic who specialised in social housing, advising the UK government and the United Nations. He died in May 2018 aged 92.
41. This song is included in the album *An Evening Wasted with Tom Lehrer* recorded in 1959. The album also includes 'Poisoning Pigeons In The Park' and 'It Makes a Fellow Proud to Be a Soldier.' Lehrer became famous in the UK as the permanent performer in the BBC satirical shows *That Was the Week That Was* and *The Frost Report*. There was a rumour that he retired from songwriting when the American warmonger Henry Kissinger was awarded the Nobel Peace Prize – beyond satire. His range of songs is readily available on the web.
42. Kennedy, P. (1988). *The Rise and Fall of the Great Powers*. London: Unwin, p. 367.
43. By the time that aid was needed in Europe, the standard 'British loaf' had gone a darker shade of grey as millers were using more of the wheat grain. The British demanded white bread. Bevin worried about this unpopularity and used his view in the acute 1948 financial crisis.
44. Ralph Miliband's sons David and Edward competed to lead the Labour Party following Labours' defeat in the 2010 election. I supported Ed, who won. In September 2013 David became President and CEO of the International Rescue Committee based in New York, giving aid in 2017/18 to 40 countries from an annual budget of some $144 million.
45. With E. P. Thompson in extra mural teaching were Richard Hoggart and Raymond Williams, each using the part-time nature of their classes to write classic contributions to the intellectual debate

of the decade. Thompson published *The Making of the English Working Class* in 1963, Hoggart's *The Uses of Literacy* was published in 1957 and Williams's *Culture and Society* was published in 1958. These are vital contributions to political debate from that time.

46. Hennessy, *op. cit.*, p. 385. My main memory of the upcoming election was the vast campaign launched by the sugar company Tate and Lyle against the prospect of nationalisation. It featured the clever logo of a happy 'Mr Cube,' an image that seemed to crop up everywhere, certainly on anything they manufactured. It caught the public's attention and was a masterly piece of marketing, although I think it probably amused people more than it affected the way they voted.
47. White Paper (1944). *A National Health Service*. London: HMSO. Cmd. 6502. The price was one shilling, with a summary version published at a price of 3d.
48. Hennessy, *op. cit.*, p. 141.
49. Fifth Series (Commons). *Official Report*. Vol 418 Col 1900–01, 1947.
50. By 2010 there were 1.6 million acres (14% of the national land area) in green belts. The new towns were Aycliffe, Crawley, Harlow and Hemel Hempstead. Later towns included Easington, Welwyn and Hatfield, then Basildon, Bracknell and Corby. Forecasts of population growth led to further towns in the early 1960s (including Redditch, Skelmersdale, Warrington and Telford). These towns now house some 1,340,000 people. The last towns were designated in 1967, among which was Milton Keynes, a highly modernistic city with large areas of linear parkland. The vast central shopping mall was opened in 1979. This was also the year the population rose to some 230,000. Many of the new towns are currently being further developed as 'eco towns,' although, as Milton Keynes' widely spread design was to accommodate widespread car ownership it now presents a greater challenge. The site was chosen to be equidistant from London, Birmingham, Leicester, Oxford and Cambridge. It was managed by the Milton Keynes Development Corporation. In 1992, the Corporation merged with the New Towns Commission as part of the rationalisation of non-government bodies. It is now part of English Partnerships.
51. Sidelsky, R. (2003). *John Maynard Keynes: 1883–1946*. London: Pan MacMillan.
52. The British Nationality Act (1948) had established the status of Citizen of the United Kingdom and Colonies (CUKCs). Until the early 1960s there was little difference, if any, in United Kingdom law between the rights of CUKCs and other British subjects, all of whom had the right at any time to enter and live in the United Kingdom. Unfortunately, many of these individuals, quite naturally, saw no need to actually obtain a new British passport for themselves or their children. From about 2017, in the face of anti-migrant feelings and a hard line Tory government, anyone in that situation who had committed any crime, often in their teens, stood a good chance of being put in detention and sent back to Jamaica, a country many had never even visited. Ministers insisted on referring to them as 'foreign national criminals,' in defiance of any logic. Given the gang culture in Jamaica, many went into hiding on arrival, and some were killed.
53. Levy, A. (2004). *Small Island*. London: Tinder Press, p. 139.
54. Robeson's passport was confiscated for eight years until 1958. His response to Senator McCarthy was, 'I have told you, mister, that I would not discuss anything with the people who have murdered sixty million of my people, and I will not discuss Stalin with you.' See Duberman, M. (2007). *Paul Robeson: A Biography*. New York: The New Press, p. 354. The cast of the 1959 Stratford production of *Othello* included Sam Wanamaker (also blacklisted by the House Committee on Un-American Activities and shadowed by M15) as a terrifying Iago with Albert Finney as Cassio. Vanessa Redgrave had a walk-on part. When Robeson was allowed back into America, 3,000 people went to Carnegie Hall for his 75th birthday celebrations, including the US Attorney General Ramsey Clark, Pete Seeger, Dizzy Gillespie, Sidney Poitier, Harry Belafonte (who also produced the show), Zero Mostel, Ossie Davis and Coretta Scott King; birthday greetings arrived from President Julius K. Nyerere of Tanzania, Prime Minister Michael Manley of Jamaica, President Kenneth Kaunda of

Zambia, Indira Gandhi, Arthur Ashe, Linus Pauling, Leonard Bernstein and the African National Congress. Robeson was too ill to attend. He died in January 1976.
55. *The People* newspaper discovered that Hutch and Edwina had been admitted to hospital, inseparable after an attack of vaginismus, although she declined to end the affair. When he died in penury in 1969, Lord Louis Mountbatten paid for his headstone. A later documentary was nothing if not prurient on the matter of Hutch's 'legendary manhood.' It was also keen to highlight his promiscuity, his neglect of his children and his dismissal of other African Americans. The documentary (*Horizon*, BBC, 25th November 2008) was less interested in what, from snatches, sounded to be a beautiful but very period-specific voice.
56. Ms Francina Blankers-Koen was 30, had had three children and became known as the 'flying housewife.' She had not been able to compete in the long-jump where she was the record holder as women were limited to three solo events. Emil Zatopek went on to break many records and win several gold medals. His last long race was in 1957. He was a democratic communist and took part in the Prague uprising, after which he was removed from all important positions and was forced to work as a low level scientist as punishment. He was rehabilitated by Václav Havel in 1990 and, following his death in 2000, was awarded the Pierre de Coubertin medal for his special services to the Olympic movement.
57. What can now be seen as extraordinary is the fact that this same Act continued funding the export of children abroad, a practice which can be traced back to the 17th century. Whilst questioning whether the emigration of children was really necessary, the Curtis Committee had recognised that 'a fresh start in a new country may, for children with an unfortunate background, be the foundation of a happy life, and the opportunity should therefore, in our view, remain open to suitable children who express a desire for it.' Tens of thousands of children in care were sent across the world, mostly by Catholic societies, to colonial and Commonwealth countries which were short of labour (South Africa and the Caribbean when slavery was abolished) or needing to build their population (Australia and Canada). The policy was justified by the possibility of a bright new future for such children, and a need to strengthen the Empire. For some the truth was unhappiness and years of hard labour with uncaring families or being kept in large uncaring institutions. These children were sometimes told that their parents had died, siblings were split up, surnames were changed and all contact with Britain broken. A single letter searching for relatives led social worker Margaret Humphries to establish the Child Migrants Trust in 1987. Research and campaigning by this Trust managed to unite some children with family members and led in February 2010 to a formal apology by the Prime Minister Gordon Brown in the House of Commons. See also Humphries, M. (1996). *Empty Cradles: One Woman's Fight to Uncover Britain's Most Shameful Secret.* London: Corgi.
58. The Children and Young Persons Act (1952) imposed a duty of children's departments to investigate reports of children at risk, an early acceptance of the preventive role for which the Kahans and others had long campaigned.
59. Goldberg, E. M. *et al.* (eds). (1959). *The Boundaries of Casework: A Symposium.* Association of Psychiatric Social Workers, 1956.
60. British Institute of Engineering Technology.
61. Among Lloyd Douglas's novels were *Magnificent Obsession, The Robe*, and its sequel *The Big Fisherman*, all of which were made into films. *The Robe* was the first film produced in widescreen Cinemascope and starred Richard Burton, Jean Simmons and Victor Mature.
62. Arthur English's broad cockney comedian act became very popular, based on the wartime 'spiv,' Prince of the Wide Boys, who could get everything at the right price. (A similar character was later exemplified as Private Walker in the TV series *Dad's Army*.) His costume included the widest and brightest possible 'kipper' tie; his catchphrase at the end of his act was 'Open the cage muvver 'ere

I come.' In the 1970s English played the caretaker in the long running series *Are You Being Served?* He died in 1995 aged 75.

63. Throughout late 1945 and 1946, troops had been frustrated at the slow pace of discharge. This resulted in some breakdown in discipline and a widespread 'strike' by RAF personnel across India. There was a fear from the more far flung colonies that whole drafts would be forgotten. There is a wonderful BBC radio play *Brecon Beacons* which captures this feeling to both comic and tragic effect. Unfortunately, I have been unable to track it down.
64. We had only recently had a telephone installed. At that time numbers were preceded by the name of the exchange, usually where it was located. This could be confusing. A friend of mine decided that he would only phone for detailed instructions to our house when he got to New Cross Station. He then had a four mile walk over a big hill.
65. Jordan, M. (1986). *An Autobiography*. Preston: Nemco Press, p. 39.
66. His fellow piano player Den Hagens was already home with his wife Pat, his son Michael and daughter Maureen. They had been to visit us and had a great time with my model trains.
67. In October 2009 Pinewood Studios (films include the *Carry On* titles and the James Bond series to *Alien* and *Batman*) submitted a £200 million expansion plan to erect a large 'media park' replicating the styles of world cities to make more realistic films. Suspicious local residents saw this as a cunning way to use green belt land for housing. The battle continued through the courts and appeals. Eventually in 2014 the government gave approval. In 2019 the studios were leased by the Walt Disney Studios.
68. Now Haberdashers' Aske's Hatcham College, one of a federation of nine academies led by a Chief Executive Officer.
69. How working-class kids 'encounter the formal, proper, posh atmosphere of the school as if it were a foreign country.' See Evans, G. (2007). *Educational Failure and Working Class White Children in Britain*. London: Palgrave Macmillan. Chris Woodhead, the controversial former Chief Inspector of Schools stated, 'The failure of white working-class boys is one of the most disturbing problems we face within the whole education system.' See Woodhead, C. (2002). *Class War: The State of British Education*. London: Little Brown. Whilst this indicates a continuing problem sixty years on from my own experience, the current debate also refers to a situation where girls outperform boys and the family and cultural pressures on Asian children ensure that they achieve well at school.
70. This was Anthony Twinner, who retired as Principal Pianist and Conductor at the Royal Opera and Ballet in 1999.
71. Kings 14:2. See the satirical show *Beyond the Fringe. The Sermon*, by Alan Bennett. Available on YouTube.
72. This was part of the very discreet naturist movement (the magazine *The Naturist* is still published at the time of writing). Some twenty years later, Paul Raymond was to publish *Men Only*, the first UK 'top shelf' magazine.
73. Much fun can, of course, be had from the whole history of school reports. Churchill at Harrow received the judgement that, 'He cannot be trusted to behave himself anywhere.' Princess Diana had been warned that she must try to be less emotional in her dealings with others. Ustinov departed with 'Shows great originality, which must be curbed at all costs.' See Hurley, C. (2002). *Could Do Better: School Reports of the Great and the Good*. London: Pocket Books.
74. Penicillin was used in the treatment of patients in March 1942 in Oxford. It was mass produced in 1945, the difficult process being developed by a team of Oxford research scientists led by Australian Howard Florey and including Ernst Boris Chain and Norman Heatley. Florey and Chain shared the 1945 Nobel Prize in Medicine with Fleming for their work. It was used towards the end of the war, not least for venereal diseases caught by troops returning home through the chaos of post-war Europe. There was a wonderful example of American marketing, a poster circulated to

all units with the warning '98% of all Procurable Women have Venereal Disease. Why bet against those odds?'

75. This might be a good place to explain some of the difficulties that faced any sexual adventure at that time. Apart from widespread ignorance, the only contraceptives available were condoms, which were not thought to be that reliable and were only available from barbers' shops. A man might be politely asked if he needed 'anything for the weekend,' but a boy would certainly not. Virginity (no man will want to marry you if you were not a virgin) was valued, and if a girl 'got in to trouble' she would normally seek an abortion from an illegal back-street amateur, or go into a home for unmarried mothers where pressure would be brought to have the baby adopted. If the boy decided to 'do the right thing,' it would mean a quick marriage with a poor prognosis. In general both parties would lose respect from their families and the local community. Young people were therefore caught between their own hormonal drives, the pressures of peer group dares, the romance of Hollywood and severe social pressures including finding a shop that might sell them the goods. For a portrayal of a woman who performed illegal 'back-street' abortions in the 1950s, see the film *Vera Drake*. Dir. Mike Leigh. London: Inside Track Productions, 2007. The film starred Imelda Staunton and Jim Broadbent. See also Szrester, S. and Fisher, K. (2010). *Sex Before the Sexual Revolution: Intimate Life in England 1918–1963*. Cambridge: Cambridge University Press.

76. The troops having returned from the war, the resumption of normal marital behaviour rather took the old sewage system by surprise. Screens that were intended to filter out such items could not cope, with the result that, caught in the general sludge, they were dumped in the estuary, but naturally floated back upriver with the incoming tide. More effective screens and methods of disposal, including incineration, were eventually introduced. The East London Sludge Incinerator was eventually built in 1997 at Crossness alongside the original pumping station. Part of this whole system is now a Trust, Chaired by Peter Bazalgette, a direct descendant of the man who built the original London sewer system. He was also responsible for the TV *Big Brother* series. See www.sewerhistory.org.

77. Over 15 million people tuned into *Dick Barton*, the adventures of the upper-class detective assisted by Snowy and Jock, as they saved the world from a variety of threats. The signature tune was catchy and the series ran for five years from 1946. It was followed by a film, stage plays and a musical some fifty years after the last broadcast. In 2008 the series was re-broadcast on BBC Radio 4 Extra. *Mrs Dale's Diary* ran for 21 years, *Woman's Hour* was first broadcast in October 1946 and is still running in 2020. In May 1950 the BBC launched *The Archers*, the 'everyday story of country folk,' which 70 years on is now the world's longest running soap story.

78. 4 mm or 1 to 76 scale.

79. It would be another forty years before this business would be closed down after 101 years of operation. By that time their cameras were treasured masterpieces. I was amazed, in the early 1980s, to find a large Gandolfi camera as a prized exhibit in the National Museum of Photography, Film and Television (now the National Science and Media Museum) in Bradford. When I asked the value, I was told it was 'priceless.' In March 1984, the brothers eventually found someone they could trust to maintain their traditions and work continued in Andover.

80. 'The Three Bells' (aka 'Little Jimmy Brown'), sung by The Browns. Available on YouTube.

81. Now brought together in Wiggins, M. (1948). *My Court Casebook*. London: Sylvan Press.

SIX

1950–1954
COLONIAL ADVENTURES

We persist in regarding ourselves as a Great Power, capable of everything and only temporarily handicapped by economic difficulties. We are not a great power and never will be again. We are a great nation, but if we continue to behave like a Great Power we shall soon cease to be a great nation. Let us take warning from the Great Powers of the past and not burst ourselves with pride.

– Sir Henry Tizard[1n]

> Show us not the aim without the way,
> For ends and means on earth are so entangled
> That changing one, you change the other too;
> Each different path brings other ends in view.
>
> – From *Darkness at Noon* by Arthur Koestler[2n]

INTERNATIONAL EVENTS

Korea

After the war, the peninsular of Korea had been divided into two by China's influence in the north and America's presence in the south. In June 1950, troops from communist North Korea invaded the south. President Truman, who was determined to show that the newly created United Nations worked more effectively than the old League of Nations, took the matter to the Security Council. As Russia was absent, due to the UN's refusal to recognise communist China, the Council voted to call for a retreat. America, who saw this as a clear justification for their newly agreed 'global strategy for containing communism,' immediately sent troops to assist the South Korean army. This was as part of a multi-national 'UN Police Force,' the first time the UN blue beret was worn in combat.

Russia vented their fury on the UN Secretary General, the Norwegian Trygve Lie, and he was forced to resign in 1952. The Council then appointed a relatively unknown Swedish diplomat, Dag Hammarskjold, who seemed to define harmless neutrality. In fact, in the single greatest misapprehension in the history of this selection process, a brilliant, fearless and deeply self-willed man became the second Secretary General who, by his actions and his eventual death in service, promoted the organisation to the status and respect that it deserved.[3n]

By August, the North Koreans had captured most of South Korea. Reinforcements were urgently needed. Responding to a perceived world status, and in pursuit of their close partnership with the USA, Great Britain dispatched a Commonwealth Parachute Brigade. Heavy air and ground support from nearby bases in Japan forced the invaders back across the 38th parallel, at which point the American General MacArthur proposed bombing supply points in China. The major powers now faced each other, both possessing atomic bombs. In a reverse of fortunes, the North Korean and Chinese forces pushed the UN forces back south, and in January 1951 the South Korean capital, Seoul, was captured. MacArthur, who had arrogantly assured his President that the Chinese would not invade, sought agreement to use an atomic weapon. News of this sent the British Prime Minister, Clement Attlee, who was well aware of the opposition to nuclear weapons, to Washington, where he achieved an assurance from Truman that the bomb would not be used. As some forty nations now formed the UN forces, and with the support of massive American air power, the North Korean forces were slowly driven back towards the border.

In April, units of the British 29th Brigade (which included Belgian, Canadian, American and Philippine units) ran into trouble near the Imjin River. The Brigade retreated, but a small unit from these nations, including a battalion of the Gloucestershire Regiment, were surrounded and outnumbered on Hill 235. In military folklore there then occurred a classic piece of Anglo-American miscommunication. Brigadier Tom Brodie told his superior officer that things were 'a bit sticky'. In English of course this meant that they were in serious trouble; to the American General it had little meaning. Eventually the besieged units had to surrender. They suffered terribly, enduring many hours every day of brainwashing as prisoners for two years.[4n] After that action the UN line held, although fighting continued for a further two years in a virtual stalemate, while the armistice negotiations took place. At the start of the age when we were all struggling with the fear of imminent extinction if either Russia or America precipitated atomic warfare, Korea had marked an emerging role for ground forces, to keep the battle rolling to prevent escalation. The idea being not to 'win' the war, but to continue fighting until a settlement could be agreed. The armistice was eventually agreed in July 1953 after Eisenhower had replaced Truman as President.[5n]

Part of the agreement was the establishment of a Demilitarised Zone each side of the 38th parallel to be manned by troops under UN control, and that is how it is maintained today, with the result that America, Russia, China and Japan could play global politics with these two small states for the next few decades, a situation which seems to have left Koreans on both sides of the 38th parallel disgusted at their treatment by the great powers. During the Korean War troop numbers in Europe were strengthened in the belief that Russian support in Korea was designed as a cover for an invasion of Europe. All of a sudden life felt very precarious.

Malaya

While the 'Glorious Gloucesters' were beginning their 're-education,' the Chinese-led incursion in Malaya was coming to a climax. In October 1951, the British High Commissioner, Sir Henry Gurney, was ambushed and assassinated. Following this, Sir Gerald Templer changed the tactics of the Commonwealth troops from the initial heavy-handed response of moving populations to cut support for the insurgents to a high propaganda 'hearts and minds' campaign alongside new military tactics. The latter put great emphasis on intensive training in jungle warfare, which also put emphasis on small patrols which relied on the initiative of ordinary soldiers, many of whom were National Servicemen.[6n] Political reform gave the ethnic Chinese more influence, and by 1955 an amnesty was offered to individual guerrillas (this was rejected, although it had widespread popular support). Complex political discussions continued led by the Prime Minister of Malaya, Tunku Abdul Rahman, who withdrew the amnesty because support for the Communist Party and its military arm, the Malayan National Liberation Army, was withering. Malaya was declared independent in August 1957 with no communist involvement.[7n]

Kenya

As the large military commitments in Malaya and Korea were drawing to a close, more resources were required in Kenya where a serious uprising led by the Kikuyu tribe was threatening the colonial administration. Although there were strong anti-colonial elements, this was a more local movement stemming from land disputes. In common with other African colonies, particularly where there was good farming land, white settlers had seized the best land, increasingly confining the native population to poor and more crowded areas. Such seizures paid scant respect for the tribal concept of land ownership based on inheritance. By the late 1940s expansion of the Kikuyu community meant that one and a quarter million people were living on 2,000 square miles while 30,000 white farmers occupied some 12,000 square miles. Tribal leaders aided by trades unions and the Kenya African Union commenced raids on local white farms. By then the Kikuyu Chief, Jomo Kenyatta, had returned to Kenya from his studies in Moscow and London where he had specialised in anthropology and written particular studies of his tribe. Kenyatta, who took up the post of Principal of the Kenya Teachers College, was also President of the Kenya African Union. Consequently he was seen as the leader of the rebellion by the authorities and eventually by the rest of the world. However, although he spoke and acted for his people, his leadership of the Mau Mau forces has always been in doubt. In October 1952, a state of emergency was imposed. In addition to direct action against insurgents, the government decided to corral Kikuyus in virtual concentration camps to deprive the Mau Mau of support.

Two elements made this dispute among the most horrific experiences of our imperial history. Membership of the Mau Mau was achieved by taking a solemn oath.

This bound one to secrecy, commitment to kill and by the very abhorrent nature of the ceremony meant that members lost the respect of family and tribe. The problem for the white community therefore was the slow realisation that no worker or servant, despite years of loyal service and mutual respect, could be trusted. The whole basis upon which the civil structure was based was thus undermined. Although, in comparison with other uprisings, the number of white farmers and workers killed was small, the killing was often horrific. Once inducted, further Mau Mau oaths comprised seven levels designed to de-humanise members and spread fear in the community. After the initial induction, which may include drinking a cocktail of blood and semen, further levels would include eating the flesh of rotted corpses or drinking the eye fluid of those murdered. Apart from the actual nature of these ceremonies the exaggerated rumours spread further alarm and disgust.

Conditions in the 'protected camps' deteriorated to dreadful levels of starvation and disease due to colonial incompetence and overwhelming numbers. Captured Mau Mau were placed in prison camps and were subject to regimes of physical and sexual abuse and torture. In the course of the emergency over 1,000 sentences of death were carried out. This extraordinary figure, together with the extreme nature of the British response, marks out the Kenyan Emergency as a shameful event towards the end of colonial rule.

In January 1955 the Rev. David Steel, father of the UK Liberal leader (at this time being educated at the Prince of Wales school, Nairobi), broadcast a sermon from St Andrews in Nairobi using the text of the massacre of the innocents to speak out against the repression. This certainly helped matters to move towards a turning point.[8n] In 1953 Jomo Kenyatta, accused of leading the rebellion, was sentenced to seven years hard labour but was released in late 1959 following petitions and international calls for his release. By this time the government had made massive land concessions. In 1960 Britain agreed to elections on the basis of one person one vote and the Kenya African Union was returned to power with a large majority. Kenya became independent in 1963 with Kenyatta as its first Prime Minister. He became President the following year.[9n]

Following some legal changes in 2003, some surviving Mau Mau members brought actions in the High Court in London seeking compensation for abuse and torture, including castration and rape. In 2010 the British government argued that the case was out of time and that in any case (based on some remote fishing dispute) responsibility for British actions passed to the Kenyan authorities on independence! In 2013 the government paid £19.9 million to over 5,000 claimants and agreed to a permanent monument in Nairobi commemorating victims of colonialism. In the 2008 American presidential campaign, Barack Obama claimed that his grandfather had been tortured by the British. Although his ancestry is not in doubt, research continues about the validity of this claim. Meanwhile, his political opponents argued that his grandfather's sympathy with such a rebellion must be evidence of Obama's 'socialist' sympathies.

Russia

Probably the most important world event during my time in the bubble of military life had been the death of Joseph Stalin on March 5th 1953. The news having been released to the world, the former political prisoner Victor Zorza listened in to hear how the Russians themselves would be told. After the playing of martial music and church bells:

> At 03.30 hrs the bells stopped … And then the majestic strains of the Soviet national anthem, which replaced the 'Internationale' during the war. The broad melody swept the vast expanses of Russia … it penetrated into the little huts in the mountain settlements of Central Asia. And far in the North, where the snow and the ice never thaw, it was heard by the camp guards who had just come back into the warmth of the guard room, having been relieved by their comrades on the stroke of three. But the camp inmates – probably did not know and if they knew were hardly in a condition to care … Five minutes and the anthem came to an end … Yuri Levitan … at the microphone. Slowly, solemnly, with a voice brimming over with emotion, he read:
>
> 'The Central Committee of the Communist party, The Council of Ministers and the Praesidium of the Supreme Soviet of the USSR announce with deep grief to the party and all workers that on March 5th at 21.50 hours, Joseph Vissarionovich Stalin … died after a serious illness. The heart of the collaborator and follower of the genius of Lenin's work, the wise leader and teacher of the Communist Party and of the Soviet people, stopped breathing … The Soviet people are united in its confidence and inspired by the warm love for the Communist Party, knowing that the supreme law governing all activity of the party is to serve the interests of the people.'[10n]

Stalin was succeeded by Nikita Krushchev. In February 1956 in a speech to the 'secret' 20th Congress he denounced the cult of personality and Stalin's illegal acts, thus starting to lift the veil on the extreme violence and degradation of the regime. The reverberations of these discoveries challenged members of the Communist Party and those who had admired the achievements of post-war Russia, causing radical reappraisals of the whole basis of the communist system. Eric Hobsbawm equals the impact of the speech to that of the initial revolution. It shook the worldwide party to its core because the extent of the horrors was authenticated by Moscow, not the hostile western press.[11n] Although great numbers left the Party, Hobsbawm remained, locked into his historian role.

NATIONAL EVENTS

The situation faced by the Labour Cabinet was somewhat mixed; the economy remained under vast strains, increased by Great Britain's commitment to the Korean war, the dreadful continuation of the 'Malay Emergency' and the build up to the uprising in Kenya. However, industry had rallied, production was increasing and there was full employment and a sense that the worst years were behind us; in fact some prospect of joy and prosperity could actually be seen appearing on the distant horizon. Unfortunately our leaders, already exhausted by war service and the immense pressures of the last five years, were to face further deterioration in the economy, dissent and division. In 1950 the Rowntree Foundation conducted the third of its social surveys in York, this time concentrating on economic conditions of 'working people' only. Absolute poverty had dropped from the 1936 figure of 18% to a very marginal figure, confined mostly to some elderly residents, and it seemed that the accumulated welfare provisions, now capped, had at long last banished poverty for the majority of citizens.[12n]

The 1951 Budget

The post-election Budget, although reducing income tax, became unpopular as it raised purchase and fuel tax, thus making most people worse off. The following month troops had to be sent in to the London Docks, which had been closed by a dockers' strike. Korea, Malaya and Kenya, the increased commitment to NATO, our own atomic weapons and the consequences of devaluation had an inevitable consequence on the Budget of 1951. (Britain's first atomic test was in October 1952 on the Pacific Montebello Islands.) The position was exacerbated by the success of the NHS which by 1949/50 was £138 million over estimate. There were understandable calls for curbs on all the welfare expenditure. Unfortunately, two more crises were in store for the extended and exhausted Attlee Cabinet.[13n]

With no warning, the Board of the Anglo-Iranian Oil Company had arbitrarily diminished the Iranian stake. The Shah's newly appointed Prime Minister Mohammad Mossadegh responded in March 1951 by nationalising the company. In the words of the American Secretary of State, 'Never had so few lost so much so stupidly and so fast.'[14n] In April the public were horrified when two senior civil servants Guy Burgess and Donald MacLean were exposed as spies and fled to Moscow.

The 1951 Budget was the final straw which broke the back of the disintegrating government. Chancellor Hugh Gaitskell announced that the Balance of Payments surplus of 1950 was now a deficit of £369 million. A wage freeze was announced, there occurred some trimming of the defence budget and the NHS bill was curbed by charges for dentures and spectacles. Bevan, the young Harold Wilson from Defence and John Freeman from Supply all resigned in protest at this betrayal of a key principle of the NHS. A government with a majority of 5 could no longer carry on.

Groundnuts

At about this time the infamous 'Groundnut Scheme' came to a head, having made the government a laughing stock for some time. Chancellor John Strachey, whose name meant austerity at home, had enthusiastically embraced a win-win scheme to clear over three million acres of bush in East Africa to grow peanuts. Roads, railways, an air-strip, settlements and a new port were all planned. The oil from the crop would solve the chronic shortage of edible oil at home, the residue and shells would make fibre for clothing and the foliage would feed local animals. Employment for the local people was a positive by-product. The fact that the area selected was waterless, fly infested and virtually unfit for human habitation was overlooked at the outset, but eventually destroyed the overambitious project at a cost of £49 million to the taxpayer. The King (himself dying of cancer) expressed his anxiety about the apparent instability of the government and followed this up on September 1st with a letter indicating that he would like matters settled before he embarked on a planned six-month tour of the Commonwealth, a tour which in fact had to be called off as his health deteriorated. Election day was fixed for October 25th 1951.

The Festival of Britain

In crude terms the Festival of Britain was an attempt to move on from the anxieties of the war and austerity, to raise morale and show the world that 'Britain can make it.' The years leading up to the exhibition had seen the world overshadowed by the fear of atomic warfare as the Cold War heated up in Korea. As we looked to future prosperity and creativity, the Arts Council was formed to be the central means of distributing funds to all arts organisations, just in time to help with the Festival. Although a national event, our focus was London where a large area had been cleared on the South Bank of the Thames, the Science Museum held special exhibitions and the Festival Gardens were opened in Battersea Park – where a whole range of entertainments were available for our amusement. In East London modern architecture was represented by the Lansbury Estate in Poplar. The whole thing was said to promise a 'Landscape for the imagination' and in the following seventy years has continued and expanded that ambition. It was great fun. I remember that in the Science Museum there was a demonstration of rather large mouse-like characters that were programmed to move around an area without colliding with other 'mice' or, if they hit the boundary, would turn round and move back into the arena. It took a further fifty years for this invention to be used in toys and in vacuum cleaners that guide themselves round the furniture!

We must have had rebated tickets to the South Bank as I was a frequent visitor quite captivated by the Pavilions showing the new inventions, old achievements and products of far-off lands. The Dome of Discovery was fascinating, but my particular favourite was the Lion and the Unicorn Pavilion featuring the zany things that were thought to represent our sense of humour and eccentricity, for example cartoons, including those I think by Ronald Searle, but also the ridiculously weird moving machines designed by Rowland Emett and the more famous Heath Robinson.[15n]

The futuristic and seemingly unsupported cigar shaped 'Skylon' pointed its light high into the evening sky as a beacon of hope for the future.[16n] I became peculiarly obsessed by a small, raised platform on which was a replica of the 1851 Crystal Palace. By pressing a button Handel's great *Hallelujah Chorus* would ring out, an experience which I repeated as many times as possible until another visitor approached. A further attraction was the Film Theatre located under the Waterloo railway bridge which showed short but great films, but, unlike any other theatre, the screen was revealed not by curtains but by raising a huge venetian blind bearing the impressive Festival logo. Near the Shot Tower (the remains of the factory where molten lead was dropped down into water thus naturally forming cannon balls) stood the Royal Festival Hall which together with the Film Theatre (now the BFI cinema) remain as the only permanent parts of the exhibition. John and I would attend the Festival Hall frequently, starting in May 1951 for a concert by the Tasmanian pianist Eileen Joyce, who I always identified with the startling 'Scherzo' by Litolff. It became my ambition to play this demanding piece, although I never progressed beyond the opening bars. John played the whole thing! An early performer was the Australian soprano Joan Sutherland who went on to great acclaim in opera and concert halls.[17n]

The Festival was a great success in terms of attendance – some eight and a half million people visited the South Bank alone, the profit being used to extend the whole South Bank area. Similar sites were established in every city and region. It can be seen as the last gift of an exhausted government to the general population which had been damaged and impoverished by the war, the end of a leftward leaning age. It convinced us that, whilst we might no longer be the most powerful country in the world we had the wisdom and the creative ideas. We could play Athens to the American Rome. Goodbye drabness, welcome to the new music of Britten, the 'angry young men' of the theatre and within a decade the explosion of pop music and culture. When it closed in September, the King was dying, Labour had lost the 1951 election and Churchill at the age of 77 returned to 10 Downing Street. One of his first acts was to order the premature clearing of the Festival site.

Elections

The initial Conservative Party lead in the polls of some 7 points indicated a Conservative government with a comfortable majority, but a fierce campaign, during which the *Daily Mirror* said that, had Churchill been in power there would have been war with Persia, threatened that lead. Although Labour actually polled more votes than any party had before, our electoral system worked against them. The Conservative Party had a majority of 26 seats with the support of six Liberal MPs. Churchill was back in power. Before Christmas the Conservatives had introduced the prescription charge that Labour had baulked at.

The Conservative regime of the next three and a half years was mainly concerned with consolidating the post-war gains, much of the extreme conflict between the parties having been mediated by the cross-party support for the welfare measures recently introduced. Early steps were taken to return the iron and steel industries to private ownership and chunks of road haulage were sold off to various bidders. The committee set up in the expectation that expenditure on the NHS was getting out of hand actually reported that more money needed to be spent.[18n]

The Labour Party in opposition suffered greatly from internal dissent, mostly around the question of whether or not the country should continue its high expenditure on defence or, by accepting a less ambitious world status, divert these funds to welfare. Given this situation and the diminution in a marked difference between the parties there was little surprise when, in 1955, the Conservative Party was returned to power, with Sir Anthony Eden as Prime Minister with a drop of 5% in those bothering to vote.[19n]

King George VI

On February 6th 1952 it was announced that at the age of 56 George VI, King of the United Kingdom and the Dominions of the British Commonwealth, had died peacefully in his sleep. He was always held in the greatest respect and love by his people. Having come reluctantly and unprepared to the throne, he had overcome personal difficulties to lead the nation through ten very difficult years. His decision that his family would remain in London throughout the war and his obvious deep concern for his suffering subjects, his early visits to the bombed out families and the closeness of his own family had made for a very popular monarch. At the time of his death his daughter Princess Elizabeth and her husband were in Kenya on the first leg of a tour to end in Australia. Having been told of her father's death Princess Elizabeth returned immediately to the UK to be greeted as Queen Elizabeth II. (See also 'Family' below.)

The Coronation

June 2nd 1953 saw the Coronation of the new Queen, an amazing, brilliant event that brought all the pageantry and tradition of the Empire to the streets of London. Every element from round the world took part in the long procession, the centre of which was the golden Coronation Coach. So began a new Elizabethan Age and a restatement of our place in the world. As the left-wing *Daily Mirror* columnist Cassandra (the journalist Sir William Neil Connor) extolled:

> I have heard the beating heart of England. I have seen the supreme moment in the history of our peoples. Who can doubt our strength and dignity and power. Richness of grace and beauty of spirit have never been surpassed as in the Coronation of Elizabeth our Queen ... It was a great and noble ceremony. But it was more than that for it was a pageant and a show too ... No one human being has ever been scrutinised with such searching vigilance by such a vast audience as was the Queen.[20]

Once inside the Abbey, greeted by great choral anthems and trumpet calls, the service commenced with the twenty-seven-year-old Queen accepting her oaths in response to the Archbishop of Canterbury's questions:

> Will you solemnly promise and swear to govern the Peoples of the United Kingdom of Great Britain and Northern Island, Canada, Australia, New Zealand, the Union of South

Africa, Pakistan and Ceylon and your Possessions and the other Territories to any of them belonging or pertaining, according to their respective laws and customs?

Will you to your power cause Law and Justice, in Mercy, to be executed in all your judgements?

Will you to the utmost of your power maintain the Laws of God and the true profession of the Gospel? Will you, to the utmost of your power, maintain in the United Kingdom the Protestant Reformed Religion established by Law? Will you maintain and preserve inviolably the settlement of the Church of England, and the doctrine, worship, discipline, and the government thereof, as by law established in England? And will you preserve unto the Bishops and Clergy of England, and to all the Churches there committed to their charge, all such rights and privileges, as by law do or shall appertain to them or any of them?[21]

There had been much debate, within the religious, royal (as so conveniently defined above) and political establishments about the wisdom or otherwise of allowing the new medium and techniques of television into the Abbey. Despite the extra heat from the intense lighting, the extra pressure on the Queen and the advice of Prime Minister Churchill, agreement was reached that the service would be shown on TV, except for the sacred anointing with oil. Some fourteen million recently purchased TV sets, most commonly with a 15 inch black and white screen, enabled some twenty million people to follow the processions, the service and all the celebrations, the appearances on the balcony of the Palace and a limited view of the celebrations across the country. The main commentary was by the imposing Richard Dimbleby.[22] It marked the coming of age of television for most people.

The return procession from the Abbey to the Palace via the West End was marred by increased rainfall which restricted views of the great and the good as carriages were closed, with the memorable exception of the generously figured, six foot three inches tall, traditionally dressed Queen Salote of Tonga, one of the remotest and smallest of the Queen's protected territories, who kept her carriage open, commenting that 'I've come 17,000 miles to see you, and I know that you want to see me too.' She got the loudest cheers.[23n] By an amazing 'coincidence' news that the British expedition to Everest had reached the summit on May 29th reached the Embassy in Kathmandu on 2nd June and arrived in London on Coronation Day, thus confirming our ability to conquer anything that stood in our way! The expedition was led by the British Colonel John Hunt, although it was the New Zealander mountaineer Edmund Hillary and Sherpa Tenzing Norgay who were the first men ever to reach the summit.[24n]

The New Government

The year 1952 promised some easing of the long period of austerity. The years between 1948 and 1952 had seen the fastest period of growth in European history. Industrial production increased by 35%. Agricultural production substantially surpassed pre-war levels.

The poverty and starvation of the immediate post-war years eased and Western Europe embarked upon an unprecedented two decades of growth that saw standards of living increase dramatically. In part this was a tribute to the Marshall Plan which had at least stimulated growth; it had perhaps achieved its aim, that of easing the financial worries of business, research and government by providing the space which allowed them to innovate and develop. Britain had used the wartime research and development programmes well. The first commercially available mainframe computer was installed, the four-engined turbo-prop Vickers Viking was sold worldwide (including 400 to America) and the beautiful revolutionary Comet, the first ever jet-powered commercial plane, was just coming into service. All this was achieved by a combination of very bright inventors and old-fashioned equipment. In these self-congratulatory times, hopefully Attlee's promised big heave had been successfully heaved. Meanwhile we had failed to notice that Germany and Japan were also recovering and of necessity had built new efficient manufacturing plants and social structures which were devoid of old class wars. Let's just enjoy ourselves for a change.

CULTURE

Billy Butlin expanded his holiday camps around the coast. With few cars on the road, cycling clubs expanded to some 300,000 members. Football games, which were local, tribal but not corrupted by excess wealth as a branch of the entertainment industry, passed 40 million spectators through the turnstiles every weekend. Dance halls were full to overflowing, which meant good work for John and Den. Humphrey Littleton and Chris Barber were livening up the jazz clubs. Aunt Lola and Uncle Jim had taken to renting a holiday place at Pagham, a small village in a remote part of the West Sussex coast near Bognor Regis. We lived in one of the former railway carriages that were available and just ran wild on the beach. The only drawback was that the loo was a bucket in a shed, emptied every few days by the 'shit man.' Happy days! We could continue enjoying the Ealing comedies. They had scored a hit with the anti-rationing in 1949 *Passport to Pimlico* followed by *The Lavender Hill Mob* and *The Titchfield Thunderbolt*, while portraying the ordinary unarmed British 'copper' (Jack Warner) on his regular beat, shot by a cornered kid (Dirk Bogarde) in *The Blue Lamp*.[25n] Given the sudden return of men from the war a rise in crime was not surprising. In late 1951 a mail van was robbed just off Oxford Street. The gang (who were never arrested) stole £287,000, a huge sum at that time. The military precision of the attack pointed to ex-servicemen or former Borstal boys, probably both. It may have been a model for the great train robbery of 1963 and two more recent well planned major crimes – the 1983 Brink's-Mat theft of gold bullion and the Hatton Garden safe raid in 1993.

SOCIAL WORK

A sign of the profession's development came in 1951 with the publication of a report on social work training by the eminent upper-class Eileen Younghusband. She had obtained a diploma in sociology from the LSE and was a tutor there, having 'slummed it in the East End doing good works and so on with some sort of *vivid socialists in the 1930s,' and worked in food and rest centres. Her formal report[26] drew together the key elements of a social work curriculum and suggested that training should concentrate on the generic elements through an Applied Social Studies curriculum. These recommendations drew hostility from Kay McDougall and Clare Britton both about the report and the fact that Younghusband was not a qualified social worker. McDougall and Britton were leading the specialised psychiatric and childcare social work courses at the LSE as well as the two professional associations. McDougall was left to pilot the new course once Younghusband had left the college. Her report had also recommended that a senior 'staff' training college was required. This eventually led to the 1961 creation of the National Institute for Social Work in London.

The qualifying courses now had a wealth of material to teach. The work on a child's intellectual development of the French philosopher and psychologist Piaget was slowly coming into fashion alongside the emotional model developed by Freud. Piaget had noticed from observation of his own young children that their intellectual interaction with the world passes through stages, each of which allow for more complexity and social awareness than the previous one. Critically each stage must be completed in sequence; a child who fails to complete a particular stage will remain intellectually stuck at that stage. For example, between the ages of seven and twelve a child will have left the egocentric stage and can think logically, but only after this age can abstract thought be employed.[27]

The work of the American sociologist Robert Merton had further developed the functionalist approach of Talcott Parsons and Émile Durkheim's concept of anomie to offer an explanation of deviance. Merton's primary aim lay in

> ... discovering how some social structures *exert a definite pressure* upon certain persons in the society to engage in nonconformist rather than conformist conduct. Thus each individual chooses either to accept or reject the many goals generally accepted by society and the means of achieving those goals. Total acceptance leads to conformity, rejection of the ordinary means may lead to innovation or retreatism or to rebellion if the means are perceived as unavailable to that individual or group.[28]

The psychologist John Bowlby had studied affectionless and institutionalised children before and during the war. He was then commissioned by the United Nations Organization to advise on homeless children in Europe after the war, a study which led to his influential publication *Maternal Care and Mental Health* in 1951. Bowlby drew on a wide range of disciplines to emphasise the centrality of the carer–child relationship.[29] His work increasingly distanced him from psychoanalytic theories, including the conclusions reached by Anna Freud from her work with refugee children and published as two papers from the Tavistock Clinic.[30]

Social work training for many years drew heavily on psychoanalytic concepts. In fact, I sometimes think that many courses were umbilically linked to the Tavistock Clinic.

Professional methodology also drew on American ideas, particularly the one-to-one work with individuals, usually referred to as casework. Significant American influences came from Charlotte Towle and Helen Harris Perlman. In 1939, Towle had addressed the indivisibility of social work from the larger social order and the insight provided by Freud. She wrote:

> The basic concepts of casework practice which have been articulated in the literature for some years have been democratic concepts in that they place the centre of activity in the client rather than the agency … In stressing the autonomy of the individual rather than the autocracy of the agency, casework today presumably affords the client a democratic experience. In other words casework today consciously aims to strengthen the ego of the individual and avoid strengthening the super-ego structure.[31]

This belief in the democratic value basis of social work led to her book *Common Human Needs* being destroyed in the anti-communist McCarthy years in America. At one point Towle's passport was withdrawn in view of her 'communist' sympathies, which she denied whilst retaining the right of any social worker to comment on matters of social concern. The National Association of Social Work responded by publishing the book themselves, and the subsequent publicity drew the attention of trainers in the UK to Towle's work.

Some idea of reality in residential childcare comes from my brother's account of life in one of the Banardo's Homes in 1951. As part of his course John had to submit a detailed 'child study.' The home was a converted manor house with extensive grounds which included cricket and football pitches, a swimming pool, trees for climbing and parts left wild for the boys to explore. The home accommodated 150 boys from 6 to 16 years of age, divided into four 'houses.' The bugle sounded reveille at 06:45 hrs followed by allocated tasks, after which each boy had to ask 'pass work please' before he could proceed to the washrooms and breakfast. Most boys then attended local schools, returning at 16:30 hrs, changing into play clothes for more jobs and tea. Prayers were said before each meal. From 18:30 hrs until lights out at 20:15 hrs the boys were free to play indoors or out. Bed was preceded by a bath every night.

The weekend routine was slightly more relaxed, but included compulsory attendance at the local parish church service. Bad behaviour was punished on a sliding scale from standing outside the office (facing the wall for a considerable time and not speaking), through loss of privilege (sweet ration or cinema trip), to extra work, fines or (rarely) the cane. The subject of John's study was twelve-year-old 'Terence' whose ability to break his glasses was causing concern. Explaining this to Head Office, the Superintendent commented:

> I do not think the little boy has any violent objection to wearing glasses. He is just full of mischief and somehow in his pranks his glasses get broken. For instance, the other day he climbed on to one of the lockers in the boot room and managed to get himself suspended upside down by his braces from one of the coat hooks. In tricks like this do you wonder that his glasses get broken?

Noting the boy's love of nature, John concluded that he would be best placed by being 'boarded out' with a family, preferably on a farm; the alternative would be to build on his love of responsibility by moving him to a smaller home where there was less competition from so many other boys.

FAMILY

John

While John was attending Goldsmiths College, weekends were spent with one or two of the student societies, and I was a regular member of the rambling group which would set out in all weathers to explore some remote but apparently 'interesting' site. During the holidays, pursuing his dissertation, John acted as assistant housemaster at the Barnardo's Home mentioned above, and there again we would sometimes join them on a day out. Two other memories stand out from this time: one was an 'open day' where Goldsmiths' science department demonstrated new techniques, the most spectacular of which was how a tomato, dunked in liquid nitrogen at minus 196 degrees Celsius, would splinter alarmingly when hit by a hammer. More alarming for Mother was the attempted importation into her kitchen of 'time and motion' techniques taught in the college or, even worse, improved hygiene regimes![32n]

School

At Aske's our uniform made us ready targets for pupils from the 'ordinary' secondary modern schools, and most days there would be a few scuffles that occasionally developed into mass fighting. The most frequent fights were with boys from the secondary school in the next road, Wallbutton Road School. There was a certain inevitability in the fact that, having successfully obtained his teachers certificate in October 1952, that was where John started his teaching career.[33n] Within my school, from the fifth form onwards, my favourite lesson was the required hour of religious instruction. This was taken by the headmaster; he used freestyle to link current affairs, philosophy and ethics, all of which I found much more interesting than my fellows. I recall that somehow we got onto the subject of atoms (pretty important at that time) and our revered Head mentioned that the idea of atoms had been developed by a Roman philosopher Democritus who somehow had his eureka moment while masturbating. Amazing ... the Head knew all about wanking! I was persuaded to read a few key books, including the philosopher Bertrand Russell's *Principia Mathematica*, which I found a step too far.[34n]

It was after one of these lessons that the Head decided that, following my truancy, I needed to be read the riot act; he told me that if I pulled my socks up in other lessons, I might prove to be quite bright. Unfortunately, in the heat of the moment he chose another tall boy with bushy hair to shout at, thus revealing to everyone the true reason for my absence, which moved me up from poor sick boy to odd but a bit admired. One of the Head's delights was mass speaking and at the least excuse he would get the class to recite poems with a wonderful rhythm. This compensated somewhat for my failure in the choir as I came to enjoy such fascinating verses as

> Now is my way clear, now is the meaning plain:
> Temptation shall not come in this kind again.
> The last temptation is the greatest treason:
> To do the right deed for the wrong reason.[35]

I can still recall an escapist verse that struck home:

> Perched on my city office-stool,
> I watched with envy, while a cool
> And lucky carter handled ice …
> And I was wandering in a trice,
> Far from the grey and grimy heat
> Of that intolerable street,
> O'er a sapphire berg and emerald floe,
> Beneath the still, cold ruby glow
> Of everlasting Polar night,
> Bewildered by the queer half-light,
> Until I stumbled, unawares,
> Upon a creek where big white bears
> Plunged headlong down with flourished heels
> And floundered after shining seals
> Through shivering seas of blinding blue.
> And as I watched them, ere I knew,
> I'd stripped, and I was swimming too,
> Among the sea-pack, young and hale,
> And thrusting on with threshing tail,
> With twist and twirl and sudden leap
> Through crackling ice and salty deep.[36]

Trips and Shows

Since John's return home we had embarked on short youth hostel trips to explore England. An early journey was to Portsmouth where we stayed on the train to the dock station. On getting out at the battered station we witnessed just piles of rubble and a few skeleton buildings as far one could see, the result of a 240-plane, bombing raid in April 1941. By contrast there was a trip to Butlin's holiday camp in Pwhelli to be followed by a week's hiking in the mountains of North Wales. At Butlins we teamed up with two girls and would sit on the cliffs and watch the sun go down in the west. We did get up to some naughty things, for example we gave them a great fright by creeping into their chalet, making up 'apple pie' beds and stuffing their knitting sets down. Wow! A small landmark was a first flight, just for 15 minutes in the scariest of small planes. My complete memory of North Wales, where we had planned to walk in Snowdonia, was grey, slate faced passes and drenching rain for seven days on end. Sixty years would pass before I changed my view. A hostel trip in 1948 took us to Stratford-upon-Avon where we sat high up in the top circle to see *A Winter's Tale*, which I remember as a pretty boring play.[37n]

My adolescent carelessness was illustrated one morning when my task was to empty the ash from the fires. All collected in an open topped bucket, disaster struck when I opened the door straight into a fierce wind! Two mornings later John received a telegram summoning us home urgently – obviously it must be Dad's health, although it seemed a bit strange as we were due home that day anyway. A rush to catch the first train and a phone call from Kings Cross revealed that the telegram should have read 'Happy Birthday!' We have always wondered what happened to the guy who should have got the urgent recall.

Mother, determined to introduce her dozy son to wider cultural horizons, led us through a programme of opera, musicals and concerts. The latter were built round the Promenade Concerts in the Albert Hall and these turned out to be quite fun. Queueing, which we had to do for anything anyway, on a cool summer evening was pleasant enough, but was enlivened by a procession of entertainers to keep us busy and provoke great conversations in the crowd. Some chanced their arm at singing or a little tap dance, but my favourites were the guys who drew elaborate patterns or pictures on large china plates blackened by candle soot, so they could wipe and start again many times. Our tickets were confined to the upper promenade area, which suited me fine. If the music was interesting, I could lean over the balcony; otherwise there was plenty of space to sit on the floor, legs outstretched and perhaps to doze quietly. One of the 'pop stars' of the day was the conductor Sir Malcolm Sargent and on at least two occasions I was swept up in the crowd of women, with Mother in the van, chasing him back to his nearby apartment! Sargent was a witty, colourful and handsome man who carried the nickname 'Flash Harry' among more conservative musicians. Among his many affairs he included Edwina Mountbatten.

Musical and opera were provided by touring companies, usually at the Lewisham Hippodrome in Catford.[38n] Of all the shows we saw, only two remain in my memory. The first was Vivian Ellis's *Bless the Bride* which has some great tunes and lyrics including the duet 'This Is My Lovely Day,' which includes the lyrics 'This is my lovely day. This is the day I shall remember the day I'm dying,' which I still wonder about. The second was when the Carl Rosa Opera Company presented Verdi's *Rigoletto*, which continues to enchant me, not that surprising as it portrays the tragedy of an outsider against the establishment.[39n] Unfortunately, I seem to have continued Mother's ambitions by dragging anyone that comes into my orbit to similar events!

If there was any chance of boredom, we would be at Tower Hill watching the escapologists or acrobats or, even more interesting, at Hyde Park Corner to hear the speakers, both sane and mad and from every political or religious persuasion, all saying whatever they wished despite sometimes being heckled mercilessly by the crowd. If we were very lucky, we could hear Donald Soper, a Methodist minister, pacifist, anti-nuclear campaigner, old Askean and wonderful radical preacher. He preached at Hyde Park Corner practically every week from the 1930s to 1993 when he was 90 years old. I don't think a heckler ever got the better of him. He died three days before Christmas in 1998.

Books and Films

Interesting things were happening further afield. To settle an argument about how the original population of the Polynesian Islands got there, the Norwegian explorer Thor Heyerdahl built the elementary Kon-Tiki raft from balsa logs and completed an 8,000 km crossing in 10 days from South America thus proving his theory.[40] He wrote a great book about it. Another great book was the powerful *Cry the Beloved Country* by Alan Paton. This told the heart-rending story of a Zulu country priest's search for his son Absolon through apartheid Johannesburg when he comes face to face with the tragic consequences of city life.[41]

In any event, in common with most of the population, I was a regular cinema goer. In 1948 I had seen Laurence Olivier's ground breaking production of *Hamlet*. The final scene stuck firmly in my mind. As they carry the dead body shoulder high Fortinbras commands, 'Let four captains bear Hamlet, like a soldier, to the stage; For he was likely, had he been put on, to have prov'd most royally.' What a waste, I thought, but I had a sneaking idea that that was a fate which if it was not mine, might be one that might befall me; after all I also remembered Hamlet's view that, 'So, oft it chances in particular men. That, for some vicious mole of nature in them leads, from that particular fault, to their downfall.[42] How true that became thirty years later. To some extent the cinema had been a source of comfort, puzzlement and interest throughout my school years. Cinemas then ran continuous programmes so once you had paid you could sit and see the whole thing as many times as you chose.[43n] One enjoyable visit was to the film of the musical *Annie Get Your Gun*, a story of sharpshooter Annie Oakley, an extremely competitive woman, never to be outdone by a man, but under all that defensive bluster waiting to be wooed and won to discover the wonderful woman underneath. It would be a few years yet before I met my Annie.[44]

Final School Years

Somehow the confidence from the Cadet Corps combined with good teaching was causing the whole educational project to make sense as my report for 1950 shows progress (it also notes only 11 boys in the Remove Form). There was praise for hard work and the comment that 'shows a brighter and more interested intelligence than most of the boys in this form,' but with the warning again that I was subject to 'occasional fits of indifference or flippancy.' Nonetheless I managed three credits and two passes in the General School Certificate 'O' level, failing in Art, History and Physics.

This result must have held out some hope of salvation, for when asked whether I wished to stay on at the 6th form my parents had told me to put my hand up. This question was, of course, put to a class full of fellow pupils and the answer took the Head somewhat by surprise as 'Remove' boys were generally expected to leave the school quietly and float away into the lesser world of commerce or semi-skilled labour. I think the exact quotation was 'What are you doing here, Jordan?' Unfortunately, I had not been prepared for the next question: arts or science? A quick look round the room showed that the extrovert sporting types were choosing arts and I was hopeless at drawing, so science it was; anyway, there were fewer boys opting for that. So my course for the next two years was determined in an instant and with no knowledge of what the consequences of such a choice would be. Had I known that 'arts' included literature, music and philosophy, subjects I had loved so much, my life may have turned out quite differently.

The school had a full orchestra, based more on enthusiasm than tunefulness. It was run by the woodwork master 'Archie' Smith who I admired not only for his robust style of teaching the crafts ('If something doesn't fit boys use the Birmingham screwdriver,' he would declare whilst holding up a large hammer), but also for his amazing dedication and skill. In the face of post-war shortages he set to and made all the violins and many cellos for the orchestra that he trained and also conducted! In general, as John commented, the performances were overambitious tackling Vivaldi, Bergmuller and Torelli with great enthusiasm. Two years later even its own write up in the school magazine describes the woodwind as failing to come up to the mark. Archie also ran the film club, introducing us to classic old films.

I was fascinated by my fellow pupils' ability to act in the plays put on every term. How do you get the confidence to say lines in public, let alone take on the role of someone else? This was so far from my own insecurities, but at least I got to hang around backstage and help with lighting or scene shifting, etc. A continuation of the service role developed in the village hall in Willian. Apart from the classic plays, the most vivid in my memory is a play, with significant verse choruses, illustrating the previous 261 years of the school. Though witty and serious, it struck a great chord with us all with a dramatic performance of 'The Re-evacuation Blues' by the typical spoken Askean and chorus:

> We had a sick fear then
> That all our history would die,
> A dizzy terror in the hearts of men
> When planes made patterns in the sky,
> Weaving grey murder in the sky ...
>
> We ran swift races on the sands.
> Grew hot and brown beneath the sun.
> And in our hands we took and held
> The promise of another dawn.

> Dawn was strange and strained …
>
> In such a time, in time of war
> Dawn is another day to live
> Dawn is another life to give
> Dawn in another gone to fight
> Dawn is a switching on of light …
>
> The lights went on and we blinked.
> We gathered on the Green to dance
> But had forgotten how to dance …[45n]

I thought that this was brilliant, and most of us shared the Head's belief that the student author Robert Furnival had a brilliant career ahead of him. Unfortunately he died, of TB I think, within two years.

Army Cadet Force

To offset academic and social difficulties, my interest in the Cadet Corps increased. Although still chronically shy and insecure by nature out of uniform, it came as a pleasant surprise to discover that, armed with a stripe, other pupils obeyed your command.[46n] Well at least on one afternoon a week they did. To cut a long story short, the Commanding Officer clearly decided to give me my head and through rapid promotion I became that feared figure, the Regimental Sergeant Major, a rank which I held for a record period of time having, with my usual naivety, refused promotion to 'Under Officer' many times. Why give up real status and power? By this means I was able to form an alternative activity and power base to rugger and cricket, and although recognition was slower, I was eventually made a prefect. Sometime in the 6th form I was awarded a prize, although I have no idea why, but when called to the stage to receive my book, a great cheer went up from the assembled pupils. Where the hell did that come from?[47]

I suspect there were several skirmishes behind the scenes between the Head, P. A. Brown, responsible for the Remove Form, and the Commanding Officer, F. W. R. Wright, whose appearance and mannerisms must have been the model for Captain Mainwaring of the much later TV series *Dads Army*! Colonel Wright became an occasional visitor at my home to discuss my future, using my first name rather than the surname then used by all masters and pupils. These visits put Mother in a spin, but they were usually managed by use of a clean tablecloth (on top of the maroon chenille one), cold sliced ham and coleslaw. With his shaved head the Colonel earned the unfortunate nickname 'Fritz,' whilst my devotion to the regiment and a tangled mass of curls meant that I was dubbed 'Fuzzie' (also there was a pop song of the time: 'Fuzzy Wuzzy was a bear, Fuzzy Wuzzy had no hair, Fuzzy Wuzzy wasn't fuzzy, wuzz he?' – not terms acceptable today). It occurs to me now that on parade my 6' 2" and his 5' 6" must have caused more than a few laughs.

The role led to some helpful privileges. I had my own office, and access to keys to various rooms including the armoury and garage, where on one great day we took delivery of a whole vehicle on which we could learn maintenance and repair. These keys, and a few window exits, were essential to winning the cat-and-mouse fight with the PE teacher as I skipped his classes – he was never able to discover where I hid, which raised his frustration to a level where his self-respect could only be saved by the eager application of a slipper to my arse. Having privileged access to the newly delivered vehicle, I set about some self-teaching before others got there. We had obviously been sold a pup as the wheels would not go round even with the brakes off so I set about dismantling them to find the cause, which I never did. As only the very well off had a car, I do not think I had travelled in one before. Of course it never dawned on me that the gear stick and clutch might be factors worth considering – what were they?

The RSM role was pivotal to the whole enterprise and all my energies went into making the Corps successful. There was much organising, timetabling, training, etc., and we managed to notch up national records with 100% exams passed and many other remarkable achievements. The production of timetables, notices, rotas and teaching aids required the acquisition of new skills, unknown in such work today. The first was typing, for which I acquired an old 'Imperial' machine. When duplicates were required one inserted sufficient 'carbon papers'; between the pages. I usually inserted too many sheets, thus jamming the machine. The alternative was to type on a thin waxed sheet, then transfer this to a silk screen on to which thick ink would be rolled, each copy having to be moved and put out to dry. Needless to say ink got everywhere. Rescue was coming for the ink spattered homework and all those fountain pens, with the 'Biro' pen slowly becoming available, although it would be a few years before the Bic Company made them ubiquitous. If tabulation or a diagram was required, I worked out that placing the top copy on, say, seven sheets, with pins pressed through to mark the points, made it easier to repeat the design accurately on every other page. All this was very time consuming and added to the general chaos in our small living room.

I note that so far in this account there has been no mention of homework, which might well explain the repeated hope from teachers that I would put as much effort in to academic work as the Corps. A particular attraction of this achievement for me was the radical reorganisation and administration of the whole training system. All new recruits were placed in one company until they had passed the first exam. They were divided into groups, each in charge of an NCO who was responsible for success and could administer defaulters. Well, in advance of the actual exam I introduced a system of individual progress reports and mock exams. A significant blow to progress concerned Ken Davies, an enthusiastic ex-pupil who had just been demobbed and was coaching myself and other NCOs on a Saturday to improve our drill and arms maintenance. These informal and friendly sessions came to an abrupt end in August when he was decapitated, having driven his motorbike round a corner and straight under a lorry. His distraught mother explained that his motorbike was scratch free, although his watch still worked perfectly. The Colonel was very distressed, as were those of us who knew Ken. I sent a small 'pillow' of flowers which I was told was buried with him; this was my first experience of a close sudden death. Somehow we pulled ourselves together as the exam result was an unprecedented 100% pass for all cadets. This earned us letters of congratulations from none other than Field Marshal William Slim of Burma and Wilson of Libya.

The techniques involved in this achievement were a fascinating challenge. More than a balance to any sanctions was a system of rewards. One was a heavy brass plaque of a complex coat of arms. I have no idea where this old thing came from, but Dad took it to work and brought it back fully restored and polished. Other prizes were books; these were paperback (the most I could afford) which I bound with a board covered in paper dipped in oil to make elaborate patterns. I found it amusing that these were modern publications such as George Orwell's *1984*[48n] or *Animal Farm*.[49] I did enjoy the subversion. I also wrote articles which appeared in the national cadet magazine,[50] and there was a personal portrait from an old soldier who had seen me on parade in the guards barracks in Birdcage Walk. To my surprise my tenure as RSM was said to mark

> … a high record of efficiency and good morale. To young cadets he is a hero, to senior cadets he is a sure and experienced guide and to the NCOs he is a stimulating companion … On parade he is 'point-device' the very man … with a presence rare in one of his years. Off parade he exhibits an infectious friendliness and enthusiasm, tempered in the presence of strangers with that attractive shyness which is often present before maturity … Malcolm Jordan found the means to express his own personality and incidentally found happiness, in the A.C.F.[51]

I think this ranks as the best testimonial I ever obtained, but the shyness never went.

Attempts were made from time to time to poach me away to other units. In particular, I recall a scheme to get me to leave school and join the Stock Exchange so that I could help develop their own cadet company commanded by an officer who could not have been more than 4' 6". Another promising career move turned down by failure to understand the potential that was being offered. Anyway there was no way that I was going to stand next to an officer nearly two feet shorter than me! All was not always well. I recall one day when a boy fell from the climbing bars in the gym and an ambulance had to be called. Just as it left, a boy fooling around in the armoury shot his friend! The Head could not believe that a more urgent ambulance was now needed. I took it upon myself to visit the boy at home once he was out of danger, an interesting illustration of how extensively I saw the caring aspect of my role.

One evening in May 1950 the school assembled to dedicate the panel commemorating the 79 former pupils who had lost their lives in the war. The cadets lined the hall and as the emotional ceremony proceeded an observant person may have noticed the Regimental Sergeant Major quietly weeping. Despite such plaudits, I only ever saw the cadets as a means to other ends, never a love of warfare or the possible start of a military career. This did not stop every master assuming the opposite, thus not offering any alternative career advice. It seemed clear to me that my role was to enable others to develop, to open up horizons and adventures for younger pupils and to help all of us develop some form of self-respect. The whole issue of leadership was fascinating. A central problem seemed to be a capacity to recognise the different characteristics of each key player while striving to act fairly and equally. I even went so far as to adapt the school motto 'Serve and Obey' to one of my own, 'Service through Leadership.' Unfortunately, it was later pointed out to me that the Royal Military Academy at Sandhurst already had the copyright on that.

It must be admitted that such a central role could be quite satisfying. Quite a kick when three hundred of your fellow pupils, including a wonderful band (where did the boy drum major get to know all that was needed for that complex role?) respond immediately to your command, even more so, for example, on Remembrance Days when I marshalled all the London contingents in the vast square behind the British Museum for the long march to the Regimental War Memorial in High Holborn and then through the City to the Tower. Once a year we marched into the forecourt of Buckingham Palace to learn more about the Guards drill, a journey via Victoria Station where commands echoed pleasingly through the whole station. All this attracted little attention as the aftermath of war was still in people's minds and boys preparing to serve their country were seen as commendable, although I suspect a few ex-soldiers gave some wry smiles. On one occasion I was talking to the front rank as we marched up Buckingham Palace Road, only to find that all the rest had stopped at the traffic lights! This was still a time when men removed their hats and faced the road if a funeral passed by or as they passed a war memorial, if you were in uniform you saluted, a tradition that I upheld punctiliously.

Other activities flowed from the Corps. Weekend and summer camps were little more than subsidised holidays for less well off pupils as well as the chance to do some serious field craft training – lots of time back close to the earth. We felt so grown up out in town for evening cinema, our little group smoking away and, if we were very lucky, getting served in pubs. We steered well clear of the unit from Borstal, the system within the Prison Service for re-habilitating boys who had got into serious trouble. My behaviour was not always beyond reproach. Power goes to everyone's head at some time. For some reason at the Marine Barracks in Deal I used my authority to hold an elaborate 'Court of Enquiry.' A minor error brought forth a wonderful 'corrective note' from an English scholar Donald LeJeune who signed himself 'Cadet of his Britannic Majesty's Armed Forces of the Crown.' The following year, now an Acting Corporal, he was in trouble again on a charge of 'Fidgeting on Parade, Insolence and Unsatisfactory Conduct!' His appeal against the length of his defaulters admitted the first charge (excessive heat and exhaustion after GCE exams); he called the second an 'insult to a gentleman Cadet' for which he needed an apology; and the third monstrous charge he said was without justification. If his appeal were rejected he demanded a Court Martial! All good fun.

At weekends we stayed at the Regimental Headquarters in the Tower of London, in my case in both the barrack room then the Sergeant's mess. (Those who had chosen to be made Under Officers lived in the Officer's mess, no doubt learning a number of the customs and rituals that would have been very helpful to me a year later.)

On a more important note I was invited as ACF representative to the service held in St Paul's Cathedral on the opening of the Festival of Britain, and I retain the photo of the King and Queen with my bushy mop just a few feet away. The opening hymn left us in no doubt about the mood, Wesley's triumphalist:

> Ye servants of God, your master proclaim,
> and publish abroad his wonderful Name;
> the name all-victorious of Jesus extol;
> his Kingdom is glorious, and rules over all.

On May 3rd 1951, at the end of the service, the King opened the Festival from the steps of St Paul's as both a celebration of the 1851 Exhibition and 'a tonic for the nation,' as Herbert Morrison put it.

Death of King George VI

A clear memory is of a sudden call to school assembly on February 6th 1952 when the Head fought through tears to tell us that King George VI had died that morning, aged 56. This was a blow; I certainly had always admired this man who had, in common with his subjects but mostly my dad, looked more and more tired and grey as the war progressed. He always seemed a very decent man placed in an impossible situation. But now it was 'Long Live Queen Elizabeth.'[52n] On February 15th 1952 our Cadet contingent duly lined the route for the King's state funeral, a long and exhausting day which started for us at New Cross at 05:30 hrs, not an hour welcomed by adolescent boys. Our position was near Paddington Station and we performed our duties with great solemnity, including the rather complex rifle manoeuvre 'rest on your arms reversed,' the consequence of which is that with your head bowed you miss the procession, although I cannot guarantee that none of us peeped up to witness the black draped coffin on the gun carriage pulled by sailors, with seemingly miles of slow marching troops and all the overwhelming sombre music. All seemed to go like clockwork, perhaps because the end of the long march was near, for at Paddington the coffin and chief mourners went by train to Windsor for the burial. Kings, queens, presidents and representatives from all round the world attended the funeral. Russia lifted the blocking of BBC broadcasts to allow people to listen and the new wonder of television managed by a great effort to extend the service over the border to Scotland. History! On a lighter note, the Brigadier in charge of our section caused us great amusement by chiding Colonel Wright about the fact that his greatcoat did not properly cover his ample waistline and ordered him to breathe in. This was my first encounter with Brigadier ap Rhys Pryce.

Slowly though, during the four years in the Cadets there was less support from new pupils to such an extent that on leaving I typed up a long and 'secret' report for the Head recommending some radical changes. It seemed to me that the Cadet Corps was losing support in the school partly because the current commanding officer was becoming an outmoded figure and hence a bit of a laughing stock, also the whole lack of choice was a major problem for many boys. My proposal was that the unit should become a Combined Cadet Force incorporating Naval, Army and Air Force sections, a structure that would dissipate the role of a single commanding officer. The Head acknowledged receipt and warned me that such a document undermined authority, but I learnt that soon afterwards all those changes had been made. What he did not say, but what I acknowledged then, was the scale of the disloyalty shown to the staff member who had done more than anyone else to support me and nurture my self-respect back to normal levels. In retrospect of course this was my first 'Independent Report.' My game of cat-and-mouse with the Games master had run its long course and eventually his frustration got to bursting point. He saved his own sense of authority by hauling me in for a thorough ritual beating which caused some pain and a short loss of dignity for me at the age of eighteen just before going off to fight for Queen and Country. I was amazed to see the scene recreated many years later in Lindsay Anderson's film *If....*, although in my case I failed to mobilise and arm the students in acts of violent revenge.[53n]

At some point during these years I became a frequent visitor to the ACF Association shop in Buckingham Palace Road. Thus I came to know Stanley White who ran the shop and seemed to have a special supply of inexpensive army boots, which were generally in very short supply. Stanley and the Secretary, Bill Newcombe, had developed the London Guide Service and invited me to help that scheme; over a very nice underage large sherry in the Officers' mess at the Duke of York's Barracks on the Kings Road.[54n] I was thus able to introduce cadets from all over the UK to the sights of London. On these occasions they would sometimes be accommodated in the Clapham deep shelters, and on more than one occasion, buried so deep down, I noted my reluctance to come back to the realities of everyday life. Another memory is of losing visiting cadets in an absolute downpour in central London. I eventually lodged them at the Nuffield Centre, just behind St-Martin-in-the-Fields[55n] to dry out, but how to restore the supreme smartness required of an RSM? All the cash I had took me only halfway home (much to the conductor's chagrin as I had to stand on the back platform with water running off me). I walked the remaining three miles home, dried, changed, borrowed some money and went back to Trafalgar Square in smart order! I also spent time at a small social centre run by a vicar in Soho, which later developed into Centrepoint, the leading charity for homeless young people. Outside London I helped to organise the vast ACF Annual National Rifle Competition camp, run at Bisley ranges.

The 6th Form

Academic progress for the last two years in the sixth form can be easily summarised. Advanced level Applied Maths and Physics were within my grasp, but Pure Maths and Chemistry were not. Having failed O level Physics, some effort was required, but at the end of the first year a score of 1% in Chemistry did not bode well. I had to fall back on my trick of surfing across these subjects and trying desperately to grasp a few principles. I eventually managed to get an A level in Physics and a continuing love of Maths. The only subjects to grasp my imagination were a sort of philosophy, taught as current affairs by the Head and general studies taught by A. K. Adams who fought an uphill battle to interest these arrogant scientists in literature and the arts. My report shows hard work in my last year and I am pleased to see that Mr Adams described me as 'Industrious and a fellow of ideas' – how generous from a master that I had come close to beheading. I remember that after the A levels he set us a test of general knowledge, among which was the simple question: 'Why does milk boil over so easily?' No one could answer it! Gradually my interest was diverted to literature, but this being Aske's I faced Dostoyevsky's *The Brothers Karamazov* and Goncharov's *Oblomov*, a novel about a young man who is content to lie abed and let the world go by.

> Lying down was not for Oblomov a necessity, as it is for a sick man or for a man who is sleepy; or a matter of chance, as it is for a man who is tired; or a pleasure, as it is for a lazy man; it was his normal condition. When he was at home, and he was almost always at home ... he lay down all the time and always in the same room at his occasional work. If he were told to do one thing or another, he did it in such a way that his superior was unable to say whether he had done it badly or well. He would just look at his work, read it through a few times and say 'Leave it, I'll look it through later, and, anyway, it seems to be perfectly alright.'[56]

Mother thought it a very appropriate book for me.

What I did get from these two years is a growing appreciation of what school should have been about. I gained a small group of friends; we renovated and ran the school library (housed in the old community air raid shelter), organised lunchtime sessions where we would listen to classical music and went to town to see arts exhibitions (including the great exhibition of Leonardo da Vinci's work, which took my breath away), theatres and cinemas. It is worth noting that all plays, broadcasts and books had to meet standards set by the censorship boards to check for any trace of obscenity, very broadly cast, sedition or religious offence. It was a pretty tough regime. The BBC guidelines were strictly enforced. Jokes about religion were forbidden, and there were no jokes about effeminacy in men, no double entendre, and no reference to ladies' underwear (e.g. 'winter draw[er]s on').

We all knew that we had two years' National Service to do before anything like a career could be started, and it was with this prospect that on our last evening a small group of us left school and walked through the twilight up 'One Tree Hill' to look over South London and say goodbye. Tears came readily at both the parting and the vague realisation at what opportunities had been missed. Here I was, a tall skinny and spotty youth with dark curly hair already flecked with grey. Chronically shy, socially incompetent, but now aware of some natural authority and capacity for leadership. As school corridors filled with boys between lessons, I was the guy who had held the door open, but then could never let go as there were always more coming! As the Head swept through, he commented that unless I wanted to make a career out of it, my role was not to open doors for other people! I had some knowledge but yearned for more, particularly to understand the underlying truths of this world. I was highly suspicious of established power structures and was willing to play politics and subvert structures if they threatened my own values and ideas. These were coming to be based on opening up opportunities for people who, like me, were left on the outside looking in on a more privileged club. How could I get others to realise their potential, have choices and be given the power to act? Perhaps just open doors for others now that I could dimly appreciate how they had been opened for me. Some insight of other people's views of me might be gained from the gifts given me in those last days by my friends, including the forgiving A. K. Adams who gave me 'Composers' Gallery'; the final Cadet Camp contingent came up with 'A Seat at the Ballet'; and the senior Cadets gave me the 1948 edition of *The Weekend Book*, all registering their appreciation for all my work.[57]

A Terrible Loss

Soon after I had left Aske's, John was away, I think acting as holiday housemaster in a Barnardo's Home, and I was using the holiday to sleep in when Mum rushed into my room in a very distressed state. She had taken the opportunity of John's absence to sleep in his room at night so as not to disturb Dad by her late night reading, but, when she had gone to call him she had found that he had died. What a terrible shock, having all survived the war. This was August 6th 1952. Thus it fell to me to deal with this dreadful emergency, to try to comfort Mum and to send for John; I seem to recall it took him two days to get home. I ran to fetch the doctor, held tight while the men from the Co-operative Society funeral service struggled with the coffin down the narrow stairs, registered the death and accompanied Mum to make the preliminary arrangements. It was a dreadful shock, but the family rallied round. Dad's workmates brought back his tools and eventually a simple service was held in St Silas Church followed by a burial at Forest Hill Cemetery. A second sudden death in a short time, but one of so much more significance.

Mother needed some recuperation so, as John had to go back to college, we spent a miserable week, in our black attire, in a small cheerless hotel in Warrior Square, St Leonards on Sea, reading, walking and occasionally actually talking. Dad was in an unmarked shared plot. I have never been able to understand, apart from the cost, why this was so. As far as I know, no one ever visited his grave. He seemed to have just left us completely. Was this what six years of war had done to us? Seven days later I was summoned for my pre call-up medical. Some fifty years later I drove round the cemetery, but once there I lacked the courage to go in to locate the grave. The location that I remembered had long since been grassed over. Perhaps one day I will. I contrast these events with the fact that I think about my dad often and have so much enjoyment handling the tools that were his, the man who could craft key machine parts to one-ten-thousandths of an inch. They are still in use, but not with that accuracy. I had forgotten about the strong smell of his roll up St Julians tobacco until it reappeared in my study fifty-six years later when I most needed support. Since then, a strangely disturbing memory lapse has come to light. My memory has always been that John's great plan to move out of London developed slowly from about 1956, but I now see in letters to me a few months after the funeral, when I was in the Army, that this plan must have been commenced within a few weeks of Dad's death. Was this a reaction to this close death, a function of John's failure to settle back to urban life or our mother wanting to get away from the house where the dreadful event had occurred? There is no way to know, but it does seem that I went along with it, although by the time it became more definite I was many miles away in the Egyptian desert. The saga featured in practically every letter that I received.

National Service

On September 18th 1952, I reported to the Tower of London to start my National Service in the Royal Fusiliers, 'The Shiny Seventh of Foot,' the City of London Regiment. I was proud to be following in the footsteps of my grandfather, father and uncles. In fact, the four years in the Cadets meant that this was not exactly a new experience, and was certainly less of a shock than to most other recruits assembling that morning in the overpowering setting of the Tower. The fact that I was here at all was due to the kindly but powerful influence of 'Brigadier ap' from his position in the War Office. Despite putting the Regiment as first choice, I had been posted to The Royal West Kent Regiment, a move which 'Brigadier ap' had managed to reverse.

The well-tuned 'basic training' was about to start with its indignities and its many painful injections, well documented elsewhere, all designed to strip a new recruit of any sense of individuality and instil unthinking obedience. To my mind this international experience is best described, if somewhat exaggerated, by John Steinbeck in the first chapter of *East of Eden*:

> They'll first strip off your clothes, but they'll go deeper than that. They'll shuck off any little dignity you have – you'll lose what you think of as your decent right to live and be let alone to live. They'll make you sleep and eat and shit close to other men … And when they dress you up again, you'll not be able to tell yourself from the others … you'll think no thoughts the others do not think. You'll know no word the others can't say. And you'll do things because the others do them. You'll feel the danger in any difference whatever – a danger to the whole crowd of like thinking like-acting men … Once in a while there is a man who

won't do what is demanded of him [then] the whole machine devotes itself coldly to the destruction of his difference ... A thing so triumphantly illogical, so beautifully senseless as an army, can't allow a question to weaken it.[58]

I have a very clear memory of our first night in that big barrack room, with its floor so well polished by generations of squaddies. Each recruit, struggling with the task of pressing, cleaning, 'Blanco-ing' and polishing strange bits of kit, all accompanied by loud obscenities or complete silence. The mix of social class and background was extraordinary. At lights out some just stripped off and slid into bed while a fair number climbed into neat pyjamas and knelt down to pray before sleep. No one laughed or made any comment. Having been identified as a potential officer, I knew that my time at the Tower would be short. My obvious familiarity with the basics of army life, and my ability to handle a rifle and machine gun, meant that I could be pulled out of training for any odd job that was going. I particularly recall acting as escort to a soldier going for psychiatric assessment as a route out of the Army. Apparently I looked more nervous than he did.

Within a few weeks came a posting to New Infantry Barracks Canterbury, where a group of 'potential officers' were to be trained together. This proved a highly enjoyable, but challenging, time with able and intelligent colleagues together in the face of constant drill, physical exercise, route marches and hard infantry exercises. It was a great gang. I recall that, in order to get sufficient cardboard required to help polish our brasses, we wrote to a major soap powder manufacturer. In due course a small lorry load of cardboard was delivered plus free packets of soap powder. Here we met with slightly more than the usual insults from the drill sergeants: 'When I am in charge you will drill until blood comes out of the welts of your boots!' And, if the brass eyes used to lace your boots were not highly polished, the painful 'I could polish those better with the end of me penis!' Sundays might well see us in the cathedral for morning service where The Very Reverend Hewlett Johnson, the 'Red Dean,' would be preaching.

> Johnson was one of the intellectuals who had visited Russia, concluded that, even under Stalin, it offered a more equal and just society, but refused to recognise the harsh realities behind the ideal, although by 1952 these were slowly becoming clear. During the war his political stance had led the War Office to ban him from preaching to the troops, although at that time he supported both Stalin and Churchill. The Dean, a friend of Bertrand Russell, joined the Campaign for Nuclear Disarmament. In 1955 he spoke at the Albert Hall with the folk singer Ewan MacColl [whose first wife Joan Littlewood was the dynamic Director of the Theatre Royal in Stratford, East London] and Harry Pollitt [Secretary of the British Communist Party]. All these individuals were monitored by MI5 throughout and after the war.[59]

Evenings were spent in the NAAFI with lots of alcohol and occasionally a trip to the cinema to see the latest films, including the wonderful *Singing In The Rain* with Gene Kelly and the very sexy Cyd Charisse, who had the longest and most elegant legs that any of us had ever seen; she was definitely the toast of the barrack room forever.[60n]

I took all this in my stride, and had no problems except that, when I was allowed a weekend leave to attend the annual Cadet competition at Bisley, the sheer joy of being free of the intense training and homeward bound, even for one night, was extraordinary. My feelings of loss and homesickness had clearly been denied during all those weeks. Trips home were achieved by 'thumbing a lift,' that is, standing by a major crossroads and signing that you wanted a lift, then discussing how far and in what direction. Cars, but more likely lorries, pulled in readily as this was a widely recognised mode of travel at a time when car ownership was low and trains infrequent. It was a very social system which seems to have suffered a sharp decline following the development of motorways (no pedestrians allowed), and increasing social isolation and fear of physical attack or false accusation of improper conduct reflecting the new culture. Perhaps in hard economic times and with environmental anxieties it will return to Europe and America, it never having left less developed and more harmonious countries.

It is interesting now to see the references written about me as I passed through the various stages of the selection process – what a reflection of class differences they highlight. My dear headmaster commented that I had '... considerable ability in many ways ... an efficient RSM in organisation, control and discipline etc.,' but then adds, 'He certainly should deserve a commission except that his voice may count against him.' My Canterbury Company Commander commented that although my manner was 'direct and convincing ... ideas are sensible ... his background is modest and he lacks polish ... further training may give him the composure and sense of proportion he needs.' The CO endorsed my lack of polish, and thought that he 'does not see why he should not develop into an average officer, though I very much doubt if he is suitable for Sandhurst.' All three referees however did have the good grace to praise my pleasant personality and sense of humour! On this basis I was allowed to progress to the War Office Selection Board (WOSB) for promotion to Officer Cadet.

In the WOSB you underwent a series of physical and mental tests, had to talk on a chosen subject for five minutes and perform those curious physical tasks whereby you had to display leadership skills in getting a heavy box across an imaginary crocodile infested river, etc. Forty years later they seem to have come back into fashion in TV game shows and management 'bonding' weekends! At the end of three days there was a long and anxious wait. It speaks volumes for a particular psychological theory of learning that I can remember perfectly the words of a risqué verse passed round in an attempt to pass the time:

> When the Lord made little girls,
> He made them all of lace.
> But He hadn't got enough, so He left a little space.
> When the Lord made little boys,
> He made them all of string.
> But He had a little over, so He left a little thing.

It is remarkable that that a group of 18- and 20-year-old men in December 1952 thought this very daring.

Eventually we were all lined up and handed the result paper upside down. At least I had been 'Recommended for OCS Training,' so the next step was to Chester and Officer Training Camp housed in Eaton Hall, the requisitioned stately home of the Duke of Westminster.

The first strange experience was the train journey across England north of London. All those geography lessons from P. A. Brown came back as the train moved slowly past huge industrial areas and vast brickyards with their tall chimneys belching out foul smoke. So this was the Black Country.[61n] Then through beautiful countryside to Chester, a remarkably beautiful town.

If I had assumed that I fully comprehended the class structure of this country and was already a tough military man, these assumptions were blown apart at Eaton Hall. Coping with the most demanding tests of physical endurance, weapons training, complex exercises and tests of leadership demanded a certain group solidarity. The general division between the public school boys and the rest undermined that and everything else for the next four months. This first dawned on my slow brain when, after the first three weeks, promotions to Senior Cadet were announced (the prefect system by another name). Having done very well so far and with the experience of proven military leadership for the past few years, I naively thought that my name might be called. No chance! They were all the 'natural leaders' from the public schools regardless of how poorly they had performed to date. In February I applied to the Regular Commission Board, one up on WOSB, which would have admitted me to Sandhurst (being ignorant of the official view that I was unsuitable), but by that time the realities of a class-bound army had eventually dawned on me, so my rejection was a natural consequence of my complete lack of commitment during the various tasks.

The sixteen-week Eaton Hall course, undertaken by an intake of sixty or ninety men from all units of the UK, colonies and friendly countries arriving every fortnight was tough, succeeding in its aim to push us all to the limits both physically and mentally. A carefully graded fitness programme plus the daily assault courses kept us pretty well exhausted. At the end of the day, as we passed one after the other of as yet unused structures of torture, we would joke about the most impossible things that they might make us do there. Sure enough, that turned out to be the horror that faced us the next day. Route marches were gradually lengthened up to a nine mile forced endurance march in full kit with rifles and machine guns. These harrowing events relied particularly on group loyalty as, when endurance limits were reached, those still able would carry the kit of those that lagged, among which were a few superior public school kids, although I never remember a thank you. That great sense of entitlement. A rather sweeping statement as some from Westminster and other more minor schools did manage to break through the barrier.

We were kept up to the mark with lessons on military history, organisation, use of air and armoured support, leadership and military law. The latter included a mock

Court Martial, whereby an officer's car met a farm cart in a narrow lane. Recognising that the farmer was a deserter, the officer's decision to arrest him was helped when the man called out 'Bollocks!' The defence was that he had actually said 'Bullocks!' as a warning that the calves were coming down the lane. I have no idea what the outcome was, but I remember there was much hilarity. Discipline was strict and punishments severe. Some way on, as I was nearing my physical and mental limits, I had to take a gamble. As I was coming down the sweeping staircase that led down to the grand hall I put my hand in my pocket for a split second to get my handkerchief. The CSM immediately spotted such slovenly behaviour and I was ordered to report for CO's orders (the morning routine to hand out punishments). I spent a pretty sleepless night imagining the potential punishment that would be the inevitable outcome. At the very least it would be hours of extra fast drill in full kit, an ordeal that I did not think I would survive. I had seen others destroyed this way. The alternative was not to turn up in the hopes that the CSM forgot. The result of that would most likely be relegation back to my unit to start basic training from the beginning. In the morning I decided to take the risk. Luckily, the gamble paid off.

There were long, 24 and 36 hour, exercises at nearby Trawsfynydd and at Okehampton in Devon, involving attacks under live ammunition and night manoeuvres when we each had to command a patrol against 'enemy' lines. Deprived of sleep but exhausted, it was our main concern to force ourselves to stay awake in case the OC crept up on us. To be caught asleep on sentry was an immediate return to your regiment in disgrace. On one occasion, try as I might, I eventually fell into a deep sleep. Luckily I awoke just as I heard footsteps approaching and managed to respond to the challenge. Okehampton Battle School was a severe test, day after day on the wet, windy moors, taking command of a section to capture an 'enemy' position on the far side of the valley. Inevitably we always found ourselves waist deep in the bog we were forced to cross!

There were final services to be attended in the ornate chapel where the Chaplain (Rev. John Davies Padre 1st Class) would often deliver sermons that produced hearty laughter. The 'passing out' prayers asked that:

> [We] may be so united in friendship and trust that we always think of those around us before ourselves. Fill us with thy good spirit that we may bear about with us the infection of a good courage … we dedicate to thee this day the years that lie before us. Grant that we may serve our fellow men with zeal and sincerity. That we may always defend the freedom of our land and the rights of our people.

In contrast, a final medical lecture, also in the chapel, was from the young unit doctor, including the inevitable advice when posted abroad to keep away from disease-ridden native women and a reassurance that no harm came from masturbation, at which point he blushed and did a hasty exit. Eventually the whole challenge was over and I passed with a quiet satisfaction and the knowledge that every muscle in my body was tuned to

100% fitness, quite an enjoyable feeling that left me wondering why I had resisted gym and games for so long at school. My report, which of course I was never shown, regretted my written work and thought that I would make a 'satisfactory officer' if only I could be 'more forceful in command' and develop more self-confidence.

Commissioned

The passing out parade in late April 1953 was a significant event and Mother came up to stay the night at a small hotel in Chester. It never occurred to me that she might just be reluctant to see her second son swept along the way to war. This was, I think, the only time I ever knew her stay away from home, apart from the enforced break in Hastings after my father's death. The parade went well and I hope she felt some pride in my excellent performance as 'Right Marker', the first to march on and from whom all the rest formed their straight lines, the qualification for which was just to be the tallest cadet. When the official commission arrived 'signed' by the Queen it was quite something:

> **Elizabeth the Second** by the Grace of God of the United Kingdom, Northern Ireland and of Her other Realms and Territories Queen, Head of the Commonwealth, Defender of the Faith. To Our Trusty and well beloved Malcolm Brian Jordan Greetings. We are reposing special Trust and Confidence in your Loyalty, Courage and Good Conduct do by these Presents Constitute and Appoint you to be an Officer in our Land Forces from the 2nd day of May 1953 …

The next step was the 'postings list.' Was I back to the regiment and thence to jungle warfare in Malaya or Korea? Some were, but in fact the end of those campaigns was in sight and there was therefore less demand for young officers as easy targets. One or two of those who had been with me from the original intake at the Tower were posted there, although returned in a short while to the Canal Zone. One, Richard Horton, was posted to the Kings African Rifles in Kenya to confront the Mau Mau. What would a regiment, which saw itself guarding a tradition equal to the Guards regiments, do with a new officer from the wrong side of the tracks whose writing was indecipherable and spelling impossible? The answer was obvious: lend him to someone else! So, with no explanation, my posting read '2059 Artisan Works Company, Royal Pioneer Corps in the Suez Canal Zone.'

The first week of embarkation leave was spent negating all that physical fitness by staying in bed, but then began the challenging task of making a small uniform allowance of 40 pounds ten shillings stretch to the demands of full officer's dress kit, desert uniform and a large tin trunk to contain it all totalling over £80, way beyond the family's exchequer. A search for cheap alternatives found 'Alkit' at Cambridge Circus, who did a cheap version of my dress blue uniform. An essential requirement was to open a bank account, and I was the first member of the family to do so. I entered the bank nervously clutching one of those meaningfully large white five pound notes with the beautiful script.

The Tower of London – Again

Eventually, in a brown suit, bought as I left school and therefore a couple of inches short in the arms and legs, and in a battered old hire car, the best in Peckham, I chugged through the main gates of the Tower on May 6th 1953 and unloaded myself in front of the Officers' mess for my brief sojourn before flying out to Egypt. Getting used to breakfast, lunch and dinner with full silver service and all the precedents of rank and tradition was terrifying, and accepting the services of a personal servant in the form of a batman was very weird. The uniform from Alkit was of course wrong, so I was in disgrace immediately. Walking out in bowler hat with a tightly rolled umbrella was very uncomfortable. In town my fellow officers would naturally hail a taxi, something that would never occur to me, and in fact still worries me.

Travelling home by bus dressed thus presented different challenges; as we went up Peckham High Street there would be several suggestions from fellow passengers about where I could put my umbrella, and had it served to hide it I would have willingly given it a try! Somehow I got through it and prepared to leave London. My only compromise seems to have been changing my low level of cigarette use for a pipe. It seemed somehow more serious, but it didn't last long. We walked round the city as preparations for the Coronation on 2nd June were complete and London was definitely in a party mood. Sadly, I was driven to the RAF station on May 30th and enplaned for Egypt. As we flew south and east, getting warmer all the time, London was experiencing a typical early summer day, overcast and raining more and more as the day progressed.

Egypt – The Suez Canal Zone

We had an overnight stop at Malta before throbbing on over the vast expanse of desert. My attention was frequently drawn to the rivets holding the wings together, which seemed to loosen and sweat in the extreme heat. Eventually we landed at Fayed and were sent off to transit camp to await collection by our unit. I had of course no idea what lay in store. I had seen films of the French Foreign Legion in their mud forts defending themselves against marauding tribes. What I had just seen of the desert seemed to confirm that fantasy, so that was obviously what awaited me. The first morning was Coronation Day and all regular units were on parade with Colours flying and medals worn. A small group of us wandered innocently into the next camp with the idea of watching the parade, but soon the heat became overwhelming so we went into the nearest Officers' mess, where we were met with due deference by black Egyptian waiters in flowing white galabeas and red fezzes. We were just finishing our cool drinks when it dawned on the more observant of us that we were in fact in the mess reserved for the Generals, who would no doubt return once the parade was over. We did a quick exit to the Officers' club, beautifully set by the shores of the Great Bitter Lake. A sure way of avoiding the heat was to run down the jetty, jump in the lake and swim. This we did except that just before jumping in I noticed the depth of water and remembered that swimming was another skill I had failed to learn, but which my colleagues took for granted. I just froze and spent an embarrassing twenty minutes sitting on the end of the pier before I could creep quietly away to hide my inadequacy.

The British were of course an occupying power, and not welcomed by an increasingly nationalistic population, so ambushes were not infrequent. Troops had given up driving around in open-top jeeps once the natives had taken to stretching thin wires across a road at neck height (shades of my school misdemeanours). I was eventually collected one evening by the adjutant and escort in two pickup trucks. My troop's skin colour ranged from black, through brown to white, reflecting the historical occupants of their islands of Mauritius, Seychelles and Rodrigues. They were all in the Pioneer Corps, the most junior regiment in the Army. Just before we set off the bright young adjutant advised us that if we fell into an ambush I should grab the escort's rifle as I was certainly a better shot than he would be.

The next ten months would be spent with a loaded pistol under my pillow every night. The man in charge of the Seychellois unit, Major Ted Ingham, was a calm, kind and wonderful example of a British officer. His disappointment at my initial interview was understandable. Could I handle the company accounts? – No. Could I be responsible for sports? – No. Would I be able to look after the vehicles? – Yes, but I can't drive. The answer was obviously to teach me both to keep accounts and drive, a terrifying process in a three ton lorry in rough desert, and settle me down in charge of the transport section until the end of my stay.

The unit was a tented camp outside the army town of Moascar, by the Egyptian town of Ismailia. Not a good place to be. Egypt was in political turmoil, and in October 1951 the Egyptian police had failed to control riots in Ismailia to the extent that British troops had to intervene. They then came under fire from the local police. As British casualties increased from this and other incidents the decision was taken to disarm the police. After many warnings and failed negotiations, the British infantry, backed up by tanks, entered the town on January 25th 1952. The initial battle cost the infantry 14 casualties but in the ensuing engagement at least 50 policemen were killed and 73 injured. The date was recognised in Egypt as 'National Police Day.'

Clearly, we were not at all popular. Those events in Ismailia had however triggered a nationalist group of Egyptian officers (the Association of Free Officers) to act against King Farouk, which they had achieved in July 1952. The officers were led by Gamal Abdel Nasser, although they installed a civilian, Muhammad Naguib, as President of the Republic of Egypt in June 1953. My recollection of these events is that most people had welcomed the change, seeing the greedy and corrupt Farouk ripe for removal. I doubt however that this was the view of the British government as Nasser was known to have support from communist Russia and some radical religio-political groups in Egypt. Nasser chaired the Revolution Command Council, which remained determined to drive the British from occupation of the Canal Zone. Nasser attempted to balance the membership of the Association of Free Officers between various political and religious interest groups. Among these was the Brotherhood, a well established Islamist Sunni political grouping.[62n]

The camp was well into the desert opposite the British Cemetery and next to the Parachute Regiment so that the mournful sounds of the 'Dead March' from the opera *Saul* would be heard every time another drop had gone wrong. Off duty was spent in the small mess shared with officers from the Mauritian unit that shared the camp. This was a total of two Mauritian and two British regular officers and four or five subalterns, all I think on National Service. Despite our remote situation mess etiquette was strict: meals were served against formally laid out menus, typically Gelatine a la Vallee de Mai; Dindonneau a la Seychelloise; Melba Angleterre; all honour met! Fun, which sometimes backfired, came from the rivalry between our British regiments of the line and the RPC officers.

Each day in camp started early but work finished at lunchtime; there was a brief visit to the mess for a meal then, while most colleagues headed for the beach, I would read and lay out in the fierce sun getting myself a very dark tan. (Fortunately this was before the ozone layer thinned.) The evening usually involved a trip to the cinema or occasional invites to parties. Military wit was often evident in the cinema; soon after the great sex scandal of the young Lord Montague and the Boy Scouts, the film *Julius Caesar* arrived. Before the last battle, Brutus (James Mason) has a gentle scene with his boy page – a joyful near riot broke out![63n] A few weeks later, in a different film, a hero succeeds in putting out some vast forest fire; he pauses, exhausted, sinks to the ground and lights a cigarette. Naturally from the back came the cry 'That's right – start another bloody fire!' At some point a senior officer brought a small group of Egyptian women in their late thirties to dinner, which was fine except for the consequence that one of our newly arrived and more naive young officers was persuaded to become engaged! Alarms all round as it was clear to everyone else that she was just after a British passport. He was quickly posted elsewhere.

The troops were exceptional, and the more one learnt, the more respect one had for these hardworking and highly skilled men, so far from home. They lived a steady and uneventful life, but the Regiment had served the Army well for many years. They had excelled themselves in the war, particularly in the North African campaign in Tripoli. It seemed to me grossly unfair that, however talented or ambitious these men were, they could only join segregated RPC units. I made good friends with my fellow officers and some NCOs and men, like Cyril Latchman, a Mauritian Captain who was de-mobbed to London, and lived in Peckham. We were reunited at his wedding and enjoyed the visits of his two young children. His CO, Major George Li Ting Ling, lived less successfully in South London and returned home to Mauritius. Before they arrived, I made some feeble efforts to campaign on their behalf and joined the ex-pat Seychellois community in London, but being faced with a room full of the most beautiful maidens all speaking Creole resulted in my early flight.[64]

In Moascar I settled into the routine of Company life, concentrating on my small group of drivers and ensuring that our six vehicles were kept regularly serviced and safe.

There was also a whole educational programme where I was required to help teach English, correct spelling(!), mark exam papers and generally attend to the welfare of the men. I went on interesting courses to help manage issues of pay and allowances and to keep accounts (double entry book-keeping). I seem to have attended a number of Courts Martial, either as an observer, to defend various soldiers on relatively minor charges, or to sit in judgement. On weekend evenings alcohol flowed quite freely in the men's canteen and slowly they would dance, to some great music, usually with a chair held in place of a girl. As various building skills were required throughout the Canal Zone, there were quite a few detachments to be visited – long tiring drives along straight desert roads with plenty of opportunity to see real mirages rather than the false one we had once made at school for a science demonstration. School habits continued as I received a number of severe warnings for driving minus my hat. The first major disruption occurred some three months after my arrival. Major Ingram was expecting his son to arrive for school holidays, but before the boy could arrive our much respected commander had a fit and was promptly admitted to hospital. He was allowed out when his young son finally arrived. Inevitably his poor health led to his return to the UK, to be replaced by Major J. S. Logan, a traditional officer of the opposite sort, a bully who made no effort to understand the culture of the Seychellois and was consequently disliked by all. We clashed fairly regularly and, as the second in command became a chronic alcoholic, life got slowly worse. The men had us sussed, nicknaming us 'Casseput' (the OC had a limp), 'Vieille pompe' (the old pump – the Captain was an alcoholic) and 'Grand-garcon' (big child).

There was a rumour that I would accompany the troops when they went to the Seychelles to be discharged or on leave for Christmas. By this time I was making considerable progress in understanding French Creole, but I still lacked the confidence to speak it. A fact, once known, that the more suspicious soldiers disliked, and for that matter so did I. I then heard that at a meeting, when asked if he could spare an officer for the Seychelles trip, the OC had said no. I was furious and told him so; he wrote to HQ saying that I was free to go, but it was too late. Somehow, I had either become more assertive or months in the desert was having its effect, or both. I wrote home that 'not only is the new OC a clot, but he now knows it.'

Mauritius

In mid December 1953, having learnt a lot about the Seychellois, I was to accompany the Mauritian troops home. In accordance with wonderful military tradition, a despatch rider screamed into the camp with the first amendment to the movement order the day before the order itself arrived. When the day came the lorries arrived, and as we headed for the station the great cheers of sheer joy that arose from the troops brought tears to my eyes, my first expression of emotion for many years. Another part of surreal military life was that the train to take us down to Port Suez was hired from the Egyptian Railway. Not exactly a friendly outfit. So, I was the 'Officer in Charge of a Train,' for which I got three pages of instruction to post armed guards at the end of each carriage and ensure that 'any suspicious person, or native vendor will be immediately turned off the train.' I signed for the whole train on Form 108 (which the army uses for everything from a lost button to a detained prisoner). We loaded the 163 Mauritians and posted the British troops, who were fully armed escorts, along the train, and the number grew to 300 as we picked up a British contingent under the command of a Guards Officer who was extremely miffed that he was not OC Train.

We eventually reached Suez and we embarked in HM Troopship Somersetshire, on its last voyage after a career carrying troops to the Middle and Far East. It would take 14 days to reach Mauritius, via Aden, Port Sudan and Mombassa. The voyage for the officers was a relative luxury of a 1930s style cruise interrupted by the military routines of kit inspection, drill and sports. For me this was a dream come true, moving slowly through the beautiful Indian Ocean, accompanied by shoals of dolphin who swam alongside from time to time. We crossed the equator (at long. 51°30'E) on December 18th with the traditional ceremony and ritual dunking.

On arrival, Port Louis Harbour was impressively full of large cargo ships taking out sugar cane. Unloading the hundreds of troops by barge was necessarily slow, but once it was all over I was driven across the island to a small camp set against the fabulous La Challand Bay complete with distant coral reef. Christmas was spent in the sun and with kind officers' families that were actually stationed in this magical spot. It was Christmas and the taxpayer was paying! Peckham seemed even further away than it actually was. The stay was short and the cruise home was going to be less restful as we would have a ship full of new recruits unused to military ways or a long sea voyage.

Departure was a rather long drawn out and at times dangerous affair. The major problem was a cross-cultural view of property so that every time the new recruits were issued with uniform or kit they were passed on to the family, the young man then coming back for more from the generous representatives of the Queen. Her Majesty's representatives were pretty tolerant, but in the end each recruit's new kit was placed in a padlocked kit-bag and kept in the quartermaster's care until on board the ship. Some of the tolerance came from a recognition that unemployment and poverty were so rife that competition to be accepted in the Army was fierce, so why not try and spread success around? The last 24 hours were marked by rather ashen faced young men now having to face the reality of leaving their beloved family and island for a completely unknown world. Marriages were solemnised, shares of pay were formalised and heart-breaking farewells endured. Our very slow train, complete with Askaris from the Kings African Rifles with fixed bayonets, was waiting among the sugar cane by the level crossings, and we eventually started our extraordinary journey around the island through pineapple, banana and sugar plantations where all tools were downed and the train mobbed. At every small halt crowds of family, friends and children threw on parcels of food and cigarettes. Our carriage was reserved for the naughty boys with police escorts, and every time we stopped some elderly mother would call for her son and entreat him to mend his ways and be a really good boy. After a few of these, the men, the sergeant-majors and I were all in tears.

As we approached Port Louis, the crowds ran into the thousands, about half of whom jumped on the train as it crawled its way to the entrance gates. Although the whole atmosphere was in good humour, there was danger of an accident and the Royal African Rifles contingent, who were supposed to be containing the crowd, were getting edgy. The order was given to close the gates once the train was through; this would have worked well had not some idiot then opened another gate so in came the crowds again. At last we sorted the men from the relatives, got them aboard and gave them their kit-bags. Of course, as the ship could not clear harbour until the appointed time hordes of small boats were launched and more gifts passed up and down on ropes. The voyage home was longer than anticipated as we had to sail east to avoid a cyclone, which meant that we were frustratingly close to the Seychelles. Mass sea sickness gave way to great fun as we hit the doldrums before transiting Aden and heading for Suez. The recruits were subject to an intensive training and inspection programme every day, mostly drill, lectures on discipline, security, personal hygiene, uniform (and its loss) and conditions in Egypt. It was my pleasure to share a cabin with RPC Captain Bill Williams who worked at HQ MELF calculating military pay. Bill was an enthusiastic artist and, on learning that it was my twentieth birthday, he gave me a painting of the bay at La Challand. It has been above my desk ever since.

At Suez some thirty lorries were lined up in wait for recruits destined for different parts of the Zone. One of my last tasks was to ensure the safe transit of our recruits through some thirty-five miles of hostile territory back to camp. For this I had nine troop trucks and one 15 cwt lorry. Using this I commenced a life threatening series of moves from back to front of the long convoy doing a masterful sheep dog act. This was followed by arrival at the unit, a smart salute to the OC and my report that men and nine lorries were all well and correct. We counted: 1, 2, 3, up to 5, then a gap then number 6, but no more. A lorry had broken down 10 miles back in the middle of the desert and with only one armed man on board! Embarrassment and a hectic drive back and essential repairs eventually saved the day. Life back at camp quickly fell into the usual routine interrupted by small adventures. This included Egyptians outside the wire, possibly patrolling for an attack or much more likely cutting copper cable for sale (we sent our guys out to arrest them) or women offering essential sexual services to frustrated soldiers (I arrested one poor guy from the neighbouring REME unit). Occasionally a few shots would be fired, but the only bullet that whizzed a few inches above my head came from some idiot soldier in said REME camp cleaning his rifle with a live round in it.

The Egyptians were definitely getting more restless, so on the occasion of our annual inspection I was asked to demonstrate how our vehicles would react if ambushed. This was great fun. As we tore across the desert at top speed, we had to jump on to the 'enemy' vehicle and kill them all. It seems to have escaped us all that because the exercise was conducted within easy sight of Moascar the real 'enemy' would observe and work out exact counter measures! One of my last experiences in the unit was discovering one of the most popular soldiers, and star football player, asleep on sentry duty when forming part of the inner security ring guarding the armoury. With the Sergeant Major breathing down my neck and a snoring soldier comfortably spread on a prepared bed of chairs, there was no option but to march him to the guardroom on a charge. Whilst accepting my actions the OC was faced in the morning with a charge that carried the death penalty as we were on 'active service' and had recently been under some direct attacks. It took quite some tricky reading and re-formulation of regulations and local orders to produce a lesser charge that could be dealt with immediately. Relief and rejoicing all round. My final report from the appalling OC was that I had carried out my duties fairly satisfactorily, but he 'tends to be careless and slovenly unless watched.' Oh dear, our battles and the number of times I had been caught without a hat had a consequence! I was very happy when I heard later that this OC had been posted home following complaints lodged by NCOs and soldiers. Justice.

It still seemed to me, from time to time, that I would make a good probation officer, having experienced my own delinquency, but that required university entrance, the essential element of which was competence in a foreign language, so that was the end of that idea. In any event in correspondence with the Berkshire Probation Service they had advised me to take 'ordinary employment that would bring me in touch with human beings' until I was at least 23 years old. This led me to think that I might be more use in poorer countries. In this I was influenced by my increasing respect for the Seychellois and their culture, anger at the lowly place allocated to them by the superior Brits and reading some, probably romantic, books about the lives of District Commissioners who were posted throughout the colonies to administer small remote outposts where they inevitably sympathised more with the natives and less with their remote masters. (In 1954 there were 18,000 overseas colonial staff.) Given my recent experience with our sleeping guard I could see myself in the sort of situation explained by Kenneth Bradley, one of the thousands of middle-class ex minor public schools, young men who fanned out across the world to administer the Empire. He recalls a case of triple murder:

> The custom was for offenders to sit by the flagpole if they felt the need to confess. One day a young man sat meekly before approaching the young District Officer to confess to the murder of three brothers by poison as they had raped his sister. He was certain that the British would hang him. Try as he may the DC could not extract any other motive for such an extreme act so, as he seemed an honest and likeable person he kept him on station for weeks talking until a man explained that he had to kill all three to protect himself and family from ancestors' spirits who would kill him for losing family honour. Reluctantly he was then sent for trial at the High Court, but word having been passed up the line, the Governor commuted the mandatory death sentence to a short term of imprisonment. All African honour respected and real justice achieved.[65]

In a more romantic mood, later in his career, as the Second World War threatened and he toured his whole District in Northern Rhodesia, camping and sleeping in the open, his musings reflected my own wonder at the desert and feeling of loneliness:

> I have the pleasant feeling tonight that I am at the world's end. To the south uninhabited bush stretches, as far as I know, all the way to the Mbozi hill, thirty miles at least. Between here and the Kunda villages of the valley only the elephant lives ... If ever tired of the world I would come and live in a village like this – so remote that few strangers ever visit it, and no white men whatever except a wandering District Officer once a year. I shall bear it in mind against Armageddon.[66]

Such ideas led to some frantic correspondence with the Colonial Office in London and Mauritius for information and job applications, but of course I had no acceptable qualifications. Letters home to announce my new ideas were met with acknowledgement of my sympathies, distress at the idea that any return home may be brief and wise counsel that it would be more sensible to come home, get a temporary job and get the right qualifications to ensure both a good job and any future promotion. In the end no job offers materialised and realisation that the family's advice was sound persuaded me to get through the rest of my service and go home. Some further fury was provoked by a letter from my Aunt Elsie (she of the small dog) (see Chapter 5) who from her deeply religious viewpoint wrote to my mother that 'By all means have a circle of coloured friends; they're human and they have souls, as well as the 'favoured' whites. I believe the Chinese peasants are very lovable, but oh so ignorant and unhygienic and how grateful they are for the healing powers of the white missionaries.' Not, I thought, an uncommon view in 1950s England.

Meanwhile, back at home, the project to move out to Kent was moving forward where a plot of land had been purchased in a prime position in the picturesque village of Eynsford on the River Darent. An architect and builder had been engaged and I was receiving detailed plans for comment in an effort to keep me involved. As the excitement of an impending move grew and the house was semi packed, models were being constructed to ensure that new furniture fitted, including a baby grand piano on which John had paid a deposit. The whole thing was apparently so tight that at one point they were designing a table suspended from the ceiling! The family had held a picnic on 'our land' and had marked out the whole site with string, including a 200 ft garden, and, wonder of wonders, Mother's birthday present had been her first vacuum cleaner. It transpired that we were all very naive.

The Sudan

Whatever one's original posting, the rule was that the last three months of National Service must be served with your own regiment. So June 1st 1954 found me flying to Khartoum to once again be confronted with the old stratified rituals of a top regiment, a situation which I quickly learnt exactly replicated the life of the Raj in India. The barracks were of brick built wide verandah type bordering the confluence of the Blue Nile and the White Nile. I was allocated as Second in Command to D Company. Relationships between officers and men were based largely on mutual respect and ability, particularly whether you had performed well in battle. If this did not apply, then what counted with the men and the NCOs were whether you had got your 'knees brown' (i.e. got some service in – I had). This put you in a better category than newly trained officers, and whether you were regular or national service. The camaraderie between the latter across all ranks and classes far outweighed any other considerations. As I cycled round the barracks doing my stint as Duty Officer the shout would come down from the balconies 'How many days, and one early breakfast before demob?'

There were many characters among my fellow officers. It came as quite a shock to experience the combination of a cut glass, English accent and the constant stream of foul language that came from the adjutant. 'Short arm' inspections were a regular feature of army life aimed at controlling venereal disease. Men 'stood by their beds' naked or scantily dressed while the medical officer inspected each soldier's genitals. It was usually quickly accomplished with a minimum of fuss. One senior officer however used to walk up and down the barrack room, using his swagger stick to lift the penises of various men whilst commenting on their attributes in what he took to be a humorous way. The soldiers really had no option but to endure this, and I can only assume that the class and rank structure and his good battle history saved him from the beating that would be given to anyone else. I had to stay well down the barrack room to contain my sense of outrage. Life was fairly peaceful; everyone was looked after by 'tea wallas' and each afternoon was siesta time. It could be a strange sight when checking each vast barrack room to be faced with 20 or more naked soldiers fast asleep, guarded by a Sudanese who served 'chai' when called. A scene which seemed to me to reflect F. T. Prince's poem of war and innocence, 'Soldiers Bathing.'[67]

The most interesting part of my duties was to deal with welfare issues, problems at home, decisions on whether to recommend compassionate leave, etc. Most found this posting more difficult than the Canal Zone as here we were in the midst of more normal family life, where wives and children abounded in the barracks or in the town. Homesickness for some turned to breakdown, and in one of my letters I report that six fusiliers had been sent home for discharge on mental health grounds. My role in the Company did not last long as some past problem between the Company CO and the troops led to a rare display of protest when the men emptied the office contents down into the yard, top secret documents and all. The Company was temporarily closed and for the last few weeks of my service I was responsible for the training of new recruits who had just joined the Battalion. In addition to getting them used to the heat, this included talking about the local culture, the need to respect it with inevitable warnings about not going into the red-light districts, which were formally out of bounds anyway.

There was also a whole programme of general education. Test papers included the following questions:

> *Arithmetic:* During service in Korea one ninth of a certain battalion were killed and one third wounded. The remainder consisted of 435 men. What was the original strength?
>
> *English:* Write 400–500 words on one of the following:
>
> (a) There are too many people in Great Britain and the only solution to the problem is mass emigration.
> (b) Choose any Arm of the Service (your own, if you wish) and describe the role it plays in peace and in war.
> (c) The miracle of Spring.

Teaching as a challenge brought a significant response from brother John who was facing the realities of teaching unwilling pupils (Warburton Road School had now been renamed Pepys Academy). He wrote that his colleague had wondered was it worth it: 'Education – just casting imaginary pearls before real swine.' One 13-year-old boy had written, 'the man fell down the stairs and eitised [hit his head]' – what happened to all those promises of a good education system! My ideas about a radical change seemed to be unsettling my brother, as he wrote of his frustration as a teacher:

> …trying to teach music and all that it can offer, confidence, poise, virility etc. to children who are controlled and civilised to think that it is unimportant compared to technical drawing, history or mathematics. It's pathetic of course to see them in the fourth year (having realised that they will never be architects or atomic scientists) – grouped round the gramophone, addicts to jazz, feet tapping because they have never learnt to move, hands in pockets having never been taught how to use them in gesture, backs bent with boredom and chests that have never been thrown out in joyful creation! And because they cannot sing they smoke. Surely how much easier it would be to get Seychellois children, in their own way to sing and dance? But does this necessarily make it worthwhile trying to help our children …

Once the new recruits had been judged ready for full duty, I was moved to be in charge of the Officers' mess, a strange role that included managing the men working there, deciding on table decorations and layouts and counting the gold and silver cutlery and the trophies after each formal dinner. I surprised the Mess Sergeant by laying all the duties and shift patterns out on a large sheet of graph paper as bar charts. 'I've never seen it done like that before,' he said. Neither had I, but I now realise that this was a self-invented flow diagram since favoured by consultants charging high fees to large corporations. The post included responsibility for all the mess staff, including Tom, my personal batman, who would make a dramatic entry into my life some ten years later.

A few habits illustrate the culture of the time. Newly arrived officers were expected to hand in their visiting card at the Governor's Palace. No luck for me there then –

I had no card. We were responsible for guarding the Governor's Palace, and part of the Duty Officer's routine was to visit the guard at all hours. This you did by climbing over the railings that were meant to seal off the gap between the building and the river. So, General Gordon's old palace was still not secure. Formal meals were of course a nightmare for me, especially when the Governor came to play cards late into the night. The slightest wrong move at table or afterwards on my part would bring complete embarrassment to my fellow officers. I remember the shock when I asked my neighbour if I could light my cigarette from his. I should apparently have asked the waiter for a light. There were party invites to the married quarters and at least one semi-formal cruise to a small island further up the Nile, naturally in the Governor's launch. These were elaborate picnic events organised by one of the resident British 'matrons' who brought along just the right number of young ladies to keep us amused, or more seriously to see whether we were marriageable material, which clearly I was not. Experience allowed me to dodge the inevitable invite to the Sergeants' mess during my turn as Duty Officer, the object of which I well knew was to get the new officer completely paralytic, and to sense the running Corporal coming up behind me as I inspected the swimming pool. Routine duties at one time included visiting each latrine to check whether the contractor had emptied the buckets as per specification. The report was inevitably headed 'Shit Rep.'[68n]

There was a good open-air cinema (The Nile Cinema) in Camp, which among other films showed Charlie Chaplin's last great film *Limelight*, a rather sad story set in a London music hall before World War One, the background music to which was impossible to get out of your head for days.[69n]

My pay came via the National Westminster Bank in Peckham who had made the crass error of making it available to me at the Egyptian Bank in Khartoum! So a lone and nervous British officer had to climb the temple like steps of this vast building every time he needed money. All my fellows of course went to the very posh Barclays Dominion, Colonial and Overseas branch. This necessity had a strange offshoot when the Under Manager invited me to his home, an invitation which I accepted without further thought (neither did I think to report this in Barracks). So one afternoon I took a solo taxi into the depths of the 'native' part of Khartoum where I shared a lovely glass of tea and pastries with this kind man, while his wife and daughters were kept well out of sight. I then had to summon a local taxi to get back to barracks, my first experience of shared 'Dolmus.' I did not stop to see what the Guard Sergeant thought of me climbing out of a taxi full of locals. I cling to the belief that the invitation was an example of traditional hospitality and commercial practice, but, given the hostile feelings brewing up at the time, I often wonder what would have happened if I had stayed longer and developed that contact.

My stay followed the time when the pride of British aviation, The Comet, had undertaken trials from Khartoum Airport. Its take off over the flat roof of the mess caused chaos. The Battalion was of course there to keep the colony in order and to guard against any signs of revolt. In case of riot there was a well rehearsed set of legal duties 'In Aid of the Civil Powers.' So one sunny afternoon the Company CO and I stood drinking whisky and ginger, mixing with the passengers on the cool flat airport roof. Our conversation however was concerned with where we would draw the line (the road) behind which demonstrators would be told to stay; where would we unveil the warning banner? In the event that they moved forward then we would have machine guns placed there and there and reinforcements stationed there and there. Having thus set the scene of battle, we had another drink and returned to base.

From time to time we rehearsed how we would deal with a hostile crowd of 'natives.' It inevitably fell to me to be in charge of the soldiers dressed up in sheets and pretending to be Sudanese. Our tactic was to throw rotten fruit at our 'oppressors' then to stage a prayer meeting at an important crossroad and go into mock prayers for as long as possible. I apologise now for all the offence this must have given to any Sudanese who watched this mockery of their religious practices. Although the battalion remained in Khartoum for a few more months, towards the end of my stay we formed the guard of honour while the Union Jack was lowered and the flag of an independent Sudan was raised. Britain and Egypt had signed a treaty under which Sudan would have full independence on January 1st 1956. Another former colony was waving the British goodbye.

Counting the days to demob went awry when there came a rumour that our draft could be delayed due to an emergency in our far-flung Empire (shades of John's posting to Palestine), but eventually the date was fixed for August 28th 1954. My stay in Khartoum came to an end soon after the last mess meeting that I attended. I retain a clear memory of that event and in particular the Commanding Officer, the understated W. A. B. Harris MC, expressing his concern that young gentlemen were not keeping fit despite the compulsory gymnastics every morning at 06:15 hrs. My experience of that had been clouded by a short combat exercise when, with a fellow officer riding piggy-back, I foolishly chose to charge the steed ridden by Lt Roper MC. Consciousness was soon regained and battle continued!

The Colonel's solution to his perceived problem was to order that within the month each officer would acquire a set of polo ponies and competition would start thereafter. As I had no idea how to ride a horse, let alone any understanding of polo, I was very relieved to leave behind the monstrous assumptions behind this initiative and start the long journey home. Despite such a short stay I had glimpsed that peculiar mixture of macho posturing, mutual respect and care bordering on love that marks the family feeling of a good British battalion. In some small way I may even have been edging into acceptance.

Demobilisation

In London we were taken to the demob centre housed in Goodge Street Underground Station.[70] There we were fitted with some civilian clothes and given the papers which moved us from the regular Army to the Territorial Commitment for the next three and a half years. My request to rejoin Aske's Cadet Unit having been refused, I was allocated to the Regiment's own Cadet Unit at Balham. It was September 21st 1954, my service had been 'Satisfactory' and I had until early 1958 before my commitment was finished. Not quite the last lap. Climbing on board the number 53 bus towards home, I stowed my kit-bag and went upstairs. The conductor took one look at my tanned features and waived the fare. Solidarity was still in place. The question was, what next? Back home the house project was running into problems as the land agent Major Bidwell was proving very elusive when anyone actually tried to get a binding document out of him. Mum had written, 'we are worn out with getting nowhere, but hope to survive to lay the foundation stone.' Sam Silkin, our MP, was engaged as solicitor.

The general feeling of the country when I returned however was one of optimism, some movement out of austerity and an expectation that, as wages increased, we might have more leisure time. The film industry was doing well and there was this new thing called television. On March 7th 1954 Roger Bannister broke the 4 minute time for a mile race, so Britain must still be great. Any summary of Part One of this book is best done by quoting extensively from an 80th birthday article written in 1952 by the mathematician, philosopher, social critic and determined opponent of nuclear weapons, Bertrand Russell (the Third Earl Russell):

My youth was passed at the very summit of the Victorian Epoch. I saw Disraeli driving to the opening of Parliament in 1879 … England in those days was still aristocratic. There was an old Duchess of Cleveland who I knew was outraged by the institution of bank holidays and exclaimed acidly, 'What do the poor want with holidays? They ought to work.

I well remember the first crack in the imposing aristocratic facade. It was when Keir Hardie came to the House of Commons in a cloth cap instead of a top hat. When it was found that no thunderbolt struck him down for his impropriety, strange new doubts began to germinate in men's mind … The landed aristocracy was reduced to a ruin which began with Lloyd George's budget. Those who felt that the poor ought to work became themselves poor.

The revolution that has taken place in the social life of England has been accomplished without the use of the guillotine or the concentration camp, though it has been more profound than anything that the guillotine achieved. … I have two entirely different versions of the future according to if I happen to feel cheerful or the reverse.

On gloomy days, I foresee a third world war in the near future lasting for years and ending in unparalleled destruction … I see Western Europe with its cities reduced to rubble and its countryside transformed into a radioactive desert … I see the United States shorn of power like the Byzantine Empire's last fading glimmer of a more civilised age, endeavouring to survive behind defensive walls and living on old ideas which the rest of the world will regard as archaic.

On cheerful days I see quite a different vision. I see Russia and America gradually growing less suspicious of each other and arriving at last at the point where genuine accord is possible … I see Communism losing its fierceness and white men learning to acquiesce in equality for those of different pigmentation. I see science at last allowed to bring to mankind the happiness it is capable of bringing … *Man has survived hitherto because his ignorance and incompetence have made his folly ineffective. Now that science has shown us how to make folly effective, we must abandon folly or perish.* (My italics.)[71]

NOTES AND REFERENCES

1. Confidential note by Sir Henry Tizard, Chief Scientific Adviser to the Ministry of Defence in 1949. Sir Henry said that his memo was greeted with the kind of horror one would expect if one had made a disrespectful remark about the King. See Hennessy, P. (1992). *Never Again: Britain 1945–51*. London: Cape, p. 41.
2. Koestler, A. (1947). *Darkness at Noon*. London: Penguin Classics, p. 193. The book examines the logic of all dictatorships. The quotation is from Lassalle, F. (1904). *Franz von Sickingen, A Tragedy in Five Acts*. New York: Labour News. Koestler's book draws on his experience in the condemned cells during the Spanish Civil War. The book ends with a gripping scene as the hero is led blindfolded to his execution and knocked semi-conscious: 'A shapeless figure bent over him, he smelt the fresh leather of the revolver belt; but what insignia did the figure wear on the sleeves and shoulder straps of his uniform – and in whose name did it raise the dark pistol barrel? A second, smashing blow hit him in the ear. Then all became quiet. There was the sea again with its sounds. A wave slowly lifted him up. It came from afar and travelled sedately on, a shrug of eternity.' Koestler was a fiery character. After the war he lived in Paris, part of the group with Camus and Sartre and had an affair with Simone de Beauvoir. He was prominent in the 1960's 'Flower Power' culture. He was fiercely against the death penalty and campaigned for its abolition following the hanging of Kevin Bentley. On February 28th 1988 he arranged a joint suicide with his wife Cynthia who was over twenty years younger and a less powerful personality. There remains controversy about this event. See Scammell, M. (2010). *Koestler, The Indispensable Intellectual*. London: Faber. My favourite book is Koestler, A. (1967). *The Ghost in the Machine*. Reprint by Penguin.
3. Traub, J. (2006). *The Best Intentions. Kofi Annan and the UN in the Era of American World Power*. New York: Farrar, Straus and Giroux. President Kennedy commented 'I realise now that, in comparison to him I am a small man. He was the greatest statesman of the 20th century.' Kofi Annan was quite clear about moral judgements. During the McCarthy witch hunts he banned the FBI from the UN building, he formed the UN Emergency Force during the Suez Crisis and negotiated a temporary resolution of that conflict, being trusted by both President Nassar and the Israeli leader Ben Gurion. He died in an unexplained air crash in 1961 while negotiating a Congo ceasefire. Investigations have never explained the crash, and in July 2012 a new body was established to start a new investigation. Hammarskjold explained his view of life as follows: 'We are not permitted to choose the frame of our destiny. But what we put into it is ours. He who wills adventure will experience it – according to the measure of his courage. He who wills sacrifice will be sacrificed – according to the measure of his heart.' (I have not been able to discover the whole of this quote, but it appeared in an article entitled 'My Hero' by Timothy Mo in *The Guardian*, 26.05.12.)
4. Brainwashing has fallen into common use in many contexts since. The process is usually characterised by isolation of an individual or group, control of all aspects of their lives, creation of uncertainty, repetition, usually of both the 'bad' ideas that required cleaning out and the new ideas to be put in their place, and emotional manipulation. During the Covid-19 pandemic of 2020 South Korea sent a large consignment of protective equipment to Gloucestershire as a thank you for their sacrifice.
5. On February 12th 1951, the publisher Victor Gollancz wrote to the press arguing against the ever-increasing amount of money directed to the arms industry as world powers competed in the arms race. Meanwhile, world poverty was increasing. He proposed a negotiated settlement in Korea and asked those who agreed to send a postcard with one word 'Yes.' The response of over 10,000 replies led to the formation of the international charity 'War on Want' which now operates worldwide

to fight poverty and injustice. It now campaigns against the effects of globalisation on both these issues. On February 12th 2011, to celebrate its 60th birthday, it asked supporters to e-mail 'Yes' to support their call to demilitarise Afghanistan and the use of development aid money in support of military objectives.

6. The force included British (including Gurka), Australian, New Zealand and Kenyan troops. Some 500 were killed during this long campaign which had little attention at home, another 'forgotten army'; 1,400 Malayan troops, 6,700 MNLA and some 3,000 civilians were killed or went missing.

7. The general view remains that the Malayan campaign developed a successful model for counter-insurgency operations. Some aspects, including the enforced containment of rural populations, were also used against the Mau Mau uprising in Kenya. Comparisons continue to be made between this and the unsuccessful American war in Vietnam where America had overwhelming force but was pitted against a stronger native force, gaining much greater material and other support from China through a shared border. Vietnam, as part of French Indochina, had sided with the Japanese against the Allies whereas British troops had had the support of Malays and fought side by side to liberate the country. In Vietnam the Americans lacked time to develop small self-sufficient jungle patrols and a campaign for hearts and minds. These issues would re-emerge sharply in Iraq and Afghanistan in the 21st century.

8. BBC interview as part of *Children of the Empire* series July 16th 2007. On July 27th, Enoch Powell spoke in Parliament to express his horror at the deaths of eleven Mau Mau prisoners for refusing to work in the Hola Camp. The veteran Labour politician Denis Healey described the speech as the 'greatest Parliamentary speech I ever heard … it had all the moral passion and rhetorical force of Demosthenes.'

9. Jomo Kenyatta has always denied leadership of the Mau Mau, and indeed there is evidence that he despised their methods and in fact cracked down heavily on them after he came to power. The early subsequent history of Kenya was a happy one. The Promised Land distribution by Kenyatta and his successor Alexander Moi favoured the Kikuyu elite so that discontent among poor Kikuyu plus inter-tribal warfare, based on traditional concepts of land ownership, brought the country to a poor economic and social state.

10. Suspicion about the cause of Stalin's death has continued ever since. Although he had spent an enjoyable evening with his closest comrades, they had left unusually early. It has also been reported that the much feared Beria, head of the Secret Service, boasted that he had poisoned Stalin, probably with warfarin. No definitive evidence has ever been discovered. For an illuminating and irreverent view of these events see the satirical, but informative film *Death of Stalin*. Dir. Armando Iannucci. Quad Productions, 2017, starring Simon Russell Beale, Steve Buscemi and Michael Palin.

11. The extent of Stalin's purges, which extended to basically any group that he became suspicious of, were unknown in the west. In the years before his death, 4.7 million people were killed, but if the earlier post-revolution years are included countless millions were murdered. See Judt, T. (2010). *Post War: A History of Europe Since 1945*. London: Vintage, p. 191.

12. Rowntree, S. and Lavers, G. (1951). *Poverty and the Welfare State*. London: Longmans. The previous surveys had been in 1900 and 1936. The 1950 report found that whereas the percentage cause of poverty due to unemployment had dropped from 28.6% to 0%, when old age was given as a cause the percentage had risen from 14.7% to 68.1%.

13. Divisions within the Cabinet were reaching crisis point. Bevin was dying (he died on April 14th); Cripps had retired due to ill health and consequently Gaitskill was untried as Chancellor. Bevan was ill, bad tempered and disgruntled; Morrison was plotting as ever; and Attlee was ill and tired beyond the telling.

14. Mossadegh (referred to by Churchill as 'Mussy Duck') became a comic hate figure in the British press. His role was ended by a CIA/MI6 engineered coup and the company, now called BP, returned with a negotiated fairer share of the profits. More than any other incident, his removal now leads Iran to support any cause against the west. Having destroyed a popular and enlightened government, Britain restored the dictatorial Shah resulting in the 1979 revolution when Iran became a religious autocracy deeply involved in Middle Eastern conflicts. See Bellaigue, C. (2013). *Patriot of Persia: Muhammad Mossadegh and a Very British Coup*. London: Viking.
15. The term entered into common parlance so that anything odd or puzzling would be called 'sheer Heath Robinson'. Emett designed a weird railway in Battersea Park, and later all the elaborate designs of Caractacus Potts in the 1968 film *Chitty Chitty Bang Bang*.
16. Some 50 years later a campaign was launched to reconstruct the Skylon and re-erect it for the 2012 Olympics. This was rejected in favour of the 'Orbit', a much higher, complex structure made from Indian steel which visitors can go up and perhaps use the restaurant at the top. The design has been described as incoherent, pretentious and profoundly ugly. We will wait and see!
17. In 2009 Joan Sutherland presented the prizes at the Cardiff Singer of the Year Competition at the age of 83.
18. Report of The Guillebaud Committee on the Costs of the National Health Service, January 1956. Cmd. 9663.
19. Attlee was elevated to the peerage to take his seat in the House of Lords as Earl Attlee on December 16th 1955. In 1958 he was, along with Bertrand Russell, one of a group of notables to establish the Homosexual Law Reform Society, which campaigned for the decriminalisation of homosexual acts in private by consenting adults, a reform which was voted through Parliament nine years later. He attended Churchill's funeral in January 1965 – elderly and frail by then, he had to remain seated in the freezing cold as the coffin was carried in, having tired himself out by standing at the rehearsal the previous day. He lived to see Labour returned to power under Harold Wilson in 1964. Clement Attlee died on October 8th 1967. His estate was sworn for probate purposes at £7,295. His ashes are buried in the nave of Westminster Abbey. His title passed to his grandson, a member of the Conservative Party.
20. *Daily Mirror*, 03.06.1953, p. 4.
21. The Coronation of Her Majesty Queen Elizabeth II, Approved Souvenir Programme, p. 31. Some evidence has recently emerged that, fearing that Elizabeth was liable to be too susceptible to the influence of the ambitious Lord Mountbatten through his nephew Philip, there was a plot to return the disgraced Duke of Windsor as heir to the throne. The Duke dithered and thus killed the plot. Wilson, C. (2009). *Sunday Telegraph*, 22.11.09, p. 19.
22. Richard Dimbleby had broadcast accounts of bombing raids during the war, including one of the first reports from the Belsen Concentration Camps. His sons David and Jonathan also became leading commentators and TV personalities.
23. *Daily Sketch*, 03.06.1953, p. 20. Tonga, situated in the Pacific Ocean, maintained its independent monarchy and governance throughout its protectorate. It was declared independent in June 1970. It became a constitutional monarchy with a fully representative election in 2010. After 3,000 years of habitation the island, along with others in the Polynesian group, are seriously threatened by climate change.
24. Hilary and Hunt were knighted by the Queen, although Tenzing was only awarded the George Medal. It was thought that Prime Minister Nehru refused to agree to a knighthood for Tenzing. Hilary devoted the rest of his life to a Trust which established schools and hospital to aid the people of remote areas of Nepal. Tenzing established a variety of organisations offering tours and trekking in the Himalayas. His son still runs these expeditions, having himself reached the summit

of Everest in 1996. Hunt became the first Director of the newly launched Duke of Edinburgh Award scheme, which is where I briefly met him.
25. Although there was no connection, this film has always been linked to the real shooting of PC Miles by two young robbers in November 1952. Both culprits were tried and convicted at the Old Bailey and the older Derek Bentley, aged 19, was sentenced to death even though he had not fired the fatal shot. The murderer was too young to face the death penalty. This caused considerable public disquiet, but a petition for clemency was denied despite carrying the signatures of 200 MPs. Bentley was hanged at Wandsworth Prison by Albert Pierrepoint on January 28th 1953. Bentley's execution played an important part in subsequent campaigns to abolish the death penalty, which was abolished for murder in December 1969 following a long campaign by Sydney Silverman MP. In 1993 in view of later evidence Bentley was granted a royal pardon and in 1998 the Court of Appeal quashed the conviction. That same year the death penalty was abolished for treason and piracy with violence.
26. Younghusband, E. L. (1971). *In Britain (2nd Younghusband Report)*. Dunfermline: Carnegie UK Trust.
27. Piaget, J. (1926). *The Language and Thought of the Child*, Third edition. San Diego: Harcourt, pp. 38–41.
28. Merton, R. K. (1938). 'Social Structure and Anomie,' *American Sociological Review*, Vol. 3, p. 672.
29. Bowlby, J. (1951). *Maternal Care and Mental Health*. Geneva: World Health Organisation.
30. *Young Children in War Time* (1942) and *Infants Without Families* (1944), in Vol. 3 of Freud, A. (1966–1980). *The Writings of Anna Freud* (8 Volumes). New York: International Universities Press.
31. Payne, M. (2005). *The Origins of Social Work*. London: Palgrave.
32. At this time, Taylorism (the scientific study of actual workplace behaviour in order to boost production, including time and motion studies) had worked its way through American and Russian industry and other workplaces, arriving at the design of fitted kitchens with the stated aim of saving the energy of housewives.
33. Wallbutton Road was a very tough school. I note that after three changes of name it closed in 2002 under the headship of Ms J. Jordan. The headline in the local paper was 'It's all over for the school of no hope.'
34. Whitehead, A. N. and Russell, B. (2018). *Principia Mathematica*. London: Franklin Classics. (First Published 1925–27.) See Alastair Cooke's chapter on Russell in Cooke, A. (2008). *Six Men*. London: Penguin. Cooke writes of this great man as follows: 'It was not possible … to look back on his career without enormous if qualified admiration. It could be said that the First Act of his life, up to the First World War, was the predictable ferment of a gifted and neurotic Cambridge intellectual who chose to throw himself into academic controversy, political protests, Fabian causes and a sequence of love affairs sparked by simple lust but rationalised, and agonised over, as experiments in human freedom. After that came the Second Act … between the beginning of the First World War and the end of the second … he withstood imprisonment, debt, the alienation of friends, Soviet Communism, a nearly mortal illness, fatherhood (at fifty nine), the shattering and remaking of his fundamental beliefs … the repudiation and then the favour of the Foreign Office, an unrelentingly vicious campaign of slander by the American academic and newspaper establishment, near poverty, "despair beyond bearing," and the ecstasy and exhaustion of five grand passions.' Until shortly before his death in 1970 at the age of 97, Russell led the Campaign for Nuclear Disarmament campaign and had time in prison.
35. Elliot, T. S. (1979). *Murder in the Cathedral*. Part I. London: Faber and Faber, p. 44.
36. Gibson, W. W. (1929). 'The Ice Cart'. *Collected Poems*. London: Macmillan.
37. Minor parts were played by Edward Purdom, Paul Schofield, Claire Bloom and Alfie Bass, who later found fame as a comic actor. In 2011 an established theatre critic, recalling the Swan Theatre, now replaced, commented that it was impossible to hear anything higher than the circle!

38. The theatre was demolished in 1961.
39. Carl Rosa formed his opera company in 1873 and at a later date toured throughout Europe bringing opera to local communities. In the late 1950s, I think it ran into difficulties, but was re-established in 1998 and continues its valuable work in schools and communities. It has a base in East London and is associated with Sadler's Wells Opera.
40. Heyerdahl, T. (1950). *The Kon-Tiki Expedition: By Raft Across the Pacific*. London: George Allen & Unwin.
41. Paton, A. (1972). *Cry the Beloved Country:* New York: Simon and Schuster. (Originally published in 1948.)
42. Shakespeare, W. (1601–2). *Hamlet, Prince of Denmark*. Act 1, Scene IV. In *The Works of William Shakespeare Gathered into One Volume* (1947). London: Odhams Press & Basil Blackwell, p. 676.
43. Cinemas were relied on to show up to date domestic and foreign news as well as entertainment. Some 4,500 cinemas were spread across the country with a regular audience totalling 30 million out of a total population of 46 million. In 1950, every adult went to the pictures at least once every ten days. As aircraft were reaching the speed of sound, I remember a startling film showing how air crew's faces were distorted by the g-forces encountered.
44. *Annie Get Your Gun*. Dir. George Sidney and Busby Berkeley. Metro-Goldwyn-Mayer, 1950. Starring Betty Hutton and Howard Keel.
45. I note that his publication *A Tale of Aske: A Tedious Briefe Historie of The Askean* is still available.
46. Bill Speakman had won the Victoria Cross during an action on Hill 217 in Korea where, while severely wounded, he defended his position, eventually relying on empty beer bottles. His biography recalled how he was taken by surprise when his fellow soldiers jumped to his order once he had a stripe. He returned to Korea in May 2010 on the 60th anniversary of the battles. See Hunt, D. and Mulholland, J. (2013). *Beyond the Legend: Bill Speakman VC*. Cheltenham: The History Press Ltd. The Kindle edition and second-hand copies can be obtained from Amazon.
47. Ponting, H. G. (1949). *The Great White South*. London: G. Duckworth and Sons.
48. Orwell, G. (2004). *1984*. London: Penguin Modern Classics.
49. This remarkable book was first published in June 1945. The author struggled against advanced tuberculosis to complete it. He died six months after publication, aged 46. In America it was seen as an attack on all left-wing politics, including the socialist government in Britain. Just after publication Orwell denied this, saying 'I do not believe that the kind of society I described necessarily will arrive, but I believe (allowing of course for the fact that the book is a satire) that something resembling it could arrive. I believe also that totalitarian ideas have taken root in the minds of intellectuals everywhere, and I have tried to draw these ideas out to their logical consequences.' See Harris, R. *This Week*, 06.06.2009. Whilst many of the character descriptions match Stalin and his associates, concern might be more relevant to the monitoring and surveillance now made possible by modern technology. Orwell, G. (2000). *Animal Farm: A Fairy Story*. London: Penguin Modern Classics.
50. *The Cadet Journal*. July and September 1951, Vol. XIII, Nos. 7 & 9, pp. 165, 218.
51. *The Cadet Journal*. March 1952, Vol XIV, No 3, pp. 1, 5.
52. In 2011, the film *The King's Speech* was released to great acclaim. It concentrated on the relationship between the King and his speech therapist up to the time of the broadcast at the start of the war. It certainly brought back those feelings that most of his subjects had for him, and by implication the role this shy man had in rescuing the institution of the monarchy from the abdication crisis and laying the foundation of his daughter's long reign.
53. *If....* Dir. Lindsay Anderson. Paramount Pictures, 1968. Starring Malcolm McDowell. The soundtrack was the *Missa Luba, A Congolese Mass*, arranged by Fr Guido Haazen. The film was released as the whole youth revolt of the 1960s was at its height. It led the pupils of Aldenham

School in Hertfordshire, where the film had been shot, to open revolt. An article by Simon Worrall, one of the ringleaders of the school revolt was published in *The Times* and reprinted in *The Week* on June 7th 2008.
54. The Barracks were sold for £94 million in 2003 and the site is now an upmarket housing estate with a public square and retail outlets. The Saatchi Gallery opened there in 2008.
55. This centre closed but the Nuffield Trust for the Forces of the Crown provides sports and recreational activities for men and women of the armed forces. See http//www.nuffieldtrust.org.
56. Goncharov, I. (2005). *Oblomov*. London: Penguin Classics. (First published in 1889 and in English in 1954).
57. Brook, D. (1946). *Composers' Gallery*. Nottingham: Cooke and Vowles; Brahms, C. (1952). *A Seat at the Ballet*. London: Evans Brothers; Meynell, F. (ed.) (1948). *The Weekend Book*. London: Nonesuch Press.
58. Steinbeck, J. (1959). *East of Eden*. London: WDL Books, p. 27.
59. Butler, J. (2011). *The Red Dean of Canterbury: The Public and Private Faces of Hewlett Johnson*. London: Scala Publications.
60. *Singing In The* Rain. Dir. Stanley Donen. MGM, 1952. Starring Gene Kelly, Debbie Reynolds and Cyd Charisse. The film includes a famous 15 minute dance sequence; in fact Cyd Charisse had little else to do but dance throughout the film. Her fluidity and grace was all the more remarkable as it grew from the fierce and determined dance lessons she had as a child after she had contracted polio, which had attacked the muscles in her legs. It was her determination to overcome this disability that shaped her famous legs, which were insured for $5 million, a world record at the time.
61. The Black Country earned its name during the Industrial Revolution as the location, generally in the West Midlands, for coal mining, coking, iron, steel and brickworks. All factories and most of the houses in the area became intensely ingrained with soot. This was still the case when I passed through, although the decline in demand had commenced, but the brickworks were still working hard. In subsequent years most of the heavy industries closed, causing mass unemployment. The last brickworks closed in 2008, a decision heavily influenced by the toxic fumes which breached environmental laws. The Black Country Museum is in Dudley.
62. The founder of the Muslim Brotherhood in 1928 was Hassan al Banna; a leading member was Sayeed Qutb. A lonely two-year visit to America as a student had reinforced his conservative Islamist views against the materialism, individualism and sexual mores among fellow students, the start of his hatred of all things western. He had been shocked whilst attending a dance in a church hall in Greeley Colorado: 'The dance hall was full of pounding feet and seductive legs ... Arms circled waists, lips met lips, chests met chests.' Ayman Zawahiri, who was to become established as a key figure alongside Osama bin Laden in Al-Qaeda, was heavily influenced by the writings and the direct influence of Muhammad Qutb. It was Zawahiri's advice that the organisation should attack major western targets that led to the aerial attacks on the east coast of America on September 11th 2001. Ironically, the same student behaviour shocked the American academic philosopher Leo Strauss into extreme right-wing morality, subsequently leading the American Republican administrations to oppose those Islamist leaders. The excellent BBC 2004 documentary *The Stuff of Nightmares* develops these histories. See also Drury, S. (1990). *Leo Strauss and the American Right*. London: Palgrave Macmillan. Hassan al Banna's son-in law, Said Ramadan, was exiled to Switzerland by Nasser, where he communicated with Malcolm X and was seen as the foreign minister of the Brotherhood. His son Tariq is Professor of Contemporary Islamic Studies in the Faculty of Oriental Studies at Oxford University.
63. *Julius Caesar*. Dir: Joseph L. Mankiewicz. MGM, 1953. Starring Marlon Brando, James Mason and John Gielgud.

64. Forty-eight years were to pass before Ann and I could manage the cost of visiting the Seychelles to be reunited with those men still alive. The sudden demobilisation of these men had caused economic disaster to these islands until the tourism industry eventually came to their rescue. The men had memorised the speech given by the Duke of Edinburgh when the Queen opened the airport on the main island of the Seychelles in 1972. According to their account he had paid tribute to the men who had served so loyally in the war and served so valiantly at Tobruk, but had explained that if they were hoping he could do anything to help them in their current depressed state of affairs, they were wrong!
65. Bradley, K. (1966 reprint). *Once a District Officer*. New York: MacMillan.
66. Bradley, K. (1966). *The Diary of a District Officer*. New York: MacMillan, p. 138. (First published 1943).
67. Prince, F. T. (1963). 'Soldiers Bathing' in Allott, K. (ed.). *The Penguin Book of Contemporary Verse*. London: Penguin, p. 249.
68. During battle, or when patrolling, the lead officer has to submit a situation report (Sit Rep).
69. *Limelight*. Dir. Charles Chaplin. United Artists, 1953. Chaplin also acted as producer and wrote the music. Starring Claire Bloom and Buster Keaton. It was while touring with his wife and four children to publicise the film that Chaplin learnt that he would be refused re-entry to America as a suspected member of the Communist Party with a leering, sneering attitude to America. Chaplin then lived in Switzerland, but returned to the USA in 1972 to receive an honorary Oscar for his life's work. His health deteriorated after this event and he died in Switzerland in December 1977, aged 88, having made two films after *Limelight*. Papers released in 2012 revealed that the FBI had asked MI5 to confirm Chaplin's communism and the fact that his name was false. MI5 replied that he posed no security risk. Other papers revealed that in 1970 Chaplin had been born in a caravan belonging to the Gypsy Queen on the 'Black Patch' in Smethwick. *The Guardian*, 17.02.12, p. 3.
70. This station had been used as a deep shelter during the blitz and then as General Eisenhower's headquarters for the launch of D-Day. At the time of my brief visit it was equipped as a hostel for up to 8,000 soldiers.
71. Reprinted in *The Observer*, 04.11.07, p. 18.

1898 London
The Jordan Family
My father, Harry Jordan, is standing on the right

c.1915
My father Private Henry George Jordan (Harry)
3rd Volunteer Battalion Royal Fusiliers
(City of London Regiment)

1916
3rd Battalion of Royal Fusiliers, France
Harry Jordan: with pipe, holding the reins
Jack Jordan: kneeling just below Harry, with a long moustache

c.1917
Jackie, Elsie and Doris
Queenie and Jack Jordan's children

c.1915
Charles Wood
Royal Flying Corp

1916 London
Woolwich Arsenal
Edith Glover: 2nd row up, 3rd in from the left

c.1916
Edie, Mabel and Lola Glover

1918
South London Telephone Exchange
My mother, Mabel Glover, worked here during the war

1922
Mabel Glover and Harry Jordan's wedding

1922
The family at Mabel and Harry's wedding

1926
Mabel, John and Harry

c.1926
Ruby

c.1932
The Family, 113 Grove Vale
South London
'The House of Horrors'

1934
Malcolm and John

1935
George V Jubilee
Family day out

1936
Malcolm and Gran

1939
John and Malcolm

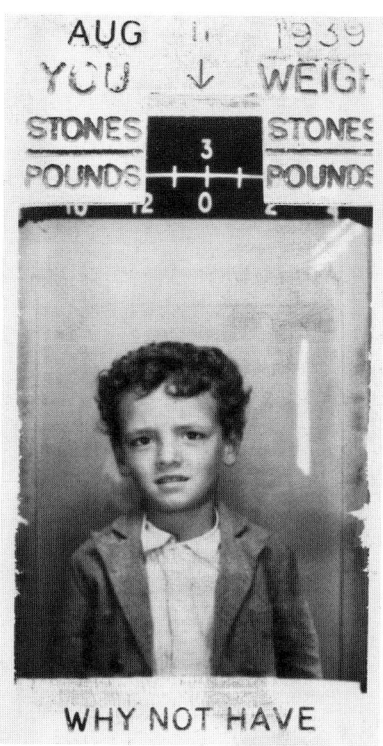

1939
Malcolm

1939 Swanage
The Four Evacuees
1st Placement with the Misses Gay

1939 Swanage
John, Malcolm and the Grant Family
2nd Placement

1940 Willian, Hertfordshire
3rd Placement
Family Visit

1940 Willian, Hertfordshire
The London evacuees, housed at The Terrace in condemned farmers cottages,
with candles, oil lamps, a coal fired stove and a shared laundry tub

1941 Peckham
The postcard sent to the evacuees reads
'Out of the shelter
Gran does come
To keep Old Hitler on the run
One eye up and one eye down
That's the way in London town
Ain't it awful !!!
Lots of love, from Old Mum'

1942
John, called up to the Royal Armoured Corp
Westminster Dragoons

Sherman Flail Tank
John was a driver/gunner throughout the European Campaign
Photo: The Tank Museum

1944 London
Embarkation leave

1945 Willian
First long trousers
Sent by Chris and Charlie Wood
in their regular aid package from the US

1945 Peckham
John and Malcolm
Digging out the Anderson shelter

1950
6th Battalion Royal Fusiliers
City of London Regiment
Cadets marching through the city and back to the Tower for lunch

1951
Malcolm
Cadet Regimental Sergeant Major

1951
Sixth Form, Haberdashers' Aske's
Hatcham Boys School
Malcolm: back row, middle

1952 Chester
Eaton Hall Officers Training Centre

1953 Peckham
Malcolm, newly commissioned
Royal Fusiliers

1953
Peckham High Street with Tower Cinema
Photo: Fred Bell

c.1954
Canal Zone, Egypt
Malcolm posted with Seychellois troops

1954
Canal Zone, Egypt

c.1954
Canal Zone, Egypt
Malcolm with camera

PART TWO

1954–1980

ENGAGEMENT

SEVEN

1954–1961
THE TECTONIC PLATES START TO SHIFT

As I've travelled around the Union I have found everywhere … a deep preoccupation with what is happening in the rest of the African continent … In the twentieth century, and especially since the end of the war, the processes which gave birth to the nation states of Europe have been repeated all over the world. We have seen the awakening of national consciousness in peoples who have for centuries lived in dependence upon some other power … In different places it takes different forms, but it is happening everywhere. The wind of change is blowing through this continent, and whether we like it or not, this growth of national consciousness is a political fact … for which both you and we, and the other nations of the western world are ultimately responsible and we must accept it as such. That means, I would judge, that we've got to come to terms with it.

– Harold MacMillan[1n]

INTERNATIONAL EVENTS

Having contributed so much to the epic victory of the major western powers, it was natural that colonies, noting the rapid rise of India and Pakistan, should press for their own independence. We were keen to oblige, the French less so. Having conceded independence to Indochina,[2n] France was reluctant to lose control of Algeria, which was constituted as an integral part of the French state. The resultant war, which spanned eight years from 1954, was the scene of bloodshed, terror and torture involving complex rival movements, including several million European settlers (the 'Pieds-Noirs') who considered that they had as much claim to Algeria as the native Arab populations. At one stage the civil war split the loyalty of the army, leading to the collapse of the Fourth Republic and the return to power of an aging General De Gaulle on June 1st 1958. As the war continued, De Gaulle was subject to several assassination attempts and military coups, the last of which was in April 1961. A peace settlement was eventually agreed in February 1962, although interracial violence continued for many years. Referendums were held in France and Algeria in the following months and independence was finally achieved in July 1962. The war had cost 300,000 deaths (about half of which were Algerians); one million Europeans were forced to flee and two million Algerians were resettled or displaced.

Impoverished Britain, having already lost major colonies, warned by Algeria and tired of uprising in so many colonies, was ready to deploy diplomatic oil on any gathering storm in the belief that friendly relations would yield future advantages. Our rush to relieve ourselves of ill-prepared countries resulted too often in tribal conflict and chronic corruption. In ten years from 1957 some twenty-three territories became independent, only Malaya, Kenya and Cyprus through bloody conflict.[3n] Many opted to join the great Commonwealth club, and a few small countries later applied to be taken back under Crown protection. Only Rhodesia (the Federation of Rhodesia and Nyasaland) and Hong Kong remained during the Conservative period of office. We still saw ourselves as a world power entitled to sit at the top table of world affairs. This belief was about to be severely dented.

The Middle East

Egypt's President Colonel Nasser's ambitious plan to control the flow of water in the Nile valley, essential for increased industrial development, by building an enormous and high dam at Aswan was to be backed by financial aid from Britain and the World Bank. These loans were conditional on financial support promised by America. Struggling to maintain some independent balance in the Cold War, Nasser recognised communist China and was purchasing arms from Russia. This so alarmed America that their financial offer was withdrawn, thus removing all other offers from the west. In my view, this single act was foolishly short sighted and lay the foundations for much subsequent conflict and turmoil in the Middle East. Nasser, a hero to Arab nationalists throughout the region, infuriated by both the deed and the tone of the notifying letter, declared in July 1956 that he would nationalise the Suez Canal, promising free passage to all ships, with the exception of those from Israel. Just compensation would be paid to shareholders, mostly Britain and France. At home the government and popular press vilified Nasser as some evil dictator and a threat to international peace whose possession of the Canal would mean that he would have his hands round the nation's throat and so would be able to squeeze off essential supplies at any time.[4n] The press campaigns reached their climax while I was with the cadets in summer camp and, in common with many others, still subject to National Service call up. Similar propaganda campaigns were launched in France, which was furious at Nasser's support for the Algerian rebels. Israel was threatened by the prospect that removal of the international buffer zone of Sinai would mean a hostile Egyptian presence on its border. International diplomacy went into overdrive. On October 29th 1956, to the surprise of the general public, Israeli forces, led by Ariel Sharon, moved into Sinai with the apparent aim of occupying the land up to the Canal. To have such a conflict threatening such a vital waterway, Britain and France called on both sides to withdraw, which of course both Israel and Egypt rejected. Thus, somehow miraculously at the ready, 15,000 British and French troops landed at Port Said and Ismailia on November 6th with the declared intention of 'safeguarding' the Canal and, it was rumoured, perhaps entering Cairo to topple the upstart. Nasser blocked the Canal by simply sinking ships. My memory is that, following Churchill's retirement, most of us respected the Prime Minister Anthony Eden's judgement as he had an exceptional record in foreign affairs and was trustworthy. Nonetheless, thousands demonstrated against the government. Having to some extent precipitated the crisis, President Eisenhower protested at military action, which he feared would drive Middle Eastern countries further towards Moscow. It came as a bitter blow when the US sponsored a Security Council resolution condemning Israel and calling on other nations to withdraw. The only option for France and Britain was to veto an American motion, leaving the US to threaten the pound with inevitable economic disaster. Faced with this, we had no alternative but to order our bewildered troops to withdraw under United Nations supervision. What a humiliation! The whole adventure, with up to 2,500 Egyptians dead, severely damaged any remaining influence that Britain had in the Middle East or world affairs.

We had been betrayed by the great power that we had assumed would always support us. All of this was bad enough, but worse was to follow. Some leaks emerged of a secret agreement between Israel, France and Britain (the Sevres Protocol signed on October 24th 1956) with the express object of giving us an excuse to grab the Canal back. The independent minded, pro-Arab, Tory MP William Yates had stated in the House of Commons as early as November 1956 that he had come to the 'conclusion that Her Majesty's Government had been involved in an international conspiracy' and accused the Prime Minister of colluding with others in order to regain control of the Canal.[5n] On December 5th, the veteran Labour leader Aneurin Bevan made what many MPs across the House considered his finest speech. He mocked the government for repeatedly changing the explanation for the invasion of a foreign country and for their apparent naivety in not anticipating Nasser's actions: 'He sank ships in the canal, the wicked man. The result is that the first objective realised was the opposite of the one we set out to achieve; the canal was blocked and is still blocked.' He continued:

> Our objective was to 'deal with all the outstanding problems of the Middle East.' After insulting the United States, after having affronted all our friends in the Commonwealth, after having driven the whole of the Arab world into one solid phalanx behind Nasser we were then going to deal with all the problems of the Middle East … These civil and political objectives in modern society are not attainable by armed force … The social furniture of modern society is so complicated and fragile that it cannot support the jackboot … If we have not learnt that we have learned nothing. Therefore, from our point of view, whatever may have been the morality of the government's action, there is no doubt about the imbecility … they have been synthetic villains … They have not only set off on villainous courses, but they cannot even use the language of villainy.[6]

Once a full copy of the agreement had been leaked, Eden and his Foreign Secretary Selwyn Lloyd, both having lied to Parliament, had no option but to resign on January 9th 1957. Eden was exhausted and seriously ill. This whole incident, followed by a wave of satirical humour now directed at those in power, marked a significant breach in our natural trust of politicians. It was clear to all, except future British politicians, that

Britain no longer had an effective or respected voice in the world. Perhaps we should at last spend our energies on Europe.

However, De Gaulle, furious that Britain had given in so soon to American pressure, was waiting to repeatedly veto our entry to the Common Market. For us it was little compensation that Eisenhower later stated that withdrawing finance for the dam and failing to support Eden had been a major policy mistake, as the humiliation of Britain had the effect that Nasser became the undisputed colossus of the Arab world looking to Russia. Russia stepped in to finance the Aswan Dam, thus giving it a strong foothold in the area. The suave and sophisticated Harold Macmillan succeeded Eden as Prime Minister. There would be a few small hurrahs left for us. We were allowed to protect the Jordanian border in 1958 when American troops landed in Lebanon to shore up the pro-western regime then led by Maronite Christians. In 1990 we were able to join the American-led invasion to expel Saddam Hussein's invasion of Kuwait (The Gulf War).

Cyprus

Both Eden and Macmillan had to deal with uprisings in Cyprus, which was carried out in a textbook example of how to deal with these 'naughty colonies.' Naturally enough, some 30,000 Cypriots, having fought through the war, sought independence – which in true tradition we refused. In 1950 the Greek Orthodox clergyman Archbishop Makarios had organised an open petition which showed that over 95% of the population sought independence, a view that the British could not accept given the vital strategic importance of the island. In 1955, allegedly supported by Makarios, the seasoned Greek Cypriot Colonel Georgios Grivas formed a resistance organisation, Ethniki Organosis Kyprion Agoniston, known as EOKA, to drive the British out. EOKA was promptly outlawed and Makarios was exiled to the Seychelles. The conflict, which claimed the lives of 371 British soldiers and over 500 Cypriots, was short lived as the indigenous Turkish minority became concerned that the independence movement sought only incorporation with Greece. The United Nations sought to resolve the situation between the three countries and independence was granted in 1960, overriding the Turkish demands that the island be divided. Britain retained two military bases and promptly returned Archbishop Makarios to be elected President of the new republic, which joined the Commonwealth the following year.

Europe

Following Khrushchev's denunciation of Stalin (see Chapter 6), dissent was growing in the now vastly expanded Soviet Union. In June 1953 strikes in East Germany were easily put down; then in June 1956 there was an uprising in Poland by citizens who, anxious to emulate the 'semi-detached' status of Tito's Yugoslavia and spurred on by appalling wartime memories and dissatisfaction with economic conditions, commenced a strike which was quickly suppressed. In neighbouring Hungary, post-war elections had resulted in a minority vote for the Communist Party. This was promptly set aside by the occupying army in favour of a faux coalition. But as time went by, the non-communist members slowly 'disappeared.' In October 1956 students posted a 14-point ultimatum calling for Imre Nagy to be confirmed as Premier. The movement had the support of József Mindszenty, the widely respected Primate of Hungary, who led a massive anti-government demonstration, a situation encouraged by western powers and press. There was widespread relief when Khrushchev agreed to allow democratic elections, but with the western powers split by the Suez fiasco, Khrushchev decided to act. Early in the morning of November 4th 1956, seventeen divisions of his tanks, infantry and artillery rolled into Budapest with heavy air support. The Hungarians fell back, holding out for a further six days, looking to the west for support. Late on November 5th the last rebel radio broadcast was received in Vienna:

> Civilised people of the world. On the watchtower of 1,000 year old Hungary the last flames begin to go out. Soviet tanks and guns are roaring over Hungarian soil. Our women – mothers and daughters – are sitting in dread. They still have terrible memories of the army's entry in 1945. Save our Souls. This word may be the last from the last Hungarian freedom station. Listen to our call. Help us – not with advice – not with words, but with action, with soldiers and arms.[7n]

They finally surrendered on November 10th. Despite significant demonstrations in European capitals, in America and outside the UN building, the west did nothing. Nagy was killed on Khrushchev's orders and Cardinal Mindszenty found refuge in the American Embassy, where he lived for the next fifteen years. The Soviet hold on Eastern Europe had been defiantly consolidated while the west had proved powerless to intervene. The inhuman power exercised from Moscow challenged loyal members of the Communist Party in the west. A sort of collective nervous breakdown seized the members as they balanced the imperial aggression of Suez against what lay closer to home. Seven thousand members left the British Communist Party. Twelve years later the crushing of the Czechoslovakia uprising decided the issue for many more.

Britain's chronic indecision over Europe was to be reignited in 1955 when the group of six nations who had formed the European Coal and Steel Community (ECSC) proposed to develop a Customs Union which would embrace atomic development, transport and energy policies. Britain sent a civil servant as observer; after all, we had the Commonwealth trade and our Atlantic alliance. The six continued to negotiate the expansion of the ECSC to a stronger economic and political union. The fact that the European markets were growing faster than our trade with the Commonwealth members, many of whom were developing their independence or looking to America, placed the UK in a difficult position. As negotiations moved towards a draft treaty to establish the European Economic Community (EEC), Britain, already worried that power had been ceded to the United Nations, NATO and the IMF, viewed the developments with the utmost suspicion. The Prime Minister Harold Macmillan was strongly advised that the proposals would remove significant powers from Parliament and the courts. The Treaty of Rome was signed in March 1957 by six countries. The EEC commenced operations in January 1958.

The Cold War and Cuba

Soviet Russia was determinedly threatening America's world domination. Significant United Nations' initiatives were vetoed – the Foreign Minister Andrei Gromyko, who used the veto 79 times, was widely known as 'Mr No,' – but much more galling for the west and America in particular was that on October 4th 1957 Russia launched the first ever satellite into space. This was the famous *Sputnik 1*, a magnificent achievement which served to increase the general level of fear that such technology could now spy on all of us and more accurately decide which of us to annihilate first. The American reaction was to assign many millions of dollars to achieve their goal to get the first man into space and on the moon. Although they lost the first, they succeeded in the second, as the Soviet Union headed slowly towards bankruptcy due mostly to the ridiculous arms and space race.

In Cuba, a newly qualified lawyer, Fidel Castro, was moving to left-wing politics. In the early 1950s he formed the 'Movement' to oppose the dictatorial President Fulgencio Batista. Following time in prison and a number of failed attempts to bring down Batista, Fidel Castro followed his brother Raúl into exile in Mexico, where a relationship had been formed with an Argentinian doctor Ernesto 'Che' Guevara. On November 25th 1956 these leaders with a group of 81 supporters set sail in an old yacht to make contact with revolutionaries in Cuba. Arriving into an ambush, only 20 survived to set up camp in the jungles of the Sierra Maestra to commence a long guerrilla war to regain control of Cuba. Castro's forces rolled into Havana among popular support on January 8th 1959 and he was sworn in as Prime Minister at the age of 32. President Eisenhower, who was nearing the end of his second term and had firmly supported the Batista government, was not pleased to have a Communist regime just 90 miles off the Florida coast. Plans were put in place to reverse the situation at the earliest opportunity. Two years later it would fall to the very new President John F. Kennedy to sanction the CIA's plans that his predecessor had laid at the cost of $13 million. These included the use of CIA trained Cuban exiles and preliminary bombing of Cuban airfields by 'anonymous' bombers. It was assumed, despite British intelligence to the contrary, that the local population would support the invaders. The invasion at the Bay of Pigs on the south of the island in April 1961 ended in disaster, partly as Kennedy had denied the air cover which had been part of the original plan. This incident caused considerable international concern, strengthened Castro's regime and earned him the much needed $53 million of farming equipment which he demanded from the US in exchange for the 1,113 captured prisoners. Kennedy accepted responsibility for his decision, although he suspected that right-wing elements in the CIA had set him up to fail.

Europe

As the obvious disparity between East and West Berliners' prosperity grew, Khrushchev repeatedly called for western troops to be withdrawn; he also commenced the construction of barricades and a wall to separate the divided city and stop the flow of people from east to west. In a sudden rehearsal for the far more serious confrontation to come, Kennedy and Khrushchev had, in October 1961, to deal with armed confrontation across the newly erected Berlin Wall. A Soviet guard at Checkpoint Charlie, the principal crossing between east and west, turned back an American diplomat wishing to routinely pass through. Within a few hours the hot-headed US General Lucius D. Clay ordered his tanks to drive to 75 yards short of the checkpoint, a noisy move immediately answered by the same number of Soviet tanks arriving on the other side. The world held its breath, but Kennedy cleverly used diplomatic channels to resolve the issue and within days carefully choreographed moves allowed one tank at a time to pull back. We could all breathe again.

America

In Montgomery Alabama there had been growing discontent at racial segregation, particularly on public transport. In 1949 a black professor, Jo Ann Robinson, had been abused for absentmindedly sitting in the wrong seat on an empty bus. An active member of the local Women's Political Council she argued for a bus boycott, but the WPC reportedly rejected the idea because it was 'a fact of life in Montgomery.' Robinson became President of the WPC and worked with the National Association for the Advancement of Coloured People (NAACP) to persuade the local council to change their policy, with no real success. Once the Supreme Court, in 1954, had unanimously ruled that segregated education was unconstitutional, the determination for a bus boycott was reignited. The search was on to find the right person. They chose Rosa Parks who presented as a humble seamstress but was in fact a well educated politically aware member of the NAACP. On December 1st 1955 she sat, with three others, on the first row of bus seats allowed for black people. Once all the white seats were full they were asked to move back a row so that a white man could be seated. They refused and were arrested to appear in court the following Monday. The black community had established the Montgomery Improvement Association (MIA), elected a local minister Martin Luther King as its President and organised a successful boycott of all buses. Negotiations with the bus company and city commissioners repeatedly failed. After thirty days King's house and others were fire-bombed and lawsuits launched to end the action.

The black community remained solidly behind the action despite the adverse effect on their ability to work, earn or shop. One small incident reported was when a white bus driver stopped to let off a lone black man in a black neighbourhood. Looking in his rear view mirror, he saw an elderly black woman with a cane rushing towards the bus. He opened the door and said, 'You don't have to rush, auntie. I'll wait for you.' The woman replied, 'In the first place, I ain't your auntie. In the second place, I ain't rushing to get on your bus. I'm jus' trying to catch up with that nigger [sic] who just got off, so I can hit him with this here stick.'[8] The boycott went to the US Supreme Court, which in November 1956 declared segregation unconstitutional. The black community returned to the buses, but faced abuse and violence for many months until the wider community started to accept the new way of life. This marked the start of the long, bitter and often violent ten-year struggle across America and the world for people who had for so long been oppressed to stand up for and believe in their own rights and status in a modern democracy. Britain viewed these developments with some alarm: the apartheid regime enforced by the Afrikaner government of South Africa was of increasing concern, and American civil rights movements could only stir up trouble elsewhere. We still saw ourselves as 'the mother country' of the Commonwealth with, in theory, a benign connection to peoples of every ethnicity across the world.

These events coincided with the early stages of the presidential election to be held in 1960 on the forthcoming retirement of the great Dwight Eisenhower. The contenders were Richard Nixon and John F. Kennedy. The latter's victory brought a ray of hope for the future of the world. A key element in this election was the black vote, organised by the early civil rights movements. The established singer Harry Belafonte had worked hard persuading first Bobby and then a more dubious John Kennedy of the significance of the campaign and the feelings behind the movement for the future of America. The new President's great charisma and clear oratory brought hope to all in the west. He seemed to promise a new and fresh world order, perhaps weaving together the cultural freedoms that had been emerging, particularly from the young, and offering a fresh form of politics. He made this clear in his inaugural speech of January 20th 1961. Referring back to America's own revolution he said:

> We dare not forget today that we are the heirs of that first revolution. Let the world go forth from this time and place, to friend and foe alike, that the torch has been passed to a new generation of Americans – born in this century, tempered by war, disciplined by a hard and bitter peace, proud of our ancient heritage, and unwilling to witness or permit the slow undoing of those human rights to which this nation has always been committed … Let every nation know, whether it wishes us well or ill, that we shall pay any price, bear any burden, meet any hardship, support any friend, oppose any foe, to assure the survival and the success of liberty … To that world assembly of sovereign states, the United Nations, our last best hope in an age where the instruments of war have far outpaced the instruments of peace, we renew our pledge of support … So let us begin anew … Let us never negotiate out of fear, but let us never fear to negotiate.
>
> And so, my fellow Americans, ask not what your country can do for you; ask what you can do for your country. My fellow citizens of the world, ask not what America will do for you, but what, together, we can do for the freedom of man.

It was certainly a contrast to the parade of elderly establishment aristocrats that continued to lead our own antiquated systems. Kennedy's pledge to pay any price was in contrast to the retiring President's advice. Eisenhower warned him that the military–industrial complex was exerting unwarranted influence in Washington and would continue to manipulate politicians into spending more and more on defence than was necessary. America has continued to spend a disproportionate part of its national wealth on military weapons ever since.[9]

Not many months would pass before Kennedy would have to act on his words, but it would be another half century before another President would make such a remarkable speech. In his first year, Kennedy had faced down Khrushchev's regime over the Berlin Wall and the failed attempt to recapture Cuba. He was not overly concerned about the French/NATO loss of Indochina, but, although anxious not to lose more territory to communism, he was reluctant to move from 'advisors' training the South Vietnamese army to putting American fighting troops on the ground. His stance was that 'to introduce US forces in large numbers … might have an initially favourable military impact, it would almost certainly lead to adverse political and, in the long run, adverse military consequences.'

South Africa

By the mid 1950s unrest in South Africa was reaching breaking point. Books, including *Cry the Beloved Country*,[10] alerted me to the reality of the 'pass laws,' which relegated any citizen who was not white to second class. By 1955 the several long-established organisations formed to represent black and coloured peoples came together to form the African National Congress (ANC), the leaders of which were arrested after the government named it as a communist organisation. In early 1959, some ANC members broke away and formed the Pan Africanist Congress of Azania (PAC). Pre-empting a plan by the ANC, the PAC organised a demonstration against the pass laws in Sharpeville for March 21st 1960. Some six thousand unarmed residents approached the local police station, where 20 staff were on duty, to offer themselves up for arrest, peacefully and in a somewhat festive mood. As the day wore on the numbers increased and the mood became more hostile, prompting the arrival of 130 police reinforcements. As missiles were thrown and scuffles broke out, the situation got out of hand. The police opened fire with rifles and machine guns, killing 89 and injuring 180, many wounds being in the back as the crowd fled. The consequences of this event, generally thought to be caused by young nervous and untrained police, were far reaching. The ANC and PAC were banned, leading them to move to armed resistance; some 18,000 people were arrested. Condemnation was worldwide, and the United Nations Security Council called upon the South African government to abandon apartheid and adopt policies which would bring about racial harmony and equality. France and the United Kingdom abstained.

One year after the massacre, the heads of Commonwealth countries met to discuss the South African situation. When it became clear that the meeting was moving decisively against his country, Prime Minister Hendrik Verwoerd withdrew his country from the Commonwealth. It remained excluded for three years. This meeting also expressed alarm at Britain's prospective membership of the European Common Market and its detrimental effect on long-standing trading within the Commonwealth.

NATIONAL EVENTS

At home, both the wartime leaders retired in 1955 – Winston Churchill in April and Clement Attlee in December. The former remained as a less than active, increasingly disabled backbencher until his final stroke ten years later at the age of eighty-four. Attlee entered the House of Lords as 1st Earl Attlee of Walthamstow, Viscount Prestwood, and remained active in politics, travelling to and fro on the underground, although in failing health. He lived to see Labour return to power in 1964, but died three years later. Churchill was succeeded by Anthony Eden and Attlee by Hugh Gaitskell. Conservatives won the 1955 election with a majority of sixty-eight seats, and consequently the government set about a gentle programme of denationalisation, releasing only road haulage and iron and steel back to full private ownership, although both remained under tight government regulation. Gaitskell, on the right wing of the Labour Party and who carried the taint of introducing NHS charges, had been elected leader by defeating both left-wingers Aneurin Bevan and Herbert Morrison. His lack of Attlee's consummate skills as moderator inevitably led to fierce splits in the party. The left fought to retain socialist policies, including 'Clause 4,' which committed the Party to keeping the means of production, distribution and exchange in common ownership. The more reformist policies set out, for example by Anthony Crosland, argued that instead of fighting over how the cake should be divided, the Party should concentrate on economic growth to achieve a bigger and better cake, provided that the economy was well regulated.

> I have never been able to see why high consumption and brotherly love should be thought incompatible – why should not the brothers be affluent and the love conducted under conditions of reasonable comfort?[11]

Unable to produce a clear manifesto and with the press constantly reporting internecine warfare, the Party were kept out of office for thirteen years and were therefore of limited interest to most people. The populace was swept along by the emergence of the teenager, their music and fashions, while respect for our elderly aristocratic leaders was undermined by the arrival of high satire both in print and on screen.

As the economy faltered, there was concern at the rising cost of the NHS. The Conservative Government appointed a committee under the chairmanship of the economist C. W. Guillebaud to enquire into the efficiency and cost of the service.[12] After three years the committee found that in relative terms NHS spending had fallen between 1948 and 1954, from 3.75 to 3.25% of GNP, and that capital spending was running at only 33% of pre-war levels, signalling a deterioration in the many old buildings inherited in 1945. They proposed an expenditure of £30 million annually for seven years. There was also a prediction that additional costs implied by an aging population could be financed easily by economic growth. In general the recommendation was that the young service needed a period of stability. One member was concerned that the existing divided management structures of hospitals, local authority services and primary care might need further considerations as hospitals would increasingly absorb the major resources. The large asylums, as they used to be called, housing mentally ill and 'mentally defective' patients (the term used at the time) were among the most neglected and accounted for almost half of all hospital beds. A unified management structure was proposed.[12] The government introduced some organisational changes and in 1957 doubled the National Insurance contribution, promising that the extra money would be spent on the NHS. Although considerable sums were allocated to improve buildings, concern was expressed that much more would be needed. The first definite link between smoking and lung cancer was published in 1954 and promptly ignored.

At the same time, changing public attitudes led to calls for the law relating to mental illness and disability (wherein many elements of the 1840 Act were still in force) to be reformed. The subject was starting to be more readily discussed in the public arena, partly due to a series of key publications. These included a pamphlet entitled *50,000 Outside the Law*, an examination of people certified for detention in hospitals for the 'mentally defective,' Maxwell Jones's *Therapeutic Communities* and Stafford Clarke's *Psychiatry Today*.[13] In 1953 the government agreed to set up a Royal Commission on the law relating to mental health and mental deficiency. The Commission first sat in 1954 under the chairmanship of Lord Percy and it published its landmark report in 1957.[14] In the run up to the publication of the report, the BBC had broken its silence by broadcasting a five-part documentary entitled *The Hurt Mind*. This coincided with important changes to the treatment of mentally ill patients, the most significant being the availability from the mid 1950s of the first effective anti-psychotic drug Largactil (chlorpromazine), a treatment which promised to control symptoms and behaviour to the extent that it might be possible to free significant numbers of patients from the asylums. Some hospitals were already developing open door policies. The Percy Report proposed that hospitals treating people who were mentally ill or disabled should be treated in the same way as all other hospitals, with the direct implication that decisions on their treatment, care, admission and discharge were the responsibility of the medical profession, not local councils, usually the Medical Officer of Health. Admission and treatment were to be more informal and flexible.

In July 1955 Ruth Ellis was hanged for murder, provoking a public outcry and reigniting the campaign that had followed the execution of the 19-year-old Derek Bentley in 1953. A campaign led by Sydney Silverman MP, and backed with publications from

Arthur Koestler and Albert Camus, led to an abolition bill in the Commons which gained a third reading in June 1956 and was then roundly defeated by a vote of 238 to 95 in the Lords. A compromise bill was passed the following year which abolished the death penalty for six aggravating circumstances.[15n]

Towards the end of Churchill's second term, the government had established a departmental committee, under the chairmanship of John Wolfenden, Vice Chancellor of the University of Reading, to examine aspects of British sex laws. To some extent this was precipitated by the trial of Lord Montagu of Beaulieu, Michael Pitt-Rivers and Peter Wildeblood for homosexual offences and the backlash when all three were imprisoned.

The committee consisted of twelve men and three women who worked diligently, peering with some trepidation into the hidden areas of sexual behaviour in post-war Britain. Faced with embarrassing language the chairman decided to refer to homosexuals as 'Huntleys' and prostitutes as 'Palmers' after the makers of the biscuits available on his daily train journey. First class of course.[16n] Despite significant cultural and personal challenges, the committee reported in 1957 that homosexual behaviour between consenting adults in private should no longer be a criminal offence because it was not the function of law to interfere in the private lives of citizens, particularly as medical evidence indicated that homosexual activity could be compatible with good mental health.[17n] Their recommendations were a shock to the conservative elements in society, although for the most part our culture had already moved towards a much more relaxed approach.[18n] It became clear that the government was, to put it mildly, in no rush to act[19n] on these recommendations despite a very positive debate. In December 1957, a group of distinguished individuals formed the Homosexual Law Reform Society which established The Albany Trust.[20n] It would take ten years of constant campaigning and a change of government before the law was passed.

The fact that most Commonwealth citizens carried a British passport was in line with the UK's historic toleration of immigration, although of course it was never expected that these citizens would actually arrive here. True, the Caribbean migrants from *SS Windrush* (1948) had met many problems (rented accommodation signs reading 'No dogs, No Irish, No Blacks'), but it now seemed to have settled down, the proviso being that the flow inwards did not rise above a small stream. Faced with an acute labour shortage, businesses, particularly London Transport, launched recruitment drives focused on the Caribbean. The result was a more noticeable flow of some 36,000 immigrants a year through the mid to late fifties. As I knew well from duties at BOAC, new arrivals headed directly to their relatives or friends already settled here, often in the rundown areas of our major cities. In London, Brixton and Notting Hill were particular favourites. There they would face violent attacks from the white 'Teddy Boy' gangs. A downturn in the economy served to bring white youths, remnants of the Mosleyites and others, into the open. In August 1958, sexual tensions in the St Ann's area of Nottingham sparked a violent racial riot at pub closing time. A few nights later a similar incident involving a Swedish woman and a Jamaican man in London's Notting Hill brought large gangs of

Teddy Boys rampaging through the area on the August Bank Holiday. Although confined mostly to West London, the attacks grew in violence to involve bicycle chains, iron bars and petrol bombs. The immediate response was one of outrage across the country; a period of national introspection ensued. The fact that such a violent incident passed relatively quietly was, in my view, due to the wisdom of the black community leaders who counselled a non-violent response. Unfortunately, on May 17th 1959 a young man, Kelso Cochrane, who lived in Notting Hill, was set upon and murdered by a gang of white youths. Suspicion fell on local groups of Mosleyites and Colin Jordan's White Defence League. The police pursued it as a robbery, despite evidence that Cochrane had no money at all. These events sharpened the community's suspicion of the Metropolitan Police and marked the emergence of a more assertive attitude by immigrant groups, although the immediate consequence was the local community's resolve to invite everyone to celebrate their culture by holding an annual carnival every August Bank Holiday weekend.[21n]

Macmillan, having been returned to power, faced both the pressure of these events and increasing unemployment. His government passed the Commonwealth Immigration Act of 1962, which restricted immigration to 40,000 a year plus dependents and imposed a quota system for those who had definite employment. The prospect of such restrictions immediately provoked a significant increase in the inflow from the Caribbean, India, Pakistan and Hong Kong. One historian has noted that between 1960 and 1963, 'more migrants had arrived in Britain than had disembarked in the whole of the twentieth century up to that point. The country would never be the same again.'[22n]

The international arms race to develop and test more powerful nuclear weapons continued to absorb vast resources, and the programmes gave rise to increasing anxiety and opposition. In May 1957 Britain tested its first hydrogen bomb, claimed to be 1,000 times more powerful than the atomic bomb. Governments seemed intent on pursuing further developments, although the concept of mutual destruction implied that any country firing the first such missile would itself be destroyed by the response. Seven months after the test, a small group of concerned citizens met to form the Campaign for Nuclear Disarmament (CND). The philosopher Bertrand Russell was appointed President, John Collins, Cannon of St Paul's Cathedral, acted as Chair, and committee members included the leading Labour politician Michael Foot, the journalist James Cameron, the activist Peggy Duff, the author J. B. Priestley and the physicist Joseph Rotblat. The first meeting was held at Central Hall Westminster in February 1958 and was attended by 5,000 people who agreed that the aim of CND would be 'the unconditional renunciation of the use, production of or dependence upon nuclear weapons by Britain and the bringing about of a general disarmament convention.' In the meantime, Britain should halt the flight of planes armed with nuclear weapons, end nuclear testing, not proceed with missile bases and not provide nuclear weapons to any other country. The first march in 1958 from Trafalgar Square to the Aldermaston Atomic Weapons Research Establishment some 46 miles west of London had 8,000 people staying in church halls and supporter's houses. In subsequent years the route was reversed so that more impact would be achieved by ending in Central London. CND rapidly became a popular mass movement. Over the next five years the numbers of marchers rose to 10,000. The aim and sense of common purpose was enhanced by the involvement of folk music and singers led by Ewan MacColl and Peggy Seeger. In preparation for my job with the Prison Commission I thought I should attend the 1960 demonstration in Trafalgar Square; it was an amazing experience, but the lasting impression on me was the carefree arrogance of the police, who, on the periphery of the square, just swept anyone standing on a windowsill off to fall painfully on to the pavement. Did I really want to be associated with the enforcement services?

After three years, some members of the CND wanted to do more than march and demonstrate, and in 1960 Bertrand Russell resigned and formed the controversial Committee of 100 to organise mass non-violent direct action. In their first action in February 1961, some 4,000 protesters sat down outside the Ministry of Defence in Whitehall. There were other demonstrations including one at Holy Loch in Scotland where the US Polaris nuclear missile submarines were based. In advance of a protest to be held in Trafalgar Square in September 1961, all 100 committee members were ordered to court, under an Act of 1361, to bind themselves over to keep the peace for a year. Thirty-two, including Russell aged 89, were sent to prison for refusing to sign. Some 15,000 attended the sit in, which was entirely peaceful. In December eight military airfields were broken into with protesters sitting on the runway. At Wethersfield 5,000 attempted to do so, but were met by 3,000 MOD police. Six young protesters were charged and imprisoned, among them Terry Chandler a classmate of mine from Aske's.[23n] In March 1962 Russell addressed 1,500 demonstrators in Trafalgar Square to protest against the prison sentences. All were arrested. After this the steam seemed to go out of the CND and the Committee of 100, although their efforts would rise and fall as threats to peace grew.[24n]

CULTURE

The significant social and political changes of this period were both reflected in and driven by new cultural influences that, for the first time, infiltrated everyone's daily lives through radio, TV, records and print regardless of social class. In these post-war years, the British film industry was obsessed with wartime daring deeds. The first film, and in my judgement the best, was *The Cruel Sea*, followed chronologically by *The Dam Busters*, *Reach for the Sky* and *The Bridge on the River Kwai*.[25] In Peckham my regular cinema attendance must have made a big impression because I vividly remember the emotional hammering of Julie Harris and James Dean in Eli Kazan's *East of Eden*.[26n] Not only did sex ooze from the screen in practically every scene, but also the family argued violently, there was a good and bad brother and their mother ran a brothel! Here was an outsider, wound up in the passionate torments of adolescence, wanting love and knowing deep inside himself that he was a hero, or at least might become one. A lifetime devotion to blouson jackets followed! Another memorable film was the wonderful *Carmen Jones*, which had an all-black cast and was a modern mildly explicit adaptation of Bizet's opera. The lead roles were taken by Dorothy Dandridge and Harry Belafonte. The music was wonderful with Pearl Bailey's memorable rendition of 'Beat Out Dat Rhythm On a Drum'.[27] Both these films showed a more daring portrayal of sex, and to a limited extent this was a subject that one could start to talk about, except of course at home. I saw these films in one of those vast Romanesque decorated cinemas, The Tower in Rye Lane. Entrance was up a majestic staircase, and more than once I had to sit on the stairs for a few minutes to recover from the emotional shock of a film.

September 1955 marked the first television broadcast by a commercial channel for the southeast regional programme. The first colour programmes followed twelve years later. Real change was also happening in the theatre. August 1955 saw the first production of Samuel Beckett's strange post-modern absurdist play *Waiting for Godot* in which two characters seem to have the sort of conversation that most of us have inside our heads. It got very mixed reviews! At the same time the 'angry young men' were emerging with more direct plays about real life, and in the lower classes at that! They were a magnificent challenge to the established round of tried and tested classics with established leading 'actors.' First to hit the stage at the Royal Court in 1956 was John Osborne's *Look Back in Anger*, followed by *Roots*, the second of Arnold Wesker's trilogy about a poor East London Jewish family.[28n] *Room at the Top*, released in 1959, has been described as one of the most emotionally devastating films ever created in the UK. It changed the face of British cinema. Its success opened the way for more 'kitchen sink dramas,' including Alan Sillitoe's *Saturday Night and Sunday Morning* and Stan Barstow's *A Kind of Loving*.[29n] Cinema was certainly changing, although these productions ran alongside the comic 'Carry On' productions laced with the sexual innuendo that we loved so much.

Somewhat different and more radical events were happening across the Atlantic where the world of the hobo, the bum and the beatnik was under threat from the rapid growth of consumerism. One of their number, Jack Kerouac, had written his autobiographical masterpiece *On the Road* in 1951. It traced 'a gentle invisible revolt' in America which, along with the works of William Burroughs and Allen Ginsberg,[30] would emerge into the colourful free-living culture of the 1960s.

> They danced down the streets like dingledodies, and I shambled after as I've been doing all my life after people who interest me, because the only people for me are the mad ones, the ones who are mad to live, mad to talk, mad to be saved, desirous of everything at the same time, the ones that never yawn or say a commonplace thing, but burn, burn, burn …[31]

John and I haunted the Royal Festival Hall; I think we attended about fifty concerts, musicals and poetry readings throughout the 1950s. We enjoyed a short 'radical opera' by Benjamin Britten at the Royal Court where the first half was spent rehearsing the audience to sing the choruses, in four parts of course![32n] In 1958, at Her Majesty's

Theatre, we thrilled to the arrival of Bernstein's *West Side Story* with the wonderful Chita Rivera as Anita. Visiting the Edinburgh Festival, my current girlfriend and I chose a wide variety of events, but the one that stands out was the remarkable Edith Piaf,[33n] who was stunning. Things were definitely changing, as talented men, mostly comedians often determined to get their own back on the 'establishment,' returned from National Service and found their place, mostly on the BBC. Arthur English, who John had worked with in Palestine, continued his act as 'The Cheeky Chappie' as did Tommy Handley in *ITMA* (*It's That Man Again*). Kenneth Horne's shows *Much-Binding-in-the-Marsh* and *Round the Horne* both fondly ridiculed service life. Comedians slowly pushed back the BBC's boundaries on sexual innuendo, a much appreciated British form of humour. Max Wall was more than once removed from broadcasting when he went too far for closing his act with lines such as 'When roses are red, they're ready for plucking. When girls are sixteen, they're ready for … Goodnight Ladies and Gentlemen!' My greatest favourites were the great Spike Milligan, Peter Sellers, Harry Secombe and Michael Bentine together as 'the Goons' who sent us all crazy every week with their surreal humour. The Goons produced their great one-reel film *The Running Jumping & Standing Still Film*. It was first shown at The Mermaid Theatre at Puddle Dock, Blackfriars, and caused a sensation. I rushed over from Victoria to see it but could hardly get near the theatre for the crowds, eventually pushing myself forward until I could just peep through a small window in a door to watch what I could. Amazing![34n]

While zany humour helped distract most from the constant threat of annihilation, others looked to religion. In 1954 Billy Graham arrived from America to hold his first 'crusade' at Harringay Arena. His 'warm up' was Roy Rogers and his horse Trigger, the heroes of many cowboy films. Graham preached in an evangelical style supported by a well-drilled organisation. He filled all 10,000 seats each night for twelve weeks. At the end of each event, participants were called to come forward and become witnesses in their local communities. The crusades continued across the country for over thirty years.[35n] Not being of a particular religious persuasion, my friends and I kept our distance.

Popular music was emerging as a defined genre, and was promoted and marketed as such, particularly now that smaller 45 rpm discs, which could hold one song each side, and the 33.3 rpm long-playing vinyl records were becoming widely available. The 45 rpm records were ideally suited to the juke boxes that were being established in coffee bars (the latest craze of the time), pubs and clubs. My recollection is that the first major UK 'pop star' was Tommy Steele who built his career on cover versions of popular American hits and was marketed as the British Elvis Presley.[36n] Steele's success was followed in the UK by others including Cliff Richard, Marty Wilde and Billy Fury. Those ultra masculine names say it all. Around these young stars emerged a small army of dubious manipulative entrepreneurs. The most well known was Larry Parnes, who had a unique ability to spot young males whom teenage girls would fancy. They were coiffured and packaged with tough names and launched into the pop music market, where the audiences would embrace the match between the lightness of the music and the freedom of their new affluence. Rich pickings for all.

Between 1958 and 1960 the BBC launched a brave series of dramas, *Play for Today*, and an innovative series of radio ballads which used the voices of working people combined with Euan MacColl and Peggy Seeger's folk songs, sound effects and instrumentals produced by Charles Parker and his daughter. The team spent time with workers and then constructed the ballads. They were very powerful. I remember 'The Ballad Of John Axon' about a train driver who gave his life saving many others by staying at the controls of his runaway freight train. 'Singing The Fishing' proclaimed the work of the herring fishermen and most memorable of all 'The Big Hewer' portrayed the work of coal miners. It confirmed my respect for miners, further strengthened when I was to spend a full day at a coal face.

Publication in the UK remained hemmed in by laws on libel, state security, blasphemy and obscenity. In the latter case, the offence was proved if the publication was judged to be capable of depraving and corrupting those whose minds are open to such immoral influence and into whose hands the publication might fall. Following pressure over many years the Macmillan government passed the Obscene Publications Act 1959 which, while retaining the general categories, required that a whole publication and the circumstances must be taken into account. It would also have to be shown that a significant number of people reading the publication would be corrupted. A defence that a publication was in the public good was allowed. The publishing company Penguin Books had been waiting for this Act to release the unexpurgated edition of D. H. Lawrence's *Lady Chatterley's Lover* (first printed 1928) for public sale. A book in which the author, dying of TB, sought to weigh off the horrors of the First World War by writing a testament to the tenderness of sex using common words. Penguin Books were taken to court, and on October 20th 1960, and for many weeks, we were all treated to massive publicity as a whole range of notable academics, including Bernard Williams, Richard Hoggart and E. M. Forster, were called by the defence whilst public humiliation was heaped on the prosecution, most notably when the chief prosecutor suggested to the jury that they should ask themselves whether this was a book that they would wish their wife or servants to read! On November 2nd the jury returned a verdict of not guilty. The book was on sale eight days later; it sold out within minutes, with two million copies sold in the first year.[37]

Information about sex and the language that would help open discussion was further helped by the work of Dr Alfred Kinsey, an American gynaecologist who, appalled by widespread ignorance about the actual physiology of sexual intercourse, embarked on an obsessive study of human sexual behaviour. His reports on the sexual behaviour in the human male, followed in 1953 by that of the female, hit the headlines, although it took a little time before the publications were readily available in the UK. In one section of both reports the researchers presented the controversial six-point Kinsey scale indicating the proportion of respondents who were exclusively heterosexual or homosexual, the majority having a more varied orientation. These findings were a direct challenge to society's long-held beliefs and prejudices, but Kinsey calmly observed that 'once you have the view of variety as your cardinal principle, you're forced into tolerance. You can't say that anything is "abnormal" or "perverted" you can only say that it is rare.' It is no great surprise that this work is credited with a significant contribution to the sexual freedom of the 1960s.[38]

In 1960 a group of Oxbridge students staged a revue show called *Beyond the Fringe*, which hit the headlines once it reached London and New York. The cast included Peter Cook, Jonathan Miller, Dudley Moore and Alan Bennett, whose mock sermon dealt a blow to the comfortable smug Church of England. The satirical political magazine *Private Eye* was launched in 1961 by the comedian Peter Cook and the following year the nation could join in licensed disrespect as the BBC launched *That Was The Week That Was* presented by David Frost specialising in an aggressive form of political satire never before seen nationwide. Trades unions did not escape attack, most notably lampooned in the hilarious film *I'm All Right Jack*.[39] It was against the backdrop of these cultural freedoms that National Service came to an end so that in May 1963, when the last man was demobbed, teenagers could pass into adult life at their own pace and style.

These young citizens had the advantage of an economy which, if not quite booming, certainly offered jobs with good wages, most of which could be spent on leisure. The fashion to emulate Edwardian dress codes, adopted at the start of the decade, spread down through the class structure to groups of older boys whom the media termed 'Teddy Boys,' the first group to be recognised as one at which marketing for clothes and accessories could be directed. From the same source came the music termed 'rock and roll,' which received a tremendous boost by the film *Blackboard Jungle*.[40n] The music, particularly the Bill Hayley and the Comets' number 'Rock Around the Clock,' blew new life into our existence.

The whole idea of teenagers imposing their opinions and fashions on to adult authority figures was both unprecedented and thrilling. When *Blackboard Jungle* was shown in the nearby Elephant and Castle, the Teddy Boys or 'Teds' as they were known caused a riot by tearing up seats and dancing wildly wherever they could. At odds with the Teds were the Mods: clean cut, Italian fashions, Fred Perry polo shirts, Hush Puppies, coffee bars and the essential zippy Italian motor-scooter with as many shiny accessories as possible. All were freed by technology from domestic routines, with an increased choice in entertainment, more TV channels (ITV was launched in 1955), tape recordings, cassette players and transistor radios. Entertainment could be personalised; rock and roll and pop were everywhere. Advertisers, building on the latest psychological insights, were increasingly able to manipulate consumer choice, particularly the young, who were quick to embrace all the new fashions, most obviously the ubiquitous blue jeans.

FAMILY

My brief welcome home sessions were to a more optimistic climate than the gloomy austerity which I had left two years previously. A choice of a career now became urgent. Any idea of further studies was blocked by the continued absence of that essential French exam. Lorry driving seemed a good idea: protected by glass and metal from the world, I could explore the country and occasionally help hitch-hikers along their way; service with a smile. Perhaps something less physical, but where I could be of service, was in order, so serious consideration was given to the secret service, which would include excitement, danger and use of my capacity to readily assume a variety of personae. As attractive as that sounded, and at a time when jobs were easy to come by, in January 1955 I was easily recruited by the British Overseas Airways Corporation (BOAC) to help passengers as they checked in on all long-distance airlines at the impressive HQ behind Victoria Station before the long coach journey to Heathrow. The attractions of this job were many. I was of service to people but protected by both a uniform and a counter; the ambience carried a certain amount of glamour and a somewhat avant-garde lifestyle; here the 50s were what others experienced in the 60s and 70s. We worked in separate female-dominated teams of about fifteen so that, with the shift system, much social life was with team members. This could be quite complicated. An early flight and overnight stay in Prestwick, officially to show us what first-class travel meant, launched a long and very enjoyable social life. Later, in 1961, our group 'did' Rome (during the Queen's visit in May), which, despite the free-flowing wine, was unbelievably wonderful. This was followed by a complimentary trip for me and three women colleagues skiing in the Austrian resort of Hochsölden. The photos of me wearing old army kit and holding wooden skis (which had to be your height plus an extended arm) were just hilarious.

BOAC offered massive discounts on the fares on all flights and the shift system allowed lots of time off. This would, of course, be a temporary short term job while I studied for my true career in social work. The rota of three days off could be used for some voluntary work and as a start it seemed sensible to fulfil my three-year reserve commitments in the local Army Cadet Unit. Something familiar that had been good to me. I had no great wish to spend the required evenings and weekends in standard TA army training, which inevitably ended in long sessions in the pub. My first posting was to the Royal Fusiliers Cadet Unit at Balham, very convenient as it entailed at least two visits a week to my Aunt Lola, Uncle Jim and their children Paul and Jayne. Lola only discovered that the woman upstairs was a prostitute when she heard two neighbours gossiping that her clientele included a young army officer who came regularly every week! There was a subsequent event when dear Jim was quietly watching television one evening when a guy crept up behind him with the greeting 'Hello darling, are you ready for me?' They abandoned the custom of the day and locked the front door after that.

The completion of one year's service with BOAC had entitled me to travel, for 10% of the normal fare, so I was soon off across the Atlantic on a fourteen-hour flight to see long-lost relatives.[41n] As a preliminary, John and I, equipped with the latest portable tape recorder (Phillips and still working), visited every available member of the extended family to record a short greeting. Grandma did the links and commentary, a role which she embraced with enthusiasm once her initial fear of the machine was overcome. The tape is now a lively part of the family archive. Being alone, in grey trousers and a Harris tweed jacket, in the vastness of New York in November 1956 was a very strange experience. Naively staying in a small hotel off 42nd Street, I based my exploration on Grand Central Station, spending three days walking the crowded streets of the city. Steam seemed to emerge from every vent, giving the whole experience a very weird feeling. The new United Nations Building seemed to reflect the hope of this great institution and, predictably enough, the great mural at the back of the Security Council Chamber, showing the poor and distressed of the world rising up phoenix like, was the most memorable part of this first brief visit.[42n]

I had booked the cheapest train ticket north to my maternal cousins, an overnight journey across the Canadian border to Hamilton. Used to the basic standards of British trains, the hard wooden slat bench was both unexpected and uncomfortable for a journey that never seemed to end, although the greeting and welcome from Cousin Dorothy and her family made up for all the pain. We travelled to Toronto to see my father's relatives who had shared the traumas of the house 'of horrors' at Goose Green but were now well established commercial photographers. The return journey to New York by Greyhound bus was very superior. A short stay in New York was followed by a flight, via the Bahamas, to Florida and an entirely different scene. My great uncle Charlie and his wife Chris, having retired, both worked occasionally as domestic staff in the Fontainebleau and Bal Harbour, the most expensive hotels along the beach. One insight into American society was afforded by the relationship between them and the rich residents, several of whom had become friends and invited them to stay in their luxury estates across the USA. Walking anywhere cast you in the role of eccentric or poverty stricken so the only alternative was a public bus where, of course, black people were confined to the back. This was another quite different insight. The facilities behind each beach were kept clean by gangs of prisoners, all black and chained together. I just could not accept any of this and was rather relieved to be on the plane home.

Browsing a bookshop for the boring return journey, I picked up *The Fifty-Minute Hour: A Collection of True Psychoanalytic Tales*.[43] What an amazing picture of the suffering and treatment of neurotic, obsessive and psychotic patients. By the end of the flight, I was completely hooked and determined that my future social work career would be in psychiatry.

At home John was deeply involved in his long punishing teaching career in inner city secondary schools. He always remained in the classroom, avoiding any participation in what he saw as irrelevant management speak. His overriding aim during school hours or extracurricular activities was to seek every opportunity to develop the imagination and self-respect of pupils through pop or classical music, where he refused to recognise any divisions. With all three of us working, these years were marked by some prosperity within the household even if our agreement to split all costs equally cast a severe limit on my social life. I think the shadow of Dad's death and John's need to get out of London continued his drive to move. The stress of teaching in a very 'tough' school and then constantly meeting his pupils whenever he was shopping or socialising was proving too much. It was particularly embarrassing when pupils failed to appreciate that their formal music teacher was also the guy in the dance band with all the popular tunes. A government minister, commenting on the poor standards in inner city schools, had described the teacher's task as a little more than baby-sitting. John was moved to write to *The Guardian*. His letter appeared in print; it simply said, 'Dear Sir, some babies.'

One evening in late 1956, at the Swanley Drill Hall, one of the BOAC managers rang to ask if I would agree to help out in the emergency in Istanbul caused by the sudden closure of Cairo Airport when our troops invaded Suez. Answer now! Quick thoughts that balanced maintaining the Unit against a new adventure led to acceptance, so in no time our team of five arrived in Turkey with the task of caring for the passengers whose flights had been disrupted. The drive into the city was unforgettable. We approached the ancient walls of the great city across rough countryside, through a narrow gate to the quaint, but historic Pera Palace Hotel.[44n] This was my first close encounter with such an ancient city and I found it fascinating in every way. Traffic mostly comprised donkey carts, horse-drawn trailers or a human with a headband, all overloaded with extraordinary mixtures of goods. Among these were a few cars and buses. In this beautiful city I had gone back a century, but at the airport the work was modern and challenging to say the least as technicians and passenger staff worked together to keep flights moving. The runways, which were not up to standard at the start of the crisis, were taking a hammering so burst tyres or damaged undercarriages were common. Captains were powerful figures and carried great presence. Unfortunately I was to be left in no doubt about the power of such figures when a particular captain's plane burst a tyre on landing twice in exactly the same place. As the plane parked, he noticed the smile on my face. Captain Norman Tebbit was far from amused. Later, as a leading Conservative MP, the Labour leader Michael Foot described him as 'a semi-house-trained polecat.' He had certainly practised on me that day! My agreed two-week posting came to an end, but there was no sign of a replacement. Desperate cables to London produced no response and it seemed to me that all that hard work developing the Unit at Swanley was now being placed in jeopardy. The only solution was to check in myself and my luggage on the next plane. There were some unpleasant interviews at HQ, but as there had been no written agreement for my posting, I narrowly escaped the sack.

All this time the search, started when I was in Khartoum, continued for a site on which to build a new house in Kent. We were directed to definite locations where John's money had been invested. We could not believe that John's money, saved from his long army service, was in the hands of a fraudster. We trailed him through the top business clubs of London when he eventually persuaded us that John's deposit was now transferred to the village of Shoreham, the mystical home of the poet William Blake and artist Samuel Palmer. One day, as we were starting to dig out the rubble from the basement of a great house, a part of which we thought we owned, the penny finally dropped that this was all a sham and John had to say goodbye to his money. We had learnt some valuable lessons and the perpetrator finally ended up in Brixton Prison on a whole range of fraud charges other than ours. John visited him from time to time, feeling sorry for the bastard.

Despite this major setback, our urge to move remained strong and our interest in the Darenth Valley continued. We saw an advert for a small cottage on the hill above Shoreham village, which was definitely worth investigating. Once there, I realised that this was the gate cottage to Stanley White's place where he, 'Ap' and I had planned the pilot King George VI (KGVI) Memorial courses (see below). We moved in on November 5th 1957 so for a few years the move meant that Mum, John and I became regular commuters back to our London jobs.[45n] For me it was often the 'workman's train' leaving the small station of Knockholt at five in the morning, but for Mother the long hilly walk to Shoreham Station added a further three mile walk and three hours travelling every day. John would add the journey to the stresses of being Head of Music at Samuel Pepys School in Wallbutton Road for eight years. A significant relief for me was the saving in travelling time from Peckham that allowed me to run the small West Kent Regiment Cadet Unit in Swanley, which I had undertaken in anticipation of the move. We tackled the house with great enthusiasm. Full of fresh ideas, John and I designed the kitchen.[46n] The first purchase was a German oven and hob combination which could be run off an ordinary socket. The oven and hob were placed horizontally over a cupboard in which all the cooking equipment could be stored. The oven opened from above and had a glass top – ultra modern. Mother immediately pointed out that every time you opened the top all the heat left! Our real achievement was to discover a cabinet maker in the East End of London who made a kitchen table covered in a Formica which looked just like wood, all done by a new photographic process. I carpeted my room with the newly marketed 'Kosset' carpet, the bed side being mottled red and black, the office side black and grey.[47n] The fact that the house stood on raised ground meant that the increasing traffic in a narrow road was undercutting our embankment. We decided to build a low concrete wall to prevent this. The local council gave their consent providing that the wall 'did not abut the road,' but as this was the whole purpose we did it anyway. One long summer after I had left, John repainted all the high weatherboarding, poised on a long ladder while Mother sat at the bottom reading *War and Peace*.

Some ten years later my mother's sister Lola and family moved from Balham into a cottage called 'Little Timberden' opposite us so that a small part of Kent became a South London enclave. A very special guest was my maternal grandfather Herbert, who lived in appallingly poor circumstances in Camberwell Green and was in poor health, his alcoholism having taken its toll. A few photos were taken with his two daughters outside the cottage, although these visits had to be kept a great secret from their mother Edith. Old wounds were still sore. Life at Darent Hulme Cottage was as near to rural bliss as one could get, and very enjoyable, although my main attention was in Swanley and London. John and Mother lived there for some twenty years. John became organist and choirmaster in the village church, roles that he embraced with enthusiasm and total commitment whilst also enjoying his membership of 'The Squires,' a lively group who played for local dances. The cottage was an attractive rendezvous for more of the extended families, especially when Lola and Jim's place was only a few yards away. It was 'just a nice drive out' from London. There were always tea and cakes waiting. My mother's commitment to keeping all parts of the extended family in touch certainly came home to roost during her time at the cottage. In addition to the many relatives from London, Sussex and Surrey were the New Zealand, Florida and Canadian branches, as well as an old family friend from British Columbia. Arriving in Southampton on the *Queen Mary* or flying into Heathrow came branches of my father's eldest sister Hettie's family who we had memorably visited in Dunedin (see below). After Hettie died, her lively husband Jack became a regular visitor, as did his daughter, also called Hettie, her husband John Miller and their family.

The main house, Darenth Hulme, was split between Stanley White's wonderful family and the Feldmars, who, despite their obvious wealth, were members of the Communist Party with an interest in the arts. Mrs Feldmar was a psychiatric social worker. They organised a visit, under close escort, of the Bolshoi Ballet during their second tour to Covent Garden. The village was invited to this amazing event; I assume that it had been selected as a safe excursion for the company to meet some locals. In reality, given that none of us could speak Russian and none of them spoke English, this proved optimistic.

Seven years working full shifts and long hours of voluntary work in Swanley proved demanding, although there was still time to relax and explore other aspects of life, where I met fascinating people and startlingly interesting women. Car hire was available at much reduced rates for BOAC staff, so five of us crammed comfortably in for a tour of Cornwall. On the return trip along the north coast, we were tempted to explore Porthtowan Beach where my good friend Roger Goom and I decided to return to the car park by climbing the cliff. Inevitably we got completely stuck on the slippery shale, our cries of help being ignored by the girls who, understandably enough, assumed we were joking. Eventually the coastguards were alerted and we were rescued, although the whole incident had jeopardised our punctual return for night duty. We found a phone and called the office to apologise for our late arrival to be told that they knew all about it as the cliff rescue photos had been on the front page of the London evening papers!

Sensing that my spell at BOAC might be ending, I took the Florida trip twice: once with my girlfriend (including a trip to see the family in Canada) and then again as a present for my mother, for whom the whole experience was memorable. It was her first flight, her first time in a hot climate and it gave her a totally new look at life. The idea was that once we got to Florida she could stay for a season with Chris and Charlie. After the Canada visit, we enjoyed Florida and took an unforgettable long trip across the peninsula to Dunedin to visit Dad's sister Hettie and her husband Jack. Entering their house took us straight back to the Victorian era; it had net curtains to keep the sun out and walls full of sepia photos. It was a brief and strange visit to this elderly couple who, having greeted us with the enquiry that we were probably thirsty, directed us to the tea shop up the road!

My plan was to head home and to get my brother John to share the party life that I was enjoying. The first chance was at a fancy dress party organised by Michael Pickles, who ran the County Youth Club and whose events were known to be a bit wild. Three of the girls from BOAC came to stay for the party; John and I were sailors, the girls were in nightwear so, all suitably made up, we headed for Swanley. Of course once they spotted the police station we had to stop while they asked the desk sergeant to light their candles! This caused a slight dent in my local reputation. The party lived up to expectations, particularly the 'animal game,' where we each had to draw an animal name from a hat, adjourn to the local field in the dark (men and women at opposite ends) and find your mate by making the matching animal call. My plan was going well – John was relaxed and happy, while a teacher and I had found a quiet room where we could get better acquainted. Unfortunately, John walked in and then out in an advanced state of shock. Lives that I had kept separate had suddenly collided. More adventures were planned, but then came a phone call from Mother announcing her arrival at Heathrow! Experiencing the banter between Chris and Charlie had I think brought back memories of her own parental split, which she found unbearable. Actually she was just homesick, but it marked the end of my campaign to help my older brother to spread his social wings. I left BOAC late in 1961, having secured a job as an Assistant Governor in the Prison and Borstal Service, a job which had been described as social work.

SOCIAL WORK AND ME

Youth Work

Demobilisation in 1954 and attempts to move out of London formed the background to the start of my youth and community work and the pattern which was to mark my future career: immersion, commitment, disaster. The first port of call was, naturally enough, the small Army Cadet Force Association offices in Buckingham Palace Road where Stanley White was busy in the 'shop' editing the *Cadet Journal* and parcelling up affordable boots, a relatively rare item at that time. This opened up a series of initiatives which I think reflected concern about the interests and activities of the young as the constraints of National Service came to an end. In the early 1950s, the Duke of Edinburgh had agreed to promote a scheme to involve young people in positive activities. Elements of physical fitness and challenge, community service and creativity were to be central. The Duke of Edinburgh's Award Scheme was launched in 1956 with bronze, silver and gold award levels; achieving the latter gave you a chance to meet the Duke for presentation of the award. The idea drew heavily on the work of Kurt Hahn, the headmaster of Gordonstoun, the Duke's old school.[48] At the same time the fund, established as a memorial to King George VI, gave a substantial grant to the Army Cadet Force Association (ACFA) to develop courses designed to strengthen and develop leadership.

Leadership

I was invited by Stanley White and Brigadier ap Rhys Pryce to help design and run the early ACFA leadership courses. On a given morning I waited at Camberwell Green for 'Ap' to pick me up for a planning meeting. What luxury to be driven in a modern car even though it was, somewhat surprisingly, French. An hour or so later we dropped down from the main A21 through a narrow country lane and up the steep drive to Darenth Hulme, Stanley's impressively turreted home in Shoreham, Kent. Four months later we set out again in the Citroën estate, joined by Stanley's right hand man Frank, on a reconnaissance journey from London to the key army base at Warminster, a mission fulfilling one of the Brigadier's principles that 'time spent in reconnaissance is seldom, if ever, wasted,' one that my family has since come to know only too well. We were worried that we had no means of identification and there was a major alert in progress as the IRA bombing campaign was directed at military camps. It was Sunday, a day of rest for all soldiers; consequently we drove in unchallenged and set about digging up the turf between two huts as the planned site for a camp fire exhibit. We had been digging for an hour before a sleepy corporal gently enquired who we were and what did we think we were doing!

It was thus my privilege to act as adjutant to the original pilot course for cadet force leaders held at Warminster in March 1955. It was a very busy week. This time the car was heavily loaded, including having a metal bullet catcher on the roof, and Ap was an imposing sight in full Brigadier uniform. His drive and enthusiasm and Stanley's quiet romanticism lay at the heart of the scheme and took the participants through a frantic week of lectures, field exercises and role-plays. Those judged worthy were granted a certificate and commended to their units; those that failed were let go. I was amazed both by the commitment of the volunteer officers, some of whom had fought and served for many years, and their willingness to take instruction from an upstart like me, even though I was covered by some of Ap and Stanley's charisma.[49] Every course had a VIP guest for an after dinner talk and discussion. For this first course the guest was Sir John Hunt of Everest fame, a charming, humble and striking leader, the art of which was the subject of his talk. While this reinforced many of the ideas I had already developed, it placed them in a more thoughtful framework which I would follow throughout my life. In conclusion he came to his own definition of leadership as follows:

> The power to inspire others to discover and give of their best. It demands that the leader operates from within the group, not from above it; setting a fine example, but not stealing initiative: taking his share of the joint task. The spirit of this is 'Let's try this' not 'You do this' … it's the attitude that the leader's job is only one of the jobs to be done; it's the art of persuading each other member of the group that his is also an essential job and it's development his own responsibility, it's the art of blending all these efforts to produce a combined result.[50n]

I helped with further courses at Chester, where Major-General William Dimoline was the guest and at Warminster, gaining many commendations and valuable ideas which I could apply in Swanley.[51n] Among many memories, two stand out. One was when a group of 'undeveloped' army recruits were used to demonstrate exercises suitable for young cadets. They were treated to a spontaneous demonstration of a Brigadier in full regalia showing them his extraordinary set of morning exercises. The other was when an 'enemy' group of older officers acting as Mau Mau took it upon themselves to dress the part, including loincloths and dozens of old bones fresh from the butcher, complete with bits of flesh and blood.[52n] Their leader, who hit the local paper, was Captain Eric Cooper, the Deputy Governor of Borstal, who was to play a significant part in my next career move.

Academic Developments

The recent changes in my family's lifestyle – full employment, modest prosperity and home ownership – seemed, in some ways, to echo the concerns highlighted in two landmark studies both published in 1957. These were the sociological study by Michael Young and Peter Willmott in Bethnal Green, East London (*Family and Kinship in East London*) and the first study of inherent cultural activity by Richard Hoggart (*The Uses of Literacy*). This gave rise to new university departments, the first of which was Hoggart's own Centre for Contemporary Cultural Studies at the University of Birmingham in 1964. Young and Willmott, pioneers in social observation, carefully examined the close and extended family, the group ties that formed the functioning life blood of the communities which faced being broken up by the centrally planned slum clearances, the building of wonderful new tower blocks and the collapse of the docks as the central working hub. Although grounded in rigorous research the book was written in an easy style which made it easily accessible. Hoggart charted the more intimate traditional local community cultures of the working and middle classes, including popular music with the power of the new mass culture promoted by radio, television and 'red top' papers. A mass culture was 'drifting in' from above; it would of necessity be bland to have the widest appeal. In the same year, Vance Packard published his study of the psychological research and subliminal techniques used by advertisers to induce us all to buy their products (*The Hidden Persuaders*). This was followed by Raymond Williams' masterly historical study (*Culture and Society*) of how culture is shaped by the economic conditions of the time.[53]

Mental Health

One of the recommendations of the Percy Committee was that if compulsory admission to hospital was required then an application should be made by a nominated person (a 'duly authorised' local authority Mental Welfare Officer or concerned relative) and the agreement of two doctors. No involvement of the legal system would be required.

Social workers thus acquired an enhanced status and were to have a key role in most compulsory admissions. Such admissions were either for observation (for a limited period) or for treatment (up to 12 months) and required the consent of two medical practitioners: one had to be approved as a specialist and the other had to have some knowledge of the patient, usually the GP. The Mental Health Act 1959 was widely welcomed and has been noted as one of the least controversial post-war bills presented to a welcoming Parliament. Local authorities were to be responsible for prevention and aftercare as all the welfare provisions of the 1946 Act (residential, day care and all ancillary services) were extended to apply to persons with a mental disorder. New definitions were available covering mental disorder, a wide generic term; severe subnormality (incapable of living an independent life); subnormality (susceptible to medical treatment, needing special care or training); and psychopathic personality (abnormal aggression or seriously irresponsible conduct requiring or susceptible to treatment). This last designation marked a change from the moral attitudes which had previously filled so many institutions; the Act specifically excluded admission 'by reason only of promiscuity or other immoral conduct.' Also, people with a diagnosis of psychopathy or subnormality could only be detained for treatment if they were under 21 years of age. One leading psychiatrist commented that a 'vice lobby' could not have achieved more sympathetic treatment.'[54]

One of the few parliamentary disagreements concerned the Committee's view that the Duly Authorised Mental Welfare Officers did not need qualifications. The relatively small Association of Psychiatric Social Workers refused amalgamation with the Association of Duly Authorised Officers, a distinction enhanced by their usual employment in child guidance clinics or within psychiatric hospitals where the Mental Welfare Officers operated in the communities and were employed as Local Authority Officers. Relationships between the two groups varied widely. The 1959 Act changed the whole culture of the asylums and community care, although there would soon be scandals along the way as old deep-rooted practices remained in badly managed hospitals. New treatments and legislation meant that long term patients could now be discharged and new patients might stay for only a short time. The institutions now had to look outwards, to find lost families, accommodation and support for discharged patients. They urgently needed qualified social workers, but few were available. Fortunately for me this was to provide my route into the profession.

Swanley

The small Army Cadet Unit that was my responsibility from 1955 posed several major challenges. Swanley lay just beyond the new London, the 'over-spill' developments of St Paul's Cray and St Mary's Cray. If I had ever thought of running a standard cadet unit, the circumstances of the town at that time changed all that. The village of Swanley had been swamped by a population migrating from London, but no thought had been given to providing any facilities for the new estates. (Sixty years later the comedian Mark Steele, brought up in Swanley, usually included the comment that 'Swanley was a shithole and still is' in his performances.) There were therefore many young people drifting around with little to occupy their time. In this new community there was the 'official' youth club run by the highly charismatic and eccentric Michael Pickles and his wife. There was also a more sedate club run by the local Methodist Church and it seemed obvious that we could be of more benefit to the community if we worked together, included other churches and shared our premises and activities as much as was appropriate. Significant joint intervention was needed!

These were busy times running both the Unit and the coordinated youth activities, and at the same time managing my demanding work pattern at BOAC. Despite the shifts, I kept a pretty tight control over the Unit, for example all lessons had to be recorded on a twelve-point pro-forma covering preliminaries, equipment, how many minutes for each section, questions and adjustments for future learning. My accountability was clear but was made harder due to the distance, our headquarters being twenty miles away in Gillingham. I kept the Commanding Officer informed and up to date with all our events, and he seemed happy enough. All the traditional aspects of the unit were going well: we drilled and paraded, boys passed proficiency exams and got promotion, and we shone whenever we were inspected. Summer camps could be quite fun. One memorable moment, which would fit in well with the TV comedy *Dad's Army*, was when a long convoy of lorries was lined up to leave camp. The stout captain in charge was a pompous guy who rushed up and down with his swagger stick, checking every detail and synchronising watches. On his command, the front truck moved out and turned right, followed by the second. The third turned left so that every following driver had to make an arbitrary choice. Hilarious!

I developed ideas from Aske's, and from my work developing the KGVI courses, giving the boys as much freedom to take initiatives and run the unit as possible. Looking back, one can see how extraordinary it all was. We established a club room/canteen, found furniture, then painted and decorated it all. The Kent Education Authority provided a library and the services of a PT teacher. There were regular film shows, thanks to the free availability of films from the British and Canadian Film Institutes and British Railways. From the BFI came my favourite *We Are The Lambeth Boys*, a perfect portrait of London teenagers and their local club.[55]

On more than one occasion I would shop in the cheap markets of Peckham High Street, shoulder a roll of lino, march to the station to take the train to Swanley and walk it down to the Drill Hall, which was right in the centre of town. As the rage of the moment was 'rock and roll,' we found groups or DJs and turned the premises over to mass madness at least once a month. This would prove a good resource for the local youth. We had our own small lorry so we could help anyone in town or go off camping, to the shooting ranges or wherever we pleased, often taking members of the other clubs with us. We were having a ball, using our own judgement of benefit and risk, and thankfully well before the modern obsession with health and safety was even recognised.

As we extended our range of activities, there was a need to recruit more adult volunteers, so Michael Pickles and I ventured to Broadcasting House to seek help for our campaign. We were received gently and they agreed to send a reporter down to do a piece to be broadcast on the south eastern regional news. I was very relieved as my enthusiasm was turning to exhaustion. The BBC visit was a great success; the reporter, Bill Grundy, made great contact with the boys and put together a really good item. On broadcast night in October 1958, we put blackboards up in the station urging all the commuters returning from London to listen in as Swanley would be on the local news. Bill Grundy struck me as a man of intelligence and integrity, a model of what a BBC reporter should be, although he fell from grace in late 1976.[56n] The broadcast paid off. We got more people involved with youth work. Pursuing the same aim, the Supporters Club was formed headed by a local worthy and we recruited some helpers to run more social activities. We were a pretty exciting place to be. Every opportunity was taken to get publicity in the local papers and the national *Cadet Journal* magazine. Unfortunately, such enthusiasm set against such a tenuous link to higher authority would prove to be my downfall, although our Commanding Officer, the sound and wise Major Pipe, seemed content to give us our head and encouraged our initiatives. Our regular inspection reports were always good and in January 1957, having reached the qualifying length of service, I was promoted to Full Lieutenant. Major Pipe wrote that I was

> an outstandingly good officer … very keen and conscientious … a pleasing personality, unfailing good humour, outstanding patience and a determination to achieve his objective … and has the gift of arousing enthusiasm and encouraging hard work from all with whom he comes into contact.

The Unit grew apace, rising to seven adults and 25 plus cadets. The Supporters Club rose in membership from 1 to 72 as we approached the build up to the celebrations to mark the 100th birthday of the ACF. Unfortunately, at this time Major Pipe retired and was replaced by Major Poole, a totally different character.

In retrospect I can see that the unorthodox way in which I ran the Swanley Unit could be somewhat alarming to a more orthodox person. I am also sure that my very frequent memos requesting supplies, more uniforms and a whole range of guidance must have felt like a never ending stream of demands to an overworked HQ. My deep involvement in the national scene may have been seen as threatening for one who had a desire for control. Nevertheless I was never aware of any hostility and I was not warned that my conduct may be causing offence, but then communications on anything from a distant HQ were pretty rare and my view was that any HQ was there to serve the front line – it was not our job to boost their egos. Wrapped up in the need to keep the local dynamic moving, I planned to launch us into the centenary celebrations with a bang.

The national celebrations would start with the Duke of Edinburgh presenting a centenary banner at the Tower of London, and this would then tour the country to mark local celebrations. The Queen held a garden party at Buckingham Palace, to which I was kindly invited. I decided that we would have our own banner and stage an event which would involve the other clubs and the whole Swanley community, hopefully also bringing in more volunteers. Following my philosophy that success came by starting at the top rather than fighting your way upwards, invitations were sent to the high and mighty asking them to present our Swanley banner in the summer of 1960. The signatures on the letters of refusal included Generals Bill Slim of Burma and Sir John Glubb ('Glubb Pasha' who had commanded Jordan's Foreign Legion) – each would gladden the heart of a collector – but eventually the Prime Minister's wife Lady Dorothy Macmillan agreed to attend. With my long term interest in film, I approached the Orpington Film Society, who agreed to make a general recruiting film that could then be used by units anywhere in the country and a full colour film of our presentation ceremony. The whole thing was a great adventure and we produced two excellent films which were widely used by units across the UK.

The ceremony was held on the afternoon of Saturday July 9th in the school grounds so I set about designing the ceremony, the official programme, the formal invitations, etc. The ceremony laid down in Queens Regulations seemed too long and formal, so I 'adjusted' it to suit. Five other units agreed to take part, as did the TA (who provided stewards and technical expertise for the day), the county padre and the regular band of the Royal West Kent Regiment. Major Poole declined to attend. The most expensive item was the standard itself, which was on blue silk bearing the ACF badge and motto, the white horse of Kent and 'Swanley.'

On Friday evening the local dry cleaning company collected over 100 uniforms, returning them next day neatly pressed and clean. Despite my best intentions, the parade programme was quite long, with some complex drill manoeuvres, but it went well. Lady Macmillan was charming and the local MP and dignitaries, including Colonel Wright from Aske's, were impressed. My greatest pride was in the fact that there had only been one adult on parade. The cadets had otherwise given all the orders and run the whole thing. We had demonstrated the Benjamin Franklin quote that was in the programme:

> Nothing is of more importance to the public weal than to form and train up youth in wisdom and virtue. Wise men are the strength of the state, far more so than riches or arms.[57]

Revenge came quickly. Triumph to disaster in one month. In preparation for summer camp, the CO had to send a pro-forma to my employer that this was part of my TA commitment. I had booked my leave and BOAC were very well aware of this annual event. The CO refused to sign on the extraordinarily thin grounds that my request was so late that he did not wish to offend my employer! This of course prevented my attendance at camp, the major training and bonding event of the year. I fired off a mildly angry note pointing this out, also dragging up all the frustrations of the previous few months. Two days later I was relieved of my command, a response out of proportion to any misdeed of mine. This plot had clearly been cooking for some time as the date of Major Poole's action coincided exactly with the time when all officers were automatically reviewed for further service. All he had to do was refuse to endorse my renewal. Shock and anger hit me and the Unit, the Supporters Club and the volunteers. Reluctantly the CO eventually agreed to meet a small delegation from the Supporters Club and parents, but found them impossible to deal with as they were so 'Jordanised.' I headed for the County HQ in Maidstone, where, during an interview, I was read some negative but minor comments from our annual inspection reports as justification for my dismissal. My disbelief was so strong that on the way out I doubled back to the secretary's office and, with a bit of charm, asked if I could just check a few points from the files now resting on her desk. My interviewer had been holding down the pages that praised the Unit as 'A plus.' I knew enough of military ways to realise that I was unlikely to win this battle, but an appeal to the Army Council eventually led to an offer of a staff car to take me to Divisional HQ where I received a verbal apology and assurances that if I asked for another command, I would be given excellent references. There had apparently been a 'clash of personalities,' although quite how this could have happened with so little awareness on my part remains a mystery. Looking back over the documents fifty years later, it is clear that the Unit that I had created clashed entirely with the traditional view of visiting senior officers. The fact that I was closely following the new post-Amery vision of the KGVI course cut no ice with the local traditionalists.[58n]

Fortunately for me, and probably for the ACF, I think I was aware that my life had fallen into a rut, rushing busily between home, Swanley, BOAC and the increasing high life in London. Having lost the Swanley Unit, my last formal contact was to address a Citizenship Day at Frimley Park[59n] in March 1961. Referring back to Octavia Hill, I emphasised that the ACF was a youth movement, not a feed for the Army. It was an organisation that used the Army ethos to make good citizens.

Having lost command of the Swanley unit I renewed my acquaintance with Eric Cooper, the Mau Mau man on the Chester course, and this led to a day tour of the original Borstal at Rochester and the chance to teach an evening class. We studied map reading and, apart from a request that I should refrain from using local maps (to avoid escapes), all went well. I was certainly impressed by the motto carved above the entrance:

> He determined to save the young and careless from a wasted life of crime. Through his vision and persistence, a system of repression has been gradually replaced by one of leadership and training. We shall remember him as one who believed in his fellow men.

Assistant Governor

A number of factors reminded me that the BOAC job was only ever supposed to be temporary. It was definitely time to start a proper social work job. The advert for Assistant Governor posts in the prison and Borstal service emphasised the welfare and social work aspects of the job, so I applied and, much to my surprise, was appointed. Goodbye to the pleasures of London and hello to Wakefield in Yorkshire and a six-month intensive residential training course at the Prison Commission's Staff College. At the age of 25, another weird but exciting period of my life was about to begin. This time the gap between enthusiasm and cull would be shorter.

The group of some 27 men and three women who assembled at the Staff College opposite HM Prison Wakefield in September 1961 were an interesting mix of former military and colonial officers, young graduates (some of whom were, of course, sons of present or past Prison Commissioners) and long-serving Prison Officers who had been deemed eligible for promotion to Governor grade. Studies covered prison and Borstal. The difference was in the practical placements. In his welcome address, the benign Principal outlined the studies that would be the main focus of our lives for the next six months. The main message was to enjoy this rare 'time out' and soak up as much knowledge as possible. (There was no fear of failure as only one person had ever failed.) Completing the full-time staff were a seasoned Principal Officer (with some similarities to Officer MacKay in the TV comedy *Porridge*) and two young Assistant Governors, who were enthusiastic to offer us a liberal educational experience. Their vision was that enshrined in the objectives of the Borstal system:

> The object of training shall be to bring together every influence which may establish in the inmates the will to lead a good and useful life on release and to fit them to do so by the fullest possible development of personal responsibility.

Further insight was in the 1959 handout that we were given on the principles of the Borstal system, from which the Introduction gives a good guide to the whole tenure:

> Here, in a hundred cities of England and Wales, gather the men and lads who are already unemployed and in danger of becoming unemployable. Their desultory conversation hovers around horses rather than football, and crime rather than cricket ... they are a group of lost opportunities. Material that could have been shaped into good men has now softened, mildew and poison have invaded the system. Instead of being merely non-contributive citizens, they become, by actual breach of the law, the enemies of society.
>
> A considerable number of lads each year are handed over by the courts ... to the care of the prison commissioners, that they may receive this Borstal training and grow to be decent men. A fascinating task and not one to be attempted by the optimist. Desires must be balanced and controlled, and inhibitions must be strengthened. The good must be developed to beat the bad, and a clear and effective knowledge of right and wrong introduced into an impulsive system. Borstal training is on the double assumption that there is individual good in each, and among all an innate corporate spirit, which will respond to the appeal made to the British of every sort to play the game, to follow the flag, to stand by the old ship.[60]

Clearly designed to give us an early warning of what lay ahead, our assignment on day one was to write a critique of Max Weber's masterly *The Protestant Ethic and the Spirit of Capitalism*.[61] A task which seemed somewhat bizarre given the wide educational background of the group let alone our forgotten ability to write an essay. After such a challenging start, there is only space to outline the highs and lows of the next six months. The very experience of living and learning together was of great value, and friendships could be enhanced or broken by the weekend experience of sharing hair raising journeys at top speed up and down the roundabout infested old A1 from London in cars which would never now pass a basic safety test. I found the city of Wakefield, evening excursions to Leeds, including the famous 'City Varieties' (where heckling was allowed, much to the disapproval of senior colleagues), the challenges offered by the Yorkshire Dales and the whole lifestyle of the north so attractive that I vowed to move to this sort of environment at some future date. The 'young gentlemen' (there were three women) received invitations to local events. I recall a preview art exhibition of the Australian artist Sidney Nolan's paintings in the local gallery featuring his 'Ned Kelly' series. For the first time I could actually watch television (black and white, of course) and there was a delicate and sensitive portrait of Paul Tortelier playing the cello. I was captivated at once by the music and the close ups of that striking face in ecstasy.

Needing to meet as many prisoners as possible meant that all new arrivals had to undergo a long interview to obtain a detailed family history. Needless to say a high proportion still believed in their innocence. Most felt very hard done by to be in prison as the initiative was never theirs.[62n]

Next we were exposed to the working lives of 'real' people by means of long day visits to observe various occupations. Close at hand were the steel mills, where we were led as close as possible to the blast furnaces for as long as possible to experience the noise and searing heat endured by the workers every day. After this we went to the mines, where we were at the deep coal-face for hours. I don't think we were supposed to find this enjoyable, but, with a reprise of those long ago lessons at Aske's and the Clapham deep shelters, I was very reluctant to return to the surface. The same was not true of the brewery visit, ending of course in free pints of perfectly pumped samples that we were obliged to drink before we left; we had a very jolly journey home although I was worried by the vast layers of chemical foam floating away down river. Top of the bill for me were the weekly sessions led by visiting lecturers from the Leeds University Extra Mural Department, a key centre for the historic Workers Educational Association. The remarkable Roy Shaw[63n] took us through issues of media studies, prejudice and communication skills. Our law lecturer was the eminent J. M. Kelly,[64n] who covered broad concepts of law and jurisprudence. Should the man who dreamed that he killed a pig and woke to find he had strangled his baby son, in bed beside him, be charged with murder? Was this just? We would then be invited to discuss various points. By now many of the class would be asleep, whilst my own lack of confidence and shyness got in the way of the participation that I longed for. Psychology was taught by the eminent John McLeish, a confirmed behaviourist, who took us through the research on delinquency and the range of tests that prisoners might be subjected to. He outlined some interesting research on group behaviour.[65n]

Good as these three were, they were dwarfed by the great Edward Palmer Thompson.[66n] This extraordinarily tall gaunt man would enter the room balancing a huge pile of dog-eared books from which he would quote as he got us to relive with him the social history of the land, from the point of view of the working class of course. His sessions entranced me, for his whole being was taken up with the process of enlightening this odd group. He drew out the key lessons and concepts with such skill and enthusiasm that I could not fail to be moved.

I particularly recall a visit to York Minster, and to the Dean's office there. The great safe was slowly opened to reveal an original of Caxton's Bible. Thompson passed it round whilst he explained the hand printing process: 'Now you have touched a page that Caxton's hand touched and been part of the enlightenment that it brought to mankind over 300 years ago.' In contrast, he laid a small bet on the first to race to Ingleton Falls and bought the first round. Great man! This was the education that I had craved since at Aske's a mere ten years earlier. It lit me up. I wanted more, and in common with many of Thompson's students still miss him dreadfully. His intellect and leadership are exactly what we need in the current crisis of capitalism.

In sharp contrast were the practical sessions on the prison policies and procedures required to manage one of Her Majesty's institutions. Corporal and capital punishment still being possible sentences, we were, behind closed doors and covered windows, taught the application of the birch and the cat o' nine tails and the details of how to hang a condemned prisoner (our job if the hangman failed to arrive). From time to time we were sent to a variety of institutions, and it was during these visits, with the lessons on punishment still in my mind, that I realised that this job was much more about containment and routine than any form of social work as I understood it. In February 1962, while working in that extraordinary Victorian prison Wormwood Scrubs, staff and prisoners stood together round a small radio in awe while the American John Glenn circled the Earth. Nothing was stolen from my pockets. My first significant own goal was failing to turn up to Harrogate for a tour of the police forensic laboratories. Travelling in my own car, I got lost in the fog and was too shy to go in late. The fact that my current girlfriend was staying in town for a few days seemed to cast doubt on my explanation. On a Borstal placement, part of an Assistant Governor's role was to pass a full assessment to the Probation Officer responsible for a boy's after-care. One file before me was empty except for the psychologist's report and I was required to pass this on. The following week several probation officers came to the college to feed back their view and one quoted this report as an example of what they did not want to hear. All the report said of the poor boy was that, 'his ineffectuality is sadly prole like.' I lacked the social courage to stand up and explain that this was a prime example of the sort of rubbish that the prison service had to put up with from psychologists.

Another black mark came when I worked at a Borstal where the accommodation and workshops had been built by past and current residents. Our neighbour in Shoreham, who was a psychiatric social worker and member of the Communist Party, had lent me a copy of *Road to Life* by Anton Makarenko,[67] a book which describes how he applied his pedagogic principles to the rehabilitation of serious young criminals after the revolution by involving them in community work and major civil engineering projects. It was only after I had waxed enthusiastic about this whole concept that I noticed the Catholic signs and icons all round the Governor's office and recalled that his nickname was Bunny due to his large family. A more serious clash occurred when I was asked to 'get to know' and write a case study on a particular boy that no one else could fathom. He was extremely withdrawn and even more lacking in social skills than me, so I reported that any attempt to befriend this boy in the few days available to me would do him far more harm than good. A broken trust was the last thing he needed. Not a welcome refusal to add to my report.

Although there was a minority of hard line staff, by far the majority of governors and officers that I met in Borstals were committed to the task of reforming their charges, despite limited resources. The gap between the world the boys and girls inhabited and the values and beliefs of the staff, particularly the principles quoted above, was considerable, a fact well developed in Alan Sillitoe's novel *The Loneliness of the Long Distance Runner*,[68] and, as is true of all residential interventions, however much progress was achieved during the sentence much was lost on return to the home environment. On discharge, Borstal lads and lasses passed to the Probation Service for a period of aftercare. In contrast, adult prisoners had very little opportunity to improve their situation and were usually discharged in the clothes in which they had been admitted with just the train fare home! There is great concern, both within the system and in society, that in 2019 with a population of over 83,000 the reconviction rate was between 24 and 31%. In every prison or Borstal we visited we asked two questions: 'Do you bake your own bread?' and 'What is your reconviction rate?' The answer to the first was usually yes; to the second, whatever regime was in place, was that about two-thirds re-offended within two years.[69n]

Despite all this, I was enjoying the sense of personal growth during these months, although pressures and puzzlements remained. There were enjoyable projects, the last of which was a design for a prison where prisoners earned a fair wage for working in a 'factory' under normal conditions, producing work of value. As the course drew to an end, I came to two opposing conclusions. I did not belong here, but I desperately needed a new car and the pay was very good. The solution was to stay for six months and then resign, having at least paid off the car and the commission for my education. In my obsessional way I tabulated all the data on a selection of cars that I could afford but, walking past a local garage, I fell for a beautiful red two-stroke Saab 90, this manufacturer having won the Monte Carlo Rally in successive years. The design was just perfect so I bought it on the spot, signing the hire purchase agreement with a flourish. The next day we were told that before the end of the week we would all be interviewed by a Senior Commissioner from London and we would be informed of our postings after we had left Wakefield. From memory, eleven of us had our contracts terminated! This infuriated me as it was a breach of trust – no mention had ever been made of assessment and we had been told to relax as no one had ever failed the course. Clearly the Commission had over-estimated the number of recruits required and had just chopped a third of the graduates, although, with so many negative reports, it was no great surprise that I was one of them. So, harking back to my recent ACF battle, another long and detailed report was written and sent to the Home Secretary, but this time of course nothing happened, which just reinforced my determination to at least ensure that the next group of students were not similarly lulled into a false position. How I could do that remained a mystery for the present.

Residential Childcare

An expensive car and no income indicated an urgent need for a job so, still determined to follow a career in social work, I secured a place as assistant housemaster at Turners Court, a residential special school for 'educationally subnormal' boys at Wallingford, near Oxford. The Principal, R. P. Menday M.C., was a charismatic man who lived on site with his charming and attractive Swedish wife. I was allocated to the small unit that specialised in older boys who had additional behavioural problems. This was run by a kindly enough ex-naval commander. His wife, as was the normal practice at the time, acted as matron to the whole establishment. They lived in the unit and I had a bed-sit along one of the corridors to the bedrooms. The unit housed about ten boys. The establishment provided care and education for about 120 boys.

Although my time there was short, it was interesting and instructive. The house was run on a routine basis. The boys attended the on-site school, horticultural training or outside employment so my days were not very demanding. My life at Turner's Court had a surreal element, as with a severe reduction in salary most of my time was spent admiring my prized car but being unable to afford to move it. By calculating the exact amount of oil and petrol required for a set mileage, I did venture once to Wallingford and, joy of joys, to Oxford, where I saw a striking performance of *Hamlet* amid the beauty of a college courtyard.

I was fortunate in that my time at Turner's Court coincided with their bi-annual public performance traditionally involving every boy in what was effectively a massive group therapy session. The year I was there the production was the story of the 13th century Children's Crusade, *The Crusaders*, written and directed by John Wiles and Richard Wade.[70n] Cast selection was carried out on the rugger pitch with boys wearing small shorts only, a technique that raised even the Commander's eyebrows! Rehearsals took the entire summer term although most staff were only vaguely aware of what was developing. At dress rehearsals our role was to shepherd in groups of scantily clad boys on the right cue. Costume costs were clearly kept to a minimum. Come the first public performance all boys had to have their hair washed with a heavy dose of conditioner and the full wonder of the thing was revealed amid clever lighting systems. Out from the massive sound system came Carl Orff's *Carmina Burana*,[71n] the first time I heard it. Forward went the whole series of tableaus of boys joining the Crusade, sailing to the Holy Land and fighting the good fight, led by the stars of the show who were the most well built and probably the most intelligent. The final scene, which had been kept secret, involved the leader dragging a heavy cross across the arena to then be crucified. The effect on the audience was stunning, and everyone went back to bed satisfied with the acclaim that they had deservedly received. It was amazing and very thrilling for everyone taking part, a wonderful memory for everyone to take away.[72n]

Oakwood Hospital

In the Spring of 1962, I managed to save enough petrol to get from Oxford to Shoreham, where I spotted an advert from our local mental hospital who were recruiting 'apprentice' social workers who they would support and finance through training. This must be for me! Driving through the impressive gates of the 135-year-old Oakwood Hospital at Barming Heath, just outside Maidstone, the only other car that I wanted to park my pride and joy near was a sparkling bright red Sunbeam Alpine racing car. The reception area was packed, and it transpired that, in the aristocratic tradition of the time, everyone had been called at the same time on the assumption that we would wait all day until the hierarchy were pleased to call us for interview. This was not at all what I had in mind and my protests eventually led to an early call for me and a dangerously fast drive back to Turners Court. My temper had been relieved by a striking woman who took it upon herself to serve coffee and get us all into conversation while the time passed. She was quite something and amazingly she was the owner of the flame red racer. This was Ann Wickett. We were both appointed and my personal and professional life for the next fifty-six years had been settled! It would not prove a quiet life.

NOTES AND REFERENCES

1. Extract from a speech given by the Prime Minister Harold Macmillan to the South African Parliament on February 3rd 1960. His grandson, who inherited the title in 1991, retained his seat as a Conservative peer.
2. The French created the colony of Indochina which covered modern Vietnam and Cambodia. Their post-war claim to the area was challenged by the communist independence movement Viet Minh which had been supported by the Allies, most notably China, to defeat the Japanese occupation. NATO forces had supported French claims, but were defeated by the Viet Minh. Independence was granted to the whole region by a United Nations agreement in 1954, but South Vietnam and America rejected the settlement.
3. The territories were Malaya (1957), Cyprus, Singapore, Kenya, Nigeria, Southern Cameroons and Somalia (1960), Sierra Leone and Kuwait (1961), Jamaica, Trinidad, Tobago, Uganda and Tanganyika (1962), Sarawak, North Borneo, Sudan and Gold Coast (1963), Malta and Gozo, British Honduras, Fiji, Vanuatu, Solomon Islands, Papua New Guinea, Nyasaland, Basutoland and Bechuanaland (1964), and Barbados and Guyana (1966).

4. Fifty years later, Nasser's daughter Hoda, a professional historian, was researching Britain's oppressive role in Egypt's history. Deprived of sources in her native land, she relied on the Public Record Office at Kew. See Steele, A. J. and Black, I. (2006). 'Act of Folly,' *The Guardian*, 08.07.2006, pp. 29–33, and Nasser, H. G. (1994). *Britain and the Egyptian Nationalist Movement, 1936–52*. New York: Ithaca Press.
5. William Yates lost his seat in 1967 after which he and his family emigrated to Australia where, following a career as a teacher, he was elected MP in the Australian House of Representatives, thus achieving the rare record of election to both Parliaments. He was later appointed as Governor of Christmas Island and died in 2010. *The Week*, 08.05.2010, p. 42.
6. 'Great Speeches of the 20th Century.' *The Guardian*, Pamphlet No 13, 2007.
7. On November 17th *Picture Post* magazine published a tribute issue entitled 'Cry Hungary' giving a pictorial and verbatim account of events.
8. *The Montgomery Bus Boycott*. http://www.watson.org/~lisa/blackhistory/civilrights-55-65/montbus.html.
9. Canellos, P. S. (2010). 'We Should Have Listened to Eisenhower.' *The Boston Globe*.
10. Paton, A. (1972). *Cry the Beloved Country*. New York: Simon and Schuster. (Originally published in 1948.)
11. Crosland, A. (1956). *The Future of Socialism*. London: Jonathan Cape.
12. Report of the Committee of Enquiry into the cost of the National Health Service (1956). London: HMSO. Cmd 9663.
13. National Council for Civil Liberties (1951). *50,000 Outside the Law: An Examination of the Treatment of Those Certified as Mentally Defective*. Jones, M. (1952). *Social Psychiatry: A Study of Therapeutic Communities*. Stafford: Tavistock Publications. Clarke, D. (1952). *Psychiatry Today*. London: Penguin.
14. *The Royal Commission on the Law Relating to Mental Illness and Mental Deficiency* (The Percy Report) (1957). Cmd 169. London: HMSO.
15. The Homicide Act 1957 retained the death penalty for murderers in the furtherance of theft, by shooting or explosion, avoiding arrest or assisting escape, murder of a police officer or prison officer or for two murders on different occasions.
16. The BBC4 (2007) documentary *Consenting Adults* portrayed the Committee at work. It starred Charles Dance, Samantha Bond and Mel Smith.
17. *Report of the Committee on Homosexual Offenses and Prostitution*. (1957). Cmd 267. London: HMSO.
18. Convictions for sexual offences remain on file so that in the so-called more tolerant years of the 21st century a person seeking to work with vulnerable people of whatever age has to declare such offences, even though the offence no longer exists. See *The Guardian*, 15.02.2010, p. 10.
19. The Lord Chancellor, Lord Kilmuir, expressed his position when he commented that he had no intention of 'going down in history as the man who made sodomy legal.'
20. The supporters included Clement Attlee, Bertram Russell, Trevor Huddleston, Donald Soper, J. B. Priestley, Barbara Wootton, Victor Gollancz and Stephen Spender.
21. The police had been slow to respond in August when the attacks started. Papers revealed in 2002 showed that the Commissioner had assured the Home Secretary that there was no racial element in the riots despite the fact that police actually involved had stated the opposite. The same denials of racial motive applied to Cochrane's murder, but at least the government established an enquiry under the chairmanship of the amazing Amy Ashwood Garvey (wife of Marcus Garvey). Suspicion by the communities and denial by the police would carry forward into the 21st century, a situation marked by outbursts of protest and riot. The White Defence League was a short-lived far-right organisation modelled on Mosley's BUF. Members emphasised patriotism and admired

22. Hitler's policies. In 1959 they held a rally in Trafalgar Square under the banner 'Stop the Coloured Invasion.' See also Marr, A. (2007). *History of Modern Britain*. London: Macmillan, pp. 192–201.
22. In 2012 Elaine Arnold, a psychiatric social worker, conducted research into the children of the early immigrants from the West Indies, most of whom (as was the custom) were left behind in the care of extended family. When they were summoned years later to join parents who they hardly knew, many suffered a greater shock than their parents. The qualifications they had gained were not recognised in the UK so careers could not be followed and younger children were sometimes classified as educationally subnormal. See Arnold, E. (2011). *Working with Families of African Caribbean Origin: Understanding Issues Around Immigration and Attachment*. London: Jessica Kingsley.
23. Terry and five others broke into the base and sat in front of a plane to prevent its take-off. Their principal defence against the serious charges was that their sole purpose was to prevent the departure of a weapon of mass destruction, thus enhancing the welfare of the state. Their appeal against imprisonment for eighteen months went to the House of Lords, where eight Law Lords found against them on July 12th 1962 on the basis that even if their peaceful intentions were accepted the consequences of their actions were otherwise. See Chandler and Others v Director of Public Prosecutions. House of Lords, July 12th 1962, 46Cr. App. R.347.
24. Probably the longest serving supporter was Pat Arrowsmith, who was imprisoned eleven times. Support for the organisation declined as test ban treaties and agreements to reduce weapon stockpiles were completed, but revived again in the 1980s, when Rev Bruce Kent became a leader and continues to campaign for the complete abolition of nuclear weapons. A reunion was held to mark the 50th anniversary of the first march and Pat Arrowsmith, still working as a volunteer, attended.
25. *The Cruel Sea*. Dir. Charles Frend. GFD, 1953. Starring Jack Hawkins, Donald Sinden, Virginia McKenna and Stanley Baker. *The Dam Busters*. Dir. Michael Anderson. Pathe, 1955. Starring Richard Todd and Michael Redgrave. *Reach for the Sky*. Dir. Lewis Gilbert. Rank, 1956. Starring, Kenneth Moore and Muriel Pavlow. *The Bridge on the River Kwai*. Dir. David Lean. Columbia, 1957. Starring William Holden, Alec Guinness and Jack Hawkins.
26. *East of Eden*. Dir. Eli Kazan. Warner Bros, 1955. Starring James Dean, Julie Harris and Raymond Massey. Dean had moved quickly from a typical American basketball-playing red-necked farm boy with bottle glasses, frequently broken in fights, to teenage star. He was recruited in the steps of Marlon Brando to fit in with the new wave of adolescent stories, among which was *Catcher in the Rye*. *East of Ed*en was Dean's first major role. He quickly rose to iconic stardom but died in September 1955 at the age of 24, driving his super Porsche Spyder 550 sports car. It took more than ten years before the fact of his homosexuality was revealed, a fact that would have never been accepted in the 1950s. See Greer, G. 'Mad About the Boy.' *The Guardian*, 14.05.2005, p. 18. Recently, the award-winning Danish director Lone Scherfig named this film as the one that changed her life.
27. *Carmen Jones*. Dir. Otto Preminger. 20th Century Fox, 1954. Libretto adapted from Oscar Hammerstein II.
28. The trilogy, all written in 1958, comprises *Kitchen Soup with Barley*, *Roots* and *I'm Talking About Jerusalem*, all hard-hitting political dramas. Wesker's plays tend to be didactic. In *Roots*, a character slams the division between 'high' culture and what the majority accept: 'The slop singers and the pop writers and the filmmakers and the women's magazines and the tabloid papers and the picture-strip love stories – those who come along, and you don't have to make no effort for them, it come easy … The whole stinkin' commercial world insults us and we don't care a damn. Well, Ronnie's right – it's our own bloody fault. We want the third-rate – we got it!' His more frequently performed plays are *The Kitchen* and *Chips with Everything*.

29. *Room at the Top*. Dir. Jack Clayton. British Lion, 1959. Starring Laurence Harvey, Simone Signoret, Donald Wolfit and Hermione Baddeley. *Saturday Night and Sunday Morning*. Dir. Karel Reisz. Bryanston Films, 1960. Starring Albert Finney and Shirley Ann Fields. *A Kind of Loving*. Dir. J. Schlesinger. Anglo-Amalgamated, 1962. Starring Alan Bates, June Ritchie and Thora Hird. In 1960 Sillitoe was celebrated by the Soviet Union as a hero of the oppressed workers and given freedom to tour. In 1968 he addressed the Soviet Union of Writers (the audience included Leoni Brezhnev, General Secretary of the Central Committee of the Soviet CP), haranguing them on the human rights abuses that he had witnessed. He pursued these objectives across the Soviet sphere of influence. He supported the Free Theatre of Belarus, including organising regular seasons in London. He died in April 2010.
30. Kerouac, J. (1957). *On the Road*, New York: Viking. Burroughs, W. (1959). *Naked Lunch*. London: Penguin Classics. Ginsberg, A. (1956). *Howl and Other Poems*. San Francisco: City Lights Books. See also the animated documentary film *Howl*. Dir. Rob Epstein. Werc Werk Works, 2011. Starring James Franco.
31. Kerouac, *op cit*. Part 1, Chap. 1.
32. Britten, B. and Crozier, E. (1949). *Let's Make an Opera – The Little Sweep*. Prod. P. Potter. The English Opera Group. The cast included David Hemmings, who went to create a lead role in the film of Britten's *Turn of the Screw* and to star in the controversial 1966 film *Blow Up*.
33. Edith Piaf was a French singer songwriter seen as the national chanteuse. In the UK her most popular songs were 'La Vie en rose,' 'Non, je ne regrette rien' and 'Milord.' She had a very unhappy childhood. Her singing career started in 1935 and was a great success. Her personal life was dogged by violence, accident and chronic illness. By the time we saw her, the effects of chronic alcoholism and medication had taken their toll, although her performance was brilliant. Piaf died in 1963. Her funeral procession in Paris drew tens of thousands with 100,000 fans waiting at the cemetery. See the film *La Vie en Rose*. Dir. Oliver Dahan. Légendre Films, 2007. Starring Marion Cotillard, who won an Academy Award for Best Actress.
34. The Goon's film, which took place in one field and cost about £70 to make, was directed by Richard Lester. It was a favourite of The Beatles, who asked him to produce their innovative films *A Hard Day's Night* (1964) and *Help* (1965).
35. In his later years he filled the role of wise pastor in America, advising presidents from Eisenhower to Bush Senior and Junior. In 2010, at the age of ninety-two he met President Obama.
36. Steele remained in the charts for many years, slowly moving to a film and stage career well into the 21st century. His most popular roles and songs were in *Scrooge*, *Singing in the Rain* and *Half a Sixpence* (1965). The latter, based on H. G. Wells's story *Kipps*, ran in London and Broadway. Steele has written several books and is a respected sculptor. His autobiography was published in 2006 and is entitled *Bermondsey Boy: Memories of a Forgotten World*. London: Joseph.
37. Lawrence, D. H. (1960). *Lady Chatterley's Lover*. London: Penguin Books. Lawrence, D. H. (1961). *A Propos of Lady Chatterley's Lover and Other Stories*. London: Penguin Books. For a powerful review of the novel and the trial, see 'Testament of Love' by Doris Lessing, published in *Guardian Review*, 15.07.2006, pp. 4–6.
38. Kinsey, A. C., Pomeroy, W. B. and Martin, C. E. (1948). *Sexual Behaviour in the Human Male*. London: Saunders. Kinsey, A. C., Pomeroy, W. B. and Martin, C. E. (1953). *Sexual Behaviour in the Human Female*. London: Saunders. *Kinsey – Let's Talk About Sex*. Dir. N. Condon. Fox, 2004. Starring Liam Neeson and Laura Linney. See also *Masters of Sex*. Channel 4, 2013.
39. *I'm All Right Jack*. Dir. John Boulting. Charter Film Productions, 1959. Starring Ian Carmichael, Terry-Thomas and Peter Sellers.
40. *Blackboard Jungle*. Dir. Richard Brooks. MGM, 1955. Starring Glenn Ford, Ann Frances and Sidney Poitier. The film featured a musical track 'Rock Around The Clock' by Bill Haley & His

Comets. The song held the 'Top of the Pops' number one position for many weeks. The group had a similar success the previous year with 'Shake, Rattle and Roll'. The plot of the film concerned a teacher who tries to achieve 'breakthrough' with a group of disengaged pupils, repeated in several later films. It was so much like my brother John who used every genre of music to make a breakthrough with his classes.

41. The flight plan was as follows: London to Shannon, 1.5 hrs 10,500 ft – Shannon to Boston, 11.75 hrs, 10,000 ft – Boston to Idlewild (NY), 0.75 hrs, 6,000 ft.
42. The Chamber was a gift from Norway and the mural is by the Norwegian artist Per Krohg. Second in impact was the long mural on the third floor by the Spanish artist Jose Vela Zanetti showing the struggle of man working towards peace.
43. Lindner, R. (1956). *The Fifty-Minute Hour: A Collection of True Psychoanalytic Tales*. New York: Bantam Books.
44. The hotel opened towards the end of the 19th century to provide high-class accommodation for tourists, particularly those who travelled on the new Orient Express that ended at the city. Ataturk was a regular guest, and a stay at the hotel inspired Agatha Christie's *Murder on the Orient Express* during the period that she 'disappeared' from London. Other guests have included Ernest Hemingway, King Edward VIII and Queen Elizabeth II. The hotel was closed for modernisation and reopened in September 2010.
45. The cottage was advertised as 15 minutes walk to the station where there were 'frequent electric trains' to London. The purchase price was £2,975 (equivalent now to about £500,000). The rateable value was £28. John (whose monthly salary as a Head of Department was reasonable) took out a mortgage with the National Union of Teachers. There was a problem when the surveyor failed the house, but the owners reported that he had been drunk! I insisted that we appeal, with the result that a new survey passed the house. We would own a house!
46. My memory is that pride in British design and manufacture was high during this period, soon of course to reach a pinnacle when the nationalised British Motor Company launched the iconic Mini designed by Alec Issigonis with a transverse mounted engine and low petrol consumption. It became immensely popular, becoming an essential style element to the 'swinging' London of the 1960s. An amazing 5.3 million cars of the original design were sold. BMC later became British Leyland, and was then bought out by British Aerospace and then by BMW. The original design continued for over 30 years, replaced by a new model in 2001. Our obsession was with the Design Centre in central London, which provoked great ideas for us to follow.
47. Kosset Carpets was launched in 1954 using nylon and polyester yarns. The firm prospered in the rush for cheaper home furnishings and it still continues. I bought a modern desk from office furnishers near Victoria Station; it is still in use over 67 years later. I think the Victoria and Albert Museum recently had an exhibition featuring British domestic rooms through the decades. I was rather taken aback to find a room very much like the Lanbury Road living room in the 1940s and my light fittings in a room of the 1950/60s. Visiting the cottage more than 60 years later it remains the same, sadly with the paint peeling off. The concrete wall is still there.
48. More than two million young people worldwide have now achieved an award. Kurt Hahn moved to Scotland, having spoken out against Hitler. He believed strongly that the educational process should equip youth to resist the corrupting influence of society. His model relied on physical fitness, intellectual rigour, expeditions and public service. He was instrumental in the establishment of the Outward Bound scheme and Atlantic College in Wales.
49. For an account of this first course, see Pigg, G. E. (1955). 'I Was There'. *Cadet Journal*, June, Vol XVII, pp. 82–84.
50. As the 1960s advanced, the concept of leadership as an important function in society, and more particularly in the management of any organisation, fell out of fashion. I am very happy to see that

it seems to be returning as a useful concept fifty years later. I note articles in the *NHS Magazine* (November 2002, 'A Lead Role for Leadership,' p. 27), *Community Care* (February 24th 2005, 'How to be a Good Leader,' p. 51) and the recent book Gilbert, P. (2005). *Leadership, Being Effective and Remaining Human*. London: Random House. Or take a glance at any management section in a bookshop.

51. Employers were required to grant leave for TA duties, and public sector employers, of which BOAC was one, were usually generous seeing this commitment as part of their general public duty. Nonetheless, this activity plus attending the routine summer camps was somewhat pushing my luck.

52. Bizarrely the photo titled 'Lessons on a Cabbage Patch' appeared on the front page of the local paper, alongside the American reaction to Russia's escalation of the nuclear threat by claiming to possess inter-continental ballistic missiles. *Chester Evening Chronicle*, 27.08.97.

53. Young, M. and Willmott, P. (1958). *Family and Kinship in East London*. London: Penguin. Hoggart, R. (1957). *The Uses of Literacy: Aspects of Working Class Life*. London: Penguin. Packard, V. (1957). *The Hidden Persuaders*. London: Penguin. Williams, R. (1958). *Culture and Society*. London: Penguin.

54. Sym, M. (1963). *Guide to Psychiatry*. Edinburgh: Livingstone, p. 752.

55. *We Are The Lambeth Boys*. (1956) Dir. Karel Reisz, Prod. Leon Clore and Robert Adams, 1956. This was part of the BFI's 'Free Cinema' programme.

56. Having moved to television as presenter of the *Today* show and fallen victim to excess alcohol, he provoked and mocked the Sex Pistols who had just risen to prominence as the leading punk band. The interview went from bad to worse, from the first word 'Fuck' to Steve Jones calling Grundy a 'dirty old fucker.' Grundy was immediately suspended and his career ruined. The full transcript of the interview is available on youtube.com.

57. Benjamin Franklin, letter to Samuel Johnson, August 23rd 1750.

58. Amery, H. (1957). *The Report of the Committee on the Army Cadet Force*. The report recommended that the ACF needed to improve the leadership and to this end a UK training centre was established. It also recommended a broader range of activities other than standard military drill, etc.

59. Frimley Park was established in 1959 as the central training place for cadet officers. It remains active, offering a range of courses for officers and cadets.

60. See 'The Principles of Borstal Training' as laid down by Sir Alex Paterson and incorporated in the Statutory Rules 1932. In Fox, L. (1952). *The English Prison and Borstal System*. London: Kegan Paul, p. 358.

61. Weber, M. (1920). *The Protestant Ethic and the Spirit of Capitalism*. Oxford: Oxford University Press.

62. In part because they had sat a long time in court listening to their defending lawyers.

63. Roy Shaw, son of a Sheffield steel worker, had been a conscientious objector during WWII and campaigned on social issues and for individuals throughout his life, including the Israeli atomic whistle blower Vanunu in the late 1990s. He was appointed Secretary General of the Arts Council in 1975 until 1983. He wrote *The Arts and the People* in 1987 followed by a devastating criticism of business and sponsorship in the arts and sport in *The Spread of Sponsorship* in 1993. He chaired the Brighton Festival in 2006 at the age of 88. He died on May 15th 2012.

64. At the time, Kelly was lecturing at Trinity College, Oxford. He then moved to University College Dublin, moved into politics and was eventually appointed as Attorney General to the Eire government. He died suddenly in 1991. He is remembered for his clarity of thought, brevity of expression and wit.

65. Born in the Glasgow Gorbals and a committed member of the CND, John McLeish spoke seven languages. He emigrated to Canada in 1969 on his appointment as Professor of Educational

Psychology. He was working on a history of science when he died at home in British Columbia in October 1998. See McLeish, J. (1981). *The Science of Behaviour*. London: Pemberton. McLeish, J. (1969). *The Theory of Social Change – Four Views Considered*. London: Routledge and Kegan Paul.
66. E. P. Thompson was born in Oxford, attended public school and fought in WWII at Monte Cassino. He attended Cambridge University and joined the Communist Party with Christopher Hill and Eric Hobsbawm. He lectured at Warwick University and in the USA, but was best known as a freelance writer and polemicist. He was a leading peace campaigner and member of the CND and worked tirelessly for the Workers Educational Association. He died in August 1993 at the age of 69. He is very much missed. See Thompson, E. P. (1963). *The Making of the English Working Class*. London: Victor Gollancz; Thompson, E. P. (1980). *Writing by Candlelight*. London: Merlin Press. See also the documentary tribute *The Poor Stockinger, the Luddite Cropper and the Deluded Followers of Joanna Southcott*. Dir. Luke Fowler. LUX, 2012. It was shown at the BFI London Film Festival in October 2012. Following his death, funds were established for an annual E. P. Thompson lecture and a memorial bursary.
67. Makarenko, A. (1936). Road to Life. Translated by Stephen Garry. London: Stanley Nott.
68. Sillitoe, A. (1959). *The Loneliness of the Long Distance Runner*. London: Plume. The 1962 film of the same name was directed by Tony Richardson and starred Tom Courtney, Michael Redgrave and James Bolam (Woodfall Films).
69. By 2013 the total was approaching 90,000. The reconviction rate is between 24 and 31%.
70. John Wiles was an experienced film and TV producer who went on to act as producer of four episodes of *Dr Who* between 1965 and 1966. Richard Wade was a scriptwriter and TV dramatist.
71. Carl Orf's *Carmina Burana* was first performed in Frankfurt in 1937, setting 24 medieval secular songs following the turns of fortune, wealth, joy and the perils of drinking, gluttony and lust to modern music for a choir and soloist. It is very impactful.
72. Soon after the final performance, the key boys, returning from a day on the producer's boat, were killed in a road accident while walking back down the narrow lane to the home. The cross that had been carried at the conclusion of the show was encased in scaffolding and erected outside the main office. Quite what the effect was on boys and social workers arriving for a first visit was never clear!

EIGHT

1961–1969

HOPE AND DESPAIR

> That once there was a fleeting wisp of glory
> Called Camelot.
> Camelot! Camelot!!
> …
> Don't let it be forgot
> That once there was a spot
> For one brief shining moment
> That was known as Camelot
>
> – From *Camelot* the musical[1]

Each time a man stands up for an ideal, or acts to improve the lot of others, or strikes out against injustice, he sends forth a tiny ripple of hope, and crossing each other from a million different centres of energy and daring, those ripples build a current which can sweep down the mightiest walls of oppression and resistance.

– Robert Kennedy[2]

> Let the sunshine in
>
> – From *Hair* the musical[3n]

INTERNATIONAL EVENTS

Cuba

President Kennedy had continued the Eisenhower policy of placing intercontinental ballistic missile bases in the UK, Turkey and Italy, all aimed towards Moscow. Premier Khrushchev, faced with a young opponent who had hesitated over Berlin and failed in the Bay of Pigs, saw an opportunity to increase pressure by installing long range missiles in the communist satellite island of Cuba. This put Washington and other major US cities well within range. The process was a long one and it was late in the day before the Americans realised that large sites capable of holding missiles had been prepared in Cuba. The first confirmed photos were analysed on October 15th 1962 and linked to other reconnaissance reports that Soviet ships were already crossing the Atlantic with large crates on deck. On October 16th President Kennedy met with his military advisers who recommended immediate invasion of the island, or at least a full naval blockade. Further consideration of the strategic balance of power convinced Kennedy to announce that the US Navy would quarantine any ship carrying offensive weapons to Cuba and seek a diplomatic solution despite Khrushchev's declaration that his ships would ignore any interference. The US put almost its entire air force and intercontinental missiles on full alert.[4n] By now the whole world was holding its breath. Ten days later American ships intercepted the first cargo ships in the Soviet convoy and diplomatic channels seemed to offer a resolution that if America declared no intention of invading Cuba the missiles could be removed. Within a few days the Soviet position hardened to a demand that American missiles in Turkey be removed, a demand to which Turkey and NATO were opposed.

Two days later a US plane was shot down and another badly damaged by missiles from Cuba. The Cold War had just got very much hotter. Luckily both sides held back from further escalation in case these incidents had been mistakes (which later proved to be the case) and, with the intervention of the President's brother Bobby, emissaries met. With the help of the United Nations Secretary General U Thant, America accepted Khrushchev's offer, and on October 28th Khrushchev announced that all missiles in Cuba would be dismantled and returned to the Soviet Union. In a less publicised move, negotiated by Bobby Kennedy, the old missiles in Turkey were subsequently removed, the US confident that their powerful submarine-based Polaris missiles would be more effective.

The general public came, not surprisingly, to the conclusion that the new young American President had saved us all from extinction. One significant practical outcome was the installation of a permanent 'hot line' between key capitals so that any further errors or misunderstandings could be immediately resolved. As far as we ordinary mortals were concerned, the most noticeable consequence was a slight warmth in east–west relations. Kennedy went out of his way to recognise the great Russian contribution to WWII and by July 1963 a treaty had been signed by the USA, the UK and the Soviet Union to ban atomic testing in the air and on the ground, but not under it. There seemed to be some optimism that the great powers would be able to work together. Hope in the west focused on the charismatic American President, his beautiful wife Jacqueline and his brother Bobby in the redecorated and modernised White House, now the centre of a great social scene, reminiscent, it was said, of King Arthur's court at Camelot.

Only a few short weeks would destroy the hope that we had placed in Kennedy's America. The relationship between the UK's Prime Minister Harold Macmillan and Kennedy was instrumental in the signing of the 1963 Test Ban Treaty with the USSR and an agreement to replace American nuclear submarines armed with American Polaris missiles at Holy Loch in Scotland. Macmillan had also agreed to powerful American bombers capable of carrying atomic bombs being based in the UK, which of course drew demonstrations from CND. In addition to the fear of direct attack, we were obsessed with the 'domino' theory of world domination: if one significant country with relationships with the west were to fall to communism then others would fall, just as in a line of dominoes. South Vietnam was coming under increased pressure from the communist

North, both directly across the border from the thousands of underground communist troops in the southern jungles and from internal conflicts that were hampering effective domestic leadership. Whilst Kennedy remained reluctant to send in American troops, he increased the number of 'advisers' and material assistance for the southern army; he also agreed to the wide scale use of defoliant (Agent Orange) in order to deny enemy use of jungle hideouts.[5n]

Kennedy and Vietnam

In November 1963 South Vietnam's President and his Cabinet were overthrown by the military and Kennedy asked for a report on the consequences of the new situation to be ready when he returned from a political visit to Dallas. On November 22nd 1963, President John F. Kennedy, who was travelling in an open car with his wife Jacqueline by his side through Dallas's Dealey Plaza, was assassinated by, so it is believed, Lee Harvey Oswald. America and the whole free world were shocked by both the fact of the shooting and the tragic images that were seen round the world. It felt a very personal loss. The hope of a new post-war politics and culture had died. Here was a young man who had launched the American Peace Corps, had stood up against the Soviet threat and had held out the possibility of a thaw in the Cold War and a safer world, had promised to end racial discrimination, approved Civil Rights legislation and provided health care for most Americans. He had committed America to land a man on the moon within a decade. His thirty-four months of office had been busy and extraordinarily promising.[6n] Two days later Oswald was shot by a local nightclub owner Jack Ruby while being led under police escort from Dallas Police Station.[7n] In addition to Jacqueline Kennedy, the two young children and other close family, the assassination left two men in particular to deal with their grief and agonise over the way forward for their country. These were the Vice President L. B. Johnson and Bobby Kennedy, the former President's brother.

Johnson was immediately sworn in as the 36th President at the age of fifty-five. A markedly different presidency had begun in a few seconds. A quick witted Catholic from an eminent Boston family had been replaced by a less charismatic, pragmatic but more experienced politician from Texas farming stock who saw that his immediate task was to calm the nation and follow many of Kennedy's domestic policies. President Johnson used the natural shock of events and subsequent national mourning to get Congress to pass the Civil Rights Bill. In November 1964 he fought an election, which he won by a large majority, and then set about his ambitious domestic programme by which he aimed to create a 'Great Society'. This included federal enhancement of education programmes, comprehensive Medicare programmes, development of depressed areas and a war on poverty. In the six years of his presidency he achieved most of these programmes to some degree. Unfortunately from the start of his term of office the situation in Vietnam deteriorated.

South Vietnam was being challenged by the Viet Cong, the insurgent troops strengthened by the communist North, which was in turn supported by China. All this despite the southern army's increased strength to nearly a million men. Some military incidents, including attacks on US troops defending supply airfields, led Johnson, supported by Congress, the Senate and general public opinion, to increase the number of military advisers. Following the domino theory, LBJ took a more determinedly offensive approach. In March 1965 a reluctant President Johnson agreed to the deployment of combat troops. On March 8th 1965 some 3,500 American Marines landed in South Vietnam. The war would last another ten years, witness untold horrors on all sides and leave some seven and a half million people dead or injured.

The long war would shatter America's image worldwide, and bring a large number of citizens into violent conflict with the government in demonstrations that spread around the world as young people raged against the pointlessness of the conflict. The President, who had initiated such great social programmes, would be haunted by demonstrations that were televised across the world with the repeated cry 'Hey, hey, LBJ, how many kids have you killed today?' Interviewed towards the end of his term of office, Johnson explained the agonising choice as he saw it:

> I knew from the start that I was bound to be crucified either way I moved. If I left the woman I really loved – the Great Society – in order to get involved in that bitch of a war on the other side of the world, then I would lose everything at home. All my programs … But if I left that war and let the Communists take over South Vietnam, then I would be seen as a coward and my nation would be seen as an appeaser and we would find it impossible to accomplish anything for anybody anywhere on the entire globe.[8]

As Johnson's term continued, his Democratic Party were increasingly divided, as was the whole country, by Vietnam, civil rights and segregation. His declining popularity was being held responsible for the economic decline. Soon after the start of the 1968 election Johnson withdrew from the campaign, which would become the most violent and controversial ever. Attention now focussed on Bobby Kennedy who, to my mind, had always had greater integrity than his brother and had far greater understanding and empathy with the disadvantaged sections of American society. In addition to the usual political calculations his agony centred on the historical divide between his liberal political beliefs and those of the majority of American voters, who believed passionately in the crude working of the market, his fears for his family and the personal difficulties of moving from the shadow of his elder brother's presidency and assassination.

The Middle East – The Six-Day War

Since the 1956 Suez fiasco (see Chapter 7), relations between Israel and its Arab neighbours had slowly deteriorated, with a more or less continuing series of military border exchanges between Syria and Israel. In time, the Arab nations of Syria, Jordan, Iraq and Egypt formed defensive alliances so that, when it was reported that Israel was amassing troops on the Syrian border, the other nations, particularly Egypt's massive forces, blocked the Straits of Tiran and positioned themselves on the Israeli border. On June 5th 1967 Israel made a pre-emptive strike which disabled the powerful Egyptian air force, thus denying the coming invasion of air superiority. By the time a ceasefire was agreed on June 10th Israel had increased its territory threefold, adding the Gaza Strip, the West Bank, the Golan Heights and the Sinai Peninsula. The six days of fighting had cost Israel fewer than five thousand killed or injured and the Arab forces nearly twenty-nine thousand.

America and Civil Rights

Martin Luther King's non-violent campaigns, based on Gandhi's teachings, continued throughout these years. In 1963 a sustained mass demonstration in Birmingham Alabama had forced the police chief to resign and all facilities be made open to black residents. In August of that year more than a quarter of a million people from many civil rights movements, led by King, marched for 'Jobs and Freedom' in a demonstration of the plight of black people in the southern states. They prepared a list of grievances, mediated by assurances from the Kennedys who were advised by the singer Harry Belafonte. Announcing his decision in March to run for President, Bobby made his views on equality and Vietnam clear:

> I run to seek new policies – policies to end the bloodshed in Vietnam and in our cities, policies to close the gaps that now exist between black and white, between rich and poor, between young and old, in this country and around the rest of the world … I run for the presidency because I want the Democratic Party and the United States of America to stand for hope instead of despair, for reconciliation of men instead of the growing risk of world war … In private talks and in public, I have tried in vain to alter our course in Vietnam before it further saps our spirit and our manpower, further raises the risks of wider war, and further destroys the country and the people it was meant to save.[9]

The largest Washington gathering in American history was topped by King's famous 'I have a dream' speech. More militant movements, including Malcolm X's Nation of Islam, had refused to join the march.[10n] In the following years marches and demonstrations continued across the nation, reaching Chicago in 1966, where demonstrations were held against violent attacks from white crowds supporting discrimination in housing and other public services. Increasingly the civil rights movement found common cause with the anti-Vietnam war movement, King pointing out that

> We were taking the young black men who had been crippled by our society and sending them eight thousand miles away to guarantee liberties which they had not found in Southwest Georgia and East Harlem … We have been repeatedly faced with the cruel irony of watching Negro and white boys on TV screens as they kill and die together for a nation that has been unable to seat them in the same schools.[11]

In March 1968 King travelled to Memphis to address a rally in support of local poor workers. He concluded his address by looking to his own future and that of the movement:

> We've got some difficult days ahead. But it doesn't matter with me now. Because I've been to the mountaintop. And I don't mind. Like anybody I would like to live a long life. Longevity has its place. But I'm not concerned about that now. I just want to do God's will. And He's allowed me to go up to the mountain. And I've looked over. And I've seen the promised land. I may not get there with you. But I want you to know tonight, that we, as a people, will get to the promised land. So I'm happy, tonight. I'm not worried about anything. I'm not fearing any man. Mine eyes have seen the glory of the coming of the Lord.[12]

Six days later, on April 4th 1968, Martin Luther King was assassinated on the balcony of his hotel. Riots erupted across the country. President Johnson declared a national day of mourning, but it fell to Bobby Kennedy, campaigning in Indianapolis, to break the news of the assassination to a mainly black crowd. It was remarkable for the way he brought the crowd from shock and anger to a future of compassion and a continuation of non-violence. Demonstrating his great respect for the audience, he quoted Aeschylus:

> In our sleep, pain which cannot forget falls drop by drop upon the heart until, in our own despair, against our will, comes wisdom through the awful grace of God.

On June 5th Bobby Kennedy made a speech in the Ambassador Hotel, Los Angeles, and was then taken by his security guards to exit through the underground kitchens, where he was assassinated by a Palestinian militant Sirhan Bishara Sirhan. This was a second terrible and historical loss to the nation. To suggest that these assassinations could be attributed to the extreme right wing, the military industrial complex or the demonic Edgar Hoover (Director of the FBI) would be wild fantasy. To my mind, having now witnessed the unthinking opposition and the vitriol heaped on former President Obama, such an attribution does not seem so fanciful. Despite the continuing emotional support following the Kennedy tragedies, the Democratic Party lost the election. Vice President Hubert Humphrey, a much less charismatic figure than the Kennedys, fought a strong campaign against the equally unimpressive Richard Nixon. The Governor of Alabama, the infamous George Wallace, split the right-wing vote by standing as an Independent, bitterly opposed to desegregation. Richard Nixon became the 37th President by 0.7% of the vote; Wallace gained a telling 13.5%.[13n]

NATIONAL EVENTS

While casting himself as the sage elder statesman whose role had been to act as wise uncle to the new young President Kennedy, the Prime Minister Harold Macmillan had continued his determined campaign not to be excluded from Europe. Worried that a growing French–German-led political bloc in Europe would cut Britain out, Macmillan invited de Gaulle to meet him at his house in Sussex. It did not go well. Macmillan pointed out the political and military threats to Europe which British membership would help resist, and de Gaulle replied that he feared that Britain and her Commonwealth would swamp the Community and increase American influence, evidence of which was Britain's refusal to share American intelligence with France. It is reported that at one point Macmillan broke down in the face of the General's intransigence. De Gaulle was able to report to his Cabinet that 'this poor man … seemed so sad, so beaten that I wanted to put my hand on his shoulder and say to him, as in the Edith Piaf song, "Ne pleurez pas, milord."[14] De Gaulle repeated his objections at a further meeting in France but, despite frantic negotiations by Macmillan's minister Edward Heath, the enlarged Treaty of Rome was signed in March 1967 with only the original six states as signatories. The Common Market had been born. Three years later Denmark, Norway, Ireland and the United Kingdom applied to join but de Gaulle refused British entry on exactly the same grounds as he had previously stated. Britain's ambivalent agony would continue well into the 21st century.

As the British economy declined due to growing consumer credit, inflation (which naturally brought claims for higher wages) and a reduction in exports, the government imposed a very unpopular wage freeze leading to a marked erosion of the Conservative majority. In a desperate attempt to turn the tide, that cool aristocrat Macmillan drew his political knife and sacked eight junior ministers. It was said that no man had so clearly laid down his friends' life to save his own.

The Profumo Scandal

As the government's unpopularity increased, it was hit with the Profumo scandal. This, in the eyes of increasingly undeferential voters remembering the lies of Suez, was further proof of a corrupt political system. These events had been orchestrated in a setting that could not have been more familiar to the Prime Minister: Cliveden, the country house of the Astor family and the setting for much plotting by the powerful. The young Lord Astor was more concerned with social life than politics and was known to host extravagant weekend gatherings, the guest list having expanded in tune with the swinging sixties. In July 1961 John Profumo, Secretary of State for War, was one such guest. In an estate cottage with free access to the house was Stephen Ward, a Harley Street osteopath who maintained a unique network of clientele and contacts. These ranged from royalty to the notoriously violent Kray brothers, whose criminal gang exercised power from Soho to East London, and a number of lively young women who embraced the freewheeling moral codes of the times. On this particular warm evening one of Ward's guests, Christine Keeler, decided to enjoy a naked swim in the pool inside the main house where she met Profumo and an affair developed. News of this relationship came to the attention of the press at Christmas 1962 when it was also revealed that one of her other lovers was Yevgeni Ivanov, a Naval attaché (i.e. spy) at the Russian Embassy. The ensuing headlines led Profumo to make a statement to Parliament, which he did, but unfortunately he lied in the process which led to his resignation. By the end of the scandal, Profumo was disgraced, Ward had committed suicide and Christine Keeler had been convicted of perjury. Faced with Profumo's denial of the affair in court, Christine's close friend Mandy Rice-Davies just said 'Well, he would wouldn't he.' This response chimed exactly with the current view of politicians and probably of men in general. The whole episode, and the ease with which our 'Supermac' Prime Minister could be lampooned, was easy meat for the cartoonists and satirists, particularly the great new TV show *Beyond the Fringe*.[15n] Macmillan had been deeply shocked by the affair. His hard military service, long political career, personal problems and a diagnosis of cancer led him to resign his office on October 18th 1963. He felt misunderstood by a culture that had moved beyond his grasp and betrayed by a close colleague and a small group of Party members.[16n] He was succeeded by Alec Douglas-Home who, as another aristocrat and with the most anaemic personality that I can remember in any politician, did nothing to restore confidence in the Conservative government. Douglas-Home's tenure at Number 10 lasted less than a year and in the ensuing election Labour were returned to power.

Election 1964

The Labour Party greatly benefitted from the scandals surrounding the Conservatives and the generally tired feelings that the government had exhibited. The election, called for October 14th 1964, was surprisingly close, giving Labour a majority of 4 seats, hardly sufficient to achieve their ambitious plans. These included renationalisation of steel and iron. Their issues were the increasingly fragile state of the UK economy bearing the cost of our nuclear armaments, our military commitments and colonies, balanced against our commitment to America, our industrial health and relations, in particular the role and power of trades unions. And Europe! Harold Wilson, the Labour leader, entered Downing Street, marking a significant change of ethos. The senior members of both main political parties were now grammar school educated, some having parents with less education than them and a load more experience of ordinary working life. Harold Wilson, a very clever grammar school and Oxford educated Yorkshire man, who had worked his way diligently and craftily through the Party machine, promised that,

> The Britain that is going to be forged in the white heat of this revolution will be no place for restrictive practices or for outdated methods … those charged with the control of our affairs must be ready to think and speak in the language of our technological age … we must use all the resources of democratic planning, all the latent and underdeveloped energies and skills of our people, to ensure Britain's place in the world.[17]

Immediately after the election the new Chancellor was met with his departing colleague's traditional message: 'Sorry to leave such a mess,' is all it said. It soon transpired that the Tories' chronic overspending had run up a deficit of £800 million pounds, which was alarming world markets and threatening Sterling. Labour's immediate plans were ruined and the need to protect the pound would haunt Wilson's entire premiership and worry his Chancellor, the loyal Jim Callaghan, for many years as he moved to the Home Office and then became Prime Minister. At one point Wilson threatened to call an immediate election on the question of 'Who governs Britain, the government or the banks?'

Despite the pressure on the currency, Labour determined to carry their plans forward. A strong Department of Economic Affairs was established and Tony Crosland accelerated the abolition of the grammar, secondary and technical school system and the establishment of a fully comprehensive mixed sex provision of secondary education. Not only was this central to Labour's policy, but also the provision of one local school was cheaper than the provision of two or three schools each for girls and boys. The government in the person of Jenny Lee, Nye Bevan's widow, established the Open University, although it would be seven long years before the first students were enrolled. The survival of the pound ensued, by now heavily dependent on America dealing with Vietnam. This support would become interlinked, although to his eternal credit Wilson refused to send troops. He was determinedly trying to cut our troop commitments east of Suez as far as possible (a policy not to America's liking) and to reduce dependent colonies to save money.[18n] The government did however offer copious words of support which only served to get them attacked by the growing anti-Vietnam activists on both sides of the Atlantic. CND's April 1965 demonstration in London involved 150,000 people. As the pressure on the pound grew and Wilson and Callaghan resisted devaluation, an election was called on March 31st 1966. Wilson's majority was increased to a safe 98 with a turnout of nearly 76%. One major headache had been removed. Now the Middle East exploded with dramatic effects on our already weakening economy.

Devaluation

In response to the perceived pro-Israel line from London to the Six-Day War, Iraq and Kuwait imposed an oil embargo on the UK that coincided with a national dock strike which closed the main ports. The effect on the economy and Sterling was very bad. By November Callaghan, confronted by clear evidence that more delays could be fatal, took his conclusion to Cabinet and after a few further days evasion the announcement was made on November 18th 1967 that Sterling would be devalued by 14% and further restrictions on credit imposed. Wilson reassured voters that the pound in their pockets had not lost its domestic value. A typically clever, basically dishonest statement. Callaghan resigned on the principle that he had promised never to devalue the pound. This action did indeed help exports. Along with massive tax rises imposed by the new Chancellor (Roy Jenkins, who by his 1969 Budget could report that the national finances were in credit), it was the only time in fifty years (from 1936 to 1988) that our gold and reserve stocks were strong and Sterling was once again a sound currency.

Liberalising Legislation

Roy Jenkins' move to the Treasury had followed a uniquely liberalising time as Home Secretary when he had given the radical cultural changes a significant helping hand, often by sponsoring private members' bills. The landmark White Paper *The Child, the Family and the Young Offender* was published in 1965.[19] Recognising the social factors behind much of crime, it placed the welfare of the child at the centre of its approach. It proposed removing the stigma of criminality for all those under 16 by the abolition of juvenile courts to be substituted by family councils comprising social workers and other relevant people. Disputed cases and those offenders between 16 and 21 would be dealt with by special family courts. The White Paper was withdrawn the following year in the face of fierce opposition from the Magistrates Association and lawyers within the Conservative Party. The 1969 Children and Young Persons Act was therefore an uneasy compromise and many of its provisions were never introduced by the next Conservative government.

The Race Relations Act 1965 was the first legislation to address racial discrimination, outlawing discrimination on the 'grounds of colour, race, ethnic or national origins' in public places, and the following year the Race Relations Board was set up to consider complaints under the Act.

Concern over the totally unregulated rental market, where the housing shortage and a high degree of criminal activity was causing concern, led to the Rent Act of 1965, which gave security of tenure and set up independent rent officers with the power to establish a fair rent, with three-year reviews on the basis of valuation and condition. It also included safeguards against eviction. The conditions in some hostels for homeless people were very poor; under the National Assistance Act only women and children could be accommodated and then only for a maximum of three months. By excluding fathers and older children, families were consequently broken up. The situation came to light at Kings Hill, a poor, hutted camp near West Kingsdown in Kent when a husband moved in and refused to leave. In 1965 a group of social activists, some previously members of the Committee of 100 (see Chapter 7) committed to direct action became involved. They rounded up husbands and older children, many of whom were sleeping rough, and brought them all into the camp and barricaded the entrance. This brought nationwide publicity to the inhumanity of the policy and as automatic eviction meant that the children were invariably taken into care, the cost to the local authorities was high. Some families were never reunited. This campaign was led by Jim Radford and Ron Bailey and at a time of acute housing shortages extended to the squatting movement designed to force authorities to use empty houses already on their books.

On November 16th 1966 the BBC broadcast Ken Loach's *Cathy Come Home*, described by some as the best TV drama ever made. It concerned a young couple with children in a downward spiral of homelessness. The play finishes as the social workers and police forcibly remove the children and leave the mother sleeping rough.[20] It certainly stunned the audience of 12 million, and subsequent discussion in Parliament led to whole families being accommodated in homeless provision. Coincidentally the Church Housing Associations established an organisation, under the leadership of Des Wilson, to raise funds and campaign on the issue of homelessness, a mission which the charity Shelter has followed ever since. Late in 1968 Shelter discussed the problem of lone mothers with informal women's groups, and in 1969 this led to the establishment of the Gingerbread organisation which slowly developed into a national network offering informal meeting groups for lone parents who could then take action on issues that concerned them. Gingerbread continues to provide advice and support across the country.

David Steel, a leading member of the Liberal Party, had campaigned for many years for a change to the archaic law concerning abortion and the damage being done by backstreet abortionists. Some 35,000 botched abortions were being treated by the NHS each year. On October 27th 1967, in the face of considerable opposition, the Abortion Act legalised abortion up to 28 weeks' gestation by providing a legal defence for doctors carrying them out. The conditions were that continuing with the pregnancy would pose a greater risk to the physical or mental health of the woman or her child than termination; two doctors must agree; and the actual or foreseeable environment could be taken into account. The operation had to be performed in government approved premises. The reluctance of doctors to discuss abortion and the inclusion in the Act of a conscience clause allowing doctors to opt out of treatment, cast doubt on the ability of many women to actually access the new services. A group of concerned women therefore decided to form the Pregnancy Advisory Service – firstly in Birmingham and then nationwide – to ensure that women seeking an abortion could be directed to the right service. The telephone calls far exceeded expectations and the service had to be rapidly expanded.

The Sexual Offences Act 1967 finally decriminalised homosexual acts in private between two men, both of whom had to have attained the age of 21. The Act did not apply to the Merchant Navy or the armed forces. The Murder (Abolition of Death Penalty) Act 1965 confirmed the abolition of the death penalty. Soon after taking office, Jenkins refused to confirm that birching was used, and this form of punishment was abolished by the Criminal Justice Act 1967.[21n]

Following a long campaign, the Theatres Act was passed on September 26th 1968. It abolished censorship of the stage so at last scripts no longer had to be sent to the censor before being commissioned. Before this the inevitable blue pencil could be applied to any dialogue or direction that might offend public decency. Very soon after, two plays appeared on the West End stage: *Hair*, an anti-Vietnam pro-hippy rock musical with nudism and frank sexual references, and *Oh! Calcutta!*, a lively revue with some very frank sexual scenes.

The Parliamentary Commissioner Act 1967 created the post of ombudsman to investigate complaints that individuals had been treated unfairly or had received poor service from government departments and other public organisations. The Divorce Reform Act of 1969 allowed couples to divorce after they had been separated for two years (or five years if only one of them wanted a divorce). A marriage could also be ended if it had irretrievably broken down. Importantly neither partner had to prove 'fault,' which brought the whole sordid process of collecting evidence to an end; not a welcome bill for the small army of private detectives and professional co-respondents who had earned a good income from such cases.

This unprecedented raft of legislation was for the large part achieved by dedicated campaigners although it is doubtful whether they or the Home Secretary anticipated the degree to which the freedoms allowed would be exuberantly and publicly embraced by those who had been forced to wait in the shadows for so long. At the very least we were becoming a more open and socially active society. The Child Poverty Action Group and the Disablement Income Group were both formed in 1965. The charity Release, offering advice to those convicted of drug offences, started in 1967, and late in the 1960s Joe Kenyon started the Claimants and Unemployed Union in Barnsley to support people on National Assistance.

Rhodesia

Southern Rhodesia, closely allied to South Africa, fell under a white supremacist government led by a determined Ian Smith. There was a long period of armed insurrection and a harsh military response which meant that both sides became locked in non-negotiable positions. Their government sought Commonwealth membership on the basis of a constitution that denied any power to the black majority. When this was rejected and further negotiations failed, Ian Smith issued a Unilateral Declaration of Independence in November 1965. Wilson then embarked on a series of sanctions, all of which failed. One crisis occurred when the Smith regime refused three Africans sentenced to be hanged leave to appeal to London. Wilson advised the Queen to pardon the three, but they were hanged anyway. Further negotiations at the United Nations, and directly between Wilson and Smith on board battleships so that neither had to set foot in the other's country, failed. Wilson refused any suggestion that force should be used, and the dispute and the guerrilla war ran on into the next government although the effects for that country (known since November 1965 as Zimbabwe) remain with us today.

Immigration

Following the large West Indian immigration of the 1950s and the early 1960s, more residents of Pakistan and India entered Britain on the basis of their British citizenship. At BOAC I had witnessed the increasing numbers of people from Pakistan destined to work in the mills of Lancashire and Yorkshire. These migrants differed from others in important ways: they were mostly Muslims; once established they used their entitlement to bring their families to Britain; and, most likely to disturb the host community, they tended to look inwards to their own culture, for example there was a reluctance to allow women to learn English. The numbers increased steadily, but in the late 1960s some 2,000 of mostly well qualified Indians resident in Kenya arrived every month following painful pressure applied by that government in an attempt to rebalance control of commerce towards the native African population. This increased racial tension in many urban areas and led to a rise in right-wing movements. On April 20th 1968 the Conservative MP for Wolverhampton South West, Enoch Powell, threw a grenade into the debate. Powell was a classist and fiercely intelligent. He had fought in North Africa, he was a good orator and he was heavily involved with the debates which surrounded the Commonwealth Immigration Act, which severely restricted the flow of immigrants, and the Race Relations Act, which outlawed discrimination. In addition to concerns raised by his constituents, Powell enjoyed the philosophical debate about whether it was right to remove a right of entry to people to whom we had given British citizenship. In this infamous speech Powell quoted a constituent who had told him that he would leave England if he could as he foresaw a time when 'the black man will have the whip hand over the white man.' Calling on a classical reference he concluded his speech by lamenting that as he looked ahead, 'I am full of foreboding. Like the Roman I seem to see "the Tiber foaming with so much blood",' unless the government started a policy of voluntary repatriation. The speech started a storm. Powell was sacked from the Shadow Cabinet although most demonstrations and letters supported his views.[22n]

Trades Unions

Throughout this government the trades unions, whose membership stood at 10 million (44% of the workforce), had leant hard on Wilson and his Cabinet, although there had been fewer strikes than in the previous decade. However, as inflation increased in the late 1960s so did the pressure from the unions. At one point when the unions threatened to use their sponsored MPs to bring down the government Wilson told them to 'get your tanks off my lawn.'

CULTURE

As the 1960s progressed, the enormous energy of the young generation, fired by global communication and radical ideas, exciting music and increased sexual freedom, started for some to coalesce in protest movements. While some bordered on revolution others promoted radical theatre formats and, most readily available, popular music. The new culture burned brightly. Hitting the headlines were the Californian 'Summer of Love' of 1964, the violent anti-Vietnam war demonstrations in America and Europe and mass hysteria for The Beatles pop group. It seemed that we suddenly threw away our reserve and determinedly let it all hang out, even if we sometimes needed the help of now widely available cannabis to relax or the mind-enhancing LSD to provide colourful visions. A culture in which deference and duty and knowing one's place gave way to claims for civic and individual rights, evidenced most clearly by the American civil rights movement. In the UK the campaigns for equality in Northern Ireland and for equal respect and recognition, particularly for women and homosexuals, led the way.

By the mid 1960s London had become the epicentre of the colourful exhibitionist facet of this brave new world. A spate of glittering boutiques and shops appeared along the Kings Road in Chelsea and spread out to high streets across the country. Mary Quant, the designer of the miniskirt and hot pants, was controversially clear about her focus on youth, whatever the age of the wearer:

> The way girls model clothes, the way they sit, sprawl or stand, is all doing the same thing. It's not 'come hither,' but it's very provocative. She's standing there defiantly with her legs apart saying 'I'm very sexy. I enjoy sex, I feel provocative, but you're going to have a job to get me. You've got to excite me and you've got to be jolly marvellous to attract me. I can't be bought, but if I want you, I'll have you.'[23]

Biba's determined ambition was to make new designs available for all and therefore less expensive than in established stores.[24n] Then Vivienne Westwood brought punk to fashion. At the centre of it all was Carnaby Street, a small space tucked between Soho and Regent Street, which became the symbol of the times where anyone could buy anything that was newly fashionable. Many of the designers of course had revelled in the creative anarchy that held sway in most art colleges across the land.

Although Cliff Richard was among the first to follow Elvis's rock and roll music, others came from UK art colleges: John Lennon from Liverpool, Ian Dury from Walthamstow, Pete Townshend from Ealing, Cat Stevens from Hammersmith and Keith Richards from Sidcup are but a few of those that carried rock music forward, each in their own very different styles. Their popularity was enhanced by the TV version of *Top of the Pops*, which started in January 1964 and had a huge weekly following. The launch of the first Telstar satellites provided transatlantic TV and instant communication, and in 1967 colour TV arrived. American influence continued to be heavy. Bob Dylan, a poet songwriter, connected popular music with protest, particularly the American civil rights and anti-war movements.

The long campaign for civil rights, to end segregation and achieve voting rights and fair housing led by Martin Luther King made progress in the face of fierce physical and political opposition. His widow Coretta continued campaigning until her death in 2006, and full achievement towards true equality still lies in the future. The influence of the civil rights campaigns spread to other countries, linking with the anti-apartheid campaign in South Africa and raising interest in Northern Ireland where generations of Catholic and Protestant citizens had faced discrimination from a small minority of mostly Protestant Unionists. The new culture of freedom and self expression provided the tinder for action. Harold Wilson had been urging the Province's Prime Minister, Terry O'Neil, to institute reforms, but these were blocked by conservative elements in his Ulster Unionist Party, including the young Reverend Ian Paisley. In 1966 community and left-wing organisations came together to form the Northern Irish Civil Rights Association; behind them more militant groups sought an opportunity to reawaken the battle for a united Ireland. When the Association's initial campaign failed they decided to copy King's example of non-violence and hold a civil rights march on August 24th 1968 with a happy carnival atmosphere. They were unable to finish the march when faced with a counter demonstration led by Paisley. A further march in Derry on October 5th was met by violence from the police, who drove the marchers back into the Catholic area of Bogside. This event hit the headlines and alerted the UK population to the fact that simmering injustices in their own country had to be faced and resolved. From the movement came the student activist Bernadette Devlin who was elected to the Westminster Parliament. A very articulate and angry 21-year-old, she made her maiden speech on the day she took her seat, April 22nd 1969. She gave her view plainly in a speech unique in modern politics:

> I remind the Hon. Member for Londonderry [Robert Chichester-Clark] that I, too, was in the Bogside area on the night that he was there. As the Hon. Gentleman rightly said, there never was born an Englishman who understands the Irish people. Thus a man who is alien to the ordinary working Irish people cannot understand them, and I therefore respectfully suggest that the Hon. Gentleman has no understanding of my people, because Catholics and Protestants are the ordinary people, the oppressed people from whom I come and whom I represent … I never thought that I should see the day when I should agree with any phrase uttered by the representative of such a party, but the Hon. Gentleman summed up the situation to a 't.' He referred to stark, human misery. That is what I saw in Bogside. It has not been there just for one night. It has been there for 50 years – and that same stark human misery is to be found in the Protestant Fountain area, which the Hon. Gentleman would claim to represent.
>
> We came to the situation in Derry when the people had had enough. Since 5th October, it has been the unashamed and deliberate policy of the Unionist Government to try to force an image on the civil rights movement that it was nothing more than a Catholic uprising … How can we say that we are a nonsectarian movement and are for the rights of both Catholics and Protestants when, clearly, we are beaten into the Catholic areas? Never have we been beaten into the Protestant areas. When the students marched from Belfast to Derry, there was a predominant number of Protestants. The number of non-Catholics was greater than the number of Catholics. Nevertheless, we were still beaten into the Catholic area because it was in the interests of the minority and the Unionist Party to establish that we were nothing more than a Catholic uprising – just as it is in the interest of the Hon. Member for Londonderry to come up with all this tripe about the I.R.A. [Irish Republican Army].
>
> I saw with my own eyes 1,000 policemen come in military formation into an oppressed, socially and economically depressed area – in formation of six abreast, joining up to form 12 abreast like wild Indians, screaming their heads off to terrorise the inhabitants of that area so that they could beat them off the streets and into the houses … There is no denying that the problem and the reason for this situation in Northern Ireland is social and economic, because the people of Northern Ireland are

being oppressed not only by a Tory Government, a misruling Tory Government and an absolutely corrupt, bigoted and self-interested Tory Government, but by a Tory Government of whom even the Tories in this House ought to be ashamed and from which they should dissociate themselves.[25]

Radical politics, civil rights concerns, the great expansion of restless student numbers in America and the zeitgeist of individual freedom of expression came together in the anti-Vietnam war movements that grew from a small demonstration in 1964 to tens of thousands of protesters in the early 1970s. The treatment of Vietnamese citizens (including the use of napalm) and allied casualties were, thanks to satellites, transmitted to TV audiences across the world, sowing doubt about the morality of the intervention and the likelihood of a successful outcome. Protests were encouraged by two intellectual giants, the great sociologist C. Wright Mills and the younger Herbert Marcuse. In *The Sociological Imagination* and *The Power Elite*, both published in the late 1950s, Wright Mills had described the centralisation of power by political, military and economic elites who consolidate their position by manipulating citizens through media and consumerism. Marcuse, a philosopher and political theorist of the new left, addressed many student protest movements, developing Wright Mills' attack on consumerism in *One Dimensional Man* and urging that young people break out of the superficial satisfaction of their needs to regain their true humanity. He also coined the concept of 'repressive tolerance', the cunning way by which governments keep radical protest repressed while giving some ground to give the appearance of tolerance. It was very popular among radical groups for the next decade.[26]

In 1965 the first self-immolation took place in America when Norman Morrison set fire to himself outside the Pentagon as a protest against the Vietnam War. The following April, 400,000 people marched to the UN Building in New York and another 100,000 protested in San Francisco, where they were addressed among others by the singer and activist Harry Belafonte and the American paediatrician Benjamin Spock, whose advice on baby and child care had acted as a guide to many post-war parents. Following the powerful 'Tet' offensive in January 1968, opposition grew when the extent and ferocity of the American and South Vietnamese counterattack became known. This included the spontaneous execution of a captured officer by a South Vietnamese general in front of TV cameras.[27n] In March of that year 200,000 people marched through London, led by the young Tariq Ali and Vanessa Redgrave,[28n] but a few thousand activists diverted into Grosvenor Square where 1,000 police were guarding the American Embassy. After both mounted and other police were attacked by stones and fire-crackers, they charged into the crowd and general fighting broke out resulting in some 300 arrests and 86 injuries; fifty were hospitalised. In August a more violent confrontation occurred in Chicago during the Democratic National Convention and the same month saw the first Woodstock Festival for 'Peace and Music'. Demonstrations continued throughout the following year by citizens, students and school children across the world, and in

November 1969 some half a million people demonstrated in Washington, by which time polls revealed that a majority of Americans thought the war was a mistake. The war finally ended in April 1975.

The many radical liberation movements, together with the civil rights movement, now turned their attention to the role and rights of women. They found that while joining in protests and demonstrations, often with the famous motto 'make love not war,' traditional domination by men was still experienced. Voices were first raised in the hotbed of liberation movements, San Francisco. The campaign was then taken up in France before arriving in the United Kingdom where Roy Jenkins's raft of liberal legislation (see above) had already addressed some of the concerns. From the late 1950s San Francisco's authorities proposed a series of plans to 'modernise' the city which were challenged by numerous community groups concerned with protecting both their heritage and natural environment. In 1962 Rachel Carson's book *Silent Spring* was published attacking the profit fuelled use of pesticides and other chemicals on the land, pointing out that 'what we have to face is not an occasional dose of poison which has accidentally got into some article of fruit but a persistent and continuous poisoning of the whole human environment.' If all was not well in the environment there were also questions to be asked about the ideal of American domestic life. Betty Friedan's book *The Feminine Mystique* pointed out the painful dilemma of American women unable to use their education or stretch their intelligence while conforming to the stereotypical role of good wife and mother.[29]

In 1966 three hundred men and women formed the American National Organisation for Women in the belief that

> The time has come for a new movement towards free equality for all women in America, and towards a truly equal partnership of the sexes, as part of the world-wide revolution of human rights now taking place within and beyond our national boundaries.[30]

The wild sweep of new freedoms, especially regarding the youth of America, allowed young women a wide choice of lifestyles, social roles and sexual partners. In September 1968 a group used street theatre techniques in Atlantic City to mock the Miss America contests which had cast women as objects in the sexual game. Leaflets were circulated inviting women to bring 'old bras, girdles, high-heeled shoes, women's magazines, curlers and other instruments of torture' to chuck into a 'freedom trash can.' A sheep was crowned 'Miss America' and a placard proclaimed that 'Miss America is a Big Falsie.' The event attracted TV coverage, and journalists reported that the women had 'burnt their bras.'[31] A whole myth was born! Various groups were formed in Britain, some seeded by American visitors and others from trade unionists demanding equal pay. The Australian author Germaine Greer's *The Female Eunuch*[32] was published in 1969 and widely read. In 1970 TV viewers of the Miss World contest at the Royal Albert Hall saw flour, stink bombs and smoke bombs thrown at the stage. From the moderate women's movements of 1950s, radical ideas from the West Coast of America and widespread social action came the emergence of an identifiable worldwide movement termed 'feminism.' Spurred on by such crusading mottos as Carol Hanisch's 'The Personal is Political,' continuing injustices and a growing theoretical base, feminism would advance as it became more confident and confrontational in the next decades.

FAMILY

Life at Shoreham, specifically the small settlement of Londoners centred on my mother, brother, Aunt Lola, Uncle Jim and their two children, was proceeding at its own gentle pace. Gran came down from Peckham on a regular basis to stay with one or other of her daughters. The visitors kept coming, and in 1962 Uncle Ernie's eldest son Alan arrived home from Canada with his wife Dini and their son Jeffrey echoing his parents' return 34 years earlier (see Chapter 2). As Alan had trouble finding work, the marriage came under strain and Dini and Alan moved into the cottage for several months. John and Mother applied themselves to counselling the parents and enjoying encouraging Jeffrey through this difficult period. They soon left for Holland and, apart from one postcard, never communicated again.[33n]

In 1965, after fifteen increasingly tough years at Samuel Pepys Comprehensive School in New Cross, John was appointed Head of Music at Chislehurst Secondary School. Life was significantly more relaxed and he was able to enjoy his seven years there. Helping their lively drama department he provided the music for the school's remarkable production of *Ross*, which tells the story of Lawrence of Arabia and included homosexual and sado-masochistic themes. I thought the staff and the young actors were amazingly brave to tackle such a subject so well. Our culture was certainly changing fast!

I was busy working and studying at Oakwood Hospital and spending more time with my girlfriend Ann. In the summer of 1963 we took the vital step of visiting her sister Joan's family at Coads Green in Cornwall; quite a challenge. Joan, who worked for the Milk Marketing Board, and Bill, who worked for Prudential Insurance, were both enjoying the mix of local characters that they met every day. They had two sons, James aged ten and Richard aged eight. It was a brief and happy visit except that my total failure to play a simple game of cricket in the back field somewhat damaged the boys' view of their potential uncle.

With a place at Birmingham University secured, the time had come to further consolidate our relationship, so on August 27th 1964, with a red rose ready in the glove box, I drove Ann to the Theatre Royal Drury Lane to see the romantic musical *Camelot*. It was very enjoyable, as was the following meal in Soho. Then it was on to my old regimental HQ, the Tower of London, for the late night six-hundred-years-old Ceremony of the Keys. Down by the river I proposed marriage, telling Ann that I thought this the most secure place from which to start our lives together. I don't recall that she ever actually said 'Yes'. We then broke the news to our families, including our intention to get married in nine weeks' time!

We set our wedding day as November 7th 1964, which of course necessitated gaining the agreement of Ann's stepfather, Hugh Adams, who was a mildly eccentric man brought up in the Chicago of Al Capone and for whom any sign of left-wing sympathy seemed a threat. At what was a fairly tense meeting I was able to reassure him that I would be selling my beloved Saab two-stroke car in order to help finance the year in Birmingham. We had agreed that Ann would then explain that she would be buying my car and selling her own prized racer! The next practicality was somewhere to live, but as my acceptance was so late we spent unhappy days looking at the dreadful remains of what every other student had walked away from. At the last minute Hugh approached his employers, the building firm Wimpey, who agreed to rent us, at a full commercial rent, a derelict house in Redditch (it was one of two in a rather up market street, which they were holding empty to provide access for a future development). We were overjoyed, although Pauline Shapiro, the senior course tutor, was not. Notifying her of my new address brought a long letter warning me of the demands of the course; was it wise to live so far (15 miles) from the university?

The house in Easemore Road was in very poor condition, but the next step was to move in, which would mark a final departure from home and Darent Hulme Cottage. On the due day all my furniture was loaded into Norman Rose's old Bedford van for the long drive from Kent to Birmingham, with Mother in what little space was left for a passenger. Unfortunately, although I had loaded everything Tetris style, I had not thought about the weight. Somehow the van got up the extraordinarily steep hill to Badgers Mount roundabout on the A21 (now an exit from the M25). We just made it with some groaning from the springs and the smell of burnt diesel coming from the overheated engine which lay between us in the cab. At least there were no more hills like that on the route. The tumble-down house was now part furnished, except for a new double bed. Other essentials were made up of old packing cases and canvas deck chairs. So, this was our first home together. It seems a good time to write a little more about my fiancée's background.

Ann Wickett

Ann was an amazingly good looking brunette with bright brown eyes – a vital, intelligent and quick-witted extrovert as opposed to my more introverted personality. I had fallen completely in love. When we first met, Ann lived with her stepfather Hugh Adams in a wing of the impressive Birchley House in Biddenden, Kent. They had not lived there long, and a significant part of Hugh's resistance to our marriage was, naturally enough, the loss of the very person whom he anticipated would keep his house for the foreseeable future. In Cornwall Ann's parents William Wickett and Violet lived in the school house. It was not a happy place to be. Tensions led to the frequent rows, often with crockery thrown across the kitchen, the situation reached a climax as Ann was rising five by her father's determination to join the Army, presumably both to meet his patriotic duty and to escape from his wife. Violet being of a somewhat volcanic temperament, promptly resolved to enrol as a nurse. This left no option but for Ann and her older sister Joan to join a rather Victorian girls boarding school. Such a sudden loss of both parents seems to have led to some extreme behaviour and regular punishments for the very young Ann. Happier times were spent with her paternal grandparents on their farm at Launceston where Ann was loved by her grandparents, her Great Aunt Bessie and cousins. She adored the animals and could ride her horse Flossy.

Ann's behaviour deteriorated after each weekend on the farm, and eventually her father determined that such visits should be stopped, which of course produced more trauma. Ann's progress in private education finished at the prestigious Roedean School in Brighton, that being the fourth school from which she was expelled. Her final school was an excellent comprehensive school at Orpington in Kent. This emotional turmoil had come to a head for Ann when, as part of her parents' divorce proceedings, she had to appear before the judge at the impressive Royal Courts of Justice in the Strand to declare which parent she chose to live with. Understandably she chose her mother. After the war Violet worked in Guy's Hospital and lived in a service apartment near the Royal Albert Hall where she met, and eventually married, Hugh Adams, a civil engineer. Knowledge of the relationship between Violet and Hugh then led to a crisis meeting at a Lyons Corner House when William declared that he would no longer pay for Ann's education. Ann told him exactly what she thought of his behaviour to date. They did not communicate or meet again for over twenty years.

Ann's great ambition throughout all this time was to become a vet, a profession where she would have been excellent, but with no financial backing she was forced to accept her stepfather's direction and was enrolled at the Domestic Science College in Leicester, which she enjoyed, and obtained her Certificate with Distinction. Her main interest at this time was sports car racing, at which she excelled at Silverstone and Brands Hatch. By now the family had moved to Cudham, very near Shoreham in Kent. Tragedy hit the family when, after a year of marriage, Violet died suddenly from 'status asthmaticus' (now known as severe asthma) while at work in Orpington Hospital. Hugh was distraught and Ann took a year out from college to drive him round all the Wimpey sites in the UK and Eire. After that, as a qualified dietician, Ann worked briefly at the BBC and the Admiralty, leaving both when molested by senior staff. Next came a post with a public schools catering company; this job enabled her to buy her first car, a flame coloured Sunbeam Alpine racer. After a short while, she worked for the London Borough of Penge Home Help Service as organiser and dietician, slowly becoming more disillusioned at other people's failure to follow her good advice, usually because their social situation prevented them from doing so. This ceased when she and Hugh moved to the village of Biddenden in Kent. Throughout this period her passion for motor racing continued. Dissatisfaction with her work as a dietician led her thoughts increasingly to some sort of social work.

Our meeting was the coming together of two vastly different cultures and personal histories. Many years passed before I saw the large Cornish farmhouse where Ann had spent her happy early years with her grandparents and their servants. It was only then that I fully appreciated the contrast between all that and our small council house in Peckham.

Marriage

A few days before our wedding, I gathered all the rose petals from the overgrown garden of both houses in Redditch, much to the interest of the neighbours, and spread them through the house and into the bedroom (where the bed had not been slept in). Then it was off to Kent for the wedding. Having made great links with the hospital chefs, Ann had got them to agree to make the wedding cake, supply the buffet and loan us all the china and cutlery. The evening before the wedding therefore Ann and I were driving backwards and forwards from Maidstone to Biddenden ferrying all the necessary food and kit. Our student grants and salary had to cover all the costs, although Hugh had eventually agreed to buy the champagne. November 7th 1964 dawned brilliantly and in the clear sun Mother, John, Gran, my dad's brother Ernie and I set out for Headcorn for the service. The sight of my beautiful bride coming towards me was almost too much, but some sort of equilibrium was restored by the broad wink that Ann gave me once the service started. Anxiety about her arrival was not entirely misplaced as in their car her stepfather kept asking her if she was sure what she was doing and even at the church door had offered her a last-minute offer of escape. John fulfilled his best man duties with great aplomb. The reception was at Birchley House, where Ann's much loved maternal grandfather Lang Tomlinson was keeping warm by the Aga watching all that went on.

The wedding day having gone well, we were both due back at work and college on Monday. I had prepared the ideal first night of married life by booking a chalet at a motel, itself a new concept in the UK, so it was there to which we drove as soon as possible once the guests had departed and we had cleared up and re-packed the stuff to return to the hospital. We arrived at the motel fairly late on a freezing November evening to find that no food was available. Outside our chalet a small container of milk had been left and inside were bunk beds and no heating! So, back to Maidstone for an expensive meal in the main hotel. Although never one to admit to any nervousness I actually joined Ann by smoking my first cigarette since my army days. We managed the night without external heating, but by early the next morning we were both in need of sustenance so we set off back to Birchley, collecting fresh eggs and milk en route. My father-in-law was delighted, assuming that his dream had come true and he had got his housekeeper back for ever!

Honeymoon

Somehow I had started the London social studies course by getting an A-level in Maths, and Birmingham University had accepted me on the graduate course before receiving the final Diploma results from London, so I had moved from lack of university entrance to postgraduate fully qualified professional (a psychiatric social worker) in three short years. Ann had been with me all the way, and we both needed to take the sort of break that made up for all the missed holidays. At the end of our time in Birmingham we summoned up our courage, collected our student travel cards and went on an eight-week delayed honeymoon starting in Rome then continuing to Greece and Istanbul, although the money ran out before we got that far. The flights were in the oldest planes I had ever seen, the boats that took us from island to island were rust buckets, all the schedules were uncertain and many questions were asked about how a grey-haired man qualified as a student, particularly with such an attractive wife. This was Ann's first trip abroad.

Unfortunately our hotel room in Rome looked out on the street where the ladies of the night played ritual games with the police, 'hiding' behind storage sacks only to reappear immediately they had passed. Ann was fascinated and had to be firmly reminded that we were actually on *our* honeymoon! We went to the open air performance of 'Aida,' horses, elephants and all. We were running late and when Ann made a dive for the toilet a great cheer went up from the audience as she had chosen the gents. Rome certainly proved a good start.

In Athens the student hostel was a nightmare, bound by rules and 'do not' notices, but the city captured us completely, although our stay was not to be uneventful. Deciding, after a great meal and some wine, that it would be fun to climb to the Acropolis by the back path, Ann tripped and broke a toe. On arrival at the hospital we were directed down darkened corridors where the wards either side were lit with blue nightlights, all very Florence Nightingale. Following a quick inspection by a nurse at the duty desk the doctor was called and we witnessed a scene so familiar to us from Oakwood, or more precisely from any comedy film. When he could eventually be extracted from the party the young suave doctor arrived, pinched the nurses' bums but expertly did what was required. His advice to return next morning was never followed. Wonderful times, and we returned relaxed and ready for a new life working in a new asylum although in some ways this was to prove just as crazy an experience as the last one. We had a hospital house, decorated to our taste, we still owned a beautiful Saab two-stroke car, and life had never been better.

Pregnancy

The Greek Islands having worked their magic, specifically Siros, the very much welcomed pregnancy was a time when we managed to put several systems to the test. Ahead of current medical, nursing and public attitudes, both of us wanted to be as involved as possible in the whole process. Although consultants tended to nod their approval, in principle the practice often fell far short. One striking example of this was ante-natal clinics where patients moved through a series of small rooms surrounding the main waiting area. Rather like a board game, if they passed the tests in each room they eventually ended up with the consultant. I was not to be allowed in the rooms and did not trust the nursing staff to call me before the final consultation so I had no choice but to sit watching the gap that separated the last but one room from the consultant's office. I was quite happily reading a book, but keeping an eye out for when Ann crossed the gap, when nurses arrived to put screens all round me on the basis that my presence was upsetting other patients, although in truth I think it was the professionals that were more upset.

Juliet

Juliet very much took her time arriving but eventually her birth seemed imminent. It seemed natural to me, and I think was accepted as professional practice, for telegrams to be sent to the patients who I was due to visit at home that afternoon to apologise that I would be unable to keep my appointment. The joy of fatherhood was overwhelming, and mother and daughter were soon welcomed home by the whole community. My father-in-law Hugh's reaction was extraordinary. The event seemed to reawaken a lost part of his life. On the positive side he would walk up and down Canterbury High Street stopping passers-by to insist that they admire the most wonderful baby ever born, but unfortunately, when taking on child care duties, he could never get the word 'No' to pass his lips. Once the initial shock of parenthood was over Ann and I wrapped up our precious bundle and headed for a quiet drink in our local pub, but full realisation that life would never be the same came when the landlord refused to serve us as Juliet was underage!

Juliet of course had no chance of avoiding her parents' occupation. The much loved Saab had been replaced with a functional but capacious Renault 4L. Ann would take our daughter with her from clinic to clinic, but even exposure to Hyatt Williams' extreme views in Maidstone does not seem to have left any lasting damage, although she was sensible enough to sleep through most seminars. Looking back on this extraordinarily happy event I see a darker side. Ann suffered badly from the birth, the baby having been pronounced five weeks late, but only later did she tell me that she had known all along that the doctor's date was wrong. Apart from the fact that nothing could persuade her to go through that again, it puzzled me how someone so used to challenging doctors in her work had not voiced her views to me or them during the pregnancy. Next time such reticence would be fatal.

Soon after our marriage, Ann's grandfather Lang, who had lived a lonely widower's life in the New Forest, died leaving his bungalow and all his effects to Ann. Clearing the place out was a very sad and distressing process. He had been an engineer and I still treasure some of his tools. The effect on our life was profound, enabling us to afford a deposit on our first house which meant that in the coming years of rising value we could afford to live a little comfortably. In addition, by very slowly nibbling away at the relatively modest value of the estate for the next fifty years we could avoid some financial crises and still pass a few of Lang's shares to Juliet.

Gran

On an early visit to Shoreham, I walked in the back door of the Darent Hulme Cottage one bright summer day cuddling my precious daughter close and was surprised to see a weak rather shrunken elderly lady tucked up asleep in bed in the lounge. Continuing through to the kitchen Mum broke the news that Gran, who had cared for me so much, had had a heart attack. I had failed to recognise her! I just broke down completely amid apologies from John and Mother that they had not warned me, assuming that we would come through the front door. The shock was dreadful. Gran's great frame recovered slowly and she was able to enjoy the flow of visitors from far and wide, jolly to the last. She loved Ann and lived to enjoy Juliet's toddler antics but died at home on September 16th 1969. She was buried in the churchyard deep in the magic valley and the blank side of her memorial book awaits a mixture of Ann and my ashes.

Pluckley

When Juliet was aged one we purchased The Mount, a three-storey narrow 15th century house semi-detached to The Black Horse pub overlooking the square in Pluckley, near Ashford, which required the installation of a complex central heating system. In a great spirit of rehabilitation it had been agreed that we would employ, under all the correct working conditions, an expert plumber who at that time was a patient in the ward for young schizophrenics. On the same basis, Jim, from the group therapy ward, volunteered to guard all the copper and iron piping and equipment in the empty house; we foolishly agreed that after his discharge from hospital we would employ him in that capacity. So whilst we were still grappling with the roles of new parents and new house owners one or other of us was also driving backwards and forwards to our new residence with a psychotic patient ('You have to keep reminding me when to take my 22 daily tablets') and leaving a guy with a psychopathic personality in the village. Eventually, long after we had moved in and despite his undoubted child care skills, Ann announced that either Jim went or she was leaving me to cope alone. Jim found accommodation and work on a hop farm some miles away. Soon after we heard that he had set fire to his shack with his military medals laid out on his bed.

A few chickens were soon installed in The Mount's small garden but the purchase of a donkey, Shadow by name, was somewhat of a surprise for me. We walked her home by the simple process of gently shaking a cornflake packet behind her, but it was only after Shadow had settled that Ann admitted that a foal was soon due! Our dinner guests were sometimes taken aback when Ann decided to show off our new acquisition by bringing Shadow in to join the party, after which I suspect that we became local characters.

Shadow spent the next few happy years moving from one friendly farmer's field to another to compensate for our sparse garden.

Pluckley was a friendly village and we joined in with the community whenever we could. It is reputed to be the most haunted village in England and one of the village ladies who came to help absolutely refused to go into the attic bedrooms. Ann was recruited, on the basis that the costume fitted, for a film made locally about the Pluckley ghosts, and I imagine that it is still being shown as the village now makes a good income from tourists drawn by its reputation as the most haunted village. Interestingly, if boys from the adolescent boys' unit, Beech House, were staying, they would often report that they were awoken by the bedclothes being suddenly pulled off in the early hours; we never told them about the ghosts!

Occasionally boys would return very drunk, having been allowed into one of the three village pubs, so that we would find horrible sick stains down the front of the house for all the village to discuss. On one occasion our dear doctor friend Masood Akhtar was so worried about a boy that he sat up all night in case he suffocated from vomiting.

In due course Juliet attended the village school which was immediately across the square, although she was not happy there, finding some of the village children less than friendly.

SOCIAL WORK

Student Social Worker, Oakwood Hospital

The decision by Oakwood Hospital in Maidstone to appoint three trainee posts and pay for their training was a very brave initiative on the part of the Hospital Board. I think that they were among the first to offer such posts, realising that the supply of qualified social workers was never going to meet the demands of hospitals now that new drugs made it possible to discharge long stay patients and actually 'cure' new admissions. Back home to live in Shoreham and, whilst the family expressed their concern and curiosity about why I would want to work 'in a place like that,' I organised myself for work and study. In addition to Ann and me, a lady of more mature years had been appointed and all three of us came under the gentle management of the resident social worker, Miss Florence Epps, a kind lady who had been the clerk to previous social workers and had served patients and hospital well for many years. What she lacked in training she more than made up for in wisdom, compassion and experience. Despite her meek demeanour she was rarely shocked, either by the extraordinary behaviours that she encountered or the often dictatorial demands of those demigods of the hospital, the consultant psychiatrists. The team was completed by an excellent secretary, Valerie, whose calm efficiency both in typing our long reports and controlling the flow of patients helped the department run smoothly. This was indeed a strange institution, but the work was challenging, the training fascinating and my fellow student gorgeous. The social work office was situated above the long main corridor and we had our own discrete front door to which we all had a key, which was very convenient later for extra-curricular activities.

The introduction to NHS psychiatry at Oakwood was quite a challenge. Patients were allocated to wards according to their diagnosis and legal status. The old stone buildings and grounds covered some 40 acres (about 20 football pitches) mostly surrounded by a high stone wall. In addition to nearly two thousand patients hundreds of staff were employed there so that with vast kitchens, workshops, sports grounds, a mortuary, administrative offices and nurses' and doctors' quarters it formed a complete world with its own rules, norms and social structures; in short, a total institution. At the top of the structure was the Board of Governors, then there were the physician superintendents, the hospital secretaries, the consultant psychiatrists and the matrons. We were still in the era when physician superintendents were local dignitaries, part of the mayor's social network, the remains of the old squirarchy. Each of the six consultants covered part of the vast catchment area each with a population of about 150,000, where they held regular outpatient clinics, and in due course each social work student was allocated to one or more areas and the relevant consultants, although some could see no point in having a social worker attend clinics in their local community.

I covered the south of the county, from the Sussex border to Dover and Deal, and my 'home' area from Sevenoaks to the London border at Orpington. Although each consultant was responsible for a group of wards, the system dictated that patients admitted with a particular diagnosis would go into a ward under the care of a different consultant. Given the idiosyncratic approaches to treatment held by each consultant, this was the cause of much conflict; indeed we quickly grasped the importance of manipulating the system to see that 'our' patients got the 'right' treatment, or at least some degree of consistency. The key to any such manoeuvres, and most of anything else that happened inside the wall, was the power held by the nurses in charge of each ward. Because of the comparatively low status of mental health nurses most had worked at Oakwood for many years with promotion often depending on retirement or death of the person next up the ladder. Similarities with the prison service were obvious. It was certainly true that nurses lived with patients year after year with no prospect of discharge for either. They now faced the prospect of change as doctors, using new drugs, were referring numerous patients from each ward to the newly enlarged social work department for discharge. This process implied a degree of threat for the established order. Our role was therefore viewed with a mixture of apprehension and acceptance, but to the credit of most staff our student status usually tilted the balance towards personal acceptance as the opportunity to teach and hand on acquired wisdom was embraced. Somehow we made good relationships across the hospital hierarchy, that is to say that Ann's more extrovert personality led the way and I followed. The position of social workers within the structure was unclear and anyway I initially lacked the confidence to communicate with such high status professions, particularly doctors and matrons. Experience and knowledge eased my shyness and when a 'proper' psychiatric social worker, Kay Sykes, arrived we were reprimanded for talking and laughing with a doctor in the long corridor that formed the main spine of the hospital! No sooner had Miss Epps recovered from the fact that her lone mission had been dramatically reinforced than she saw the chance to bring one of her long hatched schemes to fruition. Could we find a way of encouraging institutionalised patients out from behind the walls that had enclosed them for so long? Within a short time the vicar responsible for the nearby church hall had been persuaded to give us the use of the hall for one day a week and we then set about designing a programme of interesting activities and sent invitations to selected patients. Over the course of the next few weeks more and more poorly dressed and fearful individuals crept out of the front gate and crossed the road to the meeting. The next step was to ask the group for a name and within a very short time they proposed the most wonderful name, so from then onwards we had 'The Forget-me-not Club' which only closed just before Florence Epps retired because so many of the regulars had left the hospital. The small seed had blossomed and achieved its purpose.

One of my outpatient clinics was in Orpington Hospital, primarily with Dr McIlroy, an ex-army psychiatrist with a deeply intuitive insight into the problems presented to him and an esoteric understanding of the treatments available. Patients took it for granted that I sat in on all sessions. If anyone asked, Dr Mac would wave an arm airily and just say 'Oh he's learning the job you know.' After each session he would run through his diagnosis and as time went by he would invite me to give my conclusions first, an extremely effective way of learning psychiatry, even if it taught little about the rights of patients. He would then summon his faithful secretary, the lively Mrs Price, and dictate his reply to the GP. The referring letter might have just said 'Please see,' but what they got back was a flowery essay that beautifully described the patient, the symptoms, diagnosis and treatment. Each one was a literary masterpiece. If admitted to Oakwood for short term treatment some thirty miles away Dr Mac retained responsibility and this included the administration of electroconvulsive therapy (ECT) or as he described it 'plugging them into the mains.' This was the most frequently used effective treatment for severe acute depression. On the morning set aside, the patient, who had been deprived of breakfast, would come into the ward and lie on a hospital bed whilst a mild anaesthetic and muscle relaxant was administered. Once asleep, the patients had electrodes attached to each temple and a current briefly applied at the right level. In a minute or two the bed was then pushed down the ward, the screens rolled back and the next patient was shown in, well aware that behind the curtain there could be a row of up to 20 beds each with a patient in various stages of recovery. Once your bed got to the far end of the ward you got a cup of tea, a biscuit and a quick medical check before going back to the ward or home. These weekly sessions usually went without incident, but I remember one when, distracted by a private patient's striking beauty, Dr Mac forgot to ask whether she had had breakfast. Apparently she had eaten well and a minor medical emergency ensued.

To describe these individual consultants as characters is a true understatement. Dr Zavier's catchment area included all the Medway towns. He did not require a social worker in attendance at his clinics, he just phoned through his orders as and when he remembered. His more extrovert personality enjoyed the theatre of clinical teaching rounds, which we always attended. Here some distressed patient was led into a room full of people where every intimate detail of his or her personal life was discussed while we were all encouraged to ask questions which might illuminate the particular painful psychotic ideation or paranoid delusions. It seemed to us that this was designed to ensure continued confusion, but we were learning fast and had little option but to take part in as many of these as possible. Other consultants quietly got on with their demanding work trying to relieve individual distress with resources which were both limited and lacking in effectiveness, but, despite the criticisms levelled at these asylums, our experience was that the care and compassion expressed by doctors and nurses for their patients was limited only by the constraints of the institution and the limited state of knowledge at that time. Of course many of the acute patients in the new building found the quiet and beauty of the extensive grounds therapeutic in themselves; a true asylum from the very fact of removal from the pressure of their troubles.[34]

Apart from helping those patients that never came to the hospital, seeing new patients before or on admission (long social histories on each one) and visiting those who had been discharged, our main task was to rehabilitate heavily institutionalised patients back into the community. We were appalled that men and women had spent many decades in such a place. Many admissions had resulted from the application of the Poor Law which sent them to an asylum for immorality, usually illegitimate pregnancy, or as a consequence of some minor offence. There were a fair number of people who had survived the Nazi concentration camps with major mental problems and with numbers still tattooed on their arms. The task was considerable but seemed to fall differentially on Ann and myself. My memory is of long negotiations with landlords and local authorities, neither of whom were prepared for the new policy of release into the community which was expected to care. Ann often had to help upgrade a patient's wardrobe to one acceptable in the community. She was taken aback by the readiness of patients to disrobe completely without recourse to changing rooms. We soon developed a shared black sense of humour. Whether we were out in the town or driving patients to see possible accommodation I do not remember any thought given to possible risk to ourselves. Health and safety assessment would not be considered until well into the future.

I probably had something in common with the withdrawn, schizophrenic patients whose complex delusions or hallucinations had been ameliorated by the new drugs. Arthur was an ex-army cook who had suffered a severe psychotic breakdown. In our small office one day he was reminiscing about his army days and how he always made the gravy with a roux while mere housewives never bothered, just using cheap Oxo cubes. Unfortunately Ann, who was an expert cook and dietician, disagreed and a somewhat heated argument developed with Ann giving no ground. Much to my surprise this did not trigger a major relapse although Arthur never ventured to the office again and no doubt used the experience to bolster his paranoid ideas about women. It also illustrated how different our approaches were to mental illness. A further lesson in honest and open dealings with our patients came when Cecil was referred to me for rehabilitation. This was this young man's third hospital admission following public disturbances; clearly his GP was fed up with him. He had a long-standing history of behaviour problems made worse by a motorcycle accident followed by six months' hospitalisation. He had a lifelong habit of dressing up as a girl, being teased by his peers due to his effeminate gait and habits and had experienced sexual encounters with men since the age of 11. His poor school history was explained by his 'educational backwardness.' In 1960 the only diagnosis in his file was 'homosexuality' and he was now in hospital on a court order. With me he was very quick witted and as camp as any stereotype. My first move was to consult his probation officer and I approached that office with some trepidation in view of my Wakefield experience (see Chapter 7). I needn't have worried. Mike was a red-bearded florid man who was even more camp than Cecil! Trying to discuss Cecil's progress drew the response, 'I can't do anything with him. I was hoping that you had the answer! I sit here and read him the riot act about his behaviour, banging my ruler on the desk. If I pause he just leans across, raps me on the hand with my own ruler and says "Don't talk to me like that, ducky!" I am at my wits end. I look out over Cathedral Green and see him hanging round the gent's toilets; I don't know whether to call the cops or run out and take a commission.' This was not what I had expected, neither was it any help, although we eventually managed to get Cecil back home and relatively settled. My experience was fed back to the group with much hilarity and Mike became a long term valued friend.

The consultant at the Ramsgate clinic was a man of quick decisions and little empathy; if a consultation lasted more than five minutes, you were seriously ill. He took a simple approach to a young man who may be worried by his sexual feelings. My carefully researched social history was ignored and after a brief discussion the patient was sent for an X-ray and told to return in two weeks' time. A particular result earned treatment for depression, another outcome was for the young man to be told that, as his bone structure was clearly feminine, he should accept his orientation and get on with his life! (It should be remembered that homosexual acts between men were illegal until 1967.)

As part of our training we attended the Maidstone Assizes for one day in November 1962. Once the red-robed judge had been greeted by great ceremony and a fanfare of trumpets, Ann and I settled down to an interesting day in court. At first all seemed to go well. Cases of blackmail and extracting money with threats were adjourned for medical reports, and extenuating circumstances for an unmarried mother charged with infanticide resulted in two years' probation. Grievous bodily harm by two lads in a drunken brawl, and incest and indecent assault by a father, resulted in sentences of 3 years. The buggery of a 23-year-old stepdaughter resulted in an embarrassing exchange between the judge and the prosecuting solicitor about the impossibility of any physical precision in the case, and the case was dismissed. The same offence with a long history and several counts received

14 years' preventive detention.³⁵ⁿ During lunch break Ann timidly asked me if I would answer a question: 'What is buggery?' she asked. Oh dear, this needed a delicate answer.

Things took quite a different turn in the afternoon when a young country lad described as 'mentally defective with some traces of schizophrenia' was ordered, under the Mental Health Act (Sections 650 and 65), to be detained in a mental hospital with a five-year restriction order. He had been charged with arson having, accidentally we thought, set fire to a hay barn. No one was hurt and the farmer collected the insurance. We were furious, but Kent was farming territory and those interests had to be protected at all costs.

If this was my new life I also had to tackle the problem of university admission which had been a part of the employment contract and one in which I was eager to progress. Arrangements had been made to enrol us on the London University extramural course which led to a Diploma in Social Science. Fortunately the requirement of a foreign language had at last been dropped so I could achieve entrance by returning to my love of mathematics and managed fairly quickly to achieve a good A-level in Applied Maths. Gaining admission meant that one day a week Ann and I, joined by a child care worker from Kent County Council, Norman Rose, set out for Brighton, meeting up in the Tunbridge Wells Hospital car park to share the driving. There were some ten other students employed in child care and health visiting and those aspiring to work in the field. The course was demanding but interesting under the committed leadership of Mrs Graham-Stone who also took the social psychology element, standing there in long twisted tweed skirts, held roughly together with large safety pins. My favourite lecturer was Mr Ricketts who strolled in and used a piece from the morning paper or magazine to draw us into an issue of social history, policy or philosophy. We hardly knew that we were learning; shades of Richmond Coggan from Askes and Edward Thompson at Wakefield. To me this was what education was about, drawing students out, not pushing stuff in. Following Thompson's foundations I was mostly drawn to social history. In parallel we covered the development of education, health and welfare systems and the structure and functions of the state. Other sessions focused on issues of mental health, social work and the so-called problem family, provision for children and young people, the handicapped and the delinquent. All this was manna from heaven for me. I see from my notes a quote of Auden's hit the mark:

> The romantic lie in the brain
> Of the sensual man in the street
> And the lie of Authority
> Whose buildings grope the sky,
> There is no such thing as The State
> And no one exists alone;
> Hunger allows no choice
> To the citizen or the police;
> We must love one another or die.[36]

Psychology drew heavily on Freudian and Kleinian theories but included the developmental theories of Piaget as well as the standard stages of emotional and intellectual development. We then turned to clinical work, covering the ideas of Jung, Adler, Horney, Fromm and Suttie. Interestingly there was no mention of behaviourism. Social psychology and anthropology included role theory and the work of G. H. Mead on the development of self. The subject of leadership relied on Lewin, Lippitt and White's 1939 study of a group of eleven-year-olds and W. F. Whyte's 1943 study of hierarchy in the Norton Street Gang, an Italian street corner gang in Boston.[37]

In addition to the regular sessions we had summer schools in London where among our visitors was the great, if cadaverous, Richard Titmuss, a founding father of social policy.[38] There were opportunities to visit the local offices of a whole variety of agencies. I particularly recall a National Assistance Board (NAB) office where we discussed people who they saw as undeserving. Their solution was to refer them to the neighbouring office who would then send them on to another until they got so exhausted that they abandoned their claim. Another visit took us back to Camberwell Green where there was a traditional craft workshop for blind men. Although the wicker baskets that they produced were wonderful, the conditions were very basic. We were learning how the welfare system really worked, and also a bit more about the profession that we hoped to enter. One foggy evening we went to Caxton Hall for a lecture with members of the Associations of Lady Almoners and Psychiatric Social Workers. We arrived in time for the break to see a procession of ladies in large hats, pulling on their long white gloves as they swept down the stairs ignoring the two dishevelled figures waiting in the grand hall. Did we really want to join this gang? More significantly did I as a lone male?

From Oakwood there were enjoyable excuses for journeys to London in Ann's racer or the Saab, although we always had to be accompanied by her black poodle Toto, who had an extraordinary capacity to howl loudly when left alone, not a comfortable background to serious lectures. One impressive speaker was the MP for Pontypool, Leo Abse, one of Labour's greatest reforming backbenchers. What he lacked in height was compensated by his dress code, which seemed to emulate Oscar Wilde. Of particular interest to us was the fact that his view of the word was deeply Freudian. Thus he could always win his audience over by commenting that Freud's link between toilet training, obsessional personalities and power was confirmed by the fact that MPs spent their time passing motions in a chamber! Abse was a very clever man who had used his knowledge of parliamentary procedures to launch successful private members' bills. In 1961 he had introduced the Bill to legalise homosexual acts between consenting adults, and when it was talked out (allegedly because the Speaker considered it too filthy a subject to be discussed in the Chamber) he pursued the cause with great tenacity until his 1967 Bill won support.[39n]

A central part of the course was completion of three practical work placements, the first of which was with the welfare section of Brighton Council. It afforded an insight into the workings and attitudes in a local government office and the services provided to elderly and disabled people in the community. I did not settle in this authoritarian environment, particularly annoying the manager from time to time. Late on a Friday afternoon I was asked to visit an elderly man who lived at the top of one of Brighton's steep hills. This poor lonely soul was clearly in the last few days of his life – the smell was overpowering and in order to get near his bed one had to squelch across the urine-soaked carpet. All he wanted of me was that I would bring him a bottle of whisky. This posed a professional and moral dilemma, and not a little panic ensued. Humanity urged compliance but was this professional – what if it finally killed him? I ran back to the office, which was closed for the weekend, so no guidance was available. Still undecided I decided to revisit the old man to discuss his wishes a bit further and more accurately assess his condition. The day was saved for both of us as, during my absence, his GP had called and provided a full bottle of the desired relief.

As predicted by my tutor I found the residential placement in a hostel and workshop for mentally handicapped adults difficult, but I learnt a great deal, not the least of which was to lose my fear and reticence and learn to value the residents' many capacities, including a great sense of fun. The staff knew each individual so well having worked with the same group over many years. Part of my initial reluctance came from a visit that Ann and I had made to Leybourne Grange Hospital which held over a thousand children and adults with every degree of mental disability. We were horrified by the wards where severely disabled children were bed bound; some it was explained to us were so badly disabled that they would not have the mental ability to reach for food or water if they were starving. The nurses managed their challenging tasks with a mixture of care and clinical curiosity; one told us that he awaited the post mortem of a particular child to see how polished the child's brain would be as it would be devoid of any of the normal crevices. We then visited a workshop where the task was to work on a vat of toffees rejected by the local manufacturer because the wrappers had got twisted into the toffee. The job was to separate out the toffee from the wrapper. To say that the standard of hygiene was poor would be an understatement as on the day of our visit most workers had long runs of snot streaming from their noses. We were of course assured that the firm never re-used the toffee, but then why go to the trouble of separating it out? We were learning a lot very quickly.

My final placement was with the Family Service Unit at the Elephant and Castle, back to home territory and into a highly professionally competent and committed organisation. Its roots were in the pacifist units of WWII and had strong links to the Fabians and the Labour Party. There was an air of general quiet determination. Working with families experiencing great difficulties and intervening in complex situations, the balance of traditional, casework, practical help and common sense was maintained by thorough recording, close supervision and group discussion. I was allocated the case of a distressed family in darkest Deptford in order to support the lone mother and her two young children. This involved financial help, counselling, babysitting, cleaning and escorting the daughter to hospital appointments. Journeys by bus and tube and bending down to the height of a four-year-old certainly gave me a new perspective: just a sea of legs pushing and rushing by. The supreme challenge was a long day's babysitting, which naturally included feeding, nappy changing and entertainment. I was so happy to succeed without using the reserve toys and balloons hidden in my coat pocket. An all-round experience of professional social work at its best, for which I remain very grateful.

Ann's seven-week residential placement was at Blackfriars Settlement in Nelson Square (see Chapter 2), and was challenging but enjoyable for both of us. Ann's first surprise was that, in addition to an enjoyable group of fellow students, there were ex-prisoners and drug addicts sharing the accommodation. The second was that there was no way she was allowed to have her much loved dog Toto. This of course resulted in my first chance to rescue my maiden in distress, to have the dog to live with me in a house that had no experience of dogs. No hesitation of course. So the next few weeks were spent using my elementary knowledge of behaviourism to train this very spoilt animal; hours were spent up in Meenfield Woods until he obeyed most commands. He was really quite a sweetie. Ann enjoyed visiting the families of those children who had been chosen to join in the summer holiday schemes (for which the charge was a shilling a day – the equivalent of 5p today) and spending exhausting days playing games with five- to twelve-year-olds in the hilly Greenwich Park. Ann knew that several of these families had had their gas supply cut off or their cooking stoves taken in payment for debt. The following two-week camp at Deal pushed the challenges and exhaustion to new levels. Each student had a hut where they played temporary parent to a group of children who had most probably never been out of London. With children who were homesick, enuretic, or just not used to an ordered way of life, Ann rose to the challenge of twenty-four-hour care, laundry and cooking, that being the least of her problems.

Two years at Oakwood passed very quickly and enjoyably. We made many friends among nurses, doctors, volunteers and admin staff. We could call in to the comfortable Matron's quarters, where she and her assistant matrons met over elegant china tea every afternoon waited on by a loyal patient, or the junior doctors' residence where there was a minority of Pakistani immigrant doctors and we could sample the wonders of their cuisine for the very first time. From this group we particularly befriended Masood Akhtar and his Welsh wife Jen who we were to keep in touch with for many years. From the more senior psychiatrists we respected and befriended Jim Lyons who had a bad stutter and (to make matters worse) dribbled badly as he struggled for a word – his humanity and care for patients were second to none. Patients found their first encounter with Jim quite a shock and at outpatient clinics would often emerge shaking their head to reflect 'Well, I thought I was poorly until I met the doctor.'

A notable evening among these friends was a fancy-dress dance to reflect Beatlemania, all the rage at that time. Not only do I recall Jim Lyons in the 'band' and under a cleaning mop as a wig, but also that the relationship between Ann and I moved up an important gear. Ann had proved quite a challenge, being highly suspicious of anyone trying to get past the extrovert façade that she had painfully constructed for so long. For me our relationship was like the old cowboy films where the main man determinedly works with a beautiful wild horse to develop a relationship of trust. The breakthrough, which I remember so well, occurred when driving back from one of our external lectures when Ann reluctantly allowed me to drive her precious sports car and then, wonder of wonders, fell asleep. Trust at last!

Life was moving forward at a steady rate with the training programme gaining momentum, ward rounds, teach-ins and academic work together with 'working' privately in the office well after hours. Neither would I swear that visits to establishments, including the newly opened Grendon Underwood Prison, which was surrounded by some discrete woods, were entirely academic. This establishment was based on group work usually led by trainee psychologists, under the leadership of the Principal, who I had known at Wakefield. We did wonder about the effect his young female psychologists, with the fashionable miniskirts, had on men under confinement.

We became fairly regular visitors to the great Henderson Hospital in South London, also based on group therapy for young psychopaths. The centrepiece of each visit was the routine morning meeting of the total community: painful and challenging with fascinating dynamics as rage, anxiety and depression fought for democratic attention and resolution. The more local Finchden Manor, founded and run by the extraordinary George Lyward, was a more intimate version of the same methodology although based on educational theory rather than psychiatric. On arrival the door could be opened by a staff member on his knees. This was a choice he had made soon after arriving for a short visit some years previously, his thought being that such a disability would give him something in common with the residents. Casual visitors had to get used to drinking tea from jam jars. The main criteria for admission were high intelligence and major problems in behaviour, social relationships and mental health. Although the life of the establishment was based on group and individual work, it was Lyward's wisdom, patience, insight and calmness that emanated throughout every aspect of the place. Finchden Manor had much success with these highly challenging boys, and spending time there was always an inspiration. It was a fee-based school and although some boys may have been paid for by local education authorities others were from the wealthiest families of Europe and the Middle East. Others would be there solely because George Lyward felt that he could ease their pain and help them realise their potential.[40]

The rush of actual social work, psychiatric theory and practice absorbed from good doctors and nurses, heavy study at Brighton and all these amazing visits combined to prepare us well for both the final exams and many years of social work. It was a wonderful grounding. The Diploma exams were held in Brighton in May 1964 and I was as prepared as I could be, helped by stringing a 4 inch tape battery recorder under the dashboard of my car thus ramming facts and figures into my mind while driving to work every day. I suspect that I also played them at night while I was asleep. The social psychology questions included

> Consider, with examples, the bearing of a young person's physique and appearance on either his possible social behaviour or his choice of work.
> Discuss the evidence for supporting that early social relations have a bearing on tendencies to delinquency. What other factors seem to you also important?

Confident that I had passed, I learnt that, rather late in the year, Birmingham University was adding a psychiatric stream to its Postgraduate Diploma in Social Work. I was interviewed there, the interview being less stressful than overcoming my old feelings about universities. I clearly remember getting on the bus from New Street Station and whispering to the conductor that I needed a ticket to the University and would he please tell me when we were there. It seemed a form of betrayal to my whole upbringing; how dare I think of entering such a place? I was accepted in August 1963 so now important matters had to be attended to. Unfortunately Oakwood could not finance a full-time course, only bargaining on a basic qualification, so at the end of September 1964 Ann and I left that establishment.

Birmingham

Some 18 students working in probation, medical or psychiatric work or child care assembled for the start of the generic course. We launched immediately into an intensive programme of lectures, seminars and tutorials. The latter were the most feared as tutors probed and prodded each student's personal history and range of feelings in order to develop those two requirements for a good social worker: insight and self-knowledge. For many this was a very painful experience. Indeed, the degree to which tutors felt free to delve into the intimate personal history of some students caused considerable distress and served to unite the student body in a defensive mode. My own crisis came when I had been spotted in town looking in a jeweller's window. 'Was I possibly thinking of getting engaged?' was the simple question which would have been an excuse to explore my sexual history for the first time. 'Oh no,' I replied. 'I'm getting married next week.' There was a stunned silence as the implication of this sunk in and it was pointed out that had I mentioned this at interview I would never have been offered a place. The psychological burden of the course combined with marriage was bound to be excessively heavy. My reply was truly that I had never been asked that question. The next few months, spent in the condemned Redditch house, were pretty happy and exciting. Ann worked at the Child Guidance Clinic at Leamington Spa, mostly concerned with mentally handicapped children, and then at Rubery, the old asylum to the south of Birmingham.

If I had thought the part time Diploma course at Brighton was intense, then this was even more demanding, particularly the heavy load of written work and the precision required. Any slip would be liable to be interpreted under a psychoanalytic microscope. I never quite worked out whether my wonderful tutor, Pauline Shapiro (who was also course leader), was treating me more gently than other students because of my assumed 'heavy burden' or whether my defences resisted any attempts to probe.

The Birmingham course provided a background of lectures on physical medicine and genetics, social institutions and welfare services, physical and mental illness, the law relating to all welfare matters and sociology, but the main focus was on human growth and behaviour, psychiatry and of course social work, which effectively meant individual casework with a late addition of group work. There were also two long intensive placements. Physical medicine took us through all the common diseases and treatments from birth and included an up to date briefing on genetics. We had a thorough grounding of the legal systems, including the possibility that family courts might well be introduced as a less formal setting for domestic disputes and adjudications concerning children.

Much time was spent in detailed examination of the Mental Health Act 1959, but I was particularly taken with the duties imposed by the Act on the mental welfare officers employed by local authorities, usually under the authority of the Medical Officer of Health. I note that a session on the 'Professionalisation of Social Workers' by Martin Collis posed the question why America and the UK developed a focus on individuals rather than involvement in wider issues and the formation of policy? Did we think that the selection of students on to social work courses, usually by psychoanalytically trained tutors, ruled out firebrands? All questions which would certainly be embraced by myself and many others within the next decade. At this point the respected criminologist Barbara Wootton launched her carefully aimed missile at the profession. In the relevant chapter in her *Social Science and Social Pathology*, she explained that in her view the move from charity with the original Charity Organisation Society to psychoanalysis had only exchanged 'the garment of charity for a uniform borrowed from the practitioners of psychological medicine,' resulting in 'the erection of a fantastically pretentious façade' and an emphasis on certain aspects to the exclusion of all others. We were attacked for the use of the word 'client,' which she considered 'an odd word to apply to the subjects of social work … its use in this sense smacks of a deliberate attempt to pretend that things are other than they are, and looks like an illustration of the recurrent human tendency to employ words as instruments of self-deception.' Why do social workers use medical terms? she demanded. Why do they talk so much about the relationship and personality and fail to respond to the precipitating social problems? Wootton found it impossible to take seriously the idea that 'complex problems of personal unhappiness could be helped by a young woman with an academic training in social work,' and goes on to quote Virginia Woolf's comment about the 'peculiar repulsiveness of those who dabble their fingers, self approvingly in the stuff of other people's souls.' As an empiricist Wootton saw no validity in social work being a profession as it clearly lacked any specific knowledge or skill, was unverifiable and borrowed from other disciplines. Have we not just replaced the old uncooperative (or undeserving) with 'unable to benefit from therapy' and hidden moral judgements in the mysteries of casework? The real problem as Wootton saw it was that the training and practice of modern social workers deflected them from facing the real social problems that we should have been attending to: the implications of evil environments and social mores. All in all, a great start to a casework course![41]

My memory is that the most relevant contribution of sociology was the study of group functioning. F. M. Thrasher's early Chicago study of over a thousand small street gangs had shown how each developed systems of status and position where each member had a recognisable role, although all members agreed on a common code and, however strong the leader was, they must submit to what passed as democracy in that group. Other studies showed that sentiment develops in small groups in relation to the frequency of interaction, which in itself provokes more interaction and more group sentiment. Groups become more cohesive where there is acceptance of group norms and there is a clear division of labour, where there is high morale in the face of an external threat.[42]

Thankfully the experience of the preceding two years had prepared me for the gap between all these ideas and the actual practice of adult psychiatry in the NHS. Consequently one was left in a strange double world where one language, based on drug therapy or behavioural programmes, was used in the clinics and ward rounds, but quite another used with other students and when your professional supervisor went through your long verbatim process recordings of each interview, turning every phrase over to see the 'real' meaning. Only in the comfort of child guidance clinics was there a common language or at least a willingness to give credit to different approaches for the benefit of the child and the family.

With all this extensive knowledge we approached the central module of the one-year course, how we did social work or, to be more precise, individual casework which we approached historically, starting almost exclusively with American authors, the first of which was Gordon Hamilton.[43] For Hamilton, social casework was about treating the individual 'in relation to their social experience and their subjective feelings about this experience.' She saw each case as a psycho-social problem incorporating economic, physical, mental, emotional and social factors: it was pointless in her view to deal only with outer or inner problems. Clients are usually more satisfied with intervention in direct proportion to the degree to which they have a hand in shaping their own destiny. Hamilton stated that professional purpose demanded action in the interest of client and community. A social worker is obligated to continue the task of creating a better social environment. The worker needs to restrain their desire to help so that the client can develop self-help. As the work continues one should seek clarification, with interpretation kept to the minimum. A more analytic approach came from Helen Perlman, who advised that the caseworker's initial task is to select facets to work on from each complex problem. These facets could include the problem presented by the client, the possible and desirable situation as seen by the social worker, or perhaps the function of the agency. Problems, of course, are both objective and subjective, complicated by the very fact of being a client. Perlman's definition of the casework relationship was 'a purposive sharing of a problem in which the client can feel the worker's competence to help.' Pretty realistic I thought.[44]

The basis of all such work was the relationship between worker and client, and the bible for this was *The Casework Relationship* by Felix Biestek, an ordained Jesuit priest and Professor of Social Work, whose short book would remain in the syllabus for many years to come. He used a definition of social casework written by the Canadian, the Rev Swithun Bowers, in 1949:

> An art in which knowledge of the science of human relations and skill in relationships are used to mobilise capacities in the individual and resources in the community appropriate for better adjustment between the client and all or any part of his total environment.

Biestek held that, while the relationship is the medium for applying knowledge and the channel for the entire casework process, it should never seek to be as deep as in psychoanalysis:

> The relationship is the dynamic interaction of attitudes and emotions between the caseworker and the client, with the purpose of helping the client to achieve a better judgement between himself and his environment.

Above all, and rarely omitted from examinations for many years, were Biestek's seven principles of social casework:

1. **Individualisation** (The recognition and understanding of each client's unique qualities and … the rights of human beings to be individuals and to be treated not just as a human being but *this* human being.)
2. **The purposeful expression of feelings** (by the client and purposeful listening by the worker).
3. **Controlled emotional involvement** (over-involvement and the issue of transference).
4. **Acceptance** (Deal with the client as he really is, strengths and weaknesses, congenial or uncongenial qualities, constructive and destructive attitudes. Does not mean approval of deviant behaviour. The object is to help the client free himself of his defences so that he feels safe to reveal himself and see himself as he really is.)
5. **Non-judgemental attitude**.
6. **Self-determination**.
7. **Confidentiality**.

In Biestek's terms the worker is both a 'sure-footed realist and a clear-eyed idealist who, within the motive of love, strives for skill in the use of the wisdom of science to help a brother in need.'[45]

The latest American book with which we worked was Florence Hollis's bravely entitled *A Psychosocial Therapy*. Hollis followed many of the principles already covered but leant much more towards helping people to adapt to their environment. She listed the frustration of infantile needs and faulty ego or super ego functioning as issues to be addressed in the light of external pressures. Hollis included direct influence (action, advice or suggestion) as appropriate interventions, providing that the worker is clear about whose need is being met in giving advice or taking action. A whole chapter was devoted to 'The Caseworker and the Unconscious.' In addition, Hollis paid great attention to the importance of a thorough psycho-social study, a full diagnosis based on an assessment of all the external factors (including cultural, racial, class and religious norms), physical health, internal factors (libidinal characteristics, ego and super ego factors, signs and symptoms). From this comes 'the treatment plan.'[46] I felt increasing sympathy with Barbara Wootton.

Wootton was certainly a body blow to an aspiring profession. I think that as students we could agree with much of her criticism but could not allow it to shake our commitment to what we had been taught and the whole culture of the occupation that we were about to enter. However, I am quite sure that Wootton's attack played no small part in the revolution that was to change social work education in the next few years. The virtual absence of any current developments in sociology which would play such a significant part in the coming changes was remarkable but attributable I guess to the professional background of our tutors.

A latecomer to the studies, and for me the author of the most interesting work, was the psychoanalyst W. R. Bion's *Experiences in Groups*.[47] Bion worked with groups of neurotic patients who, discovering that they were all on the same footing, lost some of their self-centredness. Bion observed higher levels of feeling expressed in groups, so if one member becomes hostile the others will project their hostile feelings back onto them. Over and above their individual contributions they formed a group mentality. Conflict then develops between the group mentality and the needs of individual members, leading to differing identifiable cultures within the group, so if two people are involved in a prolonged interaction the group's unconscious basic assumption is that they are together for sex, thus the group becomes hopeful of a good outcome although the fact of pairing itself threatens the continued life of the group which can move to stop the pair. Groups who give way to a strong leader have a basic assumption of dependency, believing that perhaps 'daddy' will solve the problems. A new idea introduced to the group causes excitement, which leads to confusion as the group cannot decide whether to use the mechanisms of fight or flight. These three basic assumptions stop the group working effectively. Bion considered that the most efficient groups were between six and eight people.

My first placement was in the Professorial Psychiatric Unit located on the top floor of the Queen Elizabeth Hospital which was part of the university campus. It was presided over by an extrovert former jazz trumpet player who ran his demonstration ward reviews along Oakwood lines, although this seemed far more acceptable in a teaching unit. Ann and I had a few lively discussions about the relative workloads and status of our two units, as the location of the Professorial Unit precluded it accommodating any suicidal or dangerously manic patients who were consequently shipped out to the old Rubery Hospital. I was joined by a student from the newly instituted Certificate in Social Service[48n] course, but as far as I could see, apart from specialism, our programmes were very similar. The status of our awards were significantly different, however, both professionally and salary wise. My only recollection of direct patient care from this unit was being asked to escort a young man, said to have recovered from acute mania, on a walk to get some fresh air. The fact that he was the son of a senior member of the university probably explained why he remained in the unit. The walk was somewhat exciting as he, of course, was only interested in heading straight for his father's office, the very place which I had been instructed to avoid at all costs. There was little I could do as, apart from any professional or personal influence, he was bigger and stronger than me – I could see my whole career disappearing down the elaborate corridors. Luckily all that greeted us was a series of empty rooms and an angry security guard who had to be placated. Some extra persuasive efforts on my part restored us to the unit without alarm, an event that I don't actually recall formally recording.

The fact that I was still disadvantaged by chronic shyness stopped me elucidating a problem put before an audience of medical students by a senior psychologist. Their thorough investigation of a particular patient led to a clear diagnosis of significant deterioration of mental function, perhaps dementia, except that he passed all the tests of numerical recall, including reverse numbers, with amazing accuracy. I could not bring myself to point out the fact (which seemed obvious to me) that, as he had spent his entire working life in the stores of a major motor manufacturer, he had to remember complex part numbers all day and every day.

A more congenial placement was with the Child Guidance Clinic in Worcester where the psychiatric social worker (PSW) and the psychiatrist had run the clinic for so long that they were now starting to see the children of some of their early patients. Quite what this meant as an indicator of success was unclear, but they did intend to write up the value of service continuity over such a long period. Whether these intentions were ever realised I do not know, although I hope they were as the caring culture and sense of positive and purposeful partnership that was the hallmark of that clinic was remarkable and one that I have seldom experienced since. I enjoyed working with the families of these young children. I recall visiting a family, always by appointment of course, where the father was reluctant to let my visit interfere with his regular session in the local pub so it seemed natural to suggest that I accompany him there to finish our discussion. Reporting what I took to be normal behaviour caused quite a stir with the very insightful and caring PSW who posed questions about professional conduct, confidentiality and the real meaning of buying him a drink, all of which I must have dealt with adequately as this incident was written up in my report as a striking example of innovative practice! The gap between my view of the real world and the clinical detachment of a professional was still a worry that niggled away as something to tackle when the opportunity arose.

The end of the course came into view with considerable relief as, despite Ann's earnings, we were financially pressed to the point where I had had to approach the Officers Association for a grant to help with fuel through the winter and the Dame Eveline Fox Memorial Fund to help with book purchases. Also, Ann had been visiting her stepfather every other weekend and the joys of casseroles maturing on our one-ring Belling stove were beginning to pall. By this time bits of the house had started to fall down and we were constantly being woken by police in the early hours as they searched for anyone who may be hiding in the other half of our decrepit property. Final exams were looming and from time to time the normal stress of a new marriage complicated life. I recall that at one point, probably jealous of Ann's daily phone calls to Hugh, I determined to make a point. When it seemed that more than an hour had passed I walked up to the town square telephone box, put the receiver down and frogmarched Ann back to our house. Perhaps my tutor's dire concerns were justified. Exams were taken and passed and the search for a new job commenced. The job I really set my heart on was in the East End of London, near Oxford House. Apart from a natural desire to work in such an exciting area, the local Child Guidance Clinic had established a high reputation and had published a very good book about their experiences. Ann and I travelled down and arrived at the appointed place in good time. We waited, then we waited longer and eventually the PSW came down and called me up for interview. As we were tired and hungry I asked if there was somewhere Ann could get some refreshment; she was directed to a café that was 'somewhere over there.' There was no apology for the delay. Most of the interview was spent complaining that the local mental welfare officers (MWOs) thought the clinic was out of touch with the local cultures. Some two hours later I emerged, never having been offered a drink, to find that the café that Ann had been directed to was closed. Discussing the experience on the way home we weighed up the excitement of working in that environment and the professional attraction of working in such a good team against the lack of common courtesy and obvious disconnect with the local environment. I could see that my sympathies would end up with the local MWOs. With great regret it was goodbye to dear old London. An alternative vacancy was at St Augustine's Hospital near Canterbury, and a visit to the PSW team and interview confirmed that I could work there with proper supervision (and a salary of £1168 – nearly double my student rate but still just below the average wage for 1965). Importantly there was the offer of renting a hospital house.

When the end of the year was in sight, we invited tutors, students and Ann's medical and nursing colleagues to a wild party, at the end of which the orange box furniture would be thrown away and the condition of the house would no longer be a concern. It was quite a party and, far too late, our neighbours, who had observed the consultant's expensive cars arriving, decided that they could manage to speak to us as we may not quite be the weird hippy types they had previously despised. One last time we loaded our possessions into the faithful Saab and headed across country to the not long opened M1 and home. We revisited Redditch some thirty years later; the house was still standing and still derelict, with permission to develop still being sought.

QUALIFIED SOCIAL WORKER

St Augustine's Hospital at Chartham stood on the crest of a hill west of Canterbury just far enough from the city to feel safe. Our new semi-detached house was one of those forming 'The Crescent,' which faced the main gates leading up the grand drive to the main brick built hospital. There were fewer long corridors and an altogether less institutional feel than at Oakwood. Set in the beautiful extensive grounds was the only inpatient unit for adolescent boys in southern England and Ann was successful in getting a job there as a social worker. In the main hospital the head of the fully qualified social work team lived in a flat above the short-stay unit and had been at the hospital for many years. The other member was Miss Mitchell, a kind, hard-working and thoughtful woman who had qualified in 1945 at the first historic LSE course. She was to be my supervisor. I was to work in the east of the catchment area, between a line south to Deal and east to Margate, attending all the outpatient clinics as required and working with newly admitted and discharged patients. In addition to attending ward rounds I worked particularly in Cyprus Ward, which offered a group therapy regime for young male patients diagnosed as psychopathic or personality disordered. My year in Birmingham must have been of some value as I certainly had more confidence and was readily accepted as a reliable member of the team.

In addition to working at the adolescent unit, Ann took a part-time post at Oakwood's day hospital in Maidstone, where she worked again with Masood Akhtar and Dr Hyatt Williams.[49n] Every other week Williams held an informal seminar for local social workers who he considered to be more in the front line of complex and dangerous situations than most psychiatrists. These sessions were well attended and fun, particularly as Mike, the camp probation officer, was a regular attendee who provided a good sense of humour to our otherwise earnest discussions. Having completed a series of analyses, the last and most recent being with Melanie Klein herself, Hyatt Williams saw everything through that framework. So, he would tell us that the root of schizophrenia lay in the first few months of life (the oral stage) when the infant feels violently good or bad depending on the balance of satisfaction in their body. Disturbances of this balance cause violent internal conflict, which splits off part of the unformed personality. At puberty or soon after, this split part breaks through to shatter the personality. If the spilt part is projected on to others, a paranoid disorder is likely. Ann was teased every session as she had a smart red handbag with two small pockets on the outside with protruding brass buttons – 'Oh,' said Williams, 'and here comes the good and bad breast.' He and Ann developed a good working relationship which included some very interesting cases, although his prison work seemed to blunt his sense of danger as he would send Ann on some pretty hair-raising visits to the families of known violent prisoners in search of detailed family background. I suspect that the secret of their mutual respect was the fact that Ann had no time at all for his theories, and he knew it. The doctor ran at an extraordinary fast rate up and down the stairs, consulting as he went, in a sort of chronic manic state which was also evident in his home life where his passion for gardening would lead him to rush round Oakwood's grounds in the shabbiest of clothes pushing wheelbarrows full of all sorts of rubbish and plants. Just one of the eccentric inhabitants of the doctors' houses!

Personally and professionally life was going well at Chartham. It seemed natural enough that if a boy in the unit had nowhere to go during the school holidays they joined us for the duration. (Was this a throwback to Ann's unhappy school days?) Thus we had some challenging incidents and interesting dynamics if Ann's stepfather joined us in a cramped caravan in Cornwall. Regression and sibling rivalry between him and the boys were very evident! Opposite the crescent of staff houses was a pub which was of course a favourite place for a variety of patients, but word seemed to have got round that the social workers' house was easily found and consequently we became hosts to psychotic or neurotic individuals at all hours. From time to time some of the boys from Ann's unit would spend the evening with us, chatting and watching TV. One hilarious evening there was a film about a nudist camp where one guy was cooking sausages on an open fire. The boys were rolling on the floor, clutching themselves in terror.

One should not assume that all our visitors were patients as we soon rediscovered the level of sheer madness among the medical staff. I particularly recall the psychiatrist responsible for the group therapy ward being in a constant state of distress as he believed that his wife could never be entirely faithful to him due to the bond between her and her twin sister. In our role of extended counsellors to all, we made the mistake of inviting him to supper. He arrived more than two hours late and devoured the meal with no awareness of what it was whilst he fantasised a story of abduction in some dense woods on his way home from Dover!

We were fast learning lessons not taught on qualifying courses but, despite changing fashions, we have always maintained open boundaries between home and work – a policy which has given rise to occasional problems and was arguably to have disastrous career consequences for me much later. I was somewhat shaken when, wandering into Cyprus Ward one day, a patient sprang to attention and reminded me that he had been my batman in Khartoum (see Chapter ??)! With the wisdom of hindsight I cannot believe the risks we took out in the community visiting the acutely ill or the less easily diagnosed group of unhappy, stressed or neurotic individuals. One household displayed a wide variety of weaponry on the living room wall. Every time I called, always of course by prior appointment, the man kept me in his rifle sight as I walked up the path and then boasted about how easy it would have been to dispatch me on the spot. Risk assessments and health and safety at work being so far into the future, we had no option but to rely on instinct, a calm approach and a degree of sang-froid. I was only ever warned in respect of one patient who had been released from the high-security Broadmoor Hospital and had already severely crippled one 'official' visitor. He was a hugely built man living in a flat with his wife and child of about eight. I must have managed to project a convincingly non-threatening clinical persona and within a short while visits were relaxed, complete with the mug of strong tea made with creamy Carnation milk, which seemed to be the usual refreshment served to visiting social workers by everyone. A strong bladder was certainly an essential qualification for a day of home visiting. During my third visit or thereabouts I was shown further than the lounge – the tour included a photographic dark-room complete with strips of 35-mm film rolls hanging up to dry. We had found a common interest, that key to a good relationship, but when I casually examined the negatives they were definitely in the mildly pornographic category. My next report for the GP, whose desperate referral it had been, mentioned this activity in the best non-judgemental fashion that my training had prescribed. The next home visit was interesting as the patient's long experience of institutional life had enabled him to read reports upside down on the GP's desk. I was relieved that he accepted my judgement on the matter and visits continued in their usual comfortable style. Looking back of course I am appalled that not once did I or my supervisor consider the possibility of risk to the child, although had I seen any indicative signs from the boy or in the household I am sure I would have acted. A great gap was maintained between hospital based social workers and those in the community.

Pain and tragedy were never far away in the field of mental health and it was probably within the first year since qualification that I was assigned the most challenging case on which I would work. The patient, a young and beautiful woman, had, in the grips of an acute psychotic post-partum episode, murdered her young babies. I was asked to work with the husband. We met whenever he visited the hospital and I tried to listen to both his grief and his complete puzzlement as to how the woman that he loved could commit such an horrendous crime. Whilst the medical staff worked hard to find the right mixture of medication that would end the psychotic episode we were increasingly concerned about how his wife would react when reality returned and she had to face what she had done. Predictably a deep depression set in and as this in turn began to wane we needed to explore any possibility of the marriage continuing. The mood swings of both partners were extreme; for a few weeks the husband would express the extent of his horror that he could ever see or touch his wife again, then she would report sexual reunions in the summer house outside the ward. Eventually the mixture of medication, casework and love pulled them through to a future together, but I have no idea for how long. At Oakwood I had been shaken when an elderly couple who had never lived apart for forty years were separated on admission to the male and female sections of the institution.[50n] At St Augustine's I witnessed a different aspect of sexual mores when a pregnant teenager was admitted for assessment of her depression, the only non-physical justification for an abortion at that time. On the instructions of her and her parents the young man responsible was denied access despite his persistent hammering on the ward door and pleas that he had rights in the decision to be made. Denied any say in the matter, he hanged himself in the hospital grounds.

Within the boundaries of these more extreme situations the routine of the hospital rolled on. Very ill patients from across all social classes were admitted and were discharged at least with their symptoms eased. I was called in late one evening to talk with the distressed family of an internationally renowned pianist who had suffered an acute psychotic episode on the cross-Channel ferry, had been taken into custody and admitted to the locked ward under a detention order. The gap between their experience of the world and a hospital corridor late at night was alarming, but they had no real option but to accept my argument that, for the moment, his safety was paramount and that he was sufficiently out of touch with reality to be less aware of his environment than they were.

Group work in Cyprus Ward under the good care of the consultant psychiatrist Toby Hartigan was going so well that I decided to start a group in the neighbouring ward for young schizophrenic patients; a doubtful move. Some progress was made, but the strain on my own mental health was considerable during each session as each member counselled the other from their own individual set of delusions and fantasies. Ann's work in the adolescent unit and my work in the main hospital were becoming an established part of hospital life, but the inability to escape from constant visits after the pub closed was a constant issue. Another problem was taking its toll on me. Early on it had become apparent that the principal PSW who had lived in this institution for many years, was somewhat paranoid. Thus soon after I left any ward she would find a reason to visit. A copy of every note or report that I wrote found its way to her office, and finally I discovered that once or twice a week she would search through my desk. I doubt whether any malice was intended, it was just a way to maintain complete control. That helped me to decide to leave the hospital and, after twelve years doing community work, exploring the penal and child care world and six years of psychiatry, it seemed a change would be good.

Education having been a long-standing interest I was successful in obtaining a job as lecturer on the newly established Certificate of Qualification in Social Work (CQSW) course at Maidstone College. All my cases had to be reviewed and decisions taken about future management. Final visits had to be made to everyone and these threw up a couple of surprises as two patients, one male, one female, confessed that the reason that my visits had lasted so long was that their object had been my seduction! So much for my trained ability to understand what was really going on. Obviously, I was ready to teach others!

Social work had consolidated its professional base, acquired new powers and was a valued part of society. Important developments within the social sciences, particularly sociology, were bringing discrete disciplines together in ways which would enhance their application to practice. Ann and I were living happily in a sound marriage with a wonderful daughter. We enjoyed and respected those who we helped with no firm line between them and family life; indeed many of the boys that Ann worked with remained in contact in subsequent years. Life was good despite the painful loss of loved and valued family members. In common with the majority of people we felt more financially secure, unemployment was low and prospects were good.

NOTES AND REFERENCES

1. From *Camelot*, the musical, by Lerner and Lowe. London 1964 production starring Laurence Harvey and Elizabeth Larner.
2. Robert Kennedy's speech on Day of Affirmation, Cape Town, June 6th 1966.
3. Song from the American rock musical *Hair* written by James Rado and Gerome Ragni in 1964 to celebrate the young hippy counter-culture and sexual revolution of the 1960s. It was first performed off-Broadway in 1967 before becoming a worldwide success. It was adapted as a film in 1979, directed by Milos Forman.
4. The CIA considered that the intelligence reports from the island were unreliable, and effective air reconnaissance had been withheld following the loss of several of the American U2 super spy planes. Such a plane was not used until October, by which time many missiles were already in place. In 2012 it become known that four Russian submarines armed with nuclear torpedoes had been stationed just to the northeast of Cuba throughout the crisis. The crews suffered badly as the submarines had not been designed for tropical waters: one captain lost his temper in a dispute with senior officers and ordered the torpedoes to be armed. The presence of this threat had been discovered by the US Navy as the subs had to surface to charge their batteries.
5. The widespread use of this chemical in Vietnam was aimed at removing cover for the enemy and driving peasant farmers into urban areas where they were less likely to aid invading troops. Other chemicals were also used on food crops. In addition to the obvious environmental damage, the action caused wide suffering, death and birth defects among the population, including Vietnamese and American military. To the present day America has been faced with innumerable claims for damages from both its own veterans and Vietnamese groups and has allocated funds to clean up the worst affected areas in Vietnam. America has faced down allegations of war crimes, but compensation cases are still being fought.
6. Whilst it was generally known that Kennedy was in constant pain due to severe back injuries, the degree to which the image of a young vital man was a PR front was not known. In 1947 he had been diagnosed with Addison's disease and at one point had been so critically ill that the last rites were administered. For the rest of his life he took high doses of cortisone amid a range of other medications and a daily regime of hot baths and sleep. Given the poor prognosis for this disease any hopes for his second presidential campaign may never have been realised.
7. These events have been steeped in controversy ever since, with many subsequent conspiracy theories, books and films. These centre on disputes about how many bullets hit the President, how many gunmen there were and who was responsible if, as Oswald claimed, he was the 'patsy' set up by others. Candidates have varied from the Vietnamese, drug barons, communists, an accident caused by one of his bodyguards and American right-wing extremists with or without the collusion of the FBI and CIA.
8. Fletcher, M. 'LBJ Tape Confirms Vietnam War Error.' *The Times*, 7.11.2001. From Wikipedia.
9. Published speech by Robert Kennedy, Washington, D.C., March 16th 1968.
10. In the early 1960s Malcolm X had become the main spokesperson and public face of the Nation of Islam, a long-standing radical American Islamic movement. His exceptional oratory boosted

the movement's membership to national prominence. Unlike King he was not prepared to limit campaigns to non-violence, following the Nation's belief that black people were superior to white people and would eventually rule over them. Malcolm X recruited the world heavyweight boxer Cassius Clay to the movement when he changed his name to Mohammad Ali. Following disagreements within the movement Malcolm left to become a Sunni Muslim. He was welcomed worldwide, attracting much attention for his more moderate doctrine. In February 1965 he was violently assassinated by members of the Nation. He was succeeded by Louis Farrakhan. By 2007 Farrakhan was reducing his responsibilities to the Nation, but in 1995 he had organised the Million Man March, which he led again 20 years later.
11. Martin Luther King, speech at the Riverside Church, New York, April 4th 1967.
12. Martin Luther King, speech at the Bishop Charles Masonic Temple, Memphis, April 3rd 1968.
13. Wallace continued his campaign despite political and personal difficulties (his second wife commented during the divorce that George did not need a family, just an audience, his ego being too big for a family). In May 1972 Wallace was shot five times in an attempted assassination. He fought his last bid for the presidency with his spinal cord damaged, severely disabled and in a wheelchair. After becoming a born-again Christian he apologised publicly for his long and violent opposition to desegregation.
14. Marr, A. (2007). *A History of Modern Britain*. London: MacMillan, p. 207.
15. *Beyond the Fringe* was a fiercely satirical comedy review drawing its stars from Oxbridge students including Peter Cook, Dudley Moore, Alan Bennett and Jonathan Miller. It toured the UK and the USA to great acclaim. It specialised in humiliating politicians and the elite. When they discovered that Harold Macmillan was in the audience they taunted him directly.
16. Macmillan lived a further 23 years, the diagnosis which forced his resignation turning out to be false. A scandal that was slow to emerge was that his loyal wife Dorothy (who had presented the colour to my Swanley ACF unit in 1959) had a thirty-year-long affair with the promiscuous bisexual MP Robert Boothby, who in turn procured boys for the Kray twins. The press kept a lid on this affair partly in deference to the Conservative government but also because the senior Labour politician Tom Driberg was using the same network for his homosexual activities. Dorothy Macmillan died in 1966. Harold took his cool aristocratic view of a changing world, informed by his long experience and a very sharp wit to the House of Lords. His role as a respected intelligent and entertaining guru was much enjoyed. He died in December 1986.
17. Marr, *op. cit.*, p. 238.
18. Ten colonies were granted independence at this time: Uganda, Tanganyika, Kenya, Malta, Nyasaland, Northern Rhodesia, Botswana, and Barbados, Jamaica and Guyana.
19. *The Child, the Family and the Young Offender*, 1965, Cmnd 2742.
20. *Cathy Come Home*. Dir. Ken Loach, Prod. Tony Garnett. BBC, 1966. Starring Carol White and Ken Brooks.
21. The most famous official hangman was Albert Pierrepoint who in a career lasting 34 years executed between 400 and 600 men and women. He retired and became the landlord of the Rose and Crown pub near Preston in Lancashire. On one occasion in the 1970s he turned up at an official event at County Hall where I inadvertently shook his hand. He died in 1998. *Pierrepoint*, the excellent 2005 film, covers his career. Dir. Adrian Shergold. Redbus Film, 2005. Starring Timothy Spall and Juliet Stephenson.
22. Powell left the Conservative Party in 1974 but was returned to Parliament as an Ulster Unionist where he continued to criticise successive governments on Northern Ireland, immigration and defence matters. He left Parliament in 1987. In the late 1980s I pulled my car over in order to listen to a gripping personal radio interview. The man was recalling his service in the North African campaign of 1944 and was sobbing uncontrollably with guilt that he survived when others had

not. It took me some time to realise that this was Powell. He campaigned fiercely against our involvement in Europe, died in February 1998 and was buried in his brigadier's uniform. See the BBC documentary *Odd Man Out* (November 1995) and Shepherd, R. (1998). *Enoch Powell, A Biography*. London: Hutchinson.
23. DeGroot, G. (2009). *The Sixties Unplugged*. Oxford: Pan, p. 138.
24. Biba was founded by Barbara Hulanicki, born in Warsaw and brought up in British Mandated Palestine. Her father, a UN negotiator, had been killed by Zionist terrorists.
25. Hansard HC Deb. Vol 782 Col 281. April 22nd 1969.
26. Mills, C. W. (1956). *The Power Elite*. Oxford: Oxford University Press; Mills, C. W. (1959). *The Sociological Imagination*. Oxford: Oxford University Press; Marcuse, H. (1964). *One Dimensional Man. Studies in the Ideology of Advanced Industrial Society*. New York: Beacon Press; Wolff, R., Moore, B. and Marcuse, H. (1965). *A Critique of Pure Tolerance*. New York: Beacon Press; Marcuse, H. (1969). *An Essay on Liberation*. London: Pelican.
27. On the second day of the Tet offensive, when South Vietnam was under intense pressure, Colonel Nguyễn Loan, Chief of South Vietnam Police, was presented with a Viet Cong prisoner. In front of Eddie Adams, an AP photographer on his second term, the Colonel pulled out his pistol and shot the prisoner in the head. The Colonel explained to the shocked photographer that the man was responsible for many killings, including the beheading of the Colonel's colleague and his wife. According to some commentators this video on the evening news turned American public opinion against the war.
28. In the 1960s Vanessa Redgrave was a young and gifted actress who was a member of left-wing Marxist and Trotskyist groups. Tariq Ali was a British-born Pakistani resident in Britain. He was President of the Oxford Union in 1965 and active in extreme left-wing groups including the International Marxist Group. Vanessa Redgrave CBE continues her successful acting career and her political activism, criticising the war on terror and campaigning for universal human rights. At the time of writing Tariq Ali continues to edit the *New Left Review* and works as a journalist and TV participant on international relations.
29. Carson, R. (1962). *Silent Spring*. London: Penguin; Friedan, B. (1963). *The Feminist Mystique*. London: Penguin. In this section I have drawn heavily on Marwick, A. (1958). *The Sixties Cultural Revolution in Britain, France, Italy and the United States*. Oxford: Oxford University Press, from which the Carson quote is taken (p. 88).
30. Marwick, *op. cit.*, p. 679.
31. Marwick, *op. cit.*, p. 685.
32. Greer, G. (1970). *The Female Eunuch*. London: Harper Collins.
33. This is not quite true as in 1990 I was taken aback when Alan telephoned me to say goodbye as he had only a few days left to live. In 2015 we discovered that his son David was working in New York where Juliet was able to reconnect the families. We met David and his wife Kim there two years later and have continued to keep in touch. Jeffrey still lives in Holland.
34. For a fascinating account of this way of life, see Self, W. (2012). *Umbrella*. London: Bloomsbury. It is a complete book without chapters and very few paragraphs.
35. Preventive detention was an indeterminate sentence, release depending on the offender being fit to return to society. It was succeeded in 2012 by imprisonment for public protection. An alternative outcome might be detention under mental health legislation.
36. Auden, W. H. (1940). 'September 1st 1939,' in *Another Time*. London: Random House.
37. Thrasher, F. (1927). *The Gang: A Study of 1,313 Gangs in Chicago*. Chicago: University of Chicago Press.
38. Alcock, P. and Oakley, A. (2001). *Welfare and Wellbeing – Richard Titmuss's Contribution to Social Policy*. Bristol: Policy Press.

39. A graduate of the LSE, Leo Abse was Labour MP for Pontypool for 29 years. He pursued social issues throughout his career. These included divorce by consent (The Matrimonial Causes Act 1973) and the Family Planning Act of 1967, which allowed the NHS to offer free advice regardless of marital status. In later years his interest in psychoanalysis rather overtook him. In 2000 he published *Fellatio Masochism, Politics and Love*. He also published less than complimentary psycho-biographies of Margaret Thatcher and Tony Blair. His younger brother is the poet Danny Abse and his older brother Wilfred is a professor of psychiatry in the USA. Leo died in August 2008.
40. Burn, M. (1956). *Mr Lyward's Answer: The Story of George Lyward and Finchden Manor*. London: Hamilton.
41. Wootton, B. (1959). *Social Science and Social Pathology*. London: George Allen & Unwin, chap. 9.
42. Lewin, K., Lippitt, R. and White, R. K. (1939). Patterns of Aggressive Behavior in Experimentally Created Social Climates. *Journal of Social Psychology*, Vol. 10, pp. 271–279; Whyte, W. F. (1993). *Street Corner Society: The Social Structure of an Italian Slum*, Fourth Edition. Chicago: University of Chicago Press.
43. Hamilton, G. (1951). *Theory and Practice of Social Case Work*. Chicago: University of Chicago Press.
44. Perlman, H. (1957). *Social Casework: A Problem-Solving Process*. Chicago: University of Chicago Press.
45. Biestek, F. (1961). *The Casework Relationship*. London. Allen & Unwin.
46. Hollis, F. (1955). Principles and Assumptions Underlying Casework Practice, *Social Work*, pp. 41–55; Hollis, F. (1965). *Casework: A Psychosocial Therapy*. New York: Random House.
47. Bion, W. R. (1961). *Experiences in Groups and Other Papers*. London: Tavistock.
48. The Certificate in Social Service was introduced after pressure from employers who considered the existing qualifying courses as too academic so that newly qualified staff arrived with little idea about the actual tasks facing them. The 'education or training' issue, closely related to the claim to be a professional, has been argued among social workers for many years. My belief has always been that training for present tasks is inevitably short term and restrictive. Education should give wider perspectives and a grounding in practice-based theory, which gives the worker greater flexibility and depth. The CSS was established for social work assistants and managers of residential care. It was seen as the intrusion of managerialism into the profession. My view was that, given the similarity of the tutors and existing curriculum on both courses, and the fact that many social work assistants were often doing the same job as social workers, we should give up the dispute. The CSS was established in 1977 and after a year of dispute BASW accepted CSS students into open membership.
49. Dr Arthur Hyatt Williams died on August 27th 2009, a few days before his 95th birthday. Obituaries commented on the warmth of his personality, his boundless energy and his optimism. He had believed strongly that even the most hardened criminals, including murderers for whom there was no chance of direct reparation, could be helped to work on their sense of guilt and to modify their destructive tendencies, and he would put himself out to a great degree in order to treat them. This belief was one source of his enthusiastic campaigning, along with Leo Abse and others, for the abolition of the death penalty, which came in 1965. He was one of a relatively small group of prominent psychoanalysts who combined their high level of commitment to psychoanalysis with a passionate dedication to the public sector. Moreover, where tough work was to be done – with very disturbed adolescents, or psychotically depressed postnatal mothers, or couples involved in domestic violence, say – there he would be. He was remembered at the Cassell Hospital for changing from his suit (and his challenging work with troubled families) into his gardening clothes and producing lots of vegetables. He is said to have grown aubergines in pots on the sunny

window-ledge of his office at the Tavistock Clinic. He will be remembered above all for his gift of friendship across generations, the ever-present twinkle in his eye and his lovely, ready sense of humour.

50. In case it seems that this represents irresponsible care I recall that a 19th century physician superintendent who, when this charge was levelled at him, replied 'It has been suggested that they be deprived of this privilege. I would sooner resign my appointment than deprive my patients of privileges that are enjoyed by the ordinary citizen.' Sym, M. (1963). *Guide to Psychiatry*. London: Livingstone. I note that in 2006 Gloucestershire County Council was severely criticised for refusing a wife's request to be admitted to the same care home as her husband. They had been married for 65 years. The council gave way after the couple had been 'reassessed.' The case added pressure on the newly appointed Commission for Equality and Human Rights to protect the rights of older people. See *The Guardian*, 03.02.2006, p. 12.

NINE

1969–1975

TRANSITIONS

The cultivation and expansion of needs is the antithesis of wisdom. It is also the antithesis of freedom and peace. Every increase of needs tends to increase one's dependence on outside forces over which one cannot have control, and therefore increases existential fear. Only by a reduction of needs can one promote a genuine reduction in those tensions which are the ultimate causes of strife and war.

– E.F. Schumacher, *Small is Beautiful*[1]

At many points in this report we have stressed that we see our proposals not simply in terms of organisation but as embodying a wider conception of social services, directed to the wellbeing of the whole community and not only of social casualties, and seeing the community it serves as the basis of its authority, resources and effectiveness.

– The Seebohm Report[2]

INTERNATIONAL EVENTS

Vietnam

As anti-war protests increased across the world, the Republican Richard Nixon was elected President of the USA in June 1969 on a ticket that promised to seek greater global 'peace with honour' and reduce America's involvement in Vietnam. The policy was brought about in part by escalating costs, continuing popular opposition and the continuing isolation of America: no other country was coming forward in sufficient numbers to fight. In fact, the American policy of running a high trade deficit meant that much of the cost of the war fell on any other countries with trade relations. In 1971 the Nixon administration suspended the dollar link with gold and introduced a 10% import tax, thus adding to the economic woes currently experienced across the world, and also increasing uncertainty about the price of oil, which was fixed to the dollar. Nixon commenced a programme of staged withdrawal of American troops from Vietnam, but infuriated protesters by sending troops across the border into Laos and Cambodia on the grounds that they provided the routes from China through which the northern troops were supplied. Determined to cut that link and pursue peace, Nixon's major achievement was a state visit to China for face-to-face discussions with Chairman Mao, although no long-lasting agreements were reached.[3n] He also concluded two important arms control treaties with the Soviet Union and stopped conscription. American troop reductions continued, and in 1973 a ceasefire was agreed on the basis of complete American withdrawal, although no arrangements were made for the numerous North Vietnamese troops remaining in the South, and on April 30th 1975 they captured Saigon. The world witnessed the scene of Americans evacuating the Embassy by helicopter while crowds of screaming Vietnamese who had worked for them were left outside the gates. A very undignified defeat.

The question 'Why did America, the most powerful country in the world, lose the war?' has been much discussed. Broadly speaking the answer seems to rest on the widespread protests by students, the public and returning veterans. These protests had gained strength as the widespread use of defoliants, napalm, carpet bombing, the extension into Laos and Cambodia and torture and massacres became known. Nixon was seen to have broken his election promise to end the war.

Support had faded significantly when in 1971 Daniel Ellsberg, a former Marine and military adviser to the government, published a 7,000-page document revealing how the government had lied over the progress of the war and concluded several years earlier that it was unwinnable. These 'Pentagon Papers' provoked public outrage.[4n] Decline in support affected morale in the fighting troops, the use of cannabis became widespread and casualties increased as the Viet Cong troops ramped up the pressure to a point where the situation on the ground became unsustainable. Troops also faced confusion as extending the war into Cambodia involved a three-way war between Cambodian government troops, South Vietnamese with American troops and North Vietnamese communist troops, although the boundaries and loyalties were sometimes less than clear. Whatever horrors had been witnessed in Vietnam, events in Cambodia exceeded the soldiers' capacity to cope and many still suffer from the traumas of these experiences.

In 1973 Nixon was re-elected as President, but it would be a short term. During the campaign use had been made of his election committee to fund a variety of illegal activities which included a break-in at the Democratic Party's suite in the Watergate Offices. This incident was traced back to the President, the final evidence coming eventually from the tapes he had installed to record every word spoken in his office. Nixon resigned in August 1974 to avoid impeachment.[5n]

By 1975, under the leadership of Pol Pot, the communist Khmer Rouge (an offshoot of the North Vietnamese Army) had captured the Cambodian capital of Phnom Penh and instituted a fierce regime aimed at restoring the country to its traditional agrarian basis, involving the forced relocation of populations. The next four years were marked by starvation, the imposition of extreme torture and mass executions (known as the Killing Fields), which reduced the population by 25%.[6n] In 1979 Vietnamese forces took over control of Cambodia, although fighting continued among the various factions until 1999 when the Khmer Rouge surrendered. These events had been among the most horrific of modern times.[7n]

China

Mao Zedong had been in power in China for some thirty years when Nixon visited in 1972. Mao's communism did not offer hope of eventual prosperity for individuals in the Marxist model, but aimed for an 'ideal society united in common consensus in which the individual's self abnegation and total immersion in the collective are the ultimate goal ... a kind of collectivist mysticism.'[8] This philosophy had led China to two economic and social disasters after the harsh collectivism of the initial rise to power. The 'Great Leap Forward' of the late 1950s, which aimed to propel Chinese agriculture into increased productivity, was followed by the 'Great Famine' of 1961, with mass starvation resulting in a 57% drop in the projected population. In 1966 Mao had launched his last great programme, the 'Cultural Revolution.' The reasons for this are unclear but seem broadly to have been based on a growing distrust of an intellectual elite who, as they rose to positions of authority, lost touch with the people. The revolution quickly gained support of the young, who formed the Red Guard to eliminate any signs of elitism, urged on by Mao's comment that, 'The death of a worker weighs heavily like a mountain, while that of a bourgeois weighs as lightly as a feather.' A life and death struggle was clear in a circular issued by Mao which demanded that, 'All erroneous ideas, all poisonous weeds, all ghosts and monsters, must be subject to criticism.'[9] Schools were closed, and teachers, university professors and intellectuals were forced to work on the land or face prison where they could be re-educated. Young teenagers tore through communities viscously persecuting teachers, lynching suspected class enemies and using scissors to cut off the toes of pointy shoes and slice open excessively fashioned trousers or locks of long hair. In Beijing the young Red Guards raced through the city looting and staging public 'struggle sessions' in which victims were beaten, tortured and sometimes killed. At least 1,772 people were killed in that city alone.[10]

By the time of Mao's death ten years later, much of China's culture had been destroyed, education at all levels had virtually halted and anyone with above average skills or ambitions had been targeted. Estimates of the casualties vary, but range upwards from three million killed and one million seriously injured. Rather like the true nature of Stalin's regime (see Chapter 2), most of the disasters of Mao's three great ideas were not fully appreciated in the west. In tune with the 1960s/70s search for new ideas we were all waving the 'Little Red Book' that glorified Mao's wise sayings, most popularly that we should 'let a thousand flowers bloom.'[11n] One Marxist commentator was reassured that, 'In China there are no signs of alienation, nervous disorders or of the fragmentation within the individual that you find in a consumer society. The world of the Chinese is compact, integrated and absolutely whole.'[12n]

America's obsession with the spread of communism was not confined to the Far and Middle East but extended right across Central and South America, primarily by covert means, occasional armed action and significant financial support for those fighting to bring down any government with any taint of left-wing ideology. Their activities spread across Argentina, Brazil, Uruguay, Paraguay, Guatemala and El Salvador. Another example was the election in 1970 of the Socialist Salvador Allende as Chilean President. A complicated operation was initiated by American agents leading to a coup in 1973 and the ascension of Augusto Pinochet, who would run one of the most brutal right-wing regimes in the history of that continent.[13n]

The Middle East

Turmoil in Palestine continued as Israel continued to expand, and the constant support of America drove the Arab populations to despair, feeling that no end would ever come to their plight. The world was shocked in September 1970 when the Popular Front for the Liberation of Palestine (PFLP)[14n] hijacked five aircraft bound for New York and London, landing them at Dawson's Field in Jordan where the majority of passengers were released – the Jewish passengers and American men were detained. On September 12th all the aircraft were blown up, and all passengers and crew were eventually released. Two years later, a smaller group, the Black September Organisation, which had split from Fatah (a nationalist democratic political party) and the PFLP, carried out a terrible attack on the Israeli athletes attending the summer Olympics in Munich. Eleven athletes were slaughtered. However much I and many others sympathised and understood the chronic plight of the Palestinians faced with a rich and arrogant Israel, this attack was unforgivable. The Arab states also remained aggrieved at the loss of territory during the 1967 Six-Day War and Israel's rejection of the UN/Egyptian peace plan of 1971, which required it to move back to its pre-war boundaries. Egypt's President Anwar Sadat had supported this plan and in general followed more moderate policies than the more populist President Nasser. This included allowing Islamist groups such as the Brotherhood more cultural freedom. As the economy ran into trouble, Sadat and the President of Syria agreed to a joint attack on Israel, from north and south, to coincide with the religious celebrations of Yom Kippur. The initial attacks went well, particularly in the Sinai, but the superior fire power and training of the Israeli forces quickly drove the invaders back, the war ending nineteen days after it had started. Among the consequences of the war were the resumption of Sadat's original peace negotiations with support from the west and the further isolation of America when European states blocked its intention to rush planes and ammunition to Israel. We found it hard to accept that the need to support Israel was justified by the fight against communism; also at this time we were relying on oil for 19% of our energy. In addition, of course, was the Arab States' consequent oil embargo which quadrupled the price of oil even though the actual embargo was lighter on Europe than America. In 1977 Sadat visited Israel in pursuance of peace building and a full agreement was signed in Washington in March 1979, to the disapproval of most Arab countries. Sadat was assassinated while taking a military parade in October 1981.

NATIONAL EVENTS

The Fall of Labour

As the 1960s faded, the economy was in trouble, inflation rose and, naturally enough, trades unions sought to maintain the value of their members' income; the number of strikes increased which threatened the pound, further damaging the economy. Something had to be done and what happened was a sad landmark in post-war industrial history. Wilson's Secretary of State for Employment, Barbara Castle, a left-wing firebrand and MP for Blackburn, released a White Paper *In Place of Strife* in January 1969. This proposed that unions must hold a ballot before striking, with the establishment of an 'industrial board' with the power to impose settlements in industrial disputes.[15] The document, which would now be seen as very moderate, had been secretly prepared by Wilson and Castle and was suddenly presented to Cabinet and the unions. The trades unions, apparently blind to the public mood and wider economic considerations, were completely opposed to what they saw as an attempt to limit their power, and in this they were supported by most Labour MPs (including the future PM Jim Callaghan) and half the Cabinet. As fierce political negotiations continued through the summer the authors found themselves isolated. Wilson stormed out of Cabinet with the comment 'I don't mind running a green Cabinet but I'm buggered if I'm going to run a yellow one.'[16]

Under fire from the Tories and the right-wing press, a tired Wilson eventually had little option but to ask the electorate for support, the polls indicating a healthy Labour lead.[17] In the event June 1970 saw the Conservative Party returned to power, with a majority of 30 seats. One can well argue that had Castle, whom I admired greatly, been more diplomatic and had Wilson been less fond of political intrigue and capable of more principled leadership, the future of British politics would have been markedly different and much subsequent pain avoided.

Conservatives in Power

Edward Heath became Prime Minister in June 1970, appointing Margaret Thatcher as Secretary of State for Education, and the subsequent four years would see the emergence of a new approach to politics, although Heath's tenure would not be a happy one. He was a gifted musician and an all round 'jolly good chap' who had risen in the Tory ranks as Chief Whip and Prime Negotiator in Europe until being elected Leader of the Party against Enoch Powell in 1965. He was the first person rising to this position from outside the aristocratic Tory clique. He found interaction with the public difficult and was uneasy on television; he also lacked support of many on the right wing of his party. The Prime Minister was determined that our interests lie in joining the European Economic Community. A view derived from his long war experience, Heath believed in the 'middle way' proposed by his mentor Harold Macmillan, the centre ground of capitalism within an economy planned by the state.[18] I had some personal sympathy with him for most of the next twenty years. He seemed to lack the essential element required to be a great politician; good luck.

The new government went for urgent action to aid the flagging economy, setting up various new ministerial structures and, following the example of Roosevelt's New Deal (see Chapter 2), embarked on a programme of public infrastructure spending which included a start to the Channel Tunnel, the massive Thames Barrier (much appreciated forty years later when climate change was recognised) and the construction of a new airport on Maplin Sands on the Thames Estuary, the remains of which are still to be seen.[19n] The travel firm Thomas Cook was denationalised, and when the aircraft division of Rolls Royce was approaching bankruptcy it was virtually nationalised. Relations between the trades unions and the new Prime Minister were initially respectful. Heath, with his experience of the inter-war depression and the Spanish Civil War, recognised the unions as an estate of the realm, providing they acted in accord with that responsibility. There was no way they were going to stand in the way of one of his key policies, the transformation of British industry. My view was that most people took a balanced view on the unions, supporting them when they acted to get their members' income increased in line with inflation, even when this meant a larger than normal claim if a particular group had fallen behind, but were worried when they overreached themselves and were seen to be using their great power irresponsibly. Picking up on public opinion and regretting Wilson's failure to act, Heath published an Industrial Relations Bill which, after much opposition in Parliament and in the face of the largest ever union demonstration of 120,000 members determined to 'Kill the Bill,' became law in August 1971. Only registered trades unions would have legal rights and enjoy legal immunities. Registration was dependent on the organisation having rules which specified how, when and by whom authority was to be exercised, especially concerning the taking of industrial action. Wildcat strikes were to be limited and a National Industrial Relations Court was able to grant injunctions to prevent injurious strikes. In retrospect, most union leaders accepted that they should have accepted Barbara Castle's modest proposals.

The Clyde Initiative

In June 1971, the Upper Clyde Shipbuilders went into liquidation, dramatically threatening the jobs of all the Glasgow-based workers. Instead of striking, four young shop stewards, all members of the Communist Party, argued that as the workers knew much more about the shipyards than anyone else, they would stage a 'work-in' to keep the yards alive until a solution could be found. Eight months later Heath's government agreed to restructure the yards to form viable businesses, which were still working forty years later. The work-in was led by Jimmy Airlie (the strategist) and Jimmy Reid (the orator). Both became very popular, and in 1972 Reid was elected Rector of Glasgow University. His first speech to students was a remarkable statement of his beliefs and political foresight. It was reproduced in full in the *New York Times*. At one point Reid made the following prediction:

> Profit is the sole criterion used by the establishment to evaluate economic activity … The power structures that have inevitably emerged from this approach threaten and undermine our hard-won democratic rights. The whole process is towards the centralisation and concentration of power in fewer and fewer hands. The facts are there for all who want to see. Giant monopoly companies and consortia dominate almost every branch of our economy. The men who wield effective control within these giants exercise a power over their fellow men which is frightening and is a negation of democracy … Government by the people for the people becomes meaningless unless it includes major economic decision making by the people for the people.[20]

Decimalisation and Europe

In May 1969 Parliament had passed the final Decimal Currency Act with little serious challenge; February 15th 1971 became 'Decimal Day,' after which all the familiar calculations, coins and notes would disappear. The banks were closed for the previous two trading days and much work had gone into changing the many thousands of coin machines. Explanatory leaflets were delivered to every household. In general the transition went smoothly. My favourite story is of a vox-pop interview on the street of Darwen in Lancashire, where Ann was to love working a few years hence. Perhaps more than most this is a proudly insular town so when the radio interviewer asked for an opinion of decimalisation the answer was 'Oh I think it's probably a good idea but it'll never 'appen here.'

With de Gaulle out of the way and President Georges Pompidou apparently welcoming us, negotiations proceeded apace, and in October 1971 Heath's government introduced his first Parliamentary debate on the principle of joining the European Economic Community (EEC) which was won by a majority of 112 votes, both main parties being split. One cloud hanging over this victory was the decision, taken under pressure to cut public spending, by Margaret Thatcher, Secretary of State for Education, to save £9 million of her budget by scrapping the one-third of a pint of free milk to schoolchildren aged between seven and eleven. This was met by a wave of public, political and press outrage. The chant 'Margaret Thatcher the Milk Snatcher' could be heard in primary school playgrounds across the country.[21n] One of her first acts was to remove the compulsion on local authorities to convert all schools to comprehensives, although in fact more comprehensives were opened while she was minister than any other. While the Prime Minister pushed ahead with finalising Britain's entry to the EEC, other problems were building up.

Bloody Sunday

In addition to a sluggish UK economy, a major trauma occurred in Northern Ireland on January 30th 1972 when soldiers from the Parachute Regiment shot 26 protesters on a civil rights march in the Bogside area of Londonderry. Fourteen people were killed.

This was 'Bloody Sunday'.[22n] The IRA responded by car bombing the Regiment's barracks at Aldershot, killing a priest and five kitchen staff. Further attacks on military targets were promised. Direct rule of Northern Ireland was imposed in March 1972 with the experienced and reliable Willie Whitelaw as Secretary of State. The Northern Ireland Parliament was prorogued and all of the Unionist IMPs resigned. While we were alarmed at the bombs on the mainland and puzzled by the failure of any attempt to resolve these deeply rooted divisions, it was all, in a strange way, a bit remote, partly perhaps because the drip drip of daily news disguised the fact that between 1972 and 1976 917 civilians and 217 soldiers had been killed. A routine survey in March 1973 indicated that fewer than 10% of Britons thought this was the country's most important problem, although some of the Irish communities in England and the Orange Order in Scotland were much more involved, sometimes sending money or guns to opposing sides.[23] As the years passed, there was a growing frustration with the so-called 'Irish problem.' Apparently unable to solve the situation, many took the view that we should withdraw and leave them to fight it out. In 1973 a 'Troops Out' movement was started that gained some traction. Opinion polls taken in 1969 showed 61% in favour of military intervention, but by 1974 some 59% favoured withdrawal. It had become a dirty war, with kidnappings, revenge and random killings, undercover spies, sudden detention and degrees of torture on all sides. The Protestants, whose political mouthpiece was the bombastic Reverend Ian Paisley, and the IRA spokesmen, the quietly spoken but relentless Gerry Adams and Martin McGuinness, seemed hell bent on the maxim of 'never surrender,' and, as a consequence of Bloody Sunday, aid and funding for the Catholic cause increased from America where strong Irish-based organisations provided not only cash but also political support: very embarrassing for the government. Soon after the dreadful Sunday the Official IRA had declared a ceasefire, but the more militant provisional wing continued their campaign, although both Catholic and Protestant organisations split with a series of internecine bombings and shootings. After the failure of Heath's original peace plan and with no political initiative by the UK or Irish governments proving viable, the whole dreadful thing went on to cause more deaths, destruction and heartache.

The Miners

Their pay having fallen far behind the average, miners submitted a claim for a 43% pay rise, refusing the modest response from the Coal Board. After three months of negotiations and a long overtime ban, a national strike was called in early 1972, the first since the disasters of 1926. The miner's leader was the veteran Joe Gormley OBE, a skilled negotiator later to enter the House of Lords. Determined to block any infiltration from the extreme left-wing elements in the National Union of Mineworkers (NUM) meant alienating a key figure in the Yorkshire branch. This led in quick time to support for Arthur Scargill as a new local leader. He was a young firebrand who viewed Gormley's approach as anathema, proposing a more assertive 'new unionism' based on firm picketing with 'flying pickets' who, relying on modern communications, could be sent to any pit or demonstration where reinforcements were needed. These were effectively shock troops under orders from Scargill's HQ in Barnsley. The government viewed the prospect of a national strike with some alarm as coal and coke stocks were low and winter was approaching.

A major crisis occurred early in 1972 at Saltley coke works in the West Midlands, seen as a threat to the strike by continuing to supply fuel to the power stations. The constant stream of lorries queuing every day had to be stopped, although the drivers for the most part were non-union and many were self-employed. The system of flying pickets, mainly from Yorkshire, was used to full force, and eventually the supply was stopped by the sheer pressure of large numbers of miners, this very fact preventing the police using violence as they sought to keep the gates open and the lorries moving. On one occasion, just as the scene became violent, displaying his great sense of timing, Scargill arrived to urge his troops on. He was arrested and appeared on the front pages of the papers and TV. A scary leader, a martyr, a hero for others and a challenge for Joe Gormley; exactly where he wanted to be. Whilst there was alarm at the miners' tactics there was still widespread sympathy for them given their history, their working conditions and low pay. Although the 'Battle of Saltley Gate' remains in the memory, its effect on the strike was actually of no major significance; other miners across the country had brought the power stations' fuel and coke stocks down to ten days.

A hastily arranged court of inquiry found in favour of the miners, forcing the government to sit at the negotiating table from a weak position. In an all-night session in Downing Street, victory went to the miners; all their original demands, plus many added at the last minute, were met. We were relieved that power was now secure, the damage to the economy eased and the 1.5 million workers laid off could return to work; some justice had been done. The government set about reviewing the law on picketing, police procedures and civil contingence arrangements, just in case. Interviewed later, Dai Francis, Secretary of the South Wales Miners' Union, glimpsed the future long term consequences of Arthur Scargill's policies:

> There's no doubt that we'll see some very serious battles in the not too distant future, because they didn't take their defeat gracefully did they? The government. They may be plotting their revenge on the miner now, do you see?[24]

There would be another battle eighteen months later, but crushing revenge with devastating consequences would wait another twelve years.

Immigration

At long last, at midnight on December 31st 1972, Britain along with Belgium and Ireland joined the European Economic Community. No celebrations, large or small, were held. In any event, the Heath government had other problems to face, namely immigration and the economy, which was fluctuating between inflation and stagnation. Immigration, particularly from the Caribbean and the Indian sub-continent, had remained a hidden issue apart from the Powell 1968 rumpus (see Chapter 8). Although many of the white population were unhappy at the increasing numbers, the political elite wished to avoid the issue, thus failing to intervene. There had been no serious attempt to quantify the numbers or the implications, no attempt to legislate, provide support or avoid the new ghettos which could only grow as time passed. One of the problems arose from our past generosity in giving so many colonial citizens British citizenship so, in a replay of the Kenyan crisis (see Chapter 6), in August 1972 the upstart dictator of Uganda, Idi Amin, decided to expel all Asians, except of course those few with essential skills. The UK government was suddenly faced with some 30,000 British citizens requiring admission, having had all their wealth stripped on Amin's orders. A series of refugee camps was established as temporary holding places until they settled, often where relatives lived, Leicester being a particular favourite. It says a great deal that, despite some racial abuse, these new immigrants were welcomed, although their natural interests and skills enabled them to establish themselves in businesses; corner shops were given a new lease of life as they were willing to open all hours. Many enrolled in advanced courses and established themselves in the professions, becoming an asset to the economy.

The Energy Crisis

As prices rose so did claims for higher wages, so in November 1972 the government imposed a freeze on prices and wages in a bid to halt galloping inflation, which was hitting 8.6%. This further extended the wage freeze for public employees. In April 1973 the outdated purchase tax was replaced by value added tax (VAT) at 25%. As the year moved on the miners continued to celebrate their recent victory, the reversal of pit closures and the £1 billion investment promised by the government. This seems to have given the left-wing militants the belief that they could move further, a move which alarmed Joe Gormley and many on the National Executive. The summer conference of 1973 was a lively affair, the meeting loudly applauding the Yorkshire delegate, Arthur Scargill, when he spelt out a new ambition for the union which was 'to remove the most immoral, most corrupt government in living memory.' Good oratory but potential suicide for an established movement whose legal constitution was the representation of the membership in trade disputes, not to change governments. An overtime ban was proposed and exhaustive discussions between the government, the Coal Board and the NUM Executive failed to agree. The ban therefore came into operation on November 12th 1973, severely reducing the output of coal. As a precaution against further trouble, the government had been increasing the output from oil-fired power stations, thus enabling the stocks of coal and coke in the stations to build up. Unfortunately for the government, Egypt and Syria had chosen October 6th to attack Israel, while they were engaged in the holiest day of prayer in their calendar.

The Arab nations, perceiving the west's support for Israel, imposed an oil embargo which continued until March 1974, by which time the price of oil had quadrupled. This combination of events caused the greatest national crisis since 1945. Heath, faced with these serious threats, overworked following EEC admission and deeply involved in attempts to solve the Northern Ireland crisis, was completely exhausted. On December 13th he announced that television would cease at 22:30 hrs every night, no sport could be floodlit, petrol would be rationed and a 50 mph speed limit imposed. From January 1st 1974 the nation would be restricted to a three-day working week in order to conserve power, a great blow for the economy but necessary to get us through the winter. It was pretty devastating. Although Heath tried to keep a middle course towards the end of the broadcast, he made this call:

> At times like these, there is deep in all of us an instinct that tells us that we must abandon disputes among ourselves. We must close our ranks, so that we can deal together with the difficulties which come to us, whether from within or from beyond our own shores. That has been our way in the past, and it is a good way ... Our future and the character of our country depend on it.[25]

The actual imposition of these measures was far from effective, but by and large we fell into the old wartime mental set and put up with it. Given our poor economic situation, my main memory is the anxiety of filling our small car up for petrol, never before has each spilt drop seemed so expensive. We were urged to share our baths and clean our teeth in the dark, along with a whole list of other doubtful advice. For many workers the opportunity to spend more time with the family was quite welcome. It would be nice if one day this work pattern became the norm.

A School Strike

In counterpoint to these national industrial disputes, May 1971 had seen a lively strike by pupils at the very traditionally run Sir John Cass Secondary School in Stepney. A young idealistic teacher, Chris Searle, had arrived a few months before to inspire his pupils with a love of poetry. He decided that a selection of his pupil's poems should be published as 'Stepney Words,' and this was achieved with parental support, the works appearing in national papers and being read at the Royal Albert Hall. Within the school, alarm had been raised by his noisy classes, his 'progressive' ideas, the extra-curricular clubs he had started and the fact that he had actually chosen to live in Stepney! The governors thought the poems too gloomy and ordered Searle not to publish. He was sacked, which led his pupils to walk out of school and stand in the pouring rain all day singing and chanting in his support. Other schools joined in and there was a march to Trafalgar Square. In 1973 Searle's appeal went to Margaret Thatcher as Secretary of State who came down in his favour, but although he was reinstated he was ostracised by staff and left shortly afterwards.

Election

In February 1974, with a warmer than usual winter and fuel stocks holding up well, the miners decided to up the ante by coming out on strike, with the loss of much public support. As far as Heath was concerned this was the last straw and, in an act of supreme brinkmanship, he called an election on the question of 'Who governs Britain?' To the exasperation of the right wing of his party, Heath, determined to maintain his centrist, one-nation Tory beliefs, fought a moderate campaign, easing the 22:30 hrs TV ban and offering the miners an independent pay review. It was inconceivable to him that the electorate would not support his stance.

Harold Wilson, dogged by ill health and facing his fourth general election, was resigned to losing and fought a lacklustre campaign. The electorate were unsure, wavering between those inclined to the left, who were worried by a weak Wilson and signs that the unions were now too powerful, and those on the right, furious at Heath's concessions to the miners and love of Europe. The emergence of 'middle way' politics aiming for the comfort of the centre ground was confusing old loyalties. More people changed their minds than in any previous election, so that the outcome of the election was unpredictable. Labour gained 301 seats (32.7%), the Conservatives 296 (37.9%) with the Liberals holding 14 (19.3%) and others spread over the remaining 22%. Five days of haggling led to Heath's resignation on March 4th 1974. Wilson returned to power with a minority Labour government that relied on support from the Liberals led by Jeremy Thorpe, a colourful personality who had led his party well, although he was haunted by rumours of illegal homosexual acts in the 1960s.[26n]

On March 11th the miners returned to work having accepted a generous pay settlement, facilitated by Michael Foot, the new Secretary of State for Employment. Eight months later Wilson went to the country again and emerged (with a 72.8% turnout) with an overall majority of 3 seats (Labour 319, Conservatives 277, Liberals 13 and others 28). It would be a difficult Parliament, certainly not helped by Wilson himself who, in addition to his chronic exhaustion and love for internecine plotting, was not planning to remain PM for long and decided to lead from the back, just co-ordinating the activities of his ministers. As the years progressed his alcohol consumption increased and he became more lethargic. Not a recipe for a united Cabinet. In 1975, prompted by the European Commission, the government established a committee to examine industrial democracy, reporting in 1977 that if there were more than 2,000 employees in a company they would have a right to representation on the board. It was a mild step towards the German model which has proved so important to that country's economic success. As far as I know it has never significantly happened here.[27]

Unfortunately, three of our key problems from Heath's government promptly deteriorated. The recently established Northern Ireland Power Sharing Executive, so diplomatically constructed by Heath, fell apart under fierce opposition from the loyalists. In 1974, the IRA's mainland campaign killed 38 people and injured nearly two hundred. Bombs hit pubs in Guildford and Birmingham and a military coach on the Liverpool to Leeds road. A bomb at the Houses of Parliament caused injuries and extensive damage, as did one at the home of Edward Heath, who was not resident at the time. The economy, responsibility for which Denis Healey had inherited, was going downhill. Recovery from the three-day week and the oil crisis was restricting productivity, the exchange rate was poor and inflation rose steadily, reaching an alarming 26.9%. The strange lethargy of the new Cabinet seems to have caused a degree of blindness to what was happening. Healey's first Budget raised the higher level of income tax to 83% and increased pensions and subsidies for housing and food for those in need. The median family income fell by over 7%, although those relying on unearned income suffered slightly more under Healey's Budgets, particularly as house prices fell by about 30%. Pawnbrokers were welcoming in the rich. The numbers taking the emigration route out led, along with a fall in birth rate, to a decline in the population. As GDP fell, public expenditure increased by 12%. The sense of decline was general with a fear that the world was turning upside down. By May 1975 CBS informed its American audience that 'Britain is drifting slowly towards a condition of ungovernability,' comparing Wilson with the Chilean socialist President Salvador Allende before his downfall.[28n]

Referendum

Tony Benn's opposition to our entry to the EEC on the grounds that it took power further away from ordinary people, had led to Labour committing itself to a referendum when they were next in power. The government therefore had no option but to launch a referendum following some marginal renegotiation of terms in Brussels. It was held on June 5th 1975 with the question 'Do you think the UK should stay in the European Community (Common Market)?' It gained a positive answer from 67% of the voters with a 65% turnout. Every county voted in favour except the Shetland and Western Isles. The debate had centred on issues that may seem strange to those who faced the referendum of 2016. In 1975 many arguments centred on our relations with Commonwealth countries, particularly Australia and New Zealand, from where we imported most of our lamb and butter; why would we desert them for people we had just defeated in the war? Farm subsidies and others would be reduced as ours were more generous than Europe's and, of course, loss of sovereignty.

Devolution

The previous Labour government had established a royal commission 'to examine the present functions of the legislature and government in the several countries, nations and regions of the United Kingdom and to consider whether any changes are desirable in the constitutional and economic relationships between them.' It finally reported in 1973 in favour of devolved powers for Scotland, and six members recommended a more limited scheme for Wales and a 'special relationship' with Cornwall.[29] In September 1974 the government published a White Paper followed by separate Scotland and Wales Acts proposing agreed devolution providing referenda were held in advance. The respective Parliament and assemblies were finally convened twenty-four years later under another Labour government. Cornwall's claims have never been met.

North Sea Oil

Although Benn's commitment to his principles could sometimes lead him into difficulties, another of his personality traits was loyalty, which had enabled him to remain in Wilson's Cabinet following his demotion from Secretary of State for Industry to Energy. Despite early expectations that this placed him on the political margins, his period of office coincided with the arrival of one of the main elements which rescued us from our 'slough of despond.' This was North Sea oil and gas. First discovered in the late 1950s, it took trouble in the Middle East to spur on the complex and dangerous task of sinking wells in the deep and dangerous North Sea and bring it to land. This was achieved in November 1975, when the Queen pressed a button and oil was seen to flow ashore from the Forties field. As more fields were discovered and brought online, production grew slowly, passing a million barrels in 1978 and reaching a peak in 1985 which it then maintained. The Labour MP Laurance Reed opined: 'The 1980s will be Britain's decade. We shall become one of the most influential of nations.' Oil would end our dependence on the US and the Middle East, Britain would have a new Empire, a chance for expansion comparable to the American 'opening the west.' The treasury of course was delighted to see potential large tax revenue rolling in. The whole thing lifted the mood of the nation as we slowly emerged from the economic depths, for the short term at least. In the event we never seem to have increased our influence abroad and it seems to be somewhat of a mystery how a small island apparently floating on oil and gas and with huge reserves of coal failed to use these riches to address the many infrastructural and social issues that faced us as we still remain dependent on imported fuel.

Margaret Thatcher

The Conservative Party in opposition was scarred by both defeat and the cause of their defeat: Ted Heath's failure to face up to the trades unions, specifically the miners who seemed to believe that they ran Britain. The right wing of the party were clear about the way forward to save the country – a return to free market policies based on the ideas of Hayek and Friedman (see Chapter 4) – the question was who was to replace Heath, who had no intention of giving up the leadership and still had support from many moderate MPs and 70% of Conservative voters.[30] The few leading members who were prepared to challenge Heath came to grief early in the proceedings, leaving the wily campaigner Airey Neave to support Margaret Thatcher, who he was convinced would move to the right from the more centrist popular polices she was currently advocating. Neave persuaded his colleagues that when Thatcher lost the first round more serious men would stand; a crafty ruse. Thatcher's strange ability to charm powerful men rather obscured her history as a persistent bossy bully. It was a considerable shock to most party members then when in February 1975 Margaret Thatcher defeated Heath in the first ballot and subsequently become the new Leader of the Conservative Party. The news was greeted by a vice chairman of the party with 'My God! The Bitch has won!'[31]

Later Michael Foot would comment that, 'She has no imagination and that means no compassion.' The previous year *The Sun* newspaper had called her the 'Most unpopular woman in Britain.' Her early years as leader would not be smooth. Ian Aitken, *The Guardian*'s political correspondent, wrote,

> The Conservative Party last night shut its eyes, pinched its nose and jumped into the deep end of the women's liberation movement with an overwhelming vote of confidence for Mrs Margaret Thatcher as the first woman leader of a great national political party in the western world ... Most MPs recognised last night that, whatever the breach with tradition in terms of sex ... the result of yesterday's ballot has effectively halted the remorseless progress of the Tory Party ... towards a frankly interventionist role in economic affairs and revived its role as the historic defender of private enterprise and the free market economy.[32]

The new leader would prove to be a very quick learner. She was eternally grateful to the war hero Neave for winning more than the other four candidates put together. Heath did not take the outcome well and never forgave either of them for the defeat and the deceptive nature of the campaign. It had thus come about that behind the hallowed doors of Westminster both major political parties had set the stage for the fierce disputes of the next thirty years. Although there were dissenting Conservative voices, the fiercest fights would sadly be within the Labour Party.

CULTURE

Street Protests

Although the cause of protest varied from place to place, common concerns were civil rights, heavily influenced by the black civil rights movement, unreformed authoritarian regimes in colleges, which mirrored the society of which they had been part, the horrors and injustices of the Vietnam War and overt political repression, the clearest examples being the 'Prague Spring' of 1968 (see Chapter 5). As the 1960s ended, groups across the political divide became angry that the summers of love had not led to the desired changes in the basic structure of authoritarian governments; in other words the powerful had played the game of repressive tolerance so well described by Marcuse.[33] In Britain little real power had been gained, consequently 1970 saw the formation of the 'Angry Brigade,' a small group of anarchists who ran a brief campaign of bombing the buildings of the establishment and the embassies of far-right governments. During the same period the IRA moved its bombing campaign to the mainland; sometimes it felt like the Blitz. Some comparison with continental feelings can be glimpsed by the fact that when a leading French revolutionary came to London to meet twenty of Britain's leading revolutionaries, only three turned up and the visitors left very disillusioned.[34]

The campaign to achieve a more democratic college system started in art colleges and new polytechnics, but soon spread to other campuses. Trouble erupted at the London School of Economics in the autumn of 1966 when it was announced that Dr Walter Adams had been appointed as Director. As a former Principal of the University College of Rhodesia, he was seen as an embodiment of a faction which had declared unilateral independence from Great Britain in order to run a white supremacist regime enforcing racial segregation. When he actually took up his appointment a year later there was little sign of protest. In the autumn of 1968 students at the LSE (where a certain Jack Straw – Home Secretary nine years later – was President of the Union) had been heavily involved in the massive Grosvenor Square protests against the Vietnam War. Resolution of disputes about student involvement in governance were put aside when a student decision to close the college for a weekend 'teach-in' was resisted by the governing body. Further demands having been rejected, students and some staff started to remove recently installed iron security gates. At this point the police were called, who arrived to find that the perpetrators had adjourned to the bar. When the main culprits had been cautiously arrested and the university proceeded with disciplinary action, further demonstrations were held and the LSE was closed for four weeks until settlements were eventually reached. Public reaction to all this had been mild, if anything veering towards support for the students. Mick Jagger of the Rolling Stones joined the demonstration, threw a few stones and wrote 'Street Fighting Man,' which significantly added to his fortune. The Beatles released 'Revolution' as a reaction to all the violence of 1968, with John Lennon adding 'Don't expect me to be on the barricades unless it's with flowers.' An approach which caused a temporary breach with many of his fans.[35n]

Black Power

In America and Europe, for slightly different reasons, anger turned to violence as a primary tactic. In America the Black Panther Party for Self-Defense, formed in 1966, were originally part social workers (setting up schools, health clinics and breakfast clubs) and part a ghetto army ready to use violence to achieve their quite reasonable social objectives of better schooling, housing and employment for black people.[36n] In 1970 nine members of the UK's Black Power Party were arrested outside the Mangrove restaurant in Notting Hill during a scuffle with the police who had grown suspicious that the meetings in this cultural centre were planning terrorist attacks. One of the leaders was Darcus Howe, who took on the defence to a charge of incitement to riot. All were acquitted, Darcus Howe becoming a respected lifelong campaigner, writer and broadcaster.[37n] In March 1970 the historic number 18 West 11th Street, just off Manhattan's Fifth Avenue, exploded killing three people: the incompetent bomb maker and their accomplices.[38n] The bombers were members of the Weathermen, a somewhat bizarre group of white Americans, formed to complement the Black Panthers in 1968, who, frustrated at non-violent campaigns, ran for a decade violently attacking imperialist 'Amerika' claiming to act as shock troops for the oppressed across the world 'behind enemy lines.' Naturally enough, the Panthers distanced themselves from what they perceived as opportunist white supremacists too chaotic to be effective.

Vietnam

Towards the end of the 1960s the increased power of student protests in America was met by use of extreme force by state governors and local mayors, particularly at Columbia University in New York, at the Chicago Democratic Convention, where Mayor Daly was responsible for security, and at the University of California, Berkeley, where Ronald Reagan as Governor was starting his path to the presidency. Many tens of thousands of students and staff took part in these three events; in each case police and the National Guard used violent force, including use of tear gas and guns. California was both the home of libertarianism and substantial military industrial interests; Berkeley being dependent on financial support from that source was among the first to hit the headlines. In 1964, demonstrations by students and staff in favour of free speech and academic freedom led the Dean to authorise a dawn police swoop and the arrest of 800 students. Disciplining the student leaders led to more extensive protests, which continued for the next five years.

At the end of April 1970 the Republican President Richard Nixon announced that, far from redeeming his election promise to reduce US involvement in Vietnam, the campaign was now extending to Cambodia. On May 1st five hundred students assembled at Ohio's Kent University in protest and arranged a further protest for May 4th. Some violence and the burning of the office of the University Officer Training Corps building gave the Town Mayor and State Governor justification to mobilise the National Guard. When some 2,000 students attended the planned demonstration they were met by guardsmen with fixed bayonets and gas masks. After most students had dispersed in clouds of tear gas a group of guardsmen opened fire, killing four students and injuring nine.[39] Five days later 100,000 people protested violently in Washington and 900 colleges had to close as four million students across America went on strike in protest. In the face of these protests, President Nixon was moved from the White House to the safety of Camp David. In 2007 a researcher claimed that the only audio tape of the Kent events revealed that the guardsmen were ordered to fire, contrary to previous accounts that the soldiers had panicked.[40] Forensic tests confirmed that the order was given, but repeated demands for an independent investigation have been refused. In 2014, a request was made to the United Nations Human Rights Committee for an independent review.

Protest at the conduct of the war extended to soldiers who had served there, who campaigned as Vietnam Veterans Against the War. In April 1971 one of their leaders, John Kerry, summarised the views of many Americans when he testified to the Senate Foreign Relations Committee:

> We who have come here to Washington have come here because we feel we have to be winter soldiers now. We could come back to this country, we could be quiet, we could hold our silence, we could not tell what went on in Vietnam, but we feel because of what threatens this country, not the reds, but the crimes which we are committing that threaten it, that we have to speak out …
>
> In our opinion and from our experience, there is nothing in South Vietnam which could happen that realistically threatens the United States of America. And to attempt to justify the loss of one American life in Vietnam, Cambodia or Laos by linking such loss to the preservation of freedom, which those misfits supposedly abuse, is to us the height of criminal hypocrisy, and it is that kind of hypocrisy which we feel has torn this country apart.[41n]

Feminism

Feminism continued to gain strength and recognition in everyday life as its devotees campaigned for equal rights legislation; the Equal Pay Act, passed in 1970 by the Wilson government was implemented in 1975. The ability to control fertility (the contraceptive pill having become available), the relative freedom from frequent childbearing and the acquisition of domestic aids led to more women being able to work and enter higher education. These were great times, marked by earnest discussions about how to spread the word and enable women to exchange experiences. The first edition of *Spare Rib* emerged in July 1972 to become a well established radical and effective mouthpiece for the movement. While the women's movement shared many ideological objectives for justice at work with trades unions, these, dominated by assertive male leaders, were mostly less than welcoming. One clash occurred when a Women's Liberation Front meeting met in the building where the National Union of Mineworkers was gathered to plan their forthcoming strike, with a striptease act for evening entertainment. It was duly 'zapped' by the WLF! The movement maintained its impact throughout the 1970s, certainly altering the perception of the role and function of women in society, but when Margaret Thatcher became Prime Minister in 1979, there was a pause and a shift to specific issues including domestic violence.

Festivals

The established individualism of the age gave rise to two further developments: the rise of large open-air festivals, often free to anyone, and squatting. This often led to relatively stable counter-cultural communes, a situation caused by a shortage of housing and the number of unoccupied properties, which were often quite large and part of the hated developers' bid for profits. The first Glastonbury Festival was attended by 10,000 people in 1971. The following year the first of three free festivals were held in Windsor Great Park, a Crown Estate property, predictably leading to local and national protests at the highest levels. Before the fourth festival could be held the liberal Home Secretary Roy Jenkins decided to intervene by floating the idea that the government, alarmed by poor behaviour elsewhere, would offer an alternative site and give every other assistance that they could to events.

A large disused airfield at Watchfield, near Swindon, was selected and an eight-day festival announced, much longer than any previous rock festival. In the event, it was run by a strange political movement called the Albion Free State.[42n] It was a remarkable success, and the formal report, turning a blind eye to the extensive drug taking, promoted such events as giving inner city people the chance to enjoy the countryside so that 'People who cannot afford to go to commercial festivals should have the opportunity of attending free festivals.'[43]

The gay community held their first march in March 1970, followed by the more significant Gay Pride march in central London two years later, one of the organisers being the social activist Peter Tatchell.[44n] A large gay commune known as 'Colvillia' located in Notting Hill held firmly to counter-cultural beliefs. In the magazine *Come Together* published by the Gay Liberation Front, the squatters proudly proclaimed that 'The more we learn about each other in the commune, the higher we get: much higher than anything that came after flower power.'[45] By the mid 1970s some of the dynamism of the commune movement and specifically the GLF seems to have exhausted itself, and it and Colvillia were closed down.

The entertainment scene was bravely responding to the general cultural trends that held that nothing human was vile or should be hidden. In 1971 the editors of the Australian imported counter-culture magazine *Oz* were prosecuted with conspiracy to corrupt public morals, an offence carrying a maximum penalty of life imprisonment. They had commissioned and published a schoolchildren's edition, compiled by children which, among other things, portrayed Rupert Bear with a large erection. Defended by the eminent QC John Mortimer, the three men, Richard Neville, Jim Anderson and Felix Dennis, were acquitted by the jury on the main charge while the minor charges were dismissed at appeal.[46n]

Much more interesting was Peter Shaffer's 1973 play *Equus*, a fierce psychological battle about the hidden sexual motivations of a youth who had blinded six horses and the repressed feelings of the psychiatrist assigned to find some form of cure for the boy detained for in-patient care. The brief nudity seemed appropriate as the play asked the audience to decide which of these two were most alive.[47n]

Among the many books that I am sure Ann and I enjoyed were the first of John Updike's 'Rabbit' series and the apparently philosophical treatise *Zen and the Art of Motorcycle Maintenance*, which I enjoyed very much. It builds round a motorbike trip that the author Robert Pirsig makes with his twelve-year-old son and is at heart a search for meaning and self-discovery:

> Our current modes of rationality are not moving society forward into a better world … Since the Renaissance these modes have worked. As long as the need for food, clothing and shelter is dominant they will continue to work. But now for huge masses of people these needs no longer overwhelm everything else. The whole structure of reason, handed down to us from ancient times, is no longer adequate. It begins to be seen for what it really is – emotionally hollow, aesthetically meaningless and spiritually empty. That today is where it is at, and will continue to be at for a long time to come.[48n]

It seems that our young daughter may have restricted our cinema visits, but among the films we did manage to see were the superb *One Flew Over the Cuckoo's Nest*, set in an American asylum,[49] the historically based wonderful musicals *Fiddler on the Roof* and *Cabaret* and the sharp drama *The Sting*. We decided to give *Jaws* a miss. Our choice in popular music was casual. The Beatles were still very popular, the great John Lennon released 'Imagine' as a call for peace in late 1971, but then, reflecting the cultural changes outlined above, a more assertive style in both music and performance came into fashion through Queen and also The Blockheads led by the unique Ian Dury whose specific mix of music and sexual humour hit the top with 'Hit Me With Your Rhythm Stick' in the late 70s. Dury's poetic gifts and musical style were certainly a severe contrast to the poets Bob Dylan and, one of my personal favourites, the Canadian Leonard Cohen who was just becoming well known and whose concert I attended thirty years later. Our daughter Juliet's favourite was the gifted, androgynous David Bowie.

To our mind, assertiveness turned to aggressiveness when punk hit the headlines, determinedly rebelling against anything that was tuneful or attractive. The punks claimed to be challenging the commercialism of popular music, although as groups became more successful it might be said that theirs was just another sales pitch to make more money. It seemed that the joy of the late 1960s was turning sour. Television stations mounted an excellent series of plays, wonderful entertainment and comedy, then in 1974 we were gripped by a new type of reality show: *The Family*, directed by Paul Watson documented the day to day lives of the members of a Reading family in all its intricate interaction. It certainly held the interest of viewers and caused conflict in the media.

All this was no doubt in line with Marcuse's prediction that advanced industrial society's trick was to create affluence, so that the basic needs of the population are met to the degree that protest and critical thinking are discouraged while the idea that both the elite and the establishment watch the same TV or listen to the same music gives a false sense of equality. Perhaps popular culture reflects Huxley's administration of the drug 'soma' in *Brave New World*[50] to keep the population happy, a theme picked up by Orwell in his book *1984*.[51] Personal computers, the addictive internet and mobile phones were in the future.

The Environment

Concerns over the environment and our general city-based consumer society were slowly edging into public consciousness, assisted by a number of doom-laden publications.[52] We were all glued to both the BBC's drama series *Doomwatch* and the situation comedy *The Good Life*, where lawns in a prosperous middle-class suburb were replaced by vegetables and the back garden by hen runs and pig breeding. The millionaire Teddy Goldsmith funded the serious magazine *The Ecologist*, which first appeared in 1970 and did not hesitate to spell out the consequences of modern life. In the first edition the assistant editor wrote:

> ... it is still an open question whether (modern) man will be able to survive the exceedingly complex and unstable ecological conditions he has created, interplanetary archaeologists of the future will classify our planet as one in which a very long and stable period of small-scale hunting and gathering was followed by an ... efflorescence of technology and society leading to rapid extinction.

In contrast to this approach, which, while earnestly environmental, showed something of the huntin' and shootin' lifestyle of the Goldsmiths, the novel *Watership Down* based on the dramatic lives of rabbits when left to their natural environment was published in 1972 and became an instant bestseller. A year later a more serious call for action gained a great deal of attention: the economist E. F. Schumacher's *Small is Beautiful: A Study of Economics as if People Mattered*.[53] This remarkable man brought his extensive knowledge about and experience in so-called 'third world' countries to ask a simple question: Why are the 'developed' countries so committed to higher growth, more complicated technology and larger more remote centres of control (what he termed 'gigantism') when the resources of the planet are limited and in some cases being corrupted? His view was that systems needed to be appropriate from a human point of view. Rather than make more and more complex, and therefore expensive, technology, we should make simple technology more efficient and more productive (soft technology) to meet the needs of more local communities. His argument, which suited the popular culture, was that people can be trusted to do their own thing whereas complex technical systems were intrinsically dehumanising. Excessive consumption, clearly increased by globalisation, depended completely on fossil fuels, which are exhaustible. We needed more reliance on renewable sources (soft power), an idea that was widely dismissed at the time. Following his untimely death in September 1977, Schumacher's ideas faded. My view however is that while the fundamental ideas of the 1960s and early 70s have been taken into everyday life, Schumacher's have had the benefit of an active range of specific practical initiatives across the world which have continued to develop his ideas. As his predictions are proving real in the late 20th century, the development of alternative energy sources and the devolution of power to local areas, plus the power of the internet, we are approaching the Schumacher age.

PIE

Encouraged by the current sense of freedom, a small group of paedophiles formed the Paedophile Information Exchange (PIE) 'to provide the means for paedophiles to feel less isolated and gain a sense of community.' They talked of the right of children of any age to have a loving sexual relationship. This bizarre organisation attempted to link themselves to gay movements but were decisively rejected. The chairman and four others were tried for conspiracy to corrupt public morals and eventually the chairman was gaoled for two years and the organisation, with a membership of 450, was disbanded in 1984. None of the learned articles written at the time seems to have addressed the vulnerability of children in care homes despite the fact that one of the leaders, Peter Righton, was an experienced social worker with a long career in residential care.[54]

SOCIAL WORK

In my view the period from 1968 until 1975 was an exciting time to be a social worker; it certainly marked a high point for the profession. The 1969 Children and Young Persons Act had introduced care and control orders so that young offenders could be made subject to care orders on the same basis as children in need. The following year the Chronically Sick and Disabled Act and the 1971 White Paper *Better Services for the Handicapped*[55] charted a radical new direction for those services. Alf Morris, the MP for Manchester Wythenshawe, described as a very old style socialist and determined to help the most disadvantaged, had been elected to Parliament in 1964 and was demoted by Harold Wilson when he abstained during the vote on EEC membership three years later. His long time interest in disability led him to submit a bill in the 1969 private members' ballot for parliamentary time. Having won the ballot, he managed his bill against opposition from members in both parties to royal assent in 1970 just before Wilson's government collapsed.[56n] The 1970 Chronically Sick and Disabled Act placed a liability on local authorities to identify disabled people and provide appropriate services. Also, local and health authorities were required to establish joint consultative committees and planning teams to provide integrated care. These duties fell on the new social service departments, which had been exhorted by Seebohm to do research. Many authorities decided that the only way to collect reliable data was to do a house to house survey, and, while much good information was collected, interviewers were occasionally taken aback when a householder with a clear disability assured them that there was no one with a disability living at that address. There was much lively discussion about the nature and perception of disability.

The Seebohm Report

Major changes in the organisation of welfare were introduced by the Social Work (Scotland) Act 1968 (which established social service departments – including probation – with a duty to promote social welfare) and the Local Authority Personal Social Services Act 1970. This latter Act, which was implemented in 1971, followed the publication of the *Report of the Committee on Local Authority and Allied Personal Social Services* (The Seebohm Report) in July 1968.[57] This well written and researched report was the most significant report ever written on the subject, with enormous implications for social work. The radical nature of the recommendations can be seen in the quotation at the head of this chapter. The committee had been established in December 1965 as a result of concerns that the current services were inefficient, divided within local authorities by children's departments (headed by a recognised professional) and adult services (often still in the hands of medical officers of health), the NHS and voluntary agencies. It was too easy for people to fall down the cracks between services and anyway found it difficult to know in advance which door on which to knock. The committee had been asked to 'review the organisation and responsibilities of the local authority personal social serves in England and Wales, and to consider what changes are desirable to secure an effective family service.' In reviewing the shortcomings of the existing services and their causes, some emphasis was placed on the need for adaptability in the face of the increasing rate of social change and the fact that the existing structure meant that staff pursued the specific objectives of their separate departments instead of meeting the full range of needs of each individual or family.

It was concluded that such practices could only be achieved by organisational change, which would also provide clearer accountability, attract more resources and be more efficient. The answer was to set up a single social service department in each local authority which would incorporate the existing children's and welfare departments, education welfare and child guidance services, home helps, mental health social work, adult training centres and housing welfare. The new service would be founded on adequate housing, prevention, research and intelligence and the active role of the community, including voluntary effort. The committee placed great emphasis on the prevention of social distress, arguing that 'morally, socially and economically this makes sense. In principle, by taking timely and appropriate measures much human suffering and family breakdown can be avoided.'[58] This was followed by emphasising the part that research must play in any effective family service. Turning to 'the community' they saw community development as complementary and inextricably interwoven within the department, and defined it as

> Community development in this country is seen as a process whereby local groups are assisted to clarify and express their needs and objectives and to take collective action to attempt to meet them. It emphasises the involvement of the people themselves in determining and meeting their own needs. The role of the community worker is that of a source of information and expertise, a stimulator, a catalyst and encourager.[59]

And then pursued these ideas further:

> Implicit in the idea of a community-orientated family service is a belief in the importance of the maximum participation of individuals and groups in the community in the planning, organisation and provision of social services ... Above all, the development of citizen participation should reduce the rigid distinction between the givers and the takers of social services and the stigma which being a client has often involved in the past.[60]

The committee recognised that the role of the social worker in this context is likely to give rise to problems of conflicting loyalties and quoted the training council as advising that

> [the authority] will need to recognise the fact that some of its staff may be involved in situations which lead to criticism of their services or with pressure groups about new needs. The workers themselves will need to be clear about their professional role and this will depend on their training and the organisational structure within which they work.[61]

If the new service were to work, then training would need to be overhauled so that a family or individual in need should be served by a single social worker carrying primary responsibility and calling in more specialised workers when required, after consultation with the client. Staff would need to have the appropriate knowledge, attitudes and skill and possess a sound basic training in the light of new knowledge or changed circumstances. It was seen as essential that

> the content of professional training for social workers should be reconsidered so that attention is paid to work with groups and communities, to social planning and to the administrative structure of the organisations in which social work services are provided.[62]

From this the committee recommended experimentation with a wider conception of generic training rather than the artificial divisions which currently existed.

The report seemed to sum up all that I had ever believed and hoped for in my profession and I could not wait for its implementation. Although 1971 was the official date, it actually took some time for the new directors, staff and structures to be settled. Probation was not included, housing and education welfare were to remain outside, as were the hospital social workers, who clung to their special status for some time before being absorbed to the advantage of older and disabled people. Nonetheless, I grabbed on to the report and saw it as a new bible for my career. The longest dispute about the report centred on the term 'generic.' It seemed clear to me that if the new ambitions were to be realised then social workers needed to have a general base of knowledge, skills and outlook then develop more specialised skills later in training or practice. This was the approach adopted by most courses, but after a time as the specialisms fought back, Lord Seebohm explained that he had only meant the term to apply to each team. My view was, and remains, that if a team is to function effectively a common generic basis for all is required.

Key to the Seebohm thinking was that people in need should have only one door on which to knock. In practice, well qualified 'professional' child care officers were now joined by staff from the welfare section, few of whom were qualified in social work and had been seen more as local government functionaries. Life was not always easy in the new departments. In addition to cultural and practice differences between the constituent groups, workers were, in accord with the culture of the times, not always compliant with the new hierarchies. Wally Harbert, an early Director, recalls how staff called to his office for a welcome chat soon after appointment would often be late or just fail to show up. When asked for an explanation, one said 'I don't think you're a vital part of the department. It's people like me, at the sharp end, who really get things done.'[63]

While I respect that point of view, the worker failed to appreciate (as I learnt to my cost many years later) that the role of the director in fighting other chief officers and elected members for the resources required to sustain the workforce is key. In those early days, the large new department would have invariably been seen as a threat to all other departments. The fact that the Conservative government allocated 10% above inflation for social services departments (SSDs) for the first six years of their lives was both a credit to Sir Keith Joseph, the Secretary of State, and a cause for further jealousy. Sir William Utting put the matter concisely when he commented

> Local authorities wanted a nice, tidy, buttoned down department whose achievements and low cost would be a credit, come the next election. The workforce, on the other hand, swollen by the unqualified and politicised intake of the 1970s, wanted the New Jerusalem for their clients and themselves – and now![64]

The new departments were generally welcomed, one view being that at the very least the director's car would have its reserved place alongside all the other chief officers. Sitting at the top table must denote recognition and influence at last! There was however some cultural and practical opposition. An early study sought to clarify the differing conceptions of need by the client, the social work professional, other workers and the organisation, and the problem of recording them in a form that was useful for the latter (despite the ideology of family work, all recording was on an individual basis).[65] American studies warned that the organisation's need usually won out, with the consequence that clients were objectified, a danger that inevitably came to impinge on the social worker's view. 'If he actually tries to help his clients and "buck" the organisation he often suffers from emotional and physical fatigue and becomes cynical and defeatist about the nature of social work.' The author urges the profession to use its knowledge of bureaucracies to counter this process.[66] This ancient study should be pinned on the board of every modern office. A more positive study emphasised the benefits of teamwork as opposed to the traditional social work model. Sharing tasks in a multi-professional team was seen to aid innovation and flexibility in work with families, but also in countering the power of the organisation.⁶⁷

In 1996, the magazine *Community Care* asked workers to look back to the early post-Seebohm days of 1971. Social worker Kate Slade from Birmingham remembered:

> For a practitioner like myself, Seebohm was a positive change. It got away from exclusivity and presented a more holistic way of dealing with families and individuals. It was a real step forward. The working environment at the time was full of confidence, optimism and mutual support. Political campaigns around Vietnam, civil rights and nuclear disarmament were influencing the world of social work ... Social workers felt that they could do something useful for society. There was a feeling of change in the air. We thought we could help people. Now it feels that we are doing things to people rather than empowering them. Visiting people at home on a regular basis was an essential part of the job, but it required a great deal of sacrifice ... To try to do everything that was needed became an impossible task because of the caseload. We would work regularly in the evenings, about three or four times a week ... Appointments would be made at six, seven or eight o'clock at night. It was the only way to see the clients. But it was difficult to switch off.⁶⁸

John Crick in Hertfordshire recalled:

> People were having to let go of their pre-Seebohm cultures and there was a fear of loss of skill and expertise. At the same time there was a lot of joint work – people doing joint visits and learning from one another – and wanting to form a new culture. I believed in the Seebohm reforms so fundamentally that I used to say that my specialism was generic social work ... We were aware of the work on breakup of communities in East London and aimed to help people retain their networks of support. I remember the team allowed me to take three months without taking any referrals to survey the day care needs of people in the Hitchin area ... Another thing I did was to visit all the over sixties clubs in Hitchin and asked them if they wanted to form an over-sixties action committee. They did and I advised the committee. They organised a conference on the needs of elderly people and the local MP came along. They also got in touch with local shops to ask them to provide more seating. Others in the team developed a village hall drop-in facility for parents and children in a rural area.⁶⁹

In 1970 an informal left-wing group of radicals came together as 'CASE CON' launching a magazine of the same name along the lines of the also relatively new *Private Eye* magazine. The group's aims were in opposition to capitalism, the use of social workers as tranquilisers and agents of social control, professional exclusiveness and attacks on the living standards of the poor. They supported the democratic organisation of training courses and the restructuring of agencies based on client need rather than establishment goals. The single-page first issue is signed CASE CON Basement Flat, 110 Lansdowne Way, London SW8. Although the magazine only ran for seven years, it had a significant impact. Perhaps it deserves a blue plaque. It attacked the managerialism of the new SSDs and traditional casework. Issue after issue of lively commentary was published, often in cartoon drawings of besuited directors on their massive salaries of £5,000-plus a year heading the Seebohm factories of downtrodden workers forced to suppress needy applicants. The magazine was enjoyable for its reflection of the spirit of the age, its humour, its commitment and its effect on our outlook and practice.[70n]

Deinstitutionalisationism

The Seebohm Report was in accord with the culture of the time, as were developments in the care of people who were mentally ill or handicapped. Slowly a combination of new treatments, civil rights movements, the influence of academic works, particularly Goffman's *Asylums*[71] and financial pressures led to a determination to close these vast establishments. The long neglected hospitals for the mentally handicapped also had to face the question of why the medical profession was supervising regimes for individuals who were permanently handicapped. Over the next twenty years, interesting interprofessional wars were fought. Firstly, increased use of behaviourism saw psychologists taking a greater leadership role, but in time a new generation of nurses committed themselves to increasing the rate of discharge into the community, where a considerable minority opened small homes to continue good nursing practice in the community. In 1970 the psychoanalytically trained social worker Jane Mattinson published research recognising the rights of those with learning disabilities, concluding that marriage usually meant that couples functioned better, giving each other support, a challenging conclusion at the time.[72]

Domestic Violence

In late 1971 a women's group led by Erin Pizzey was meeting in Belmont Terrace, Chiswick, when a badly bruised woman, Jenny Smith, knocked on the door and became the first admission to what was to become the Chiswick Refuge, the first domestic refuge in the western world. Despite the strength of the women's movement, the plight of women battered in their own homes had been far from well recognised. Jenny had suffered two years of severe assaults from her violent husband, culminating in near strangulation. Repeatedly advised by professionals to go home and make peace, she heard of the group and was instantly admitted. She became a lifelong campaigner against abuse within the home and helped in the expansion of the hostel and Pizzey's European campaigning. In 1974, the hostel developed into the Women's Aid Federation who lobbied for the passing of the 1976 Domestic Violence and Matrimonial Proceedings Act, and for having women and children at risk of domestic violence to count as homeless under The Housing Act 1977. The work of the refuges is continued by the national charity Refuge, which now accommodates some 3,000 women every night in addition to a national range of support services.[73] Though of central importance, the Chiswick hostel was only one of a wide range of local initiatives during the late 1960s and 1970s.

They have come to be seen as part of a 'survivor movement.' One was the Mental Patients Union established in England, another the Protection of the Rights of Mental Patients in Therapy, and all were established and run by service users.[74]

Professionalisation

Following the Seebohm Report, it made sense for the various professional associations to come together, and the British Association of Social Workers (BASW) was formed in 1970.[75n] The new association fought hard to maintain a professional qualification for membership, but the fact had to be faced that with so many groups brought into the SSDs qualified staff were in the minority. After many fierce debates, the BASW allowed established unqualified staff to join as full members on grounds of equality. Also bowing to the spirit of the age and financial stress from a small membership of some 10,000, it moved from the fashionable Bedford Square to New Street, Birmingham. It left that office forty-seven years later. It quickly published a draft Code of Ethics (Discussion Paper No 2) which included the following statement of principles:

> Basic to the profession of social work is the recognition of the value and dignity of every individual human being, irrespective of origin, status, sex, age, belief or contribution to society. The profession accepts responsibility to encourage and facilitate the self-realisation of the individual person with due regard for the interest of others.

In October 1971 the Central Council for the Education and Training in Social Work (CCETSW) took over the responsibilities of the existing councils and subsequently certificates in child care and social qualifications were merged into a generic qualification, the Certificate of Qualification in Social Work (CQSW). The new Council faced a tough challenge. The previous councils had spent many years adapting to the growth and changes in both care and education, adjusting the curricula, the entry age and requirements and future employment opportunities. All this had to be melded into one qualification to suit the new departments whose needs had yet to be clearly identified. In addition, the Council faced the rapid expansion in further and higher education, the boom in social work recruitment and problems with its own constitution. The Seebohm Report (paras 533 and 641/643) had pointed to the need for 'some more visibly effective machinery ... for co-ordinating all those aspects of policy and practice which would affect substantially the working and development of the new departments.' It then went on to list the stakeholders that should be represented and emphasised accountability to the minister. As no other body existed, the CCETSW was established with a board of over sixty members including about eight from BASW and eleven civil servants; luckily the senior of these was Robin Birch who quickly embraced a sound understanding of the issues faced by this new organisation and thus made a substantial contribution to social work history.[76] In the midst of all this, the new Council was faced with the first major media and public outcry following the death of Maria Colwell, a foster child who had been returned to her parents in Brighton.

Maria Colwell

Maria died in January 1973 at the hands of her stepfather William Kepple, who was jailed for eight years for manslaughter. Social workers and others at that time were less informed of child abuse, and battered baby syndrome had not been identified. There was much criticism of the SSD's decision not to object when Maria's mother applied for a revocation order, a significant influence being Bowlby's late 1950's research into attachment.[77] In findings which were to become all too familiar in future tragedies, the inquiry discovered that, although many professionals had witnessed Maria's distress and received many complaints from concerned neighbours, there had been a lack of communication and co-ordination between the SSD, the NSPCC, the police, the housing department, teachers and medical staff. Although one of the social work professionals, Olive Stevenson, agreed with most of the report, she dissented with a narrative section arguing that the committee had failed to understand the complexity of the role performed by social workers. She also emphasised the need for inter-professional working.[78]

The impact of the Colwell tragedy and the media attacks on social work caused some division in opinion. Arguments within the profession arose between those who favoured more investment in early intervention to prevent abuse by using the wider kinships available for children at risk, and those that favoured an early move to a permanent new home.[79] Faced with continued pressure from the press, the shortage of babies for adoption and the Colwell Report, the government appointed a committee to review the provision of adoption services and make recommendations. The outcome was a move away from the wide variety of adoption agencies provided by voluntary and religious organisations towards a secular specialist service run by local authorities. The committee also recommended that 'on reaching the age of majority an adopted person should not be denied access to his/her original birth records. This should apply to all adults in England and Wales whenever adopted.'[80]

The government brought these recommendations into law in the Children Act 1975 and the Adoption Act 1976, which implemented a more focussed and assertive child protection system together with a duty on each local authority to provide a comprehensive service to all those involved in adoption. This should include children, parents and guardians, as well as adopters and prospective adopters, and provide a service for those who have a personal connection with adoption if they have unresolved issues and counselling needs.

Residential Care

The focus on professional and organisational change for social workers somewhat obscured significant changes happening in the structure and culture in the residential sector. New departments were faced with the management of a wide variety of residential settings, including, since the 1969 Act, the old approved schools, now called 'community homes with education' (CHEs) but with a shortage of senior managers with experience and knowledge of this sector. Since the late 1950s the traditional pattern was that homes were led by a husband and wife team (often as manager and matron) and an almost exclusively female staff, some of whom would be resident. Now there was a need for separate roles and a balance of male and female staff, most of whom were non-resident and working shift systems. Very few staff were qualified. In retrospect the confusion from such changes was complicated by the wider cultural and social influences of the 1960s, which promoted changes in sexual attitudes and emphasised the individual rights of adults and children. Boundaries and strict rules and sanctions were having to be re-thought at a time when lines of accountability were often unclear and managers preoccupied with other pressures.

FAMILY

Pluckley

For our small family the years in Pluckley were enjoyable; with our bright daughter Juliet growing fast they could not be other than magical. We were in a compact, friendly village set on a hill overlooking the Kentish Weald with a variety of clubs and village fetes to meld us all together. The problem of finding grazing for our donkey, Shadow, continued. Much effort had to be devoted to begging for the use of every spare piece of land in the village and ensuring that hay bales and supplementary food were always available. We soon had one donkey, one foal, two dogs and several chickens. All new to me, but recreating the Cornish farm of Ann's childhood.

All this added to the pressure to move, and luckily a pair of houses suddenly came on the market at the end of a short footpath from the village square. These houses were relatively modern and were near the site of an old windmill that had stood on a bluff overlooking the Weald. The elderly couple wanting a very quick sale were delightful, we agreed the purchase price and soon both houses were ours. We lived in the house called 'Oxendene.' The couple explained that the other house was let, but failed to mention that the tenants had proved very difficult neighbours who were waiting to buy the properties but were away for three weeks! Not a good beginning of our relationship. The rent was controlled at a pittance for a three bedroomed house and, although we did everything we could to keep the house in good repair and improve it, we were constantly bombarded with requests and legal demands, including the relaying of a new water supply from the centre of the village (very expensive).

Despite this our house served us well; Ann loved the place. We had a modern single-storey extension as a kitchen and I gained some local notoriety by building three large garages on a deep concrete raft which compensated for the drainage and fall of the land. It was quite a one-man operation and would certainly not pass modern building regulations, partly because I had not always put sufficient mortar between the blocks.

The locals nicknamed it the 'Aertex building.' I can however confirm that, despite hurricanes and terrible storms on this exposed site, still they stand! I spent months levelling the ground for a lawn, but I think the animals made short shrift of that. My pride and joy, however, was a great tree house where Juliet and her friends could hide out.

Buoyed up by all this happiness, the atmosphere of professional practice and the radical ideas of the times, I took up my new post as lecturer for the Certificate in Social Work (CSW) course at the Medway and Maidstone College of Technology in 1969.

At Oxendene we entertained many friends from the village and neighbouring towns. Ann's stepfather Hugh, now settled in Ashford, called round most days, mostly to admire and help care for his granddaughter. Juliet was in the Brownies, enjoying making friends and in due course riding her friends' horses round the hop fields and orchards. The question of her future schooling caused a bit of a stir. As time went by, Juliet was not happy at the village school; should she continue there and go to one of the good secondary schools in the area, or move to the private Ashford Girls School where she could start straight away? The argument went backwards and forwards, my position being that such a step would severely limit her social circle for life and anyway how could I reconcile my politics with sending my daughter to such a school. I could see the counter-argument that my child should not suffer from my politics, but then I made a tactical mistake by adding that my mother would obviously support my view. Of course, when the question was put to her she called me an idiot and voted for Ashford! It appears that I had completely buried my own experience at this age (see Chapter 5). Juliet embraced the new school, which she joined in 1973, and received a good education until she was eleven when the question had to be faced again. In the meantime we could enjoy village life: sledging down the steep hill in front of the house by moonlight in winter and discussing the meaning of some interesting poems, which were part of Juliet's homework. We now seemed to be breeding donkeys as well as chasing them round the village. The postman would knock early in the morning to tell us that they had wandered into the next village again or, on one occasion, that Juliet's large white rabbit was dead, it having failed to greet him at the gate!

In case this idyllic scene seems too remote from the political and professional turmoil outlined above, in fact the contrast was not that great. While work at Maidstone was keeping me incredibly busy and somewhat stressed, Ann was accomplishing wonders both professionally and in the villages in addition to caring for Juliet, her friends and our menagerie of animals, the dogs and donkeys having been joined by hens and guinea fowl, the most annoying of creatures.

Beech House, the residential psychiatric unit for boys, was enlarged to twenty-four beds with plans for a girls' unit, and Ann worked part-time there for a few years in addition to continuing her work based at Oakwood's day hospital at Woodside where Dr Hyatt Williams continued to trust her with complex, edgy cases. By 1974 Ann was also developing the University of Kent's external studies programme for social work, in conjunction with the Oxford University Extra Mural Department. Ann's natural concern for the less advantaged members of the community inevitably led to organising the monthly Derby and Joan Club in the village and this led, through a link with the Women's Royal Voluntary Service, to a situation where in her final few years in Kent Ann was organising the voluntary programmes in twenty of the local villages. She was both busy and very fulfilled. In March 1973 we managed to persuade Hugh to visit his relatives in America and with great trepidation we got him to Heathrow and on to the plane for three weeks, which he very much enjoyed.[81n]

Eastbourne

At about the same time, my mother and brother announced their intention of selling Darent Hulme Cottage, our first ever house purchase, and were thinking of moving to Eastbourne. We tried hard to persuade them to join us in Pluckley, where there was a suitable house for sale in the middle of the village; why would anyone not want to join our idyll? There followed one of the most painful scenes between Mother and I as she quietly but steadfastly refused my entreaties to be near the family and see her granddaughter grow up. They moved to Eastbourne in 1975. Two lessons came from this: firstly, I should have appreciated the central schism in my mother's relationship with the world – although she was the central communicator of family relationships, writing many letters a week, she had a deep reserve which prevented too close a personal connection; secondly, fate dictated that two years later we would move to Lancashire so we would not have been nearby for long. I had also forgotten the fierce determination that had seen her through the Great Depression and two world wars!

Mother and John moved into a small house on Grassington Road, Eastbourne, and in 1975 my brother John retired from his long and arduous full-time teaching career and opted for occasional work as a supply teacher in local schools. This was a great relief to him and allowed him to pursue his interests in family history, filmmaking, the work of church organist and his musical studies at Sussex University, where he had enrolled on an MA in musicology. In time he brought his early film and technology studies to an early exploration of how the new technology of computers could be used in music and education. Mother really enjoyed the whole seaside scene: the band concerts, the processions, the annual pre-Wimbledon tennis, but above all the walks. Whatever the weather, she took long walks along the front and up towards Beachy Head, where, if the sun was shining, she found a nook in the cliffs and indulged her passion for reading. This was her ideal. Letters to relatives around the world and writing her own autobiography were winter tasks, but the constant stream of family visitors meant that there were few free weekends.

Family reunions were always large and fairly regular. One was the golden wedding anniversary of my Aunt Elsie and her husband Harry in Worthing in April 1975, and the following year saw us all gathering in Eastbourne, when my Great Uncle Charlie and Chris visited in September. The final one was in 1981 when we organised a surprise 80th birthday get together for Mother. The surprise was essential given her abhorrence of any fuss about her and her dislike of hotels. At that time she had developed the strange habit of taking the kitchen waste in a small bag and dropping it into a public waste bin. On the day this meant that she walked into the room clutching her bag of rubbish! Naturally, all such events were filmed and photographed to exhaustion.

In addition to our regular trips to Eastbourne and summer holidays in Cornwall with Ann's sister and family, we developed a love for the New Forest, and my brother and Hugh would join us for a short while. The Forest was certainly a place to relax, usually staying at the magical Bramble Hill Hotel. We had many happy times there, despite one traumatic day when Juliet broke her leg. We rushed her to the local hospital where a wonderful duty GP applied a cast leading to a full recovery. During an early visit there, Hugh gave Juliet a small padded dog standing on four castors, made by the patients at Woodside Day Hospital, and as I write this over fifty years later, it lives in New York, presumably waiting for Juliet's own grandchildren.

SOCIAL WORKER – EDUCATOR

Buoyed up by the joys of Pluckley, the atmosphere of professional practice and the radical ideas of the times, I took up my new post as lecturer for the Certificate in Social Work (CSW) course at the Medway and Maidstone College of Technology in 1969. The CSW course was led by Jean Bevan, a psychiatric social worker, and the Certificate in Child Care course was led by Pearl Jones, a qualified and experienced child care officer. Pearl was very ably assisted by Joan McIver, previously a senior manager in Kent's Children's Department. Reflecting the traditional tone of a college whose experience was in engineering and technology, these courses ran quietly along with curricula built around a psychoanalytic base, as was the case with most courses at that time. My new colleagues were delightfully relaxed and effective teachers, who cared for their students and were committed to producing high quality social workers in the best pre-Seebohm traditions. Something had to change.

As far as this book is concerned, the historical process will be postponed while I recount the events at the social work qualifying course for which I was responsible in Maidstone. Hopefully, this will illustrate the optimism, madness and progress of the profession during this period as it reflected the wider society and the challenging ideas current in education in general.

NOTES AND REFERENCES

In this chapter I have drawn on the following publications: Beckett, A. (2009). *When the Lights Went Out*. London: Faber & Faber; Judt, A. (2005). *Post War: A History of Europe Since 1945*. London: Heinemann.

1. Schumacher, E. F. (1973). *Small Is Beautiful: A Study of Economics as if People Mattered*. New York: Blond & Briggs.

2. *Report of the Committee on Local Authority and Allied Personal Social Services* (The Seebohm Report) (1968). London: HMSO, Cmnd 3703, Para 474, p. 147.
3. By the early 1980s composer Richard Adams, attracted by the dramatic scope and mythology of the situation, decided to write his first opera on the occasion. *Nixon in China* was first performed in Houston in 1987 and in London in 2000. Ann and I saw the production in London and enjoyed both drama and music. It has not yet been shown in China.
4. It was the President's use of burglary against Ellsberg's office which led directly to the Watergate scandal and Nixon's downfall. See Sheehan, N. (2017). *The Pentagon Papers: The Secret History of the Vietnam War*. New York: Racehorse Publishing.
5. See Woodward, R. and Bernstein, C. (2006). *All the President's Men*. New York: Simon & Schuster. A film adaptation was released in 1976. Dir. Alan Pakula. Warner Bros. Starring Robert Redford and Dustin Hoffman. President Ford pardoned Nixon in 1974 and, although he issued a statement of regret, Nixon never admitted to a crime. In 1977 the British TV personality David Frost staked his considerable fortune on obtaining an interview with Nixon, who still harboured feelings of injustice that his achievements had not been recognised and that he had been brought down by the puritanical American conscience manipulated by his political enemies. In a historic bout, Nixon resisted any culpability on the grounds that he had not acted from bad motives until right at the end when he said, 'I had let down my friends, I let down the country, I let down our system of government and the dreams of all those young people that ought to get into government but will think it is all too corrupt and the rest.' See David Frost and Richard Nixon, in the pamphlet 'Great Interviews of the 20th Century.' *The Guardian* (2007).
6. Recent research has uncovered 20,000 mass graves and estimated the total deaths at between 1.4 and 2.2 million people.
7. The United Nations had played a significant part in bringing peace to Cambodia, and in 2006 tribunals were established to try leaders of the Khmer Rouge for crimes against humanity and genocide. Many of the leaders have died or are sick, but although the process is painfully slow, two sentences of life imprisonment have been handed down since 2013.
8. Hobsbawm, E. (1964). *Age of Extremes: The Short Twentieth Century 1914–1991*. London: Abacus, p. 467.
9. Judt, A. (2005). *Post War: A History of Europe Since 1945*. London: Heinemann, p. 453.
10. Phillips, T. (2016). 'Fifty years on, one of Mao's 'little generals' exposes the horror of the Cultural Revolution.' *The Observer*. 08.05.2016, p. 27. This concerns Yu Xiangzhen, who ran a blog reviewing her experience as a Red Guard.
11. The real title of the 'Little Red Book' was *Quotations from Chairman Mao Tse-tung*, published from 1964; worldwide sales ran to several million copies. A new edition was published in November 2014 but will be edited and only partially red.
12. Judt, *op. cit.*, p. 406. Very shortly after Mao's death the four leaders of the Cultural Revolution, including his wife, were denounced. In 1981 they received long prison sentences.
13. See Agee, P. (1975). *Inside the Company: CIA Diary*. New York: Farrar Straus and Giroux. Also see *Missing*. Dir. Costa-Gavras. Polygram Pictures, 1982, a film based on a true story which portrays a group of Americans trapped in Chile by events and their painful discovery of the extent of American influence in the ensuing violence. Starring Jack Lemmon and Sissy Spacek.
14. The PFLP and Fatah were two large elements of the Palestinian Liberation Organisation, a political grouping led by Yasser Arafat. It was recognised as the representative of the Palestinian people and has observer status at the United Nations.
15. *In Place of Strife, A Policy for Industrial Relations*. (1969). Cmnd 3888. London: HMSO.
16. Marr, A. (2007). *A History of Modern Britain*. London: Macmillan.
17. Marr, *op. cit.*, p. 311.

18. Macmillan, H. (1938). *The Middle Way*. London: Macmillan and Co.
19. It would be 1988 before serious tunnelling commenced under the Channel, and the Maplin project had to be abandoned as the costs rose and the economy dived. See Beckett, A. (2009). *When the Lights Went Out*. London: Faber & Faber, pp. 35 et seq. Successive governments have revised the concept of a new airport at the Thames Estuary, the latest being Boris Johnson's ambitious scheme of 2014.
20. See the New Left Review website: http://newleftreview.org.
21. Free milk for all schoolchildren had a long history, finally becoming law in 1946. It had been abolished for secondary school children in 1968. The original justification had been as an essential dietary supplement for disadvantaged children, and in 1971 this same argument was used against this cut. Mrs Thatcher later commented that the furore had taught her a valuable lesson: that public odium was out of all proportion to small financial gain. Some local authorities ignored the ban, others added a small amount of cocoa powder so that what they issued was not milk!
22. The city's Coroner, retired British Army Major Hubert O'Neill, issued a statement on August 21st 1973, at the completion of the inquest into the people killed. He declared: 'It strikes me that the army ran amok that day and shot without thinking what they were doing. They were shooting innocent people. These people may have been taking part in a march that was banned but that does not justify the troops coming in and firing live rounds indiscriminately. I would say without hesitation that it was sheer, unadulterated murder. It was murder.' The government launched an immediate inquiry under Lord Widgery which supported the army's view and was rejected by the IRA. In 1998 the then Prime Minister Tony Blair launched a Commission of Inquiry under Lord Saville which reported in May 2010, concluding that, 'The firing by soldiers of 1 Para on Bloody Sunday caused the deaths of thirteen people and injury to a similar number, none of whom was posing a threat of causing death or serious injury.' They also concluded that an IRA sniper did fire, but were unable to confirm whether this was before or after the army. The Prime Minister David Cameron concluded his statement to the House of Commons by saying, 'What happened on Bloody Sunday was both unjustified and unjustifiable. It was wrong.'
23. Beckett, *op. cit.*, p. 120.
24. Quoted in Kellaway, R. (2010). *Re-examining the Battle of Saltley Gate: Interpretations of Leadership, Violence and Legacy*. Best Graduate Dissertation, Bristol University.
25. Beckett, *op. cit.*, p. 133.
26. In August 1978 Jeremy Thorpe and three other men were charged with conspiracy to murder a male model, Norman Scott, who had previously claimed to have had an affair with Thorpe at a time when homosexual acts were illegal. This claim had lost Thorpe the leadership of the Party after a gunman had been hired to shoot Scott's dog. All four men were acquitted in 1979, by which time Thorpe had lost his parliamentary seat in the general election. See the four-part TV series *A Very English Scandal*. Script Russell T. Davies. Dir. Stephen Frears. Blueprint Pictures, 2018. Starring Hugh Grant and Ben Whishaw.
27. *Report of the Committee of Inquiry on Industrial Democracy* (The Bullock Report). (1977). Cmnd 6706. London: HMSO.
28. Beckett, *op. cit.*, p. 177. For most of his premiership, Wilson had been the victim of an illegal campaign of destabilisation by a group of senior right-wing military and retired MI5 personnel, prompted by the CIA, who had the idea that Wilson was a Soviet agent! As society began to unravel serious consideration was given to a coup d'état with a military takeover. A formal inquiry found no basis for this conspiracy, but further investigations, including the controversial book *Spycatcher* by a former Assistant Director of MI5, have strengthened the existence of this group. See Wright, P. (1987). *Spycatcher*. Sydney: Heinemann.

29. *Royal Commission on the Constitution 1969–1973, Volume I, Report* (The Kilbrandon Report). (1973). Cmnd 5460.
30. Marr, A. (2007). *The History of Modern Britain*. London: Macmillan, p. 357.
31. Foreman, A. 'Why the Iron Lady was the Ultimate Women's Libber.' *Daily Mail*, 03.02.2012.
32. Aitken, I. (1975). 'Iron Lady will put the Tories right.' *The Guardian*, 12.02.1975.
33. Marcuse, H. (1965). *Repressive Tolerance*. The full text can be found at https://la.utexas.edu/users/hcleaver/330T/350kPEEMarcuseToleranceTable.pdf.
34. DeGroot, G. (2008). *The Sixties Unplugged*. London: Pan Macmillan.
35. Given the colossal worldwide impact that The Beatles had in the turbulent 1960s, the release of 'Revolution' caused a split in their fans. The record seemed a departure from their early promotion of 'love one another and world peace' to a more radical stance. The more extreme activist groups leading demonstrations across the world considered that the record had fudged the issue. Lennon's view had for some time been to ask if anyone could point to a violent revolution, but had not been followed by a more violent response. He asked those advocating revolution what was their constructive plan for after the revolution? The quote comes from a continuing 1980 dialogue with the left activist magazine *Black Dwarf* edited by Tariq Ali. Specifically, Lennon was replying to an article by John Hoyland that the record was 'no more revolutionary than Mrs Dale's Diary.'
36. In 1972, three prisoners in a tough Louisiana prison formed a Black Panther chapter. When a guard was murdered in 1972, the three were accused and two were sentenced to solitary confinement; they remained in their cells for 23 hours a day for 40 years. One died; another was released in 2016, his conviction having been overturned and the third spent 29 years in solitary until his conviction was overturned. See the 2014 documentary film *Herman's House* by Angad Bhalla.
37. Darcus Howe, originally from Trinidad, was based in Brixton. He joined the British Black Panthers and led several significant local and national protests. He edited *Race Today*, which was praised for its poetry, and was a frequent broadcaster throughout his life. He died in April 2017.
38. The area was home to many past and present stars of stage and screen. In 1882, Oscar Wilde had lived at number 18 after his successful tour of America. The wealthy owner in 1970 was unaware that his daughter had turned part of it into a bomb factory. See DeGroot, *op. cit.*, p. 426.
39. Goldburg, S. (2017). 'Tape "Reveals Order" to Shoot Vietnam Protesters.' *The Guardian*, 02.05.2017.
40. Sheeran, T. (2007). 'Kent State Audio Tape Released.' *Washington Post*, 02.05.2007.
41. In January 2013, John Kerry sat in same seat to be endorsed as US Secretary of State for Foreign Affairs in the Obama administration.
42. This movement argued for a vast expansion of free festivals as a network of independent collectives operating outside the established society. See Beckett, *op. cit.*, p. 244.
43. Beckett, *op. cit.*, p. 257.
44. Peter Tatchell moved to London in 1971, following a history of campaigning since his schooldays. He became a leading member of the Gay Liberation Front. He joined the Labour Party and stood for the Bermondsey constituency. He has continued as a campaigner and activist ever since.
45. Beckett, *op. cit.*, p. 217.
46. John Mortimer also successfully defended the novel *Last Exit to Brooklyn* and many others. He later turned to writing, particularly the series *Rumpole of the Bailey*, which ran from 1975–1992, starring Leo McKern. Richard Neville continued to work as a journalist worldwide, returning to Australia as a controversial presenter. He co-founded the Australian Futures Foundation. Jim Anderson sought therapy in different countries before settling in California for many years. In the 1990s he returned to Australia to work as a writer and photo artist. Felix Dennis, a Londoner,

47. *Equus*. Dir. Sidney Lumet. United Artists, 1977. Starring Richard Burton, Peter Firth, Joan Plowright and Jenny Agutter. In 2007 the play was revised with Richard Griffiths as the psychiatrist and the 17-year-old Daniel Radcliffe as the boy. It was very well received, attracting new young audiences as both stars had been in the highly successful *Harry Potter* film series.
48. Pirsig, R. (1974). *Zen and the Art of Motorcycle Maintenance. An Inquiry into Values*. Ealing: Corgi, p. 110. Pirsig had many bad times in his life before the book was published in his early forties. It had been rejected by 121 publishers, but then sold five million copies. His son Chris was stabbed to death by a mugger outside the Zen Centre in San Francisco at the age of 22 while his father was in England.
49. *One Flew Over the Cuckoo's Nest*. Dir. Milos Foreman. United Artists, 1975. Starring Jack Nicholson; *Fiddler on the Roof*. Dir. Norman Jewison. United Artists, 1971. Starring Zero Mostel; *Cabaret*. Dir. Bob Fosse. Allied Artists, 1972. Starring Liza Minnelli, Michael York and Joel Grey; *Jaws*. Dir. Steven Spielberg. Universal Pictures, 1975. Starring Roy Scheider, Robert Shaw and Richard Dreyfus.
50. Huxley, A. (1932). *Brave New World*. London: Chatto and Windus.
51. Orwell, G. (1950). *1984*. London: Signet Classics.
52. Schumacher, *op. cit.* See also Kumar, S. (Ed.) (1980). *The Schumacher Lectures*. London: Blond and Briggs; McRobie, G. (1981). *Small is Possible*. London: Jonathan Cape.
53. Schumacher, *op. cit.*
54. Wolmar, C. (2000). *Forgotten Children: The Secret Abuse Scandal in Children's Homes*. London: Vision Paperbacks.
55. *Better Services for the Handicapped* (1971). Cmnd 4683. DHSS.
56. Alf Morris became the first Minister for the Disabled in 1974, introducing mobility allowances; he continued to campaign and support further bills for disabled people until he retired thirty-three years after his first election and campaigned until his death in 2012. In his first party conference speech in 1957 he railed against 'a society which allows people to make millions of pounds in a day and other people to exist without even the price for coal.' In 1981 he opened the UN discussion which established the International Year of the Disabled. In 2004 he set up an inquiry into the damage to the health of veterans of the Gulf War. His niece Estelle Morris became Secretary of State for Education and Skills in 2001.
57. *Report of the Committee on Local Authority and Allied Personal Social Services* (The Seebohm Report). (1968). HMSO
58. The Seebohm Report, *op. cit.*, para 427.
59. The Seebohm Report, *op. cit.*, para 480.
60. The Seebohm Report, *op. cit.*, para 491/492.
61. The Seebohm Report, *op. cit.*, para 494.
62. The Seebohm Report, *op. cit.*, para 557.
63. Harbert, W. (1998). From the Barricades to the Boardroom, Viewpoint, *Community Care Magazine*, May 7/13th, p. 9.
64. Sir Willam Utting's 2002 speech to BASW Conference. *Professional Social Work*, June, pp. 10–11.
65. Smith, G. and Harris, J. (1972). Ideology of Need and Organisation of Social Work Departments, *British Journal of Social Work*, Spring, Vol. 2(1).
66. Wasserman, H. (1971). The Professional Social Worker in a Bureaucracy, *Social Work*, January.
67. Rice, R. M. (1973). Organising to Innovate in Social Work, *Social Casework*, January.

68. Then and Now, *Community Care*, April 25th–May 11th (1966), p. 20.
69. Then and Now, *Community Care*, April 11th–17th (1966), p. 22.
70. See Weinstein, J. (2011). *Case Con and Radical Social Work in the 1970s: The Impatient Revolutionaries in Radical Social Work Today, Social Work at the Crossroads*. (Ed. M. Lavalette), Bristol: Policy Press. Jeremy Weinstein was one of the original CASE CON group.
71. Goffman, E. (1961). *Asylums*. London: Penguin.
72. Mattinson, J. (1970). *Marriage and Mental Handicap*. London: Duckworth.
73. Pizzey, E. (2011). *This Way to the Revolution – An Autobiography*. London: Peter Owen Ltd; Pizzey, E. (1979). *Scream Quietly or the Neighbours Will Hear*. London: Penguin Press; Smith, J. (2014). *The Refuge: My Journey to the Safe House for Battered Women*. London: Simon & Schuster.
74. Morrison, L. J. (2005). *Talking Back to Psychiatry: The Psychiatric Consumer / Survivor / Ex-Patient Movement*. New Approaches to Sociology. London: Routledge.
75. The BASW was formed by the amalgamation of the Institute of Medical Social Workers, the Association of Psychiatric Social Workers, the Association of Social Workers (mostly employed by local authorities), the Association of Child Care Officers, the Association of Moral Welfare Workers, the Association of Family Caseworkers and the Society of Mental Health Workers. Probation officers remain with their own national association on the grounds that they are related more to the criminal justice system and residential child care staff remain with the Residential Care Association (later the Social Care Association).
76. Summary of Central Council Activities 1947–1971 (internal paper) and History and Achievements 1971–2001, CCETSW.
77. Bowlby, J. (1971). *Attachment and Loss. Vol 1 Attachment*. London: Pelican.
78. Field-Fisher, T. G. (Chairman). (1974). Report of the Committee of Inquiry into the Care and Supervision Provided in Relation to Maria Colwell. London: HMSO.
79. Rowe, J. and Lambert, L. (1973). *Children Who Wait*. London: Association of British Adoption Agencies.
80. Houghton Departmental Committee Report. (1972). Cmnd 5107. HMSO
81. In 2011, Juliet, my grandson Duke and I took old photos and memorabilia to the surviving relatives. While they certainly carried the family likeness, they seemed to have lost most of their ancestors' adventurous spirit, being content to work and enjoy life in their town by the Mississippi.

TEN

1969–1976
RADICAL SOCIAL WORK EDUCATION (MAIDSTONE)

In memory of Laurie Almark, David Pithers and Norman Rose – gifted educators

The new education has as its purpose the development of a new kind of person, one who – as a result of internalising a different series of concepts – is an actively enquiring, flexible, creative, innovative, tolerant, liberal personality who can face ambiguity without disorientation, who can formulate viable new meanings to meet changes in the environment which threatens individual and mutual survival.

– Teaching as a Subversive Activity[1]

In problem-posing education, men develop their power to perceive critically the way they exist in the world with which and in which they find themselves; they come to see the world not as a static reality, but as a reality in process, in transformation.

– Pedagogy of the Oppressed[2]

If there is one charge which I feel must be given to our profession, it is that those responsible for social work, education in all parts of the globe, must submerge themselves in the life of their own societies, must feel viscerally, as well as intellectually, what the human and social aspirations and needs of the people are; and accept the challenge of working creatively and courageously at devising and inventing approaches which will not only be effective in their own countries but will serve as an inspiration to each of us in our search for solutions.

– Education for Social Work[3]

THE CQSW COURSE AND OTHER EVENTS

Introduction

It is too often said that if you remember the 60s you weren't there, presumably due to the wide availability of hallucinogenic drugs, but, as has been shown in the previous chapter, any lasting social and cultural changes took root in the 1970s. This chapter will attempt to explain the events external to the social work courses in Maidstone, our objectives, the staff and students involved, the content and methods, and the internal and external conflicts that were faced. In addition to the historical interest of the course itself, it seems to me that it reflected the confusions and achievements of social work and social workers in those turbulent times. In accord with the principles of the course, drafts of this chapter were discussed at a small reunion of former students and staff held in Maidstone in November 2015. As some forty years had passed we were a somewhat venerable group, but we were at least able to look back over our entire careers.

Educator

Having joined the staff at Maidstone in January 1969 I was immediately seconded to the six-month 'Fellowship' course at the National Institute of Social Work (NISW) in Tavistock Place, London, designed to introduce social workers to the skills and demands of teaching. Here a small group of international students enjoyed the supportive culture of the Institute and the leadership of Peter Leonard[4n] and Peter Righton,[5n] enhanced by others including the determined researcher Tilda Goldberg[6n] and visiting professors including Henry Meyer from the University of Michigan, whose excellent six-year research project *Girls at Vocational High* had just been published.[7] This was reported to be the first research to show clearly that social work intervention was effective. The two Peters could not have been more different in personality and style. Peter Leonard followed a Marxist approach and argued fiercely that social work should have a more radical place in society. Peter Righton led discussions on the philosophical underpinning of the profession and our value base, also drawing on his experience of residential childcare to argue for an approach which would give 'touch hungry' children the love that they had previously been denied. Why, he would ask, was it wrong to cuddle a child if that is what they most needed. I don't recall the group seriously questioning this – after all it was a great theme of the 60s, and it certainly chimed with my experience of residential care where children would throw themselves at staff whether demanding close contact play-fighting or just invading your space on the settee.

I very much enjoyed the rare opportunity of this demanding course which took us through the principles of curriculum design, a significant political act in itself, teaching methods and, of course, the present state of social work.[8] While I was able to clear some confusion left from my own patchy education and experience, I was stimulated by the remarkable changes in the social sciences. In the few years since I had qualified in Birmingham, the clear boundaries between the disciplines of psychology,[9] sociology and social administration had eroded. In particular, sociology had moved from structures, statistics and institutions to the cultural and personal experiences of everyday life.[10] These changes and the current social protests and upheavals had given the social sciences a more political edge. All this challenged the profession of social work, and there was much talk of a new 'radical' form more suited to the issues of the day and the opportunities provided by the new powerful departments.[11] The increased overlap between the academic subjects militated against the established professional specialisms and laid the foundations of a generic model. The importance of research to validate practice and the opportunities afforded in our daily work to garner information, which could be taken to the new directors and government to urge policy change for the benefit of those who used the services, were seen as critical.[12] Whilst at the Institute we could choose which courses to visit, there were presentations to be made and teaching practice to be reported on, but by June of 1969 our course was over, we were 'Fellows' of the Institute and, with the final experience of the rock musical *Hair*, I was fired up and ready to change the world, or at least my small bit of it.

Medway and Maidstone College of Technology

My main contact with the College had been for teaching practice and selection of students for the autumn 1969 intake; neither had been incident free. Given my long-standing interest and experience at St Augustine's I had chosen the topic of group dynamics for my first teaching practice at the Maidstone campus. I walked into the hut, confident and stress free, sat down, swept my arms in greeting and a full box of 144 chalk sticks fell to the floor and smashed! Of more lasting consequence, although not without its humorous side, was an encounter during a selection interview. Given the College's lack of tutorial rooms, I was directed to use the unoccupied boardroom, which I rearranged as best I could with a large notice indicating that we should not be disturbed. I was halfway through a personal interview when a man walked in and demanded to know what was going on. I think it must have been the shock, professional offence and lack of familiarity with my surroundings that led to one of my very rare rages! I followed the guy into the adjoining office and continued to point out the crassness of his actions when, as the red mist eased, I realised that he was sitting in the Principal's chair with his feet on the desk. He proved to be the Deputy Principal, a nice enough guy who never held the event against me. When I apologised to the students waiting anxiously in the distant front lobby, explaining that there had been an 'administrative problem,' they just said, 'We heard!'

The autumn of 1969 involved me teaching full time on two courses, soon to be combined as the new generic Certificate of Qualification in Social Work (CQSW). Very soon these changes, exhaustion and difficult relations with the College witnessed the departure of the three tutors who had so diligently taught the separate courses. I was consequently left responsible for the combined course and the recruitment of the staff who would join in the creation and development of an exciting course incorporating the vision of Seebohm and the demands of the age. This had to be accomplished against several significant changes.

In advancing the principle that universities 'should be available to all who were qualified for them by ability and attainment,' the 1963 Robbins Report (commissioned by Macmillan's government but implemented by Wilson's) had led both to new universities and an expansion in further education colleges.[13] Some universities now offered students a greater individual choice by abandoning rigid subject boundaries and embracing programmes designed on a modular basis. These changes had been driven by a new generation of lecturers educated in the left-wing spirit of the post-war years and anxious to attract students, many of whom were well aware of the major changes demanded by the worldwide student protests, the very protests in which many of the staff had been involved.

Formed in the 1890s, Medway and Maidstone College of Technology had a long history of meeting the needs of the Chatham dockyards, industry and established trades, providing a range of courses run on traditional models. They had accepted a course for health visitors, presumably embracing the natural science basis as being within their tradition. In response to the growing demand for qualified social workers, the Central Council for the Education and Training in Social Work (CCETSW) had noted the desert in the southeast and set about establishing courses at the very new University of Kent in Canterbury, although they recognised the difficulties that could arise. Our informal culture and need for one-to-one tutorials all presented problems; the very expensive input from a famous psychoanalyst was an added issue.

As the CQSW course embarked on a more challenging agenda, there were many heavy arguments. In our favour was the relatively high status of the course, which was of financial benefit to the College. To be fair as our numbers (and income) grew they provided the staff and facilities required, year by year. More and more mobile units (each adapted for three tutors' rooms) were added to the original Hut D for lectures and student gatherings. However, two chronic problems remained, both of which had driven my predecessors away. The most annoying was the requirement that we called the register at every lesson. In practice this meant that tutors spent hours every year end marking up estimated attendances. This was related to the measurement of contact hours. Our students, of course, spent months out of college, and tutors therefore spent a lot of time travelling with only a relatively brief contact. Recognising and resolving this issue was very time consuming as was the relatively low salary that our staff merited according to the existing rules. It took us some time to realise why this was not seen as such a problem for some other staff in our department. They could most helpfully meet the needs of industry by running intensive weekend courses which used up almost all of their contact hours, thus leaving them free to accept lucrative consultancies during the week.

While the main college was based in the Medway Towns the social work courses were located in a country park site in Maidstone next to a progressive art college and only a stone's throw from Oakwood Hospital where Ann and I had first met. In these huts we would not contaminate the mainstream, a pattern which I have seen so many times since in colleges and universities. It did however mean that radical developments were fairly free from interference. We were lucky in our head of department, the wise J. E. Bateson – a kind man who had the daunting task of mediating between our experimental practices and the traditional powers at HQ. For me the stress of handling these conflicts was eased a little by a close association with the degree/CQSW course just established at the University of Kent under the tutorship of Nancy Hazel and Brian

Munday in the department led by Vic George.[14] We established a Joint Committee on Social Work Education which not only mediated any issues about student placements but also supported a number of initiatives.

In September 1971, following discussion with the University, I wrote a paper on how, given that almost all of the existing practical placements were based on individual casework, we could meet the Seebohm vision. We proposed 'multi-faceted community-based' placements which would offer the student the opportunity to explore a range of interventions in a given local community. This would effectively be a student unit where the leader would be a 'central person' for the student's learning experience. They would gain knowledge of the local area in order to locate others who would be significant supervisors in any specialist activity. The central person would be responsible for ensuring that the students' diverse experiences were shared by the group, and this would form the basis of teaching, enhanced by the involvement of tutors and lecturers. We would explore the possibility of 'continuous placement' so that community projects carried out by one student group would be sustained by the next. These situations opened up rich grounds for research. Between the University, the College, the local authority and the CCETSW, finance was made available, and my memory is that we established units for the use of both courses in the Medway Towns, West Kent (based in West Malling), the Probation Service and Canterbury Social Services. We also had a unique and valuable informal unit in Guys Hospital.

Whilst the Social Services Act had become law in 1971, the actual process of establishing the new departments took some time, with wide differences between authorities. This led to a long period of uncertainty as staff sought either to stay put and hope for the best or move in order to find promotion in a department seen to be more ambitious or better led. The key position of director was causing significant chaos as applicants toured the country in the hope of an appointment. One applicant, not untypical, made 42 applications and published his experiences, shedding some light on the approaches of different authorities. He found that some sent no particulars and no job description, and many omitted key information. Some application forms were all-purpose for anyone from cleaners to chief officers; closing dates were often a week from receipt of the forms. Interview panels usually comprised between 10 and 20 councillors, often advised by management consultants who had no knowledge or experience of social services. The questions posed during interview led to his conclusion that 'provided you had run any department of a few hundred staff without having a nervous breakdown and without causing a public scandal, then you were destined for a top job.' The author was eventually appointed, but after many interviews could see 'no logic either in the criteria or salary related to the vast differences in the population size.'[15]

A few authorities went through a short process to appoint their existing Medical Officer of Health but central government strongly discouraged such appointments. Conservative minded Kent initially appointed a lawyer and former town clerk who set about modernising the services for the elderly and learning disability clients, leaving the better run children's section under the leadership of Elizabeth Harvey. In 1974 the Rev Nick Stacey, whose previous post had been Deputy Director of Oxfam, was appointed. Stacey had built a reputation as an Olympic athlete, a naval officer and as a somewhat radical clergyman in the 1960s under John Robinson, the outspoken Bishop of Woolwich.[16] There was much to admire about Nick Stacey. He was fearless in driving through important changes in a traditionally conservative authority, and he was out and about meeting staff, clients and anyone who he thought had a good idea. He was well known to children in care, who nicknamed him 'Colombo' after the fictional detective as Nick usually wore a light raincoat, smoked a fag and had untidy hair and a slight stoop. He was sociable, could swear like a trooper and regularly stated that his remaining ambitions were either to become editor of *The Times* or Archbishop of Canterbury. One of his first actions was to close the appalling homeless provision at King Hill camp with its dreadful workhouse regime and the rule that brought children into care if a family had not been re-housed in three months (see Chapter 8). As much as I empathised with his maverick approach, I was never quite certain how to deal with him. As a man of action he was generally hostile to 'academics.' He and Nancy Hazel clashed over aspects of her innovative special fostering scheme, although he constantly supported it.[17n] He served the people of Kent well in his eleven years, although it took Kent until 1991 to appoint a director with a social work qualification.

Planning

The effect on social workers of all this uncertainty was unsettling, and anxiety levels were very high as staff having widely different experiences, qualifications and cultures were learning to work together. Once the director was in place and area directors were appointed, staff morale went up or down according to individual situations. Student placements were difficult to arrange throughout this period; experienced staff were already too stressed to take on more responsibility for prolonged periods and, as we went round pleading our case, we often found ourselves used as independent listeners onto whom all these anxieties could be unloaded. It was a difficult time, leading us to launch a major research project on the whole situation (see Chapter 11).

In the meantime, the task was to bring my experience of community work, residential institutions, teaching and social work together with the inspiration of the Fellowship course to consider what to do. Given the need for 'generic' workers, the turmoil in the organisational setting and the revolution in social sciences, how could we design a course that would equip students for the demands that they would face? Once we knew what our objectives and methods were, we needed to recruit staff to implement our ideas and then select students who we thought could most benefit from two years with us, make a valuable contribution to the profession and serve their clients well. Some task!

Student Selection

Between 1968 and 1971 the two courses had passed 92 social workers as competent to practice, but from 1971 onward the demand for qualified staff escalated in order to meet the needs of the new departments. In 1971 Kent County Council decided to move the one-year Residential Child Care (RCC) course, long established in Sidcup, South London, and now led by Laurie Allmark, to join us in Maidstone. This course had covered the physical, psychological and emotional development of the child, practice in crafts, hobbies and activities for children and some theory relating to professional practice. The basic entry requirements were below those for CQSW courses. By 1978 the national student annual output was equal to that of doctors at 4,000. By 1975 the annual intake to our CQSW course was 50 students. Taking these numbers into account I would estimate that we passed at least 400 students during my leadership. Our criteria for admission remained relatively simple. We required some experience in social work or a related field, some evidence of academic ability, intelligence (as evidenced by the IQ test administered at the College), but above all applicants had to demonstrate a capacity for empathy and have the ability to express themselves clearly. By the time the sessions dealing with these issues had been completed and students had been coached in Laurie's series on essay writing, it was impossible to tell those students who already had a degree, including social science, from those who had had no further or higher education.

With an age range between nineteen and forty-five our student group brought a wide range of personal and professional experience to the dynamic of the course. Kent very courageously decided to second some newly recruited education welfare officers to the course.[18] The arrangement was that candidates would be interviewed for the three jobs in the morning then the top six candidates would come to the College in the afternoon for our selection. I drove to County Hall late in the afternoon to discover that we had chosen the exact opposite three! A sharp and significant row then developed, the education staff insisting that they were right and that anyway, as a council employee, I had no choice but to do as I was told! Unfortunately for them, all constitutional and academic arguments were with me, so the dispute was quickly solved. It was however an interesting insight into the failure of that department, so used to recruiting ex police or military men, to keep up with the times.

The Curriculum

The CCETSW had introduced the new Certificate in 1971 with the first awards in 1973. Our response was to establish a series of curriculum study groups commencing early in 1971. They started with a blank page: all staff, students, fieldwork supervisors and employers (via training officers) would be involved. It would be honest and open. Whilst applauding the Seebohm concept of generic social work, we would encourage students to choose a specialist area of practice in their second year. Early meetings were spent drawing elaborate diagrams to indicate the key role sets for each client group and how they would relate to a community worker, group (field or residential) or individual caseworker. This led to a list of generic knowledge and skills required to assess and decide on the most appropriate level of intervention, followed by the requirements for specific effective interventions. In addition to the CQSW it was proposed that the College could issue diplomas for chosen specialist practice. We interpreted Seebohm as referring to generic teams. The concept of a generic social worker was impossible given that different students had different interests and capacities which led them to work better with specific client groups.

Our objective was to give students a generic base which could be shared with colleagues and from which each member could choose a specialism. It was agreed that, apart from formal practice placements, the experience of students during the course should also offer opportunities to model such interventions and that the interactions within the student body, between students and staff, and between differing values and academic disciplines, should allow for conflict and the resolution of such conflict if possible. Use would be made throughout the course of fiction in print and film. A research attitude would be inculcated throughout the course. In October 1971 the students formed themselves into an organised body including sports and entertainments committees. By now staff and student groups were on a roll, though anxious, urged on by events beyond the campus, new staff and a variety of relevant publications about adult education.[19]

In early 1972 thirteen joint task groups were established to review every aspect of the course. This followed a staff meeting which agreed that

> Staff are committed to exploring ways in which staff and students can move towards equal membership in the educational community. This places a responsibility on each staff member to develop student participation in all areas of teaching, planning and administrative duties.

The diagram attached to the statement recognised that, in addition to wide areas of shared responsibility, there remained other duties that lay entirely with students or staff. The latter included accountability to College management and the CCETSW to maintain the high standards required for recognition and ultimate qualification into the profession. Student meetings then took some key decisions. All lectures would be optional and examinations would be abolished. Staff would circulate extensive notes in advance of each formal teaching session so that the 'lecture' time would be used to explore and debate the subject together. All staff were summoned to a student meeting to give their individual views on 'social work education,' with special attention given to 'their notion of what the goals of this course are at the present time.' By a majority vote, students favoured coursework assessment and, to my amazement, there was a unanimous vote that the tutor's report would form part of the assessment, although an appeal system was proposed, which seemed very sensible given the subjective nature of tutor's assessments.

By May 1972 draft proposals were prepared for a generic social work course, the aim of which would be

> To produce a critically thinking, enquiring, innovative, sensitive social worker/change agent who is flexible, creative and concerned for the value of the individual. He/she should be able to facilitate change in individuals, groups, organisations or communities. He/she should understand the process of change and be able to operate and support others under stressful conditions.

It is interesting to note that social work was not alone in seeking radical initiatives. The legal profession (most notably the community-located Law Centres movement), medicine (putting the patient at the centre of treatment and the barefoot doctor movement in China) and architecture (post-modern designs and new estates built for pedestrians rather than cars) were all seeking similar changes. Common themes seemed to be to challenge the existing professional elite. At the same time trades unions were in a militant phase, and BASW itself was clear about what it required of its members:

> The Social Worker ... has the right and duty to bring to the attention of those in power and of the general public, ways in which the activity of government, society or agencies, create or contribute to hardship and suffering or militate against their relief. Social workers are often at the interface between powerful organisations and relatively powerless applicants for service. Certainly social workers are accountable to those under whose authority they work, and responsible for the efficient performance of their professional task and for their management of the organisation's resources. In view of the applicant's lack of power, social workers have a special responsibility to ensure the fullest possible realisation of his rights and satisfaction of his needs.[20]

A small survey of BASW members showed that members believed that the Association should take a stance on social issues: 78% supported lobbying and a further 46% supported direct conflict such as squatting or 'sit-ins.'[21n]

All in all, our aims seemed reasonable and very much in accord with the Seebohm vision. Our proposal recognised two radical elements: firstly that 'learning is most fruitful when the learner participates directly in creating the educational experience.' Thus an outline curriculum presented and followed in the first term would then be negotiated and detailed by staff and students and seen as an ongoing process throughout the course. We would include service users wherever possible. Secondly, the ethos of the Seebohm Report required such a wide range of knowledge and skills that a three-year course was essential. We could not see how the required breadth and depth could be achieved in two years. The first year would examine the 'social process perspective,' the second 'institutions, organisations and superstructure' and 'the community in depth.' Each of these would be accompanied by seminars and tutorials on philosophy, research and 'sensitivity training.' There would be some concurrent practice placements in the first two years, but the third year would be spent in two placements along the lines of the multi-faceted community-based placement outlined above. Soon after the start of the course the group would reside together in a deprived area of the county, perhaps in some condemned houses. The proposal to make the course extend to three years met considerable national opposition and was impossible to achieve, so we reluctantly trimmed it down to two years whilst keeping all the essential elements.

The Staff

This might be a convenient time to mention the staff group, officially divided between social work tutors and subject lecturers, although that division became blurred partly because our geographic isolation meant that our subject lecturers were not often called upon to service courses elsewhere in the College, but, more importantly, because the whole dynamic of the course negated such separate roles. The staff group who brought their experience, knowledge and energy to this whole process for successive student groups, and who led the way through the complex negotiations to achieve the best outcome for our students, was comprised as follows:

Philip Lee[+]	Lecturer in Sociology and Social Administration
David Pithers	Philosophy and Residential Child Care
Myra Garrett	Social Work
Laurie Allmark[+]	Residential Care
Mary Gordon	Social Administration and Social Work
John Durham	Social Work (Community Work)
Kathleen Ralphs[+]	Social Work (Child Care)
Norman Rose[+]	Social Work (Child Care)
Bram Bottle[+]	Social Work (Adults)
Fred Winkless	Social Work (Probation)
Jackie Sandford	Social Work and Residential Child Care
Freda Ruddle	Social Work (Adults)

[+] These staff completed the NISW Fellowship Course in Adult Education
(There was a small turnover of staff so not all of these were with us the whole time.)

I have listed these staff according to my estimation of how much they were initially committed to the development of a radical course. Of these twelve staff, not all of whom were present throughout the whole time, four had post-graduate degrees and eleven had social work qualifications and experience. Once the course took off, they all set to with enthusiasm, although it will be clear from the information given above that conflict between staff, and between staff and students, was not only inevitable but also seen as an essential element in the educational process. Most staff took the outline given above and drove through the two-year course that was eventually delivered. It was my job to give them all the support they required, confirm the final submission for approval by the

CCETSW, keep the team and the College management happy, fight off opposition, agree final assessments and, of course, teach and tutor students. The permanent staff were strengthened by regular visiting lecturers, including the psychoanalyst Dr F. Castillo, psychologist Helen Penn, statistician David Thomas and social researcher Dianne Cunningham, plus a significant number of occasional speakers and activists. These ranged from community workers Peter Beresford and Suzy Croft to drama and group activist Ed Berman and musician Roderick Swanson.[22n] Child and adult psychiatrists and a consultant physician made regular contributions. The whole operation rested on sound administration, and we were very fortunate that our team was led by Brenda Smith, who worked, at different times, with Nan Bridges, Janet Baker, Joan Helbran and Elizabeth Lane. Their workload was steadily increased both by the escalating number of applicants and by the requirements of pre-lecture notes and extended comment on all essays and continuous assessment.

In what ways did the Maidstone course justify the term 'radical' in relation to education and practice? I think that the information given above and the quotations at the beginning of this chapter help answer that question about the real radical nature of our educational experience. The influence of Paulo Freire and the liberation movement rapidly developing in South America was important. Central to this approach was the concept of conscientisation, which challenged the traditional authoritative practice where the teacher sees the pupil as a passive vessel to be filled. Freire's education was a process through which teachers and learners together move towards a critical consciousness; this enables those involved to challenge the oppressional forces that inhibit their freedom of thought and action. His approach was summed up in the phrase 'Liberate the imagination – Imagine the liberation.'[23n] His colleague Alfero explains it as a 'human process in which … consciousness becomes reflective and allows for a deepening awareness' of one's self and the world.[24] Our medium was certainly going to be the message.[25] The same question in relation to practice, and the knowledge and skills required, is more difficult to answer, although the course objective quoted above goes a long way towards doing so. We supported Roy Bailey and Mike Brake's view that 'Radical work is … essentially experiencing the position of the oppressed in the context of the social and economic structure in which they live and are taking action.'[26]

While some courses went no further than a generic programme, others combined subjects in a similar way to us but claimed radicalism by adding community work as an optional sequence. I suspect that we alone extended the community and political interventions to every level of social work practice, including residential care. Ours was a moral, social and political project, never just a tool kit. At Maidstone we went the whole hog! A number of unique factors enabled us to achieve our goals. Our very committed staff were able to use the rush of new developments and closer relationships between academic disciplines to craft a challenging curriculum, and we did this with as much involvement as possible of a great mix of students and based on full, open and honest communication. I think the sociology of deviance, the concepts of role and systems theory were key factors in helping us see the connections which enabled the change from a person-centred pathological stance to wider social perspectives being accepted.[27] We took full advantage of our geographical and educational isolation in a minor technical college in a county relatively isolated by sea, rivers and concrete. We linked with the University (at one stage holding what, with my immature humour, was termed the 'Inter-Course Conference') and had regular dialogue with CCETSW although they themselves were swamped by the demands of national expansion and pressure from employers. In 1974 it introduced the employer led Certificate of Social Service with its emphasis on training rather than education.

Our direction was not always welcomed by employers, and as our students returned to their work a few decided to second no more staff members to the Maidstone course, although the number of applicants continued to rise. At one point we heard that Kent had decided against seconding staff to the course. Given that we had maintained friendly relationships with the staff and training officers my thought was to attribute this to Nick Stacey's visit. I was furious. We had been 'blacklisted.' I discussed this recently with Don Brand, who had been a training officer and has written a biography of Stacey, and he gave a more diplomatic explanation. It was not Stacey but the Principal Training Officer, a somewhat traditional psychiatric social worker, who had led the team to review the variety of courses to which they seconded students and spread the load more equally. An interesting decision given that places outside Kent would be more expensive.

Revised Student Selection

The course proceeded with these ideals, although each year the process evolved at a rapid rate. Selection of students for field and residential courses presented a major problem and consumed high levels of resources. We took the view that the inequality of criteria between residential and fieldwork staff was wrong. While we could not alter the unfair salary structure of these two branches of social work, we could raise the qualification, status and morale of these workers by merging them into the CQSW course. We achieved this from 1973, despite howls of protest from the CCETSW. It was achieved by 'failing' to find any suitable candidates for the RCC course, but instead some excellent residential workers who we thought would survive the full two-year course. Given the expansion of social work at the time, the ratio of applications to acceptances rose from six-to-one to ten-to-one. The initial sort was by form, personal statement and essay. Those invited to attend had to provide three references and attend the College for a full day, complete standard IQ tests and the 16PF Questionnaire[28n] (see Chapter 11) and spend time with current students. The practice of individual psychoanalytically based interviews was replaced by a small panel of staff, practice teachers and a student representative, including group assessment. The criteria for success reflected the course objectives of 'concern for others without being overwhelmed,' ability to think imaginatively, ability to tolerate uncertainty, awareness of self and others, commitment and decisiveness, integrity and experience of life. Successful applicants were then sent a preliminary reading list which included suggested novels and texts.[29] If they had no experience of social work, a preliminary four-week observational placement was arranged.

The First Year

In welcoming students on their first day, we confirmed the objectives, teaching methods and general programme for the course, the balance between college and practice placements and the heavy commitment expected from students throughout the two years. I warned them that the voyage would not be calm as change and conflict were inevitable. That on this course excitement and anxiety could reach high levels. Our belief was that if students survived these two years the move into practice would be less stressful as it was unlikely to be as challenging as the course! It was, however, the staff's role to ensure that they all arrived safely at the end of the two years and were fit to practice in their chosen field of social work. Tutors would always be available for advice and support. At our reunion students expressed surprise, having arrived from a traditional setting and expecting a normal course, on discovering the responsibility given to students: to find their own resources, to invite speakers, to create positive interventions on placements. The whole experience was enormously empowering; students saw that everything and anything seemed possible. In retrospect, perhaps we were all in a naive bubble, but it reflected a time when the social work role was fluid as it needed to establish itself in the large new bureaucracies.

For the first few weeks the emphasis was on experiential teaching; this was led by David Pithers and Phil Lee as 'Thinking About Thinking' (TAT) – or 'Seeing and Understanding.' TAT aimed to provide students with the conceptual tools of analysis that would enable them to make better sense of the conflicting theories encountered during the course.[30] Discussions in initial sessions concentrated on the nature of knowledge, the context of its generation and cultural relativity. What do we each know and how did we come to know it? How are we ever certain, a very rare thing indeed in social work? What is time? What is pain? What is education? The groups then discussed how one argues while avoiding cross purposes, and this led to study techniques from listening to reading, making notes, writing and critical learning in all the media used. What are models, theories and laws? Former students at the reunion recalled being encouraged to question everything, never to make assumptions and having to find new ways of doing things. You could never say a thing without someone saying 'Yes, but…'. Some reported that TAT was the biggest thing that helped them in their career. Given the style of the course, the issue of conflict was given much thought; perhaps our view was best summed up by John Galtung:

> It is not just a question of 'learning how to live with conflict.' That is like the official Victorian attitude to sex – something you must tolerate but not enjoy. In conflict as in sex toleration is not enough: you must like it, love it too. Both are the salt of life. They enrich our experience – if we have the courage and maturity to meet the challenge fully – and even joyfully.[31]

We never managed the initial residential experience in condemned houses, but we certainly had some challenging 72-hour sessions in the local Aylesford Priory. The one that remains most vividly in my memory was when we all put ourselves completely in the hands of Don Bannister and Fay Franscella, who had just published their book advancing the ideas of Kelly's personal construct theory.[32] We all arrived with no knowledge at all of what lay in store. The initial exercise was to stand in a limited space, close our eyes and move around, feeling each other as appropriately as possible in an attempt to identify the gender of each individual with whom we collided! Terrifying, especially for those like me who were by nature extremely shy. I seem to remember that most of the women did well by peeping at the shoes, the men apparently being too naïve or literally minded to 'cheat'. My only other memories are the intensity of the three days and the odd experience of a Carmelite Friar manning the bar before the reign of silence commenced, I think, at 9 pm.

One afternoon a week for six weeks group experiences led by Ed Berman of the consultancy Inter-Action were attended by staff and students.[33n] These sessions complemented the more academic work and aimed to explore different ways of expression through non-verbal communication, sensitivity to self and others in a group and links between this experience and social work intervention. One issue of the course magazine included the following poem, which I think illustrated the feelings experienced by many students.

INTERACTION

Another world of inter-action
of being slowly taken apart.
Broken into so many pieces
some I didn't know belonged to me.

In my small group I feel safe,
they will be gentle.
Their arms protect me as I pass from one to another.

But where do I belong now?
Are these people really friends?
What shall I do, were shall I go?
Home?
To a man who is kind and caring,
but he does not know that I am feeling broken.
I feel his love but not his understanding.

Thursday morning – will the pieces fit together?
Reading poetry – everyone so restful, trusting.
Now I am healed by the knowledge of communion.

– *Sue Austin*

These weeks also saw the start of individual or group tutorials, a new experience for many students as well as staff; the principle was that the tutorials should be used to share ignorance as well as wisdom. There was involvement in the twice weekly student meetings (often followed by separate student/staff meetings) and an opportunity for students to choose optional sessions within the main sequences. These ranged from Professionalism, Theatre Workshop, Women's Estate and Research to Commitment and the Philosophy of Being, Authority, Ideology and Role of the British Working Class. Students were encouraged to create their own options.

David Pithers, Helen Penn and I ran the introductory sequence, Self and Society, with a number of visiting speakers. This sequence explored the language of mental events, the problems of verification and the contribution of the diversity of psychological disciplines. The problem of motive was addressed by Phil Lee as a bridge, with Sociology examining motivation of deviant individuals using Matza's statement that

> ... the search for adventure, excitement and thrill is a subterranean value [which] often exists side by side with the values of security, routinisation and the rest. It is not a deviant value, but must be held in abeyance until the proper moment or circumstance for its expression arrive. The delinquent, for example, is no respecter of the proper time and place as he drifts between criminal and conventional action.[34]

Students worked in pairs or in small or large groups, and towards the end of the sequence were required to present examples from art or literature which had informed their understanding of personal identity.

Students then had to select which course in human behaviour to follow in depth, choosing between Psychoanalysis, Behaviourism, Existentialism or Humanist Schools.[35] Those students who chose the psychoanalytic module had, I think, a unique experience as for one afternoon a week Dr Castillo took them through the theories of Sigmund Freud, Melanie Klein, Anna Freud and the stages of human development from those perspectives. Castillo was a charming, gentle man of Mexican descent who followed a didactic session with open discussion around case histories. At the end of each year his group was invited to his elegant family home in the exclusive Brompton Square.[36n] As time went by, these sessions, which had been inherited from the calm days of the Child Care course became ridiculously out of step with the rest of the course; challenged by staff, students and, given the exorbitant cost, the College. It was a sad day when these sessions came to an end, but it was not before time. Different schools of psychoanalysis remained on the curriculum which also covered behaviourism, specifically the basic theories and procedures relating to operant and classical conditioning. We examined the limits of a theory that ignores internal unobservable phenomena, particularly the work of the linguist philosopher Noam Chomsky who noted that 'as long as we restrict ourselves, conceptually, to the investigation of behaviour, its organisation, its development through interaction with the environment, we are bound to miss these characteristics of language and mind.'[37]

The first-year sequences on Social Administration considered the development of the welfare state: the ideas, social and political controversies and fears and hopes of those involved.[38] Phil also led the Sociology sequence followed by a brief introduction to traditional macro-sociology with a study of socialisation, which combined with the Self and Society sequence. This led into a consideration of the family, the sociology of education and institutions. During and after the placements, issues of law, the sociology of politics, power and authority concluded with combined sequences on Communities.[39] Linked with this was an introductory sequence on Social Research to consider its uses, evaluation and methods.[40]

Building on all these sequences was the Principles and Practice of Social Work, the core sequence bravely run in the first year by Norman Rose, Jackie Sandford and Kathleen Ralphs. This was now contested ground. A comment from one of Phil Lee's papers illustrates the point, as well as the tensions within the staff group:

> I want to end up by analysing the fact that social work exists, despite its desire to ignore the fact, in the muddle of a mosaic of moral problems. The 'escape routes' by which the practitioners of social work avoid the inherent moral problems are what largely account for the present form and existence of social work – like men fumbling and playing blind-man's bluff.[41]

Similar issues were raised by John Ward in a 1972 paper:

> In the fight against poverty and social injustice the social services cannot be on both sides at the same time … The professional go-between is an easier role to play, working in the no man's land ministering to the casualties, and appreciated by both sides. Is it possible to remain neutral in such a fight, especially when it is clear that all the casualties are on one side? Workers in the social services smart at the suggestion that they are pimps of poverty, but how can they continue to live on their increasingly comfortable incomes, growing professional status and expanding career opportunities without taking sides?[42n]

This module offered a broad introduction to field and residential practice, the social and political implications of intervention and the values, knowledge and skills available to a generic practitioner. Issues of agency, client's rights, specific methods, recording and evaluation were considered. Following a critical paper of mine, the traditional approach using case histories was replaced by consideration of generic roles including those of communicator, advocate, care and support person, researcher and employee. Once these were considered, students had to choose between two options. One examined the roles of counsellor, educator, promoter of change and enabler or the roles of reconciler of conflict, intermediary and innovator. The operation of such roles were placed in the context of an open system rather than in a hierarchical model.[43]

Students were cautiously introduced to the systems approach as a possible aid to assessment prior to a decision concerning at which point to intervene in a complex situation and also provide a linking tool between the various models and methods available. Although this approach provided a limited snapshot of situations, it certainly offered a break from the traditional developmental models. My introduction explained that

> I am concerned to offer a model, a framework, an analogy that will help us to clarify phenomena so that we can use our knowledge and skills effectively. The systems approach in this limited sense enables us to develop our own hypothesis, create our own insights and put a definition on reality that is hopefully appropriate for a particular situation … if used imaginatively and with care this approach is likely to be more helpful than harmful and have fewer concealed value judgements within it that others …

Some difficulties were encountered in using the definition of the primary task of every system as that which it must achieve in order to survive. I hoped that some examples, already familiar enough to students, would help:[44]

> A tramp has repeatedly visited the casualty department of a busy general hospital and each time presents with symptoms that are serious enough not to be ignored but are thought to be hysterical in origin. The primary task of the unit is to treat acute illness. The primary task of this particular patient may be to obtain comfort and attention. If the hospital social worker is called in, what is her primary task?

I would like to pay a fulsome tribute to the teamwork between all the staff who committed themselves to this work for so many years. While it is difficult to single out just one member, I particularly appreciated the dynamic understanding of Phil Lee, who broke through the traditional antipathy between sociology and social work. Thirty years earlier the great Wright Mills had dismissively identified social workers as having 'an occupationally trained incapacity to rise above a series of cases.'[45] I hope we buried that charge. The reunion meeting considered how the student experience of the whole course could be influenced by the way in which individual tutors ran tutorials. Experience ranged from those that proceeded on fairly traditional lines of teaching and counselling through Phil Lee's intense sessions to John Durham's concentration on local communities and Myra Garret's tutorials, which were always conducted in a group. She would never see a student alone. Students felt this odd at first but then felt 'special.'

Students were able to change tutors, given reasonable grounds, and quite a few did. This raises the difficult issues of personal relationships within such an intense pressurised experience where people could grow or be damaged. There was certainly a lively social scene throughout the two years, and I am not convinced that we always made the boundaries between staff and students clear enough. The reunion group talked about the effect that this had on their own families. One student remembered that when he applied to the course he was advised that 'If you are in a relationship either get married or break it off as the course will change you.' The poem above raises the same point. My experience is that this is common to most social work courses and some serious research is very overdue. On the other hand some relationships led to long term commitments.

My memory is that before or in the early stages of the first long placement, the whole course participated in a massive exercise in the main hall, organised by Bram Bottle, called 'Conflict and Coalition.' The purpose was to explore how key people within a community achieve change in establishing a provision for their community. The available resources (different colour Lego blocks) were money/credit; knowledge/expertise; information; popularity/esteem and social standing; personal energy; legitimacy/legality; political influence. Some 24 roles were randomly assigned from local authority chief officers; local politicians; MPs; community workers; representatives from local media; the unemployed; physically disabled people; a young delinquent and his mother; a claimants' union worker; and someone from a tenants' association. At the start of the game each had the appropriate mix of resources, which they then had to use to get want they wanted. Participants were initially offered five projects. Once the start whistle went it was up to them to form coalitions in order to get a particular project approved. At the end of the first fiscal year (60 minutes) a list of projects that had been agreed was posted for all to see. Now that everyone knew the opposition, the fight for final acceptance occupied the second period. It was an exhausting, tense and amusing seven-hour day and, I hope, a very useful learning experience for everyone involved.

All the above college work took some 24 weeks (59%) of the first year, leaving 41% available for practice placements. The first assessed placement was four weeks' observation in a school, the purpose of which was to observe child development and the dynamics of the establishment. Early in the second term a residential placement had to be completed. This was followed by a 14-week placement in a student unit or local community agency with concurrent college work varying from one to three days a week. In this sequence students could work individually or in small groups, either within the agency or unit or based in college, to develop projects in the same area as their peers. The intention was to make clear links between formal and informal structures within a given community to enhance a full understanding of the interaction between the different players, time being allowed in college for groups to discuss and compare their experiences.

Practice Teachers

All this time we had taken great care to inform and involve fieldwork teachers and project supervisors, without whom we could not proceed. In March 1973 all were invited to a full day meeting to discuss our plans with a presentation and discussions in plenary and small group sessions of teachers, students and staff. We were anxious to share our plans 'to liberate students from the restrictions of a formalised, highly structured model of education with all the implications this has regarding such matters as role boundaries, the sharing of power, course planning, etc.' My circulated paper included several quotations from the Seebohm Report, particularly the need for local authorities to recognise that staff may become involved in groups critical of services. Interestingly, in view of how the Seebohm vision was soon drowned, I included a quote from the USA commenting that 'many professional altruists have become political activists, and this is a transformation that Government will neither accept nor forgive.'[46] We were clear about our position: that, although we lagged behind the continent in only allowing a two-year course, we had to ensure that by the end of the course the student had a deep understanding of all the forces bearing on the client and the profession. They would have a thorough understanding of the ethical base for their practice, have the knowledge and skills that are central to practice with individuals, groups, residential work and community work, and have received an introduction to their chosen specialism.

Given the breadth of the task confronting a generic social worker our only option in two years was to teach the broad vision and principles first and then the narrower specialisms. The reverse was not educationally possible. Therefore employers had to accept that it was their responsibility to train newly qualified workers in their own policies and procedures as well as provide supervisors and managers with time to complete the specific training that we had started. We always made this clear in our brochures and communication. I reassured the supervisors that although they would hear a great deal about student participation the final accountability for all aspects of the course, including assessment, remained with the staff and practice teachers. All information, personal files, correspondence and reports would be open to students. We hoped that those present would accept our position and, to their everlasting credit, the vast majority agreed to go along with the vision and the practicalities. Perhaps the organisational chaos and disputed objectives in their own agencies may have persuaded them that anything was worth trying! Some idea of the changes in the pattern of placements is shown in the following table:

Distribution of Fieldwork Placements by Agency

	1968–1972	1972–1975
Local authority departments	59%	25%
Probation Service	8%	17%
Psychiatric hospitals	3%	10%
General hospitals	7%	13%
Child guidance clinics	16%	10%
Volunteer agencies /community placements	7%	25%
Total	100%	100%

Students and staff owed a great deal to the practice teachers who took on the extra workload with little recognition from their agencies. In recognition of this we invited them to day conferences at least once a year, which we hoped they and our own staff and students would find of value. One memorable day R. D. Laing, whose ideas chimed well with the psychedelic fashions of the day, gave an address followed by one from his main challenger, Peter Sedgwick. This was, given Laing's status as a cultural icon of the day, very well attended with high expectations. He had agreed to attend providing that he was driven from his home in Hampstead and back, a task which fell to me accompanied by David who I think anticipated some deep conversations en route. The seventy-mile journey via Rochester meant a very early start, but we arrived more or less on time for a brief glimpse into a home enhanced by the chaos of young children. The journey to Maidstone went badly due to excessive traffic with 'the man' quietly in the back with his young PA who seemed to spend the time feeding pills to our Glaswegian speaker. Meanwhile the audience waited patiently. Phil Lee, apologising for the delay, was taken aback by the great cheer that greeted his announcement, his on-stage stance naturally replicating the lithe Mick Jagger. Once the great man took to the stage his accent and wandering presentation meant that it was almost impossible to follow his argument. He certainly lost quite a few followers.[47n] Peter Sedgwick, a radical lecturer in Politics and Psychiatry and a dedicated libertarian Marxist, therefore had an easier time presenting his research into Laing's life, writings and ideas, gently taking them apart as confused, logically redundant and pursued with a dogmatism which ignored the selection of his patients and the temporary nature of his 'cures.' He was concerned that the much vaunted anti-psychiatry movement would be used by governments to cut NHS provision for psychiatric services.[48]

An equally exciting day was a duel between Rhodes Boyson, the verbose Head of a comprehensive school in North London and a mix between the late comedian Jimmy Edwards and Boris Johnson,[49n] and the Professor of Education at Oxford. Speaking second, the professor won his audience over by commenting that 'now comes the quiet voice of reason.' Another popular speaker was Roy Bailey of Sheffield Polytechnic and a member of the National Deviancy Conference, who, with Kenneth Irwin, Director of Camden Social Services, addressed the issue 'What is a social problem?' by arguing that such problems should not be seen as pathological aberrations, indicative of disturbed personalities. The Principal of the College chaired the day. The conference that puzzled the audience most was a demonstration by an American new-age therapist, I suspect from the newly established Esalen Institute in California. My main memory is of her asking for a volunteer who would have a conversation with an empty chair. I was so relieved when an experienced probation officer not only stepped forward but also poured out his ambivalent feelings towards his father to this piece of furniture. Victory for the new 'encounter' techniques, but probably not a technique that many present would use.[50]

The Second Year

The summer holiday included preparation of the extended essay that students would have agreed at the start of the second year and complete halfway through that year, 56% of which would be spent on a practical placement/project. This lasted for 23 weeks, four of which would be full time, the rest for three days a week. These placements reflected the student's choice and were usually related to the specialism that they wished to pursue, but had to be different to those undertaken in the first year. For the final four weeks students could choose a special placement, often residential (the Henderson or Cassell Hospitals, Grendon Underwood Prison, Mr Lywood's Finchden Manor or a special project based perhaps on a welfare rights stall or welfare pressure group). Some students arranged an attachment to a GP practice. As the issue of homelessness, centred on nearby Kings Hill, became a national issue, students and staff hired a coach in order to join the protests in Whitehall. Students also organised a five-day visit to Denmark to examine services for the under fives.

The TAT sessions continued throughout the second year. In many ways their dynamic carried them through, but there were sessions on moral judgements in the language of therapy to existentialism and freedom. David tabled a series of papers extensively examining selected philosophers from Marx to Max Stirner. He and Phil introduced a major essay, posing the question 'Radical residential child care – Trojan horse or non runner?'.

The second-year sequence delivered by David and myself on Self and Society commenced with a review of the first-year material examined through different perspectives and evaluating their implications for practice. This was followed by consideration of the causes, treatment, and personal and social issues of mental illness and disability in children and adults.[51] John Bazalgette, from the Grubb Institute,[52] ran experiential group sessions examining how we interact in groups and organisations and how this affects our internal and external life. The works of Wilhelm Reich, Carl Jung, Eric Fromm and Harry Stack Sullivan[53] were examined, as was the whole question of 'cure' in these areas.[54] There was also a short course on Social Research run by Phil and me with input from David Thomas from the Maths Department. This considered the use of research, evaluation and methods of research that students might find useful in their projects, placements or employment.[55]

The Principles of Practice and Social Administration sequences were combined to study professional practice and the settings in which it operated in order to respond to a range of personal and social problems. Initially the sequence considered people with physical or mental disabilities, care of the elderly, dying and delinquency. This was followed by addressing preventive work in family and community situations, child care and the special needs of minority groups. This sequence was run by Kathleen Ralphs, John Durham and Fred Winkless.[56] Given all that had gone before, these sequences were more down to earth given the imminent placements and employment. This naturally led to some problems of organisations raising the issue of how they define their actual aim, whether they actually follow it by structure, policies and procedures, whether all this results in the desired practice and how the failure to clarify aims leads to diverse problems and a range of unintended consequences. This and the associated issues of authority and power were intensely studied in seminar groups, particularly how the culture of an organisation spills over to the clients and how the personal distance found in most organisations relates to practice. Given that organisational politics lean towards inertia, how can staff counter this? From this came consideration of the unique position of social workers as 'inside-outsiders' and their potential for effective research which could be used to assist both clients and policy. Is there always a need for action or is non-intervention an option? This discussion centred around Schur's writing on delinquency; given the huge resources entailed in dealing with large numbers of minor offenders, why don't we just leave kids alone?[57]

This module was cross-referenced with Phil's Sociology sequence which concentrated on the development of self and its relation to social structure related to the sociology of deviance. The sequences ended with a critical investigation of the contribution of sociology to social work.[58] The emergence of a very personal focus and the related studies in deviance in the late 1960s were of particular interest to social work, and certainly fascinated me. We considered the emergence, transmission, maintenance and modification of social meanings, which sees social structures as a vast shifting complex of these meanings. Harold Garfinkel's writings combined critical analysis of social situations with an imaginative writing style explaining how ethnomethodology seeks to analyse how people go about finding meanings in their everyday interactions and then interpreting that phenomenon. Garfinkel described his approach as 'an organisational study of a member's knowledge of his ordinary affairs, of his own organised enterprises, where that knowledge is treated by us as part of the same settings that it also makes orderable.'[59] Perhaps Garfinkel was particularly attractive for students as he dealt with 'the world of tricky harassed little devils' that were all of us. The sociology of deviance certainly opened the eyes of social workers and many others, marking a radical change from focussing on the deviant individual or group to the interaction of the person with society. In doing so Goffman extended the ordinary understanding of that term to embrace criminality, mental illness, homosexuality in all its forms, weirdoes or geniuses. Such richness was very inviting, casting deviance not as the quality of the act that a person commits but as a consequence of rules and sanctions created by others. A deviant is someone to whom that label has been applied, often confirmed and exacerbated by the media. In relation to mental illness, Szasz commented that,

> When one speaks of mental illness the norm from which deviation is measured is a psychological and ethical standard. Yet the remedy is sought in terms of medical measures that – it is hoped and assumed – are free from wide differences of ethical value.[60]

Alongside these sequences, a number of voluntary study groups were available that were run by staff, students or visiting specialists and open to all. These included Social Work with the Dying, Work with Offenders and Drug Abusers, The Morality of Caring, Adolescent Pregnancy and Sign Language. I enjoyed the latter, which was run by a student who was qualified in this skill although pressure of work as final assessments loomed meant that I had to withdraw prematurely. Norman ran a popular option group on

The Arts in Social Work, which considered the role of the artist in society, the therapeutic use of drama, music, painting and drawing and whether certain works of art could illuminate key social work concepts. A student ran a sequence on Documentary Films to prompt discussion on social problems and I showed some major relevant dramas whenever there seemed a space in the hectic schedule. Naturally one of these was the 1966 docudrama *Cathy Come Home*, which had caused such a furore when first broadcast.[61n]

Assessment

At the end of each placement the fieldwork teacher was responsible for the production of a comprehensive report, which concluded whether the student had passed or failed. The latter meant either failing the course or, in exceptional circumstances, completing another placement. Teachers referred to the standards that our students were aiming for; in turn, students (if they were failing a grade) had the right to challenge a teacher's decision via a separate report. Failing grades were not given unless the student and the College had been warned and discussions held in good time so that every step could be taken to rectify the situation.

The final tutor's report was required to provide an overall picture of the student's personal qualities, specialism and achievements in all areas of the course. The summary had to show areas of strengths and weaknesses, levels of attainment, special aptitudes and potential for development in future practice. In order to obtain the CQSW, students had to pass the fieldwork final report, achieve a positive tutor's report, pass the extended essay, have successfully presented an assigned paper to a seminar or tutorial group, and received a 'pass' in four essays. The term 'essay' is misleading as students could choose the medium. In practice, although most submitted written work we did have to assess some beautiful drawings, poems, plays and sculptures. Much of this was inspired by Norman Rose's sequence outlined above which used the facilities of the art college which shared our campus and our view of adult education.

Much of the final hassle around the assessments was contained in the last three weeks when students were back in college and the final board was held, usually a week before the final day. This was usually chaired by our ever-patient Head of Department and included tutors, lecturers, one student representative and two external assessors who then met the student group for an open discussion; this was often a very challenging meeting when students who had perhaps failed one of the nine elements would be fought for by staff and usually the student rep. These final boards were always tense, especially as some staff were opposed to the whole concept of assessment. I found my last board particularly challenging as, apart from the fact that it was our Head of Department's last one before retiring, Myra Garret decided to knit her way through it and when called upon to respond to the blank spaces she had left in the various lists just said 'Pass, I guess.' Each board was followed in due course by the external assessors' report. Our assessors during this period were Peter Righton, Roy Bailey, Head of Department at Sheffield Polytechnic, and Sarah McCabe, Reader in Criminology at the University of Oxford. In 1972 they commented positively on the move from 'pre-digested' essays to lively work showing critical thinking and freedom of expression. Tutors' extended comments on essays were welcomed, as were improvements in the extended essay. The variety of placements was commended, as were the final reports, which were of exceptional quality (although perhaps sometimes too long). They had seen an interesting course providing continuous stimulation and challenge and a high level of student performance. In 1973 more progress was noted, as were the tension and stress inevitable with continuous assessment, but students had produced good work, of originality in some cases and of reasonable scholarship in others. The work showed a strength, cohesion and balance between the main sequences. Fieldwork reports were still improving, as was student input, and discussion was clearly of value in furthering the student's forward learning.

By 1976 examiners commented on the impressively high standard of work and the beneficial, if painful, result of the extensive comments made by tutors and the subsequent disagreements. They considered that in general the course seemed to be highly successful in its aim of developing a critical approach to social work and the social sciences and that students had the capacity to express authentic feelings even when they were ambivalent or confused. 'Students who come to this course expecting to be fed with intellectual or practical certainties run a considerable risk of feeling cheated. The assessors find this course to be innovative and stimulating. It was clear that students leave the college not only challenged and stretched to the limits of their ability – in their general education as well as in their professional training – but with the zest to continue learning after departure.'

As this is part of my story, I should mention a formal letter sent by the assessors in 1974 congratulating us on achieving

> ... the most difficult balance between the training of 'professional social workers' and the wider education of an intelligent and well motivated group of human beings. That this is a difficult task was borne out by the manifest anxieties expressed in our last meeting with the students and individual meetings. The intellectual and emotional uncertainty that is the price – and the reward – of free intellectual discourse seemed to be the main problem which found vocal expression. For that, you and we and they should be profoundly grateful since no educational process worth its salt produces unquestioning commitment to any single view of the human situation. The assessors however spotted a significant problem in that in their view students had not seemed to have worked out the logic of their demands upon the course and the tutors. While students claim and are present at all aspects including assessment they failed to pursue this argument to its conclusion by excluding staff when the assessors met the students. Unless such issues were resolved democratic ideals in educational establishments were put at risk. The letter should be passed to students.

It certainly was.

The departure of a group of students was always difficult and emotional given the history that we had shared for two intensive years and the relationships that we had all formed. Feelings of success and loss competed with one another in a great tangle. The situation was well commented on by a personal paper by David:

> It is into a climate of moral, political and theoretical dispute, confusion and confrontation that our students go when they leave college. Increasingly they will be called upon to justify their behaviour and their values to a better informed, less respectful public who will not be subdued by cliches, no matter how well worn they may be. We are not training people for a trade, where the objects even if abused are yet uncomplaining. Our students are bound for creative engagements with distressed people, often in an environment of unremitting hostility, where solutions are unavailable and experience tragic. Here bureaucratic systems and social engineering are as irrelevant as they are undesirable.

The following is another extract from the course magazine:

TRAD. COURSE HYMN

When this weary course is over
Oh, how happy we shall be
We'll take our little bits of paper
and flush them down the lavotree

No more hamming up from Norman
No more flashing from Phil Lee
No more quotes from rotten Nietzsche
from existential Pithers D

We are pissed with epistomology
We've had our Phil of Philosophy
And as for ethnomethodology
We'll leave that up to Phil Lee

We'll make lots of banal statements
Chocletics we will eat
David Pithers will ignore us
Delivering papers in the street

No more booze ups down the Admiral
No more ping pong in Hut D
Malcolm can we stay here longer
Instead of two years make it three

— *Anon*

At our small reunion one former staff member explained a significant change in her attitude. In the past when a client suggested that if she really wanted to help she should be on the town hall steps in protest, she had felt this would have been unprofessional. Not now; in fact it was she who had organised the coach to London for the homeless demonstrations. Emphasising a theme of the meeting, a student who had completed a successful career in the Probation Service explained that, 'One of my strongest memories of learning from the course is to question everything, never make an assumption and assess/analyse everything, back to last principles. This has always stood me in good stead, regarding family assessment, using differing psychological therapies etc. and developing family therapy, as previously our service had only been doing individual therapy/counselling. It was also possible to integrate mental health services across health and social care.'

OTHER ACTIVITIES

By 1972 we were venturing beyond our campus to debate with the outside world. Nancy Hazel and I launched a series of 'Canterbury Consultations,' essentially five intensive seminars to discuss a selection of papers circulated in advance exploring recent developments in social work and education. Ken Irwin, Director of Camden Social Services, commenced with a search for a definition of social work. The second session was on Systems Theory led by Mr W. Lawrence from the Tavistock Institute and the third addressed by Steve Box was on Deviance, Reality and the Social Worker. Professor Barbara Tizard from the Institute of Education started a day on A Sociological Approach to Residential Care, and the final session was kicked off by Peter Leonard on The Application of Theory to Social Work Practice. Following each initial presentation, Nancy and I ran the seminars for the rest of the day. It was an exhausting but really interesting project. In April 1973 Rev Peter Absolon, one of our valued community practice teachers, addressed a Social Services Conference held at the University describing the network of community groups that he had established in the Medway Towns. He concluded a moving address with an aim for community action 'to help the weak realise their strength and to help the strong realise their weakness.'

After a controversial article on Behaviourism in Social Work in Residential Care, David addressed Guy's Hospital's Department of Community Medicine on the Origins and Nature of Conflict in Social Work.[62] I went to war in the pages of *Social Work Today* to challenge an article on 'Staff tensions in social work education,'[63] which described tutors as non-graduates and non-teacher-trained who seem to enjoy telling practitioners how to run their departments instead of developing radical ideas on the courses. It also charged that tutors carried over their 'therapeutic' activities to students, denying that education was essentially a process involving the whole person. In the same year I published an article in the same magazine commenting on the similarities and differences in the two processes.[64]

DEPARTURE

In early 1976 I discussed with Laurie that I thought we had achieved much of our original ambition regarding the basic values of the course: transparency, honesty, mutual involvement of students and staff and a good network of practice teachers who were committed to us. The course dynamic was running well and although there would be changes made to content and methods there was a strong group of staff who would carry the ideals forward. We had somehow managed to avoid problems that had been encountered elsewhere. Students at the University of Sussex had been promised democracy but then found that tutors and the whole system worked to restrict it. When they rebelled, tutors looked for individual pathology, leaving a chronic sense of impotence and frustration. It seemed to me that we had reached a plateau where I needed to take personal stock; I realised that although the task was not finished, in fact it could never be said to be finished.

Achieving this, as well as the busy research work (see Chapter 11) and my own MA, had taken a very heavy toll on me and my family. Managing tensions between the College hierarchy and our culture, the lengthy discussions between both of those and the CCETSW and facing the conflicts that arose most weeks within the staff and students, let alone coping with my direct teaching load, had frankly exhausted me. My main issue was the peculiar circular nature of academic life. You welcomed new students, engaged with them through challenging times, and over two years we knew each other well. However, from early in their first term you were moderating the 500 applications for the next intake, then interviewing and starting the whole process all over again – very emotionally wearing! Added to this was the fact that, unlike some courses, the fast changing nature of our course meant that virtually all of our teaching notes had to be re-written every year. It was clearly time for a change. I considered other academic posts but then by chance came the opportunity for something new. I applied for a post with the Department of Health and Social Services in the Social Service Inspectorate's Development Group promoting new policies and practices across the country. I naively became a civil servant, a situation which would not last long. It was a very sad farewell; depressingly, my resignation letter to the Principal raised exactly the same concerns as those of the previous course leaders who had left six years previously.

NOTES AND REFERENCES

1. Postman, N. and Weingartner, C. (1971). *Teaching as a Subversive Activity*. London: Penguin Educational Special, p. 204.
2. Freire, P. (1972). *Pedagogy of the Oppressed*. London: Penguin Books, p. 56.
3. Blackley, E. (1968). 'Building the Curriculum: The Foundation of Professional Competence,' in *Education for Social Work, Readings in Social Work, Vol. IV*. E. Younghusband, Ed. London: George Allen and Unwin, p. 15.
4. Peter Leonard began his career armed with two degrees and a post-graduate diploma from the London School of Business when he set out to contribute to making British social services progressive for the people. He was the youngest member of the Seebohm Committee and a Founding Professor of Applied Social Sciences at the University of Warwick before moving to McGill University in Montreal as Director of the School of Social Work in 1987. Peter died in Canada in 2013.
5. Peter Righton had a long career in residential child care and had lectured in child protection for the Open University and Birmingham colleges. He was Director of Education at the NISW

and held this post for some years. He was a founder member of the Paedophile Information Exchange (PIE). In the 1980s he wrote in favour of consensual sexual relations between adults and children, and in 1992 he was convicted for importing child pornography and was warned in relation to a previous assault. In 2012 it was alleged that he was centrally involved in sexual abuse of children by prominent members of the establishment staying at a guest house in southwest London. It later emerged that in the 1980s newspapers wishing to publish these scandals had been served with D-notices preventing publication on grounds of national security. During 2014/15, while the government struggled to establish a wide ranging national inquiry, it was revealed that many of the relevant files were lost or incomplete. Peter died in 2007. In 2019 the identity of the man who had made these allegations was revealed. He was charged with perverting the cause of justice and fraud, convicted and sentenced to 18 years imprisonment. His allegations had caused immeasurable damage and acute distress to many honourable prominent members of society.

6. Tilda Goldberg left Berlin in 1933, studied at the LSE and qualified as a psychiatric social worker in 1936, editing that association's journal from 1961 to 1965. As Director of Research at the NISWT she had the opportunity to encourage social work colleagues and students to evaluate their work, to be rigorous in their approach to their data and back up their views with clear research data. See Goldberg, E. (1970). *The Families of Schizophrenic Patients*. London: Bedford Square Press; Goldberg, E. et al. (1970). *Helping the Aged. A Field Experiment in Social Work*. London: Allen & Lane.

7. Meyer, H. J., Borgatta, E. F. and Jones, W. C. (1965). *Girls at Vocational High. An Experiment in Social Work Intervention*. London: Sage.

8. Cooper, D. (1969). *The Dialectics of Liberation*. London: Penguin; Illich, D. (1973). *Celebration of Awareness, A Call for Institutional Revolution*. London: Penguin; Jeffreys, M. (1966). *Personal Values in the Modern World*. London: Penguin; Lyons, J. (1970). *Chomsky*. London: Fontana; Marcuse, H. (1969). *Eros and Civilization*. London: Sphere; Marcuse, H. (1968). *One Dimensional Man*. London: Sphere; Walker, K. (1962). *Diagnosis of Man*. London: Pelican.

9. Berne, E. (1967). *Games People Play. The Psychology of Human Relations*. London: Pan Books; Eysenck, H. (1962). *Sense and Nonsense in Psychology*. London: Pelican; Fromm, E. (1970). *The Crisis of Psychoanalysis*. London: Pelican; Harris, A. (1973). *I'm OK – You're OK (Transactional Analysis)*. London: Pan; Jehu, D. (1967). *Learning Theory & Social Work*. London: Routledge & Kegan Paul; Laing, R. and Esterson, A. (1970). *Sanity, Madness and the Family*. London: Pelican; Laing, R. (1969). *The Self and Others*. London: Pelican.

10. Becker, H. (1963). *Outsiders. Studies in the Sociology of Deviance*. Toronto: Collier Macmillan; Becker, E. (1970). *The Birth and Death of Meaning*. London: Penguin Education; Berger, P. and Luckman, T. (1967). *The Social Construction of Reality*. London: Penguin; Garfinkel, H. (1967). *Studies in Ethnomethodology*. Englewood Cliffs, New Jersey: Prentice Hall; Goffman, E. (1969). *The Presentation of Self in Everyday Life*. London: Allen Lane; Goffman, E. (1969). *Where the Action Is*. London: Allen Lane; Plant, R. (1970). *Social and Moral Theory in Casework*. London: Routledge & Kegan Paul.

11. Alinsky, S. (1971). *Rules for Radicals. A Pragmatic Primer for Realistic Radicals*. New York: Vintage Books; Lees, R. (1972). *Politics and Social Work*. London: Routledge & Kegan Paul; Leonard, P. (1966). *Sociology in Social Work*. London: Routledge & Kegan Paul; Polsky, L. (1962). *Cottage Six*. New York: Wiley (Russell Sage Foundation); Timms, N. (1968). *Language of Social Casework*. London: Routledge & Kegan Paul.

12. BASW (1970). *Research and Social Work*. BASW Monograph No 4; King, R., Raynes, N. and Tizard, J. (1971). *Patterns of Residential Care*. London: Routledge & Kegan Paul; Mayer, J. and Timms, N. (1970). *The Client Speaks, Working Class Impressions of Casework*. London: Routledge & Kegan Paul.

13. *Committee on Higher Education: Report of the Committee appointed by the Prime Minister under the Chairmanship of Lord Robbins* (1963). London: HMSO, Cmnd. 2154.
14. See George, V. and Wilding, P. (1985). *Ideology and Social Welfare (Radical Social Policy Series)*. London: Routledge; Hazel, N. (1981). *A Bridge to Independence*. London: Blackwell.
15. Anon (1970). 'The Making of a Director'. *The Hospital Journal and Social Services Review*, November 21st.
16. Robinson, J. (1963). *Honest to God*. London: SCM Press; Stacey, N. (1971). *Who Cares. The Autobiography of an Impatient Parson*. London: Hodder & Stoughton; Brand, D. (2008). *Nick Stacey and Kent Social Services (A Study in Leadership)*. London: Brand Book.
17. Hazel, N. (1990). *Fostering Teenagers: Two Innovative Schemes in Kent*. London: National Foster Care. The Special Family Placement Project was established as a pilot to examine whether a community based fostering scheme based on the Swedish model could be established. Can 'ordinary people' in their own homes provide effective help to teenagers with severe problems if you spent as much money as it costs to provide residential care? Nancy and Rosemary Cox worked semi-independently within the Social Services Department to recruit suitable foster parents who were prepared to undertake training and become the child's focal therapist. These families formed local groups to support and develop each other. Careful matching was achieved between the 'professional foster families' and the young person. Once the placement was made, the foster parents and child had open access at any time to support and advice from key people, the local group, other children in the project, social workers or the family of origin. It worked on the basis of a written contract defining the tasks to be undertaken and a time scale. Remarkable success was achieved with very challenging adolescents and the scheme was eventually absorbed into the department.
18. The Ralphs Report (1975). *Report of the Working Party on the Role and Training of Education Welfare Officers*. London: Local Government Training Board.
19. See Ball, C. and Ball, M. (1973). *Education for Change*. London: Penguin; Friere, P. (1972). *Pedagogy of the Oppressed*. London: Penguin; Friere, P. (1972). *Cultural Action for Freedom*. London: Penguin; Postman and Weingartner, *op. cit.*; Reimer, E. (1971). *School is Dead. An Essay on Alternatives in Education*. London: Penguin.
20. BASW (1975). *Code of Ethics, Objectives*. Birmingham, para 9.
21. Lees, *op. cit.*, p. 78. Ray Lees was a member of staff at Maidstone.
22. Helen Penn has maintained a special interest in early childhood education. She has a brilliant academic career and is currently Professor of Early Childhood at the University of East London. In 2007 she launched the International Centre for the Study of the Mixed Economy of Childcare. Thomas was Senior Lecturer in the Department of Mathematics at the Medway College. David Lambert followed his experience in residential child care and as leader of the Sidcup course. He was later appointed as an Inspector for the Department of Health and Social Services and was appointed as Assistant Chief Inspector for the London Region, and was awarded the CBE in 1998. He died in December 2010. Peter Beresford and Suzy Croft were radical, very active community workers living on benefits in Clapham, South London. They published local advice sheets. They developed particular interests in user involvement, disability and mental health. Peter is currently Director of the Centre for Citizen Participation at Brunel University and Chair of Shaping Our Lives, the national disabled people's and service user's organisation. He was awarded an OBE in 2007. Suzy Croft has continued in community involvement and social work practice since the early 1970s. She has been a pioneer in the development of user involvement in social work and social care policy and practice, influencing policy and practice both through her role as a trustee of national organisations and through her writing and research and has also been active in international organisations and activities. Since 1993 Suzy has been closely involved in palliative

care at St John's Hospice, where she is team leader. She has published widely, is a research fellow at Brunel University and was a board member of the College of Social Work. Roderick Swanson was a professor at the Royal College of Music and is a celebrated broadcaster, lecturer and writer. He was President of the Incorporated Society of Musicians for 2008.

23. This summary comment was written by Paolo Freire in David Pither's copy of *Pedagogy of the Oppressed*.
24. Alfero, L. (1972). 'New Contributions to Social Work Education.' Paper presented to the XVIth International Congress of School of Social Work, August, 1972, The Hague.
25. Mcluhan, M. (1964). *Understanding Media. The Extension of Man*. New York: McGraw.
26. Bailey, R. and Brake, M. (1975). *Radical Social Work*. London: Edward Arnold, p. 9. See also Corrigan, P. and Leonard, P. (1978). *Social Work Practice Under Capitalism: A Marxist Approach*. London: MacMillan.
27. Taylor, L. (1971). *Deviance and Society*. London: Michael Joseph; Cohen, S. (1971). *Images of Deviance*. London: Penguin; Buckley, W. (1967). *Sociology and Modern Systems Theory*. New Jersey: Prentice Hall; Banton, M. (1965). *Roles*. London: Tavistock.
28. The Sixteen Personality Factor (16PF) Questionnaire had been developed by the psychologist Raymond Cattell since the 1940s in an attempt to measure the source traits of human personality based on multiple factor analysis. The test followed the demand for a test which would give the fullest information in the shortest time. Students were asked to avoid the in between response wherever possible and to go through the questions quickly and honestly. We used the 1957 edition with 1964 updates.
29. Axeline, V. (1971). *Dibs; In Search of Self*. London: Penguin; Salinger, J. (1951). *Catcher in the Rye*. London: Penguin; Greenberg, J. (1964). *I Never Promised You a Rose Garden*. London: Pan; Kesey, K. (1962). *One Flew Over the Cuckoo's Nest*. New York: Viking; Malcolm X. (1965). *Autobiography of Malcolm X*. New York: Grove; Beedell, C. (1970). *Residential Life With Children*. London: Routledge & Kegan Paul; Timms, N. (1967). *Social Work: An Outline for an Intending Student*. London: Routledge & Kegan Paul; Koestler A. (1967). *The Ghost in the Machine*. London: Hutchinson.
30. Hospers, J. (1967). *Introduction to Philosophical Analysis*. London: Routledge & Kegan Paul; Wilson, J. (1963). *Thinking with Concepts (Part 1)*. London: Cambridge University Press; Berger, J. (1972). *Ways of Seeing* London: Penguin.
31. Galtung, J. (1969). 'Conflict as a Way of Life,' *New Society*, October 11th, No 368.
32. Bannister, D. and Fransella, F. (1971). *Inquiring Man, The Theory of Personal Constructs*. London: Penguin.
33. Ed Berman was heavily involved in alternative theatre in the 1960s and 70s. He formed Inter-Action as a creative game method in 1968 to explore new approaches to motivate learning in disadvantaged inner-city areas. This led to street theatre with Dogg's Troupe, City Farms, the Fun Arts Bus and many other community projects. Ed was awarded the MBE in 1979. See http://www.inter-action.uk.com.
34. Matza, D. (1964). *Delinquency and Drift*. New York: John Wiley.
35. References included the following: **Novels:** Dostoevsky, F. (1880). *The Brothers Karamazov*. London: Penguin 1966; Camus, A. (1946). *The Outsider (The Stranger)*. London: Hamilton; Burgess, A. (1967). *The Clockwork Orange*. London: Heinemann. **Texts:** Skinner, B. (1971). *Beyond Freedom and Dignity*. New York: Hackett; Ryle, G. (1949). *The Concept of Mind*. London: Hutchinson; Freud, S. (2002). *Civilisation and its Discontents*. London: Penguin; Rogers, C. (1961). *On Becoming a Person*. London: Penguin; Erikson, C. (1965). *Childhood and Society*. London: Hogarth; Laing, R. (1965). *The Divided Self: An Existential Study in Sanity and Madness*. London: Penguin.

36. Fortunato Gabriel Castillo had studied in Mexico and Illinois before taking a teaching fellowship at Harvard. Moving to London, he worked at St Mary's Hospital and then as a consultant psychiatrist to the USAF at Lakenheath. He was a member of the British Psychoanalytic Society, having been sponsored by Anna Freud. At the time of his work in Maidstone he was a teaching consultant at the Hampstead Child Guidance Clinic.
37. Chomsky, N. (1970). 'Language and Freedom,' in *For Reasons of State*. New York: The New Press, p. 185.
38. Bibliography included Martin, I. (1971). *From Workhouse to Welfare: The Development of the Welfare State*. London: Penguin; Dangerfield, S. (1971). *The Death of Liberal England*. London: Paladin; Townsend, P. (1959). *The Last Refuge*. London: Routledge & Kegan Paul; Orwell, G. (1937). *The Road to Wigan Pier*. London: Gollancz; Disraeli, E. (1987). *Sybil or the Tale of Two Nations*. London: Penguin; Dickens, C. (2012). *Little Dorrit*. London: Penguin Classics.
39. Mills, C.W. (1959). *The Sociological Imagination*. Oxford: Oxford University Press; Cotgrove, A. (1967). *The Science of Society*. London: Allen & Unwin; Reisman, D. (1950). *The Lonely Crowd*. New Haven: Yale University Press; Laing, R. (1970). *The Politics of the Family*. London: Tavistock; Jackson, B. and Marsden, D. (1973). *Education and the Working Class*. London: Penguin; Goffman, E. (1968). *Asylums. Essays on the Social Situation of Mental Patients and Other Inmates*. London: Penguin.
40. Miller, E. and Gwynne, G. (1972). *A Life Apart*. London: Tavistock; Timms, N. (Ed.) (1973). *The Receiving End*. London: Routledge & Kegan Paul; Tripoldi, T., Fellin, P. and Meyer, H. (1969). *The Assessment of Social Research*. Ithaca, NY: Peacock.
41. Lee, P. (1975). 'The Social Work Profession, Welfare and Fairy Tales,' Draft Paper, May 15th.
42. Ward, J. (1969) 'The Haves and Have-nots – A Policy for Change.' Ward was Head of Training, National Council for Social Service and Chairman, Association of Community Workers.
43. Biestek, F. (1961). *The Casework Relationship*. London: Allen & Unwin; Bartlett, H. (1970). *The Common Base of Social Work Practice*. London: NISW; Halmos, P. (1970). *The Personal Service Society*. New York: Constable; Hamilton, G. (1940). *Theory and Practice of Social Work*. New York: Columbia; Wootton, B. (1959). *Social Science and Social Pathology*. London: Unwin; Beedell, C. (1970). *Residential Life with Children*. London: Routledge & Kegan Paul; Reid, W. and Epstein, L. (1972). *Task Centred Casework*. New York: Columbia; Satir, V. (1967). *Conjoint Family Therapy*. New York: Science & Behaviour; Goetschius, G. and Trash, M. (1967). *Working with Unattached Youth*. London: Tavistock; Leaper, R. (1968). *Community Work*. London: NCSS; Rice, R. (1973). 'Organising to Innovate,' *Social Casework Magazine*, January; Cartwright, D. (1949). 'Achieving Change in People: Some Applications of Group Dynamic Theory,' *Human Relations*, Vol. II, No 3, pp. 253–267.
44. Heam, G. (Ed.) (1969). *The General Systems Approach (A Contribution to the Holistic Conception of Social Work)*. London: C.S.W.E.; Emery, F. E. (1969). *Systems Thinking*. London: Penguin; Hartman, A. (1970). 'To Think About the Unthinkable,' *Social Casework*, October; Allport, G. (1960). 'The Open System in Personality Theory,' *Journal of Abnormal & Social Psychiatry*; Vickery, A. (1972). 'Systems Approach to Social Work Intervention,' NISW Paper.
45. See Berger, P. (1978). 'Sociology and Freedom,' *American Sociologist*, Vol. 6, No 1, p. 197 also in Webb, D. 'Developing a Client Centred Sociology,' *Community Care*, February 22nd.
46. Specht, H. (1972). 'The Deprofessionalisation of Social Work,' *Social Work*, Vol. 7, March, pp. 3–15.
47. R. D. Laing fell out of fashion, partly as the swinging sixties gave way to a more materialistic culture, but also because some bad incidents occurred at the Kingsley Hall commune where his schizophrenic patients could express themselves freely in pursuit of relief. More recently, following the unfortunate death of his son Adam, Adam's half-brother Adrian described their father as a

depressive alcoholic who had no interest in his own family, ironic in the extreme as his fame was as a family psychiatrist. (See *The Observer*, 01.06. 2008, pp. 4–5.) Against this has to be weighed the freedom that Laing's campaigns gave to patients to speak out. It could well be argued that without Laing the emergence of mental health service user groups would have been long delayed.

48. Sedgwick, P. (1982). *Psychopolitics (The Politics of Health)*. London: Pluto Press.
49. Rhodes Boyson, who was a leading member of the Conservative Party and intolerant of homosexuality, became Minister of State for Higher Education under Mrs Thatcher. He created a storm by cutting grants to universities, an act which, it is thought, lay behind Oxford University's refusal to grant Mrs Thatcher an Honorary Degree. Boyson was knighted in 1987 and died in 2012 at the age of 87.
50. See, for example, Schutz, W. (1973). *Joy – Expanding Human Awareness*. London: Pelican. For this we drew on visiting adult and child psychiatrists Drs S. Shere and John Clouston. References include the following: Mayer-Gross, W., Slater, E. and Roth, M. (1969). *Clinical Psychiatry*. London: Tindall & Cassell; Stafford Clarke, D. (1964). *Psychiatry Today*. London: Pelican; Stengel, E. (1964). *Suicide and Attempted Suicide*. London: Pelican; Tredgold, R. F. and Soddy, K. (1972). *Textbook of Mental Deficiency*. London; Baillière, Tindall and Cox.
51. Barker, P. (1971). *Basic Child Psychiatry*. London: Wiley; Tizzard, J. (1964). *Community Services for the Mentally Handicapped*. London: Oxford University Press.
52. See https//www.grubbinstitute.org.uk.
53. Reich, W. (1989). *The Function of the Orgasm*. London: Souvenir; Reich, W. (1997). *The Mass Psychology of Fascism*. London: Souvenir; Fromm, E. (1965). *The Art of Loving*. London: Unwin Books; Sullivan, H. S. (1955). *The Interpersonal Theory of Psychiatry*. London: Tavistock. See also a quote from Fromm, E. (1964). *The Heart of Man: Its Genius for Good or Evil*. New York: Harper Collins. '… freedom requires that the individual be active and responsible, not a slave or a well fed cog in the machine … It is not enough that men are not slaves; if social conditions further the existence of automatons, the result will not be love of life, but love of death.'
54. Storr, A. (1966). 'The Concept of Cure,' *Sunday Times*, 09.10.1966.
55. Madge, J. (1967). *The Tools of Social Science*. London: Longman; Mayer, J. and Timms, N. (1970). *The Client Speaks*. London: Routledge & Kegan Paul; Bott, E. (1968). *Family and Social Research*. London: Tavistock.
56. Bibliography included: Foren, R. and Bailey, K. (1968). *Authority in Casework*. Oxford: Pergamon; Reid, N. and Shyne, A. (1969). *Brief and Extended Casework*. New York: Columbia University Press; Parad, H. (1965). *Crisis Intervention*. London: FSAA; Caplan, G. (1961). *An Approach to Community Mental Health*. London: Tavistock; Hardiker, P., Yelloly, M. and Shaw, M. (1972). *Behaviour Modification in Social Work*. New York: Wiley; Timms, N. (1964). *Casework in the Child Care Service*. London: Butterworth; Butrym, Z. (1967). *Social Work in Medical Care*. New York: Bell; Shibutani, T. (1972). *Society and Personality*. New York: Prentice Hall; Szasz, T. (1972). *The Myth of Mental Illness*. London: Paladin; Matza, D. (1964). *Delinquency and Drift*. New York: Wiley; Becker, E. (1973). *The Outsiders: Studies in the Sociology of Deviance*. New York: Free Press; Smith, G. (1970). *Social Work and the Sociology of Organisations*. London: Routledge & Kegan Paul.
57. Schur, E. (1973). *Radical Non-Intervention. Rethinking the Delinquency Problem*. New Jersey: Prentice Hall.
58. Ruddock, R. (1969). *Roles and Relationships*. London: Routledge & Kegan Paul; Mead, G. (1967). *Mind, Self and Society*. New York: University of Chicago Press; Marcuse, H. (1969). *Eros and Civilization*. London: Sphere; Marcuse, H. (1968). *One Dimensional Man*. London: Sphere.
59. Garfinkel, H. (1967). *Studies in Ethnomethodology*. New York: Prentice Hall; Goffman, E. (1967). *Where The Action Is. Three Essays*. London: Allen Lane; Goffman, E. (1969). *Presentation of Self in*

Everyday Life. London: Allen Lane; Berger, P. and Luckmann, T. (1966). *The Social Construction of Reality*. London: Penguin; Freud, S. (2002). *The Psychopathology of Everyday Life*. London: Penguin; Cohen, S. (1971). *Images of Deviance*. London: Penguin; Taylor, L. (1973). *Deviance and Society*. London: Nelsons University.
60. Szasz, T. S. (1962). *The Myth of Mental Illness*. London: Secker and Warburg.
61. Directed by Ken Loach and produced by Tony Garnett, this was part of the outstanding 'Wednesday Play' series on BBC TV. It was the first docu-drama and dealt with the terrible effect of the housing crisis on a family whose circumstances deteriorate until they become homeless, at which point, in the final scene, the police accompany social workers to remove the children. It was watched by 11.8 million viewers and eventually led to legislation. In that year 4,000 children had been received into care as a result of homelessness.
62. Pithers, D. (1974). 'The Origins and Nature of Conflict in Social Care.' Paper read at Guys Hospital Community Medicine, December 3rd.
63. Jordan, M. (1972). 'The End of the Grand March,' *Social Work Today*, Vol. 3, No. 6.
64. Jordan, M. (1972). 'Education and social work,' *Social Work Today*, Vol. 4, No. 5.

ELEVEN

1969–1976
RESEARCH ON A SHOESTRING

During the two-year CQSW in course in Maidstone we sought to interest students, and staff, in the value of research for method and ethics as well as its relevance to practice. It was hoped that this would encourage them to carry out research projects in their subsequent practice as an aid to advocating on behalf of individuals, groups or communities to managers, local or national government. Three members of staff claimed a teaching hours allowance in order to carry out research; this was entirely nominal as we were all working far too many hours anyway. Their work was on Task Centred Social Work, The Arts in Social Work and Clients' Perception of Social Workers, which was part of my work for an MA.

In addition to this a joint student–staff group undertook overambitious pieces of research into the experience of the differing groups being swept up by the Seebohm changes and an examination of the results of the 16PF personality tests undertaken by all applicants. It is to my great shame that, despite the heroic efforts of all concerned, none of this work has ever been published. This chapter is therefore an attempt partially to expiate this guilt by offering a brief summary of results that can now be retrieved from the files.

CHANGE IN THE SOCIAL SERVICES 1969–1974

The group were well aware that the implications of the 1969 Children and Young Persons Act, the Chronically Sick and Disabled Act, the Green Paper on reorganisation of the NHS and the Seebohm Report were causing high levels of anxiety among staff of all grades. We therefore designed a three-part survey by postal questionnaire to all social workers in a selected English county. Following a trial survey with workers in a neighbouring county we launched our surveys in 1970 (when the actual Seebohm change was yet to be implemented), in 1972 (when it was all happening) and in 1974 (when we hoped that our participants could look back). We defined social workers as those professionally employed as such in any agency in the county. Questionnaires were dispatched under a personal letter of explanation and guarantee of confidentiality. With great regret we excluded residential workers as we had no way of finding staff lists, and inclusion of the vast number of staff involved would have made the material unwieldy. There were eight students and two staff involved in this work, although we also had support from David Thomas, a Senior Lecturer in Mathematics at the College and Diane Cunningham from the Centre for Research in the Social Sciences at the University of Kent at Canterbury, who took our results, fed them into vast computers and returned with miles of data sheets. By any lights this was research on a shoestring!

FIRST SURVEY: 1970

The first survey sought to answer the following questions: Who are the social workers, and what were their social and educational backgrounds? In what structures do they work and what is their workload? What was their view of the impending changes? Did they see themselves as having had any part in forming the changes and how well informed were they of what would happen? In July 1970, 355 overambitious and complex questionnaires were sent out; 245 came back and were accepted for analysis, an average positive response rate of 69%.

Although the general response rate was high, the most usual reason for declining to take part was the personal questions included in this first document, especially the request for details of father's occupation and place of birth. Several declined because they did not trust the guarantee of confidentiality, but on the other hand 13% went out of their way to identify themselves! We checked the information given against published information about the age, qualification level, etc. of social workers at that time, and we were satisfied that our sample was not significantly skewed although it was possible that our samples were slightly weighted by more senior or long-serving staff. My view is that the differing response rates related to levels of anxiety, although of course at this stage only the Children's Department and Health and Welfare were directly involved in creating the Social Services Department. The crude age, gender and marital status distribution was as in Table 2.

The most significant findings seem to be the high proportion of older men working as education welfare officers (EWOs) and the higher age ranges of women in the hospital and voluntary sectors. In general the popular image at the time of social workers as elderly spinsters did not seem to be supported, with the possible exception

Table 1 Response rate by agency

	Total	Children's Department	Education Welfare Officers (EWOs)	Health and Welfare	Hospitals and Child Guidance	Probation Service	Voluntary agencies
Questionnaires accepted	245	69	26	49	31	47	23
Response rate	69%	80%	65%	66%	70%	63%	64%

Table 2 Crude age distribution, sex and marital status of respondents

	Average	Children's Department	EWOs	Health and Welfare	Hospitals and Child Guidance	Probation Service	Voluntary agencies
Percentage of staff under 30	16	28	0	24	16	9	9
Percentage of staff over 30 but under 45	32	41	12	34	13	51	18
Percentage of staff 45 and over	52	31	88	42	71	40	73
Approximate ratio male to female		1 to 2	4 to 1	2 to 1	all female	5 to 2	1 to 3
Approximate ratio married to single		2 to 1	12 to 1	5 to 1	3 to 2	8 to 1	2 to 1

of the hospital groups, presumably reflecting the historical roots of those services. Pushing our luck as naïve researchers, we then asked about the occupation of the workers' fathers.

Further analysis revealed that a significantly higher proportion of female respondents than male came from classifications 1 and 2, while the reverse was true of classifications 5 to 7. Subsequent questions sought to show the father's upward social

Table 3 Father's occupation at respondent's birth

Socio-economic classification (shortened*)	Percentage of all respondents
1. Professional workers	11
2. Employers/managers & self-employed	20
3. Skilled workers & foremen	15
4. Intermediate & junior non-manual	15
5. Service workers, semi-skilled & agricultural	17
6. Armed forces	13
7. Unskilled	5
8. Not known or no answer	4

*See *Classification Manual for Household Interview Survey in Great Britain*, 1969, Social and Community Planning Research

Table 4 Age at leaving school as a percentage in each agency

Age at leaving school	Children's Department	EWOs	Health and Welfare	Hospitals and Child Guidance	Probation Service	Voluntary agencies
14 and under	3	20	10	6	17	44
Over 14 but under 16	42	58	42	26	40	26
16 and over	55	22	48	68	43	30

mobility related to the age of respondents. The least mobile (15%) concerned the oldest respondents, while the youngest had 40% of fathers showing upward mobility. We then looked at educational and qualifying achievements starting at the age of leaving school (Table 4).

These tables have to be read in relation to the period involved, including two world wars and a severe economic depression. They also give some indication of possible difficulties in bringing staff together in one department, particularly the fears that more 'high powered' groups would dominate both initial appointments and future promotion. For further information, and you may now be beginning to understand why some people objected, we then asked about careers before social work. Fewer than 10% had held blue collar jobs and a further 10% were in the armed forces, but over 70% had remained in white collar jobs throughout their previous career. Most women (92%) had only held white collar jobs. Turning to careers in social welfare we related qualification to level of seniority, dividing respondents roughly into senior managers (central office), middle managers (area) and social workers/trainees. We also asked about length of service and salaries.

Table 5 Relevant qualification achieved by agency

	Average	Children's Department	EWOs	Health and Welfare	Hospitals and Child Guidance	Probation Service	Voluntary agencies
Social science degree	14	28	0	5	16	15	13
Professional post-graduate	5	8	0	0	13	4	0
Professional certificate or diploma	34	35	8	42	42	37	39
Total qualified	53	71	8	47	71	56	52

Table 6 Qualifications related to position held

	Central office	Area	Social worker/trainee
Professional qualification	60%	62%	28%
Relevant degree	10%	13%	25%
No FE qualification	30%	25%	47%

Table 7 Length of service in present post

	Central office	Area	Social worker/trainee
3 years or under	61%	58%	50%
4 years up to 5 years	0	11%	10%
5 years up to 10 years	39%	18%	25%
10 years and over	0	13%	15%

Table 8 Gross annual salary by gender and agency as a percentage

	Total	Male	Female	Children's Dept	EWOs	Health and Welfare	Hospitals and Child Guidance	Probation Service	Voluntary agencies
£1,000 or less (£15,580)*	6	4	10	3	0	5	15	0	25
£1,001 to £1,250 (£19,480)	14	5	17	19	6	10	20	5	23
£1,251 to £1,500 (£23,370)	32	30	36	26	84	29	26	16	43
£1,500 to £2000 (£31,160)	37	43	31	46	5	36	31	57	9
£2,000 and over	11	18	6	6	5	20	8	22	0

* Equivalent values in 2020 are given in parentheses

Consideration of Tables 6, 7 and 8 indicates some tentative conclusions in addition to the obvious discrepancy between male and female staff. It appears that service users would be most likely to be seen by unqualified staff with little experience, although short times in the most senior positions is surprising. This may be counterbalanced by the fact that central office and practitioners also have the highest number of staff with more than five years' service. All this, of course, is before the organisational changes. It is also worth noting that although most staff fall within the second and third levels, staff in the two male dominated agencies take most of the two higher salary levels despite the fact that the EWOs were the least qualified. We then attempted to look at staff stability, asking whether respondents had applied for other jobs. Not surprisingly the youngest staff had applied for other posts (35%) falling to 23% for the oldest group. These figures held for all agencies except the EWOs when it fell to 7.5% and voluntary agencies where the figure was nil.

Our next questions concerned workloads in terms of the number of cases carried and the number of clients seen in the last week before the question was answered.

We thought the only conclusion that could be drawn from Tables 9 and 10 was the widely differing types of tasks being undertaken, for example between EWOs and the more highly qualified and specialised agencies. It is noted that the traditionally more specialised voluntary agencies seemed to concentrate on fewer clients while carrying higher total caseloads.[1]

Having established the best baselines we could to inform the whole project, we then went on to address the issues at hand. The statistical section asked how workers were getting information about the two major legislative based changes and then invited

Table 9 Workloads by agency as a percentage

Caseloads	Children's Dept	EWOs	Health and Welfare	Hospitals and Child Guidance	Probation Service	Voluntary agencies
1–49	42	25	18	33	41	25
50–99	58	25	32	48	48	64
100 plus	0	50	50	19	11	11

Table 10 Number of clients seen in the previous week by agency as a percentage

Clients seen	Children's Dept	EWOs	Health and Welfare	Hospitals and Child Guidance	Probation Service	Voluntary agencies
Fewer than 10	3	0	4	6	5	28
11–19	46	0	25	31	20	34
20–29	31	10	45	27	32	19
30–39	16	20	21	21	30	7
40–49	2	25	5	5	8	6
50 plus	2	45	0	10	5	6

general comments. In respect of the 1969 Children and Young Persons Act although 27% of our sample were unable to cite any clear source of information on either subject, it was noticeable that over 50% of these were in the 45–60 age group. Perhaps less surprising was the fact that over 50% of health and welfare workers were unable to mention any source of information on this subject. Only 28% of all respondents identified departmental newsletters and memos as their prime source of information, whereas 32% relied on professional journals. Only 11% mentioned staff meetings, while the remainder relied on mass media. In summary, 36% cited internal sources and 52% relied on external sources. The Probation Service appeared to be most efficient, while Health and Welfare staff relied more on informal networks, colleagues and gossip as their prime source. The situation for the overriding Social Services Act was less satisfactory: 15% were unable to cite any source, 45% relied on journals.

We then ended this initial part of the survey with a question that would make 'proper' researchers blanch!

'There are frustrations in every field of work, e.g. too much administrative work, inefficient administration, lack of supervision, responsibilities etc. What do you consider to be the main ones in your job and how do you think the proposed changes might affect them?'

Given the time that has elapsed since this project it may help to sketch in a brief context. The Authority was conservative in both senses of the word. The two services central to the reorganisation were, markedly different. The Children's Department had a good sense of professionalism with a good manager. This did not of course eliminate the fact that in the County Council's view they were local government officers first and foremost. The Health and Welfare Service was less professional, more bureaucratic and led by a Medical Officer of Health for whom welfare was a secondary consideration. This marginalisation was also a feature of the Education Welfare Service, where many officers were ex-policemen managed within the Education Department. Although the Probation Service was well led, many of its staff saw their role very traditionally. Hospital and Child Guidance social workers were among the most qualified and established, although their work and management varied in relation to each hospital and the attitude of medical consultants. Voluntary agencies varied: they were fairly prolific and enthusiastically run by volunteers managed by lone social workers. The background in terms of economic conditions was difficult, and a recent rise in the birth rate was putting more pressure on all services.

It was remarkable that 173 of our respondents gave us their comments. For many it gave them a chance to abreat in situations where supervision and staff meetings were rare events. Those running things were 'the administration' and as the same term was often used for immediate clerical and support staff it was sometimes difficult to interpret responses. Only one person in all the thousands of questions used the word management. I have however attempted to reflect these feelings in the following.

The Children's Department (68% answered the question)

The most frequent complaint concerned poor resources to enable the social workers to see clients. This increased the existing pressure from too heavy caseloads (see Table 7), crowded offices, lack of privacy and clerical help and too much minor administration falling to professional staff. The hierarchy was seen to have too many layers and, with very little decentralisation, small issues could not be resolved quickly. Some complained that communication of ideas upwards was impossible. Some felt that they were seen as a local government officer first, social worker second. There was 'a lack of interest in recruitment of trained officers at basic level, administrative training for seniors, staff development, full consultation/supervision and good relations between field and residential staff, foster parents and volunteers.'

A close second issue was a high level of concern at the lack of resources for clients in terms of reception and assessment centres, children's homes, hostels, and foster parents. Putting aside the increase in child population, this severely restricted good practice, children having to be put in the one bed available regardless of appropriateness – and this sometimes meant splitting up siblings. One worker commented that, 'Nothing is more detrimental to good social work than having to put a child in the only hole available.' The credibility of the department was at risk. Staff were expected to do the whole range of child care work, which was sometimes overwhelming; more specialisation was required. Staff time was increasingly spent on marginal tasks such as 'loan collection, loan guarantees, delivery of equipment and insignificant escort duties only remotely related to caring for children.' Although the establishment of the new department was imminent, many complained that they had little information about this massive change to their work.

Given this list of concerns, many in the hands of those controlling the council's finances, expectations for the great new department were not high. One respondent felt that 'despite good will, actual improvements would be limited due to complete lack of understanding by both councillors and central government.' It was felt that the existing low morale would be raised if the new director were a qualified social worker with an understanding of the need to decentralise and to improve service to clients; if a non social worker was appointed then the situation would become untenable. There was some hope that a large new department might have more weight and thus be able to obtain more of the much needed resources; on the other hand a larger department could lead to more empire building and bureaucracy. Most hoped for more professional supervision and more specialisation with a much increased ability to liaise with colleagues and to co-ordinate services to avoid duplication. Problems were anticipated in integration as fewer staff in the Health and Welfare Department were qualified.

Health and Welfare Staff (48% answered the question)

The concerns about the conditions of work, lack of clerical support, issues with administrators and feeling of remoteness from senior management expressed by child care staff were much more acutely felt by these staff. It seemed that the lack of clear role definitions meant that the department never made up its mind whether our respondents were social workers or administrators. What office support existed was described as inefficient or chaotic, as were work records. Delegation was very poor and communication with headquarters was described as a battle. Senior staff were seen as lacking in any dynamism, and middle managers were usually ignored. Social workers felt isolated and resented being directed by administrators. Waiting for decisions from above ruined any work and self-respect. Workloads were overwhelming and there was considerable concern about lack of resources such as day centre places. One respondent simply stated that they were 'very happy.' There was little or no information about the forthcoming changes.

Most respondents were hopeful of the new department, that professional supervisors and enlightened managers must improve the service to clients, that such a department must be more efficient. It was hoped that more specialisation might be possible and caseloads might be better managed. Much of this would depend on the right appointments being made and more finance being made available to improve the service to clients. A minority had no hope of change as the council would remain the same. One respondent explained that 'There is nothing in the Act which requires a backward administration to provide a better service ... it is extremely doubtful whether it is realistic to expect that a "new" department will be controlled by an administration that will include more physical resources and more qualified staff in the list of top priorities.'

Education Welfare Officers (81% answered the question)

There was a different tone in these responses as most EWOs did not hold a social work qualification and, given their past careers, were used to working independently with discretion on how they worked in their given area. There were similar complaints about lack of clerical support, excessive paperwork and very high caseloads, with more expected once the school leaving age increased to 16. There was little time for thinking about complex cases, and liaison with other departments was difficult. There was national uncertainty about whether or not these staff would be included in the new departments, and our respondents complained about the anxiety that this caused, as did the lack of any information from senior managers about their future. The Education Department 'does schools, not individual cases' said one respondent.

There were mixed expectations about the new department. Paperwork might be more streamlined, and the stress of integration might highlight important issues. Easier liaison and clearer roles would end the ability of other people to pass the buck. More time and supervision might mean more time available for complex family issues, although there was a fear that this work might be taken away. One respondent hoped that they could persuade such an organisation to set up an 'At risk' register to safeguard children in such families. One respondent commented that probation should be included in the new department and thought that 'Health Visitors should be abolished' as their role was ambiguous and EWOs could do that work which would add status.

Hospital Social Workers (47% answered the question)

Although it was legally possible, there was certainly no rush to incorporate these workers into the new departments. Many of these mentioned a sense of isolation, no supervision and annoyance at being at the whim of local medical management and consultants. They often had no clerical help. One complained that nurses and junior doctors had no understanding of patients' real needs. Conferences were often relegated to meetings in corridors. Their isolation meant that they had little contact with local authority workers and were unable to influence them for the benefit of patients. They had very little information about the changes, and this seemed to reflect confusion of thought and lack of direction.

There were mixed feelings about the new department. One respondent commented that there was a fear that 'a big department takes on a life of its own and people get very involved in that life to the detriment of clients.' It was believed that if the director were a dynamic qualified social worker such a department might offer better clerical assistance and better grades with opportunities for career progression. Communication with other social workers would be much easier, but on the other hand the close link with hospital teams would be weakened. Questions were raised, such as Would doctors and ward sisters work with outside social workers? and Perhaps some workers could remain based in hospitals?

Probation Service (87% replied to the question)

The response from this group was higher than expected as it was never suggested that this group would be part of the new department. Most concerns were similar to those received from local authority groups, e.g. lack of clerical support, therefore recording and report writing getting in the way of work with clients. High caseloads meant no time for good work even though there was no cap on the hierarchy, which was growing all the time. The question arose: Are we social workers to the courts or general social workers doing after-care etc., which is problematic as it depends on other departments? There was a sense of isolation from other social workers, lack of stimulation, lack of recognition and limited promotion prospects. A cap of 40/45 cases was suggested. A shortage of hostel places etc. was a problem.

It was thought that the implementation of the Children and Young Persons Act should reduce workload, although the Children's Department did not seem ready. Less juvenile work implied more work with recidivists. The new department should very much help with liaison and co-ordination of work with families, although there were dangers in a large organisation. 'I don't feel the changes will be based on requirements but on polarised attitudes towards offenders and other users of the services,' said one respondent. Clients might be sacrificed to administrative convenience.

The Voluntary Sector (39% answered the question)

The new department would only affect these social workers indirectly. Their comments mostly concerned the difficulties posed by managing large numbers of volunteers while working alone with no professional supervision. This was experienced as an inefficient way to work when most committee members were volunteers. This was exacerbated by the need to spend so much time raising money for their agency. There were difficulties in liaising with other social workers. While the new organisation with a good director should improve co-operation and might lead to better grants, there was a fear that such a large group of fellow professionals might make these workers more isolated.

THE NEW DEPARTMENT

In fact the new department commenced work in late 1972 with a legally qualified director. Faced with a Children's Department that was in good hands, and a Health and Welfare Department losing its nominal leader and clearly less efficient, the director decided to give the latter area the highest initial priority. A very early initiative was to decide upon a standard for social work staffing. This examined sample workloads, and some national agreements, except for child care, where a maximum case load was already set in the county.[2]

Calculations were aimed at a good but not exceptional service. Social work assistants would do 25 visits per week, each lasting 40 minutes. Travelling time does not seem to have received much attention. On this basis the following figures for caseloads were derived:

One social worker helped by a social work assistant can carry:

Mentally ill, or community care	46 cases
Child care	50 cases
Elderly	103 cases
Cases on the physically handicapped register	119 cases
Cases on the blind, partially sighted and deaf registers	120 cases
Mentally handicapped cases	142 cases
Miscellaneous visits, including to nurseries & child minders	828 per year

or

Mental health statutory admissions	460 per year

or a combination of the above.

Comparing these figures with the existing workloads it was deduced that a further 54 additional social workers would be required. No account appears to have been taken of the impact of new legislation being implemented or anticipated, or of the increase in population. This director was soon succeeded by Rev Nick Stacey, who offered good leadership for eleven years. Education officers and welfare and hospital social workers were eventually incorporated into the new department.

SECOND SURVEY: 1972

This survey was intended to gather the reactions of those in the midst of change. About 96% had indicated their willingness to be followed up in this way, although many of the original respondents had left the county, suffered ill health or retired. A comparison of the response rate is shown in Table 11.

Unfortunately it has not been possible to reproduce as much detail from this second questionnaire despite the fact that there were only 17 questions compared with the original 25 so the following figures should be treated with some caution. We asked how many moves each individual had made in the previous two years. Details of workload in the new position were sought and we then repeated the original questions about sources of information, staff meetings, associations, in-service training, salary, etc.

Turning to the responders' experiences of the major changes, we asked about career opportunities and their views about the changes in general for the post they were

Table 11 Response to first and second surveys by agency

Response date	Total	Children's Dept	EWOs	Health and Welfare	Hospitals and Child Guidance	Probation Service	Voluntary agencies
1970	245	69	26	49	31	47	23
1972	182	58	19	41	20	38	6

Table 12 Workload by number of respondents

	Number	Children's Dept	EWOs	Health and Welfare	Hospitals and Child Guidance	Probation Service
Active workload	Below 50	13	0	17	6	8
	50–99	25	0	2	1	0
	100 plus	1	9	0	0	0
Clients seen last week	Fewer than 10	12	1	9	0	4
	10–19	12	1	5	6	4
	20 or more	16	7	7	6	13
Clients not seen for 8 weeks	Fewer than 10	10	1	3	2	7
	10–19	6	0	0	0	3
	20 or more					

previously holding, the degree of responsibility or caseload, contact with other social workers and the degree of specialisation. Key questions addressed whether the changes would result in a better service and standard for the clients and whether respondents felt that they had had any influence on the changes. The final question was an open invitation to comment.

Table 13 How have the changes affected your career prospects?*

	Children's Dept	EWOs	Health and Welfare	Hospitals and Child Guidance	Probation Service	Voluntary agencies
Better	12	4	13	1	4	0
Same	24	7	5	6	24	1
Worse	5	0	1	2	1	1

* Average C & YP and Social Services Department (SSD) by individuals

Table 14 Personal view of changes*

	Children's Dept	EWOs	Health and Welfare	Hospitals and Child Guidance	Probation Service	Voluntary agencies
Favourably	39	11	27	11	25	1
Neutrally	12	8	12	8	12	4
Unfavourably	0	0	0	1	0	0

*SSD only by individuals answering this question

Table 15 Knowledge of change and expectations so far*

Responsibility		Caseloads		Contact with other social workers		More specialisation		Has the standard of service offered since 1970...	
More	45	Heavier	35	Yes	53	Yes	30	...greatly improved?	2
Same	58	Same	51	No	35	No	116	...improved?	60
Less	11	Lighter	9	Don't know	25	Don't know	36	...stayed the same?	9
Don't know	28	Don't know	21					...declined/seriously declined?	0

*SSD only

Table 16 Staff meetings per month

	Children's Dept	EWOs	Health and Welfare	Hospitals and Child Guidance	Probation Service	Voluntary agencies
Formal staff meetings						
1	2	0	8	1	5	5
2	17	1	6	1	2	10
3	21	3	8	2	4	19
Don't know	13	9	10	1	10	5
Which was more supportive?						
Formal	3	2	5	0	1	10
Informal	39	10	20	4	11	22

Table 17 How many social work posts applied for in the last two years?

	Children's Dept	EWOs	Health and Welfare	Hospitals and Child Guidance	Probation Service	Voluntary agencies
Within the county	1	0	12	0	0	1
Outside the county	22	1	10	5	3	8

Table 18 Involvement in professional associations

	Children's Dept	EWOs	Health and Welfare	Hospitals and Child Guidance	Probation Service	Voluntary agencies
Membership	22	8	20	4	17	4
Active or very involved	6	7	6	0	2	3
Not very involved or inactive	18	4	15	4	16	1
Attends local branch						
Regularly/occasionally	17	10	13	2	10	1
Seldom/never	7	2	6	1	3	2

This Authority was late establishing its SSD under the leadership of a non social worker. This may account for the high number of staff seeking jobs outside the county and the difficulties, reported below, in attracting qualified and experienced staff, although there was also a national shortage. It is very difficult, without further work,

Table 19 Did respondents feel that they had any influence on the changes?*

	Children's Dept	EWOs	Health and Welfare	Hospitals and Child Guidance	Probation Service	Voluntary agencies
Yes	2	1	3	0	1	1
No	6	1	3	0	3	5
Don't know	45	12	26	5	15	3

*SSD only

to make comparisons between these two sets of tables, and I have already cautioned against these numbers. It appears that caseloads had fallen, a fact very much disputed in the comments that follow; also, participation in associations seems to have fallen and involvement dropped. However, two respondents indicated that it was this involvement that enabled them to have some influence in the establishment of the SSD. The general comments by department follow.

Former Children's Department (78% answered the question)

Only two staff considered they had been able to influence change. One senior member of staff said that they had helped by telling the new director about social work. Others, not included in the numbers above, had used their professional associations; some signed a protest letter written by the Association of Child Care Officers (ACCO) to their MP; others had been able to influence policies and practices at local level; some formed a group of basic grade staff to evaluate new policies.

The SSD had changed everything, although, as one respondent stated: 'I still hope it will be OK. We are suffering for being late in the search for talent, especially senior staff, this makes it difficult to change to new methods; staff were anxious and looked to middle managers who are not yet appointed, this produced crisis at client level.' Existing senior staff therefore looked inwards rather than at basic grades and clients. The lack of experienced senior staff resulted in changes being a more traumatic and frustrating experience for all. There was no real integration yet – everything was in a state of change from day to day. If you asked for help, you might find that the person or indeed the whole department had vanished. This shortage of senior staff and stress meant the buck was passed down to field staff. Internal communications were poor. There were more and more meetings about very little and the clients suffered. There were too many new brooms, too many unproductive meetings and too many people in transit.

Existing skills were threatened and not utilised to teach others, and there was too much emphasis on being generic. The shortage of qualified staff and the need to be generic slowed everything down, so a poor service resulted. There was uncertainty about how to cope with the less qualified Health and Welfare staff. One comment raised the worry that 'We used to be able to co-operate with them over families, but it now seems more difficult.'

The new department raised public expectations, but there was no finance to match those expectations, let alone to correct the long-established shortage of resources and staff. The recent Chronically Sick and Disabled Act and the 1969 Children & Young Persons Act had exacerbated the situation. Social workers were required to increase output and expected to carry out a wider field of work in the joint department, but there was no continuity and there was a shortage of senior staff. Those promoted were anxious, and that affected teams. Area directors were bemused: the top was now further removed from the front line. Experienced staff only functioned by knowing the ropes in order to find a place or resources for a child or family. The pressure prevented any community initiatives or new developments.

Former Health and Welfare Staff (95% answered the question)

Few staff considered they had had some influence over decisions, through professional associations which contacted the director or joined in policy discussions at divisional level. Others in a more senior position could write new policies and structures; others felt that their feelings must have reached HQ.

While one person exclaimed that this was the opportunity to do the work for which they were trained, it was conceded that the priority given to generic work and increased pressure made it difficult. Some complained that within local offices all health and welfare cases were sent to the one worker from that section while the three child care officers could share their cases. This was made worse by an instruction that all request for aids must come to ex health and welfare staff as others had been handing them out 'willy nilly'. The Chronically Sick and Disabled Act was increasing demand without any extra staff. The qualified child care staff were getting the promotions. There was much uncertainty about future prospects and specialist skills gained over many years. Inexperienced staff took time away from seniors, so a reduced service to clients resulted. There was suspicion that some people at HQ were not really interested in integration.

It was a challenge coming to grips with new roles, new identities and new organisational structures. There was, it was perceived, too much talk, not enough action and little sense of urgency. Too much time was taken up in local meetings; before reorganisation: 'We could write to others (e.g. voluntary agencies) directly, now it was in the third person to be signed only by the team leader. Impossible to offer continuity for clients.'

Education Welfare Officers (26% answered the question)

These staff were not initially incorporated in the new department. They therefore felt that things were either the same or getting worse. Previous easy communication about families with child care staff had been lost and was now only allowed through team leaders. Staff in the SSD did not seem able to take positive action and there were too many changes of staff. EWOs were left with more complex problems, made worse by newly complicated benefit rules but inadequate flow of information and poorer co-operation from SSD staff.

Hospital Social Workers (95% answered the question)

One respondent was very worried that, 'This new vast machine seems to be suffocating itself with paper. We can't contact social workers, only through duty officers, and clients get lost in the system.' There seems to be general confusion and lack of communication. 'Why not leave the generic element until later?' it was asked. Life was made difficult due to the lack of social workers, and those in the new department showed a lack of courtesy. There was great uncertainty about their future, combined with initial chaos and teething troubles. *'Leave us Out.'* The obsession seems to be that, 'We all become "jack of all trades". Stimulation came when we manage to meet other specialist workers.' There was a view that, 'If we are to become a profession we must specialise.'

Probation Service (89% answered the question but only 29% referred to issues other than those related to probation)

Work was being held up while the two Acts were fully implemented. There was regret at losing juvenile work. Minor frustrations were experienced when SSD staff could not do the duties that they should. This caused uncertainty about the basic aims of social work. There was a danger that probation officers would become isolated and that those at the top would lose touch with the pressing human needs of clients. It seemed that SSD seniors lacked understanding about probation work.

Voluntary Sector (50% of respondents answered the question)

These staff complained of a lack of communication from SSD managers. The unrest in social work was affecting voluntary agencies, who seemed to be losing their identity. There was too much pressure to bring them in line with SSDs. They experienced a lack of flexibility which caused uncertainty about the future.

THIRD SURVEY: 1974

Former Children's Department Social Workers

Naturally enough, most of the comments concerned the different experiences of a newly established, rapidly growing hierarchical organisation. A sense of depersonalisation was reported as the department now numbered some 4,000 staff. Comments were more extensive than previously.

Senior staff were frustrated that the size of the department and divisions now restricted their ability to get out on the front line to see what was really happening, particularly with innovative projects. It was distressing to see social workers overwhelmed

Table 20 Response to third survey of original subjects by agency

	Total	Children's Dept	EWOs	Health and Welfare	Hospitals and Child Guidance	Probation Service	Voluntary agencies
Second survey	182	58	19	41	20	38	6
Third survey	122	32	11	25	16	27	11

by too many trivial referrals with no time to think or help clients properly. Resources were scarcer than before and the bureaucracy slower (nine months to get an estate car so that an occupational therapist could deliver aids); on the other hand, policy decisions were now taken after proper consultation and discussion. An important section of the 1969 Act, for example intermediate treatment, remained inactive due to lack of staff or finance to set it up. Too much legislation but no money and genericism resulted in a wider range of issues falling on the same group of trained staff. Thus, 'A social worker knows that a child committed to care may wait two months for a placement and also knows that an adapted bathroom for a disabled man will take two years to be installed.' Was a cumbersome, male dominated local government suitable for social work? Clients are now seen as 'cases,' mere facts for a computer.

A widespread view was that communication was more difficult due to staff expansion, the breadth of work now faced and the frequent changes of personnel. Team leaders' expectations that communication with HQ would be improved were foiled by the sheer pressure of work in the teams. Decentralisation to divisions complicated the relationship between senior practitioners and central office. The old frustrations and increased pressure of referrals meant that, 'Most of us have little energy or inclination to alter things.' Everything 'at the top' seemed to be done in the interest of smooth admin. Changes in caseloads for administrative reasons was deplorable. Where 'courageous' divisional directors developed intake teams, individual workloads had been reduced. There remained no vacancies in homes or day centres, and holidays for children with learning disabilities had been reduced with bad consequences for both children and family.

Uncertainties had been replaced by a feeling of being trapped in terms of promotion as replacement was impossible – it was easier to attract a trained person from outside to the higher post. Staff felt that access to team leaders was more immediate even if formal supervision was less frequent. There were too few trained workers and higher caseloads.

Former Health and Welfare Staff (48% answered the question)

The view from this group was that there were too few social workers to cope with the increased demand. They were still doing work more suited to occupational therapists or social work assistants. For them the larger organisation meant there was a lack of understanding about roles and corporate management. Political considerations were taking precedence, hence there was inefficiency and lack of understanding of the needs of staff trying to deliver a high standard of service. The previous wish to expand their areas of work proved too soon for many; there was never enough time to do all the teaching and support work required. The unequal team balance between qualification and experience proved difficult. More demand meant more hands but no time to supervise. There was a lack of continuity as specialisation gave way to generic work and new staff joined, went on courses or were promoted. One responder explained, 'Although I feel that they were now more imaginative, the responsibility is focussed on pressure points ... and the department would grind itself to a halt because our will will be sapped ... lack of communication will mean that others will not be able to take over.'

They were barely coping with the crisis of demand and raised expectations just as government had reduced expenditure. There was some optimism about the future. Residential resources were gradually becoming more available, and one comment read that, 'On every side great efforts were being made to improve the service – there were new ideas and fresh approaches to the many problems but it is an uphill battle and we have a long way to go.' There was a need to recognise the limits of responsibilities in respect of police, hospitals, etc. Unfair criticism in the media was not helping.

Education Welfare Staff (55% answered this question)

During the preceding four years, as a consequence of new legislation, staff had to make more evening visits in order to see the families, who then resented comments made about their child care. Dealing with the new SSD was frustrating, but that maybe was due to the ability of EWOs to work with individual authority where now they have to consult and discuss. Their increased need to liaise with the SSD showed them to be ineffective as the SSD had a long-winded procedural approach to problems. There seemed to be a tendency to want to ease parental responsibilities. There was a case for a more selective method of dispensing welfare. The old problems of too much inefficient admin had become worse.

Hospital Social Workers (73% answered this question)

In this sector there was a general feeling of being in limbo, not yet belonging to any department and the refusal of medics to allow psychiatric social workers (PSWs) to give their views on their future was still seen as undemocratic. It was impossible to attract qualified PSWs. There was no support from divisional offices. The previous smooth flow of hospital work had been lost in a larger organisation which meant delays and frustrations. Long discussions and delays, which led to hospital staff joining the SSD on April 1st 1974, had meant that apprehensions remained unresolved as the county seemed to have no understanding of the work of hospital social workers and their place in the hospital system. Preparatory training had raised expectations, but significant frustrations remained. Contact with HQ had been less than reassuring. PSWs in child guidance clinics joined the new department later so this questionnaire was not so relevant. They formed a group to represent them, and there was a fear that the essential team feeling of child guidance could be lost. It would be the end of the traditional role of the PSW, '... as the product of the LSE, the Maudsley and the Child Guidance Training Centre ... The new generation will have to look at their clients in a different way and provide community facilities for them.'

Probation Service (67% answered the question)

The view of one respondent was that the 'SSD seemed to have so much on their plate that there was no time left for creative or experimental work, all available resources appeared to be stretched to meet emergency situations.' While court reforms had helped the Probation Service, easing caseloads, the shortage of resources remained and the lack of action regarding persistent offenders was a worry. The uncertainty, frustration and lack of purpose before the decision whether or not to join SSDs had passed, and witnessing the results meant that they would resist further changes towards bureaucracy. The role of the SSDs had increased but unfortunately their standards had lowered due to lack of trained personnel.

Voluntary Sector (36% of respondents answered the question)

As reorganisation was complete communication had improved. Previous uncertainty had caused a lack of interest in the voluntary sector.

NEW STAFF

To add to our troubles our ambition then led us to survey the social workers who had joined the county since 1970. Unfortunately I now have only limited data, but some gross comparisons are possible: two hundred and fifty people responded.

Of the 179 respondents answering the question about spouse's occupation, 83% were in full- or part-time work. Of the 144 who gave further information it seemed that 85% of the spouses were in white collar employment; 57% of the workers' fathers had been in white collar employment when they were born and there was slight evidence of social mobility to the present.

Table 21 Age, gender and marital status comparing new staff in 1970 and 1974

	1970 new staff	1974 new staff
Under 30 years of age	16%	35%
Between 30 and 45 years	32%	39%
Over 45 years	52%	26%
Male to female ratio	1.4 to 1	1.3 to 1
Married to single ratio	4.5 to 1	3 to 1

Of the 250 respondents, 54% had attended grammar schools and 27% public schools, 60% remaining to the age of 17 or over although 16% left by the age of 15 years. Of the 200 who gave information about ongoing education, 44% had attended university and 42% college. Of 139 respondents who gave answers about academic achievement, 48% had first or post-graduate degrees, 52% had diplomas in social science, social work or related areas. By far the majority of respondents had worked in manual, intermediate or junior non-manual work before entering social work, with the next largest group having experience in the professional or managerial occupations.

Two hundred and thirty-three of the respondents had previously held their posts for less than three years; the majority employed as social workers, assistant social workers or probation officers. Workloads varied from below 50 to 149, but the practice of the different agencies, particularly EWOs, distorted these figures. During the week before the survey most respondents had seen fewer than 20 clients; the next largest group recorded seeing up to 39.

THE 16 PERSONALITY FACTOR QUESTIONNAIRE

If the above project was overambitious in terms of scale and duration, this project surpassed it in its naivety and relative disregard of the rigid scientific basis of this well established and validated test.[3] We thought that, given the vast resources involved in our annual selection process, it would help if such a test could help us predict the most promising applicants.

By 1969, when the course was formally divided into Child Care and Certificate in Social Work, we received about 500 completed applications for 50 places. Tutors then selected some 200, who were asked to submit an essay selected from three possible titles. In the belief that this gave some indication of educational ability, this resulted in 100 applicants, many of whom were experienced social workers. They were then invited for a full day in the college, which would include completion of a standard IQ test and a 16PF pro-forma and interview by two tutors or fieldwork teachers. The 16PF results were not used in the selection, but each interviewer was asked to complete their estimate of what the candidate's profile would look like. Applicants had the option to be sent a copy of their profile. The research project was established to examine the following questions:

> Were there any profile patterns that would enable us to identify successful candidates?
> Were there typical patterns emerging that would indicate a typical social worker's profile?
> Were profiles different for Child Care or CSW applicants?
> Did a comparison between test and subjective assessment differ between interviewers of different genders and levels of qualification?

In due course we extended these questions to include the wider generic intake and we also asked students to complete the test again at the end of the course.

Our results for the 1969 intake are not easy to summarise. Over all the tests that were administered it seemed that most applicants lay within the median scores. Otherwise they were of above average intelligence,* slightly more assertive, imaginative and free thinking than comparative groups. A few factors were however worth further consideration. Given the ten-point scale between 'opposite' traits these were:

Factor C
Affected by Feelings (emotional, easily upset) vs.
Emotionally Stable (faces reality, calm)

(Low Ego Strength)	(Higher Ego Strength)
Test Scores: CSW = 4	Child Care = 7

Interviewers favoured those with higher scores

For the 50% of all students completing the test at the end of the course, this difference had settled around the median

Factor G
Expedient (disregards rules) vs.
Conscientious (persevering, staid, moralistic)

(Weaker Super-Ego Strength)	(Stronger Super-Ego Strength)
CSW = 3	Child Care = 6

Interviewers favoured those with lower scores

For the 50% of all students completing the test at the end of this difference had vanished, with all registering a score of 3

Factor Q3
Undisciplined Self-Conflict (follows own urges) vs.
Controlled (socially precise)

CSW = 4	Child Care = 7

Interviewers favoured those with lower scores

For the 50% of all students completing the test at the end of the course this difference had settled around the median

---

* This factor in the 16PF indicates a measure of general ability rather than the narrow result in traditional time-tested IQ tests. In the standard IQ test 17% of applicants scored IQs of 126 and over.

Factor Q4
Relaxed (tranquil, unfrustrated) vs. **Tense** (frustrated, driven)

CSW = 3	Child Care = 7

Interviewers favoured median scores

For the 50% of all students completing the test at the end of the course this difference had settled around the median

Calculations were also made of four derived general characteristics placing a high percentage of the applicants indicating low anxiety levels, tending towards extraversion, high on tender-heartedness and above average for independence. In fact this factor was the most marked for accepted students. It was therefore tempting to say that in general social worker students were of above average intelligence, had low anxiety levels, were slightly more assertive and extrovert, independent and free thinking, as well as being imaginative and tender-hearted.

For this report I have to re-emphasise the point that these results should not be relied upon given the time lag since the information was collected. At the time, given the outline above we decided to end the search for a more objective and less expensive selection method. It would certainly be interesting to know whether any related research has been carried out since then.

SOCIAL WORKERS AND CLIENTS: EXPECTATIONS AND EXPERIENCE

This was a small exploratory research project that I undertook in late 1974 as it seemed to me that, although a few retrospective studies of the client's experience of social work intervention were emerging,[4] it would be interesting to get to the clients before they met their worker and ask what they expected before any possible influence occurred. I think this was the first such research and I was lucky to be conducting this at a time when the profession had virtually no media presence so that expectations would be relatively naïve. I wanted to explore the experiences of people who came for help to professional social workers and the views of the social worker who sought to offer this help. I wanted to explore whether the integrity of each was valued: How did clients experience the value base of the social workers? Further, was disagreement or disappointment handled without loss of respect? I had been very interested in a paper written in the 1950s by Helen Harris Perlman raising the question of why one in three people never returned after first contact with an agency, a serious loss given the anxieties to be overcome in approaching the agency in the first place.[5]

It proved impossible to interview the worker before contact, but a later interview relied on the referral form and detailed recording of the case. Delicate negotiations led to an arrangement whereby as soon as the office had a referral an intermediary visited to explain the situation and offer a fee of £1 for the participant's time. If at that point the situation required immediate intervention or there was no agreement, I withdrew. If the client agreed I visited before the social worker arrived. I then recorded a semi-structured interview which was transcribed. The process was repeated eight weeks later. I then interviewed the social worker, resulting in three transcripts to consider for each case. There were fifteen clients ranging in age from 21 to 87.

All the clients in the study were described as 'crisis' referrals. However, for two of these the referral followed a period of extreme concern, while they were at risk, but it was not until the last straw broke that they were directed to social services. One, an elderly lady who had fallen and broken her ankle, managed to put a 'HELP' sign in the window which was seen by a passing delivery man who phoned social services. The other, a 21-year-old couple, discovered that the woman's father had died during the night and got to social services via the doctor, the registrar and the housing department. All but this couple had been in touch with a range of health and social agencies during the chronic stage of their problem. It was generally assumed that they were all part of 'the welfare,' so that at the point of crisis the realisation that they were not all in harmony and, in the case of the council's housing and SSD in conflict, produced confusion and occasional anger. Although, in the Seebohm phrase, there was only one door for people to knock on, the route to it was often confusing and difficult. One subject, needing urgent financial assistance, recalled her contact with Social Security and a charity.

> Well I went to see them, first they said 'Oh, you can borrow from your neighbours.' I'm not asking, I'm demanding money, I'm entitled to it, so they gave me some … it was all very degrading. I can stand up for my rights but I always end up crying … they treat you as if, well, as if you are delinquents.
>
> The woman they sent down, well she was the wife of a doctor and she used to wrangle every time. She'd never done a day's work in her life – she'd got no idea – she treated me as if I was a charity case. I said you know what you can do with that money!

In general, subjects expected their social worker to be kind, to listen and be understanding with them and to use their professional knowledge of situations and the system but also have some authority. A single mother having trouble with her teenage son was quite clear:

> Somebody who could give him a sort of 'man to man' talk … he wants someone to take a firm line and say, 'All right, no work, no money, NO NOTHING' … I mean you have got to get through to him very carefully in the first place … the social workers they're trained to help you and, you know, a talk from these, not a brutality but a firm straight talk.

A mother desperately living with her large family in overcrowded accommodation put her finger on what she was expecting:

> They've really got to *listen* to you, what you're talking about. They've got to listen and look around and see what your place is like and look at you and see what you're talking about and really *understand*. Not to say 'We understand' ... Really look as if you *do* understand and make you feel as if you do care, otherwise it's just like going to the council officials.

Asked about training, all but one of the subjects assumed a sort of very broad apprenticeship model giving 'A basic knowledge of more or less everything,' 'Trained over a broad spectrum,' 'Trained to cope with all different classes.' One subject expected that they would have 'two or three years of a social science degree, or maybe less for a diploma,' but thought that this would probably only apply to the ones in charge.

When asked what help they required, all expected information about what to do, what was available and how the system worked. They expected befriending and support, inexpensive aids to help with a disability, expensive or complex resources or advocacy with regards to another organisation or authority. These expectations, the problems about access and the attitudes of other officials produced a general feeling of confusion as they waited for their first visit. One was 'all at sea,' while another explained 'I haven't got a clue.' When asked what they expected the social worker to do they said they 'didn't really know ... I don't know what they do or anything. I just went down because I was told to.' For all the subjects, familiar with health, council or voluntary contacts, the expected visit was new ground. Two examples illustrate the actual experience.

Example 1: Mrs A

Mrs A had approached the SSD for help getting her mother into a home as the overcrowded situation in the house was becoming unbearable. The social worker gave the subject and her mother lots of information about the council's homes, concentrating on a new home opening soon, which he highly recommended. He called again and completed an application form, commenting that it was not right for the mother to remain in the house as it was having a detrimental effect on the grandchildren's schooling. Although the social worker did not talk about alternatives, the client thought he was 'as helpful as he could be and didn't hold anything back.' As time went by and no further visit or contact was made it became clear that the social worker had failed to adequately address the subject's main issue, the immediate pressure and tension in the family caused by her mother's presence and behaviour, neither had he indicated when this home was opening or confirmed that her mother had a place booked. Many attempts were made to contact the social worker, but he was never available so the family was forced to make independent enquiries in order to get the reassurance and information required for them to make some short term decisions. In the end the hope given in the initial visit was replaced by frustration born of lack of information: 'If only we knew something.'

Example 2: Mr and Mrs L

Mr and Mrs L and their four children lived in poor, privately rented accommodation. The children slept in an overcrowded attic room, which the health authorities had condemned. Following the landlord's decision to sell the property a notice to quit was issued placing the family in crisis. The GP had declined to help but a local newspaper had published a short piece on their predicament. Because they had not lived in the area for long the local housing department could not help. When Mrs L asked the manager what she should do he had replied, 'I don't care what you do, you're not on my list,' but the receptionist had suggested that she approach social services. Following this experience Mrs L was concerned about the reception she might get at social services but just wanted to know whether they would understand her situation and whether they could help. Perhaps they might have the power to influence the housing department, but she was concerned that they might want to take the children away. Practical advice about what to do if they became homeless would help. She expected the worker to be trained and have 'a great deal of knowledge.' Mrs L was asked to call at the office three days after my initial interview. Unfortunately after an initial discussion and completion of forms the social worker was taken ill, but after a short delay he made further visits in a short period of time but, in the subject's view, had not been much help as 'they can't solve it,' although Mrs L saw that 'they still *want* to help but everything is the same in the end. They think we might get a place but the council still says no.' There was a lot of talk and form filling, but there was 'nothing really *done* about it, although the worker was very nice and pleasant.' The only practical steps were to contact the health department again, and to make contact with her local councillor and a local self-help group.

Matching these accounts against those of the social workers was an interesting experience. Mrs A's social worker, Mr Caulton, identified his client as the mother but gave both mother and daughter the details. When further questioned, he agreed that his information was confined to council homes but he had mentioned that there were private homes which 'we more or less recommend.' On the second visit, three days later, he completed the application forms insisting that he did this with the mother alone, with Mrs A bringing them tea when they finished. He explained that he tried to make the procedure 'as relaxed as possible – I try to make it a general conversation and bring the questions in as we go along. It doesn't look as much as though you are authoritarian … just having a little conversation.' Over tea there was a general discussion, described as 'all very airy fairy.' He marked the application as urgent with a note to visit monthly. Mr Caulton had appreciated the strain on the family and on Mrs A; he thought the usual thing was for a family to take an elderly relative in when they were ill but then return them to their own home when they were recovered, arranging for home help and other support services, but this family chose not to do that.

He thought that Mrs A would be satisfied with his intervention although they would get more dissatisfied 'if they have to wait two or three years … which is more than likely unless she is suddenly brought forward.' He felt sorry for the situation they were in and thought the idea of sending mother home would not be right as it would be too traumatic for his client. Social workers were in an unsatisfactory position:

> We can see the urgency, but you can't put the urgency on paper, you can only put facts on paper. When someone asks for a place we say 'Yes, OK,' but then when you go back six months or so later and they haven't heard anything you are absolutely deflated. There is not a damn thing you can do about it ... but you can't say 'Well, I'm sorry but you will have to wait quite a few years.' I feel that the client won't accept that there aren't enough homes when they get to 85, 86 or 90 they should *make* a space for them ... They're always on television or the wireless saying to approach the social services, yet the minute you go down you have to say 'Ah well, it may say that but we don't do it.' It makes it very hard, very hard indeed, you've got to keep covering up.

The L family's social worker Mr Adamson saw the initial problem as just a housing problem as the family basis was good, although 'something else might develop in time.' He visited the family and thought that the accommodation was 'pretty grotty ... the room where the children slept was very overcrowded.' He advised Mrs L to contact the local councillor and to join the local action group which was putting pressure on the council, and also to keep in touch with him. He advised them to stay put as once the initial year passed the housing department was more subject to pressure. He was aware of his own powerlessness in not being able to offer an alternative: 'They've got a roof over their head which is more than we could offer in some tatty B & B. If they were to move or be moved outside the borough they would lose all the benefits where they are now ... even if they are evicted social services could not help their case.' Given this impossible situation Mr Adamson saw his main role as supportive for at least a year, as 'living in conditions like this mother may become more depressed and the kids might well get into trouble, they certainly are at risk.' This social worker felt he had no control at all:

> If I took action, a positive step, and say that this situation is impossible for these children the result would probably be far more disastrous. I wouldn't be prepared to take that risk because I have no control. If I had I would be prepared to force the issue but then you are in the hands of other people, so *many* other people so *far* removed ... Since being a large department ... there are so many people in the pipeline and it doesn't help one little bit. Of course the client has the greatest need but it's now equally frustrating for the social worker who wants to get something done.

Mr Adamson felt that in this situation no one was likely be satisfied. From now on he would respond to pressure from the client and in turn would put pressure on the system. 'That's how it works.'

These interactions, where most applicants and social workers remained unsatisfied, had to be viewed against the major changes in social work following the Seebohm Report. This study shared with others the lack of any clear objectives for the new departments with the consequent uncertainty for staff which, given the extreme pressure on workloads, led to some confusion about what actually was expected of them. This was exacerbated in the fleeting encounters in this study. Unable to deal adequately with immediate expressed need the workers used their training to apply the art of consolation or, in Goffman's great phrase, they had to 'Cool the Mark out.'[6] In some cases this resolved into mutual consolation for workers seen to be doing their best. In this situation the social worker came to rely on fleeting contacts to help to reaffirm their identity. Unfortunately this study indicated that when difficult access is followed by low level contact a process of disenchantment and alienation develops, well described by Goffman:

> When the encounter fails to capture the attention of the participants but does not release them from the obligation of involving themselves in it, the persons are likely to feel unhappy; for them the interaction fails to come off.[7]

Behind all this of course was the failure of successive governments to provide the resources to back up new compassionate legislation, thus leaving local authorities and their staff to handle the painful gap between raised expectations and lack of resources. At the time of this study the major issue was shortage of housing and the facilities to deal with the consequences. My colleague Bram Bottle emphasised this factor in a study published by BASW and Shelter in 1974:

> Where housing departments are unable to provide accommodation, they often refer families to the social services department, leading to an expectation on the part of the client that we will solve their problem. Anxieties are raised to an intolerable level when they find that all we have to offer is bed and breakfast and the result is breakdown in marital and child/parent relationships ... [resulting] in loss of faith and increasing frustration for the family and no job satisfaction for the social worker.[8]

In conclusion I argued that these failures of professional identity and security, of effective encounter, of clear objectives and immediately available resources underlay the failure in the careers of the interactants. They prevented both professionals and clients from having an honest, efficient and satisfying encounter that offered congruent experiences for both parties. This eroded the professional integrity of the worker. Considering the wider aspects of this work I argued whether, given these failures, social work could be classed as a profession, particularly as it was now located in large bureaucratic organisations which themselves had limited control over available resources. In this situation social work may, like the medical profession, produce its own iatrogenic problems. If the Seebohm vision of community and consumer involvement in the services were to be realised, many of these tensions might be eased by restoring respect and dignity. A process which would require social workers to develop roles such as community innovator, mediator, advocate, researcher and educator should result in more open and honest interactions towards resolving the powerlessness of so many applicants.[9]

NOTES AND REFERENCES

1. See Grey, E. (1969). 'Workloads in Children's Departments.' Home Office Research Studies. London: HMSO.
2. Grey, *op. cit.*
3. Cattell, R. and Eber, H. (1964). *Handbook for the Sixteen Personality Factor Questionnaire*. (1964 Revision). Champaign. Illinois; Saville, P. (1972). *The British Standardisation of the 16PF Test*. Windsor: NFER Publishing Company.
4. Mayer, J. E. and Timms, N. (1970). *The Client Speaks* London: Routledge & Kegan Paul; Timms, N. (Ed.) (1973). *The Receiving End*. London: Routledge & Kegan Paul; Rees, S. (1974). No More Than Contact, *British Journal of Social Work*, Vol. 4, No 3, pp. 255–279; Glampson, A., Glastonbury, B. and Fruin, D. (1977). Knowledge and Perceptions of the Social Services, *Journal of Social Policy* Vol. 6, No 1, pp. 1–16; Lishman, J. (1978). A Clash in Perspectives? *British Journal of Social Work*, Vol. 8, No 3, pp. 301–312; Reid, F. (1974). Expectations of the Social Services by the Client. Address: Directors of Social Services Annual Conference, 1964.
5. Perlman, H. (1962). Intake and Some Role Considerations. In Kasius, C. (Ed.) *Social Casework in the 1950s. Selected Articles 1950–60*. NY: FSAA, pp. 163–174.
6. Goffman, E. (1952). On Cooling the Mark Out: Some Aspects of Adaptation to Failure, *Interpersonal and Biological magazine*, Vol. 15, Issue 4.
7. Goffman, E. (1957). Alienation from Interaction, *Human Relations*, Vol. 10, No. 1.
8. Bottle, A. B. (1974). *Homelessness in Kent: A Survey*. Maidstone: Shelter, p. 66.
9. Jordan, M. B. (1976). *Social Worker's and Client's Expectation and Experience*. MA Dissertation, University of Kent at Canterbury.

TWELVE

1977–1980
THE COUNTER REVOLUTION – MONETARISM

I think we have gone through a period when too many children and people have been given to understand 'I have a problem, it is the Government's job to cope with it!' or 'I have a problem, I will go and get a grant to cope with it!' 'I am homeless, the Government must house me!' and so they are casting their problems on society and who is society? There is no such thing as society! There are individual men and women and there are families and no government can do anything except through people and people look to themselves first. It is our duty to look after ourselves and then also to help look after our neighbour and life is a reciprocal business and people have got the entitlements too much in mind without the obligations, because there is no such thing as an entitlement unless someone has first met an obligation.

– Margaret Thatcher[1n]

We are not here in this world to find elegant solutions, pregnant with initiative, or to serve the ways and means of profitable progress. No. We are here to provide for all those who are weaker and hungrier, more battered and crippled than ourselves. That is our only certain good and great purpose on earth, and if you ask me about those insoluble economic problems that may arise if the top is deprived of their initiative, I would answer 'To hell with them.' The top is greedy and mean and will always find a way to take care of themselves. They always do.

– Michael Foot, Labour leader, from his 1983 campaign speech

INTERNATIONAL EVENTS

Iran

The Cold War between a more confident Soviet Republic (led by Leonid Brezhnev) changed as America (under Jimmy Carter), counting the cost of Vietnam, let their initiative slip. Russia spread its influence across Africa, backing revolutionary groups in Angola, Mozambique, Guinea and Ethiopia, mirroring the American history in some South American countries. From the early 1970s secular and religious opposition to the Shah of Persia had been growing due to his expensive expansion of the military (encouraged by the UK and the USA), with the consequent suppression of the population, his modernisation programmes (for example, improving the position of women) and the obvious western influences. When the final revolution came it came quickly and surprised observers across the world. In January 1979 millions of citizens spilled on to the streets and on January 16th the Shah went into permanent exile in America, who accepted the Shah (who was dying of cancer). Fifteen days later, the radical exiled Shia clergyman Ayatollah Khomeini, who had been promoting the revolution from abroad, landed in Tehran to a rapturous reception and immediately established his own government, appointing Mehdi Bazargan as Prime Minister with the following declaration:

> I hereby pronounce Bazargan as the Ruler, and since I have appointed him he must be obeyed. The nation must obey him. This is not an ordinary government. It is a government based on the Sharia. Opposing this government means opposing the Sharia of Islam ... Revolt against God's government is a revolt against God. Revolt against God is blasphemy.[2]

It took ten days for the Khomeini government to establish itself, February 11th being celebrated ever since as the Islamic Revolution's Victory Day. America and the UK finally decided to refer to this country as Iran, the historically correct title for which the Shah had campaigned for forty years. By November 1979 the Sharia government was well established and anger grew against America, including their role in destroying the previous nationalist government under Prime Minister Mosaddegh in 1953, so on November 4th student protesters invaded the American Embassy and held the staff hostage. After many attempts at a diplomatic resolution failed, President Carter authorised a rescue in April 1980 by helicopters launched from ships in the Mediterranean. The mission had to be aborted after three of the eight aircraft failed and then a fourth caught fire, killing eight servicemen. This chaotic failure was said to be a significant factor in Carter's loss of the presidency in January 1981 when he lost to the Republican Ronald Reagan, thus setting the scene for Reagan and Thatcher's mutual support.

Afghanistan

Happy to have ousted America from an important foothold in the Middle East, the Soviet Union, having encouraged a coup in Afghanistan, decided to invade that tribal country in December 1979. In common with so many previous invaders (see Chapter 1), their nine-year occupation would not be easy. In the face of international opposition, their justification for the invasion was that the government had invited their presence. This had some legitimacy as the new communist government had lost support due to its violent suppression of local tribal leaders, mostly devout Muslims supported by more radical Mujahideen insurgents. America's reaction was to support the diverse Mujahideen groups, including many Arab volunteers who had now based themselves in Northern Pakistan. Among these groups was the Al-Qaeda organisation led by the rich Saudi Arabian Osama bin Laden. They were supplied, to the tune of billions of dollars, with ammunition: light and heavy arms including Stinger missiles capable of destroying Russian helicopters and aircraft. As the situation in the country disintegrated and insurgent attacks increased, the number of Russian troops increased from the original 30,000 to over 100,000. The war caused immense destruction within Afghanistan, with estimates of several million people killed. A third of the population fled to Pakistan and Iran.[3n]

The Soviet Union

While Moscow's international initiatives advanced or retreated, its domestic economic and social policies were meeting increased resistance following the 1968 Prague Spring. In devoutly catholic Poland, resistance to Moscow increased, boosted by the first Polish pope Karol Wojtyla (Pope John Paul II) and a series of strikes by the national workers union Solidarity culminating in a total strike in the Lenin Shipyard at Gdansk, where thousands of workers locked themselves into the yard (following Jimmy Reid's example in Scotland) (see Chapter 9). Days of negotiations with a weak communist government led, on August 31st 1980, to the signing of an agreement which promised free independent trades unions, the release of political prisoners, uncensored media and the right to strike. Within days similar agreements were signed across the country, and nine million workers joined Solidarity. The Gdansk strike was led by the mischievous Lech Wałęsa, who eventually became president of a free Poland. Although the final victory took another nine years and the election of the relatively liberal Mikhail Gorbachev, the events at Gdansk, the last grand uprising of the workers, showed that the Soviet system could be challenged; this led, bit by bit, to its collapse in 1991.[4]

My memory is that events in Iran made more impact in the UK than did the Afghanistan war, which, while it clearly indicated a warming up of the Cold War, did not directly affect us. The exception to this was the 1980 Summer Olympics in Moscow, which, as part of the sanctions imposed on Russia for its aggression, was boycotted by western nations led by the USA. Fierce debates gripped the press between the politicians and the athletes who argued that the 'purity' of sport should not be used for political ends although, of course, the opposite argument had been deployed for the anti-apartheid campaign against South Africa. For different reasons, China, Japan, Argentina, Iran, Germany and Canada gave their full support. France, Australia and Great Britain supported the boycott but left it to the respective national athletic committees to make the final decision. In the event Great Britain sent a team of 326 people, supporting 170 athletes who won six gold medals. The government refused to allow British Airways to carry anyone to or from the Games so the individual teams had to be ferried in and out just for their events, not as a team.

The Iran–Iraq War

The Middle East erupted again in the autumn of 1980 when Iraq invaded Iran. This resulted from historical rivalries and disputes, brought to a head not only by the rise of the Khomeini government, but also by repeated Iranian calls for the Shia population in Iraq to rise up against the secular Ba'athist regime of Saddam Hussein. Iraq launched its massive air and ground offensive in late September 1980 to start the longest and most murderous war since WWI. Despite the insecurity of the new Iranian government, the population rallied to the cause, the Iraq invasion was held and 80% of its naval and radar targets were destroyed. The war then developed into long drawn-out trench warfare: the Iranians using mass ground attacks, the Iraqis using heavy weapons and poison gas. By 1982, however, Iraq was losing men, equipment and air power at too high a rate to be sustained, a situation which America was not prepared to tolerate. President Reagan therefore poured arms and ammunition into Iraq, quickly followed by the French, who sold helicopters, missiles and fighter aircraft to Iraq. Unfortunately this increased armament was met with massed infantry led by the Iranian Revolution Guard leading to stalemate for another five years, by which time populations on both sides were weary of war and governments sought a way out of the impasse. (In mid 1987 the Security Council called for a ceasefire and a return to the original boundaries, although Iraq, boosted by even more powerful weapons of mass destruction from the west, was ready to drive the Iranians into submission. It was during this final phase that mustard gas and cyanide weapons were used extensively. On August 20th peace was restored and UN Peacekeepers arrived. The military and civilian casualties of this terrible deadly war were very high at 1.5 million deaths. The consequences would bug the whole of the Middle East and key world powers for decades.)

Zimbabwe

Throughout this period the deadly civil war in Ian Smith's white governed Southern Rhodesia dragged on while the country was subject to severe sanctions. As neighbouring Angola and Mozambique gained independence from Portugal, the Smith regime became more isolated. In response to increased pressure from the Zimbabwean guerrillas, led by Robert Mugabe and Joshua Nkomo, Smith signed an accord in 1978 which gave 78 seats to Africans and 28 to whites in the parliament of Zimbabwe–Rhodesia, voted for on separate rolls. The deal was rejected by Mugabe and not recognised by the UK and the UN. Following further pressure from Commonwealth countries a constitutional conference was held in London which resulted in a ceasefire and a transitional period during which sanctions were lifted. Free elections were held in 1979, and in 1980 Zimbabwe became independent with Robert Mugabe as prime minister.

NATIONAL EVENTS

Previous chapters have outlined the drift of the individualised libertarian 1960s culture into the mainstream and the raft of liberal legislation which had carried forward the post-war welfare responsibilities of the state to which we had become accustomed. Alongside the youthful discontents expressed on the streets there developed widespread concerns at the increasing power exercised by the trades unions, the expansion of the public sector and, for those of a moderate disposition, a general move to the left of the Labour Party.

The journalist Paul Johnson described worries about 'The burgeoning bureaucrats of local and central government; the new breed of "administrators" who control schools, hospitals and even the arts; sociology lecturers ... so called social workers with their glib pseudo-solutions to non-problems.'[5] Such concerns were shared by the International Monetary Fund as they viewed the recessive effect on economies of the rise in oil prices and the cost of the Vietnam war alongside inflation, increased union power and increased public spending. The position of Britain was a particular worry; we were seen as 'the sick man of Europe.'

These concerns took some time to penetrate through to the general public, who still enjoyed the happy atmosphere of the early 1970s. However, by the middle of the decade this had given way to the concerns expressed in The Strawbs' song 'Part Of The Union,' which stayed at number 2 in the charts for three weeks.[6] It was to become the marching song for protesters in the coming years and, forty years later, for social workers in their anti-austerity protests (in which I would be heavily involved).

In late 1975 an amazing Anglo-French enterprise launched Concorde, the first commercial plane to break the sound barrier. Inflation rose steadily to a painful 26%, and in November 1975 the Irish Republican Army (IRA) assassinated Ross McWhirter, a leading Conservative[7n] who had argued for fierce restrictions on all Irish people living in England and had offered a large reward for the arrest of the notorious IRA Balcombe Street Gang, whose members were subsequently convicted of his murder.

The Sick Man

The assertive Dennis Healey, having grasped the role of Chancellor by late 1974 and realising just how bad the economy was, had restricted public spending, restrained wages and fought a long fight with the unions. By late 1975 his policies were slowly but surely working. Inflation fell, wage restraint broadly worked and public spending was reducing. More cuts were made, share prices rose and, thanks to some cash-rich workers, pension money made the city happy. On March 16th 1976 the Prime Minister, Harold Wilson, took all his Cabinet and the public by surprise by announcing his resignation now that the economy was on the up. He never explained his sudden decision, but I agree with those that think he must have realised his declining powers. His parting honours list was a notorious two-fingered salute to the establishment. Wilson nominated the very experienced Jim Callaghan as leader of the party and he was duly appointed by a narrow majority after three full voting rounds, becoming Prime Minister on April 5th 1976.

For the next three years 'Sunny Jim' Callaghan faced governing the country with a tiny parliamentary majority (which would soon disappear altogether) and chronic economic difficulties. Divisions in the Commons were characterised by pulling in MPs who were sick, on trolleys or near death. There was one incident when the Whips took a member's pulse to check that he was alive enough to vote! Retaining Dennis Healey as Chancellor meant that the two most powerful offices were held by individuals moving away from Labour's traditional Keynesian policies towards a need to control the money supply. A 'compact' was signed with the unions which tied them to accept low wage increases despite high inflation to help get the country back on its feet. During these years old divisions in the Labour Party re-emerged, resulting in an increased support for a more left-wing party, among which was the Militant Tendency, a Trotskyist group which gained seats in local council elections, particularly in the North West. The young Neil Kinnock, recently elected from South Wales, was a strong supporter of trades unions, and both he and Tony Benn had noted the continuing rise of Arthur Scargill within the National Union of Miners. A small group of leading Labour MPs, concerned about recent events and the direction in which the party might be moving, were thinking of forming an alternative political party.

What went wrong was largely due to the domestic and international commentariat, who, having largely swallowed the monetarist pill, portrayed us as a country on the edge of disaster with an unsustainably unbalanced budget, even though in fact government spending was far less important than the rise in oil prices and the wage inflation that naturally followed. However, these external pressures became so intense that the government feared a run on the pound and decided to seek a loan from the IMF to allow the existing policies to continue their work. The last three months of 1976 were marked by a very disputatious Labour Party Conference in Blackpool, continuing speculation from the media and markets, and finally prolonged negotiations with the IMF against a deadline of December 31st when we were due to repay existing loans to various central banks (which would have made our reserves dangerously low). The IMF team arrived at the end of October, but agreement was not reached until late November on terms much less favourable than the original demands, settled at £2.5 billion over two years. A series of Cabinet meetings ran until December 14th when the offer was agreed by a majority of five ministers, and the final deal was confirmed in Parliament on December 21st, a very close call. Some £320 million would be spent to stimulate employment, £945 million on defence, housing, roads and industry, and £217 million was earmarked for food subsidies. Welfare and NHS cuts would be very small. When the borrowing requirement turned out to be just over half of the projected figure given to the IMF, it became fairly clear that senior officials in the Treasury and Bank of England had manoeuvred the figures to ensure the imposition of budget cuts that they could not otherwise have achieved.[8] In fact, the Callaghan government only used half the IMF loan and paid it back ahead of schedule.

In August 1976, tucked away in the residential streets of Willesden, North London, an incident in a relatively small company owned by three entrepreneurs sparked a national debate, the lessons from which would shape much of the next decade and beyond. From the owner's surnames they contrived the name Grunwick. The company processed photographs, and as cameras became cheaper and colour photography more popular it expanded into a very profitable enterprise. The workers were mostly drawn from the local Asian communities and they were managed in traditional hierarchical fashion which, as the pressure of work grew, bore down more heavily on the workers, resulting in petty restrictions and compulsory overtime in the busy summer seasons. On August 20th an unreasonable order, from a known to be heavy-handed manager, led to a walk out by five employees who were summarily dismissed for their action. There being no union representation in the factories, these five ex-employees asked other employees to sign a petition and were eventually advised to seek the help of APEX, the trade union representing professional, executive, clerical and computer staff. The local activist Jack Dromey was asked to assist.[9n]

Unbelievably, the subsequent strike lasted for some 24 months as every move made by the unions, including mass picketing (including by miners led by Arthur Scargill), sympathetic strikes by postal workers (which blocked the post on which the whole business depended) and clever public relations was matched by Grunwick's managing director George Ward, who recruited key right-wing organisations to assist (by subscription, by driving the non-striking workers by bus and finally the fatal blow of organising a 'Pony Express' which stormed into the works at night, collected all the outgoing mail and drove into the countryside where a fleet of small vehicles waited to distribute the post outside London). The dispute itself, the idea of poorly paid Asian women being oppressed by bullying managers and the pictures spreading round the world of the mass picketing and police actions caught the public attention, gaining support on both sides from all ethnic groups. A special Cabinet committee was formed, meeting daily to monitor events. In June 1977 Lord Scarman was appointed to lead a court of inquiry into the origins of the dispute and the issues between Grunwick and APEX. In August the inquiry published its recommendations that the full-time strikers be reinstated and that the company should allow APEX to represent the workers. The strike struggled on until the summer of 1978. Ward ignored all the recommendations, whilst the company survived and prospered. Lessons were certainly not lost on the political right.[10]

In the summer of 1978 the Labour government was doing well in the polls, the economy was seen to be recovering, inflation and unemployment were falling, and people could see the results of Healey's determined management. Most of the Cabinet expected an autumn election in order to restore a workable majority. Fatally the Prime Minister decided to delay until the spring of 1979. He did not trust the polls and could see no reason why the economy would not continue to improve, so a spring election might bring a higher majority. For the third year the unions were tied to a wage increase of 5%; however, over this time workers had seen inflation eat away the value of their income and it became almost impossible to hold the line. No sooner had the election announcement been made than a dispute arose in the Ford factories. The company had had a profitable year, their directors had been well rewarded so the 5% offered to workers was, not surprisingly, rejected. The Transport and General Workers' Union put in a bid for 30%, and 57,000 workers came out in support for the next five weeks, eventually settling for 17%.

In the following months, oil tanker drivers, haulage drivers, British Leyland car workers, dock workers, water and sewage workers and BBC electricians all came out on strike, all settling for an average of about 20%. The disruption caused by these strikes caused great distress: the army was put on standby, but the most damage was done by the media coverage and tales of impending disaster. 'Sunny Jim' did not help matters when in January, returning from an international conference in Guadeloupe, he dismissed the idea that the country was in chaos. His response was twisted by *The Sun* newspaper to make the headline 'Crisis? What Crisis?' In January the public sector workers, who had suffered most during the recession, took action. The National Union of Public Employees called random stoppages of a million manual staff from caretakers, cooks, ambulance men and refuse collectors, demanding a minimum wage of £60 a week. The final straw came when the parks and cemetery staff in Liverpool walked out, refusing to bury the dead. At one point 150 unburied bodies were left in plastic bags in a disused factory in Speke with 25 more being added every day.

The removal of all the 'taken for granted' services hit the public hard, although there had always been food in the shops and no one had died of hunger, but of course the media had a field day. By March most of the disputes had been settled, but on March 28th 1979, despite frantic searches for allies and sick MPs being brought to the Commons in wheelchairs and sick beds, the government lost a vote of confidence against the Conservatives, Liberals, Scottish Nationalists and Ulster Unionists. Jim Callaghan was consequently the first prime minister since 1924 to ask for a dissolution on the grounds that his government had lost a vote in the commons. Two days later Parliament and the nation, but particularly Mrs Thatcher, were shaken by the death of her favourite MP Airey Neave, whose car had exploded as he drove into the Commons underground car park; the Irish National Liberation Army claimed responsibility. The bombers had attacked the heart of government!

The election campaign was short. Callaghan was generally liked, his approval rating against Thatcher in the polls increased from 39% versus 33% to 44% versus 25%, and he could point to his achievements in managing the economy after the oil crisis and his support from the unions – although more recent events caused some doubt about who held the power in that relationship. Apart from industrial disputes there was a positive feeling in the air. For the first time since the war housing needs had largely been met, unemployment was low and inflation was dropping. A woman contender was something quite new, but Margaret Thatcher quickly mastered the media, easily winning the TV war. Callaghan and his team were understandably battle scarred and tired. On May 3rd 1979 the Conservative victory was clear, with 339 seats taking 61 from Labour. Nonetheless, the winners had only 43.9% of the vote, the lowest for a winning party since 1945. The Labour vote had increased by 75,000.

Margaret Thatcher

On May 4th 1979, Margaret Thatcher stood proudly on the steps of No 10 Downing Street and uttered what to my mind is the most hypocritical victory speech ever. Quoting St Francis of Assisi, she said

> Where there is discord, may we bring harmony. Where there is error, may we bring truth. Where there is doubt, may we bring faith. And where there is despair, may we bring hope.

The new Prime Minister quickly signalled the change in her relationship with the unions and set about organising a Cabinet of loyal supporters to launch her monetarist regime.[11n]

The politics of Britain would never be the same, although the pressures in the economic and social situation would suffer many crises; unemployment would rise to unprecedented levels and unrest would continue well into the mid 1980s. The fate of the other main parties was not good. The Liberals and Scottish Nationalists had been routed, Labour moved further to the left against strong opposition from Healey, who was fiercely attacked for his policies, and when Callaghan eventually resigned the leadership in October 1980 they took their revenge. They elected a committed socialist, the highly literate and sparkling speaker Michael Foot (MP for Plymouth, Devonport) as leader.[12n] Although a fierce campaigner and, in strictly political terms, the right man of the moment, his somewhat dishevelled look was seized on by cartoonists, and this gave plenty of opportunities for the right-wing press to attack. All in all it was not a wise choice. Had Dennis Healey won, Labour would have had a leader tough and determined enough to equal Margaret Thatcher who he termed the 'Great She Elephant.' In view of the clear leftwards move in the Party, four moderate senior members, Shirley Williams, David Owen, Bill Rodgers and Roy Jenkins, decided in March to form the Social Democratic Party, taking nine other members with them and winning by-elections against both Labour and Tory seats.[13n]

Margaret Thatcher, the daughter of a Lincolnshire grocer with a strong Methodist background, who had studied Chemistry at Oxford (where she became President of the Conservative Association), was much influenced by the writings of Hayek and general arguments against state intervention. In 1951 she had married Dennis Thatcher, a wealthy businessman, and then became a barrister, entering Parliament in 1959. Those in the know had some idea of what we were in for. During a visit to Iran in 1978 she discussed with the Ambassador that there were some people in her Party who still believed in consensus politics; she described them as 'Quislings, traitors [and] I mean it.'[14]

Her maiden speech was in support of a Bill to make all local council meetings open to the public and subsequently supported the return of birching to the penal system. Margaret was a very determined, hard-working woman who would drive her monetarist ideas forward, perhaps with a narrow focus ('Blinkered and proud of it,' she once remarked) as against some of her colleagues' more strategic approach. It was said that she came not with a list of policies but enemies including trades unions, miners, teachers and single mothers. We are indebted to the ninety-year-old Harold Macmillan for a clear explanation of the two competing economic theories. In a long wandering speech he explained:

> Then the prime minister tried to slim the public sector, and of course it was very disagreeable ... It had to be done and it still needs to be done. The question is what do we do now? ... As always, there are broadly two answers ... Many of your Lordships will remember that it operated in the nursery. How do you treat a cold? One nanny said 'Feed a cold!' – she was a Neo-Keynesian. Another nanny said 'Starve the child!' – she was a monetarist.[15]

Once inside No 10, all did not go smoothly for Thatcher. Among her Cabinet of 21 she appointed the very experienced Willie Whitelaw as her Deputy, Geoffrey Howe as Chancellor, Michael Heseltine (Environment), Patrick Jenkins (Health and Social Security), Keith Joseph (Industry) and Lord Carrington (Foreign Secretary). The first two problems on her agenda were money and the unions. The answer to the first was to restrict the money supply by raising interest rates, cutting income tax, but raising VAT to 15%. These steps, combined with oil wealth, raised the value of Sterling to the detriment of industry. Unemployment rose above 2 million by the end of 1980, and this was especially hard on the youth. Government spending was cut in all departments, including the Foreign Office and Defence. Between these two departments it was decided that the cost of keeping a permanent naval patrol in the South Atlantic could not be justified. Generals in Argentina took this as a sign that we had lost interest in our Falkland Islands which lay just off that country's coast.

Despite protests from 364 leading economists, the government proceeded to raise taxes further, thus precipitating a rise in unemployment to three million by Christmas 1982. Union reform was dealt with by three Acts in four years. These restricted lawful picketing to six strikers, action was confined only to the actual employer, the definition of a trade dispute was narrowed and employers were no longer required to recognise trades unions. Employers could obtain injunctions and sue unions for damages.[16]

As Thatcher's popularity fell steeply, Cabinet ministers and others (she would term them the 'Wets') suggested that she should resign, but, supported by the loyal William Whitelaw, she was able to resist (later she was to remark that 'Everyone needs a Willie'). The need to regain popularity and ideology were combined in the 'right to buy' policy (Housing Act 1980) which allowed council house tenants to buy houses at discounts on the market price from 33 to 50% depending on the length of the tenancy. This was classic Thatcherism, appealing to the typical British belief in the ownership of one's own house, relieving central government of the cost of subsidies and leaving local authorities to face the consequences while depriving them of the funds to build more houses. Home ownership was predicted to ensure more Tory votes.

Plans by the National Coal Board to close several uneconomic pits provoked a strong reaction from the National Union of Miners. Faced with no preparation by the Department of Energy and the general recession there was no alternative but to submit. The closure plan was withdrawn, subsidies were increased, imports restricted and redundancy terms increased. The fig leaf for this U-turn was that the miners were a 'special case.' The media wondered whether this was the end of the Thatcher experiment. Otherwise, with inflation raging, recession biting and credit restrictions loosening, the money supply could not be controlled. The economy was shrinking and businesses were going bust at a high rate. Challenged at the 1980 Brighton Conservative Party Conference Thatcher replied with a carefully prepared phrase that marked her period of office: 'You turn if you want to. The Lady's not for turning.' Later in that speech, prioritising the economy she summarised her basic beliefs:

> Without a healthy economy we cannot have a healthy society. But it is not the state that creates a healthy society. When the state grows too powerful, people feel that they count for less and less. The state drains society, not only of its wealth but of its initiative, of energy, the will to improve and innovate as well as to preserve what is best ... There is not a generation gap in a happy and united family. People yearn to be able to rely on some generally accepted standards.[17]

Later she was to explain,

> This is the road I am resolved to follow. This is the path I must go. I ask all of you who have spirit – the bold, the steadfast and the young at heart – to stand and join with me.

The government was now below Labour and the new SDP in the polls.

With local businesses closing and prices rising, a series of strikes and riots broke out across the country. In 1981 in Brixton, where 60% of black youths were unemployed, rioters burnt 200 shops and streets were barricaded, with 200 people, mostly police, injured. Lord Scarman was once again asked to investigate. Norman Tebbit (who Foot had described as a 'semi-house-trained polecat') had more immediate simple advice: 'I grew up in the 1930s with an unemployed father. He did not riot. He got on his bike and looked for work and he went on looking until he found it.' Four months later Southall erupted with petrol bombs, arson and a series of serious attacks on the police. Rioting spread to Leeds, Birmingham, Glasgow and the Toxteth area of Liverpool. This was the most violent, with protesters fiercely attacking the police and their vehicles and setting fire to many properties in the very run down area of the borough. The police resorted to deploying CS gas (for the first time in the UK) and driving Land Rovers into the crowds. Some 700 buildings and 100 cars were destroyed and 1,000 people were injured, the numbers shared equally between police and protestors. Michael Heseltine decided he needed to investigate; his view coincided with Scarman's that the underlying causes were unemployment, poverty and hard line police attitudes, particularly against young black men. Thatcher saw it as lack of initiative through years of dependency on welfare. Heseltine, however, following what he saw as the best traditions of the Tory party, stuck to his guns and managed to gather private businesses and public funding for investments, housing and job creation programmes topped off by the transformation of a household tip to a great Garden Festival, which went some way to raise morale and brought in over three million visitors. It certainly started the regeneration of the Liverpool waterfront.[18n]

It now transpired that new calculations had shown that the next Budget would require further cuts worth £5 billion. Fresh from Liverpool, Heseltine and several other members of the Cabinet were horrified, leading to one of the most angry Cabinet meetings ever, resolved by the Prime Minister reshuffling the Cabinet – out went the 'Wets' (not quite all of them, of course, that would be bad PR). At this low point Mrs Thatcher was the most unpopular prime minister since polls began; the protesters and strikers united in the cry 'Maggie, Maggie, Maggie. Out, Out, Out!' We were about to learn that when cornered Mrs Thatcher just fought even harder.

Northern Ireland

The late 1970s and 1980s saw a strange change in the cultural climate of the UK. The free individualism of the 1960s remained the accepted norm of most social interaction, but the harsher economic and political experiences outlined above added an angrier and more commercial element. The IRA continued its bombing campaign both in Northern Ireland and on the mainland, despite two attempts to negotiate a ceasefire in 1972 and 1975. The campaign seemed to last forever, the government being unable to act on demands that troops remain in barracks followed by withdrawal and a release of Republican prisoners. The long war of national independence would last for the next twenty years, and was aimed at killing as many British Army personnel as possible. This meant a sustained bombing campaign, designed to make the six counties of the Province ungovernable and to terrorise people into a peace which would force a complete British withdrawal from Northern Ireland, leaving the Irish people free to manage their own affairs. Between 1976 and 1980 there was only one IRA bomb on the mainland, although the Loyalist Ulster Defence force bombed two pubs in Glasgow frequented by Irish Catholics.

In August 1979, just off the western coast of Southern Ireland, the IRA assassinated Lord Mountbatten, second cousin to the Queen. The radio-controlled bomb had been placed in the unguarded boat the previous night. Two teenagers, Nicholas Knatchbull, one of Mountbatten's grandsons, and a crew member, were also killed; Lady Brabourne (aged 83) died the following day. All others on board were seriously injured. This was a major blow, which drew international attention to the events in Ireland and led to widespread mourning for a man who had served the country so well. Paramilitary prisoners were confined in the Maze prison, and by 1975 there were 1,981 internees, the vast majority being Catholic nationalists. Since 1972 the majority were deemed to have 'special category' status, which allowed them extra privileges. Prisoners were housed in dormitories under the command of their own senior members. In 1976 the government embarked on a policy of criminalisation. Terrorists would now be treated as common criminals and housed in H blocks (this name referring to the layout of the buildings within the prison). Prisoners protested at this change of status by refusing to wear prison uniforms, and within two years 300 prisoners wore only blankets, which quickly escalated to the 'dirty protests' of refusing to wash or use the toilets and of smearing their cells with excrement. In October 1980 six prisoners went on hunger strike, an extreme form of protest which would last for twelve months during which time nine died. The leader, Bobby Sands, was actually elected to Parliament in a local by-election but died a month later in May 1981. These events drew international pressure on the government to change its policy, with no effect at all.

We somehow grew accustomed to adding fear of random bombing to the ever-present nuclear threat which was warming up again. Then in April 1980 six armed men from Iran invaded the Iranian Embassy in London, holding 26 people as hostage for the release of prisoners in a southern province of Iran. The siege lasted six days, ending with a memorable seventeen-minute assault by the SAS who rescued 24 of the hostages. Apart from the courage and skill of the special forces, the extraordinary thing was that the whole thing was captured on live TV. Millions were gripped. Mrs Thatcher's poll ratings rose!

CULTURE

Punk's angry performers were now joined by proponents of alternative comedy, a movement that was a long way away from long-established British humour relying on sexual innuendo and increasing racism. From this new movement, the TV show *The Young Ones* hit the screens with a bang. Its four main student characters attended Scumbag College, shared a flat and were stereotypes of the day: one a budding businessman, one a punk, one a vegetarian hippie and another an anarchist. Starting in November 1982, each of the twelve episodes featured disputes between the residents which quickly deteriorated into extreme verbal and physical violence. It was a spectacular success; we never missed an episode![19n] We were also addicted to the dark comedy of the American series *M*A*S*H*, which was set in a mobile army surgical hospital behind the front lines in Korea. Each episode was introduced by a gripping helicopter ballet bringing wounded and dying soldiers into the tented hospital. There among the blood, guts and tragedy the black humour and sharp comment on the stupidity of war mingled with the eccentric characters and their relationships to make believable drama.[20n]

Sharper competition and the prospect of high earnings were changing young peoples' view of the world; it seemed that anyone could do anything. Not as in the 60s, to creatively express ourselves, but now in pursuit of wealth in the global markets, trading currency, bonds and shares, or through popular music. We were to use our talents for our own advantage as wealth started to push out class as the key social gauge. One of the early examples of this was the new wave band Spandau Ballet, formed by five 'ordinary' guys from North London who built on the New Romantic fashion to rise to the top of the international charts with many awards and a degree of wealth that initially took them somewhat by surprise. These singers and bands, along with the extraordinary David Bowie from the previous decade, would keep us entertained for the next few decades and be worshipped by our daughter Juliet.

The most popular entrepreneur of the times was Richard Branson who in his teens had set up several ventures including Virgin Records. In the 1980s he began an airline business which started when he and all other passengers were stranded on a Caribbean island by repairs to their flight. The young Branson hired anther plane and sold tickets to the stranded passengers at a profit.

Two major events, in some ways contrary to the prevailing culture, marked this period. Peter Gabriel, who had been the lead singer of the rock group Genesis, pursued his long-standing interest in world music and founded WOMAD, this organisation eventually spreading to 27 locations around the world. Theatre was slow to respond to the new politics, but in 1977 Mike Leigh brought the priceless *Abigail's Party* to the stage. This play cruelly satirised the pretensions of the middle class seeking to be part of the new regime. Howard Brenton brought *The Romans in Britain* – against the imperial echoes of British troops in Northern Ireland causing an uproar,[21n] and he and Tony Howard brought *Short Sharp Shock* to Theatre Royal, Stratford. The play attacked the promotion of self-interest and unemployment caused by the policy of de-industrialisation. Although the play broke box office records, the Minister for the Arts was called to the Commons to explain how such a play could be put on in a subsidised theatre.

SOCIAL WORK

Through the early years of the new government social workers were left in relative peace to care for the casualties of the recession and monetarist policies, although more 'scandals' would soon provide the opportunity for action. In 1982 ministers had been asked to submit their proposals for abolishing the Welfare State. These included the need to encourage mothers to stay at home to strengthen the family's responsibility to care for children or elderly, disabled and unemployed members; single parent families were to be made more self-reliant. The 'helping professions' were to have their power reviewed by changes in their training and the establishment of watchdog councils. The 'safety net' was to be tightened and prepared to be handed over to the private sector. In general the objective should be to counter 'those factors which tend to undermine or even prohibit the exercise of personal responsibility and a sense of an individual self-respect.' The strategy would be to achieve 'a change in social values so that wealth-creation becomes more acceptable.'[22]

Having generally supported the increased power and status of the new Social Service Departments (SSDs), doubts soon emerged about the effect of managerialism and bureaucratisation on actual profession practice. Social work, in the view of many left-wing members, was becoming more and more concerned with control of clients rather than support and therapy. These elements brought into focus the growing anxieties about the actual tasks expected of social workers in these large organisations. This led to increased membership of the local government trade union NALGO (now UNISON). Arguments about new grading levels and the disadvantage of central negotiations for night and weekend cover were linked to the fact that these periods were getting busier, as the expectations raised by SSDs was rapidly increasing. Workers wanted local negotiations. The first social workers' strike, which dragged on for 42 weeks in 1978/79, was nationwide, although it only affected a minority of authorities.[23] It was divisive as workers found themselves caught between their duty to clients and their conditions of work; the press had a great time attacking the strike as harmful to dependent people. A settlement finally resulted in increased allowances and a grading system that promised a career ladder which might help keep qualified staff on the front line. The damage to the profession was that social workers were now seen by many as just another group of public sector workers.[24]

A year later, a book entitled *Can Social Work Survive?* launched a broadside attack on the profession, similar to that from Barbara Wootton twenty years earlier, and a study into the task of social work carried out in 1976.[25] The book was the work of a peripatetic doctor/journalist Colin Brewer and social worker June Lait and it aimed to answer the question 'Does it deserve to survive?' The peculiar nature of this publication was the thoroughness with which it marshalled evidence, together with the arrogant and snide way in which the authors attacked the profession and its members, who for them were embraced in the term 'personal social services.' Much of their argument follows Wootton's against the broad claims and training of the profession with very little evidence of its efficacy. The problem of what social workers should and did do, and what was more effective, had become more urgent as the new departments expanded. The tasks allocated included a whole range of administrative and legal detritus that an untrained worker could do. One chapter was titled 'Bureaucrat, psychotherapist or child minder?' The authors placed considerable blame for this situation on the original Seebohm Committee's failure to do any serious research to back up their conclusions. Social work training and radical social work naturally draw particular fire:

> We do not think Marxist theoreticians disguised as social work teachers pose a threat to any save the lunatic fringe of students, or to society, since even the lunatic fringe tends to abandon theory when confronted with the complex real world. But we do think that having to regurgitate these tedious and irrelevant nostrums to obtain a certificate in applied social studies is a substantial waste of time and an outrageous waste of public money.[26]

The authors' consideration of actual practice drew fierce critiques based on the wide range of tasks now being assigned, the lack of evidence-based practice and the failure to prioritise by matching needs to skills:

> However, if social workers are spending a significant part of their time in energetic attempts to treat problems which are actually untreatable then it represents a useless and inefficient diversion of their energies away from areas where they might prove more effective … We sympathise with the natural and understandable feelings in such cases that 'something must be done' but feel that one of the hallmarks of a professional is that his actions are governed by his knowledge and experience rather than instinctive or emotional reaction. Social workers seem even more reluctant than doctors to admit defeat, and one explanation for this may be [that] social workers seem to have remarkably little interest in the evidence for the effectiveness or ineffectiveness of their work. If, as it seems, they do not seem to care very much whether they succeed it is hardly surprising that they are equally oblivious to failure.[27]

The authors conclude by suggesting the establishment of an independent commission of inquiry to establish what exactly social workers did and to define what exactly their role and task should be. They then indicate what conclusions such an inquiry should reach. The ensuing furore and personal attacks on the authors were extensive, particularly against the breadth of their attack, the nasty tone of the writing and the total dismissal of any compassionate and empathetic element in social work. Others, recognising the chaotic range of duties and legislation that fell on to the new departments called on central government to remove issues of school non-attendance and welfare rights and put them back in the right departments.[28]

Social Worker – Civil Servant

Towards the end of my time in Maidstone I was attracted by an advertisement for the post in the Social Work Advisory Service of the Department of Health and Social Security. This was in the Development Group, a small section of the service charged with promoting and developing good practice in social work. In due course, I was interviewed by the redoubtable Barbara Kahan, then Assistant Director of the service, but previously one of the original children's officers who had an interest in delinquent children. I was then formerly appointed into the civil service, through extensive security clearance and, as I soon discovered, as one of Barbara's 'edgy young men'!

To say that life in the ministry was a contrast to Maidstone would be a major understatement. The first thing was an introduction to my 'clerk,' a professional, if junior, civil servant. This helpful person took me to get a security pass and library ticket, where all questions about me were directed to her as part of the establishment and of sufficiently lowly rank to deal with such mundane matters. With such a strictly hierarchical situation, life here was not going to be easy. The four-person Development Group itself was led by Jim Hodder, a qualified and experienced residential worker who had worked out highly defensive and personal methods of dealing with the establishment and the tasks in hand. Joan Thurman and David Stapleton made up the quartet. The group was semi-detached to both the main hierarchy of the service led by Joan Cooper and later Bill Utting, and the traditional ladder of senior civil servants from the Under Secretary to wise and knowledgeable Principals. At first glance the differences between experienced professionals committed to their specialist field and the civil servants who would be handling child care today but defence tomorrow seemed to militate against progress. Despite occasional tensions and personality clashes, the system did however seem to work well. This was a wonderful insight into the working of government; the pressures from the political arena, the highly analytic and long-term view of the senior civil servants and the professional advisers among whom any power or influence in the social work field was outweighed many times over by the power of medical and nursing colleagues. At the time I joined the department it was involved in an exercise to forecast the shape of services, including social work, up to 2007. In general terms the project expected that the functions of social work would be refined as professional tasks were separated from others. Social workers would be left to

> ...stand for the disadvantaged in terms of supporting, speaking for, and campaigning for them, and in terms of sustaining with them the role of scapegoat which might be thrust upon them and on social workers by a careless or uncomprehending society.

In terms of training, the project members thought that

> Training would differentiate between social work proper and other tasks in personal social services. Courses would be flexible, perhaps modular, and so allow for both general, basic, training and for later specialisation ... Training would have to take account not only of social work but also of the kind of techniques necessary to the successful manipulation of corporate management (especially middle management) on behalf of the clients of social services ... Training would have to strengthen social workers for an unpopular role, which might involve them as scapegoats at worst and at best would leave them in an equivocal position between society and its casualties or victims.[29]

I was grateful to Norman Tutt, who at that time was a Principal Advisor in Child Care (responsible for the 1969 Act and the implementation of the White Paper 'Children in Trouble'), for a summary of the whole experience. After a few months, ducking out of that terrible building for a quick lunch, he retold the joke about the poor soul touring Hades with a choice of torture chamber in which he wanted to spend eternity. He views a room where the condemned stood up to their waists in faeces drinking tea. No sooner had he opted for this than the foreman ordered 'Right, tea break over, back on your heads!' Inside our rabbit warren, colleagues seemed to be divided into two groups: those who were attracted to this level of analysis and the chance to influence government policy and those who looked for an early chance of escape. Norman and I were already in the latter group. At an early stage, Barbara carefully explained that although the wheels of the civil service ground slowly they eventually came up with the right answer. I was not convinced.

One of the nice things about my new post was the large office overlooking the main junction at the Elephant and Castle where traffic negotiated the complex networks and where my great grandfather had spent his working life in all weathers, manually changing the points in the tram tracks to ensure that each tram followed the correct route. The office was equipped with IN and OUT trays, which enabled the 'messengers' to move papers from desk to desk. My aunt Lola had been one of these messengers in the Home Office. After a few days Joan Thurman wandered into my office to talk about IT. I thought perhaps this was an exciting venture into computerisation, so it was a while before it became clear that the group's mission at that time was to promote and develop 'intermediate treatment', a product of the 1969 Children and Young Persons Act, but which had not been fully grasped by local authorities and practitioners. The government was anxious to spread good practice in accordance with its policies of community based work as opposed to prison or the old 'approved schools' (recently renamed as community homes with education, CHEs). My first job with the group was to help with this project, in addition to supporting the ongoing concerns to bring child care within CHEs in line with modern child care practice. The modus operandi of the Development Group was to hold conferences, seminars and joint working groups in specific geographical areas and then write these up as a report, occasionally published by HMSO, which in turn was used to promote policy and practice.

As part of my induction I spent an enjoyable period in the Manchester office, and here one could appreciate the close links between the issues facing local authorities, SSDs and the concerns of central government and individual MPs. The team here seemed to me more realistic, more in touch with reality, and were giving good service to local practice and policy. Information and advice in response to a question about to be raised in Parliament were dealt with accurately and with speed. Apart from the happy atmosphere of the office, I was very impressed with the ease of travel on the motorway networks in the North West. I never visited Lancashire HQ, but I did visit Red Bank, the large and well established former approved school at Newton-le-Willows, which, under its authoritarian principal, was having some problems adapting to the ethos required by the Act. This establishment would embroil me in many future encounters.

Whilst I was well equipped to run conferences, seminars and to write reports, I was less comfortable being boxed up in Alexander Fleming House.[30n] The chance to bring together good practitioners with academic and strategic thinking in a dialogue which would inform both seemed a worthwhile process. The most enjoyable aspect of this work was scouring the country visiting local projects and spending time with the social workers and young people. Selected groups were then scooped up into regional conferences or to feature in the IT film which we had commissioned. Making the film was a fascinating experience, and in mid 1978 we viewed the rushes followed by the final cut attended by Barbara for the OK. We were particularly anxious about one scene where two young country lads were rabbiting. We saw them catching the animal, then killing and skinning it. We waited for her decision. It was OK, but there was to be no skinning!

I can recall two memorable experiences from that time. The first of these was a slow cross-country train journey from Hull to Carlisle across the beautiful northern countryside while gripped by Geoffrey Pearson's wonderfully written *The Deviant Imagination*, a masterly work addressing the central question posed by deviants in our society: Are they men and women not unlike ourselves who live life in a fully human but different way or pests to be purged from social life? It seemed quite relevant to our work.[31] The second was a large conference held in the massive Grand Hotel at Scarborough to which I invited practitioners, along with the young people they worked with, in addition to the usual raft of speakers and managers. It certainly went with a bang! There was an odd note in that my clerk, now a young man studying for an A-level in Sociology, turned up for work looking dreadful. During the conference he told me just how many varieties of drug he was smoking, sniffing and swallowing. As he played a large part in organising all these events, Jim Hodder's final speech to the conference drew attention to what a fine example of modern youth he was. Hilarious! The government aided our work by making funds available to authorities who wanted to move from residential care to intermediate treatment, and the concept of spreading good practice by imaginative practitioners in one area via books, pamphlets and film seemed sound to me.[32]

Alongside the IT project, we worked at the invitation of a particular SSD to develop CHEs (we were greatly helped by the staff of Dartington Hall Research Group[33n]) and then pressed from outside by research results and academics, including David Thorpe at Lancaster University. We were involved in CHEs in Bedfordshire, North London and Kent. The Bedfordshire project at Carlton CHE was the longest, running from 1975 to 1978.[34n] The model used by the Development Group was to hold a local opening event to involve a cross section of the key people involved and to spell out the programme. From this would be launched a series of working groups examining every aspect of the home, from direct work with the young people, staffing, management and the role of the council. Each group had a cross section of staff and was led by a member of the Development Group.

As these groups progressed, sometimes for many months, we co-ordinated progress and gradually drew out the key issues and recommendations for discussion at a further general meeting. The outcomes of this meeting would or would not lead to further working groups, but would also be passed to the local authority for consideration by the Chief Officers and elected members. This could involve the Treasurer and Architect Departments for specific projects, often supported by our own commissioned architects. A plenary meeting was then held to finalise the work and agree specific recommendations, which should not come as a surprise to the authority, which was expected to take matters forward. Progress was then monitored by our regional colleagues, possibly leading to a follow up in the course of time. This was extensive and exhausting. In many cases the recommendations were so demanding that closure followed.[35] This was an exciting programme, but in respect of CHEs it always struck me as dubious, as the hidden purpose of many events was to give the local Director of Social Services the evidence and excuse to close the establishment.

Our next project, where I took the lead using the same methodology, was an examination of the care of elderly people in Brighton. This formed one part of the Department's review into how they could use resources more wisely in view of changing demographics. After the initial conference, which gathered the experiences and views of staff, we set about gathering the views of elderly people in the community and in residential care, and detailed studies of dependency levels in residential and day care. I very much enjoyed interviewing 15 elderly people on the waiting list for admission to long term care. The most depressing aspect was that such a move was seen as a one-way ticket; alternatives were seldom offered. The other was the acceptance of whatever was on offer. I asked a gentleman whether he could take some of his own furniture and belongings with him.

> 'Well there's one or two little bits but I'll be contented not to take them,' he replied. 'I don't mind forfeiting a lot of things if I can go somewhere relatively comfortable and feel that I'm being looked after.'
>
> I continued: 'Several times you said you'd put up with anything they wanted you to do, you know…'
>
> 'Yes,' he said, 'Rather than cause any trouble.'
>
> I was moved by the pathos of this, so I asked: 'So you would give up some things for companionship?'
>
> 'I'd give up *anything* for it,' he said, 'Cos when people call here half the time I don't know how to talk.'[36]

We took over a large hotel on the sea front for a two-day role play run with us by Tom Douglas. I have a vivid memory of Pam Emy, who was a social worker in the Elderly Policy Division of the Department, playing the role of an irascible resident who insisted on attending an event despite the lack of any facilities for her wheelchair. Those playing the roles of carers had eventually to find a path via the hotel kitchen in the basement while all the time my colleague kept up wails of pain and distress. It brought tears to my eyes and changed my view of policy makers on the spot.[37] In addition to her responsibilities for all regional work, Barbara Kahan presided over these and many other projects, protected the group from critics and fought the interests of children with her powerful personality. The greatest torture was her insistence on perfect English in all publications. The slightest sign of carelessness or the use of a hyphen would be greeted with 'No jargon!' and 'No telegraphese!' 'English!'[38]

After some fifteen months, it was clear that any future for me in this claustrophobic setting would be highly problematic. I have never had any time for inter-departmental politicking, or for people who build their own personal empires against others and thus the objectives of the organisation. I badly needed to get back to where the action really was. The search for a new job commenced. Two opportunities presented themselves in quick succession: the post of Deputy Director of Social Services in Lancashire (with the principle brief of personnel and training) and Chair in Social Work at the University of Lancaster. I prepared my applications and in due course found myself shortlisted for both.

Social Worker – Deputy Chief

The selection process in County Hall, Preston, was somewhat of a shock. Candidates spent a long morning together as we each had a thirty-minute interview with elected members of the Social Services Committee. There was then a long wait, not necessarily an indication of the difficulties of decision making, but due to the fact that the Chief Executive had to read out each of our references. Why these could not be read in advance by the selection panel remains a mystery to this day. By early afternoon I was offered the job of Deputy Director and we adjourned for a celebratory lunch in the County Mess with senior staff and I actually met the Director for the first time. I remember sensing quite a lot of tension at that table, but my own excitement (and some tears) at the scale of all this rather limited my appreciation of the dynamics. Immediately after lunch I was able to phone home and break the news that pursuing my commitment to training and development now meant uprooting ourselves from Kent to realise my long-standing wish to come north where the people and the environment promised a great life.

The next step was to call at the Education Office and to join the queue to explain that I was moving to Lancashire and needed some information about secondary schools for my daughter. The response brought home the fact that this was more than a geographical move; before any sensible advice could be given, I had to declare whether I was Protestant or Roman Catholic! On August 16th, my last day in the civil service, my colleagues in the Development Group presented me with an engraved picture of the view from my office window across the city, so this memento of my time there and my great grandfather has been with me ever since.

As it was high summer and as there had been little follow up after the interview, I decided to make an informal visit to check on schools etc. I was invited to a small-scale sports meeting for children with learning disabilities. As it was a scorching Saturday, I dressed in my trademark open sandals, shorts and T-shirt. The Director of Social Services, Rex Johnson, arrived with the Director of Education, both in heavy suits, and proceeded to ignore me. After I had actually taken up my appointment (on August 18th 1978 at a salary of £10,449 (equivalent to £46,114 in 2021),[39n] I spent a long time looking for the social workers until it eventually dawned on me that they too wore suits. I clearly had a wider cultural divide to cross than anticipated. As a temporary measure I stayed at the Department's residential training centre in Kirkham, then run by Mr and Mrs Allen, both former members of the Salvation Army and very hospitable, although I thought it wise to decline Mrs Allen's repeated offer of massages.

Having received no welcoming letter, joining instructions or any details about the location of the office, my hosts had very kindly driven to the Headquarters' offices, which then were at the top of Duchy House, a modern and boring office block by the old open Preston Market, in order to draw a very detailed map. Thus I was able to take my large bronze coloured Ford estate car directly into the appointed spot in time for my first Monday. Unfortunately the Director had exactly the same model and colour so Lèse-majesté on day one, hour one! The first few weeks could, in an understated way, be described as 'interesting,' made bearable by my excellent secretary Audrey Harrison who guided and protected me with such kindness and consideration. People and papers came and went in a somewhat bewildering fashion as I tried to get to grips with the size and scope of this vast organisation of 9,000 staff and a gross budget of just over £34 million serving a population of 1.3 million spread over some 1,182 square miles. It was the largest SSD in England.

At that time the Department was divided into six geographical areas each managed by a Divisional Director who was responsible for all services in that area. Social workers operated from 31 small area teams operating on the 'patch' system, later recommended by the Barclay Report of 1982. At Headquarters, apart from the Director there were Assistant Directors for Service Delivery, for Planning and Research along with Personnel and Training. There was also a Professional Advisory Group consisting of consultants for each 'client group'; part of their role was to warn of forthcoming policy issues and maintain practice standards throughout the Department – a sort of local team of inspectors and certainly seen as that by workers in the field. The Assistant Directors for Planning and Research and Personnel and Training reported directly to me. The management process was, in theory, headed by the Headquarters team, forming a Policy Steering Group (PSG), then a regular meeting with all six Divisional Directors as a management team. A standard structure which was no surprise as the former Director, John Ward, and Rex Johnson, who had been his deputy, had both moved from the DHSS. It made perfect sense for staff to see me as another bloody civil servant who knew little about real life, and a southerner too!

In an effort to gain further understanding, I asked Rex if I could accompany him on his frequent forays into the divisions, social work teams and the many residential establishments. Whilst these journeys achieved little for my education, they, and the next seven years, did endanger my health as Rex was an established chain smoker. His was the only car I have ever known where the complete covering of brown tar on the inside prevented any clear view of the road ahead. PSG meetings in our small conference room where the majority smoked was another torture. Apart from this habit Rex always appeared relaxed and in no way weighed down by his wide-ranging responsibilities. He was a psychologist who had worked with his wife Mary for many years in the old approved school system where they eventually ran a much respected assessment centre. He relied upon a high intelligence and easy interpersonal relations to see him through all situations, and these qualities enabled him to communicate with staff and elected councillors at all levels. Commitment to high level policies of his own determination was not his strong suit, and this resulted in some clinging on to past cultures and a tendency, which was deeply resented by his managers, to suddenly adopt an idea fed to him by any member of staff, particularly if they were female. Rex was undoubtedly a people person.

Starting a career in local government as a Chief Officer presented a few challenges. One had to come to terms with the role of elected members and the whole committee system as well as the power relationships between the various departments of the council and in particular the Chief Executive and County Treasurer. Papers coming up from the Department were put before the Social Services Committee and thence to the County Council. At the time I joined there was a certain inevitable process behind all this. As one development, perhaps a day care centre or increase in domiciliary care, was achieved in one division, so the money appeared for the pattern to be repeated in the others. Routine reports came to committee from the research and statistics section and quality control.

The Director's main role seemed to be to monitor and regulate these reports in accordance with his estimate of how politically acceptable they would be. In all this the key person was the Committee Chair; at the time of my appointment this was David Murray, a senior member of the Conservative administration and a consultant anaesthetist by profession. In addition to the papers put to committee I was amazed at the large number of 'special case' items that had to come all the way through the system for approval by the Chair. Anything outside the ordinary, however small the resource implications and how individual the situation, had to be argued through. If all went well the case would be agreed, but many had the expenditure reduced (often by a token amount) or rejected. It appeared that David's political reputation depended in some way on his thorough examination of these minutiae. I soon learnt that the skill in these situations was not to see them as a routine detailed professional matter (which they were) but as full of political threat so that the Chair had to be involved early, fully briefed and never surprised by an issue. As he lived in Blackburn, we were frequent visitors to each other's homes when urgent decisions were required.

The corporate management of the Council came as a considerable surprise. Rex was a member of the County Management Board where all the Departmental Directors met under the chairmanship of the Chief Executive, Brian Hill, a powerful figure whose expertise and assertive style held councillors and officers in thrall. This was shadowed by the Standing Conference of Deputies, whose agenda echoed their masters and dealt with many more detailed issues. So within a short space of time my social work expertise was stretched to issues confronting the county's libraries, schools, policing, roads, bridges or finances. All valuable learning! The particular bane of my life was the monthly meeting of the County Personnel Committee who had to approve any increase or significant change in any departmental personnel. For the first few years growth was steady so appearances before the Committee were frequent and demanding. If one got a proposal through the departmental system and agreed by the trade union then each minor change had to be checked out by the 'time and motion' experts in the County Personnel Officer's section and then by the accountants answerable to the Treasurer. Progress was never fast, and any problem could easily result in the proposal being put back to the next committee cycle. Client needs seemed a very long way away, and with a low priority, in the hallowed halls of County Hall.

These constant tensions brought into full play the rivalries and differing professional perspectives of each department. The reports that went before the Personnel Committee were therefore quite technical, often too much so for many elected members. I was summoned to each committee, asked to wait outside until they got to my items and then I would be shown in to sit on a low level as a supplicant to argue the case for the Department's needs. For many years the Committee was chaired by a highly eccentric but likeable woman, and one example may serve to illustrate the problem. I was arguing for some extra residential child care staff to deal with the more disturbed children now 'cascading' down the system from prisons and CHEs to local homes. At some point during an increasingly bizarre discussion I mentioned the word 'Borstal,' when the Chair intervened to explain that she had such a meaningful experience of abortion. As all the 'professionals' exchanged questioning glances, the item was voted through on a complete misunderstanding.

It would be misleading to say that my very early days were marked by general rejoicing and a warm welcome by all. Personnel and Training was managed by John Read, a man of a determined intellectual disposition who did not suffer fools gladly; after a short period he gained a post as Deputy Director in Cornwall. He was succeeded by Tom Groves, who was an excellent, hard working officer who added the management of the HQ establishments to his role. Within this section there were divisional and central Training Officers and a highly competent Personnel Section headed by Jim Thomas, who could be relied on to outwit the investigators from central personnel, talk sense to the unions and advise on disciplinary issues with great care. Tom Atkinson headed the Planning and Research sections; he was a remarkably able man who could handle vast projects and great volumes of paperwork with consummate skill. I could never understand why I had been appointed as Deputy while his application had not even made the shortlist. His Principal Research Officer, Mike Derbyshire, held a doctorate in statistics and was an invaluable resource both in defending the Department's performance against all the questionable comparisons published by government and later in questioning the government statistics on which our resource allocation came to be based. The Service Delivery section was headed by Len Meadwell, a manager whose heavy workload was handled by a harassing style which bore heavily on his staff. In addition to having operational responsibility for 12 specialist residential units (totalling some 700 beds), Len was in a chronic state of conflict with the Advisory Group (who were seen as out of touch with the real world) and the Divisional Directors who tended to resent any operational intrusion from Headquarters. Within his group I came to work with Margaret Phillips, Bryan Hughes and Dick Tomlinson. The former could use her long experience with challenging children to mediate between heads of homes and any problems that may cause concern. Bryan Hughes was a wonderful example of a sensitive and knowledgeable officer in all aspects of the care for mentally handicapped adults. Dick Tomlinson could have come straight out of Catch 22 or any military unit. If you wanted something without going through the tedious system you asked Dick and it appeared. A very valuable asset.

Lal Kennedy, another former DHSS advisor, headed the Consultancy Section and had the greatest difficulty in coming to terms with my appointment as it was rumoured that she had seen herself as Rex's natural deputy. Enabling and underlying all this was the Finance and Administrative Group led by the irrepressible Wilf Twist and his excellent Finance Officer Colin Spencer who was as ready to protect and enhance the Department's resources as the Treasurer's department was to reduce them. These then were the key people who managed this large and unwieldy department including some 71 day and 72 residential establishments managed by the divisions.

It was an impressive monster of a system where nothing happened very quickly, although my own view, which never changed, was that 99% of staff at every level worked very hard, well beyond the call of duty and all for the benefit of the community or individuals that we served. It was this ethos that seemed to me to mark out the Social Service Department. Other departments had excellent and conscientious staff but they were more bureaucratic, probably because for the main part they were not drawn from the professionals that carried out the day to day work. The most obvious example of this was the Education Department where one was faced with a tribe of administrators rather than teachers. My attention was drawn to a helpful definition informally being passed round staff:

> The heaviest known element has recently been discovered. It is called 'administratium' and it possesses one neutron, 8 assistant neutrons, 10 executive neutrons, 35 vice-neutrons and 256 executive neutrons. The whole structure is kept in place by particles called morons. Administratium is completely inert, although it can be detected chemically because it impedes every reaction with which it comes into contact.

It took some time to, as one would now say, 'get my head around' all these processes, probably not helped by my retiring nature which made it difficult to find an entry point into the existing work and friendship networks built up by everyone else over long careers within the Department. They had many shared years and did not quite know what to make of this strange creature parachuted in from central government. There was no knowledge of my more radical ideas and the achievements before that brief period as a civil servant. So for many weeks my lunch would be taken wandering around Preston and finding a sandwich in any small coffee bar or shopping centre. The only way through this, it seemed to me, was to learn as much as I could as quickly as I could and to get on with the strange range of duties that came my way – certainly nothing that gave any clear identity to the role of Deputy Director, which had been advertised mainly as a training post.

In addition to those items already mentioned, the issues that took time in the early years were hearing disciplinary cases against staff, visiting and coming to terms with the large and complex residential establishments managed directly from HQ and chairing a remarkable group named the Standing Committee on Forms and Procedures. All these duties, with all the associated documentation, took some fifty to sixty hours work a week, so I was back to Maidstone demands. On top of that I determinedly followed the policy that my door was always open. As hard as one worked there was very little chance of getting through to the workers at the coal face, but this was not our role. In a highly parochial county, where some of the main towns had previously had their own departments, each population saw their Divisional Director, or sometimes the local Area Team Manager, as their 'Director' and they would be described thus in the local press. Whilst this drove Rex into a rage, I saw this as understandable and beneficial. The nearer the ground the better. Of course, wherever I could I took opportunities to meet staff in training and discussion groups, but there was a significant gap between my open style and what staff in this very traditional and hierarchical system could use. It was also part of my job to hold quarterly liaison meetings with the police, magistrates, probation services, education, voluntary agencies, professional associations and trades unions.

I was probably seen as remote, but it transpired that such views would be breached by odd incidents rather than any determined efforts of mine. If staff misbehaved and the offence was serious enough it came to Duchy House to be heard by me, or they went to a sub-committee of elected members where I acted as a professional advisor. These were always difficult. Fairly early on I issued a final warning to a member of staff who had acted against the interests of a man with learning disabilities who attended a day centre. I was furious that he should take advantage of such a vulnerable individual and I made my feelings very clear at the end of the session, just managing to hold back tears of anger. Word was passed back that I really did care and was not quite the cool academic that I appeared to be. These things could get out of hand, and later in my tenure I supported the sub-committee hearing of a case of a social worker who had developed much too close a relationship with a client. The defence brought witnesses from afar but by about 7pm it was suggested that we should adjourn. This was met with statements from the trade union that there was no way the witnesses could return and pleas that we continue. By the time the verdict of dismissal was handed down it was about 2.30am and all the facilities at County Hall had been closed for hours. This led to a further hearing of unfair dismissal to the industrial tribunal, who instructed that we re-instate the social worker, partly because no sensible decision could be reached at that hour. Our argument that Parliament passed most legislation at that hour was ignored. Despite this reversal I refused to reinstate this person in a social work role and luckily the Committee backed me.

The Standing Committee on Forms and Procedures at least dealt with issues of practice. It consisted of Divisional Directors and a small cross section of staff. There were plenty of strong feelings from the traditionalists, usually led by the powerful figure of Jack Robinson, Divisional Director for Blackpool (and former Director of his own department), and those who felt that our function was to give practitioners a framework from which they should be trusted to use discretion and professional judgement. Each word of a procedure would often be fought over. Over time I think I managed to turn things my way and in the process earned the respect of Jack and many of his colleagues. At one of these meetings I rolled up my shirt sleeves, a common enough style for me, to reveal arms badly scratched by a weekend gardening. Thus it was revealed that I was an ordinary guy who got stuck into to manual tasks: another myth had been dispelled.

Looking back on this some twenty years later, some of my former colleagues responded to my request for an honest appraisal. They were united in their anxiety about the arrival of someone with no operational management or local government experience but soon appreciated a much needed fresh perspective, although they were apprehensive that the weight of tradition would prove intractable. My sensitive handling of some complex personnel issues was welcomed as innovative. In succession, the Department had had a Director committed to clear management by structure, policy and procedure, and consequently not appreciated by social workers, and not a good communicator in committee, followed by almost exactly the opposite, although lacking respect from departmental staff. So there was some hope that the arrival of a 'change agent' would move the Department forward. At least I was prepared to listen, had a good sense of humour and gave a fair response which quickly earned me acceptance and enabled me, against expectations, to slip into this complex system, appreciating the nuances of all the internal politics. My only response to this was to appreciate how the basic knowledge and skills of social work apply, as I had always fought for organisations and political action.

All this was small beer compared with the residential establishments managed directly from HQ. Lancashire provided the whole of the northwest, and most of the rest of the country, with secure and open places for delinquent children and children needing intensive care. We had six CHEs and four regional assessment centres with a total of 550 beds. These were all managed by powerful principals, who were often answerable to their own management boards who resisted any interference from outside. They were, to differing degrees, total institutions of the type that the Development Group had been closing down. In addition there were three residential nurseries with forty-two beds. Coming to terms with these heavyweight establishments took time, and it seemed to me that they were all going to have to face up to new approaches and a sharpening of their task. Children could be sent to a CHE for minor misdemeanours committed in local children's homes or if they were just too troubled. Once they had arrived, too often the pressure was taken off their social worker so the child could stay away from their home area for years. Staff therefore found themselves dealing with a wide range of needs, from those few who were seriously disturbed and/or delinquent to those who just needed care. In any event the costs of each place were very high and out of all proportion to the needs of the latter group. The largest unit, Red Bank at Newton-le-Willows, was a monster of a place and included a secure unit, as did two other CHEs. The regimes in these secure units in the county were more intense and more child centred than their host establishments, but they also needed to come into line with what I saw as modern child care. Early action was needed.

Lancashire was a truly great authority, respected by many because it had a reputation for playing issues straight down the middle. After a couple of months I was able to review my position and think of things that needed to be done. The first conclusion was that such a large department had a life of its own and would run for quite a long time under its own momentum if Rex and I, plus most of HQ, were not there. Rex seemed pretty happy with the way things ran and was disinclined to rock any boats; his role to reassure elected members only required him to intervene occasionally. Apart from that he was happy pursuing small projects which seemed to me to be on the edge of the main game but were suggested to him by the small group of female acolytes who spent so long hanging around his office. My role was sufficiently ill defined to open the way for me to create my own agenda. Three areas of work seemed to demand my attention. They were the over provision of CHEs and the total lack of any alternatives, the sad position of social work and the provision for adults with a learning disability.

Starting in the autumn of 1978 the CHE issue would be my first attempt at achieving change and finding some money for alternative approaches. Both Rex Johnson and Lal Kennedy were pretty well steeped in the approved school culture and could see no strong reason to change. The main process in my favour was the increasing financial pressure on all local authorities by central government; we needed to demonstrate some savings. It so happened that Lancaster University, where Norman Tutt had been appointed Professor of the Applied Social Studies Department, was the main base for those researchers who were providing the evidence for change from institutional to community care. David Thorpe was the key person and he had carefully examined the unit costs of CHE care and noted how few of the residents actually warranted such expenditure.[40]

My experience so far was that although Rex would never directly oppose any of my initiatives he could be relied upon to savage anyone who I introduced to support or explain new 'radical' ideas. The most embarrassing of these so far had been Andrea Kelmanson of the Community Service Volunteers (CSV – now known as Volunteering Matters) who came up from London at my request to strengthen the community orientation and voluntary element of the service which we provided. Once she had made some introductory comments at a full management meeting, Rex launched a highly personal attack on the whole issue of volunteers. There was quite a bit of north–south divide behind all this. David Thorpe's appearance followed the same pattern. Rex's argument was that any of his findings were invalid because the high degree of needs of the children in CHEs skewed all the results. I was getting really fed up with apologising to people whom I respected! The only way out of this, as far as I could see, was to check the national research findings against the population in our own CHEs.

In January 1979 the PSG agreed to my proposals to establish a working group to 'consider all aspects of the problem of juvenile delinquency, suggest a suitable strategy and role for the department and indicate where areas of departmental policy and practice need to be changed and developed.' The group examined a wide range of publications and visited community provisions in other authorities, which had policies designed to divert young people away from the criminal justice system, and undertook a series of studies indicating the significant savings to be made in residential provision and the low costs of community care. A research project led by our excellent research section set about examining the files of a random selection of children in each establishment. The 60 files were then considered individually by five experienced staff members (of which I was one) outside of that establishment. These were then brought to a meeting chaired by the Principal Research Officer and ranked on whether the children required the expert and intense service that a CHE should provide or whether they could be cared for in the community; otherwise, an uncertain verdict was reached. This exercise involved a great deal of extra work for all concerned and I often found myself leaving home very early to collect sealed packs of files to be delivered to the next assessor. Much to my relief the final result supported other national studies. The boys' study showed that 60% could be placed in the community; a later girls' study produced similar results.[41]

The working group's report was published in late 1979, making 32 recommendations that the county should adopt a full diversionary policy to tackle juvenile crime locally wherever possible as a primary alternative to residential care, which in any case should be short term. Volunteers would have significant roles to play in the new system and they and the professionals should be fully trained. The report[42] was sent out for consultation and in due course appeared on the agenda of the County Management Team, to which I was invited. Brian Hill went round the table asking for comments; they were pretty balanced. Rex's contribution was to recall a weekend visit to an army cadet unit and to praise the role of discipline in the lives of young people. Revealing something of my origins I just had to say that I had spent much of the weekend in Blackburn Police Station trying to extricate a young black man who had accompanied a relative of mine in stealing a car in Blackpool and was chased down the motorway until forced off at the Blackburn junction! Brian Hill summarised the discussion by giving the report a weak endorsement but commenting that all this research stuff made it somewhat academic. However, on that basis we started intermediate treatment in Lancashire.

An Intermediate Treatment Officer (ITO) on a senior grade was appointed to each division and the social work element of each area team increased. In addition, a residential IT centre was opened in Blackburn. This was achieved by the process of closing some 100 beds and one CHE. The element of all this of which I am most proud was that each divisional ITO and the residential unit had a small but significant budget (I think £5,000) which they could spend as they thought fit with only minimal accountability. A major innovation in centralised, treasurer-dominated Lancashire.

The first idea about how to change the routinised regime of day and residential care for adults with a learning disability came whilst I was in London at a conference when Rex phoned to say that there was some sort of meeting about sports for people with a learning disability going on in Lowestoft. If I was interested I should call in there. Whilst I have never had much interest in sports I was intrigued, and this marked the Department's involvement in the American based Special Olympics movement, or to be more precise a group that started out as a British alternative: the United Kingdom Sports Association for People with a Learning Disability. I started in a small way to encourage these activities, very much helped by Bryan Hughes, and by 1980 we had assembled a Lancashire team to take part in the second 'Mini Olympics' in Lowestoft in September. This was a five-day event which Ann and I attended and learnt a great deal from our team of some twenty athletes. There were some 800 competitors for events ranging from snooker and darts through football, equestrian sport and swimming to a small range of track and field events. The commitment of the organisers, staff and all the athletes was very impressive. We were overwhelmed. There was an embarrassing moment after the closing ceremony when clearly champagne was indicated but in our ignorance we wondered whether this would be appropriate. Of course it was, and all enjoyed the toast! The signed programme is a great memento. The occasion also marked a memorable family event (see below).

FAMILY

Working in South London had meant commuting most days, from the quiet of Pluckley Station to hectic Charing Cross and a change in family dynamics as my travels across the country and frequent three-day conferences kept me away from home. Not nice at all particularly as, settled in the village and our new home, this was one of those magic times when Juliet was enjoying a relatively uncomplicated life to the full. She had a good number of friends at school and was an enthusiastic pupil eagerly learning about the world and its ways. Her particular joy was riding a friend's horse through the hop fields and apple orchards that surrounded the village. Ann was hectically busy with her unbelievable range of voluntary work caring for the elderly across the area and running a busy programme of extramural conferences and seminars at the University from extended courses on counselling, volunteers and professionals working together and the process of supervision, to workshops on communicating with adolescents and social work and mental illness. Her diary was packed, and we spent enjoyable evenings dining in hall. We had many friends in the village so there were meals together, occasional parties and a busy programme of theatre visits to the Marlowe in Canterbury and in London. Ann's stepfather continued as a significant presence in all that we did. Juliet's babysitter Anne was married to Bob Hills and had two baby boys who we spent a lot of time caring for as Anne, in particular, was wont to take spur of the minute sunny breaks to Spain. She would arrive with baby, cot and essential equipment and announce that she was off; would we mind? We never did. Later our nephew Richard White lived with us while he obtained a place at Wye College. The donkeys produced foals, the hens thrived and the awful guinea fowl were a constant annoyance, having to be rescued frequently from our close friends the Reeces who lived across the valley. During the summer holidays we were home to two horses from the nearby children's home. This was a delightfully busy close family time from which I hated to be absent but delighted to return. I kept in touch as much as possible although this was of course well before mobile phones.

There were frequent journeys to Eastbourne to see Mum and John, where there were usually other family members gathering. A total reunion was Aunt Elsie and Harry's 50th wedding anniversary in Findon, just north of Worthing. Summer holidays were spent in Cornwall, renting various cottages on the Lizard Peninsula. These were wonderful times as Juliet's summer school break lasted some nine and a half weeks. I would join them for as long as I could, arriving at Redruth Station with bags full of fresh salads and vegetables from the garden. Determined to take Juliet abroad, we boarded the cross-Channel ferry for Boulogne with my brother John – the shortest sea route as both Ann and John suffered from seasickness. The outward trip was quite rough, surprisingly, so Ann and John spent time below decks in the cafe while Juliet and I had a high old time on the top deck revelling in the storm. France did not go well – we took a wrong turning and ended up in the industrial area of the town so had little time for the charming shopping area. All was OK until Juliet noticed the butchers selling horsemeat. We left with her judgment on the trip and the French: 'It's just like Folkestone but they eat horse!'

Ann and I had long discussions about the situation I found myself in at the DHSS and we talked through the fact that my application could mean moving up to Lancashire. Ann had no reservations about backing a move north; what an amazing wife I had! We discussed this with Juliet who was not very happy but was quite clear that as she was now about to move to secondary school she would prefer to move out of the private sector. In July 1978 when I opened my suitcase there was a sweet card from Ann and Juliet pledging their support for my interview in Preston. The period from then until I took up my post in late August was one of turmoil at home and at work but in late July we based ourselves at Junction 32 on the M6 and spent a long weekend searching for a house. Juliet's sole criterion was that any property must have good stables! I think we saw 45 houses within a reasonable distance of Preston. We saw immediately how heavy industry, or its remains, and attractive rural cottages could exist side by side. A house in the midst of the moors above Darwen was rejected on grounds that it would be entirely cut off in the winter. One that met all our requirements turned out to be right next to the proposed Leyland car and lorry test track. We also realised, rather late in the day, that the lush green that makes the North West so attractive results from more rain than we had ever experienced in our lives. In despair we visited an old college friend of Ann's and she knew immediately of a suitable house in the village of Balderstone in the Ribble Valley. This was Jenny's Barn. The major issue was a school for Juliet who very much wanted out of the private sector. During a preliminary visit I had toured all of the available schools in and around Blackburn – it had not been encouraging. The best school in Clitheroe was oversubscribed and refused my pleas for help. The main comprehensive was on a split site and the buildings were overlooked by dirty industrial sites. I took photos and after discussion it was agreed that changing from the hop fields of Kent to such an environment plus a change of location would be too much for Juliet. We therefore enrolled her in Westholme, a fee-paying school for girls where luckily she settled and made good lifelong friends. For the few weeks between the end of term and our house move Juliet stayed with our dear friend and solicitor Trevor Carney.

We moved into the Barn with Hugh who had a lounge, small kitchen and his own facilities, but we were quite cramped. A house named after another woman was not working for Ann, so it was promptly renamed 'Brock Barn.' The vendor turned out to be a difficult man who would phone and bully my secretary Audrey, shouting that I must speak to him immediately, never mind whatever meeting in which I was engrossed. He would then bully me, so an early perception of me by my new colleagues was of someone who shouted down the phone quite a lot. Too close to the house was a rotten tree which a friend offered to cut down for us, leading to some mild protests from the parish council. We made some alterations to the house in order to ease Hugh's situation and built a concrete raft on which went a stable, so in due course we were joined by the horse and donkeys. In that short space of time we had met the owner of a chainsaw, Tom Woods, who would become a firm family friend, and the builder Rod Wilkins with whom we became close friends, although his views on the role of women and a clash of personalities between him and Ann led to some lively encounters. Within two years a much larger house, Higher Studlehurst, became available in the neighbouring village of Osbaldestone so we moved in and lived there for most of the next twenty-one years. Hugh helped invest in that project, where he had a whole self-contained wing with a large lounge, kitchen and good bedroom. This was farming country and we became very close to the remarkable Brian Brocklehurst and his family whose farm we adjoined. In a very short time we had three families through whom we embraced the routine of the farm and appreciated the wonderful character of Lancashire. For some time Ann commuted back to Canterbury to complete the extramural courses that she had already planned. My mother and John approved, although infuriatingly they only made day trips from far off Eastbourne.

In the summer of 1980 Ann and I drove to Felixstowe to support Lancashire's 'Mini Olympic' team. Driving back through Suffolk, Ann casually mentioned that her father lived nearby and with a little persuasion by me we diverted to his house. It was some time since we had briefly met him and his partner Bay, but she was thrilled to see Ann and showed us into the comfortable lounge where Ann's father was playing the piano. He welcomed us warmly and we chatted away while Bay prepared a celebration tea. As time went on there was a growing tension so, as we had a long drive home, we made to leave. As we shook hands her father said, 'It's been very nice seeing you but please could you tell me who you are.' We made a rapid exit, both sincerely wishing we had never bothered.

These five years marked massive changes in society and family. As far as social work was concerned, the issues of definition had always been difficult. My former boss Bill Utting, whose work I admire greatly, bemoaned

> As a class of public servants they are patronised by professionals in the law and in medicine; they are vilified by the popular press; they are disliked by sections of the public who misunderstand, or are ignorant of what social work is about; their failings are constantly highlighted while similar or worse acts of negligence by other professionals go unremarked.[43]

Life in the UK had changed dramatically to the advantage of some and the detriment of many. The carefree individualism of the 1960s and early 1970s was being corrupted by the neo-liberal and monetarist beliefs of Thatcherism. It would soon become evident that success did not lead to concern for the less fortunate. Those less successful were increasingly insecure and fearful in the face of these changes and those that had looked to the Labour Party or their trade union saw them pushed to the margins. The immediate future looked pretty grim.

NOTES AND REFERENCES

1. Interview with *Women's Own* magazine 23.09.1987. Some of the wording is disputed. This is taken from the Margaret Thatcher Foundation.
2. Khomeini, *Sahifeh-ye Nur*, Vol. 5, p. 31, translated by Baqer Moin in *Khomeini* (2000). London: Bloomsbury, p. 204.
3. For these paragraphs I have drawn on Hobsbawm, E. (1995). *Age of Extremes*. London: Abacus, supplemented by Wikipedia and my own memory.
4. Ascherson, N. 'The Workers United,' *The Independent*, 30.08.2010.
5. Beckett, A. (2009). *When the Lights Went Out: What Really Happened to Britain in the Seventies*. London: Faber & Faber, p. 288.
6. Beckett, *op. cit.*, p. 293.
7. Brothers Ross and Norris McWhirter founded the *Guinness World Records* publications and the associated *Record Breakers* TV show for children. They founded The Freedom Association, which describes itself as 'non-partisan, centre right and libertarian,' but by others as 'a charmless libertarian pressure group.' It was they who organised the 'Pony Express' at the Grunwick dispute.

8. Beckett, *op. cit.*, p. 355.
9. Jack Dromey rose to be Deputy General Secretary of the TGWU and was elected as Labour MP for Birmingham, Erdington in May 2010. He held shadow offices under the leadership of Ed Miliband. He is married to Harriet Harman, who held Cabinet offices under Tony Blair and was later acting Leader of the Labour Party and Leader of the Opposition under Jeremy Corbyn. He would play a role in the critical debates about Brexit in 2019.
10. For an extended history of this dispute, see Dromey, J. and Taylor, G. (1978). *Grunwick: The Workers' Story*. London: Lawrence & Wishart, chap. 15; Ward, G. (1977). *Fort Grunwick*. London: Maurice Temple Smith.
11. Monetarism claims that the economic role of government is to control the supply of money rather than fiscal measures such as interest rates and taxation.
12. Michael was the fifth child in a remarkable family. Three older brothers had been MPs and Hugh was Governor of Cyprus and the UK's representative to the UN until 1970. Paul Foot, the campaigning journalist, was Michael's nephew.
13. Although the new party gained much popular support, it soon became victim of internal feuding, and in 1988 it merged with the Liberal Party to become the Liberal Democrats.
14. Marr, A. (2007). *A History of Modern Britain*. London: Pan Macmillan, p. 386.
15. Hansard HC Deb. Vol 148 Col 1251 et seq March 27th 1905.
16. 1980 Employment Act; 1982 Employment Act; 1984 Trade Union Act.
17. *The Guardian* (2007). 'Great Speeches of the 20th Century. Margaret Thatcher: The lady's not for turning,' delivered October 10th 1980.
18. The gardens fell into dereliction by 1997 but with a grant from the North West Development Agency were restored to their former beauty with free access to local residents.
19. *The Young Ones*, written by Ben Elton and Rick Mayall. Dir Paul Jackson, Geoff Posner. Starring Adrian Edmonson, Rick Mayall, Nigel Planer, Christopher Ryan and Alexei Sayle. BBC 1982.
20. *M*A*S*H*, created by Larry Gelbart and Gene Reynolds. Starring Alan Alda, Loretta Swit, Wayne Rogers, McLean Stevenson and Jamie Farr. 20th Century Fox, CBS 1972.
21. One scene depicting anal rape by a soldier on a druid, against which Mary Whitehouse brought a private prosecution, had to be withdrawn.
22. Dean, M. (1983). 'Ministers rethink Welfare State.' *The Guardian*, 17.02.1983, p. 1.
23. Bamford, T. (2015). *A Contemporary History of Social Work*. Bristol: Policy Press, pp. 29–30.
24. Birch, R. (1976). *Manpower and Training in the Social Services*. London: HMSO.
25. Brewer, C. and Lait, J. (1980). *Can Social Work Survive?* London: Maurice Temple Smith; Lait, J. (1978). 'Social Work: Retreat from Reality,' *World Medicine Magazine*, 11.01.1978; Lait, J. (1979). 'The Unnecessary Profession,' *Community Care Magazine*, 05.01.1979.
26. Brewer and Lait, *op. cit.*, p. 114.
27. Brewer and Lait, *op. cit.*, p. 166.
28. Cassam, E. (1981). 'Other People's Failure,' *Community Care Magazine*, 02.07.1981.
29. Social Work Service Draft Document, 1976/77.
30. The building gained a Civic Trust Award in 1964. In the early 1990s it became the victim of 'sick building syndrome,' by which faulty ventilation, heating systems and mould caused staff sickness. It was converted to 400 apartments and is now known as Metro Central Heights; it was awarded Grade II listed building status in 2013.
31. Pearson, G. (1975). *The Deviant Imagination*. London: Macmillan Press.
32. *Intermediate Treatment Project Development Group Report*. (1973). London: DHSS/HMSO.
33. The Dartington Hall Research Group, linked to Bristol University, then led by Roger Bullock, was concerned with providing independent social research for policy makers. It is now a charity, called the Dartington Social Research Unit, with offices in London and Glasgow. Dartington Hall

now hosts 'Research in Practice' and 'Research in Practice Adults,' which continue the work of the original group.
34. Carlton Approved School hit the national headlines in August 1959 when major riots broke out and many boys escaped. This was a significant incident in a series of disturbances that focussed on the population and regimes across the country, and later fed into the 1969 Act.
35. *Social Work Service Development Group: Community Home Exercise at Carlton.* (1978). DHSS; *Approved School to Community Home, St Christopher's Hillingdon.* (1973). DHSS; *Developments at St Christopher's.* (1976–1977). DHSS; *Residential Child Care Policy in Kent, With Particular Reference to Northdowns Community Home.* (1975). DHSS.
36. Jordan, M. (1977). *Report on Interviews with 15 Clients in the Community.* Development Group, DHSS.
37. DHSS Development Group. (1980). *Growing Old in Brighton.* London: HMSO.
38. DHSS Development Group. (1977). *Records in Social Services Departments.* London: HMSO.
39. It is interesting and somewhat worrying to note that in nine years this salary had practically trebled due to national negotiations.
40. Thorpe, D., Paley, J. and Green, C. (1979). 'The Making of a Delinquent, *Community Care*, 26.04.1979.
41. Derbyshire, M., Barrow, S. and Jordan, M. (1980). 'Care and Control for Boys in CHEs: The Scope for Transferring Resources,' *Social Work Service Magazine*, September, DHSS; Derbyshire, M., Barrow, S. and Jordan, M. (1981). 'Alternatives to CHEs: Divergence and Agreement in a Lancashire Study,' *Social Work Service Magazine*, September, DHSS.
42. Lancashire County Council (1979). *Report of the Working Party on Juvenile Delinquency.* Lancashire County Council SSD.
43. Quoted in 'Preaching what we Practice' by Sir William Utting, reported in *Professional Social Work Magazine*, June 2002.

1956 Prestwick
BOAC Training
First Flight

1957 Shoreham
Darent Hulme Cottage

1958 Hochsolden, Austria
Ski Trip

c. 1958 Swanley
Army Cadet Unit
Royal Engineers
BBC interview with Bill Grundy

1960
Herbert Glover
with Mabel and Jackie Jordan

1963
Darent Hulme
Jack Leopold visits from Florida

1964
Ann Wickett

1964
Edith Glover

1964 Headcorn, Kent
Ann & Malcolm's wedding

1966
Juliet arrives

1967
Darent Hulme
Family Fun

1971 Kent
Juliet and the donkeys

1970's Maidstone
CQSW course
Student and Staff group

1972 Maidstone
CQSW course
Norman Rose

1970's Maidstone
CQSW course tutorial

c. 1976 Pluckley, Kent
Oxendene and Mill House

c.1979
Family

1982
Special Olympics programme

PART THREE

1980–2021

PUSHING ONWARDS

THIRTEEN

1980–1987

TRAUMAS

The media these days has a great line in hunting 'extremists.' When they dislike anyone's ideas, they set them up ... and pelt them. They did it to Mr Benn and Mr Livingstone, and now with Bruce Kent and the peace campers at Greenham Common.

Yet if I look around this country the most extreme people in our public life are Mrs Thatcher and her circle ... They are bent (under cover of the cry of 'freedom') to strengthen all the powers of the over mighty central State: to increase the powers of the police and the surveillance of citizens: ...to sell off the nation's assets: to interfere with our university's autonomy: to interfere with our trade unions: to weaken the powers of our local authorities.

In short the Falklands war, coming at a time when our economy and social life were visibly falling apart, was the greatest and most undeserved bonus which the Militant Faction of the Tory Party could get. And it made them more militant, more factional and more extreme.

– E. P. Thompson[1]

Too much is generally expected of social workers. We load upon them unrealistic expectations and we then complain when they do not live up to them... In order to cope with the demands that parliament has laid upon social service authorities, large departments have grown up in which social workers find it difficult to come to terms with the complex pressures which surround them... They operate uneasily on the frontier between what appears to be almost limitless needs on the one hand and an inadequate pool of resources to satisfy those needs on the other.

In spite of all the complexities and uncertainties surrounding the functions of social workers, we are united in our belief that the work that they do is of vital importance in our society... It is here to stay and social workers are needed as never before. But it is important that we use a scarce and costly resource – the trained social worker – in a creative and effective manner.

– P. Barclay[2]

INTERNATIONAL EVENTS

The Middle East

At the close of 1979 and into January 1980 we read with horror of the siege of the Grand Mosque in Mecca by about 500 Islamic fundamentalists and the fierce fighting to recapture this holy shrine. At least 255 people were killed and over 560 injured. The consequences of this bloody battle would emerge across the whole Middle East and cause untold horrors over the following decades. Michael Hayden, a former Chief of USA intelligence has written that:

> After the attacks, the Saudis made a deal with the devil. They decided that, with the Wahhabists, no one is going to be on our religious right. That has left them supporting a violent interpretation: let me say this carefully – of one of the world's greatest monotheisms. That has spread a poison throughout the Middle East... At a minimum you've got the Wahhabist philosophy theology which posits a permanent state of animosity between Islam and the rest of the world.[3n]

The Falkland Islands

In December 1981, as successive governments in Argentina had failed to ease chronic economic and civil unrest, control fell to yet another military junta. General Leopoldo Galtieri, Brigadier Basilio Lami Dozo and Admiral Jorge Anaya took power. They later led a campaign to end the long dispute with Britain over the sovereignty of the Falkland Islands by military means. They saw a chance to capture a patriotic spirit and thus divert attention from domestic chaos and regain the Islands from a country 11,522 miles away and in so much economic decline they had withdrawn Naval protection. Thus, they rescued Margaret Thatcher's premiership and consolidated the most significant change in economic, political and cultural change in this country for fifty years.

On March 19th 1982 members of the Argentinean military posing as 'scrap merchants' landed on South Georgia, an uninhabited British territory some 800 miles east of the Falkland Islands. They then hoisted the Argentinean flag. This was quickly followed by an invasion of the main island of East Falkland, quickly overwhelming the Governor and the small population of under 3,000, most of British descent. The UK government was taken completely by surprise, although they had sent two submarines towards South Georgia in March. Despite mayhem in Whitehall, Thatcher saw the ultimate threat to her position and brought her blinkered approach to drive through an immediate response, backed by the Chief of Naval Staff, Sir John Leach, who promised that within 48 hours he could assemble a task force ready to sail. Once the order had been given, ships and submarines from around the world were ordered to head for the Falklands. Two aircraft carriers left Portsmouth on April 5th and then the requisitioned cruise ships SS *Canberra* and *Queen Elizabeth 2*, all to resounding cheers. We were back in full war mode with the majority of the population supporting action against the invaders. The Commons authorised the action and the whole episode allowed Margaret Thatcher to don a Churchillian stance, using every PR trick to support her image, driving around in a large fast tank, waving the Union Jack. A small war Cabinet was formed, excluding the Chancellor Geoffrey Howe. The task force eventually consisted of 127 ships supported by helicopters, RAF fighters, and with a total manpower of over 25,000 troops.

In the background of the conflict, diplomatic channels were busy trying to find a peaceful solution. Our actions threatened the close relationship between the Prime

Minister and President Reagan, for whom the Argentinean generals formed an important element in his undeclared war on Communism throughout South America. Eventually America came to our aid providing intelligence and diplomatic support and continued to sell the Sidewinder Missiles used by the RAF. No deal was ever accepted by Argentina.

The operation facing the UK was alarming. In addition to the difficult terrain and near Antarctic weather, we were outnumbered three to one in the air making cover for troop landings very dangerous. The Argentinean fighters and their submarines were equipped with modern French Exocet missiles, and our supply lines were extraordinarily long. Approval for a landing was given on May 18th 1982, and three days later 4,000 troops landed under heavy Argentinean air attack which sunk or severely damaged six ships including a destroyer and a container ship full of supplies. The *QE2* with another 3,000 troops on board was in jeopardy. Had the Argentinean bombs been properly fused and had they had more Exocets these first days could have seen the end of the mission. If Argentina had then bombed the supply and troops ships, they would certainly have won. It took the hard-pressed troops 23 days of heavy, heroic fighting and demanding marching across boggy moorland to recapture the island and declare a cease fire. During that period nearly a thousand troops had been killed (255 of ours), over 2,500 wounded (775 ours) and we had lost 7 ships and 35 aircraft. The country was relieved, although not all responded to Mrs Thatcher's command to 'Rejoice, Rejoice, Rejoice.'

Two issues tarnished her victory. One was the fact that the troops had fought almost to the last rounds of ammunition, placing them at great risk, and the second was the late sinking of the Argentinean ship ARA *General Belgrano* with the loss of 323 men. The final order for our submarine to sink the ship had come directly from the Prime Minister when it was thought, and later established, to have been sailing away from the battle zone. Appearing on TV during the forthcoming election, Mrs Thatcher was furiously attacked for this act by a well-informed teacher Mrs Diana Gould, but, despite handling the surprise incident in her usual style, many viewers retained reservations about the decision. However, the incident did not significantly damage her enhanced reputation as a victorious leader of the nation. Confrontation was now confirmed as the Prime Minister's primary style.

AIDS

In 1981 rumours started to appear concerning a devastating disease found among the gay community on the west coast of America; a year later it gained the term AIDS (acquired immunodeficiency syndrome). It was caused by a retrovirus spread by unprotected sex, dirty hypodermic needles and infected blood transfusions. It could take up to three years from infection to the appearance of signs and symptoms, by which time, in these early days, the most severe cases had a life expectancy of six months. This became a global epidemic, mostly affecting Sub-Saharan Africa and South and South East Asia and killing some 39 million people worldwide. There was an urgent search for a cure. Although effective anti-retroviral treatments to slow the effects of the disease were discovered, no cure has yet been found. It took no time at all for the media to headline the terrible nature of this fatal disease and cause general panic in the population (improperly terming the disease the 'Gay Plague') from which a whole range of ideas spread, mostly about bodily contacts, kissing, sharing a drinking vessel or using a public lavatory seat.

Within social work, concerns naturally focussed on residential care across all age groups. New policies and procedures were quickly issued. I recall a manager of a girls' home explaining an embarrassing incident when, seated with a group of girls. they were sharing a Mars bar by passing it round for each to take a bite. Better not to encourage that particular bonding behaviour again. Fear and concern about infection had driven another nail in the personal care of needy young people. As the disease spread, the government launched a series of public health warnings on TV. Thus the conservative Margaret Thatcher oversaw the most frank and detailed programmes about sex and drugs ever screened.

The Middle East

In this same period the Israeli–Arab conflict had been increasing, and in June 1982 Israel's ambassador to London was seriously injured by a marksman from the Abu-Nidal terrorist organisation. Israel used this provocation to invade Lebanon where the PLO and other Palestinian organisations were based. Their initial response was a prolonged air attack centred on the PLO camps at Sabra and Shatila, killing some 200 people. Following an accord agreed in late 1982, large numbers of PLO and Fatah fighters moved out of Lebanon. The American envoy gave an assurance that the refugee camps would be safeguarded by US Marines but, following the assassination of the Syrian President in September, the Israeli forces re-entered Beirut; Ariel Sharon authorised their allies, the Christian Militant Phalangists, to enter the Sabra and Shatila camps, and up to 3,500 Palestinians were massacred. These events, along with the subsequent Syrian occupation of Lebanon and the creation of the Iranian supported Hezbollah organisation, further aggravated the long-standing violence in the region into the 21st century.

Russia

On March 15th 1985, much to most people's surprise, the passionate reformer Mikhail Gorbachev was elected General Secretary of the Soviet Communist Party. He was determined to bring to an end the chronic corruption within the system and respond to the growing calls for the radical reorganisation needed if the Soviet Union were to survive as a world power. The campaign was launched with the twin slogans 'perestroika' (restructuring of the economy and political systems) and 'glasnost' (freedom of information) and was initially directed at ending the Cold War, which was haemorrhaging the Soviet economy. Gorbachev was soon very popular in the west because he had started the withdrawal from Afghanistan and promoted a policy to ban the feared intermediate range nuclear weapons from Europe.

Gorbachev adopted more peaceful policies, reducing nuclear weapons and forming working relationships with western leaders including Ronald Reagan and Margaret Thatcher, who famously decided that they could 'do business together.' Faced with an effective defeat and the rising costs of the Afghanistan campaign, Russia decided in July 1986 to withdraw from that country. It is considered that the combination of the cost of this prolonged war, the impact of a military defeat and the subsequent division between military and political leadership were major contributory factors to the dissolution of the Soviet Bloc into its constituent States from the late 1980s. In 1986 Gorbachev and President Reagan met in Iceland and agreed an absolute limit on the number of nuclear warheads, with the aim of eliminating all nuclear weapons by 1996.

Chernobyl

On April 26th 1986 Europe experienced a massive threat when the Chernobyl Nuclear Power Plant near Pripyat in Ukraine exploded scattering deadly debris and radioactive fallout across Belarus and far beyond. The buildings and immediate area were immediately subject to five times the fatal dose of radiation, and the explosion eventually released 400 times more radioactive material than the Hiroshima bomb. Thirty-one people on the site were killed. The next day the population of Pripyat was evacuated, followed by the whole 30 km area around the site. This area remains deserted to this day (in 2022 the Russians invaded Ukraine threatening an atomic power station in the south of the country as shells threatened to exterior safety wall). The wind swept most of the contamination northwards, with Belarus, Russia, Scandinavia and Austria being the worst affected. It is understood that the flora and fauna of all affected countries will retain the radiation for 100 years. As alarming as this disaster was, it was naively thought that the UK would escape the effects, but traces of fallout were discovered in Scotland, Northern Ireland, Wales and England. Restrictions (finally lifted in 2012) were placed on the movement of over four million sheep. President Gorbachev announced that the equivalent of $30 million had been spent on containment and decontamination, virtually bankrupting the Soviet Union.[4n]

NATIONAL EVENTS

Campaign for Nuclear Disarmament

1981 saw the start of a nineteen-year campaign, led by the Campaign for Nuclear Disarmament (CND), by women campaigning against the presence of nuclear missiles and nuclear submarines, the principal land site being Greenham Common in Berkshire. They fought back against legal interventions by the local council and the RAF police who guarded the airfield behind banks of razor wire. In December 1982 an 'Embrace the Base' protest was organised and some 30,000 women arrived to join hands around the perimeter wire. The following year 70,000 women formed a chain from Greenham to the atomic research station at Aldermaston. It certainly hit the media. If background anxiety was rising, anger at the effects of a depressed economy and a struggling government was expressed not only in the riots detailed above, but also in comedy and popular music.

Northern Ireland

Despite her Falklands victory and a ten-point lead in the polls (overtaking Labour for the first time), Mrs Thatcher's difficulties were not over. With the publicity following the death of Bobby Sands,[5n] the Irish Republican bombing campaign increased as new volunteers joined the cause. On October 10th 1981 a nail bomb outside Chelsea Barracks, aimed at a bus load of Irish Guards, killed 2 people and injured 50. This was followed by another attack a year later when two nail bombs directed at passing soldier formations exploded in Hyde Park and Regents Park. Eleven soldiers were killed and many civilians were serious injured; seven horses of the Blues and Royals were also killed, provoking a massive public reaction against such heartless terrorists. In December 1983 a nail bomb exploded outside Harrods killing 6 people and injuring a further 90. Thatcher's Northern Ireland secretary Willie Whitelaw met with Gerry Adams, the head of the IRA's political wing, but no compromises that would show a way forward were available. Lengthy discussions were also proceeding with the Government of Ireland and in 1985 the Anglo-Irish Agreement was signed, giving that government an advisory role in the North, a fact that horrified the Unionists. In fact, this was the first step in a long peace process which would occupy the next 22 years, although it seemed a lot longer.

Housing

The effects of the 'Right to Buy' your council house were slow to take off but with various incentives sales rose rapidly so that by the end of 1987 over a million houses had been purchased under the scheme. Local councils could keep 50% of the income but could only use it to repay debts, mostly to the Treasury. The inevitable result was a sharp fall in public housing, driving people into renting from private landlords, who then raised the rents, disinclined to accept people (particularly young people) on benefits. By 1988 the pressure group Shelter estimated that millions of people, including some 256,000 households, were homeless, with young single people forced on to the streets. There was a short moratorium on house building by local authorities, while housing subsidies would drop by 70%, saving the Treasury a sum which would form 75% of the planned reduction in government spending. In the decades that followed, this policy, enhanced by the austerity of the late 2010s and cuts to income support, would devastate public housing, create many millionaires and increase the level of homelessness to historic levels.

Europe

Mrs Thatcher had long been a supporter of our membership of the European Economic Community but after entering Downing Street her attitude became more ambivalent. Determined to defend this country, she set herself against the centralisation of power in Europe, the whole complex bureaucracy and the Commission, while supporting any economic policies that promised growth and development. Her presentation in this country portrayed her as a brave Boadicea fighting those foreigners. Her first major fight was a bid to increase the rebate that the UK received from the EEC by £1 million. Her slogan was 'We want our money back,' and, with her metaphorical handbag swinging, she went into battle. I can do no better than quote from the account given, I am sure from his good contacts, by Andrew Marr to illustrate the new style of politics.

> Doing so involved an anti-diplomatic brawl that careered from Dublin to Luxembourg to Brussels ... she would not back down. The German Chancellor, Helmut Schmidt, pretended to go to sleep and the French President, Valery Giscard d'Estaing, began to read a newspaper, then got his cars outside to rev their engines – not a subtle hint. She was entirely unfazed. In an epic four hour meeting over dinner, she simply refused to shut up. Diplomats from all sides suggested interesting side deals, trade-offs, honourable compromises. She brushed them all aside. Astonishingly in the end she got three-quarters of what she had first demanded. Astonishingly she then said 'No'. It was only when almost her entire cabinet were in favour of the settlement that she grudgingly agreed, like some bloodied prize fighter desperate for just another slug, hauled away by worried friends. She may have had the mother of all makeovers – softer voice, softer hair, better teeth but she was a raw, double-or-quits killer when she was cornered.[6]

Not surprisingly, the Cabinet was soon reshuffled to bring in Norman Tebbit, Cecil Parkinson and Nigel Lawson. The ground was prepared for the battle against the miners. A new political climate was developing in Britain as Margaret Thatcher's style took root. Many responded to her straight-talking clear leadership ('What a girl' she was), and somehow her aggressive approach to issues trickled down to work and even family life. It just seemed the right thing to do regardless of the fact that unemployment had now reached three and a quarter million and the economy was in a poor state. On a darker side, a good friend of mine who was a senior officer in the largest police force in the country explained that if it was known that he read *The Guardian* newspaper his promotion would be blocked.

The resurgence of the Left, led by Labour's 'Militant tendency,' a Trotskyite group which campaigned for exit from the European Community, state control of all industries and the abolition of the House of Lords, and which had been infiltrating the Labour Party since Wilson's day, had been championed by Tony Benn. They had managed to reformulate policy and rules at party conferences to increase the influence of local constituency parties. There were heavy tactics and physical threats involved in these manoeuvres and at one conference the miners' leader Arthur Scargill came to blows with Neil Kinnock, the young MP for Islwyn and Bedwellty in South Wales. During the early 1980s Militant had gained control of the youth wing of the party and established control in several local elections, in particular Liverpool where they implemented aggressive anti-Thatcher policies.

Those who looked to the Labour opposition to offer an alternative to Thatcher were met with a party in turmoil under the leadership of the great parliamentarian and committed socialist Michael Foot. The heavily coiffured, perfectly tailored leading lady was pitted against the untidy guy who wore a black duffle coat to the Remembrance Day parade at the Cenotaph. Admired for his brilliant performances in the Commons, particularly at Prime Minister's Questions, Foot lost out to a media campaign that ridiculed his intellectualism and his shabby appearance. Although he is generally remembered as the only man who could have actually held the Labour Party together, the manifesto he prepared for the forthcoming election, promising to nationalise the banks, to leave the EEC and to aim for unilateral nuclear disarmament was so out of touch with the times that one of his senior colleagues described it as 'The longest suicide note in history.' When the election came in June 1983 Labour managed to hold on to its place as the main opposition to the rising SDP–Liberal alliance but gave way to an increased Conservative majority of 184. Foot resigned immediately and Neil Kinnock became Leader of the Labour Party.

Coal

The government now turned its attention to the coal industry, appointing Ian MacGregor as head of the National Coal Board (NCB) following his success returning British Steel to profit by halving the workforce. The cost of deep mining had been exceeding that of imported coal for many years, and a programme of pit closures had succeeded by moving miners to viable pits. As the issue of rising subsidies became more acute, government promoted a clear policy to support the service sector, which could compete in the new global marketplace, against the industrial sector which was struggling to do so in the face of global competition. The consequences of that policy wrecked many towns in the Midlands and in the North. The devastation would continue well into the 21st century and would continue to complicate politics throughout that time.

In March 1984 the NCB announced plans to close 20 coal fields with the loss of 20,000 jobs. The miners' leader Arthur Scargill said that he knew the government planned to close 75 pits, a claim which MacGregor and the government denied publicly and in a letter to every miner. (Papers released in 2014 proved Scargill was right; they also revealed that the government had an informant inside the TUC throughout the strike.) Such a programme epitomised the neo-liberal beliefs adopted by the Conservative Party in defining value in purely monetary terms with no regard to the loss of social value, particularly key to the mining communities. In a PR attempt to counter the historic respect for the miners, Mrs Thatcher referred to them as 'the enemy within.' Strikes commenced at threatened pits, mostly in Yorkshire where many still had many years of coal to mine. On March 12th 1984 Scargill declared that the strikes were now national and called miners across the country out on strike to fight a proposed small pay rise and pit closures. This was to become the most divisive, violent and longest dispute since the general strike of 1926.

The full strike lasted for twelve months, during which time the public attitude waxed and waned. Unlike the previous government, Thatcher had ensured that there were high coal stocks at power stations. Support for the miners had a long tradition and now they were fighting massive threats to their jobs and their whole communities so I think the majority felt some sympathy; on the other hand most people supported the government's determined attempts to clip the power of the unions. Others were puzzled about why such a valuable asset was being left in the ground; we had always believed that our 'green and pleasant land' covered sufficient fuel to last forever and now we had oil as well, so how come coal imported from Australia was cheaper? (The answers seemed to be opencast mining and the low cost of shipping by vessels paying their crew very low wages.) Despite recent legislation, the National Union of Miners embarked on a carefully organised programme of 'flying pickets' to support threatened pits across the country; the government's response was to deploy police from non-mining areas and employ checks on approaching roads, often many miles from the pits. This raised numerous concerns about the extension of police powers and public liberty.

Many of these factors swirled around the 'Battle of Orgreave,' which certainly hit the headlines and became the defining event of the strike. By June 1984 heavy industries were running short of fuel, and the coking plant at Orgreave, near Rotherham, was asked to supply British Steel in Scunthorpe; 35 lorries were due to be loaded. In answer to the call, some 7,000 loyal pickets arrived at the plant to prevent the lorries leaving. As each full lorry emerged the pickets used mass attacks with bottles, stones and broken fences, held back by some 1,700 police from 13 forces using full riot gear. After each affray miners escaped into the fields pursued by mounted police and dogs. Much of the picketing was reasonably peaceful but when Scargill and the TV crews arrived violence escalated to demonstrate the power of the NUM and the extreme violence of the police. Twenty-eight miners and 41 police were injured during that one day. Scargill called on all his members and the whole trade union movement '... to come here in their thousands in order that we can make aware to everybody that we're not prepared to see this kind of brutality inflicted on working men and women.'[7]

I don't recall many responding well as Scargill's extreme rhetoric was making people wary, and in any event this was not a total strike. Flying pickets were dispatched to mines where work was continuing, the objective being to keep miners out of the pit and the coal in. The uncertainty of miners in Nottinghamshire and Derbyshire about the strike increased, and in August 1984 they formally declared their opposition, significant issues being the failure of their area to support the initial call, the intervention of flying pickets in their area and the fact that the national strike was unconstitutional and illegal as there had never been a ballot for a national strike.

In the autumn the number of strike breakers increased, and on March 3rd 1985 the strike was formally called off. Ten years later the remaining mines were privatised.

In 1983 there had been 174 working pits; closures came quickly and the last deep mine was closed in December 2015 with only a few open-cast pits still working. The miners returned to work with pride in their long campaign, cheered on by their loyal communities which had given and suffered so much in support of their men folk. The wives had formed a courageous force, feeding the strikers at home and on the picket lines, where many had suffered from police action. They had kept their communities alive and now faced the slow destruction of these loved communities with very little financial help to survive and cope with the massive changes to their family life. The cost of policing the strike was £200 million, which central government sought to lay at the door of local government despite the fact that policing the strike had been organised on a national basis, sometimes approaching a militarisation of the police force.

Brighton

In the autumn of 1983 Brighton hosted the annual conference of the Labour Party. Under Kinnock's leadership the fight against Militant was pursued by the expulsion of individual members and the whole editorial board of the magazine *Militant*. In 1984 the Conservative Party arrived for their conference full of confidence, having defeated both Argentina and the miners although still well aware that unemployment was over 11%. Members of the Cabinet were accommodated at the Grand Hotel. At 02:54 hrs on October 12th a large IRA bomb exploded in the hotel as a response to the government's Northern Ireland policy in general and against the hunger strikes in particular. The plan was to kill the Cabinet and thus force a retreat from Northern Ireland. In the event, five people were killed, including one MP, and 34 were injured, including Norman Tebbit's wife who was paralysed in the attack and for whom he cared diligently in the years to come. At the time of the explosion the Prime Minister was working on her big speech and, owing to the structure of the Victorian hotel, she and the Cabinet escaped serious injury. Thanks to the local Marks and Spencer they were all able to appear smartly dressed as usual at the conference where Thatcher told her stunned audience and the world that 'The fact that we are gathered here now … is a sign not only that this attack has failed, but that all attempts to destroy democracy by terrorism will fail.' The IRA's response was that 'Today we were unlucky, but remember we only have to be lucky once. Give Ireland peace and there will be no more war.' At the end of the day however it was Margaret Thatcher that emerged triumphant to great acclaim. Could anyone defeat her? Once the celebrations were over it was back to face the poor state of the economy, rising unemployment, particularly for the young, disaffection by black youths facing clear discrimination from the police and growing discontent in her Cabinet.

The Prime Minister had set herself firmly against the power and influence of local authorities and a series of laws were passed forcing them to put a variety of functions out to tender, whilst spending caps and auditing programmes were re-introduced under the banner of the 'three Es' – economy, efficiency and effectiveness. The Greater London Council, led by Labour's Ken Livingstone, had become an embarrassment to the government when they started displaying a massive banner on the side of their offices facing Parliament, recording the unemployment figures every week. The GLC was abolished, along with metropolitan county councils, in the Local Government Act, narrowly passed in July 1985.[8n] The rioting of the late 1970s continued sporadically. In 1981, there were race riots in Brixton where a householder had been shot during a house search, and then in October 1985 serious riots broke out in the Broadwater Farm Estate in North London when police called at a flat searching for stolen goods. They entered without warning and Cynthia Jarrett, who was watching TV with her children, died of a heart attack. A massive disturbance followed and continued throughout the night led by some 500 mostly young black men. In the late evening one police officer, PC Keith Blakelock, became isolated and was set upon and killed by rioters using machetes and knives. He was the first policeman killed in a riot since 1833. The media led a moral panic, putting pressure on the police who arrested hundreds of young men.[9n]

Dissent

Six years into her premiership, Mrs Thatcher increasingly relied on a small group of advisers, much resented by her Cabinet ministers. Early in 1986 the first public display of these splits arose between the Prime Minister and her defence secretary, the ambitious and charismatic Michael Heseltine. The question was whether replacement military helicopters would be built by a European consortium based in the Westland factory in Yeovil or by an American backed consortium. Heseltine was convinced that the European Westland option would be technically best but was aware that Thatcher's unelected advisors favoured the American option. The dispute dragged over several Cabinet meetings but came to a head in January 1986 when it was clear to Heseltine that he had been outmanoeuvred. He walked out of Cabinet and Downing Street to the delight of the waiting photographers. He then issued a statement criticising the Prime Minister's management style, stating that she was a liar who lacked integrity. Heseltine later wrote: 'I saw many good people broken by the Downing Street machine. I had observed the techniques of character assassination: the drip, drip of carefully planted, un-attributable stories that were fed into the public domain, as colleagues became marked as "semi-detached" or "not one of us".'[10]

Murdoch

The printing trade had been embedded in Fleet Street since the early 1500s; the skill of compositors setting the type in metal was part of the old guild system. By the 20th century it was overcrowded by the offices of most of the nation's newspapers. In the process the trades unions had gained unprecedented power. Extraordinarily, the owners had delegated to the unions decisions on whom and how many typesetters and others worked in the presses, their conditions of service and a complicated system of payments, bonuses etc. In the early 1980s, News International, owned by the Australian Rupert Murdoch, had, with others, decided that it was impossible to produce a profitable paper in these circumstances. He therefore built a new HQ in Wapping where the government was encouraging the development of a new business zone at Canary Wharf. He told his staff that it was to produce just one of his many publications. In January 1986 Murdoch announced that *all* his printing would be moved to Wapping where new offset litho machines were waiting. The old skills were no longer required and journalists could type in their own stories, bypassing the old processes. More than 5,000 staff went on strike only to be served with dismissal notices. Business was transferred to Wapping forthwith, where new staff, electricians and those familiar with new technology were already engaged. Strikers demonstrated at the Wapping offices for many months and there were severe clashes with police, but by February 1987 the strike was called off. Whilst recognising that new technology was now essential, the arbitrary way in which Murdoch, supported by the government, had lied to his staff and his disregard for their hard won skills did not earn him much support. All other newspapers changed to the new technology but accomplished the changes by retraining and respecting their staff. Given that my grandfather, father and cousin had worked 'in the print' this seemed a personal loss, and I have never bought any publication or subscribed to anything from the Murdoch empire since that time.

The Big Bang

A similar story applied to the City of London where the bowler hatted, rolled umbrella cosy traditions still reigned while the New York Stock Exchange prospered. Things began to change in the 1960s when America decided to tax overseas investment, thus opening the way for London to step in; also the Soviet Union favoured London as a place to invest rather than the 'evil' USA. As the City began to prosper it argued that exchange restrictions, some imposed in WWII, should be eased, and in October 1979 Geoffrey Howe, Mrs Thatcher's Chancellor, removed all these restrictions. This gradually opened up the money market for free trade. After 1983 the government embarked on a programme to reform the old Stock Exchange which was now falling behind the global markets. In October 1986 the 'new' Stock Exchange opened for business. The busy personal interaction of the trading floor was replaced by computer screens, and business that would previously have taken at least a quarter of an hour could be done in seconds. This, the 'Big Bang,' was the essential mark of the Thatcher era. It was de-regulated, and loans as well as domestic, business and international deals were readily available. Many of the people behind the screens became obscenely rich in a very short time and paid their tribute to Margaret Thatcher and her successors for many years. Those that rushed to get mortgages in excess of the value of their property, however, would pay the price, and many tears would be shed as the economy fell in future years. Twenty-one years later, the whole system would collapse with devastating consequences, but for now it was boom time. The money and credit flowing into the economy gave a sense of optimism which further fuelled the markets. The unemployment rate, which had reached three and a quarter million in July 1986, slowly began to fall.

Election

The time came to call a general election with the aim of getting Mrs Thatcher a third term. This time she would be up against Neil Kinnock who had been busy sorting out the Labour Party ready for such an event. For the first time, I was having some concerns about our Prime Minister's state of mind. Her eyes had that fixed, staring quality, perhaps associated with hyperthyroidism, and her voice was becoming hoarser and more strident. How, I wondered, could any one person hold this office with the relentless demands of globalisation and instant international news for 24 hours a day, seven days a week?

Kinnock, a passionate socialist, had gathered a strong Shadow Cabinet around him in a determined attempt to develop clear policies, to win back those who had drifted away during Foot's time and to restore unity to the party. He loathed Thatcher and hated Scargill's foolish leadership of the miners' strike and the far-left ideologies of the Militant tendency. In Liverpool, where they held power, their anti-government policies, in particular frantic house building, resulted in an illegal budget and the bankruptcy of the Council. In that position the only option was to sack staff. That would confront Thatcher with the effects of her policies and bring down the government! On October 1st, at the Labour Party's annual conference, in a typically discursive speech Kinnock took them on. Calling for unity and realism, which would win the coming election, he continued with increasing passion and anger:

> If socialism is to be successful in this country, it must relate to the practical needs and the mental and moral traditions of the men and women of this country ... We must not dogmatise or browbeat. We have got to reason with people, we have got to persuade people. That is their due ... There is anger in this country brought about by these last six years of Tory government, but strangely that anger is mixed with despair ... If our response to that despair ... amounts to little more than slogans. If we give the impression that ... we believe that if we can just make a loud noise the Tory walls of Jericho will fall down, they are not going to treat us very seriously at all.
>
> Because you are from the people, because you are of the people, because you live with the same realities as everybody else lives with, implausible promises don't win victories. I'll tell you what happens with impossible promises. You start with far fetched resolutions. They are then pickled into a rigid dogma, a code, and you go through the years sticking to that, outdated, misplaced, irrelevant to the real needs and you end up with the grotesque chaos of a *Labour* council hiring taxis to scuttle round a city handing out redundancy notice to its own workers. I am telling you, no matter how entertaining, how fulfilling to short term egos – you can't play politics with people's jobs and with people's services or with their homes. Comrades ... the voice of the real people with real needs ... is louder than all the boos that can be assembled ... The people will not, cannot abide posturing.
>
> Comrades it seems to me lately that some of our number become like latter-day public school boys. It seems it matters not whether you won or lost, but how you play the game ... Those game players get isolated, hammered, blocked off ... and then they claim a rampant

victory ... Comrades, these are vile times under this Tory government, and we have got to secure power to restore real local democracy.[11]

This was a great speech broadcast live on TV and marked the beginning of the end of the Militant groupings within the party. For once the overwhelming press coverage was positive, membership increased and the opinion polls started to rise.

The election was called for June 11th 1987 and it was a good contest. Labour, with the help of Peter Mandelson, ran an excellent media campaign but never managed to break the media's portrayal of Kinnock as an accident prone 'Welsh windbag.' More importantly the voters were beginning to sense the promise of home ownership and prosperity promised by the market and felt they could see an end to the depressed economy; they were just not willing to trust a party still committed to nationalisation. In any event, Mrs Thatcher's reputation of a determined leader who won any challenges, saved the Falklands and escaped an assassination attempt won her the day. Labour did gain 20 seats and the Conservatives lost 21, their majority cut to 101. Mrs Thatcher had her third win, something almost unprecedented in British politics. Although I am sure she would never have admitted it, it was a tired Margaret Thatcher that returned to Downing Street. Her work ethic and self-belief carried her through, and she set about, in her own words, 'pulling the State off people's backs,' which in reality seemed to involve removing power from local authorities (who, being locally elected, she could not control) and to force the so-called efficiency of the market on public services while bringing more power to her central government. This, of course, required a willing Cabinet, which, although appointed by her, never quite matched her ambitions and to whom she felt able to be as rude and demeaning as she could. The first targets would be education and the NHS.

CULTURE

This section has no option but to start with one of the greatest tragedies of the times: the untimely murder of John Lennon, the great musician and peace campaigner, on December 8th 1980. Lennon was shot and killed outside his New York apartment, beside his wife the artist Yoko Ono, by a deranged fan Mark Chapman. As news of this tragedy spread across the world there was a universal outcry of grief which reflected not only the joy that he had given so many as part of The Beatles, but also the admiration of so many for his attractive 'laid back' personality.

In 1981 the BBC TV series *Boys from the Blackstuff*, following the lives of five Liverpool unemployed men, struck at the heart of the failing economy. It was a touching insight into the effects of economic policies on individuals at a time when the jobless total was rising rapidly. The main character, Yosser Hughes, a powerfully built man who had lost everything in his life, caught the nation's heart with his desperate cries of 'Gis a job' and 'I can do that' as he went for any type of work despite his total unsuitability. His cries became catchphrases adopted across the country.[12]

He was echoed by the boastful cockney plasterer created by Paul Whitehouse and Harry Enfield whose only joy in life was 'loadsamoney.' In popular music Duran Duran hit the headlines while the New Romantics morphed into Culture Club with their lead singer with a soulful voice, Boy George, who dressed in a decidedly flamboyant style. Lads from the working classes had found a means of expression which would tumble them into wealth. Red Wedge, a collective of groups and performers who were determinedly anti-Thatcher and who gave their support to the Labour Party, achieved several *Top of the Pops* appearances with their lead singer Billy Bragg. 'Alternative,' that is to say non-racist, non-misogynistic comedians were bringing a tougher, more 'in your face' comedy to the screen. Among them were Alexei Sayle, Ben Elton, Jo Brand, Eddie Izzard and Harry Hill. In 1984 these stars were matched by the comedy puppet show *Spitting Image*, which tore mercilessly into politicians of all parties and celebrities of all sorts. Most of their ire was directed at the Conservative Cabinet and Margaret Thatcher in particular. They certainly got the climate of Cabinet meetings right in their famous sketch in which the Prime Minister was seated at the head of a restaurant table. The waitress asks for her choice, to which she replies 'Steak,' but when asked about the vegetables she looks down the table and says, 'Oh they can make their own choice.'[13]

Not surprisingly, the current events and the political climate, together with economic depression, chronic unemployment and poverty, were all reflected in the culture of the 1980s which seemed to extend from violence to escapism. Professional football was still being played in shabby grounds that showed ample evidence of lack of investment. The mid 1970s had seen rising hooliganism gradually infiltrated by organised gangs, but now it accelerated to an alarming extent, threatening and killing many ordinary fans. In May 1985 a 15-year-old boy was killed in Birmingham when a wall collapsed under pressure from fans. Two weeks later, Liverpool fans arrived at the Heysel Stadium in Brussels for the European Cup final to support their team against Juventus. Many were on the end of a two-day alcoholic binge and found themselves crammed into an overcrowded area of the ground. Next to them was a vacant 'safe' area which somehow accommodated a few Juventus fans. The Liverpool fans commenced to tear down the thin wire fence to gain more space and reach the rival fans. Police had withdrawn to get reinforcements as the two groups of fans met at a wall which collapsed under their weight. Riot police arrived and indiscriminately wielded their batons, apparently not fully realising that there were casualties buried under the wall. The riot caused the deaths of 38 fans, all but one of whom supported Juventus. Riots also broke out in Germany as English hooligans disrupted further European games. The result was that English fans were banned from European games until the end of the decade. We were all infuriated in 1986 by the World Cup semi-final game against Argentina when England lost by one goal, scored by Diego Maradona using his hand to flip the ball into the net. The Tunisian referee said he saw no offence.

Hooliganism was a feature of life across the country throughout the 1980s. Clearly unemployment and depression were contributory factors, and the appearance of 'yuppies' (young urban professional people), usually associated with aspirational workers in the finance industry, helped emphasise the social divide. Many had experienced the slow erosion of the reference points by which they had negotiated behaviour, and the new regime called for competition in an aggressive marketplace. The police rose to the challenge of rioters and hooligans, thus reinforcing their ingrained racism and ability to bring corrupt charges. The trade in illegal drugs now left the casual scene of previous decades and became significant business. This was particularly evident in the use of cocaine, the pure stuff for the yuppies, the contaminated for the rest, and for the really poor and young solvent sniffing from adhesives in the DIY stores had to suffice.

From the poor yet aspiring South London came a remarkable film, *My Beautiful Laundrette*, which focussed on an Asian family committed to the Thatcherite doctrine who encourage their young son to take over a local laundrette, which he does despite violence from local racist gangs. He recruits his friend and lover Omar and together they redecorate the laundrette in a somewhat flamboyant style. It challenged on so many levels, and included the first gay kiss in a UK film.[14] There were some other great films too. Most memorable for us were Richard Attenborough's *Gandhi*, a hard hitting portrayal of this great man's fight against British Imperialism.[15] Otherwise we were entertained by musicals including *Cats* and *The Phantom of the Opera* for those anxious to escape the realities of the times.

If hooliganism was one answer to the oppression of unemployment for some young people, then music and dance were others. Michael Jackson hit the UK with his remarkable show *Thriller*, which caused a wave of new dances across the country, and pop-up raves, where non-stop rock and punk music blared out into vast indoor (and some outdoor) arenas with young people losing themselves in energetic wild dancing all night.

In 1983 the northern states of Ethiopia suffered one of that country's regular famines caused by lack of rainfall and land reform following the revolution that ousted Emperor Haile Selassie. The famine caused half a million deaths. The effects of the famine and the camps for desperate refugees, filmed by cameraman Mohammed Amin and reported by the BBC's Michael Buerk, showed the most devastating biblical scenes. The film burst on to our TV screens in October 1984 with tremendous power and called for something to be done to save these destitute and dying people. The rock star Bob Geldof and singer/producer Midge Ure called fellow stars together to produce a hard hitting single 'Do They Know It's Christmas?' to raise money for the relief of the famine. It became the fastest selling single produced in the UK and raised £8 million. The following year, following on from an idea by Boy George, the first Live Aid concert was organised. This was an amazing event staged in London and Philadelphia with supporting events in Australia and Germany. It played to a global TV audience of 1.9 billion who were spellbound by the music, the technology of the transatlantic performances and the cause. It raised £150 million.

Ann and I were embracing the rich culture available in Manchester from the Halle Orchestra to the major theatres. We enjoyed Joe Orton's satire *Loot* which teases the Roman Catholic Church and gives a poor view of the police, a revival of Pinero's farce *The Cabinet Minister*. We took Juliet and her friend Melissa to Southport to see a rumbustiously hilarious New Vic production of *Canterbury Tales* where the action was not confined to the stage. At the Palace Theatre we enjoyed Lauren Bacall in Tennessee Williams' *Sweet Bird of Youth* directed by Harold Pinter. A good friend organised us to see a memorable performance of *The Life and Adventures of Nickolas Nickleby*, a full-length version of Dickens' novel. I think it went on for eight hours with a meal break at the halfway point. It was amazing. We decided to see Rudolf Nureyev with the Northern Theatre Ballet but wished we hadn't as it was just too late for him to live up to his reputation. Into Blackburn King George's Hall came the dream jazz trio of Kenny Ball, Acker Bilk and George Melly, who was Ann's favourite. Our real find however was the annual Buxton Festival. For a year or so John joined Ann, me, Juliet plus her current boyfriend at the delightfully old fashioned Old Hall Hotel to enjoy the fun classic and jazz music. Those were wonderful days in a glorious setting and the hotel even treated us to a real-life version of Victoria Wood's iconic comic sketch known as 'Two Soups.'[16]

SOCIAL WORK

The experience of social workers in this period was mixed. To some extent the personal social services were protected from the worst excesses of the fierce cuts on public spending, not by any wish of central government but by local authorities which decided to protect these services within their own budgets. The Prime Minister's view was that the primary agency for personal individual care for people who had a disability or the elderly was not the state but the family or charitable agencies and, if that was not possible, then the private market. Considerable suspicion surrounded the role of social workers: were they motivated to encourage their clients to conform to social norms or to challenge them? Alarm was raised in Cleveland in 1987 when an extraordinary number of children were taken into care on suspicion of child abuse. The cause of this was the use of new diagnostic tests by two paediatricians in the local hospital. When it was known that 200 children had been taken into care a media storm broke over the actions of the social workers who were seen as carelessly interfering in family life.

On the other hand, when another child, Jasmine Beckford, died at the hand of her parents in 1984 social workers were attacked for *not* taking action. The 1989 Children Act tilted the responsibility for children firmly towards the parents and set out the primacy of the welfare of the child. Even when a child had been taken into care, responsibility was shared with the parents. In 1980 a BASW initiative had led to the Secretary of State asking the National Institute for Social Work to inquire into the actual roles and tasks that defined professional social work. As part of this the Institute undertook its own surveys into the reality of life in SSDs. The findings were quite alarming, showing how far the Seebohm vision was losing the battle with bureaucracy. Seventy-five percent of workers were dissatisfied with the way that their departments were organised, 67% wanted less central control and more area autonomy, 90% wanted more emphasis on specialisation and 70% would welcome the involvement of more volunteers. Some 58% did not wish to be promoted to senior management positions. Among their expectation of the review was 'a constructive and positive clarification of the role of social work in our society,' recognition that management and bureaucracy had got out of hand and a coherent and positive statement of what social work is about. Asked to define their role, respondents offered:

> To provide an input to client's lives, to help them help themselves to alleviate or avoid the most crushing events. Social work *cannot* transform but it can assist individuals and families to retain their cohesion.
>
> Doing the best you can in a professional role to serve others willingly and with warmth and sympathy, to make material resources available where appropriate and to relieve, where possible, confusion of thought, fears and anxieties.
>
> To strive at all times to leave things better than you find them.
>
> To work through personal contact with individuals, groups and communities to maximise their potential for achieving full and effective membership of the society in which they live.[17]

My view was that, although these quotations represented a good range of views from the front line, they did little to help clarify a sharp definition of where social workers actually wanted to go. The inquiry was chaired by Peter Barclay, whose long interest in social policies had led to his appointment as the President of the National Institute. The report was published in 1982. It proved controversial in favouring a community approach as against individual casework, seeing the social work role as both 'social care planning' – designing care packages based on local networks – and counselling. This led to the concept of 'patch work,' small teams based in areas of deprivation and drawing on the resources of that neighbourhood. Local networks could 'mobilise individual and collective responses to adversity.'[18] The general tenet of the report was positive. However, the committee's conclusion was ambiguous, finding themselves faced with the BASW's arguments for a professional regulatory and registration council along with NALGO's view that social workers were like any other local authority staff.

Not surprisingly, my reaction to this report was one of frustration. In many ways it repeated key aspects of the Seebohm Committee Report fourteen years earlier. It certainly fell far short of all the radical work that we had achieved in Maidstone (see Chapter 10), and more importantly it confused rather than clarified the central issues of the role and tasks of social work, which was the reason why the government had supported its establishment. We remained a vulnerable occupational group, with the door open to a more targeted investigation. In fact the most significant intervention came from a more general review, although powered by the prevailing political drivers.[19] As local authorities were forced to stop building new residential homes for the elderly, provision by the private and voluntary sectors increased. Costs from the government's social security budget rose from £10 million in 1979 to £2.5 billion 14 years later. The Residential Care Act of 1984 was long overdue in requiring local authorities to establish inspection and regulation regimes for independent sector homes. In 1986 an Audit Commission report pointed out the illogicality of this rise due to allowing free choice rather than any assessment of need as the government's distrust of local authorities had effectively ruled them out of the system. In fact, in Lancashire, where most elderly people saw admission to residential care as a right after retirement, we had, by moving responsibility to the individual, successfully moved the housing element of the costs to central government, saving the ratepayers some £3 million a year.

Social Worker – Deputy Chief

Ann was very busy serving on social security appeal panels and enjoying her victories on behalf of claimants. Meanwhile she continued to work in the Darwen social work team which she enjoyed very much although it did lead to a couple of amusing incidents. On one occasion, whilst attending a conference in the training centre, a visiting speaker made some detrimental reference about those self-serving people who work at HQ. Ann was on her feet immediately, pointing out the error of his ways, much to the surprise of the audience. More seriously a decision had been taken to move a disruptive young teenager from the children's home (which he was wrecking) to a secure unit. By the time it was arranged it was a dark evening and the only person available as escort was me. I was assigned to the back garden in case he made a bolt for it. In the event all went well but had there been a fight my presence would have raised so many difficult questions, let alone why I was facilitating a boy into a secure unit when it was well known that I thought such units were inappropriate for young children.

Sports

I resumed my extra-curricular interest in sport for adults with a learning disability with the help of Bryan Hughes and a committed sports adviser from the special needs section of the Education Department, and the whole thing grew and grew. County sports were organised between divisional adult training centres and then regional competitions until there was a whole annual and bi-annual series of competitions at every level. Each year more sports were added and the level of skill increased, as did the sophistication of the methods used to classify competitors according to the degree of their disability. Thus individuals who had severe and complex disabilities came to play a full part. I spent some period as chair of the regional committee although I did little but offer some high-profile influence with other authorities. One thing I could not do was hand out medals as the joy on the recipients' faces brought me to tears of joy; how weird it would be to get your award from a guy in tears! The work was mainly done by tireless volunteers, and it never failed to impress me to the point of tears that for each meeting a whole army of judges and officials all expert in their event or sport, but willing to adapt to any special circumstances, just materialised and stayed until all the work was done. In June 1984 we held a 'June Spectacular' with teams from fourteen local authorities and over 100 competitors.

I have many other memories of these events, in particular the commitment to sports. Committee meetings were usually held in the sports centre at Kirby, and often it was raining so heavily that it was difficult to see the road but *always* every outdoor hard football pitch would be fully occupied, floodlights ablaze. Whilst the sports went well and the whole movement took off, it was not without some opposition. These activities were detracting from the tedious 'industrial' contract work which was the main focus of many adult training centres at that time. Work was falling behind, attendees were less committed and contracts were not being met. Clearly this needed to be got hold of, but it took some time and a great deal of re-training to enable all managers to throw away these old practices and to run more flexible, client centred facilities which would act as a base for a wide variety of activities out in the community.

Although the years from 1978 to 1980 had been exceptionally busy with a steep learning curve, I had found a way of moving things forward despite some reactionary elements within the Department. Whilst funds were available in 1982, I engineered the appointment of three Special Project Officers – Steve Barsby, Phil Southern and Roisin Miller, roughly one for each initiative. I took care to select staff who were intelligent, able to read the internal politics of the Department and confident in their professional ideas. Steve energetically pursued the change from institutional to community care for young offenders, Phil worked hard to introduce new technology to our management and communications systems and Roisin focussed on care of the elderly. Each of these was directly accountable to me and I could therefore deploy them as required. This proved to be somewhat subversive as these great professionals would go round the Department communicating directly with frontline staff thus opening up a two-way avenue which was quicker than the tired old methods of sending ideas up and down (often sticking at one level where it was not favoured). These three were a great help in achieving change much more quickly than relying on the formal structures. Other key people that I looked to were Marion Penny, the Senior Training Officer, internal consultants Joyce Thom, care of the elderly, Agnes Shepardson and David Halpin, the brave wheelchair user (disabilities). Margaret Phillips from the Operations Group could be called upon at any time if there was a crisis in a residential unit.

Within the county Labour in opposition was quite a powerful force, led by Lousie Ellman[20n] who argued point by point in every committee meeting, her eyes flashing passionately. In 1981, after I had been in post for some three years, Labour were returned as the largest party but with no overall control, a situation which lasted for four years.[21n] The Conservatives under Pat Case held the second highest number of seats but Labour with the largest number held all the chairs so Jack Bury became Chair of the Social Services Committee. Life was never going to be the same again. We were into unknown territory. After extraordinary scenes at the main council and in committees some new rules of procedure were agreed pressed by the Liberals, under the leadership of Tony Greaves. In particular they objected to the tradition whereby the Deputy Chair of any committee or the council itself automatically became Chair the following year. They won the battle and in future elections would be held each year. Might that policy apply to Departmental Officers where traditionally Lancashire always promoted the Deputy?

Jack Bury

Although the actual programme of steady development went on more or less as before, the culture changed more in favour of social issues, so that personnel committee meetings were easier and there was less detailed questioning about every penny of each 'special case.' Jack Bury was in the mainstream of traditional Labour and a Blackburn man through and through. He had been a postman and served in the Navy, having been torpedoed in the Mediterranean and suffered a damaged spine. Through many years in local politics Jack had honed his political skills to be a very shrewd operator both within his own party and in the broader political field. He clearly intended to become much more closely involved in the day to day issues confronting the department and set out to find himself an office next to Rex and myself, a move which infuriated the Chief Executive who ordered my boss Rex to move Jack out. Elected members should never be allowed that close to day to day management. It never happened but Rex did have to suffer being sent up at the next Chief Officer's Dinner when the resident comedian colleague did a skit on members' relationships with their chief officers:

> There's a member living in Rex Johnston's office!
> He's never Bury, Bury far away;
> Rex says he can use the loo, if he'll let him use it too,
> Sometimes he stays up all night, until the morning,
> Allocating cheap passes for the bus.
> If Rex knew he was there, he'd just go ruddy spare.
> And he does.

Jack cared deeply for the people that we served and always spoke well at any public event. Early on he was opening a grand new day centre in Preston and I typed out a speech for him but the delivery was just too painful. Jack was great left to himself. Following our long-established family policy of an open house and lack of boundaries Jack, as well as David Murray or any staff member, might call if it was convenient, but as time went by Jack became a regular caller on Sundays. Within a short while discussion about work was relegated in favour of the snooker games that we then held for our neighbours. Higher Studlehurst always had a relaxing atmosphere and it took quite a while and some determined interventions from Ann to persuade Jack to drop the pushy politician persona and relax.

Unfortunately from this time onwards the policy of central government called for cuts every year so that there was the agony of annual plans to shave off a proportion of the service. We drew up priority lists after battling with the treasurer and the committee then had to decide where to draw the line; obviously we designed the cuts with the least possible damage to frontline services and prioritised in relation to which proposals the committee might reject or favour. Each list was a prolonged game of chess. In addition, each department had to establish a member led committee to discover how the work could be done with more efficiency, economy and effectiveness. Some members struggled with the complexity of the task but by 1986 the three Es had become the major battlefield over the reorganisation of our Department.

Change

Work in these years was hectic, with the three Special Project Officers allowing us to increase the speed of change and intervene by a series of day events aimed to stimulate change. In particular I remember using the International Year of Disabled People in 1981 to gather service user groups, voluntary groups and staff from Education and the SSD to review the whole range of needs and provision required in the future. Working groups throughout the county were brought together in a large day workshop and drew up sixteen hard hitting recommendations which led to radical changes in the relationship between service users and professional staff. A week in June 1986 was set aside to explore the potential of play and the creative arts for young people involved in intermediate treatment (IT). It was held at the large residential IT centre in Blackburn and co-ordinated by Margaret Phillips from the Operations Group. It brought together muralists, photographers, video makers, kite makers, game makers, musicians, percussion groups, play therapists, makers of instruments created out of junk, Chinese dragon makers and the famous Lock Stock and Barrel Community Theatre. It was a fascinating week; by the last day Rex was invited for the grand finale and was surprised to be seated on a large throne as the 'Big Chief' while all the young people paraded past to act out, demonstrate and exhibit the result of the work to him. It went on for hours. After some initial anxiety, during which I held my breath, Rex enjoyed the whole thing and I certainly admired his ability to do just that, not at all sure that I could have coped. By early 1982 we completed a massive county wide, year-long exercise designed to make the residential care of elderly people into a more pro-active stimulating regime. This raised many major issues, among which was the classification and lack of qualification of most staff. Quiet, calm and routinised regimes were to be replaced by active, participatory days where residents had a choice of interesting and challenging activities. The 25 recommendations were passed into policy except for the proposal to make one home in each division a specialist place for mentally infirm residents and the request that all staff were given the title of Residential Officers rather than remain categorised as manual staff. This needed more thought!

In 1986 as part of the annual review of the 1981 Delinquency Plan we undertook a close study of the position of young women. This was led by the experienced Child Care Manager Ev Newby and supported by Roisin. The group decided to follow the career paths as young women passed through the system. Alarmed by some of the case histories they examined, they made 14 recommendations which called for Family Resource Centres in each division to offer preventative work and to keep young women in their home communities, and the establishment of 'gate keeping' groups to monitor progress through the system. It was agreed that a Principal Officer post should be created to promote the care of this group, to create policies and practice guides for all staff, to promote research and make annual reports to the Director.

Advanced Management Programme

In 1983 I was selected to attend the Advanced Management Programme (ADMP) for Chief and Senior Officers run by the Institute of Local Government (INLOGOV) at Birmingham University. This was the precursor of the modern MBA, very expensive for the county, highly regarded and run in a series of one- and two-week residential blocks covering some twelve months. This was an exciting and challenging programme covering every aspect of the knowledge and skills required in the management of local government. It was a chance to meet with colleagues from a wide variety of professions and types of local authority. Learning was by a good balance of lecture, seminar, exercise, role play and presentation. By the end of the course a sound network of contacts had been developed; one in particular was Peter Claydon, a senior administrator from Yorkshire who subsequently became a senior executive and Director of the Yorkshire Enterprise Board, one result of the Thatcherite drive to get local authorities to promote local entrepreneurs. I enjoyed the course and got very good reports. I was certainly put through the mill with a view to my expected promotion to Director of Social Services. The joke that ran through my entire stay was that halfway through *every* evening meal the telephone would ring and the call would go out 'Malcolm, it's your chairman!' Jack would need to go over the events of the day and be reassured that he had done the right thing, which he usually had.

In the summer Jack's wife Fe who suffered from emphysema joined him on a Sunday, her delight being to sit out in the garden to enjoy the flowers and watch the birds. She had a mobile oxygen set and from time to time she would remove her mask to take a drag on her fag. They were a close but unusual couple. Late one January evening we were summoned to the infirmary where Fe was painfully breathing her last. We stayed until the end, after which Jack asked if I and Ev Newby would arrange a non-religious service for her funeral. We put a service together, and Jack and his daughters chose the music. We entered to 'Kumbaya', then 'Solitaire' followed by 'Mother Of Mine.' We sang 'Jerusalem' and exited to 'Bridge Over Troubled Water.' The service went well, attended by senior councillors from all parties. Ev and I managed this highly unusual request tolerably well, telling the congregation what we had gathered of her life with Jack who she termed her 'curly haired little bugger.' I declined the undertakers' request for my business details just before one of my colleagues, more experienced than I in the ways of local government, patiently explained that I had just committed professional suicide!

When Labour regained control in 1985 it seemed that Jack's first priority was to get a new Director. His main problem was that Rex had no intention of retiring before he was 65. Rex and I had many long discussions during which Rex had explained his fear of retirement and repeated his determination to stay in post as long as possible. For Rex, retirement was synonymous with death, a feeling with which I could empathise; in many ways he was enjoying life although at the same time he was frightening the assistant directors and myself by arriving at committee and whispering that he had not even read the agenda. Nonetheless this did not stop him speaking to items and charming the committee. The battle was to be long drawn out. Many of the newly elected councillors were new to social services so I undertook to devise a training day which gave us the opportunity to show the breadth of the Department's activity and make a determined bid to change the archaic structure of the sub-committees which had occupied all the councillors' attention only on the establishments run by HQ. It was a good day. For the first time, I thought, we ran an interactive session which involved councillors in the wide range of the Department's activities and the value of the social work and care staff. They agreed to a new committee structure on client groups, but my planned masterly conclusion was ruined by the speaker before me ran twenty minutes over time. No chance to impress.

It took Jack months to wear down Rex's resistance, to the point where he was within reach of his sixty-fifth birthday. So a date was set: we were to have a new Director. A few weeks later Jack told me that at the next committee meeting I would be nominated as the next Director. This was not right, and I told him that if that was put to the meeting I would decline. He was not at all happy. It was nine years since my appointment and in that time the whole ethos of management in local authorities had been transformed. MBAs had been up and running and there was a significant number of very able young social services managers who should be considered. Reluctantly Jack agreed to open up the competition. In many ways promotion to Director was attractive but I lacked Rex's ability to make it up as it went along and I knew that my obsessional drive would result in years of stress as I tried to move this great Department to a more radical view of community orientated social work. Nonetheless I applied for the job, just in case all the applicants were less capable than me. As an alternative, and as an opportunity to explore pastures new, I applied for the directorship in Cumbria.

The processes went through their usual phases over the next six months. Eventually the selection day dawned and we assembled in County Hall for what felt like an exact replay of my appointment: the same formalities; the same set questions; and no doubt the ritual reading out of references. Jack was in the chair. There were six other candidates, only a few of which I knew. It was all so dreadfully old fashioned.[22] I thought that my thirty-minute interview went well. I committed myself to a highly decentralised Department with more delegation of power to integrated teams which involved their local communities in how services were delivered. This was my ambition and I knew it would be well received by Labour and Liberal members. When asked about health I explained that I had submitted to a full medical exam at my own cost, a step that I thought the county should have done before appointing at this level. The leader of the Liberal group, Tony Greaves, described later as the 'Hairy man of grassroots Liberalism,'[23n] came in just before the end of my presentation, not anything I attached too much significance to as my vision exactly matched the Liberal Party's policy at that time. Having committed myself to the race, I was determined to win but as the day wore on it was clear that the appointment committee was running into trouble. Eventually the clerk was sent out to send visiting candidates home and take Tom Foster, a local Director, in to be offered the job. I was then called in to be told of Tom's appointment and took the opportunity to assure the councillors that I would of course support the new Director; after all, it was my plan that the best person be appointed. The drive home and breaking the news to Ann was very painful, complicated by Jack's self-invitation to call in and commiserate. It was a peculiar evening, Jack tearfully apologising and Ann angrily denouncing the committee, the Council and regretting that she had not realised that my appointment could go wrong. Jack after all had chaired the meeting! Lancashire had always appointed the Deputy to take the Chief Officer's job. I had scored a first!

So what went wrong? Participants had never been entirely forthcoming, but, in addition to any errors or shortcomings of mine, it seems that I was beaten by straight politics. I have been told that the first count gave me the job by a majority of one, but Pat Case, as leader of the Conservative group, then imposed a party whip which left the way open for the Liberals who, as they had done on other occasions since they held the balance of power, decided to break the tradition that deputies move up to the top job. The following days were somewhat tense as staff expressed surprise and alarm at the turn of events. There was much distress, but my main thought was that, although Tom Foster had completed the INLOGOV course and had been Director of Tameside Metropolitan Borough for 13 years, preceded by a steady rise with five jobs, each lasting between two and three years, I had never heard of him, even though I would have said that I knew every Chief Officer in the region either directly or by reputation. It was decidedly odd.

An immediate decision had to be taken about the Cumbria post for which interviews had been set a few days later. In the interval I attended a regular briefing session with Pat Case when she took me aside to say that not achieving the directorship had nothing to do with any lack of ability and she was absolutely sure that I would get the Cumbria job, then in the formal meeting she proposed a county wide policy that deputies should never be promoted to the top job at any level, a stupid idea that would kill any ambition! In the face of such hypocrisy I withdrew from Cumbria at once. News that made me very angry was that more than one of the younger Directors who I would have loved to have been appointed had not applied on the assumption that I would clearly be appointed. I felt so bad for them.

One of the final jobs that I undertook was to organise Rex's farewell party which was held in the NALGO club in County Hall. It went fairly well and we managed to keep up a party spirit, each of us doing a turn until his usual circle of women brought in a stripper who went through her whole routine. Ann, my secretary and I left. Whilst this seemed totally inappropriate and robbed the whole event of any dignity, it certainly said something about the later years of Rex's reign. He was a highly intelligent man who could cut to the centre of any issue, easily relating it to a range of personal encounters, but having a great strategic vision and the determination to achieve it were not strong points for him. I had grown very fond of him, although some perspective was given some three years later when for the first time I met the previous Director for whom Rex had been Deputy. He just asked me 'Malcolm, did you ever discover what Rex did all day?' Unfortunately Rex's health fears had been well founded and he died soon after he left his post.

Tom Foster's first day as Director of this vast Department was in July 1986. I had managed to work through my feelings of anger and injustice that stemmed, not from my rejection but from the method by which it had been achieved. As far as I was concerned, a well trained, tried and tested man was coming and my job was to support him all the way. I was on hand daily for any advice or information that Tom needed, but the most obvious first impression was of a very nervous man who constantly wrung his hands and sniffed, using up boxes of tissues every week. I think we got on well and I certainly came to respect him as a professional social worker with an extensive knowledge of his specialist field of mental health and learning disabilities, which was his special interest. Tom faced two massive tasks for which he had my sympathy: one was moving from a small Department catering for a population of some 250,000 to a large organisation meeting the needs of 1.3 million people, and the other was the quiet opposition to his appointment from most of the professional staff. As the weeks went by I could not see much hope of Tom making this leap. Rumours started to circulate that his previous employers had been preparing a case to force his early retirement. My hopes that the Council would appoint a high flier from whom I would learn and who had the drive and imagination to kick this Department forward were fading fast. Jack adopted a more aggressive approach; he clearly saw the appointment as a blow to his chairmanship and political reputation, and not one which he could accept. His disappointment was fuelled by Tom's apparent inability to take a decision; coffee time became increasingly embarrassing as Jack would taunt Tom every time he hesitated on a choice of which biscuit to choose from the plate held before him. Having to defend himself from these attacks must have been a hugely distracting drain on Tom's energy.

Tom decided that the Department needed to be reorganised and promised the three Es committee that he would bring forward an early plan to meet the requirements of effectiveness, efficiency and economy. This rather underestimated the size and complexity of the task. I tried so very hard to advise him, as did many of the senior staff, but he seemed deaf to any input. He would change his plans, and at one critical point when his latest plan was to be put to a meeting of the Divisional Directors to seek their agreement, he decided not to attend, leaving me to sell his project. He decided that the Deputy role should carry more operational responsibility. In May 1984 he took his plan to the cross party 3Es committee who rejected most of it, calling for a radical re-think. When asked about the Deputy role he said it would probably mean two deputies. The councillors, who were looking for cuts, were not impressed. I sent him a list of comments and recommended a more consensual consultative approach. About a third of my ideas were accepted. Most advice from my colleagues was that, if there was a problem it was about process, not structure. Moving the boxes around on the management was not enough. Eventually Tom sent his latest plan to County Hall without circulating it to senior staff. All this indicated an uncertain future through which this great Department would just drift.

After some six months of this obduracy and indecision, I came to accept that my position was impossible. I would end up disagreeing with the Director, but any opinion that I offered would too readily be seen as disloyalty driven by my own rejection. The fate before me seemed, at a local and personal level, to reflect the position that Edward Heath held in relation to Mrs Thatcher who had sunk his premiership. Nothing Heath said was seen as other than sour grapes. Time to look for a change of scene. My options were very limited. We had no wish to move from our lovely home in the Ribble Valley and Juliet was studying in Sheffield. The first wonderful opening was Director of the Central Council for Education and Training in Social Work (CCETSW) based, of course, in London. Two days of selection in London were interesting and challenging and a complete contrast to Lancashire's archaic methods. One day was spent having a complete psychological assessment from a specialist agency. My result showed that I was a '... stable and relaxed personality which can tolerate stress to a high degree. He is a free thinking individual, not constrained by convention. He has an open and forthright personality which is trusting of others and unlikely to be manipulative.' It went on in the same vein! In sharp contrast, the next day was a disaster. There was a group discussion, a situation so familiar from my time in Maidstone, but this time it included Tony Hall, already a board member, so articulate and energetic that no one was able to stop his domination. The first question from the high powered interview panel focused on my submission, which drew attention to the similarities between the process of teaching and social work. I stumbled so it was no surprise not to be selected. We were allowed to return for feedback of our psychological assessment and it was no consolation to be greeted by the assessor with the words 'Congratulations on your appointment, you were our chosen candidate!'

Len Meadwell, a retired Assistant Director from Lancashire, was working on an occasional basis for David Rattray, who had a commercial company called Care Concern that provided residential care for adults with a severe learning disability. His provision was far from any modern ideas, consisting as it did of large institutional care which included a small village community. Neither he nor the provision had a good reputation. He was not unique, having moved from authority to authority across the country gaining rapid promotion at each move until he was the Assistant Director in Wrexham in North Wales. It was there he had spotted a commercial opportunity when a children's home had come on to the market. He had leapt in and gone from strength to strength, moving from child care to adults with a learning disability as a more viable commercial venture. His five establishments had rapidly filled up in those terrible years when hospitals were closing and, more often than anyone would have admitted, coach loads of patients were being taken round the country to be offloaded to whoever would take them.

Len asked me if I would consider working for David who now wanted to bring his provision up to modern standards and expand into the rest of the country. I agreed to meet him and consider the move, providing that I could first see the units in North Wales. It was an interesting trip, posing as someone looking for a placement when only the Head of Service John Donovan knew my true interest. The units were not in a good state and the degree of challenge in the behaviour of some residents was extreme, but the commitment and enthusiasm of the senior staff were impressive. I guess that the other factor, the long-standing policy to close long-stay hospitals and move *all* the patients into small houses in the community, was a growing worry. In the hurly burly of premature closure, insufficient support had been given to patients with more than an ordinary level of disability, and many went straight into the care of the prison service. The people I saw in Care Concern seemed happier that they would have been as guests of Her Majesty. The visit gave me grounds for much thought and I eventually agreed to meet David.

The meeting necessitated a flight to the Isle of Man where Care Concern was registered for tax purposes. I was at the bar when this charming elegantly dressed man walked in. I bought him a drink and we had a very enjoyable evening meal. This man and his plans to improve and expand his organisation were impressive. He offered a good salary (£35,000 per annum – equivalent to £87,540 today) and a company car (with telephone) with no direct responsibility for unit management. Above all he would be happy for me stay based in Lancashire. I was left to think things over and discuss them with Ann, who wrote down two points. Against was the fact that the business would be difficult, although with my patience I would soon get on to the right wavelength; in favour was 'a laughing, happy at work husband able to make decisions without the hierarchy intervening.' When I phoned the following day to say that I would accept the post of Director of Development and Training, David, with typical charm, pronounced himself honoured!

Unfortunately, Lancashire, in common with all North West authorities, were, as was I, very firm believers in the whole normalisation policy. Care Concern was on the verge of being blacklisted for their poor care standards; in particular Lancashire's Education Department was about to stop all referrals to the residential school Hengwrt Hall run by Care Concern near Dolgellau in North Wales. I chaired the regular liaison meeting between the Education and Social Service Departments which endorsed the blacklisting. As we left the meeting, I told my colleagues that I was joining Care Concern as soon as possible. I later drove over to see Jack to tell him that I would be resigning the next morning. The last weeks with Lancashire were strange as I tried to close files and delegate my various roles; it was all quite unreal. I had asked not to be put through any of the ritual farewell sessions and in particular I requested no speeches. I opted instead to entertain staff at Higher Studlehurst at three successive tea parties. My luck finally ran out when the heads of the CHEs treated me to a very nice evening meal and Tom Groves gave a moving tribute to my constant support, availability and commitment. Finally I could say goodbye to Lancashire, my last day being October 9th 1987. I had provided just over nine years of challenging commitment.

These years had included the heart of the Thatcher regime which changed the culture of our society. The post-war consensus of mutual support with the state playing a key role was squeezed out by the neo-liberal belief in a small state, expecting families to care for themselves. In these years state expenditure fell from 43% to 38% of GDP. Unfortunately Margaret Thatcher's belief in Victorian values of thrift, family support and continuity had been supplanted by an economy that relied on the 'spend, spend, spend' drive to keep the wheels of a service based economy turning. Our economy had been turned from making things to making money, inevitably leading to a loss of democratic control as power flowed to a global elite who, through successive mergers, would control markets for their own benefit. Large swathes of our national assets would be owned by foreign agencies with uncontrollable consequences to our economy and way of life, particularly the cost of housing. Trades unions had been dealt massive blows, not only by legislation, but also by the collapse of industry from which most of their members were drawn. Many families who had relied on the dignity of manual work were losing their bearings in this rapidly changing world – their community culture and the moral codes therein were weakening. Many were led to protest and riot against the seemingly inevitable advance of the hostile culture that was being imposed on them from a political class that seemed remote and uncomprehending. In May 1987 I published a rather mournful conversation piece called 'The End of the Grand March?'

> The debate is about the romanticism or reality of the Grand March, the sense of solidarity that forever binds together the generations that struggle to improve their life chances in any unequal society. Are such messages of hope available to the generation that has been brought up in the dogma of Thatcherism? ... For previous generations the purpose of work, apart from survival, is the assumption that the next generation will start the race a little better off. It is a message of hope and commitment to the march of social progress...

Presumably the long term effect of low income is to reduce the spending power of large sectors of society and is self defeating... It seems inevitable that future generations will start even less well off than their parents, relatively even below that of their grandparents. I am quite clear that social work has a duty to address these issues and find ways in which they can be placed for discussion without falling into the trap of sterile political debate.[24]

All the work and innovations that we made in Lancashire were willingly shared on a mutual basis with any other authority, but we were now actually wondering whether we should place a value on our work and charge for it! Had I become Director, I know that with the support of the controlling Labour group I would have fought the government cuts and social policies with every resource available to me. It would have been Liverpool without Militant and most likely ended in tears. I comforted myself that with Bill Utting in central government, David Jones at BASW and Tony Hall at CCETSW the profession was in good hands and would lead us rationally and intelligently but just as passionately as I could ever had done.

In the coming years, market values, disguised within the political dogma of choice and freedom, would quickly extend over most of the world and traditional welfare agencies were forced to justify themselves by the narrow ethics of the market. In this period the income of the bottom 10% of the population fell by 17%, and our streets were frequented by homeless and vulnerable beggars. It is worth remembering Alvin Toffler's brief summary that 'The market is a tool, not a religion, and no tool does every job.'[25]

FAMILY

This decade was not going to be the best. In January 1980 my mother's sister Lola died. This was a great loss. Her determined joy in life had brought great happiness to the family throughout my life. This left my uncle Jim alone in his cottage at Lower Timberden to be supported by his many friends in the village and his daughter Jayne and family in Sevenoaks. He continued commuting to Charing Cross to manage Hamblings model railway shop where he had worked since the age of fourteen. In 1982 Ann's birth father William Wicket died, leaving his long term partner Bay as a widow. As a former county councillor, headmaster and Chair of the County British Legion his funeral was a ceremonial affair with banners on display and a guard of honour. It went well despite some inevitable tensions within the family. Ann's step-father Hugh Adams died on June 25th 1983. He had been unwell for some time, then after suffering strokes had moved to a nursing home in Blackburn where we visited him every day. We fought the home over their care as he had been found lying on the toilet floor, where he had been for some time; it was very distressing. I collected his belongings and met Juliet from school at the top of our lane to break the news. It was a beautiful day and I could see her coming along, making a daisy chain and singing away. She got in the car, took one look at the luggage and we both burst into tears. His ashes were placed under the altar in the village church and stayed there until the prospect of moving house prompted Ann to take a decision. So we travelled to Ipswich where his family had bought a plot many years before and buried him there, checking all the other graves in the hope of finding that of his schizophrenic brother Bernard. We were sad to see that his grave had been left without a headstone, a fault we determined to rectify.

In 1975 Mother and John had moved to Eastbourne where John had bought a small semi-detached house near the prestigious Eastbourne College. In 1980, after much reluctance to admit to her illness, Mum had been diagnosed with cancer of the uterus and endured the whole painfully exhausting programme of surgery, radiology and chemotherapy. She recovered well, but by this time John had had enough of teaching and took early retirement. They settled well there in a relaxed if rather eccentric lifestyle. Mum determinedly walked the long promenade westwards where she would settle into a small space in the chalk cliffs and read extensively. Of course visits from the extended family continued, including a long visit from Charlie and Chris from Miami, but at least there were more activities, fitness classes, the beach, bandstand performances and all the fun of the English seaside.

Mum's health deteriorated from 1982. Her determination to live normally at home, to keep walking and to entertain the family was interrupted from time to time by hospitalisation. John of course cared for her obsessively and determinedly. Frequent trips down from Lancashire were difficult but I visited as often as possible. In a late bow to alternative medicine, washing-up liquid was replaced by soda, washing powder with soap and meals became plainer and more sparse. As the demands on him grew, John developed phlebitis so he would drive himself to hospital, get into a wheelchair, which he had equipped with a wooden plank to hold his bad leg, and push himself into the ward to visit. He was a hero. Eventually Mum was admitted to the local hospice where she was made comfortable for the final two weeks of her life. John and I visited constantly and then, on April 4th 1984, we sat either side of her as she quietly faded away. Our dear mother's life came to a peaceful end in the early afternoon. We kissed her goodbye and wandered out to the town in a daze of sadness and loss through which came all the memories of her long hard journey, balanced by her heroic joy of life. She had fought for us and any other family member forever. It was Friday as we did the rounds of registrars and the Co-op to arrange the funeral. John, who was often anxious about his health, casually mentioned that he thought he may have something wrong with his blood. I suggested that he see his GP but perhaps it was the blood thinning pills he was taking for his phlebitis? We went home and discussed the old will in which Mum had left her small estate to John. We went through a list of relations who we thought she would have liked to benefit. That evening I wrote a long letter home to Ann and Juliet:

> I feel very sad that we have lost such a loving and central person in our lives but also relieved that her long period of suffering is over. There was so much love expressed for her and that continues *for ever* ... as age creeps on figures from our history are constantly with us. A job

well done or badly done I still measure against Dad's standard of work ... What richness this generation brings to our experience of the world, what struggle and compassion has been demanded of them ... a generation of fighters all of them. Hard work, with no modern conveniences or means of communication but all the suffering of an unhappy century and a not very well off family ... The new generations build on these experiences to forge their careers and lifestyles that are the stronger for the family history. Belonging is freeing not limiting, enabling not restricting. The family tree and photos are pointers to the future, not the past. John is not well and very very tired and more distressed than he shows. I think he will take time to sort things out and may be willing to spend time with us. He will need gentle convalescence and to be kept busy with plenty of time to talk and evolve a new lifestyle.

The funeral was set for the following Thursday and John was left to phone everyone as I had to return north. He reported that he had been to the GP who had given him the most thorough examination from top to toe that he had ever had; he was probably coming down with flu.

On Wednesday April 11th we all drove south and stayed at the same hotel as for the 80th birthday party. Ann had brought down some food for the reception to be held afterwards at the house but there was more to be done. I went to see John's GP to explain the situation and our concern about his obvious ill health. The GP had ruled that with such a severe dose of influenza John must not leave the house. We arranged that we would meet on the doorstep at 8.30 the following morning for an opinion as to John's fitness to travel in the car home to Lancashire where we could nurse him back to health. Mother had been the focus of the extensive family networks for so many years that her passing was going to be a loss greater than our personal grief; it was the passing of a generation and there was a fear that those ties which had bound us together for as long as I could remember would now inevitably loosen unless we made major efforts to persevere. The formalities of these dreadful occasions are a help, but it was troubling to have a funeral service without the principal mourner. By the time we arrived back at the house, John's condition had deteriorated but we reckoned that the combination of his infection and his extreme loss and frustration at being denied the final act were the cause. Ann positioned herself by John's door and regulated the flow of relatives and the time that they could spend with my dear brother. At last the final mourners had gone and we could pause to consider our circumstances, knowing that I had arranged the GP to come within the next twelve hours. As usual there was no food in the house at all and we were emotionally and physically exhausted. We decided to go to a nearby restaurant for a quick meal hoping that it would revive us and give us time to talk things through with Juliet who was in the midst of her A-level exams.

We returned after about an hour to an empty house! Neighbours told us that an ambulance had arrived and taken John to the local hospital. It appeared that Sister Kate, a Macmillan nurse who had cared for Mother, had called for a routine follow up visit, taken one look at John and had him whisked to hospital. We were stunned. By the time we got to the ward the first medical had been completed and we were able to talk things through with John and the ward nurses who recognised him as the man who only a couple of weeks ago had visited his mother in his adapted wheelchair. Routine tests would continue and we were reassured that an early visit next morning would be OK. It seemed sensible to try and get some sleep, particularly as Juliet's care and upcoming A-level exams were at the forefront of our minds. As we left the ward John smiled and waved as he was taken off to X ray in a wheelchair. It was about 2.30 the next morning when we were woken by a very bad tempered night porter putting the hospital telephone call through to our room. Ann and I left Juliet asleep and drove to the old hospital. We could hear John's breathing from the car park! He was in the third bed on the left in a full ward and was obviously very ill. We were told that he had been diagnosed with leukaemia and was critically ill. I asked what would happen in the morning – would it be possible to have him moved to a specialist hospital? But eventually Ann managed to get through to me that what the nurses were really saying was that he would not survive the night. I had cremated my mother and now my wonderful brother was dying before our eyes; how could this happen to the kindest, most caring and sincere man? We sat by his bed holding his hands and telling him how very much we loved him. There were no curtains round us. The noise and the drama were keeping everyone else in the packed ward awake and I knew how John would have hated this disturbance to the peace of others. The nurse approached, as another had approached Mother only seven days ago, and gave him an injection that would 'help with the pain,' and with that euphemism he opened his eyes and died just nine days after our mother. In shock we drank the tea offered by sympathetic nurses and sat as a porter wheeled a rough zinc box on wheels right past us. I think the shock lasted until early next morning when we had to tell Juliet that her lovely uncle had died. The diagnosis was acute myeloblastic leukaemia. That empty feeling lasted while we repeated the rounds of registrar and funeral parlour, exactly as we had done the previous Friday for our mother. Ann held me back from the GP's surgery where I was determined to confront the GP who had so culpably missed a diagnosis which could have saved this gentle man's life with a condition where every hour counted. By the afternoon I fell apart and stayed that way for a very long time.

However deep my grief, some things managed to get through the black clouds that enveloped me. Despite our idea that it was too much to ask relatives to travel twice to Eastbourne in quick succession, everyone turned up at the same crematorium. Ann, Juliet and I followed the coffin in for a repeat ritual, but it was not quite to be as the preacher, Canon Denys Giddey, gave such an amazing, appropriate and hopeful sermon that it lifted us all up and by some divine act actually put a smile on my face for the next hour at least. I could only hope that, given John's deep religious belief, it gave peace to his soul. Unfortunately my peace was short lived as I was swept with bitter feelings of guilt (What could we have done differently?), the loss of the major role model of my life, fury at the incompetence of the GP (who we were told had come out of retirement as a locum and was 'a bit doddery') and the lack of dignity and privacy of that dreadful hospital ward. Was that really the level to which the NHS, which promised so much in 1945, had sunk? Unfortunately, although I am by no means an orthodox religious person, I found myself weeping all over our local vicar asking him why my mother had pulled John up to heaven for her comfort so soon and so selfishly. What a terrible calumny on my amazing mother.

I thought of all the times since my BOAC days that I had tried unsuccessfully to get John a separate life, but he was always drawn back. The thing that I could most usefully do to help myself was to write and tidy things up. I wrote an immediate and rushed account of everything that had happened and every word of that wonderful sermon; I drew a huge and detailed family tree and filled in a pro-forma for every one of my relatives in case I lost any of the hours and hours that John had spent on his research. As Christmas was rapidly approaching and we could not face it at home all three of us flew to Miami for a week to see a better life and to introduce Juliet to her great great uncle Charlie and aunt Chris who reminisced about watching the troops return from the Boer War. It helped, except for the fact that when Juliet returned home she discovered that all her jewellery had been stolen from her hotel room!

In the summer we held a good memorial service in Shoreham Church where Mum and John's ashes were interred and where Grandma had been buried. Members of the choir said nice things and the counter-tenor Mark Deller of the famous Deller family sang beautifully. After that we walked through the village to the pub where the branches of the family had gathered and we could check photos and versions of the family tree. We established a bench seat, in the remote place in the cliffs where mother used to read as a memorial, and the JJ Trust, for the benefit of young people who could not be helped from elsewhere, as a memorial for John. The seat was vandalised within a few months to be replaced within the tennis club. John's trust has helped countless young people and is still running.

The Eastbourne house was eventually sold at a discount after the agent had pointed out that the decor and furniture were far below the local middle-class standards. Once all the relatives that John and I had discussed had been sent appropriate funds, we realised that we could put Higher Studlehurst in better order. The home scene had been changing throughout this period. Juliet was working her way steadily through school, enjoying history, English, art and the history of art. She had made a number of close friends and increasingly the house seemed to attract boys! They were out and about at those pubs which did not worry too much about the legal age limit; clubs were enjoyed most weekends and we were kept busy providing a taxi service whenever required, usually in the early hours, but then the young men could often be roped in to help with the larger DIY jobs that confronted me.

We were close to the Brocklehurst family and seemed to be additional minor parents to young Ian Clarkson who lived in Mellor and Juliet's best friend Melissa Holden stayed to study for a while following a small fire at her house. Also our animal population had increased to three dogs, a horse, two donkeys, hens, ducks with a large pond and a peacock! Juliet developed an interest in journalism and media and we thought about appropriate universities. Eventually she settled on Sheffield and a course covering the history of art and media studies, so in September 1984, just a short time after the deaths of Mother and John, she drove out through the gates in her much loved Morris Minor. Ann and I just sat and wept. Ann managed to keep me from total breakdown, although it was a pretty close call for many months. Somehow the relentless pressure of work helped. It was more than two years before some sense of equilibrium was restored, when I would not burst into tears as random thoughts or external events reminded me of John's sudden loss. By then other things were going badly wrong.

NOTES AND REFERENCES

1. Thompson, E. P. (1983). 'A Choice Between Two Britains.' *The Guardian*, 07.06.1983, p. 19.
2. Barclay, P. (1982). *Social Workers, Their Role and Tasks*. London: Bedford Square Press, pp. vii, xi.
3. McGreal, C. (2016). Interview with General Michael Hayden. *Guardian G2*, 10.03.2016, p. 14. See also Hayden, M. (2016). *'Playing to the Edge: American Intelligence in the Age of Terror*. London: Penguin. The attack came towards the end of a massive restoration/reconstruction of the Grand Mosque, the environment and access roads by the massive Bin Laden construction corporation and it was one of their employees who managed to phone the government before all the lines were cut. Regaining the Mosque was complicated in spite of the religious rules against violence in the vicinity. At one stage French special forces were brought in, converting to Islam on a temporary basis. At one point Osama Bin Laden was arrested in error. He later came to see the rebels as true Muslims whose beliefs he would follow. It was during this siege that Soviet Troops entered Afghanistan and Bin Laden went there immediately to fight the infidel with the support of American arms. See Wright, L. (2007). *The Looming Tower. Al-Qaeda and the Road to 9/11*. New York: Knopf, Chap. 4.
4. There had been several serious accidents at nuclear power points since their installation in the 1950s. The most serious was at Three Mile Island in Pennsylvania in 1979. The most recent was in 2011 at the Fukushima plant in Japan, which was struck by a tsunami. An area of 30 km^2 was prepared for evacuation for fear of contamination. Estimates have been made that nearly one million cases of cancer can be traced back to exposure from all these nuclear accidents, so it is hardly surprising that fear and opposition to their continued construction is widespread. In the UK plans are well advanced for the construction of an additional large nuclear power point at Hinkley Point in Somerset. It seems remarkable to many people that such a project is being pursued right on the coast given the projections of rising sea levels and storms due to climate change. Work continues at pace and June 2026 is the projected completion date. In 2001 it was our great pleasure to host three teenagers from Belarus (see Chapter ??) and to visit that country in 2014. All their parents were doctors and we had an extensive tour of the cancer hospital where most of their equipment had been donated by Japan and Germany.
5. Bobby Sands was a member of the Provisional Irish Republican Army. In 1977 he was convicted of possession of a firearm and sentenced to 14 years in prison. In 1980 he was nominated as the commanding officer of the IRA prisoners in the Maze prison. Mrs Thatcher had removed these prisoners' political status with the comment that 'Crime is crime. It is not political, it is crime.' Prisoners protested by refusing to wear prison uniform and conducting a series of 'dirty' protests. In March 1981 Sands commenced a hunger strike, which others followed. On April 9th he was elected to Parliament as the 'Anti H-block/Armagh Political Prisoner.' As attempted negotiations failed, Sands' health declined and he died on May 5th 1981 at the age of 27, sixty-six days after starting his strike. Nine other prisoners also died.

6. Marr A. (2007). *A History of Modern Britain*. London: Macmillan, pp. 391–2.
7. *The Guardian*, 30.05.1984.
8. Powers were delegated to the many small London boroughs already having to contract services out to tender. In 2000 the Labour government created the Greater London Authority with greater geographical coverage but with more strategic powers, including transport. Ken Livingstone was elected as the first Mayor of London.
9. Despite hundreds of arrests and many trials, no one has ever been convicted of PC Blakelock's murder. As late as 2014 the incident was still being investigated. In that same year the Metropolitan Police Commissioner made an unreserved apology for the Brixton shooting which had sparked these riots.
10. Marr, *op. cit.*, p. 420.
11. Naughtie, J. (1985). Kinnock Rounds on Left's Militants. *The Guardian*, 02.10.1985.
12. *Boys from the Blackstuff* by Alan Bleasdale, starring Bernard Hill, Michael Angelis, Alan Igbon and George Georgeson. 1980. BBC Birmingham.
13. *Spitting Image* created by Peter Fluck, Peter Law and Martin Lambie-Nairn. 1984. Produced by Central Independent Television. First shown on ITV on 26.02.1984.
14. *My Beautiful Laundrette*. Dir. Stephen Frears, written by Hanif Kureishi. Starring Daniel Day Lewis, Gordon Warnecke and Saeed Jaffrey. 1985. Working Title. This was one of the first films from Working Title Films.
15. *Gandhi*. Dir. Richard Attenborough. Starring Ben Kingsley, Edward Fox, Candice Bergen, John Gielgud, Trevor Howard and John Mills. 1982. Goldcrest Films.
16. 'The Waitress' (more commonly known as 'Two Soups'). Written by Victoria Wood. Starring Julie Walters, Duncan Preston and Celia Imrie. 1986. BBC. (Easily found on YouTube.)
17. Harbridge, R. (1981). What Social Workers Think: A Survey of Fact and Opinions. *Community Care Magazine*, April 16th.
18. Barclay, P. (1982). *Social Workers, Their Role and Tasks*. London: Bedford Square Press.
19. Griffiths, R. (1998). *Community Care: Agenda for Action*. London: HMSO.
20. Louise Ellman became Chair of the County Council in 1981 and was then elected Labour MP for Liverpool Riverside in 1997. In 2016 she became Chair of the All Party Select Committee on Transport.
21. In 1985 Labour took control and held it for twenty-four years. In 2009 the Conservatives took power but in 2013 the Council reverted to no overall control.
22. Westland, P. (1986). 'The Day of Reckoning,' *Insight, Journal of Social Services Management*, Vol. 1, No 29.
23. Profile. *The Independent*, 12.09.1987, p. 10. Tony Greaves had joined the Liberal Party in 1961 and was committed to local community politics. In 2000 he entered the House of Lords as Baron Greaves of Pendle.
24. Jordan, M. (1987). 'The End of the Grand March,' *Soapbox. Social Work Today BASW*, May 25th, p. 20.
25. Toffler, A. (1970). *Future Shock*. New York: Random House.

FOURTEEN

1987–2001
RADICAL CHANGES

One side effect of the new economic era is that a sizeable minority see their incomes rise and also enjoy a fair amount of security, but the majority have to struggle to keep incomes stable, and may experience declining incomes along with greater insecurity. More importantly people no longer live in the same universe of opportunity ... Widening income differentials result in a serious disjunction to the values and institutions of society ... An underclass emerges, consisting of people who live their separate lives often characterised by a combination of destitution, dependence on welfare payments and other benefits, occasional windfalls, petty or not so petty crime and apathy. The underclass may not be a new phenomenon but its size, its visibility, and its presence in otherwise wealthy societies is an indictment of communities professing to espouse citizenship for all.

– R. Dahrendorf et al.[1]

The 1990s have often seemed to be a sort of virtual decade, in which history has been abolished, tradition counts for nothing and everything is in a state of flux. For our fortunate elite – the well heeled, the able, the peripatetic intelligentsia with their Rhodes scholarships and their PhDs from Harvard and Stanford – it has all been hugely exciting ... They have travelled the world (club class at the very least) like latter day Richard the Lionhearts, suffused with a crusading spirit. In place of a lance they have had a laptop, instead of a shield they grasped a mobile phone and a flipchart containing one word: change ... Rarely a day goes by without the public being told that they have to change, change the way they communicate, change the way they show their emotions, change the way they look after their bodies, change the way they think about welfare. Everything, in short, can and should be changed about the way we live our lives except, of course, from the economic system.

– L. Elliot and D. Atkinson[2]

INTERNATIONAL EVENTS

Russia

The late 1980s proved to be a period of political upheaval from Russia to China. In 1988 the General Secretary of the Soviet Union, Mikhail Gorbachev, announced the relaxation of control over the countries of Eastern Europe, leading to the restoration of independent nations, for the most part without violence. In October 1989, faced with mass demonstrations, the East German leader Erich Honecker resigned, and on November 9th the Politburo authorised free movement to the west to commence on the 17th.

However, the official who announced the decision got it wrong, stating that it was effective immediately. November 9th was a night to remember as thousands flocked into West Germany. This was all going far too well; at long last the nuclear threat that had hung over us for forty years was easing and Soviet power was decreasing.³

Unfortunately, Gorbachev's urgent domestic policies – to introduce free and fair elections, massively reducing the influence of the Communist Party, to restructure the economy and form a voluntary union of Eastern European states – were meeting with opposition, and by 1990 both the old guard in the KGB and those that urged immediate change to a market economy were ready for a coup. On December 25th 1991 Gorbachev resigned his post, handing over power to Boris Yeltsin, who proceeded to introduce some capitalist freedoms into Russia which meant that a large part of the assets and wealth of the country fell into the hands of the elite kleptocracy leading to corruption on a grand scale. His frequently drunken appearance and erratic behaviour, and the consequent economic collapse, led to a challenge by parliamentarians, leading Yeltsin to shell government buildings. He survived this upheaval and struggled on, in practice in the hands of the rich oligarchs until 1999 when he handed control to the Prime Minister and former security chief Vladimir Putin.

South Africa

As the firm hand of the Soviet Union weakened, upheavals in Poland, Hungary, Bulgaria and Romania followed, only the last being met by violence. In South Africa the illness of the hard line President Botha led to the appointment of F. W. de Klerk, who realised that the long-standing policy of apartheid could no longer be sustained either at home or in the light of international pressure and sanctions. Discussions therefore commenced between the government and the leader of the African National Party, Nelson Mandela, who had been in prison for 27 years, mostly in the harsh regime of Robben Island. On February 11th 1990 Mandela was unconditionally released from prison. With supreme dignity this 71-year-old great man walked out of prison with his wife to great acclaim in front of TV cameras from all round the world. In 1994 he was elected President of South Africa, a post which he held for five years seeking reconciliation with past political leaders and establishing the countrywide Truth and Reconciliation Commission with the lively Archbishop Desmond Tutu as its Chair. After retirement he continued to be active as a greatly respected politician on the world stage as well as establishing a number of philanthropic agencies. He died in December 2013.

China

The terrible effects of Chairman Mao's regime (see Chapter 9) were still being felt, particularly in the economy. The government decided to allow the development of some profit making enterprises but, as in Russia, this led to corruption as the elite made big profits, leaving the majority of the population behind. Inflation rose and the gap between the rich and poor increased leading to widespread discontent. A student movement, attracted by Gorbachev's reforms and western lifestyles, decided to campaign for a more transparent democracy. In late April 1989 thousands of students demonstrated peacefully across the country including in Tiananmen Square in the heart of Beijing. As the numbers increased, and filmed by TV companies from around the world, the government declared martial law and mobilised some 30 military divisions. As they moved into the city, they met sustained opposition from the population who were sympathetic to the students' cause; many were killed, never believing their comrades would actually open fire. Early on May 4th troops arrived in the Square and started pushing the students back without violence, but this quickly turned to severe beatings and later to shootings. On June 5th demonstrators were confronted by tanks. This led to the iconic picture of a single brave protester standing in front of a tank, forcing it to stop, taken just before he climbed up to talk to the soldiers. This photograph was seen around the world, though no one has ever established this man's identity. He is universally known as the 'tank man.' By the time order was restored, several hundred protesters had been killed; naturally the ringleaders were later rounded up and faced long terms in prison.

International reaction was very critical; bank loans were withheld and with the loss of tourist income China's economy was significantly damaged. Despite many fears, the process by which the major British colony of Hong Kong would be passed over to China as a highly autonomous special administrative region, proceeded, optimistically on a principle of 'one country two systems.' The final handover took place on July 1st 1997. In December of that year, the Kyoto Protocol, the first worldwide agreement on climate control, was signed and later ratified by 192 countries. The USA, however, never ratified it, and in 2001 President George W. Bush withdrew from the Protocol.

The Middle East

For a short time it seemed that peace was coming to the Middle East as secret talks between Israel and the Palestine Liberation Organisation meeting in Oslo led to an accord which recognised the PLO as its formal partner in continuing negotiations and established the Palestine Authority having some powers over the Gaza strip and the West Bank. In December 1994 the Prime Minister of Israel Yitzhak Rabin and the Palestinian leader Yasser Arafat were awarded Nobel Peace prizes for their part in the peace process. A year later Rabin was assassinated by a member of a right-wing Israeli group. This progress led to high expectations for a Summit of the main parties hosted by President Clinton at Camp David in July 2000 but it failed to reach any agreement on the key points including governance of Jerusalem, Israeli settlements and the return of the many thousand Palestinians previously forced from their homeland. Almost immediately the bombastic right-wing Israeli politician Ariel Sharon made a provocative display of entering the Temple Mount, a site revered by both Jews and Arabs, and announcing that the shrine would remain in Jewish possession for ever. This led to

Palestinian protests and rioting, severely put down by Israeli troops and the start of the second Intifada (uprising) against Israel which lasted for eight years with over 5,000 fatalities (1,000 being Jewish).

Al-Qaeda

In parallel with these events, a large number of insurgent Muslim groups, growing from the Egyptian Brotherhood (see Chapter 9) and the experience and teachings of Sayyid Qutb (see Chapter 4), had been developing across the Middle and Far East and were now actively spreading discontent across the world, including in the inward looking United States. Many had come together in fighting the Soviet invasion of Afghanistan in the 1980s as members of the Mujahideen. One of these was Al-Qaeda, led by the rich Saudi Arabian Osama bin Laden. In 1993 this organisation financed an attack on the World Trade Center, which stood in the Financial District of Lower Manhattan. (This was eight years before the infamous attack on 9/11.) The World Trade Center was seen as an arrogant statement of the power of America and in particular its wealth. (Interestingly, when Ann and I visited New York in 1999 and took the free ferry across to Staten Island we commented that the 'Twin Towers' looked as if they were making a great V sign to the rest of the world.) The 1993 attack took place in February; a very large bomb laced with cyanide exploded in the basement car park, creating a large crater and destroying six floors on the southern corner of the building, although it failed to seriously damage the main infrastructure as intended. Six people died and 1,042 were injured, far fewer than the 250,000 that the bomber had hoped for if both towers had collapsed as planned. The lesson was that more power was required. In 1998 various insurgent groups formed a coalition and issued a fatwa which ruled that it was the 'individual duty for every Muslim in every country to kill Americans and their allies – civilian and military in any way that they can do it.' That same year there were two serious attacks against American assets. The first was on the American Embassy in Nairobi and the second on the modern guided missile destroyer USS *Cole*, which was refuelling in the bay at Aden. These attacks caused 230 deaths and over 4,500 injuries, as well as a significant blow to American pride (extraordinary efforts only just prevented the *Cole* from sinking, which would have been seen as an even bigger PR disaster). Although these incidents hit the world headlines, as far as I recall no mention was ever made of Al-Qaeda; we will never know whether this was deliberate or reflected the fact that the CIA throughout these years had been poorly equipped or unable to monitor or fight these organisations.[4n]

In April 2001 a western supported tribal leader from Afghanistan, Ahmad Shah Massoud, addressed the European Parliament in Strasbourg and specifically warned American officials of Al-Qaeda's plans to attack America as 'another Hiroshima.' By then the plans were already in operation. In mid 1999 the two leaders of Al-Qaeda met in Kandahar to select the targets for their great plan in the belief that if these were struck America would stumble and fail to be a world power. The targets were finally whittled down to the White House and Capitol, the Pentagon and the Twin Towers of the World Trade Center. The key requirements were pilots, although it took some time to find the right combination of young men who could carry out the plan and were willing to become martyrs. Eventually two small teams were established, one based in Malaysia and the other in Germany. Having obtained US visas, Nawaf al-Hazmi and Khalid al-Mihdhar, neither of whom spoke English, arrived in Los Angeles. At this stage the CIA were aware that 'something big' was in the air and recognised Hazmi but failed to pass any of this information to other US agencies, most notably the FBI. By mid 2001 the key Al-Qaeda operatives were enrolled in flight schools in America. An FBI agent in Phoenix sent a message to his HQ expressing the view that Osama bin Laden was sending members of his organisation to America to learn to fly. The receiving official threw the message in the trash can explaining that they had not got the resources to check all 30,000 flight schools in America. This was followed by another alarm from Minnesota that Arab trainees were asking suspicious questions about airline security and fight patterns around New York.

The attack which shook the world commenced early on the morning of September 11th 2001 when 19 hijackers took control of two fully fuelled long distance aircraft from Boston, one from Washington and another from New Jersey. The two planes from Boston were flown into the Twin Towers of the World Trade Center; the Washington plane was crashed into the Pentagon. The New Jersey flight destined for the Capitol failed as passengers, hearing news from New York and realising they were about to be killed anyway, attacked the hijackers causing the plane to crash in Pennsylvania. The total casualties on that day were nearly 3,000 dead and 6,000 injured. The collapse of the World Trade Center and the dreadful images associated with it were immediately sent around the world causing much horror and fear and widespread offers of support to America. President George W. Bush gave immediate assurances to citizens and concluded by promising that America had 'stood down terrorists before and we will do so this time.' Tony Blair's response was to assure Bush that we stood 'shoulder to shoulder' with America, and eleven days later when Bush addressed Congress he commented that 'America has no truer friend than Great Britain.' We were irretrievably bound together to face the world-changing consequences of the events of 9/11.

NATIONAL EVENTS

Education

The Prime Minister Margaret Thatcher was not happy with the curricula in schools across the country where she was convinced that poorly trained teachers, many of whom she was sure were of a left-wing persuasion, were not acting in the way demanded by the new wealth economy. The government therefore created a national curriculum to be taught in all schools. Maths, Science and British History would be important and assessments would be required of all pupils at the ages of 7, 11, 14 and 16. The Education Reform Act (1988) brought all these policies into effect. Peter Wilby, a respected commentator, summed up the changes as follows:

> 1988 has been an educational watershed as perhaps no other year has been in this century. [The Act] has irrevocably changed the balance of power. It provides that local authorities will lose control of the polytechnics and larger colleges next year. Gradually, too, councils will lose control of schools ... The curriculum will be determined by statutory orders made by the Secretary of State for Education ... Thus Heads in future will take their cues from parents and central government rather than from their own town and county halls. Since their funds will be tied by law to the number of pupils they can attract they will be operating rather as if they were running small businesses. The cultural change for head teachers – many of whom are temperamentally opposed to the very idea of marketing – will be enormous.[5]

Universities, having demonstrated their disapproval of Thatcher in 1985 when Oxford refused to grant her an honorary degree, felt at war with the government. Their funding was cut year by year, the tradition of tenure for staff was to be replaced by open competition and student maintenance grants were squeezed. Controversy and confusion followed the passing of the Local Government Act (1988), including Clause 28, which decreed 'that expenditure by local authorities for the purpose of promoting homosexuality would no longer be permitted.' Following the relaxed 1960 and 70s some local authorities, in particular the Greater London Council, had included discussion of homosexuality in their sex education and published some pamphlets on the subject. The word 'promote' was legally vague, but the central issue was whether the ban actually applied to schools and other education institutions within an authority. In practice teachers and counsellors curtailed their work just in case they would fall foul of this law. As a consequence there was a chronic rise in bullying, mental health problems and suicide among gay, lesbian and bisexual young people.[6n]

The NHS

Change for the NHS was proposed in a White Paper 'Working for Patients'[7] and implemented in the 1990 NHS and Community Care Act. This divided services into purchasers or providers, forming an internal market. Purchasers would be district health authorities and general practitioners. The providers of service would have to rely on these for their funding, thus costs would be driven down and the quality of service increased. The motto was that 'The money follows the patient,' who would in theory have a degree of choice. The obvious problems were the increased administrative costs (particularly the central system created to monitor and control the changes) and the introduction of commercial principles to public healthcare, where all staff worked on a public service ethic, and it created a two-tier level of GP services between those that opted to be fundholders and those that declined.[8] All these changes were sold on the basis that competition and profit motives would produce better outcomes than a traditional public service ethic and gave users the power of choice. No evidence has ever been produced to support these claims.

The Poll Tax

Local authority finance was to be the last major problem tackled by Thatcher. The long-established arrangement was based on the rateable value of houses in each council area. The balance between this income and expenditure fell to central government. This meant that the majority of voters in local elections could vote for popular policies, leading to increased government spending. After much consideration the government decided to change this situation so that everyone entitled to vote would pay towards the cost – a single flat tax for everyone. The result would be a reduction for home owners but a new tax for some twenty million citizens. The intention was to introduce this system over a ten-year period but the 1987 Tory Conference pushed for immediate implementation and the Prime Minister agreed. This would be a regressive tax and, although exceptions were made for the unemployed and low paid, 80% of people would be paying more. Attempts to divide the 'community charge' into three bands were rebuffed. On March 31st 1990 there was a massive demonstration in Trafalgar Square which ended in a violent riot with demonstrators, including my daughter and son-in-law, being run down by mounted police. There was widespread resistance to this 'poll tax,' with many supporting the demonstrators and objecting to the police tactics. Thatcher was not moved, although some Tory MPs were, and talk began that perhaps Margaret's time was running out. Michael Heseltine did not disabuse those that wondered whether he might be a suitable replacement.

Cabinet battles built up over Europe, the long-running great divide in the Tory Party. Thatcher was firmly set against increasing federalisation where power could be imposed from Brussels. She saw the establishment of a European Exchange Rate Mechanism (ERM) designed to increase monetary stability by keeping all European currencies within a restricted range. Put together they would be stronger against the dollar and currency speculators. The ERM was a precursor of a single currency and the Prime Minister objected to her Chancellor Nigel Lawson's determination to join. She was finally persuaded by the Chief Secretary to the Treasury, John Major, so in October 1990 Great Britain became part of the ERM.

The Fall of Thatcher

Thatcher fought back by reshuffling her Cabinet, sacking her Deputy Geoffrey Howe and making it so intolerable for her Chancellor that he resigned in October telling her she should treat her ministers better. Eventually she was challenged in a leadership election and, although she survived, sixty Tories either voted against her or abstained. On November 13th 1990 the unassuming Geoffrey Howe made his dramatic resignation speech in the Commons, which had so recently agreed to the installation of TV cameras. His dispute was Europe, more particularly the ERM and the prospect of a single currency, triggered by the Prime Minister's recent impassioned cry of 'No! No! No!' After rehearsing the long history of his work in European negotiations, Howe continued:

> We must at all costs avoid presenting ourselves yet again with an over-simplified choice, a false antithesis, a bogus dilemma … We commit a serious error if we think always in terms of 'surrendering' sovereignty and seek to stand pat for all time on a given deal. What kind of vision is that for our business people who trade there each day, for our financiers … and for all our young people of today … How on earth are the Chancellor and the Governor of the Bank of England … to be taken as serious participants in the debate against that kind of background noise? I believe that both … are cricketing enthusiasts so I hope that there is no monopoly of cricketing metaphors. It is rather like sending your opening batsmen to the crease only for them to find, the moment the first balls are bowled, that their bats have been broken before the game by the team captain … I no longer believe it possible to resolve that conflict from within this government. That is why I have resigned. In doing so, I have done what I believe to be right for my party and my country. The time has come for others to consider their own response to the tragic conflict of loyalties with which I have myself wrestled for perhaps too long.[9]

In parliamentary terms this was a clarion call for action and another leadership election quickly followed between Thatcher and Heseltine. In the first round Thatcher did not quite reach the required majority, thus a final ballot was called. The Prime Minister emerged from a summit in Paris and announced to a bemused BBC reporter that she would fight on. Returning to London she summoned her Cabinet members one at a time, all of whom warned her that if she stood again she would lose; it would be better to resign. This she did on November 28th 1990, having drummed up sufficient support to scupper Heseltine's chance of success in favour of the relatively unknown John Major, our next Prime Minister. Major was the son of a music hall entertainer from Brixton whose young political ambitions had been inspired by Harold Macmillan and Clement Attlee. Michael Heseltine was appointed as his Deputy.

It seemed that the mild mannered Major inherited a generally more prosperous country than was the case when Thatcher came to power eleven and a half years earlier, a country remarkably changed by her neo-liberal policies and forceful personality. In that time she had changed the political, economic and cultural landscapes of the United Kingdom. Entrepreneurship, competitiveness and individualism had become more important than the public and community service ethic that had held sway for generations. The nation's prosperity now rested on the finance and service sectors, which were mainly based in London, while the dirty, heavy northern industries had been cruelly neglected. We had seemingly embraced the global markets enthusiastically so that during Thatcher's premiership social inequality increased to a greater extent than in any other country in Europe.

The very pattern of our everyday lives had been changed. With a fluid economy came job insecurity; continuity of work and the mutual loyalty between employer and employee had been eroded as sessional and agency work came to shatter the trust within a long-established workplace. All new experiences for the white-collar middle-class workforce. Respected skills and experience were sacrificed to cut staff costs, to keep staff on their toes by threat of dismissal in the knowledge that the trades unions had been robbed of much of their power. The social consequences of the Thatcher years have been well recorded. A 1993 report by UNICEF commented that child welfare had slipped backwards so that the 1980s had seen child poverty rise by 40% (defined in relation to median net disposable income).[10] In a 1992 submission to the UN Committee on Economic and Social Rights the organisation Justice stated that 1 in 3 children in the UK were living in poverty and that 4 out of every 10 adults were living below what the EU defined as the 'decency threshold.'[11] Two reports from the Institute for Fiscal Studies showed that the number of people living in poverty had risen from 3 million in 1977 to 11 million in 1991, and that between 1979 and 1991 the income of the poorest section of society had fallen by 5% while that of the richest had increased by 58%.[12] The percentage of GDP spent on the NHS fell from 6.3% in 1983 to 5.2% in 1987, in the face of demand, the increased cost of drugs and a growing elderly population.[13n] In that same period the percentage of GDP allocated to public spending had fallen from 46% to 38%.

John Major

John Major somehow managed to retain his sangfroid throughout his time in office. He declared that his aim was to create a society where opportunities were open to all and where the privileges once available to the few would be available to the many. He believed that the UK must be in the heart of Europe. His first major challenge was the drive within Europe to form a more solid federal structure. This infuriated the right wing of his party whose members brought great pressure to bear fearing his pro Europe stance. The issue came to a head in the Belgian town of Maastricht where a great treaty was to be finalised in December 1991. Major proved a skilful and determined negotiator, politely wearing his eleven fellow leaders down and gaining opt out clauses for the UK in monetary and all the social chapters. He returned home as a hero.[14n]

On that basis, a general election was called for April 1992. The Conservatives won the greatest percentage of votes of any party since the war, although they obtained an overall majority of only 21 MPs. The Labour Party put up an excellent fight under the leadership of Neil Kinnock who, it is said, threw the election away with an over triumphalist final speech. He resigned immediately, blaming the press for the defeat. (*The Sun* newspaper had carried the headline 'Will the Last Person to Leave Britain Please Turn Out the Lights' against a picture of Kinnock.) His resignation was followed by the election of the respected John Smith, who won much public support. Tragically, having abolished the block vote of trades unions within the party and committing the party to establishing a Scottish Parliament, Smith suffered a fatal heart attack on May 4th 1994. He was succeeded by Tony Blair.

The economy hit yet another crisis and interest rates rose towards 15%. As the pressure from the dollar increased we sought comfort in the ERM's mechanism, but none came as Germany feared any hint of higher inflation. Consequently the Chancellor Nigel Lawson, in an undignified step late on September 16th 1992, withdrew the UK from the ERM. Once that drama was behind him, Major proceeded to implement a range of Thatcherite policies, spurred on from his own experience of using public services where staff were rude – one usually had to queue to get attention and action was painfully slow. League tables and output based targets were imposed across a range of public services from education to health and the police. Thirty-one coal pits were closed and more universities were created, largely by allowing polytechnics to upgrade. An early policy was the privatisation of the railways, a complex division whereby the tracks were sold off for private ownership to Railtrack, while other companies bid for a number of national and regional franchises to run the trains. These programmes, in particular the disastrous rail privatisation, launched an army of regulators, monitors and financial and legal contract writers, the cost of which has, to my knowledge, never been calculated.

Major went on to offend many traditional members of what was, after all, the Conservative and Unionist Party by announcing that if both parts of Ireland voted for reunification Britain would not stand in their way, an extraordinary declaration which had grown out of long behind the scenes discussions with Albert Reynolds, the Irish Taoiseach. This included a pledge that if the IRA renounced violence, participation in legitimate politics would be open to them. This was achieved in August 1994. The government's attention was then directed towards the Balkan States, where, following the breakup of Yugoslavia, Slovenia, Croatia and Bosnia, the Serbian invasion of Bosnia had precipitated fierce fighting. Horrific TV images of 'ethnic cleansing' were beamed back across the world, particularly from Srebrenica where some 8,000 Muslims were slaughtered. There were pressing calls for intervention from the west. Major eventually sanctioned the dispatch of 1,800 troops to protect the refugee convoys seeking to escape the conflict – too little, too late.

After some four years of hard, determined work as he successfully negotiated his way through party, economic and international crises, John Major's luck started to turn. The economy started to prosper slowly during this time but now a sense of distrust and sleaze crept into the public perception. Rumours of sexual affairs, even involving the Prime Minister, were rife. One commentator wrote that our politicians were no more than a collection of perverts, liars and actors. While they promoted family values, one minister had five mistresses and one seduced a married woman and both her daughters.[15]

By 1995 growing anger was being expressed at the high salaries commanded by those leading the newly privatised utilities. At a time of public pay restraint, the CEO of British Telecom was drawing £650,000 (equivalent to £1.3 million in 2020) and that of British Gas £475,000, while the head of Powergen scooped £1.2 million in share options without ever risking a penny of his own money.[16] There was a major scandal when it was discovered that some companies had been exporting arms to Iraq against United Nations sanctions following Saddam Hussain's gassing of 5,000 Kurds. Then Neil Hamilton, MP for Tatton, was discovered taking cash in brown paper envelopes for asking specific questions in the House of Commons.[17n] The culture of suspicion of politicians at all levels would bug the country for many years ahead and spread to some branches of the public services.

Bovine Spongiform Encephalopathy (BSE)

In the mid 1990s a severe outbreak of BSE was discovered in cattle in the UK.[18n] This deadly disease spread quickly and the decision was taken that all affected cattle would be slaughtered and burnt on site. Every evening our TV screens carried pictures of dying, distressed cattle and black smoke rising from more than four million carcasses piled high for incineration, alongside dreadful scenes from the Balkans. It felt as though death was invading our very souls, particularly as a variant of the disease spread to humans. Immediately the epidemic broke, British beef was banned from export, thus contributing to another downturn in the economy. Meanwhile the Labour Party was storming ahead in the polls and was slowly winning by-elections until Major's majority of 21 had been wiped out.

Election

As the five-year limit of power approached there was no alternative but to call an election, and so on May 1st 1997 the Conservative Party suffered the worst electoral defeat since 1832 retaining only 165 seats, with 179 members losing their seats. It was a sad irony that John Major, one of the most straightforward and hard working politicians, left office when depression, corruption and sleaze had made the electorate suspicious and distrusting of politics and politicians, although in fact the economic indicators were good and we were emerging to slightly better times. The Labour Party took control.

Violence

These were years when violence seemed to be a constant feature of our society. The IRA campaign continued. The secret peace negotiations faltered so bombing resumed in order to pressure the government to finally settle the dispute. November 1987 saw eleven people killed and 63 injured as they participated in a Remembrance Day parade in Enniskillen. Two years later, 11 Royal Marines were killed and 22 were injured by a bomb in the music section of the Deal Barracks. In February 1991 a prepared van, parked near the Ministry of Defence, was used to launch mortars on 10 Downing Street where the War Cabinet was known to be meeting. They fell at the back of No 10, thus failing in the attempt to assassinate the Prime Minister and others. In March 1993 a bomb hidden in a waste bin in Warrington killed two children aged 3 and 12 years.

The following month a massive car bomb in Bishopsgate, London, resulted in one death and 44 injuries. Intense negotiations involving the Eire and UK governments, the IRA and mediated by the USA finally led the IRA to call a ceasefire in August 1994, although it would be a further four years before a final agreement was reached.

In late December 1988 the Middle Eastern conflicts came home when a bomb placed on a Pan American plane exploded over the small Scottish town of Lockerbie killing everyone on board and eleven residents, a total of 270 people.

Violence within our home communities was also growing, reflecting the harsh economic and political policies, continued aggravation from the police (mostly against young black men) and conflict over race, the drug trade and territorial boundaries. A study by the left-wing think tank Demos revealed a number of complex issues at play. The report identified a band of 'under-wolves' – young people disconnected with society, living in unstable environments with chronic relationship breakdowns, with uncertainty about jobs and profound disconnection from political processes. The report contains a telling quote from David Cannon:

> [The] young people's list of 'What not to trust' has grown very long indeed. You cannot trust your parents to stay together, you cannot trust that your education will lead anywhere and you cannot trust your employers to provide secure jobs for either you or your parents.[19]

In March 1993 the country was shocked by the horrible murder of the two-year-old James Bulger in a railway cutting near Walton in Liverpool. Two ten-year-old boys had persuaded him to move away from his parents in a shopping mall and then calmly walked him several miles to the spot where they tortured and killed him. His mutilated body was found two days later. The combination of the ages of the victim and the perpetrators combined with the horror of the attack hit the public hard. How could this happen? Why did it happen and what did it say about our society today? The boys were convicted and sent to custody until they were at least aged 18, when they could be released with new identities on lifelong licence.[20n]

Britain's worst racial attack occurred in April 1993 when a teenage black architectural student Stephen Lawrence was killed by a gang of young white men while waiting for a bus in Eltham, South London. This blatant racial crime shocked the nation and led to a long campaign for justice as his alleged killers avoided arrest and conviction. Their cocky behaviour in court demonstrated to most people that these young men clearly felt themselves to be above the law. A major inquiry was commissioned into the murder and the conduct of the police. The report, published in February 1999, advised that the recommendations of the Scarman Report (see Chapter 12) be implemented. Examining police conduct, the inquiry found that the Metropolitan Police was 'institutionally racist' and made a number of clear recommendations for action. This included a change in the law to allow 'double jeopardy' so that anyone found not guilty by a court could be charged again if new evidence became available. Later reports investigated claims about police corruption and found devastating evidence.[21n]

As the decade progressed, gang dynamics became more complicated, depending on location, the traditions that they espoused and whether they had a single or mixed racial membership (some estates in deprived areas having experienced significant social change). As older, perhaps more prosperous, white residents moved out, their place was taken by younger, poorer families with more children, eventually leading to estates with a high concentration of teenagers, young adults and single pensioners linked neither by kinship nor friendship. Gang membership replaced these links for the young. The hierarchy within a gang often led to the junior members recruiting children as sub gangs which were seen as immune from prosecution, and thus gang culture infiltrated schools.[22] On December 8th 1995 a small incident between two young boys in St George's RC School in West London led to another violent murder which shocked the country. The Filipino 'victim' of the incident contacted his gang leader, a member of the Woo-Sing-Woo West London gang which claimed allegiance with the Triads, which were drawn mostly from the Filipino community. At the end of the school day the gang waited at the school gates to 'punish' the offender. As the fight developed, the headmaster Philip Lawrence intervened to protect the child who was being beaten with an iron rod. The local gang leader, 15-year-old Learco Chindamo, fatally stabbed the Head in front of a crowd of young pupils.[23n]

National Tragedies

On April 15th 1989, just after the start of the FA Cup semi-final between Liverpool and Nottingham Forest at the Hillsborough ground in Sheffield, late-arriving Liverpool supporters were directed into the back of an already overcrowded area. They pushed forward, causing those at the front to be trampled on as they sought escape over the boundary fence onto the pitch. Ninety-six Liverpool supporters, aged from 10 to 67, were crushed to death.[24n]

When the decade was in its closing years, the nation was hit with the shocking news that united most communities. At the age of 36, the sparkling and popular Princess Diana had been killed in a car accident in Paris on August 31st 1997. Diana Spencer had won hearts when she had married Prince Charles sixteen years earlier and then gave birth to two sons. She had experienced difficulties in relating to the close core of the royal family, where her instinctively expressive personality was never going to mix with the traditional stiff upper lip of disciplined royals. The marriage had run into difficulties in the early 1990s, in part due to Charles's continuing relationship with Camilla Parker Bowles. By and large the public sided with Diana as the situation deteriorated, and this continued after the divorce in August 1996. By this time Diana had a high standing in public perceptions due to her wide range of charity work from children, to AIDS victims, to mine clearance. Her personal life had become the subject of widespread gossip, and at the time of the accident she was linked with Dodi Fayed, son of the owner of Harrods. The crash occurred in an underpass in the centre of Paris.

The funeral on September 6th was televised and watched by over 23 million viewers. Crowds lined the route of the procession and watched as the coffin drove past. Many people (including my daughter and granddaughter, both anti-royalists) threw flowers on to the hearse. Diana's brother's impassioned address at the funeral drew attention to the fact that her extraordinary appeal to tens of millions of people watching across the world meant that they felt that they had lost someone close to them. Diana, he said, was 'someone with a natural nobility who was classless and who proved in the last years that she needed no royal title to continue to generate her particular brand of magic.'[25n] In a breach of protocol the congregation and the thousands outside Westminster Abbey broke into applause.

Labour

Since his appointment as leader in July 1994, Tony Blair, who hailed from a Christian family, had committed himself and his party to defining a 'New Labour' which would end the long period of Conservative power. The project aimed to break away from the traditional left vs right identities and, in the face of globalisation and a modern economy, declare the class war over. The team (including the MPs Gordon Brown, Peter Mandelson, 'Mo' Mowlam, Jack Straw and journalist Alistair Campbell) sought advice from those behind Bill Clinton's American election in 1993. A key part of this was thought to be the concept of 'communitarianism' developed by the sociologist Amitai Etzioni, who argued that individual and family progress should be placed in the local community, the role of the state being to support such communities. The size of the state was less important than the fact that it needed to be reconstructed and operate efficiently and effectively in pursuing its social agenda. Ideas from the London School of Economics (LSE), particularly by Anthony Giddens, emphasised the importance of the devolution of democratic power.

> It quickly became apparent that Labour's new leader was an unabashed social moralist determined to restructure British along 'communitarian' lines. What this meant in practice, beyond a sort of compulsory togetherness presided over by social workers, was not easy to discern. Some derided him as a 'preacher man,' others derided him as sanctimonious, these criticisms were like pellets from peashooters bouncing off the sides of the thundering Blair bandwagon.[26]

A Blair government would focus on social justice and equality, resting, as Blair so memorably exclaimed, on 'Education, education, education.' With these policies hammered into a manifesto, Tony Blair deployed his undoubted charm and charisma to win over the public who, rather tired of the 'ordinary' John Major, perhaps anticipated a return to the livelier politics of the Thatcher years.

As the election approached, Labour published a 'pledge card' which listed five pledges: to reduce class sizes, to speed up punishment for young offenders, to cut NHS waiting times, to ensure there was no rise in income tax and keep inflation as low as possible, and to get a quarter of a million young people off benefits and in to work. Their well planned, rather slick campaign attacked Major's lack lustre Thatcherite record and emphasised its own 'New Labour' face. The result on May 2nd 1997 was a landslide for Labour, which won 418 seats against the Conservatives' 165. The Liberal Democrats won 46 seats, the largest of a third party since 1929. The Labour members included 101 women. Blair (the youngest Prime Minister since 1812) had won a spectacular victory for his party and took power as the economy was slowly improving and the possibility of a settlement to the long Northern Irish troubles was in sight. It was noted that these young politicians took globalisation and open markets as given, something that raised concern with traditional Labour voters.

The new government certainly hit the road running, deploying a good range of Cabinet ministers including, of course, Gordon Brown as Chancellor. Tension between Blair and Brown about the leadership had bedevilled the party for some time and had apparently been resolved in favour of Blair, who was far more suited to the celebrity media image of the times, on the basis that Brown would have complete authority over the Treasury (which in his view meant most of domestic policy) while Blair concentrated on strategy, presentation and foreign affairs. Three days after the election Britain took the first steps to join the European Union's 'Social Chapter,' which guaranteed enjoyment of life without discrimination or invasion of civil and economic rights, quickly followed by the Human Rights Act (1998) which effectively incorporated the European Convention on Human Rights into UK law. Brown also stopped the political manipulation of interest rates by giving the independent Bank of England total responsibility for fixing that rate to keep inflation at a set level. In an extraordinary historic irony, Blair's most memorable and widely approved speech occurred on the fateful August 31st 1997. Woken in the early hours of the morning to be told of Princess Diana's sudden death and learning that neither the Queen nor any of the household planned to make a statement, Blair decided that he should step up to the mark. A few hours later, still visibly shaken and emotional, he said that he:

> ... felt like everyone else in this country today. Our thoughts and prayers are with Princess Diana's family – in particular her two sons, her two boys – our hearts go out to them. We are today a nation in a state of shock ... She touched the lives of so many in Britain and throughout the world with joy and with comfort. How many times shall we remember her in so many different ways with the sick, the dying, with children, with the needy? With just a look or a gesture that spoke so much more than words, she would reveal to all of us the depth of her compassion and her humanity.
>
> People everywhere, not just here in Britain, kept faith with Princess Diana. They liked her, they loved her, they regarded her as one of the people. She was the people's Princess and that is how she will stay, how she will remain in our hearts and our memories for ever.

The Prime Minister's popularity was never going to equal his standing on that sad day.

Building on the hard work by previous governments, Blair was able, by persistent diplomacy and personal charm, matched by his down to earth, straight talking Secretary of State Mo Mowlam, to bring the Ulster Unionists onto the path towards the much longed for peace in Ireland. Agreement was finally reached on Good Friday 1998 and was eventually ratified by both countries, although sporadic violence would continue for many years, the worst being a bomb attack in August 1998 by a splinter IRA group in the centre of Omagh killing 29 and injuring 200. Bills were launched for Scotland and Wales to achieve devolved powers and their own Parliament and National Assembly; this gained royal approval in November and July 1998.[27n]

In December 1998 Blair agreed with President Clinton that the Iraqi President Saddam Hussein's continued cat and mouse game with the United Nations over his production of weapons of mass destruction should be challenged by missile and bombing attacks on 250 key targets, dubbed Operation Desert Fox. The operation drew considerable opposition at home and abroad. Evidence pointed to the fact that Hussein had already disposed of his weapons, so the bombing could only have been an attempt at regime change as well as a convenient distraction for Bill Clinton who was facing impeachment.

Meanwhile the ethnic and political conflicts within the Yugoslavian states were building up to full-scale war between Serbia, led by Slobodan Milošević, and the oppressed Albanian population in Kosovo. By early 1998 America and Europe were recognising that the resulting war would threaten more than the region. The NATO Council, in support of American and United Nations resolutions, prepared to intervene, action which Tony Blair fully supported. In March 1999 NATO aircraft commenced the bombing of military targets with limited success; consequently Blair pressed for ground troops to be deployed and in June a peacekeeping force entered, allowing more than a million Albanian refugees to return home to Kosovo and an uneasy peace to be established. Both these military excursions confirmed Tony Blair's belief in 'liberal intervention' which he felt to be a moral imperative for western democracies. He spelt this belief out clearly in a speech in Chicago in April 1999 – the virtue of being proactive, the case for intervention as a just war which does not seek territorial gain but seeks to spread western values of 'liberty, the rule of law, human rights and an open society.'[28] Blair doggedly pursued this belief throughout his premiership. It would come to overwhelm whatever progressive domestic and foreign policy he achieved for the next seven years of his office.

Soon after Blair took office, work had started on a White Paper[29] that outlined proposals for a Freedom of Information Act (passed in 2000) allowing members of the public access to information held by public bodies. It was a heavily used tool, putting the civil service and administrators under considerable pressure, but was of particular interest to journalists. Tony Blair later commented that this was one of the biggest mistakes of his premiership. The Cabinet struggled to keep their commitment to continue John Major's financial cuts, and the party became restless as time went by as public expenditure fell by over 4% of GDP. Gordon Brown was sticking firmly to his guiding principle of 'prudence.' One welcome mechanism, founded by the previous government, was the 'Private

Finance Initiative' (PFI) by which private finance could be used to finance capital projects such as schools and hospitals. The great advantage was that the large sums involved did not appear as expenditure in the public accounts; the great disadvantage was that the high fees and interest payments would be a burden on these services and future governments for the next fifty or more years. I came across this when I was acting as a consultant advising a medium sized private company who wished to get into the health and care sector (see below). I struggled with all the complex paperwork, which would clearly rack up large legal fees, and advised against getting involved.

It was this same period that saw the launch of key social policies which could be built on later. The first of these was the establishment in 1997 of the 'Social Exclusion Unit,' a powerful multi-dimensional long term project involving both government departments and all those involved in the delivery of public services.

> The Unit was ... concerned with combating, in the present and for the future, a variety of problems, in a variety of ways, for a variety of reasons. The problems included a lack of individual self belief and self reliance. Remedial action included not just employment and educational programmes but also measures to combat racial prejudice and the worst instances of urban degeneration ... The mix of motives included social justice (ensuring equality of opportunity), economic efficiency (the utilisation of all the talent) and social cohesion (strengthened communities). Immediate problems, such as rough sleeping and teenage pregnancy, had to be addressed. Most important however was the breaking of the cycle of deprivation by which children might be condemned through their parents' circumstances to life long poverty.[30]

This initiative formed a key driver for a number of initiatives prompted both by the government's core beliefs and a response to a damning report by the European Community which showed the UK as being near the top of a list of countries for the number of teenage pregnancies, homelessness and child poverty. At the same time the government launched Early Excellence Centres to co-ordinate local agencies with a particular emphasis on early education; these were followed by Sure Start Centres with a wider community social brief (see below). The number of children in poverty had increased threefold since 1979 until in 1998 a third of UK children, some 4.5 million, were deemed to be in poverty. Gordon Brown set objectives to reduce this by a third by 2004 and to halve it by 2010, with final eradication by 2020. Immediate changes in the family tax system increased the income of poor families by between £1,300 and £3,000.[31] In 1999 the Disability Rights Commission Act established a commission to work towards the elimination of discrimination against disabled persons.

The new government were slower to deal with the poor state of the NHS left by the Conservatives, although this was well known to the electorate. In late 2000 the medical fertility consultant, television personality and Labour peer Robert Winston broke ranks to complain about the very bad treatment of his mother in what he described as the worst health service in Europe. Within days Blair had appeared on a TV chat show to announce that expenditure would be raised to the European level, which entailed an annual rise of 6% above inflation. There had been no prior consultation with the Chancellor.

A rise in fuel prices had brought to the fore the government's annual rise in the VAT element which represented 81.5% of the price of every gallon. In September 2000 lorry drivers and other commercial users blocked fuel terminals, thus depriving motorists of petrol. As this short protest spread across the country, it became clear that the drivers were being encouraged by the owners of large fleets who aimed to damage the government. The action petered out when the Chancellor hinted that the tax would be reduced in the forthcoming Budget. After three years in government another blip was that Ken Livingstone won the election as the first Mayor of London whilst having been expelled from the Labour Party.

The majority of the population had for some time been concerned about the 'millennium bug,' which, due to the lack of foresight by computer manufacturers, meant that they would all collapse at midnight on December 31st 1999. Complete chaos would result. In fact some minor adjustments in a few machines were all that was required to avoid Armageddon! That night saw another blip when the government's main project, the Millennium Dome, opened. In my view it was a great project, but some technical hitches which forced the elite guests to wait outside in the cold gave the mostly hostile media a further excuse to shout incompetence by the government. When everyone's computers remained working well after the dreaded hour, many people's faith in 'experts' and 'scientists' fell to the same level as for politicians, a fact that would re-emerge in the debates around Brexit and climate change some seventeen years later.

Despite these blips the political and economic climate was positive, unemployment was down, the economy had grown at an average of 2.1% every year and people could see some improvement in social and educational provisions. In these four years the number of people in poverty had fallen by three percent. Blair therefore decided to call an election in June 2001, which Labour won, losing only five seats, although the turnout fell to a low 59.4% – was this a sign of contentment or apathy? Tony Blair thus became the only Prime Minister ever to lead a Labour Party to re-election. William Hague handed over leadership of the Conservative Party to Iain Duncan Smith, a man somewhat lacking in charisma but supported by Margaret Thatcher as a determined anti-European. Once in post he gave the shadow transport brief to the little known Theresa May, who would slide unelected into the prime ministership fifteen years later.

The renewed government could now build on its social agenda, benefitting from an increasingly prosperous economy. The future looked good, but then, as mentioned earlier, on September 11th 2001 terrorists flew commercial airliners into the Twin Towers of the World Trade Center in New York. The horrific scenes of the disaster unfolding live on TV caused widespread shock and support worldwide. Tony Blair immediately ordered the closing of air space over London and nine days later was in New York to join President Bush, where he pledged his support to his friend and to the nation.

Our world changed. We became aware and wary of this remarkable terrorist organisation Al-Qaeda, based, it was said, in Afghanistan. I think that in this climate there was widespread support for Blair's actions, although as time passed and warfare spread, his perceived loyalty to Bush would cost him dear and ruin his political reputation.

CULTURE

The decade saw a strange change in cultural activity as the effects of the Thatcher years morphed into the early 'Cool Britannia' years of the Blair premiership. Somehow competitive individualism turned to a determination across the media to broadcast on its own terms. In the same period the cult of celebrity expanded, confusing the boundaries between transient media personalities and establishment figures who in general we looked to for rationality and stability. Blair was by no means the first inhabitant of Number 10 to enhance his image by being seen with the popular stars of the day, but he went further than others in entertaining and involving them in projecting the image of a young, cool Britain. His director of communications, Alastair Campbell, developed the techniques of 'spin,' which sometimes blurred the line between fact and fiction, and in her turn Princess Diana, as a senior member of the normally remote royal family, was intent on breaking down the old barriers. It was all quite confusing.

As professional football developed as a worldwide money machine, the top players joined in the celebrity culture with gusto, each becoming a recognised brand; this included one of the very best, David Beckham, who had great success at Manchester United. In 1998 he became engaged to the equally famous Victoria Adams, who had been part of the brilliant Spice Girls, an all female pop group. Their marriage, late in 1999, combined two rich brands to the advantage of both. They have, of course, gone on to develop their own brilliant careers and with their three sons and a daughter they are now an iconic family across the world.

Our TV viewing embraced endless games of snooker and the drama of Formula 1 racing, from the terrible death of Ayrton Senna on the Imola track in 1994 to the arrival of a new super driver Michael Schumacher in that same race. Winning the TV audience however was a Thatcherite comedy series *Only Fools and Horses*, featuring the endearing but incompetent entrepreneurs who ran TIT (Trotters Independent Traders) from their flat in the high rise Nelson Mandela House in Peckham; their battered Reliant Robin three-wheeler van became an iconic symbol of the working-class would-be entrepreneur.[32] Coming from left field was *Bread*, written by the great Carla Lane, telling the day to day survival techniques of a lovable Liverpool family as they skived and manipulated the benefits system. It combined humanity with hilarity.[33]

Later came another more extreme family comedy, *The Royle Family*, who sat together round a TV set exchanging and commenting on their sad experiences.[34] This was preceded by the quieter but equally funny *One Foot in the Grave*, which portrayed an elderly guy beset by the problems of everyday modern life, baffling his patient wife and alarming the neighbours.³⁵ In severe contrast was the gripping political drama *House of Cards*, whose characters relentlessly climbed the greasy pole seeking ultimate power.³⁶

Outside TV the cultural scene seemed wilder and harsher. On one hand, raves, usually fuelled by drugs, would pop up suddenly in unguarded fields creating noise and sleeplessness for rural communities. Certainly we could hear the music from the one that settled over a mile away from us. Unfortunately many ended in violence as police arrived to stop the fun.

The artist Damien Hirst pickled a shark as an exhibit entitled 'The Physical Impossibility of Death in the Mind of Someone Living,' an example of the brilliant 'Young British Art' movement which had been developing since 1988. This was followed by a series of confessional art by Tracey Emin (a graduate of Maidstone College of Art) which hit the headlines in 1998 with her exhibit 'My Bed,' a shocking mess from many days and nights during a depressive period. Two years earlier Danny Boyle's excruciatingly honest account of poverty and heroin addiction in the poorer areas of Edinburgh, *Trainspotting*, shocked cinema goers.³⁷ In the background the Internet was arriving in the home, opening up a whole new world of connections and increasingly interesting games. The first PlayStation games console was marketed in 2000. A small group of committed gamers in Edinburgh, including Sam and Dan Houser, creators of 'Grand Theft Auto' and 'Red Dead,' were experimenting with more ambitiously complex plots and structures and launching Rockstar Games in December 1998, a company which would significantly impact on our whole family nine years later.

Against this backdrop we continued to follow our own eclectic cultural choices. In the North, we had a range of theatres and concert halls in Manchester, there was the Lowry Centre in the newly developed media centre in Salford and we took excursions to Leeds and London. In 1993 my depression was lifted by a revival of the variety show *Me and My Girl*, which I had seen at the Victoria Palace just after the war with the great Lupino Lane and George Graves as stars. This musical includes the songs 'The Lambeth Walk,' 'The Sun Has Got Its Hat On' and 'Leaning on a Lamp Post.'³⁸ This show was in the same theatre which had hosted the iconic 'Crazy Gang' with Bud Flanagan and Chesney Allen who wrote and performed such numbers as 'Underneath The Arches,' 'Run Rabbit Run,' 'We're Going To Hang Out The Washing On The Siegfried Line' and 'The Umbrella Man,' which I had also seen immediately after the war. Other excursions included those to the great *Les Miserables*³⁹ and *The Rocky Horror Show*⁴⁰ and the wonderful environmental *Yanomamo* (which had the strap line from an ancient Amazonian Indian legend 'The trees support the sky. Cut down the forests and disaster follows.'⁴¹ⁿ After Sondheim's off beat *Company*⁴² and the Irish *Stones in his Pockets*,⁴³ we saw *Soul Train*⁴⁴ and a programme of Kabuki theatre.⁴⁵ At the end of the decade, despite a prolonged campaign of denigration by the press, we enjoyed a day in the Millennium Dome on the Greenwich Meridian and built on the abandoned peninsular of South Greenwich. Of the fourteen exhibition areas we mostly enjoyed 'The Body,' 'Faith,' 'Rest' and 'Home Planet,' each in vivid colour explaining their subject in depth through interactive exhibits. The day ended with the breath-taking 'Millennium Show' performed by a cast of ninety in the central area the size of Trafalgar Square rising fifty metres to the top of the Dome.[46n]

SOCIAL WORK

Now that the Griffith's report had come off the shelf and the main recommendations had been woven into the 1990 National Health Service and Community Care Act, social work had to come to terms with the implications for practice and answer to the question 'What is the role of the social worker?' The emphasis of legislation and guidance was that social workers, in their key role of assessors or planners of services for people, must involve the users of that service and those members of the family who may be already caring for or supporting that person. This was, of course, all part of the belief, introduced by the Thatcher and Major governments and supported by the centrist Blair, that competition in the care market would reduce costs and provide choice for those needing services. This would be achieved by the purchaser of the services being separate from those providing services (no longer the main function of local authorities). In social work this rested on a full assessment which would specify the range of services required. This process would be entrusted to a 'Care Manager.' The same principles would apply to children's services, with the added requirement to involve the family. The Guidance and Regulations for the 1989 Children Act emphasised two important requirements. While the requirement that 'The prime duty of the local authority is to safeguard and promote the interests of a child' was a very welcome clarification, the second requirement that 'When a child is being looked after by the local authority, the local authority is required to make arrangements for that child to live with a member of his family unless to do so would be impractical or inconsistent with the child's welfare'[47] was more problematic, as was the requirement that children should be placed near their family wherever possible.

Guidance for all this came in 'Purchase of Service' under the logo 'Caring for People,' the fourth section of which explained that:

> Whatever contractual arrangements are entered into by SSDs for the provision of services the ultimate liability for the performance of these functions rest with the local authority ... should a breach of contract occur ... the SSD remains responsible for ensuring that its statutory functions are performed.
>
> When care managers assess the needs of clients or carers, individual care plans will be produced. These may include a number of agreements which will have the force of contracts.[48]

This was followed by the Central Council for Education and Training in Social Work (CCETSW) training manual on the subject, emphasising that these processes must be carried out within the professional values of respect, dignity, privacy, confidentiality and choice. Emphasis was also placed on 'an awareness of structural oppression, counteracting stigma, combating racism, demonstrating anti-sexism and promoting non-discriminating and anti-oppressive policies.' It would be a somewhat confusing time for most social workers and their managers.[49]

It seemed to me that in these few paragraphs we see the hollowness of the conceit that the ethics and culture of the market could ever be compatible with the ethos of public service, that the project, based on the need to reduce the statistics showing how many people are employed by the state, ignored how any revenue savings are reduced by the massive legal work, paper and administrators required to set contracts and monitor subsequent performance. These contradictions were acute in education, medicine and social work, but only in the latter were the professionals actually involved on a daily face to face basis in assessing the needs of service users and negotiating, with them and a range of others, the details of each individual contract. A virtual overhaul of traditional social work was required, a task that would take some time. The need to involve the service user, family and wider community was welcomed as empowering, as was the implied decentralisation of power from senior management nearer to the front line, even if it took some time for the change in the power relationship to be fully accepted.

A central problem would, however, never go away. The process of assessment and involvement of all parties and the relationships involved was the most time consuming and arguably the most important part of the process, but it was impossible to measure and thus invalidate any measurement that relied on outcome only. The pragmatic side of the profession came to the rescue as workers and managers devised ways of complying with the process without necessarily subscribing to the underlying political belief systems. I doubt whether the whole thing would have worked if it were not for the introduction of complex computer programmes which depersonalised the process of case recording and allowed practitioners to distance themselves from the 'business' ethos now thrust upon them. The key argument that the market gave service users choice usually proved false as, with services and funds being cut every year, choice was severely limited or non-existent. Cooling the mark out[50] became an everyday activity, a distasteful role for any social worker. Not surprisingly, a study carried out in 1996 concluded that role confusion, partly due to resistance to what was seen as an alien culture, was widespread and that staff at many levels were unable to articulate the values that now underlay their practice.[51] It is no wonder that social workers showed interest in how chaos theory might help their plight.[52n]

The National Institute for Social Work (NISW) sought to clarify these dilemmas in a series of papers, one of which was aimed at a new agenda for social work, which, it argued, could no longer be seen in isolation as an elite occupation but rather as a small part of a much larger arena of social care. It drew attention to the increasing power of service users and the influence of the 1998 Human Rights Act, quoting a service user's comment: 'We don't want care, we want rights. We want to change the nature of our relationship with ... social workers from one based on welfare to one based on social justice.' It sketched out a list of social work values and skills including 'being honest, reliable and showing respect: listening to service users and starting with their agendas;

providing information and advice on all the available resources and demonstrating the personal qualities highlighted by service users and open relationships with them based on these.'[53]

Throughout this period the NISW had a central role in the campaign to clarify the role of a social worker, and to achieve this as a protected title with national registration and the power to remove an individual from the register. The Institute launched an action group in 1991 which worked with other groups to set standards for conduct. Despite setbacks by government the Labour Party eventually promised to establish such a council in their election manifesto. In 2000 the Care Standards Act was passed which extended the scope by forming the General Social Care Council (GSCC) and establishing the national registration for all residential and domiciliary care facilities. The Institute issued a Guide to the Act the same year and the Council started work in 2001. I was appointed to the Council the following year.[54]

Although much residential care had been privatised, starting with individual nurses and some doctors running their own small homes but now part of national commercial companies, domiciliary care had not been widely privatised. Charities responded to the new scenario with some reluctance as their whole ethos was threatened by the ethics of the marketplace, but bit by bit they surrendered in favour of a more commercial approach. Having closed most of their children's homes, local authorities had little option but to place the children now requiring such provision with commercial companies. In 1978 some 9% of adults needing residential care were in private provision, but by 1993 this had grown to 35% and would steadily increase. A similar trend was evident in provision for children, and local authorities were encouraged to contract private agencies to find, approve and monitor foster care placements.[55] By the end of this period social workers were clear that where previously 20% of their time was spent in the office and 80% talking with service users, the position was now reversed. This was great news for the statisticians harvesting the computer data but not exactly efficient for the purpose of social work and service users, whose personal interactions could not be measured. Inevitably the volume of data generated was so overwhelming that I doubt whether any of it was ever used constructively.

Victoria Climbié

While all these high level issues were proceeding another extreme case of child abuse was developing in North London. An eight-year-old girl, Victoria Climbié, in the care of her great aunt Marie-Thérèse Kouao, first came to the attention of the authorities some eighteen months after their arrival in the UK in April 1999. In the following ten months as they moved from place to place, the last with Marie's boyfriend, Carl Manning, Victoria's abuse increased from slaps to punches and burns. All this occurred during the time that the child was seen by a whole variety of social workers, nurses, doctors, police and the NSPCC. Victoria died on February 25th 2000, the day after being admitted to St Mary's Hospital, Paddington. The pathologist found 128 injuries on her body; it was the worst case of child abuse he had ever seen. Kouao and Manning were both sentenced to life imprisonment for murder and child cruelty. The judge commented that the services had been 'blindingly incompetent'. The last social worker having responsibility for Victoria was the young Lisa Arthurworrey who was crucified in the press. Several papers commented on alleged racial aspects of the case. As the case developed, Lord Laming, former Chief Inspector of the Social Services Inspectorate, had been commissioned to fully investigate the case. His report, discussed in the next chapter, was published in early 2009.

A DIFFERENT SORT OF SOCIAL WORKER
Care Concern International

On October 12th 1987 I pulled up at Mannanan House to the west of Chester, entered a modern office block, which was the headquarters of my new employer, and met the principal administrator and accountant and John Moss, the maintenance and building supervisor.[56n] I had a good but spartanly equipped office and very soon met Vernon Jones, a newly recruited psychologist. Vernon had specialised in the care and treatment of people with a severe learning disability and had been the Senior Advisor for Clywd County Council. The early weeks were spent, often with Vernon, visiting the residential units owned by the company. In addition to the residential special school (see Chapter 13) there were three 'traditional' units, housed in large old buildings, each with approximately twenty residents. Further to the west and hidden in the countryside was 'The Village' where 120 adults lived in a variety of houses around central facilities. In total there were some 210 adults and children in our care. All the units were under the management of John Donnavon, who had held that post for some time.

The population of each unit varied according to the physical and intellectual capacities of the residents, allocation being decided by John Donnovan. It took us some time to assess the residents, the standards of care and the capacities of the managers and staff. Many of the residents had lived in the units for a long time. We made various recommendations to John and the unit managers but with little effect. Managers seemed to have lost confidence that extra staffing or resources would ever be made available so had fallen back on 'just carrying on.' It was safer. We initiated some training for senior staff but to moderate effect, and unfortunately a senior member of staff had to be rushed to hospital from one session and we had to break the news that he had died. The omens were not good. Our routine was interrupted by two excursions to seek expansion, both illustrating how far this organisation was from current accepted philosophy and practice. One was to buy up a small, isolated group of houses in Lancashire where my former colleagues, steeped in normalisation, refused point blank to approve any such scheme, just as I had predicted. The other took us to Yorkshire to inspect an old institutional children's home (a CHE I think) which was equally isolated and unsuitable. I was later to learn that the continuing financial viability of the company rested on one of these schemes working.

As the months passed, Vernon and I realised that we were both angry at the lack of support from David Rattray and his lawyer/adviser on the Isle of Man, despairing at the limited care available to residents and pupils and frustrated that our advisory positions made it impossible to achieve rapid effective change. We also discovered that we shared radical left-wing political beliefs. In short, we found ourselves asking the same questions: What were we both doing here and what could be done? We composed a memo to David outlining our concerns and the actions required to bring the company up to date. We were summoned to the Isle of Man, basically to be told that no such memo should ever be written in a commercial company and there were no resources available anyway.[57n]

While attending a residential care conference in Bromley, I met a former colleague from the DHSS who was now working for a financial company in the City. After a brief conversation and a phone call to my old friend and solicitor Trevor Carney, it seemed that the option to buy out David, the present owner, might be possible, if risky. Vernon agreed to join the attempt and I then recruited Peter Claydon, who I had met on the AMDP course and was now business manager for Yorkshire Enterprises. The three of us then entered the weird and wonderful world of Thatcher's city finance where money was being thrown at any likely proposal, providing of course that there was good profit in it! Ann and I had recently seen the play *Serious Money*, which sent up the drive for profits. It featured a trading room where all the men wore white shirts and red braces – little had I thought that I would soon be visiting these extraordinary places.[58]

There was a small glitch when John Donnavon and the managers met me to explain that if Vernon became a director they would immediately resign. I told them that they would easily be replaced, but I was impressed by their fear of Vernon's expertise and assertive personality. We spent many a long day and night preparing extensive financial projections and, armed with Trevor and a brilliant accountant from the top London accountants KPMG, we prepared to tour city banks to seek finance for an offer of £5 million. There were some lively meetings where I think we matched their cunning and eventually got a deal in place. These were mad days when I was driving very fast up and down the M6 taking difficult phone calls and making quick decisions.

At this point I made a bad mistake: anticipating success, I met a journalist and briefed him on our ambitions to change matters and revealed more details than I should have. It seemed to me that we would need as much good publicity as possible. The fact that this was a mistake, and the awful consequences from a libelled David Rattray, dawned on me the next day, but the magazine refused to hold the article. Once again Trevor came to the rescue with an emergency injunction!

Decision day came in June 1989 when a middle man (who was set to earn £70,000 on the deal) in the City negotiated with David while we three waited in Lancashire. Despite the fact that he must have known the parlous state of the company, he refused our offer. For us it was despair and the prospect of high legal and accounting bills from our advisors, and, for me, unemployment and no car!

Consultancy

I faced three immediate issues. Shock and debt, no transport and unemployment, the debt being a concern in view of Ann's need for security, although she was receiving regular fees for her tribunal work. To me, unemployment meant a visit to the local exchange in Blackburn where a very kind and polite youth carefully explained that they would never have anything to match my qualifications and experience. His kindness brought me near to tears. The only alternative therefore was to become self-employed as The Rowan Consultancy (Rowan being the name of our company had the deal materialised). Lack of a car was solved by the purchase of an old Volvo for £1,150. It rattled and the windows did not close properly so that a man who had never willingly worn a hat had to wear a beret in the style of the comedian Frank Spencer. Over the 30,000 miles that I travelled looking for work in the next year it had more punctures than all my previous cars put together; it was a horror. The first person who came to my aid was a guilt ridden Jack Bury, who, having at last forced poor Tom Foster out of office, put me in touch with ETI & AHP Services.

This was a 'not for profit' care company with links to the Catholic Church. They provided homes for adults with a learning disability across Liverpool and were interested in expanding to other areas. I was to act as a management consultant and inspector of standards on an occasional basis at £110 a day. The work with the directors Tony Crisp and Les Roche, an ex-docker, was interesting and enjoyable. As an illustration of the difficulties faced by the de-institutionalisation and community care of the period, I recall a visit that Tony and I made to a hospital which had reduced its population to the point where it needed to close. We met the parents and guardians of the remaining patients to tell them about AHP's provision. This included photos of the houses, equipped as usual with domestic furniture, carpets etc. They were incensed. How could we be stupid enough to think that their sons or daughters could tolerate such conditions? Did we not know that they needed lino or tiles and plastic furniture? We were laughed out of the meeting, horrified that institutionalism had so corrupted their view.

Faced, as were Vernon and Peter, with bills from the City of £5,700 (kindly moderated by Trevor), I was broke. In order to keep going I had to seek a personal loan of £5,000 from my friend Tom Woods. The first thing to do was to advertise myself. This took the form of letters to all local authorities and probation offices in the country, to professional associations as well as to established consultancies and the Social Service Inspectorate at the DHSS. I was offering expertise in health, social care and special education; social work practice, residential care; all aspects of personnel practice and management; purchaser/provider contracts; and staff training at any level. Irresistible! The first months were very tough. It seemed that my 'desertion' to the private sector in general and to Care Concern in particular had put a black mark against my name; consequently I had to rely on people who actually knew me. A former senior manager from Lancashire SSD who had been appointed as Director in Cumbria asked me to review the structure and standards of residential care in his Department, a job which certainly added to my mileage across that beautiful county. Also two former Lancashire training officers, David Walton and Sheila Udall, who had struck out on their own, offered me the facilities of their office in Preston. This was a boon, the only disadvantage being that, as I didn't want to get in their way, it meant arriving about 5.30 am or in the late evening.

The Health Advisory Service

In late May 1990 the DHSS recruited me into the Hospital Advisory Service (HAS) which paid well and slowly rescued me from the brink, although it entailed long periods away from home. A team consisting of a consultant psychiatrist, a consultant gerontologist, a senior nurse and an allied professional, a manager and an experienced social worker would descend on a health district (which in those days were relatively small) for three weeks to visit all facilities for the mentally ill and the elderly. We had the full authority of the Secretary of State to visit any facility caring for elderly and mentally ill people at any time of the day or night to check on care and examine any files. The last week was spent in the HQ in Sutton hammering out an agreed report for the government. The teams were never the same.

To my mind this was one of the best mechanisms for monitoring the care of these groups. It was personal, very intense, highly professional and a great advance on the modern system of inspection by tick boxes designed by a distant body. Over the next three years it was my privilege to join some ten of these inspections across the country, all challenging because of the variability of services and the ability of the managers to accept our advice. In all the teams which I joined I had the greatest respect for all my colleagues. I remember accompanying a gerontologist on a visit to see a ward where we were shown into the office when his opposite number boasted on the excellence of his service. As we left we called the responsible consultant over to explain that the elderly lady visiting her bedridden husband had been standing there all this time and no staff member had had enough care to offer her a seat!

These were of course times of organisational and philosophical change from psychiatric hospitals towards community care. It was often a shock for a hospital or care home to have a knock on their door at 2.30 am, but these were the times we often found really bad practice and more than once had the manager summoned and the staff member immediately suspended. Talking of doors, we visited a large psychiatric hospital in South London where they had just suffered an extraordinary burglary. One evening, men dressed in the appropriate gear had spent hours removing all the new kitchen equipment then, while we were there, another gang arrived at night and removed the vast main oak doors that had stood for at least 100 years! This same visit split the team when community psychiatric nurses told us that, faced with a patient in the grips of an acute psychotic episode, all they needed was the use of a hotel room for a few nights rather than admit them to hospital. Our psychiatrist was horrified; I was supportive.

In Wolverhampton, where distressingly I had previously visited my cousin suffering terminal depressive dementia, I remember the wonderful support organised by a local ethnic community group where we spent an intense evening discussing philosophies of care and sampling their excellent catering.

Devon was, to my mind, one of the most interesting visits, particularly in view of the wide differences in philosophy and practice and the dreaded reputation of one psychiatric unit where a number of suicides had prompted more than one intense investigation. In general, thanks to sensible planning and sharing of funds, community health care and social services were well integrated and offered very good services. The psychiatric in-patient unit however was very anxiety inducing. My memory is that staff were mixed between community nurses coming in and their in-patient colleagues. Management and practice were confused, both in accountability and philosophy, and the ward therefore lacked any clear leadership, a fact which clearly impacted on patients. Each visit ended with a final meeting where the team presented our views to the assembled health services, social services, community groups and patient representatives. The dynamics were always interesting.

An extract from my contribution to the final meeting in Devon hopefully illustrates the inter-professional nature of the HAS team and the honesty with which we presented our findings. As we were approaching Christmas I held up one of those glass paperweights full of snow and shook it to illustrate what I saw as total confusion in some areas. They needed time to stop and think:

> My colleagues – and others before us – have drawn attention to problems currently being experienced within the Mental Health Services – and these seem to arise in a significant part from early attempts to resolve critical issues of conflict – a failure to sustain a consistent strategic view and lack of time to think things through clearly. A notable feature of HAS work is that within a tight timescale it gives a snapshot across a wide range of hospital and community services ... we are therefore privileged to experience the gaps between the language and the daily reality. We may wonder why systems that are stuffed full of talk about quality control can miss the blatantly improper practices that my colleagues have described ... We have identified specific examples of practices that are totally unacceptable ... they are known to all the professional groups, including social workers and yet they have continued. Even more unbelievable is that other bodies have drawn attention to poor practices and yet there has been no significant response from service managers and their leaders. If empowerment of users and the responsibilities of purchasers mean anything it is at least questionable whether, given available choices, patients would not opt for a more humane experience.

Following this visit, we sent an urgent letter to the Secretary of State, as we could have done at any time.

My last enduring memory is a similar final presentation in Sussex which was mild in comparison. The Chair of the NHS Trust was a gentleman from Eastern Europe. He ushered us into his office, white with fury that anyone should 'attack' any of his wonderful staff: 'This is a very interesting report,' he said. 'I will accept it and shove it straight into the dustbin!' Luckily we had an experienced psychiatric nurse with us who skilfully calmed him down and got him to concentrate on the recommendations for improvement, rather than criticism. We loved him for his passionate belief in his staff. Back in Sutton for our final week the intense inter-professional discussion group dynamics were sometimes challenging but always interesting! Despite the fact that the HAS was criticised as costly, and the fact that, however severe their reports (which were always published locally and nationally), there was no early follow up, it remains my view that it has never been bettered. It was disbanded in 1997 to be replaced, in accordance with New Labour's ideas, with a more managerial approach to quality control; no room for professional expertise, experience and judgement.

Other friends offered me employment. Barbara Kahan, former Assistant Director of the Social Work Advisory Service, asked me to report on the care and structure of a Save the Children's home for the care and rehabilitation of refugee children displaced by the Vietnam War. Senior staff in the Local Government Unit at Birmingham University employed me as a tutor on some of their courses and I expended a lot of energy, in a voluntary capacity, constructing a catalogue of resources for BASW which was entitled *Search*. In that project I worked with Professor Malcolm Payne at Manchester University and Sally Arkley of BASW. It sustained a couple of editions and then I think it was sold to an outside agency.

By late 1991 Vernon was back in touch to say that Care Concern was drifting into deeper financial problems. He thought that they may be prepared to sell their school at Dolgellau; might I still be interested? After some thought, mostly a mixture of revenge on Care Concern and relief from the uncertainties of my present work, I said yes. The only problem was that knowledge of my involvement would kill the deal so it was agreed that Vernon would negotiate with his wife as partner and I would put in my share of the cost once the deal was done. We gave little thought to the fact that I was now fifty-seven years of age, and I certainly did not anticipate the nine years of high anxiety that would follow.

Aran Hall School

This establishment stands on high ground, just outside the town of Dolgellau, on the west coast of North Wales. It is an imposing stone built structure built in the 1920s which was first opened as a residential school by Care Concern in 1976 when it was known as Hengwrt Hall School. (One of our first initiatives was to ask the staff to vote for a new name.) It had been approved for 'physically and mentally handicapped children categorised as having Special Educational Needs.' Apart from the front tower, it was a three-storey building which held the residential accommodation, kitchen and offices. The ground floor had a large entrance hall and three large lounge areas. The boys' bedrooms were on the first floor, the girls' on the second. There were small bedrooms on the top 'servants' floor. The education facilities were based on temporary housing at the back with facilities for art and craft. There were ample grounds. In 1983 its registration had been revised for 19 pupils with severe learning disabilities and challenging behaviour. At the time we purchased it there were eleven pupils on a 52-week residence, it was not well staffed and the fabric was in poor repair. Its registration had been withdrawn in March 1989 following reports of poor care and concerns by the fire inspectors about safety, a frequent device used when standards of care were in doubt when the physical requirements of fire regulations were more easily and practically measured. We paid £480,000 (a bank loan of £300,000, with us making up the difference) for the business. We each had to take out large mortgages on our homes. We naively believed that with some £5,000 to improve the structure and staffing, our experience, knowledge and professional reputation we could improve the life of children and staff and get full registration back. The manager of the Wrexham branch of Barclays Bank was Mr Bellis, an excellent manager in the traditional sense that he saved our bacon many times by using his own judgement to support and encourage us without constant referrals to head office.

Having moved quickly from a large local authority to the freedom of a private company, the step to owning our own school was remarkable. If action was required for individual children or staff, or a new vehicle was required, or the fence needed repair or the kitchen upgraded, the decision was just taken and the work was done, often by us. Success or failure was entirely in our hands, certainly a very stimulating feeling! There being no way for the school to pay us both a reasonable salary, it was agreed that I would be paid as a consultant and split my time between the school and other work. The headteacher at that time was Sarah Britton, and the Heads of Care and Education were responsible to her, with two team leaders responsible for all care issues. We were faced with three major battles. By far the greatest was to upgrade the care and educational provision for the children, whose behaviours and degrees of disability ranged from very to slightly less severe. This of course required a great deal of staff training and support. Alongside this were the necessary improvements to the building, the decoration and furnishing of lounges and bedrooms, many of which were shared. The third, and most concerning, was resisting the pressure of ongoing demands from the Fire and Social Service Departments of the local authority and inspectors from the Welsh Office. Although the latter accepted our genuine professional desire to vastly improve the whole ethos, regime and structure of the place, they did not always appreciate the financial pressures upon us. Not surprisingly, therefore, soon after we arrived the pupil numbers declined to nine, threatening bankruptcy, which was only avoided by cutting all salaries, including our own, and starting a drive for new admissions. Although we were unregistered, local authorities could still place children if they were satisfied that we could meet their needs. The driving factor for them, of course, was that we were the only place that could care and educate the child that they could never provide for locally. We therefore embarked on a large recruitment drive.

Our contributions to the management of the school were markedly different. Vernon lived locally and spoke Welsh, had a great presence, and his knowledge, experience, skill and understanding of these children enabled him to support staff and construct behaviour programmes which would help both children and staff. Added to this, his enjoyment of high-quality DIY repairs and construction meant that the everyday challenges were overcome, rooms were divided so that each child had his or her own room. All went ahead at a pace. My drive from home was 110 miles, some two and a half hours each way, mostly through Welsh lanes. This meant that in the early days I stayed overnight in one of the 'servants' rooms on the top floor, These were disturbing times, firstly because quite frankly some of these children frightened me and sleep was not easy given the loud night noises coming from below. I spent time with the night staff and embarked on training the care staff, laying out routines and procedures, supporting staff and ensuring that the care aspects of the process were heard in all our management meetings.

The first action for the care staff was to ensure that they saw themselves as professionals, doing a professional job, not 'just the carers' at the bottom of the pile. I guess I worried more about our weekly accounts, trying to balance the budget and possible bank concerns with Vernon's 'can do' approach to get things done as soon as possible. My participation was not helped when in 1992, when failure was staring us in the face, I developed a depression which slowed me down considerably. I think this was a degree of mourning left over from the sudden death of my brother but it was induced by high levels of anxiety about the real prospect that we would lose our home. This would be a devastating blow for Ann for whom I had pledged lifelong security, therefore of course I could not let her know how precarious our situation was. Eventually she sent me to our GP who, in a memorable session said, directly I sat down, 'Malcolm, you look dreadful. What is the matter?' It was such a relief. I walked out in tears and with a box of pills, only a few of which I ever took. At times this really got to me, and as I drove at high speeds up and down the M6 I frequently thought how easy it would be just to touch the steering wheel and send myself into the solid concrete of one of the numerous bridges. Of course, the immediately following thought was the effect on Ann and Juliet, but nonetheless it was frequently quite tempting. The other boost was Vernon. At the school, when I apologised for having a breakdown, he said 'You are not broken, you're here and functioning.' In such matters Vernon was usually right, and anyway he freely expressed his feelings immediately and openly whereas I needed time to think and kept my feelings close. Professionally and personally, we were a great team!

The next few years were very hard as we slowly improved the whole place. The young people presented new challenges every day, the old building produced its own severe problems, as did the constant flow of visitors, parents, social workers, fire and health inspectors. Education and social services inspectors were welcome, but led to many challenges. The staff complement was slowly increased, as was the training schedule, taking advantage of the newly introduced NVQ levels of qualification. Above all, one or other of us were there for a high percentage of the time, a major difference from the previous remote owners. It was obvious that we were all in this together.

The water supply came from a spring in a field on higher ground and pretty frequently cows got too close so all the water had to be boiled. We had permission to draw water from a nearby fast flowing stream, so we installed an expensive powerful pump to bring it right up to storage tanks in the tower. The next big flood washed it away! The upstairs WCs relied on macerators before the solids were sent down a narrow pipe. Unfortunately the mechanism could not cope with the plimsolls and other strange objects that our residents put down there. After several sessions with our arms buried in shit we decided to extensively redesign the whole system. As health and safety pushed the fire officer to demand more intrusive equipment, we challenged them with such questions as 'Do you have a bloody great fire extinguisher in *your* lounge?' We had no reserve water tank in case of fire. This saw me hanging around Lancashire tanker depots until I found a very large stainless steel tank being removed from a lorry. Off it went to the school to be installed by a huge crane. Social work was never quite like this! More seriously, we repeatedly challenged the inspectors on whom restoration of our approval depended. Their difficulty was that, as our establishment was unique they had no comparative model by which to judge us and anyway both directors and senior managers knew more about the best regime for our exceptional pupils than anyone else. There were frequent disputes!

The first three years were very stressful as numbers varied, as did our balance sheets. For the first five years our accounts were a nightmare. We certainly appreciated the services of our accountant Mike Coxey, whose advice was invaluable and who, as the years rolled by, had a remarkable ability to recall specific details of previous entries when he quizzed us as to why such and such an item of expenditure had changed. Whilst an income of £760,000 seemed attractive, staff costs were never less than 70% of that and increased as we built up the staff. If you add on all the running costs there was very little left to invest. It was 1994 before we showed our first profit. It was £8,000. Much more worrying were the large negative balances in our revenue budget. The pathway between the visiting social worker and the treasurer's department was bureaucratic and time consuming, leading to long delays in fee payment by the placing authorities. As local authorities started to face annual budget cuts this problem worsened and we had no option but to fall back on threats. In extremis Vernon would phone the social worker, point out how late the payment was and announce that at the end of that month their pupil would be driven back home where they would have to provide the intensive care required. That usually worked, but what a waste of time and energy. In these matters we were fortunate that the traditional responsibilities delegated to local bank managers still held sway in Wrexham. We were called in for frequent meetings with Mr Bellis, during which he would express his concern about the appalling state of our overdraft (whilst welcoming our contribution to their profits). Tea and coffee were served and we would recount some recent hilarious high jinks from the school. We would be sent on our way with imprecations to try to do better; of course what saved us was the knowledge that in the end public authorities would eventually pay their dues. We were apprehensive when Mr Bellis retired, but although his replacement was more in the modern mode, he retained the humanity essential to a good understanding of our work, only occasionally referring matters to higher authority. Looking back I am sure that had the more modern, high risk averse, impersonal banking culture been in place we would have been closed down very early on.

On July 15th 1996 the Welsh Office granted us general approval, allowing us to admit pupils without the painstaking and off-putting procedure of obtaining approval for each individual child. Although there was more work to be done, we were finally properly open for business. A major report published in 2001, whose authors never visited the school or sought our participation, expressed the view that, given the income, 'surprise may legitimately be expressed that it took so long to remedy the obvious physical defects at Hengwrt Hall School.' I suggest they bloody try it. The task had, at various times, driven Vernon and me to the edge of mental and physical exhaustion.[59n]

Now that we could breathe more easily it was time to sort out the management of the school and other long-standing problems. We poached Duncan Pritchard from his management post in Care Concern as Head of Care, and in due course persuaded Mark Ferguson to leave his post as deputy head in a local secondary school to join us as Head. We confirmed Lois Hubbard as Head of Education. If you add Vernon and myself we had one of the strongest and best qualified management teams in the sector. All staff were encouraged to gain qualifications at higher levels and in this we worked in close cooperation with Prospects Children's Home and the North East Wales Institute of Higher Education (NEWI, now Wrexham Glyndwr University) in Wrexham where John Bates and Neil Thompson were based and were very helpful.[60] We became concerned that we had some pupils who had reached the age of eighteen; of course, local authorities had no way of making provision for them. In particular we worried about Michael, a boy with severe handicaps who needed constant one to one care. He had been at the school from an early age and had harvested much love for his gentle soul. Never to be put off by our negative balances, we resolved to establish a new company, Aran Care, to provide staffed houses in Wrexham to continue the care of our ex-pupils who could not return home. So we now started searching for a suitable house, bought it (more debts), made the adaptations required, recruited staff and gained registration. Although this was exactly in line with the national policy and practice of normalisation and community care, we faced concern from neighbours who did not like 'people like that' living next door, and, of course, the health and safety inspectors replaying the arguments when their institutional requirement contradicted the whole normal domestic environment that we required. I left Vernon (who was more than eager) to assertively express his opinion and bat away such stupidity. Eventually we had four houses accommodating twelve residents.

Slowly, over the next four years, our anxieties diminished slightly as we could step back from the day to day management of the school, although we had weekly meetings with the management team. Vernon launched a massive building project to build an extra room in the tower, thus bringing our capacity to 21. (Up to that point, our original estimate of £5,000 to upgrade the building had reached £500,000.) It usually fell to me to visit prospective pupils, a somewhat disturbing learning experience. I think the last pupil I visited was a well built girl of thirteen who was accommodated alone in a house and requiring the supervision of two care staff. On the day of my visit she was described as unpredictable and very violent; the two male staff, who could well have been members of the local rugby team, shadowed her, both in her personal space all the time. All the windows were boarded up so very little daylight got through. There was no way I was going to leave her there so she was admitted a few days later. Determined to make her mark and, I think, excited by the relative freedom, she hugged the tall team leader who greeted her, lifted him off his feet, hit his head on the door jamb and knocked him out! She was certainly challenging but had great gifts and eventually became school captain. The greasy spoon transport cafe which had served for director's meetings was replaced with a neat office where our secretary and bookkeeper were based as we now had two companies to manage.

The school was as settled as possible with such volatile residents and our staffing and procedures had won us an award from the Investor in People organisation. In late 1997 and early 1998 we were subject to two detailed inspections, which concluded by recognising the environment, ethos, management, care and education of the residents as 'very good.' We had achieved our ambition that, after seven years of high risk, blood, sweat and tears, our school was recognised as a centre of excellence. It took quite a time to sink in. As I was now approaching sixty-five, the stresses and demands of those years, and the vast driving distances, had certainly taken their toll on me and the younger Vernon so, after long discussions and consultations, we decided to start the long process of selling the business. We offered the Head, Mark Ferguson, the opportunity to buy us out if he was interested. He came back fairly quickly to say he had found some investors that would join him, so negotiations commenced and were completed in April 2000 when we were able to pay off the personal mortgages that had weighed so heavily on us. A fair sale price was agreed, a little in excess of twice the purchase price. Vernon bought me out of Aran Care soon afterwards.

Before embarking on this extraordinary project, I would have opposed private provision both politically and professionally, seeing it as primarily a profit making enterprise where the care of residents came way down the list. Whilst I retain my general political view, our experience was exactly the opposite. The care of the pupils was always our first consideration, and profits were reinvested in the environment, recruitment of good staff and training. When I think about my eventual share of 'the profit,' I see it in relation to the eight years of severe anxiety and total commitment involved and the reward it gave Ann and me for all those years. Her initial comments that working in the private sector would give her back a happy and carefree husband had never been realised until now. As a consequence, while I listen to academics and fellow professionals rail against profit making care, I accept their general ignorance and ask myself the question 'Have you ever risked your home, your security and your health to achieve a centre of excellence for some of the most challenging people in our community?' I fear that there are few such establishments left, as time has seen them bought out by large consortia, often owned by equity firms.

Rowan

While all this was going on I was, as per our agreement, having to build up my consultancy to secure a reasonable income. Whilst the HAS visits continued I was undertaking work from the Isle of Man to Kent and in the process working through two more junk cars, each lasting just a year. These were mostly consultancies on management issues and inquiries into poor practice in social services and health related work. This included a project in Kensington and Chelsea looking at the roles of social workers and occupational therapists. In 1990 I started working as external examiner for social work courses, a role I enjoyed as it revived the exciting days in Maidstone (see Chapter 10). It was demanding and very poorly paid but at least seasonal. In the next few years I acted in this capacity for universities in Paisley, Plymouth, Sheffield and Durham. Sometime in 1992 Trevor directed me towards the role of expert witness, a demanding role which called on both my professional knowledge and the obsessional aspects of my personality. About this time, while sunning himself in Spain, Vernon met a guy whose firm awarded British Standards certification, among which was the BS5705 for efficient management.[61n] One night at the school saw me writing all the names that indicated quality and expertise and when Vernon arrived we toyed with Ashley or Maynard for our new consultancy, eventually deciding to combine them as Ashley Maynard Associates. The first task was to adapt the industrial specifications for the health and care sector which the main national company approved so that we could then accept customers referred to us by the firm. These visits, which ranged across statutory services, voluntary agencies, the NHS and private hospitals, were very interesting indeed. The process was two-fold, first to go through the maintenance procedures ensuring a safe environment then the management systems. The overriding purpose was to ensure that all potential issues that could damage residents, staff or the organisation were eliminated. These steps could lead the organisation to reduce anxiety and streamline their management. Developing the necessary steps before our final accreditation visits had gone one of two ways. Some produced a thick file of detailed processes; others had slimmed down to a thin all-purpose system. While both could gain the prized award, our favourites were the latter. We certainly remember an NHS hospital in South London which took some days to evaluate; we eventually faced the Chair of the Management Board to tell him the good news. His immediate reaction was to pick up the phone to Downing Street with the message 'Tell Margaret we've got it!'

As I think we were one of very few expert witness companies in the field of social care and special education we were very busy indeed; consequently, we recruited a small team of experts within specific areas of work and distributed the work among us. This was well paid work, and between 1993 and 2001 some 155 reports were completed. I should explain that the work was very time consuming due to the large files of care and legal papers all of which had to be combed in great detail to provide an accurate and foolproof report. On more than one occasion files arrived in large boxes loaded into a white van! Also cases would drag on year after year with revisions along the way as the legal arguments changed or more evidence was discovered. My records show that we won 138 of these cases, which ranged from abuse of residents, through injuries of residential care staff to industrial tribunals, etc. Very few required appearance in court to give evidence in person, but when they did I discovered, much to my surprise, that I found the cut and thrust of argument both exciting and very enjoyable, especially if a barrister could be put down. I remember one unfortunate lawyer in a case centred on the restraint of a child. He must have noted my age and smart suit – obviously completely out of touch. 'Mr Jordan, can you please tell the court the last time that you actually restrained a child?' Thanks to Aran Hall I was able to reply 'Last week, sir.'

We were involved in some high profile cases, three of which reflected the massive changes in residential child care. As social service departments implemented plans to close local children's homes and look to family or foster care they had no option but to send the few children presenting challenging behaviour or requiring specialist care to specialist establishments, often a long way away from their families. Whilst Aran Hall School was one of these it was unique in having a long experience in such care. Unfortunately other establishments admitted these children without preparing or training staff or reviewing their care policies and provision to match the new situation. This was behind some issues at Hawksworth Hall in Yorkshire run by SCOPE (formerly the Spastic Society). We prepared reports for parents of children who had been abused by a particular member of staff. Difficulties also occurred at Stoke Place in Buckinghamshire where lax registration had enabled the admission of adults aged from early 20s to over 70.[62n] Both these situations hit the headlines as national scandals, but underlying them were the cracks between the three responsible elements: the placing authority whose social worker was required to visit to check the welfare and progress of individual residents; the registering authority who was responsible for approving the physical environment and all aspect of the care provision; and the organisation which owned and managed the day to day care.

In 1998 Vernon and I decided to try our hand at mediation and enrolled on a residential qualifying course held in Switzerland with the Centre for Effective Dispute Resolution (CEDR). Off we went with our wives, and we managed to explore the area as well as pursue our qualifications. The group of some twenty-five students roughly divided themselves into two camps: those with some general interest in the humanities and lawyers, who had great difficulty leaving their contested court room behind. Nonetheless we anticipated that as mediation became more accepted it would be the lawyers who would dominate the market, which has proved to be correct. Before that

I had carried out some corporate mediation and later specialised in disputes between parents seeking special provision for their child with disabilities.

As the reader may have realised, I needed more support, so I sought a part time secretary who could keep records, work the computer, deal with the post, answer the phone, etc. etc. After a couple of false starts the good humoured Steven Primrose-Smith arrived, straight from a demanding job in technical design in Germany. Among other achievements he designed an amazingly good brochure for the school.[63n] In turn he was replaced by the excellent Pat Rostron, a former maths teacher who patiently organised all my files, tracked progress and sorted all my work for many years ahead, including the early chapters of this book. In this same period I combined with others, including Vernon and Ann, Phil Lee (from the Maidstone years), Sheila Udall and David Walton (former Lancashire training officers), David Gambe (writer and principal social worker) and Robert Adams (author and professor of social work) to submit proposals for a review of the Diploma in Social Work for CCETSW. No stronger team could be assembled (even if, given the location of the participants, our submission was compiled in the service station on the M62). We also sought to carry out the Department of Health's ambition to set national standards in social services. Both had very positive feedback but we lost both bids! Two further projects illustrate the extraordinary scope of the work I was undertaking.

Royd Edge School

I was appointed by the Area Child Protection Committee (ACPC) for Kirklees to run an inquiry into the circumstances in which a member of staff had abused children in the Royd Edge School, along with the management context and the care arrangements in the school, and to make recommendations. The excellent Stephen Sharp from Leeds worked with me. (I had previously worked with Sheila Poupard, Director of Wandsworth SSD, examining the employment by Sheffield of a staff member who had abused children in his care. In both these cases the offender had already been convicted.) Before we started, a TV crew was dispatched to Higher Studlehurst to film me 'working' and calling for witnesses wishing to discuss any issues about the school to come forward on the confidential phone number provided. I also emphasised the promise already announced by the local authority that our report would be published as soon as possible. The inquiry covered an intensive six months of interviews from the painfully related experiences of the young children to staff at all levels, including departmental managers and directors. We discussed progress with a small group from the ACPC and submitted interim reports as we went along. The core of our findings was the fact that this large residential school, managed by a powerful head teacher, had been allowed to become isolated from the normal management processes, despite clear warnings that things were going seriously wrong. A second key factor was the lack of care staff with any qualifications and their poor morale as a direct result of their treatment by the Head. He had been able to manipulate different sections of the council's main departments to avoid serious intervention. Our final recommendations concentrated on correcting these management failures and implementing child protection arrangements. When we presented our final report to the Chief Executive he was extremely angry and announced that the report would be kept in his safe never to be seen again! In view of the frequent interaction with the ACPC, where previously no significant issues had been identified, this response came as a considerable shock. We realised that it was likely that the report would never be published, despite the great promises that had been made Our report was not the only one to experience this fate. In particular, John Jillings had conducted a much larger inquiry into abuse at a number of care homes in Clwyd. The suspicion in both cases was that the powerful insurance company covering most local authorities was threatening to withdraw cover if critical reports were published. In subsequent correspondence with John, he sent me a quote from Bernard Shaw's *Saint Joan*: 'He who tells too much truth will surely be hanged.' Barbara Kahan subsequently became involved in correspondence with central government to stop this iniquitous use of financial threats.[64n]

Royd Edge School was closed in September 1995. I think our report was eventually used in court cases by the abused children. I campaigned in writing to Herbert Laming, who was then the Chief Inspector at the Department of Health, by sending long letters to *Community Care,* by speaking at the National Conference for Health and Social Services, held in Bath, called 'Inspection 2000,' and also at a very badly attended workshop at the annual SSD Directors Conference. The underlying theme was my anger at the fact that, by and large, all the many investigations highlighted the same issues and nothing was being done to tackle them on a national scale. The whole thing is now in the hands of the major established Independent Inquiry into Child Sexual Abuse launched by the government in March 2015.

Paydens Ltd

In Lancashire we had been advising our builder friend Rod Wilkins and his wife – they had developed their small home for elderly people into facilities for independent living and were now interested in building a purpose built home for the care of elderly people. Rod accomplished this in fine form on a site very close to the main hospital in Blackburn. It provided excellent care. In Kent Trevor was providing legal advice to Dennis Pay who wished to build a residential home for elderly and infirm people in memory of his grandmother Betsy Clara. Trevor suggested that he come to Lancashire to learn what he could from Rod's home, and in due course I met Dennis and his architect Alvin in Preston, where I piloted them through Rod's establishment for the day and took them back to the station late in the evening. They were very impressed. Paydens was a large, wholesale chemists which imported and exported a wide range of pharmaceuticals and associated personal grooming products. They also owned a number of chemist shops throughout Kent. Thus started a long, exciting and challenging association.

Once plans were drawn up for the difficult site in central Maidstone, we arranged an appointment with the Deputy Director of Kent SSD who was somewhat overwhelmed that such a great purpose built project was about to land on his doorstep and indicated that he would have no difficulty in using the facilities. Betsy Clara House was eventually opened in May 1995. Feeling a bit out of my depth I sought out the knowledgeable and outspoken Jim Kavanagh from the old Health Advisory Service teams, and we worked together over the next few years carrying out inspections and supporting managers. Our main problem was the exhausting travelling from our homes in Lancashire and Rochdale to Kent.

Two years before Betsy Clara House opened Dennis phoned me to say that he had bought a property and would appreciate my opinion on its viability as another residential home. This turned out to be a large old vicarage in Grange Road, Eastbourne, just a few doors away from where Mum and John had lived. The first shock was noticing that their little semi-detached house was still called 'The Jordans'! The property had been used as a base for a number of therapeutic businesses but was now empty. The architect was doubtful and I agreed that this was not a suitable building for elderly people. However, on the long journey home I thought that, within current policies, the new purchaser/provider split, the ability of GPs to buy services, plus referrals from private insurance companies and a few self-payers, might mean it would be possible to open this place as a community facility with some beds for the care and treatment of people with a mental illness. I put these thoughts together on a one page note to Dennis and received the brief reply 'Get on with it'! So, in addition to Aran Hall and all the other activities outlined above, it was my responsibility to get this whole project launched, help design the facility and its procedures, recruit staff, obtain registration and make it a viable business, all at a distance of 300 miles. I certainly managed to sample many of the local cheap local hotels on my many visits.

The process was demanding. Once the costly design, decor and furnishings had been approved, the issues of registration, staffing and publicity had to be tackled. The first blow was the requirement to install a lift, despite our protests that our patients would be young and fit. It was duly installed at great expense and delay. Interviews for the manager, senior nurse and staff were completed, and it was good to experience Ann, Dennis and Jim working together, although it all took a lot of time. I found an excellent logo designer in Brighton who produced three options, one of which was adopted immediately. Finding a local doctor for medical checks on admission and routine physical care was not too difficult, but, as I had expected, recruiting consultant psychiatrists was a nightmare. Under their NHS contracts they were allowed a percentage of their time for private practice. We argued and bargained away both on the level of their remuneration and how it was paid to avoid excessive tax. The whole thing annoyed Dennis who had never encountered such medics or such personalities before, but they and he both knew we could not open without them. Eventually we held a reception for local medics, hospital managers and the press before the grand opening on December 13th 1993.

To say that admissions were queuing up would be a great overstatement – in fact they dribbled in, forcing the managers to design innovative short term treatments that would be of interest to local GPs, including for alcoholism, drug abuse and anxiety reduction techniques. We were registered to admit a wide range of psychiatric patients and were accepted on the list of approved suppliers by all nearby health authorities. In the beginning hospitals only used the clinic when it suited them, which meant when an acutely ill patient arrived, perhaps in the early hours, and they were short of staff. Many months went by as the losses piled up but Dennis was pretty patient, only occasionally determining the need to cut expenditure and rev up our publicity. At these meetings we always asked Dennis how many chemist shops he now owned, the numbers growing from the 20 or so to over 60 over just a few years. His wholesale export and import business, his retail outlets, Betsy Clara House and now the Eastbourne Clinic represented a complex and large company and yet if one visited his headquarters in Maidstone you would find him tucked modestly away in a makeshift office in the corner of the warehouse. He was a kind and modest man with a wonderful family with whom I stayed happily from time to time. Jim and I had an ongoing responsibility to support the managers, monitor standards of care and report regularly to Dennis. Slowly the clinic became established and showed a profit, at which point Dennis talked about setting up another one. We also explored sites for a secure mental health unit and a residential unit for challenging young people, but none of these happened before I retired, although I notice that the Eastbourne Clinic has since become a clinic specialising in the care and treatment of mothers and babies.

FAMILY

As will be clear from previous chapters, family life had been under a lot of strain, but Higher Studlehurst was a haven for me, although once I started the consultancy work it very much intruded. Ann provided extraordinary support, as did friends who all helped nurse me through my depressed period, but above all the house and its surroundings were both restful and distractingly busy. At that time everything at home and work seemed devoid of feeling, slightly at a distance, as though on the far side of a glass wall. The horse, donkey, hens and geese kept us busy, and the dogs, the loveable Scoobie and the mischievous Lizzie, were great company. We were at home with the surrounding farmer's families, the Taylors and Hewitts down by the river, and, of course, the Brocklehursts with whom we were closely involved. Incredibly, as Brian Brocklehurst's wife Jill's undiagnosed health continued to deteriorate he found her a hospital in London where she could get special pressurised oxygen treatment. He would drive down to London to be with her for the treatments, sleep in the car, drive home in time to do the early milk rounds and run the farm; devoted madness. His mother, the lovely Annie, cared for her grandchildren with some help from us although she herself was not in the best of health. As our finances improved, we had the great 'George,' an ex-submariner, to help us with our large garden. He specialised in cutting the lawns, often in the pouring rain! We also recruited a local woman to help with routine cleaning and, in a sign of the times, eventually coached her in setting herself up as a small business offering a range of domiciliary care to a large catchment area.

Our friends the Schofield twins could not have been more different in personality. Colin, who occasionally worked for us, was a quiet, kind man, while his brother Gordon was fiery with a tendency to be paranoid, although, as it turned out not without cause. He and his wife accompanied us to a performance of *The Rocky Horror Show* and on the way home we were pleased to see that they were holding hands, a peaceful act in a very stormy marriage. The next morning Gordon was on the phone in a great rage to tell us that his wife had left him and had told him that she had been having an affair for some time. Help! Ann, who was always fearlessly magnificent in a crisis, grabbed a bottle of whisky, well aware that there were guns and hunting knives in the house. He had to be calmed down and restrained at all costs. It transpired that the arrangements for his wife and lover to meet had gone wrong and the lover had phoned the police fearful for her safety when she failed to turn up. The consequence was the arrival of two policemen at the house to find a very angry man and Ann, who they naturally assumed to be the wife being held against her wishes! All was finally explained to their satisfaction.

A variety of professionals seemed to drift towards our house when in trouble including good social workers who had been dismissed or denied promotion for clearly unjustified reasons. Other distress calls were less dramatic although they were emotionally desperate in different ways. These included a well qualified medical consultant fighting a discriminatory campaign to have him dismissed from the local hospital. During the 1992 general election Ann's friend Diana, a rather snobbish controlling woman who Ann always mocked by addressing her in person or by letter as 'Lady Diana,' was desperate to join a major rally of faithful Tories where her idol, the charismatic Michael Heseltine, was speaking to a members only gathering. So off we went to the appointed place. Heseltine arrived by helicopter and entered the tent to great acclaim. My joy was to see the disbelieving reaction to my presence of the top county Conservatives who had shafted me out of the directorship basically on the assumed grounds that I was a loyal Labour Party member. Once the speech was over we made a quick exit.

Juliet, having successfully graduated, remained in Sheffield. In due course she met Rod Edge, a fellow graduate in arts and media, and eventually she drove across the Pennines with him to meet us. It did not go well. Ann and I had developed good relationships with most of Juliet's previous teenage boyfriends but she had developed the habit of suddenly dropping them so that the good relationships we had made were suddenly lost. We had decided never to make that mistake again with any future boyfriends. On this occasion, however, Juliet had taken the precaution of warning us that Rod was 'very sensitive' so we were to be very careful how we treated him. The weekend is remembered by Rod as 'the weekend when nobody spoke to me,' a wild exaggeration about which we have since shared many a long laugh, especially when retelling it to their teenage children.

They moved to London, where Rod had spent his teenage years as a member of a small but committed punk band, before heading to Sheffield where he was sent for six months to the world famous Polish Film School in Lodz, then under the direction of the great Andrzej Wajda. In London they slowly and painfully managed to find work in the media industry. In June 1991 their daughter Aella Jewell Anne was born, of course as a natural home birth, against the advice of the GP for a first baby. At that time they were living in a ground floor flat in West London and we were invited down for the event. By the time we arrived Juliet had been in labour for some time and had exhausted herself in the deep water pool they had purchased for the event. We moved to the lounge where the heating was full on and the lighting dim, but at least there were two midwives present to ensure that all was well. As the hours went by and our precious daughter was exhaustively writhing and pushing we were getting increasingly worried. There was a selection of herbal unguents in the kitchen and from time to time Rod, now stripped to his waist, was sent to apply them to the naked form on the floor. Ann sat rigidly with a determined look sending powerful mental messages to the baby to come out. At one point I was dispatched to make tea for all except Juliet but as the kitchen was dark I failed to notice that I was pouring banana milk into the cups! By the early hours it was becoming clear that this could not go on so a midwife called an ambulance and we followed it to Edgware Hospital. It was a tremendously emotional experience; the tears fell as Juliet placed the newborn on her chest and sung 'You Are My Sunshine.' Then a very sleepy young gynaecologist arrived to repair the damage and Juliet asked for an ambulance to return home; it was 02:30 hrs and we were all completely exhausted. But we were grandparents!

This role brought a hilarious incident some weeks later when Juliet and baby were staying with us. Earlier, at the request of the police, we had entertained a visiting group of seven female police officers from Bahrain. They walked down the drive, led by the captain, in order of seniority. The idea was that they sample an English home and tea. Of course, I was banished to the billiard room! Some days later Juliet arrived with the new baby and we were invited to a thank you party at police HQ in Preston. Ann was not at all well and Juliet badly wanted to meet up with her friends for an evening as a first escape from intense baby care. I therefore volunteered to take the baby with me to the party. All the essential baby products were packed into a bright pink basket and we set off in a taxi. Arriving at the club Juliet got out and suddenly sprayed me all over with her scent 'so that the baby won't worry.' Consequently I arrived at this impressive building, where I had previously arrived with the authority of a Chief Officer, with a small baby and a bright pink plastic basket with bottles, nappies etc. and smelling delightfully of Chanel No 5. I think I was promoted to be an honorary woman and, of course, Aella was passed round, enjoying all the attention. We had a memorable evening! A few months later, I was in London doing a Health Advisory Service visit when Juliet needed help making a pop video with Sinéad O'Connor and Jah Wobble in a nearby studio so I was on duty again, sitting quietly above the work nursing my lovely granddaughter.

By 1993 Rod, Juliet and Aella were living off the Finchley Road near Swiss Cottage; the following year, while Rod's career as a film director was progressing, Juliet was accepted into the National Film and Television School near Beaconsfield for a two-year course, although it was a long journey from their home. This was an amazing opportunity, which she made the best of for her future career; quite how they both managed, particularly Rod, with a lively three-year-old and the need to accept every job available, amazes me to this day. We travelled down there whenever we could. Juliet made wonderful films which drew on her natural talent to quietly develop the trusting relationships required for a true documentary. She completed three excellent films: one on the timeless World Conker Championships in the village of Ashton in Northamptonshire; another on an investigation of a woman's unit of the Territorial Army entitled *A Weekend Away*; and an intimate portrayal of a traditional English village, part of the estate of the delightful Dame Miriam Rothschild MBE, but facing the arrival of new families who commute out to work every day.

Juliet's final production was a tribute to my brother, her Uncle John. This involved researching the large amount of film and video that he had left and some painful interviews with Ann and me. I also think it was challenging for Juliet as her emotional involvement made it difficult to cut and edit her work into a coherent film for the fast approaching Diploma Show at the BFI cinema on the South Bank. In 1997 we arrived at the cinema to see all the students' final films, quietly nursing our beautiful new grandson Duke Stanley Spencer Jordan-Edge who had arrived quickly and without drama early in the morning of June 4th in the Royal Free Hospital, Hampstead. Suddenly there on the large screen was my brother, our old house in Lanbury Road, Higher Studlehurst, and Ann and I sobbing quietly away. Shocking and amazing at the same time, but a wonderful tribute to John and an achievement for Juliet who had determinedly completed the course and the film in the face of emotional and physical exhaustion. The film gained an award as the most outstanding student film in the ethnographic tradition from the Royal Anthropological Society.

In 1994, we decided that, having been broke for our 25th wedding anniversary, we could now afford to treat ourselves to a long break as a reward. Consequently we left Heathrow on a flight to Egypt on the first stop on an individually planned itinerary. Arriving in Cairo at night we wondered how we might see the pyramids but pulling the blinds back next morning there they were, right next to us! We had a great guide round all the sites, including the main museum where you could almost touch the golden masks and statues on show. Ann fell in love with Cairo – I suspect it was the eccentric driving and the jostling between cars, lorries and donkey carts on the roads. We then did a fascinating cruise from Luxor to the Aswan Dam before jetting off to Nairobi, where we had a few eventful days in town and an exhausting but exhilarating safari in the Masai Mara. Our small plane back allowed me to film the pilot landing us in Nairobi to add to all the videos so far taken. Our last stop was in the Seychelles islands, and a chance to meet up with the guys from my national service days (see Chapter 6). There were plenty of reunions, and Ann and I had a magical time totally relaxing on the beaches. Once news of our arrival spread, old friends from 1952 came along to reminisce. When those units had been disbanded the islands had suffered badly from unemployment and since then the government had been as near communist as it is possible to get. The lads had clear memories of the opening of the airport in March 1972, which had been built to open up the tourist trade and save the economy. It was opened by the Queen and Prince Philip on a brief stop en route to Mauritius. They recalled Prince Philip recognising their great contributions to the war, particularly in the fiercely fought North African campaign, but he had also pointed out that if they expected any help from him there was nothing he could do – they then climbed back into the plane and flew away!

Back home the busy life resumed. Ann was now on the board of the North West Regional Health Authority, which she was enjoying. She loved having contact with GPs, dentists and opticians in addition to the routine work of planning hospital services. She was the only female on the board and, of course, spoke up using her extensive experience. Unfortunately, this attracted some pretty misogynistic comments from the Chair. I have lost count of the number of apologetic letters that she received. One of the main decisions taken by the Authority was which of the two large hospitals for people with a learning disability they would have to close, given the few patients remaining. After much agonising, and I suspect a lot of lobbying from Calderstones Hospital where staff had achieved national recognition for their work with the normalisation campaigns, Brockhall Hospital with its extensive grounds was put up for sale. As the process was beyond recall, the well known property tycoon Gerald Hitman pointed out that, overlooked by the NHS, he owned a lease on the main driveway into the site, and that consequently it had to be sold to him for a much reduced price. He subsequently built a large, gated housing estate which includes his magnificent house 'The Old Zoo,' the training ground of Blackburn Rovers and a small hotel. Gerald and the hotel would intrude into our lives eight years later.

As our finances improved we settled back to improving the house and gardens, as well as going on theatre visits and regular trips abroad with Ann's sister Joan, visiting Turkey, Northern Cyprus and Spain. We had an enjoyable time with Brian Brocklehurst and Ian Clarkson in Istanbul including a hilarious time in the historic Turkish Bath. We also resumed our large New Year parties when all the local farming families and other friends joined us to celebrate. In these years Ann and I went to Barcelona and also took a long tour of America by car, train, boat and aircraft from Niagara Falls, through Boston, to New York and down to New Orleans, then round the pan handle to St Petersburg in Florida, where we spent time with my elderly cousin Hetty Miller.

A remarkable event was the news that Jack Berry, having become Mayor of Blackburn in June 2001 and still a regular Sunday billiards visitor, had gone on a cruise – to my mind anything less suited to Jack was hard to think of. I had worked closely with Jack for many years, and I'd noted his tight hair and attributed his light tan to a touch of malaria during the war. It later transpired that his grandmother had been the first black woman to arrive in Blackburn with her Irish husband who had freed her from slavery, and apparently his brother's local nickname was 'Blackie'! His 'cruise' was a trip to trace his grandparents' story. And you think you know people.

Once the final proceeds from the sale of the school and Aran Care were in we could think about options, including increasing our security by increasing our pension funds. During a regular holiday in Cornwall, I drew Ann's attention to a small advert for a house for sale right down by the cove in Cadgwith, which had been our main holiday destination for nearly forty years and was where her father had been headmaster. We checked it out, only to find that it was very liable to severe flooding, the walls were made of asbestos and the thatched roof needed repair. Not for us, but of course the thought had been planted so we checked out the agents in Helston and lo and behold there was a modern house for sale a little further away from the cove. We liked it and bought it, and it has provided endless enjoyment for our families and friends ever since.

For some time we had been thinking of moving south, both to be nearer our family in London and to gain a few valuable degrees of temperature, as Ann was beginning to feel the cold badly. In November 1998 we sold Higher Studlehurst and moved into a smaller modern bungalow, Elker Lodge, near Whalley. We spent money on acquiring extra land, tunnelling out the mill stream that ran through the garden and making a large pond for the geese and ducks. There was a large boarded attic which I thought would make a great office so Colin Schofield and I set about covering the rafters with 6 x 8 ft sheets of plasterboard. It nearly killed us both. In theory we were well matched by my height and Colin's slighter build, but holding the heavy sheets high up while the other put sufficient fixing to take the weight was just too much. Once finished though it made a spacious and convenient office.

In early 2001 in a tribute to our gardener George I promised to take him to Faslane for the centenary celebration of the submarine service so, joined by his nephew and Colin, we headed for Glasgow and found a welcoming pub for B & B. After quite an alcoholic evening and a true Scottish breakfast we drove to Faslane. It was a busy, interesting day as submarines from round the world were there, many open to visitors. George, proudly displaying an array of medals, caught the eye of the Navy News and was interviewed on television. A great day for a gallant man.

We then started to look for a suitable house in an area roughly bounded by Bristol in the west, Swindon in the east and south of Cirencester. This seemed to us to be near, but not too near, the family in London and not that far from our newly acquired Cornish house. After a few trips we found a good agent in Malmesbury who came to appreciate what we were looking for, and eventually we settled on a smaller version of Higher Studlehurst in Lower Stanton St Quintin, just north of the M4, junction 17. Having sold Elker Lodge we set off early on September 11th 2001 and drove south with our personal possessions in a small white van with no radio. Hence we drove all day completely ignorant of the terrible events that would change the world for the foreseeable future.

Meanwhile, the immediate future was not looking good. The fall of the Berlin Wall had, with the help of neo-liberalism, given the green light to globalisation and the dominance of free market philosophy into every aspect of our national life. In this situation the gap between the very wealthy and the poor steadily increased, both in financial and cultural terms. In Britain the wealthy saw the top marginal rate of tax fall from 82% to 40%. Greed was seen as good. Meanwhile the growing underclass were portrayed as the victims of their own inadequacy and welfare recipients as undeserving of help. By and large, social attitudes swung with the government; if we are individuals fighting to get rich then the phrase 'I'm alright Jack,' naturally followed. For those at the bottom of the social scale insecurity could lead to unrest, violence and distrust of the police. Here 32% of children would live in poor households compared with 13% in Germany and 12% in France.[65] Child poverty trebled in 20 years.[66]

NOTES AND REFERENCES

1. Dahrendorf, R., Field, F., Hayman, C. et al. (1995). *Report on Wealth Creation and Social Cohesion in a Free Society*. London: Commission on Wealth Creation and Social Cohesion, p. 15.
2. Elliot, L. and Atkinson, D. (1999). *The Age of Insecurity*. London: Verso, p. 250.
3. Hobsbawm, E. (1995). *Age of Extremes 1914–1991*. London: Abacus, p. 479.
4. This section has drawn on material from Wright, L. (2006). *The Looming Tower: Al-Qaeda and the Road to 9/11*. New York: Knopf.
5. Marwick, A. (1996). *British Society Since 1945*. London: Penguin, p. 360.
6. The Clause was eventually repealed in September 2003. In 2009, David Cameron, the Conservative Prime Minister apologised that his party had passed the law and said that it was a mistake and offensive to gay people. Within the next few years it became clear that many of the new academies set up by the government were effectively reintroducing the policy.
7. Hansard HC Deb. Vol 152 Col 1013–1100. May 11th 1989.
8. Lowe, R. (2005). *The Welfare State in Britain Since 1945*. London: Palgrave Macmillan, pp. 326, 354–357.
9. Hansard HC Deb. Vol 180 Col 461–465. November 13th 1990.
10. UNICEF (1993). *Progress of Nations*. New York: UNICEF.
11. I found this information in a 1992 publication called 'Poverty Undermining Rights in the UK' published by Justice. It seems this is not available in the Justice archives.
12. I found this information in a 1991 publication called 'For Richer or Poorer' published by IFS. It seems this is not available in the IFS archives.
13. Marwick, *op.cit.*, p. 356. Hidden in these figures is the cost of state pensions which the government had treated relatively well, this section of the population being more inclined to vote Conservative. The effect on the NHS was therefore more severe.
14. The treaty was signed on February 7th 1992 and became effective in November 1993. It established the European Union, led to the Euro as a single currency and defined three pillars covering the economy, foreign policy and justice and home affairs. It took many months of tense parliamentary debate, with reluctant Tories (urged on by an angry Mrs Thatcher) joining with Labour, before the Treaty could finally be ratified. In an interview John Major referred to the right-wing committed anti-Europeans as 'those bastards.'
15. Turner, A. (2013). *A Classless Society; Britain in the 1990s*. London: Aurum Press.
16. Marwick, *op. cit.*, p. 408.

17. Hamilton took legal action against *The Guardian* and Mohamed Al-Fayed (the owner of Harrods) and lost both cases. In 1997 he and his wife Christine started careers as TV personalities. He became a leading member of the United Kingdom Independence Party (UKIP) under Nigel Farage and played a significant part in the campaign for the UK to leave Europe in 2016. That same year he was elected as a member of the Welsh National Assembly.
18. Bovine spongiform encephalopathy (BSE), which was commonly known as mad cow disease, could be transmitted between cattle and in some circumstances to humans. The disease attacks the brain and spinal cord and incubates for several years before signs appear. Although it spread worldwide, Europe was hit hardest due to the fact that it relied to varying degrees on mass produced cattle feed which contained the ground up bones of dead animals. The UK infection rate of 183,841 far exceeded that of any other country (France had 900 cases and Ireland 1353) due to our intense dairy farming practices. Some time after I left Lancashire, I was told that Tom Foster had very tragically died of BSE. I do wonder therefore whether some of the events that happened in Lancashire were caused by the early, unrecognised effects of the disease. It's a very distressing thought.
19. Wilkinson, H. and Mulgan, G. (1995). *Freedom's Children: Work, Relationships and Politics for 18–34 Year Olds in Britain.* London: Demos.
20. Public pressure led to the Home Secretary increasing the minimum time in custody to 15 years, although this was overturned by the House of Lords. Subsequent appeals to the European Court of Human Rights criticised the process by which eleven year olds were tried in an adult court. One of the boys was held at Red Bank secure unit. Both boys were released in 2001. In 2010 one was returned to prison on charges of child pornography. See James, D. J. (2011). *The Sleep of Reason: The Bulger Case.* London: Faber & Faber; Thomas, M. (1993). *Every Mother's Nightmare: The Killing of James Bulger.* London: Pan.
21. Macpherson, W. (1999). *Inquiry Into the Matters Arising From the Death of Stephen Lawrence.* National Archive, Cmnd 4262. Ellison, M. QC (2012). *Stephen Lawrence Independent Review.* On February 7th 2008, the Stephen Lawrence Centre was opened in Lewisham. Stephen's parents have, over the years, acted with great dignity, and his mother Doreen has run the Stephen Lawrence Charitable Trust. In 2012 Doreen was awarded a Lifetime Achievement Award at the 14th Pride of Britain Awards. In 2013 she was appointed as a baroness, sitting on the Labour benches in the House of Lords. New evidence resulted in two of Lawrence's assailants being imprisoned at Her Majesty's pleasure. In July 2016 the police, still investigating other members of the gang who were not convicted, released a new video image in a call for witnesses. In 2018, the Prime Minister Theresa May declared that April 22nd would become Stephen Lawrence day, an annual commemoration of Stephen's death. That same year Doreen Lawrence launched The Stephen Lawrence Day Foundation, a charity structured around classroom, communities and careers.
22. From research by Prof. John Pitts, published in *The Guardian* 11.12.1966, p. 11.
23. Philip Lawrence was granted the Queen's Gallantry Medal in June 1997; an awards charity was established by his wife to honour outstanding achievement by young people between the ages of 11 and 20.
24. Four days after the incident, *The Sun* carried a headline blaming the deaths and other criminal acts on drunken Liverpool fans. The story was based on information given by a Conservative MP who said the police had told him 'the truth.' Most newsagents in Liverpool boycotted the newspaper. Fifteen years later after full inquiries had been completed *The Sun* apologised without reservation. In December 2009 the Labour Home Secretary formed a panel to oversee the complete disclosure of all evidence. It was chaired by the Bishop of Liverpool. In September 2012 the panel concluded that no Liverpool fans were responsible for the events. They concluded that 41 of the dead would have been saved if the emergency services had acted properly and that there was widespread evidence that police records and witness statements had been interfered with.

The Hillsborough Support Group called for new inquests and prosecutions of all those responsible. New inquests were concluded in 2016 with a verdict of unlawful killing. The senior police officer Norman Bettison resigned. Prosecutions against senior police and other key people all failed. *The Sun* remains boycotted in Liverpool.

25. Diana's brother's eulogy reflected public anger at how the royal family had treated her. Following the funeral, the royal family retreated north to Balmoral in order to protect and support Diana's sons, but, as the banks of flowers grew outside Buckingham Palace, the public interpreted this as a failure to recognise their expression of grief, particularly as the Union Jack was not at half mast. Eventually the Queen returned to see the flowers and speak to members of the public. These events, and the public appearances of Prince Charles and Camilla Parker-Bowles, provided a minor constitutional crisis. As time has passed, and Charles and Camilla were married, careful and highly skilled PR has done much to retrieve the crown, helped enormously by celebrations for the Queen's Diamond Jubilee in 2012 and later her 90th birthday in 2016. Shining through all this has been the maturing of her sons William and Harry who seem to command public respect. There is much speculation about whether, when the Queen dies, Charles or William will be accepted as King.
26. Elliot, L. and Atkinson, D. (1998). *The Age of Insecurity*. London: Verso, p. 211.
27. Mo Mowlam was no ordinary politician; she used all her qualities to bring both sides of the Northern Ireland conflict together. Faced with intransigence on either side, she could swear with the best of them and if desperate she would whip off the wig that covered her loss of hair due to her treatment for a cancerous brain tumour. When it was clear that a hard core of prisoners in the notorious Maze Prison was causing a blockage she bravely entered the prison to hammer out a deal. As Blair and Clinton met during the final stages, she reverted to pouring the tea, commenting to Clinton that she was the new tea girl. She died in August 2005. See *Mo*, a much acclaimed docudrama film about Mo Mowlam shown on Channel 4 in January 2010 with Julie Walters playing the politician.
28. Speech in April 1999 to the Economic Club; see www.pbs.org.
29. *Your Right to Know*, Cm 3818.
30. Timmins, N. 'The Five Giants,' quoted in Lowe, *op. cit.*, p. 387.
31 Lowe, *op. cit.*, p. 407.
32. *Only Fools and Horses*, written by John Sullivan, starring David Jason, Nicholas Lyndhurst and Buster Merryfield. It ran from 1981 to 2003 on BBC1.
33. *Bread*, written by Carla Lane, starred Jean Boht and Peter Howitt. It ran from 1986 to 1991 on BBC1.
34. *The Royle Family*, written by Caroline Aherne, starring Ricky Tomlinson, Sue Johnston and Caroline Aherne, ran from 1998 to 2000.
35. *One Foot in the Grave*, written by David Renwick, starring Richard Wilson and Annette Crosby. It ran from 1990 to 2000 on BBC1.
36. *House of Cards*, written by Michael Dobbs, adapted by Andrew Davies, starred Ian Richardson and Susan Harker. Directed by Paul Seed. BBC 1990.
37. *Trainspotting*, from a book by Irvine Welsh, starring Ewan McGregor, Ewen Bremner, Robert Carlyle and Jonny Lee Miller. Produced by Channel Four Films. Released in 1996.
38. *Me and My Girl*, by L. Arthur Rose and Dougles Furber. Manchester production, directed by Mike Ockrent, starring Gary Wilmot and Jessica Martin.
39. *Les Miserables*, based on a novel by Victor Hugo, music by Claude-Michel Schoneburg. Premiere 1980. Manchester performance directed by Trevor Nunn with Jeff Leyton as Javert.
40. *The Rocky Horror Show*, by Richard O'Brien, was launched in the Royal Court in Sloane Square in 1983. The Manchester show starred Peter Blake and Kate O'Sullivan. By the time we saw it, audience participation was high!

41. *Yanomamo, Songs of the Forest*, by Peter Rose and Ann Condon, was performed by Bury Youth Orchestra and Choir. This tribe is now at the forefront of the Amazonian battle between the indigenous people, illegal loggers, the mining operations and President Bolsonaro's policy to commercialise the rain forest, on which the world relies as a carbon sink to prevent climate disaster.
42. *Company*, by Steven Sondheim, first performed in 1970. The Manchester production was directed by Roger Haines and starred Eric Loren and Gillian Kirkpatrick.
43. *Stones in his Pockets*, by Marie Jones, was first performed in 1999. The London production was directed by Ian McElhinney and starred the promising Conleth Hill and Sean Campion.
44. *Soul Train*, by Don Cornelius, was first performed in 1971. The Manchester production by Mark Clements starred Sheila Ferguson.
45. Kabuki Japanese dance drama presented by the Chikamatsu-za company with *Love Suicides at Sonezaki* and *Tsuri Onna*, a comic tale.
46. The political and media events surrounding the construction and opening of the Millennium Dome have been dealt with above. The architect was Richard Rogers and the structure was built at a cost of £789 million, although this covered the cost of clearing the neglected and corroded site. This project was intended to develop this neglected part of London. It was meant to carry on the tradition of the Great Exhibition of 1851 and the Festival of Britain in 1951. It ran into significant financial problems due to lower than expected footfall (6.5 million against a projected 12 million), no doubt due to the adverse press campaign, although, in tune with our experience, visitor feedback was very positive. After the closure of the Millennium Show it limped on until 2001 when it was taken over by the Anschutz Entertainment Group, renamed O2 and the whole site was heavily developed with a variety of entertainment venues. It has since been used for major pop concerts, sports events etc. It is a popular and profitable enterprise.
47. The Children Act (1989). Guidance and Regulation, Vol. 3. Family Placements, HMSO.
48. *Purchase of Service Practice Guidance and Practice Material for Social Services and other Agencies.*
49. *Purchasing and Contracting Skills.* 1994 CCETSW.
50. Goffman, E. (1952). On Cooling the Mark Out: Some Aspects of Adaptation to Failure. *Psychiatry*, Vol. 15, No. 4.
51. Baldwin, M. (1996). Is Assessment Working? Policy and Practice in Care Management. *Practice*, Vol. 8, No 4.
52. Bolland, K. and Atherton, C. (1999). Chaos Theory: An Alternative Approach to Social Work Practice and Research. *Families in Society: The Journal of Contemporary Human Service*, Vol. 80, No. 4, pp. 367–373. Chaos theory, better named as the 'complexity analogy,' rejects linear cause and effect explanations and argues that social and family situations are more complex. Also, that, given the interdependence of all participants, the cause of a significant event may be found in a tiny episode buried in the situation. It gave rise to the illustration that the beating wings of a butterfly in Thailand can set off a chain of reactions that result in a shortage of taxis in London on a given Tuesday. The paper recognised that this complexity was well known to social workers who were, however, forced to express their findings in traditional linear terms. Chaos theory would require them to think outside the box.
53. *National Debate on the Future of Social Work – Creating a New Agenda.* NISW Briefing Paper 28 (1999).
54. Brand, D. and Fletcher, P. (2000). *A Guide to the Care Standards Act 2000.* London: NISW.
55. Hinchcliffe, D., MP (1995). *Social Care Sell Off.* London: The Labour Party.
56. This had been announced in a light interview printed in *Care Weekly* magazine headed *Blue Sky Social Worker*, Issue dated 09.10.1987, p. 5.
57. Whenever Care Concern was attacked in the press, attention was always drawn to the large yacht that David was building on the island. When he visited Chester, arrangements were always made for his hired aircraft to land at the nearby RAF station. David once explained to me the thrill he got

when, needing a particular pot of paint for his boat from the continent, he could get immediate delivery by private plane to the island. The power of wealth.
58. *Serious Money,* by Caryl Churchill, 1978.
59. *The Report of the Macur Review. An Independent Review of the Tribunal of Enquiry into the Abuse of Children in Care in the Former County Council Areas of Gwynedd and Clywd since 1974.* (2001). London: HMSO HC201, Chap. 38, 39, para 38.16, p. 115. By repeating the past history of the school before we were involved the report repeated past allegations of abuse. Our only contact with the enquiry was the sudden arrival of one of the officials demanding that we hand over all records from the foundation of the school. These were to be scanned, together with those of all other establishments, at a high cost. We were happy to comply, but they were stunned when Vernon refused to release all the files as some pupils were privately placed and needed parental consent. This was a revelation. We wrote a note of protest when the report was published, not that we disagreed in any way at the recommendations but how they could imply abuse at the school when none had ever happened. We also noted their call for all establishments to have a whistle blower's charter. Had they asked us, we could have told them that it was one of the first policies we introduced at Aran Hall.
60. See Thompson, N. (2015). *The Professional Social Worker: Understanding Social Work* London: Palgrave.
61. These standards originated in the military and aviation industries where every chance of an error occurring had to be foreseen. It was later used in medical settings, particularly operating theatres. This particular standard concerned management processes and was developed in the electronics industry. It is now BS6001.
62. For a brief review of these scandals, including Stoke Place, see Wetherall, J. (2007). *Community Care*, issue 10.01.2007, available online. I campaigned in speeches, articles and letters to draw attention to the few key factors which lay behind most issues of abuse to children and staff. One article in *Community Care* started with the fact that the case papers on my desk were 1.6 metres high. My letter in *The Guardian* (19.06.1996) also made the point so that many of these issues resulted from local authorities placing very challenging children in local homes which lacked the expertise and experience to look after them.
63. Steven later took to touring by bicycle. See his books *Hungry for Miles: Cycling Across Europe on £1 a Day*; *No Place Like Home, Thank God*; and *George Pearly is a Miserable Old Sod*.
64. As the extent of child abuse in the 1970s and 1980s became apparent, the abused seeking recognition and compensation found themselves facing battles both in court and with the insurance companies. They devoted large sums of money to fighting the cases which were forced into court by the companies forbidding the organisations facing allegations to make no admission and no apology. This situation led to the establishment of the Association of Child Abuse Lawyers. See 'Sorry State' by Christian Wolmar in *The Guardian* 10.3.99, p. 8. See also Gosling, P. and M D'Arcy, M. (1998). *Abuse of Trust*. London: Bowerdean.
65. A UNICEF study for the Institute of Public Policy Research released on 17.03.2000.
66. *The Guardian*, 20.03.2000, p. 1.

FIFTEEN

2001–2008

CLOSING TIME

We will direct every resource at our command – every means of diplomacy, every tool of intelligence, every instrument of law enforcement, every financial influence, and every necessary weapon of war ... to the destruction and to the defeat of the global terror network ... And we will pursue nations that provide aid or safe haven to terrorism. Every nation in every region now has a decision to make: *Either you are with us or you are with the terrorists...*

This is not, however, just America's fight ... what is at stake is not just America's freedom. This is the world's fight. This is civilization's fight... This is the fight of all who believe in progress and pluralism, tolerance and freedom... As long as the United States of America is determined and strong, this will not be an age of terror. This will be an age of liberty here and across the world.

– George W. Bush, September 20th 2001[1]

And I loved you when our love was blessed
And I love you now there's nothing left
And I just don't care what happens next
Looks like freedom but it feels like death
It's something in between I guess
It's closing time

– Leonard Cohen, 'Closing Time'[2]

INTERNATIONAL EVENTS

Afghanistan

The worldwide shock at the destruction of the Twin Towers of the World Trade Center was sustained but it is interesting to consider the varieties of perceptions across the globe. For Osama bin Laden and Al-Qaeda, who had been under attack by American forces in Afghanistan for some time, it was a brilliant success: a lot of people were killed, it raised their profile and succeeded in drawing America and its allies into a bloody war against the Taliban, Al-Qaeda and other Islamist terrorist groups, which would inevitably lead to more recruits to their cause. It was the inevitability of this consequence that had divided Bin Laden's advisers who had counselled against the plan.[3] Across the Middle East there was some public rejoicing.

For America the immediate consequence of this humiliating attack was to reclaim its world status by instantly declaring war on terrorism, as illustrated in the above quotation, and to launch a military campaign in Afghanistan aimed at the destruction of Al-Qaeda and its hosts, the Taliban, which controlled that country. All this was in line with the 'Project for the New American Century' drawn up some years earlier by individuals who were now Bush's key advisors.[4n] Initially they were supported by the UK, the Afghanistan Northern Alliance, Canada, Australia and Germany. On October 7th 2001, bombs and missiles from UK and US ships and submarines were directed to the main headquarters of Al-Qaeda and the Taliban. Three cities and the airport were also targeted. Special forces were also deployed.[5n]

The British perspective was more nuanced – with the exception of the Prime Minister, Tony Blair, who gave immediate full support without reference to Parliament. He seemed to have been in the grips of a fierce crusade backed by his personal religious beliefs when he addressed the Labour Party conference three weeks after the attack:

> ... out of the shadow of this evil, should emerge lasting good: destruction of the machinery of terrorism wherever it is found; hope amongst all nations of a new beginning where we seek to resolve differences in a calm and ordered way; greater understanding between nations and between faiths; and above all justice and prosperity for the poor and dispossessed, so that people everywhere can see the chance of a better future through the hard work and creative power of the free citizen, not the violence and savagery of the fanatic.
>
> The starving, the wretched, the dispossessed, the ignorant, those living in want and squalor from the deserts of Northern Africa to the slums of Gaza, to the mountain ranges of Afghanistan: they too are our cause.
>
> This is a moment to seize. The Kaleidoscope has been shaken. The pieces are in flux. Soon they will settle again. Before they do, let us re-order this world around us ...Today, humankind has the science and technology to destroy itself or to provide prosperity to all. Yet science can't make that choice for us. Only the moral power of a world acting as a community can.

There was of course general horror at the attack, sympathy for America's hurt and a need for revenge, but, in common with many in Europe, I wondered whether our great ally had got what it deserved for its arrogant determination that its values and way of life were so desirable and that its consumerist culture and capitalist philosophy must be exported worldwide. Also, while I sympathised with those in pain and suffering, I noted that the death toll of 3,000 was less than that of the IRA campaigns (highly financed from America) and not to be compared with the WWII blitz. Nonetheless, by and large it seemed to me that we were prepared to shelve such reservations and support the action in Afghanistan. The assumption was that the conflict would be properly managed and when our troops were exposed they would be well equipped and supported. We also assumed that all our experience and understanding of the tribal nature, political structures and cultures of that country, let alone our own and Russia's failures there, would be made available to our allies. None of these assumptions turned out to be the case.

In the event Kabul fell within five weeks. British forces advanced painfully across Afghanistan, gradually introducing relative peace, some degree of local democracy and increased opportunities for women. The UK forces were responsible for the southern district of Helmand which proved to be the most challenging. Gradually, key people in the Taliban and Al-Qaeda were killed, and on May 2nd 2011 Bin Laden was located in a small village in Pakistan by American special forces and killed. By then 2,850 coalition forces and some 12,000 civilians (5,100 by insurgent actions) had died.

By that time our attention had been refocused on a more controversial American fight. It seemed to me that American imperialism was running riot. With such huge numbers of civilian casualties, did America and her allies not understand why they were hated? Did they not consider the inevitability of revenge at some point? Had we not convinced our allies from our long history that democracy, now inevitably linked to a belief in the power of the market, does not come from the end of a gun?[6n]

Iraq

Since the end of the Gulf War in 1991 evidence had built up that, under Saddam Hussein, Iraq had been manufacturing weapons of mass destruction (WMD) including biological weapons. During these years his regime continued to commit gross crimes against humanity which had been a constant feature of his reign. Saddam had attacked the northern Kurdish community with poison gas (including Sarin), had tortured and executed thousands of citizens and notably drained the southern marshes, thus destroying the whole culture and livelihood of the local Arab population. In 1998 the US passed the Iraq Liberation Act which authorised the removal of Saddam Hussein from power, an objective never authorised by the United Nations. One month after the Act was passed, the US and UK completed a four-day bombing campaign on the suspected sites of weapon constructions, an action designed to weaken Saddam's grip on power. Following the attack on 9/11 preparations were made to attack Iraq as well as Afghanistan as both countries were thought to be harbouring Al-Qaeda bases. There was no evidence that this was the case in Iraq and in fact it was well known that Saddam was in conflict with Al-Qaeda politically, theologically and militarily.

On September 12th 2002 President Bush made his first call for action against Iraq in an address to the UN Security Council. Whilst the Council was prepared to approve action to remove weapons of mass destruction, it was not prepared to approve action intending to achieve regime change. Nonetheless America continued its planning towards this aim under the guise of fighting terrorism and destroying weapons of mass destruction. In Bush's first crisis meeting after the 9/11 attacks the US Secretary of Defence, Donald Rumsfeld, when challenged about his call to attack Iraq, had said 'There just aren't enough targets in Afghanistan. We need to bomb something else to prove that we're big and strong and not going to be pushed around.'[7n]

The United Nations commissioned a group of experts to inspect the sites where weapons were supposedly being manufactured and also imposed severe economic sanctions on Iraq. This led to a prolonged game of cat and mouse between Saddam, the inspectors and the UN until in 1998 Saddam expelled all inspectors. Meanwhile President Bush and Tony Blair, buoyed up by early indications of success in Afghanistan, jointly pursued plans to invade Iraq, which decision would inevitably weaken the forces in Afghanistan and provide an opportunity for a Taliban resurgence. In the UK Blair was coming under increasing pressure from public demonstrations and Parliamentary opposition to any further involvement in Iraq (see below). In communication with President Bush in July 2002 he used the phrase 'I will be with you, George, whatever.' (A commitment not shared with his Cabinet.) He pointed out the need for a coalition to defuse anti-American uprisings and the need to stay in for the long term to bed down any new regime, and also that approval must be sought from the United Nations. This debate occurred in November 2002, resulting in Resolution 1441 which warned that Iraq would face serious consequences if it did not cooperate with weapons inspectors, which it failed completely to do. In February 2003 the US Secretary for Foreign Affairs gave a detailed illustrated account to the Security Council indicating the sites where weapons were apparently being built. Nine days later the inspectors reported that they had been unable to find any such weapons. On February 15th 2003 a worldwide protest against the invasion in 600 cities was declared the largest in history. Some three million people demonstrated in Rome, three million in Spain, over a million in Britain, and New York had over a million marching along with 150 other US cities.

In March 2003, exasperated by delays, the two world leaders, despite advice to the contrary and opposition from many countries, commenced the invasion named 'Shock and Awe'; given the TV pictures of the heavy missile bombing, this was aptly named. Within twenty days Baghdad had fallen and Bush declared that the mission had been completed! The American diplomat Paul Bremner was appointed to supervise the transition to a democratic state. A series of terrible bombings drew attention to the fact that the invasion had been launched with very little understanding of the deep religious and tribal rivalries within the country. There was little consideration of the Sunni population, which had been oppressed by Saddam's Shia leaning Ba'athist minority, or the whole sense of the *ummah* which pervades the whole Muslim community, such that an attack on one is felt by the whole. Once that central power had gone, conflict was inevitable. If lack of understanding had preceded the invasion it then became clear that no thought at all had been given to how to govern the country post conflict, thus giving rise to Bremner's fateful decision to disband the Iraqi army, police and civil service which created large numbers of disenfranchised angry Shias.[8n]

Bremner was also responsible for the distribution of funds (including $20 million from Iraq oil exports and $300 million from the US treasury) for reconstruction by a range of American and Iraqi contractors. Extraordinary sums of money, up to $600 million, were moved around and distributed in cash with very few details recorded. When Bremner left Iraq in 2005 it was estimated that most of these funds, or the work that should have been completed, was untraceable. The consequence was years of deadly conflict between religious factions in addition to the understandable guerrilla tactics against the invading troops. A sort of hell had been let loose throughout the land which the invading troops, trained to fight but not police, were ill equipped to handle.

Saddam Hussein's two sons were killed in July 2003, and their father was captured in December then tried and hanged three years later. By 2005 Iraq was deeply mired in inter-tribal and religious conflict in order to gain control of the country and drive the invaders out. President Bush admitted that the invasion was the result of faulty intelligence, but argued that the invasion was justified. The following year, in the face of declining popularity, the Republican Party lost control of both houses of Congress. By 2007 the US sent 20,000 troops to Iraq in an attempt to halt the increasingly violent insurgencies. This slowly restored some order to areas near Baghdad, but the southern town of Basra, which was under UK control, was besieged. This lasted nearly a year, during which time the military slowly lost control of the area to competing local militias. British troops withdrew from the town under cover of darkness on September 3rd 2007, returning to the safer base at the airport. This was not a good moment in UK military history. The following year an agreement was signed with the Iraqi government that all coalition troops would leave Iraq by 2011.

During these four years the coalition forces suffered some 4,500 deaths (of which 170 were British). Civilian casualties are difficult to estimate, but a figure of 1,000,000 has been suggested. As tragic and extreme as the numbers of casualties on all sides were, as the conflicts progressed the extent of the barbarity of the extremists became known. This had caused disruption to normal military codes of conduct and had highlighted the interpretation of western standards of civilised behaviour.

Many individual incidents of cruel or murderous behaviour on the battlefields were reported, with offenders brought to justice. In Iraq the first major scandal broke over the appalling treatment of prisoners at the large Abu Ghraib Prison which was used to house criminals, suspected leaders of terrorist groups and individuals who had attacked coalition forces. There were about 7,500 prisoners housed in tents and in the main prison. It was these prisoners who were subject to brutal and humiliating treatment, often stripped naked and abused by women officers, a particularly dreadful insult to any Muslim. Horrifying photos were published in 2004 and the subsequent inquiry found that abuses included torture, rape, sodomy and murder.

Following the attack on the Twin Towers, America established an extensive operation of 'black ops' by which terrorist suspects from anywhere in the world could be abducted and transported by specially commissioned aircraft to 'black sites' where they could be interrogated and tortured.[9] This involved special permission by a large number of governments for the flights to transit without being registered. Interrogation was usually by American specialists but where appropriate other national interrogators, including British, took part. High profile prisoners were flown to Cuba and held on the American leased property at Guantanamo Bay. Here up to 780 prisoners were held in cage like structures, dressed in orange jump suits, shackled and held indefinitely without trial. The whole situation was a stain on the reputation of the great United States of America and its allies. In 2022 a small number of prisoners remain.

International Terrorism

Although these conflicts were our main focus during this period other concerns were attracting attention. Libya was building up a range of chemical and biological weapons and North Korea admitted developing nuclear weapons – they later launched their first test of an intercontinental ballistic missile. In late October 2002 forty rebels from the 'Islamist Militant Separatist Movement' captured the Dubrovka Theatre in Moscow and held some 900 people hostage for four days before Russian forces stormed the building, having first infiltrated a soporific drug into the building. In a couple of hours all the rebels had been killed and some 140 hostages, unable to cope with the gas, had died. Two years later a similar group invaded a school of 800 pupils in the small town of Beslan in the Caucasus and held all the children, staff and some parents hostage for three days. Despite some successful negotiations, firing alerted the rebels who it is thought set off a bomb that caused the roof of the sports hall, where most of the hostages were being held, to collapse. Many of the children, already weakened by the refusal of the terrorists to allow any food or water into the school, were killed. This left the troops no choice but to storm the building. In total, 385 people (including 186 children) died and there were over a thousand casualties. Extra restrictions were imposed on all cities and airports, although when Ann and I arrived in Moscow some months later our passports were not even checked.

Barack Obama

There was a brief period of relief from the daily bombardment of news reporting these atrocities when the two main leaders of these wars were replaced. The fierce disputes around the Iraq war and a dip in the economy slowly ate away at Tony Blair's popularity. In my view (as had been the case with Mrs Thatcher), after eleven years in power his eyes showed that staring quality of one totally exhausted and approaching mania. Two years later, and for similar reasons (although the collapse of the world economy was also starting in the USA), George W. Bush resigned from the presidency leaving the Republican John McCain to fight the Democratic candidate Barack Obama. The result on November 4th 2008 gave Obama 52.9% of the popular vote against McCain's 45.7%. America had appointed Barack Obama as its first African American President, a young, intelligent and dynamic individual who had worked as a community organiser in Chicago's South Side and as a civil rights lawyer. Faced with great racial prejudice and opposition, his rallying cry for change was 'Yes we can,' and his message was 'Hope.' When referring to the difficulties of the past he just said 'Enough.' It felt as though change in this embattled world might actually be possible.

NATIONAL EVENTS

Throughout this period three themes dominated the political debate. The first and most significant was opposition to the Iraq war; second was the growing tension between the Prime Minister and his Chancellor Gordon Brown; and the third was the continued success of the government's social policies. Beyond all this people were losing faith in politicians and the process and were becoming concerned at the implications of globalisation. May 1st 2001 saw the first worldwide anti-globalisation protests; there were large demonstrations in Berlin, New York and London.[10n]

Iraq–UK Politics

The public was always divided over invading Iraq and as time went by 85% were against the conflict. Tony Blair therefore found himself caught between his unequivocal commitment to President Bush and the views of the UK electorate and Parliament. His task was therefore to convince both parties of the rightness of his cause. He succeeded in reducing some opposition by his insistence that the agreement of the United Nations was required before an invasion could take place.

The second tactic was to commission an authoritative dossier that would prove the virtue and necessity of action backed by a ruling that an invasion would be legal. Blair asked the Cabinet Office to draw up a document for public consumption, although the timing and form of its release would be decided by Alistair Campbell, Blair's press secretary. The document was assembled on the available evidence, some of which had not been fully confirmed. Blair's foreword stated that the fact that Saddam possessed WMD had been established beyond doubt, as was the fact that he was continuing to develop nuclear weapons. Neither of these were later found to be true. It should be noted that Blair's experts were not being helpful. They pointed out that as far as international peace was concerned Iran, Libya and North Korea were higher priorities than Iraq. With no WMD to be found, the British Intelligence communities were not co-ordinating their assessments and not raising concerns as the political spin distorted their professional view.

The dossier was launched in Parliament in September 2002 when the Prime Minister drew particular attention to the conclusion that Saddam's weapons could be launched within 48 hours. This proved to be a myth. The public opposition to war grew during the succeeding months as the dossier's claims came under scrutiny. The Attorney General, Lord Goldsmith's, initial view in January 2003 was that the relevant UN resolution (1441) did not give authority for invasion unless there was concrete evidence that

Saddam had failed to comply with the UN resolutions. No such certain evidence existed. By March, following visits to the USA, his opinion was that action could be legally justified by Iraq's material breach of previous UN resolutions, although he couldn't be sure that a court would agree with his argument. (His American colleagues explained that 'We put him right on a few things.') The day before the debate in Parliament he hardened up his advice.

The whole thing came to a head on March 18th 2003 in a ten-hour Parliamentary debate. Although there was a general view to support the motion, a quarter of Labour MPs and all Liberals opposed the invasion. The respected Foreign Secretary Robin Cook resigned with a brilliant speech, during which he pointed out that in reality we were being asked to embark 'on a war without the agreement of any of the international bodies in which we are a leading partner – not NATO – not the European Community and not the Security Council.' Why, he asked, was it urgent now to take military action to disarm a military capacity that had been there for 20 years and which we helped create? 'Why must we take action this week when Saddam's ambition is being blocked by the weapons inspectors?' The debate raged on with passionate arguments on both sides but just before 22:00 hrs the motion was carried by 412 votes to 149. Bombs fell on Baghdad the following morning. It would not be long before the first coffins bearing the bodies of fallen soldiers from Iraq and Afghanistan would arrive not far from my home at RAF Lyneham to be paraded through the main street of Wootton Bassett where flags were dipped and tributes given. In late September 2011 the repatriations returned to Brize Norton where, to the relief of the government, the TV cameras seldom came.[11n]

The election of 2001 returned a victory for Labour although they lost five seats and subsequently the reputation of politics and politicians in general. Tony Blair's Cabinet in particular had suffered. Also there had been a very low turnout, falling to an alarming 34.1% in the Riverside, Liverpool constituency. One local voter spoke for many when she said, 'It's all lots of suits and men and your "Ra Ra Order," on the telly.'[12]

A fascinating study that revisited the East London study, published in the iconic 1957 study by Peter Willmott, warned that the long term effects of slum clearances, which had broken up the natural support networks, the effect of a rights policy on housing allocation and the gentrification of large swathes of the area had led to an angry, anxious and racist white working class ignored by local and central government.[13] In a decade, sections of the population seemed to have gone from heroes, celebrated as such in TV dramas and films, to a despised group associated with dangerous dogs, binge drinking, scratch cards and chips.[14] This group was increasingly turning to right-wing political groups. By 2008 Barking and Dagenham Council had 12 British Nationalist Party members and Stoke, loyally Labour for 60 years, had elected nine British National Party councillors and Labour members had declined from 60 to 15. They were not alone among the electorate which saw MPs as in it for themselves. If MPs were not committed to their constituents, why should voters be committed to them?

It has always seemed to me a great pity that there was almost exclusive TV attention paid to the cock fighting of Prime Minister's question time rather than the hard disputes where the work was being done in committees. Voters were getting tired of the highly developed 'spin' process used by the government on any significant issue – what was true and what was spin? In addition to the confines of the two-party system that restricted the influence of individual MPs, it was becoming clear that Europe held much of the power. However, the really significant power seemed to rest with the few multinational agencies that manipulated globalised trade. How did the promotion of democracy as a universal religion match the reality of global free trade? What value could now be placed on the public good as against easy consumption? Were we citizens or just consumers? On a day to day basis the twenty-four-hour impact of worldwide news coverage was too much for most people; entertainment was far less stressful, and the culture of vacuous 'celebrity' was growing in influence. This fact of course was not wasted on Tony Blair who, more than most prime ministers, loved sharing the glamour, holding frequent receptions in Downing Street while polishing his own performances. Post-modern relativism was coming home to roost. In these ways the gap between voters and their MPs became greater and the connection between them less clear. Polls revealed that trust in MPs and the political process was falling fast.

> We in Britain do not merely live our part in this general global decline in trust. We also live in a country in which levels of trust are particularly – perhaps even uniquely – low. If British exceptionalism could be summed up in a single word that word would not be the tolerance, fairness or liberty hymned by Brown. It would be mistrust.[15]

All this despite the fact that over this period crime was falling, the provision of housing and schools was increasing and unemployment was at its lowest for 25 years. As the lack of trust extended to such reliable statistics the government never really got the credit for their positive social programmes. The gap between the real achievement of government and the recognition of how this came about was alarming. Anyway, it all happened in London. The most significant response to these concerns was to establish mayors as a more local focus in twelve cities, but very noticeably six of these were won by local people with no political allegiance. I don't think many people really got New Labour's much publicised 'Third Way,' which seemed to mean that the sharp difference between the main parties was now very fuzzy. So the traditional tribes loyal to old Labour and the Tories seemed no longer to apply and with this went a significant proportion of many people's identity and their ability to achieve change by voting for a representative with whom they could identify. This seemed to me to be a reflection of a more important issue that for a younger generation tradition had been replaced by the freedom to choose a whole range of new values and beliefs.

On July 18th 2003 the country was shocked by the news that the respected, quiet expert in biological weapons had been found dead, apparently having committed suicide near his home. Dr David Kelly, DPhil (Oxon), CBE, had been one of the chief weapons inspectors searching for Saddam Hussein's WMD. More recently Kelly had been asked to check some sections of the Iraq Dossier, after which he queried the claim that weapons could be launched within 45 minutes. As soon as he was able, he went to examine the mobile laboratories from which the attack would have originated. He later met off the record with the BBC journalist Andrew Gilligan who then quoted 'a scientist and biological weapons expert' as saying that the laboratories could only have produced hydrogen gas to fill balloons. Kelly reported his contact to his superiors at the Ministry of Defence who accepted his account that the words used were not his. The announcement that one of their employees had come forward made it certain that Kelly would be identified and he was therefore called to appear before the Foreign Affairs Select Committee which was investigating the run up to the war.

The proceedings were televised and all could see how stressed this mild mannered man was. He was questioned aggressively, and he was finally told that he was the fall guy, sent to divert the investigation. I was horrified that this man, who had given his life to government service (including communicating with journalists), was being crucified by unqualified MPs. David Kelly's death was attributed to the effects of 29 co-proxamol painkillers and an incision on his left wrist on top of a mild heart disease. The public outcry included many who did not believe that his death was suicide, arguing that this was a government plot to silence a person who doubted the validity of the case for invasion. The subsequent inquiry into the death was seen as a whitewash and it was requested that the inquest papers be sealed for 70 years. The dispute rumbles on.

The Labour Party, building on many years of social progress, a sound economy and falling unemployment, won their third election on May 5th 2005, the first time they had achieved three terms in power. However, many of the concerns outlined above, particularly the invasion of Iraq, lost them 48 seats although the Conservatives gained only 33. The Liberal Party won 62 seats, the highest gain since the 1920s. Interestingly, the swing to the Tories was lowest in the higher classes (classification AB) with the highest swing being in the third tranche (classification C2). Labour could continue with a good working majority and ignore the fact that most of the four million lost votes were from angry working-class voters now feeling alienated by the growing gap between them and the wealthy. The fact that those that did vote went to growing nationalist or right-wing parties was largely ignored. Blair faced significant challenges, including the continuation of his radical public service reforms (based on market models) which many of his 40 new MPs opposed. Among the new MPs were Sadiq Khan (who became Mayor of London in 2016) and Ed Miliband (who became Leader of the Labour Party just five years later). Blair now had to face a more confident opposition and Gordon Brown, who Blair needed beside him, despite Brown's frustration that Blair was delaying his departure to block his succession. Mr Blair's long, reluctant goodbye would be dragged on for a further two years.

Terror

On July 6th 2005 London won its bid to host the 2012 Olympic Games. At 08:26 on the following morning four young men gathered on the forecourt of Kings Cross Station; they quickly said their goodbyes and, less than 30 minutes later, three of them blew themselves up on separate rush hour underground trains, all between stations to cause maximum impact and fear. The fourth, 18-year-old Hasib Hussain, failed to get on the tube but caught a No. 30 bus, taking a seat on the top deck. As it approached Tavistock Square (immediately outside the British Medical Association HQ) he detonated his bomb. In the carnage below and above ground 52 people died and over 700 were injured. Everyone was horrified at both the number of casualties and the extent of the operation, which implied careful planning. The other bombers were later identified as Mohammad Sidique Khan, the 30-year-old ringleader, who was married with one child and worked as a classroom assistant in a primary school; Shehzad Tanweer, a 22-year-old who worked in a fish and chip shop; and Germaine Lindsay, a 19-year-old who had a son and a pregnant wife. Three lived in Leeds, and Lindsay came from Buckinghamshire. The whole area round Kings Cross and Tavistock Square was cordoned off for many days; it took me a hell of a time on the next day to reach my young granddaughter Aella who was having dancing lessons in the next street. As the initial shock and horror faded, it became apparent that this atrocity had been caused by young men who had lived peacefully among us. 'How could this happen?' we asked ourselves. A month later Al-Qaeda claimed responsibility and it was understood that the four had acted independently under the direction of an Al-Qaeda mentor. Later investigations revealed a picture which has become familiar as attacks by militant Islamists have continued. These young men were described by family and friends as quiet, apparently happily and living normal lives, although in retrospect some signs of radicalisation could be seen. One investigation found that the influence was more likely to be a close friend or family member than the internet, although for all those investigated the narrative was the same – that Muslims were under attack from the west and it is therefore every Muslim's duty to protect themselves by fighting back.

> The single narrative, like some secular political ideologies, exposes the problem and crucially offers a programme, a strategy and a solution ... Ahmed and Mohammed on the street corner in Walthamstow are both convinced that the 9/11 attacks were the work of the Israeli secret service and that the 7/7 London bombing was probably a British government plot aimed at facilitating the global repression of Muslims. There's an agenda against Muslims. They want to keep us down, keep us poor, humiliate us, they call us terrorists but they are terrorists too.[16]

As time went by we would learn to face smaller attacks inspired by radicalised young Muslims despite the fact that our security services were effective in pre-empting many plots.

Peace in Northern Ireland

Twenty-one days after the London bombings, as a weird counterpoint to these new threats, came the news that, after twenty-five years of discussions and agreement to decommission their weapons, the IRA and Provisional IRA ended their armed campaign. This was followed later by a similar statement from the Loyalist Volunteer Force. In July 2007 the last military unit left Northern Ireland and at midnight on July 31st the Union Flag was lowered on the closure of the last headquarters. This thirty-eight-year engagement had been the longest in military history, at one time deploying 25,700 troops. There had been over a thousand military and police fatalities[17n] and the deaths of 730 active Catholic and Protestant fighters and some 1,900 civilians. The military had learnt important lessons to assist in the Afghanistan and Iraq campaigns. Between January 2005 and December 2007 some 5,500 troops had also been withdrawn from Iraq.

The fact that the terrible events in Northern Ireland were now over and our troops were coming home was a weight off all our shoulders, particularly those of the military families. Anxieties were however raised again when it transpired that a senior Russian dissident Alexander Litvinenko had been poisoned by Russian agents by the administration of a small quantity of the highly radioactive polonium-210 on November 1st 2006. He was rushed to hospital but it proved impossible to correctly diagnose his illness. He was seen on TV answering questions and looking sicker each day. He died 22 days later, just as the extremely rare cause of his decline had been discovered. In a posthumous statement he accused the Russian President Vladimir Putin of his murder. Investigations, which revealed a trail of the poison across London, led to the identification of the agents responsible although they remain protected in Russia. What was shocking was the fact that such an act could be carried out in London in plain sight, although in fact this was not the first.[18n]

A New Prime Minister

In late June 2007 Blair finally resigned in favour of Gordon Brown, his brilliant but less naturally charismatic Chancellor. I think it fair to weigh up Tony Blair's ten years in power. His first achievement, in light of the post-Thatcher economic and political climate, was to move the traditional Labour Party away from classic socialism and into New Labour, that is to say into the centre ground of modern politics which he termed the Third Way, an uneasy mix of market driven philosophy and social justice. As popular as most of the domestic policies and practices launched in these years were, the long term effect, of course, was to leave those committed to the political left gasping for breath and unable to fight a resurgent Conservative Party. Membership of the Labour Party crumbled. By 2007 the economy was in good shape; the NHS, education and social care had been massively improved. New hospitals, schools and public buildings had been built which served to enhance the morale of the staff and improve the service to the public. Powers had been devolved to Scotland and Wales and peace restored to Northern Ireland. The Human Rights and Freedom of

Information Acts were passed. The link between poverty, education and career achievement had led to many initiatives, the most engaging being Sure Start. However, despite all of this, the gap between the poor and the rich had widened and chronic deep poverty remained as it had at the start of Blair's premiership. Liberal interventionism had worked to good effect in Kosovo and Sierra Leone, but this, along with a subservient relationship with America, had led him to Iraq, the disaster which blighted all his other achievements, heightened the distrust of politicians and the political process and would ultimately be his legacy. In my view the negative side would be the wholesale adoption of the market model and managerialism in the public services which found themselves bound to doubtful achievement targets, which though meaningless in terms of human relations, were used as a measure of financial control and therefore had to be achieved by whatever means possible. One example of this which came my way was the target to reduce the number of children in care. Knowing the day on which this would be measured, at least one authority reduced the number by sending children back home for the night, thus placing them back into risk situations from which they had been removed. By thus lowering the numbers left in care they avoided a £750,000 penalty so that future services were protected. Another example encountered was the practice of police forces to meet government targets to clear up juvenile offending by replacing warnings with convictions, thus sucking many very young offenders (the 'low hanging fruit') into the criminal justice system. Then of course we had the high usage of the Private Funding Initiative (PFI) by which private companies built those hospitals and schools, thus keeping the capital expenditure off the government's books. The contracts negotiated between commercial companies and inexperienced civil servants always benefitted the companies. The 750 PFI deals undertaken in this period resulted in massive debts which would take generations to repay.

In February 2007 UNICEF released its 'Innocenti Report Card 7' which reviewed child wellbeing over six dimensions in 21 rich countries. This dealt a blow to the government's aim to abolish child poverty by 2012 by placing the UK at number 21 in terms of overall child wellbeing, family relationships and risky behaviour and at number 18 in child poverty.[19] To be fair, as the government was quick to point out, the report was four years out of date and much of the data was subjective, but that had been the same for all the countries. In commenting on the report, the Children's Commissioner Sir Al Aynsley Green drew attention to the report's suggestion that the problem was less to do with political initiatives and fiscal structures than the way in which children in the UK were brought up. He said,

> There is a crisis at the heart of our society and we must not continue to ignore the impact of our attitudes towards young people and the effect it has on their wellbeing ... It is time to stop demonising children and young people for what goes wrong and start supporting them to make positive choices, to bring an end to the confusing messages we give them about their role, responsibilities and position in society and ensure that every child feels valued and has their rights respected.[20]

I wrote to Gordon Brown, the Prime Minister in waiting, to ask for an assurance that when UNICEF repeated the exercise we would be no lower than eighth on the list. After an edgy follow up no such guarantee was forthcoming. A year later the Children's Commissioners for the four nations of the UK prepared a report on progress with the UN convention on the rights of the child for the UN inspectors. Their report was highly critical, highlighting as it did a punitive justice system, public attitudes which demonised teenagers, a lack of protection against physical punishment in the home and child poverty. More specifically, they criticised physical restraint in the prison system, the high level of bullying of children with a learning disability, institutional discrimination in the NHS, poverty and the government's recent decision to check the age of refugee children by X-raying their teeth. They described this latter practice as unethical, unlawful and no more accurate than non-invasive methods.[21]

Crash

As Gordon Brown took office, he was hit by a series of disasters, including terrorist attacks, extensive flooding and a new outbreak of foot and mouth disease, all of which were handled well. He then had to consider whether to call an election to consolidate his position. He consulted and dithered for too long, eventually deciding, in the face of popularity and prosperity, not to go to the country.

The next problem that would blight subsequent generations was developing in the southern states of America. Encouraged by government policies aimed at helping poorer people buy their own house, financial institutions had been lending money in situations where it was pretty obvious that the loan exceeded the value of the property. It was deemed to be OK as house prices were rising. But then the bubble burst and house prices fell. Historically, trading managers had a daily report showing the value of their investment at risk (VAR) but as computerisation enabled vastly increased daily trades managers had lost touch with their trading floors. Once their investments started to devalue, organisations borrowed more. The banks, for example J. P. Morgan, became aware of the threat and sought out safe trades, which then failed. At one point they had $51 million in play in an increasingly uncontrollable market which led to the death of this venerable institution.

Had this confined itself to America, the damage might have been limited but it transpired that, in the global economy, these risky loans had been bundled together with others and had, with the help of clever computer programmes and post Bush and Thatcher deregulation, been sold on and on as low risk assets across the world, but particularly into the voracious UK financial sector where huge profits and bonuses increased. The extraordinary levels of excitement and danger involved led to the suggestion that the heavy use of cocaine in those circles may have been an element in the subsequent crash. The enormous size of the US housing market heightened the risk. As it became clear that the number of householders failing to make their mortgage payments was rapidly rising, investors sought to sell off their stock and borrow from the banks, thus causing a massive run on the banks to the tune of trillions of dollars.

The contagion spread fast as billions of dollars were wiped off shares across the world. Investment banks found themselves with insufficient reserves to meet demand and the larger investment/retail banks found themselves raiding customers' accounts. Both business and private customers suddenly found that withdrawing money was impossible and their credit card limits were reduced. First to go was the 158-year-old Lehman Brothers bank based in New York. Immediately afterwards, banks across America, the international Royal Bank of Scotland (RBS), Bradford and Bingley, and Alliance and Leicester announced themselves near collapse. The UK had the advantage of a good Chancellor, Alistair Darling, and a Prime Minister whose whole career had prepared him for such a crisis, which was the worst since the 1930s. The government was well advanced in its plans to prevent the whole financial system collapsing when, during the early morning of October 7th 2007 the Chancellor was called out of a meeting to take a call from the Chairman of RBS who was concerned about how fast customers were withdrawing money. The answer to the question 'How long can you hold out,' was 'Two or three hours and that's it!' Later that morning the government announced a £500 billion fund to bail out RBS and six other banks, while the Bank of England launched a £450 billion fund to help investment banks. Thus, at the height of neo-liberal policies, the UK and US governments and many others around the world had effectively nationalised a large part of their economy. Suddenly we were all back to Keynesian economics.

The economic and social consequences of these disasters would last for generations although those countries less affected, most notably China, were ready to prosper. As one financial analyst explained:

> What we are living through now will reverberate through the rest of the century ... We are witnessing a very real power shift. Money is now moving eastwards – while they're creating wealth we are losing it hand over fist. Where it ends no one knows.[22]

An urgent meeting of the G20 finance countries, nicknamed Bretton Woods II, was held in Washington, D.C. in November 2008 (see Chapter 4). They agreed on the causes of the crisis and proposed common principles for reforming the financial markets. These included strengthened transparency and accountability, enhanced regulation, the promotion of integrity, increased international cooperation and reformation of the international financial systems. Quite a package.

In the UK the stock market fell, house prices slumped, 100,000 people lost their jobs and the populace lost faith in the banks. For the moment people applauded our brilliant Prime Minister for his expertise and quick action. Quite quickly however they cursed the lack of regulation and the fact that no action was taken against the rich bastards whose greed and incompetence had brought the country to this place. What had globalisation done for us? The speed at which the gap between ordinary working people and the rich was growing was increasing, and in January 2008 the former Education Secretary David Blunkett proposed a series of steps to stop the formation of an entrenched underclass which seemed to being taken for granted. He saw sections of society leading increasingly separate lives and proposed a series of financial supports coupled with celebration of achievements and a more holistic approach to this group.[23] My understanding is that absolutely no action was ever taken, resulting, among other things, in the outcome of the historic referendum of 2015 and the election result of 2017.

Having closed down the mines, mills, shipyards and engineering industries in the face of global competition (with an ongoing cost in welfare benefits of £20 to £30 billion), the UK had bet our future on the City (where in 2007 annual bonuses ran to £14 billion), where higher taxes enabled all those positive social policies and public buildings but involved unforeseen levels of risk. Almost unnoticed, the wealth gap between the North and the South East grew (with London becoming culturally and economically separate from the rest of the country). Globalisation was well established. In 2015 a group of Swiss researchers traced the vast networks of transnational financial and business networks. They discovered over a million ownership ties which narrowed down to 737 top holders, but this could be reduced even further to an extraordinary group of 147 companies which controlled over 40% of the total value of all the transnational companies, most of which were financial institutions. These, it turns out, were the elite of the elite who pull the strings of the major banks, media outlets and governments. The world seemed to have turned upside down, a thought brilliantly expressed in a short letter by Joseph Nuttgens published in *The Guardian Weekend* on June 28th 2008,[24] which simply asked: 'Since when have the providers of what we need become the deciders of how we live?'

SOCIAL WORK

The campaign to create a register of qualified social workers had lasted for some fifty years until a government keen on regulation and spurned to action by yet another major child abuse scandal decided to act. Hence, as a consequence, the Care Standards Act 2000, the General Social Care Council (GSCC) and the Social Care Institute for Excellence (SCIE) were formed in October 2001.[25n]

In general this was a welcome boost to morale, particularly as 'social worker' was now a protected title. It was hoped that this would give protection to those using our services and also put an end to press and media reports which too readily called anyone found guilty of bad practice a social worker just because that was what they chose to call themselves despite having no qualifications. Very soon the professional qualification became a three-year course at degree level.[26n]

It was noticeable that neither the GSCC nor the SCIE was led by a social work professional, although the SCIE Chair was Jane Campbell, a respected campaigner on behalf of service users. She saw SCIE's role as the 'missing link' which would draw examples of excellent frontline practice, formal research and the experience of service users who she saw as 'not a stakeholder, she or he is *the* stakeholder.'[27]

In January 2001 Ann and I joined some two hundred people gathered in Kensington Town Hall to pay tribute to Barbara Kahan, one of the great figures in post-war child care, remembered for her fifty-year career, her pioneering work as the Director of the Oxfordshire Children's Department, the Assistant Director of the Social Work Service in the DHSS and Chair of the National Children's Bureau, as well as for her key role in the 1990 Staffordshire Child Care Inquiry and subsequent work *The Pindown Experience and the Protection of Children*.[28n] Barbara had recruited and managed me in the DHSS and had always been a dynamic and committed campaigner for children.

My former colleague and friend Norman Tutt and I and our wives had stayed with Barbara in the delightful Oxfordshire house that she had enjoyed with her husband Vladimir. One evening, while we were enjoying dinner, a young man knocked at the door begging for money. For the first time I saw Barbara in a flurry and undecided as to quite how to react. She could not refuse, but feared that any money she gave him would be put to a bad purpose; what to do? After some discussion it was agreed that he could have a good meal in the kitchen and was then sent on his way. Barbara, of course, was only one of many great pioneers of child care and social service who had served children so well in the post-war period. Their impact had been tremendous.

As a further response to the Climbié Inquiry,[29] the government issued its landmark broad brush Green Paper 'Every Child Matters' with a neat summary document and an emotional foreword by Tony Blair. The aim was '... to ensure that every child has the chance to fulfil their potential by reducing educational failure, ill health, substance misuse, teenage pregnancy, abuse and neglect, crime and anti-social behaviour among children and young people.'[30] These ambitions were to be achieved by providing advice to parents, by targeting support where required and compelling intervention by the use of 'parenting orders' as a last resort.

Early intervention would be facilitated and shared by agencies, with the school as the key agency. With the introduction and development of a common assessment tool for all agencies and the direction of a lead professional, accountability would be ensured by a director for developing children's Trusts, a local councillor for children and a Minister for Children, Young People and Families. In addition was the establishment of local children's commissioners (a response to an adverse critical UNICEF report). The existing Area Protection Committees would be replaced by Local Safeguarding Committees with increased powers. Unfortunately the youth justice system remained outside all this, accountable to the all powerful Home Office.

In case this was just too much good news, the final dismemberment and death sentence on the grand Seebohm vision of generic social work practice and organisation was pronounced in November 2003 by the NHS and Social Care (Community Health and Standards) Act and the Children's Act 2004 which split local authority departments into children and adult services, each with its own director to be run as multi-disciplinary Trusts. Children's departments became responsible for *all* children in their area and were answerable to the Department of Education (with inspection by Ofsted). Given this brief it was noticeable that most directorships came from an education background. Adult services would, from 2009, be inspected by the Care Quality Commission (CQC).

These initiatives stemmed from the Lamming Report into the death of Victoria Climbié, which highlighted, as had many previous inquiries, the failure of agencies to communicate and work closely together. The Trusts would cross the boundaries between education, social care, health and other agencies as appropriate. I wondered when we would see the first disaster caused by a family falling down the gap between the two departments and that the expansion to all children would lose focus on the most vulnerable. Denise Platt, Chief Inspector of Social Services, warned that social workers would find themselves working in a whole new range of environments and 'working with a range of professionals, and they'll need to be confident in their skills and what they have to offer'. That didn't seem to me like anything very new.[31]

In fact this reorganisation heralded a whole new era for social workers; they would increasingly find themselves working in multi-agency settings where the challenge was to maintain their role and professional values against more powerful professions. Education focussed on schools, classes and achieving standards on a long timescale; health focussed on the specific illness when a treatment is given to a patient usually over a short time. Social workers see the whole person in the family and community context, they work with people on multi-dimensional issues. Strong highly competent workers with a clear self image were now needed to work in a whole variety of changing situations working to targets based on outcomes. This period saw growing numbers of social workers establishing themselves as independent practitioners where they could use their specialist skills to best effect outside the hustle and pressure of the over bureaucratised offices. More importantly of course was the increasing development of user determined services, supported by the government and the profession as enhancing self respect through choice, where the user had funds which, in theory, enabled them to determine the service and the method of delivery that would best meet their needs. This placed the social worker in the role of assessor and then broker who organises the diverse services to meet the agreed needs. Certainly in the early days there was very little local choice of agency, although detailed issues of delivery could more easily be negotiated.

Voluntary Agencies

During this period, the status and role of voluntary societies were significantly changing as a consequence of the open market system which opened them up to competitive contract for the provision of services and the whole red tape, target and value for money systems. All this was undermining the voluntary ethos of the sector, its autonomy and its campaigning ability. It was also being attacked for the City level salaries of some chief executives, notably in the social housing sector. The development of organisations registering as charities but operating as profiteering companies was confusing the borderline between established charities and private companies. This sector was marked by companies training staff or service users across the world making millions for their chief executives.[32n]

The extent of these practices was revealed by a Charity Commission survey which showed that over two-thirds of the largest charities received at least 80% of their funding from the government for one-year contracts, 43% failed to receive full cost of the service and only 26% still felt free to make decisions without pressure from statutory funders. The downside of this for some charities is that they ended up subsidising the work from voluntary contributions, a fate which brought the well established charity Scope to near collapse.[33] Further complications arose as the government, particularly in their 2005 manifesto, promoted the development of 'social enterprises,' heirs to the mutual and co-operative societies of the 19th century.

Social enterprises could take various forms, including non-profit or for-profit, but they had to have a social aim, often to improve a local community or environment, democratic ownership (similar to a co-operative) and had to plough most of their profits back into that community. They were an avenue by which local people could use their entrepreneurial ambitions to trade in goods or services for the benefit of the community. The emergence of this middle way, between charitable and for-profit organisations, became very popular, often gaining contracts from local authorities to run local leisure, medical, community or social services. Their flexibility has proved very attractive, and by 2012 some 70,000 registered social enterprises were contributing over £18 billion to the economy.

An outstanding example of confusion and complexity between a charity and government spans this period. Kids Company was founded in 1996 in South London to cater for vulnerable children at risk, mainly relying on self referrals. It was founded and led by the determined, colourful and fierce fighter Camila Batmanghelidjh to provide a creative and child centred facility in which young people could build on their own strengths. In a crisis it gave money to individual children for specific purposes. It had considerable success and was funded by private and government donations, Camila having the extraordinary ability to deal face to face with a challenging child one minute and mix with top government officials and bankers at an elaborate reception a short taxi ride later. She was a considerable force, not to be denied. In time Kids Company had eleven centres in Greater London as well as centres in Liverpool and Bristol and a staff of 180, plus 1,500 volunteers. The annual number of children helped rose from 11,000 in 2007 to 36,000 in 2011, although this figure was frequently disputed. Its annual budget rose from £5 million to £23 million. This highlighted the gap between its somewhat freewheeling style, which matched the needs of the children with the increasing target-setting and value for money demanded by both Labour and Conservative governments. From late 2008 onwards concerns focussed on the financial stability of the company and three trustees resigned at Camila's reluctance to heed the warnings. The final crisis came in the summer of 2015 when the Conservative government's patience ran out and it withdrew an emergency £3 million grant as the conditions had not been met. Kids Company closed on August 5th 2015.[34n]

In 1998, drawing on their commitment to 'education, education, education' and the work of the Danish sociologist Gøsta Esping-Anderson,[35n] the government had launched the Sure Start programme, a welcome initiative for social workers interested in community development and family work, and one of which the government should always be very proud. The programmes were located in the most deprived areas. The concept was to bring together multi-disciplinary teams to help children under five and their parents to meet educational, health, parenting and family problems both directly and through community involvement. It was an expensive, centrally funded programme, but in 2005, apparently in an effort to ground them more firmly in local communities, responsibility was delegated to local authorities and the budget was not ring-fenced so the coherence was lost. From 2010 up to 1,000 centres were closed although a few have survived until the present day under different names. In 2021 the government announced the creation of 70 'children's hubs' across the country as multi-disciplinary centres.

Baby P

One of the most damaging cases for social work commenced on August 3rd 2007 with the death of Peter Connelly (known in the media of the time as Baby P), a seventeen-month-old child in the London Borough of Haringey. Public outrage was fuelled by the unbelievable severity of the injuries, the length of time over which they had been inflicted and the failure of a range of services to take action. Social workers were, of course, the main target for attack. Peter's young mother, overjoyed at the birth of a boy after three daughters, had ensured that he attended all his health checks, immunisations etc. and for the first six months all seemed well. By early November 2006 the GP's concern at repeated injuries and the mother's unsatisfactory explanations was so great that a referral was made to paediatricians who referred the case to Social Services. The boy was placed with a childminder known to Peter's mother. All went well and the baby was returned to his mother in January 2007. During the following months social workers, a home care worker and health visitors visited, both by appointment and unannounced. Somehow they were unaware that the mother's boyfriend (with a history of child abuse) and, for a shorter time, the boyfriend's brother with four children and a Rottweiler dog, were living in the house. The social workers, who were visiting regularly, came to accept the mother's explanation that Peter was a very active child and therefore suffered bruising by banging into things. Their work tended to focus on the chaotic and dirty state of the house and the mother's poor parenting skills (neighbours later reported that she lay on the couch all day while the boyfriend did the housework).

In the following months the GP once again referred the child to specialists and Baby P spent a night in hospital. Eventually, during an unannounced visit bruising and scratches led to another specialist medical examination and Peter was placed with a childminder for ten days while police and social services made further investigations. Peter's health continued to deteriorate badly with infections all over his body, which his mother showed to various doctors who separately prescribed different antibiotics. On July 25th the social workers placed all their evidence and concerns before the Council's lawyers, who ruled that the threshold for care proceedings had not been reached. The police concluded that their investigations had proved inconclusive, so no charges could be brought. On August 1st Peter was taken by his mother and childminder to hospital where he was examined and given further referrals which the mother did not keep, saying that she did not want to see anyone else for two weeks. (That doctor failed to notice a broken back and three broken ribs.) Two days later Peter's mother called an ambulance which took Peter to hospital, where he died. Asked if he had been unwell his mother said that he had been poorly during the night but she didn't seek help because she kept getting accused of hurting him. When told of his death she was reported as saying 'Oh God, don't take away my baby boy; I've been waiting so long for a boy.'

The fallout from this case was exceptional. The public, politicians and professionals were horrified that another child had died so soon after, and in the same authority as, Victoria Climbié. It was unbelievable that this had happened after health and care professionals had visited 60 times in eleven months with so many examinations by medical experts. The leader of the media pack was *The Sun* under the leadership of Rebekah Brooks, a close friend of David Cameron, who, as leader of the Conservative Party, was running a campaign on 'Broken Britain.' He broke parliamentary bi-party agreement and tore into the Labour Party and in particular Ed Balls, the Secretary of State for Children, Education and Families. This led 'Bully Boy Balls,' after a brief inquiry by the education inspectorate (Ofsted), to appear on television and, in a brilliant example of irresponsible opportunism, publicly order the dismissal of Sharon Shoesmith, Haringey's Director of Children's Services, without compensation. She was dismissed by the Council seven days later and rapidly became the public's number one hate figure. She was hounded by the press, received death threats and was driven to the brink of suicide.[36n]

Peter's mother, her boyfriend and his brother were all imprisoned, the brother being released after six years. Some councillors and others resigned. Three social workers and a manager were sacked by Haringey but the two registered by the GSCC were suspended. The last paediatrician to examine Peter was struck off. He and the registrar eventually left the UK. Participants in other agencies were reprimanded. Noticeably the senior managers in all the agencies remained unpunished. The social workers continued to be hounded by the press. Much of the responsibility for leading this long disgraceful witch hunt rests with Ed Balls, Rebekah Brooks and David Cameron. The tragic fact is that familial child deaths are frequent in this society. Politicians who, after each death where social care staff are involved, assure the public that their intervention will ensure that 'This will never happen again' need to appreciate both the facts of life of those involved and the social and economic circumstances and moderate their self serving comments.

Beyond that the effect of financial cuts, the consequent shortage of staff, the increasing use of agency staff, the time taken on tick box bureaucracy (increased by the Lamming Inquiry into Victoria Climbié), lack of supervision, overbearing computerisation with macho managerialism and continued failure of interagency communication all played a part in this tragedy. These tragedies underlie the main issue of modern social work. Staff need time to build relationships, which means more time with service users and much less time in the office. A combination of social work anxiety and public pressure predictably led to a large increase in the number of children taken into care (some areas saw an increase of 66%) and it became more difficult to attract social workers into children's services, placing more financial pressure on hard pressed local authorities as the government raised court fees from £150 to £4,000. Brilliant![37n]

In early 2006 the Department of Health and the Department of Education and Skills commissioned an investigation into the roles and tasks of social workers. It marked a change from the endless debates of the 1980s and 1990s about the nature of social work in that it asked, in accordance with the managerial culture of the time, two simple questions: What tasks do social workers actually do and what are they equipped to do? And therefore: What can managers expect of them? The work was led by the GSCC, the SCIE and three other organisations, and included a reference group of 50 people representing the profession (frontline, managers and academics), employers and service users. I mention it because it seemed to be to be very well run as an appreciative evaluation, was communicated to all stakeholders clearly and produced a report couched in simple but effective language which clarified most of the old arguments. It was short and generally welcomed by all parties, with very few reservations, a very rare situation. My own reservations were its refusal to see a wider view of social work and extend the profession's view to cover social exclusion, poverty or, for example, what lies behind gang culture, etc.

The project worked intelligently through online consultations, focus groups, academic research and informal discussion. The reference group's early report identified important themes for social workers including 'providing continuity in a journey of change,' 'needing positive language' and 'being uniquely human and a mental gymnast.' We were, it thought, 'a key cog in the multi-disciplinary team' as we were non-judgmental and saw the whole picture. The introduction to the final consultation paper contained the following statement:

> Social work does not claim to be unique in its values or purposes, but it makes a distinctive contribution to public well being. At its best it can change lives, help people to overcome

the problems which cause them difficulty and distress and promote social inclusion and community safety. Social work supports policies for valuing, diversity, challenging discrimination and promoting equality and human rights. It does this by:

promoting a particular cluster of roles, some defined by law,
being employed in a range of characteristic situations,
drawing together and integrating a range knowledge from a variety of academic and professional disciplines and people's own experiences, and
working in partnerships of respect with frequently disadvantaged and marginalised people to increase their choice and control over their own lives.

One of the most remarkable things about this was that when the final report was presented to the government it attracted no welcome, no fanfares and no publicity. There were mumbles that it might be useful in preparing upcoming green papers. Of course it went to be buried on the shelves. As the great Peter Beresford (that determined campaigner for service user involvement), who was present, commented, it was 'Less like a launch and more like an illicit attempt at a burial.'[38]

Around all this was the problem of low morale linked to work pressures and the growing percentage of time that social workers had to spend in the office doing administrative duties, filling in endless computer files. A study coordinated by the Conservative Shadow Minister for Children, Tim Loughton, showed the high level of sickness – three times more than teachers.[39]

One interesting statistical fact produced good news and a warning. It showed that since 1850 the average life expectancy for women had gone from 38.5 to 82 years and for men it had increased from 36.8 to 77 years. As remarkable and positive as these figures are, they gave us an indication that, if this trend continued, the demands on health and social care would exceed any expectations of the founders of the welfare state and pose massive financial problems for future governments.

SOCIAL WORKER – REGULATOR/VOLUNTEER

The move to Wiltshire marked, if anything else ever has done, a scaling down in my career. Some expert witness and mediation work continued, which included NHS complaints. In January 2002 I was appointed to the board of the newly created quango (a quasi-autonomous non-governmental organisation)[40n] the General Social Care Council (GSCC) based on London's South Bank near Southwark Cathedral close to my boyhood in the Peckham Diocese. The fee was just over £5,000 per annum for three days work a month. It turned out to take at least double that time.

Soon after moving I started to work as a volunteer with young offenders. The chance to get back to the start of my long career was too good to miss. I continued this face to face work until 2021. Throughout this period my expert witness work and Ann's membership of the North West Strategic Health Authority and Mental Health Tribunals (which was descending into chaos) kept us financially afloat.

The GSCC

The GSCC (known simply as the Council) was housed in modern offices overlooking the Thames. The chairman was Sir Rodney Brooke, a kind and able man with a long experience in local government.[41n] Its creation had been welcomed by the profession as 'social work' was now a protected title, the Council being responsible for registering all qualified social workers.[42n] The GSCC was also responsible for approving qualifying and post-qualifying courses, promoting the profession, and holding conduct hearings when complaints were received. It was also required to issue codes of practice. The staff were impressive and the facilities, modern furnishing, etc. had been acquired with full regard to the needs of people with a disability. Establishing the organisation, clarifying our scope and laying out basic policies and procedures was challenging stuff. The statutory Codes of Practice for Social Care Staff and Employers were issued late in 2002. They were generally welcomed and would form the basis against which conduct would be judged. The main problem was that while workers could face action, including deregistration, no sanctions were available against managers and employers. If we were sufficiently concerned about their behaviour we could send a report to the Secretary of State for investigation by the Chief Social Worker. In 2008 the Council sought power to make the employers' code a statutory instrument, but this was to no effect.

I enjoyed this work and sat on both the Education and Conduct Committees. As time went by the work on the board became more routine – developing our work and planning for the future where there was discussion on the next group of care workers to be registered. Whatever we chose, the sheer scale of the challenge, the costs involved and the knowledge that the workforce was somewhat transient were all practical issues beyond our decision making abilities. My argument was that we should concentrate on domiciliary workers who worked unsupervised in vulnerable people's homes. In 2004 the Council announced that they were the next group due to be registered.

I battled against the Council's objective to 'promote' social work. My idea was that this should be an active role, through press and TV, promoting dramas and documentaries on TV, etc. The chair ruled that the Council was not a campaigning organisation. My involvement became more concerned with the increasing number of conduct hearings, initially in London but then in Rugby which at least allowed me to drive up the old Roman Fosse Way through beautiful countryside. This was interesting and challenging work with social workers who had done stupid things for which they had already been disciplined by their employers, to serious cases of bad practice and neglect. For each there was a panel of three members, one of which was an expert in the relevant field of social work; we were advised by a barrister and the process went through the usual presentations by the barrister representing the Council and the legal or other representative for the worker. Many were represented by BASW's Advice and Representation Service or trades unions. When all was done and all questions asked, we adjourned to consider our findings. To my mind, although I am sure we usually reached the right conclusion, this was the weakest point in the process. The discussion, which was supported by our wise lawyers, sometimes relied on the relevance of the 'expert,' and on many occasions when asked for information on, say, the correct procedure in a child care case it would turn out that their expertise was mental health! In these rare cases, and when there was a historical element, my wide general experience was called for, despite its limitations. The other issues were the different approach and personality of the independent panel leader, who might encourage full discussion or push us to make an early decision. I believe, as we reported on these issues, the choice of leaders and relevance of experts was improved.

Most frustrating to me was the impossibility of dealing with managers whose failings were too often made clear during the hearings. I have a memory of one of the last panels I attended: this was to review the sanction placed on the social worker most involved with Baby P. She had suffered directly from the tragedy itself, from the way she was thrown to the wolves by management and had been constantly abused in the press. We were informed that our chairperson (the recently appointed Rosie Varley) was waiting for our decision in order to inform the Secretary of State. Our panel, together with a medical adviser, sifted through the history and the updated evidence, then, after much deliberation, we restored this social worker to the register subject to some re-training and increased supervision and support. I was delighted.

NHS Complaints

Working as an independent lay chair for local NHS complaints was always interesting and often distressing. The local staff handling the complaints would call to discuss a case that they were unable to resolve, or one for which it might be inappropriate that they were involved. I could then give advice or agree to take the case forward. In the latter case I would review the records and documentation, interview the complainant, obtain independent medical advice and then write a report to the relevant senior manager giving a view on the standard of care and liability. Reports ranged from some three to ten pages. On rare occasions this would proceed to a formal panel, which I chaired, usually accompanied by independent consultants and a senior nurse. I saw it as the most extended method of dealing with grief yet invented. One such hearing concerned a wife who had died in hospital under distressing circumstances. The complaint was lodged by her husband, her brothers and her in-laws. The men were all police detectives, the woman a nursing assistant. They had forensically examined all the records and were convinced that there had been errors in her care. The panel was protracted and the junior doctor highly distressed, being strongly advised by the panel consultant never to repeat the stupid mistake that he had made. He was severely reprimanded. In an effort to answer all the detailed complaints and to forestall further expensive legal action for all parties, my report was forty pages long. It was accepted by all parties.

In 2003 the government established the Healthcare Commission,[43] which was charged with reviewing healthcare provision throughout the UK, regulating the independent sector, investigating serious failures in healthcare and independently reviewing complaints not locally resolved. By 2004 this new body turned its attention to the existing system in which hundreds of volunteers like myself had been working for many years. Conflict was unavoidable. We were expecting local consultation sessions. In January, with three days notice, all lay chairs, NHS board members and CEOs in the south of England were invited to a meeting in Bournemouth. The meeting would start at 10am and end at 3.30pm. No expenses would be paid and anyone who registered and failed to attend would be fined £50. Did they really expect volunteers from Kent or Cornwall to give up a day, or two, at their own expense? I wrote a fierce letter to Lord Warner, a minister in the Department of Health asking whether anyone in the department had ever read Titmuss's *The Gift Relationship* on the value of altruism?[44n] I never received a reply, but later in the year they launched 'roadshows' to tell us about themselves and to seek our ideas and comments. Our group gathered in Bristol to hear the party line. Apparently the government had been worried by the wide variation in the lengths of reports written by lay chairs. It showed too wide a standard! The one piece of clear advice we gave was that they should be well prepared for the large wave of complaints that their centralised system would receive from across the country.

Those interested were invited to work for the Commission from their regional offices. Interestingly our contracts described us as 'lay reviewers/investigators/advisors and associate case managers.' Anyway, we signed up at £150 a day. Nothing happened except that there were press reports that thousands of complaint files were stacked in a warehouse awaiting attention. By March 2006 the Commission admitted that 'they had received a larger volume of complaints than they had anticipated' and were looking for a system that would be fair to complainants and was as an 'efficient use of public resources as possible.' Clearly no one had believed our advice and if resources were a problem why abandon the volunteer element? It then transpired that in order to deal with complaints we would have to attend the regional centre, which in my case was Manchester, to read the documentation! My protests that I regularly received highly confidential records as an expert witness and other NHS work, all securely packed and signed for, was ignored for the next two years. The next good idea to maximise our so far unused expertise required us to send in a list of our particular areas of interest and expertise in order to construct a national database so that we could be used on investigations other than complaints. Nothing happened.

It was some time before I was summoned to Manchester and accommodated in a fairly expensive hotel. On arrival at the office I was shown to my desk, as were several other people, and handed a pile of files to work through. In many ways this was helpful. I could read a file, decide a course of action, phone or e-mail the parties, come to a conclusion, write a report and write to the parties. These, how could I be so old fashioned, were templates in case we used any wrong words. On the other hand the complaints would be minor, for example parking charge disputes, impoliteness, or an improper attitude to a patient. All significant to the complainant, but hardly the serious issues that I had previously dealt with. All this structure, all these buildings, all the staff and costs just for this! It was a disgrace. I resigned in August 2006. The Commission was abolished two and a half years later, its responsibilities being passed to the Care Quality Commission who deal with complaints in relation to their inspection programmes.

Mediation

In early 2000, Neil Thompson, John Bates and I, at the request of an East London council, established an independent referral unit as an external investigation and mediation facility for their staff. The concept was good but personally I found the environment and the work too challenging. It was difficult to get to the right building; when you got there no one expected you and consequently the parties to the dispute were not available. Policies for equal opportunity and anti-discrimination were well in place, but despite this our involvement usually concerned bullying, harassment, victimisation and discrimination in the workplace. By the time a complaint reached us, it had been through the department's extensive grievance and resolution processes – therefore we had a lot of history to examine and many people to interview. Despite the value of our work and the challenges presented I found myself railing against the intense self-awareness of staff, their rights and ability to play the system to their advantage; our investigations were often prolonged by constant challenges and delays to our notes and draft reports. I fully recognised the immense pressure of work on the council, the effect of a target driven system, which, combined with the internal culture seemed, to have robbed managers of the ability to lead and take decisive action. Despite my career-long involvement and loyalty to trades unions I could not cope with a culture so focussed on rights and privileges. I just wondered how anyone ever got any meaningful work done.

Continuing Care

A much more worthwhile but distressing involvement with the local NHS was to chair the local strategic health authority's appeal panels about the dreaded issue of funding for continuing care. This happened when the cost of a relative's residential care became excessive due to escalating health issues. The question then arose whether the home could manage the extra care or should the NHS accept the cost? Faced with endless conflicts on this very personal issue, the government issued complex guidance which basically confused everyone. Specifically the decision rested on whether the health issues were now primary, intense, complex and/or unpredictable enough to qualify or whether the person was in the final stages of a terminal illness. We became involved when the district health authority had turned down an application.

The panel consisted of a doctor and a nurse from other authorities and we were advised by an independent medical consultant with relevant expertise. We had a full set of records and the special assessment that had been made against the criteria for funding. The appellant and their advisor attended to present their case, as did a senior member of the organisation being appealed against. I tried to make it as informal as possible and to make absolutely sure that every possible chink in the regulations had been thoroughly explored. The issue which obsessed every hearing was the appellant's focus on the distressing diagnosis and the consequent intensity of the treatment required. A question then arose as to whether the home, with qualified nurses and visiting doctors, could meet the need. These personal and emotional issues had to be weighed against the cold criteria outlined above and the work achieved by the original panel. Decisions were complicated by the fact that our advising medical consultants had differing views. We had been forced to turn down some appeals where the patient was diagnosed with dementia, then one consultant confirmed that this was a terminal diagnosis. Even so, what had to be decided was whether the patient was in the final stages. We granted as many appeals as we could, whereas others were referred back to the original panel for a re-think; others had to be refused. The next step was to present the case to the Health Ombudsman, who had the power to examine our work and outcome. It was tough work.

Jack Bury

On January 2nd 2005 we heard that my former chair, friend and bête-noire Jack Bury had died in a Blackburn hospice, after losing his fight with cancer. This was sad news indeed, and our thoughts went out to his daughters and grandson. I had been appointed as trustee of his estate in accordance with his will. Then I heard that, as a former Mayor of Blackburn, he was to have a non-religious service of celebration held in Blackburn Cathedral and I was asked to do a reading of my choice! The ceremony took place on January 10th 2005, and it was a very cold day indeed. The clergy welcomed the 200 people attending and then withdrew and let proceedings commence, the first item being me. I had agonised over this and had eventually settled on a quote from *Our World is Our Weapon*, an account by Subcomandante Marcos of his anti-government armed resistance in Mexico.[45] It was a stirring socialist tract of how the oppressed need to be led by lions. It seemed appropriate for a man whose political campaign covered more than 30 years. It was a good ceremony; Jack would have loved it. As we emerged from the cathedral former colleagues and friends, wrapped up tight against the weather, came up to embrace me. Seeing a familiar face, I gave one such mourner a big hug, only then realising that this was Pat Case who had blocked my appointment as Director! Ann was not happy.

CULTURE

Live 8

The wonders of Manchester were replaced by those of London, but more frequently by those of the cooler Bath. At the Theatre Royal our choice varied from the mix of African and East End cultures of *Elmira's Kitchen*[46] through the classic *The Rivals*[47] to a frightening production of *The Birthday Party*.[48] There was much laughter and enjoyment during Michael Frayn's *Noises Off*[49] and a tribute to the great comedian Tommy Cooper.[50]

In addition to these personal choices, in July 2005 we were stunned by the worldwide rock festival Live 8, which was a global cry to 'Make poverty history.' This coincided with a meeting of the G8, the eight richest countries, which was held in Edinburgh. The delegates were faced with many thousands of demonstrators. Live 8 was an unprecedented technical achievement, with concerts linked in London, Tokyo, Berlin, Rome, Paris, Moscow, Johannesburg, Philadelphia and Ontario. Not only was this a wondrous event with a great cause, but also this was a chance for us and for millions of people around the world to hear some of our most popular music legends. Unlike the original Live Aid twenty years earlier, this was not a fund raiser but rather an awareness event. As one of the organisers, Bono, of the rock band U2, explained 'We're not asking you to put your hands in your pockets but your fists in the air.' 'Get angry' was the theme. Among the stars in London were Bob Geldof, Paul McCartney, Elton John, David Bowie, Joss Stone, Madonna, Robbie Williams and Pink Floyd. It was indeed a powerful representation of the popular music of the decade. The UN Secretary General, Kofi Annan, and the great philanthropist Bill Gates both made appeals.

Our eclectic choices included the wonderful *Slava's Snowshow*, where we were taken aback by the performers sitting on the stage until the last members of the audience left. Next was Mathew Bourne's new all male production of Tchaikovsky's *Nutcracker* ballet; amazing. In Stroud we regularly attended performances of The Capella Singers, in which my nephew Richard White's wife Sarah sang. One of our final events to raise our ambitions was a performance of Wagner's Ring Cycle in the striking Wales Millennium Centre in Cardiff. We had forgotten that our names were on the waiting list, then one day in late November 2006, while I was mowing the lawn, my mobile rang and I was asked if we still wanted the tickets. I nearly collapsed when I was told the cost, but the chance to attend such a unique event was too much to resist, so off we went to Cardiff for four nights of opera and three days of touring the excellent shops in the city gathering Christmas presents. It was an exceptional experience. The sheer length was incredible, but also during all of the performances we sat in the same seats, so we could chat amongst ourselves and ask for advice and information as it continued. We were amused by the fact that there were subtitles in English as well as subtitles in Welsh. For the last night's performance the Prince of Wales attended and the Welsh version was raised to the top![51]

These are just a selection of our cultural adventures. Many would include family members or good friends from the village. In addition to our regular new year parties, we also started a monthly film show for the village. In complete contrast, my family marched me off to the 2008 Womad Festival, held a few miles from my house. The weather was good, the site vast and it suited me to wander from stage to stage to sample the music that met my mood, and it was wonderful to have Juliet and my grandchildren with me.

Spending Christmas with the family in Brooklyn, I was taken to a production of Tennessee Williams' *A Street Car Named Desire* starring Cate Blanchett in the role of Blanche Dubios. She portrayed that fragile sad lonely figure not so much with the brilliant dialogue but as a subtle posture or the slightest movement of her shoulders; a truly memorable performance.

FAMILY

Wiltshire

We, that is the humans, donkeys, hens, cockerel, ducks and my faithful collie Cassie, soon to be joined by geese, quickly settled into Croft Barn with the help of our loyal friends from Lancashire. We enjoyed the village life despite the fact that, with the title Lower Stanton St Quentin our village experienced a certain sense of inferiority to the actual Stanton St Quintin a couple of miles away. Halfway between the villages was a run-down village hall and I was soon involved in the campaign to upgrade it. We enjoyed frequent trips to London to see the family to enjoy the various school plays and concerts in which Aella and Duke took part. It was all very exciting. From Cornwall we found a contractor to install a new kitchen in Croft Barn, and when Ann discovered that one of the staff built and raced his car on the Castle Coombe circuit near our new home, she invested a small sum in the team. While I remained very busy, Ann remained a member of the North West Strategic Health Authority; sitting in on mental health reviews, she was shocked at the very poor reports submitted by social workers, usually because they had been handed the case only a few days before the hearing. Sometimes they had never met the patient who was applying for his or her freedom! She was furious. Her trips to Lancashire included accommodation at The Avenue, a small hotel on the edge of the private housing estate built by Gerald Hitman on the site of the old Brockhall Hospital. These excursions would have a significant consequence.

Luke and Andrea

The family often came to visit, as did Rod's nephew Luke, who became a close and valued family member, insisting a few years later that I was his nominal grandfather. My dear cousin Edna and her husband Bob also came to visit, preceded by cousin Andrea from Canada, soon after we had moved in. I persuaded her to stay for a week and we along with our DIY man Colin Schofield decided that we would down tools and explore Wiltshire and Gloucestershire. It went very well. This included a meal at the Vine Tree pub nearby which, unbeknown to me, was a favourite haunt for Prince Harry and his young friends. He strolled in and leaned casually against my chair. Andrea was overwhelmed.

Colin

Tragedy hit us during one visit to Cornwall when our dear helper and friend Colin Schofield was obviously unwell. Colin had recently had a serious operation for cancer and, although this was supposed to be a convalescence, he was becoming more and more lethargic. Ann tried everything she knew to boost his energy – special meals, tasty egg custards, etc. – but we reached a point where more help was required. An appointment was made with the local GP who examined him thoroughly and advised that he return home immediately to be with his family. He died a week later. It was a great loss. We missed his straightforward views on life and that wonderful acerbic Lancashire humour.

Three Special Visitors

Early in 2002, when booking her stay at The Avenue, Ann was told that on her next chosen dates the hotel would be full of young people from Belarus making an annual visit paid for and arranged by Gerald Hitman, whose ancestors came from that country, more recently devastated by the effects of the explosion of the Chernobyl atomic energy site – nothing that would deter Ann. In September Hitman changed his approach and brought over three teenagers to study for a year at Blackburn College. Soon after the start of term Hitman phoned to ask if we would agree to host these three young people over Christmas as his family could not accommodate them and anyway they needed to see more of England than Lancashire. We agreed, providing we had a chance to meet them first, perhaps over breakfast or mid-morning coffee? That was brushed aside; Gerald never rose early. He insisted on an evening meal, so, on a date on which we had already invited our close friends Wendy and Jeff to a meal, along came Gerald and three interesting visitors – Yulia, her brother Sacha and the effervescent Olga. Once we had agreed to host the visitors, Gerald departed, leaving me to pay the bill, which included his 'special' meal prepared by the chef just for him. So that's how you become a millionaire!

We all had a great Christmas, and they visited during every subsequent college holiday and the summer before they had to return home. It was the start of a life enhancing adventure. These three teenagers, whose English was perfect, were entertaining, charming and mischievous. Croft Barn suited them well; they could live in their own space upstairs and swoop down on us whenever they chose. Our family adopted them, as did the village, who invited them to all events. Our friends Dave and Mary Haines and the wonderful Smith family set up BBQs in their honour. The same went for the entire village of Cadgwith in Cornwall, although the age of the residents made life a little more difficult. Having handed the food around at a party arranged for the neighbours to meet them, Sacha commented 'They are all talking about their cats. No one asks about me or my country.'

We visited the sights of London and took them to all the local places of interest too. When in Lancashire, we would visit the house that Gerald had assigned them. This was a run-down cottage near Blackburn Rovers' training ground, beset with rats and many other problems. Ann had no problem tackling Gerald on such issues. As payment, the three had to do tasks in Gerald's house and gardens. They entertained us to tea or supper many times, entertaining us with their good humoured banter at tea or supper many gaining support from each other and us. As the time to return to Belarus approached, a difficult problem developed. We learnt that Yulia had been having an affair with an older man, Joseph, whose shoulder she had cried on when she last flew back to London. This caused us concern. Were we in loco parentis? What was to be done? We arranged to meet him in a very nice Asian restaurant on Edgware Road.

This placed Sacha in an impossible situation; he was embarrassed and upset by his older sister's behaviour and felt that, as his father's representative, he should not meet and certainly not accept hospitality from this man. Ann talked him into coming by promising that they would sit opposite each other and as far away from the happy couple as possible. The meal went well, but directly it was over Sacha stood up and announced that we were leaving! The last days of their stay were spent in Cornwall, where yet another issue came up. On touring the Blackburn markets and shops they had stacked up a lot of clothing, plus all their study books and papers. They arrived at Redruth Station with about twelve heavy cases. Luckily we had taken two cars so could cope with the vast amount of luggage.

The last episode was a flood of phone calls from Gerald, who had just learnt about the affair. We had to ensure that Yulia got on the plane home. Her visa was about to run out and he would be financially liable if she did not leave. We managed to get through this and he agreed to pay for getting the luggage to the airport and the majority of the inevitable excess baggage charge. We arranged for a friend who drove his van to London regularly to take all the luggage from Paddington to the boyfriend's and leave it for him to get it to the airport. Eventually we all arrived at Gatwick Airport, the lovers canoodling in a corner while the check-in just accepted all the luggage (their most frequent customers were students) and off they all went with many many tears from all. We noticed that Joseph was on the same train back to London so on arrival we hijacked him into tea and cakes at the hotel. We were naturally upset by the whole thing, but he assured us of his true love and explained that Yulia would come back to London as soon as possible and attend college, while he would leave his wife and children. Wow! All we could do was warn him of what might be in store from this obsession. In London, at college surrounded by students of her own age, would Yulia really stay with a man who was older than her father? It could all end in disaster. How wrong we were.

Belarus and Russia

In September 2004, after surviving visa difficulties, we kept our promise and flew to Belarus. We were met by Olga and Sacha, Sacha's father and a friend who had driven from their home town. Sacha was shyly holding a bouquet of gladiolus, the national flower of Belarus. We were driven to our hotel in the centre of Minsk and they promised to pick us up next morning, which they did. The route to Babruysk was fascinating. We saw a busy heavily forested modern country with many lakes; as time went by we established that the trip was some ninety miles. So they had driven there and back late the previous night and were now repeating the journey! We stayed a week in a small basic hotel where, of course, no one spoke English. It was a good job that we were seasoned travellers.

Our young hosts proudly showed us around their town. The trips by tram were fun, and we visited the markets, a new paved area with coffee and ice cream shops and young people sitting around gossiping round the outside tables. Ann as usual wanted to know what they were all saying. This was, of course, a communist dictatorship where corruption was rife. All the youngsters' parents were doctors, so as they were driving us around town we would always be stopped by the police on some pretext and cash had to be handed over. We visited churches, memorials and, embarrassingly, an English class at their old school. Everyone was very welcoming and kind. We were invited for dinner at their parents' comfortable flats and taken to nice restaurants. As the parents were consultant doctors (who were paid less than the police) we were able to visit their clinics, including the modern oncology unit of the main hospital. It was well equipped with the best equipment, donated by Japan following the Chernobyl disaster.

We had a very nice day in Minsk enjoying the main sights and statues, including that of the great poet Yakub Kolas. We noticed that, after a marriage ceremony and before the meal, married couples went to the local war memorial to pay tribute to the war heroes. It was a great visit, the only difficult part being having to explain as best we could what had happened with Yulia to her parents and that we had no knowledge of the relationship until it was too late. It was all very distressing, especially for poor Sacha, who, sitting on the floor, had to translate everything. It was a very emotional session, by the end of which we were all in tears. After a week we travelled to Russia and St Petersburg together as tourists.

The flight was via Moscow, and much to our surprise our passports were never checked. We just got straight off the plane, picked up our baggage and went into the busy terminal. This was a few months after the terrible Beslan school siege. We sat and discussed our situation; should we raise our concerns or keep a low profile? We chose the latter, caught our connecting flight and arrived at our hotel in St Petersburg late in the evening. Passports were surrendered … and then the trouble started. Without a landing document the hotel could not allow us in! A long negotiation ensued between the manager and our companions, with Ann getting more and more upset. Eventually it was agreed that we could stay the night but we must get the right documents early next morning. Back at the airport our dilemma was explained and, behold, a beautiful, fashionably dressed young woman took our passports and returned minutes later with the correct papers. Despite the poor and rather dirty hotel, complete with a security guard on every floor, our visit was a delight. St Petersburg is a beautiful city to wander around; we spent a long time in the famous Hermitage Gallery and we visited interesting museums, but the centrepiece was a hydrofoil trip on the Baltic to the amazing Peterhof Palace with its lakes, extraordinary fountains, statues and glorious palatial interior. We wandered round the gardens, where Ann picked up an acorn as a souvenir. The next day we said goodbye to Sacha and Olga, who, at their parents' insistence, were homeward bound on a very long train journey. We flew home.

We kept in touch with Yulia and I recently visited her, Joseph and their daughter in North London where they are happily settled. Yulia gained her qualifications as a chartered accountant, and all are deeply involved with the local community with her mother visiting regularly. In 2016 I had the great pleasure of attending Olga's wedding to Anders in the small town of Nykarleby in northern Finland. It was a magically enjoyable time and I was glad to meet up with her father who I had last seen twelve years previously in Belarus. They now have a son, Alfred.

Rod and The Wedding

In London, Juliet and Rod were settled with their two young children. Juliet abandoned her career to care for them and Rod was working hard searching for work as a director – a tough time waiting for the phone to ring and then weighing up whether to take a short film or wait for a longer job to turn up. It was constant stress. At that time, Rod worked for Lonely Planet, which, of course, meant travelling far and wide, but he very much disliked leaving his family. His very personal film, made in Poland under the tutorship of the great Andre Wajda, *A Fly Went By*, was broadcast in the autumn of 2003.

Pursuing my determination to bring the reality of social work to TV, I asked Rod and Juliet to film the Intensive Support and Supervision Programme for young offenders in Birmingham. It took a few days but far from the excitement expected of such a volatile group they all behaved like angels, thus robbing the film of any drama and narrative. Rod had to rely on the staff's car running out of petrol in the middle of Birmingham as the only point of drama. The finished short film and music were excellent, but the film did not appeal to any production companies, although I did use it to try to tempt the BBC to pick up the challenge, but to no avail.

Rod then started directing some major TV series, which were all very successful. One, *Make My Day*, was a particular challenge to film owing to the unpredictable nature of the participants and the number of hidden cameras. These followed the nominated 'victim,' perhaps on the way to work. Their attention 'happened' to be drawn to a car which had broken down and just 'happened' to be driven by their favourite pop star. The star would then turn up to their work with some thank you flowers, and so the day would continue with extraordinary events ending in an invitation to join the pop star for an evening event where the plot and the day's filming would be revealed. One of the most memorable ended on the ferry across the Mersey accompanied by the iconic song. His next series was *Crisis Command*, in which a group of volunteers had to stop a potentially devastating military attack on the UK. It starred Gavin Hewitt, a leading BBC correspondent. Rod's reputation was growing; he was definitely getting noticed! This was a very stressful period for the family, so we planned a trip to Rome which was enjoyed by us all, particularly the grandchildren who thoroughly embraced the vibe of that magical city.

In early February 2006 Juliet and Rod were in Northern Ireland, their first real break away from the children, when Rod had a phone call from the directors of Rockstar Games in New York inviting him over for a discussion. He went a few days later when he realised that this was not an interview but just to decide when he could start work! By the end of February Juliet had flown over and Rod had started his career as the film director working on the *Grand Theft Auto* series and subsequently many others. There were many things to be organised, most importantly schooling for Aella and Duke and a marriage, without which the family could not reside in America. It was all hands on deck to gather all the evidence to confirm that Rod's unique talents were not available in America, along with all the other documents and preparation for the wedding.

The wedding took place on August 11th 2005 at the impressive Marylebone Town Hall. I just managed to escort my beautiful daughter into the ceremony before the tears started. After the ceremony a red bus took all the guests to the old 20th Century Theatre in Westbourne Grove where many relatives and friends sat down to a good meal and speeches, including ones from Aella and Duke. As the theatre staff, caterers and others needed payment in cash, all my pockets were stuffed with notes. I felt a lot safer when the last person had been paid. It was a wonderful and memorable day, by the end of which we were all exhausted. In August 2006 we stood on the platform of the picturesque Brunel built Kemble station to wave goodbye to Juliet and our grandchildren as they started their journey to New York and their new life experiences. It was pretty devastating. Moving 90 miles away from them was one thing, but now it would be 3,000 miles!

Ann and Joan

Disaster struck late in the morning of Wednesday 26th October 2005 when we were sitting in the kitchen and Ann said 'I've got something to show you and you're not going to like it.' She took her bra off and there was a growth the size of a small egg on her left breast. I was stunned by thoughts of why she had kept this secret for so long, how come I didn't know and angrier feelings of horror at the consequences of that delay, but those thoughts had to be subdued – this was not the time. I gave her a comforting cuddle and phoned the GP to arrange an emergency appointment for that afternoon. He was clearly as shocked as I had been, muttering something to the effect that we were all now in a game of 'catch up.' He dispatched an urgent referral to a unit at Frenchay Hospital near Bristol, a ramshackle wartime building with long corridors leading to other old buildings. It did not take long to be told that this was a cancer gone beyond surgery, so we were transferred to the Bristol oncology department under the care of the excellent Dr Braybrooke.

It appeared that we were on what the NHS was pleased to call a 'pathway.' This was a rather intriguing concept as one imagines a smooth pathway leading into the future but with no clear destination. As it turned out the path was long, with steep emotional and physical ups and downs and the occasional bottomless crater. We were accompanied all the way by a variety of nurses and doctors who explained every step, and who remained kind, considerate, honest and invariably hopeful. Either side of the route were our family, our extended family, our long-time friends and the villagers who supported us with love and extraordinary kindness, while being ever ready to step onto the path to support us if we stumbled. Ann, of course, embarked on the journey with her usual determination, courage, intelligence and pragmatism. Standing a little back, although regularly in touch on the phone, was Ann's sister Joan who had recently had a mastectomy, and, although she had recovered well, she was now showing signs that all was not well.

We were both very anxious arriving for Ann's first chemotherapy treatment. An introduction to our key nurse, who proved such a help throughout the coming months, was reassuring, as was the kindness of the nurses and the positive ethos of the whole unit, and of course our own long experience of hospital cultures and routines. Ann had blood and general health tests before being connected to the chemo which would drip in for the next hour or so. We could read the papers, chat with the patients and staff and discuss where we went from here. These visits would continue for many months on a three-weekly cycle: a week to recover from the effects of the chemo, a week to build yourself up and a week feeling relatively strong, despite the increasing pain, before you were hit again. It was an increasingly distressing time as repeated blood tests proved difficult and Ann was soon covered in slow to heal bruises as the chemo dosage was increased. We were faced with managing the long list of daily medications: steroids, anti-emetics and antibiotics. Visits, telephone calls, messages, cards and letters poured in. The family came down for Christmas, which was very much enjoyed.

By this time Ann had lost all her hair, which was very distressing indeed for her. For most of January 2006 Ann was very depressed and often in floods of tears. Despite my reassurances that she looked wonderful with a bright headscarf she found a top wigmaker, Raoul, near Paddington Station, who made wigs that boosted Ann's confidence and fooled most people. Whenever Ann was strong enough, trips to Cornwall were a boon.

In February 2006 a clot was found on Ann's lung which necessitated a painful course of warfarin and more blood tests! Unfortunately there was a violent reaction with her other mediation and Ann, very ill by this time, was admitted to hospital. To make matters worse, she was placed in a room at the end of a corridor in which the only window was too high to see out of. This was partly because the hospital had been hit by the dreadful norovirus (the winter vomiting infection) – it felt like a punishment cell to be endured. It took all of Juliet's and my efforts to keep Ann's spirits up for the eight days until she got home to slowly regain her strength. Juliet and I caught the bug, but Ann never did. In the interim Ann decided to join the newly established advisory group whose aim it was to gain real-time feedback from patients. Inaugural meetings were attended, discussions were held and regular meetings scheduled. Ann was determined to match her experience on health boards with her current experience as a patient. She spotted the gaps in any presentation and weighed into the discussion.

Eventually treatment could be resumed and it was back to the chemotherapy with those dreadful three-week cycles. In August 2006 we were strong enough to attend Rod and Juliet's wedding in London (see above) and in November of that year, determined to see where our family was living, we managed a quiet trip to Brooklyn. Aella had dived into the new environment and was doing well at the United Nations International School, but Duke's more conservative nature had found the loss of Fitzjohns School and his friends more unsettling, and his new, laid back, 'hippy' type school, quite a puzzle.

All this, of course, demanded careful management of Ann's treatment regimes. By the end of 2006 we seemed to be winning as the tumour was shrinking to about a third of its size and for a brief period treatment moved to radiotherapy. By spring 2007 Ann was back on the chemo, although of a different sort, which continued throughout that year. During this time Ann experienced painful dry eyes. This was well treated in the new hospital in Swindon, with a warning against animals and dust for a month, an impossibility living in a stone barn with a loving dog, donkeys and fowl.

Ann's sister Joan's health had been slowly declining and her family were considering the need for a nursing home when in August she fell at home and had to be admitted to hospital. We drove down to Derriford Hospital, Plymouth, as soon as we could, but were warned by the staff that she had 'pulled down the shutters' and was not responding to anyone. We sat with her, bringing her up to date with family news, but there was no noticeable response, so we kissed her and left. The drive home was very quiet. Dear Joan died on September 23rd 2007, the death certificate showing cancer as the cause. The funeral on October 2nd at St Stephen's-by-Saltash was attended by family and friends, and we carried her casket to the thanksgiving service before she was buried next to her husband. It was very distressing indeed, lifted only by the intense reminiscing over the old family photos with their cousin Shirley who had shared those happy childhood days on the Launceston farm.

Juliet was visiting us in February 2008 when we thought that Ann had suffered a mild stroke. We drove her to Bristol Royal Infirmary where we experienced the bad and the good of the NHS. On asking for a wheelchair, I was told none were available. However, a young patient gave up hers, thus we got Ann into the assessment unit where tests and a scan were quickly completed. On her way back from the toilet Juliet heard the consultant advising the very young doctor assessing Ann to 'tell them the truth,' so she was slightly more prepared for the explanation that the scan, revealing that multiple sites of the bloody cancer had got into my wife's brain. The next weeks marked the worst experience of the whole regime.

As the hospital was now in the grips of the MRSA virus, Ann was placed in a 'closed' ward with limited access requiring complex anti-infection procedures. The ward was busy with restricted visiting times, which meant that Ann was bored and restless as her eight-bedded section was shared with the demented and dying. I stayed for as long as I was allowed and took over basic nursing. As the nursing point was directly outside the bay, Ann could easily hear all the nurses chatting and details being passed at handover. Ann found this very distressing indeed. Too late, I discovered that the next section had housed two charming men who were completely compos mentis. Why did the nurses not introduce them to Ann or vice versa and relieve Ann of so much distress?

By far the worst days were when we had to attend radiotherapy, which was buried in the dingy basement. Delays were endemic, made far worse by the fact that we were shut in a small side room to prevent cross-infection, thus denying us any chance to see how long we had to be confined. Ann's anxiety was such that she hated me leaving her side to ask about progress. By far the most terrifying thing was Ann's fear of the close head mask that had to be worn once in the therapy room. She hated it and always emerged in tears, clinging to me until we were calm enough to head back to the ward. The treatment however did significantly help the effects of the cancer and, once home in late March, Ann came under care of the physiotherapists from Chippenham Hospital who visited daily. They were amazing – Ann enjoyed their visits and responded remarkably. Her natural courage and determination meant that she religiously followed every exercise to exhaustion, and, bit by bit, most of the impairments were substantially eased. It was an amazing achievement.

Unfortunately, I seemed to enter some sort of grey world or dissociative state around this time, so what follows is somewhat vague. We enjoyed short shopping trips where Ann enjoyed the attachment to the wheelchair and the wide swings from aisle to aisle. We had frequent visitors and the animals brought Ann much pleasure. Somewhere along the line Ann became weaker and spent more time on the sofa or in bed; next she needed help to get out of bed for the toilet; and then came the realisation that I did not have the physical strength to support her. Our friends Dave and Mary from the village were able to help – Dave came daily to help with the lifting and Mary brought garden flowers and delightful cakes. Juliet and Rod arrived whenever they could to help and to talk with Ann and read her stories. By this time a hospital bed was needed and was delivered without delay. Macmillan nurses from the local hospice were regular visitors, as was the counselling specialist who talked with us all, offering good advice.

As the start of summer arrived, the family arrived, although Aella, completing her first year at Sussex University, was in Paris. Ann's strength was slowly ebbing away and she now needed sedation, administered by our GPs, Drs Wilkinson and Ingham, who visited daily, consulting the nurses in hushed tones over exactly how much of each ingredient was appropriate for that day. While our attention was on Ann, Duke naturally, at the age of eleven and sensing that this was a long term problem, asked if he could stay with friends for a while. This was quickly arranged. I think it was on July 10th while I was in bed, holding tight to Ann's hand, that Juliet snuggled in beside me followed by Rod, and then the faithful dog stretched herself out at the foot of the bed. A memorable night. The following morning, as everything seemed stable with no sign of alarm, Juliet and Rod decided to go to the shops leaving Dave and I to care for Ann. Dave walked outside for a quick smoke, a few minutes later I crossed the corridor for a quick pee, heard a deep sigh, stepped back into the room and realised that my darling wife had just died. How the hell did that happen? Dave briefly did what was essential and, as the light of reality swept away my defences, I sat in the corridor and howled as never before. Rod and Juliet had got no further than petrol pumps less than a third of a mile away! The GP attended and in the early evening we stood silently holding each other tight as the funeral director carried my lover, wife, carer and manager of forty-six years to the hearse. Just short of the three-year prognosis given on our first visit to the GP. It was July 11th 2008, the day before Juliet's birthday.

Juliet and I did the legal rounds and then turned our minds to the funeral. Attending previous funerals, Ann had expressed her view that once life had left the body it was of no value, and this led us to decide on a private cremation immediately followed by a service of thanksgiving for her life. Our short convoy set out through the pretty country lanes to the local crematorium where Rod, nephews Richard and Jonathan, and I carried the casket in for the short service. We then went back to our local church, Saint Giles in Stanton St Quintin, which was packed with many close relatives, family members and friends who had travelled from far and wide. It was a wonderful service. Elegant tributes were given by Juliet, Aella and me. As we left the church, Duke gave vent to his grief at full throttle. We moved back to Croft Barn for a reception organised by Juliet and her best friend Melissa from Lancashire. There were snacks, a hot meal and time to reminisce and catch up with relatives and friends. Eventually people drifted away and we were left to be hit by the absence of the central person in all our lives. We were comforted by the knowledge that this was not over, that the following spring we would scatter Ann's ashes in her beloved Cadgwith where she could finally rest.

Eventually the family had to return to New York and the half of me that was left was alone in this large house to work out what had happened. Was smoking for over thirty years to blame? Was it the pill or stress? Perhaps genetics had played a part, after all her sister had died of the same disease. There was no clear answer to these questions, or to the mystery of her fatal decision to hide her cancer until it was too late. Her only explanation was that she did not want to cast a cloud over the wedding, but that had only spanned a few weeks and the cancer that she revealed in that dreadful morning had been there much longer. Perhaps there was some deep element in the insecurity and lack of self value that I know lay behind the extrovert personality that faced the world. I had tried so hard, so many times, to get Ann into the Queen's Honours List for her years of public service, but despite brilliant references and support I never succeeded. It would have meant so much to her. A few months later I visited Ann's friend Jane Elvy, still grieving from her husband's recent death, in Scotland. She sent me the following verse from Marjorie Pizer's *The Existence of Love*:[52]

> I had thought that your death
> Was a waste and a destruction,
> A pain of grief hardly to be endured.
> I am only beginning to learn
> That your life was a gift and a growing
> And a loving left with me.
> The desperation of death
> Destroyed the existence of love,
> But the fact of death
> Cannot destroy what has been given.
> I am learning to look at your life again
> Instead of at your death and your departing.

We decided that Ann's memorial must be in Cornwall, and, after some hilariously Cornish procedures, it was decided to replace the badly deteriorating 'stick' in Cadgwith Cove. Thus, a twelve foot long, four inches thick plank of hard wood was installed by our builder Richard Woods outside the cafe. A discrete bronze plaque memorialises two Cornish sisters.

> A loving family tribute to Ann Jordan, and sister Joan White. Forever Cornish.
> Daughters of W.W. Wicket, headmaster of Ruan Minor School 1927–31

Easter 2009 saw us carrying small bouquets of wild hedgerow plants including forget me nots down the steep hill to the Cove and up the far side to the Huer's Hut where we scattered Ann's ashes while the wonderful Fisherman's Choir sang the old songs that we knew so well. While the ashes were being scattered, a rare Cornish chough flew right overhead. We recalled the sisters' connection with the village going back over a hundred years and how the church roof had been raised at the thanksgiving service by a great rendition of the Cornish anthem 'Trelawney'. While the ashes were scattered the choir sang 'Cornwall My Home' with the chorus:

> And no one will ever move me from this land
> Until the Lord calls me to sit at his hand
> For this is my Eden, and I'm not alone
> For this is my Cornwall and this is my home.

Juliet read an extract from Emily Bronte's *The Loving Spirit*:

> Alas – the countless links are strong
> That binds us to our clay;
> The loving spirit lingers on,
> And would not pass away.

By now we were all in floods of tears and clinging to each other for strength. The Fisherman's Choir finished with Edwin Ufford's hymn:

> Throw out the lifeline
> Throw out the lifeline
> Someone is drifting away
> Throw out the lifeline
> Throw out the lifeline
> Someone is drifting away
>
> When our eyes behold through the gath'ring night
> The city of gold, our harbour bright
> We shall anchor by the heav'nly shore
> With the storms all past for ever more

All that was left was to walk back to the Cove and christen the 'Stick' with beers all round and some further spontaneous singing. Then, back to our house, leaving the new 'Stick' with its bronze inscription to two remarkable women who both left such great memories and extraordinary descendants to carry their genes forward.

NOTES AND REFERENCES

1. President George W. Bush's speech to a joint session of Congress on September 20th 2001.
2. 'Closing Time' from the 1992 Album *The Future* by Leonard Cohen.
3. See Bergen, P. (2011). *The Longest War: The Enduring Conflict Between America and Al-Qaeda*. London: Simon & Schuster.
4. The document drawn up in 2001 by Dick Cheney and Lewis Libby (Vice President and Chief of Staff), Donald Rumsfeld and Paul Wolfowitz (Defence Secretary and Deputy) and Jebb Bush was entitled 'Rebuilding America's Defences.' It envisaged military control of the whole Gulf region

and the enlargement of American bases in the Middle East and the Far East in order to discourage advanced industrial nations from challenging America's leadership. The UK was seen as the most effective and efficient means of exercising American leadership. See Meacher, M. (2003). 'This War on Terrorism is bogus,' *The Guardian*, 06.09.03, p. 21.

5. Following agreement between the UN and NATO, forces (18 countries) took over responsibility for security based in Kabul and led the International Security Assistance Force (ISAF).
6. In February 2006, Congress received a report on the military's four-year strategic review, which concluded that America 'faced a ruthless enemy intent on destroying our way of life and an uncertain future.' The term 'The long war' replaced 'The war on terror.' Beyond Afghanistan and Iraq, the commanders envisioned 'a war unlimited in time and space against global Islamist extremism. The struggle ... may well be fought in dozens of other countries simultaneously and for many years to come.' Reported in Tindsall, S. and MacAskill, E. (2006). 'America's Long War,' *The Guardian*, 15.02.06, p. 19.
7. 'A strange kind of discourse has developed in the US. The idea appears to be that it is necessary to turn everyone into Americans so that Americans are able to live in safety in a world without borders.' See Stuart Jeffries' article 'Risky Business' presenting a preview of a lecture given by Ulrich Beck in the LSE on 15.02.06.
8. I am indebted to the rough summary of events on Wikipedia for the basis of this introduction.
9. Summers, A. and Swan, R. (2012). *'The Eleventh Day: The Full Story of 9/11*. New York: Ballantine Books, pp. 175–176.
10. 'How did the neo-conservatives end up overreaching themselves that they risk undermining their own goals? How did a group with such a pedigree come to decide that the "root cause" of terrorism lay in the Middle East's lack of democracy and that the US had the wisdom and ability to fix this problem?' See Fukuyama, F. (2006). 'Neo conservatism has evolved into something I can no longer support,' The Guardian, 22.02.06.
11. In recognition of the many years of voluntary effort in giving these tributes, the title 'Royal' was awarded to the town, thus becoming only the third Royal town in the UK.
12. *The Guardian*, 25.11.03, p. 7.
13. Dench, G., Gavron, K. and Young, M. (2006). *The New East End: Kinship, Race and Conflict*. London: Profile Books.
14. Anthony, A. (2008). 'How Britain turned its back on the white working class,' *The Guardian*, 02.03.08, p. 31.
15. Kettle, M. (2006). 'We can't just blame our lack of trust on Tony Blair's lies,' *The Guardian*, 30.12.06, p. 31.
16. Burke, J. (2006). 'Omar was a normal British teenager who loved his little brother and Man Utd. So why did he want to blow up a nightclub in London?' *Observer Magazine*, 20.01.06, pp. 15–24.
17. This includes 100 soldiers who committed suicide during or shortly after service and 100 who died as a result of accidents.
18. In 1978 the BBC journalist Georgi Markov, a severe critic of the Russian regime, was stabbed by an umbrella which administered a dose of the poison ricin while walking across Waterloo Bridge.
19. UNICEF (2007). Innocenti Report Card 7: *An Overview of Child Wellbeing in Rich Countries*. February, 2007.
20. Johnson, P. (2007). 'Crisis Point over Britain's disaffected youth,' *The Daily Telegraph*, 15.02.07.
21. Carvel, J. (2008). 'Dossier prepared for UN details grim plight of many young people in Britain,' *The Guardian*, 09.06.08, p. 4.
22. Springer, S. (2008). CEO Napier Scott, quoted in *The Guardian*, 21.09.08, p. 37.
23. Wintor, P. (2008). 'Blunkett sets out scheme to stop formation of an underclass,' *The Guardian*, 07.01.08, p. 13.

24. Vitali, S., Glattfelder, J. and Battiston, S. (2015). 'The Networks of Global Corporate Control,' PLoS ONE network, 26.10.15. An article by Vivienne Westwood, 'Who Are Our Masters?' in *My Greenpod* magazine, drew my attention to the work of Karen Hudes who was a whistleblower and former senior counsel at the World Bank who set out to expose the corruption at the heart of world finance showing a conspiracy against national sovereignty. There was a great deal of support for her analysis, although many of her later allegations were much less secure.
25. Three similar bodies were established in Wales, Scotland and Northern Ireland.
26. In 2012 under the coalition government the GSCC was closed, losing its functions to the Health Professions Council, and SCIE was subsumed within the health focussed National Institute for Clinical Excellence (NICE).
27. Revens, L. (2001). 'The hub of all that's best,' *Community Care*, 08.08.01.
28. Kahan, B and Levy, A. (1991). *'The Pindown Experience and the Protection of Children. Report of the Staffordshire Child Care Inquiry*. Staffordshire County Council. Pindown was a regime developed in North Staffordshire which claimed to be based on behaviourist principles but came to be applied in a harsh and abusive way.
29. Laming, H. (2003). *The Victoria Climbié Inquiry*. Report of an inquiry by Lord Laming. Cmnd 730 London HMSO.
30. Department for Education and Science (2003). *Every Child Matters – Summary*, Crown Copyright, p. 7.
31. Revens, L. and Pearce, J. (2001). 'Cross-border raiders,' *Community Care*, 22.08.01.
32. Report by Steve Davies of Cardiff University commissioned by the Public and Commercial Services Union. Its General Secretary Mark Serwotka called this 'soft privatisation with the voluntary sector opening up services for contests which could subsequently be won by the private sector'. See Henke, D. (2006). 'Government turns charities into multimillion-pound businesses,' *The Guardian*, 03.07.06, pp. 8–9.
33. Charity Commission (2007), *Stand and Deliver: The Future of Charities Delivering Public Services* and Gillan, S. (2006). 'Government has abused our charitable status,' *Community Care*, 08.02.06, p. 15.
34. The final £3 million grant had been opposed by senior civil servants but had then been approved by two senior ministers, a tribute to the power and influence of Camila Batmanghelidjh. See *Kids Company: The Inside Story*, a 2016 documentary following the demise of the organisation. BBC, Lynn Alleway. Exec Producer Katie Bailiff.
35. Esping-Anderson has argued that the social and educational advantage of the well off came not from their wealth or better facilities but from the development of advanced cognitive skills in early childhood. Therefore governments who wish to enhance potential and increase equality should invest in intense education before the age of five. See Esping-Anderson, G. (1990). *The Three Worlds of Welfare Capitalism*. New York: Princeton University Press.
36. My memory is that Shoesmith had been Director of Education and had no detailed social work knowledge or experience and had only been in post a short while. Nonetheless she was seen as an effective manager. In the years following her dismissal, she won a number of court cases against her persecutors and received some compensation. Eight years later she completed a book and used her experience to examine the extraordinary response to the tragedy of Baby P and to put this in the perspective of the estimated 2000 other familial child murders that happened between the Climbié and Baby P deaths. For an excellent read, see Shoesmith, S. (2016). *Learning from Baby P: The Politics of Blame, Fear and Denial*. London: Jessica Kingsley. See also *The Last Days of Baby P*. Special Issue, *The Independent*, 16.11.08.
37. Butler, I. and Drakeford, M. (2005). *Scandal, Social Policy and Social Welfare*. Bristol: Policy Press, explored the close involvement of a black family and black staff, and the tendency of others to be

wary of involvement was to be repeated ten years later in the dreadful Rotherham scandal. See Chapter 16.
38. GSCC (2008). *Social Work at its Best: A Statement of Social Work Roles and Tasks for the 21st Century*. London: GSCC.
39. 'Tories lament social work stress', *Professional Social Worker Magazine*, July 2008.
40. In the early 1980s governments took to creating 'arms length bodies,' of which quangos were one example. Whilst they were financially supported by government, who therefore exercised some control, they were usually expected to raise their own funding over time, thus they were seen as reducing the cost to the Treasury. Their staff were not counted as civil servants, thus defending accusations of escalating bureaucracy. In addition to these rather questionable reasons, the fact that they were responsible for the success of their work meant that any failures could not be laid at a minister's feet.
41. Rodney Brooke had been the CEO of Westminster Council during the scandal caused by the 'Homes for votes' policy of the Leader, Dame Shirley Porter. This involved selling off public housing, in particular a large block of council flats, all of which inevitably drove the inhabitants out of the borough to be replaced by homeowners, more likely to vote Conservative. Brooke explained that although Porter had great charisma and drove the policy through, she was also unpleasant and vindictive. (See Guardian.co.uk.) He resigned, and later the policy was declared illegal by the district auditor, who imposed a surcharge of £42 million on Dame Shirley. In 2004 she paid an agreed settlement of £12.3 million.
42. Councils continued in Wales, Scotland and Northern Ireland.
43. The Health and Social Care (Community Health and Standards) Act, 2003.
44. Titmuss, R. M. (1970). *The Gift Relationship: From Human Blood to Social Policy*. London: Allen and Unwin. Titmuss argued that man is inherently altruistic and the role of government is to create the social and economic climate which best channels man's drive to work together for the common good. It is recognised as a classic text in social policy and was nominated by the *New York Times* as one of the most important books of the year.
45. Subcomandente Insurgente Marcos and Ponce de Leon, J. (2001). *Our World is Our Weapon*. New York: Selected.
46. Kwei-Armah, K. *Elmina's Kitchen*, starring Shaun Parkes, Paterson Joseph and Dona Croll.
47. Sheridan, R. B. *The Rivals*, starring Nicholas Boulton, Jasmine Hyde, Stephanie Cole and George Baker.
48. Pinter, H. *The Birthday Party*, starring Geoffrey Hutchings and Eileen Atkins.
49. Frayn, M. *Noises Off*, starring Cheryl Campbell, Philip Franks and James Albrecht.
50. Fisher, J. *Jus' Like That*, starring Jerome Flynn as Tommy Cooper.
51. Wagner's Ring Cycle by the Marininsky Opera. Conductor George Valery.
52. Pizer, M. 'The Existence of Love.' In *To You the Living. Poems of Bereavement and Loss*, from *Selected Poems 1963–1983*. Sydney: Pinchgut Press.

SIXTEEN

2009–2019

ON THE EDGE
(MAKING US GREAT – AGAIN)

All of us share this world for but a brief moment in time. The question is whether we spend that time focused on what pushes us apart, or whether we commit ourselves to an effort – a sustained effort – to find common ground, to focus on the future we seek for our children, and to respect the dignity of all human beings.

There is also one rule that lies at the heart of every religion – that we do unto others as we would have them do unto us. This truth transcends nations and peoples – a belief that isn't new; that isn't black or white or brown; that isn't Christian, or Muslim or Jew. It's a belief that pulsed in the cradle of civilization, and that still beats in the heart of billions. It's a faith in other people, and it's what brought me here today.

We have the power to make the world we seek, but only if we have the courage to make a new beginning, keeping in mind what has been written.

– President Obama, in Cairo, 2009[1n]

But for too many of our citizens, a different reality exists: Mothers and children trapped in poverty in our inner cities; rusted-out factories scattered like tombstones across the landscape of our nation; an education system, flush with cash, but which leaves our young and beautiful students deprived of knowledge; and the crime and gangs and drugs that have stolen too many lives and robbed our country of so much unrealized potential. This American carnage stops right here and stops right now.

For many decades, we've enriched foreign industry at the expense of American industry; subsidized the armies of other countries while allowing for the very sad depletion of our military; we've defended other nation's borders while refusing to defend our own; and spent trillions of dollars overseas while America's infrastructure has fallen into disrepair and decay.

We've made other countries rich while the wealth, strength, and confidence of our country has disappeared over the horizon. One by one, the factories shuttered and left our shores, with not even a thought about the millions upon millions of American workers left behind.

From this day forward, a new vision will govern our land.
From this moment on, it's going to be America First.

– President Trump, Inaugural Speech, 2017[2n]

We hate you first and foremost because you are disbelievers: you reject the oneness of Allah... We hate you because your secular, liberal societies permit the very things that Allah has prohibited while banning many of the things that He has permitted.

We hate you for your crimes against Islam and wage war against you to punish you for your transgressions against our religion. We hate you for invading our lands and fight you to repel you and drive you out. The fact is, even if you were to stop bombing us, imprisoning us, torturing us, vilifying us, and usurping our lands, we would continue to hate you because our primary reason for hating you will not cease to exist until you embrace Islam.

– *Isis Magazine*, 2016[3]

INTERNATIONAL EVENTS

The aftermath of the 2007/08 financial crisis was experienced throughout the world although each country dealt with it differently, on different timescales with different social consequences. In general, the west followed fashionable neo-liberal financial policies although others followed the more Keynesian lead of the British Prime Minister Gordon Brown. This involved pouring billions of pounds into the banking system and stimulating the economy at the same time as cutting back on social spending. In the early years the impact on the majority of the population was marginal, but in the long term the effects of austerity measures hit the poorest citizens hardest. In addition, America, Europe and the UK cut their interest rates to unprecedented levels and then resorted to printing money under the heading of 'quantitative easing.' China, having accrued vast reserves by satisfying western consumers and finding that their goods were no longer required, diverted vast sums to major infrastructure projects to sustain levels of employment, thus preventing social unrest. (China's currency reserves grew from $156.6 billion in 2000 to $3.14 trillion in 2012. The US deficit grew from $99 million in 1989 to $22.6 billion by 2019.)

Unrest occurred in the countries of southern Europe where there were already high levels of unemployment among the young. This particularly applied to Spain, Portugal, Italy and Greece. On 16th November 2019, obvious fraud in the Iranian presidential election led to extensive protests in which the young demonstrated how authoritarian responses could be subverted by noisy protests at night from rooftops cleverly coordinated by means of social media. Six months later the invasion of Gaza by Israel brought Muslim youths and many others on to the streets of the main cities of Europe and further east. Common to most of these protests was the realisation by millions of educated but unemployed youth that, seen most clearly after the crash, their futures were imperilled while the wealthy and powerful were unscathed. Right across the world it became clear that those whom globalisation had left behind had been forgotten by the political and economic elite.

North Africa

Action was required. It commenced in the authoritarian and often corrupt regimes of North Africa and the Middle East in a series of events known as the 'Arab Spring.' Popular non-violent demonstrations against the oppressive and corrupt Zine El Abidine

Ben Ali, President of Tunisia, hit the headlines with the self-immolation on December 17th 2010 of a poor 26-year-old vegetable seller Mohamed Bouazizi in the remote city of Sidi Bouzid. This event, the local protests that followed, and the violent police response were filmed and distributed on social media, leading to massive demonstrations supported by the police and the army in the capital and the threat of a general strike. The main drivers of the protests were corruption, unemployment and poverty, the latter deriving from austerity measures imposed by the International Monetary Fund. On January 14th 2011 the President fled to Saudi Arabia. A National Unity government was established, although it took a further nineteen months and further protests before truly democratic elections were held with the moderate Muslim Ennahda party gaining a working majority. During the following seven years Tunisia suffered terrorist attacks, further demonstrations and nine changes of government but retained its democratic system, if only by a thread.

Libya

As the world looked on, thanks to mainstream and social media, the next thirteen months saw the fall of President Hosni Mubarak in Egypt and the death of President Muammar Gaddafi of Libya, whose appalling suppression of protesters led to intervention by the UN Security Council and the subsequent bombing programme by US and NATO forces to safeguard the civilian population and assist the rebels. Gaddafi was found and killed in October 2011. Since Gaddafi's death, Libya has had a disastrous history. Although an elected government was formed in August 2012, it has been continually attacked by armed groups representing various tribal and religious factions, many of whom were backed by the Islamic State group (IS). Continued fighting has enabled many people smugglers to be based there and nearly a million refugees were dispatched from Libya to Spain and Italy. This increased the corruption in the area while many migrants drowned at sea or met hostility if they landed. The UN has more recently supported the legitimate government, particularly against the most powerful group calling themselves the Libyan National Army (LNA). In June 2019 government forces successfully attacked the LNA. Late in 2019 Turkey stated that they would send arms and troops to support the government.

Egypt

The most dramatic conflict occurred in Egypt where, as in Tunisia, a distant event led directly to major protests. In April 2008 the population of the Nile Delta city of El-Mahalla protested for three days against rocketing food prices and the suppression of a strike in the city's textile mill. This led to the establishment of the Youth Movement. Social media networks enabled this and other groups to build. The storm broke on January 17th 2011 when, inspired by events in Tunisia and six local incidents of self-immolation, tens of thousands of protesters arrived in Tahrir Square to air grievances about the price of food, particularly bread. The general feeling was that the young and the politically active had had enough of the government. The ensuing battle was characterised by police and army threats against the masses, while the protesters remained fluid with excellent communications via Facebook and Twitter, sending out carefully coded fake messages to confuse the state and help co-ordinate the protesters.

The government were constrained both by the size of the crowds occupying the square night and day for 27 days and by the fact that the action was watched live across the world, broadcast as it was over social media, radio and TV channels, in particular the Qatar based Al Jazeera. On February 11th 2011, amid great rejoicing, President Hosni Mubarak stepped down. Some 846 people had died since January 17th. The elections that followed gave power to Islamist parties, significantly the Freedom and Justice Party, basically the reformed Muslim Brotherhood who nominated Mohamed Morsi as the first democratically elected President of Egypt in June 2012. Morsi's biased attempts to draw up a national constitution led to further mass protests and he was forced to resign after a year in power. He was succeeded by the military chief Abdel Fattah al-Sisi whose military and oppressive government remains in power. In the immediate crackdown, over 4,000 people were killed, a process which continues in the face of any protests. These events would feed into the horrors of Iraq, Syria, Yemen and Islamic State.

West Africa

In December 2013 a case of a viral disease called Ebola was diagnosed in the West African country of Guinea. Within weeks the virus had spread to the neighbouring countries of Sierra Leone and Liberia with disastrous results. With local health provision disabled by sheer numbers and lack of information, UN and western agencies were slow to respond. Voluntary agencies such as Médecins Sans Frontiers were among the first to assist and uncover the horror of the situation. The rapid spread of the disease was accelerated by the widespread poverty in the region, and civil wars had made the population wary of officialdom, particularly when it came clothed head to toe in clinical anti-infection wear! A further factor was the local custom of the family ritually washing the dead, the surest way to pass on the infection. Thus, whole families and rural communities were lost.

The disease had peaked by mid 2014 by which time, partly due to pressure exerted on western governments by the tragedy unfolding on TV, more effective help was established locally to administer what few treatments were available. An intensive community programme was launched in which local volunteers, often recovered patients, provided advice on the need to wash thoroughly and give up local funeral customs. Urgent global research was also devoted to discovering an effective vaccination, which was achieved just as the epidemic was fading in mid 2016. During these two years over 28,000 cases had been reported with over 11,000 deaths. Some 15% of these were health workers, doctors and nurses. It is further estimated that the closure of hospitals to other patients probably caused at least a further 11,000 deaths. The social and economic impact on these countries was severe and long lasting. I watched these events with my dear friend Finda Dunbar who is from Sierra Leone and who has many family and friends there. I think the speed with which such a powerful virus struck with such horrific effects certainly raised the general anxiety level around the world.

Iraq and Islamic State

The internecine conflicts within Iraq continued their bloody course, although much diminished following the US troop surge of 2007. It was announced that all US troops would leave by the end of 2011. This led to the government, whose authority was gradually increasing, and a small group of militant Sunni terrorists to face each other on the ground. These Sunni groups had been forming since 2004 with the aim of restoring losses that had occurred since the fall of Saddam Hussein. This was to become the infamous Daesh (in Arabic), known as the Islamic State of Iraq and Syria (in English), which had its roots in the Brotherhood and Al Qaeda. Its leader from 2010 was Abu Bakr al-Baghdadi who had been allowed to travel between US detention camps ostensibly to resolve disputes between detainees, but in reality he was gathering recruits to IS.[4n]

The enduring purpose of IS was to establish a caliphate, a radical Sunni Islamist state led by religious authorities under a caliph believed to be the successor of the Prophet Muhammad. Documentary evidence was said to exist that al-Baghdadi was a direct descendant of the Prophet. The aim of IS was to turn Iraq into a Sunni Islamic State, initially by establishing control of Baghdad and provinces in the north west, then to neighbouring countries. In the two years following the US withdrawal, IS had achieved a strength of some 2,500 fighters. Many were former members of Saddam's forces, others were young zealots drawn from across the world. The development of the organisation was greatly assisted by advisers from Syrian intelligence services. By 2011, having bombed, killed and beheaded Shia and non-Muslim groups in Iraq IS had gained effective control of the north west provinces and imposed strict barbaric regimes. They were ready to transfer their techniques to Syria where a civil war was under way.

Syria

Soon after the events in Tahrir Square the first pro-democracy secular protests started in the southern city of Daraa and spread rapidly across the country. These were essentially the same group of young unemployed, students, the poor and the oppressed. At one point local police and military joined the protests. The reaction of the government of Bashar al-Assad was extreme, precipitating a prolonged civil war inevitably drawing in major world powers to change the balance of power in the Middle East. Faced with such a violent reaction the protesters took up arms, initially to defend themselves but also to drive the government out of their localities. Within two years the secular protesters had formed themselves into the Free Syrian Army (FSA) while the Islamist and Jihadist groups formed separate organisations. As the scale of the revolution and the violence escalated, the UN, UK and US expressed concern, calling for peace and the resignation of Assad. Russia, who had military bases in Syria, supported Assad. While anxious to support the rebels, the western powers were uncertain quite which group to support. The US and the UK came under increasing pressure to intervene, particularly if chemical or biological weapons were used, although, given the disaster of Iraq, many voices were raised against any such step. Pulling together resolutions in the UN and Congress, President Obama made the following statement at a Press Conference on August 20th 2012:

> I have, at this point, not ordered military engagement [in Syria]. But the point ... about chemical and biological weapons is critical ... We cannot have a situation where chemical and biological weapons are falling into the hands of the wrong people ...We have been very clear to the Assad regime, but also to other players on the ground, that a red line for us is we start seeing a whole bunch of chemical weapons moving around or being utilized. That would change my calculus significantly.[5]

On August 21st 2013 Assad's forces launched a chemical attack on the opposition controlled area round Ghouta, a suburb of Damascus, killing just under 2,000 residents. The violent build up to this event, the film of the attack – including close up pictures of women and children stricken by the deadly sarin gas – and the live scenes on TV placed enormous pressure on governments across the world.[6n]

The British Parliament was recalled for an emergency debate on August 29th, a few days before UN inspectors were due to conclude their report on the incident. It was widely assumed that both US and UK governments were ready to launch air attacks against the Assad regime within days as Obama's red line had definitely been crossed. It was clear that neither government would act alone. President Obama therefore waited for the outcome of the UK debate before initiating attacks. The debate lasted from 14:36 until 22:34 and was an excellent example of parliamentary democracy in action.

The debate was opened by the coalition Prime Minister David Cameron and closed by his deputy Nick Clegg. The Labour leader at the time was Ed Miliband. The government motion seeking authorisation for military intervention was, to put it mildly, rather vague. It deplored the war crimes and supported a strong humanitarian response which may, if necessary, include the use of military action that must be proportionate and focussed on saving lives. It noted the failure of the UN to take action over the previous two years but considered that a UN process must be followed as far as possible. The opposition motion was not opposed to action and agreed with many of the government's arguments but sought actual evidence that the chemical attack was directly attributable to the Assad regime. Also that any action must be lawful with due consideration given to the consequences in the region and have precise and achievable objectives. MPs were therefore faced with a number of questions and dilemmas. Why had they been brought back from holiday just days before the inspectors' report was due? Why was the motion so vague? Surely this implied that both the US and UK military were briefed and ready immediately the motion was agreed?

Although the attack had horrified everyone in the country, the previous reckless and impulsive Iraq disaster meant that the majority of the population were very wary of another intervention in the Middle East. Only 11% were said to be in favour. Paul Flynn (Labour) argued that, given the long history of chemical weapon use, 'Is not the real reason we are here today not the horror at these weapons – if that horror exists – but as a result of the American President having foolishly drawn a red line, so that he is now in the position of either having to attack or face humiliation? Is that not why we are being drawn into war?' Others feared that any intervention would further alienate Muslim communities abroad and at home. The debate revolved around these issues all day, but it slowly became clear that the feeling of the House was moving away from the government motion in favour of delay to gain clear evidence and certainty about the exact limited achievable objectives of action. When the vote was called, the government was defeated by 13 votes. The Prime Minister walked out in disgust. The immediate result was to prevent America from acting alone, to strengthen Assad and hand the Middle East initiative to Russia.

In the following years the conflict in Syria became more vile and complicated. Western powers supported the rebels including the FSA and Kurdish forces (which Turkey viewed as hostile) but were very wary of supporting the Islamist and Jihadist forces fighting on the same side. Russia continued its total support of Assad, as did Iran which supplied finance and technical support plus their proxy army, the Hezbollah. Alliances between and inside these groups confused loyalties and made western support uncertain. Alongside all this was a strengthened IS nominally against Assad but also likely to attack others they deemed to be infidels. IS captured large areas of land in the east and north of Syria including valuable resources and important towns. By 2014 it was thought that IS had some 20,000–31,000 fighters in Iraq and Syria although other estimates put 50,000 in Syria alone. Among these were several thousand foreign fighters from around the world, mostly young men, their motivation varying from religious commitment, through anti-imperialism, to the need for adventure. This included between 600 to 1,000 from the UK and 250 from America.

IS had a full command and a civil service charged with road and hotel building, resource management, public health and antiquities (although their policy and practice was to destroy any historic monument or building that they saw as 'un-Islamist'). In addition there was an expert PR department promoting their radical beliefs worldwide and spreading horror through live videos of individual and mass beheadings and torture, all of which, expertly spread through social media, aided recruitment. They exercised total control of the civilian populations estimated at 8 million by 2014. By late 2014 difficulties posed by the long supply and command requirements and internal ideological and strategic divisions were seriously weakening the organisation. That year it was declared that the caliphate had finally been established. That proved to be the summit of the organisation's achievement in Syria and Iraq.

In August 2014 IS perpetrated genocide on the population of the northern town of Sinjar, mostly inhabited by Yazidis, a relatively small monotheist sect. One prolonged vicious attack included the burying alive of many women and children and the massacre of thousands of men. Surrounded by IS forces, a large group of survivors became isolated on a local mountain. Deprived of water and food, they were driven to near starvation. The campaign killed some 4,500 while up to 11,000, mostly women, were abducted, sold into slavery or subject to brutal brainwashing to accept radical Islamic beliefs. This terrifying incident was broadcast around the world, creating a significant backlash and marking the point at which IS terror overreached itself.

President Obama ordered immediate retaliation to protect civilians. Aid was dropped and air strikes commenced from August 9th and the following day five additional strikes enabled up to 30,000 civilians to be rescued by Turkish forces. France and Britain decided to join the operation in Iraq against IS. Faced with increasing losses of land, President Assad requested help from Russia who immediately deployed significant air, sea and land forces to fight the rebels and restore a fully functioning government to Syria. My view of the conflicts from 2015 looked like this. A coalition of forces led by America were supporting the Iraqi government and attacking IS in Iraq and Syria. America was supporting rebel groups, including the Kurds fighting Assad's regime. Russia was using its air power against rebel groups, nominally IS, which it saw as a potential threat, although a majority of strikes were against some of the rebels supported by America. Turkey supported action against IS but was opposed to any help for the Kurdish rebels in Northern Iraq and Syria. Iran, through Hezbollah, directly supported Assad. Many of these groups were riven with internal divisions and were hostile to other groups. Despite the effects of this lack of cohesion, by the end of 2017 IS had been all but driven out of Iraq and Syria, although they had increased their presence and influence elsewhere.[7n]

In early 2018 Turkish air and ground troops launched attacks on the Kurdish enclaves in a bid to drive a 'terrorist' group from near the Turkish border. This created a situation where one NATO state (Turkey) was attacking forces supported by another (USA). With all these interests it is not surprising that repeated attempts to resolve the situation diplomatically failed. In September 2017 it was reported that more than half of Syria's pre-war population had been killed or forced to flee their homes, with 5.2 million leaving the country. It was also reported that over a million citizens had left Iraq. These population flows put tremendous burdens on all the countries bordering Syria and Iraq, particularly Turkey and Jordan. By late 2019 Syrian forces with intense Russian air power closed on Idlib, the last remaining 'rebel' town in Syria. By February 2020 over

800,000 refugees had fled the city only to find the Turkish border closed to them. They therefore had to camp out in open countryside in sub-zero temperatures. Many children and vulnerable adults froze to death.

Turkey

During these early years of the 21st century Turkey faced tumultuous times, calling into question the secular basis of the state established by Ataturk in 1923 (see Chapter 2). Turkey has been caught between a desire to join the European Union in the west and a long-standing conflict with the Kurdish Workers Party (PKK) in the south east; caught between USA and Russia, and threatened by wars in Iraq and Syria. In 2001 a number of conservative parties came together to form the Justice and Development Party (AKP). They won the 2002 election and have held power virtually ever since. During these years, led by Recep Tayyip Erdoğan, the party has moved from an economically liberal westwards looking group to an increasingly authoritarian regime with strong Islamic tendencies. Between May and August 2013 some three and a half million protestors took to the streets throughout Turkey, specifically in Istanbul's Taksim Square, to protest against growing centralist authoritarianism, restrictions on press and internet freedoms, police brutality and violations of democratic rights. The government responded by making arrests and mandating increasingly restrictive legislation.

On July 15th 2016 the Turkish armed forces mounted an extraordinary coup d'état against the Erdogan government citing declining secularism, erosion of democracy and attacks on human rights. It was a very brief and badly managed coup with some 300 people killed and more than 2,000 injured. Parliamentary buildings and the Presidential Palace were bombed. Within hours it was possible for Erdogan to get back into Istanbul, organise those military forces not involved in the coup and mobilise thousands of citizens to overcome the rebels. So brief and easily defeated was the attempt, it has been suspected that the event was staged by the government to justify its severe response. Some 40,000 people, including the coup leaders, 10,000 soldiers and 2,745 judges were arrested. Some 36,000 teachers and education staff were suspended and this regime continues to this day. There has been a sharp decline in relations with the US, with several American journalists being arrested.

Greece

The 'infection' of political protest crossed the Mediterranean, then the Atlantic, initiated in Europe by the poor and forgotten, led by unemployed young people further stimulated by the austerity programmes imposed after the 2007/8 financial crash. Within the Eurozone these impositions were felt most strongly in the southern states of Portugal, Spain and Italy, and worst of all in Greece, a country with low reserves mostly due to the cultural habit of non-payment of taxes. It was Greece that became the focus of world attention. As the Greeks increasingly threatened the whole European project itself, the militantly neoliberal International Monetary Fund (IMF) and the European Central

Bank (ECB) imposed their single response whenever it got a chance, regardless of context. This comprised privatisation, cuts to wages, pensions, benefits and social services and reducing the size of the state. The crisis in Greece's economy (with the budget deficit rising from 12% to 150% of GDP) posed a serious threat to the euro so in May 2010 the ECB bailed Greece out to the tune of €110 billion. As conditions deteriorated one response would be devaluation but this was not available to a country trapped inside the Eurozone. The result was increased recession and eventually the urgent need for another bailout on harsher terms.[9n]

As the situation drifted into crisis in May 2010, 100,000 protesters gathered in Syntagma Square in Athens, ramping up opposition to the government's fierce austerity programme to coincide with a national strike. This crippled the infrastructure, schools and hospitals. Several buildings were set on fire. Disputes continued throughout the following year as the austerity measures came into effect and rumours abounded either that the EU would expel Greece or that Greece would leave. The UN Commissioner for Human Rights warned that the austerity measures could result in a violation of human rights such as the right to food, water, adequate housing and work. May 2011 saw further mass demonstrations throughout Greece, markedly free of political party or trade union involvement. Protests continued to bring pressure on the Prime Minister who stepped down on November 11th 2011 leaving a caretaker coalition government in power. With the EU still pressing for more austerity and with Greece in need of a further bailout of €130 million, austerity measures were agreed on February 13th 2012, but a month later Greece announced that it was in default and rejected the bailout.

It took nearly four more years of turmoil, with unemployment over 25% and youth unemployment double that, before the radical left coalition group Syriza gained power and established a government not tainted by the regimes that had led Greece for so many years. In the same election the ultra-right, nationalistic Nazi-leaning Golden Dawn party gained 17 seats to become the third largest party. Prime Minister Alexis Tsipras and Finance Minister Yanis Varoufakis brokered a more moderate deal with the EU and the IMF but also sought major loans from international banks which proved more onerous. Unfortunately the political and economic power of the IMF and ECB, together with the lack of an independent Greek banking system, inevitably defeated the new government, who were forced to accept loans with far worse terms than previously. Varoufakis resigned.[10n] By September 2015 70% of the population opposed the deal and 79% opposed Tsipras himself. Super-state neoliberalism had won. The Greeks faced years of impoverishment. In the elections held in July 2019 Tsipras lost control to the centre right New Democracy Party and the Premiership.

Italy

The common factor in all these protests was the anger felt by those groups most affected by the financial crash and unemployment, either consequent on the crash or by the closure of industries when companies moved production eastwards where lower wages and fewer regulations prevailed. Throughout Europe these factors combined with fear of the influx of migrants, who were seen as a threat to wages and established cultures.

The situation in Italy was complicated by the chronically unstable political situation, the country having had 62 changes of government since WWII. A coalition government took power in 2006 and handled the initial financial crisis fairly well but two years later lost power to the right-wing party of Silvio Berlusconi which imposed cuts on public services, particularly schools and universities. It took less than two years for Berlusconi to resign. This led to the establishment of a broadly based, 'technocratic,' government to deal with the industrial and financial crisis. This also lasted for less than two years. With wages stagnating, services cut and youth unemployment hovering around 29% it is not surprising that large protests and strikes continued throughout this period. The most severe were the anti-austerity protests in October 2013 when one protester summed up the frustrations of protesters worldwide:

> I'm here to protest because it's always the same people paying for the crisis, always the workers. It has been happening for many many years. Centre right, centre left. All the measures, liberal or social democratic, have all been unsuccessful.[11]

In the same month two extensive strikes and protests were held in Rome over two days. One spokesman complained that even after austerity had been proven to be disastrous, with debt rising, the economy crumbling and unemployment soaring, they (all the different governments) still continued with the same policies!

Spain

May 2011 saw the first mass protests across Spain, with the same demographic mix and the same pressures of youth and adult unemployment, austerity and rising prices. Spain had been particularly hit by the collapse of a long property boom, significantly due to the sale of holiday lets and timeshare properties by uncontrolled credit. The tax income from this had long sustained the government against chronic problems with other aspects of the economy so that when the boom collapsed the capacity to respond was limited. Thousands of protesters demonstrated across Spain, often listening to speeches in the afternoon and camping out in the style of the Occupy Wall Street movement. Protester numbers increased until, after five days, some 80,000 people were on the streets.

In mid June 2011 a massive demonstration commenced involving some three million people in 80 cities; from June 20th protesters commenced a month-long march across the whole country ending in Madrid. On July 23rd four massive demonstrations were held under the banners proclaiming 'Error de Sistema' or 'It's not a crisis, it's the system.' On July 25th they were joined by the economist and Nobel Prize winner Joseph Stiglitz. The elections held in November 2011, with a 69% turnout, resulted in a landslide win for the People's Party (PP), a centre right group which, a month after election, agreed a massive austerity programme. Not surprisingly the 'Indignados' resumed their protests. February 2012 saw police reacting violently against a large demonstration by school and college students in Valencia, and two months later young people, this time backed by trades unions and public employees, gathered over one million demonstrators across Spain, during which more violence was experienced. The government passed legislation imposing further austerity. A movement towards a new left-wing party developed from these prolonged protests, and in January 2014 Podemos, led by Pablo Iglesias, was formed. In the 2015 general election Podemos won over a fifth of the vote, and his party became the third largest party in the new Parliament.

America

This was not going to be a good decade for America. In addition to the now routine riots following the police shooting of a young black or Latino youth, the country suffered some extreme effects of climate change, including drought, forest fires and hurricanes. A major hurricane hit New Orleans on August 2005 causing extensive damage to property and infrastructure and killing nearly 1,500 residents. Given the extent of the disaster, federal responses were slow and communication between different agencies poor. The effects of the hurricane and the poor response fell more heavily on poor black communities. Riots and looting continued for several days requiring the import of 6,500 National Guard.

Assange

In December 2006 a tiny organisation, led by the journalist and publisher Julian Assange, named Wikileaks started to release hacked information. Many governments and global organisations around the world experienced embarrassment, although America suffered most from its activities. In subsequent years Wikileaks released confidential information about American military procedures, activities in Iraq and Afghanistan and many diplomatic cables. In 2010, some 400,000 documents relating to the Iraq war were released as well as 251,287 diplomatic American cables. In 2016, 20,000 emails and 8,000 files were released from personnel in the Democratic National Committee, a process which continued during Hillary Clinton's presidential campaign, allegedly affecting the results. Consequently Julian Assange was questioned by various security agencies when in 2012 he gained asylum in the Ecuadorian Embassy in London. He stayed there until 2019, by which time his physical and mental health had deteriorated, as had his relationship with the Ecuadorians. A criminal change in Sweden has been dropped but he now faces charges of espionage in America (which carries a death sentence). This would mean him being extradited from the UK. At the time of writing leading journalists are campaigning against the charge facing the journalist. He is currently in Belmarsh prison in poor health. This case has dragged on and on, and meanwhile Assange's health continues to decline. In December 2021 a High Court judge ruled that Assange could be extradited to America under certain conditions. (In June 2022 the Home Secretary Priti Patel authorised Assange's extradition to the USA. Leave to appeal to the Supreme Court is pending.)

Occupy

In September 2011 the 'Occupy Wall Street' movement was founded. Its first meeting was held in Zuccotti Park at the bottom of Wall Street in Manhattan. It was concerned about income inequality in the US, a reduction in the influence of major corporations or politics, bank reform and foreclosure of people's homes. I attended this meeting and enjoyed a very lively day with many very articulate famous speakers. The square was surrounded by police and, as no loudspeakers were allowed, those at the front loudly repeated whatever each speaker said. This of course increased the whole sense of solidarity. Much information was gained from speakers and information booths. As already mentioned, Occupy initiated action across the world. Its call was summarised in Issue 5 of its journal *Occupied*:

> We the people of the global Occupy movement embody and enact a deep democratic awakening with genuine joy and fierce determination. Our movement – leaderless and leaderfull – is a soulful expression of outrage at the ugly corporate greed that pushes our society and world to the brink of catastrophe. We are aware that our actions have inaugurated a radical enlightenment in a moment of undeniable distrust and disgust with oligarchic economies, corrupt politicians, arbitrary of law, corporate media and weapons of mass distraction. And we intend to sustain our momentum by nurturing our bonds of trust, fortifying our bodies, hearts and minds and sticking together through hell or high water in order to create a better world through a deep democratic revolution.

US 2016 Presidential Election

In June 2016, as preparation for the end of Obama's presidency, the long drawn out process of an election commenced against a background of protests from the poorer areas where unemployment was high and when many areas across America were suffering from factory closures. At the end of a series of difficult primaries, presidential candidates had been narrowed to three. Senator Bernie Sanders, an independent democrat, campaigned fiercely on a platform for social and economic justice and had marshalled a following of younger voters. Hillary Clinton led the Democratic Party's campaign relying on her vast political experience and hoping that the time had come for a woman president. Donald Trump from a big business background and some TV popularity was a surprise candidate who expressed his support for the poor and forgotten, explaining their problems as being due to immigration and the companies that had exported manufacturing abroad. He promised both to improve their lot and attack the 'swamp' of the political establishment. The final battle was between Clinton and Trump who had been informally adopted by the Republican Party. It was a fiercely fought campaign, Trump denigrating his opponent as never before and accusing her of a variety of criminal acts and allegations of misdemeanours created with Russian help (see below). He exposed himself as a populist nationalist prepared to lie and bully his way to power. This approach, combined with his racist policies, was supported, understandably enough, by the same groups that had been behind the Arab Spring and the UK's EU vote, as well as the Republican tribe. Much to the surprise of many, including himself, Donald Trump, a man with no knowledge or appreciation of politics or the working of government, was elected President of the United States on January 20th 2017. If the outcome of a presidential election depended on the sum of the popular votes Hillary Clinton would have won by over 2.8 million, but the result is determined by the votes of elected delegates from each state casting votes in accordance with the majority voting in that state. Trump therefore won by an Electoral College vote of 304 against 228. Trump's egoistical narcissism subsequently led him to deny the fact that Clinton had more popular votes. He also continued to believe that attendance at his inauguration was the biggest ever recorded, despite clear photographic evidence to the contrary. I was in America for the final count and the new President's inaugural address, part of which is quoted at the beginning of this chapter. This speech revealed a man obsessed by a depressive dystopian view of the world. My family and their networks across the American seaboard states were shocked, depressed and fearful for the future.

President Trump

Inauguration day was marked by fierce riots across America but particularly in Washington where violence broke out and police used pepper spray, stun grenades and tear gas to arrest 200 people. My favourite placards were the popular 'Trump – Not My President' and 'Welcome to the Dark Ages – Refuse to Normalise Hate,' a poster that correctly predicted the behaviour of this divisive president. In response to promises made during the election, which were seen as threatening to human rights, and particularly his misogynist attitudes, the day after his inauguration saw people joining women's marches across the world – five million across America, 500,000 in Washington alone. It was the largest single day protest in American history. This was not an anti-Trump demonstration but a positive demonstration of a coalition united to protect the rights of women, the vulnerable and anyone else who was fearful of the impact of the new president's policies.

My daughter Juliet was among the 400,000 protesters in New York. These were peaceful, well organised and co-ordinated events. Many wore pink knitted 'Pussyhats' in protest against Trump's recorded boast that you could 'just grab women by their pussy.' While the events were peaceful, many of the signs were not. In addition to 'We are Better than This' was the red hand logo with 'My Body My Rights,' 'Fuck Off,' 'DUMP TRUMP Fight Bigotry,' and 'We want a leader not a creepy tweeter.' Following this demonstration of power, women would concentrate on local action, entering local and national politics, putting themselves forward for office and communicating with similar groups across the country. On the first anniversary of the inauguration some 1.5 million women marched again across America, more aware of the discriminatory policies already enacted. Action was focussed on the mid-term elections of 2018.

I was in America again and caught up with the sad state of American politics in March 2018, fourteen months after Trump's inauguration. Although, as promised, he had issued many executive orders, many undoing the good work done by Obama, he had only managed to get once piece of legislation implemented, the one that reduced the taxes on the rich (including his family) by millions of dollars whilst easing the burden of those on lower incomes by a few cents a week. In addition the Bill added $2 trillion to America's $20 trillion national debt, well over 100% of GDP!

The most worrying aspects of his term so far for America and the rest of the world had been his decimation of the departments of state, his constant lying (calculated as an average of 9.2 lies a day), his lack of any clear policies and, when faced with a choice of policy (for example immigration and gun control), his ability to change his mind from hour to hour. Consequently neither the House nor the Senate could proceed on any course as the chances were that, however hard they worked to produce a Bill, the likelihood was that the President would refuse to sign it.

Fourteen months into this presidency there was clear evidence of Russian interference in the elections to an alarming degree, itself a terrible attack on American democracy. Trump had a bill to authorise sanctions on his desk but refused to sign it or say anything negative about Russia or Vladimir Putin. This of course confirmed suspicions that he relied on Russian help to win the election. Trump appeared unable to manage his own White House staff, afflicted as they were by his rages, his constant tweeting and his lack of clarity or understanding of government. Very soon some 9,239 senior staff had left or been fired from his service; consequently it became very difficult to recruit. Why would anyone want to work for an organisation in complete chaos where backstabbing and internecine warfare prevailed?

Unfortunately this turned out to be just a local example of Trump's strategy of disruption – which became worldwide. Personal initiatives in North Korea, Syria, Turkey and Iran, his withdrawal from many key trade or climate treaties and his personal interventions in the political life of other countries, including the UK, went against all diplomatic normative behaviour. He was the great disruptor. While his threats to engage in nuclear warfare with North Korea and his arbitrary launching of an international trade war with China received most attention worldwide it was the internal incompetence of Trump's regime that may have been the most dangerous threat to stability. America deserved much better.

Events in South America led in 2018 and 2019 to a large increase in those seeking safety and work by entering the US via the American southern border, despite the President's efforts to build an impenetrable wall. Large tented sites were set up for those individuals and families who managed to cross the border. Conditions deteriorated beyond anything seen in peacetime. Children were separated from their parents and then the system failed to find them, while scenes from inside the tents showed people without space to lie down, in deteriorating sanitary conditions and with water in short supply. It was a terrible stain on the USA.

In October 2019 Trump apparently arbitrarily withdrew American troops from their duties on the Turkey/Syrian border, thus exposing the Kurdish troops who had fought with America to defeat IS to a Turkish invasion which Trump knew would follow. It was a terrible betrayal of an ally.

Impeachment

In mid 2019 details of a phone call came to light between Trump and the President of Ukraine, asking the latter to investigate a Ukraine Company that employed the son of Joe Biden, the leading Democrat contender for the presidency in the 2020 election. In order to force the request, Trump withheld a large consignment of military aid, approved by Congress, at a time when Ukraine was defending itself against Russia. If proved, this was a breach of American law which led the Democrat Party, after much consideration, to commence proceedings against the President. Despite fierce opposition from Trump and other Republicans it proceeded apace. Under the American constitution the initial charge was that the President had committed 'Treason, Bribery or High Crimes and Misdemeanours.'

I was in New York for the second week of the questioning. It was an extraordinary event. Twelve witnesses, mostly committed impartial senior civil servants, managed to appear despite the President's efforts to stop anyone attending. They answered all questions clearly and honestly, the six women being by far the most effective. Their evidence of fact confirmed beyond any doubt that Trump had originated and organised this personal scheme. To summarise, he had sent his personal lawyer, the devious Rudy Giuliani, on a political assignment to smear the US Ambassador to Ukraine to enable the scheme to go ahead. The politically appointed Ambassador to the EU (who had achieved the post by donating $1 million dollars to Trump's campaign) and the similarly appointed departmental heads were shown to be aware of the project but, of course, the career civil servants were not and were proceeding to implement US foreign policy. By the end of the hearing the duplicitous nature of the situation was clear to all, and anyway there had never been any doubt as the President had boasted about it on TV.

Withholding arms to an ally fighting your enemy for personal/political gain was considered to be a high crime. Whilst Democrat members of the committee were polite and to the point with their questions, the Republicans used their allocated time to avoid asking questions, to smear the witnesses and promote their political issues and to attack the hearing and the motivation of the Democrats. At the conclusion of the formal hearing voters were left either believing the facts or the propaganda. Much of this reminded me of our experience during the referendum campaign to leave the EU and subsequent parliamentary debates. By late November it was noticeable that some of Trump's devoted supporters started to distance themselves from him, and in November two traditional Republican seats were won by the Democrats.

On December 18th 2019 the House committee agreed (by its democratic majority) Articles of Impeachment for abuse of power and obstruction of Congress. These were delivered to the Republican dominated Senate on January 16th 2020. The trial was to be headed by a Supreme Court judge, with 100 senators (53 Republicans and 47 Democrats) as the jury. Senior Republicans and their lawyers had visited the White House to agree how the trial would be run. This meant calling no witnesses and getting it over as soon as possible, definitely before Trump made his State of the Nation speech, his great opportunity to boast of his achievements as he eyed up the November elections when he was sure a 'stable genius' like himself would win a second term. The behaviour of the Republican senators was a disgrace to the process and to democracy. All the senators took an oath to judge independently the evidence before them, but this did not stop the Republicans announcing before the trial that Trump was innocent, failing to ask any pertinent questions and always voting as their leader told them. The first day was taken up by a fierce argument about whether witnesses would be allowed. This was of great importance as after January 16th key witnesses had come forward with damning evidence against the President. The answer, of course, was not to allow witnesses. Therefore the arguments for and against would be entirely in the hands of the lawyers.

The result, completely predicted from the start, was a Republican vote against impeachment, so America now had a president who had confirmation that his office allowed him to do anything he wanted. He therefore continued to interfere in ongoing court cases, causing his Attorney General to resign and, more importantly, unveiled his 'peace plan' for the Middle East. This essentially gave Israel everything it wanted and the Palestinians a bit of bare desert space. No other countries or international bodies, as far as I know, were involved. Trump was in charge of the world. Palestinians immediately rejected the plan, but the Israelis immediately started acting on it.

Meanwhile, the race to the November 2020 election was starting up as the Democrats commenced their long process of selecting a suitable leader to face the populist Trump. By February 2019 the early primaries had reduced the number of candidates to six. Bernie Sanders, a radical liberal and great orator, was improving his lead, closely followed by Pete Buttigieg, a gay, former small town mayor. Joe Biden, for whom Trump's smear campaign had caused so much trouble, was on a downward path. Elizabeth Warren, a popular liberal, was holding her place. In the wings, not participating in the early primaries, the multibillionaire, former Mayor of New York, Michael Bloomberg was gaining more interest. The great dilemma for the party was clear. Who could beat Trump? *versus* Who had the best policies? For my money, while Sanders' oratory and policies were what America needed, his label as 'socialist' (in America meaning Communist) made his bid problematic; the same applied to Buttigieg – because it was believed that a high proportion of the black electorate would be unlikely to vote for a gay man. Warren, a really good candidate, would probably run into the same storm that hit Hillary Clinton. This left the experienced Biden as a moderate or the left leaning Bloomberg for whom some of Trump's followers might support an alternative powerful rich leader.

Displaced People

By 2017 it was estimated that there were over 65 million political or economic refugees in the world. A small proportion of these were homeless within their own country; a larger proportion were living in neighbouring states, in vast refugee camps in Africa and Western Asia. The main causes of this upsurge were civil wars in the Middle East and Africa, widespread poverty and climate change, whereby environmental conditions and the effect on food supply made life intolerable. Within these mobile populations were genuine asylum seekers in fear for their lives fleeing war zones or oppressive governments. They all sought survival and safety. This phenomenon offered rich pickings for people smugglers who became wealthy by offering desperate people guides or boats to cross borders. As far as I can ascertain between 2007 and 2017 a little over five million refugees and asylum seekers entered Europe. The two main routes were from Afghanistan, Iraq and Syria via Turkey and Greece and from Africa via Libya and into Italy or Spain. Needless to say this faced the EU with enormous political and practical problems which were addressed differently by individual countries.

In general terms Eastern European countries moved swiftly to block access, erecting border fences and implementing controls contrary to EU directives. Germany, in a brave political stance, admitted over a million refugees against much public pressure. The UK admitted over 250,000, relying on the Channel to keep others out and causing chaos in the Calais area by refusing to admit young people who had gathered there. From early 2015 it became clear that disputes over immigration were forcing political debate to become more tense with occasional violence with a move to the right and extreme right, especially in Eastern Europe. Trump's emphasis during his campaign on immigration, particularly from Mexico and Muslim countries, marked a sharp move to the right and the so called 'alt-right' in America.

As for those countries directly involved in the Arab Spring, the protests and hopes of the young also resulted in the establishment of more despotic right-wing governments. These have not been good years for most of the impoverished members of the global society.

Climate Change

The hope that progress would be made in the 16th Annual United Nations Conference on Climate Change held in Copenhagen in 2009 was not to be realised. The final statement was weak, although it did confirm the requirement that global temperature increases must be kept below 2 degrees. These conferences, involving virtually all countries in the world, had been slowly grinding their way forward to near universal agreement to limit the damage that mankind was causing the natural world. The task had been to agree by a series of compromises the willingness of large and small countries to reduce the emissions causing the problem against the widely agreed doom laden scientific projections and the early consequences already witnessed.

Other voices, particularly that of James Hansen, a pre-eminent climate scientist, disagreed with the incremental approach inherent in achieving political compromises across a world obsessed by constant economic expansion. Where, he asked, was a world leader willing to stand up and tell the truth? Not surprisingly, no leader prepared to severely cut their country's industrial production in a competitive global market stepped forward.[12] In June 2015 the Pope issued an encyclical letter *Laudato si'* calling on the world to trust scientific reason and faith while angrily blaming the indifference of the powerful in the face of evidence that humanity is at risk.[13] In early December that year the 21st UN Conference was held in Paris and an accord was reached on climate change reduction. This set a target to hold the increase in global temperatures well below 2 degrees (and if possible to 1.5 by 2050) to increase our ability to adapt to the adverse impacts of change and make the financial flows consistent enough to achieve that. These agreements were subsequently adopted by countries responsible for 55% of greenhouse gas emissions. Unfortunately just before leaving for Paris the UK Chancellor had removed £1 million from a carbon capture scheme in addition to previous cuts to solar and wind power and home insulation projects, leading to a loss of 11,000 jobs in the sector.[14]

In the run up to the 2017 US presidential elections one of the leading Democrat candidates, the passionate and articulate Bernie Sanders, announced urgent plans for $16 trillion to avert catastrophe. This included 100% decarbonisation for electricity generation and transport by 2030 and complete decarbonisation by 2050. A vast challenge which, if instituted, he was confident America could achieve, as it had done when previously threatened. It was also an initiative not heard in any other country, certainly not the UK. When elected the isolationist Republican President Donald Trump withdrew from the accord along with many other international treaties. He believed that that the terrible droughts, floods and forest fires being experienced in his country were all natural phenomena, not attributed to whatever the world's experts said. Sanders believed most countries would need to change their whole way of living to achieve that goal.

1. First, to abandon the use of coal and to make fuel, transport and housing completely carbon neutral.
2. To abandon our obsession with GDP as the only indicator of progress, along with high consumerism and its consequent waste.

3. Populations must learn to be fully conscious of the effect on the climate in their daily lives: recycle rather than buy, buy, buy.
4. To preserve and increase the number of trees which are our most helpful ally in soaking up greenhouse gases and seek to avoid the rapid decline in flora and fauna.

These are vast challenges to governments and people, requiring a near reversal of the economic model that has been followed since the industrial revolution. The cost is eye-wateringly high and the planning and persuasion required extraordinary. The transition will be painful. Vested interests will fight back, for example the 20 top global fossil fuel companies that are responsible for a third of greenhouse gas emissions.

Not surprisingly, most governments, including the UK's, take steps not to make all this clear, let alone take action. However by the early years of the 21st century, people started to notice the increase in flooding, weather no longer following the usual seasons and the loss of birds, insects and other animals. On a very mundane level some 30 years ago summer driving would cause your windscreen to be covered in dead insects; now there are practically none. These direct observations in the UK and across the world were boosted by brilliant documentaries directed by David Attenborough. Through these we witnessed the worldwide effects on wildlife, observed the rapid loss of ice at the poles, saw the dying coral reefs and forests which we all rely on to clean the air.[15n] Awareness was slowly growing that if things did not change the survival of future generations would be threatened.

In the slightly hippie market town of Stroud in Gloucestershire a small group of people, including the social activist and biophysicist Gail Bradbrook and Roger Hallam, an organic farmer who lost his farm when the climate went weird and then studied civil disobedience, met with others to form Extinction Rebellion (XR), a worldwide non-violent protest movement following the examples of Gandhi, Martin Luther King and Occupy. Their demands were simply put:

1. **Tell the truth** – declare an emergency, work with others, be transparent.
2. **Act Now** – to halt biodiversity loss and reduce greenhouse gases to net zero by 2025.
3. **Create a Citizens' Assembly** – advised by experts to lead government on climate and ecological justice.

The first demonstration was held in Parliament Square on October 31st 2018 when 1,000 people announced a 'Declaration of Rebellion' that they refused to bequeath a dying planet to future generations by failing to act now. I joined the Chippenham group of XR in 2019 and experienced the movement at work. It is a very decentralised system, leaving each group to carry out local actions as they think fit. The movement spread across the world like wildfire with over 70 active countries. In November 2018 members in the UK launched a massive demonstration, blocking five bridges in London and

Oxford Circus with a large pink boat. All demonstrators followed the non-violent ethic, were cooperative with the police and allowed emergency vehicles to pass. There was a great deal of singing. It was a great success. In May 2019 the House of Commons passed a token vote to end the climate emergency by 2050. In July youth groups were formed, participating in demonstrations but also focussing on the global south and indigenous peoples. In September coordinated XR demonstrations were held across the world and in most cities and towns in the UK. Tens of thousands of people in London blocked bridges and major squares, demonstrators glued themselves to the tarmac and to cars and trains. Unfortunately there was a very small group that failed to follow the rule of peaceful protest. Opposition came from the few climate deniers, suspicion of the political agenda behind the protests and the many millions of pounds it cost the police to control the dispersed sites and deal with all those arrested. But by early 2019 climate change had become one of the top concerns cited by citizens.[16n]

By early 2019 the world recognised the name of Greta Thunberg, a 15-year-old Swedish girl who, upset when learning about climate change at the age of eight, sat alone calling for climate change outside the Swedish Parliament on strike from her school every Friday for many weeks. Slowly joined by other pupils, she formed the school activist movement called 'Fridays for Future.' The impact of this student, diagnosed with Asperger's syndrome, has been extraordinary. Within a year, thanks to coverage by social media, television and newspapers, she became a key figure as a climate activist. She has had an interview with the Pope and has addressed the UK Parliament and the United Nations Climate Summit. She travels only by low carbon means, speaks concisely and bluntly, and refers to climate denier speeches as bullshit. On September 23rd 2019 she spoke with near venom to the United Nations:

> My message is that we will be watching you.
> This is all wrong, I shouldn't be up here. I should be back in school on the other side of the ocean. Yet you all come to us young people for hope. How dare you!
> You have stolen my dreams and my childhood with your empty words. And yet I am one of the lucky ones. People are suffering. People are dying. Entire ecosystems are collapsing. We are at the beginning of a mass extinction, and all you can talk about is money and fairy tales of eternal economic growth. How dare you!
> For more than 30 years the science has been crystal clear. How dare you continue to look away and say that you are doing enough, when the politics and solutions needed are still nowhere in sight.
> You say that you hear us and that you can understand the urgency. But no matter how sad and angry I am, I do not want to believe that. Because, if you really understood the situation and still kept failing to act, then you would be evil. And that I refuse to believe.
> The popular idea of cutting our emissions in half in 10 years only gives us a 50% chance of staying below 1.5 degrees, and the risk of setting off irreversible chain reactions beyond human control...

So a 50% risk is simply not acceptable to us – we who have to live with the consequences…

You are failing us. But the young people are starting to understand your betrayal. The eyes of all future generations are upon you. And if you fail us, I say, we will never forgive you. We will not let you get away with this. Right here, right now is where we draw the line. The world is waking up. And change is coming, whether you like it or not.

President Trump was present and as they both left the chamber the look she gave him should have done him serious damage. Of course there are many other young people around the world speaking up just as loudly to their local communities. Also in September 2019 Thunberg's organisation brought out six million students and adults across the world in a call for action.

For many years concern had been rising about the effects of plastic netting and webbing on sea creatures, causing as it does terrible suffering and death when they ingest or become entangled in it, but it was only around 2015 that most people became aware of the extent of the added problem caused by the vast number of plastic items tossed into the sea as waste. Currents carry this waste around the world, resulting in miles-wide floating 'islands' of plastic. Research then revealed that some of these plastics become microplastics which pollute the seas at every level. These materials are not bio-degradable and are entering fish and other animals which we, in turn, eat; apparently a minimum of 50,000 microplastics each! A report in June 2019 found that microplastics had been found in snow worldwide indicating that they have entered the atmosphere thereby posing significant health risks to everyone.[17]

In line with increasing concern about the environment, campaigns were launched to ban single-use plastics, reduce all other plastics and review how they were disposed of. Supermarkets were urged to stop covering everything in plastic, started charging for plastic bags and supplied eco-friendly nets for fruit and vegetables. This continues as an active campaign.

Russian Expansionism

From the early 2000s, under the influence of Vladimir Putin, Russia sought to spread its influence wherever there was an opportunity. Putin's greatest success was the Middle East, particularly Syria, and the consequences of that civil war where the errors of western powers, particularly America, allowed Russia to become the predominant foreign power throughout that region. Elsewhere, countries with ethnic Russian populations were targeted. The strategy was to sow division, send in military 'advisers,' create an excuse to invade and then claim territory. The most significant target was Ukraine, which was showing some interest in joining the European Community.

The financial crisis of 2008/09 hit Ukraine badly and precipitated a series of political upheavals which, with the help of Russian influence in the media and vote rigging, brought Viktor Yanukovych to power in 2010. By 2013 it was clear that he was moving away from association with Europe in favour of Russia; significant violent street protests across the country occurred, except in the mainly Russian speaking eastern provinces. In January 2014, in the face of new anti-protest laws, violence broke out, government buildings were entered, 98 people were killed and some 15,000 were injured. Yanukovych fled to Russia. These events had an impact on the 2016 election of Donald Trump. American political advisers Paul Manafort and Rick Gates, after a career advising some of the worst most despotic leaders in the world, had been recruited by Yanukovych to get him into power. They achieved this and were very well paid. In all these matters the rule seemed to be 'Say Ukraine, mean Russia.'[18n] When their client fled to Russia their income ceased. Manafort then had dealings with the Russian oligarch Oleg Deripaska who had direct links with the Russian President.

Manafort later returned to America having seen how Russia influenced elections; why not use this in America? Although he declared himself short of money, it was believed that he had many millions of dollars hidden in off-shore accounts, for example in Cyprus. Soon after his return, Manafort took an expensive apartment in Trump Towers and with that assumption of wealth met with Donald Trump and was appointed to manage his election campaign for free – although his appointment was short lived. He handed the job over to Rick Gates who continued in the role throughout the whole campaign. It was Manafort who, together with Donald Trump Jr and others, met with senior Russian representatives who promised to provide incriminating evidence against Trump's opponent Hillary Clinton.

In May 2014, Special Counsel Robert Mueller was appointed to investigate possible Russian interference in the election of Donald Trump. By February 2018 Mueller issued indictments against Manafort and Gates charging them with conspiracy against the US and money laundering totalling $75 million. Later they were both charged with fraud having given false information to US banks in order to raise loans of $30 million. Gates pleaded guilty and charges were reduced on the basis that he would cooperate with the Counsel's investigation. Manafort followed suit a few months later, having already been convicted of serious fraud charges and facing long term imprisonment.

In February the Ukraine Parliament voted to remove Yanukovych and set elections in favour of the pro-European candidate Petro Poroshenko who resolved to take action against unrest in the east and to mend fences with the Russian Federation. Vladimir Putin's response was to use Russia's naval base at Sevastopol to take control of the Crimea, a large southern peninsular of Ukraine. This was achieved by March 2014 when a fake 'referendum' showed that 97% wished to join with Russia; the 'Republic of Ukraine and Sevastopol' was then incorporated into the Russian Federation. The UN, most western countries and Japan imposed sanctions on Russia and individuals which stand at the time of writing.

The eastern provinces of Ukraine, where there are a higher proportion of ethnic Russians, came under shellfire from the northern border with Russia in July 2014; this was followed by Russian 'civilians' entering the country, arming and stirring up trouble between Ukrainian and Russian residents. In late August 2014 a 'humanitarian convoy' crossed the border with more 'assistance' for the pro-Russian insurgents. Following more and more incursions, including convoys of Russian tanks and some vicious fighting, a large proportion of these provinces were declared a 'People's Republic.' Western powers did nothing. Military responses by Ukraine secured a significant proportion of the area under Russian control.

On July 17th 2014 a civilian aircraft en route from Amsterdam to Kuala Lumpur was shot down while flying over the area, killing 298 crew and passengers. This created outrage across the world; each side blamed the other, but there was much doubt that only the insurgents had the capacity to attack a plane at such height. Russia denied any responsibility despite photos of their rocket vehicle in exactly the right place on the day of the disaster. Russia continues to deny responsibility. Fighting continues to the present day. (In late 2021 Russia placed large forces on Ukraine's borders as an 'exercise.' On February 24th the following year Russian troops invaded Ukraine with terrible consequences to that country. At the time of writing, supported by modern weapons, the fiercest battles are continuing in that same industrial eastern region.)

Nelson Mandela

December 5th 2013 brought the very sad news that Nelson Mandela, an icon whose life from terrorist to statesman had earned him world acclaim, had died. In his statement to the court that imposed his life sentence he committed to the achievement of a democratic society where all were equal, living together in peace and harmony (see Chapter 14). He remained in prison from the age of 44 to 71 never once deviating from this ideal, never losing his temper, just quietly and intelligently pursuing his ultimate aim. He served as President of a new South Africa for five years and in retirement enjoyed worldwide respect and honour.

Myanmar

This country, as Burma, gained independence from the UK in 1948, a situation negotiated by Aung San, leader of the Burma Independence Army. Aung San was assassinated in July 1947. His daughter Aung San Suu Kyi was later employed in the United Nations to assist the Burmese Secretary General U Thant. In 1962 the army carried out a coup d'état but in 1988 another military led coup took place and the State Law and Order Council was formed. This confirmed the name of Myanmar and elections were held in 1990. Aung San Suu Kyi's party won 80% of the seats but the military refused to recognise this, having previously put her under house arrest. She remained thus restricted for nearly 15 years gaining international support as an emblem of gentle, non-violent democracy.

In 2015 Aung San Suu Kyi's party won a landslide victory and took the key parliamentary posts, with their leader effectively becoming Prime Minister. The fact remains, however, that real power sits with the military. Since independence the military have earned a fearsome reputation by oppressing the wide range of tribes and ethnic groups that form the population. The UN General Assembly have repeatedly called for the military junta to respect human rights. They have a long history of forced labour, human trafficking, child abuse and torture. The 1.3 million Rohingya people, who live mostly in the northern area near the border with Bangladesh, are Muslims. They are denied citizenship, are unable to travel or own land and are constricted to having two children. In 2017 an Islamist group attacked two military posts in the area. This was used by the military as an excuse to attack the Rohingya by setting fire to their villages, committing random killings and driving some 742,000 people across the border towards already overcrowded refugee camps in Bangladesh. The media, including phone pictures and social media, brought these atrocities and ethnic cleansing to the attention of the world. Late in 2019 Myanmar, represented by the much diminished Aung San Suu Kyi, was tried by the International Court of Justice. On January 23rd 2020 the Court issued instruction to the country to prevent any further abuse to the Rohingya people. This ruling goes to the UN Security Council and all other UN agencies to enforce. (In June 2022 Aung San Suu Kyi was placed in solitary imprisonment.)

NATIONAL EVENTS

The themes mentioned above were mirrored at home, although, with our physical, cultural and emotional boundaries so fragile, the very concept of stability was under threat. Our own local events did however add to feelings of distrust, insecurity, fear of the future and conflict. In short, a more angry culture developed as the years rolled by and the effects of a fierce austerity policy and questions about our future as a nation took hold. Two elections and a referendum accompanied by lies and deception, worries about migration, terrorist attacks and increasing concerns about climate change were unsettling. An aggressive isolationist America led by a hopeless president, a mischievous Russia and Middle Eastern wars added to a sense of insecurity. Many of our long-held assumptions about how the world worked were being challenged.

Austerity and Protests

In May 2010 the UK voted in a Conservative led coalition government with the Liberal Party. The leaders were David Cameron and Nick Clegg. The former had benefitted from displays of environmental concern and interest in youth; the latter had bought student votes with a promise not to raise student fees. Within weeks the government announced a severe programme of austerity and tripled student fees. The government held to the false argument that the vast public spending required to save the banks and the world economy was a sign of Labour's profligacy which had to be met with decades of austerity. The burden would fall on ordinary citizens whose real income would fall and the essential services which they relied on would be systematically cut. The bankers who had caused the crash and consumed billions of public money would by and large continue to prosper. David Cameron would abandon his ever thin liberal views which had shown him driving huskies as a sign of his concern about climate change, and turn away from his 'hug a hoodie' policy for dealing with social unrest to get into line with his old pals from the famously elite Bullingdon Club. The Toffs were back and very soon what little respect was due to politicians would be lost by the discovery that many were boosting their salary by fiddling their expenses.[19n]

Protests occurred in many UK cities, their numbers increased by college and sixth form pupils who saw their whole future threatened by the high fees. Protests ranged across London from Trafalgar Square to Parliament Square, some violent, others suffering from the police tactic of 'kettling' them into tight spaces for long periods of time. In early November 2010 student protesters trashed the Conservative Party's offices in Millbank Tower. The organisation UK Uncut, targeting austerity and tax avoidance, managed to close stores whose owners were guilty of not paying tax. Slowly the trades unions joined in and called a day of action against the cuts for March 26th 2011. It became the biggest trade union organised demonstration in history with an estimated attendance of up to 500,000.

In October the UK Occupy movement, in response to corporate capture of politics and the system by the top 1%, mounted a large demonstration outside the London Stock Exchange. Some 3,000 then moved to St Paul's Cathedral and set up camp on the steps. This certainly captured media attention and posed a challenge for the cathedral Dean. Canon Giles Fraser accepted people's right to protest and food and water was organised, but as the occupation continued the Church Chapter resolved to remove it. Fraser resigned. Following a number of strikes by public sector workers, whose income was virtually frozen for six years in the face of rising prices, their unions organised a major demonstration in October 2014. Some 60,000 marchers assembled in Trafalgar Square and Hyde Park and speakers highlighted the poverty of the workers against the escalating income of the rich.

While these protests were taking place pressure was growing in the Conservative Party to hold a referendum on continued membership of the European Union. By and large these were the same right-wing members who, swayed by memories of Empire and British power, had caused trouble for every Conservative prime minister since we applied to join in 1975. In 1993 the even-tempered Prime Minister John Major had been moved publicly to refer to them as 'The Bastards.' They were determined to see Britain as it was at the end of WWII, in short 'great again,' swashbuckling our way around the world capturing rich trade deals everywhere. In the run up to the 2015 election, having seen the newly formed United Kingdom Independence Party (UKIP) success in the 2014 EU elections (they gained 27% of the vote adding 14 MEPs at the expense of the Conservatives), David Cameron, confident that he could silence his dissenters and halt UKIP, gave a commitment to hold a referendum subject to changes in our relationship with the EU which he hoped to negotiate. These were focussed on controlling migration and easing the power of the European Court of Human Rights to influence UK law. His negotiations fell far short of expectations. It is quite a thought that had the EU made some concessions then, at least some control of immigration, the subsequent years of agony caused by our attempts to leave would have been avoided.

The law enabling a referendum was passed in June 2015 but contained no requirement for the result to be implemented; legally it was intended to gauge opinion, to give advice to the government. To be non-binding. Careless Cameron, apparently unaware of the feelings of loss and betrayal demonstrated by the protests, had no doubt that the government would easily win the vote. The most important poll since 1945 would be held on June 23rd 2016; it was a straight in or out choice, with no space for a moderate middle way. The government led 'Remain' campaign was far outweighed by the bizarre untruths, preposterous promises and massive financial interests of the 'Vote Leave' campaign. The issue of immigration became central; fears of 'swarms' of migrants crossing the Channel to steal our jobs were played on to the full.

The fact that the vote was confined to a straight yes or no question meant that, free of the constraints of any party loyalty, each individual vote counted. It was a gift to those millions of citizens resentful of austerity, chronic unemployment and, especially in the north, a feeling that they had been left behind in a globalised market where the power bases were far away in London. It was time to attack the government. On the day a huge turnout of 72.2% produced the result that although 48.1% wished to remain 51.9% voted to leave – a margin of 5.8%. It seemed that, aided by elderly voters and dreams of the 'old Great Britain,' the dispossessed had made their mark. The divisions between these and younger voters, who felt that their future had been jeopardised, and the fact that the result varied widely from place to place, would continue to raise fierce disputes for many years.

In the days following the result David Cameron resigned and the leaders of the Leave campaign went to ground. It transpired that neither had any plans about how to implement such a result, let alone of the complexity of the practical conundrums to be faced. The Leave campaign's declaration that extracting ourselves from Europe would be a 'walk in the park' proved baseless. Most politicians, trapped between honesty and democracy, chose to see the result as a definitive vote upon which they must act. It became their unobtainable holy grail from which to approach the impossible task of squaring a circle. This whole period would see the impact on all sections of the community of both continued austerity policies and the negotiations to extract us from the EU, eventually blocking out progress on other domestic policies. The progress and pain of these and other phenomena are dealt with below.

Social Housing

Previous decades had seen major changes in the provision of local authority housing for the less well off. Post-war provision proceeded apace, but in 1980 the Thatcher government introduced the 'right to buy' policy (see Chapter 12), which immediately removed some 1.5 million houses from public ownership. This policy, together with severe restraint on any local authority building, reduced public housing from 6.5 million in 1979 to 2 million by 2007. In September 2017 new subsidies were introduced so that for every one house sold one had to be built for an 'affordable rent,' a term which depended entirely on the market, which was rising steadily.

Over this time period, former council houses were sold on at a profit, but increasingly this was to corporate buyers who came to dominate certain neighbourhoods where rents were then increased to block off low paid families. This whole process in turn boosted the housing market, thus making a farce of the term 'affordable rent.' In the same period the role of housing associations significantly increased. By the time the austerity policy was having its full impact the number of homeless households had increased to approximately 82,310, which included 123,600 children in England alone by 2018. Many of these families were housed in cramped rooms in former office blocks or cheaply converted shipping containers. Landlords, fully aware of the need and security of payment by the local authorities, increased their charges to the maximum. In 2017/18 a group of 156 of the largest private landlords in this sector collected profits of £215 million.[20]

Those not officially classified as homeless were reduced to sleeping rough – in 2018 there were some 4,500 – or to 'sofa surf' with relatives or friends, in squats or other insecure accommodation not included in that figure. (If a proper count had been made it is estimated that it would increase that figure by over 60%.[21]) Desperation resulted from evictions, delays in receiving Universal Credit or the inability to settle pay-day loans carrying exorbitant interest rates.

Among the deleterious effects of all this was the demonisation of those on low pay or benefits and the related 'gentrification' of whole areas previously dominated by council houses. The big increase in rents forced low-income citizens out from the centre of towns and cities to the periphery, destroying family connections, schooling and social integration. In fact there has been evidence in London of 'social cleansing' of whole areas using the distressing circumstances described above but in order to import people on higher incomes, more likely not to vote Labour. All this was clear in the horror of Grenfell Tower before and after the fire.

Grenfell Tower

This 24-storey block of flats stood within the London Borough of Kensington and Chelsea. The top 20 floors were residential with six flats on each floor and lower flats added later. The block housed an estimated 600 residents. It had been opened in 1974 and upgraded in 2016 to provide a new heating system, replace windows and increase thermal efficiency. As part of that project the whole building was clad in an aluminium composite over Celotex thermal insulation. Just before 01:00 hrs on June 14th 2017 a fire in a kitchen on the fourth floor awoke the resident who immediately called the fire brigade which arrived within five minutes. The design of the flats, supported by the fire authority, meant that fire could be contained within that flat. Unfortunately in the brief time between the start of the fire and the arrival of the fire fighters the fire had burst out of the window and ignited the cladding. Within 30 minutes the fire had spread to the top floor. It raged for 24 hours watched by horrified TV viewers across the world. It was unbelievable. It was impossible to know how many people were in the flats that night, but 72 people died, 65 were rescued by fire crews and the rest managed to make their own way out. The final death figure was delayed by several weeks due to the extreme heat of the fire having cremated the victims. The exact number is still disputed. The firemen had followed the procedure that people should stay in their own flat to await rescue, although some residents on higher floors disobeyed that instruction and got out before the acrid smoke filled the stairwell. Others, some too disabled to use the stairs, perished. It was an hour and three quarters before the strategy was changed, allowing residents to flee, but for many that was too late.

The sheathed tower stands as a tribute to the horror of that night and when it is finally demolished a memorial, agreed by the survivors, will be erected. Anger was immediately directed at the local council, the manufacturers of the cladding and the government's austerity policy which had made savage cuts to both the authority and the fire service. It soon emerged that in 2012 the residents' group had commissioned their own safety inspection which found significant neglect throughout the building. This and many other issues of concern had been raised by this group over many years and had received no response. In January 2016 the residents' association had warned of the fire hazards in the building and accused the council of being an evil, unprincipled, mini-mafia. They had issued the following warning to the management agency (Kensington and Chelsea Tenant Management Organisation, KCTMO) employed by the Conservative council:

> ...only a catastrophic event would expose the ineptitude and incompetence of KCTMO and bring an end to the dangerous living and neglect of health and safety legislation. We predict that it won't be long before the words of this blog come back to haunt the KCTMO management and we will do everything in our power to ensure that those in authority know how long and how appallingly our landlord has ignored their responsibility to ensure that the health and safety of their tenants and leaseholders. They can't say that they haven't been warned.

The victims organised themselves into the Grenfell United survivors group and informal assistance poured in from all over London and beyond. The government established a full public inquiry and a £5 million fund to assist victims directly and with their rehabilitation. They would be rehoused as near to the site as possible but certainly within the borough. A national minute's silence was held on June 19th and responsibility for managing the aftermath was removed from the borough whose initial response was judged inadequate. The CEO of the council, the Chair of the local Conservative party and the CEO of KCTMO all resigned. Protests were held across the country as the fire was taken as an example of how austerity had cut back local services leading to poor service for public housing tenants and a high degree of discrimination against them, many of whom were immigrant families. The fact was that Kensington and Chelsea was among the wealthiest boroughs in the country and had the highest gap between rich and poor in the country. In June 2017 the police opened criminal investigations into the borough and KCTMO on possible grounds of corporate manslaughter.

Action may not be taken until after the final conclusion of part two of the public inquiry, due in 2022 which will deal with the events and responsibilities leading up to the fire. Part one of their report was issued on October 30th 2019. While paying tribute to the courage and devotion to duty of the fire fighters and emergency staff, the inquiry was critical of the management of the incident, reporting on systemic system failings and lack of compatibility in communication systems.

Austerity

The press of austerity would continue throughout this period, slowly eating away at the very fabric of society way past the point where it became counterproductive. Just 33 days after taking office as Chancellor, George Gideon Oliver Osborne (independently educated, an Oxford graduate and a Bullingdon Club member) presented his dramatically entitled Emergency Budget. It was introduced as a tough budget caused by the inherited high deficit in public finances, the implication being how foolish Gordon Brown had been and ignoring the fact that much of the deficit was caused by rescuing the banks after the crash (an event for which no senior banker has ever suffered). Apparently, this was a budget designed to 'raise us from an economy built on debt to a new balanced economy ... where prosperity would be shared among all sections of society and all parts of the economy.'[22]

Growth would rise to 2.9% of GDP by 2013 and there would be a balanced budget by 2015/16. This would be achieved by lower spending rather than higher taxes and as the speech went on it became clear who was meant to pay for the financial crash. NHS and Overseas Aid would be protected and pensions would rise according to the existing formula, although the pension age would be delayed for most people until age sixty-six. The greatest 'savings' would come from departmental and local authority functions. A cap would be imposed on local authority spending. This included all welfare and social security expenditure. Thus, blame for the ensuing pain could be directed at local councillors rather than central government. Public sector pay would be frozen for two years and tax credits, which had so successfully pulled so many out of poverty, would be focussed on those in most need. Maternity grants would only be paid for the first child and child benefit would be frozen for three years. The Disabled Living Allowance would be subject to medical assessment and VAT was increased to 20%. Towards the end of his speech, the Chancellor stated

> I cannot disguise from the House that the combined impact of the tax and benefit changes that we make today are tough on people. That is unavoidable ... My priority in putting together this budget has been to make sure that the measures are fair ... Too often when

countries undertake major consolidations of this kind, it is the poorest – those that had least to do with the cause of the economic misfortunes – who are hit the hardest ...This coalition Government will be different ... Today we have paid the debts of a failed past and laid the foundations for a more prosperous future ... Prosperity for all: that is our goal.[23]

Oh yes?

Osborne presented seven more budgets over the next six years, each repeating the same theme and making minor adjustments in order to trim the campaign. It took some time to realise that, however clear the presentation seemed, the actual programme of cuts was reinforced and written into legislation for implementation for years ahead, with every new measure added to the already continuing programme. Step by step the policy of cutting back the welfare state and a whole range of services to achieve the original fantastic economic targets were being realised. None of the targets were ever met.

In 2017 Osborne was succeeded by Philip Hammond, less arrogant but initially continuing the same policies. It is worth taking a look at the question of our national debt and annual deficit. It had been highest at the end of the war but by careful management and a prosperous economy the debt had been slowly reduced over some forty years to 25% in 1992 and fluctuating since then at about 40% of GDP. In 2010/11 it stood at some £1,216 billion (76% of GDP) and the deficit stood at £142 billion (10% of GDP). Thank you, bankers. In 2017/18 the debt stood at £1,764 billion (86% of GDP) and the deficit at £41 billion (3% of GDP). Much of this situation had been due to the failure of the government to support and stimulate industry and not sufficiently appreciate the levels to which austerity itself has inevitably constrained people's ability to spend money.

The NHS

By 2018 the consequences of the cuts were glaringly obvious. The public mood had changed from reluctant acceptance to distress and anger. Faced with rapidly reducing resources most public services responded by raising the bar to service, thus destroying preventive work which inevitably resulted in more serious problems later. The NHS was in a dire state, the majority of trusts were heavily in debt or facing bankruptcy. As GP services declined, patients flocked to A & E departments and waiting lists grew across every service, causing months of pain for many. Couples seeking IVF treatment found the age bars raised, thus denying them a chance of parenthood; many were forced abroad. Cancer patients found their treatment delayed. Services for people with a mental illness, especially children and teenagers, were devastated to the extent that the government were forced to provide an emergency rescue package later in the year.

Criminal Justice

The criminal justice system, never a vote catcher but usually a strong Conservative concern, deteriorated to third world levels. Police forces lost virtually all their important first level community police and finally refused to investigate a whole range of 'minor' crimes (including burglary, assault and drug possession), concentrating instead on the rise in gun and knife crime. In late October 2019 the ONS reported that these crimes rose to 44,076, the highest recorded since 2010. In that same month Scotland Yard's senior officer made the link with austerity, commenting that the link was obvious. The prison service, having lost some 8,000 officers, but faced with an increasing prison population, had no alternative but to keep prisoners locked up for longer periods and deprive them of educational and therapeutic facilities. Staff were unable to tackle the import and trading of drugs; the regime became more violent, prisoners and staff suffered injuries, and the ability to replace staff was limited. The disaster of privatising the Probation Service caused collapse, resulting in excessive caseloads, supervision by phone and an increase in re-offending which led to that service being brought back into central government. Throughout this period, unemployment, casual work, low wages, savage cuts and reforms to the benefit system caused great distress and increased poverty across the country. Before 2008 there had been a handful of food banks confined to the most deprived areas; by 2018 there were more than 2,000. Indeed, hardly any communities existed, however superficially prosperous, that did not need a food bank. What a terrible state for the fifth largest economy in the world. By 2017 there were 14 million people in poverty in the UK, including some 4 million children, 400,000 more than five years earlier.[24]

In 2017 the Institute of Fiscal Studies predicted that child poverty would rise from 27% to 36% by 2022.[25] As the benefit system became increasingly hostile, staff were given targets to apply sanctions for the slightest perceived infringement of the system, thereby putting the system of appeal under pressure. By December, just under 70% of the appeals had been upheld. It is worth considering the costs here: the distress experienced by the claimant deprived of benefit until the hearing and the financial cost of the process, estimated at £100 million![26]

Local authority services faced tremendous cuts through their rate support grant (which was sequentially reduced over the period) and an expectation from government that the end to austerity was coming. In the meantime, most councils were facing bankruptcy, many having to be put into special measures. All sectors of education had to be cut back with further education colleges (the ones that train skilled staff for industry) taking the largest cuts. Schools had to cut teaching for subjects other than those in core areas, extra-curricular activities (most damagingly, music) depended on the availability of volunteers, and parents were approached to help provide basic equipment. Teachers, particularly heads, became stressed by limited resources and the demands of constant examinations and left their posts, which were then difficult to fill. Added stress came from pupils arriving in school clearly hungry and in need, so that food and sanitary products had to be provided by the staff. The number of teaching assistants fell, with consequent difficulties for pupils with special needs and their families.

Under pressure from the culture and fear of Ofsted downgrading, more pupils were excluded to face agencies increasingly unable to help. Youth services and clubs that previously would have been available had been decimated; 600 clubs had closed. There followed an increase in gang culture and the number of younger people involved in the drug dealing networks rose. In November 2017 5,000 head teachers endorsed a letter to the Chancellor Philip Hammond, demanding more money to stop the cuts in school funding that had forced many to increase class sizes, reduce support staff and reduce the curriculum to core subjects only. Extraordinarily the summer of 2018 saw some 2,000 head teachers from across the country waving their placards in front of Parliament, forced to demonstrate to stop the cuts.

In August 2018 the Conservative run Northamptonshire County Council, which was technically insolvent, voted to find up to £70 million more cuts in order to balance the books. This followed the government's imposition of special commissioners to run the county in May, which in turn followed the revelation that it had refused to raise rates, despite years of increased demand in social care, the budget for which rose from £3 million to £32 million in four years. Instead, the council had drawn recklessly on reserves and employed accounting trickery. The consequence was dire to all services including child and adult care services. Already 25% of social work posts were vacant. It became clear that Northamptonshire was not the only Conservative council in such difficulties. East Sussex faced a very similar scenario, and many others were preparing contingency plans. In practically all of these cases the most significant issues were the failure to fund social care for the increasing population of elderly people and the increasing demands on child care services.

In her speech to the Conservative Party Conference in October 2018 the Prime Minister Theresa May danced up to the podium for her rallying speech during which she plainly said 'A decade after the financial crisis people need to know that the austerity it led to is over and that their hard work has paid off.' A couple of things struck me about this. She did not say 'so the distress and suffering is at an end'; rather, she was calling it 'hard work,' as if, like in wartime, we had all volunteered to put in the extra effort, instead of having a political policy imposed at great cost to all but the elite. How dare she call all the suffering 'work'! Also, it was patently a lie as so many of the cuts were already programmed into the system for the next five years. The budget speech which followed three weeks later confirmed my fears. Under the guise of a massive increase in funding for the NHS there was no relief for departments or local authorities or the school heads who had protested outside Parliament. In response to their call for a stop to staff cuts, so that children's education could be saved, they were offered a one-off capital allowance of £400 million (approximately £50,000 per secondary school) to buy new whiteboards or paltry bits and pieces. A complete insult.

Leaving the European Community (Brexit): High Political Drama

Once the referendum was announced for June 23rd 2016 both sides launched their campaigns. The government-backed Remain campaign was relatively low key, relying heavily on expert analysis rapidly put together to compensate for lack of early preparation. The official Vote Leave campaign was led by two leading Conservative politicians – Boris Johnson (formerly Mayor of London) and Michael Gove (former Justice Secretary). There was also a 'Leave.EU' group, well funded by a determined businessman Arron Banks and led by the UKIP leader and MEP, the ebullient disrupter Nigel Farage. Banks and Farage gloried in their own description of themselves as 'the bad boys of Brexit.' All campaign groups were regulated by the election commission and limits were put on expenditure. There were many other smaller groups campaigning on both sides. After voting the Electoral Commission raised some concerns about the conduct of both sides, but in November 2018 they referred Arron Banks' financing of his campaign, in particular a sum of £8 million (the biggest single political contribution in UK history), to the National Crime Agency for criminal investigation. He was later cleared.

The year-long campaign leant heavily on emotional persuasion. The fault in the government's campaign became evident when voters airily dismissed any expert opinion, a tendency very much encouraged by the Leave campaigns. In retrospect, one does worry why such a traditional approach was adopted as it became clear very early on that the emotional Vote Leave campaigns were benefiting from the natural anger, depression and frustration directed at the elitist view of the government. The months of campaigning proved very divisive in all areas of the UK, with extreme political groupings within communities and families. Demonstrators clashed and parliamentary debates became angry; unlike in a general election, most of the population felt directly involved in the issues. Although one could apply the usual degree of scepticism to many of the arguments and their presentation, many people shared my view that many of the Leave campaign's tactics went beyond the pale. Johnson's big red campaign bus was plastered with false claims about how much EU membership cost, all of which could reportedly be used for the NHS when we left. Farage meantime used hoardings with false pictures of long lines of immigrants who were said to be heading for the UK. In fact, the main issue that was debated was relatively simple: control immigration. Unfortunately some areas of the country had received more than their fair share of European migrants seeking and finding work. In these circumstances successive governments had made no effort to help communities by providing more school places, housing or NHS facilities. This left the field open for right-wing activists to spread false stories, which they did in abundance.

Another Leave argument was the need to 'take back control' from the over powerful Brussels bureaucrats who imposed ridiculous regulations on our daily lives. This had been the favourite theme of our right-wing press for many years, with no regard for accuracy. Considerable hate was directed to the power and cost of the immense civil service implementing these regulations. They were seen as unaccountable. This rather ignored the fact that they served the decisions of the European Parliament to which we sent 73 elected members. Of these 24 were members of UKIP – a high proportion, resulting from, I think, the low turnout in EU elections. Much resentment came from the perceived distance of this centre of power. If those voting Leave thought that

London was too remote, Brussels didn't stand a chance. Personally I was very happy that access to the European Court of Human Rights was to be retained. The ECHR stemmed directly from the post-war European Convention on Human Rights and had served UK appellants well when they disputed our more conservative high courts. It is independent of the EU.

Although the national referendum result favoured leaving the EU by 4%, further analysis produced some interesting results. Most of Northern Ireland voted Remain, as did the west coast of Wales and the whole of Scotland, giving rise to renewed calls for independence. In England most cities, apart from those in the northeast, voted Remain, especially London and the home counties up to the Midlands. It seemed clear that the North, and particularly the North-East, the areas experiencing loss of industry and subsequent neglect, had used their dissatisfaction with the London elite to vote Leave. The other general belief was that older voters had mostly voted Leave, thus angering younger voters who, naturally enough, saw the vote as about their future. Further analysis shed some doubt on the detail of that analysis.

Jo Cox

The increasingly angry level of argument now splitting the country was very worrying. No longer on traditional party lines, but rather whether you were a Leaver or a Remainer. Over the course of these few years the level of serious crime such as domestic abuse, hate crime against perceived immigrants or foreigners, street crime (especially knife attacks) and murders rose. People witnessed angry political debates with violent use of language, which somehow enabled them to act out their frustrations. There was a sense of being trapped in a never-ending process with no way out. On June 16th 2016, one week before the referendum, Jo Cox – a new Labour MP for Batley and Spen (West Yorkshire) – who had a long history of campaigning on social issues and peace in the Middle East, was assassinated. She was shot, then stabbed, in broad daylight outside her constituency library. A 52-year-old member of extreme right-wing groups carried out the attack shouting 'Britain First.' Jo Cox was the first sitting MP to be killed since 1990, when Ian Gow had been assassinated by the Provisional IRA. The nation was shocked and appalled by the event and sympathised publicly with her husband and their two young children. Four months later, the Labour MP Tracy Brabin was elected to the constituency, the main parties having agreed not to contest the seat as a mark of respect.

The Referendum Result

The government now set about taking the steps required to act on the referendum result. There were however two significant challenges to the belief that this could be done by the Executive without further legislation. A leading social activist and investment manager Gina Miller considered that such a significant constitutional event must be considered by Parliament. The Scottish Government, furious that their virtual 100% vote to remain in Europe was being ignored, together with the Welsh and Northern Ireland Assemblies, sought to ensure that no step to leave was taken without their agreement. The case escalated to the Supreme Court. On January 24th 2017, the Court found in favour of Miller's argument, but against the Scottish and other governments. Consequently, on February 1st 2017 the European Union (Notification of Withdrawal) Bill was brought before the Commons. It was a long debate, one of the best in recent history, I think. Ed Miliband, the clear sighted and honest leader of the Labour Party, laid out the dilemmas facing MPs on the second day:

> I want to say at the outset that this is clearly a fateful moment in this country's history ... We should all respect the way in which colleagues on both sides of the house are wrestling with their consciences as they decide how to vote on the Bill.
>
> I did not want the referendum ... I believed that with the many other problems the country faced the referendum would become as much about the state of the country as about Britain's place in Europe. Indeed I believe that is in part what happened ... I said that I would accept the result which I do and that is why I will be voting for the Bill's Second Reading tonight, not least because I feel the referendum stemmed in part from the sense of disaffection and deep frustration about politics that exists in this country. A heightened reason for saying that the process must begin is that we do not want to give the people who voted for Brexit a sense that they are being ignored once again.
>
> It is deeply problematic that the Government are embarking upon this process without any objective economic analysis of its implications, without clarity on key issues such as the customs union and without any sense of what transitional arrangements might look like, on the basis of what I believe is the fanciful proposition that all future arrangements can be tied up within 18 months.[27]

The vote at 19:32 hrs was passed by 329 to 112.

Two months later, the Prime Minister Theresa May informed the House that the legal document informing the EU of our intention to leave (Article 50 of the 2007 Lisbon Treaty) had been submitted. She explained:

> Perhaps now, more than ever, the world needs the liberal, democratic values of Europe – values that the United Kingdom shares. That is why, although we are leaving the institutions of the European Union, we are not leaving Europe. We will remain a close friend and ally. We will be a committed partner.

We would leave the EU at 11 pm on Friday March 29th 2019.

The Prime Minister then took the extraordinary step of calling an election for June 8th, presumably hoping to strengthen her position. This was not achieved. With a high electoral turnout, the Conservatives lost 13 seats and Labour gained 30 under the leadership of Jeremy Corbyn. Having lost her overall majority, May faced calls for her resignation and was forced into a cooperation agreement with Northern Ireland's ten Democratic Unionist Party MPs in order to get a slight majority. The deal included

£1 million for Northern Ireland despite the fact that the Assembly and Executive remained suspended due to a dispute between Sinn Fein and the DUP.

All that remained now was to negotiate our way out, a task that the Leave campaigners had said would be 'a walk in the park': done and dusted within 18 months. A department for Exiting the EU was established and a minister, David Davis, appointed. The European Council of 26 government heads appointed a senior French politician, Michel Barnier. The UK recruited thousands of extra civil servants to help in these complex negotiations at an estimated cost of £1 billion by 2019. Thousands of staff were allocated to a command-and-control centre with dire warnings that more would be needed with an increase in the consequent cost. The task before them was vast; over the previous forty-seven years of our membership, practically every aspect of our lives was tied into European rules, regulations and procedures. All farming, retail, financial and fishing activities were both subsidised and regulated, as agreed with the EU.

As industries had modernised, they had become intimately linked to Europe by the requirements of the 'just in time' system which required manufactured parts to arrive at assembly factories in the UK every day, thus avoiding the need for large warehouses. This was only possible if they passed through countries with no customs delays. A further key issue was the fact that leaving the EU meant that the somewhat weak, friendly border between Northern Ireland and Eire would become a significant international border, and a very busy one at that. Further, the terms of the Good Friday Agreement of 1998 (see Chapter 14) guaranteed free travel between Northern and Southern Ireland and stated that there would never be a hard border. Most of these clauses seemed to come as a surprise to the UK negotiators.

Theresa May and her team had 24 months to complete the deal, but to my mind the path ahead was going to be a cross between the heavy burden of *Pilgrim's Progress* with a prolonged spell caught between the Scylla and Charybdis monsters, with the complication that the final destination was unclear. The Prime Minister's oft repeated chant that 'Brexit means Brexit' presumably meant a total schism. The voters who voted to leave were given no clear picture of what that actually meant and subsequent discussion had only further confused matters. Our negotiator David Davis hacked his way along the path, finally resigning when he realised that the PM was going over his head. In her five years as Home Secretary, May had shown herself to be determined and courageous, revelling in the detail in an obsessive way. Not strong on charisma, she was an able politician with a daunting task. She was faced with a skilled negotiator working on behalf of a powerful block of 26 countries and experienced staff, some of whom would be glad to see her fail. As is the nature of complex negotiations, both detail and progress rely on trust between the parties, in turn implying a high degree of confidentiality.

Naturally enough this infuriated MPs and the public. On the right of the path were the angry voices of the powerful group of MPs determined on a total break into the promised land of free trade, making our own way in the world and making trade deals wherever we want (rather neglecting the fact that such deals usually take many years to conclude). As the months went by, they became more frustrated and abusive towards their own Prime Minister in terms never heard before. The Labour Party on the left of the path were less noisy and their attacks had less focus, although they finally produced six issues which had to be met if they were to support the final deal which was due to be put to Parliament before Christmas 2018. The tests were: to ensure good relationships with the EU; fair management of migration; to protect national security and deal with cross border crime; to deliver for all regions and nations of the UK; to defend rights and protections to prevent a race to the bottom; and to deliver the exact same benefits as we had under the single market and customs union. As reasonable as this seemed, the last point was of course logically and politically impossible! As we progressed along the road, lack of information caused rumour and misinformation, which was reflected in a hostile press that constantly denigrated the government and the PM for incompetence, mostly because they were not seen as standing up to M. Barnier. Not surprisingly, the public became fed up with the whole process and there was a widespread feeling that the government should just get on with it. Get it done. Stop this storm of speculation and uncertainty.

In early July 2018 the Cabinet met at Chequers, basking in the exceptionally warm summer, to review the negotiation progress and agree a plan spelling out what our future relationship with the EU would be. The meeting took twelve hours. The plan proposed common trade standards with a frictionless UK–EU border for Northern Ireland and a joint framework to resolve disputes. This would allow the UK to develop its own trade deals across the world. Free movement of people would cease so that the UK had control of its borders. Three ministers, including the Foreign Secretary Boris Johnson and the minister responsible for leading the negotiations David Davis, resigned immediately after the meeting. These were followed by five other ministers.

Debates in Parliament were fiercely divided; in particular a significant number of Conservative MPs stated that they would refuse to accept a deal based on the plan. During the summer and autumn of 2018 negotiations with the EU continued based on the plan, a sign of the Prime Minister's dogged obsessionalism. Critics accused her of lacking an overall vision and creativity, while Michel Barnier continued to be frustrated by having never had a clear picture of what the UK actually wanted. As the date for a final EU summit to agree a deal approached, the sense of crisis grew. On October 18th May met the 26 leaders of the EU for a working dinner. It did not go well. They claimed to be no wiser about our position and by the time the PM left the meeting an unfortunate photo gave the impression that she was being shunned. Later that month she announced that 95% of the Withdrawal Agreement had been agreed, the most significant issue outstanding being the Irish border. The Cabinet met on November 6th 2018 and agreed that a final deal should be reached before the end of that month. This allowed for a major publicity drive leading up to a final vote in Parliament before the Christmas recess. Immediately after this the Minister for Transport Jo Johnson (Boris's brother) resigned in a letter which castigated the Prime Minister's whole approach to Brexit. He was followed by ten other ministers.

Jo Johnson's argument was that the proposed Withdrawal Agreement to be put before the Commons left so many issues to be decided during the following long transition period that we would be at the mercy of EU rules and regulations with no power to challenge them. He could not accept the government's position that to offer a deal, consequent upon which we would be worse off, or no deal, the consequence of which would be chaos and economic collapse, was a proper path to take. Jo Johnson considered that the only option was to run a second referendum with three options: accept the deal, stay in the EU, or leave with no deal. At least voters would be faced with clear facts rather than the lies and manipulations of the 2016 vote. A YouGov poll on October 9th had shown that 40% thought the UK was right to want to leave the EU; now 47% thought it was wrong. Other polls taken at this time which asked how people would vote in a second referendum showed majorities of 7% to 17% in favour of remaining.

Some two and a half years after voting to leave, the public were getting very impatient and were constantly demonstrating outside Parliament. In January 2019 the Prime Minister submitted her agreement (585 very detailed pages plus a further 14 offering a vague non-binding 'Political Declaration' about future relations). The debate was fierce. Although the opposition parties objected to parts of the deal, the main opposition came from the right wing of the Conservative Party, in particular the European Research Group (ERG), who, as far as I understand, never did any research, were totally committed to leaving the EU at any cost and included Jacob Rees-Mogg, a very rich money trader with many offshore accounts. Their main objection was that many of the terms, but particularly the short Declaration, would keep us too closely aligned with Europe in terms of customs and trade. In particular they opposed the 'Irish Back Stop,' an open-ended clause that the EU required as an insurance policy against any failure to solve the critical issue of the border between Northern Ireland and the Republic, which remained in the EU.

The unresolved issue of the Irish border, hardly mentioned until that point, would form the greatest area of conflict throughout the year. At the end of the debate the government lost the first 'meaningful vote' by the unprecedented number of 432 votes against and only 202 in support. Theresa May resolved to think again, promising to consult with senior parliamentarians, a task which ran against her political and personal instincts and, as far as I know, nothing serious ever happened. Around this time there were rumours that the government had prepared studies of the likely effects of a no-deal exit. They were said to predict shortages of essential food and medical supplies, to threaten industries relying on imported goods and potentially cause a drop of up to 9% in the GDP.

On Monday February 18th 2019 seven members of the Labour Party appeared at a press conference to announce their resignation from the Party and to start a new movement. They were highly critical of the Party's leadership and their handling of Brexit. Angela Smith, MP for Penistone and Stocksbridge, pointed to the 'level of alienation from the political process on the part of the people [being] at a record high, with the chaos and conflict characterising Brexit encapsulating perfectly the sense of deadlock and hopelessness which pervades our political culture.' Gavin Shuker, MP for Luton South, attacked the anti-Semitism which riddled the party, and the most senior, Chuka Umunna, MP for Streatham, promised that he would 'treat the people like adults and be honest about the tough choices facing Britain,' stating that '… politics is broken, it doesn't have to be this way. Let's change it.'[28] This group became The Independent Group for Change, later Change UK. In June the original Labour members left to join other parties. With five members, it was led by the outspoken former Conservative MP Anna Soubry until it was disbanded in December 2019.

The new legal date to leave was set for October 31st 2019. Amended scripts were brought back to Parliament on March 19th and 29th, the day we had been due to leave the EU. There were two more 'meaningful votes,' all fairly marginal changes to avoid the ruling that motions could only be debated once. The debate on March 19th had been rowdier than before and ended with another defeat of 391 to 242 votes. The final debate in June was lost by 344 to 286. Before this vote MPs had managed to take control of the Commons agenda in an effort to test out possible solutions that would actually get approval. This would answer May's call that rather than keep saying 'No,' could someone say what they did want. Nine 'Indicative' Motions were selected for debate. These were put in place to forbid leaving with no deal. They were to support continued membership of an adapted Common Market, and to remain in the Custom Union. The Labour Party's alternative proposal was Revoke Article 50, and supported carrying out a second referendum on the proposed agreement or aim for a 'managed' no deal. These motions were massively defeated, although those tabled by two parliamentary veterans, the moderate Conservative Kenneth Clark for a customs union and Labour's Margaret Beckett for a referendum, were defeated by only 3 and 12 votes, respectively. On Saturday March 23rd over a million people from across the country marched peacefully across London to demand that, now that we knew a great many more facts, a second referendum must be held.

All these proceedings brought forth from the Attorney General Geoffrey Cox the demand 'What are you playing at? What are you doing? You are not children in the playground, you are legislators. We are playing with people's lives.'[29] It seemed to me that this summed up the deep frustration and general anger and puzzlement of the population, who saw 650 people trying to solve an impossible question while going round in circles and using weird procedural tricks to outwit each other. Patience was running out. We needed a way out of this dilemma so that we could all relax a bit instead of being on a constant knife edge. Our reputation of being a fairly sensible people with the 'Mother of Parliaments' to govern us was being eroded around the world day by day. These feelings were pinpointed by the European President Donald Tusk who commented that 'I've been wondering what the special place in hell looks like for those who pushed for Brexit without even a sketch of a plan to carry it through safely.'[30] Some assumed that he meant the UK Parliament!

MPs were increasingly receiving vile hate mail and death threats and therefore required extra personal security. In 2017 a member of the banned neo-Nazi far-right organisation National Action, Jack Renshaw, was overheard in a pub boasting that he had bought a sharp knife in order to kill the Labour MP Rosie Cooper. He was arrested and, in common with Jo Cox's murderer, was sentenced to imprisonment for life. More than one MP was severely crowded and filmed by right-wing groups as they walked into Parliament. All MPs were advised not to walk alone, only go out in groups – an unheard of situation.

On the July 24th 2019 an exhausted Theresa May resigned after three years as the Prime Minister who had faced the impossible conundrum left by her predecessor, been vilified in Parliament and beyond, and hassled by vast demonstrations and an increasingly hostile press. This was the woman who, as Home Secretary, had developed the Hostile Environment policy, sending vans round specific areas urging 'illegal migrants' to go home before they were arrested, a policy which has continued ever since. Her initial promise as PM, which I think was sincere, was to establish a strong and stable government concerned with banishing injustice and social deprivation. Her promises, along with every other urgent domestic issue, had no hearings in the House of Commons as Brexit sucked everything up. Her major mistake was to call a 2017 election in the expectation of gaining a majority but instead ending up reduced to a majority of one, meaning that she had to rely on the small Northern Ireland DUP party. Her personality sought certainty rather than flexibility so from the start of her EU negotiations she hobbled herself by fixing ideological 'red lines,' refusing any aspect of a customs union or a common market or any role for the European Court of Justice. The Irish border became a key issue. This all pointed to the fact that she was concerned more with appeasing the right wing of her own party than with a broader consideration of a divided country. These personal character traits, along with the hostility heaped upon her as Parliament descended into near chaos and vilification by the ERG group with their dreams of past misogynistic glory, led eventually to May's downfall. This was the fifth UK Prime Minister to be brought down by Conservative disputes over membership of the EU. It was a perfect Greek tragedy. Theresa May bravely remains as a backbench MP.

During this same period the Labour Party had not covered itself in glory. Jeremy Corbyn looked weak and somewhat frail as the broad church that was his party failed to clarify or agree their position. They remained committed to a deal that would protect jobs and civil rights across the whole of the UK, retain the trading benefits of the EU, protect EU citizens resident in the UK and maintain managed immigration. Unfortunately, amid the rush of the need for clarity from the media and within politics the obvious question was, 'So does this mean you'd rather stay in the EU or will you agree with the millions that voted to leave, a high proportion of which are in traditional Labour voting areas?' This discussion went round and round the opposition MPs. A few voted for May's deal; others might settle for no deal. In any event the whole situation was about to get much much worse!

Faced with the necessity to elect a new leader, the Conservative Party set their processes in train. This meant that the future of the UK would be decided by however many of the 160,000 Party members would vote, removed by age, education and class from the rest of the population. Thirteen MPs put their names forward, reduced to four in the fourth round – Sajid Javid, Michael Gove, Jeremy Hunt and Boris Johnson (who had always been the favourite and whose ambition to be PM had propelled him from an early age). Predictably Johnson won with 92,153 votes in the final postal round. We now had a Prime Minister who, according to my understanding, was a proven serial liar, adulterer, messily dressed ex Eton man whose capacity for never answering a direct question was legendary. He had been sacked from several important posts as a journalist as well as from the position of Mayor of London. He had survived by promoting a sense of bonhomie and constant optimism whatever disasters lay around him. He needed love and to be known as Boris, the politician with a cuddly name. It was noticeable that throughout the campaign he had given no interviews with journalists or commentators; his handlers, fearing his reputation for gaffes and his ability never to answer a question would damage him.

Alexander Boris de Pfeffel Johnson entered 10 Downing Street on July 24th 2019 accompanied by his 'special advisor,' the political anarchist Dominic Cummings, who had led the misleading Leave campaign. Here was a man who held politicians and the establishment and normal conventions in disdain, whose modus operandi was aggressive interaction, creating a tense and fearful working environment and was held in contempt of Parliament for failing to attend a committee meeting investigating that campaign. He was immediately given a full security pass for the whole building. Johnson's Cabinet was mostly packed with loyal Leave campaigners with only one-third women as opposed to the opposition's 60%. We were about to see a political drama never witnessed before. Johnson then removed all existing ministers who had campaigned for any other candidates, replacing them with more right-wing individuals. Finally he imported his current partner Carrie Symonds, despite his still being married to his wife Marina Wheeler with whom he had three children and who was having treatment for cancer. One Conservative MP commented that, 'Those of us who have worked alongside of him and had a chance of watching him can see for ourselves his modus operandi and his capacity both for deception and self deception and those are two ingredients of charlatanism.'[31]

Whether by luck or design, parliamentarians adjourned for their summer recess on July 25th, but Johnson had time to announce that the UK would leave the EU on October 31st 'do or die.' While stating that he preferred a deal it was widely believed that in reality he would push for a 'no deal,' which, it was predicted, would seriously damage the UK economy. At least the opposition parties recognised what was to come and moved towards a combined approach to counter Johnson's dangerous ambitions. Senior members of all parties met throughout the summer to agree effective political and legislative moves. Bouncy Boris, freed from his parliamentary inquisition, was touring the country getting photo opportunities instead of, as one fierce heckler pointed out, going to Brussels.

It was becoming quite clear that part of the PM's plan was to call an early general election, probably in October near the date when he was due to put his final proposal to EU leaders. He would campaign on the argument that MPs and/or Europe had prevented him from carrying out the will of the people at the referendum. On August 28th 2019 the Prime Minister announced that the Queen had given her consent to prorogue Parliament from September 9th–12th and this was to last until the opening of the next session on October 14th. This gave MPs a maximum of five days to take action. The explanation given for this unprecedented act was that the government required time to prepare for the Queen's speech at the opening the next session of Parliament. This spanned the normal two weeks when Parliament would normally be suspended for party conferences, but it was quite possible that MPs would have decided to stay in Parliament for those dates. There was widespread condemnation at this obvious trick to avoid debate; no one in the UK believed the reason, it was just another Johnson lie. A series of court cases were launched on the basis that Johnson had deceived the Queen and therefore the prorogation was unlawful.

MPs returned to the Chamber on September 3rd, with five days to decide a way forward. The Prime Minister reported on the G7 meeting held in Biarritz on August 24th. It was a pretty bumbling presentation with little content, but missed out the pat on the head he got from President Trump and the commitment made at his press conference with Angela Merkel. During their exchange on resolving the Northern Ireland issue, looking at the time already spent, Merkel said 'Well we could resolve this issue in maybe two years or 30 days.' Action Man Johnson immediately rose to the issue and announced that he would do it in 30 days! During his speech the Conservative MP Phillip Lee walked across the Chamber and joined the Liberal Party, thus removing the government's majority. That evening the House debated on a Conservative/Labour motion to enable the Commons to control the parliamentary timetable. The government lost by 27 votes. To cries of 'Traitors!' Johnson removed the whip from 21 of his party who had voted against him. This included Father of the House Ken Clarke, Churchill's grandson Nicholas Soames and Dominic Grieve a former Attorney General. They were also barred from standing for Parliament in any future election. The violent language once again raised the temper of the debates.

The following morning, Sajid Javid, the new Chancellor, a former top banker whose wealth was believed to be hidden in several tax havens, presented an early spending review, which, in the expectation of an early election, was very generous – apparently lots of money had just been found. The NHS was promised £6.3 billion, which may have gone part way to repairing the damage done by ten years of cuts. Nothing was allocated to deal with the historical levels of poverty, the dependence on food banks and homelessness, except to announce that 'austerity has ended,' which was patently untrue. The Commons then debated a motion to prevent the government leaving the EU without a deal known as the Benn Act, sponsored by Hilary Benn (Labour – son of Tony Benn, see Chapter 13),

Philip Hammond (former Chancellor) and David Gauke (former Lord Chancellor). It required that, if no deal had been agreed to leave by October 19th the Prime Minister must ask the EU for an extension to allow further negotiations. It was passed by a large majority.

Johnson then called for a general election on October 15th, an event which would see Parliament closed at a critical time. Jeremy Corbyn and the opposition parties refused this trap, although welcomed an election later in the year. An election required a two-thirds majority, which the government significantly failed to achieve by 236 votes. Hence Johnson had suffered three defeats on key issues bringing his total defeats to six since coming to power. On Thursday September 5th the Prime Minister's brother Jo Johnson resigned from the government, citing unresolvable tension between family loyalty and the national interest. He informed Downing Street the previous evening. Looking distressed, the Prime Minister set off to launch his election campaign in Wakefield the following day against a background of police trainees, having agreed that he would just announce the money for more recruits. When he took his place it was obvious that all was not well; he waffled on for an hour, hardly coherent, and an officer right behind him fainted. It was a PR disaster, and the Chief Constable said that he regretted that the Prime Minister had failed to keep to their agreement.

This had been a terrible week for Johnson although his optimism never quite failed. One of the remarkable aspects, apart from the heckling that the PM received wherever he went, was that for all the weeks and weeks that Brexit had been debated protesters of various persuasions had kept up fierce nonstop demonstrations outside Parliament. Sometimes they could be heard in the Chamber and every interview with the world's press had been conducted against this wall of noise. The BBC Parliament channel recorded its highest viewing figures: why would anyone want to watch fiction when this was all so absorbing and directly affected the future of all our families? Politics was alive, and, in my opinion, whatever the preceding chaos MPs had gained back some respect during this remarkable week.

On September 11th the Scottish High Court delivered their verdict that Johnson's prorogation of Parliament was unlawful, but in view of the forthcoming hearing at the UK Supreme Court they did not issue an injunction that MPs must return to work. On the 15th, before a meeting with the EU Commission, the PM told *The Mail on Sunday* that he saw himself as the 'Hulk' because the madder the Hulk gets the stronger he gets and '... he always escapes no matter how bound he was.' Thus he could break free of the European shackles. Brilliant for cartoonists and demonstrators, although, as the Hulk actor Mark Ruffalo pointed out that the Hulk only fights for the good, works best as a team player and his rages are balanced by the science of reason. The lunch meeting in Luxembourg did not go well, and as Johnson walked out for an open-air press conference a handful of British ex-pats were holding a noisy demonstration at the gates. Johnson walked out, leaving the Prime Minister of Luxembourg to address an empty podium. Yet another PR disaster.

Between September 17th and 23rd Scottish parliamentarians, submissions from Wales and Northern Ireland, the campaigner Gina Miller and a former Conservative PM John

Major presented their arguments on the decision to prorogue to all 11 High Court judges, sitting together for the first time. The Scottish QC Aidan O'Neill concluded his plea that Johnson and his government could not be trusted not to engage in low dishonest and dirty tricks. The fact was that 'The mother of Parliaments is being brought down by the father of lies'.

At the same time, in an unplanned coincidence, the former Conservative PM David Cameron launched his memoir. So, we had Cameron and Major both, in turn, naming Johnson as a liar. It occurred to me that most ordinary men faced with so much failure would just resign, but Johnson, with his determination to fulfil his lifelong ambition, could not countenance facing reality. In fact throughout this whole period it was the chronic feeling that Johnson could not be trusted that, in my view, lay behind most of the arguments within Parliament and without. There were now, by my calculation, only six days left to meet the PM's challenge of sorting Brexit in 30 days. He apparently decided to reveal his master plan bit by bit. The first outline of a plan for Northern Ireland, so vague it was officially termed a 'non-paper Paper,' was dispatched on September 19th.

On September 24th the Supreme Court delivered their unanimous devastating judgement that the decision to prorogue Parliament was unlawful because it had the effect of frustrating Parliament. The decision meant that the order to prorogue might just as well have been a blank piece of paper. It also implied that Johnson's declared motives were untrue and that he had misled the Queen. His response was to declare that the court had got it wrong, and he carried on as if nothing had happened. Downing Street's arrogant plots had resulted in attacks on two elements of the constitution: parliamentary sovereignty and the rule of law. With the Commons back in session, the fierce and divisive debates resumed with Johnson increasing the tension by the use of terms such as surrender, traitors and betrayal in his speeches, which the EU's Michel Barnier considered would make it much more difficult for MPs to agree a deal; thus making any further concessions would be a waste of time.

With October 31st fast approaching – the date on which, without a deal, we would leave the EU with catastrophic consequences – the IFS calculated that the public debt would rise to a level last seen 50 years before. On October 2nd the Prime Minister used his speech at the Conservative Party Annual Conference to outline his new plan. This introduced a complex trading deal for Northern Ireland with an effective border down the Irish Sea (a proposal previously rejected by the Irish leader and many MPs). It seemed to me either to be a rather childish attempt to be seen to do something different (although 95% of this deal had already been rejected three times) or a stupid bit of theatre contrived to fail, meaning that the true aim of leaving without a deal was inevitable. The EU was very cautious in its response. Negotiations were intensified and on October 17th Johnson announced that 'a great deal' had been agreed.

In a further desire for drama, the PM decided to present his plan for debate on a Saturday, October 19th, the first such sitting for 37 years (when one had commenced for the Falkland invasion). The 150-page detailed deal had only been made available to MPs the evening before. This was also the date set by the Benn Act, when Johnson must ask for a delay to the deadline if no agreement was made. The drama was not disappointing as speeches from all factions were met with counter arguments and a million people packed into Parliament Square protesting to remain in the EU, an increasingly popular idea. They could be plainly heard inside the Chamber. In particular, Labour's shadow Brexit Secretary Kier Starmer presented a forensic analysis of the Bill pointing out that all the clauses from the May agreement which guaranteed protection for consumers, workers and the environment had been deleted and moved to the ambiguous political declaration. Late in the day, despite great pressure not to act, the loyal Conservative Oliver Letwin tabled a motion that discussion should be delayed until full details of the new deal were available. This was passed by a majority of 16 votes. Having repeatedly declared that he would rather 'die in a ditch' than ask the EU for a further delay, Johnson had no option but to write the letter. Once again he displayed his disdain for Parliament and his own childishness by copying and pasting the letter contained in the Benn Act, attaching a personal note saying that he did not agree with the letter and instructing our EU Ambassador to ask the EU to neglect it. Not surprisingly the wise and experienced EU negotiators accepted the letter that was in the Act.

There then followed a period of political chess. The EU waited to see what happened next in Parliament, arguing that it was pointless to give more time unless it would lead to a definite result. Johnson, who now operated with a minority of 41 votes, optimistically brought forward his deal again, and the opposition parties drew closer together. Who would move first? When MPs reconvened, the Bill was presented but, after another acrimonious debate, including the revelation that ships crossing to and from Northern Ireland would have to complete customs procedures, making it effectively a separate part of the UK, the Bill was passed in principle so that it could be debated or amended at the next stage. At that point, in one of the most condescending statements I can remember, Jacob Rees-Mogg as Leader of the House announced that instead of the scheduled debate on the Queen's speech Johnson's Bill would be represented on Monday and the House would have a maximum of three days to debate and then vote. There was uproar in the house, during which Rees-Mogg walked out.

Some options were left. Labour, still anxious not to call an election before the EU agreed to avoid a no deal outcome, would have preferred time to properly debate and significantly amend the Bill, but Johnson, fearing that outcome, planned to push on. On October 28th, I assume with much use of the usual 'back channels,' the EU announced an extension until January 31st 2020, and the following day, despite over 100 Labour MPs abstaining, the Commons voted by 438 to 20 to hold an election on December 12th.

General Election 2019

This was the first December election for 96 years and posed major challenges for all parties. Five weeks were left for campaigning before a decision that would probably depend as much on the weather as anything else. This would certainly be an historic event, initial feedback indicating that with the usual tribal loyalties split by Brexit a huge amount would depend on local campaigning and MPs' performances in recent votes. In the early days the Conservatives behaved badly, having been caught re-editing an interview to make the shadow Brexit Secretary look like an idiot and, during a Corbyn speech, posing as a fact checking site while actually promoting their own propaganda. By November 22nd both parties had produced their manifestos. As far as Brexit was concerned the situation was clear. The Green and Liberal Democrat parties were proposing to remain in the EU; the Conservatives were for Leave as soon as possible; and Labour's position, much criticised, was neutral. Labour hoped to preserve votes from both their Leave and Remain constituencies, promising a referendum once their deal had been agreed. Beyond that parties produced fairly standard programmes for a five-year Parliament. Liberals promised: £50 billion for public services and to tackle inequality; that 80% of electricity would be produced by alternative sources and that low-income households would be insulated by 2020; £40 million to education; and reform for the voting system to give more power to the people. The Green Party promised £100 billion for climate change (including the planting of 700 million trees) and to introduce a basic income.

The Conservatives' manifesto was full of rhetoric and extravagant promises. For example, they vowed to recruit 50,000 nurses (which actually included 19,000 retained after retirement and 12,000 from overseas and with few migrants able to meet the new financial requirements for admission) and the pledge to build 40 new hospitals (although at least six were upgrades and the rest were scheduled to start building in 2025–2030, so presumably they would open about ten years later). Reductions in carbon emissions would be achieved by 2050 – too late according to the majority of scientists. Above all, Johnson promised to get Brexit done by Christmas, a remarkable claim given that Parliament had only agreed to his plan in principle and it was known that most MPs wished to significantly amend it. Labour on the other hand met the main concerns of the population head on with a hopeful tone running into 2050 and beyond. Climate change, youth and education would receive £12 billion, with projects completed by 2031. Health and social care would receive an extra £17.7 billion, culture £2.6 billion, peace and the Ministry of Justice £1.4 billion, and pay increases for the public sector of £15.6 billion. The total was to be met by taxing the better off, raising the sum of £82.9 billion. Key industries would be nationalised. It was an exciting document that aimed to transform our society. An ambition to achieve a four-day working week was a long term goal.

The general public greeted many of these extraordinary sums of money with some anger and curiosity – why had they endured so many years of austerity now to be faced with such generosity? There was a marked feeling of cynicism. Nonetheless there was a strange idea that out of the parliamentary chaos new feelings of hope were dawning. At least three of the opposition parties had recognised the science of climate change and taken notice of the millions demonstrating for urgent action. Issues of inequality and the role of robotics in industry were surfacing at last.

As the election campaign proceeded a sort of pattern emerged. Party leaders toured the country, naturally concentrating on seats where they perceived their presence might help. It seemed to me that the main difference with the Conservative campaign was that Johnson's visits were short, unannounced and had minimum contact with the public who might be hostile, ask questions or lead the candidate to give an unfortunate answer or seen to be flustered. On November 19th both Johnson and Corbyn appeared on stage to answer questions from the public. This was broadcast live on ITV and the majority considered that Corbyn had won by answering questions, keeping calm and defending the NHS. Johnson failed to answer questions and blustered his way through. Lord Heseltine, former Deputy Prime Minister to Margaret Thatcher, quite clearly advised voters not to vote Conservative but to support the Liberal Democratic Party.

Terror

On November 29th 2019 a terrorist attack during a conference of academics and ex-prisoners held in the Fishmongers Hall on the north end of London Bridge shocked the populace. The attacker had been released from prison, was on a tag and attended the conference with permission. He sat through the morning session before launching his fatal stabbing attack on two young attendees and wounding three others, then ran across the bridge. Within a short distance he was stopped and disarmed by brave members of the conference and others. The police arrived, saw that he appeared to be wearing an explosive belt and shot him dead on the spot. The victims' families asked to be left alone and begged that the event should not be politicised in the election campaign. The Prime Minister ignored that request. On December 1st Johnson, having refused to be interviewed by the abrasive Andrew Neil, was interviewed on TV by Andrew Marr. It was a car crash. Marr was criticised for interrupting the PM, but it was difficult not to when faced with evasions, bumbling and distractions. Johnson's repeated assertions that Brexit was 'oven ready' and could be settled quickly was followed by a number of lies. He portrayed himself as a new broom unbound by previous Conservative policies and he certainly never supported the austerity regime, despite being a senior member of the government that imposed it. It just went on and on. It should be mentioned that before the election started the government had blocked the release of investigations into the economic impact of Brexit and the findings of a Parliament report on Russian influence on the 2016 election.

As predicted by many and feared by some, the Conservative Party won 365 votes. Labour totalled 203, and other parties shared 82, giving Johnson a working majority of 80. The turnout was 67.3%. It seemed that, as in the referendum's 'Take back control' rhetoric, Johnson's short 'Let's get it done' approach had resonated with the majority of the population. Labour's manifesto had seemed too long and too radical, while Corbyn's ambiguous stance on the EU and his perceived weak leadership had been seen as not strong enough to push through the radical agenda outlined in the manifesto. Despite the promised joyful celebrations on Brexit Day, December 31st

2019, the official events fell flat and most people stayed at home, no doubt worrying what the next years of negotiations would bring before deciding whether or not there was anything to celebrate. In the second week of February Johnson, with his chief adviser Cumming's assistance, confirmed his new Cabinet, basically dismissing any critics and appointing loyal Brexiters. All did not seem to go that well as, faced with a demand to sack all his advisers, the much praised Chancellor Sajid Javid resigned to be replaced by Rishi Sunak. This created a great stir, although it seems highly likely that it was all pre-planned. The final Cabinet was generally seen as a determination to ensure complete control by Johnson. In the following weeks two worrying things were noted. Johnson continued his reluctance to be challenged in public or even in press briefings, where media who were thought to be critical were excluded. Unprecedented for this country. A second trend reflecting a Trump style was the ministers trained to brush off questions. Very early on this government increased the drive to deport foreign criminals. An outcry resulted from the determination to deport a number of 'foreign nationals' to Jamaica. A number of these were men who had been brought here as small children, had lived here ever since but never bothered to get a passport; some were now married with children. They had committed pretty minor offences in their teens and had now been rounded up. Faced with these facts ministers would just keep repeating they were foreign nationals and criminals. They arrived in Jamaica, never having visited that country before, leaving wives and children behind. Most went into hiding as the island was in the grips of violent drug wars. The policy, the refusal of ministers to admit the truth and the consequences on all involved demonstrated an horrific view of this new government.

SOCIAL WORK

Frontline

Following an initiative at the University of Bedford the government decided to support new intensive training programmes for social work. These were short, specialised courses with more emphasis on the practical aspects of social work and less on the history and theory of the social sciences. 'Step Up for Social Work' launched in 2009; this was followed by 'Frontline' four years later and 'Think Ahead' more recently. The first two focused on work with children, or more specifically child protection, the third on mental health. The titles convey a message of a future that will be made better than anything that social workers already have. Given the blurb that accompanied the launch of Frontline, rapid promotion was assured: Learn how to be a social worker and get inducted to management all within fourteen months! The government invested heavily in these initiatives which cost about three times as much per trainee as did three-year undergraduates on a qualifying course. This is all the more surprising given that the entry criterion for the fast-track courses was a 2:1 degree, although some flexibility was later allowed. This was a divisive initiative threatening to create different levels of social work and also inserting narrowly trained specialist workers among those with a wider more generically trained approach. There has never been any comprehensive independent evaluation of this new system, including how trainees fare once in employment or retention rates. It was certainly far removed from the free-flowing creative mixture of high-level education and training practiced in Maidstone in the late 1970s which aimed to develop competent, critically thinking and creative social workers. (See Chapter 10.)

In 2016 Parliament's Education Committee, examining the Social Work Reform agenda, were ambiguous in their view of these initiatives. They supported the need for generic training as opposed to these specialist courses which should be a post-qualifying event. They noted the contrast between the £19,000 bursary for fast-track students compared to the student loans for university students and recommended a full review. In an effort to reconcile these approaches they suggested that future Frontline contracts should include a university partner and asked the organisation to submit proposals for working together. I do not recall that anything much happened as a result of this publication although the financial incentives built into the fast-track courses eventually led to most universities embracing them.[32]

The College of Social Work

The traumas from the death of Baby P and the subsequent media and political storms eased, so that early in this period good things started to happen, although it would be only months before another storm hit the profession. The Social Work Task Group, established as a positive move by Ed Balls, Secretary of State for Children, Schools and Families immediately after the tragedy, published a substantial Interim Report in July 2009. It was led by Moira Gibb, a highly respected social worker. It sought to improve the quality and status of a profession which needed a voice. They recommended a Royal College of Social Work on a par with other professions, to promote the profession, improve the education and training of social workers, and to prevent the high turnover of staff and loss of experienced workers. The government responded well, putting in £109 million of funding, £58 million of which was for recruitment and retention. It seemed to me that this was a very valuable report, but I urged that instead of being focussed on individuals and families it should have promoted the wider traditional view of social work, which embraced prevention through community work and social action. It never did. The final report pursuing these ideas was released in late November and was generally welcomed. Welcoming the report Ed Balls said:

> Sometimes issues of jargon and introversion can blind the profession, let alone the outside world, to what it's supposed to be doing … I think there has been a culture of not enough voice, not enough representation and not enough of the social work profession itself shaping the future, saying these should be our professional standards, this is how we do it and this is how we should reform.[33]

Moira Gibb was appointed to lead the Social Work Reform Board to further develop the Task Group's proposals and pursue them into action and legislation.

At the same time, BASW, under the leadership of former MP Hilton Dawson, was considering how it could best support members who were in difficulties facing disciplinary action either locally or with the GSCC. Although it had an excellent Advice and Representation (A&R) Service staffed by social workers who were also qualified trade union officials, they were at a disadvantage as employers would not accept representation by a professional association in internal disputes or negotiations. It was therefore decided to form the Social Workers Union, subtly linked with BASW but sufficiently independent to be recognised as such by the Trade Union Certification Officer. It was launched in October 2011 and I was elected to the Executive the following year.

Child Abuse: Edlington

The warm glow that might have been engendered by the Task and Reform initiatives was soon punctuated by another media storm caused by the terrible torture and sexual abuse to near death, on April 4th 2009, of a nine-year-old boy by two brothers aged 10 and 11 in Edlington, South Yorkshire. It sadly paralleled the case of the Bulger murder in 1993 (see Chapter 14). The brothers had terrorised their local community for a long time in response to living in a home where they received little or no sustenance, love or care from their addicted mother and cruel father. On January 23rd 2010 the brothers were sentenced to indefinite detention.[34n] A notice outside their house had read 'BEWARE OF THE KIDS.' They had been taken into care just three weeks before the assault. Criticism of the social workers, working in an overstressed, badly managed department, was that, given the domestic situation, they had not been removed earlier. The headline in *The Observer* was 'Take more babies away from bad parents,' and was based on an interview with Martin Narey, the CEO of Barnardo's, who argued that workers should stop trying to fix families that couldn't be fixed and be braver about removing children at risk.[35] Placing young children into a permanent foster care placement was known to succeed. That is of course if there were sufficient families readily available, which meant that while waiting for such a family children may experience numerous changes of placement. This does great damage, especially to such chronically damaged children whose behaviour is unlikely to change quickly.

Child Abuse: Rotherham

As tragic as the events in Edlington were, to my mind the worst example of child abuse was happening just ten miles away in the town of Rotherham. Details emerged in the press of terrible torture and abuse of at least 1,400 children over a 16-year period by taxi drivers, usually at night. The vast majority of these men were of Asian descent and a few were from Eastern Europe. Girls, mostly white and some as young as 11, were abducted, groomed and gang raped then trafficked to nearby towns under threat of being shot or set on fire after being doused in petrol. It was horrendous. Nearly a third were in care or on child protection registers. It transpired that this had been widely known about for many years but dismissed by an incompetent local authority, the police and health workers. It was unforgivable. The drivers concentrated their attentions on vulnerable young girls, often with a history of domestic or sexual abuse, picking them up outside care homes and accommodation for care leavers as well as online.

The situation was so gross that the media focussed their attacks on the local council and the police; the role of social workers drew less attention although the whole care sector was targeted. The Children's Commissioner, reporting that such events were not confined to Rotherham, found that in a 14-month period over 2,400 children had been subject to such abuse and an estimated 16,500 children were at risk of abuse by gangs.[36] The press and a thorough investigation by Professor Alexis Jay identified some of the key causes of the disaster. The initial focus was on some reluctance of agencies to pursue reports in case they were seen to be accused of racial discrimination. Professor Jay drew attention to a Home Office Report in 2002 commenting that it dealt with 'the topic of sexual exploitation at a sensitive time with a politically inconvenient truth.' Jay reported no evidence of discrimination in social worker's case files.

These events, of course, were against the background of the 2001 terrorist attacks in the USA and consequent riots in some northern towns. The Labour council was well aware of the feelings of the majority indigenous population and the balance required between them and the minority black and ethnic populations. It is notable that, following these events, 500 BNP supporters paraded through the town, and elsewhere in the UK won sufficient seats to become the main opposition party. The report described the council as poorly rated with a macho culture of bullying and sexism. It failed to see work with very vulnerable children as a priority, tending to view the girls concerned as young prostitutes and therefore victims of their own fate. By 2016, the council had lost 33% of its spending power since 2010 under the Conservative austerity policies, this for a council faced with high levels of poverty and consequent high levels of demand on its children's services.

The last major question was how did this happen to children who were placed in residential care so that they could be safe? For this we have to go back to the history of residential child care. From my memory it was in the mid 1970s that the issue of the rights of the child became established; this was followed by the inability of care staff to safeguard children by locking the doors. As one worker explained it to me, 'They go out of the doors and any window, I just can't contain them.' The solution was to rely on the close relationship between staff and these naughty children. In subsequent years however, as a consequence of social work policies to keep children in their local communities, either with their own family or in foster care, the children assessed as needing residential care had more complex and extreme needs. Financial pressures meant that no extra staff were provided although some training was given in some authorities.

Thus staff were faced with greater challenges by the behaviour of young people and their ready exercise of their rights. The Jay report commented that:

> The sanctions available to children's social care are limited in relation to persistent runaways ... Underage girls who stay out all night and engage in overtly sexualised behaviour pose severe problems for those responsible for their care ... the impotence of children's services in dealing with absconders ... damaged belief in the effectiveness of intervention. Parents who felt that their children would be protected and secure in placements became disillusioned. This was mirrored by the victims themselves, who had no confidence in the ability of the police or social workers to protect them against their abusers.[37n]

It was reported that the police developed a low opinion of these girls whilst ignoring the role of the men and the violence involved. They were slow to respond to the continuous rise in reports that children had absconded from care. Some young girls who complained were told they were wasting police time.

Once these events had come to public notice there was a fierce reaction. The leader of Rotherham Council and the CEO resigned, as did other key players including the Director of Children's Services. Twenty-two men and two women have so far been convicted. The men have been jailed from between 4 and 19 years, with one ringleader receiving a sentence of 35 years. The women, who were involved in grooming, were sentenced for 4 years and 18 months suspended. (In late June 2022 the Independent Office for Police Conduct (IOPC) issued their final report on these events. The report concluded that 47 police officers had been investigated although none had been dismissed. It also revealed that police were continuing their investigation and still arresting offenders. There was criticism from victims and others that no one in the police force had been held to account.)

BASW and The College

Relief for social workers came in 2011 with the release in May of Professor Eileen Munro's *Review of Child Protection*. Her report charted the way in which recommendations from a whole series of reports on child abuse had resulted in restrictive bureaucratic processes that prevented social workers exercising their professional skills. This was made worse by very high caseloads, insufficient resources and high turnover of staff. This, and the importance given to targets and performance indicators, had created a defensive system (as reported in point 3 in the Executive Summary) 'that insufficient attention is given to developing and supporting the expertise to work effectively with children, young people and families.' Further,

> Practitioners and their managers have told the review that statutory guidance, targets and local rules have become so extensive that they limit their ability to stay child-centred. The demands of bureaucracy have reduced their capacity to work directly with children and

families. Services have become so standardised that they do not provide the required range of responses to the variety of need presented. This review recommends a radical reduction in the amount of central prescription to help professionals move from a compliance culture to a learning culture, where they have more freedom to use their expertise in assessing need and providing the right help.

The report also recommended the designation of a principal child and family social worker responsible for practice in each local authority along with the appointment of a Chief Social Worker to advise the government on social work practice.[38] This was a great boost to the morale of social workers. The government supported the report and appointed chief social workers in the Departments of Education and Health. Looking back at these recommendations in the light of the terrible austerity regime I am uncertain how many of the practice recommendations have survived. What I do know is that, as cutbacks have taken their toll, the emphasis on protection has changed the view of social workers in communities. They are no longer widely seen as helping families but more like police, wading in to remove children from their families.

Following the recommendations of the Social Work Task Force, the College of Social Work opened its doors in 2012. It claimed to be established to promote social work, provide an independent voice in the media and represent the views of the profession in relation to government proposed changes. It was to be entirely independent, being funded by its members although given a generous grant by the government to which it continued to be linked through its funding and policy. It aspired to become the media's preferred source of expert comment and opinion as the authoritative voice of the profession.[39] The Task Force had hoped that the College might be merged with BASW. However, these ambitions and the force with which they were expressed caused conflict, not least because BASW covered the whole of the UK whereas the College was confined to England. There was also concern that for the first seven years of its membership the Board would be unelected and appointed by government.

The College, anxious to secure independent finance and frustrated by the reluctance of social workers to join, struck a deal with the trade union Unison so that joining would significantly reduce the College membership fee. This posed a further complication for BASW who had just formed their own trade union. Oddly in 2013 the College registered itself as a charity with far narrower purposes than the aims outlined above. Tensions were aired in front of a meeting of the Education Select Committee which commented adversely on the link between the College and Unison as an effective closed shop. Despite all this, BASW started negotiations in good faith, controversially seeking to secure its own finances despite the taint of government links, which was balanced against the desire to create a single powerful voice for social work. Mediators were appointed and in due course a memorandum of understanding was signed which envisioned a UK based organisation with federal links to independent Colleges in the three other countries. The assets of both would merge into a new company with an elected Board. In the meantime a Joint Working Group would be formed to a timetable ending in 2012. The SWU and the BASW A&R service would be hived off into a separate organisation. I lived through all these stressful times and know how BASW's staff suffered under the pressure of the negotiations. Suddenly, with no notice whatsoever the College withdrew from all further contact with BASW. The shock was felt very badly, but was mixed with relief that these poisonous negotiations were at an end. The College limped on with fewer than half the membership it had anticipated and consequent financial difficulties. I conducted a lively correspondence with my local, senior, Conservative MP, arguing that giving more taxpayer money to this organisation would be a waste. Finally the government refused to bail it out and the College closed in June 2015, a victim of overambitious management, government interference and the basic false assumptions of its foundation. This was of course costly to the taxpayer and the profession, although membership of BASW rose significantly in subsequent years, in part by the attraction of its A&R service jointly run by BASW and SWU.

More Austerity

From May 2010 the Conservative and Liberal Democrat coalition led by David Cameron and Nick Clegg, with George Osborne as Chancellor launched an agenda to cut public expenditure and impose a programme of austerity on the contested ground that it was essential to reduce the country's debt and running annual deficit. One of their first targets was to cut a long list of public funded organisations. The GSCC was included; its duties would be transferred to the Health Professionals Council (HPC) which already regulated a rage of health-related occupations. It was renamed The Health and Care Professionals Council (HCPC). The complex process caused many headaches as the processes of the two organisations were incompatible. The GSCC finally closed on July 31st 2012. The closure cost £17.6 billion plus the cost of upgrading the HCPC. This was a significant loss to the profession although in recent years, following the Baby P scandal, it had attracted a great deal of criticism as it failed to deal with delays in hearings caused by the steep increase in disciplinary referrals. See below for an account of my somewhat unworthy fight with the GSCC.

The effects of the austerity policy were very soon evident, and by 2013 councils were cutting right across their services, including care for adults, youth services and libraries, some of which lost 50% of their support. Councils warned that as this policy continued they would lose more than a third of their funding, already viewing the cuts that they were forced to make as horrendous.[40] As cuts hit the NHS the trusts were already piling up debts as their static income failed to keep up with increased costs. One trust financial manager commented that in addition to cuts the constant reorganisation and the £1 million a year spent drawing up contracts was wasteful. He described a Maoist permanent revolution from the top in a service starved of funds, harried by the regulator and bullied by the Care Quality Commission demanding the impossible. After 34 years of service, he was leaving. This situation was typical across the whole education, health and care sectors. Understandably there were calls for the care of elderly people to be better co-ordinated between NHS and care services. During 2015, 156 Sure Start children's centres were closed, thus knocking the bottom out of vital care and preventive services for some of the most vulnerable in society and inevitably leading to higher costs later. If only retiring Social Service Directors were as outspoken.[41]

With the rising cost of renting, poorer families (particularly in London, where 50% of the 2.3 million families in poverty were in work) were moved out, often long distances away, thus breaking up family and friendship networks and school continuity. I heard that one London council had bought my old barracks in Canterbury in order to house 200 homeless families. The accusatory term 'ethnic cleansing' was being used more and more often. Meanwhile by late 2016 the number of children in care had rocketed to nearly 7,500 and, with the cuts to legal aid, parents were finding it difficult to argue their case in court. The President of the Association of Directors of Children's Services commented that 'The number of children in public care is a national disgrace,' a particular concern being the postcode lottery behind that figure. The rate at which children were removed from their families varied from 30 per 10,000 to 180 per 10,000. Sir James Munby, a worthy President of the Family Division of the High Court, warned that the relentless pressure of care applications, estimated to reach 20,000 by 2020, was breaking the family court system, itself already facing cuts. Figures released in March 2019 revealed that over four million children were living below the relative poverty line (one in three of the child population). Child poverty had fallen while Labour was in power but since 2010 the figures had risen steadily until in 2014 70% of these children were in working families struggling on low and insecure pay.

The austerity policy hit the most vulnerable in society very hard, not least those in residential care where market forces had resulted in significant changes in provision. Local small homes had been bought up by large companies seeking profit and often loaded with debt while their fee income was threatened by local council's budget cuts. Southern Cross collapsed in 2011 from exactly that fault. Four Seasons, with 2,000 beds, went into liquidation in 2015 to be followed by Terra Firma, the finance company, which no longer saw this sector as profitable. These were followed by smaller organisations. A survey reported that 48 authorities had been faced with private contractors handing back their contracts. This meant stress of insecurity for the residents and more responsibility on local authority staff to find alternative accommodation. It was a reflection of the banking crisis where enriched equity leaders took the profits and the taxpayer was left to clear up the mess. Local authorities found themselves caught between the NHS wanting to discharge elderly patients, often with complex needs, and providers unable to provide care. In one of the most ridiculous examples of the competitive market in social care, one local authority was 'fined' £100,000 for failing to provide care for patients due for discharge. One broken system penalising another broken system! The government gave an emergency injection of £2 million which was immediately lost in the real costs involved. By 2017 the number of homes graded as outstanding by the Care Quality Commission had fallen below 1%.[42] The whole situation showed loss of leadership and understanding by successive governments. Radical solutions had been promised by successive governments for many years, and there is currently no sign of effective political action.

Defending the Profession

Under the leadership of Ruth Allen as CEO and Guy Shennan as Chair, BASW faced many challenges following the College of Social Work fiasco. In 2016 the government tabled The Children and Social Work Bill in the House of Lords. There had been no prior consultation although there had been warnings in previous ministerial speeches. In 2013 Michael Gove had commented, 'In too many cases social work training involves idealistic students being told that the individuals with whom they will work have been disempowered by society. This analysis is, sadly, as widespread as it is pernicious.' This was later supported by Martin Narey, who claimed that social work degree courses put too much emphasis on 'inequality, empowerment and anti-oppressive practice.' The Chief Social Worker at that time was Isabelle Trowler. Whilst the many clauses in the Bill, including offering extended care, were welcomed (although there were no extra funds for their implementation), two others caused controversy. One section allowed periods of six years when Children's Departments could apply to opt out of some key policies and procedures that impeded staff exploring innovative ways of service delivery and practice. It was argued by some (extraordinarily including a group of Conservative MPs) that this offered a wonderful opportunity to free social workers to develop their professional practice. BASW, the Association of Lawyers for Children and many academics argued that it was very risky to start removing laws and guidance designed to protect vulnerable children and young people. The facts as I saw them were that previous child abuse failures had laid more and more restrictions on social work to a point where they constrained practice, so a review of the whole situation was long overdue. Had the budgets not been cut by up to 40%, causing high stress levels and high caseloads, I may have supported these experiments, but not now, particularly as the clauses opened the doors to work being outsourced to outside agencies, including private companies.

In 2014 the government established the 'Children's Social Care Innovation Programme' led by a consortium of commercial interests and including the Chief Social Worker for Children, Isabelle Trowler. It had a grant of £200 million. The government, not seeming to have learnt from the failure of the College, proposed to take direct control of social work regulation, including training and qualification. The Bill proposed that, 'The Secretary of State may, for the purpose of regulating social workers in England, make regulations ... to determine and publish (a) professional standards for social workers in England and (b) standards of conduct or ethics for registered students.'

BASW, supported by SWU, SWAN and education professionals totally opposed this attempt at direct political interference in an independent profession. After a long campaign, helped by Labour's shadow minister Emma Lewell-Buck, the government withdrew these clauses and on October 1st 2019 Social Work England came into operation, well led by good powerful staff but with no qualified social workers on the Board.[43]

Even More Austerity

The terrible impact of austerity and the cruel amendments to Universal Credit (UC), resulting in severe poverty for vulnerable families and children, were becoming more obvious to everyone. Between 2010 and 2015 the number of families living in temporary accommodation such as B&Bs had increased by 300% and now affected some 93,200 children. In April 2016 the Institute for Fiscal Studies reported that benefit cuts were forcing thousands of children into poverty. A report by the State of Hunger organisation (a specific research arm of the Trussell Trust) successfully showed the link between changes to both UC and the bedroom tax and the re-emergence of extreme poverty in the UK. One in fifty UK households used a food bank in 2018–19, and the average income for these families was £50 a week after rent, compared with the poverty line of £262 per week. Nine out of ten people referred to food banks were destitute, meaning that they struggled to eat regularly, or to clothe or clean themselves or their families. Two-thirds of food bank users blamed problems with welfare payments, mostly the long delays, UC sanctions, reduced benefits or loss of entitlements.[44]

In 2019 the Department for Work and Pensions paid the *Metro* newspaper (circulation 2.5 million) at least £250,000 to run a six-week series of wraparound advertisements promoting the 'facts' about UC but omitting mention of the DWP. Among the statements were that, 'People move faster into employment on UC than the old system,' 'If you need money your Job Centre will urgently pay you an advance' and 'Your Job Centre can pay your rent directly to landlords.' When the true authors were unveiled and MPs' questions to the responsible ministers proved fruitless, activists collected copies of the *Metro*, dumped them in dustbins and arranged bulk deliveries to the Secretary of State. Many referrals were also made to the Advertising Standards Authority which found that all these assertions were false. In plain terms the government had lied. The department was directed that in future it must provide evidence and detail any conditions on any such advertisements. Faced with this ruling the Secretary of State responsible, Amber Rudd, blamed officials, a move which seemed to be more common with this Cabinet than ever before.[45]

Social Action

The welfare services were suffering serious cuts, for example Ofsted reported that 33% of children's services had been graded 'inadequate.' In October 2016 BASW launched a pilot group in London involving professionals and service users which was then established under the meaningful but long title of Social Workers and Service Users Against Austerity (SWASUAA). It worked with similar groups from other professions to run campaigns. The group was chaired by Guy Shennan. Websites and a very large banner were made. By the following April a 100 mile walk from Birmingham to Liverpool under the sobriquet 'Boot Out Austerity' was extremely well organised by Guy. Walkers were seen off from the new BASW office on April 19th 2017 by musicians from the Royal Birmingham Conservatoire and Ruth Stark, President of the International Federation of Social Workers.[46n] They walked for seven days, travelling through countryside and towns waving their banners, holding morning rallies and evening seminars every day. Visits were made to established agencies, voluntary workers, food banks and organisations under threat. Music and poetry were composed and performed every day. One early poem tackled the effects of prolonged austerity head on:

> The deadly suck of austerity
> Sucked the social work out of me
> But that's not how it's s'posed to be
> I started in 1983, striving for equality
> But then austerity stole my soul
> But will I moan and mope and stare
> Or get myself out there to fight against austerity
> Changing the social worker in me
> Up North to launch Austerity Packs
> Get this monkey off our backs
> The writings on the wall we say
> Austerity has had its day
> Speak up for the oppressed many
> Do something extraordinary
> Join us, join us, banners high
> Austerity, the end is nigh[47n]

The central core of eight walkers was joined by others every day so in total over a hundred people took part. There was a highly effective communication operation to press and local radio throughout, and messages were sent and received from supporters, including Labour leader Jeremy Corbyn. People stopped to tell the walkers their own stories. One young mother with a disabled child was waiting for a care reassessment, which always resulted in less not more care; she added that every time she saw her social worker he looked like he was going to burst into tears, and that she just felt sorry for him.[48] Churches opened their doors to the marchers, providing food and overnight accommodation, albeit on chairs or floors. From Wolverhampton to Penkridge they followed in the steps of the great George Orwell as recorded in *The Road to Wigan Pier*, so naturally they shared a pub lunch near to where Orwell stopped and read the relevant extract.[49]

The walk ended on Liverpool's magnificent waterfront in front of the iconic Liver Building where a considerable crowd gathered to welcome the somewhat exhausted walkers as they approached with their banner held before them. The next morning they were welcomed to BASW's AGM, where two motions were readily passed, both marking a more activist role for BASW. These recognised the debilitating and oppressive effect of austerity measures, with the IFSW statement on the role of social work in social protection systems to be used to build evidence for social workers to 'help change happen with the aim of ensuring that people are included in society and get the social justice, dignity and respect that is their right.' The walk had demonstrated to social workers the need to be poverty aware in their practice and that if they joined together action was possible. At the same time it proved to service users that social workers were prepared to act.

The march was followed by the establishment of the anti-austerity group 'Boot Out Austerity Marches On,' which was a joint BASW/SWU group bringing together the eight core walkers and service user representatives. Among many other activities it commissioned two key publications. These were 'The Campaign Action Pack' released in 2018 as a guide for social workers and others who wished to actively campaign for action on a local or national subject. It included practical advice as well as guidance on both employment and public law. The 'Anti-Poverty Practice Guide for Social Work' was launched in 2019 and urged social workers to incorporate poverty and austerity in their assessments and to take this forward rather than leave it as normalised background. It offered practical advice on how to deal with this difficult issue. Taken together these publications were a powerful incentive to workers to the benefit of their clients.[50] In early 2019 SWU took over the finance and management of the group which was renamed Austerity Action Group, a more activist title.

Bob Holman

In June 2016 I was very sad to learn of the death of Bob Holman, a true social work pioneer who in 1989 gave up his professorship in Bristol to move with his family to the Easterhouse Estate some 6 miles east of Glasgow. He lived among the community there, committed to his Christian beliefs, until 2004, making himself available to residents and establishing several major community projects in the belief that the best help comes from the local community. He was an admirer of the Labour politician George Lansbury. He published many reports on his work and campaigned against inequality all his life. Following his appointment as Secretary of State for Work and Pensions, Ian Duncan Smith was invited to Easterhouse by Bob and stayed for a week facing the difficulties experienced by families on welfare benefits. This experience reduced the politician to tears and he resolved to sort out the whole system. The eventual result of this was the establishment of the Universal Credit system, a genuine attempt to simplify an overcomplex system to the benefit of claimants and staff. In time, it wrought so much pain and poverty on millions of citizens. Bob said he couldn't even recognise Duncan-Smith as the same man who pursued his political career. Bob was a remarkable, fully committed social worker who I was proud to meet several times at conferences where we were both presenting papers.

Criminal Justice

After nine years the wide corrosive effects of austerity and privatisation policies in society at large and in the public services and their interaction, were becoming painfully obvious. A significant example of this was the criminal justice system and in particular the Probation Service. Traditionally probation officers were part of the social work community and were trained on generic courses. This changed during the Labour Justice Secretary Jack Straw's time in office (2007–2010) when training was placed under Home Office management as part of the criminal justice system. In 2006 the relationship between probation and other welfare agencies was disrupted by the justice system, being reorganised into 32 area trusts coterminous with police boundaries. Within these were 35 probation services, all of which reached a good inspection standard.

In 2014, under the Conservative Justice Secretary Chris Grayling, the trusts were broken up into a politically decided division to create two systems. Offenders assessed as having a low or medium level of risk would be supervised by private companies, while officers supervising high-risk offenders remained in public employment. The difficulties of such an arbitrary division were obvious to anyone who had ever worked with offenders. In 2018 the Conservative MP Robert Neill outlined the difficulties of the probation system: 'This has a negative impact on the number of individuals who go on to reoffend. Hard working and dedicated staff are doing their best with a probation system that is currently in a mess.'

Officers were now working in a centralised organisation which, being unable to measure actual results, imposed complex target systems based on progress. Fifteen minutes was allowed for each contact between offender and officers. The political culture remained based on the erroneous creed that 'prison works,' thus belittling the work of the service for which rehabilitating people within their own neighbourhood was a key objective. One chronic offender expressed his frustration with the new system, explaining that previously if he faced a problem he could phone his own probation officer direct but he now had to go through a call centre with the inevitable long delays. Recruitment was proving difficult as the workloads were too high and the pay level was poor.[51] One officer confirmed that they were no longer able to protect society although they would inevitably become scapegoats. Since 2014 there has been a 50% rise in serious crimes, including three murders by people under supervision.

The effects of the chronic austerity policy for citizens and services in the justice system were becoming clear to those at the frontline. As levels of poverty increased, stress caused the breakup of families, drug use increased and education failed the most vulnerable. The virtual disappearance of the youth service and all the community support services had severely weakened any prevention or early intervention services.

Crime rates rose and towards the end of this period knife crime increased at a frightening rate. Unfortunately the court system had faced a 35% budget cut, and 50% of magistrates' courts, 133 Crown Courts, along with family and tribunal buildings, were closed with a loss of one-third of the staff. All these changes were instrumental in removing the service from local communities with the consequent loss of knowledge of local customs and populations. It was a long way from my early view of magistrates' courts (see Chapter 5). In practical terms of course these closures meant extended travel and extra costs for offenders, victims, police and lawyers. Wasted time for all. Not only was access to justice made impossible for some, but also the increased use of video links to replace personal appearances in court added another step to the depersonalisation of justice. The system was in chaos. Long delays in the system meant that young offenders arrested as children had turned 18 years of age before getting to court, as a consequence of which they faced adult courts led by magistrates and judges untrained in the skills of family courts. The prison system had lost a significant percentage of its staff, who now had to face a rising prison population (93,000 in 2018), many of whom were elderly, suffering from mental illness or destitution, and all requiring extra care. Among the worst affected were young people in detention where staff cutbacks had resulted in many spending 23 hours a day in their cells. Attacks on staff, self-harm and suicide were on the rise. Drug use in prisons had been allowed to become endemic through lack of investment and staff shortages. The rise in population, despite overcrowding and consequent restriction of prisoners in their cells, was of course welcome to those running the eleven prisons run by private companies.

The police had suffered the loss of 20,000 officers and the same number of support staff since 2010, inevitably resulting in the rise of thresholds before they committed resources; hence minor crimes, including minor thefts on the street or burglary, drew no response. The cutbacks in community services including the NHS meant that much of police time was spent on dealing with the failures of those systems. The most worrying was the number of mental health cases being dealt with by the police, which led to mentally distressed people spending far too long in police cells. The Chief Constable of Bedfordshire called for his officers to be given the resources to allow them to concentrate on hard-core criminals not on the fallout from the damage caused to the social fabric.[52]

In 2019 the new Prime Minister Boris Johnson promised to replace the 20,000 police officers 'on the local beat,' although considerable doubt later emerged about the accuracy of this statement. In addition, more prisons would be built. It seemed remarkable to me that given the experiences outlined above there was no mention of resurrecting swathes of local public services that would restore hope for young people rather than relying on the criminal justice system to pick up the pieces. In February 2020, following an attack in Streatham by Sudesh Amman, a known terrorist who had been recently released automatically having completed half his sentence, Johnson's immediate response was to propose that terrorists should serve two-thirds of their time in prison, to be released only if agreed by a board. Not only was this a weak response, placing more pressure on an already overcrowded system, but also the intention to make this retrospective was illegal.

Working Conditions

In late 2016 SWU held discussions with Dr Jermaine Ravalier at Bath Spa University on the possibility of research into the working conditions of social workers, a challenge that he was happy to accept. Following an exploratory survey in 2017, a more detailed questionnaire was completed by over 3,000 social workers in 2018. The situation had deteriorated within that short period and was very disturbing. Measured against the Health and Safety Executive's Management Standard Indicators social workers presented with the highest levels of stress and sickness absence of all care sectors across the country. Job satisfaction varied from just 18% to 26%. Some 66% of social workers planned to leave their posts within the next few months and 50% planned to leave the profession altogether. The survey revealed average working weeks of up to 11 hours above contract and the numbers of staff working when ill (presenteeism). The causes of stress were high workloads, lack of managerial support, too much time spent on repeatedly over-recording the same information and hot-desking. There was a marked increase in bad behaviour towards social workers.[53] Stories from front-line workers supported these findings. Some felt that they were feeling less like a social worker and more like a 'report writer' or 'data input clerk.' One said, 'Sadly process drives out practice and the voice of the child is lost in the unending forms, paper work and statistics.' It was said that their team had 'name and shame' trackers to make sure that visits are recorded, whereas the quality of the direct work was never raised. One social worker talked about how the strain was taking its toll: 'My caseload has been around 40 for about five months and this is certainly not manageable or safe. I'm exhausted. I feel guilt that I'm not doing a good enough job.'[54]

Others commented that social workers are 'caught in the middle, between individuals asking for more support – and indeed they need it and the local authority panel asking social workers how funding can be reduced.' Finally, 'I challenge any politician to spend a week in a front-line team, as the work comes in, no PR cover up for cameras, and I wonder what their views will be thereafter. This includes them working 60 hours weekly, including weekends and only getting paid for 36.'

Concern was growing at the increasing hostility faced by front-line social workers, both within the office but more frighteningly on home visits. Surveys reported that in Northern Ireland 82% of workers had experienced intimidation and 50% had encountered physical violence. Workers had been stalked and abused online, with comments such as 'knowing where you live' or 'knowing where your child goes to school.' Several had received threats of death, rape or torture. In a time when the social environment was increasingly hostile, social workers had to recognise these threats rather than see them an accepted risk intrinsic to their work. The situation for residential care workers was worse.

In 2019 the GMB Union obtained details under the Freedom of Information Act which showed that between 2013 and 2018 over 6,000 workers had experienced violent assaults, 1,026 of which were life changing. Staff shortages and lack of status and respect for care workers was widespread, and it was alarming that in most private homes absence due to sickness or injury was unpaid.[55] It was quite clear that staff and employers needed to develop clearer 'no tolerance' policies towards any aggression and improve their risk assessments.[56]

In 2018 Parliament debated the issue of attacks on emergency workers, focussing on police, fire and ambulance services. SWU and BASW campaigned to have social workers included in the protection offered by the Police, Crime, Sentencing and Courts Bill as, in relation to mental health and child care services, they worked in close conjunction with emergency services. The Scottish Act in 2015 had included social workers, however the government did not accept the arguments. The Scottish Act came into force on November 13th 2018.[57]

Following these results, BASW and SWU launched a 'Respect Social Workers' campaign and intensively lobbied Parliament. This resulted in an excellent 90-minute debate in the House of Lords. Three Lords and Baroness Walmsley placed a question to ask the government what strategies they had considered to alleviate the workload demands faced by social workers in the light of Dr Ravalier's research. These four members then directed a whole series of very pertinent questions to Baroness Manzoor, the government whip. Unfortunately her reply was a defensive list of all the alleged improvements that the government had already made and a reference to the Green Paper. She did however agree to meet with representatives of SWU at any time.[58]

They continued to press for a Commons debate and further action. Dr Ravalier published a 'Social Worker Wellbeing and Working Conditions: Best Practice Toolkit' early in 2020.[59] The Education Select Committee finally recommended that the government, in co-ordination with the social work profession, should consider how success in social work can be measured and promoted. They recommended the launch of a national public awareness campaign to celebrate the positive aspects of social work and explain its complexities to boost the profile of the profession. Social workers, through BASW and SWU, will certainly keep pushing.[60]

In 2018, Neil Thompson drew attention to the circular effect of stress across all levels of the structure. As staff go sick or burn out, they are replaced by agency staff who quickly leave the toxic environment. This creates more stress that further damages the service to those in need of help.[61]

Special Needs

As the austerity policy reached nine years, how far it had eaten into the fabric of all our lives was clear. As public services grew weaker with tattered edges they were kept going by heroic staff who soldiered on through exhaustion and stress. They were sometimes forced into a terrible game of passing delicate problem parcels from one service to another with limited chance of success. Some fell down the widening cracks now appearing in the welfare state. Social work often found itself in the middle of many of these transactions, in danger of becoming public scapegoats. A good example was the education of children with special needs. As schools and local authorities protected their dwindling budgets, several obstacles were placed in the way of parents seeking a joint assessment. This embraced their child's Education, Health and Care Plan (EHCP) required for the school to provide appropriate individual support for their child. Many disputes ended up in court. Whilst many primary and secondary schools fought to accept and retain pupils with special needs, whether they had an ECHP or not, budget and consequent staff and equipment cuts led in far too many cases to schools refusing admission or excluding these vulnerable pupils. They were taken off the school roll and sent for home tuition and support. This helped schools to attain their place in the league tables and ensure their income. If the child was at a late primary or early secondary stage, home tutors might be available depending on location, but the few available hours resulted in parental pressure, possible loss of earnings and difficulties with Universal Credit. Older children would get bored, wander into town and meet others who had been excluded from school for anything from an incorrect dress code to violent behaviour. Minor crime and drugs might be tempting. In these situations it was doubtful whether they would pass the social care threshold for intervention, in which case they were left at risk, increasing the stress on the families.

If they were accepted by a social services children's department, they either received support or were placed in a foster home or residential care, either of which might be many miles from home. In all the latter stages of this process they might be spotted as vulnerable by the sophisticated gangs of drug dealers and recruited into the County Lines structure where there was a high risk of abuse and certain exploitation. Of course at any stage after exclusion they could come to the attention of the police, themselves overstretched with a possible destination of custody in another overstretched and short staffed public service. Some facts behind this disgraceful farce are as follows.

In 2010 immediately after being appointed Secretary of State for the Department for Children, Schools and Families, Michael Gove deleted children and families from his brief thus abandoning the previous overarching strategic view coherent future policy embracing how closely related these issues are for parents and children. In December 2017, after 26,000 school inspections, the Chief Schools Inspector, Amanda Spielman, gave a speech fiercely denouncing the treatment of vulnerable children in the school system. She said, 'Off-rolling is an invidious example of where schools have lost sight of the purpose of education ... the job of education is to do what's right by children. That does not mean passing the job to parents, without professional expertise, to home educate their children. Children with special educational needs are not a problem to be pushed out of sight and out of mind.' In May 2019 the head of a secondary school in Gloucestershire who had built an excellent reputation for his inclusive school with special interest in SEN children, announced that she was now refusing admission to four children with EHCPs. She was devastated that government policies and funding issues had compromised her previous welcome of such pupils.[62]

By 2018, 7,900 pupils were permanently excluded and 80% of these were from vulnerable backgrounds. This issue was brought to public attention by the innovative Intermission Youth Theatre who produced a play simply called *Excluded*, a fate which most of the young cast had experienced. It was performed for ten nights in Saint Saviour's Church in southwest London. Each performance was followed by a discussion with the cast. Excellent! By October 2019 the Local Government and Social Care Ombudsman reported that the number of complaints received had gone up by 45% in two years, mostly from parents seeking help for children with special needs, particularly those who had experienced difficulties in obtaining EHCPs. It revealed the number of obstacles being imposed by local authorities in an attempt to reduce demand. The fact that over 87% of complaints were upheld indicated a major crisis in the system, where some parents waited over a year for assessment while the child remained out of education, to be followed by the challenging task of finding a school place.[63]

In late April 2019 school governors from all across the UK gathered in Westminster to protest against school budgets, which had been cut by 8% in real terms since 2010. In a debate about exclusions and knife crime, a parent commented on the link between budget cuts and exclusions, explaining 'There used to be a unit where pupils with problems could be worked with to try and resolve their social-emotional problems. Now kids with problems are problem kids and are shown the door a lot sooner.' In April 2017 a year long survey into child social care in England reported that 90% of Directors of Children's Services said that they were finding it increasingly difficult to fulfil their legal duties to children who needed support. In 2019 the Children's Commissioner reported that the number of teenagers in care had increased by 21% between 2013 and 2017. They were significantly more likely than younger children to be vulnerable to sexual exploitation, running away, gangs, trafficking and drug use. In August 2017 Judge Sir James Munby, Head of the High Court's Family Division, commented adversely on the fact that in 2016 the average maximum wait to be seen by a community mental health team was 30 months. He was outraged that the lack of a bed for a suicidal teenager would mean that the failing authorities would have blood on their hands. If the current state of child and adolescent mental health services is the best we can do, what right does the state have to call itself civilised?

In August 2017 a report, based on freedom of information figures by the Action for Children charity reported that 140,500 children referred to services for help for neglect or abuse were refused because they did not meet the statutory criteria for help.[64]

Spending on child early years care decreased by 62%; this particularly affected Sure Start and similar community preventive services. Up to a thousand had been closed by 2019 but many more had been hollowed out by staff reductions, shorter opening hours and the collapse of outreach services. By that year research by the Institute for Fiscal Studies showed that in deprived communities Sure Start had significantly reduced hospital admission thus saving the NHS millions of pounds.[65] Far too late, in October 2019, the Home Office announced a £20 million investment, although principally to combat County Lines, a minor contribution set against all the billions already removed.

Social Work England

The new regulator Social Work England commenced duties on December 2nd 2019. It seemed to rectify gaps that had been evident in the previous two years when its Practice Code addressed the relationship between employer and employee. It stated: '... social workers will challenge unethical practices and report concerns including a duty to tell employers of any resourcing or operational difficulties that might prevent safe practice.'[66n] In June 2019 Directors of Adult Services expressed concern about the residential and domiciliary care sector, revealing that in the year 2017–2018 £335 million had been spent on recruiting agency staff and pointed out that many services were near collapse. There were over 100,000 staff from the EU working in the sector whose future was being adversely affected by Brexit. If a significant proportion of the 80% of services now being profit driven collapsed, local authorities would be in no position to cope.[67] By March 2019 the Ministry of Housing, Communities and Local Government reported that 84,740 families were deemed to be homeless, including 126,020 children. Although this represented a rapid increase, it failed to give a true picture of the problem as it did not count people who were staying with relatives or friends or 'sofa surfing' in new places every night. The whole situation was a disgrace, reflecting the horrors of the Universal Credit system and the fast rise in evictions due to a big rise in rents in the private sector and lack of public housing.

In 2019 a House of Commons report on funding for children's services concluded that the £9 billion spent was clearly insufficient for a system at breaking point and called for a £3.1 billion core grant to bridge the funding gap. It urged the government to conduct an urgent consultation to better understand the pressures facing social workers and to fund a national recruitment agency. It stated that government should review the key factors driving demand and whether it could be reduced. If not, then local government must be appropriately and flexibly resourced.[68]

The 2014 Care Act had been an attempt to pull together relevant legislation from the past and produce a clear way through. It gained assent in May of that year and was seen as prescriptively detailed in how staff should proceed in dealing with and assessing potential service users. It spelt out six principles: Empowerment, Protection, Prevention, Proportionality, Partnership and Accountability. An intriguingly ambiguous mixture of positivity and threat given that one of the aims was to prevent need for care or support. It placed a duty on all local authorities to promote the wellbeing of each individual. In June 2017 the National Institute for Health and Care Excellence, with the Chief Social Worker for Adults, Lyn Romeo, held an event to explore what a strengths-based approach really meant for practitioners. Nearly two years later, following a process which seemed to me to be a compressed version of our Development Group work (see Chapter 14) only much more politically driven, the department published a practice framework and handbook.[69] Were it not for the underlying agenda to reduce demand on services, I would have wholeheartedly supported this initiative which, in addition to the six principles, is defined as holistic and multidisciplinary, focussing on 'What matters to you and what is strong.' It identifies personal, family and community strengths, supporting community development. It comments that 'While a reduction of packages of support is generally a collateral benefit it should not be the outcome we are seeking.' I think that depends on who 'we' are!

My Fight With The GSCC

In July 2010, as part of a bonfire of the non-government agencies, the government announced its intention to abolish the GSCC and transfer the function to the Health Professions Council (HPC), a body with no expertise in social work and limited capacity to accept the work. Social work had been demoted once again. In preparation for this change GSSC managers decided to change some criteria for Conduct Members, in particular the definition of Lay Member, i.e. that the definition of 'lay' must mean no previous professional experience. To be fair I had always had doubts about my definition as a lay person, based solely on the fact that my qualifications and experience were so long ago that I could not be registered. I had however been reconciled by my Panel experiences when the Professional Member had very little experience of the actual field of work that the accused was in. In these circumstances my wider experience often came into play. However, I decided to apply for the new role which would make me eligible for non-social work cases. In any event the decision was made that all of our contracts would be cancelled and we would have to apply for new jobs with the HPC. There was uproar at what was seen as an insult to our long experience. The Council offered us a six-month extension so that hearings could continue. They also explained that selection for the new posts would be by selection centre, then interview if you passed that.

On the assessment day there were three of us attending and the various tasks were undertaken under supervision of the assessor. In addition, there were two staff members at a distance completing assessment sheets as the day proceeded. Both of these had recently clashed with me over administrative issues. The most difficult thing, we all agreed, was having to complete a handwritten assessment of a given problem. Used to years of computers our wrists were hurting. I awaited the outcome with mixed emotions – these were still the years of mourning and I saw the world through different eyes. I was told that I had failed but by a very small margin. Did I really care? But we had all been so cross with the managers that it seemed worth pursuing further, and anyway I was intrigued. I asked the assessor about the scoring and could not believe the reply. On each day she calculated the average of the scores and anyone below that failed. Not only did this mean that there was no fixed standard, the pass score depending as it did on who else was present on a particular day, but also I didn't see how it worked with only three people present. It was crazy. I sent in a formal appeal which, after a long time and the employment of an expensive senior barrister by the Council, I won outright.

This whole incompetent and expensive procedure not only resulted in the organisation losing 23 experienced members whose competence had never been questioned, but also, by labelling them incompetent, had opened the possibility of numerous appeals to previous decisions. It also had the effect of further delaying hearings for which the Council had already been criticised in Parliament. I was very angry so, stupidly, I decided to cost the Council a bit more by pushing on for a formal interview which, not surprisingly, sealed my fate. All seemed to be going well until we reached the question of equality and discrimination; we seemed to be speaking different languages. Having promoted the doctrine of equality throughout my career and having devoted my life and career to anti-discrimination, my answers reflected that perspective. However, all the interviewers were interested in was specific actual examples of when and exactly how I had dealt with this issue. My explanation that I could not recall a clear example as I dealt with things naturally and seemingly successfully as they came up apparently did not fit the two remaining boxes to be ticked so it was with some relief that I, along with many other respected colleagues, said farewell to the GSCC. The GSCC closed in 2012. The celebration that our profession had been clearly recognised had been short lived.

Social Worker – Trade Unionist

As stated above, the Social Workers Union (SWU) was formed in June 2011, and I was elected in 2012. It was interesting, challenging and frustrating in the early days. The procedures for establishing a trade union were complex. We could not be certified as a trade union unless we were independent, yet we were financially and organisationally dependent on BASW. Their CEO was our General Secretary. Unbelievably it took a few years to crack this dilemma, not helped by the whole College of Social Work fiasco as outlined earlier. Negotiations continued and reached a point where a draft agreement was reached. Then, and my memory may be wrong, only when BASW was actually preparing to sign an agreement did they get a message to say that the College would not proceed! Once this had been resolved we could move ahead, although the complex co-operation agreement with BASW was not finally signed until March 2018!

Anti-Austerity March

As SWU's representative on SWASUAA (see above), I was involved in the idea of a march against austerity. After much reconnaissance and planning this became the 'Boot Out Austerity' walk from Birmingham to Liverpool. Not strong enough to march, I volunteered to act as back-up driver. Consequently, at a ridiculously early hour at BASW's old HQ in Kent Street a whole load of kit, including about 100 T-shirts, portable amplifiers, etc., was loaded into my small car. I then made my way to the grand new premises in Waterloo Street where a sort of mediaeval scene of a small army preparing for a campaign slowly formed. About 30 people gathered, and it was difficult to differentiate the walkers from the spectators. The radical Banner Theatre group arrived, my colleague Angi Naylor produced her guitar, and finely judged speeches were made.

Following an inspiring percussion-based piece specially composed for us by Danny Blanco Albert, a student at the Royal Birmingham Conservatoire, Jon Dudley gave the word and the whole group moved off heading northwest and out of Birmingham. It was a great start.

Following these events, BASW formed the Anti Austerity Group (AAG), in which Angi and I represented SWU. This group, supported by BASW senior staff, worked hard until it dissolved itself in November 2018. It commissioned and published a great 'Campaign Action Pack' supporting and offering practical, professional and legal help for social workers wishing to launch community action. We also commissioned an 'Anti-Poverty Practice Guide' to encourage social workers to include poverty in the assessments and other work instead of normalising it as a constant background. In 2018 we organised another, shorter march in South Wales ending in Cardiff, the location of BASW's AGM. We finished the group because of uncertainty where we stood in relation, particularly to BASW's powerful Policy, Ethics and Human Relation (PEHR) committee, which was focussing on poverty, the diminishing practical support from BASW staff and the end of Guy Shennan's term of office. Although we could have become a sub-committee of PEHR, we feared that this would involve us too much in BASW's complex systems and limit our autonomy.

In February 2019 SWU considered a proposal to re-establish the AAG by providing the finance and professional support. Following discussions with BASW and the construction of a budget, SWU decided to formally adopt the proposal. The group therefore held its first meeting on September 5th, renaming itself the Austerity Action Group (AAG) committed to working with service user groups standing side by side for social justice and as a determination that 'Boot Out Austerity Marches On.' The group is co-chaired by Angi Naylor and a service user representative, includes senior BASW representatives who were on the original march and others including the 'Poet Austeriate' Peter Unwin. We are well supported by key BASW officers.

Restorative Justice

I had volunteered to work with young offenders since 2002 – it has always been interesting and sometimes challenging. The young people are convicted and given a Referral Order. A panel of three volunteers then meet with the offender and a family member to try to agree a contract of issues that can be worked out with the professional staff, both to prevent further offending and to ease any other problems. I also visited victims to obtain their view of the offence in the hope that they would attend the Panel meeting to enhance the restorative process. In recent years attendance or representation has thankfully increased. Our work, of course, is underpinned by an excellent administrative and professional staff. The offences continue to vary from minor shoplifting through excess alcohol to serious assaults, although of late there has been a steady increase of sexual offences. However well prepared the young person is, it's an ordeal and the reaction varies from aggression (often because they think the Court has been unjust) through silent resistance, to tears. We volunteers have a great deal of experience between us, and it is very rare that we fail to agree a contract. Given that the first item for the meeting is that the young person has to tell us about the offence, a serious issue is the long delay between offence, arrest and trial. The consequence is that often they have completely forgotten the event. (Across the UK the delays in youth courts have increased by 40% since 2010 with the slowest being 491 days – see the report above.)

Other frustrations arise when we are faced with a child whose family, care and education are in chaos and we only have a three-month order. An especially aggravating issue is when a special residential home, practically all of which are commercial, have called in the police for a broken window or damaged furniture, etc. The child then gets a criminal record, has to face court and then us, with all the consequent costs for the team. I can appreciate that these events may well be the last straw, but these places are paid handsomely to help these vulnerable and sometimes violent young people in accordance with the claims they make in their expensively produced brochures and, presumably, in their contract with the local authority. It is a disgrace. Our training was regularly updated and we are regularly briefed on all child protection programmes, for example the government's 'Prevent' programme and County Lines. Interestingly, while 'Prevent' was established to counter Muslim extremism, its attention is now focussed just as much on far-right groups, being countered by organisations such as Small Steps.[70n] At least we can now recognise the tattoos and graffiti warning signs.

Some difficulties have arisen recently as the whole justice system has been slowly falling apart under austerity policies. So many local courts have been closed that young people, their supporters and professional staff have to travel many miles where, contrary to policy, young people are not kept apart from adult offenders. In her 2019 report, the Children's Commissioner Anne Longfield commented, 'We have seen first hand what is largely chaos and dysfunction. It was not an efficient or indeed child-friendly environment where you could really help a child.'[71] Sometimes the required documents were not available and the whole process had to be repeated. These time-consuming events put increased pressure on the work schedules of the professional team that deal directly with the young people, the families and everyone involved.

FAMILY

Following my wife's death, my time in the grey tunnel continued. By 2010 it was lighter but still I experienced dark spells of unreality. Living alone in the house was not easy, although our lovely spaniel, Lady, offered some continuity. My family were equally affected but offered constant support from New York, as did friends in the village. In November 2008 my friend Nigel had kindly agreed to take me to Leonard Cohen's concert in Cardiff. It was magnificent and the tone just right, although being driven home at 90 mph along the M4 was quite terrifying. I also became a regular attendee at the excellent, if rather exotic, choir concerts given in the Stroud area where my nephew Richard's wife Sarah was a member. Very calming and thoughtful as we were invited to hear music from the late 1600s onwards.

Trips, Family, Friends and Reunions

In subsequent years I was invited to join my family on a trip to Mexico which included the amazing Chichen Itza with the impressive pyramid like structures built originally by the Mayan people between the 6th and 9th centuries AD.

At the end of 2008 I was invited to join the group of family and friends which, for many years, had met every New Year in various locations across the British Isles. Having started as a small group of friends it had grown as children arrived, then partners of children, and were on the brink of the children having children. The group was now reaching twenty. The whole event was fun and joyful, relying on a system of rotas that meant meals were prepared and domestic chores completed by a much tested formula which kept everyone happy. Excursions were organised and proven group games were eagerly anticipated. Ages ran from my eighty-five to four.

In the Spring of 2009 I had the great pleasure of attending of Aella's graduation ceremony held in the UN General Assembly Hall, a wonderful achievement for her and memorable for all of us. Aella started at Sussex University in the UK in the autumn of 2009. Just before that we had all attended my son-in-law's niece Nicole's wedding to John Brooks in Cyprus. It was held near Ayia Napa and, despite some complaints about excessive travelling, it was a joyous occasion, particularly because the whole party were together for a week, time to get properly acquainted in contrast to the usual one-day events.

In April 2009 Juliet, Duke and I visited our Canadian relatives in Hamilton to attend my cousin Dorothy's 96th birthday, which included fascinating family history and a memorable resolution of a long-standing dispute. Further trips were to Florida for a luxurious time. In March 2010 we were joined by the New Year gang in the family's new brown stone house on Clinton Street, Brooklyn, to celebrate Rod's 50th birthday. If all this wasn't enough, in the summer of 2011 we went briefly to Venice then sailed down the beautiful Croatian coast led by nephew Richard (a qualified master mariner) and his wife Sarah, both experienced in all the techniques at sea that kept us fed and happy.

It was a uniquely wonderful occasion. Between 2008 and 2019 my year ends fell into a pattern of alternate trips to New York or to the UK gatherings. The generosity of my son-in-law Rod has been and continues to be overwhelming.

In the summer of 2013 I had the great pleasure of attending the annual WOMAD festival, held just north of Kington, with an old family friend Hamish, his wife and two boys, who were all over from Australia. This friendship went back to the 1970s in Pluckley and Cornwall. That same year Aella and her partner Lizzie were in Edinburgh putting on their own show at the Edinburgh Festival where it got good reviews. At this period Aella was working freelance in the media industry living in various small flats in East London, a precarious existence, but she progressed to producing and then directing pop videos first for rising stars and then well established names. In that same year Aella took me to see *The Book of Mormon* in London, an hilarious satire on the Mormon religion. At last she was able to write and direct her own great short film *Unclasped*, an account of teenage embarrassment and its consequences when a mother takes her daughter for her first bra fitting.[72] We all went to see the preview at the Rio Cinema in Dalston, premiered at the London Independent Film Festival to a great reception. Aella has used her courage and determination to establish a fine group of friends and work colleagues. She has a great, caring, bubbly personality and looks amazing. Aella has continued writing and directing excellent films and in 2021 was awarded a rare place at the National Film and Television School.

Meanwhile, six years younger, Duke, of a less extrovert nature, was working his way through the structure, style and content of the American school system. It was not an easy path, but characteristically he worked hard, got good grades and developed a group of friends as he negotiated the differences in the American idiom and faced the long series of exams, new to his parents, with their unfamiliar scoring systems. It was all very anxiety inducing, although the embrace of his family and friends, the events described above, and particularly the gatherings with the New Year group and regular time in beautiful Cornwall all helped. In his mid teens Duke decided to take up body building, and in his customary way of thorough research and careful consideration he went for it like a lion. The training seemed to be an extreme series of physical and dietary drill, the latter programme of severe intakes followed by restriction of food, painful for both him and the family. He did eventually reach his desired degree of muscle, body profile and arm circumference. Thankfully, although he still attends the gym regularly, that intense episode is behind him, but that was some massive achievement. In 2016 Duke was offered a place at the University of Chicago to study finance. By that time he was a much travelled young man. In 2017 Juliet and I went to visit him and, although he was studying well, it was clear that he was not happy in the circumstances he found himself: too much time in his room, poor food and viewing fellow students as somewhat parochial, mostly from local small towns. At the end of the year he came home and spent some time working out a future but, following a lifelong obsession with screens and video games, he was offered the job of his dreams at Rockstar Games, which he loves.

Creativity was prospering in Brooklyn where both Juliet and Rod were reaching new heights. Juliet's style of documentary making – intimate and sensitive studies of communities and individuals – was evidenced in a film about home births (a relatively rare thing in America), which had its premiere in November 2015 at the New York Documentary Film Festival. This had entailed being on call 24 hours a day and involved detailed negotiations with a variety of ethnic, cultural and religious groups, each with their own distinctive rituals around birth. One call out was to a somewhat hippie couple in Lower Manhattan who had chosen not to move out of their apartment in the face of the warning that Hurricane Sandy was on its way. Of course the event happened at the height of the storm when that area was already flooded and all the power lost. Juliet and Miriam, the midwife, managed to talk themselves through various police lines as both the bridges and surrounding area were closed. There was a challenging climb up a dark emergency stairway, with all the filming equipment, into a candlelit apartment with a mother in an advanced state of delivery. All went well and the whole episode made for great filming.[73]

Rod meanwhile had embraced his managerial role in the pressured Rockstar Games, principally, in my language, as film director and playing a key role in the production of the magnificent series of games, including the *Grand Theft Auto* series, and he was in demand throughout the world. In October 2018 they launched *Red Dead Redemption II* which surpassed previous games, particularly in its detailed visual beauty. It was a perfect cross over between the world of games and mainstream cinema. It was a magnificent achievement.[74]

Death of John and Lady

In mid-December 2010, I learnt that John Vaughan. our dear friend and financial advisor who had offered his wise counsel over so many years, had died unexpectedly in hospital. His wife and children were deeply distressed by the loss and the suspicion that something had gone seriously wrong. Acting on their behalf I went through all the records, communicated with the health authority and eventually they conceded that an error had occurred. The NHS followed their usual delaying tactic during the time after I had handed the issue back to the family lawyer. A carefully judged financial claim was submitted, then more years went by before there was no option but to accept the pathetic nominal sum offered. There was no justice there. The family remain among my most valued friends. In May 2011 I accompanied my dear friends Tom and Vera Pearson to visit one of their sons and his family in a small traditional French village. I went shopping with them in the local antique markets, fetching a carefully selected haul back home to be cleaned and sold on the internet. It was great fun. One evening we visited a local restaurant where I anticipated a tasty local meal. It was not to be. Although there was a menu, the order was fish and chips. It turned out that virtually all the customers had the same order on this particular day of the week!

If I had thought that my mourning period might be coming to an end, it then happened that our dearly loved spaniel, Lady, suddenly deteriorated. She would leave the house to be found walking through the village where Ann had taken her every morning.

Unfortunately that was followed by her wandering across the busy main road, luckily avoiding an accident, to be walked home by the villagers. Then she started behaving very oddly in the house where I eventually found her in a corner upstairs clawing and throwing herself at the walls. It was very distressing and in June 2012 the last living link in the house died.

Moving House

During the early years of my bereavement I was frequently visited and much comforted, deciding to keep busy and to try to get on with work on the Board of the GSCC and with my voluntary work with young offenders. I continued to be involved with the project to upgrade or rebuild the village hall. It slowly dawned on me that, in addition to lacking any cooking skills, I could no longer manage the stone-built Croft Barn and started to consider alternatives. One of which was a co-housing project in Stroud, which seemed just the right balance of privacy and companionship until I realised that all the shops were down a very long hill and parking was near impossible. Optimistically in the summer of 2009 I put the house up for sale and started casting round for somewhere else to live. The viewings were sparse and interest rare; it became more and more difficult until, as the agent said, it just needed the right people to come. It was finally sold in July three long years later to a couple returning from Australia who loved the house and had the imagination and budget to modernise it. There then followed, with family help, endless trips to charity shops, the tip, the nearby auction and, on incredibly early mornings, to the main boot sale where we could practice our sales pitches, which really meant practically giving stuff away. My ambition was to move to the village of Kington St Michael two miles further south across the M4. It had a reputation as a good community where I might be happy and for that reason houses for sale were few and far between.

I agonised over houses within the town of Chippenham but then one day I decided to swing through Kington, and there was a for sale notice new that day. It was a semi-detached house, with three bedrooms and an office room which I could turn into a downstairs bedroom. It had just been extended and modernised, but if I had any doubts they were swept away by the view from the front where there was no vehicular access and a magnificent countryside view stretching for miles. I shook hands on the deal and finally moved there in July 2013. Settling in took some time given the limited space compared with Croft Barn but with some ingenuity it was sorted. It was time to pick up life with family and friends.

Big Brother

In 2012 Rod's nephew Luke had come down to stay for a while. Luke, who declared himself my nominal grandson, was on the TV show *Big Brother*, a real horror event. Such was the tension that the whole extended family watched every episode as the population in the house steadily declined by viewer vote. Luke seemed OK, often seen cooking or repairing people's clothing and doing well at the variety of imposed challenges. It became clear that the editors had spotted someone who they could manipulate as they wished. The crunch came towards the end with three residents in the 'white room,' in which, as the name implies, absolutely everything was white. One contestant soon left, leaving Luke and another guy. The final task was to face a screen where an amount of money was quickly rising. The final total was, if my memory serves me right, a possible £50,000. Each had to decide to press their button at the sum they wanted. It was an extremely tense game. Luke stood relaxed with his hand behind him, his opponent with his hand on the button. He pressed the button at £50,000. Luke was devastated. He had been given the impression that his opponent had indicated that he would let him win.

That loss did however guarantee him a place in the final of the show. He then found a job hosting and chatting to callers on a TV station in central London in a late evening show. He stayed with me and moved with me to Kington. Quite soon he lost the job due to a row behind the scenes which unfortunately was heard through the thin scenery. So unfortunately I had a rather depressed young man caught between looking for another job and creating a project to run a trendy coffee bar, which had been a long-standing ambition of this born entrepreneur. It was a tough time, and I learnt a lot about coffee. His natural charm worked well for him when, unbelievably, with no experience at all he was interviewed by a major bank searching for a regional manager for a new car leasing business in the UK and got through to the final three! Luckily, that having failed he was contacted by a previous employer who offered him a job managing the Red Door cocktail bar in Chester, an industry in which he had lots of experience and a good reputation. He now co-owns the Lono Cove bar in Chester and in late 2021 opened a similar bar in Manchester.

NOTES AND REFERENCES

1. Extract from a speech made at Cairo University by Barack Obama in June 2009, shortly after his historic election. The speech clearly laid out the main sources of tension between America and the Muslim world from violent terrorism, the Israel/Palestine conflict, nuclear power and globalisation, to the role of women. Above all it was a call for tolerance, peace and democracy instead of dictatorship. The extract is taken from the conclusion of his speech.
2. Inaugural Address of President Donald J. Trump, 20.01.2017. An outstanding example of patriotic nationalism based on false truths and ignorance.
3. *Dabiq* online magazine, 15th issue. Summer 2016.
4. Chulov, M. (2014). 'Isis: the inside story.' *The Guardian*, 11.12.2014, pp. 37–40. The question has been posed as to whether the US authorities were naively unaware of this process or not.
5. Farley, R. (2013). 'Obama's Blurry Red Line.' factcheck.org.
6. It was known that sarin gas had been used in local attacks, possibly by both sides, but the extent of this attack led most observers to conclude that it could only come from Assad's forces. Russia argued that it came from the rebels. The UN appointed inspectors' report was finally published on September 16th 2013. It confirmed the use of sarin and drew attention to Russian and other shell markings and the calculated trajectory that indicated that the most likely source was from Assad's military locations.

7. As ISIS lost ground in Iraq and Syria, it strengthened its influence in Libya, Egypt, Algeria, Yemen, South Asia, Nigeria and the North Caucasus.
8. Roberts, R. (2016). 'The UK has taken just 18% of its "fair share" of Syrian refugees, report shows.' *The Independent*, 16.12.2016.
9. See Mason, P. (2012). *Why It's Kicking Off Everywhere*. London: Verso, which I have relied on for this section.
10. Varoufakis was immediately engaged as a speaker on economics across the world. In Britain he appeared regularly on TV and during the European Referendum he campaigned to remain in the EU while excoriating the power of their financial institutions. I had the great pleasure of hearing him speak in June 2017. See Varoufakis, Y. (2017). *Adults in the Room. My Battle with Europe's Deep Establishment*. London: Random House.
11. Anti-austerity protests in Italy bring transport chaos to Rome. 18.10.2013, CNBC Europe News.
12. Goldenberg, S. (2009). 'Copenhagen must fail – top scientist.' *The Guardian*. 03.12.2009, p. 1.
13. Kirchgaessner, S. (2015). 'Francis issues a passionate call for action on climate change.' *The Guardian*, 19.06.15, p. 9.
14. McKie, R. (2015). 'Osborne has undermined UK role in climate talks.' *The Guardian*, 29.11.2015, and Harvey, F. (2019), 'Big fall in jobs in renewable energy sector after cuts to incentives.' *The Guardian*, 31.05.19.
15. David Attenborough's career commenced in 1969 with a TV documentary. His massively popular series include *Planet Earth* (2006), *Frozen Planet* (2011), *Blue Planet* (2017) and *Climate Change – The Facts* (2019).
16. Some material in this section has been drawn from an article in *The Week* magazine dated 12.10.2019, p. 13.
17. Carrington, D. (2019). 'Microplastics in snow point to significant air contamination.' *The Guardian*, 15.08.19, p. 22.
18. A major theme in Trump's position was reluctance to blame Russia for interference in his election. Despite repeated presentation from all his security agencies, with hard evidence, that it was Russia, he and all Republican politicians always blamed Ukraine.
19. It is interesting to note that some of this derived from advice given by Mrs Thatcher in 1984, who, fearful of awarding MPs a rise in their salary, commented that they could always use their expenses.
20. Wall, T. (2019). 'Corporate landlords rake in profits from housing crisis.' *The Guardian*, 13.10.2019, p. 2.
21. Durham Action on Single Housing. See www.dashorg.co.uk.
22. Hansard HC Deb Vol 512 Col 166 22.06.2010.
23. Hansard HC Deb Vol 512 Col 179/180 22.06.2010.
24. Report of the Joseph Rowntree Foundation in *The Guardian*, 04.12.2017.
25. Hood, A. and Waters, T. (2017). *Living Standards, Poverty and Inequality in the UK: 2017/18 to 2021/22*. London: Institute for Fiscal Studies.
26. Hansard HC Deb Vol 620 Col 1030–1031 10.12.2017.
27. Hansard HC Deb Vol 624 Col 252 29.03.2017.
28. Marsh, S. (2019). 'In their own words: why seven MPs are quitting Labour.' *The Guardian*, 19.02.2019, pp. 6–7.
29. Crace, J. (2019). 'Incredible Sulk's anger is compounded by ranting of Geoffrey Cox.' *The Guardian*, 25.09.2019.
30. Boffey, D., Rankin, J. and Stewart, H. (2019). 'Tusk warns of 'special place in hell' for those who backed Brexit without a plan.' *The Guardian*, 06.02.2019.
31. Stewart, H. and Mason, R. (2019). 'Boris Johnson: new PM takes his revenge and sacks over half the cabinet.' *The Guardian*, 27.07.2019, p. 3.

32. House of Commons Education Committee. (2016). *Social Work Reform. Third Report of Session 2016–17*. HC201.
33. Wintour, P. and Cutis, P. (2009). 'Balls unveils pay rises and Royal College to boost social work status.' *The Guardian*, 28.11.2009, p. 2.
34. Their appeal against their sentence was rejected, but they were granted lifelong anonymity in 2016 and later released with new identities saying that they had benefitted from professional help in secure accommodation and now felt like different people. The judge commented that the elder brother's ambition to go to university was 'genuinely capable of realisation.'
35. McVeigh, T. (2009). 'Take more babies away from bad parents says Barnardo chief.' *The Observer*, 06.09.2009, p. 1.
36. Topping, A. (2014). 'Child sexual abuse is endemic, says charity.' *The Guardian*, 28.08.2014, p. 9.
37. For this section, in addition to coverage in the media, I have relied on Jay, A. (2014). *Independent Inquiry into Child Sexual Exploitation in Rotherham 1997–2013*. Rotherham Metropolitan Borough Council.
38. Munro, E. (2011). *The Munro Review of Child Protection: Final Report. A child-centred system*. London: HMSO, Cmnd 8062.
39. The College of Social Work Two-Year Report (2012).
40. Taylor, M., Butler, P. and Burn-Murdoch, J. (2013). 'Councils reveal shock toll of cuts as axe looms again.' *The Guardian*, 26.03.2013.
41. Toynbee, P. (2016). 'If the way the NHS is organised seems absurd, that's because it is.' *The Guardian*, 06.02.2016, p. 16.
42. Tickle, L. (2016). 'Safety in numbers.' *The Guardian*, 26.11.2016, p. 39.
43. Shahid, N. (2017). 'Ministers' U-turn on innovation is testimony to power of profession.' *Professional Social Work Magazine*, April, 2017.
44. Sosenko, F., Littlewood, M., Bramley, G., Fitzpatrick, S., Blenkinsop, J. and Wood, J. (2019). *State of Hunger*, November 2019 Report. The Trussell Trust.
45. Chakrabortty, A. (2019). 'This government uses your money to gaslight poor people.' *The Guardian*, 06.11.2019, p. 1.
46. In 2019, Ruth was made Chief of the Matheng section of the Lokomasama chiefdom in Sierra Leone. She was styled 'Ya-Bomposseh Kunk Bana The Third'. This was in recognition of her 'down to earth' style as a social worker during her work for global social work. IFSW Press Release, 20.10.2019.
47. Peter Unwin is the 'Poet Austeriate' following his participation in the 2017 BASW/SWU 100 mile walk. He is Principal Lecturer in Social Work at the University of Wolverhampton and is currently promoting the 'Writing stories, poems and songs' project with the SWU/BASW Austerity Action Group.
48. Shennan, G. and Unwin, P. (2017). 'The important thing is to keep fighting, and to fight with care, love, respect and a passion for justice.' *Professional Social Work Magazine*, Oct., p. 28. Birmingham BASW.
49. Orwell, G. (2001). *The Road to Wigan Pier.'* London: Penguin Modern Classics.
50. These documents can be obtained from https://www.basw.co.uk/what-we-do/campaigns/anti-austerity-and-anti-poverty.
51. Robins, J. (2019). 'We're poorly paid and the caseloads are unmanageable.' *The Guardian*, 31.07.2019.
52. Dodd, V. (2019). 'Police left to tackle impact of breakdown to social fabric, says chief constable.' *The Guardian*, 31.07.2019.
53. Ravalier, J. and Boichat, C. (2018). *UK Social Workers: Working Conditions and Wellbeing*. Bath: Bath Spa University.

54. McNicoll, A. (2018). 'Paperwork is killing social work.' *Professional Social Work Magazine*, May, p. 2, Birmingham BASW.
55. Doward, J. (2019). 'Revealed: 6,000 residential care workers suffer violent attacks.' *The Guardian*, 09.06.2019, p. 10.
56. McNicoll, A. (2018). 'Violence and abuse "not part of the job".' *Professional Social Work Magazine*, June, pp. 15–16.
57. The Assaults on Emergency Workers (Offences) Act 2018.
58. Hansard LC Vol 791 Col 747 16.05.2018.
59. Ravalier, J. (2020). *Social Worker Wellbeing and Working Conditions: Best Practice Toolkit*. Birmingham: SWU/BASW.
60. BASW submission to the Education Select Committee on Social Work Reform, March 2016. Birmingham BASW.
61. Thompson, N. (2018). *The Managing Stress Practice Manager*. Wrexham: Avenue Media Solutions.
62. Tickle, L. (2019). 'Cleansed by cuts. Desperate heads refuse school places to pupils with special needs.' *The Guardian*, 07.05.2019, p. 36.
63. Weale, S. (2019). 'Support for children with special needs, says ombudsman.' *The Guardian*, 4.10.2019, p. 17.
64. Marsh, S. (2017). 'Vulnerable children "fall through cracks in social services".' *The Guardian*, 14.08.2017, p. 10.
65. Cattan, S., Conti, G., Farquharson, C. and Ginja, R. (2019). 'The health effects of Sure Start.' Report, Institute of Fiscal Studies, 03.06.2019.
66. Shahid, N. (2019). BASW responds to Social Work England consultation on rules and standards. *Professional Social Work Magazine*, 14.05.2019, pp. 22–23. In June, BASW and SWU expressed concern that the duty to report resourcing issues could penalise practitioners.
67. The Association of Directors of Adult Services Annual Conference, 26.06.2019.
68. Funding of local authorities' children's services. 14th Report of Session 2017–19. House of Commons Housing, Communities and Local Government Committee. 01.05.2019, HC 1638.
69. SCIE (2019). *Leadership in Strengths-Based Social Care*. Practice Framework and Handbook, 01.10.2019. Department of Health and Social Care.
70. See smallstepsconsultants.com. The Prevent programme was introduced by The Counter Terrorism and Security Act 2015. It places a duty on local authorities, prisons, NHS trusts, schools, colleges and universities to report any suspicions to the Prevent teams. Soon after its introduction teachers reported that a 10-year-old boy wrote 'I live in a terrorist house,' misspelling 'terraced.' He was interviewed by police and social services and his home was searched. There is, of course, a fierce debate, particularly in education, about the implication of this on free speech.
71. Pidd, H., Parveen, N., Wolfe-Robinson, M. and Halliday, J. (2019). 'Children suffer in "chaotic" justice system.' *The Guardian*, 04.11.2019, p. 6.
72. http://vimeo.com/298212033.
73. *Miriam: Home Delivery*. dog-rose-film.com.
74. rockstargames.com.

SEVENTEEN

2019–2021

ALARM

Although the United Kingdom is the world's fifth largest economy, one-fifth of its population (14 million people) live in poverty, and 1.5 million of them experienced destitution in 2017. Policies of austerity introduced in 2010 continue largely unabated, despite the tragic social consequences ... Food banks have proliferated; homelessness and rough sleeping have increased greatly ... life expectancy is falling for certain groups; and the legal aid system has been decimated.

The social safety net has been badly damaged by drastic cuts to local authorities' budgets, which have eliminated many social services, reduced policing services, closed libraries in record numbers, shrunk community and youth centres and sold off public spaces and buildings. The bottom line is that much of the glue that has held British society together since the Second World War has been deliberately removed and replaced with a harsh and uncaring ethos. A booming economy, high employment and a budget surplus have not reversed austerity, a policy pursued more as an ideological than an economic agenda.

– Philip Alston, United Nations High Commissioner for Human Rights[1n]

I have not had an affair with Petronella. It is all complete balderdash. It is an inverted pyramid of piffle. It is all completely untrue and ludicrous conjecture.

– UK Prime Minister, Boris Johnson[2n]

INTERNATIONAL EVENTS

The Arab Spring – The Backlash

Tunisia

By 2020 it was clear that the country that had started the spread of resistance was the only one to have a positive outcome, retaining an effective democracy thanks to its small apolitical army and the fact that immediately after the revolution the Islamist movement was moderate and signed an agreement of shared principles. It had been scarred, however, by some assassinations and attacks from IS inspired terrorist attacks.[3n]

Libya

Progress here was slow due to rivalry between various Islamist groups and others under the control of powerful warlords based in the main cities and a weak central government supported by the United Nations. Civil war decimated the country until, following intense diplomatic intervention, elections were held in July 2012 and a Congress was formed. This was charged with the very difficult task of forming a government. Islamist groups immediately attacked certain historic sites, and in September 2012 the American Embassy was attacked, resulting in the death of four people including the ambassador. Slowly the central government won through, although the country remains chaotic with badly damaged infrastructure. Amid this, people smugglers have established trade routes for migrants wishing to reach Europe, bringing disruption and corruption to the country. More than 700,000 migrants landed in Italy while some 17,000 had drowned by the end of 2019.

Egypt

Egypt continues to be under the rule of President Abdel Fattah el-Sisi, who operates a dictatorial regime that tolerates no dissent, starting with the killing of 529 Brotherhood members and the imposition of indefinite detention for dissidents, 'disappearances' and extensive torture, including young children.

America

At the conclusion of a bruising campaign, the result of the US presidential election, announced on December 14th 2020, gave the victory to Joe Biden by a significant majority of both electoral colleges and with 81 million votes, the highest number of votes ever cast in a presidential election. Alongside him was his Vice President Kamala Harris (the first African Asian American to hold such a senior position). The narcissistic Trump, who falsely believed that he had won everything all his life, could not accept such a conclusive public result. He launched more than a hundred legal challenges at state and supreme court level, all of which were rejected. Trump used the weeks between the result and the inauguration to launch a campaign describing Biden's forthcoming government as illegitimate. On January 6th, two weeks before the ceremony, Trump addressed his supporters (many of whom were already wound up by his tweets) from outside the White House, encouraging them to march on the Capitol. These were his words:

> We will never give up. We will never concede. It doesn't happen. You don't concede when there is theft involved ... We're gathered together in the heart of our nation's capital for one very, very basic and simple reason: To save our democracy ... And you have to get your people to fight.

Shortly after what turned out to be a very long speech, several hundred people walked to the Capitol and, finding it weakly defended, rushed up the steps and entered the building where a joint session was formally verifying the result of the election in Biden's favour. The Capitol police, concentrating on moving members to safety, left few of its force to counter this incursion, and the armed protesters were soon in the chamber causing damage to the building, occupying offices and screaming for the Vice President, Mike Pence, and the Chair of the House, Nancy Pelosi. With help from reinforcements, the rioters were ejected. Some 140 people were injured and there were five deaths associated with the event. Condemnation was widespread and Trump was impeached again.[4n] He declined to attend Biden's inauguration. The inquiry into these events is continuing and criminal charges are still being pursued.

In the first 100 days of Biden's presidency, Biden and Harris reversed most of Trump's executive orders, rejoined the Paris Accord on climate change, organised a climate summit pledging to reduce US emissions by 50% by 2030, and called for unity across the country in order to achieve progress. They also set up a $1.9 trillion budget to fight Covid and to oversee the delivery of 200 million injections. A similar sum was devoted to economic relief. Positive changes were made to Trump's cruel immigration rules and they committed to withdraw from Afghanistan by September 2021. Two trillion dollars were targeted at improving America's poor infrastructure and $1.8 trillion were designated for education and childcare. This is just a brief summary of some of the changes that were made, and they serve to highlight that normal positive America was back.

China, the Virus and the WHO

At the end of 2019, China notified the World Health Organization (WHO) that a new virus had been identified, with a cluster of cases occurring in the city of Wuhan. This was a holiday period, and residents from Wuhan were travelling across China and worldwide. It is possible that the Chinese had taken some time to process this before releasing the news to the WHO. They then took some time to do their checks and risk assessments. On January 12th 2020, China released the genetic code of the new virus, which identified it as another type of coronavirus. On the following day, the first death outside China was confirmed. The WHO issued technical guidance on how to deal with infected patients using their experience of the previous coronavirus epidemics of SARS and MERS. SARS had been reported in Asia in 2003; it travelled to 26 countries causing 774 deaths. The MERS epidemic occurred in Saudi Arabia and spread to 17 countries, mostly in the Middle East, causing 866 deaths. The UK was only marginally affected by these viruses. The WHO followed the technical guidance of January 10th with other news releases, leading to a meeting of their Emergency Committee on the January 22nd, when delegates from around the world were faced with a lack of clear evidence to act. They reconvened eight days later and declared a public health emergency with a very high risk assessment. Further developments led the WHO on March 12th to declare this virus as a pandemic. The organisation continued to issue advice, including hand washing and keeping one metre distance from person to person. On March 16th, the Director General held a press conference to confirm their advice, adding

> ... the most effective way to prevent infections and save lives is breaking the chains of transmission. And to do that you must test and isolate. You cannot fight a fire blindfolded. And we cannot stop this pandemic if we don't know who is infected. We have a simple message for all countries. Test, Test, Test.[5]

In the early days, we knew little more than the facts that the virus was very powerful and very small – packing a couple of trillion together would fill a pinhead. Viruses rely on the availability of a host to replicate. They transmit very quickly and this one targeted the lungs and could be fatal. Older people and those with weakened immune systems were particularly vulnerable, and we soon discovered the frightening fact that a significant number of people could have the disease with no symptoms. This made immediate regular effective testing essential.

Where did this terrible virus come from? We still have no definitive answer to that question. The circumstances in Wuhan were the first obvious suspect. Covid is common in bats, a delicacy in China which were sold in the wet fish markets local to Wuhan. This may have led to direct transmission to a human, or the virus may have been transmitted via a pangolin, a mammal also sold in the market for medication. Also in Wuhan was an Institute of Virology. Perhaps the virus had escaped from there? Other clues are available. From September 2019, a lung cancer screening exercise took place in Italy. In late 2020, scientists re-examined the samples and found traces of what was by then known as COVID-19. In June 2020, cases of SARS-CoV-2, which causes COVID-19, were diagnosed in mink – the virus was observed to mutate as it moved from animals to humans and back again. Denmark subsequently culled 17 million farmed mink.

NATIONAL EVENTS

Brexit

In July 2019 Teresa May, low in charisma but sharp on detail, handed over the premiership to Boris Johnson, whose strengths lay in optimistic bluster and grand visions, no friend of the truth but a long-established aversion to detail and reluctance to study his brief. What a Populist!

Labour suffered badly from their ambiguous stance on Brexit. With his majority, Johnson was able to pass the Act by which we would formally leave the European Community on December 31st 2019. The following year would need to see a very complex treaty concluded to meet Johnson's determination to finally cut all our ties with the EU by January 31st 2021.

COVID-19

The virus arrived in the UK in January 2020 at a very inconvenient time. As outlined in the opening quotation, social and health services had been brought to their knees by ten years of enforced austerity. While some token money had recently been given to rescue the NHS, all local authorities were impoverished and their care and key public health services were severely reduced. The social care sector had suffered badly with financial cuts, but was additionally suffering from lack of clear policy about its role in society and its financial support. Prime ministers since Blair had promised the radical review required, as had both May and Johnson, but absolutely no effective conclusion had ever been reached. The long Brexit dispute had divided the nation and most people had lost patience with political conduct and conflict. During the winter of 2019–2020, repeated serious flooding had caused severe damage and disruption, mainly in the North East and the Midlands.[6]

The virus was initially described as remarkably intelligent and devious. It spread by close contact between people and was mostly passed by expelled droplets through breath, sneezing, etc. The first symptoms were a fever, a continuous dry cough and fatigue. Later, loss of taste and smell were noticed. Sometime in the early weeks, we learnt that people were most infectious during the first few days before symptoms were evident. Once in the body, the lungs, heart and kidneys were usually attacked and an overreaction by the immune system was a complicating factor. It was quickly established that elderly people were most at risk, as were people who for whatever reason had impaired immune systems. My own position was that, in my late 80s and with many other ailments, I isolated myself immediately the threat appeared. We have since learnt that men have a significantly higher risk factor than women and anyone over 80 years of age is more than 70% more likely to die than a man under 50. As time went by, we learnt that children seemed to be in much less danger than adults and that if someone had a mild dose of the disease or recovered from treatment, we did not know whether this made them immune or for how long. The same applied to thousands of people who tested positive and had no symptoms at all. By May, we were discovering that people from the black, Asian and minority ethnic (BAME) community, many of whom worked at the frontline in health and care services, were particularly susceptible. Over the following months, new mutations would emerge in the UK and across the world.

January to June 2020

The Prime Minister was slow to react to the impending crisis. In the early days of 2020, his attention remained on Europe until he signed the legal Withdrawal Agreement on January 14th. Between late December 2019 and the end of February 2020, he spent significant periods away from Downing Street. By the end of February, the government had published a sketchy four phase plan of response to the virus. These were: CONTAIN – to track cases and isolate contacts to prevent the spread; DELAY – to slow the speed of infections in order to prevent the NHS becoming overwhelmed and to get us through to the summer when the virus might be less active; RESEARCH – to learn more about the virus and pursue effective drugs and vaccines; MITIGATE – to provide the best care possible for people who became ill and to maintain essential services. On March 5th, the same day as the first recorded death in the UK, Johnson was interviewed on the ITV programme *This Morning* by the hosts Phillip Schofield and Holly Willoughby. He was in a remarkably ebullient mood, chatting away, but giving us very little information.

Confirming that the aim was to avoid an early high spike which could overwhelm the NHS, he said:

> ... and that's where a lot of the debate has been and one of the theories is, that perhaps you could take it on the chin, take it in one go and allow the disease, as it were, to move through the population without taking any draconian measures ... But I think it would be better if we take all the measures we can now to stop the peak of the disease being as difficult for the NHS as it might be.[7]

This was seized on by many as promoting the policy of 'herd immunity,' the effect of which (it has been claimed) would have resulted in 500,000 UK deaths. Placed in the context of the whole interview, I think this was an unfair interpretation. Elsewhere in the interview, he downplayed how serious the impact would be, and what I *do* think is that the imposition of what he called 'draconian measures' was anathema to his libertarian beliefs. This meant that for a while longer he relied on advice rather than instruction.

Appreciating the urgency, COBRA met five times between January 24th and February 28th. Under pressure and domestic politics, Johnson attended only the February meeting, which focussed on the disastrous flooding in the north. During the following weeks, as alarming data continued to come in from Europe, pressure grew on the Prime Minister to act. He was, at last, briefed by officials on the situation and chaired a COBRA meeting on March 2nd 2020. After that, he announced that the Cabinet would be following advice from SAGE (the Scientific Advisory Group for Emergencies). There was, he said, no need to cancel sporting events at this stage. Three days later, the Prime Minister announced that we were facing the worst public health crisis for a generation and that we were already in the second, delay, phase, meaning that the steps required would cause severe disruption for many months. Anyone displaying symptoms should isolate themselves for seven days and, he said, 'many will lose loved ones before their time.' Parliament was still sitting, with MPs closely packed on the green benches, and Johnson was shaking hands enthusiastically, as was his style. On March 12th, the NHS stopped testing as the numbers were becoming overwhelming. On the same day, medical officers raised the UK risk to high.

On March 16th, the first daily briefing was broadcast from Downing Street. These briefings were led by the PM or senior ministers from a lectern displaying the government's motto 'STAY HOME: SAVE THE NHS: SAVE LIVES' and were backed by senior scientists, usually Professor Chris Whitty, the Chief Medical Officer, and Sir Patrick Vallance, the Chief Scientific Adviser. Whilst these events were very interesting and informative, they also emphasised that the government was relying on and following scientific advice. This posed the question of who would take the blame when things went wrong. By mid March, as the effect of the pandemic on the economy was being appreciated, The Bank of England dropped the interest rate to 0.1% and the pound fell below $1.18, its lowest since 1985. The Chancellor, Rishi Sunak, just over a month in post, took extraordinary steps to support the economy. Various support schemes were launched including loan guarantees, direct loans and interventions, the most impressive being a furlough scheme by which firms could lay off staff and the taxpayer would pay 80% of their wage up to £2,500 a month until the end of July. It was later extended to October in a slightly modified form; the total cost was estimated at £132 billion. Meanwhile, supermarkets were besieged by shoppers seeking to stockpile essential goods – it turned out that toilet paper was high on the list, resulting in many angry confrontations!

On March 16th, Johnson advised against non-essential travel, contact with others and making visits to pubs, clubs and theatres. Two days later, schools, colleges and universities were closed except for pupils of key workers and vulnerable children. On Monday March 23rd, the Prime Minister announced a compulsory lockdown. Everyone was to stay at home except for basic shopping, one form of exercise, medical needs and to work when absolutely necessary. We were to distance ourselves from other people by two metres. This became law on March 26th, and police powers were increased to enable them to enforce lockdown. The following day, Johnson and the Health Secretary Matt Hancock both tested positive and self-isolated.

Late on March 27th, Johnson's political adviser Dominic Cummings received a phone call from his wife to say that she was unwell with COVID symptoms. He ran out of Number 10 to go home to her and their four-year-old son. Feeling that there was no alternative, he drove the family 246 miles to Durham, where he moved into a house in the grounds of his father's estate. On April 12th Cummings drove his family 30 miles to Barnard Castle, then left the car for a brief walk before driving back to the estate. His subsequent explanation was that he needed to test his eyesight before heading back to London two days later. This was a significant political time bomb, which would explode on May 22nd when a joint investigation by *The Guardian* and the *Daily Mirror* was published. This incident and the subsequent pathetic explanations badly damaged the government.

From March 16th, the government issued daily briefings to a set formula. The figures for the number of cases and deaths were of limited value. The number of cases were drawn from some testing and notification by GPs and hospitals. The figures for deaths included only those who had been tested. From late April, this figure included deaths in care homes. The Office of National Statistics (ONS) recorded all deaths when COVID-19 was mentioned on the death certificate and also the number of 'excess deaths.' These were calculated by checking the current deaths over the average for the same period for the previous five years.

Approximate Daily Data on the 14th of Each Month

	March	April	May
Cases (UK)	1,161	5,252	3,560
Deaths registered by gov't	65	78	428
ONS Excess deaths each month	4,995	11,507	4,385

April proved to be the darkest month for the UK in this phase of the pandemic, both for the process of the disease and potential political issues. The relevant figures for mid April are given above. These high numbers continued for some six days before the 14th, then slowly diminished. That same month it emerged that care homes, particularly those for the elderly, were suffering alarming numbers of deaths and that the staff were also suffering. It transpired that hospitals were discharging patients to care homes without testing for the infection! The Health Minister stated that the government had put a protective ring around care homes since the start of the infection, but no homes could be found that benefitted from such a ring. By late April, care home deaths were included in the daily figures. On April 18th Care England revealed that 122,347 care home residents had died as a result of the virus, a terrible verdict on the past neglect and the lack of care for this sector.

The next issue was the shortage of personal protective equipment (PPE), essential for any frontline staff dealing, in different degrees, with infected or potentially infected people. Week after week followed in which ministers leading the daily briefings explained how many millions of pieces of kit they had dispatched to hospitals and care homes, while frontline staff reported a continuing lack of PPE where it counted. This issue dogged the government until the numbers of people needing treatment or care declined. One significant factor in this was how slow the government had been to look to domestic suppliers of PPE. Once the situation was realised, local clothing manufacturers, small businesses and community volunteers rose to the supply challenge. The whole PPE saga, the repeated assurances that kit had been dispatched against the high risk to NHS and care staff when it failed to arrive led to, I think, the first significant loss of public trust in the government.

On April 4th, Hancock promised that by the end of the month there would be 100,000 tests a day, and later Johnson promised 200,000 tests a day. There then followed confusion as the goalposts were changed to mean capacity or actual tests carried out. On May 1st, Hancock announced that over 120,000 tests had been carried out the previous day. It then transpired that this included home testing kits that had been posted, with no idea as to how many were ever returned, and large numbers sent for use in a variety of research programmes. This left 82,000 tests that were actually completed. Another step taken towards public distrust. The previous day, following careful planning and army manpower, the first field NHS Nightingale critical care hospital was opened in the Excel Centre in London, with a capacity of 500 beds and a possible extension of up to 4,000 beds. A large mortuary was also built nearby. Much smaller emergency hospitals were opened in Sunderland and Bristol and other larger hospitals (with capacities of up to 5,000) in Birmingham and Cardiff. Many other sites were planned, totalling some 5,700 beds. The capital costs ran to half a billion pounds.[8]

Given the extraordinary efforts made by existing hospitals to adapt their buildings and recruit staff (mostly recently retired or student doctors and nurses), the Nightingale hospitals were seldom used, and by June they were all placed on standby in case of a second wave in the autumn. Later, some helped to deal with the vast treatment delays for non-Covid patients.

On April 5th, the Queen made a very rare broadcast to the nation, paying tribute to all the key workers and warning that we may have more to endure. Earlier that day, Johnson had been admitted to hospital and then to intensive care. He was discharged after seven days, but his first public statement came on April 27th, when he said that we were at 'the moment of maximum risk' and urged people not to lose patience with the restrictions. He looked very pale and weak and seemed to have lost weight. It took him some weeks to regain his bounce. On April 6th, a 99-year-old army captain, Tom Moore, resolved to raise money for the NHS by walking 100 lengths of his 25-metre garden with the aid of his walking frame every day until his 100th birthday on the 30th. His aim was to raise £1,000. This caught the attention of the public so that by his birthday he had raised £30 million, which eventually rose to £38.9 million for NHS Charities Together.[9] He was knighted on May 20th. He died five months later, but to this day his charity continues to raise and distribute funds. This inspired several others to copy Moore's example, including two very young children with severe disabilities.

As the months went by, crises continued to be documented, including: the supply of PPE, most of which had been handed to private companies contracted through a privileged route to ministers; the poor availability of PPE to care homes, the reliability of daily government statistics; the inability of relatives to be with dying relatives in hospitals and homes; and the ongoing general confusion surrounding unclear or contradictory advice. In time, politicians started to fall back on well practised phrases, which dented credibility. Weekend briefings stopped on June 5th 2020, and on Tuesday June 9th a nadir was reached when the Business Secretary, Alok Sharma, failed to answer, by my count, any of the sixteen questions asked of him in the Commons.

July to December 2020

The gradual easing of the lockdown that started in mid June was extended until July 4th, when most restrictions were removed, except for in Leicester. Elsewhere that Saturday was seen as 'Independence Day,' and people went wild. London's Soho district saw extraordinarily crowded scenes. Too much too soon. Pursuing the sense of freedom, the government announced a list of 73 countries worldwide which could be visited without the need to isolate on return. More positivity was sensed when it was announced that vaccines were now in their final trials. Perhaps this was countered twenty days later by the ruling that the wearing of facemasks was compulsory in all shops. Then in early August the Chancellor's 'Eat Out to Help Out' scheme was launched and over a hundred million meals were served at half cost in restaurants, which were often packed with people not wearing masks or social distancing. However, by this time a worrying rise in the number of cases was being noticed, among which was a new mutation in Kent, characterised by its increased transmissibility. With cases back to 3,000 a day and the re-infection rate (R-rate) climbing from 1.2 towards 1.6, tensions were evident in government. Scientists were raising the need for another lockdown and the PM was fiercely resisting. The government's response in mid October was to impose a confusing four-stage tier system, varying the restrictions according to the level of reported cases. Nineteen days later, as the pressure on hospital admissions meant that ICUs were nearing their limits, a second lockdown was imposed. Johnson explained this was 'for four months ... to prevent a medical and moral disaster for the NHS.'

On December 2nd, the Pfizer vaccine was approved by the regulator and was immediately distributed via a programme which prioritised the elderly and vulnerable and then moved down through the age groups. A month later, the Astra Zeneca vaccine became available – rich rewards for the vast sums invested by the government. For the first time, I think, the government handed the implementation over to the NHS, Public Health and Primary Care rather than to the commercial sector. Being able to benefit from their local knowledge, the rollout of the vaccines went like a dream. In mid December, the lockdown reverted to the tier system, but with large parts of the country in the top Tier 4. On December 16th the four home countries agreed that some restrictions could be relaxed for five days over Christmas, but warnings were given to stay local and think carefully before meeting up with relatives! This then changed right at the last minute to no travelling and families could only be together for the 24 hours of Christmas day.

If we needed any more proof about the effect of the Kent variant, some 40 countries suspended flights to or from the UK. On December 23rd 2020, NHS England issued a letter instructing hospitals not to admit non-Covid patients for treatment as every available bed was required for Covid patients. The consequence of this would be dire. Just before Christmas, a new variant was discovered in the UK with its origins in South Africa; similar to the Kent variant, it spread more quickly. Intense test and trace systems were deployed wherever it was located. By the end of the year, daily cases had risen to 55,892, the largest number so far experienced, while hospitals warned that the next few weeks would be 'nail-bitingly difficult.'

January to April 2021

As the number of virus cases, hospital admissions and deaths continued to rise over the new year, two new medications were introduced to hopefully cut down the fatalities. On December 8th the first person in the world had been vaccinated in the UK. By the end of January, over half a million people had been vaccinated, but we had also picked up another mutation, this time from Brazil. It was now a race between the spreading virus and the lockdown. Soon the number of cases, admissions and fatalities began to fall. All but one of the Nightingale hospitals were closed, and in February the optimistic Prime Minister disclosed a five-stage path by which the lockdown could be ended. The gamble was that, although cases were still high, the rapid decrease would continue; and this was indeed to be the case for the next two months. Firstly, students could return to all education establishments, but regular tests would have to be taken. People could exercise outdoors, with others, but they must observe the regulation distance (up to two metres apart, with slightly different rules across the UK countries). The data would be closely examined in the next five weeks and if all was well stage 2 would be implemented, so that from March 29th people could meet outside in small groups and open-air sports facilities, including outdoor swimming facilities. The 'stay at home' instruction would end, but people were asked to work from home wherever possible and be cautious at all times. If the data were OK, then from April 12th all shops, gyms, etc. could open, as could open-air attractions such as zoos. May 17th would see more facilities open and a review of social distancing. June 17th would see the end of all restrictions, but with the warning from the PM that, 'the virus will remain a part of our lives, we are going to have to live our lives differently to keep ourselves and others safe.'

This period saw the gradual emergence of a new strategy by the government – a greater reliance on citizens making their own informed choices rather than to rely on government edicts. So far, the existing vaccines have, to different degrees, been effective against all Covid variants. However, I think we can foresee the arrival of new variants of the virus given the long delays in getting the vaccines to the poorer countries where health systems are limited, giving plenty of time for more complex variants to develop. While this government is in office I suspect that many more confusing messages will be announced.

The next restriction to be issued before the summer holidays was about travelling abroad. The red list showed the forbidden destinations. No one was allowed to holiday in countries on either the red or the amber list. People were free to travel to green list countries, but in real terms for most people this meant just Portugal. Confusion developed over the amber list, which listed many established holiday resorts. Although it was legal to visit an amber country, the government said that people must not go there on holiday. At the same time, it became clear that many people were ignoring the government. The only penalty was the standard 10-day isolation and the cost of tests.

CULTURE

If I define culture as the beliefs, social forms, traditions and accepted expression of creative expression of a social group, it will be clear that two years of Covid restrictions hit our culture hard on many levels, chiefly by the oft-stated instruction to stay at home. Alongside this we learnt, thanks to Donald Trump, that instead of lies there are such things as 'alternative facts' and this, in a minor way, applied to our own Prime Minister who was said to have 'a distant relationship with the truth.' Many citizens who had been free to travel all over Europe to share their rich culture were now faced with a load of bureaucratic hurdles. Slowly the effects of closed theatres, cinemas, sports grounds, pubs, etc. became more powerful; we were limited to TV and online entertainments.

On the positive side, we learnt more about the four home countries, and how different and often how clear and decisive their responses to the pandemic were. Confined to home, we had much more appreciation of work/life balance, and many resolved to keep working from home. Many houses suffered a thorough spring clean, then redecoration or possible DIY extensions. If you were among the lucky ones to have a garden, they were re-planned or just tidied up. Relationships with neighbours developed, many on the basis of regular tea or coffee gatherings within the regulations for personal distance and masks. There was a clear appreciation of 'we are all in this together' and a sense of community developed. People realised, often for the first time, the extent of poverty, particularly the widespread use of food banks, which led to an increase in volunteers willing to help.

Wherever possible, TV companies responded with exciting dramas, nature programmes and, of course, drama serials, and much appreciated exercise and cooking programmes. Programmes for children were increased to help ease the pressure on parents coping with (and having to teach) bored children. Online gaming increased to record levels, as did the use of emails.

There was, of course, another far less positive experience for those millions of families who found themselves trapped on the upper floors of tower blocks with no communal space and for whom life, especially with young children, was extremely stressful. They more than most suffered mental health issues often combined with deteriorating interpersonal relations and abuse, the full extent of which would only be discovered when all the restrictions were finished.

SOCIAL WORK

Before we get to social work itself, it might be worth taking a look at the fate of associated services and their experience of Covid and austerity

The NHS

On top of all the effects of austerity, Covid hit the NHS like a sledgehammer. From March 2020, the speed with which the infection spread led to rapidly growing admissions and the need for properly equipped staff and ICU units. There were many delays in supplying staff with the right standards of kit, and improvisations came into play with fatal consequences. More and more wards were converted to ICU units, and staff were called from the rest of the hospital, thus closing down routine wards. Staff were stressed and exhausted, especially those facing the rapid numbers of painful patient deaths, particularly of the elderly, with no relative allowed to be beside them. It was traumatic. In 2020, 150 nurses, 99 nursing assistants and 33 doctors, most from black Asian and minority ethnic backgrounds, had died.[10]

Education

Covid was a disaster for education at all levels. Schools and universities closed for months on end, except for some vulnerable pupils or if a parent was working in a key job. Strong efforts were made to teach online, but this presented pupils, parents and teachers with challenges. In schools, teachers were devising Covid-safe environments to teach the small numbers of pupils attending and, at the same time, preparing and delivering online material. It was exhausting and very stressful. Under the leadership of Gavin Williamson, the Department of Education did not handle the situation well. Throughout 2020, schools were subject to contradictory instructions to open or close. Eventually, caring local authorities would decide, given the data, to close schools, only to be threatened with legal action by the government. All the uncertainty put strain on children and parents who had to suddenly adjust their work and home commitments and turn again to home schooling. On top of this came chaos in relation to exams. From the start of the pandemic, all summer sittings of GCSE and A-level examinations were cancelled for 2020. They would be replaced by teacher predictions plus a computer programme that would monitor results. When these results were announced, all hell was let loose as the grades bore little relation to the known ability of the pupils. After weeks of protest and argument, it was decided that just the teacher assessment grades (TAGs) would stand. To say that this traumatised parents and pupils, clearing houses and universities would be a considerable understatement.

Universities already had their own challenges in the form of being 'home' to thousands of students, a significant proportion of which were from overseas. When lockdown was imposed, students found themselves confined indefinitely to their small single or shared rooms.

Social Care

The effects of prolonged austerity followed by Covid were horrendous on a system that largely relied on cash-starved local authorities paying private or charitable home owners to care for what were acknowledged as the most vulnerable citizens in our society. Across the country, homes had been forced to cut their staff and levels of care despite the commitment of their staff. Significant numbers of individual and corporately owned establishments, finding the task impossible, handed the keys back to local authorities and got out of the industry. The failure of successive governments to produce a solution to the whole basis of the UK care system did not help a provision where funding was a complex mixture of personal (people selling their own homes) and central funds fed through local authorities. Wages were poor, staff were often tempted to leave to join an agency for better pay, and carers found the regular situation whereby they could be sent into any home when colleagues were absent or sick incredibly difficult. In February 2020, as the pandemic started to bite in the UK, homes started to prepare by searching for the right masks, uniforms, etc. They found the market sparse and the cost high;

the government focussed on the NHS and were very slow to supply homes. Some were reduced to using black bin bags and homemade masks for their protection. In May 2020, the Secretary of State announced that 'right from the start we have put a protective ring around care homes was seen as an insult.'[11n] Already between mid March and mid June 19,286 deaths had been recorded in care homes.[12] These deaths, as in hospitals, denied any relative or loved one present to comfort the dying. Nursing or care staff carried out this function, causing them more pain and distress beyond that already imposed by their job. More than 470 care workers died from Covid-19 between March and December 2020, the majority being men.[13]

Social Work

The Covid lockdown in March 2020 hit social workers hard. It forced most to work from home, where isolation from service users was difficult and face-to-face support from colleagues was not easily available when complex or stressful critical situations arose. Stress could not be shared at home. Above all, except in rare cases, they lost the most central and valuable aspect of their work: face-to-face interaction with service users to mutually achieve a sound relationship. If working online was available, body language and sense of environment were not. Those working with abusive families, where children or frail elderly people were at risk, suffered long term anxieties about what was happening. How was lockdown affecting them? If a home visit was essential, then protective equipment was rarely available. Managers were important in this situation and unfortunately their response, under pressure from their legislative duties and target driven seniors, varied from supportive to bullying. In addition to this, they were distressed by the knowledge that services relied on by families were falling away; more were relying completely on their local food banks, which were struggling.[14]

On April 23rd 2020, under the cover of Covid, the government issued a Statutory Instrument which removed over sixty protections for children in care in England. It was to be implemented the following day and expire six months later, but could be extended. This was a rehash of the proposals put forward in 2016 and withdrawn under pressure. This time it again met fierce opposition led by the charity 'Article 39' (Sir Bill Utting as Patron). The initial response from their Director, Carolyne Willow, was as follows:

> The idea that local authorities have been clamouring to remove fundamental legal protections from vulnerable children during the middle of a global pandemic is just not creditable. This is deregulation on steroids. It is soul-destroying that so much time and effort has been put in to systematically eroding the rights of children. Most of this disrupter's wish list has been in the public domain for years. It is an insult to children to suggest that COVID-19 is the cause of this.[15]

Among the clauses were the replacement of a social workers' duty to visit a child one week after a placement and then every six weeks 'as soon as reasonably practical.'

The contact could be achieved by phone or electronic means! The 'soon as' phrase was then used in relation to six month' reviews, care standards and the twice yearly visit by Ofsted. Local authorities were no longer required to establish adoption panels, and checks of the suitability of foster carers no longer required health or criminal record checks. Other loosening of regulations occurred. The lessons learnt, so painfully, from recent inquiries exposing the failure of social services to properly supervise children had all been completely ignored. Fierce campaigning and Article 39's successful appeal to the High Court once again led to the withdrawal of this Statutory Instrument. The government's Chief Social Worker, Isabelle Fowler, had argued that social workers had asked for these changes to free them from bureaucracy, a strange stance to take, but there were quite a few questions for Ms Fowler.[16]

In December 2020, BASW published the result of a survey that asked members to reflect on their experience of Covid-19. Feelings of loneliness and isolation appeared, along with having to cope with deaths, particularly of clients in residential homes and of close relatives, especially when no one was able to hold their hand at the last. Also reported were the experiences of not being able to prevent mental health breakdowns of friends, colleagues and service users and the failure to be recognised as frontline workers. One respondent was hurt by 'social media, the rise in toxic lies and bullying and the ... growth in people not taking any responsibility for being vile and abusive.' On the positive side, there was recognition of resilience – communities coming together to support the vulnerable and finding the strength to carry on despite the losses, deaths and gloom. And that there is a willingness of all people to do the right thing, even when it's the hardest. The future looked bleak for families, social workers and society. Everyone had been in survival mode, but once anything near normal arrived, the trauma will come to the surface. The fallout will start and the repercussions will last for years. The effect on the economy will inevitably lead to pay cuts, more austerity and a widening of the income gap. More poverty with an unsympathetic government.[17]

As the months went by, the levels of stress and mental health challenges for social workers, care and NHS staff naturally increased to epic proportions. Surveys of social workers revealed that six out of ten workers experienced burnout between November 2020 and January 2021 and that stress was increasing. Home working was causing feelings of isolation, dangerous in a workforce relying on relationships and social interaction. As one respondent who had worked through the AIDS epidemic in Africa and had reached the point where the situation became really scary commented, 'I thought we had reached that point in January 2021. I had lost two members of staff to Covid. My staff had experienced multiple losses. The mood music was really low.' Another commented, 'My confidence has vanished underneath me. It has had a massive impact mentally and physically.' In another survey, 70% of workers agreed that working from home made it difficult to switch off.[18]

From these distressing positions, social workers strived to provide the best service they could to meet the needs of individuals and families. Having been urged to include poverty as a factor in their assessment, they were now facing increasing levels of poverty. Research by the House of Commons Library revealed some figures. Between 2019 and 2020, relative child poverty stood at 4.3 million, an absolute disgrace in a rich country.[19] Within those figures was the terrible experience of food poverty, a blight on communities and an abuse to a citizen's fundamental right. Research showed that some 4.7 million people were in food-insecure households, 26% of which included children.[20]

In response to these situations, the number of operational community-based food banks in the UK rose to some 2,200, a sad indictment of our society. In the October 2020 edition of the magazine *Professional Social Work*, a then student social worker wrote of what food poverty meant to him as a single parent bringing up his daughter on a deprived estate in Kent. For him, food poverty was 'as pernicious as it is widespread.' The government's approach to all this was largely to ignore it, its website only commenting on poverty abroad. This was significantly challenged by the 22-year-old footballer Marcus Rashford, who was born in Manchester and played for Manchester United and England. Among other issues and while making philanthropic donations, in March 2020 he campaigned on the controversial issue of children eligible for free school meals receiving no help during the holidays, especially the long summer ones. There was widespread public support for his campaign and the government came under considerable pressure. On June 15th Rashford wrote an open letter to the government calling for an end to child poverty. The following day, the government reversed its policy so that these children would receive meals throughout the summer holidays. Rashford subsequently launched a petition for end of child poverty, an expansion of free school meals and activities for children in the holidays. It received over 200,000 signatures on the first day. It was discussed in Parliament in October 2020, where the Labour motion was defeated by 61 votes. It showed, Rashford said, a total lack of humanity.

On August 12th 2021, *The Guardian* reported on their survey of children's services during the previous 18 months in some of England's most deprived communities. It broadly supported the situation outlined above, but it is worth further highlighting some of their findings. Such local authorities were expecting to overspend by up to £12 million with no reserves available. Middlesbrough and Rochdale reported an increase of 40% and 35% referrals in the previous year. In Hull, a shortage of foster parents meant that fifty-five looked after children were moved to seven or more placements in the same year. London authorities reported a shortage of 500 foster homes, forcing councils to use more expensive private provision, some costing up to £10,000 a week. Residential care costs much more than that. Two children in Gateshead were placed at a cost of over a million pounds for a year. In Liverpool, the number of children entering into care because of parental neglect or alcohol abuse almost doubled. Blackburn with Darwen reported a recent trend of 'large groups of brothers and sisters needing to be looked after because of compromised parenting capacity, maybe because of substance abuse.' And the government does not see social workers as frontline staff.

All these processes required court action, but court proceedings had been severely cut resulting in delays of up to a year, which greatly increased the stress on all concerned.[21]

BASW sought to support its members throughout these many months. They had issued press statements and written to the government directly on a number of issues of concern. In June 2021, the Association launched a new 'Professional Support Service.' This was not a counselling service but rather an opportunity to work with a coach to talk about an individuals' issues, reflect together and structure a way through towards a resolution. A peer-to-peer service to 'support you while you support others.' In March the word Ubantu – we are because you are – was adopted as a useful community expression and a response to the populism now spreading across the world to disguise the new right-wing movements. The UK being one example.

Social Worker and Trade Unionist

A long-standing problem soon for both the Social Workers Union (SWU) and the Anti Austerity Group (AAG) emerged as we sought to involve people with lived experience or the volunteer groups that represented them. Our policy was to pay expenses and, where appropriate, to compensate for loss of earnings or interruption of their work. The difficulty was that any financial assistance we paid immediately led to difficulties with Universal Credit or other financial assistance. Research quickly revealed that this was a widespread problem affecting many agencies who wished to involve people with lived experience in their committees, working groups, etc. It was an intractable problem that needed to be resolved once and for all. We engaged the Campaign Collective group to carry out further research and to develop a plan to bring this issue to Parliament to lobby for a resolution between departments, declaring that such involvement was essential against the actual consequences. Once awareness of these initiatives spread, our campaign garnered support across the country and it became a major piece of work which continues.

Recently, SWU has taken two central initiatives. As membership rose towards 15,000, the fastest growing union in the country, and we celebrated our 10th anniversary, we made a formal request to become a member of the Trade Union Council. Apart from the advantage to our members of belonging to such a powerful organisation, we hoped it would help resolve the long-standing problems we were having with some of the big unions, most notably UNITE and UNISON (formed from NALGO, the local government union) which refused any attempt at cooperation and took every opportunity to dismiss us when seeking new members. It was no surprise that our application was summarily rejected, blocked by these two big unions and the GMB, the general workers' union. As of April 2022, we are appealing their decision on the grounds that their decision was based on false information.

In August 2021, SWU founded and financed the 'SWU Campaign Collective' in conjunction with the national Campaign Collective. This enabled any member who wished to launch a campaign, whether local or national, to access the expertise and support of Campaign Collective. A brilliant opportunity.

Restorative Justice

Whilst I remained committed to all these activities, following the long march I was increasingly aware that, at the age of 87 and accumulating a number of medical issues some of this might have to end. As time went by, with the practical implications of Covid, I had to withdraw from the youth offending work after nineteen years but remained active in SWU, SWAN and the AAG. I could see my 68 years in social work coming to an end.

FAMILY AND FRIENDS

Like every other family on the planet, we were affected by the Covid virus, the reaction of our governments and how they managed this deadly pandemic. In America, President Trump was dismissive of what was plainly happening in his own country, which largely left state governors and city mayors to do what they could, initially with little backup from the central government. During the early months, New York became a hotbed of infection. My family remained indoors as much as possible, working online, not easy for a family of film and game makers. The pressure on my son-in-law as Rockstar's local director was immense. Excellent and honest city leadership eventually brought the situation under control. My daughter, who was very cautious, reported that when she went out practically everyone wore a mask, a major contrast with those in London. Nonetheless, the games had to be made and, after much research and consultation, the studio was brought back into action in 2020. A village of caravans was assembled in the studio grounds to accommodate the actors and a slimmed down crew. Strict regulations were imposed and policed, and testing was an ever present routine. In general, all went well in this bubble. One advantage for my grandson Duke was that he was required to quickly learn a lot of new skills, in addition to his normal specialist role. The experiment was repeated some months later without the caravans, but each person had a personal taxi and they were tested on arrival and throughout the day. Unfortunately Juliet was less lucky as she had no option but to suspend her documentary about the people of Brooklyn, but that film is now in post production.

Aella, living in London was in trouble, as her work making music videos dried up, leaving her reliant on casual research work, etc. Not to be beaten, with her close friends she directed and launched two excellent short films, *Remember That* and *Misnomer*.[22] As restrictions were being eased, she decided to broaden her experience and, with the help of a friend, she worked at studios in Uxbridge and around the UK where Netflix were shooting instalments of their popular series *Bridgerton*. She was one of the Covid team, laying down the procedures to be followed and then enforcing them. Not always a popular job, but it gave her access to all areas and a golden opportunity to see how filming a big project worked. It was a good networking and learning opportunity. By December, Aella had had enough and handed in her notice. At the same time, she had decided to make her second application to the two-year director's course at the National

Film and Television School (NFTS). In January 2021 she was contacted by some friends from the Netflix shoot to say that a well-known director was being flown in from America and needed an assistant. Joy of joy, after a brief online interview, she got the job which she very much enjoyed even if it was exhausting. A few weeks later, Aella was invited for an interview at NFTS and shortly afterwards was told she had gained a place. More extreme joy and a well earned development in the career which she loves so much.

One family member that did not escape the virus was my dear niece Joanna White who lives with her teenage daughter in Saltash, the Cornish side of the River Tamar from Plymouth. Not long before the pandemic started, she gave up her job as a teaching assistant and started work at Derriford Hospital in Plymouth as a nursing assistant. For all three waves of the virus Jo was in the Covid wards and was fully enveloped in the horrors of overflowing wards, and in caring for the dying and distressed and experiencing more deaths than anyone should ever face. The shifts were 12 hours long by the end of which she and all her colleagues were physically and emotionally exhausted – and this went on day after day after day. To my mind, Jo and all of them deserve every tribute available.

In early May 2021 Juliet was contacted, using the DNA tracing part of the Ancestry family history programme, by Laura and Geoffrey, relatives of mine. This turned out to be the family of my father's elder sister, Annie Bullard, who had died on December 20th 1920 while giving birth to her daughter Ruby. This meant that Ruby added to the already overcrowded 'house of horrors' where the family dealt with the consequences of war and the economic depression. My mother had taken care of Ruby until poverty forced a return to her father, a soldier. We arranged a visit, and on the memorable Saturday June 19th Ruby's son Geoffrey and his daughter Laura walked in, sat down and were clearly full family members. There followed a very enjoyable but exhausting day exchanging stories, poring over the full family tree, photos, etc. We were left with some mysteries around Ruby. She had very much remained involved with the family, and had been a very welcome guest at my mother's 80th birthday in 1981, but we then lost track of her. After the memorable day, we trailed through family members asking for information and advice. Information along with some further mysteries came in slowly, and in the end I sought solutions from Debbie Winter, a professional ancestry consultant whom I had used many times before, and we now await another meeting to discuss her report.

My response to the pandemic was simple. Stay indoors and only venture out when essential and then well masked and keeping the two metre distance. In some ways I guess I thought of myself as independent, but on second thoughts that was far from the case. I was supported by daily transatlantic calls from my daughter, as well as by calls and visits from friends and family, including my wonderful neighbours, Phil and Gina Bussey, who take my waste bins out and are always on hand for any help needed, and Anne Raines, who my dog Jessie looks to for titbits and a good chat. My garden is tended by Flea and Pete Haddrell, and my house is cleaned by the lovely Finda Dunbar.

In Cornwall Malcolm and Lorraine Scott have cared for our house in Cadgwith very diligently. These four people have been with us before I moved to this address. The life of my Cockapoo dog has been transformed by the amazing Thompsett family who walk her every afternoon, usually up on their father's farm where she runs with the small pack of dogs there, returning home late in the evening exhausted and much loved. So, I now have a 'teenage' dog who comes home only for food and sleep. If fish and chips or an Indian takeaway is on the agenda, I am included, just as I am if it turns out they have catered for too many for their evening meal. Their friend Dotty loves baking so any excesses come my way. This they do for others in the village too. Village life. They all help me a great deal.

Despite the necessity to abide by Covid rules, my family have managed to be together as a family every Christmas, New Year and summer. A masterpiece of planning! On these occasions, and at home, Rod is a fierce cyclist, exploring the hidden byways of The Lizard peninsular, returning home covered in mud and stung all over by nettles. In 2019, he and his sister Anne completed a 225-mile cycling trip ending at Land's End.

In addition to all this, lockdown offered the opportunity to work full time on this book, which was badly needed. Among other skills developed was the use of WhatsApp which came into its own as the family were all communicating more than usual from across the world, a great way to share our Covid experiences and watch the young grow, greet new additions and enter the challenging home-made quizzes. Throughout this period I had been increasingly suffering from angina, which limited my ability to move around but increased my ability to fall downstairs! Eventually, under considerable pressure from my family, and in the face of increasing delays in the NHS, I agreed to accept their kind offer to go private. Consequently I experienced an early admission to hospital for the insertion of two stents into my arteries in 40 minutes and returned home by teatime. Now come daily exercises to get some strength in my limbs and I'm feeling fine. The situation as I see it is that we have all come through these dreadful months and are now ready to face the future, unfortunately that includes the yet appreciated problems of Brexit, the very urgent challenge of climate change followed by the war in Ukraine.

NOTES AND REFERENCES

1. The Special Rapporteur on extreme poverty and human rights, Philip Alston, undertook a mission to the United Kingdom of Great Britain and Northern Ireland from November 5th to 16th 2018.
2. Reported in *The Mail on Sunday* November 7th 2004. In Gimson, A. (2006). *The Rise of Boris Johnson*. London: Simon and Schuster. I have used this quote to illustrate the style of Johnson's rhetoric and readiness to lie, even though the affair with two pregnancies was well known in Westminster circles and beyond. At this time, Johnson was married with four children.
3. In the 2019 elections, with a low turnout and a lively campaign, the parliament had a more religious element. Subsequently, as the pandemic struck there were signs of discontent. In July 2021, President Kais Saied sacked the Prime Minister, closed parliament and completed a coup, ending Tunisia's democracy.

4. The impeachment was for 'incitement of insurrection.' Despite fierce arguments, during which several Republicans supported the motion, it was lost, having failed to achieve a two-thirds majority.
5. WHO Director (2020). General Press Conference, Geneva, March 16th 2020.
6. PA Media (2019). 'Flooding chaos in northern England to continue until Tuesday.' *The Guardian*, 17.11.2019.
7. Boris Johnson: UK will 'Take it on the chin.' See www.youtube.com.
8. Carding, N. (2021). 'Revealed Nightingale hospitals to cost half a million pounds in total.' *Health Services Journal*, Jan. 20th.
9. See captaintomfoundation.org.
10. Mitchell, M. (2021). 'Covid-19: New nurse death figures prompt call for investigation.' *Nursing Times*, Jan. 25th, p. 1. Godlee, F. (2022). 'Remembering the UK doctors who have died of Covid-19.' *British Medical Journal*. bmj.com, 12.04.2022.
11. In June 2021, when asked about this statement, Matt Hancock explained that he meant once there was a proper test system, which, to put it kindly, was mid May 2020.
12. Scobie, S. (2021). 'Covid-19 and the deaths of care home residents.' nuffieldtrust.org.uk online blog, 17.2.2021.
13. See the following articles in *Professional Social Work*. McNicoll, A. (2020). 'The impact of outbreak.' *Professional Social Work*, Apr., pp. 14–15. Miljkovic S. and Hill J. (2020). 'Child protection in a pandemic.' *Professional Social Work*, May, pp. 14–15.
14. Navid, S. (2020–2021). 'Covid 2020.' *Professional Social Work*, Dec. /Jan., pp. 15–17.
15. Navid, S. (2021). 'The cost of caring during Covid.' *Professional Social Work*, June, p. 16. Ndluvu, T. (2021). 'Everyone is grieving.' Workforce Focus, *Professional Social Work*, June, p. 18.
16. See Sen, R. and Smith, R. (2020). 'Who's guarding our guardians?' *Professional Social Work*, Sept., p. 18.
17. BASW (2022). The BASW Annual Survey of Social Workers and Social Work 2021. Summary Report.
18. Cook, L. and Zschomler, D. (2020). 'Virtual home visits during the Covid pandemic: social workers' perspectives.' *Practice*, Vol. 32, pp. 401–408.
19. House of Commons Library (2021). *Poverty in the UK: Statistics*. Briefing Paper 7096, 31.03.2021.
20. House of Commons Library (2021). *Food Poverty: Households, Food Banks and Free School Meals*. Briefing Paper 9209, 30.04.2021.
21. Marshall, P. (2021). 'Revealed: the pandemic boom in child poverty, neglect and abuse.' *The Guardian*, 12.8.2021, pp. 1–8.
22. See aellajordanedge.com.

1980
Malcolm M.A. (Social Work)
John M.A. (Education)

1980
Mini Olympics
Lowestoft

1981
Eastbourne
Mabel Jordan's 80th

Mid 1980s
Lancashire SSD management

Late 1980s
Vernon Jones, Malcolm and Peter Claydon
planning to take over Care Concern

Late 1980s
Higher Studlehurst, Lancashire

1991
London
Baby Aella arrives

1991
Aran Hall

1995
Lancashire
Wendy Brocklehurst and Aella

1990s
Lancashire
Ann in the kitchen

1996
Jack Bury, OBE

1997
London
Baby Duke arrives

1999
River Ribble, Lancashire
Aella, Juliet, Luke, Duke and Nicole

2001
Faslane Submarine Base
George

2002
London
Yulia, Olya and Sacha with Malcolm

2003
Croft Barn, Wiltshire
Malcolm and Duke

2003
Croft Barn, Wiltshire
Ann and the donkeys

2004
Bobrusk, Belarus

2009
Brooklyn, New York
Duke and Malcolm

2012
Michigan USA
Malcolm and nephew James White

2014
Jessie the Cockapoo

2017
Cadgwith, Cornwall
Aella, Malcolm and Nicole with George and Nancy

2017
Birmingham to Liverpool
SWU and BASW's 100-mile Walk Against Austerity

2019
London
Aella. Extinction Rebellion protest

PART FOUR

THE LAST POST
2021–2022
SEPT 2022

CLIMATE CHANGE

THE PANDEMIC

BREXIT

THE PRIME MINISTER, HIS CABINET
AND HIS PARLIAMENTARY PARTY

FAMILY AND FRIENDS

UKRAINE

EIGHTEEN

WHAT FUTURE?

It ought to be remembered that there is nothing more difficult to take in hand, More perilous to conduct or more uncertain in its success than to take the lead in the introduction of a new order of things. Because the innovator has for his enemies all those who have done well under the old conditions, and lukewarm defenders in those who may do well under the new. This coolness arises partly from fear of the opponents, who have the laws on their side and partly from the incredulity of men, who do not believe in new things until they have a long experience of them.

– Machiavelli (1532)[1]

For generations, we have assumed that the efforts of mankind would leave the fundamental equilibrium of the world's systems and atmosphere stable. But it is possible that with all these enormous changes (population, agricultural, use of fossil fuels) concentrated into such a short period of time, we have unwittingly begun a massive experiment with the system of this planet itself. Recently three changes in atmospheric chemistry have become familiar subjects of concern. The first is the increase in the greenhouse gases- which has led some to fear that we are creating a global heat trap which could lead to climatic instability. We are told that a warming effect of 1°C per decade would greatly exceed the capacity of our natural habitat to cope. It is noteworthy that globally the five warmest years in a century of records have all been since 2010, though we may not have seen much evidence in Britain.

The second matter under discussion is the discovery by the British Antarctic Survey of a large hole in the ozone layer which protects life from ultra-violet radiation. The third matter is acid deposition which has affected soils, lakes and trees. Extensive action is being taken to cut down emission of sulphur and nitrogen oxides from power stations at great but necessary expense. Even though this kind of action may cost a lot, I believe it to be money well and necessarily spent because the health of the economy and the health of our environment are totally dependent upon each other.

In studying the system of the earth and its atmosphere we have no laboratory in which to carry out controlled experiments. We need to consider in more detail the likely effects of change within precise timescales. And to consider the wider implications for policy, for energy production, for fuel efficiency, for reforestation. This is no small task, for the annual increase in atmospheric carbon dioxide alone is of the order of three billion tonnes. And half the carbon emitted since the Industrial Revolution remains in the atmosphere.

– Margaret Thatcher (1988)[2n]

Tell the Truth. Act Now.
Extinction Rebellion[3n]

FACING CLIMATE CHANGE

This book has traced the issue of climate change from Rachel Carson's 1962 blockbuster to the present day and reluctantly I have to admit that my arch enemy with her scientific background got it right, although sadly, in my view, hardly any action followed and widespread concern only began in the early 2020s when the population in the developed world noticed changes in the weather patterns and the media gave more attention to the subject, prompted by the United Nations framework convention on climate change series of conferences. In Naomi Klein's latest book she comments that:

> It's our greatest collective misfortune that the scientific community made its decisive diagnosis of the climate threat at the precise moment when an elite minority was enjoying more unfettered political, cultural and intellectual power than at any point since the 1920s.[4]

In early 2020 we saw the frightening wild fires on the western coast of America and in Australia, then the droughts and fiercer hurricanes in the mid west of those countries and across Africa and the Far East. The UK and Europe had experienced increased heavy rainfall and damaging flooding. The Irish writer Mark O'Connell drew attention to a situation where we are shocked at these events and may well correctly embrace them in the short term, but it doesn't feel like that on the nerve ends. Thus we might get used to large parts of the planet in flames and even more horror under water and we might harden our hearts against the people who live and die in the floods and the fire. In short the danger is that our moral judgement will slowly atrophy. That would mark the real apocalypse.[5]

The UN Conferences of the Peoples (COP) commenced in 1995 in Berlin, then continued annually. In the 1997 Kyoto meeting a protocol was adopted outlining greenhouse gas emission limits for the biggest economies of between 6% and 8%. All counties signed but the American Congress refused to ratify the treaty and in 2001 the Bush administration rejected it. These COPs were for open discussion and to review how far countries had progressed. The 2005 meeting in Canada and subsequently was attended by 10,000 delegates.

Four years later in Copenhagen there was little agreement among the 192 attending countries; led by President Obama and others the difficult issues were delayed. The following year in Mexico the delegates agreed to recognise that climate change represented an urgent and potentially irreversible threat to human societies and the planet. The 2011 COP in South Africa set out an agreement to start negotiating a legally binding deal to be adopted to be adopted after 2020.

This sad story reflects a battle between the increasing alarms from climate scientists and the diversity of experience, political and economic, of participating countries – from small Pacific islands who experience the direct effect of rising sea levels through to the majority of countries where citizens are concerned, to the richer western nations who are concerned about keeping their economy healthy, particularly in the face of massive expenditure on Covid. Then, in 2021, came COP26 in Glasgow.

Shortly ahead of that meeting the science based Intergovernmental Panel on Climate Change (IPCC) issued a report entitled 'Climate change widespread, rapid and intensifying.' It reported that strong and sustained reduction in emissions of CO_2 and other greenhouse gases would limit climate change; even so it would take 20–30 years to fully stabilise. Only urgent action to achieve such reductions would enable the rise in global temperatures to remain below 1.5°C, the current goal. Even then there will be increasing heat waves, with longer warm and shorter cold seasons. Further warming will increase flooding in some regions and severe droughts in others. Coastal areas will see continued sea level rises and further warming will increase the thawing of permafrost (which will release massive amounts of CO_2). Glaciers and ice sheets will melt (increasing sea levels) and the oceans will acidify. Cities will become overheated to unbearable levels. It was there for all of us to see and understand.[6]

This vital conference hosted by the UK was attended by 197 countries and expertly chaired by Alok Sharma, Secretary of State for Business, Energy and Industrial Strategy, who had spent the previous year visiting countries around the world discussing their situations and expected contributions. Our Prime Minister greeted arrivals and spread a feeling of bonhomie and hopefulness as is his trademark. Faced with growing citizen concern and the IPPC report it was seen as a 'make or break' meeting, one in which it was essential to get real agreement on immediate action to keep temperature to 1.5°C. The speakers were sharp and intense, including the highly respected David Attenborough, the People's Advocate:

> Is this how our story is going to end? A tale of the smartest species doomed by that all too human characteristic of failing to see the bigger picture in pursuit of short term goals ... We are, after all, the greatest problem solvers to have ever existed on Earth. We now understand this problem. We know how to stop the numbers rising and put it in reverse ... We must fix our sights on keeping one and a half degrees within sight. A new industrial revolution, powered by millions of sustainable innovations, is essential, and is indeed already beginning ... It comes down to this. The people alive now, the generations to come, will look at this conference and consider one thing. Did that number stop rising and start to drop as a result of the commitments made here? .... That desperate hope ... is why the world is looking at you and why you are here.[7]

With this, he pointed a challenging finger at his audience!

After 13 days the meeting ended with a crisis and a mixed result. At the very last minute, with some delegates having signed up to the final agreement, the Indian delegation demanded that in the agreement on coal reduction the words 'phased out' must be replaced by 'phased down.' The chairman left the dais for an urgent discussion and returned in tears of frustration and exhaustion. On the positive side was the first ever mention of fossil fuels which were to be only 'phased down' for power and 'phased out for inefficient fossil fuel subsidies.' The parties accepted that 'rapid, deep and sustained reductions in all global greenhouse gas emissions are required,' but the target of 1.5 degrees was left until another year! A revised version of the rule book laid out how countries would be helped to account as they deliver on their commitments. In total, 140 countries signed a pledge to halt deforestation, with no mechanism for enforcement.

Meetings were proposed between the global north and south although wealthier nations did agree to help poorer countries to become more resilient against weather caused by climate change; however, no fund was established. Our Prime Minister declared the outcome as 'truly historic' and 'game changing' although he did admit the notable failings. So, Alok Sharmer retains his chair for twelve months to pursue the shortcomings and help countries to prepare the comprehensive statements all must have ready for COP27 all in a world battling Covid. It seems to me that in order to achieve real progress governments need to tell their citizens the full truth about the actual effects on everyday life and the essential changes to the very basis of how a country is run of committing to the 1.5 degree target. This is spelt out clearly by Ed Miliband in his 2021 book *GO BIG*.[8] In order to achieve this we need clear, consistent and committed leadership which earns the respect and loyalty of voters. Unfortunately the Johnson government has none of these characteristics.

As we entered 2022, I became aware that news on progress on these goals was hard to find. Then, of course, the war in Ukraine preoccupied the government and climate change slipped further down the agenda. In May the government issued a statistical newsletter on the subject: it was not encouraging. While six out of ten UK adults fully expected that climate change would affect their lives within the next eight years, less than a quarter of big businesses had plans to help. Tree planting rose, as did the trend for farmers to change their practice to limit the release of CO_2.

On June 30th in America the Supreme Court issued a ruling severely limiting the government's ability to control emissions of CO_2 in the second largest polluter on the planet. The action was brought by the coal producing companies in the Republican state of Virginia, arguing that the power to impose restrictions by the Environment Protection Agency were unlawful. The Court, packed with right-wing justices appointed by President Trump, found in favour of the Virginian coal industry. This finding hobbled President Biden's ambitious plans, although Democratic states would no doubt continue to act for climate change. The fact that such a small group of people could negatively affect the entire population of Earth was totally unbelievable. President Biden pursued a programme of climate change legislation until 0n August 16th 2022 he signed a bill on climate change valued at $391 billon.

THE PANDEMIC IN THE UK

At the start of 2021 the country was in lockdown as the number of cases reached higher levels and deaths reached over 100,000. Thankfully effective vaccines became available, and the impact of the virus slowly reduced – by the end of February over

20 million people had been vaccinated and the fall in GDP was the largest on record. In May a variation in the virus from India was discovered, and in response the gap between first and second vaccinations was reduced to eight weeks. Surge testing for areas where vulnerable citizens were identified was introduced. In mid May the PM said that people should not travel to countries on the 'amber' list. He was immediately contradicted by a minister who stated that it was a matter of individual responsibility. In late May Johnson's former adviser Dominic Cummings gave evidence to a Parliamentary Committee alleging that tens of thousands of people died due to Johnson's mistakes, his failure to follow scientific advice and delayed decision making, and that he was not fit to hold office.

In early June, before the UK hosted the G7 summit in Cornwall, Johnson received a letter urging him to show historic leadership by sharing vaccines with other poorer countries. Six days later he announced that the UK would donate 100,000 vaccines in the next year. By late 2021 only 20% had been delivered and he was warned in Parliament that at this rate his promise would be broken. On June 2nd COVAX, the body responsible for securing vaccines for poorer countries, held a virtual summit which raised a total of $9.6 billion for vaccines and a further $775 million for delivery. As far as I can ascertain the UK was not involved and made no donation although Dominic Raab, the Foreign Secretary, commented how proud we were to have sponsored the AstraZeneca vaccine.[9]

Later in June there was a significant rise in cases, attributed to a new variation of the virus identified in India and named Delta. This variant proved to be more infectious and dangerous but, despite warnings from the British Medical Association, on the announced date of July 19th Johnson removed all restrictions, with the wearing of masks becoming optional in England, unlike in the three other home countries. From then onwards the daily case numbers declined.

On July 13th 2022 the Commons voted, by 319 to 245, to support legislation requiring the compulsory vaccination of care home staff from October. Were they just hitting a soft target? Once the requirement to wear masks had been lifted it was noted on TV that, in the poorly ventilated House of Commons, no Conservative MP wore a mask. The Leader of the House, Jacob Rees-Mogg, later explained that they didn't need to as they all knew each other!

In August vaccines were made available for sixteen- and seventeen-year-olds. Concern was now growing about the damage Covid hospitalisations were having on the treatment of other serious illnesses. The NHS reported a waiting list of 5.45 million people, many of whom would be in chronic pain and fear of premature death. An urgent inquiry was held into the excessive cost of PCR tests among 'exploitative practices' by manufacturers. It was slowly becoming apparent that the pandemic was badly affecting the supply chain; the 'just in time' process was no longer possible. Shortage of labour was causing chaos at container ports where the shortage of lorry drivers was leaving container stacks overflowing. In the UK the construction industry was particularly badly affected; houses could not be built and the cost of materials was rising to ridiculous levels.

This process spread throughout the economy and as skilled labour, particularly fully licensed lorry drivers, became short workers demanded higher wages which employers had no option but to pay, as importing drivers from Europe was no longer possible due to Brexit. When short term visas were eventually offered there was minimal take up. Consequently prices went up across the board starting an inflationary spiral. Alongside these events the question of 'passports' to confirm vaccination and allow the holder into public events was being raised. This highly controversial step never happened because an increasingly vocal right wing of the Conservative party set against such an invasion of individual liberties. This group increasingly restricted the Prime Minister's ability to act on scientific advice. By September vulnerable people and those over 70 were being called for a third 'booster' inoculation. Johnson reassured us that the extra vaccines would not affect 'our massive commitment to the rest of the world.' More fantasy.

In October a joint report on the handling of the pandemic by two cross-party parliamentary committees was published. It was pretty damning. They described the delay in imposing the initial lockdown as 'one of the most important public health failures that the UK has ever experienced.' They blamed failures on 'group think' by ministers, scientific advisers and civil servants. Allowing thousands of infected patients into care homes showed that the safety of residents was an afterthought. MPs were appalled to learn that DNRs, 'do not resuscitate' notices, had been issued inappropriately to some patients with a learning disability. In addition, the test and trace system had been an expensive failure. In contrast the vaccine programme was one of the most effective initiatives in UK history and praise was due to government for developing new treatments for Covid.[10]

On December 15th 2021 it was announced that Baroness Heather Hallet would chair an inquiry due to commence in 2022. Baroness Hallet is a crossbench peer, having been a member of the Court of Appeal with a long experience in chairing complex inquiries. Early in 2022 she intends to consult with those who have lost loved ones and other affected groups to help in establishing the terms of reference. My expectation is that as the members of her team are announced concerns will be raised about the degree of independence, especially given the delay in starting the process. I anticipate the Prime Minister will take every opportunity to ensure that the findings are not published before the next election, due in May 2024. At the end of March 2022 the Parliamentary and Health Ombudsman submitted their comments on the terms of reference, stating that a full 'robust and forensic approach,' should be extended to consider events after December 2021 and should cover events outside hospitals.[11]

In late November fears emerged that a significant mutation of the virus had been diagnosed in southern Africa and, given our lax border controls, was inevitably found here three days later. This was named the Omicron variant. Its confirmed characteristic was its speed of infection, doubling every 36 hours, although the fact that it led to less serious illness was not confirmed for some months. The government's response was to rapidly promote the availability of vaccines and urge the public to take advantage of new vaccine centres to get themselves thoroughly vaccinated, advice which was quickly followed. As the year ended it seemed that, thanks to the amazing NHS organisation the public were feeling protected, despite the very rapid rise in cases. In addition, most infected people experienced only the same symptoms as a bad cold. However, a significant number of those admitted to hospital were unvaccinated as were those who did not survive. This enabled the government to avoid any significant restrictions until 2022. On December 31st 2021, 162,572 cases were reported with 12,000 patients in hospital and 154 deaths. As the population felt free of restrictions, with mask wearing and testing being a minority activity, cases started to rise steadily until in late June 2022 some 251,980 cases were reported.

BREXIT

After five years of titanic negotiations and damaging political events at home, the UK left the European Union on December 31st 2020 at the conclusion of a transitional year. This was Johnson's beautiful 'oven ready' deal. Unfortunately, but not surprisingly for a man who has never bothered with detail, it proved to have many holes. Consequently chaos immediately descended on the ports where lorry drivers delivering to the EU were faced with complex pages of documents required by the treaty but their employers had either not known about them or had not had time to learn. Although further negotiations eased that situation, the most serious issue remains the trade border between mainland and Northern Ireland, which remained in the EU trading area.

Having been forced to accept this solution because a land border was politically impossible, Johnson dismissed any difficulties as of no significant consequence for businesses. Exactly the opposite proved to be the case. The EU, protecting the integrity of their border, imposed strict custom regulations for which the vast majority of mainland companies were totally unprepared. Eventually the EU eased their requirements to avoid shortages of food and associated issues. Negotiations, led for the UK by the uncompromising Lord Frost, continued, with a new leader, into 2022. At the time of writing, the government is preparing to break international law by arbitrarily changing the treaty.

Throughout the year, many thousands of EU citizens working in our key industries left the UK. Transport, hospitality and farming were badly affected. Delivery shortages led to unfilled shelves in supermarkets, empty petrol pumps and farmers seeing their crops rot in the ground, while lack of abattoir staff meant animals were overstocked and had to be culled. In addition to the direct effect of the virus and consequent closures, the hospitality sector struggled to recruit staff. By year end the two wonderful tiki bars that my grandson Luke established were in danger. Faced with demands for temporary visas to be issued the government response was ridiculously inadequate so that UK workers could then demand higher pay which inevitably led to higher prices: 2022 has already been called the year of the squeeze, costing households at least £1,200 extra per year.[12]

The further we got from the final separation the more we gradually realised how many lies we had been told both in relation to the deal itself and the consequences. A more serious problem comes from the political classes having to bend and twist to cover up their lack of truth; this sharpens the political debate and slowly destroys public confidence in the whole process.[13]

SOCIAL CARE AND SOCIAL WORK

Social Care

2021 was not a good time for social care and social work. Frontline staff and those responsible for their supervision and welfare were under intolerable pressure. Especially as they were already suffering from the erosive effects of ten years of austerity. Local authorities had previously lost 40% of their government income and were in no condition to face the pandemic and its legacy. Care homes suffered the terrible effects of over 38,000 excess deaths as a result of government incompetence, low pay (in the face of general pay rises, see above) and low morale. Then, as the super infectious Omicron variant swept across the land, staff were falling ill and having to isolate. This meant that bed numbers had to be reduced with inevitable financial consequences. The public had been offered a small glance of the real situation in a poignant and angry TV play *Help* that was broadcast on Channel 4 on September 21st.[14]

Home care was similarly affected resulting in reduced hours for vulnerable, elderly and disabled service users, and causing distress and financial challenges to families or voluntary agencies who had no option but to undertake often very challenging personal intimate work. Over all this hung the promise of the 2019 Conservative election manifesto that they would seek a cross-party consensus to reform how people pay for adult social care so that no one would have to sell their house. In reality the actual proposals fell short of this ambition. It introduced a cap of £86,000 on the amount anyone in England could spend on their personal care in a lifetime. This did not include housekeeping, which included food set at £200 per week. The point at which one becomes eligible for financial support from their local authority would rise from £23,250 to £100,000. This is to become live in October 2023. It was quickly pointed out that these proposals would considerably benefit the wealthy while the rest of society could lose 80% of their assets with no protection.

Social Work

For most of the pandemic social workers were denied the key element of their practice, face to face meetings with service users. During lockdowns their nightmares have been about the abuses possibly taking place behind the doors of families stressed out by the very fact of being confined with small children or poorly elders. However inventive and expert the phone or video contacts were, doubts remained. Pressure from management remained a significant concern for many, as did staff shortages and absences due to isolation. For the most part the profession suffered in silence. Concerns included the media reaction to any failings, the government's refusal to include them in the definition of frontline workers, the MacAlister review of children's social care and the Competition and Markets Authorities review of the market in child care. Both these reports were published in the Spring of 2022. While these reviews were generally welcomed, considerable concern was expressed about the leadership and the team (consisting of civil servants) who produced the MacAlister review. His previous work had led to the decimation of social work education by establishing Frontline short training courses and other initiatives as part of a network of political and financial interests.[15]

In the meantime social workers were developing ways of working with families and communities to explore the help and support available to those in need. Rather than looking back to previous patterns new ideas were developing. One SWU initiative in 2021 was to give social workers the opportunity to run a campaign backed by the excellent Campaign Collective and paid for by SWU. The political activist Gorge commented that during the pandemic, 'Power has migrated, not just from private money to the state but from both market and state to … the commons.' A survey reported that 81% of respondents considered that the pandemic would leave behind a society that has learnt a good lesson that 'we are all in it together.'[16] In October 2020 Isabel Martin's call to arms reminded us that

> Social work cannot mend the destruction caused by this pandemic but can certainly help towards the inevitable recalibration of society's priorities. It can strengthen the value placed upon the marginalised in our society who are not able to benefit from what has been our finance obsessed economy. It can also strengthen the inspirational individual and social resources which humanity has relied upon for generations.[17]

Finally, in a leap forward of 50 years Maris Stratulis predicted Equalities and Social Justice Hubs in every community wherein the workforce would report to local citizens to decide, among other things, which needs can best be met by a member of staff or an android. Those formerly known as social workers are called 'Freedom Enablers,' responsible for ensuring that every child, young person and elder person has the freedom to flourish and to lead their lives free from oppression, discrimination and abuse.[18] Two more contributions to our future can be found in the radical Social Work Action Network's journal *Critical and Radical Social Work*.[19]

Against all this hope came, in mid December, the trial of Emma Tustin and Thomas Hughes for the killing of their six-year-old son Arthur Labinjo-Hughes. Over a period of at least a month they had poisoned him, denied him food and drink and beat him regularly. They were jailed for 29 and 21 years, respectively. It was stated that social services, the school and the police had all missed a number of 'red flags.' An inquiry was launched with a broader brief covering services in Solihull. Their report published in February 2022 confirmed that social workers had visited the home two months before Arthur's death but found no safeguarding concerns. Such a conclusion was seen as over optimistic and lacking in professional curiosity. The situation of social work and policing in the borough was severely criticised.[20]

THE PRIME MINISTER, HIS CABINET AND HIS PARLIAMENTARY PARTY

Boris Johnson entered 10 Downing Street as Prime Minister on July 24th 2019. I cannot imagine how much this achievement of his long-held ambition meant to him. He was generally described as a one nation Conservative being socially liberal. His reputation as a popular Mayor of London, a position from which he retired three years earlier (where he had been supported by strong deputies), was that he was one for broad popular schemes but not concerned with detail and the processes required to match vision with action. Other aspects of his personality caused some concern. He was an easy liar, a misogynist with an unknown number of children and was skilled in deploying bluster when refusing to give a straight answer to a question. Reflecting on my own career I recalled the warning that the higher up you went the more your arse was seen by others.

It was a great historical irony that five months later the UK was hit by the worst pandemic in modern history – an issue that called for urgent action, clear leadership and full grasp of detail from the government, hence the excess deaths referred to above. Johnson appointed his Cabinet mostly from those close to him from the Brexit campaign, none of whom had experience of government. He and his chosen advisers settled into Downing Street away from contact with their own parliamentary party. In complete contrast the Labour Party elected Kier Starmer, an experienced lawyer and skilled interrogator as their leader. Their challenges included all the issues discussed above. The next two and a half years were going to be interesting!

It took both leaders quite a long time to sort out Prime Minister's Questions (PMQs) every Wednesday. Starmer would ask his six questions, and Johnson would seldom answer any, just relying on bluster and deflection or counterattack using false evidence. Serious straightforward Starmer found this very difficult and frustrating, however entertaining it appeared. Another tactic much favoured by the PM was to deploy three-word catchphrases such as 'Hands, face, space' when referring to the virus, 'Eat-out to help-out' – the £10 per head discount to help restaurants survive – and 'levelling up,' a phrase which came to mean anything from renewed transport links in the north of England to an increase in national insurance to pay for social care. Very few of these phrases were backed by a policy statement or any actual details. The situation in the Conservative Parliamentary Party was becoming clear by late 2020. Within the government's 80 majority were the new MPs from the so-called 'Red Wall' of previous Labour strongholds. These were seeing little legislation that helped their constituents, for example the changes to the northern transport plan which would undermine the promises on which they were elected and make them one-term MPs. Also a significant number of right-wing members began chafing at the Covid restrictions on the grounds that people should be left to decide on their own precautions, not have them imposed by the state.

Early in the pandemic the government had to invest huge amounts of money to acquire protective equipment for NHS and care staff, etc. True to Johnson's character he created a 'red carpet' system by which certain people, especially if they donated to the Party, could have privileged access to the departments awarding contracts. Some of these bidders had no experience in this field or indeed were newly created organisations in order to get a contract. As details of these schemes became known several high-quality law firms sought disclosures and possible prosecution of the parties concerned. There followed allegations that peerages were being bought for contributions to the Conservative Party. Questions arose about payments for the PM's Caribbean holidays and the expensive refurbishment of his flat, over which the PM declared himself unaware.

A crisis developed, as it had before, over the question of how much money and time Conservative MPs were using in doing jobs other than those covered by their MP salaries. Many were investigated but in particular Owen Paterson, a friend of the Prime Minister, was alleged to have lobbied in parliament on behalf of his private business. This was clearly a breach of the rules for which the Standards Committee had recommended suspension for 30 days. Paterson denied the offence and criticised the process. In early November the standard motion to agree the suspension was debated in the Commons. A Johnson-backed motion was put forward to delay the vote and set up a new committee to examine the whole process. A three-line whip was issued in a bid to save Johnson's friend. The motion was passed by 18 votes, showing that 100 Conservatives had disobeyed the Whip, a severe blow to the PM's standing. Faced with this defeat a further debate was scheduled which would have confirmed Paterson's suspension. He resigned, triggering a by-election which was fought on December 16th 2021 with 14 candidates competing. The Tory Party had held the seat for well over 100 years. The result, with a turnout of 46.3%, was a clear win for the Liberal Democrat Party, a swing of 34.2% away from the Tories.

Such a disaster, mostly caused by Johnson's attempt to change the whole system to save his friend, gained the PM no ground with his party who he could no longer trust to support him. Over the same period a series of stories, with supporting photos, appeared to show that whilst the population at large were obeying the rules imposed by lockdown in 2020–21 MPs and staff at Number 10 were holding seasonal parties with no regard for social distancing. The last that I can remember was an aerial shot of the garden in Downing Street where staff with the PM's wife and baby were sitting close together drinking wine and eating snacks. Questioned about that the Deputy Prime Minister Dominic Raab explained that it couldn't be a party as they were wearing suits! These events led to the major 'Partygate' scandal involving police investigations into some eleven events in Downing Street. Eighty-three individuals were fined, with 28 receiving between two and five fines. Johnson received one conviction, being the first Prime Minister to be convicted of a criminal offence.

While all these events were holding the public attention more serious issues were appearing on the parliamentary agenda. The Home Office, under the leadership of Priti Patel, who is on the right-wing 'Thatcherite' side of the party, produced legislation on immigration which made no sense at all, although it had terrible effects on those involved. Despite a number of initiatives, attempts failed to stop thousands of migrants crossing the English Channel in thin rubber overloaded boats, some of which never made it leading to rising public concerns. Under Patel's policy all such arrivals were criminalised because they had not come through the formal channels, although no such effective facility existed. This meant that tens of thousands of 'illegal' migrants were held in poor accommodation while awaiting the result of their application to remain. They were forbidden to use their skills to work even though our economy was short of those very skills. The government became worried about the increasing number of migrants arriving by boat every day. Consequently on April 14th 2022 it was announced that such migrants would be sent to Rwanda, over 4,000 miles away, on a one-way ticket! The government convinced themselves that this would stop the 'evil' smugglers from operating in France. The first flight was scheduled to depart with eight people on board on June 14th, but emergency court cases slowly reduced this number and eventually, just before take-off, the European Court of Human Rights intervened. At the time of writing no more flights have been scheduled although Patel was determined to proceed. The set-up cost was £120 million and the cost per migrant was estimated at £15,000.[21] Patel's other legislation was the Police Bill, which among other things allowed public protests providing they did not inconvenience anyone in any way.

All these events and the public reaction to the Partygate photos enabled Labour to run a campaign in Parliament and beyond with the theme of lack of clear leadership, right-wing drift, sleaze and the hard-hitting obvious point that the Tories believed in 'one rule for them and another for everybody else.' This chimed exactly with the general public's view and by the end of December 2021 the Labour Party were ahead by eight points in the opinion polls while the government was left with a Prime Minister who had lost any respect or authority. The crisis came in the first week of July 2022 when the political climate rose unbearably against the Prime Minister. The TV pictures of the morning Cabinet meeting revealed a set of very gloomy faces. Once again Johnson's handling of a senior appointment was being severely criticised. His Deputy Chief Whip (who had the role of supporting and caring for MPs) resigned on June 30th after admitting that he had drunk too much at a private members club the previous evening. Allegations then emerged that he had made sexual advances to several people. The question then arose as to why the PM had appointed him in the first place as the MP's behaviour had been well known for years. Johnson, as usual, claimed he knew nothing about all that. It was immediately proved that he had indeed known. Immediately two of the most senior Cabinet members resigned. The following day, July 6th, a flood of resignations started to pour in to Downing Street. By 6 pm the total resignations from government had risen to 38. Johnson was still claiming that he could turn it round. Eventually nearly 60 people resigned. Running the government was impossible. Early on the morning of July 7th 2022 it was confirmed that Johnson had decided to step down, and later he emerged to address the nation, summarising his achievements and blaming the 'herd mentality' that had overcome his MPs. He declared he would remain in post until September to give his Party time to elect a new leader.

PRESIDENT PUTIN OF RUSSIA

If my personal future was uncertain as the age of 88 approached, the expectation of the future was not clear to anyone. We assumed that the virus would at the very worst become endemic with probably an annual vaccination to protect us. Additionally the complexities left by Brexit really had to be sorted out, especially in Northern Ireland where letting the situation fester could lead to pressures for reunion with Eire.

Perhaps Johnson's luck would run out as blunder after blunder robbed him of any respect and, in any case an election is due in 2024. I did not look forward to the next few years with much optimism. And then events in Russia started to alarm Europe. In the summer of 2021 Putin published a long and discursive essay entitled 'On the Historical Unity of Russians and Ukranians.' Towards the conclusion he wrote:

> I am confident that the true sovereignty of Ukraine is possible only in partnership with Russia ... Our kinship has been transmitted from generation to generation. It is in the hearts and memory of people living in modern Russia and Ukraine, in the blood ties that unite millions of our families. Together we have always been strong and will be many times stronger and more successful. For we are one people.[22]

Commentators drew attention to the many historical errors and the faulty reasoning. Others saw it as a clear threat from a tiring and increasingly isolated man in the grips of an obsession and challenged by the poor state of the Russian economy. In mid December tens of thousands of troops were deployed to the Ukrainian border to engage in frenzied exercises.

On February 24th 2022 Russian troops invaded Ukraine from the south and north. It did not go well. The northern invasion, aimed at Kyiv to decapitate the government, was foiled by fierce opposition from Ukrainian forces. At the time of writing, over eight million civilians have left Ukraine for neighbouring countries. Russia has relentlessly pursued its strategy of completely destroying cities and towns by prolonged missile attacks before their troops enter whereby the Ukrainian forces engage them in battle. These battles seem to be settling into a long war of attrition. Western nations have increased their supply of equipment to Ukraine to include modern mobile artillery and missile launchers with a greater range than those of the Russians, along with tanks, ammunition, and aerial defences. The event has strengthened Western political unity and NATO has been greatly enhanced, including the likely admission of Finland and Sweden. Troops are being deployed in NATO countries that border Russia. It is considered that the timing of Putin's invasion relied partly on his belief that Western countries, particularly those in the EU and America, were weak.

FAMILY AND FRIENDS

My family and friends, in common with many others, have experienced the effect of the pandemic throughout 2021. I live alone in the village of Kington St Michael; it lies five miles north of Chippenham and one mile from the M4 motorway. Its most recent claim to fame was that Jeremy Corbyn spent some early years here. My granddaughter Aella lives in London, and the rest of my family are in Brooklyn, New York. My second eldest nephew lives in nearby Stroud and other families live in Scotland, the North, the West Midlands, London, Kent and Cornwall. Other family and friends are scattered across America, Canada, Spain and Australia.

The virus and my ongoing ill health have kept me indoors. I have experienced a long period of low blood pressure resulting in fainting and falling, at least twice down the stairs with A & E to follow. As my low blood pressure got worse, the problem was solved in early 2022 by having a double stent inserted. A more positive effect of the virus and my subsequent isolation has been the increased interaction I have had with those distant members of the clan from whom a Christmas card was previously the only contact. We have transatlantic quizzes, great conversations and photos shared, all of which deepen the relationship between us all. In that way, 2021 was an incredible year.

In the UK five families have fallen victim of the Delta or Omicron variants and one member of the much loved Jones family of Blackburn, Evie, suffered horrendous life-changing injuries in a road accident.

At the end of the 2021, following all the rules, the family flew in and we had a magical Christmas in Cadgwith followed by the glorious biannual meeting of the families from Lancashire and the Midlands, this time in Devon. All were tested the day before arrival and the week was full of love for the four generations gathered. In particular it was a joy to see Evie, the life and soul of any party enjoying the event but still suffering times of dreadful pain.

2022 has not been such a good year. Juliet, Rod, Aella and Duke all caught Covid, taking them out of action for ten or more days. Unfortunately Juliet then developed 'long Covid,' an enervating condition which, at the time of writing, has also given her recurrent shingles, a painful and worrying condition. Despite this she is determined, with her best women friends and relations, to take part in the large summer swim from Marazion round St Michael's Mount, a distance of a mile and a half in open water. This is in aid of prostate cancer research. A long week of practice is planned.

NOTES AND REFERENCES

1. Niccolo Machiavelli (1532). *The Prince*. Partly quoted in Miliband, E. (2021). *GO BIG. How to Fix Our World*. London: Bodley Head, p. 202.
2. Edited version of a speech by Mrs Thatcher to the Royal Society on September 27th 1988. A similar but more powerful version was given to the United Nations General Assembly on November 8th 1989.
3. Two key demands of the Extinction Rebellion movement, founded on October 31st 2018.
4. Klein, N. (2014). *This Changes Everything: Capitalism vs The Climate*. New York: Simon & Schuster.
5. O'Connell, M. (2020). 'Pictures of the world on fire won't shock us for much longer.' *The Guardian*, 13.1.20, p. 3.
6. The 6th Report of the IPCC, released on August 9th 2021. 'Climate change, widespread, rapid and intensifying.' See www.ipcc.ch.
7. See www.rev.com.
8. Miliband, *op. cit*.
9. See gavi.org.
10. Clemence, H. (2021). 'A damning verdict.' *The Week*, 16.10.2021, p. 6.
11. See the Consultation on the UK COVID-19 inquiry draft terms of reference: Submission from the Parliamentary and Health Service Ombudsman, 31.03.2022. ombudsman.org.uk.
12. Bell, T., Corlett, A., Marshall, J. and Slaughter, H. (2021). *Labour Market Outlook Q4 2021. Wages and the cost of living in 2022*. London: Resolution Foundation.
13. Oborn, P. (2021). The Assault on Truth: Boris Johnson, Donald Trump and the Emergence of a New Moral Barbarism. London: Simon & Schuster.
14. *Help* by Jake Thorn starring Jodie Comer and Stephen Graham. Dir. Marc Munden.
15. See Jordan, M. 'Looking back over 50 years; in Bamford, T. and Bilton, K. (2020), eds. *Social Work Past, Present and Future*: Bristol. Policy Press.
16. Palfreyman, L. (2021). *Social Work Today*, Dec., pp. 24–25.
17. Martin, I. (2020). 'Social work's voice needs to be much louder to fight for a fairer future after the pandemic.' *PSW magazine*, Oct., p. 12.
18. Stratulis, M. (2020). 'Imagining social work in 2070 after 50 years of rapid, radical change.' *PSW magazine*, July/Aug., p. 55.
19. Gupta, A. and Morris, K. (2021). 'Post-pandemic: moving on from "child protection".' *Critical and Radical Social Work*, Vol. 9 no 2, Aug., p. 151. Larkins, C., Satchwell, C., Davididge, G. and Carter, B. (2021). 'Working back to the future: strengthening radical social work with children and young people and their perspectives on resilience, capabilities and overcoming adversity.' *Critical and Radical Social Work*, Vol. 9 no 2, Aug., p. 185.
20. Child Safeguarding Practice Review Panel (2022). 'National review into the murders of Arthur Labinjo-Hughes and Star Hobson.' Department of Education, 26.05.2022. www.gov.uk/government/publications.
21. Walsh, P. W. (2022). 'Q&A: The UK's policy to send asylum seekers to Rwanda.' The Migration Observatory, University of Oxford. migrationobservatory.ox.ac.uk, 10.06.2022.
22. See the article by Vladimir Putin 'On the historical unity of Russians and Ukranians.' en.kremlin.ru.

The cartoon below is reproduced by kind permission of Peter Rigby

Have you tried turning it off and back on again?

ABOUT THE AUTHOR

Malcolm was born and raised in 1930s Peckham, South London, with the exception of five wartime years as an evacuee, running wild in the countryside. Having no effective education during evacuation, life drastically changed on his return to London, as he was sent to 'posh school' (which he hated) for years. Over seven decades Malcolm's career in social work has spanned the prison system, community work, psychiatric social work, teaching, central government, senior management roles, residential school and consultancy. He has worked within the public and private sectors, in both the north and south of Great Britain. A career-long trade unionist and member of BASW, Malcolm is an executive of SWU and the Austerity Action Group In September 22 he was appointed as Hon President of SWU He is an active member of SWAN and the Social Work History Network, the Parliamentary Labour Social Work Group and XR (Extinction Rebellion). During the last 15 years, he has volunteered with the Youth Offending Service. During her lifetime, Malcolm's wife Ann was also a social worker and NHS board member. Malcolm has a daughter, two grandchildren, seven great grandnephews and nieces, and a close network of family and friends.

Publications include:

Growing Old in Brighton (DHSS, 1980)
'Piggy in the Middle: Social Work Education – A View from the Field' in *Theory and Practice in Social Work*, Eds. Roy Bailey and Phil Lee.
Wiley and Son (1982).

'Looking Back' in *Social Work Past, Present and Future*, Eds.
Terry Bamford and Keith Bilton, Policy Press, (2020)